VAT and the City: Banking, Finance and Insurance
Seventh Edition

VAT and the City: Banking, Finance and Insurance
Seventh Edition

a Wolters Kluwer business

This publication is sold with the understanding that neither the publisher nor the authors, with regard to this publication, are engaged in rendering legal or professional services. The material contained in this publication neither purports, nor is intended to be, advice on any particular matter.

Although this publication incorporates a considerable degree of standardisation, subjective judgement by the user, based on individual circumstances, is indispensable. This publication is an aid and cannot be expected to replace such judgement.

Neither the publisher nor the authors can accept any responsibility or liability to any person, whether a purchaser of this publication or not, in respect of anything done or omitted to be done by any such person in reliance, whether sole or partial, upon the whole or any part of the contents of this publication.

Legislative and other material

While copyright in all statutory and other materials resides in the Crown or other relevant body, copyright in the remaining material in this publication is vested in the publisher.

The author has asserted his moral rights in accordance with sections 77 to 80 of the Copyright, Designs and Patents Act 1988.

The publisher advises that any statutory or other materials issued by the Crown or other relevant bodies and reproduced and quoted in this publication are not the authorised official versions of those statutory or other materials. In the preparation, however, the greatest care has been taken to ensure exact conformity with the law as enacted or other material as issued.

Crown copyright legislation is reproduced under the terms of Crown Copyright Policy Guidance issued by HMSO. Other Crown copyright material is reproduced with the permission of the controller of HMSO. European Communities Copyright material is reproduced with permission.

Telephone Helpline Disclaimer Notice

Where purchasers of this publication also have access to any Telephone Helpline Service operated by Wolters Kluwer (UK), then Wolters Kluwer's total liability to contract, tort (including negligence, or breach of statutory duty) misrepresentation, restitution or otherwise with respect to any claim arising out of its acts or alleged omissions in the provision of the Helpline Service shall be limited to the yearly subscription fee paid by the Claimant.

© 2012 Wolters Kluwer (UK) Limited

Wolters Kluwer
145 London Road
Kingston upon Thames
KT2 6SR
Telephone: (0) 844 561 8166
Facsimile: (0) 208 247 2638
E-mail: cch@wolterskluwer.co.uk
Website: www.cch.co.uk

ISBN 978-1-84798-438-8

All rights reserved. No part of this publication may be reproduced or transmitted in any form or by any means, or stored in any retrieval system of any nature without permission, except for permitted fair dealing under the Copyright, Designs and Patents Act 1988, or in accordance with the terms of a licence issued by the Copyright Licensing Agency in respect of photocopying and/or reprographic reproduction. Application for permission for other use of copyright material, including to reproduce extracts in other published works, shall be made to the publisher. Full acknowledgement to author, publisher and source must be given.

No responsibility for loss occasioned to any person acting or refraining from action as a result of any material in this publication can be accepted by the author or publisher.

British Library Cataloguing-in-Publication Data

A catalogue record for this book is available from the British Library.

Typeset by Innodata Inc.
Printed by in the UK by Hobbs the Printers Ltd

About the author

Julian J.B. Hickey
LLM (Tax), PhD (Lond), CTA (Fellow), Partner, Bird & Bird LLP

Julian is Head of the International VAT Group at Bird & Bird LLP. He advises corporate clients on direct tax and VAT matters. In recent years his practice has focused on providing VAT advisory services to a range of clients (often with a cross-border element). During his career he has advised on a broad range of tax matters, with a particular focus on the financial services and commercial sectors. He has experience of tax dispute resolution work, having acted as Solicitor-Advocate before the High Court and Court of Appeal. He has a PhD in tax and is a contributor to a number of tax publications. Julian is a Fellow of the Chartered Institute of Taxation.

Contributing author

David Southern MPhil MA D Phil FTII FIIT

David is a barrister at Temple Tax Chambers. He has a broad experience of tax litigation and advice, principally in relation to business taxation and VAT. Before beginning independent practice at the Bar, he worked in the Inland Revenue Solicitor's Office and in the tax department of Lloyds TSB Bank. He represented the taxpayer in Fleming (t/a Bodycraft) v R & C Commrs [2008] STC 325 in the House of Lords and in three lower levels of courts. The case was described by the Financial Times as 'the VAT case of the decade'. A special Fleming Repayment Unit had to be set up in consequence, and the consequent tax refunds have been put at £13.1 billion. More recently he represented BAA in its successful appeal to recover VAT on takeover costs.

David is a Bencher of Lincoln's Inn and past Treasurer of the Bar Council. He is Director of the School of Tax Law and Visiting Professorial Fellow at Queen Mary, University of London. He is also the UK National Reporter at the 2012 IFA Congress in Boston on the subject of 'The Debt-Equity Conundrum'.

Foreword

As long ago as 1994, in the landmark case of *Card Protection Plan,* Sir John Megaw recognised that 'special difficulties arise in the mystic twilight of VAT legislation'. That case concerned whether a package of benefits available when a customer lost his credit card was a multiple supply or a single supply of insurance related services. His observation still resonates for anyone doing business in the banking, financial and insurance sectors, where VAT is a perennial headache. Since Big Bang, globalisation and increased regulation of financial markets have served only to multiply complexity. The courts grapple courageously with concepts such as payments and transfers, intermediation, outsourcing and click-through insurance. And yet the legislation always seems to lag one step behind technical developments. It is difficult to disagree with Sedley LJ's observation, in the *Royal and Sun Alliance* case, that 'VAT is a kind of fiscal theme park in which factual or legal realities are suspended or inverted'.

As with previous editions, this new updated edition of *VAT and the City* brings us off the Big Dipper and back to earth with our stomachs intact. The work can be read as a complete treatise, taking the reader on a journey from the origins and concept of VAT to the treatment of the latest electronic transactions. More likely, however, it will come into its own as a work of reference. Its chapters are, to a large extent, self-contained. The reader will find all that is necessary under a particular subject heading. Technical explanation of the legislation is interspersed with succinct case summaries, tabulations, flowcharts and 'practice points'. There are helpful summaries of the European Commission's latest proposals on financial and insurance services, including outsourcing, currently in the form of a draft directive amending the Principal VAT Directive. Other useful material, such as extracts from legislation, HMRC manuals and guidance and Statements of Practice, is included in the Appendices.

Chapter 9 (Insurance) and Chapter 10 (Commodity Derivatives and Financial Derivatives) have been extensively updated. Chapter 11 (Mergers and Acquisitions) is new and explores the practical problems arising from cases like *SKF AB v Skatterverket* and *BAA Ltd* on recovery of input tax on deal costs. Chapter 12 (Electronic Banking, Finance, Insurance and Related Services) is also new and helps to de-mystify the many acronyms and virtual concepts, such as 'electronic money'.

Tax is once again in the news. The Chancellor of the Exchequer has publicly condemned tax avoidance schemes which are 'morally repugnant', whether practised by corporates or individuals. Legislation introduced in 2004, which requires disclosure of designated schemes, has been found inadequate. The government is to introduce a GAAR (a statutory general anti-abuse rule) for direct tax and plans further measures to target 'cowboy advisers'. Meanwhile, case law on the prevention of abuse in the field of VAT (enunciated by the European Court in the joined cases of *Halifax, Huddersfield and BUPA*) is developing apace.

In today's enforcement climate, therefore, it is essential for all businesses to ensure the correct classification of their transactions for VAT purposes and prioritise their compliance

Foreword

obligations. This is nowhere more important than in the industry sectors covered by this book, where large sums of VAT are at stake as well as reputational issues. Where VAT planning is employed, businesses must ensure arrangements are so structured that they comply with the spirit and not just the letter of the law.

VAT and the City is the invaluable vade-mecum for the practitioner and in-house expert alike.

Michael Conlon QC
Hogan Lovells International LLP
London
November 2012

Preface to the Seventh Edition

It was a daunting task to take on the seventh edition of this title from Peter Landon, who has successfully navigated it through six editions. However, it has been a joy to update, and deal with a relatively short period in the history of VAT development, which has seen material changes since 2007, such as the introduction of the VAT Package (and the impact on place of supply rules), EU Council Implementing Regulation No. 282/2011, and case law developments on the interpretation of Group 5 Sch. 9 of VATA, and Art. 135 of the VAT Directive: such as *AXA UK PLC*, *Proceedings brought by Nordea Pankki Suomi Oyj*. Other cases of particular note, which are reflected in this edition, include: *Deutsche Bank AG*, *Skatteverket v AB SKF*, *Airtours Holidays Transport Ltd*, *Volkswagen Financial Services Limited*, *BAA Limited*, *GFKL Financial Services AG*, *CGI Group (Europe) Ltd*, *Christel Schriever*, *Everything Everywhere Ltd (formerly T-Mobile UK)*, *Insurancewide.com*, and *Purple Parking Ltd, Airparks Services Ltd*. Additionally, the *Finance Act* 2012 has finally seen the UK implement the VAT Directive exemption for cost sharing.

The opportunity has also been taken to introduce two new chapters on: (1) Mergers and Acquisitions (Chapter 11), and (2) Banking and Electronic Services (Chapter 12). The appendices have also been expanded to include updated materials published in connection with the progress of the EU's proposals on the exemption for finance and insurance.

The material problem which has to be dealt with in the application of VAT to financial services and insurance is the fact that financial sector businesses are still predominantly VAT-exempt and the prime concerns, as always, are with the recovery of input VAT and the avoidance of unnecessary VAT cost. How far one can legitimately go to mitigate the impact of VAT tends to be the major objective, particularly in the context of outsourcing. Cases like that of *Arthur Andersen & Co* in 2005, however, have done little to temper the feeling that the balance is somehow being tilted unfairly in favour of the collectors of tax and not just in the UK: as illustrated by the decision of the Court of Justice in cases such as *CGI Group (Europe) Ltd*, *AXA UK PLC* and *Nordea Pankki Suomi Oyi*.

Planning or tax mitigation is still not ruled out, of course (a point emphasised by the CoJ's rulings on the concept of abuse of rights: notably in *RBS Deutschland Holdings Gmbh and Weald Leasing Ltd*), but we now have very detailed and complex legislation, with specific anti-avoidance measures built-in and disclosure requirements if an avoidance scheme is involved. As Peter mentioned in the sixth edition, often though, the answer to getting the best result in terms of VAT is fairly simple. The key to getting the correct end-result is usually:

- to know, first of all, what a particular transaction actually involves; and then
- to fit that transaction within a generally fairly straightforward legal framework.

It is surprising how easy it is, sometimes, for simple misunderstandings to arise or for steps to either go too far, or, more likely, not far enough. What I have tried to do in inheriting Peter's

Preface to the Seventh Edition

mantle, as he did, is to provide some perspective and to give, not just a guide to the relevant provisions of UK and EU law, but to show how they relate to the different types of transactions commonly encountered.

Many difficulties arise because situations are not understood or are looked at globally, rather than by analysing the individual components involved, the contractual arrangements and the cash-flows. Strip away the jargon, know the rules and you are half-way there.

As with all editions, preparing this one has been a mammoth task. I am particularly indebted to David Southern of Temple Tax Chambers, who has taken on and updated Chapters 9 and 10, but has also contributed Chapter 11 on Mergers and Acquisitions.

I would like to thank my colleagues, Adam Singer, Caroline Brown and Karen Aswani, for their helpful comments on the manuscript.

Responsibility for any errors and ommissions is mine. While all reasonable care has been taken in the preparation of this edition, this book should not be relied upon as a substitute for legal or other professional advice which should be obtained before implementing any new transaction and business structure. Tax laws and practice can change rapidly and the application of tax law to any particular situation may not be straightforward. The authors would be happy to assist in these situations.

I hope, in the end – as Peter intended in previous editions – that we have been able to make it that much easier for those working in or advising the industries covered by this book to plan their affairs more effectively.

The authors would also like to acknowledge Peter's ongoing contribution to this book through its format of a blend of VAT laws and technical analysis, which was his original idea, and what has made it such a popular and respected work for the past 25 year since he wrote the first edition.

Julian Hickey, Head of International VAT Group, Bird & Bird LLP
London
November 2012

Contents

About the author	vii
Foreword	ix
Preface	xi
Abbreviations	xix

1 Introduction — 1
   Context of VAT — 1
   Scope of VAT: who and what are affected? — 7
   What is a supply and what is the nature of the supply? — 10
   The place of supply — 17
   The place of acquisition — 17
   Taxable persons — 17
   Business — 18
   How the tax is collected — 27
   Avoidance (see also 40–000) — 34

2 Registration — 37
   Introduction — 37
   The general rule — 37
   Voluntary registration — 39
   Exemption from registration — 40
   De-registration — 40
   Groups — 41
   Overseas traders and representative offices — 60

3 Outputs and Output VAT — 63
   Outputs and meaning of supply — 63
   Standard-rated supplies — 67
   Zero-rated supplies — 68
   Exempt supplies — 69
   Outside the scope — 70
   Fiscal neutrality — 72
   Place of supply and belonging — 73
   Imports, acquisitions and dispatches — 100
   Time of supply or taxpoint – the taxable event — 101

Contents

Time of acquisition and dispatch	107
Transfers of business	108
Consideration and value	118
Single or multiple supplies	130
Invoicing	142
Bad debt relief	146
4 Input VAT and Partial Exemption	**153**
The meaning of inputs and input VAT	153
Exclusions: blocked input VAT	180
Self-supplies	186
The right to recover	187
Recovering input tax – partial exemption	193
Recovering input tax – special situations	233
Accounting generally and records	241
5 Services from Abroad – The Reverse-Charge	**247**
The general concept for imported services	247
What is covered?	250
Points affecting particular supplies	253
Implementation	256
6 Groups and Connected Parties	**261**
Introduction	261
Central administration: cost-sharing	261
Employment	268
Consortia and joint ventures	269
VAT groups	272
Cost sharing arrangements	273
7 Banks and Financial Institutions	**279**
What is involved?	279
General VAT liability issues	280
Monetary financial services	281
Non-monetary services	294
Points affecting particular supplies	300
Banks	344
Credit and charge card companies	347

Contents

Finance houses	358
Equipment leasing and rental	361
Factoring	373
Outsourcing	375

8 Securities, Property and Investment — **397**

What is involved?	397
General VAT liability issues	398
Financial investments	398
Property	417
Points affecting particular supplies	440
Brokers and dealers	461
Investment managers	465
Investment and unit trusts	472
Funded pension schemes	473

9 Insurance — **481**

What is involved?	481
General VAT liability issues	481
Providing or arranging cover	483
Other insurance-related activities	501
Points affecting particular supplies and claims costs (other than points specific to Lloyd's – see also 90-300)	507
Insurance and reinsurance companies	523
Lloyd's	527
Insurance intermediaries (other than Lloyd's) and outsourcing	532

10 Commodity derivatives and financial Derivatives — **549**

What is involved?	549
The commodities, products and markets	553
The parties and the capacities in which they act	555
The contracts and their place of supply	556
Zero-rating and the Black Box	565
Other supplies involving deliverable hard and soft commodities	567
Financial futures and options and other intangibles	572
Electricity and gas trading	578
Emissions allowances and other environmental products	585
Points affecting particular supplies	587

11 Mergers and Acquisitions — 595

Mergers and acquisitions: general — 595
Economic activity — 597
Activities of holding companies — 599
Share purchases – acquisition of a business — 601
Share sales – disposal of a business — 602
Business combinations – impact of grouping — 603
Business continuity — 604
Share purchases – use of an SPV — 606
Direct and immediate link — 608
Share issues — 610
Abortive supplies — 611
TOGCs — 612
Supplies to third parties — 612
Maximising VAT recovery — 612

12 Electronic Banking, Finance, Insurance and Related Services — 615

Introduction — 615
Electronic banking and associated services: the e-commerce context — 615
Electronic services related to banking, finance and insurance — 616
Classification of exempt and standard rated supplies: electronic messaging and payment services — 618
Classification of exempt and standard rated supplies: internet based services of an intermediary/comparison web sites — 622
Electronically supplied services — 624

Appendix 1: Important HM Revenue & Customs Notices and Leaflets — 635

Appendix 2: VATA 1994, s. 43 — 637

Appendix 3: EU Proposals — 641

Appendix 4: VATA 1994, Sch. 4A &SI 2012/2787 — 687

Appendix 5: The EU Member States — 695

Appendix 6: VATA 1994, Sch. 9 — 697

Appendix 7: CTA 2010, s. 1122 — 699

Appendix 8: Value Added Tax Regulations 1995, Pt. XIV and XV — 701

Appendix 9: Customs Industry Agreements — 719

Appendix 10: Examples of Typical Banking and Financial Services — 737

Appendix 11: Extracts from the Financial Services and Markets Act 2000	741
Appendix 12: VATA 1994, Sch. 9, Grp. 5	769
Appendix 13: Liability of Money Brokers' Services	773
Appendix 14: VATA 1994, Sch. 9, Grp. 1	775
Appendix 15: Lloyd's VAT Arrangements	779
Appendix 16: VATA 1994, Sch. 9, Grp. 2	789
Appendix 17: Extracts from Notice 701/21 Gold (October 2011)	791
Appendix 18: Value Added Tax (Terminal Markets) Order 1973 (SI 1973/173)	795
Appendix 19: VATA 1994, Sch. 9, Grp. 15	797
Appendix 20: VAT: Guidance on the VAT treatment of certain Islamic products	799
Appendix 21: Flowchart for Specified Bodies	807
Appendix 22: VAT Finance Manual, para. VATFIN7650 – 'The Retail Distribution Review'	809
Appendix 23: Council Directive 2010/45/EU of 13 July 2010	813
Appendix 24: Revenue & Customs Brief 23/12 and VAT Information Sheet 07/12	821
Appendix 25: VATFIN7280 - Intermediaries: When is someone acting as an intermediary?: Flowchart-determining whether someone is acting as an intermediary	849
Appendix 26: VAT Finance Manual, para. VATFIN5260 – 'Actively Marketed'	851
Appendix 27: Council Regulation (EU) No 967/2012	853
Appendix 28: Subsection 3 & 4 of the EU Implementing Regulation	867
Appendix 29: Guidance on the Application of Para 8A of Schedule 6 of the VAT Act Valuing Reverse Charge Supplies Due Under Section 43(2A)	871
Appendix 30: Business Brief 30/12	877
Case Table	881
Legislation Finding List	891
Official Publications	899
Index	901

Abbreviations

The following abbreviations are commonly used throughout this publication.

AC	Law Reports, Appeal Cases, from 1891–(current)
A-G	Attorney-General
AIM	Alternative Investment Market
All ER	All England Law Reports, from 1936–(current)
All ER	Rep All England Law Reports Reprint, 1558–1935
App.	appendix
App Cas	Appeal Cases
art.	article(s)
ATC	Annotated Tax Cases
AVC	Additional Voluntary Contributions
BB	Customs and Excise Business Brief
BN	Budget Note
BTC	British Tax Cases (CCH), 1982–(current)
CA	Court of Appeal
CA 2006	Companies Act 2006
CCAB	Consultative Committee of Accountancy Bodies
CCH	CCH Editions Limited (or associated CCH companies)
C & E	Commrs Commissioners of Customs and Excise
CEMA 1979	Customs and Excise Management Act 1979
cf.	compare with
Ch	Law Reports, Chancery Division, from 1891–(current)
Ch.	Chapter(s) (of a statute/SI etc.)
ChD	Law Reports, Chancery Division, from 1875–1890
cl.	clause(s)
CoJ	Court of Justice (Europe)
col.	column(s)
Commr;	Commrs commissioner; commissioners
Conv.	convention
CS	Court of Session
CT	corporation tax
Dir.	EC directive(s)
DTI	Department of Trade and Industry
EC	European Community/Communities
ECJ	European Court of Justice
edn.	edition
EEC	European Economic Community
EEIG	European Economic Interest Grouping
e.g.	(exempli gratia) for example
ESC	extra-statutory concession
etc.	(et cetera) and so on
et seq.	(et sequens) and the following
EU	European Union
EU Implementing Regulation	EU Regulation 282/2011 (15 March 2011)
EWHC	Law Report for the High Court of England and Wales
FA	Finance Act
FTT	First-Tier Tax Tribunal

Abbreviations

GAAP	generally accepted accounting practice
Grp.	Group
HC	High Court
HL	House of Lords
HM	Her Majesty
HMIT	Her Majesty's Inspector of Taxes
HMRC	Her Majesty's Revenue and Customs
HMSO	Her Majesty's Stationery Office
ICAEW	Institute of Chartered Accountants in England and Wales
ICAS	Institute of Chartered Accountants of Scotland
ICTA 1988	Income and Corporation Taxes Act 1988
i.e.	that is (id est)
IR Commrs	Commissioners of Inland Revenue
IRDec.	Inland Revenue decision
IRInt.	Inland Revenue interpretation
IRRA	1890 Inland Revenue Regulation Act 1890
KB	Law Reports, King's Bench Division 1900–1952
LIFFE	London International Financial Futures and Options Exchange
LJ; L JJ	Lord Justice; Lord Justices
LR	Law Reports, from 1865–(current)
LT	Law Times Reports 1859–1947
Misc.	miscellaneous items (denoted by number)
MR	Master of the Rolls
NB	(nota bene) note well
O.	Order(s)
OJ	Official Journal of the European Communities
Ors	others
p.; pp.	page; pages
p.a.	per annum (each year)
para.	paragraph(s)
PC	Privy Council
PN	Customs and Excise Press Notice
PR	press release(s)
Pt.	Part(s)
PVD	Principal VAT Directive (Council Directive 2006/112)
QB	Law Reports, Queen's Bench Division 1891–1901; 1952–(current)
QBD	Law Reports, Queen's Bench Division 1875–1890; 1952–(current)
QC	Queen's Counsel
r.	rule(s)
R & C Commrs	Revenue and Customs Commissioners
reg.	regulations
RPI	retail prices index
RSC	Rules of the Supreme Court
s.	section(s)
SAO	Senior Accounting Officer
Sch.	Schedule(s)
SI	statutory instrument
Sixth Directive	Council Directive 77/388
SLR	Scottish Law Reporter 1865–1924
SLT	Scots Law Times, from 1893–current
SP	Inland Revenue statement of practice

SR & O	statutory Rules and Orders
STC	Simons Tax Cases, from 1973–(current)
subcl.	subclause(s)
subpara.	subparagraph(s)
subs.	subsection(s)
TFEU	Treaty of the Functioning of the European Union
TLR	Times Law Reports, 1884–(current)
UCITS	Undertakings for Collective Investment in Transferable Securities
UEL	Upper earnings limit
UK	United Kingdom
UTT	Upper Tier Tribunal
VAT	value added tax
VATA/VATA 1994	Value Added Tax Act 1994
VAT Directive	Directive 2006/112 (also referred to as the Principal VAT Directive)
VATTR	Value Added Tax Tribunal Reports
VCT	Venture Capital Trust
VC	Vice Chancellor
vol.	volume(s)
WDA	writing down allowance
WDV	written-down value
WLR	Weekly Law Reports, from 1953–(current)
WN	Law Reports, Weekly Notes 1866–1952
¶	CCH paragraph

1 Introduction

> **Overview**
>
> This Chapter considers:
>
> (1) The general scope of VAT, including;
>
>   (a) what constitutes a supply;
>   (b) the place of supply.
>
> (2) Taxable persons and what constitutes a business.
>
> (3) Compliance.
>
> (4) Planning and avoidance.

10-000 Context of VAT

The introduction of Value Added Tax on 1 April 1973 saw a major change to the UK tax system. VAT, being an indirect tax on consumption, affected everyone (or nearly everyone) carrying on business in the UK. Before then, its predecessor, Purchase Tax, affected only the few; it applied only to goods and then only at the wholesale stage. VAT, on the other hand, can be applied to everything; supplies of goods and services alike, so that the immediate impact was widespread. Of course, there were (and still are) exceptions. However, these are strictly limited and are not always easy to define. They are also the cause of many of the complications affecting the sectors covered by this book.

The application of VAT requires an understanding of the 'economic realities' of the circumstances of the supply or supplies (as the CoJ has recently commented in *Revenue and Customs Commissioners v Loyalty Management UK Ltd; Baxi Group Ltd v Revenue and Customs Commissioners* Joined Cases C-53/09 and C-55/09 [2011] BVC 1 (at para. 39), see further the discussion at 10-100). In this regard it is necessary to understand the nature of a supply chain for the purposes of properly applying the VAT rules.

VAT as a concept was not, of course, new. Having its origins in France, it forms one of the cornerstones of the Economic Union and is one of the bases for assessing contributions to the Community Budget. Its original enactment in the UK in the *Finance Act* 1972 (FA 1972) was essentially in preparation for the UK's entry into what was then the European Economic Community. The principles of the new tax were initially modelled on the Second VAT Directive (Directive 67/228). On 1 January 1978, this was updated as part of a continuing process of harmonisation on the introduction of the Sixth VAT Directive (Directive 77/388). Now, from 1 January 2007, this process has continued with the introduction, on 28 November 2006, of a revised (re-cast) EC VAT Directive (Directive 2006/112) to replace both the First and the Sixth EC VAT Directives. This new Directive is not, however, meant to change existing EC law, but to make it easier to access and to comprehend, although it was substantially revised to deal with the changes in place of supply rules (see **Chapter 3**). The EC VAT Directive is the subject of Council Implementing Regulation (No. 282/2011 of 15 March 2011) which has direct effect in each Member State of the EU, from 1 July 2011. The objective of the Regulation is to ensure the uniform application of the Directive in relation to its implementation on a range of matters, such as the place of supply of taxable transactions, taxable persons and the supplies of specific types of goods and services.

Article 113 of the *Treaty on the Functioning of the European Union* ('TFEU') imposes an obligation on the Council of the EU to adopt provisions for the harmonisation of turnover taxes (such as VAT) to ensure the establishment and the functioning of the single market within the EU. In particular, the Council is authorised, acting unanimously and after consulting with the EU Parliament, to issue directives for the approximation of laws on turnover taxes. Generally therefore, EU laws on VAT take the form of directives. The directives are then implemented into the domestic laws of a Member State.

VAT is a common tax imposed in all Member States of the EU. The countries which comprise the VAT territory of the EU are: Austria, Belgium, Bulgaria, Cyprus, Czech Republic, Denmark (excluding Busingen and the Isle of Heligoland), Greece, Hungary, the Republic of Ireland, Italy (except the communes of Livigno and Camione d'Italia and the Italian waters of Lake Lugano), Latvia, Lithuania, Luxembourg, Malta, the Netherlands, Poland, Portugal (including the Azores and Madeira), Romania, Slovakia, Slovenia, Spain (including the Balearic Islands but excluding Ceuta and Melilla), Sweden and the United Kingdom (including the Isle of Man). Some territories are not within the VAT territory of the EU, and accordingly supplies from these territories will be treated as being from third countries outside the EU. The territories are: Andorra, the Åland Islands (Finland), the Channel Islands (Jersey, Guernsey, Sark), the Canary Islands (Spain), the overseas departments of France (Guadeloupe, Martinique, Reunion and French Guiana), Mount Athos (Greece) and Gibraltar. To check on any alterations in the extent of the VAT territory see www.hmrc.gov.uk, and the *Value Added Tax Regulations* 1995, SI 1995/2518, reg. 136–139.

Many of the provisions in domestic law relating to VAT are derived from Directives. Accordingly, each Member State will implement the relevant provisions into their domestic laws, and may prepare their own national guides for the application of VAT rules. A list of the web addresses of the Member States tax authorities where national guidance may be available can be found at the following website: http://ec.europa.eu/taxation_customs/common/links/tax/index_en.htm. The present UK law on VAT is in the *Value Added Tax Act* 1994 (VATA 1994 or VATA) and its attendant Regulations and Treasury Orders. The *Value Added Tax Act* 1994 is, itself, a Consolidation Act, which had effect from 1 September 1994. The VAT Regulations were also consolidated from 20 October 1995 and are now found in the *Value Added Tax Regulations* 1995 (SI 1995/2518).

Current EU developments

In 2007, the Commission adopted a proposal for a Directive (COM/2007/747) on the future VAT treatment of financial and insurance services. Since their implementation, those provisions in the Sixth VAT Directive governing financial services and insurance have been considered by the courts but have not been revisited legislatively for over 30 years. The purpose of the proposed Directive is to achieve three objectives:

(1) to increase legal certainty for both businesses and national tax administrations within the EU;

(2) to ensure consistent application of the tax treatment of financial and insurance services in the EU; and

(3) to allow businesses to manage the impact of non-deductible VAT on their business activities.

A draft proposal for the new Directive (amending Council Directive 2006/112/EC as regards financial and insurance services) was published on 28 November 2007. This is set out in full in **Appendix 3** and commented on, where appropriate, in later Chapters. The proposed Directive was also supplemented by draft Regulations (see COM(2007) 746). The latest version of a new compromise text for the Directive (FISC 122, published on 30 September 2011, is also provided in Appendix 3). Details relating to the current position on the proposed Directive are available at the European Parliament website via the following link: www.europarl.europa.eu.

The Council of the European Union have been consulting on amendments to the proposals as regards insurance and financial services, and the current status of these discussions can be accessed on the European Council Register Consilium website (http://register.consilium.europa.eu). Appendix 3 also contains a compromise text proposed by the Council of the European Union on the VAT treatment of insurance and financial services, which reflects proposed amendments to the text published on 28 November 2007 (the text is sourced from Interinstitutional File 2007/0267 (CNS): LIMITE FISC 11 (1 February 2011)). The following EU documents are of interest: FISC 11 discloses proposals relating to the scope of the original concepts, and provides further clarification on key terms contained in the draft proposed amendments. LIMITE FISC 127 (Interinstitutional File 2007/0267 (CNS)) (7 October 2011) provides an update on progress in connection with the Draft Directive, and identifies four major outstanding issues of political importance, namely the treatment of: (1) transfer of insurance and reinsurance contract portfolios, (2) outsourcing, (3) management of investment funds and (4) derivatives. These issues are referred to in FISC 127, which is also reproduced in Appendix 3. Since there are no final draft proposals, this edition will not comment on the amendments due to the developing nature of the draft provisions. However, it is possible for the reader to track the progress of evolving discussions by referring to LIMITE FISC 100 (11 July 2011), LIMITE FISC 124 (30 September 2011), LIMITE 141 (14 November 2011) and additional papers as they are released onto the Council website. On 14 December 2011, the Council of the European Union published a Presidency progress report (FISC 170) noting that further work should continue on the proposals.

On 6 December 2011 the European Commission announced their approach to the future of VAT in a Communication (COM(2011) 851) which sets out the fundamental characteristics that must underlie the VAT system, and priority actions to create a simpler and more efficient VAT system in the EU. Details of the Communication can be obtained at: http://ec.europa.eu/taxation_customs/resources/documents/taxation/vat/key_documents/communications/com_2011_851_en.pdf.

1 Introduction

The main objectives expressed in the Communication are as follows (which will form the basis of priority areas for further work):

- To create a simpler more transparent VAT system for businesses: to be achieved, among other things, by expanding the one-stop shop (OSS) VAT registration for cross border transactions, standardising VAT declarations and providing access to the details of all national VAT regimes (via a central web-portal). A mini OSS for EU providers of telecommunications broadcasting and electronic services which are provided to final customers within the EU will enter into force in 2015. From this date the Commission envisages a managed broadening of the regime. The OSS currently applies to non-EU suppliers of electronic services, but is being extended to EU business suppliers of electronic services, broadcasting and telecommunication services. The OSS allows businesses to declare and pay VAT in the Member State where they are established instead of where their customer belongs. The nature of the OSS is considered in Chapter 12. The Commission also anticipate that it will propose in 2013 a standardised VAT declaration which should be available in all languages and optional for businesses throughout the EU.
- The Commission will review exemptions and reduced rates applied by Member States with a view to broadening the tax base so that Member States achieve sustainable economic growth.
- To ensure VAT fraud is stopped by developing a better way of responding to suspected fraud.
- VAT should be collected in the country of destination (i.e. where the customer is located), and the Commission will seek to develop a VAT system based on this principle.

Subsequently in May 2012, the European Council has adopted (PRESS 198, 9733/12) the following action points:

(a) a simpler VAT system: the Council takes note of the Commission's view that, in a VAT system based on taxation at destination, a One-Stop-Shop is a crucial instrument to facilitate access to the single market. The Council calls on the Commission to further clarify the legal status of the information, as well as content, form, roles and responsibilities in connection with the proposed EU VAT web portal and invites Member States to collaborate on the design of such a portal, which should not impose disproportionate administrative burdens on national authorities nor duplicate work;

(b) a more efficient VAT system: The Council takes note that the Commission favours a restricted use of reduced rates in order to increase the efficiency of the VAT system, and that it intends to launch in 2012 an assessment of the current VAT rates structure in the light of the various guiding principles set out in its Communication. The Council has committed itself to examine the findings of that assessment;

(c) a more robust and fraud-proof VAT system: The Council takes note of the intention of the Commission to come forward with a concrete proposal for a Quick Reaction Mechanism which, with a view to combating sudden fraud, will enable the adoption at national level of temporary measures derogating from the Directive, pending the outcome of the procedures for the adoption of appropriate measures at EU level;

(d) a VAT system tailored to the single market: The Council invites the Commission to proceed with in-depth technical work and a broadly based dialogue with Member States to examine in detail the different possible ways to implement the destination principle.

Context of VAT 10-000

In the text of this new edition, references are to the relevant passages in Directive 2006/112 ('the VAT Directive'), with cross-references to the earlier legislation where necessary or appropriate. On the 1 January 2010 the 'VAT Package' was introduced across the EU, which made a number of changes, the most important of which was a new general default rule that supplies of services between businesses are deemed to be where the recipient belongs (B2B supplies), and supplies made to non-business customers are deemed to be where the supplier belongs (B2C supplies). However, these are subject to certain exceptions. The nature of these rules are particularly considered in Chapter 3. In 2011 Council Implementing Regulation 282/2011/EU provided specific implementing measures for the VAT Directive (2006/112/EC) on the common system of value added tax (OJ L77/1, 15/03/2011, pp 1–22). Although directives are not generally 'directly applicable', Art. 397 of the VAT Directive allows the Council to adopt measures necessary to implement the VAT Directive. Such measures include the EU Implementing Regulation, which has been adopted to provide binding rules on the application of certain provisions of the VAT Directive and to give legal certainty to a number of non-binding guidelines previously agreed by the EU concerning VAT.

Interpretation of UK laws

If there is an inconsistency between the domestic laws of a Member State and any Directive, a UK court will give effect to the Directive (provided it has 'direct effect') in any dispute between a taxpayer and the national tax authorities. A directive is only of direct effect if in connection with its subject matter the terms of the directive are unconditional and sufficiently precise (*Becker v Finanzamt Munster-Innenstadt* (Case 8/81) [1982] ECR 53, at paras 17–25). There is an additional concept of 'indirect effect' by which a court is required to interpret the laws of a Member State as far as possible to be consistent with EU law (*Von Colson and Kamann v Land Nordrhein-Westfalen* (Case 14/83) [1984] ECR 1891). The nature of indirect effect is that through the interpretation of the courts the provisions of a directive may be given effect 'indirectly'. In this respect, the ECJ has held that a national court is obliged, to the extent possible, to interpret domestic legislation in the context of the wording and the purpose of an applicable directive in order to secure the result sought to be achieved by the directive (*Marleasing SA v La Comercial Internacional de Alimentacion SA* (Case C-106/89) [1990] ECR 1-4135, at para 8). In addition, where a treaty Article has direct effect, a UK court must seek to interpret any domestic legislation as if its provisions were without prejudice to the directly enforceable rights conferred by the treaty Article. The approach of a UK court in construing domestic legislation in conformity with a directive concerning VAT was considered in *R & C Commrs v IDT Card Services Ireland Ltd* [2006] BVC 244; ([2006] EWCA Civ 29). In this case the Court of Appeal made the following comments in relation to VATA 1994 and the Sixth Council Directive 77/388/EEC (now replaced by the VAT Directive – see below) (at para. 68 of the judgment):

> 'There are two different levels at which the court undertakes the task of interpretation in this case. The first level is that of the Sixth Directive, because, although that has no legal force as such in the United Kingdom, it is now well-established that the court must interpret domestic legislation in accordance with any applicable European directive. So the Court has to satisfy itself as to the meaning of that underlying legislation. The second level at which the court must undertake the task of interpretation is at the level of the VATA 1994. This of course is domestic law. The former task must be carried out in accordance with the principles laid down by the Court of Justice, which is the final arbiter on what Community legislation means. The latter task, however, is

conducted under the principles of domestic law but for the purpose not of interpreting the statute in the ordinary way but of fulfilling the requirement of European Union law that a national court should interpret a statute which implements a directive, so far as possible, in the light of the wording and purpose of that directive.'

Where VATA 1994 is not capable of being given a conforming interpretation in accordance with the VAT Directive then a taxpayer is entitled to rely on the provisions of VATA where the domestic legislation confers on the taxpayer greater rights than were intended to be available under the directive. A Member State cannot claim that its domestic laws fail properly to implement a directive as a justification in not conferring rights on a taxpayer, since to do so would mean that it is pleading its own failure to discharge its obligation to implement the Directive.

Exempt supplies

In the context of the banking, financial and insurance sectors, most of the supplies made (outputs) will be exempt from VAT rather than taxable. That is not to say, however, that these businesses will be *outside the scope* of VAT, they will not. Most will be liable to be registered; all will be charged tax (input VAT) on many of the costs they incur. Input VAT is, in principle, generally deductible but restricted when outputs are exempt. How much can be recouped in particular cases will often be as significant, if not more so, than accounting for output VAT.

What is taxable and what is exempt, largely follows principles now applied in the VAT Directive 2006/112. The significance of these two categories and of transactions or activities which are *outside the scope* of VAT is important. It determines not only whether output VAT has to be charged but also the extent to which input VAT can be recovered.

In addition, it is important to remember that VAT does not just apply to revenue matters. It also affects capital transactions, including investment, the raising of finance and the issue of shares and other securities.

Administration of VAT

The tax is administered in the UK by HM Revenue and Customs (HMRC) an agency created in April 2005, following the merger of the separate Inland Revenue and HM Customs and Excise Departments. HM Customs and Excise, rather than the Inland Revenue, have, historically, controlled and supervised VAT through local and regional VAT offices, a system which continues under the new arrangement. Disputes or complicated issues which cannot be settled locally will often, however, be referred to HMRC Headquarters. The normal procedure is for the taxpayer to be able to ask for HMRC's original decision to be reviewed by another HMRC officer who has not previously been involved in deciding the issue. Alternatively for any unresolved matters, recourse is by appeal to the Tax Chamber of the First Tier Tribunal and thereafter to the Upper Tribunal (Tax and Chancery) and then with the possibility of appeal to the higher courts. Increasingly, there is a tendency for fundamental disagreements on interpretation of European law to be referred to the Court of Justice (CoJ (formerly known as the European Court of Justice (ECJ)) and for this to be instigated at a lower level in the appeal process. Most decisions of HMRC are capable of being challenged by using the appeal process, e.g. on matters relating to registration (including refusal to allow a group registration), assessments, input tax repayments, application of VAT schemes, valuation, claims, penalties, etc.

For convenience, and, hopefully, to minimise the risk of confusion, all references to HM Customs & Excise, or Customs have, where possible, been changed in this edition to HM Revenue and Customs, HMRC.

Explanations and information on how the law is seen as operating are available in a number of booklets (Notices) and leaflets available free of charge on the HMRC website at *www.hmrc.gov. uk*. HMRC also issue press releases on important new developments and, until December 2006, published a series of regular *Business Briefs*. *Business Briefs* were originally published by the former HM Customs & Excise and dealt with changes in indirect tax policy. In the former Inland Revenue a similar publication *Tax Bulletin* covered direct tax matters. HMRC have taken the opportunity, from 1 January 2007, to combine the two publications into a single online only bulletin *Revenue & Customs Brief*, to appear in the library section of the HMRC website.

A list of the HMRC publications of particular interest to the banking, finance and insurance sectors is to be found at **Appendix 1**.

10-050 Scope of VAT: who and what are affected?

As noted earlier, VAT is essentially an indirect tax on consumption affecting all forms of supply. The initial, if not the main, impact, however, is largely on businesses, who have the responsibility for charging and collecting the tax, and for accounting for it to the authorities. The principle of VAT in the EU is stated in art. 1 of the VAT Directive:

> 'The principle of the common system of VAT entails the application to goods and services of a general tax on consumption exactly proportional to the price of the goods and services, however many transactions take place in the production and distribution process before the stage at which tax is charged. On each transaction, VAT, calculated on the price of the goods or services at the rate applicable to such goods or services, shall be chargeable after deduction of the amount of VAT borne directly by the various cost components. The common system of VAT shall be applied up to and including the retail trade stage.'

The effect of art. 1 is to emphasise that VAT is a tax applied to the price of goods and services supplied to the end consumer; but only after deduction of the amount of VAT which has been incurred directly in connection with the cost components of the goods and services supplied. The main principle of VAT is that it will be borne by the final consumer. This is why a supplier who incurs VAT on components used for the purposes of making a supply is generally entitled to deduct 'input tax' from the tax charged on supplies made by it, known as 'output tax' (but the ability to deduct input tax is dependent on a supplier making non-exempt supplies).

To determine how VAT is imposed on the supply of goods and services it is of fundamental importance to identify the economic reality of the supply chain, and in particular to identify the nature of the transactions made by a supplier. In *R & C Commrs v Loyalty Management UK Ltd & Anor* (C-53/09 and C-55/09) [2011] BVC 1 the CoJ emphasised that 'where a transaction comprises a bundle of features and acts, regard must be had to all the circumstances in which the transaction in question takes place in order to determine, firstly, if there were two or more distinct supplies or one single supply and, secondly, whether, in the latter case, that single supply is to be regarded as a supply of goods or services' (at para. 60 of the judgment). It is always important to clearly understand the factual position in order to determine the VAT treatment of supplies.

The charge is introduced in Directive 2006/112, art. 2(1) (art. 2 of the Sixth VAT Directive (Directive 77/388)) by subjecting to VAT:

'(a) the supply of goods for consideration within the territory of a Member State by a taxable person acting as such;
(b) the intra-Community acquisition of goods for consideration within the territory of a Member State by:
 (i) a taxable person acting as such ...
 (ii) in the case of new means of transport, a taxable person ...
(c) the supply of services for consideration within the territory of a Member State by a taxable person acting as such;
(d) the importation of goods.'

The corresponding provisions in UK law are found in s. 1 of VATA 1994. The charge arises in relation to:

- *supplies* of goods and services in the UK;
- *acquisitions* of goods in the UK received from other Member States; and
- *imports* of goods into the UK from outside the EU.

Thus, there are, to start with, three basic concepts: supplies, acquisitions and imports. Each has to be approached on a country-by-country basis; each Member State looks to tax transactions arising within its own boundaries. The concept of consideration is discussed at 30-500.

In this connection, for all practical purposes, the same rules apply to the Isle of Man as apply to the UK. Although the Isle of Man is not part of the EU, there is a common purse arrangement with the UK. This has the effect that, for VAT and customs duty purposes, it is treated as if it were part of the EU and, to an extent, as if it were part of the UK. The Isle of Man has, as a result, enacted VAT law corresponding to that in the UK, the two systems being treated in many respects as one (see *Value Added Tax (Isle of Man) Order* 1982, SI 1982/1067).

The same does not apply, however, to the Channel Islands, which remain outside the EU.

Supplies

The scope of VAT is set out in art. 2 of Directive 2006/112, which provides that:

'(1) The following transactions shall be subject to VAT:
(a) the supply of goods for consideration within the territory of a Member State by a taxable person acting as such;
(b) the intra-Community acquisition of goods for consideration within the territory of a Member State by:

(i) a taxable person acting as such, or a non-taxable legal person, where the vendor is a taxable person acting as such who is not eligible for the exemption for small enterprises provided for in Articles 282 to 292 and who is not covered by Articles 33 or 36;
(ii) in the case of new means of transport, a taxable person, or a non-taxable legal person, whose other acquisitions are not subject to VAT pursuant to Article 3(1), or any other non-taxable person;
(iii) in the case of products subject to excise duty, where the excise duty on the intra-Community acquisition is chargeable, pursuant to Directive 92/12/EEC, within the territory of the Member State, a taxable person, or a non-taxable legal person, whose other acquisitions are not subject to VAT pursuant to Article 3(1);
(c) the supply of services for consideration within the territory of a Member State by a taxable person acting as such;
(d) the importation of goods.'

For UK purposes, this is enacted in VATA 1994, s. 4. This causes VAT to be due (s. 4(1)) on:

'... any supply of goods or services made in the United Kingdom, where it is a taxable supply made by a taxable person in the course or furtherance of any business carried on by him.'

Specifically excluded is any supply made in the UK which is exempt (s. 4(2)). Thus, there are now four further points to consider:

- *taxable supplies*, which is where the main VAT charge arises (see 10-100 later);
- the *place of supply*, e.g. whether it is in the UK (see 10-150 later) and **Chapter 3**;
- *taxable persons* (see 10-250 later); and
- *business* (the carrying on of a business (referred to as an 'economic activity' in the VAT Directive 2006/112) is critical to the recovery of input VAT costs in the supply of goods or services: see 10-300.

Acquisitions

Acquisitions are a concept that arose as part of the Single Market changes from 1 January 1993. These are dealt with in art. 20–23 of the VAT Directive (and for UK purposes in VATA 1994, s. 10). The term denotes what were formerly *imports* of goods from other Member States, where there is the right to dispose of those goods as owner. It need not involve a supply. An acquisition may, for example, simply amount to the transfer of an asset from one branch to another. It will be chargeable, broadly, if it is taxable (i.e. not exempt), takes place in the UK, is not in pursuance of a taxable supply (in the UK) and is by a taxable person. Thus there is now a further concept: the place of acquisition (see 10-200 later).

There are special rules for goods subject to excise duty, distance selling (e.g. mail order) and new means of transport. However, these are not within the scope of this book.

Imports

Imports now only refer to goods received from outside the EU. These are covered by art. 2(1)(d) of the VAT Directive (and for UK purposes in VATA 1994, s. 1(4)), tax being charged and payable *as if it were a duty of customs.*

10-100 What is a supply and what is the nature of the supply?

VAT thus centres round the concept of *supplies*. Being widely drawn, the term includes all forms of supply goods and services. Article 14 of Directive 2006/112 provides, for example, that:

> '1. "Supply of goods" shall mean the transfer of the right to dispose of tangible property as owner.'

and art. 24:

> '1. "Supply of services" shall mean any transaction which does not constitute a supply of goods.'

In the UK, this is given effect by VATA 1994, s. 5(2), but, unless otherwise stated, it does not cover anything provided otherwise than for consideration (i.e. free).

A distinction is also drawn between goods or services, services being anything other than the supply of goods which is done for a consideration. The term *services* especially includes the grant, assignment or surrender of any right. This distinction between goods and services is important for various reasons, in particular:

- where a supply takes place (see 10-150 and **Chapter 3** at 30-250); and
- the time of supply (see **Chapter 3** at 30-350).

From basic principles, therefore, this definition of a supply will exclude any transaction occurring between separate parts of the same legal entity or person (e.g. between branch and head office). In reality there can, of course, be no actual supply; you cannot provide a service (or anything else, for that matter) to yourself. Equally, you cannot pay yourself anything, which means there can be nothing that could be construed as consideration.

> *Practice point*
>
> As a general principle, it should always be assumed, in the first instance, that anything received in a business context is *consideration* for something supplied. There will be exceptions, as will be seen later, with things like the issue of shares and the receipt of dividends. But usually, there will be a *quid pro quo* and deciding whether that exists, and what it represents, will be important.

- Interestingly, this issue has now come before the ECJ in the case of *Ministero dell'Economia e delle Finanze and Agenzia delle Entrate v FCE Bank plc* (Case C-210/04) ECR I-2803 [2009] BVC 692. This concerned *supplies* from a UK bank to its Italian branch and in dispute was whether the branch had to account for Italian VAT. It had, in fact, done so in accordance with Italian law, but, on a Reference to the ECJ, the Court was asked if transactions between two establishments of a single legal entity can be regarded as supplies for VAT purposes. In a Ruling in March 2006, the Court concluded that the branch of a non-resident company is not independent and therefore there is no legal relationship between them. They must be considered as one and the same taxable person within the meaning of art. 4(1) of the Sixth Directive (art. 9 of Directive 2006/112). FCE IT was, therefore, a part of FCE Bank. It followed that the Italian administrative practice of recognizing a supply in this situation was incompatible with the Sixth Directive.

Supplies between companies which are members of a VAT group are also generally to be disregarded (see **Chapter 2**). The concept of supplies is considered in more detail in **Chapter 3**.

> *Practice point*
>
> As will be seen in a number of passages in this book, the concept of a VAT group can play an important part in the planning or administrative strategies of many businesses in the finance and insurance sectors. It creates, for VAT purposes, a single taxable person and can achieve, for separate related corporate entities, the same end result as that in *FCE Bank*.
>
> In industries that tend to be largely VAT-exempt, with sometimes limited scope for recovering input tax, this can clearly be a considerable advantage.

It is important to identify the factual nature of the supply which is being made in order to determine the correct VAT treatment. In other words, it is of critical importance to identify the supply chain between the parties. The nature of what is being supplied can normally be determined by referring to the contract between the supplier and customer. Normally, the parties will have entered into a written contract which will determine all the rights and obligations that arise between them in relation to a supply of goods and/or services. However, it is possible that the nature of the rights and obligations between the parties will be determined by their conduct (i.e. by what is done and said) to the extent that the written contract does not cover all the supplies made between the parties. Additionally, it is possible for the terms of a contract to be disregarded where the parties by their actions fail to operate in accordance with the terms of the contract. In this situation, the rights and obligations of the parties will be determined by what actually happens, rather than by the contractual terms which are not applied.

The decision in *A1 Lofts Ltd (and related appeal)* [2010] UKFTT 581; [2011] TC 00831 illustrates the approach to be adopted in determining the nature of a supply for VAT purposes. In this case, A1 Lofts Ltd carried on a loft conversion business, and the issue was whether the company either supplied a complete package to a homeowner consisting of a finished loft conversion, or only project management services with the individual tradesmen (fitters, plumbers, electricians, etc.) making separate supplies to the homeowner. The tribunal held that A1 Lofts supplied the whole package. A1 Lofts appealed on the basis that it was only providing project management services. The judge summarised the correct approach to determining the nature of the rights and obligations between parties for the purposes of determining the nature of a supply for VAT purposes. The judge commented as follows (at para. 47 of the judgment):

> '(i) Where two or more persons (call them A and B) are involved in the supply of goods or services to an ultimate consumer (call him C) different contractual structures may entail different VAT consequences ...;
>
> (ii) Those consequences will follow whether C knows about the contractual arrangements between A and B or not ...;
>
> (iii) The starting point for determining the true relationship between A, B and C is an analysis of the contractual arrangements between them ...;
>
> (iv) Where the contractual arrangements are contained wholly in written agreements, this will be a question of construction of the agreements. But a contract may be partly written and partly

oral, in which case what the parties said and did may throw light on the extent of their contractual obligations ...;

(v) The apparent contractual arrangements will not represent the true relationship between A, B and C if the contractual arrangements are a sham; or if the parties have failed to operate the contractual arrangements; or if the evidence is wholly inconsistent with the apparent contract ...;

(vi) The identification of the true rights and obligations of the parties will be the same, whether the question arises in the context of VAT or in the context of an action for breach of contract; and is the same whether the question arises in a domestic or a European context ...;

(vii) Having identified the true rights and obligations of the parties, it will then be necessary to decide how those rights and obligations should be classified for the purposes of VAT ...;

(viii) Sometimes this will be concluded by the terms of the contract themselves; but it may not be ... If it is not then the classification of the parties' rights and obligations for the purposes of VAT may involve the application of particular deeming provisions of the VATA ...; or deciding whether the nature of the supply falls within a particular description ...; whether there is one contract or more than one ...; or in some cases deciding whether on the true construction of a single contract there is one supply or more than one ...;

(ix) Depending on the true relationship between A, B and C the conclusion might be that A makes a supply to B, who makes an overall supply to C; or A and B may make separate and concurrent supplies to C ...'

The High Court remitted the case for a rehearing to the tribunal. The High Court considered that at the original hearing the tribunal had adopted an unstructured approach to the question they were asked to decide. At the rehearing the tribunal upheld its previous decision that the taxpayer was not an agent for the self-employed tradesmen, and the taxpayer was accordingly liable to account for VAT on the full amounts charged to customers. The tribunal considered that several matters in the contract were inconsistent with agency, e.g. there was no evidence that quotes were obtained from different parties so as to provide the client with the best price. In an agency relationship an agent would normally agree the level of his commission and then go out and find the best price for the works from builders and other tradesmen. The taxpayer agreed the price for the whole works and undertook that the work could be done at that price regardless of the fact that no tradesman had yet agreed to do the job at that or at any price. The taxpayer was held to be supplying a complete service of loft conversion by reference to the following additional factors: there was no written contract between the client and the contractors; that the taxpayer undertook to remedy delay by the contractors, which pointed to the contractors supplying their services to the taxpayer; that the documentation signed by clients on completion stated that the works 'have been completed by A1 Lofts' and the fact that the taxpayer guaranteed the work, indicates that A1 Lofts undertook to supply a completed loft conversion.

Practice point

To determine the correct VAT treatment it is necessary to start with identifying the true factual nature of the supply (i.e. the economic realities). The correct approach is to: (a) construe the contract between supplier and customer; and then (b) ask whether in the light of the facts, does the written contract represent the true contract between the parties or is the contract a sham or is it otherwise superseded by some different contract. Once you have

> determined the legal rights and obligations of the different parties, only then are you in a position to classify the supplies for the purposes of VAT. It is always important to ensure that any form of supply is properly and comprehensively referred to in the contract in order to create certainty of VAT treatment.

The decision of the Upper Tier Tribunal in *Secret Hotels2 Ltd v R & C Commrs* [2011] BVC 1,700 provides additional guidance on how contracts should be construed for VAT purposes. The case concerned supplies of hotel accommodation through a website; and the issue arose as to whether the person operating the website was acting as agent of the hotel operators (whose accommodation was booked via the website). The Tribunal provided the following guidance ([2011] UKUT 308 at para. 88 to 90):

> 'When construing a written agreement, the court has regard to all of the provisions of the contract. The court construes the agreement against the relevant background. The material which is admissible in relation to that background is everything which a reasonable man would regard as relevant and which would have affected the way in which a reasonable man would have understood the language used in the document: *Investors Compensation Scheme Ltd v West Bromwich B.S.* [1998] 1 WLR 896 at 912–913. The relevant material is restricted to the material which would have been available to the parties. At the risk of stating the obvious, this last proposition means that the court cannot be influenced, when construing a written agreement, by material which would not have been available to the parties when they entered into that agreement. The court may also be assisted by considering the commercial purpose of the agreement. In some cases, the ordinary literal meaning of the language used will be in accordance with the apparent commercial purpose of the agreement. If the ordinary meaning of the language appears to convey a meaning which does not make reasonable commercial sense, then a court will look more critically at the wording to see if the ordinary meaning is really what the parties must be taken to have intended. In a case where the ordinary meaning of the language is in serious conflict with commercial sense, then the court may conclude that the language has not been well chosen and may choose a possible meaning (even though it would not be the most likely meaning of the language in other circumstances) which fits better with commercial sense. In some cases, the parties purport to state the legal effect of their agreement. They may, for example, state that the agreement is a licence in relation to land and not a tenancy. They may do this even where there is no question of the agreement being a sham. They may act in this way through a misunderstanding of what is involved in the legal concept to which they refer or for other reasons. Notwithstanding this, the court will examine the substance of the agreement to determine its legal effect: see, for example, *Street v Mountford* [1985] AC 809. This will often produce the result that the court finds the parties have correctly described the legal effect of the agreement but in other cases the court will determine that the description used by the parties is incorrect and is overridden by the substance of what they have otherwise agreed.'

As discussed in the context of the decision of *A1 Lofts* it is necessary to consider the nature of what has been agreed in the contract between the supplier and customer to identify the supply. However, the law allows consideration to be given to other factors in identifying the chain of a supply. In this regard, the recipient of a supply of a service is the person who instructs the supplier, and who is liable to pay for the service (*C & E Commrs v Redrow Group plc* [1996] BVC 96). But the CoJ has formulated an approach whereby the chain of supply is determined by the 'economic reality' of the arrangements, and not solely by the contractual arrangements. The approach here is likely to be to consider the nature of the overall arrangements, the identity of the parties who choose the supplier, nature of the supply, and who pays for the supply and/or incurs the commercial risk associated with the supply (*R & C Commrs v Loyalty Management Ltd* [2011] BVC 1). Although in *Secret Hotels2 Ltd v R & C Commrs* [2011] UKUT 308 at para. 112 Morgan J commented in relation to the *Loyalty Management Ltd* case that:

> 'There is, no doubt, scope for argument as to how ... [it is] ... to be interpreted and applied. But, whatever its meaning, I do not think that an approach which uses a contractual analysis to determine the identity of the supplier of hotel accommodation and which results in that supplier, rather than someone else, bearing the liability to account for VAT, in any way lacks economic reality. It is quite possible in a case like the present for the relevant parties to adopt different legal structures to produce similar (but not identical) economic results.'

The issue in *Revenue and Customs Commissioners v Loyalty Management UK Ltd* (Case C-53/09) related to the VAT classification of the consideration for payments made by the operator of a loyalty rewards scheme to the redeemers who supplied the loyalty rewards to customers, and by the trader to the operator (namely LMUK) of the loyalty rewards scheme supplying such rewards. In essence the case concerned input VAT deductibility on fees paid to redeemers under the scheme. The case is of interest since it illustrates the difference in approach in determining how VAT applies between an approach of identifying the economic reality, and one which looks to the contracts which are the links of a supply chain (as in *Secret Hotels2 Ltd*). The material facts in relation to *Loyalty Management* ('LMUK') were as follows:

- LMUK operated a customer loyalty rewards scheme, which enabled customers to earn points which they could redeem for loyalty rewards (in the form of goods or services). Points accrued to a customer when they purchased goods or services from retailers participating in the scheme.
- There were four participants in the scheme, namely (i) the sponsors (i.e. the retailers seeking to encourage customers to buy more from them), (ii) the customers, (iii) the operator of the scheme concerned (i.e. LMUK), and (iv) the redeemers (i.e. the companies which supplied loyalty rewards to customers in return for their points).
- Sponsors awarded points to customers for each purchase on the basis of the amount of money spent. A customer who accumulated a sufficient number of points, would receive a loyalty reward in return for those points, either for no payment or at a reduced price. The loyalty rewards were obtained by the redeemers.
- The sponsors paid to LMUK a specified sum of money in respect of each point issued, and also paid an annual fee for the marketing, development and promotion of the scheme in question.
- The redeemers received a fixed amount of money from LMUK for each point redeemed (the sum being described as a 'service charge'). The redeemers issued an invoice to LMUK in respect of the 'service charge' which was inclusive of VAT.
- LMUK sought to deduct the input VAT attributable to the 'service charge', but HMRC decided that the tax paid constituted a tax on a charge which represented a payment made as the consideration for transactions carried out by the redeemers, not for the benefit of LMUK, but for the benefit of the customers (although payment for those transactions was made, wholly or in part, by LMUK). HMRC considered that the charge was third-party consideration for the supply of loyalty rewards to customers and, consequently, that LMUK was not entitled to deduct the input tax paid on that charge.

What is a supply and what is the nature of the supply? 10-100

- LMUK appealed to the VAT and Duties Tribunal, who decided that the supplies of goods to customers made by the redeemers in return for points had to be considered to be supplies of services to LMUK (see [2005] V&DR 377).
- The High Court ([2006] EWHC 1498) reversed the decision of the Tribunal, deciding that the redeemers were supplying loyalty rewards to customers and that the charge concerned was consideration paid by a third party, namely LMUK, for that supply.
- The Court of Appeal ([2007] EWCA Civ 965) reversed the judgment of the High Court, deciding that LMUK paid the charge to the redeemers as consideration for the service supplied by them to LMUK. Accordingly, LMUK was entitled to deduct the VAT payable on that charge.
- The House of Lords then referred the matter to the COJ on the interpretation of the Sixth Directive. In the context of LMUK, the House of Lords asked the CoJ whether, with reference to a customer loyalty reward scheme, 'payments made by the operator of the scheme at issue to redeemers who supply loyalty rewards to customers must be considered as third-party consideration for a supply of goods to those customers, and/or, as the case may be, for a supply of services made by those redeemers for the benefit of those customers, and/or as the consideration for a supply of services made by those redeemers for the benefit of the operator of that scheme'.
- The CoJ emphasised that '*consideration of economic realities is a fundamental criterion for the application of the common system of VAT*' (para. 39 of the judgment, emphasis added).
- The Court turned to consider the nature of the transactions carried out within the context of the loyalty rewards schemes. In this regard, the Court made the following observations:
  - The loyalty rewards schemes were designed to encourage customers to make their purchases from particular traders. To that end LMUK provided a number of services linked to the operation of those schemes, but 'the economic reality is that, under those schemes, loyalty rewards, which may consist of both goods and ... services, are supplied by the redeemers to the customers.' (para. 42 of the judgment).
  - To determine whether the transaction, consisting of the supply of loyalty rewards, was subject to VAT, it was necessary to consider whether it was a supply of goods or services effected for consideration within the territory of the country by a taxable person.
- The relevant Direct provisions: Art. 5(1) of the Sixth Directive provided that a 'supply of goods' is to be understood as meaning the transfer of the right to dispose of tangible property as owner (and that this 'covers any transfer of tangible property by one party which empowers the other party actually to dispose of it as if the recipient were the owner of the property (see *Staatssecretaris van Financiën v Shipping and Forwarding Enterprise Safe BV* (Case C-320/88) [1990] ECR I-285, para 7, [1991] BVC 119, and *Auto Lease Holland* (para 32))' (para. 45 of the judgment). Art. 6(1) of the Sixth Directive defined 'supply of services' as any transaction which does not constitute a supply of goods.
- What was the nature of the transactions? Based on the order for reference the CoJ concluded that it was evident that (para. 47):
  - LMUK entered into contracts with the redeemers under which, when the redeemers supply loyalty rewards (e.g. goods) to customers in return for points, LMUK paid to those redeemers an agreed value for those points.

1 Introduction

- Under the contract entered into by LMUK with each redeemer, the possibility of the redeemers receiving any payment from LMUK was in fact conditional on the supply by the redeemers of loyalty rewards to the customers, rewards which could take the form not only of tangible goods but also of services. Only in this way could the redeemers obtain points which then gave rise to the making of payment by LMUK.
- The Court held that the redeemers supplied to the customers goods, within the meaning of art 5(1) of the Sixth Directive, and also supplied to them services, within the meaning of art 6(1) of the Directive.

• Were those transactions carried out for consideration? The CoJ made the following comments:

- The sale of goods and the supplies of services giving rise to the award of points to customers, on the one hand, and the supply of loyalty rewards in exchange for those points, on the other hand, are two separate transactions (para. 55).
- For a supply of goods or services to be effected 'for consideration', within the meaning of Art 2(1) of the Directive, the consideration for that supply is not required to be obtained directly from the person to whom those goods or services are supplied. Article 11A(1)(a) of the Directive provided that the consideration may be obtained from a third party. Accordingly, the exchange of points by the customers with the redeemers gave rise to the making of a payment by LMUK to those redeemers. The amount of that payment was the sum total of the charges, which were of a fixed amount for each point redeemed against all or part of the price of the loyalty reward. Therefore that payment corresponds to the consideration for the supply of the loyalty rewards (para. 57).

• The CoJ concluded that payments made by the operator of the scheme to redeemers who supplied loyalty rewards to customers must be regarded, as being the consideration, paid by a third party, for a supply of goods to those customers or, as the case may be, a supply of services to them. However, it was for the UK court to determine whether those payments also included the consideration for a supply of services corresponding to a separate service.

• The effect of the CoJ decision appears to be that the claimant was not entitled to input tax recovery in relation to the third party consideration.

The ramification of the CoJ decision in *LMUK* is that tax authorities of the Member States are likely to take a broad approach to analysing the nature of a supply chain for VAT purposes with a view to examining the 'economic realities'. The effect of the decision, in the circumstances of the case, is that the finding of the payment as being third party consideration prevents the payer (i.e. LMUK) deducting the cost as input VAT.

The decision in *LMUK* was also heard with another case *Baxi Group Ltd* (C 55/09). The principal distinguishing feature of this case was that a company acted simultaneously as the operator of the customer loyalty rewards scheme and as the redeemer. Baxi was the sponsor of the loyalty reward scheme. HMRC permitted Baxi some recovery of input VAT in respect of fees made to the operator of the scheme, on the basis that part of the payment was for operation of the scheme; but not allowing deduction for that part of the payment which represented reward items.

10-150 The place of supply

Where a supply takes place will, by and large, determine whether it is to be taken into account for VAT purposes. Following from Art. 2.1(a) of Directive 2006/112, tax cannot be chargeable in the UK, for example, unless a supply takes place in the UK (VATA 1994, s. 7(1)) (goods), s. 7A(1) (services)). Different rules apply, however, according to whether the supply is of goods or services.

- In the case of goods, the issue is essentially governed by their physical location.
- For services, the basic rule looks to the location, or rather establishment of a business, to which services are most directly provided where those supplies are made business to business (known as 'B2B' supplies). In terms of the VAT Directive, the businesses are taxable persons. In this situation the place of supply is where the recipient is located, unless there are overriding rules.
- The place of supply of services may, however, in some cases be varied by looking more to concepts like the location of the supplier where supplies are made to a non-business recipient (known as 'B2C' supplies) or the place of enjoyment (e.g. in the case of electronic and telecommunication services).

The place of supply for financial and banking services is where the customer belongs; provided the customer is either (a) outside the EU, or (b) receives the supply for the purposes of a business. In all other circumstances the place of supply of financial and banking services is where the supplier belongs. This issue is considered in more detail in **Chapter 3**.

10-200 The place of acquisition

Where goods are imported from another Member State by someone who is VAT registered, tax is accounted for on what is termed an acquisition. As with supplies, the place of acquisition (VATA 1994, s. 13) must be in the UK if tax is to be accounted for here. This is determined by the physical location of the goods and their destination on removal. This is considered in more detail in **Chapter 4**.

10-250 Taxable persons

The term 'taxable person' in terms of Directive 2006/112 (art. 9(1)) (art. 4(1) of Directive 77/388)) means:

> '......any person who, independently, carries out in any place any economic activity, whatever the purpose or results of that activity. Any activity of producers, traders or persons supplying services, including mining and agricultural activities and activities of the professions, shall be regarded as "economic activity". The exploitation of tangible or intangible property for the purposes of obtaining income therefrom on a continuing basis shall in particular be regarded as an economic activity.'

and is defined in UK law in VATA 1994, s. 3:

> 'A person is a taxable person ... while he is, or is required to be, registered under this Act.'

1 Introduction

i.e. where he makes taxable supplies and becomes registrable in accordance with the provisions in Sch. 1–3 of VATA (see later at **Chapter 2**). A taxable supply is, it will be remembered, any supply made in the UK other than an exempt supply.

Essentially, therefore, this means someone who is carrying on any activity which can be described as a business. However, it is important to appreciate that UK law must be construed in conformity with EU law, and accordingly anything which is an 'economic activity' will also be a business for the purposes of VAT in the UK.

The term 'taxable person' is also extended in VATA 1994, Sch. 2 to include persons, not otherwise liable to be registered under the Act, who make taxable acquisitions from other Member States above a given value. The level set is determined according to the Sixth VAT Directive. In the UK the figure is presently set at £77,000 (01/04/12) (Sch. 3, para. 1). It also includes (Sch. 2) persons engaged in distance selling (e.g. by mail-order) from another Member State, although this is unlikely to be of great interest, if at all, to businesses covered by this book.

10-300   Business

The *Value Added Tax Act* 1994, s. 94, defines business as including any trade, profession or vocation. As illustrated by the early VAT decision in *C & E Commrs v Morrison's Academy Boarding Houses Association* (1977) 1 BVC 108, this does not necessarily require the activity to be carried on at a profit. What it does call for is, according to the tests put forward by Gibson J in *C & E Commrs v Lord Fisher* (1981) 1 BVC 392, that:

(1)   The activity should be a 'serious undertaking earnestly pursued' or 'a serious occupation not necessarily confined to commercial or profit making undertakings'.

(2)   The activity should be an occupation or function actively pursued with reasonable or recognisable continuity.

(3)   The activity should have a measure of substance to the extent that such measure should be shown in VAT returns.

(4)   The activity should be conducted in a regular manner and on sound and recognised business principles.

(5)   The activity should be predominantly concerned with making taxable supplies for a consideration.

(6)   The taxable supplies made should be of a kind which, subject to differences of detail, are commonly made by those who seek to profit by them.

- In *C & E Commrs v Apple and Pear Development Council* (1984) 2 BVC 200,029, Woolf J also said that:

    'a business for the purposes of value added tax requires the carrying on of an occupation, function or activity which includes the making of some supplies recognised for value added tax purposes.'

which underlines, perhaps, that *taxable supplies* in the sense of the Lord Fisher tests are *economic activities* as in art. 9 of Directive 2006/112 (the Sixth VAT Directive (Directive 77/388), art. 4), rather than simply supplies subject to a positive rate of tax. This does not automatically mean, however, that everything done by someone who is in business is itself treated as a business activity, as illustrated by the observations of Fox LJ in the later Court of Appeal decision in the *Apple and Pear* case.

What this has meant in practice is that some activities or transactions, particularly in the financial sector, may not be recognised as *economic activities* in the VAT sense.

- The *National Society for the Prevention of Cruelty to Children* [1993] BVC 701 was a good illustration of this. It was essentially concerned with the recovery of input VAT. The critical point was the treatment of investments and whether they amounted to business activities. The conclusion of the Tribunal was that they were not. This was really because they fell within the range of things a charity would do in carrying out the everyday investment management necessary to support its charitable role. The realisations of investments and the obtaining of an income from investments by the Society did not, therefore, amount to 'supplies in the course or furtherance of a business'.
  In the Society's case, the day-to-day management of the investments was delegated to outside investment managers, although it did have its own investment group providing an overall supervisory function. The Tribunal's conclusions were largely coloured by the decision by the ECJ in the Polysar case.
- *Polysar Investments Netherlands BV v Inspecteur der Invoerrechten en Accijnzen, Arnhem* (Case C-60/90) [1993] BVC 88 was concerned with a holding company with no commercial activity other than the holding of shares in subsidiaries and which had, no doubt, been installed in the group for purely fiscal reasons. It had been taking place about the same time as the *National Society for the Prevention of Cruelty to Children* case and, in support of its conclusion, the Tribunal had cited an extract from the unofficial translation of the Court's judgment. The official version, in substance the same, reads:

  'Article 4 of the Sixth Council Directive 77/388 of 17 May 1977, on the harmonisation of the laws of the member states relating to turnover taxes – common system of VAT: uniform basis of assessment, must be interpreted as meaning that a holding company whose sole purpose is to acquire holdings in other undertakings, without involving itself directly or indirectly in the management of those undertakings, without prejudice to its rights as shareholder, does not have the status of a taxable person for the purposes of VAT and therefore has no right to deduct tax under art. 17 of the sixth directive. The fact that the holding company belongs to a world-wide group of undertakings, which appears outwardly under a single name, is not relevant to the company's classification as a taxable person for the purposes of VAT.'

It is interesting, though, to note the comments in para. 5 of the Opinion of the Advocate General (Mr W van Gerven) on which the Court's conclusion appeared to have been based:

'On the basis of the wording of art. 4 of the sixth VAT directive (art. 9 of Directive 2006/112) and the wide interpretation which the court has given of the term "taxable person", there can be no doubt, according to Polysar, of its status as a taxable person on the ground that it carries on business independently and exploits property (in particular its holdings in subsidiary companies) for the purpose of obtaining income (in particular dividends) therefrom on a continuing basis.

Polysar's contention is based on the premise that the mere investment of financial resources in itself constitutes an "economic activity" which, in my view, cannot be inferred from the case law of the court, in particular from the judgments in *Rompelman* and *Van Tiem*. Both judgments were concerned not only with an investment, that is to say the acquisition of property (in the former case, future title to an apartment, and in the latter, title to a building plot), but also with the property acquired subsequently being *made available* to a third party for consideration (in the former case by the letting of the apartment, and in the latter by the grant of building rights over the plot). The mere acquisition of a holding in a company does not entail making it available in that way. The dividends which may subsequently be payable to the shareholder are, in my view, not to be regarded as "income ... on a continuing basis" from the "exploitation" of property; they are merely benefits which the owner may receive from property and which are yielded by the mere holding thereof. If a different view were taken, any holder of shares or securities would have to be regarded as a taxable person.

The position would be different only where a company engages in share transactions which go beyond the activities of a normal investor in connection with the usual management of his assets, for instance where a company regularly buys and sells shares as profit-making transactions. In such a case, repeated transactions which involve buying and selling may be regarded as economic activities. That situation does not arise, however, in the case of a holding company such as Polysar, which forms a "link" in a group of companies and which has acquired shares in its subsidiaries with a view to retaining them.'

Thus, whilst the disposal of securities may well, in one sense, involve a supply, it remains necessary to show that the transaction is in the course or furtherance of a business (or, in Directive 2006/112 terms) represent an *economic activity* within art. 9(1). This should not be a difficulty in the case of established unit and investment trusts (see **Chapter 8**) or insurers (see **Chapter 9**).

- Interestingly, the same approach was later followed in *Wellcome Trust Ltd v C & E Commrs* (Case C-155/94) [1996] BVC 377. Here the Tribunal again found it hard to see the investment activities of a company acting as sole trustee of a charitable trust as an *economic activity*. The problem in this case was with the *predominant concern* test propounded by Gibson J in *Morrison's Academy* (as put forward by Gibson J in *Lord Fisher*). The emphasis was slightly different, though, to that in the NSPCC case in that the Trust was trying to recover part of the VAT incurred on the costs of realising what was, in effect, a substantial part of its endowment. The appeal resulted, in the end, in a Reference to the ECJ, whose judgment was delivered on 20 June 1996. The Opinion of the Advocate General, released in the early part of December 1995 was pretty clear:

  '"Economic activities" did not cover sales of shares and securities by a person who is not a dealer in shares and securities but is acting in the management of his own assets.'

  The Court, in due course, took much the same line. The concept of economic activities in art. 4(2) of the Sixth VAT Directive (Directive 77/388) (art. 9(1) of Directive 2006/112), was to be interpreted as not including an activity consisting in the purchase and sale of shares and other securities by a trustee in the course of the management of the assets of a charitable trust.

  It was clear that the Trust did not have the status of a professional dealer in securities in the UK. However, that did not necessarily mean the acquisition and sale of shares and other securities, could not, in some cases, be treated as an economic activity within the meaning of art. 4. According to ECJ case law (as in *Polysar*) this was to be taken to have a very wide meaning in terms of VAT. Nonetheless, it was also clear that the mere exercise of the right of ownership by its holder could not, in itself, be seen as such an economic activity. This was evident from the earlier rulings in relation to financial holdings acquired by holding companies in other undertakings, in particular in the judgments in *Polysar* and in *Sofitam v Ministre Chargé du Budget* ((Case C-333/91) [1993] ECR I-3513, para. 12).

It was true that, by virtue of art. 13(B)(d)5 of the Sixth VAT Directive (art. 135(1)(f) of Directive 2006/112), transactions in shares, interests in companies or associations, debentures and other securities may fall within the scope of VAT. This will be the case, in particular, where such transactions are effected as part of a commercial share-dealing activity or in order to secure a direct or indirect involvement in the management of the companies in which the holding has been acquired. However, as was clear from the Order for Reference, the Trust was forbidden to engage in precisely those activities, being required to make all reasonable efforts to avoid engaging in trade when exercising its powers and being precluded from taking majority holdings in other companies.

Consequently, irrespective of whether the activities were similar to those of an investment trust or a pension fund, the conclusion had to be that a trust such as that existing in the present case must be regarded as managing an investment portfolio in the same way as a private investor.

Neither the scale of a share sale, nor the employment, in connection with such a sale, of consultants could be a basis for distinguishing between the activities of a private investor, falling outside the scope of the Sixth VAT Directive (now Directive 2006/112), and those of an investor whose transactions constitute an economic activity. Furthermore, as the Advocate General had observed (in para. 27 of his Opinion), to treat the Trust's activities as an economic activity would place it at an advantage vis-à-vis other private investors. Also, whether or not the sale of shares and other securities was the predominant concern of the activity in the course of which the sales in question took place could not affect the classification of the investment activity for the purposes of art. 4.

Following the ruling by the ECJ, the matter eventually came back to the Tribunal ([1995] BVC 1,011), where the taxpayer tried to bring more evidence about the function of trustees, which it felt the Court had misunderstood. It also argued that as the trustees had involved themselves in the management of Wellcome Foundation Ltd from the outset, its activities should be an exception to the general rule. None of this was of any avail, however, as the Tribunal felt bound to follow the ruling of the Court.

- In a similar vein, the ECJ in *Harnas & Helm v Staatssecretaris van Financiën* (Case C-80/95) [1997] BVC 358 held that the same rule applied in the case of the acquisition and holding of Bonds. Any income resulted merely from ownership, rather than the exploitation of property.

- Likewise, in *Empresa de Desenvolvimento Mineiro SGPS SA (EDM) v Fazenda Pública* (Case C-77/01) [2006] BVC 140 the Court held that the mere sale of shares, or securities (or the receipt of interest on securities) may not, in itself, constitute an economic activity or supply for VAT and may thus be *outside the scope*.

The question, of course, is ultimately how far this principle will be taken. There was some suggestion in the Advocate General's Opinion in the *Wellcome Trust Ltd* case that the actions of the trustees of a pension fund might be distinguished, something that is of interest, perhaps, in the context of *Willis Pension Trustees Ltd* [2006] BVC 2,045 (see later at **Chapter 8**). Quite possibly, the link with the employer will be sufficient to impart the necessary *business* flavour. Investment by an insurance company should also not be an issue, given the extent that this is inextricably linked with the whole business of underwriting premiums and claims. There will remain, of course, a potential risk for companies which are pure holding companies in the *Polysar* sense, although in the UK, these tend to be very much a rarity.

- *Floridienne SA & Berginvest SA v Belgian State* (Case C-142/99) [2001] BVC 76 gives a further interesting angle on this business/non-business point. This was essentially a dispute over what companies can omit from the denominator of a standard partial exemption calculation. It concerned dividends and interest received by a holding company from its subsidiaries.

  Briefly, Floridienne is a holding company at the head of an essentially taxable chemicals group. Berginvest is an intermediate holding company in that Group heading up the plastics division. Both are directly or indirectly involved in the management of their respective subsidiaries, to which they make taxable supplies of administrative, accounting and IT services. They also provide inter-company loans on which interest is received and, from time-to-time, get dividends on their shares.

  Both companies habitually recovered input tax in full. However, the Belgian authorities took the view that both the dividends and interest represented exempt supplies and were to be taken into account in the standard pro-rata partial exemption calculation in art. 17 of the Sixth VAT Directive (Directive 77/388). When the matter was referred to the ECJ, however, the Court considered that the effect of art. 19(2) of the Sixth VAT Directive (dealing with the exclusion of the value of certain *incidental* supplies) was that:

  - dividends paid by a subsidiary to a holding company in this situation were to be excluded; and also that
  - interest paid by those subsidiaries to the holding company on loans made to them could likewise be excluded, where the loan transactions did not constitute an *economic activity*.

The ruling on dividends followed the line adopted in earlier cases like *Sofitam* and the ECJ said these were *outside the scope* of VAT as they were not consideration for any supply. The position with interest, however, is different. This *is* normally seen as an economic activity (and within the scope of VAT). Generally, HMRC do not see interest received by holding companies as *incidental*, but now it may, arguably, be possible to ignore such receipts if they are not income received as a result of supplies in the course of a business in the sense adopted in *Floridienne*.

- In *Trinity Mirror plc v C & E Commrs* [2001] BVC 167 the Court of Appeal held that the issue by a company of its own shares is a supply of services by that company and accordingly the input tax attributable to shares issued to EU residents was attributable to an exempt supply and thus irrecoverable. However, this has now been overturned by later Rulings of the ECJ, which indicated that the issue, as opposed to the sale, of shares is not a supply at all.

- In *KapHag Renditefonds v Finanzamt Charlottenburg* [2005] BVC 566 decided in June 2003, the issues concerned the concepts of *economic activity* and whether there was a supply of services for consideration when a partnership admitted a new partner in return for a contribution in cash. The finding of the Court was that the mere acquisition of financial holdings in other undertakings did not amount to the exploitation of property for the purpose of obtaining income therefrom on a continuing basis because any dividend yielded by that holding was merely the result of ownership of the property. It followed that the entry of a new partner into a partnership in consideration for a contribution in cash, in circumstances such as those of the main case, did not constitute an *economic activity* within the meaning of the Sixth Directive, on the part of the partner. If the taking of shares did not in itself constitute an economic activity within the meaning of the Sixth Directive, the same had to be true of activities consisting in the transfer of such shares. The admission of a new partner into a partnership did not therefore constitute a supply of services to him. In that context, it was irrelevant whether the admission of the new partner was regarded as the act of the partnership itself or as that of the other partners, since the admission of a new partner did not, in any event, constitute a supply of services for consideration for the purposes of the directive.

- *Kretztechnik AG v Finanzamt Linz* (Case C-465/03) [2006] BVC, decided in May 2005, involved a company increasing its capital by the issue of bearer shares. The dispute was over whether there was a right to deduct input tax under art. 17(1) and (2) of the Sixth VAT Directive (now art. 168 of Directive 2006/112) (see **Chapter 4**) in respect of the associated costs of advertising, agent's fees, and legal and technical advice. Adopting the same approach (as in *KapHag*), the Court concluded that a company that issued new shares was increasing its assets by acquiring additional capital, whilst granting the new shareholders a right of ownership of part of the capital thus increased.

- From the issuing company's point of view, the aim was to raise capital and not to provide services.
- As far as the shareholder was concerned, payment of the sums necessary for the increase of capital was not a payment of consideration but an investment or an employment of capital.

It followed that a share issue did not constitute a supply of goods or of services for consideration within the meaning of art. 2(1) of the Sixth Directive (art. 4(1) of Directive 77/388). That being the case, it followed that the costs of the supplies acquired in connection with the issue formed part of the company's overheads and had a direct and immediate link with the whole of its economic activities.

> **Practice point**
>
> Although this has not been decided on, it is likely that the same general principles would apply to other issues, such as those involving bonds, debentures and loan stock, as well as other financial instruments.

An interesting application of the *Lord Fisher* case is provided in *Cadbury Ireland Pension Trust Ltd v Revenue Commrs (Ireland)* ([2007] IEHC 179) which is a decision of the Irish High Court and relates to investment management services supplied from the UK. The taxpayer was the trustee of a pension fund and a company limited by guarantee not having a share capital. The principal object of the taxpayer was to act as trustee of any non-contributory or contributory pension or superannuation fund. The taxpayer outsourced the management of their investments to a company based in the UK. The Irish tax authority concluded that the taxpayer was liable for VAT in connection with services received by the taxpayer in the course of business which were subject to a reverse charge. The activities of the taxpayer, either directly or indirectly, comprised the purchase of investments, the sale of investments, the holding of investments, the receipt of contributions from approximately 500 members and from Cadbury, the receipt of income from the UK investment manager, the payment of benefits to approximately 900 pensioners, the payment of expenses, the carrying out of secretarial, administrative and accounting procedures to record, monitor and control these activities including payroll systems, bank records, accounts preparation, actuarial reports, tax returns, regular meetings with the UK investment adviser and the preparation of reports. The investment advisers activities involved the collection of pension contributions, collection of dividend income, the paying of benefits, the making of investments, the realisation of investments, the acquisition of properties, the provision of secretarial, recording and accountancy services, the furnishing of reports and the provision of advice. The High Court concluded that the investment management services received by the taxpayer were for the purposes of a business. The memorandum of association of the trustee provided that its affairs should at all times be conducted with a view to avoiding the acquisition of any profit or gain of any kind and, if any profit or gain should nonetheless be acquired, that it should be applied in reducing charges made by that appellant for its services. The Irish tax authority considered that the input tax attributable to the services was not reclaimable. The services were provided by the investment adviser to the taxpayer, and not to Cadbury. The High Court considered that the test in the *Lord Fisher* case was one which could be applied in Ireland in determining whether the supply of goods or services was 'in the course or furtherance of business', or whether services were received 'for the purposes of business' carried on by the recipient. It was immaterial that the appellants were not paid a fee and were precluded from making a profit. They were paid for the performance of their functions in the management and administration of the pension schemes; they didnot provide them gratis. The Irish High Court considered that it was immaterial that payment was achieved through the medium of the contribution of Cadbury, as certified by the actuary in accordance with the provisions of the trust deed, rather than by a payment by Cadbury to the taxpayer.

In *Skatteverket v AB SKF (Case C-29/08)* [2009] ECR I-10413; [2011] BVC 359 was the parent company of an industrial group, and it performed an active role in the management of its subsidiaries and made supplies to them for consideration (the services included management, administration and marketing policy). The services were subject to VAT, which was accounted for by SKF. SKF subsequently decided to restructure its group (which was to involve the disposal of the business of one of its wholly owned subsidiaries via a share sale; and the sale of a 26.5 per cent shareholding in another company, which was in the past wholly owned. The disposals were designed to obtain funds to finance other activities of the group. To further these disposals SKF proposed to acquire supplies of services relating to valuation of shares, assistance with negotiations and legal advice (all such supplies to be subject to VAT). SKF sought advance clearance from the tax authority that it would be able to recover the VAT costs, and the clearance was refused. The ECJ decided that where a parent company disposes of all the shares in a wholly owned subsidiary and of its remaining shareholding in a controlled company which was previously wholly owned by it, and where it has supplied to those companies services that are subject to VAT, that disposal is an economic activity coming within the scope of the VAT Directives. However, in so far as the disposal of shares is equivalent to the transfer of a totality of assets or part thereof of an undertaking (within art. 19(1) of the Directive), and where the Member State concerned has chosen to exercise the option provided for by those provisions, that transaction does not constitute an economic activity subject to VAT.

The CoJ has recently reaffirmed the principles in respect of economic activity and holding companies in *Portugal Telecom SGPS SA v Fazenda Pública* (C-496/11). The Court reiterated (at para. 32 to 34 of the judgment) the following material points:

- mere acquisition and mere holding of shares cannot be treated as an economic activity for the purposes of the VAT Directive;
- mere financial holding in other undertakings does not amount to the exploitation of property for the purpose of obtaining income therefrom on a continuing basis because any dividend yielded by that holding is merely the result of ownership of the property;
- if the holding in another company is accompanied by direct or indirect involvement in the management of the company in which the holding has been acquired, without prejudice to the rights held by the holding company as shareholder then such circumstances can constitute an economic activity;
- the type of activities which should constitute an economic activity are: the supply by a holding company to its subsidiaries of administrative, financial, commercial and technical services.

Subject to this, in practice most activities carried on by companies will be seen as economic activities and, in the case of an intending trader, this will apply where there is a clear and firm aim of making business supplies (see *Merseyside Cablevision Ltd* (1987) 3 BVC 596).

Avoidance (see also 10-400 and 40-000)

Nonetheless, the issue of whether something is carried out in the course of a business is something that has, in recent years, arisen in the context of VAT avoidance. In several cases, the Tribunal has taken a robust line, dismissing an appeal on the basis that what was being done was not undertaken in the course of a business. Whilst, in the event, these were decided on other grounds, in at least one case, this approach was not entirely ruled out.

- *Halifax plc v C & E Commrs* [2002] BVC 370 (see 10-000) was one case, which took most by surprise. Transactions were routed via subsidiary companies to achieve the recovery of input tax by a bank on the costs of constructing a number of new call centres. The Tribunal chairman took an unusually robust stance in dismissing the appeal by concluding that what was done by the subsidiaries was not undertaken in the course of a business. This case later went to the High Court on appeal, where the matter was remitted back to the Tribunal because the Court felt there was doubt as to whether the Tribunal had asked itself the right question.

    Ultimately, though, the matter went to the ECJ, *Halifax plc, Leeds Permanent Development Services Ltd, County Wide Property Investments Ltd v C & E Commrs* (Case C-255/02)

[2006] BVC 377, where the Court decided against Halifax but did not go as far as to endorse the non-business argument. Halifax lost because the Court preferred to see this as a case for applying the principle of *Abuse of Rights*.

The position taken by the Court was that the transactions concerned did constitute supplies of goods or services and an *economic activity* within the meaning of the Sixth Directive provided that they satisfied the objective criteria on which those concepts are based. And this was so, even if they were carried out with the sole aim of obtaining a tax advantage, without any other economic objective. However, the Directive must be interpreted as precluding any right of a taxable person to deduct input VAT where the transactions from which that right derives constitute an abusive practice – i.e. where:

- the transactions concerned, notwithstanding compliance with the conditions laid down by the relevant provisions of the Directive and of national law, result in the accrual of a tax advantage the grant of which would be contrary to the purpose of those provisions;
- it is also apparent from a number of objective factors that the essential aim of the transactions is to obtain a tax advantage.

Where an abusive practice has been found to exist, the Court said the transactions involved must be redefined so as to re-establish the situation that would otherwise have prevailed.

- *BUPA Hospitals Ltd and Goldsborough Developments Ltd v C & E Commrs* (Case C-419/02) [2006] BVC 377 concerned a different avoidance scheme involving substantial prepayments for drugs and prostheses. This also ended up before the ECJ, where the Court decided that the prepayments made (whereby lump sums were paid for goods referred to in general terms in a list which could be altered at any time by agreement) were *economic activities*. However, there had been no tax point/chargeable event, and no supply. What stopped the scheme, therefore, was the inherent uncertainty.

Although, the non-business argument did not prevail, this was not ruled out in *Halifax* and the Tribunal in the *BUPA* case gave a useful indication of what the objective criteria referred to were. Citing the *Rompelmann, Wellcome Trust* and *Breitsohl* cases, what it said was:

'Those cases illustrate a self-evident feature of business. Its character as such will be determined as much by objective characteristics such as its categorisation and its object clause as by subjective characteristics such as the particular motive or purpose of its decision makers. The same goes for the character of a particular transaction or activity of a person who is admittedly carrying on a business. Thus motive or purpose of a person effecting a transaction will be relevant to the question of whether that transaction is disqualified from ranking as an economic activity on the grounds that, on a proper analysis of the evidence, there was no motive or purpose other than the avoidance of tax. Thus when determining whether a person is carrying on an economic activity, his motive or purpose cannot be ignored.

So, bearing in mind that the person seeking to deduct input tax has the burden of showing that he is carrying on an economic activity, it will be incumbent on the Appellants to demonstrate that they are not excluded on the grounds that tax avoidance was the motive or purpose for which the transactions in question were effected.

If the transaction in question is carried out for avoidance of tax and, viewed alone or as part of a wider arrangement, has no demonstrable commercial or business purpose, those features will disqualify it from ranking as an economic activity or as a supply (as the case may be).'

And the conclusion in the *University of Huddersfield* case rested solely on whether these criteria were met, which they appear to have been.

- *R & C Commrs v Debenhams Retail plc* [2005] BVC 425 was lost by Debenhams before the Court of Appeal because the facts just simply did not stack-up. Debenhams, a retailer with a number of department stores, had put in place a scheme designed to change the terms on which the group accepted credit cards in order to reduce its liability to VAT. The idea was that the customer would enter into two contracts when making a purchase:

    - one with Debenhams for the goods or services at 97.5 per cent of the retail price; and
    - another with a subsidiary, DCHS, under which 2.5 per cent of the retail price became payable to that company for exempt card-handling services.

Notices to that effect were posted in Debenhams' stores and the customer signed a till-slip purporting to agree to the 2.5 per cent being paid to DCHS.

The Tribunal had dismissed Debenhams' appeal on a number of grounds, including the non-business argument. However, the Court of Appeal, where the matter rested, said that:

(1) The proper approach under Community law to the identification of any supply and consideration depended, save in exceptional cases, upon the objective character of the transaction. When the ordinary customer shopped in a retail store, he or she expected to pay the ticket price and, the general understanding of the public was that when a customer signed the voucher he had discharged his obligations to the supplier and that he paid for the goods or services he had obtained when he paid the card-issuing company. In this case the contractual position under domestic law was the starting and finishing point for the VAT analysis.

(2) There was nothing in the till slips, read against the background of the notification words, which showed sufficiently clearly that the customer was required to enter into some separate contract with DCHS. There was only one contract between Debenhams and the customer whereby at most the customer was required and agreed to pay 2.5 per cent of the total consideration to a third party, DCHS. The taxpayer was deemed to have made a taxable supply of goods for a consideration consisting of 100 per cent of the total paid.

(3) Even if there were a separate contract between the customer and DCHS, Debenhams should be regarded as stipulating for and obtaining consideration consisting both of the 97.5 per cent of the price paid to it directly and the 2.5 per cent paid at its insistence to DCHS.

On that analysis, the question of abuse did not arise. However, if, on the facts, DCHS were regarded as having contracted with the Debenhams' customers, it was clear there was no other economic justification for interposing DCHS, or for causing it to contract as it did, other than that of creating a tax advantage.

10-350 How the tax is collected

For businesses, VAT is, in principle, non-cumulative and largely self-assessed. As a tax aimed essentially at the ultimate consumer, it is collected at each of the intermediate stages of supply. Taxpayers account for any output VAT due on any *taxable supplies* or *outputs*; from 1 January

1 Introduction

1995, VAT is also accounted for on *taxable acquisitions* from other EU countries. The non-cumulative effect is then achieved by the deduction of any VAT (input VAT) paid by them on business purchases (inputs). Any excess of input VAT over output VAT is repaid.

As will be seen later, however, this process can be complicated, particularly in the banking, financial and insurance sectors. Many activities will be exempted, *outside the scope* or otherwise relieved of VAT. The result, especially with exemption, is to limit how much input VAT is recovered. This is explored more fully in **Chapters 3** and **4**.

If the business decides to be represented by a third party in relation to its tax affairs then appropriate authorisation must be given to HMRC, otherwise they will not respond to the representative's correspondence (see www.hmrc.gov.uk/agents).

(1) The VAT return

The collection process is essentially one of self-assessment, involving the regular submission of VAT returns by persons who are registered for VAT (see **Chapter 2**). Most persons have to submit their VAT Returns online and pay VAT electronically. The requirement to do so applies to all businesses (for all accounting periods starting on or after 1 April 2012), except for a very small number who are exempt. VAT return shows:

- the total output VAT due;
- the input VAT claimed; and
- the net balance due or repayable.

In addition to dealing with normal supplies, they also cover tax due on acquisitions and on certain services from abroad, where responsibility for accounting falls on the recipient by a form of reverse-charge (see **Chapter 5**).

As well as showing figures for input and output tax to give the net VAT due or repayable for the period, returns must also provide details of the total values of inputs and outputs in the period (net of VAT, and of goods acquired from, or despatched to, other Member States).

Returns must generally be completed for what are known as *prescribed accounting periods*, usually at quarterly intervals but in some cases monthly. The latter are primarily for repayment traders i.e. those whose recoverable input VAT typically exceeds output VAT due. For financial and insurance sector businesses, the periods for which quarterly returns are submitted are usually in practice calendar quarters i.e. ending on 31 March, 30 June, 30 September and 31 December. However, this is not an invariable rule and return periods may be staggered to avoid bunching, ending, for example, on 30 April or 31 May. Arrangements can also usually be made to allow VAT periods to coincide with those for financial accounts purposes.

As might be expected, there is a time-limit for submission. Returns submitted online must be completed and returned by the end of the month following the period to which they relate (*Value Added Tax Regulations* 1995 (SI 1995/2518), reg. 25). They must also be accompanied by a remittance for any tax due which must be paid electronically. A further seven days' grace is available for payment where, with HMRC's prior approval, this is by BACS Direct Credit or Bank Giro Credit Transfer.

There is an annual accounting scheme which allows eligible businesses to submit one VAT return each year, instead of the usual four. However, the scheme is open to businesses who expect to have taxable supplies of up to £1,350,000. Interim payments are made electronically, based on actual or estimated annual VAT liability.

For businesses with an annual net output VAT liability of £2m or more there is also a system of monthly payments on account where VAT returns are submitted quarterly (governed by the *Value Added Tax (Payments on Account) Order* 1993 (SI 1993/2001) (as amended by SI 1995/291, SI 1996/1196 and SI 1997/2542) and also by *Part VI of the Value Added Tax Regulations* 1995 (SI 1995/2518)). This arrangement was designed to overcome the Government's cash flow reversal on the change in the taxation of movements of goods between Member States from 1 January 1993. Because of the way it works, it can easily apply to some of the larger financial institutions.

(2) Statistical information

Businesses are also required to provide further information on intra-EU acquisitions and dispatches. These are partly for control purposes; partly to replace the wealth of statistical detail no longer available following the abolition of the single administrative document for intra-EU movements of goods. Two extra boxes are included on the VAT returns for acquisitions and dispatches. In addition, businesses must also supply *EU Sales Listings* (otherwise known as Aggregate Sales Listings), which must be submitted on a calendar quarter basis (the Listings show details of each customer in the EU and the value (in sterling) of the supplies made to them in the period), and Supplementary Statistical Declarations (SDs), which are due monthly. The latter, however, apply only where acquisitions and dispatches exceed certain thresholds (see generally HMRC Notice 60). The exemption thresholds currently (2011) for arrivals is £600,000, and for dispatches is £250,000. The threshold applies on a calendar year basis, and once exceeded the it is necessary to continue to submit SDs until the end of the calendar year.

(3) Sanctions

As might be expected with a system of self-assessment, failure to comply with the requirements, particularly on registration and returns, invites penalties. In practice these will not tend to be of as great concern within the banking, finance and insurance sectors. Many of the activities will be exempt, zero-rated or outside the scope rather than taxable at the standard rate so that little tax may be at risk.

(a) Late notification (FA 2008, s. 123)

In the case of late notification in connection with obligations to notify liability to register and notify material changes in the nature of supplies, there is a penalty set by reference to three categories. Details are provided in Sch. 41 to FA 2008. For further details see www.hmrc.gov.uk/vat/managing/problems/penalties.htm. Further guidance is available in HMRC's Compliance Checklist series (CC/FS11).

1 Introduction

(b) Regulatory offences (VATA 1994, s. 69)

Regulatory offences can attract daily penalties for matters such as failing to notify the end of a liability to be registered or to provide records or information. In this case, the penalties range from £5, £10 or £15 a day for non-monetary offences to one-sixth, one-third or one-half of one per cent per day in other cases.

(c) Late returns or payments (VATA 1994, s. 59 and 76)

Late returns or payments can give rise to default surcharge and default interest. The default surcharge arises under s. 59. It is currently set at fixed rates rising from two per cent to now 15 per cent for successive defaults after the third. Before it can be imposed, however, the defaulting business must have been issued with a Surcharge Liability Notice. Default interest (s. 76) is set at prescribed rates and can arise where VAT is underpaid or over-recovered and results in an assessment.

(d) Error in VAT return (FA 2007, s. 97)

In the case of errors in a taxpayer's VAT return there is a penalty set by reference to three categories. Details are provided in Sch. 24 to FA 2007. For more details see: www.hmrc.gov.uk/vat/managing/problems/penalties.htm.

(4) Power to assess

In the event that returns are not made or, if made, are incomplete or incorrect, VATA 1994, s. 73 allows HMRC to assess the amount of any VAT due (either output VAT under-declared or input tax over-deducted). This must be done *to the best of their judgment* and must be notified to the taxpayer. Any such assessment must also not be made after the later of:

- two years after the end of the prescribed accounting period; or
- one year after evidence of facts, sufficient in the opinion of the Commissioners to justify the making of the assessment, comes to their knowledge.

However, where further evidence comes to their knowledge after an assessment is made, a further assessment is permitted. All this is subject to further time limits in VATA 1994, s. 77. These have the effect that any assessment must be made not more than four years after the end of the prescribed accounting period concerned.

VATA 1994, s. 74 contains provision for interest to be charged on any VAT so recovered.

(5) Repayment supplement

The measures are not all one way, however. There is a repayment supplement (VATA 1994, s. 79) where refunds of VAT are unreasonably delayed. This is at a fixed rate of the greater of £50 or five per cent of the tax involved. It applies, broadly, where refunds are not made within 30 days of a return being submitted. This 30-day period is suspended by time taken by HMRC in making reasonable enquiries. However, as this includes internal enquiries within HMRC, the benefit of the 30-day measure may sometimes be relatively illusory.

Apart from this, VATA 1994, s. 78 allows interest to be claimed, where tax has been overpaid through official error.

Whether the interest must be calculated on a simple, compound or other basis has been the subject of extensive litigation (see *Littlewoods Retail Ltd and Others v Her Majesty's Commissioners for Revenue and Customs* (C-591/10). The CoJ in *Littlewoods* has confirmed that it is for national law to determine, in compliance with the EU principles of effectiveness and equivalence, whether the principal sum must bear 'simple interest', 'compound interest' or another type of interest.

(6) Recovery of tax overpaid

There is also provision (in VATA 1994, s. 80) for the recovery of VAT overpaid. This requires a quantified claim to be made by the taxpayer and is subject to the defence, on HMRC's part, that this would lead to the claimant being *unjustly enriched*. As with the rules on assessments, there is a four-year time limit on all claims for overpaid output tax. There is no mechanism for the courts to waive or extend the capping provision (see the First Tier Tax Tribunal decision in *GF Mercer Ltd* [2011] UKFTT 539; [2011] TC 01386). This time period also applies to input tax (*Value Added Tax Regulations* 1995 (SI 1995/2518), reg. 29). The effect is that a claim for deduction under VATA 1994, s. 25(2) shall not be allowed more than four years after the date by which the return for the prescribed accounting period in which the taxpayer was entitled to claim that input tax. As a matter of good practice, it is important to ensure that claims are made in good time. However, in relation to claims for input VAT attributable to services, there is a time limit of six months before the date from which the taxable person was or was required to be registered for VAT purposes (*Value Added Tax Regulations* 1995 (SI 1995/2518), reg. 111(2)(d)).

(7) Unjust enrichment

A further complication to the recovery of VAT incorrectly charged is the rule in VATA 1994, s. 80(3) on what is termed *unjust enrichment*. HMRC can use this as a defence to deny a refund, where they consider that tax has been incorrectly charged and where there are inadequate procedures in place to ensure the sums involved are passed on. This can effectively prevent repayment in many cases.

However, where reimbursement is permitted, the principles for reimbursement arrangements under which businesses can claim overpaid VAT from HMRC and then pass it back to their customers are set out in section 80A of VATA 1994 and Regulations 43A to 43G of VATA Regulations 1995.

- In *C & E Commrs v National Westminster Bank plc* [2003] BVC 633, for example the Bank had initially won before the Tribunal, but lost on appeal to the High Court, where their argument that they had been treated differently from their rivals was not sufficient to help win the day. Within the National Westminster VAT group were companies (the Lombard Group), whose activities included the purchase of cars for leasing to business customers. Manufacturers paid Lombard periodic manufacturers' bonuses, initially treated as consideration for taxable supplies of services. Subsequently, following the ECJ decision in *Elida Gibbs Ltd v C & E Commrs* (Case C-317/94) [1997] BVC 80), it was decided that the bonuses should be treated as discounts on the purchase price. This had the effect of reducing the amount of VAT subject to the input tax block (see later in **Chapter 4** at 40-050), which HMRC acknowledged in *Business Brief* 16/97. Affected businesses were invited to claim repayment of VAT wrongly accounted for, which National Westminster did, but was only paid in part, the balance being refused on the basis of unjust enrichment (VATA 1994, s. 80(3)).

The Court had started with no presumption of unjust enrichment, but found that, on the facts, Customs (HMRC) had established that it was more probable than not that the tax had been passed on and not borne by Lombard. The Tribunal's reasoning in holding otherwise was flawed and amounted to an error of law. Whilst there was ample material upon which the Tribunal could conclude National Westminster had been treated differently from its rivals, the Tribunal had no jurisdiction to decide on the question of unfair treatment and, in any event, a case of unfair treatment had not been made out. What the Tribunal had failed to do was consider that what it was ordering was payment of a sum which would enrich the taxpayer at the expense of the general body of taxpayers.

However, there are also cases where a taxpayer has been able to recover and retain tax overpaid.

- *National Provincial Building Society* [1996] BVC 2,783, where the issue concerned VAT wrongly charged on deeds production fees (i.e. fees charged to solicitors on the supply of title deeds).

The taxpayer, like all other building societies, took money deposits from the public and made loans on property secured by mortgages. Generally, the Society held the borrower's title deeds and, if a mortgagor wished to inspect those deeds, and/or copy them, he could (on payment of the Society's reasonable costs and expenses). These charges (called *deeds production fees*) were, in common with other building societies, accounted for on the basis that they were subject to VAT– until that is, HMRC, in early 1990, agreed tax was not due. Hitherto, none of the Society's borrowers had asked for tax invoices and, after the new ruling on the VAT liability, the level of fees charged remained the same.

When the Society asked for the tax it had accounted for to be given back, HMRC refused, but the Tribunal, on appeal decided for the Society on the basis that:

- claims under VATA 1994, s. 80 ought to be considered under that section and not under the general law of restitution in force in England and Wales or Scotland, each of which differs from the other;
- the burden of proving unjust enrichment lay on the Commissioners;
- there must be a real link between the tax and the price paid to establish that the VAT was passed on to the customer;
- in fixing its deeds production fees the appellant was concerned only to fix a price which would be acceptable to the market and the supposed impact of VAT merely reduced the amount which it would otherwise have received by the way of fees. In other words, the Society had suffered loss by being compelled, as it thought, to account for VAT on fees which it had fixed without reference to VAT;

- in the instant case the VAT element of the deed production fees was not *passed on* to the borrowers and the borrowers were not overcharged because the deed production fees were expressed as a single inclusive amount.

The Society stated that, if the appeal was successful, it did not propose to pay back the VAT accounted for in respect of the deeds production fees to the relevant borrowers. It considered it was justly entitled to retain the VAT and since the average sum to be returned was £1.05 per fee paid, and there had been 374,000 fees involved, the cost of inviting, receiving, verifying and satisfying claims would exceed the amount which would be repayable. The Society therefore proposed, if the appeal succeeded, to place the moneys received in its general reserves to be applied from time-to-time with the rest of its reserves for the benefit of its members.

(8) Senior accounting officer obligations

The senior accounting officer ('SAO') of a qualifying company is required to take reasonable steps to ensure that his or her company establishes and maintains appropriate tax accounting arrangements (see generally FA 2009 Sch 46, para. 1). This includes tax liabilities relating to VAT. For the purpose of these rules, a qualifying company is one which meets the conditions of para. 15(2) Sch 46 FA 2009 (namely the company satisfies either or both of the following: (i) relevant turnover is more than £200 million, and/or (ii) relevant balance sheet total is more than £2 billion). For these companies they must establish and maintain their tax accounting arrangements, and their SAO is responsible for ensuring that they do (HMRC's Senior Accounting Officer Guidance at SAOG01000). Particular points are:

- An SAO's main duty is to take reasonable steps to ensure that the company establishes and maintains appropriate tax accounting arrangements. As part of this duty, an SAO must monitor the arrangements and identify any respects in which the arrangements fall short of the requirement (Sch 46 FA 2009, para.1).
- Tax accounting arrangements are (Sch 46 FA 2009, para.14):
    - the framework of responsibilities, policies, appropriate people and procedures in place for managing the tax compliance risk, and
    - the systems and processes which put this framework into practice.
- Reasonable steps are the steps a person in this situation would normally be expected to take to (SAOG14410):
    - ensure awareness of all taxes and duties for which the company is liable,
    - ensure that risks to tax compliance are properly managed and
    - enable the various returns to be prepared with an appropriate degree of confidence. The steps that are reasonable will depend on the particular circumstances within which tax accounting is taking place.
- An SAO must provide a certificate to HMRC after the end of a financial year of a qualifying company (Sch 46 FA 2009, para.2). In the certificate an SAO must state that either:
    - the company had appropriate tax accounting arrangements throughout the financial year, or
    - the company did not have appropriate tax accounting arrangements throughout the financial year and give details about the respects in which the arrangements were not appropriate.

- Failure to comply can result in penalties being imposed (including on the SAO) (Sch 46 FA 2009, para.4, 5, 7, 9).

10-400 Avoidance (see also 40–000)

Given the spate of VAT avoidance cases of late, it is hardly surprising that something would be done to curb the tendency to what might be described as aggressive planning. For years, many have relied on the oft-quoted remarks of Lord Tomlin in the House of Lords in the *Duke of Westminster* case in 1935:

> 'Every man is entitled if he can to order his affairs so that the tax attaching under the appropriate Acts is less than it otherwise would be. If he succeeds in ordering them so as to secure this result, then, however unappreciative the Commissioners of Inland Revenue or his fellow tax-payers may be of his ingenuity, he cannot be compelled to pay an increased tax.'

and where he went on to say:

> 'This so-called doctrine of "the substance" seems to me to be nothing more than an attempt to make a man pay notwithstanding that he has so ordered his affairs that the amount of tax sought from him is not legally claimable.'

Or those of the Lord President (Clyde) in the Scottish Court of Session in *Ayrshire Pullman Motor Services* a few years earlier, in 1929:

> '... No man in this country is under the smallest obligation, moral or other, so to arrange his legal relations to his business or to his property as to enable the Inland Revenue to put the largest possible shovel into his stores.'

sentiments leading many to argue avoidance is perfectly legal. But times have changed. Whilst not embracing entirely the doctrine of substance over form, the Courts in this country are nudging closer all the time, where artificial avoidance is concerned.

The Government's (or rather HMRC's) position on avoidance was set out in a special report *Protecting indirect tax revenues* in the Pre-Budget Report in December 2004. It stated the following:

- every business has the right to plan its tax affairs efficiently so that they do not incur higher tax liabilities and compliance costs than they need to, or leave themselves at a competitive disadvantage compared to other businesses;
- however, it is not acceptable for businesses to use artificial schemes and devices for the purpose of reducing or delaying their liabilities, and thereby seek an unfair advantage over their competitors;
- it is therefore vital to tackle tax avoidance, not just because of the revenue at stake, but because businesses who pay the amount of tax they are liable to pay and make their fair contribution to the tax system should not be placed at a competitive disadvantage, or drawn into following suit, by those seeking to exploit the rules, abuse the tax system and avoid their liabilities.

Avoidance 10-400

As the Report pointed out, they had successfully tackled the most abusive and artificial schemes in recent years, challenging them through assessments and (if necessary) through the courts, and tightening loopholes in the law. They now proposed to allocate additional resources to this over the following three years. The Finance Bill 2004 also saw the announcement of new rules on disclosure, from 1 August 2004, of schemes designed to achieve a tax advantage. These are found in VATA 1994, s. 58A and Sch. 11A (as inserted by FA 2004, s. 19 and Sch. 2), the *VAT (Disclosure of Avoidance Schemes) Regulations* 2004 (SI 2004/1929) and the *VAT (Disclosure of Avoidance Schemes) (Designations) Order* 2004 (SI 2004/1933). There is commentary on the requirements in HMRC Notice 700/8 of February 2006 – Disclosure of VAT avoidance schemes. The meaning of *tax advantage* and *notifiable scheme* are defined in the law and the duty to notify and penalty provisions, are prescribed in: Sch. 11A. There are certain *listed schemes* and *hallmarks* described in the *VAT (Disclosure of Avoidance Schemes) (Designations) Order* and the time of notification, and information to be notified, is prescribed in the *VAT (Disclosure of Avoidance Schemes) Regulations*.

Practice point

Whilst planning is undoubtedly a legitimate and necessary pursuit for taxpayers, it can pay to remember that much of the best strategy is down to good house-keeping and knowing the rules; and having a detailed understanding of the nature of the supply chain for goods and services, and the participants involved in making the supplies. Artificial avoidance is, these days, seldom a good idea and it can be important to bear in mind that:

- it is better to do something in a way that can be commercially justified than to go all out to secure the maximum VAT advantage;
- there can always be potential direct tax implications to consider; and
- a short-term gain may be won at the price of long-term grief and a more difficult VAT regime for the company or group concerned – and generally.

Letting the tax tail wag the commercial dog can also be the surest way to invite a successful challenge. It is unlikely that HMRC will one day persuade the Courts that *Furniss (HMIT) v Dawson* [1984] AC 474; [1984] BTC 71 should apply to VAT. The decisions of the courts in the *Halifax* and *BUPA* cases are pointing in a different direction, namely at the concept of 'abuse of rights' (see 40-000).

As it happens many of the schemes objected to have been artificial and apt to fail on basic technical grounds anyway, as with *Thorn Materials Supply Ltd, Halifax, BUPA and Debenhams*; *Shamrock Leasing Ltd* only really succeeded by default.

1 Introduction

> **Summary**
>
> This Chapter has outlined the basics of VAT, from being a tax on consumption, to the mechanics of how it is operated in practice and collected.
>
> In concept, it is not a difficult tax; indeed, when it was first introduced into the UK, it was hailed as simple. It's not quite that, but as later Chapters will hopefully show, the key to getting the correct end result is usually:
>
> - to know, first of all, what a particular transaction actually involves; and then
> - to fit that transaction within a generally fairly straightforward framework.
>
> That may seem obvious, but in practice, many difficulties arise because situations are looked at globally, rather than by analysing the individual component transactions involved, the contractual arrangements and the cash-flows. Strip away the jargon, know the rules and you are half-way there.

2 Registration

> **Overview**
>
> This Chapter considers:
>
> (1) The general rules on registration, plus:
>
> (a) voluntary registration;
> (b) exemption from registration; and
> (c) deregistration.
>
> (2) VAT groups:
>
> (a) membership;
> (b) their advantages;
> (c) their use in planning;
> (d) transfers of businesses.
>
> (3) Overseas traders and representative offices.

20-000 Introduction

The liability to be registered, rather than actual registration, initially decides whether VAT is to be accounted for in the UK. Being registered, however, is what initiates the requirement for VAT returns and what makes it possible to recover input VAT.

It is this ability to recover input tax that tends to be important for those in the banking, financial and insurance sectors. In practice, most of the supplies (income or other outputs) in those sectors will be VAT-exempt, with the ready implication that any related or underlying input VAT will not be deductible so that this has a direct bearing on costs and profitability. How much input VAT can be recovered, though, is another matter, which is discussed later in **Chapter 4**. But the timing (i.e. when you register) is also important.

As has been seen (in **Chapter 1** at 10-250), a taxable person (VATA 1994, s. 3(1)) is someone who is *or is required to be* registered.

20-050 The general rule

(1) Registration

For most businesses, whether to register is fixed by VATA 1994, Sch. 1, para. 1. This simply requires someone in business, but not yet registered, to review the level of past and future taxable supplies. As now amended from 1 April 2012 by the *Value Added Tax (Increase of*

Registration Limits) Order 2012 (SI 2012/883), it provides that someone making taxable supplies, but who is not VAT-registered, now becomes liable to registration:

'(a) at the end of any month, if the value of his taxable supplies in the period of one year then ending has exceeded £77,000; or
(b) at any time, if there are reasonable grounds for believing that the value of his taxable supplies in the period of 30 days then beginning will exceed £77,000.'

These turnover figures, and those for de-registration, assume no tax is chargeable – i.e. they are VAT exclusive (Sch. 1, para. 16).

For businesses transferred as going concerns (para. 1(2) – see **Chapter 3** at 30-450), the transferee, if not already registered, becomes liable to be registered at the time of transfer if:

'(a) the value of his taxable supplies in the period of one year ending at the time of the transfer has exceeded £77,000; or
(b) there are reasonable grounds for believing that the value of his taxable supplies in the period of 30 days beginning at the time of the transfer will exceed £77,000.'

For this purpose, the effect of VATA 1994, s. 49(1)(a) is to treat as the transferee's taxable supplies those previously made by the transferor from the business acquired. The result, therefore, is usually that the transferee must register immediately.

Having said this, for test (a) in both of the above situations, registration may not be insisted on if HMRC are satisfied that taxable supplies in the next 12 months will not exceed £75,000 (see HMRC's Supplement to Notices 700/1 and 700/11 (April 2012)).

Even if registration is not, in the event, required, a business exceeding the monetary thresholds must still notify HMRC within a specified time-scale.

(2) Notification and when registration begins

All businesses exceeding the initial tests for registration must inform HMRC within a relatively short period of time. Failure will invoke penalties (FA 2008, Sch. 41, para. 1) and will not stop the clock running for the payment of tax.

- Where the monthly rule in para. 1(1)(a) applies (see 20-050(1) earlier), HMRC must be told within 30 days of the end of the relevant month. Registration is then normally from the end of the month following the relevant month, unless an earlier date is agreed (VATA 1994, Sch. 1, para. 5).
- Where an immediate liability arises under para. 1(1)(b), HMRC are to be told before the end of the 30-day period. Registration is then from the beginning of the 30 days.
- For businesses transferred as going concerns and where the transferee is not already VAT-registered, notification is to be made within 30 days of the transfer. If registration is needed, it takes effect from the transfer date (VATA 1994, Sch. 1, para. 7).

Where both para. 1(1)(a) and para. 1(1)(b) or para. 1(2) apply, the date of registration is decided by the second of the two rules above (VATA 1994, Sch. 1, para. 8).

Practice point

Over the last decade, there has been increasing emphasis on the part of HMRC towards combating MTIC (Missing Trader Intra-Community) VAT fraud.

Consequently, the process of actually being registered and obtaining a VAT number has tended to become longer than previously experienced due to the level of checks that now have to be made. This should not affect the actual date of registration. However, it does mean that taking steps to apply to be registered is something that should normally be done at an early stage.

(3) Non-established taxable persons

A non-UK established business (i.e. one which has no establishment in the UK) is subject to registration for VAT in the UK if the conditions of Sch. 1A to VATA 1994 are met. The Schedule is introduced by the *Finance Act* 2012, and has the effect that the VAT registration thresholds (as discussed above) are removed for non-UK established businesses (with effect from 1 December 2012). Under Sch. 1A, a non-UK establishment is subject to VAT registration where the following four conditions are met (see para. 1 of Sch. 1A to VATA 1994):

Condition A is that:

(a) the person makes taxable supplies, or
(b) there are reasonable grounds for believing that the person will make taxable supplies in the period of 30 days then beginning.

Condition B is that those supplies (or any of them) are or will be made in the course or furtherance of a business carried on by the person.

Condition C is that the person has no business establishment, or other fixed establishment, in the United Kingdom in relation to any business carried on by the person.

Condition D is that the person is not registered under VATA 1994.

The Schedule also contains provisions specifying the time scales for the notification and execution of various matters relating to registration, de-registration, cancellation of registration, and exemption from registration (e.g. where the person makes or intends to make zero-rated supplies). For further guidance see Revenue & Customs Brief 31/12.

20-100   Voluntary registration

Not all businesses must exceed the registration limits before they can register. They can do so voluntarily and often the ability to recover input VAT (**Chapter 4**) makes this an attractive proposition. This is particularly so in the early stages of a business, when substantial sums may be being spent on capital expenditure, such as computers and other equipment or on professional fees. Early registration, or even just registration itself, can then give cash flow advantages or even secure relief which might otherwise be lost. Possibilities for those not liable to be registered fall under two headings:

- for taxable businesses with turnover below the registration threshold; and
- for intending traders – i.e. new businesses not yet making taxable supplies but anticipating doing so.

In either case, registration (Sch. 1, para. 9) is at the option of the taxpayer. Subject to satisfying HMRC on the intention to make taxable supplies, it is, moreover, entirely unconditional. The present rules followed *Merseyside Cablevision Ltd* (1987) VATTR 134; (1987) 3 BVC 596. However, a registration will not be backdated more than four years.

VATA, Sch. 1, para. 10 also permits voluntary registration, inter alia, for representative offices – i.e. non-trading branches of business with trading establishments elsewhere (see 20-300(2) later).

20-150   Exemption from registration

In some cases, however, businesses liable to be registered may apply to opt out. VATA, Sch. 1, para. 14(1) allows HMRC to exempt from registration someone making taxable supplies if they are satisfied that any such supply is, or would be, zero-rated. In practice this has, at times, been interpreted by HMRC as meaning *all* taxable supplies. However, small levels of standard-rated supplies may be permissible, provided, generally, that the business would be in a net repayment position (HMRC Notice 700/1 (October 2012) para. 3.11).

The effect of exemption from registration is, of course, to prevent input VAT being recovered. However, some businesses will find this an acceptable alternative to the administrative costs of otherwise complying. Any exemption from registration under para. 14 is subject always to a requirement for notification. HMRC must be told of any material change in the nature of supplies made or in the proportion which fall to be zero-rated. Where the former applies, notification is to be made within 30 days of the date of the change (or, if there is no identifiable date, at the end of the calendar quarter in which it occurs); where it is the proportion which alters, notification must be by 30 days after the end of the quarter concerned.

20-200   De-registration

De-registration may be applied for (VATA 1994, Sch. 1, para. 13) where a business' taxable turnover falls, or is likely to fall, below £75,000 (£2,000 less than the annual registration limit). Again this is on a VAT-exclusive basis (para. 16). De-registration is only compulsory, however, if the Commissioners are satisfied that a person, who is registered, has ceased either to be liable or entitled to be registered. If taxable supplies or the intention to make taxable supplies cease, notification must be given to HMRC within 30 days (VATA 1994, s. 11 and 12).

20-250 Groups

Many VAT problems (and, indeed, planning opportunities) arise in the context of groups. This will be particularly so in the industries covered by this book. Intra-group transactions and shared administration, for example, can easily create an internally generated VAT cost or two or more supplies instead of just one. This is where the VAT grouping provisions become important.

Article 11 of Council Directive 2006/112/EC (previously art. 4(4) of the Sixth VAT Directive (Directive 77/388)) provides the basis for the UK rules and, in particular, that:

> 'After consulting the advisory committee on value added tax (hereafter, the "VAT Committee"), each Member State may regard as a single taxable person any persons established in the territory of that Member State who, while legally independent, are closely bound to one another by financial, economic and organizational links.
>
> A Member State exercising the option provided for in the first paragraph, may adopt any measures needed to prevent tax evasion or avoidance through the use of this provision.'

In UK terms, this is translated into what is now VATA 1994, s. 43. The text of this is reproduced in full at **Appendix 2**. The section achieves the intention of art. 11 (art. 4(4)) by means of a combined VAT registration. Its scope is limited, however, to groups of companies and does not extend to other forms of operation such as partnerships.

Practice point

Holding companies

Looked at, on their own, holding companies can often be non-registrable and thus unable to recover any underlying VAT. They may not make taxable supplies, but may simply exist to acquire and hold investments and/or to provide intra-group finance. Pure holding companies are especially at risk following the ECJ decision in *Polysar Investments Netherlands BV v Inspecteur der Invoerrechten en Accijnzen, Arnhem* (Case C-60/90) [1993] BVC 88. However:

- whilst the levels of holding company input VAT may not always be high, having a VAT group with trading subsidiaries often allows some, at least, to be attributable to the taxable activities in the rest of the group;
- the recovery of VAT on acquisition costs is easier to justify if the target company is included from the outset. It should then be possible to argue that any VAT can be attributed to its own future taxable supplies within the VAT group. But this does require forethought and generally needs to be applied for in advance; and
- making management charges to subsidiaries can create taxable supplies.

But it is clearly hard to argue, for example, that the tax on acquisition costs is really attributable to the charges made to the target. To that extent, therefore, this is generally a less satisfactory option.

> To an extent, some of the difficulties or concerns may be removed by what is said in HMRC [News Release 59/93 of 10 September 1993]. However, this is not the most clear of statements and, ultimately, how much input VAT will be recovered will depend on the overall partial exemption position (see **Chapter 4**).

(1) Eligibility and Membership

Although art. 11 of Council Directive 2006/112/EC authorises joint treatment for any persons who '...while legally independent, are closely bound to one another by financial, economic and organisational links,' VATA 1994, s. 43, as presently drafted, applies only to companies, or bodies corporate.

The present rules on eligibility and membership are now to be found in VATA 1994, s. 43A–43D. For two or more companies to be eligible to be treated as members of a group (VATA 1994, s. 43A(1)), each must now be *established* or have a *fixed establishment* here and must also be under common control – i.e. where:

- one of them controls the other(s); or
- one person (whether a body corporate or an individual) controls all of them; or
- two or more individuals carrying on a business in partnership control all of them.

Control in the sense used in VATA 1994, s. 43 (s. 43A(2)) looks principally to the *Companies Act* 2006 criteria for holding companies. However, this test (the *Companies Act* 2006, s. 1159) is applied for this purpose equally to control by individuals and individuals in partnership as it applies to companies. One company can also be controlled by another as the result of the exercise of a power conferred by statute.

This can, therefore, include companies from outside the UK, but (s. 43A(1)) only so long as they are established or have a fixed establishment in the UK.

Applying the *Companies Act* 2006 test, a company will now be a holding company of a subsidiary (and exercise control) if it:

- holds a majority of the voting rights in it;
- is a member of it and has the right to appoint or remove a majority of its board of directors;
- is a member of it and controls alone, pursuant to an agreement with other shareholders or members, a majority of the voting rights in it; or
- the subsidiary is itself a subsidiary of a company which is a subsidiary of the holding company.

Under the *Companies Act* 2006, s. 1159– meaning of 'subsidiary' etc., reads:

> '(1) A company is a "subsidiary" of another company, its "holding company", if that other company–
>
>   (a) holds a majority of the voting rights in it, or
>   (b) is a member of it and has the right to appoint or remove a majority of its board of directors, or

(c) is a member of it and controls alone, pursuant to an agreement with other members, a majority of the voting rights in it, or if it is a subsidiary of a company that is itself a subsidiary of that other company.

(2) A company is a "wholly-owned subsidiary" of another company if it has no members except that other and that other's wholly-owned subsidiaries or persons acting on behalf of that other or its wholly-owned subsidiaries.'

Control can thus be direct or indirect. There is also no requirement that the person with control must also either be UK resident or have an established place of business in the UK. To that extent, the composition of a VAT group is considerably more flexible than group treatment for direct tax purposes in for example, CTA 2010, Part 5, Chapter 5 (Group Relief).

There are further eligibility conditions (see (b) below) applying to *specified bodies* and which affect VAT groups with turnover over £10m per year.

> **Practice point**
>
> VAT groups are often the most useful means of avoiding or minimising VAT costs for associated companies. They will often, for example:
>
> (1) help avoid the internally generated VAT cost on, say, staff secondment or administration, something that is even possible where the VAT group as a whole is fully exempt; and
>
> (2) help in the recovery of residual input VAT (see **Chapter 4** at 40-200) by;
>
> > (a) bringing a much wider range of taxable activities into what is then a single registered unit; and
> >
> > (b) offering a greater chance of disregarding potentially distortive transactions as *incidental* in a residual input tax calculation (see **Chapter 4**) (e.g. the sale of centrally-owned group premises or subsidiary companies).
>
> If the criteria are met, it is generally sensible to assume that an application for grouping should be made. The question should always be, *if not, why not?*

(a) Established and having a fixed establishment

The current test in s. 43A(1) requires a company to be either *established* in the UK or have a *fixed establishment* in the UK. What this means, according to Section 6.4 of the September 2011 edition of HMRC Notice 700/2 on group treatment, is that:

'*Established*

A company is "established" in the UK if it has its principal place of business or registered office in the UK, which means if:

- the central management and control of the company are carried on in the UK; or
- its headquarters or head office are in the UK.

A company will, generally speaking, be "established" in only one country.

2 Registration

Fixed establishment

A company has a "fixed establishment" in the UK for VAT grouping purposes if it has a real and permanent trading presence in the UK, for example, if:

- it has a permanent place of business which comprises the necessary human and technical resources to carry on its business activities; or
- it has a branch or office in the UK, which comprises its own staff and equipment.

For the purposes of VAT grouping, a company does not have a "fixed establishment" in the UK purely by virtue of the fact that:

- it is incorporated and has its registered office in the UK;
- it has a simple brass plate presence in the UK;
- it has a UK based agent.'

> ### Practice point
>
> Overall, this idea of a *fixed establishment* is likely, in practice, to follow reasonably closely the permanent establishment concept for direct tax, something with which many practitioners should be familiar.
>
> The consequences in terms of actual liability to tax are not necessarily the same, however:
>
> - direct tax liabilities depend, broadly, on the activities giving rise to profits or gains arising at or through the permanent establishment;
> - for VAT, liabilities turn on the more artificial rules on the place of supply described later in **Chapter 3**.
>
> Nonetheless, the significance of this concept should not be overlooked.

Although this extract from Notice 700/2 seems to exclude agency, it is interesting to compare this with what emerged in the *DFDS* case, an appeal on the meaning of fixed establishment in art. 9(1) of the Sixth VAT Directive (Directive 77/388).

- This case, *C & E Commrs v DFDS A/S* (C-260/95) [1997] BVC 279 ended up being referred to the ECJ. The ruling, which went in favour of HMRC, was given in February 1995 and concerned a company trading through the agency of an affiliate in the UK. The taxpayer, *DFDS*, was a Danish tour operator selling package tours through a UK subsidiary. The latter had, since 1989, acted as agent for its Danish parent and HMRC sought to tax DFDS under the Tour Operators Margin Scheme. In this connection, art. 5 of the *Value Added Tax (Tour Operators) Order* 1987 (SI 1987/1806) modifies the normal place of supply rules in VATA 1994, art. 5(2) providing that:

  > 'A designated travel service shall be treated as supplied in the Member State in which the tour operator *has established his business* or, if the supply was made from a *fixed establishment*, in the Member State in which the fixed establishment is situated. [emphasis added]'

  The same phrasing is found in the corresponding provisions of art. 307 of Council Directive 2006/112/EC (art. 26(2) of the Sixth VAT Directive (Directive 77/388)), and also in art. 43 of the Directive (art. 9(1)), dealing with the basic rules for the place of supply of services.

Before the Tribunal, DFDS had won, the decision being given that the place of supply was intended to be the place where the supplier had a readily visible presence. The Tribunal went on to say that the expression 'established [its] business' referred to a centre, headquarters or main seat of economic activity, although it was not essential that the services were actually supplied from there. It also concluded that a 'fixed establishment' had to be that of the person supplying the services. In other words, it could not be achieved by looking at an establishment of a third-party. However, on appeal by HMRC, the High Court was less sure and the reference to the ECJ produced the ruling that:

> '…art 26(2) of the 6th Directive is to be interpreted as meaning that, where a tour operator established in one Member State provides services to travellers through the intermediary of a company operating as an agent in another Member State, VAT is payable on those services in the latter state if that company, which acts as a mere auxiliary organ of the tour operator, has the human and technical resources characteristic of a fixed establishment.'

Potentially, the decision in DFDS could be relevant to situations where, say, within an international group, a UK company were to provide an active dealing desk for an overseas affiliate to enable trading to take place after hours. This is fairly common in the financial sector with banks and broking firms and, where the UK company has power to bind the overseas affiliate contractually, the affiliate might be held to belong in the UK by reason of a dependent agency, with a possible knock-on effect for the treatment of any brokerage or fees.

(b) The rules on 'specified bodies'

From 1 August 2004, there are two further tests to be met by companies or bodies corporate known as *specified bodies*. These are designed as an anti-avoidance measure to prevent partly exempt purchasers of services setting up joint ventures within their VAT group, whereby third-party suppliers can effectively profit from the provision of taxable services to the group VAT-free. The statutory provisions are found in the *VAT (Groups: eligibility) Order 2004* (SI 2004/1931) and are covered in Section 3 of HMRC Notice 700/2 (September 2011). A flowchart explaining how these provisions are to be applied is found in paragraph 3.7 of Notice 700/2 and is reproduced at **Appendix 21**.

Briefly, where a company or body corporate is a *specified body* it may only be a member of a VAT group if:

(1) it meets the benefit test (para. 5 of the *VAT (Groups: Eligibility) Order*) – i.e. that no more than 50 per cent of the benefits generated by the business activity accrue to third parties; and

(2) the group accounts consolidation condition (art. 6 of the *VAT (Groups: Eligibility) Order*) is satisfied, namely that:

  (a) under generally accepted accounting practice (GAAP), a person controlling the VAT group consolidates the specified body as a subsidiary in his consolidated group accounts; and

  (b) there is no third-party, who, under GAAP consolidates the specified body as a subsidiary in his consolidated group accounts.

If more than one person controls the VAT group (eg there is a series of holding companies), then the first requirement need only be met by one of them.

A *specified body* exists, in this context, if all the following apply:

(1) the VAT group turnover exceeded £10m in the last year or is expected to exceed £10m in the coming year;

(2) the body corporate concerned is partly owned by a third party, or the business activity is managed by a third party, or the body corporate is the sole general partner of a limited partnership; and

(3) the body is not specifically excepted from being a *specified body* – i.e.:
   (a) it controls all the other VAT group members;
   (b) its activities are ones that another body corporate is empowered by statute to control;
   (c) its only activity is acting as a pension fund trustee; and
   (d) it is a charity.

(c) Fully exempt groups

A frequent misconception is that grouping under VATA 1994, s. 43 is confined to companies making taxable supplies. However registration is simply a procedural mechanism for recognising a VAT group exists. The importance of s. 43 is that it simply enables companies to be treated as members of a group, with all that that entails. Subject to issues like protection of the revenue, which is discussed later, there is nothing that restricts or prevents membership by reason of the type or liability of supplies a company may make.

Knowing this can be useful for some groups providing totally exempt services within the UK – insurance, consumer credit or finance, for example. When administration or accounting is organised centrally, perhaps using a service company, inter-group charges tend to be taxable at the standard-rate. The result can then be an internally generated VAT cost, which can avoid unnecessary VAT expense. Being registered, the companies will be expected to complete the usual quarterly returns, but these are simply filled in on a *nil* basis.

(d) Membership of more than one VAT group

In theory, it is clearly possible to envisage situations where a company might satisfy criteria for membership of more than one VAT group. To prevent opportunities for mitigating the effect of VAT beyond that envisaged by what is, after all, a facilitation measure, VATA 1994, s. 43D provides that a body corporate may not be treated as a member of more than one group at a time.

(e) Limitation

HMRC do, nonetheless, have some say in the composition of a VAT group. Until 1995 their powers were somewhat limited. They could only refuse permission for a company to join a VAT group or not allow the choice of a representative member and could only do this if it was necessary for the *protection of the revenue*. As a result of *Thorn EMI*, these powers were extended to cover applications to de-group. This aspect is discussed in (3) (anti-avoidance) later.

What HMRC cannot do is to refuse permission to de-group, where the VAT group is broken up on a change in ownership. However, they can dictate when such a change will take place, a view supported by the Court of Appeal in a decision given on 17 October 2001 involving Barclays Bank.

- In *C & E Commrs v Barclays Bank plc* [2001] BVC 606, the Court, ruling for HMRC, overturned the previous decisions of both the VAT Tribunal and the High Court that a company ceased to be a member of a VAT group by operation of law when the criteria for membership ceased to be satisfied (by, say, a change in ownership). The Tribunal had earlier taken the view that the power in VATA 1994, s. 43(6), under which HMRC could direct de-grouping, was needed to cope with situations where there might be two views as to who actually exercises control but did not otherwise apply.

   The Court of Appeal, however, considered that, unless HMRC's contentions were correct, s. 43(6), as it then was, was redundant. A company that had been sold could thus remain in a VAT group with the vendor until such a time as HMRC were satisfied that it had ceased to be controlled by the vendor and issued a notice notifying the vendor that the company was to be removed from a date that they, HMRC, could specify.

   Leave to the House of Lords was refused.

The *Barclays* appeal concerned s. 43(6), as it then was. The corresponding provisions in what is now s. 43C(3) require HMRC, by notice, to terminate a company's membership of a VAT group from a specified date where it appears to them that it is not, or is no longer, eligible to be included. This date may be earlier than the date on which the notice is given but shall not be earlier than:

- the first date on which, in HMRC's opinion, the company was not eligible to be treated as a member of the group; or
- the date on which, in their opinion, it ceased to be eligible to be treated as a member of the group.

The termination date might, conceivably, therefore, be later than the date on which the ownership of a company changed hands, something that could be unattractive for both the vendor and the buyer. What HMRC said on this in *Business Brief* 30/02 was that:

> 'Businesses and tax advisers are concerned that keeping a company in a VAT group after the company has been sold to a third party may cause commercial difficulties. In practice, it would be rare for Customs to set a later date for cases. Normally Customs policy will be to agree the date requested by the selling group. Customs will set a later date only if VAT avoidance is involved or is likely to arise through obtaining an earlier date.'

Nonetheless, this is clearly something to watch.

In short ...

Subject to satisfying the *control* and *established/fixed establishment* tests, as a broad proposition, the composition of a VAT group is infinitely variable. As many or as few eligible companies can be included as the group decide; there can even be more than one VAT group in place within a commercial group.

Guidance on eligibility for membership of a VAT group can be found in HMRC VAT Information Sheet 07/04.

(2) The consequences

At one time, the HMRC view was that a group registration under VATA 1994, s. 43 was little more than an administrative arrangement; something designed merely to provide simplified accounting procedures, whereby supplies of goods and services between members of the group were disregarded for VAT purposes. It did not create, nor was it intended to create, a single taxable person for VAT. However, as was been made clear in *Kingfisher*, this was not correct.

- In *C & E Commrs v Kingfisher plc* [1994] BVC 3, the issue was the treatment, under the retail scheme rules, of a credit card scheme. The scheme was operated by a group finance company and was used for purchases from a retail company in the same group. *Kingfisher* maintained the effect of the VAT group was that, as representative member, it was entitled to be treated as carrying on both the credit card and retail business. This was important because Notice 727, HMRC's retail scheme booklet, allowed a sale subject to self-financed credit to be accounted for as and when the money is received, rather than in the period in which the sale is actually made. The Tribunal and the Court agreed with Kingfisher, an approach followed subsequently in the appeal by *Midland Bank plc* [1991] BVC 749.

What *Kingfisher* does not mean, however, is that the VAT group creates a single business. This distinction can be important in the case of special purpose companies, particularly when it comes to partial exemption and the recovery of input VAT (see **Chapter 4** at 40-200).

Subject to this, the effect of creating a single person for VAT means (VATA 1994, s. 43(1)) that one company, the representative member, assumes overall responsibility for the VAT group and that, in broad terms:

- any business carried on by a member of the group is regarded as carried on by the representative member;
- any supplies of goods or services by one VAT group member to another are disregarded;
- any supplies of goods or services (which is a supply to which the previous bullet point does not apply) by or to any member of the group are regarded as made by or to the representative member;
- any tax paid or payable by a member of the group on the importation of goods is treated as paid or payable by the representative member, who will also be treated as having imported them; and, similarly
- any tax paid or payable by a member of the group on the acquisition of goods from another Member State is treated as paid or payable by the representative member, who will be regarded as having acquired them.

Whilst the primary responsibility thus rests with the representative member, how any VAT liabilities or repayments are shared within the group is for the group itself to decide. Normally, this will be according to the members' respective contributions to input and output VAT and, where appropriate, will reflect differing partial exemption calculations applicable to each. However, each member of the group can be held jointly and severally liable for any tax due.

It is also worth bearing in mind that:

- it is necessary to ensure that the representative member has all the necessary information to submit a VAT return for the group by the due date;
- the partial exemption *de minimis* limits apply to the group as a whole, not to the members individually;
- the limit for voluntary disclosures applies to the group as a whole (see **Chapter 1** at 10-350); and the cash accounting and payment on account limits also apply to the group as a whole.

Although, the primary focus of a VAT group is thus on the representative member, this does not mean the interests of other members of the group are set aside. This was made clear by the decision in *J&W Waste Management*.

- *J&W Waste Management Ltd; J&W Plant and Tool Hire Ltd* [2003] BVC 4,102 was a case where HMRC had sought to deny a right of appeal against a VAT assessment by members of a VAT group where the representative member of that group was in liquidation and did not, itself appeal. They had argued the appellants had no legal standing. The VAT group amounted to one legal entity and was to be treated as a single person, the right of appeal being that of the representative member or the liquidator.

    J&W Waste Managements' response was that there could not be joint and several liability without joint and several rights of appeal. And the Tribunal agreed. Section 43 does not mention rights of appeal. What it said was that the members of the group shall be jointly and severally liable for 'any VAT due' from the representative member. But this raised two questions:
    - whether 'any tax due' did or did not mean an unconditional and absolute liability on the members for 'any tax due'; and
    - whether it meant any tax Customs say is due, or just tax established as being due.

    The Tribunal took the latter view on both. That tax should be payable on demand without the possibility of any appeal was not warranted by the text and it was wrong that the right of appeal against the demand for tax, a right of a fundamental nature, should be deemed to be abrogated by implication in a text which relates to group registration, and does not refer to appeals.

> **Practice point**
>
> If grouping is not be possible – for example, where there isn't the requisite degree of common ownership, the impact of irrecoverable input VAT can sometimes be averted or minimised if:
>
> - the inter-company charges can be treated as exempt *intermediary services* for the provision of insurance or finance;
> - the arrangements can be structured as cost-sharing or joint employment; or
> - the company with the highest use provides the taxable services to the others, rather than vice versa.

(3) Anti-avoidance and the prevention of abuse

The ability to group for VAT purposes is clearly valuable and, for these reasons can invite exploitation for reasons for which the facility was not intended. To recognise this, there are a number of measures that may be applied:

(a) Protection of the revenue

Firstly, VATA 1994, s. 43B and 43C give HMRC the power to prevent a company joining a VAT group and to remove an existing member from a VAT group, where this is considered necessary for the *protection of the revenue*. They will not normally do this, however, where the revenue loss follows from the normal operation of grouping – in other words, where VAT is eliminated on the value added, when a supply takes place between two group members. This effectively recognises that the same equitable result should be allowed to arise as if the VAT group were, instead, a single legal person.

Understandably, the *protection of the revenue* test can be difficult for HMRC to apply. In practice, therefore, this power has rarely been resorted to, although, in the present climate, there has been growing evidence of enquiries being made at the time of application. As noted in Section 4.2 of Notice 700/2, the meaning of *protection of the revenue* was discussed in the VAT & Duties Tribunal in the case of *National Westminster Bank plc* [1998] BVC 2,264. Paragraph 72 of the decision says that:

> '… the protection in question under section 43(5A) may be against any loss of revenue which is not de minimis whether or not it follows from the normal operation of grouping. It certainly covers an artificial avoidance scheme but it also covers a straight forward case which would not be characterised as avoidance or as abusive.'

In Section 4.2 of Notice 700/2 HMRC go on to observe that paragraph 74 of that decision says:

> 'the phrase "necessary for the protection of the revenue" must be considered as a totality and involves a balancing exercise in which the Commissioners must weigh the effect on the appellant of refusal of grouping against the loss of revenue likely to result from grouping.'

If they have concerns that the revenue loss goes beyond the accepted consequence of grouping, HMRC will ask for relevant information about the administrative savings that grouping brings, and an estimate of the revenue impact. Understandably applications for group treatment may be refused where proposed group members have a poor compliance record which might pose a threat to their ability to collect the revenue (for example, where they have consistently failed to pay VAT debts).

In *Business Brief* 30/02 HMRC made a useful observation that:

> 'As a general principle, Customs consider that the VAT grouping of two corporate bodies (A and B) is acceptable where A's corporate group either receives or has the ability to control 50% or more of the "economic benefits" of running B's business, provided that the determination of the "economic benefits" is not manipulated to divert benefits to a third party through, for example, high management charges; special dividend payments or other charges, payments or arrangements.
>
> Customs will consider challenging any grouping structure which does not meet this general principle, unless the amount of VAT revenue at stake is nil or too low to justify action.'

Any decision by HMRC to refuse permission on these grounds can, in any event, be subject to appeal.

Practice point

Best practice when it comes to applying for a VAT group clearly involves being open about things and not economical with the truth. Presentation and timing is also likely to be important.

(1) *Presentation*, because there will always, or nearly always, be a significant benefit to the taxpayer, usually involving a saving in tax. It can be important to get across the fact that this is a housekeeping benefit and not part of some unacceptable avoidance scheme.

(2) *Timing*, because it is always better to be open from the start and avoid HMRC coming to any preconceived conclusions based on what they may have learned from elsewhere.

Taking the initiative means there is a better chance of retaining control. Responding quickly invites a quicker answer, and can be an indication that the applicant is co-operating and has nothing to hide.

- The case of *Prudential Assurance Company Ltd* [2006] BVC 4,093 offers a reminder that HMRC are not always right, when it comes to judging whether a refusal is justified on these grounds. The appeal concerned the refusal of an application by Prudential for the grouping of a wholly-owned subsidiary intended to become 50 per cent owned on the grant of regulatory consents. The company had entered into a joint venture through a jointly-owned company with a South African insurer to market health insurance. Its partner needed approval from the South African Reserve Bank before investing, so, in the meantime, Prudential set the vehicle company up as a wholly-owned subsidiary, applying to include it in its VAT group for the time being. This was refused on the grounds of the *protection of the revenue* as HMRC maintained the delay in creating the joint venture had been contrived to avoid a substantial VAT cost. This failed to impress the Tribunal as, in reality, there was nothing artificial in the timing of the ending of grouping. The Commissioners could not reasonably have been satisfied that there were grounds for refusing the application and, therefore, the refusal of grouping was irrational.

(b) Removing companies from a group

Under VATA 1994, s. 43C(1), HMRC can direct that a member of a VAT group be removed, where it appears necessary for the protection of the revenue, although they cannot do this retrospectively. They can also direct, under s. 43C(3) that a company be removed from a group if it is not, or has ceased to be, eligible for inclusion. A direction issued under this provision can, however, have effect retrospectively from the date on which the group member ceased to be eligible.

Whether the power in s. 43C(3) is, strictly speaking, justified seems debateable, since a company either meets the eligibility requirements or it does not. The consequence of the Court of Appeal's decision in the *Barclays* appeal (see (2) earlier) has, though, made this a potentially important issue when companies are sold, as it can be unfortunate if a failure to notify HMRC in time causes the company to remain in the VAT group of the Vendor, with the continuing joint and several responsibilities that entails.

> ### *Practice point*
>
> Timing can be important when a company leaves a VAT group by reason of a change in ownership. The Court of Appeal in the *Barclays* case ruled that grouping did not automatically cease on Completion. This can potentially give problems for both the seller and the buyer. By not taking steps in time to remove it from the seller's VAT group, the company being sold could remain treated as part of that group subsequent to the transfer date.
>
> - This would clearly be unwelcome for the seller, who would not wish to retain a joint and several liability for post-transfer transactions of the company sold.
> - Equally, the buyer would not want to have to disclose the post-transfer transactions to the seller for VAT reporting purposes.
>
> This is, to some extent, now dealt with by the changes to VATA 1994, s. 43, in that s. 43C(3) now requires HMRC by notice to terminate the company's membership of the VAT group from a specified date, where it appears to them that it is not, or is no longer, eligible to be included.
>
> However, the potential problems remain. They can be avoided, though, if applications for the company to be sold to leave the vendor's VAT group and join that of the buyer on Completion are made under VATA 1994, s. 43B(2) prior to completion and conditional on the sale taking place.
>
> Applying in good time for the company to join the VAT group of the buyer from the outset could also have advantages in terms of recovering input tax on any acquisition costs.

(c) Exit and entry schemes and Sch. 9A

The scope of VATA 1994, s. 43 has, tended to be continually under review and was brought even more into focus as a result of an aggressive VAT avoidance scheme adopted by companies in the Thorn EMI Group.

- The arrangement in *Thorn Materials Supply Ltd & Thorn Resources Ltd* [1996] BVC 2,095 was centred around the ability to ignore intra-group supplies, being aimed at circumventing the block on the recovery of input VAT on the purchase of cars under art. 7 of the *Value Added Tax (Input Tax) Order* 1992 (SI 1992/3222). Other assets were also included in the scheme but the tax on these was not critical. The scheme operated on the premise that the purchaser of the vehicles, Thorn EMI Home Electronics (UK) Ltd (Home), bought the vehicles from associated group companies, Thorn Materials Supply Ltd (Materials) and Thorn Resources Ltd. All three were initially members of a VAT group. On the first occasion, the cars (and the other assets) were ordered on 29 November 1993 by Home from Materials, at which time 90 per cent of the purchase price was paid. On 6 December, Materials, on its own application, left the Thorn VAT group. It then proceeded to purchase the cars and the other assets, which it delivered to Thorn, recovering the VAT in the process. The input VAT on the cars was, it was alleged, largely saved since Materials had bought the vehicles for resale; it was not subject to the block. So far as Thorn was concerned, it had avoided paying tax on 90 per cent of the price because, to the extent of the advance payment, the supply was to be disregarded. The Tribunal agreed with Thorn.

Not surprisingly, HMRC appealed and the matter proceeded, by leapfrog, to the Court of Appeal and, ultimately, to the House of Lords [1998] BVC 270, where Thorn eventually lost.

In the meantime, steps were taken in the *Finance Act* 1995 to radically amend VATA 1994, s. 43 to prevent the abuse continuing. Initially, these included measures to inhibit the ability to disregard intra-group supplies unless actual performance or delivery took place before the VAT group relationship was broken, a change that was coupled with further powers to allow HMRC in future to refuse permission for companies to leave a VAT group.

With the exception of the power to refuse permission to de-group, these changes were, however, short-lived. From 29 November 1995, VATA 1994, Sch. 9A has allowed HMRC powers to counter the use of VAT group treatment for avoidance purposes. Provided certain conditions are met, they can issue Notices of Direction to:

(1) Include a company in a VAT group (providing the company is eligible).

(2) Exclude a company from a VAT group.

(3) Re-regard a disregarded intra group supply where a *relevant event* has occurred and there *is or may be* a supply on which VAT *has been, or will or may be*, charged otherwise than by reference to its full value and where:

    (a) at least part of the supply is not or would not be zero-rated; and
    (b) the charging of VAT on less than full value would give rise to a tax advantage,

a tax advantage in this sense being seen as arising if, and only if, a person has become entitled (para. 1(4)).

However, the measures will be applied only if the condition that there *is or may be* such a supply would not be fulfilled apart from the occurrence of the relevant event. They will also not be applied if the transaction in question had, as its main purpose or, as the case may be, as each of its main purposes, a genuine commercial purpose unconnected with the tax advantage.

A *relevant event* for this purpose, is something that occurs (para. 1(2)) when a company:

'(a) begins to be or ceases to be, treated as a member of a [VAT] group; or
(b) enters into any transaction.'

Full value in this context is not taken to mean open market value. It means the value of the supply on the assumption that nothing fell to be disregarded as a result of VATA 1994, s. 43 itself.

In short, HMRC are now to be able to effectively negate the benefit of an avoidance exercise involving companies moving into or out of a VAT group or transactions, such as the transfer of a trade into a VAT group after the three year period critical for VATA 1994, s. 44 (see (6) below). It is not the intention, however, that the measures should be used beyond that, something confirmed by the then Paymaster General, Mr Heathcoat-Amery, in a statement to the House of Commons on 6 February 1995 when he said that:

'Customs and Excise measures – taxing supplies in the group or de-grouping, would be used only to recoup the tax that was avoided.'

HMRC themselves also say in Notice 700/2 that it is not their intention to attack the more usual benefits of grouping. Nothing, of course, is cast in tablets of stone.

(d) Special purpose companies

As was made clear in the *Kingfisher* case.

- In *C & E Commrs v Kingfisher plc* [1994] BVC 3, the issue was the treatment under the retail scheme rules of a credit card scheme. The scheme was operated by a group finance company and was used for purchases from a retail company in the same group. Kingfisher maintained the effect of the VAT group was that, as representative member, it was entitled to be treated as carrying on both the credit card and retail business. This was important because Notice 727, HMRC's retail scheme booklet, allowed a sale subject to self-financed credit to be accounted for as and when the money is received rather than in the period in which the sale is actually made. The Tribunal and the Court agreed, an approach which was followed subsequently in the appeal by *Midland Bank plc* [1991] BVC 749.

What *Kingfisher* does not mean, however, is that the VAT group creates a single business. This distinction can be important, particularly when it comes to partial exemption and the recovery of input VAT (see **Chapter 4**).

Whilst HMRC did not appeal *Kingfisher*, they remained, however, concerned about the way the rules were used. As a result, VATA 1994, s. 43(1AA) now prevents such advantages being gained in the case of *special status* companies where:

'it is material, for the purposes of any provision made by or under this Act ("the relevant provision"), whether the person by or to whom a supply is made, or the person by whom goods are acquired or imported, is a person of a particular description.'

This effectively prevented any further benefit being gained in similar situations.

In announcing these measures, HMRC cited examples of supplies of insurance and education. At the time, insurance was generally only exempt from VAT when provided by *permitted insurers*; education is normally only exempt when supplied by *eligible bodies* (VATA 1994, Sch. 9, Grp. 2 and 6). Where VATA 1994, s. 43(1AA) applies, the VAT liability is decided by looking at the status of the group member actually making the supply, even though for other VAT purposes the representative member is treated as making the supply.

- The need for the new rules on special purpose companies was illustrated in the case of *Canary Wharf Ltd* [1997] BVC 2,058.

  Management services were supplied under a tripartite agreement between a landlord (Canary Wharf Ltd), a management company (Canary Wharf Management Ltd) – both companies being part of the same VAT group – and a tenant (Barclays Bank Plc). HMRC's main contention was that, looked at as a whole, CWM made supplies of management services as principal to the appellant and not to Barclays as the appellant had an obligation under the lease to repair and to keep the demised premises in 'good and substantial repair and condition'. The management services were thus re-characterised as part of an overall exempt supply of an interest in land.

  The Tribunal felt, though that s. 43(1) did not go so far as to lay down, as a statutory hypothesis, for the character of any supply to a third-party to be determined as if it were part of a single supply by the representative member. Supplies had to be looked at on ordinary principles and standard-rated supplies of services made to an entity outside the group were not transformed into part of an exempt interest in land simply by virtue of the fact that the representative group member deemed to supply it was the landlord.

  The Tribunal went on to comment that the logical extension of the HMRC argument was that, where exemption was conferred on account of the particular status of the supplier, e.g. an 'eligible body' in the field of education or enrolment in a medical register in that of health, the character of the supply altered according to whether the representative member had the required status. Hence the need to make this clear.

(e) Group supplies using an overseas member

Since 1996, there has also been a tax charge for the representative member of a VAT group, where certain supplies are purchased by an overseas member of that group and on-supplied to another, UK member of that VAT group. These measures are to be found in VATA 1994, s. 43(2A) to (2E). The supplies affected are those to which VATA 1994, s. 7A(2)(a) applies (namely services treated as being made in the UK due to the recipient of the services being a UK 'relevant business person'). Services which may be subject to this provision include the assignment of copyright, advertising services, data processing and legal services, amongst others. They were introduced as an anti-avoidance measure to prevent services being routed tax-free via an overseas branch of one of the companies forming the VAT group. The *Finance Act* 2012 legislates to preserve the treatment of an Extra-Statutory Concession (January 2012), number 3.2.2, which applies to partly exempt VAT groups with overseas members that make supplies to the UK group. The relevant provision concerns how the reverse charge applies to an intra-group supply, and how such a supply should be valued (Sch. 6, para. 8A to VATA 1994, applying to supplies made on or after the date of Royal Assent (17 July 2012)). The provisions set out that where the value of the brought-in supply or supplies is at least open market value then the value of the intra-group supply is the value of the bought-in supply or supplies. Where the value of any bought-in supply is less than its open market value, then HMRC may direct that the supply is valued taking an open market value (see generally VATA 1994, Sch. 6, para. 8A). HMRC's guidance on how the new rules apply in practice will be available in their VAT valuation guidance (a copy of their standalone guidance, pending incorporation into HMRC guidance is provided at Appendix 29).

The general idea is that, services subject to VATA 1994, s. 7A(2)(a), might be provided VAT-free to the non-UK branch as a person belonging outside the UK and then transferred without any further VAT consequence to the ultimate user within the VAT group. Most commentators regarded this type of arrangement as likely to be ineffective but HMRC had obvious concerns and what happened in the Shamrock Leasing case clearly prompted the introduction of the change in the law.

Whilst only a few schemes had been found in operation, the measure was particularly intended to prevent attempts to circumvent the rules introduced from 1997 for telecommunications services provided by non-UK service providers.

- Briefly, *Shamrock Leasing Ltd* [1999] BVC 2,032 was a case involving the exploitation of the inter-action of the rules on the place of supply of services and the grouping provisions in VATA 1994, s. 43. Equipment leased to a contractual customer within the VAT group, but belonging outside the EC was then leased back to a UK end-user within the same VAT group under a sub-lease. The idea was that the first lease, a head lease to a US-based company with no presence in the UK, was not subject to VAT by reason of the rules on services supplied where received in art. 16 of the *Value Added Tax (Place of Supply of Services) Order* 1992 (SI 1992/3121) (see **Chapter 3** at 30-250). The subsequent under-lease, being within the VAT group, was disregarded under the rules in VATA 1994, s. 43(1) so that, in theory, the end-user, a partly exempt bank (see **Chapter 4**) effectively enjoyed the equipment VAT-free instead of incurring a substantial amount of irrecoverable input tax.

HMRC issued an assessment in respect of the period ending 31 August 1996, on the basis that the initial supply under the head-lease was within the scope of UK VAT, as it was to be treated as made to the representative member of the VAT group, a company having a business establishment in the UK. In the event, they lost the appeal, not because their point was incorrect, but because the inclusion in the VAT group of the US company was invalid. The initial supply was thus correctly outside the scope, but not for quite the reason the taxpayer anticipated. The subsequent intra-group supply was, by the same token, not relieved by VATA 1994, s. 43(1) and was, in theory, taxable under the reverse charge (see **Chapter 5**). Unfortunately, it seems, by the time the decision was given, HMRC were too late to issue an amending assessment.

In short, the appeal succeeded because of what the Tribunal held was an invalid approach to membership of a VAT group. In a sense, therefore, *Shamrock* appear to have won by accident rather than design.

(4) Timing

The other main constraint is timing. Historically, up to 90 days prior could be required under the old VATA 1994, s. 43(7) before a change took place. In practice, the actual interval was often less, although delays were increasingly common as more attention came to be given by HMRC to the *protection of the revenue* issue. As shown by the decision in *C & E Commrs v Save & Prosper Group Ltd* (1978) VATRR 11; ((1978) 1 BVC 179)) grouping could also be agreed to retrospectively, but, only in exceptional cases would permission be given in practice. Changes also technically could only be made at the beginning or end of a VAT period. This, again though, has not generally been an issue.

The present emphasis is changed, however. As a result of VATA 1994, s. 43B(5), grouping applications will be given immediate provisional effect from the date received. HMRC will then have 90 days within which to decide whether to refuse the application on protection of the revenue grounds. Their power to remove a company from an existing VAT group for the protection of the revenue is not subject to any such 90-day limit.

HMRC's current policy on this is set out in Section 2 of Notice 700/2. Taxpayers are advised to apply for grouping as soon as possible to ensure registration by their preferred date. The aim is to respond within 15 working days to acknowledge receipt and to provide any new VAT registration number. At the same time, they aim to confirm that the application has been approved or advise that further enquiries need to be made, which is where the 90 day period now comes in.

If an application is refused, though, it will effectively be set aside and will be deemed never to have been allowed or effected. This may mean that:

- the applicant will have to notify a liability to register for VAT in the normal way; or
- HMRC will reinstate the VAT registration number previously held and with effect from the date on which it was earlier cancelled; and
- the representative member of the VAT group will have to submit a Voluntary Disclosure to reverse the VAT accounting done while the change had provisional effect.

When a decision is made to remove a company from a group, HMRC will give written notice specifying the date from which the company is to be removed but this cannot be retrospective. They will also normally provide sufficient notice to allow a company time to reorganise its affairs.

Practice point

Obtaining a group registration after the event remains possible, but is still difficult to achieve.

The stated policy on this, is that, normally, a registration may be backdated, but only up to 30 days prior to the application being received and only if the requested date corresponds to the commencement of the current accounting period of: the existing VAT group or of any of the companies involved.

Beyond that, any further extension must rely on factors where HMRC are at fault.

(5) Transfers of business

As noted at 20-050(1) earlier, for businesses transferred as going concerns (para. 1(2) – see **Chapter 3** at 30-450), the transferee, if not already registered, becomes liable to be registered at the time of transfer if:

'(a) the value of his taxable supplies in the period of one year ending at the time of the transfer has exceeded £77,000; or
(b) there are reasonable grounds for believing that the value of his taxable supplies in the period of 30 days beginning at the time of the transfer will exceed £77,000'

For this purpose the effect of VATA 1994, s. 49(1)(a) is to treat as the transferee's taxable supplies those previously made by the transferor from the business acquired. The result, therefore, is usually that the transferee must register immediately.

Having said this, for test (a) in both of the above situations, registration may not be insisted on if HMRC are satisfied that taxable supplies in the next 12 months will not exceed £75,000.

Even if registration is not, in the event, required, a business exceeding the monetary thresholds must still notify HMRC within a specified time-scale.

This is generally straightforward. However, there are two types of situation, which raise potentially important considerations.

(a) Acquisitions by partly exempt VAT groups

Where there is an acquisition of a business by an exempt or partly exempt VAT group, VATA 1994, s. 44 creates a deemed self-supply of most, if not all, of the chargeable assets acquired – i.e. those on which VAT would normally have been chargeable. However:

- this does not apply where the assets were acquired by the transferor more than three years prior to the transfer;
- HMRC may also reduce the VAT chargeable where it can be shown that the transferor had been unable to obtain credit for the full amount of input tax on his own purchase, import or acquisition of the assets concerned; and
- the charge does not extend to any assets subject to the capital goods scheme (s. 44(4) see **Chapter 4** at 40-150(7)). This applies to individual items of computer equipment costing over £50,000 and land and buildings costing over £250,000. Where the exclusion applies, the transferor will make no final adjustment; instead, adjustments will be made by the transferee for the remainder of the five or ten year period.

This section (an anti-avoidance measure) was designed to prevent input VAT on assets such as computer equipment being recovered in full by a wholly or largely taxable business with the assets subsequently being enjoyed VAT-free by an exempt business into which they had been merged. The provisions have the effect of restoring the cost in terms of irrecoverable input VAT. This can, on the face of it, be overcome in some cases to the extent the transfer takes place more than three years after the original acquisition by the transferor of the assets concerned.

This is considered further in **Chapter 3** at 30-450(2) and in **Chapter 4** at 40-150(9).

(b) Transfers involving tenanted property

Transfers involving tenanted property can be a particular problem where the landlord and the tenant or the purchaser and the tenant are members of the same VAT group. In *Kingfisher plc*, referred to earlier, the Court decided that members of a VAT group are to be deemed a single taxable person for VAT. With this in mind and given what was said by the House of Lords in *Thorn Materials Supply*, also mentioned earlier, the question arises as to whether there can be a transfer of a going concern when the sole business activity constitutes supplies from one group member to another.

HMRC's position on this (Section 4 of Notice 700/9 of April 2008) is that:

'**4.1 Transfers of businesses between members of the same VAT group**

The formation of a VAT group creates a single person for VAT purposes and as such any supply by a member of a VAT group is considered to be made by the representative member of the group. Therefore any assets transferred by a group member as part of the transfer of a going concern are considered to be transferred by the representative member.

The transfer of assets within a VAT group, like most supplies between the members of a VAT group, is disregarded for VAT purposes.

4.2 Transfers made to persons outside the VAT group

There cannot be a TOGC when the sole activity of the business transferred is the making of supplies from one group member to another. However, if supplies are also being made to businesses outside of the VAT group, a TOGC is possible.

4.3 Transfers made to a VAT Group

Where a business is sold and the buyer is part of a VAT group and uses the new acquisition simply to make supplies to VAT group members, the business has effectively ceased and it cannot be treated as a TOGC. However, if supplies are also being made to businesses outside of the VAT group, a TOGC is possible. For example:

The purchaser of a property rental business is a member of the same VAT group as the existing tenant	Not a TOGC
A VAT group member sells a property currently being rented to a another group member to a third party	Not a TOGC
A property rental business is sold where the tenant who is a member of the outgoing landlord's VAT group is only one of a number of tenants	Can be a TOGC.
A property rental business is sold where the tenant who is a member of the purchaser's VAT group is only one of a number of tenants	Can be a TOGC'

20-300 Overseas traders and representative offices

(1) General

Just because a company is incorporated or operating abroad does not mean it may not be subject to UK VAT and liable to be registered here if the goods or services it supplies are regarded as made within the UK (VATA 1994, s. 7 to s.7A, and the *VAT (Place of Supply of Services) Order* 1992 (SI 1992/3121) – see **Chapter 3** at 30-200).

Branches of non-UK companies are an obvious example. When carrying on business in the UK they are treated no differently from any other UK trader; no differently, that is, apart from their relationship with the separate parts of the same entity abroad. For direct tax purposes, a UK branch will generally be treated as if trading at arm's length with its head office or with other branches overseas. There is, however, no such concept for VAT. There can be no supplies of goods or services. There can be no consideration, a basic requirement under VATA 1994, s. 5(2)(a); but equally there can, in reality, be no supply at all – a person cannot supply anything to himself (see *Ministero dell'Economia e delle Finanze and Agenzia delle Entrate v FCE Bank plc* (Case C-210/04) ECR I-2803; [2009] BVC 692). This applies also to the imported services rules (see **Chapter 5**).

With one exception in the case of imports of goods (or, from 1 January 1993, acquisitions from other EU countries – see **Chapter 1** at 10-050), inter-branch transactions will not attract VAT.

Whether a supply is made in the UK or not is not always easy to decide especially if more than one branch of a company is involved in the transaction. In practice, however, it tends to be easier for an insurance company than, say, a bank.

- If a loan, for example, is arranged in the UK but is eventually booked abroad, is the supply a UK supply or must it be treated as made elsewhere? In many cases the answer will be straightforward and in the affirmative. What one cannot say, however, is that a supply which is substantially performed here is made abroad merely because it is booked abroad or invoiced and paid for abroad.
- The greater autonomy implied by insurance company law and regulatory requirements, though, usually means supplies are identified with a substantial presence with the necessary involvement and mind and management.

As will be seen at **Chapter 3**, the place where the recipient of services belongs is the location of the place of supply if they are supplied to a relevant business person; but in other cases, it will be where the supplier is *established* where the supply is made to a non-business recipient. However, these are not always the tests.

- The place of use and enjoyment may be important in some cases.
- In others, especially where the service is related to land, it may be the location of the subject matter.

Generally, though, the need for a company established overseas (and not in the UK) to be registered may in practice now be dispensed with in relation to the supply of services. This is as a result of the reverse-charge to services supplied in the UK, allowing any tax due to be accounted for by the relevant business recipient (VATA 1994, s. 8 – see **Chapter 5**).

> *Practice point*
>
> In some cases the concern may be to ensure a supply is specifically *not* seen as made in the UK.
>
> Where the place of supply is judged by where the supplier or recipient is established, care may need to be taken, for example, over the use of dependent agencies or trading desks in the UK acting on behalf of overseas affiliates so that it might be argued that *DFDS* applied.

(2) Representative offices

In other cases, an overseas company may, initially at least, simply establish a representative office here, often as a pre-cursor to opening a fully operational trading branch. This is especially common in the case of banks, where it can take some time to achieve Bank of England approval. The representative function will involve simply a promotional and administrative activity, with possibly the gathering and provision of information or customer liaison. What will generally not happen is the receipt of income from dealings with third parties – except possibly to some limited extent for the receipt of interest on surplus funds or rents from sub-letting accommodation.

Although income in normal VAT terms will be absent, these offices are, nonetheless, business establishments in a real sense. They frequently incur considerable costs on capital equipment and telecommunications, for example – and much of this bears VAT. Whether or how much of this VAT is recovered can then become important.

The existence of a place of business in the UK will effectively prevent the recovery of this VAT under the special rules for companies established abroad – i.e. Directive 2008/9 (replacing the 8th Directive) and the 13th VAT Directive (Directive 86/560). Relief is often, however, still possible. Provisions in what is now VATA 1994, Sch. 1, para. 10 permit voluntary VAT registration where such supplies, as are made outside the UK, would be taxable if made in the UK (under the normal place of supply rules). However, to the extent that some of the non-UK supplies would be VAT-exempt (e.g. finance provided to a customer in another Member State), some restriction on partial exemption lines is to be expected.

Where registration on this basis is applied for, the company will be sent a VAT return form (VAT 100) like any other VAT trader. This should be completed in the normal way, except that no entries are to be made in boxes 1 or 8, unless actual supplies have been made in the UK in a given VAT period.

As an alternative to this procedure, it may, on occasions, be appropriate to consider registration as part of a VAT group with any UK affiliated companies. This is now possible following the extension of the rules on VAT grouping (see 20-250(4) earlier) to include branches of companies incorporated abroad.

(3) Anti-avoidance: assets supplied in the UK by overseas businesses

Schedule 3A to VATA 1994 is aimed at preventing the avoidance of UK VAT by certain foreign-based businesses making claims for the recovery of UK VAT under Directive 2008/9 or the Thirteenth VAT Directive (Directive 86/560).

Typically, the companies affected are those carrying out the cross-border leasing of equipment or vehicles. Having no established place of business in the UK and making no supplies in the UK other than those that are treated as made where received (i.e. under the VATA 1994, Sch. 4A – see **Chapter 3** at 30-250, companies in this position have hitherto not generally been required to be registered for UK VAT.

- Any disposals here of assets leased to their UK customers have usually been disregarded for registration purposes on the basis that they represent the disposal of capital assets within Sch. 1, para. 1(7).
- The companies have thus not been required to be registered here and the disposals have thus been VAT-free.
- In the meantime, any UK VAT on the cost of those assets or on their import into the UK may have been recovered under Directive 2008/9 or the Thirteenth VAT Directive (Directive 86/560), thus giving a potentially substantial saving overall.

However, Sch. 3A, which, unlike VATA 1994, Sch. 1, has no registration threshold, and requires any business affected to become registered for UK VAT. Once liable, it must notify HMRC within 30 days of the day when it first expected to make relevant supplies. Registration will not be required, however, if the overseas business does not make or intend to make a claim under Directive 2008/9 or the Thirteenth VAT Directive (Directive 86/560) refund arrangements, as the supplies are not then *relevant supplies*.

There are also rules to cover situations where the business concerned is transferred to another company as a going concern.

Summary

This Chapter has aimed to outline the basic rules on VAT registration.

For most of the readers of this book, the registration limits themselves will be relatively academic. What will be important will be the facility that registration gives for the recovery of input tax and the possibilities within the rules on VAT groups for minimising unnecessary VAT cost.

Registration should not, though, be looked at as a simple administrative issue as how it is approached and timing can play an essential part in the eventual outcome.

Later Chapters will explore the implications for particular industry sectors and Chapter 6 looks at the issues affecting connected parties.

3 Outputs and Output VAT

> **Overview**
>
> This Chapter considers:
>
> (1) Outputs and meaning of supply, including:
>
>   (a) standard-rating;
>   (b) zero-rating;
>   (c) exemption;
>   (d) *outside the scope*; and
>   (e) fiscal neutrality.
>
> (2) The importance of the place of supply.
>
> (3) The effect of imports, acquisitions and dispatches.
>
> (4) The importance of the time of supply – *taxpoint*.
>
> (5) The special implications of business transfers.
>
> (6) Relief for bad debts.

30-000 Outputs and meaning of supply

With limited exceptions, tax is charged in respect of what are termed *supplies* resulting from what art. 9 of Council Directive 2006/112/EC (previously art. 4 of Sixth VAT Directive (Directive 77/388)) refers to as *economic activities*.

Article 14 of the Directive provides that:

> '(1) "Supply of goods" shall mean the transfer of the right to dispose of tangible property as owner.
>
> (2) In addition to the transaction referred to in paragraph 1, each of the following shall be regarded as a supply of goods:
>
>   (a) the transfer, by order made by or in the name of a public authority or in pursuance of the law, of the ownership of property against payment of compensation;
>   (b) the actual handing over of goods pursuant to a contract for the hire of goods for a certain period, or for the sale of goods on deferred terms, which provides that in the normal course of events ownership is to pass at the latest upon payment of the final instalment;
>   (c) the transfer of goods pursuant to a contract under which commission is payable on purchase or sale.
>
> (3) Member States may regard the handing over of certain works of construction as a supply of goods.'

3 Outputs and Output VAT

and art. 24 that:

> '(1) "Supply of services" shall mean any transaction which does not constitute a supply of goods.'

For UK VAT law purposes, *supply* is defined in VATA 1994, s. 5. In particular s. 5(1) and (2) provide:

> '5(1) Schedule 4 shall apply for determining what is, or is to be treated as, a supply of goods or a supply of services.
>
> 5(2) Subject to any provision made by that Schedule and to Treasury orders under subsection (3) to (6) below-
> (a) "supply" in this Act includes all forms of supply, but not anything done otherwise than for a consideration;
> (b) anything which is not a supply of goods but is done for a consideration (including, if so done, the granting, assignment or surrender of any right), is a supply of services.'

Schedule 4 goes on to provide:

> '(1) Any transfer of the whole property in goods is a supply of goods; but, subject to sub-paragraph (2) below, the transfer-
> (a) of any undivided share of the property, or
> (b) of the possession of goods,
> is a supply of services.
> (2) If the possession of goods is transferred:
> (a) under an agreement for the sale of the goods, or
> (b) under agreements which expressly contemplate that the property also will pass at some time in the future (determined by, or ascertainable from, the agreements but in any case not later than when the goods are fully paid for),
> it is then in either case a supply of the goods.'

These are distinctions and concepts, which will be important for many of the supplies and transactions covered in this book.

A *supply*, though, normally only arises if something is being done for a *consideration* i.e. where something, not necessarily money, is given as a *quid pro quo* in return.

What is meant by consideration is considered later in this Chapter at 30-500, along with the related issues of free supplies and valuation.

Whilst most activities carried out by companies in the sectors covered by this book will tend to give rise to supplies for VAT purposes, not all of these will be subject to VAT as discussed later. However:

- from basic principles, it is clear there can be no supply between separate parts of the same legal entity or person. You cannot pay yourself anything or, for that matter, actually supply yourself with anything that is already yours. This has now been confirmed in

March 2006 by the ECJ in *Ministero dell'Economia e delle Finanze and Agenzia delle Entrate v FCE Bank plc* (Case C-210/04) [2009] BVC 692. The case concerned the supply of management, consulting, data processing, employees' training, and the supply and management of software, from the Head Office of a UK bank, FCE Bank plc, to its branch in Italy. Under Italian VAT law, these services were liable to Italian VAT, which the branch could not fully recover. FCE disputed the charge to tax and, on a Reference to the ECJ, the Court ruled that:

> 'a fixed establishment, which is not a legal entity distinct from the company of which it forms part, established in another Member State and to which the company supplies services, should not be treated as a taxable person by reason of the costs imputed to it in respect of those supplies.'

Accordingly, any apparent inter-branch supplies are, on this basis, generally ignored. That debit notes or adjustments may be made for management accounting or tax purposes is irrelevant. This can be important, for example, for many international banks, like FCE, operating on a branch basis. There is, however, a deemed supply for intra-EU acquisitions or dispatches of goods (VATA 1994, Sch. 4, para. 6 (see later at 30-300));

- there is a further exception for VAT groups. Transactions between members of the group (see **Chapter 2** at 20-250) are also not usually recognised. The VAT group is effectively treated as a single person in the form of the representative member. This can need to be qualified, however, to the extent that particular transactions are primarily motivated by avoidance, where certain supplies are purchased by an overseas member of a VAT group and used for making supplies to a UK member of the VAT group. This is discussed earlier in **Chapter 2**.
- special rules also apply to transfers of assets as part of a business disposed of as a going concern. This is discussed later at 30-450;
- certain transactions or receipts do not involve supplies or are otherwise *outside the scope* of VAT altogether. This is discussed at 30-200.

Examples of where this is likely to be important will be with the making of capital contributions to partnerships (see *KapHag Renditefonds v Finanzamt Charlottenburg* (C-442/01) [2005] BVC 566, discussed later in **Chapter 4** at 40-000), the issue of shares and arguably other securities (see *Kretztechnik AG v Finanzamt Linz* (C-465/03) [2006] BVC 66 also later in **Chapter 4** at 40-000), the participation in hedging transactions in foreign exchange and certain other financial products by persons other than banks (see *Willis Pension Fund Trustees Ltd* [2006] BVC 2,045, considered in **Chapter 7** at 70-200) and the assignment of debts and receivables under a securitisation arrangement (see *MBNA Europe Bank Ltd v R & C Commrs* [2007] BVC 3 and *Capital One Bank (Europe) Plc v HM Revenue & Customs* [2006] BVC 2,148 discussed in **Chapter 7** at 70-200).

- Transactions that are not in the course of a business or, *in* Council Directive 2006/112/EC terms, an *economic activity* will not be subject to VAT because they are outside the scope of VAT.
- In *Blackqueen Ltd* [2002] BVC 2,221, this was an issue in a VAT avoidance scheme. The scheme involved a circular series of transactions within a group for the purpose of obtaining full input tax credit, whilst paying output tax only on the margin. It also involved a claim for the refund of VAT under the Eighth VAT Directive (Directive 79/1072 (now

replaced by Directive 2008/9). Before the Tribunal, it was held that the supplies to and by the appellant were not, in fact, *economic activities* and were therefore *outside the scope* of VAT. This conclusion was consistent with the findings of the Tribunal in the appeal by Halifax plc (a finding later not followed at by the ECJ (see **Chapter 4**). The Tribunal also concluded that the principle of *abuse of rights* was applicable.

- Interestingly, neither the *non-business* nor the *abuse of rights* approach was followed in *RBS Property Developments Ltd; The Royal Bank of Scotland Group plc* [2003] BVC 2,074, where a group property developer was used to recover input tax on the construction of a new building. Initially, the intention was that the development would be sold or let to third parties, but it was later decided that the buildings would be occupied by RBS in a way that caused RBS to only incur an irrecoverable VAT cost for three years while the buildings were regarded as *new* for VAT purposes (see **Chapter 8** at 80-150). The Tribunal in this case found the transactions were not carried out with the sole intention of obtaining a tax advantage and that there were real and understandable business purposes for the structure used. The concept of *abuse of rights* also had no application in the present appeals. There was nothing improper, illegal or artificial about the transactions in question.

However, although the non-business approach adopted by the Tribunal in *Blackqueen* (and also, incidentally by the Tribunal in the *Debenhams Retail plc* [2003] BVC 2,543) did not in the end find favour, any arrangement that is contrived or artificial must, in the present climate, be viewed with caution.

What you cannot do, as confirmed by the VAT Tribunal in the *Co-operative Insurance Society Ltd* [1997] BVC 4,100 is to manipulate the rules to create taxable supplies where they otherwise would not exist.

- The *Co-operative Insurance Society Ltd* [1997] BVC 4,100 appeal concerned the supply of hotel accommodation to employees of CIS when travelling away from the office on business. CIS had argued this was provided by the hotel to CIS and then by CIS to the employee. The benefit to CIS, a partially exempt business, would have been to increase its recoverable input tax by linking the VAT incurred on hotel accommodation to the onward taxable supply to its employee. Because the employee did not pay CIS for the accommodation no output tax was due on the onward supply, but the taxable supply would, nonetheless, have still existed by reason of the rules in VATA 1994, Sch. 6, para. 10. The Tribunal held that, in reality, there was no supply of hotel accommodation by CIS to the employee.

Another important rule to observe is to recognise that all supplies will be taxable (and subject to VAT) unless specifically exempted (VATA 1994, s. 4(2) and s. 31 and art. 131 to 137 of Council Directive 2006/112/EC (art. 13 of the Sixth VAT Directive (Directive 77/388)) or *outside the scope* because of the rules on the place of supply (VATA 1994, s. 7, s. 7A and s. 9. (art. 31 to 59 of Council Directive 2006/112/EC)).

Normally *taxable* means subject to VAT at the standard-rate, currently 20 per cent (2012). There is, however, an important further category of taxable supplies, zero-rated supplies, where the rate of VAT is nil (VATA 1994, s. 30) and a lower rate of five per cent, which applies to domestic fuel and certain other supplies covered in VATA 1994, Sch. 7A none of which are really within the scope of this book. Where applicable, zero-rating always overrides both standard-rating and exemption (VATA 1994, s. 30(1)). European laws do not refer to zero-rating (a UK concept) but simply has different types of exemptions. It is only an exemption with a right of recovery for input tax, which is comparable to zero-rating under VATA 1994.

The distinction between taxable and exempt supplies and supplies which are *outside the scope* can be important, not just in terms of whether tax has to be accounted for, but for the recovery of input tax. In many respects, this can be one of the main concerns for businesses in the sectors covered by this book and is discussed later in **Chapter 4**.

Practice point

It can be important to examine each situation where something is provided or made available or where money is given or payment made. It is generally best to assume, in the first instance, that a supply may be involved, but to be aware of the possibility that there may not.

30-050 Standard-rated supplies

Although most of the supplies by the sectors covered by this book will be basically exempt, this is a departure to the general rule. It should always be assumed, therefore, that tax is due at the standard-rate, unless there is a clear indication to the contrary. In the context of the financial and insurance sectors standard-rating will apply, in particular, to transactions such as:

- advisory services;
- certain benefits or facilities afforded to staff;
- equipment leasing (see **Chapter 7**);
- freehold sales of most new (or partly complete) buildings, supplies of land or buildings pursuant to developmental tenancies, leases or licences or lettings or other disposals of land and buildings where the option to tax has been exercised (see **Chapters 8** and **9**);
- investment management (see **Chapter 8**);
- management and administration;
- most supplies of fuel and power;
- sales of assets such as plant and equipment;
- sales of goods under a hire-purchase, conditional sale or credit sale agreement (apart from the finance element) (see also **Chapter 7**);
- supplies of staff; and
- transactions involving hard or soft commodities (unless covered by specific and limited rules involving certain approved UK terminal markets) (see **Chapter 10**).

Charging VAT can, of course, be a disadvantage. It does, however, mean underlying input VAT can be recovered and is not an expense (**Chapter 4**).

As noted, though, exemption tends to be the norm for the sectors covered by this book. But there is also the very important further exception of zero-rating.

30-100 Zero-rated supplies

Zero-rated supplies are taxable supplies for which the rate of VAT is nil (from the perspective of the VAT Directive these are exempt supplies with a right of recovery). As a category these are particularly useful, since, being taxable supplies, they confer the same benefit as standard-rated supplies (i.e. the right to recover input VAT) but without the need for output VAT to be charged. As such, they are one of the more important areas to be considered in the context of finance and insurance and the rules, VATA 1994, s. 30 and Sch. 8, cover, among other things:

(1) Exports of goods (VATA 1994, s. 30(6) and (8)) and, from 1 January 1993, dispatches of goods to taxable businesses in other Member States (s. 30(8) – see 30-300 later).

(2) Various supplies of goods or services within categories listed in VATA 1994, Sch. 8 (s. 30(2)). The Schedule contains some 16 different categories, of which the following will be of particular interest:

   (a) Groups 5 and 6 – land including supplies of major interests in, or involving the construction or demolition of, new or protected dwellings or relevant residential or charitable buildings. This will be especially relevant in the context of investment (see **Chapter 8**);
   (b) Group 7 – certain international services (see **Chapter 7**);
   (c) Group 8 – transport, including the leasing or chartering of large ships or commercial aircraft. This is of special concern to leasing companies and is considered in more detail in **Chapter 7**;
   (d) Group 10 – supplies of gold between Central Banks or between a Central Bank and a member of the London Gold Market (see **Chapter 10**); and
   (e) Group 11 – the issue of bank notes.

(3) Transactions in certain hard and soft commodities dealt with on specified UK terminal markets (VATA 1994, s. 50). Relief in this case is under the *Value Added Tax (Terminal Markets) Order* 1973 (SI 1973/173). It is, however, strictly limited and is considered in detail in **Chapter 10**.

Colloquially, the term *zero-rating* is also used to refer to certain services for which the place of supply is outside the UK by reason of art. 43 to 59 of Council Directive 2006/112/EC or in UK terms, by reason of s. 7A of VATA 1994. These are, strictly speaking, *outside the scope* of UK VAT, but, like zero-rated supplies, can, in certain situations, confer the right to recover underlying input tax. What the place of supply rules involve is explained at 30-200 and 30-250 and their effect in terms of input tax recovery in **Chapter 4**.

Zero-rated supplies therefore are, understandably, attractive, but a number of conditions may, however, need to be met:

- For exports of goods to third-countries or the dispatch of goods to taxable businesses in other Member States, this usually means holding the relevant commercial and shipping documentation. Typically, these will include customer correspondence and orders and bills of lading and air way bills. All must generally be obtained within a relatively short time following export or shipment. For dispatches, the invoice must also show the customer's overseas VAT number.

- For services, it is generally important to show where the customer or the recipient of a supply *belongs*. If this is in another Member State, the relief, in the case of services within VATA 1994, s. 7A (see **Appendix 4**), depends on the recipient of the supply being in business. In practice, it can be most easily shown by the customer's overseas VAT number. In the case of services, however, this is not mandatory if other evidence is available (see 30-250). A list of countries which are currently members of the EU is to be found at **Appendix 5**.

In *Vogtländische Straßen-, Tief- und Rohrleitungsbau GmbH Rodewisch (VSTR) v. Finanzamt Plauen* (C587/10) the CoJ decided that a Member State cannot make zero-rating conditional on the supplier having the customers VAT number. The case was decided in the context of intra-Community supplies. The CoJ noted that whilst a VAT identification number provides proof of the tax status of the taxable person and facilitates the tax audit of intra-Community transactions, it constitutes only a formal requirement which cannot undermine the right of exemption from VAT where the substantive conditions for an intra-Community supply are satisfied. Accordingly, where a supplier, acting in good faith and having taken all the measures which can reasonably be required, is unable to provide the VAT number but provides other information which is such as to demonstrate sufficiently that the person acquiring the goods is a taxable person acting as such in the transaction then that will be sufficient for the purposes of the VAT Directive.

30-150 Exempt supplies

Exempt supplies (art. 131 to 137 of Council Directive 2006/112/EC (art. 13 of the Sixth VAT Directive (Directive 77/388)) and VATA 1994, s. 31 and Sch. 9) are supplies specifically not chargeable with VAT.

Not charging VAT is, in itself, often a distinct advantage where customers are private consumers or otherwise not in business and able to recover input tax. However, in this case, as a *quid pro quo*, there is generally no corresponding relief for input VAT (VATA 1994, s. 26 – see **Chapter 4**).

In practice, the main categories of interest in the context of this book are, looking at VATA 1994, Sch. 9:

- Group 1 – transactions involving land or buildings (art. 135(1)(j), (k) and (l) of Council Directive 2006/112/EC). This covers both the sale or letting of property. It applies equally to a business' own premises as to land and buildings held as investments. The latter will be of a special interest to insurance companies (see **Chapter 9**) and investors such as funded pension schemes (**Chapter 8**). In many cases, however, exemption is replaced by standard-rating. This applies particularly to freehold sales of new or partly completed new commercial buildings. It also affects many other sales or lettings, including, in particular, cases where the option to tax is exercised.
- Group 2 – insurance and insurance-related services (art. 135(1)(a)). These are also discussed in detail in **Chapter 9**.

- Group 5 – finance (art. 135(1)(b) to (g)). This will cover in particular transactions involving money, credit or securities and is explored later in **Chapters 7** and **8**.
- Group 14 – supplies of goods where input tax cannot be recovered. This was introduced following the ECJ judgment in the case of *EC Commission v Italian Republic* (Case C-45/95) [1997] BVC 536 over the implementation of art. 136 of Council Directive 2006/112/EC (art. 13(B)(c) of the Sixth VAT Directive (Directive 77/388)) and mainly affects the VAT treatment of the disposal of business assets, primarily cars or goods purchased for the purposes of business entertainment, where the recovery of input tax is specifically blocked (see later in **Chapter 4** at 40-050). Group 14, which is set out in full in **Appendix 6** was introduced with effect from 1 March 2000 by the *Value Added Tax (Supplies of Goods where Input Tax cannot be recovered) Order* 1999 (SI 1999/2833) (art. 136 of Council Directive 2006/112/EC (art. 13(B)(c)). The effect of these provisions in relation to property is discussed later in **Chapter 8** at 80-150.

It can be important, on occasions to consider exemption in the context of single and multiple supplies (see later at 30-550), where the aim may be to limit the amount of consideration received on which output tax needs to be charged or accounted for. Cases to consider in this area will include *C & E Commrs v Primback Ltd* (Case C-34/99) [2001] BVC 315, *Card Protection Plan Ltd v C & E Commrs* [2001] BVC 158, *Muys' en De Winter's Bouw- en Aannemingsbedrijf BV v Staatssecretaris van Financién* (Case C-281/91) [1993] ECR I-5405 and *Everything Everywhere Ltd (formerly T-Mobile UK) v R & C Commrs* (Case C-276/09)[2011] BVC 44.

Exemption is thus by no means the same as zero-rating – or exemption in the sense of art. 138 to 164 of Council Directive 2006/112/EC (art. 14 to 16 of the Sixth VAT Directive (Directive 77/388)).

30-200 Outside the scope

The phrase *outside the scope* refers to payments or transactions to which VAT, or at least UK VAT, does not apply. It is not the same as exemption and covers, in terms of payments, for example:

- agency payments, i.e. pure disbursements;
- compensation, damages and liquidated damages;
- discounts on bills of exchange;
- dividends;
- foreign exchange;
- group relief payments;
- the issue of shares and securities;
- profit shares;
- payments on the redemption, but not the purchase for redemption, of shares and other securities;
- salaries – but only as between employee and employer;
- settlements in a joint venture; and

- subventions, all of which are not in themselves normally consideration for anything supplied (VATA 1994, s. 5(2)(a)).

However:

- transactions between two parts of the same legal entity – e.g. between a branch and head office are, on basic principles, not supplies of services (see the decision of the ECJ in the case of *Ministero dell'Economia e delle Finanze and Agenzia delle Entrate v FCE Bank plc* (Case C-210/04);[2009] BVC 692);
- as *C & E Commrs v Tilling Management Services Ltd* (1978) 1 BVC 185 showed, VAT can still be a problem with group relief. This case involved an agreement for the surrender of group relief. On its own, this would have been harmless enough. However, the surrender was expressed to be *in return* for the procurement of management services, which created a taxable supply of management services;
- compensation or liquidated damages can also give rise to taxable supplies (and a liability to VAT) if they are part of an agreement conferring some right or other benefit;
- profit shares are sometimes no more than payment by results for something that is really a taxable, or exempt, supply. They will only be otherwise if they are genuinely a distribution in something like a partnership or joint venture.

In short, providing goods or services will not be VAT-free merely because the consideration is expressed in terms of the kinds of payment listed.

The phrase *outside the scope* also covers:

- gifts of services (except where the *VAT (Supply of Services) Order* 1993 (SI 1993/1507) applies for bought-in standard-rated services put to free private use);
- small-value gifts of goods (usually costing less than £50 – VATA 1994, Sch. 4, para. 5(2));
- most transfers of businesses on a going concern basis (art. 5 of the *Value Added Tax (Special Provisions) Order* 1992 (SI 1992/3129) – see 30-450 later); and
- supplies made or treated as made abroad – i.e. outside the UK and Isle of Man by reason of the place of supply rules, in particular those in VATA 1994, s. 7A and Sch. 4A – (see art. 43 to 59 of Council Directive 2006/112/EC). This is discussed at 30-250 later;
- supplies resulting from transactions that are not undertaken in the course of a business or, in terms of art. 2.1(a) of Council Directive 2006/112/EC (art. 2(1) of the Sixth VAT Directive (Directive 77/388)) undertaken by a taxable person acting as such. The significance of this is illustrated by cases such as:
  - *Wellcome Trust Ltd v C & E Commrs* (Case C-155/94) [1996] BVC 377 where the disposal of shares owned by a charitable foundation was held not to amount to a transaction in the course of a business.
  - *Harnas & Helm v Staatssecretaris van Financiën* (Case C-80/95) [1997] BVC 358, where the same rule applied in the case of the acquisition and holding of bonds.
  - *Floridienne SA & Berginvest SA v Belgian State* (Case C-142/99) [2001] BVC 76 where share dividends were said not to be consideration for any supplies and interest on loans to subsidiaries from funds derived from dividend income were not the result of an *economic activity*.
  - *Empresa de Desenvolvimento Mineiro SGPS SA (EDM) v Fazenda Pública* (Case C-77/01) [2006] BVC 140 where it was held that the mere sale of shares, or securities

3 Outputs and Output VAT

(or the receipt of interest on securities) may not, in itself, constitute an economic activity or supply for VAT and may thus be *outside the scope* of VAT.

Examples of where this is likely to be important will be with:

- the making of capital contributions to partnerships (see *KapHag Renditefonds v Finanzamt Charlottenburg* discussed later in **Chapter 4** at 40-000),
- the issue of shares and arguably other securities (see *Kretztechnik AG v Finanzamt Linz* and later in **Chapter 4** at 40-000),
- the participation in hedging transactions in foreign exchange and certain other financial products by persons other than banks (see *Willis Pension Fund Trustees Ltd* [2006] BVC 2,045, discussed later in **Chapter 7** at 70-200); and
- the assignment of debts and receivables under a securitisation arrangement (see *MBNA Europe Bank Ltd v R & C Commrs* and *Capital One Bank (Europe) Plc v HM Revenue & Customs* discussed at 70-100 in **Chapter 7**, where the assignment was seen as little more than security for loans).

The *KapHag* and *Kretztechnik* decisions have now effectively negated the earlier decisions in cases like *Trinity Mirror plc v C & E Commrs* [2001] BVC 167, *Southampton Leisure Holdings plc* [2003] BVC 4,010, *Water Hall Group plc v C & E Commrs* [2003] BVC 4,085 and *Actinic plc v C & E Commrs* [2003] BVC 4,096.

Some, but not necessarily all, of these will cause problems over the recovery of input VAT (see **Chapter 2**).

30-225 Fiscal neutrality

The VAT treatment of output supplies must meet the requirements of fiscal neutrality (the principle is to be found in the preamble to the VAT Directive (see paragraphs 5 and 7)). This means that two identical or similar supplies from the perspective of the consumer must not be treated in a different way for VAT purposes. The way in which this principle applies is illustrated by the decision of the Court of Justice in *R & C Commrs v The Rank Group plc* (Cases C-259/10 and C-260/10) [2011] BVC 389 . The case involved supplies relating to mechanised cash bingo and slot machines which were treated differently for the purposes of exemption from VAT. The difference in treatment existed despite the fact that the machines were comparable/identical from the consumers point of view. The taxpayer argued that the difference in treatment was contrary to the principle of fiscal neutrality. The court held that (at para. 36 of the judgment):

> '... the principle of fiscal neutrality must be interpreted as meaning that a difference in treatment for the purposes of VAT of two supplies of services which are identical or similar from the point of view of the consumer and meet the same needs of the consumer is sufficient to establish an infringement of that principle. Such an infringement thus does not require in addition that the actual existence of competition between the services in question or distortion of competition because of such difference in treatment be established.'

In relation to the scope of the application of the VAT exemption imposed on supplies relating to some of the machines (the exemption under art. 13B(f) of the Sixth Directive (now art. 135(1)(i) of the VAT Directive)) the CoJ noted that the provision leaves a broad discretion to the Member States as regards the exemption or the taxation of the transactions concerned since it allows the Member States to fix the conditions and the limitations to which entitlement to that exemption may be subject. However, in determining which transactions are subject to VAT, each Member State must respect the principle of fiscal neutrality. In relation to the approach on similarity of services, the CoJ commented (at para. 44 of their judgment):

> 'Two supplies of services are therefore similar where they have similar characteristics and meet the same needs from the point of view of consumers, the test being whether their use is comparable, and where the differences between them do not have a significant influence on the decision of the average consumer to use one such service or the other ...'

Where there is a breach of the concept in circumstances where one service is subject to VAT, and the other is not, then the taxpayer is entitled to claim repayment of the VAT, and for the services to be treated in the same way for VAT purposes.

30-250 Place of supply and belonging

In **Chapter 1** reference was made to the basic concepts which determine whether or not something may be subject to VAT. Perhaps the most important is the *place of supply*, because the incidence and burden of VAT is based on territory. Council Directive 2006/112/EC provides in art. 2(1)(a), for example, that:

> 'the supply of goods for consideration within the territory of a Member State by a taxable person acting as such;'

shall be subject to VAT and, similarly, in art. 2(1)(c) for services:

> 'the supply of services for consideration within the territory of a Member State by a taxable person acting as such'

although it is as well to bear in mind that this principle does not just apply to supplies that are taxable, in the sense that they give rise to a liability to VAT. It also applies to supplies that are VAT exempt.

For UK VAT purposes, therefore, a supply, whether taxable or exempt, will generally only be counted as a UK supply if it takes place in the UK; otherwise it is *outside the scope*.

Whilst this same general proposition applies, to both goods and services, however, it is important to note that there are quite different rules that apply to each. For goods, it is also necessary, in the case of intra-EU movements, to consider the place of *acquisition* or *dispatch*. The latter are discussed later at 30-300.

(1) Goods

For goods, the test on the *place of supply* is essentially physical. The place of supply is decided by VATA 1994, s. 7 and the corresponding rules in art. 31 to 36 of Council Directive 2006/112/

EC (the Sixth VAT Directive (art. 8)). A summary of the place of supply rules is provided in the Table shown below. The result is to look to where the goods are at the time of supply or appropriation. Where contracts are signed or accepted (or where the supplier may be established) is rarely a factor. Therefore, the place of supply is *in the UK* if:

(1) the goods are in the UK; or

(2) the supply involves:

    (a) installation or assembly in the UK;
    (b) exports from the UK; or
    (c) dispatches from the UK to other Member States;

The place of supply is *outside* the UK if:

(1) the goods are outside the UK; or

(2) the supply involves:

    (a) installation or assembly outside the UK;
    (b) imports into the UK; or
    (c) acquisitions in the UK from other Member States.

In the latter case, although the supply may be outside the UK, the actual act of importation or acquisition into the UK generally triggers a VAT charge (VATA 1994, s. 1(1)(a) and (b)).

The exceptions are few and tend to cover matters such as distance selling, which are of generally less relevance to the sectors covered by this book.

- *Auto Lease Holland BV v Bundesant fur Finanzen* (Case C-185/01) [2005] BVC 182) was an interesting case, perhaps, in this respect. The company leased motor vehicles and also offered the facility of a fuel management agreement. This enabled lessees to buy fuel using a credit card issued in Auto Lease's name. Auto Lease paid the credit card company for the fuel and spread the cost, so far as the lessees were concerned, in equal instalments over a year, with a settlement at the end, based on actual consumption. The question put to ECJ was whether this:

    - represented a supply of goods (at the place where the fuel *was physically supplied*); or
    - was included in Auto Lease's supply of vehicle leasing (at the basic place of supply of services, where the supplier, Auto Lease *belonged* or *was established*).

    The Court ruled that the fuel management agreement was not a contract for the supply of fuel, but a contract to finance its purchase.

The question was not, therefore, so much one of the place of supply as of what was being supplied and to whom, but the importance of the decision is evident when it is remembered that the fuel was purchased in Germany and Auto Lease was based in the Netherlands.

Place of supply and belonging   30-250

A summary of the place of supply rules for goods is provided below.

Summary of place of supply rules for goods

Goods	Place of supply	VATA 1994/VAT Directive
Goods not removed from the UK that are in the UK when supplied.	Goods supplied in the UK.	s 7(2) (VAT Directive, arts 31 and 32)
Goods not removed to the UK that are outside the UK when supplied.	Goods supplied outside the UK.	s 7(2) (VAT Directive, arts 31 and 32)
Goods installed or assembled at a place in the UK to which they are removed.	Goods supplied in the UK.	s 7(3)(a) (VAT Directive, art 36)
Goods installed or assembled outside the UK at a place to which they are removed.	Goods supplied outside the UK.	s 7(3)(b) (VAT Directive, art 36)
A supply involving the removal of goods to the UK by or under the directions of the person who supplies them; the supply is a transaction in pursuance of which the goods are acquired in the UK from another Member State by a person who is not a taxable person; the supplier is liable to be registered under VATA 1994; and the supply is neither a supply of goods consisting in a new means of transport nor anything which is treated as a supply of goods by virtue of being a deemed supply of assets from a business or transfer of own goods (whether for consideration or not).	Goods supplied in the UK. This place of supply rule applies unless any of the preceding rules apply.	s 7(4) (VAT Directive, arts 33 and 34)
A supply of goods that does not consist of a new means of transport, where the supply involves the removal of goods, by or under the directions of the person who supplies them, from the UK to another Member State; the person who makes the supply is taxable in another Member State; and the provisions of the law of that Member State corresponding, in relation to that Member State, to the rules referred to in the row above (for s 7(4) regarding supplies to non-taxable customers) make that person liable to VAT on the supply in that Member State.	Goods supplied outside the UK. This place of supply rule applies unless any of the preceding rules apply. This rule does not however apply where the VAT liability of the person in the other Member State depends on the exercise by any person of an option (to tax in the Member State of destination whatever the value of supplies) in the UK, under specific rules which treats supplies as being made outside the UK.	s 7(5) (VAT Directive, arts 33 and 34)

3 Outputs and Output VAT

Goods	Place of supply	VATA 1994/VAT Directive
A supply of goods, where the supply involves the goods being imported into the UK from somewhere outside the EU by or under the directions of the person who supplies them. Where, or to whom, the goods are delivered in the UK following importation does not affect the position.	Goods supplied in the UK. Again, this place of supply rule applies unless any of the preceding rules apply. Effectively, under this rule the place of supply is determined by who acts as the importer. So, if the supplier imports the goods into the UK, the supply to the UK customer is treated as taking place in the UK and the supplier may be liable to register for VAT in the UK. However, if the UK customer imports the goods, the supply is treated under s 7(7)(b) (see below) as taking place outside the UK.	s 7(6) (VAT Directive, art 32)
Goods removed from the UK without also involving their previous removal to the UK, eg goods removed from the UK to another Member State (other than supplies to private/non-taxable customers under s 7(5) above), and an export of goods from the UK to outside the EU.	Goods supplied in the UK. However, the VAT liability should be zero-rated. The supplier would need to complete an EC Sales List for supplies of goods to a VAT registered business in another Member State.	s 7(7)(a). See also s 30(8). (VAT Directive, art 32)
Goods removed to the UK from another Member State (other than supplies to private/non-taxable customers under s 7(4) above), or imported from outside the EU to the UK where the UK customer (rather than the supplier) is the person responsible for the importation.	Goods supplied outside the UK.	s 7(7)(b) (VAT Directive, art 32)

(2) Services

The rules on the place of supply of services will be the main concern for the businesses covered by this book.

To some extent, the test here is also a physical one – the basic rule is fixed by where the supplier of the service is located in relation to supplies to non-business customers ('B2C'); and where the recipient, if a 'relevant taxable business person', of the supply of services is located ('B2B'). However, this is just the starting point. Other rules place greater emphasis on exactly what is provided, to whom it is provided, and where, which will override the general rules as discussed below.

As with supplies of goods, where contracts are signed or accepted is also rarely a factor.

A summary of the place of supply rules for services is provided below.

(a) The basic rules

This is really the fall-back position, or starting point, and is that found in art. 44 of VAT Directive 2006/112 in connection with business to business supplies. This reads:

> 'The place of supply of services to a taxable person acting as such shall be the place where that person has established his business. However, if those services are provided to a fixed establishment of the taxable person located in a place other than the place where he has established his business, the place of supply of those services shall be the place where that fixed establishment is located. In the absence of such a place of establishment or fixed establishment, the place of supply of services shall be the place where the taxable person who receives such services has his permanent address or usually resides.'

Where supplies are made to a non-taxable person the fall-back position, or starting point, is that found in art. 45 of VAT Directive 2006/112. This reads:

> 'The place of supply of services to a non-taxable person shall be the place where the supplier has established his business. However, if those services are provided from a fixed establishment of the supplier in a place other than the place where he has established his business, the place of supply of those services shall be the place where that fixed establishment is located. In the absence of such a place of establishment or fixed establishment, the place of supply of services shall be the place where the supplier has his permanent address or usually resides.'

This is reflected in the UK in what is now VATA 1994, s. 7A(2), which provides that:

> 'A supply of services is to be treated as made -
> (a) in a case in which the person to whom the services are supplied is a relevant business person in the country in which the recipient belongs; and
> (b) otherwise, in the country in which the supplier belongs.'

Where a person *belongs* is then defined in VATA 1994, s. 9 for both the supplier and the recipient of a service.

Put another way:

- a supply to someone in business in the UK is always a UK supply;
- a supply to a private individual or to someone not in business in the UK by a UK supplier is always a UK supply;
- a supply by a UK supplier to a private individual or to someone not in business and who, in either case, is established or belongs in another EU country is also always a UK supply;
- a supply by a UK supplier to someone in business and who is established or belongs in another EU country will take place in the Member State concerned and will be outside the scope of UK VAT;
- a supply by a UK supplier to someone in business belonging or established outside the EU will be outside the scope of both UK and EU VAT altogether.

Who is a relevant business person, and where does such a person belong?

If the recipient of services is a relevant business person then the place of supply is where the recipient belongs (unless overriding place of supply rules apply in Sch. 4A to VATA 1994 (which are summarised in the Table below)). A person is treated as a 'relevant business person' if that person:

(a) is a taxable person within the meaning of art. 9 of the VAT Directive (2006/112/EC) (broadly, any person who, independently, carries out in any place any economic activity, whatever the purpose or results of that activity);
(b) is registered under VATA 1994;
(c) is identified as a taxable person under the law of another Member State, or
(d) is registered under an Act of Tynwald (Isle of Man) for the purposes of any tax imposed under that Act which corresponds to VAT, and the services are received by the person otherwise than wholly for private purposes. (VATA 1994, s 7A(4)).

In relation to identifying who is a 'relevant business' for the purposes of (a) above, art. 9 of the VAT Directive provides a 'taxable person' means 'any person who independently carries out in any place any economic activity ... whatever the purpose or results of that activity'. An economic activity is defined as 'any activity of producers, traders or persons supplying services' (art. 9(1)) (see generally 10-300). A person who carries on an economic activity under a contract of employment does not carry on the activity independently (art. 10). Any state, regional or local authority governed by public law is not, unless otherwise provided for, a taxable person in respect of activities carried on by it as a public authority. This prohibition applies even where the public authority collects fees, contributions or payments in respect of those activities or transactions (art. 13(1)). However, a public authority is treated as a taxable person where it would lead to significant distortions of competition (art. 13(1)). Where any of the following activities are carried on by a body governed by public law it is treated as a taxable person in respect of the activities, provided it is not carried out on such a small scale as to be negligible (see art 13(1)), which include:

(a) telecommunication services;
(b) supply of new goods manufactured for sale;
(c) running of trade fairs and exhibitions;
(d) activities of commercial publicity bodies;
(e) activities of travel agencies;
(f) transactions (other than those specified in art 132(1)(q)) of radio and television bodies (art 132 relates to the exemption of specific activities in the public interest, such as 'activities of public radio and television bodies other than those of a commercial nature').

The evidential circumstances in which a person can be considered to be a taxable person are considered below. The place where a 'relevant business person' is treated as belonging for the purposes of VATA 1994 must be construed in accordance with the EU Council Implementing Regulation (No. 282/2011 (15 March 2011)). For the purposes of the place of supply rules, under VATA 1994, a 'relevant business person' is treated as belonging in a 'relevant country', which means: (a) if the person has a business establishment, or some other fixed place of establishment, in a country (and none in any other country), that country; or (b) if the person has a business establishment, or some other fixed establishment or establishments, in more than one country, the country in which the relevant establishment is located (this means whichever of the person's establishments is most directly concerned with the supply) (VATA 1994, s 9(4)), or (c) if none of the foregoing apply, the country in which the person's usual place of residence is located (VATA 1994, s 9(3)). The business establishment for a person is the principal place of business for that person, and is regarded as being the head office, headquarters or 'seat' from which the business is operated (HMRC Notice 741A (January 2010), para. 3.3). There can only be once such place, such as an office, show room or factory (HMRC Notice 741A (January 2010), para. 3.3).

Relevant business person: business establishment

Under the EU Council Implementing Regulation the place where the business of a taxable person is established is the place where the functions of the business' central administration are carried out (this is directly relevant to the application of art. 44 and 45 of the VAT Directive) (art. 10(1)). To determine this location the following matters must be taken into account (art. 10(2)):

- the place where essential decisions concerning the general management of the business are taken;
- the place where the registered office of the business is located; and
- the place where management meets.

Where the foregoing criteria do not allow the place of establishment of a business to be determined with certainty, the place where essential decisions concerning the general management of the business are taken will take precedence (art. 10(2)). However, the mere presence of a postal address may not be taken to be the place of establishment of a business of a taxable person (art. 10(3)).

Relevant business person: fixed establishment

The EU Council Implementing Regulation (art. 11(1)) provides that in the context of the place of supply rules to a taxable person, a 'fixed establishment' means any establishment, other than the place of establishment of a business (referred to above), characterised by a sufficient degree of permanence and a suitable structure in terms of human and technical resources to enable it to receive and use the services supplied to it for its own needs. The EU Council Implementing Regulations (art. 11(2)) provides a similar definition of fixed establishment in connection with the application of art. 45 of the VAT Directive (supply of services to a non-taxable person). The EU Implementing Regulations also provide that the fact of having a VAT identification number is not of itself sufficient to create a fixed establishment for a taxable person (art. 11(3)).

Essentially, therefore, the test is whether, and, if so, where, the relevant business person has a *business establishment* or some other fixed establishment. . In the absence of such an establishment, a body corporate (e.g. a company) will have its usual place of residence where it is legally constituted (s. 9(6)).

3 Outputs and Output VAT

Who is a non business person, and where does such a person belong?

Under VATA 1994, a person who is not a relevant business person is treated as belonging in the country in which the person's usual place of residence is located (VATA 1994, s 9(5)). The 'usual place of residence' for a body corporate is treated as being the place where it is legally constituted (VATA 1994, s 9(6)). However, it is necessary to construe VATA 1994 in accordance with the EU Implementing Regulations, which provide that the place where a natural person 'usually resides', whether or not a taxable person, is the place where that natural person usually lives as a result of personal and occupational ties (art. 13). Where the occupational ties are in a country different from that of the personal ties, or where no occupational ties exist, the place of usual residence shall be determined by personal ties which show close links between the natural person and a place where he is living (art. 13).

Articles 44 and 45 of the VAT Directive also refer to the concept of 'permanent address' (as referred to above in the articles). The EU Implementing Regulation provides that the concept of 'permanent address' of a natural person, whether or not a taxable person is to mean 'the address entered in the population or similar register, or the address indicated by that person to the relevant tax authorities, unless there is evidence that this address does not reflect reality' (art. 12).

In *1st Contact Ltd* [2012] UKFTT 84; [2012] TC 01780 the First-tier Tax Tribunal was asked to consider whether individuals belonged outside the UK who received supplies of foreign exchange (FOREX) and money remittance services. The FOREX services were exempt supplies under Sch. 9, Group 5, item 1 of VATA 1994. The issue was whether the individuals belonged outside the UK for the purposes of s. 9(3) of VATA 1994 (which turned on the individual's usual place of residence) and art. 56 of VAT Directive 2006/112 (previously art. 9(2)(2) of the Sixth Directive). If the individuals did belong outside the UK then the taxpayer would be able to claim the input tax attributable to the supplies in accordance with art. 3(a) of the *Value Added Tax (Input Tax) (Specified Supplies) Order* 1999 (SI 1999/3121). The First-tier Tribunal decided that the individuals did not on the evidence belong outside the UK, with the consequence that the taxpayer was not entitled to relief for input VAT. Section 9(3) of VATA 1994, as then in force, provided that:

> 'If the supply of services is made to an individual and received by him otherwise than for the purposes of any business carried on by him, he shall be treated as belonging in whatever country he has his usual place of residence.'

The taxpayer's customers were young people, typically aged 21–30, from Australia, New Zealand and South Africa who came to the United Kingdom on a 'working holiday' or 'overseas experience' (OE). They have flexible work/travel arrangements and no fixed plans. They were usually interested in temporary work, predominantly 3-6 month contracts. The Tribunal made the following comments:

> 'an ordinary tourist in the UK for a period of days or weeks clearly could not generally be said to have their ordinary residence here. A typical tourist would normally have a home and employment in their country of origin. Typically, a tourist would not rent their home out while on holidays, and would be on annual leave from their employment at home and would not be taking up employment in the UK. However, each case would depend on its own facts. A person

who spent a year in the UK without working, and who spent the year in the UK travelling and sightseeing, might well be described as a "tourist". However, if the person had no home or employment in their country of origin, and if they rented a home in the UK for the year as a base from which to conduct travels and sightseeing, the conclusion might be reached that the person is ordinarily resident in the UK for the year in question (para. 50 of the judgment).

- the nature of customers' work while in the United Kingdom (whether in the "finance" industry, or in unskilled labour) has no material bearing (para. 53 of the judgment).
- the taxpayer's customers came to the UK intending to have an experience involving a combination of travel and work known as a "working holiday" or "overseas experience", and that they would typically stay some 18 months. They remained regularly in the UK for that period, with temporary absences visiting other countries (including short trips back to their home countries), even if their living arrangements were short term and transitory. The purpose of having such a "working holiday" or "overseas experience" could itself be a "settled purpose" (para. 54 of the judgment).
- the fact that the taxpayer's customers intended that they would be in the UK only temporarily and would return to their "normal" lives in their home countries at the end of a working holiday does not mean that they could not be ordinarily resident in the UK (para. 56 of the judgment).'

Determining the status of the customer: whether a taxable person

Under the EU Implementing Regulation , a supplier may regard a customer established within the EU as a taxable person (subject to any information to the contrary) (art. 18(1)):

(a) where the customer has communicated his individual VAT identification number to him, and the supplier obtains confirmation of the validity of that identification number and of the associated name and address;

(b) where the customer has not yet received an individual VAT identification number, but informs the supplier that he has applied for it and the supplier obtains any other proof which demonstrates that the customer is a taxable person or a non-taxable legal person required to be identified for VAT purposes and carries out a reasonable level of verification of the accuracy of the information provided by the customer, by normal commercial security measures such as those relating to identity or payment checks.

Under the EU Implementing Regulation (art. 18(2)), a supplier may regard a customer established within the EU as a non-taxable person (subject to any information to the contrary) when he can demonstrate that the customer has not communicated his individual VAT identification number to him.

A supplier may regard a customer established outside the EU as a taxable person (subject to any information to the contrary) (art. 18(3)):

(a) if he obtains from the customer a certificate issued by the customer's competent tax authorities as confirmation that the customer is engaged in economic activities in order to enable him to obtain a refund of VAT under Council Directive 86/560/EEC (arrangements for the refund of value added tax to taxable persons not established in Community territory);

(b) where the customer does not possess that certificate, if the supplier has the VAT number, or a similar number attributed to the customer by the country of establishment and used to identify businesses or any other proof which demonstrates that the customer is a taxable person and if the supplier carries out a reasonable level of verification of the accuracy of the information provided by the customer, by normal commercial security measures such as those relating to identity or payment checks.

Further guidance on where the recipient belongs

The conditions referred to in VATA 1994, s 9 relate to identifying a business establishment or some other fixed establishment, or place of residence, for the place of belonging rules of a relevant business person. The rules for a person who is not a relevant business person focus exclusively on that person's usual place of residence (VATA 1994, s. 9(4)). Identifying whether the person is in business or not is usually relatively clear, although, as cases like that of *Polysar Investments Netherlands BV v Inspecteur der Invoerrechten en Accijnzen, Arnhem* (Case C-60/90) [1993] BVC 88 and the *Wellcome Trust Ltd v C & E Commrs* (Case C-155/94) [1996] BVC 377 illustrate, it is not always possible to take things at face-value. Applying the belonging rules is not always straightforward.

Securities and place of supply

Transactions involving securities, for example, can be difficult and often the position can be hard to decide with any degree of certainty. To overcome this, a practical balance of probabilities approach has evolved, which is effectively codified in a special HMRC easement (referred to in para 6.16 of Notice 701/49 of November 2011). This is important in the context of what is discussed in Chapter 8 and what it says is:

'If:

- your place of belonging is the UK
- you sell securities to a customer, and
- you cannot identify your customer or their place of belonging

you may

- treat the supply as being in the UK and exempt, or
- use the place of belonging of a nominee account for the purchaser to determine the place of supply, or
- use a special rule known as "the easement". This works by using the following tests in sequential order:
    (a) Where the place of transaction, that is the relevant security exchange, is known then a sale transacted:
        - in the UK is treated as made to a person belonging in the UK and exempt
        - in any other EU Member State is treated as made to a taxable person belonging in that Member State, and is outside the scope of UK VAT, but without recovery of your related input tax
        - outside the EU is treated as made to a person belonging outside the EU and is outside the scope of UK VAT. You can recover related input tax subject to normal rules.
    (b) Where the place of the transaction is not known, then the place of supply is deemed to be a place where the security is listed.

(c) Where the place of transaction is not known and the security is not listed or is listed on both a EU and non-EU exchange, then the place of supply is deemed to be the place where the last known broker in the transaction "belongs".'

How do you attribute supplies to a particular establishment?

In most cases, the question of where someone *belongs* will be easy to decide. A company or unincorporated business will usually have a branch or office somewhere. All that remains, therefore, is to consider whether that location or some other is most directly concerned with a given transaction. Guidance on how to attribute supplies to a particular establishment is provided by the EU Implementing Regulation (No. 282/2011 (15 March 2011): see generally art. 4, Subsection 3).

Taxable person located in multiple countries with a fixed establishment: determining location of the supply

The following principles apply to determine in which country a supply is taxable where a taxable person is established in more than one country (EU Implementing Regulation No. 282/2011 (15 March 2011), art. 21):

- the supply is taxable in the country where that taxable person has established his business,
- where the service is provided to a fixed establishment of the taxable person located in a place other than that where the customer has established his business, that supply is taxable at the place of the fixed establishment receiving that service and using it for its own needs,
- where the taxable person does not have a place of establishment of a business or a fixed establishment, the supply is taxable at his permanent address or usual residence.

The following principles are applied to determine the identity of the fixed establishment to which a service is supplied (EU Implementing Regulation No. 282/2011 (15 March 2011), art. 22):

- the supplier is required to examine the nature and use of the service provided to the taxable person,
- where the nature and use of the service provided do not enable the supplier to identify the fixed establishment to which the service is provided, the supplier, in identifying that fixed establishment, is required to pay particular attention to whether:
  - the contract,
  - the order form, and
  - the VAT identification number attributed by the Member State of the customer and communicated to the supplier by the customer

identify the fixed establishment as the customer of the service, and whether the fixed establishment is the entity paying for the service.

Where the customer's fixed establishment to which the service is provided cannot be determined in accordance with the foregoing principles or where services are supplied to a taxable person under a contract covering one or more services used in an unidentifiable and non-quantifiable manner, the supplier is entitled to consider that the services have been supplied at the place where the customer has established its business (No. 282/2011 (15 March 2011), art. 22).

There are further rules on who accounts for VAT where a taxable person has a fixed establishment. These are that where a taxable person has a fixed establishment in the territory of a Member State where tax is due then the supplier is treated as a taxable person who is not established within that Member State when it makes a taxable supply in that Member State and any fixed establishment 'does not intervene in that supply' (VAT Directive, art. 192a). In the application of this article, a fixed establishment of a taxable person will only be taken into consideration when it is characterised by a sufficient degree of permanence and a suitable structure in terms of human and technical resources to enable it to make the supply of goods or services in which it intervenes (art. 53(1) EU Implementing Regulation). Where a taxable person has a fixed establishment within the territory of the EU where the VAT is due, that establishment shall be considered as not intervening in the supply of goods or services, unless the technical and human resources of that fixed establishment are used by that person for transactions inherent in the fulfilment of the taxable supply of those goods or services made within that Member State, before or during this fulfilment (art. 53(2)). Where the resources of the fixed establishment are only used for administrative support tasks such as accounting, invoicing and collection of debt-claims, they shall not be regarded as being used for the fulfilment of the supply of goods or services (art. 53(2)). However, if an invoice is issued under the VAT identification number attributed by the Member State of the fixed establishment, that fixed establishment shall be regarded as having intervened in the supply of goods or services made in that Member State unless there is proof to the contrary (art. 53(2)). However, where a taxable person has established its place of business within the territory of the Member State where the VAT is due then the foregoing does not apply irrespective of whether or not that place of business intervenes in the supply of goods or services which are made in that Member State (No. 282/2011 (15 March 2011), art. 54).

What is a fixed establishment?

The concept of fixed establishment is interpreted by HMRC as (HMRC Notice 741A (January 2010), para. 3.4):

> **'What is a fixed establishment?**
>
> A fixed establishment is an establishment other than the business establishment, which has both the technical and human resources necessary for providing or receiving services permanently present. A business may have several fixed establishments, including a branch of a business or an agency.
>
> If you have a temporary presence of human and technical resources, this does not create a fixed establishment in the UK. For example, an overseas television company sending staff and equipment to the UK to film for a week does not constitute a fixed establishment in the UK.
>
> 3.4.1 Examples of fixed establishment
>
> - An overseas business sets up a branch comprising staff and offices in the UK to provide services. The UK branch is a fixed establishment.
> - A company with a business establishment overseas owns a property in the UK which it leases to tenants. The property does not in itself create a fixed establishment. However, if

Place of supply and belonging   30-250

the company has UK offices and staff or appoints a UK agency to carry on its business by managing the property, this creates a fixed establishment in the UK.
- An overseas business contracts with UK customers to provide services. It has no human or technical resources in the UK and therefore sets up a UK subsidiary to act in its name to provide those services. The overseas business has a fixed establishment in the UK created by the agency of the subsidiary.
- A company is incorporated in the UK but trades entirely overseas from its head office in the USA, which is its business establishment. The UK registered office is a fixed establishment.
- A UK company acts as the Operating Member of a consortium for offshore exploitation of oil or gas using a fixed production platform. The rig is a fixed establishment of the Operating Member.'

The issues surrounding the concepts surrounding belonging, established, having an established place of business are set out in some detail in section 3 of Notice 741.

Summary of place of supply rules for services

Services	Place of Supply	VATA 1994/VAT Directive
Business to Consumer (B2C)		
Supply of a service by a supplier who belongs in the UK to a non-business person (i.e. a private individual, charity, government department or other body that has no business activities)	Service supplied in the country in which the supplier belongs (unless an overriding place of supply rule applies in Schedule 4A to VATA: see below). UK VAT is due where the supplier belongs in the UK.	s 7A(2)(b) (Art 44 VAT Directive)
Business to Business (B2B)		
Supply of a service to a 'relevant business person' by a UK supplier	Service supplied in the country in which the recipient belongs (unless an overriding place of supply rule applies in Sch 4A to VATA 1994: see below). If the customer is in the UK then UK VAT is due. If the customer is outside the UK then the supply is outside the scope of UK VAT; and if outside the EU then the supply is outside the scope of EU VAT. If the customer belongs in another Member State (and is VAT registered), no UK VAT is due but the supply is subject to VAT in that Member State (due to the effect of the reverse charge (see Chapter 5)).	s 7A(2)(a) (Art 45 VAT Directive)

Services	Place of Supply	VATA 1994/VAT Directive
General exceptions (overriding rules)		
Land		
Services relating to land, including (a) the provision in a hotel, inn, boarding house or similar establishment of sleeping accommodation or of accommodation in rooms which are provided in conjunction with sleeping accommodation or for the supply of catering and (b) services such as are supplied by estate agents, auctioneers, architects, surveyors, engineers and others involved in matters relating to land.	Supply treated as made in the country in which the land is situated.	Sch 4A, para 1.
HMRC Notice 741A (January 2010), para 6.4/6.5 • Within exception: Legal Services such as conveyancing, the supply of warehouse space • Outside exception: Advice or information relating to land prices or property markets (since the information does not relate to specific sites)		
Passenger transport		
A supply of services consisting of the transportation of passengers (or of any luggage or motor vehicles accompanying passengers).	Made in the country in which the transportation takes place, and, in a case where it takes place in more than one country, in proportion to the distances covered in each. There are special rules for passenger transport which leaves and re-enters a country, which can treat the transportation as taking place wholly in that country.	Sch 4A, para 2
Hiring of means of transport		
A supply consisting of the short-term hiring of a means of transport Short-term hiring means transport which is hired for a continuous period not exceeding (a) if the means of transport is a vessel, 90 days and (b) otherwise 30 days. Any hire beyond this point is a long-term hire of the means of transport.	Made in the country in which the means of transport is actually put at the disposal of the person by whom it is hired (this treatment applies for both B2B and B2C supplies). However, (a) if the hiring of a means of transport would otherwise be treated as being made in the UK, and the services are to any extent effectively used and enjoyed in a country which is not a Member State, then the supply	Sch 4A, para 3 (EU Implementing Regulation, Arts 38–40)

Services	Place of Supply	VATA 1994/VAT Directive
	is to be treated to that extent as being made in that country and (b) where a supply consists of the hiring of a means of transport which would otherwise be treated as made in a country which is not a Member State, and the services are to any extent effectively used and enjoyed in the UK the supply is to be treated to that extent as made in the UK.	
	Without prejudice to point (b) from 1 January 2013, the supply is not subject to VAT if the supplier demonstrates that the place of supply it outside the EU (as determined by Section 4(3) and (4) of Chapter V of the EU Implementing Reg (Art 3). See Appendix 28).	

NB: The place where the means of transport is put at the disposal of the customer is the place where the customer or a third party acting on his behalf takes physical possession of it.

HMRC Notice 741A (January 2010), para 7

- Within exception: Ships, boats, yachts, barges, aircraft, cars, trucks, lorries, motorcycles, cycles, touring caravans and trailers, railway wagons
- Outside exception: Freight containers, static caravans, racing cars (where the provision of the car forms part of a supply of sporting activities)

EU Implementing Regulation, Art 38: -

'Means of transport' includes vehicles, whether motorised or not, and other equipment and devices designed to transport persons or objects from one place to another, which might be pulled, drawn or pushed by vehicles and which are normally designed to be used and actually capable of being used for transport.

- The means of transport includes, the following vehicles: (a) land vehicles, such as cars, motor cycles, bicycles, tricycles and caravans, (b) trailers and semi-trailers, (c) railway wagons, (d) vessels, (e) aircraft, (f) vehicles specifically designed for the transport of sick or injured persons, (g) agricultural tractors and other agricultural carriages, (h) mechanically or electronically propelled invalid carriages.

Hiring of goods		
A supply of services consisting of the hiring of any goods other than a means of transport which would otherwise be treated as made in the UK, and the services are to any extent effectively used and enjoyed in a country which is not a Member State.	Subject to the use and enjoyment rule, with the result that the supply is made in a non-EU country to the extent it is effectively used and enjoyed in that country.	Sch 4A, para 7(1)

Services	Place of Supply	VATA 1994/VAT Directive
A supply of services consisting of the hiring of any goods other than a means of transport which would otherwise be treated as made in a country which is not a Member State, and the services are to any extent effectively used and enjoyed in the UK.	Subject to the use and enjoyment rule, with the result that the supply takes place in the UK to the extent it is effectively used and enjoyed in the UK during the hiring period.	Sch 4A, para 7(2)
Telecommunications and broadcasting services		
A supply of services consisting of the provision of: (a) telecommunications services, or (b) radio or television broadcasting services. 'telecommunications services' means services relating to the transmission, emission or reception of signals, writing, images and sounds or information of any nature by wire, radio, optical or other electromagnetic systems, including (a) the related transfer or assignment of the right to use capacity for such transmission, emission or reception and (b) the provision of access to global information networks.	Covered by the general rules described above (until January 2015 – see Note below). Subject to the use and enjoyment rule with the result that where (a) the supply of services would otherwise be treated as made in the UK and (b) the services are to any extent effectively used and enjoyed in a country which is not a Member State, the supply is to be treated to that extent as made in that country. Where (a) the supply of services would otherwise be treated as made in a country which is not a Member State, and (b) the services are to any extent effectively used and enjoyed the UK, the supply is to be treated to that extent as made in the UK. However, from 1 January 2015 (without prejudice to the use and enjoyment rule), a B2C supply of these services is not subject to VAT if the supplier demonstrates that the place of supply is outside the EU in accordance with the EU Implementing Regulation (Art 3).	Sch 4A, para 8
NB: From 1 January 2015, B2C supplies of these services will move from the current general rule (location of supplier) to where the customer is established, has their permanent address, or usually resides. The 'one stop shop' registration scheme discussed in Chapter 12, which is available to non-EU suppliers in respect of electronically supplied services to EU private consumers, will be extended to both EU and non-EU businesses, and be widened to include telecommunications and broadcasting services (see Appendix 27).		
Exceptions to place of supply of services relating to supplies made to a relevant business person (B2B). **Electronically supplied services**		
Provision of electronically supplied services to a relevant business person. Examples (para. 9(3) Sch 4A):	Subject to the B2B general rule, but this is subject to the use and enjoyment rule.	Sch 4A, para 9

Services	Place of Supply	VATA 1994/VAT Directive
• website supply, web-hosting and distance maintenance of programmes and equipment; • the supply of software and the updating of software; • the supply of images, text and information, and the making available of databases; • the supply of music, films and games (including games of chance and gambling games); • the supply of political, cultural, artistic, sporting, scientific, educational or entertainment broadcasts (including broadcasts of events); and • the supply of distance teaching. (see also EU Implementing Regulation, Art 7 which provides a full definition and illustrations of services within the concept): See generally Chapter 12.	If there is a supply of services consisting of the provision of electronically supplied services to a relevant business person which would otherwise be treated as made in the UK, but the services are to any extent effectively used and enjoyed in a country which is not a Member State, then the supply is to be treated to that extent as made in that country. If there is a supply of services consisting of the provision of electronically supplied services to a relevant business person which would otherwise be treated as made in a country which is not a Member State, but the services are to any extent effectively used and enjoyed in the UK, then the supply is to be treated to that extent as made in the UK.	
NB: Where the supplier and customer communicate via e-mail, this does not of itself mean that the service provided is an electronically supplied service.		
Admission to cultural, educational and entertainment activities	[omitted]	
Transport of goods	Where: (a) a supply of services to a relevant business person consisting of the transportation of goods would otherwise be treated as made in the United Kingdom, and (b) the transportation takes place wholly outside the member States, the supply is to be treated as made wholly outside the member States.	The Value Added Tax (Place of Supply of Services) (Transport of Goods) Order 2012, SI 2012/2787, para. 9B

Services	Place of Supply	VATA 1994/VAT Directive
Ancillary transport services 'ancillary transport services' means loading, unloading, handling and similar activities.	(1) Where: (a) a supply of services to a relevant business person consisting of ancillary transport services would otherwise be treated as made in the United Kingdom, and (b) the services are physically performed wholly outside the member States, the supply is to be treated as made wholly outside the member States.	The Value Added Tax (Place of Supply of Services) (Transport of Goods) Order 2012, SI 2012/2787, para. 9C
Exceptions relating to supplies not made to a relevant business person (B2C)		
Intermediaries		
A supply to a person who is not a relevant business person consisting of the making of arrangements for a supply by or to another person or of any other activity intended to facilitate the making of such a supply. This also covers the services of intermediaries acting in the name and on behalf of the recipient of the service procured, and the services performed by intermediaries acting in the name and on behalf of the provider of the services procured.	Made in the same country as the (underlying) supply to which it relates. Most B2B intermediary services are subject to the general B2B rule and are supplied where the recipient belongs, (ie, subject to any specific exceptions such as land-related services).	Sch 4A, para 10 (EU Implementing Regulation, Arts 30–31)
Transport of goods: general		
A supply of services to a person who is not a relevant business person consisting of the transportation of goods (but not Intra-Community transport of goods).	Made in the country in which the transportation takes place, and (in a case where it takes place in more than one country) in proportion to the distances covered in each. B2B supplies of these services are subject to the general rule and supplied where the recipient belongs.	Sch 4A, para 11
Intra-Community transport of goods		
A supply of services to a person who is not a relevant business person consisting of the transportation of goods which begins in one Member State and ends in another.	Made in the Member State in which the transportation begins.	Sch 4A, para 12
Ancillary transport services	[omitted]	

Services	Place of Supply	VATA 1994/VAT Directive
Long-term hiring of means of transport		
A supply to a person who is not a relevant business person ('the recipient') of services consisting of the long-term hiring of a means of transport.	Made in the country in which the recipient belongs, unless the hire is a long-term hire of a pleasure boat.	Sch 4A, para 13A (with effect in relation to supplies made on or after 1 January 2013)
The hiring of a means of transport is 'long-term' if it is not short term (see above)	A supply to a person who is not a relevant business person ('the recipient') of services consisting of the long-term hiring of a pleasure boat which is actually put at the disposal of the recipient at the supplier's business establishment, or some other fixed establishment of the supplier, is to be treated as made in the country where the pleasure boat is actually put at the disposal of the recipient.	
	B2B supplies of long-term hiring of a means of transport remain subject to the general rule for B2B supplies and supplied where the recipient/customer belongs. However, the long-term hire of a means of transport is also subject to use and enjoyment rule, where the supply is B2B or B2C.	
	In addition, from 1 January 2013 (without prejudice to the use and enjoyment rule), the supply of B2C long-term hiring of a means of transport is not subject to VAT if the supplier demonstrates that the place of supply is outside the EU in accordance with the EU Implementing Regulation (Art 3).	
Valuation of, or work carried out, on goods	[omitted]	
Cultural, educational and entertainment activities etc	[omitted]	

3 Outputs and Output VAT

Services	Place of Supply	VATA 1994/VAT Directive
Electronic services		
A supply consisting of the provision by a person who belongs in a country which is not a Member State (other than the Isle of Man) of electronically supplied services (see below for meaning) to a person ('the recipient') who: (a) is not a relevant business person and (b) belongs in a Member State.	Made in the country in which the recipient belongs. Without prejudice to the place of effective enjoyment rules where the place of supply is outside the EU (Art 59a of the VAT Directive) from 1 January 2015, the supply is not subject to VAT if the supplier demonstrates that the place of supply it outside the EU (as determined by Section 4(3) and (4) of Chapter V of the EU Implementing Reg (Art 3)	Sch 4A, para 15
	Where supplied to a non-taxable person who is established in more than one country or has his permanent address in one country and his usual residence in another, priority is to be given to the place that best ensures taxation at the place of actual consumption when determining the place of supply of those services.	(EU Implementing Regulation, Art 24(2))
	(See above on changes being introduced in 2015 for the place of supply of cross border B2C supplies of telecommunications, broadcasting and electronically supplied services)	
Other services provided to a recipient belonging outside EC		
A supply consisting of the provision to a person ('the recipient') who: (a) is not a relevant business person and (b) belongs in a country which is not a Member State (other than the Isle of Man),of the following services:	Made in the country in which the recipient belongs.	Sch 4A, para 16
(a) transfers and assignments of copyright, patents, licences, trademarks and similar rights;	However, as noted earlier, the B2C services listed at (h), (i) and (j) are subject to the UK's use and enjoyment provisions (see HMRC Notice 741A, para 14.6).	
(b) the acceptance of any obligation to refrain from pursuing or exercising (in whole or in part) any business activity or any rights within paragraph (a);	Without prejudice to the place of effective enjoyment rules where the place of supply is outside the EU (Art 59a of the VAT Directive), the supply is not subject to VAT if the supplier demonstrates that the place of supply it outside the EU (as determined by Section 4(3) and (4) of Chapter V of the EU Implementing Reg (Art 3)	

Services	Place of Supply	VATA 1994/VAT Directive
(c) advertising services;		
(d) services of consultants, engineers, consultancy bureaux, lawyers, accountants, and similar services, data processing and provision of information, other than any services relating to land;		
(e) banking, financial and insurance services (including reinsurance), other than the provision of safe deposit facilities;	(See above on changes to be introduced in 2015 for the place of supply of cross border B2C supplies of telecommunications, broadcasting and electronically supplied services)	
(f) the provision of access to, or transmission or distribution through: (i) a natural gas system situated within the territory of a Member State or any network connected to such a system; (ii) an electricity system; or (iii) a network through which heat or cooling is supplied, and the provision of other directly linked services;		
(g) the supply of staff;		
(h) the letting on hire of goods other than means of transport;		
(i) telecommunication services (until January 2015);		
(j) radio and television broadcasting services (until January 2015); and		
(k) electronically supplied services (until January 2015)		
NB: the text of EU Implementing Regulation (Chapter V, Section 4, Subsections 3 and 4): Determining the place of supply is reproduced in Appendix 28.		

(b) The exceptions

In practice, the basic rules will apply to many of the services supplied by the business covered in this book. However, there are a number of special rules found in VATA 1994, s. 7A and Sch. 4A . Taken in their probable order of importance and relevance they are as follows:

(3) Services related to land

Important in the context of the businesses covered here are the categories of services connected with or related to land. Under art. 47 of VAT Directive 2006/112, these are taken to be supplied where the property is situated, a principle now reflected in VATA 1994, Sch. 4A, para. 1.

Thus, whether the supply is within the scope of UK VAT depends on whether the land is here, not on whether the service is physically performed in the UK or whether the supplier or recipient of the service belongs here. Applying the general principles of land law, this will extend to services to do with anything permanently attached to and forming part of it, including growing crops, buildings and other fixed structures.

What is interesting is that art. 47 of Council Directive 2006/112/EC is expressed in terms of services *connected with* the land. Paragraph 1(2) of Sch. 4A of VATA 1994, however, specifically covers:

'(a) the grant, assignment or surrender of any interest in or right over land, (b) the grant, assignment or surrender of a personal right to call for or be granted any interest in or right over land, (c) the grant, assignment or surrender of a licence to occupy land or any other contractual right exercisable over or in relation to land (including the provision of holiday accommodation, seasonal pitches for caravans and facilities at caravan parks for persons for whom such pitches are provided and pitches for tents and camping facilities), (d) the provision in an hotel, inn, boarding house or similar establishment of sleeping accommodation or of accommodation in rooms which are provided in conjunction with sleeping accommodation or for the purpose of a supply of catering, (e) any works of construction, demolition, conversion, reconstruction, alteration, enlargement, repair or maintenance of a building or civil engineering work, and (f) services such as are supplied by estate agents, auctioneers, architects, surveyors, engineers and others involved in matters relating to land.'

It thus extends to supplies *of* the land, which, on the face of it, appears arguably, perhaps, incorrect.

Section 3.4.1 of Notice 741A (January 2010) comments on whether land is capable of being a fixed establishment as follows:

'Examples of fixed establishment

- ...
- A company with a business establishment overseas owns a property in the UK which it leases to tenants. The property does not in itself create a fixed establishment. However, if the company has UK offices and staff or appoints a UK agency to carry on its business by managing the property, this creates a fixed establishment in the UK.'

However, the wording of art. 47 of VAT Directive 2006/112 and of para. 1 of Sch. 4A of VATA 1994 must make the existence of a fixed establishment largely irrelevant.

The rule in para.1 will be of particular interest in the context of insurance valuations, etc. covered in **Chapter 9**. It will also cover legal conveyancing work, but not similar services in effecting a charge over land in order to secure a loan.

In *Revenue & Customs Brief* 22/12 (2 August 2012) HMRC have published their view as to when services will be connected to land. HMRC state that:

'When is a service related to land?

In order for a service to be land related for determining the place of supply it must have a sufficiently direct connection with a specific piece of land.

This will include services:

- derived from land and where the land is a central and essential part of the service
- intended to legally or physically alter a property

Examples of services relating to land which are subject to VAT where the property is situated

- Construction or demolition of a building or permanent structure (such as pipelines for gas, water or sewage). Surveying and assessing property.
- Valuing property, including for insurance or loan purposes.
- Providing accommodation in hotels, holiday camps, camping sites or timeshare accommodation.
- Maintenance, renovation and repair of a building (including work such as cleaning and decorating) or permanent structure.
- Property management services (but not the management of a property investment portfolio).
- Arranging the sale or lease of land or property.
- Drawing up of plans for a building or part of a building designated for a particular site.
- On-site security services.
- Agricultural work on land (including tillage, sowing, watering and fertilization).
- Installation and assembly of machines which, when installed, will form a fixture that cannot be easily dismantled or moved.

The granting of rights to use all or part of a property (such as fishing or hunting rights and access to airport lounges).

Legal services such as conveyancing and drawing up of contracts of sale or leases.

- Bridge or tunnel toll fees.
- The supply of space for the use of advertising bill-boards - for example the leasing of a plot of land or the side of a building to allow a billboard to be erected.
- The supply of plant and equipment together with an operator, to allow the customer to carry out work on land or property where the supplier has responsibility for the execution of work.

Examples of services not relating to land

- Drawing up of plans for a building or part of a building that do not relate to a particular site.
- Arranging the supply of hotel accommodation or similar services.
- Installation, assembly, repair or maintenance of machines or equipment which are not, and do not become, part of the land or property.
- Management of a property investment portfolio.
- Advertising services that involve the use of a billboard.
- The supply of equipment with an operator, **where it can be shown** that the supplier has no responsibility for the performance of the work.'

(4) The hiring of a means of transport, passenger transport, and hiring of goods

- For passenger transport (para. 2, Sch. 4A of VATA 1994) a supply of services consisting of the transportation of passengers (or of any luggage or motor vehicles accompanying passengers) is treated as made in the country in which the transportation takes place, and in a case where it takes place in more than one country, in proportion to the distances covered in each;
- For a supply consisting of the short-term hiring of a means of transport (para. 3, Sch. 4A of VATA 1994) the supply is treated as made in the country in which the means of transport is actually put at the disposal of the person by whom it is hired; but (a) if the hiring of a means of transport would otherwise be treated as being made in the UK, and the services are to any extent effectively used and enjoyed in a country which is not a Member State then the supply is to be treated to that extent as being made in that country; and (b) where a supply consists of the hiring of a means of transport which would otherwise be treated as made in a country which is not a Member State, and the services are to any extent effectively used and enjoyed in the UK the supply is to be treated to that extent as made in the UK. The place where the means of transport is put at the disposal of the customer is the place where the customer or a third party acting on his behalf takes physical possession of it (EU Implementing Directive, art. 40). For this purpose, a 'means of transport' includes vehicles, whether motorised or not, and other equipment and devices designed to transport persons or objects from one place to another, which might be pulled, drawn or pushed by vehicles and which are normally designed to be used and actually capable of being used for transport. The means of transport includes, in particular, the following vehicles: (a) land vehicles, such as cars, motor cycles, bicycles, tricycles and caravans; (b) trailers and semi-trailers; (c) railway wagons; (d) vessels; (e) aircraft; (f) vehicles specifically designed for the transport of sick or injured persons; (g) agricultural tractors and other agricultural vehicles; (h) mechanically or electronically propelled invalid carriages. But vehicles which are permanently immobilised and containers will not be considered to be means of transport (EU Implementing Directive, art. 38). In practice, this heading will cover most means of transport and will include ships, boats, yachts, barges, aircraft, cars, trucks, lorries, motorcycles, cycles, touring caravans and trailers, railway wagons. It will not include freight containers, static caravans, racing cars (where forming part of a supply of sporting activities);
- For the position on the supply of a long term hiring of a means of transport see the Table above.
- For the transport of goods and ancillary transport services the following place of supply rules are effective from 20 December 2012 (by virtue of *The Value Added Tax (Place of Supply of Services) (Transport of Goods) Order 2012*, S I2012/2787 (See Schedule 4). These place of supply rules apply where the services are supplied to a relevant business person, specifically that:
    - *Transport of services*
      Where:

      (a) a supply of services to a relevant business person consisting of the transportation of goods would otherwise be treated as made in the United Kingdom, and

(b) the transportation takes place wholly outside the member States, the supply is to be treated as made wholly outside the member States.

- *Ancillary transport services*
  (1) Where:
  (a) a supply of services to a relevant business person consisting of ancillary transport services would otherwise be treated as made in the United Kingdom, and
  (b) the services are physically performed wholly outside the member States, the supply is to be treated as made wholly outside the member States.
  (2) In sub-paragraph (1)(a) 'ancillary transport services' means loading, unloading, handling and similar activities.

- For the hiring of goods, the position is as follows:
  - a supply of services consisting of the hiring of any goods (para. 7(1), Sch 4A of VATA 1994) other than a means of transport which would otherwise be treated as made in the United Kingdom, and the services are to any extent effectively used and enjoyed in a country which is not a Member State will be treated as made in the non-EU country to the extent it is effectively used and enjoyed in that country;
  - a supply of services consisting of the hiring of any goods (para. 7(2), Sch 4A of VATA 1994) other than a means of transport which would otherwise be treated as made in a country which is not a Member State, and the services are to any extent effectively used and enjoyed in the United Kingdom will be treated as made in the UK to the extent it is effectively used and enjoyed in the UK. However, from 1 January 2013 (without prejudice to the use and enjoyment rule), the supply is not subject to VAT if the supplier demonstrates that the place of supply is outside the EU in accordance with the EU Implementing Regulations (art. 3).

With cross-border leases to a taxable person between one Member State to another, there is the basic rule in art. 44 (VATA 1994, s 7A)– i.e. looking to where the recipient is *established* or *belongs*. The following cases were decided under the former place of supply rules, i.e. services supplied where the supplier has established its business or has a fixed establishment from which the service is supplied (i.e. the old art. 43 of the Sixth Directive). However, the cases are of assistance in illustrating the concepts of business establishment and fixed establishment.

- In the case of *ARO Lease BV v Inspecteur der Belastingdienst Grote Ondernemingen, Amsterdam* (Case C-190/95) [1997] BVC 547 the question was posed as to whether an asset can itself constitute a sufficient presence for this purpose. The ECJ held it could not.

ARO was a car leasing company based in Holland. It had no office in Belgium but, in the period concerned in the appeal, had agreements for some 800 cars to be leased in that country, in addition to 6,000 leased in Holland. These agreements were for periods of three to four years and, for Belgian customers, were entered into through self-employed intermediaries established in Belgium, acting on commission. Belgian customers generally chose the cars themselves from local dealers, who delivered them to ARO. ARO then paid for the cars, which were registered in Belgium, and made them available to the customers. The intermediaries had no further role to play. The customer paid for the cost of maintenance and Belgian road tax and ARO for repairs and breakdown or accident assistance and also insurance.

ARO had always accounted for Dutch VAT on the vehicle rental payments, even for cars leased in Belgium, assuming art. 9(1) (the old art. 43: services supplied where the supplier has established its business) applied. It also sought to recover, under the Eighth VAT Directive (Directive 79/1072 (replaced by Directive 2008/9)) (see **Chapter 4** at 40-400), any Belgian VAT on the cost of the cars and on repairs. However, the Belgian authorities said this was wrong. The mere presence of a fleet of cars in Belgium owned by ARO meant, it was argued, that ARO had a fixed establishment there from which the cars were supplied. ARO had, therefore, to pay VAT in Belgium. ARO initially went along with this. However, the Dutch authorities then objected. As ARO had no staff or technical facilities in Belgium, in their view, it had no fixed establishment there through which the agreements were concluded.

The Dutch Courts then referred the matter to the ECJ, which ruled in favour of the views of the Dutch authorities. What the Court said was that the place where the supplier, ARO, had established its business was a primary point of reference. Unless this did not lead to a rational result or created a conflict with another Member State, there was no point in looking for some other establishment from which the services might be supplied. An establishment other than the main place of business could also only be relevant if it had a minimum degree of stability derived from the permanent presence of both the human and technical resources necessary for the provision of the services and this could not be found with the agencies employed in this case. The matter might well have been decided differently, of course, had the intermediaries in Belgium been *dependent* agencies, as in *DFDS*, and their role somewhat more extensive.

- *Lease Plan Luxembourg SA v Belgian State* (Case C-390/96) [1998] BVC 412 raised a similar issue. This case, which, like ARO, was referred to the ECJ, mainly concerned refunds under the Eighth VAT Directive, but had essentially the same end-result. Like ARO, it also involved a company which leased cars to persons in other Member States. Most of its contracts were with Luxembourg companies under comprehensive contracts. Lease Plan paid for insurance and maintenance using garages established in Belgium which rendered invoices with Belgian VAT. Lease Plan also bought some cars (10 out of a fleet of 1,000) for leasing to clients established in Belgium.

A car leasing business which hired cars to clients in another Member State did not thereby acquire a fixed establishment in that other State within the meaning of art. 9(1) of the Sixth Directive. Since Lease Plan had no staff or permanent structure in Belgium the mere leasing of cars under contracts made in Luxembourg did not constitute a fixed establishment.

(5) Telecommunication and broadcasting services

A supply of services consisting of the provision of: (a) telecommunication services, or (b) radio or television broadcasting services (Sch 4A, para. 8 of VATA 1994) is treated as supplied where (a) the supply of services would otherwise be treated as made in the UK, and (b) the services are to any extent effectively used and enjoyed in a country which is not a Member State, then the supply is to be treated to that extent as made in that country. However, where (a) the supply of services would otherwise be treated as made in a country which is not a Member State, and (b) the services are to any extent effectively used and enjoyed the UK, the supply is to be treated to that extent as made in the UK. For this purpose, 'telecommunication services' means services relating to the transmission, emission or reception of signals, writing, images and sounds or information of any nature by wire, radio, optical or other electromagnetic systems, including (a) the related transfer or assignment of the right to use capacity for such transmission, emission or reception, and (b) the provision of access to global information networks.

From 1 January 2015, B2C supplies of these services will move from the current general rule (supplier establishment) to where the customer is established, has their permanent address, or usually resides, and the special registration scheme discussed in **Chapter 12**, which is available to non-EU suppliers in respect of electronically supplied services to EU private consumers, will be extended to both EU and non-EU businesses, and widened to include telecommunications and broadcasting services, called the 'One Stop Shop' (OSS) by the EU.

For further information on the nature of the proposals in connection with non-established taxable persons supplying telecommunications services, broadcasting services or electronic services to non-taxable persons see EU Council paper 6872/12 FISC 29: see http://register.consilium.europa.eu/pdf/en/12/st06/st06872.en12.pdf.

(6) Electronically-supplied services to a relevant business person

The provision of electronically supplied services to a relevant business person is treated as being supplied as follows (Sch 4A, para. 9 of VATA 1994):

- a supply of services consisting of the provision of electronically supplied services to a relevant business person which would otherwise be treated as made in the UK, but the services are to any extent effectively used and enjoyed in a country which is not a Member State, then the supply is to be treated to that extent as made in that country;
- a supply of services consisting of the provision of electronically supplied services to a relevant business person which would otherwise be treated as made in a country which is not a Member State, but the services are to any extent effectively used and enjoyed in the UK, then the supply is to be treated to that extent as made in the United Kingdom.

Examples of such electronically supplied services are (Sch 4A, para. 9 of VATA 1994):

- website supply, web-hosting and distance maintenance of programmes and equipment,
- the supply of software and the updating of software,
- the supply of images, text and information, and the making available of databases,
- the supply of music, films and games (including games of chance and gambling games),
- the supply of political, cultural, artistic, sporting, scientific, educational or entertainment broadcasts (including broadcasts of events), and
- the supply of distance teaching.

NB: Where the supplier of a service and the supplier's customer communicate via e-mail, this does not of itself mean that the service provided is an electronically supplied service (Sch. 4A, para. 9(4) of VATA 1994).

For further information on the nature of the proposals in connection with non-established taxable persons supplying telecommunications services, broadcasting services or electronic services to non-taxable persons see EU Council paper 6872/12 FISC 29: see http://register.consilium.europa.eu/pdf/en/12/st06/st06872.en12.pdf.

For the position for supplies from 1 January 2015 see the Table above, and the discussion in **Chapter 12**.

(7) Supplies to person who is not a relevant business person

The place of supply for services made to a person who is not a 'relevant business person' are summarised in the Table shown above.

There are also exceptions to the basic place of supply rules in connection with supplies of restaurant and catering services, EC on-board restaurant and catering services, admission to cultural, educational and entertainment services; but these are beyond the scope of this book (see Sch 4A of VATA 1994).

The place of supply is not, however, looked at in isolation. It must also be viewed in the context of the time of supply, a topic discussed later at 30-350.

30-300   Imports, acquisitions and dispatches

Occasionally, you need to look at something other than supplies. Importing goods from abroad, for example, will, in itself, create a taxable event for VAT, irrespective of whether the importer is a business or there is a supply (VATA 1994, s 1(1)(c)). Acquiring goods from another Member State, likewise, becomes a taxable event, but this time, only where the person receiving the goods into the UK is a business (VATA 1994, s. 10).

(1) Imports

When the origin of the goods is outside the EU, the matter is relatively straightforward. Value added tax is payable, not on a supply, but as a duty of customs (VATA 1994, s. 1(4)). When due, it is payable immediately on entry of the goods into the UK or, in the case of imports by businesses, may be deferred, by arrangement with HMRC, to the fifteenth day of the following month.

(2) Acquisitions

There are different rules for goods coming from other Member States. Goods brought to the UK by persons not in business can generally be brought in without charge. If tax is due on their supply, this will be at the rate in force in the country of origin (unless the supplier is required to register under the distance selling rules). However, when the person bringing the goods to the UK or taking delivery of them from another Member State is a business registered for UK VAT, there is what is termed an *acquisition*. Tax is then due here, rather than in the other Member State.

Acquisitions, for this purpose, are, like imports earlier, not confined to transactions involving actual supplies and, as defined in art. 20 of Council Directive 2006/112/EC (Sixth VAT Directive (Directive 77/388), art. 28A(3)), mean the:

'... acquisition of the right to dispose as owner of movable tangible property....'

VAT can thus be due here when goods are received into the UK from a branch of the same company in another Member State, in contrast to the rules on *supplies* earlier.

Where the acquisition takes place is determined by rules in VATA 1994, s. 13. This provides, as a primary rule, in s. 13(2) that:

'The goods shall be treated as acquired in the United Kingdom if they are acquired in pursuance of a transaction which involves their removal to the United Kingdom and does not involve their removal from the United Kingdom, and (subject to the following provisions of this section) shall otherwise be treated as acquired outside the United Kingdom.'

There is also a secondary rule (s. 13(3)), which can treat the place of acquisition as in the UK if the goods are not sent to the UK but the acquirer has made use of a UK VAT number to secure a VAT-free dispatch from another Member State. This can, however, be overridden to the extent that acquisition VAT is accounted for by that person in the Member State in which the goods have actually been received.

With acquisitions, the taxing mechanism differs from that for imports. Tax is not payable on entry into the UK or by deferment. Instead, it will generally be accounted for through the acquirer's normal VAT return.

(3) Dispatches

Dispatches are the other side of the coin to acquisitions. As with acquisitions, a *dispatch* to another part of the same entity, which cannot be a supply for consideration, is deemed to be a supply for the purposes of these provisions (see VATA 1994, Sch. 4, para. 6). There is thus a specific departure from the normal rules on supply discussed earlier. However, art. 138 of Council Directive 2006/112/EC (art. 15 of the Sixth VAT Directive (Directive 77/388)) makes the event free of VAT.

The rules on the place of dispatch are as for the supply of goods as also described earlier.

30-350　Time of supply or taxpoint – the taxable event

The taxpoint determines when a supply takes place for VAT purposes. It will also effectively decide when, or even sometimes whether, VAT has to be accounted for. In the event of a rate change, it may also decide what rate, if any, is to be applied.

The rules, VATA 1994, s. 6 and Pt. XI of the *Value Added Tax Regulations* 1995 (SI 1995/2518), apply equally to taxable and exempt supplies. To that extent, the term *taxpoint* is thus misleading. Whilst primarily concerned with outputs and output VAT, the rules are also important for input VAT – when, for example, you can, or should, claim input VAT relief (reg.

29 of the *Value Added Tax Regulations* 1995); also, in the case of partially exempt traders (see **Chapter 4**), possibly how much relief is available and in what VAT year.

In terms of EC law these rules are found in art. 62 to 71 of Council Directive 2006/112/EC (art. 10 of the Sixth VAT Directive (Directive 77/388)).

As with the place of supply, there are different rules for goods and for services.

(1) Goods

(a) The general rule

In the case of goods (VATA 1994, s. 6(2)), the basic rule is that the supply occurs:

'(a) if the goods are to be removed, at the time of the removal;
(b) if the goods are not to be removed, at the time when they are made available to the person to whom they are supplied;
(c) if the goods (being sent or taken on approval or sale or return or similar terms) are removed before it is known whether a supply will take place, at the time when it becomes certain that the supply has taken place [e.g. when the goods have been adopted] or, if sooner, 12 months after removal.'

art. 62 of Council Directive 2006/112/EC puts this succinctly as:

'chargeable event" shall mean the occurrence by virtue of which the legal conditions necessary for VAT to become chargeable are fulfilled;'

and art. 63 goes on to provide that:

'The chargeable event shall occur and VAT shall become chargeable when the goods or the services are supplied.'

As with the place of supply, therefore, it is looked at from an essentially practical viewpoint. This basic taxpoint can, however, be superseded:

- if it will be advanced by the earlier of the receipt of payment or the issue of a tax invoice (to the extent covered) (VATA 1994, s. 6(4)); or
- if neither happens, it will be delayed up to 14 days by the subsequent issue of a tax invoice (longer periods may be agreed) (VATA 1994, s. 6(5)).
- *Cumbernauld Development Corporation v C & E Commrs* [2002] BVC 384 was a case that considered the application of these rules in relation to property. It concerned an agreement for transfer of land, where the transferee was given occupation some ten months before the date on which title passed. The land was development land and the supply was taxable (see later in **Chapter 8** at 80-150) and the transferor was assessed to VAT on the basis that the supply took place on Completion. The taxpayer, however, sought to avoid this by arguing that the supply took place earlier, when the land was made available to it – i.e. when it entered into occupation, so that the assessment was out of time.

  The Tribunal refused the company's appeal and the matter then went to the Court of Session (Inner House, Second Division) in Scotland, where the same conclusion was reached. The legislation was concerned with the supply of 'goods'. By the extended definition of that term in VATA 1994, Sch. 4, 'goods' included 'a major interest in land'. That expression had to be interpreted to mean ownership of the land and not any lesser interest such as a right or a mere licence to occupy. Although the land itself was initially made available to the transferee in the sense it was given the occupation and use of it, title to the land remained, for the time being, vested in the transferor until completion, when the property was actually conveyed.

Potentially, of course, the rules for the variation of a taxpoint can be used to create an advantage, as was attempted, unsuccessfully, as it transpired, in the *BUPA* case.

- *BUPA Hospitals Ltd and Goldsborough Developments Ltd v C & E Commrs* (Case C-419/02) [2006] BVC 377 concerned a company that ran a large number of private hospitals. Until 1997, its supplies of drugs and prostheses to patients were zero-rated, rather than VAT-exempt as healthcare. This allowed it to recover the related input VAT incurred on the purchase of those goods. When the Government announced its intention to change this and take away the zero-rating, BUPA decided to use a prepayment scheme. It contracted with another group company, BUPA Medical, for the future purchase and supply of the drugs and prostheses and made a prepayment of £60m, plus VAT, for the drugs and £40m, plus VAT for prostheses. These payments were made before the change in the law, anticipating that, by advancing the tax-point, the supply of drugs and prostheses could still be zero-rated, but the VAT charged by the supplier would be deductible by BUPA Medical.

HMRC, needless to say, refused to allow the repayment of the tax and the High Court eventually referred to the ECJ the questions of:

- whether BUPA Medical carried on any *economic activity* and made supplies for VAT purposes; and
- whether the principle of *abuse of rights* was applicable in respect of transactions designed to obtain a tax advantage.

Whilst the Court, ruled for BUPA on the first point, it went on to hold that payments on account of supplies of goods or services that have not yet been clearly identified could not be subject to VAT. Accordingly prepayments of the kind at issue, whereby lump sums were paid for goods referred to in general terms in a list which might be altered at any time by agreement, did not fall within the scope of the second sub-paragraph of art. 10(2) of the Sixth Directive (art. 65 of Council Directive 2006/112/EC).

In other words, the taxpoint was not advanced and the scheme failed through uncertainty.

(b) Property

There is a special rule for property (in reg. 84 of the *VAT Regulations* 1995) designed to prevent avoidance, where someone (the grantor) grants or assigns the fee simple in any land, and at the time of the grant or assignment, the total consideration for it is not determinable. The supply, which is technically of goods for VAT, is treated as separately and successively supplied at the following times:

(1) the time determined in accordance with s. 6(2), (4), (5), (6) or (10) of the Act, as the case may require, and

(2) the earlier of the following times:
- (a) each time that any part of the consideration which was not determinable at the time mentioned in sub-paragraph (a) above is received by the grantor; or
- (b) each time that the grantor issues a VAT invoice in respect of such a part.

This is, however, subject to certain exceptions (para. 84(3) to (5)). It does not apply to a grant or assignment falling within item 1(a) of VATA 1994, Grp 1, Sch. 9 (supplies of a new or uncompleted building), which is neither designed as a dwelling or number of dwellings nor intended for use solely for a relevant residential purpose or a relevant charitable purpose or an uncompleted or new civil engineering work where:

(1) the grantor;

(2) any person who, with the intention or in the expectation that occupation of the land on a date before a date ten years after completion of the building or civil engineering work would not be wholly or substantially wholly for eligible purposes:
- (a) provides finance for the grantor's development of the land; or
- (b) has entered into any agreement, arrangement or understanding (whether or not legally enforceable) to provide finance for the grantor's development of the land;

(3) any person who is connected with any person of a description within the previous sub-paragraphs,

intends or expects to occupy the land on a date before a date ten years after completion of the building or civil engineering work on the land, without being in occupation of it wholly or mainly for eligible purposes.

For the purposes of these regulations:

- Note (2) to Sch. 9, Grp 1 to the Act applies to determining when a building or civil engineering work is completed;
- Sch. 10, para. 3A(8) to the Act shall have effect for determining the meaning of *eligible purposes* and *occupation* (see later in **Chapter 8**);
- the grantor's development of the land means any acquisition by the grantor of an interest in the land, building or civil engineering work and includes the construction of the building or civil engineering work;
- providing finance has the same meaning as in Sch. 10, para. 14(3) to the Act, subject to any appropriate modifications, but does not include paying the consideration for the grantor's grant or assignment within paragraph (3) above;
- any question whether one person is connected with another shall be determined in accordance with ICTA 1988, s. 839.

(2) Services

For services (VATA 1994, s. 6(3) and art. 63 of the VAT Directive), the basic rule is that supply occurs when they are performed. It is equally, therefore, a practical, common sense idea. As with goods, this can be superseded by:

- the earlier receipt of payment or the issue of a tax invoice; or
- delayed by the subsequent issue of a tax invoice – usually, within 14 days.

Historically, the VAT Regulations have envisaged that a tax invoice could not be issued for an exempt supply – or, with the exception of certain intra-EU supplies, for one that is zero-rated. In such cases, the matter of the time of supply will have been decided under this basic rule by payment or performance.

However, following the commencement of formal infraction proceedings by the European Commission (on the grounds that the UK had not fully implemented the VAT Directive), certain changes have now been made by the *VAT (Amendment) (No 5) Regulations* 2007 (SI 2007/2085), to impose invoicing requirements for certain intra-EC exempt or reverse-charge supplies. This change, which had effect from 1 October 2007, is discussed later at 30-550.

(3) Special situations

Although the rules in (2) and (3) above are the norm, there are a number of special situations in which different principles apply. These are found in what is now Pt. XI of the *Value Added Tax Regulations* 1995 (SI 1995/2518). These override the usual rules in VATA 1994, s. 6 and can be especially important for many of the supplies made in the financial and insurance sectors.

(a) Continuous supplies

Regulation 90 of the *Value Added Tax Regulations* 1995 in particular applies to continuous supplies of services. There is no basic taxpoint and the rules are much simplified:

> 'Subject to paragraph (2) below, where services except those to which regulation 93 applies [supplies in the construction industry] are supplied for a period for a consideration, the whole or part of which is determined or payable periodically or from time to time, they shall be treated as separately and successively supplied at the earlier of the following times -
>
> (a) each time that a payment in respect of the supplies is received by the supplier, or
> (b) each time that the supplier issues a VAT invoice relating to the supplies.'

This is modified, however, to cover cases where agreements, for equipment rental, for example, provide for successive payments, with a global VAT invoice being issued in advance for a period not exceeding one year. In such cases, the taxpoint is when payment is received or due, whichever is earlier. Where the supply is exempt, as in the case of interest or many property rents, there can be no tax invoice. The receipt of payment is again always the deciding factor.

Similar rules apply for other supplies such as lettings of property, power and heating, royalties and construction services.

(b) Special rules for construction

There is also a further special rule in reg. 90(1) and 93 of the *Value Added Tax Regulations* 1995 (SI 1995/2518) introduced to counter avoidance by companies in the VAT exempt sectors. A number of businesses within these sectors had been exploiting the continuous supply rules for construction services by interposing associated construction companies between themselves and the construction company actually carrying out the construction work. These interposed *construction companies*, which were not grouped with the VAT-exempt employers, paid the real construction companies, recovering the VAT charged on the work. The VAT-exempt employer

3 Outputs and Output VAT

could then defer payment to the interposed associate, sometimes for many years. The result was that payment of VAT was avoided, giving a significant cash flow disadvantage to the Exchequer.

As a result, all construction businesses now have to account for VAT no later than 18 months after they complete their work. But they will still have to account for VAT when they receive payment or issue an invoice, if either happens earlier.

(c) Connected parties

Companies in the sectors covered by this book can also, following the *Svenska* case, be affected by special rules on connected parties, where supplies are made between members of a group.

- The case of *Svenska International plc v C & E Commrs* [1999] BVC 221, concerned continuous supplies of management services supplied by UK subsidiary of a Swedish bank to the London branch of its parent company. The branch, which was partly exempt, eventually became part of a VAT group with the bank. In the meantime, the bank provisionally recovered in full the input tax on the costs of providing the management services on the basis that the tax was attributable to VATable supplies. No payment was received, or invoices raised, however, until after the branch joined the bank's VAT group. Consequently no taxpoint had occurred and, once the VAT group had been created, the matter was, on the face of it, thereafter disregarded on the basis of the rules in what is now VATA 1994, s. 43.

The point at issue was whether HMRC could assess the Bank to recover input tax credited correctly at the time as attributable to intended taxable supplies, but which, in the event did not take place. The matter eventually reached the House of Lords where, dismissing *Svenska's* appeal, it was held that:

- There was a continuous supply of services within reg. 23 of the *Value Added Tax (General) Regulations* 1985 (SI 1985/886) (now reg. 90 of the *Value Added Tax Regulations* 1995 (SI 1995/2518)), with the result that no supply should be treated as having been made until there had been a payment received or a tax invoice had been issued.
- However, the tax on costs relating to the intended management services could not be recovered in full as the intended taxable supplies never took place. Once the VAT group was created, the partly exempt supplies of the branch became those of the bank, as representative member of the VAT group. In other words, the tax on costs incurred by the bank before the branch was included in the VAT group were to be treated as used by the bank after that date in making the partially exempt supplies to third parties made by the branch before grouping occurred.

From 1 August 2003, the *VAT Regulations* 1995 (SI 1995/2518) were amended by the addition of reg. 94B by *The VAT (Amendment) (No. 5) Regulations* 2003 (SI 2003/2318). The rules, described in VAT Information Sheet 14/2003, are designed to ensure that taxpoints will be created periodically, in most cases based on 12-month periods, so that accounting for VAT cannot be indefinitely or excessively delayed.

The Regulation applies only where the supplier and recipient are connected or are group undertakings. And then only if:

- the supply is liable at a positive rate of VAT (in other words is not exempt or zero-rated); and
- the recipient is unable to fully recover all the VAT on the supply as input tax.

If a VAT invoice is issued or payment received for the supplies in question within six months of the annual taxpoint date, the date of issue or receipt becomes the taxpoint, overriding the earlier annual taxpoint.

(d) Imported services

For imported services (see **Chapter 5**), the rules, reg. 82 of the *Value Added Tax Regulations* 1995, provide that:

(i) Such services (excluding those supplied for a period for a consideration the whole or part of which is determined or payable periodically or from time to time) are treated as made when the services are performed;

(ii) Such services that are supplied for a period for a consideration the whole or part of which is determined or payable periodically or from time to time are treated as separately and successively made at the end of the periods in respect of which payments are made or invoices issued, and to the extent covered by the relevant payment or invoice;

(iii) When in the case of a service to which (i) applies, a payment is made in respect of the supply before the time specified in (i) the time of supply is treated as made at the time the payment is made;

(iv) Where in the case of services to which (ii) applies, and either (a) a payment is made at a time that is earlier than the end of the period to which it relates or (b) a payment is made which is not made in respect of any identified period the time of supply is treated as made at the time the payment is made;

(v) Where the supply of services to which (iii) applies (a) commences before 1st January and continues after 31st December of any year, and during that year no invoice is issued that has effect for the purposes of (iii) above and no payment is made in respect of that supply then the services supplied during that year are treated as being supplied on the 31st December of that year to the extent that the recipient has received the benefit of them.

30-400 Time of acquisition and dispatch

The rules on the intra-EU movement of goods also include provisions on when a taxable acquisition or dispatch is to be accounted for (art. 67, 68 and 69 of Council Directive 2006/112/EC) (art. 10 of the Sixth VAT Directive (Directive 77/388)).

In the case of *acquisitions*, the rules in VATA 1994, s. 12 are that the acquisition is regarded as taking place at the earlier of:

'(a) the 15th day of the month following that in which the event occurs which, in relation to that acquisition, is the first relevant event for the purposes of taxing the acquisition; and

(b) the day of the issue, in respect of the transaction in pursuance of which the goods are acquired, of an invoice of such a description as the Commissioners may by regulations prescribe.'

3 Outputs and Output VAT

For *dispatches*, the time of the actual or deemed supply, VATA 1994, s. 6(7) and (8), is the earlier of:

'(a) the 15th day of the month following that in which the removal in question takes place; and
(b) the day of the issue, in respect of the supply, of a VAT invoice or of an invoice of such other description as the Commissioners may by regulations prescribe.'

30-450 Transfers of business

Special rules apply to the acquisition or disposal of the assets of a business as a going concern (art. 19 and 29 of Council Directive 2006/112/EC).

(1) The general rule

Article 5(1) of the *Value Added Tax (Special Provisions) Order* 1995 (SI 1995/1268) provides that, subject to para. 2, a person shall be treated as making neither a supply of goods nor a supply of services on the supply of the assets of a business where:

'(a) their supply to a person to whom he transfers his business as a going concern where -
  (i) the assets are to be used by the transferee in carrying on the same kind of business, whether or not as part of an existing business, as that carried on by the transferor, and
  (ii) in a case where the transferor is a taxable person, the transferee is already, or immediately becomes as a result of the transfer, a taxable person or a person defined as such in section 3(1) of the Manx Act.'

Similar rules, art. 5(1)(b), apply in the case of the transfer of part of a business, with the further proviso that the part transferred is capable of separate operation.

The requirement that the transferee is or becomes a taxable person does not apply to an acquisition from someone who is not registered – either because he is fully exempt or because he is excused from registration under VATA 1994, Sch. 1, para. 14 (see **Chapter 2** at 20-150).

Article 5(1) only applies to asset transfers where a 'business' is transferred. In *Kenmir v Frizzell* (QB (1968) 1 WLR 329) the judge commented that the approach to be taken in determining when a transfer of a business occurs is as follows:

'In deciding whether a transaction amounted to the transfer of a business, regard must be had to its substance rather than its form, and consideration must be given to the whole of the circumstances, weighting the factors which point in one direction against those which point in another. In the end, the vital consideration is whether the effect of the transaction was to put the transferee in possession of a going concern, the activities of which he could carry on without interruption. Many factors may be relevant to this decision though few will be conclusive in themselves.'

As typical examples of where the rules can be applied:

- In *Baltic Leasing Ltd* (1986) VATTR 98; (1986) 2 BVC 208,097, for example, the transfer of all or part of a leasing company's portfolio was held to be within these rules.
- In *Hallborough Properties Ltd* [1994] BVC 1,377 it was also held that the rules similarly applied to the transfer of a property with the benefit of an existing tenancy.

Sometimes, however, there can be unexpected difficulties. It can be important, for instance, to watch how such transfers are structured.

- In *Kwik Save Group plc* [1996] BVC 4,004, the taxpayer acquired a number of businesses, contracting in its position as the parent of the group. Some of the businesses were then immediately transferred to a trading subsidiary by a sub-sale. Unfortunately, as the companies were not grouped for VAT (see **Chapter 2** at 20-250), the last leg of the transfer could not be disregarded. The assets had not been used in the transferor's (i.e. Kwik Save's) business. Probably, the first leg was not, strictly, covered either!
- In *Associates Fleet Services Ltd* [2001] BVC 4,150 the VAT Tribunal confirmed the treatment as a going concern under the *Value Added Tax (Special Provisions) Order* 1995 (SI 1995/1268), art. 5 of the sale of assets of a leasing business notwithstanding that, amongst other things, there was no transfer of goodwill, business name or staff, no purchase of premises and no restrictive covenants imposed on the vendor. The circumstances of the case made it clear that the purchaser was put in possession of part of the vendor's leasing business, and, although not mentioned, the decision clearly follows the line adopted in the *Baltic Leasing* case.
- In *Royal Bank of Scotland Group plc v C & E Commrs* [2002] BVC 2,213 the issue was the outsourcing of the bank's cheque clearing and processing functions to EDS, an independent data processing company. Staff and premises were transferred, but some contracts and assets were retained. On appeal, it was held that the factors which weighed in the appellant's favour outweighed those identified by HMRC as pointing to a taxable supply. Those carrying the most weight were:
  - the transfer of the whole of the staff involved;
  - the sale or lease of the properties in which the activities were carried on;
  - the supply of the equipment and intellectual property required to continue the activity; and
  - the intention of the parties to transfer the activity as a going concern.

  There was no doubt that the cheque-clearing facility was capable of separate operation and that the clearing activity was carried on without interruption in the same way as before, was capable of separate operation and did, in fact, operate as an independent business subsequently.

- In *Winterthur Swiss Insurance Co* [2006] BVC 2,376, the position was more unusual and was a situation where the requirements of the TOGC rules in art. 5 were not met. Winterthur, a Swiss insurer with branches in the EU and a UK subsidiary, Churchill Management Ltd, entered into an agreement with Prudential Assurance Co Ltd for the acquisition of Prudential's reinsurance business. The day-to-day administration was to be handled by CML, which took over the assets and employees involved; Winterthur took over the actual business, paying £350m for goodwill, including renewal rights. Subsequently, the company found that Swiss regulatory problems made it difficult to operate the business in Switzerland, so decided to transfer it to a group company based in Bermuda.

  There were three issues:

  (1) Was the transfer of Prudential's general insurance the transfer of a going concern for VAT?
  (2) If it wasn't, where was the place of supply?
  (3) If the supply was taxable, could Winterthur recover the VAT under the EC Eighth Directive (Directive 79/1072 (replaced by Directive 2008/9))?

Winterthur ultimately failed on the first point as, although the transfer from Prudential involved an identifiable part of the Prudential's business and was capable of separate operation, the assets weren't, in the event, used by Winterthur in carrying on the same kind of business as Prudential and, anyway, Winterthur was not a taxable person for UK VAT.

On the second and third points taken together, however, Winterthur succeeded. The supply of goodwill by Prudential was not within art. 9(2)(e) of the Sixth Directive (VATA 1994, Sch. 5 and art. 56 of Council Directive 2006/112/EC). However, Winterthur, which was VAT-registered in other EU Member States was able to claim back the VAT charged by Prudential because nothing in the Directive prevented this.

The part of a business that is transferred must make supplies before it is transferred. In *FMCG Home Services Ltd* [2004] BVC 4,037 (LON/00/529) (VAT Decision 18377) Prudential transferred cash collection activities relating to its life assurance/financial services businesses to FMCG. As these services had only ever been an overhead cost of the business the transfer did not constitute a transfer of a going concern. The activities only took the identity of a business (i.e. making supplies) after the transfer. The assets transferred included staff, customer lists, a licence to use specialised equipment, goodwill and the agreement that it could act on behalf of the Prudential in respect of collecting money owed and handling complaints. The Tribunal held that for a transfer to qualify as a TOGC the part of the business transferred must have operated as a business.

> *Practice point*
>
> In practice, an assets deal will often have a number of attractions over an acquisition by way of shares.
>
> - In purely VAT terms, it can avoid, for example, inheriting unquantified or undisclosed liabilities.
> - In relation to direct tax, it can also offer the acquirer a number of advantages, including capital allowances on plant and equipment.

There are also a number of other considerations to bear in mind when looking at business transfers.

(2) Transfers including land

The rules in the *Value Added Tax (Special Provisions) Order* 1995, art. 5 are further modified (art. 5(2)) to the extent that one or more of the assets transferred is either:

- a grant of a fee simple which falls within paragraph (a) of item 1 of Group 1, Sch. 9 of VATA 1994 (which means, a new freehold building or civil engineering work (VATA 1994, Sch. 9, Grp. 1, item 1 exception (a)). (This covers, in particular, commercial, non-residential, non-charitable buildings (see **Chapter 8** at 80-350)).
- any grant in respect of land which would but for an option which the transferor has exercised, would fall within item 1 of Group 1 of Sch. 9 of VATA 1994 (which broadly means any other grant of commercial, non-residential, non-charitable land or building where the transferor has opted to tax rather than treat any supplies as exempt (VATA 1994, Sch. 10, para. 2–4) (see **Chapter 8** at 80-350).

In either case, the transferor will be required to account for VAT on the land or building concerned unless certain conditions are satisfied. These are that the transferee has, no later than the relevant date:

(1) exercised an option in relation to the land which has effect on the relevant date and has given any necessary written notification of the election to HMRC; and

(2) notified the transferor that the following does not apply:

    (a) the supply of the asset to be transferred would become, in relation to him, a capital item as described in reg. 113 of the *Value Added Tax Regulations* 1995 (see **Chapter 4** at 40-200) if the supply of that asset to him:

        (i) were to be treated as neither a supply of goods nor a supply of services; or

        (ii) were not so treated; and

    (b) his own supplies of that asset will, or would fall, to be exempt by virtue of the option to tax being disapplied by virtue of para. 12 of Sch. 10 of VATA 1994 (i.e. where the person making the grant giving rise to the supply is a developer of the land, and at the time when the grant was made the grantor or development financier intended or expected that the land would become exempt land, or would continue to be exempt land).

This is an anti-avoidance measure to prevent input tax on a new development or refurbishment by the transferor with the property subsequently being let VAT-free by the transferee. It will apply, for example, to transfers of pre-let buildings such as office blocks, but also covers other commercial and industrial premises.

These conditions apply to all supplies of land and buildings for which an option to tax has been exercised (freehold, leasehold, licences etc), or where the property is less than three years old (VATA 1994, Sch. 9, Group 1, Note (4)).

- Previously, for the sale to qualify as a VAT-free TOGC, the transferee had also to opt to tax the property and notify HMRC *before* the transaction occurred. Failure to do this meant the transferor was required to charge VAT on the sale.
- However, in addition to opting to tax, the transferee also needs to notify the transferor, before the transfer takes place, that the transferee's option to tax will not be disapplied.

If the transferee cannot make this notification, the transaction cannot be VAT-free.

The significance of the need for the transferee to opt became especially evident in the *Higher Education Statistics Agency Ltd* case.

- The *Higher Education Statistics Agency Ltd* [2000] BVC 150, concerned the purchase of a property at auction, where it was held that the payment of a deposit, rather than Completion, fixed the time by which an election to tax had to be made. The property was adjacent to the HESA's existing premises and was bought as an investment. A deposit of ten per cent of the purchase price had to be paid to the auctioneer. As it happened, the vendor, Royal and Sun Alliance, had elected to tax the property (see **Chapter 8** at 80-150) and, by letter to the Commissioners dated 23 December 1997, the HESA purported to make and notify an election. Completion of the sale took place on 8 January 1998, with payment made of the balance of 90 per cent of the purchase price on that date.

Shortly thereafter, the HESA's accountants wrote to HMRC for confirmation that the acquisition of the building represented the transfer of a business, or part of a business, as a going concern, so that no VAT was chargeable on the transaction. HMRC did not dispute that part of a business was transferred as a going concern. They maintained, however, that, as the notification of the election had not been given to them *before* the exchange of contracts on the property, there was no valid election at the time of the grant of the interest in land. VAT was thus chargeable on the sale.

The HESA argued, against this, that HMRC's reliance on Notice 700/9/96, para. 2.3 in stating that the 'time of supply' and the 'grant' of the interest in land were the same was misplaced; alternatively, a UK rule requiring a bidder at an auction to make an election *before* the date of the auction where a deposit *might* be made if the bidder was successful, offended against the fundamental concept of Community law outlawing the distortion of competition.

Unfortunately for the HESA, both the Tribunal and the Court disagreed, with the result that the relevant date was the date the deposit was paid.

HMRC had originally argued that this notification had to be actually *received* by them by the relevant time. However, in *Chalegrove Properties Ltd* [2001] BVC 2,279, the Tribunal held it was sufficient to show that, on or by the relevant date, the transferee had properly addressed, pre-paid and posted the letter. Making sure the requisite proof is held could, therefore, be vital.

> ### Practice point
>
> It must be remembered that Completion under the agreement for the transfer or sale is not necessarily the date to go by. In the *Higher Education Statistics Agency* case, for example, what would normally have been the time of supply of the property was advanced by the payment of a deposit. Leaving things to Completion could easily, therefore, be too late anyway.
>
> VAT can be easily overlooked in the heat of the moment when there are *more important* matters to attend to. It is sensible, therefore, not to leave such things to chance in the first place.
>
> - There is no particular reason why opting to tax and notifying HMRC cannot be done well before anything like a time of supply occurs.
> - This can always be conditional on completion eventually taking place and at least then one major potential problem will be out of the way.
> - The same is equally true of applications for joining or leaving a VAT group.
>
> In this context, there is a useful statement of practice (Notice 700/9 at para. 8) for situations where a nominee purchaser acquires legal title for a named beneficial owner. HMRC have said that, for the purpose of establishing the transfer of a property letting business as a going concern, they will consider the named beneficial owner of the land to be the transferee, and not the nominee acquiring legal title.
>
> This, optional, practice allows a person transferring an interest in land to a nominee for a named beneficial owner, with the agreement of that nominee and beneficial owner, to treat the named beneficial owner as the transferee for the purposes of establishing whether there has been a transfer of a going concern.

In the case of transfers involving let property, what HMRC say (Section 4 of Notice 700/9 of April 2008) is that:

> '**4.1 Transfers of businesses between members of the same VAT group**
>
> The formation of a VAT group creates a single person for VAT purposes and as such any supply by a member of a VAT group is considered to be made by the representative member of the group. Therefore any assets transferred by a group member as part of the transfer of a going concern are considered to be transferred by the representative member.
>
> The transfer of assets within a VAT group, like most supplies between the members of a VAT group, is disregarded for VAT purposes.
>
> **4.2 Transfers made to persons outside the VAT group**
>
> There cannot be a TOGC when the sole activity of the business transferred is the making of supplies from one group member to another. However, if supplies are also being made to businesses outside of the VAT group, a TOGC is possible.
>
> **4.3 Transfers made to a VAT Group**
>
> Where a business is sold and the buyer is part of a VAT group and uses the new acquisition simply to make supplies to VAT group members, the business has effectively ceased and it cannot be treated as a TOGC. However, if supplies are also being made to businesses outside of the VAT group, a TOGC is possible. For example:
>
> | | |
> |---|---|
> | The purchaser of a property rental business is a member of the same VAT group as the existing tenant | Not a TOGC |
> | A VAT group member sells a property currently being rented to a another group member to a third party | Not a TOGC |
> | A property rental business is sold where the tenant who is a member of the outgoing landlord's VAT group is only one of a number of tenants | Can be a TOGC |
> | A property rental business is sold where the tenant who is a member of the purchaser's VAT group is only one of a number of tenants | Can be a TOGC' |

A particular issue that arises in the context of land transactions is whether the grant of a lease can benefit from being treated as a transfer of a going concern.

In *Finanzamt Lüdenscheid v Christel Schriever* (C-444/10) the CoJ decided that the transfer of fittings and stock qualified as a transfer of a going concern due to the fact that the buyer had possession of retail premises (achieved by the grant of a lease) which was needed to carry on the seller's business. The issue related to the transfer of going concern provisions under art. 5(8) of the Sixth Directive (now art. 19 of VAT Directive 2006/112). The facts of the case were as follows:

- Ms Schriever (S) ran a retail business, selling sports equipment from premises that she owned.
- S sold the stock and fittings of the business to Sport S. GmbH ('Sport S'). At the same time, S granted a lease of the premises where the business was carried on to Sport S. The components of the business therefore, included both moveable and immovable assets.

3 Outputs and Output VAT

- The lease was granted for an indefinite period (but it could be terminated by either party to take effect at the end of the calendar quarter following that in which notice had been given).
- S treated the transfer of the stock and fittings as a non-taxable transfer of a business in its entirety. The tax authority decided that there was no transfer since the conditions for a transfer of a business in its entirety were not satisfied due to the business premises, which constituted an essential component element of the business, were not among the items sold to Sport s.

The CoJ decided that there was a transfer of a going concern of the retail business on the particular facts. The reasoning of the court was as follows:

- To be within the transfer of going concern provisions there must be a transfer of a business, or of an independent part of an undertaking, so that all the elements transferred must, together, be sufficient to allow an independent economic activity to be carried on (para. 25 of the judgment).
- The court emphasised that in applying the provisions of the Directive, the question is whether there must be both movable and immovable assets among those elements transferred, and this must be assessed in the light of the nature of the economic activity at issue (para. 26 of the judgment).

In this regard, the court commented (para. 27 to 29 of the judgment):

> 'Where an economic activity does not require the use of particular premises or of premises equipped with fixtures necessary for the pursuit of the economic activity, there may be a transfer of a totality of assets for the purposes of Article 5(8) of the Sixth Directive even without the transfer of property in an immovable asset.
>
> However, where the very nature of the economic activity entails the use of an inseparable bundle of movable and immovable property, such a transfer cannot be considered to have occurred if the transferee has not taken possession of the business premises. In particular, if the business premises are equipped with fixtures necessary for the pursuit of the economic activity, these immovable items must form part of the elements transferred in order for the transaction to qualify as the transfer of a totality of assets, or of a part thereof, for the purposes of the Sixth Directive.
>
> Equally, a transfer of assets may also take place if the business premises are made available to the transferee by means of a lease contract, or if the transferee itself has appropriate premises to which all of the goods transferred can be moved and where the transferee may continue to carry on the economic activity concerned.'

- The CoJ emphasised that 'an overall assessment must be made of the factual circumstances of the transaction at issue in order to determine whether it is covered by the concept of the transfer of a totality of assets for the purposes of the Sixth Directive. In that context, particular importance must be attached to the nature of the economic activity which it is sought to continue' (para. 32 of the judgment).
- On the particular facts, the purchaser needed to carry on the retail business which had been sold to it. In this regard, the continuation of the economic activity in question required that the transferee use the same premises as were used by the transferor, and there was no reason in principle why possession of those premises could not be transferred by means of a lease (see para. 36 of the judgment). In this regard, the facts submitted by the referring court stated that 'the transfer of the stock and fittings of the sports equipment retailer

concomitant with the conclusion of a contract of lease of the business premises did indeed allow the purchaser to continue the independent economic activity previously carried on by the seller' (para. 39 of the judgment).

The decision of the CoJ is a useful illustration of how to approach the application of the going concern provisions. However, it does not necessarily support the view that the grant of a lease can be a transfer of a going concern of itself in the context of a property rental business. This is because in the context of the particular facts of the retail business in the case, the transfer could not be regarded as a mere sale of stock: both the stock and the fittings of the business formed part of the assets transferred. It was critical to the case that the purchaser had sufficient possession of the premises in order to carry on the retail business. The CoJ did not say in the judgment that the grant of the lease itself formed part of the 'totality of assets'.

A recent UK case of particular interest is *Robinson Family Ltd* ([2012] UKFTT 360) [2012] TC 02046 in which the First Tier Tax Tribunal held that the creation of a sub-lease should be treated as the transfer of a business as a going concern. It will be interesting to see whether this case is appealed by HMRC since it challenges HMRC's treatment of the grant of a lease as not being capable of being a TOGC. This case was heard before the release of the CoJ decision in *Schriever* (discussed above). Accordingly, whilst there is no reference to *Schriever* in the decision it is consistent with the CoJ decision. These cases illustrate why it is necessary to understand the precise nature of what is occurring in order to properly understand how VAT should be applied in particular circumstances (in particular, these decisions echo the comments of the CoJ in *R & C Commrs v Loyalty Management UK Ltd; Baxi Group Ltd v R & C Commrs* (Joined Cases C-53/09 and C-55/09 [2011] BVC 1 at para. 39) that it is necessary to understand the 'economic realities' of the circumstances of the supply or supplies (see further the discussion at 10-100).

The facts of *Robinson Family Ltd* can be summarised as follows:

- The Appellant bought a site from Belfast Harbour Commissioners ("BHC"). The title was held by the Appellant under a lease ("the Head Lease") directly from BHC with a term of 125 years. The Head Lease contained restrictions on transfer (e.g. a prohibition against sub-division of the site other than by way of creation of sub-leases in accordance with specific terms in the Head Lease). The site was subsequently redeveloped to comprise of 6 commercial Units.
- The Appellant disposed of one unit to the purchaser by sale by way of sub-lease for the entirety of the term of the Head Lease less a nominal reversion of three days.
- The Appellant treated the disposal as a TOGC.
- HMRC considered that the grant of the sub-lease, which was used to transact the disposal was a "new" lease, therefore it was not a TOGC.
- HMRC had accepted that sufficient preparatory acts had been undertaken by the Appellant to constitute a letting business, and that on the proposed sale of the Unit to CJ Higgins that the conditions for a TOGC would be fulfilled (if there had been a sale of the Unit).

The First-Tier Tax Tribunal decided that the sale by way of sub-lease should be treated as a TOGC. The reasons for the Tribunal decision can be summarised as follows:

- The Tribunal noted that the sole question was whether or not there was a sale of an asset (namely the creation of a new sub-lease in respect of the Unit) or whether the Appellant had disposed of part of its letting business as it related to that Unit.
- The Tribunal placed particular emphasis on the fact that it was "cogniscent of the fact that the Appellant was constrained by the title which it held from Belfast Harbour Commissioners on foot of the BHC Standard Lease. That form of lease requires all developers within Belfast Harbour Estate to conduct transactions in a particular manner – namely by way of the creation of sub-leases." (see para. 60 of the judgment).
- It was noted that the Tribunal was required to have regard to the substance rather than the form of a transaction (para. 70 of the judgment).
- The Tribunal concluded that the business had been transferred. It identified the nature of the Appellants business in the context of the transfer by way of sub-lease as follows (para. 78 to 79):

> 'To use the language then of Article 5 of the Order, what were the assets which were required for that business? In short they consisted of the unit which was to be sub-let or occupied. In the case of Unit 3, that meant that ownership and possession would need to have transferred to C.J. Higgins Limited as transferee. Again, the Tribunal finds that that transfer was effected – albeit on foot of the sub-lease which was created. That sub-lease did not in any material respect constrain C.J. Higgins from carrying out the business and was ... an outright disposal. The particular nuances around the resultant pyramid title structure were simply a result of the requirements of Belfast Harbour Commissioners. In substance the assets which constituted the core of the lettings business were transferred with the transferor retaining only a notional interest (ie. the reversionary interest of 3 days) but otherwise disposing of the economic activity which was to be carried on from or in relation to that Unit.
>
> ... the transferor did, in addition, retain a small economic interest (in effect a profit rent). The Tribunal does not find that that in any way alters the substance of what was happening. It is true that the payment of the profit rent would have to be factored in as an expense of the business being carried forward by the transferee, but it does not impact on the substance of what was happening. The letting business was being transferred and the transferee was free to conduct it as it saw fit (subject only to the confines of the sub-lease and ultimately the requirements of BHC as reflected in the Head Lease).'

The Tribunal adopted a clear approach of examining the substance over form of the transfer in reaching its conclusion. The current trend in case law would tend to indicate that the substance of a transfer should be examined for the purposes of applying VAT, and that the mere legal form should not interfere with the economic realities.

HMRC have decided not to appeal the First-Tier Tax Tribunal decision, and in consequence of it, have changed their position (reflected in *Revenue & Customs Brief* 30/12 (16 November 2012) (see **Appendix 30**)). In essence, HMRC now accept that:

- where a transferor of a property rental business retains a small reversionary interest in the property transferred then there may be a TOGC (subject to other relevant conditions being satisfied);
- HMRC accept that the creation of a new asset (a lease or sub-lease) and the retention of the original asset (the freehold or a superior lease) is not automatically incompatible with TOGC treatment;

- A reversion retained by a transferor is a small interest if the value of the retained interest is no more than one per cent of the value of the property immediately before the transfer (disregarding any mortgage or charge).

The change in HMRC policy is to be welcomed. However, nonetheless, in light of the CoJ decision in *Christel Schriever* (C-444/10) and the requirement to have regard to the 'economic realities' of any situation (*LMUK* (C-53/09)) it is arguable that TOGC treatment should be available in a wider variety of circumstances than identified by HMRC in Brief 30/12.

(3) Acquisitions by VAT groups

Whilst most transfers of assets as a going concern can be made VAT-free, there is an important exception in the case of an acquisition by a partly exempt VAT group. In this case, as an anti-avoidance measure, a charge to tax can arise for the transferee group under VATA 1994, s. 44. This applies where the taxable assets transferred were originally acquired less than three years before the transfer date, the aim being to stop input tax being substantially recovered by a transferor on assets, which will then be used in an exempt or partly exempt business (see **Chapter 4**). Where the section applies, VAT is accounted for on the open market value of the chargeable assets acquired. These will include:

- plant, machinery and equipment;
- stock-in-trade and work-in-progress;
- patents, licences, copyright, know-how, etc.;
- motor vehicles (but not cars);
- freehold interests in new or partly completed new commercial buildings, civil engineering works; and
- leasehold interests in such buildings or freehold or leasehold interests in any other commercial building or land where, in either case, the transferor has opted to tax.

Section 44 could, in theory, also extend to goodwill. However, by concession HMRC do not take the point (HMRC Notice 700/9 para. 5.2). It will not, in any event, cover transfers of:

- debts;
- land and buildings other than those referred to above; or
- shares in companies,

where the supply is exempt.

Open market value will generally be the same as that adopted in a sale/purchase agreement.

> ### Practice point
>
> There could be a problem if undue emphasis is placed on certain assets as opposed to others in the context of the agreement as a whole – e.g. if the purchaser wants to place too low a value on plant and too high a value on an exempt property (VATA 1994, s. 19(4)).
>
> There may also be difficulties where the transfer is not at arm's length – e.g. within a group. However, where the vendor has been unable to recover all the VAT originally incurred on the assets, HMRC may allow some abatement.

There is a further modification to these rules to the extent the taxable assets acquired are subject to the capital goods scheme (VATA 1994, s. 44(4)) (see 40-300(7)). The assets are then excluded from the charge to tax. The transferor will make no final adjustment and the transferee effectively takes over the transferor's position.

(4) Registration and records

To some extent registration and records are dealt with elsewhere in **Chapter 2**. However, on the acquisition of a business, there are modifications to the normal rules.

Where a taxable business is acquired by someone not already VAT-registered from someone who is, the transferee can have an immediate obligation to register. The present rules (VATA 1994, Sch. 1, para. 1(2)) make the transferee liable to be registered at the time of the transfer if:

- his taxable supplies in the last year have exceeded £77,000; or
- it is likely that his taxable supplies in the next 30 days will exceed £77,000.

The effect of VATA 1994, s. 49(1)(a), is to treat, for this purpose, the relevant supplies previously made by the transferor as having been made by the transferee. Thus, for the first of these two tests, the transferee will need to take account of those supplies in addition to any taxable supplies actually made by him before the transfer date. Notification is required, in either event, within 30 days. However, if HMRC are satisfied that taxable supplies in the following year will not exceed £75,000 registration may be dispensed with. If there is a liability to be registered, registration will take effect from the transfer date.

Acquiring a business has, historically, also generally caused the transferee to be required to preserve the transferor's VAT records (VATA 1994, s. 49(1)(b)). This can be for up to six years. Again, this was not a necessary obligation and could be avoided by agreement between HMRC and the transferor. However, these record-keeping requirements were brought into line with other tax and regulatory regimes in the Budget for 2007. From 1 September 2007, s. 49 and reg. 6 of the *VAT Regulations* 1995, were amended by the *VAT (Amendment) (No 5) Regulations* 2007 (SI 2007/2085) so that:

- the seller will keep the business records in all but a few specified cases (where, because the buyer retains the seller's VAT number it is essential for VAT compliance purposes that the records are passed over); but
- the seller must make available to the buyer information necessary for the buyer to comply with his duties under VATA.

HMRC may disclose to the buyer information it holds that is needed by the buyer to comply with his duties under VATA for this purpose.

30-500 Consideration and value

As has been seen earlier at 30-000, the essence of VAT is that it is a tax on supplies. For the most part, these will be supplies for consideration, a term which, in this context, is very wide.

This is expressed in art. 73 of Council Directive 2006/112/EC (art. 11(A)(1)(a) of the Sixth VAT Directive (Directive 77/388)) as:

> 'In respect of the supply of goods or services, other than as referred to in Articles 74 to 77, the taxable amount shall include everything which constitutes consideration obtained or to be obtained by the supplier, in return for the supply, from the customer or a third party, including subsidies directly linked to the price of the supply.'

In other words, subject to the other Articles, the taxable amount for a transaction is the consideration actually received. This Article has direct effect (see Case 62/00 *Marks & Spencer* [2002] ECR I-6325, para. 7). The reference to 'in return for' means that there must be a direct link between the supply and the consideration (see *C & E Commrs v The Apple and Pear Development Council* (Case 102/86)).

Article 78 then goes on to provide that:

> 'The taxable amount shall include the following factors:
> (a) taxes, duties, levies and charges, excluding the VAT itself;
> (b) incidental expenses, such as commission, packing, transport and insurance costs, charged by the supplier to the customer.
>
> For the purposes of point (b) of the first paragraph, Member States may regard expenses covered by a separate agreement as incidental expenses.'

and art. 79:

> 'The taxable amount shall not include the following factors:
> (a) price reductions by way of discount for early payment;
> (b) price discounts and rebates granted to the customer and obtained by him at the time of the supply;
> (c) amounts received by a taxable person from the customer, as repayment of expenditure incurred in the name and on behalf of the customer, and entered in his books in a suspense account.
>
> The taxable person must furnish proof of the actual amount of the expenditure referred to in point (c) of the first paragraph and may not deduct any VAT which may have been charged.'

In short, therefore consideration can be anything, not, necessarily money, that is given as a *quid pro quo* for something done, but subject to discounts, taxes and other adjustments.

The UK rules, VATA 1994, s. 19, provide, in particular, that:

> '19(2) If the supply is for a consideration in money its value [i.e. the amount on which tax is charged] shall be taken to be such amount as, with the addition of the VAT chargeable, is equal to the consideration.'

and:

> '19(3) If the supply is for a consideration not consisting or not wholly consisting of money, its value shall be taken to be such amount in money as, with the addition of the VAT chargeable, is equivalent to the consideration.'

and are supplemented, where necessary, by special rules in VATA 1994, Sch. 6 for special situations, like discounts, free supplies and connected party transactions.

(1) Monetary consideration

The position with monetary consideration is usually fairly straightforward, subject to the particular implications that can arise from situations like:

- subsidies (see (3) later);
- compensation (see (4) later); and
- connected party transactions (see (7) later).

It will not include returnable deposits or something provided by way of security (see *Cross Border Lease Management Ltd* [2007] BVC 4,035. However, where something is retained as a cancellation charge, this will be regarded as payment for something supplied (*Societe thermale d'Eugenie-Les-Bains v Ministere de l'Economie, des Finances et de l'Industrie* (Case C-277/05)).

(2) Non-monetary consideration

Non-monetary consideration, which arises when something is done in return for something else can be more problematic. Often, one part of the exchange is ostensibly provided *free* – in the sense that there is no money payment required and the temptation is to say this is not a supply. But in business you rarely find something given away for nothing. Usually, something is expected in return and, in reality, there are often reciprocal supplies of one kind or another (a barter).

Soft commissions – e.g. services or facilities without charge and the free use of equipment are a particular case in point. A broker or agent, for example, may supply introductory services and, instead of (or possibly in addition to) a normal percentage commission, will be offered a valuable benefit or facility. Both sides of this barter transaction, may then need to be recognised, although, these will not necessarily give rise to equal and opposite VAT liabilities:

- the taxable supply of the use of a computer, say, may be wholly or partly in return for services;
- VAT-exempt financial or insurance brokerage services.

On occasions with banks, you can also find customers being offered goods or services without charge (so long as a sufficient interest-free deposit is maintained).

Not recognising this sort of situation could create an unexpected added cost for one or other of the parties concerned – or, perhaps even, for both. (See, for example, *Naturally Yours Cosmetics v C & E Commrs* (Case 230/87) (1988) 3 BVC 428 and *Empire Stores Ltd v C & E Commrs* (Case C-33/93) [1994] BVC 253 and *C & E Commrs v Euphony Communications Ltd* [2004] BVC 473).

Sometimes there is an added complication in that what appear to be two quite separate supplies by the same party are somehow linked.

- In *Exeter Golf and Country Club Ltd v C & E Commrs* (1980) 1 BVC 385, for example, the members were required to provide interest-free loans, these being repayable if membership ceased. Part of the consideration for annual membership was seen as non-monetary in the form of the use of the money by the club for the forthcoming year. This was valued at the amount the club would otherwise have had to pay.
- However, the later Tribunal appeal in February 1996 by the *Arsenal Football Club plc* [1996] BVC 2,775 brought quite the opposite result and was in contrast to the earlier, 1978 decision in *Dyrham Park* (see below). The club in this case offered bonds for subscription to finance the building of their new North Bank Stand. The bonds-securities in the context of VATA 1994, Sch. 9, Grp. 5, item 6, were again interest-free but were generally repayable only after 150 years. Each conferred the right, however, to buy, or to nominate someone to buy, one North Bank Stand season ticket, such tickets only being available to bondholders or their nominees. These tickets represented a substantial discount from the normal match-day price and, as the bonds stripped of these rights were virtually worthless, this discount, so HMRC argued, was effectively non-monetary consideration attributable to the bonds. The Tribunal, though, disagreed even though the discount was greater than that which might otherwise have been given in the absence of the issue.
- In *Dyrham Park Country Club Ltd* (1978) VATTR 244; (1978) 1 BVC 1,099 members were required to subscribe for interest-free bonds – this time, securities for money within what is now VATA 1994, Sch. 9, Grp. 5, item 1 – and the Tribunal decided that the character of the initial transaction was a composite supply of the bond (exempt) and the right of membership (standard-rated). The subscription price thus fell to be apportioned under what is now VATA 1994, s. 19(4).

The principle in art. 73 can also apply where there is a straight exchange or swap of one thing for another without any monetary adjustment between the parties. In the case of *Cumbernauld Development Corp* [1997] BVC 4,043, the agreement for an exchange of land between a golf club and a property developer even expressed the consideration as *nil*. But this did not prevent the supplies that were made being recognised for VAT at their respective subjective values.

In assessing the value of consideration, the VAT Directive makes no reference to objective criteria. The test is based on subjective criteria, due to VAT being imposed on the consideration actually received in exchange for the supply. To determine the value of the transaction it is necessary to examine what is agreed upon between the parties. An early case which illustrates this concept is *Naturally Yours Cosmetics Ltd v C & E Commrs* [1988] ECR 6365 where the ECJ examined a contract between the supplier and an individual beauty consultant. Under the agreement, a pot of cream would be supplied materially below the wholesale price, on condition that the beauty consultant arranged for a party to be held (via a party hostess). In the event of no party being arranged, the pot of cream had either to be returned or paid for at the retail price. The ECJ held that in these circumstances the value of the consideration should be fixed as the difference between the wholesale price and the cost price, because this difference, although not paid in monetary terms, was paid for by the provision of a service, i.e. procuring arranging a party for the purposes of selling beauty products.

Where an exchange or "barter" takes place, the value of the supply is calculated by the value of the consideration provided by the other party. In other words, it is necessary to determine the value assigned to the supply by the parties. For example, if the consideration represents a supply of services in exchange for goods, the value of the consideration is the cost of the goods; because that represents what the recipient of the services was prepared to pay. The point is illustrated by *Empire Stores Ltd v C & E Commrs* [1994] ECR - I 2329 where the ECJ held that the consideration on an exchange must be ascertained in the following way (para. 19 of the judgment):

> 'Where that value is not a sum of money agreed between the parties, it must, in order to be subjective, be the value which the recipient of the services constituting the consideration for the supply of goods attributes to the services which he is seeking to obtain and must correspond to the amount which he is prepared to spend for that purpose. Where, as here, the supply of goods is involved, that value can only be the price which the supplier has paid for the article which he is supplying without extra charge in consideration of the services in question.'

The *Empire Stores* case is a useful illustration of how VAT can be charged on the exchange of goods for services, or services for services. In *Empire Stores* a retailer sold merchandise through a catalogue. In order to acquire new clientele it operated various schemes. Under one scheme, a 'self-introduction scheme', a person would provide personal information about themselves, including the implicit right to use the information to check creditworthiness. The customer list could then be sold by the catalogue retailer. The information provided therefore had economic value. Additionally, the retailer received the real advantage that if a person introduced themselves to the catalogue that the person would make purchases. Once the information was provided and accepted (i.e. after a credit check) a 'free' gift would be sent to the person providing the information. Under a second scheme, 'introduce-a-friend scheme', Empire Stores offered an article to established customers who recommended one of their friends as a potential customer; the article was supplied once the new customer had completed a form, had been approved by the retailer and had made a first payment relating to an order. Under each scheme, Empire Stores accounted for VAT in respect of the articles on the basis of the cost price of it. The UK tax authority argued that the VAT treatment should be the tax exclusive cost price plus 50%, being the tax authority's estimate of the prices which Empire Stores would have charged for the articles if they had been offered in its sales catalogue.

The issue was whether VAT was chargeable, and if so what the amount was. In essence the retailer undertook to provide goods in exchange for the supply of information. The gift was intended as the quid pro quo for an advantage provided to the retailer by a person introducing a potential customer, and not in return for the purchase by that customer of goods offered in the retailer's sales catalogue. In the judgment of the ECJ in Empire Stores there was a direct link between the provision of the introduction of a customer because for the retailer it had an economic value. The value in this case had a subjective value, because the retailer was prepared to give an article for which it had paid the cost price. The ECJ's conclusions were as follows, as to the nature of the supplies, and the value of those supplies for VAT purposes (at para. 111 of the judgment):

> 'The link between the supply of the article without extra charge and the introduction of a potential customer must be regarded as direct, since if the service is not provided no article is due from or supplied without extra charge by Empire Stores.
>
> Moreover, since the services provided to Empire Stores are remunerated by the supply of goods the value of the services can unquestionably be expressed in monetary terms.

As for the determination of that value, which is the substance of the second question, the court held in Naturally Yours Cosmetics (1988) 3 BVC 428, [1988] ECR 6365 at 6390, at para. 16, that the consideration taken as the taxable amount in respect of a supply of goods is a subjective value, since the taxable amount is the consideration actually received and not a value estimated according to objective criteria.

Where that value is not a sum of money agreed between the parties, it must, in order to be subjective, be the value which the recipient of the services constituting the consideration for the supply of goods attributes to the services which he is seeking to obtain and must correspond to the amount which he is prepared to spend for that purpose. Where, as here, the supply of goods is involved, that value can only be the price which the supplier has paid for the article which he is supplying without extra charge in consideration of the services in question.'

Accordingly, it is always important even in the absence of monetary consideration to consider whether there is nonetheless a non-monetary value which is capable of being attributed to a transaction.

(3) Subsidies

Problems can sometimes arise where there is the appearance of a subsidy – i.e. where part of the price is borne by someone other than the recipient of the supply.

- The question of subsidies was considered by the ECJ in the case of *Office des produits wallons ASBL v Belgian State* (Case C-184/00) [2001] ECR I-9115[2003] BVC 650. The taxpayer was a non-profit-making association, which advertised and sold agricultural and other products. It received an annual operating subsidy from the Walloon Region administration, which the Belgian authorities said was subject to VAT. The Court decided that, for a subsidy to be *directly linked to the price* of a supply (and therefore taxable) it had to be paid *specifically* to enable the recipient to provide the particular goods and services concerned. The purchase price also had to be fixed such that it was reduced in proportion to the subsidy (showing that the subsidy constituted an element in determining the price) and the subsidy had to allow the recipient to sell the goods or services at a lower price than would otherwise have been the case. However, there did not have to be an exact correlation between the subsidy and the reduction in price, but there did have to be a significant relationship.
- In *Keeping Newcastle Warm Ltd v C&E Commrs* (Case C-353/00) [2003] BVC 283 the company received £10 by way of a grant from a third-party each time it provided energy advice to a householder. It was agreed that the £10 formed part of the consideration for the supply. However, the company claimed that, not being linked to the actual price of its supplies, the subsidy therefore didn't form part of the taxable amount. On a Reference to the ECJ, the Court held that this was not a correct view.

(4) Compensation

Compensation in the true sense is generally not regarded as consideration for any supply, but merely recompense for damage or inconvenience suffered. Before any such payment or receipt is taken to be VAT-free, however, it is always important to consider the circumstances in which it arises.

- In *Lloyds Bank plc* [1996] BVC 2,875, for example, a payment described as compensation was made in the context of the termination of a lease carried out by way of a Deed of Variation. In 1974 Lloyds had entered into a 25-year lease for two floors of a building in Birmingham. The landlord subsequently opted to tax this and other leases, which it had granted to the bank. In 1994, when a rent review was due to be carried out, Lloyds decided to seek alternative accommodation. At the same time, the landlord set about refurbishing the building and the parties entered into discussions with a view to terminating the lease. In doing so, they focused on appropriate compensation for the landlord for loss of rent for the remaining term of the lease, taking into account the benefit of vacant possession. It was suggested by the landlord that it would be best from a VAT viewpoint to have a notice of termination rather than surrender. The parties accordingly entered into a deed of variation of the lease giving the landlord, for no consideration, the right to determine the lease on 25 March 1995 subject to giving notice in writing of the exercise of the right at any time prior to September 1994. This would be in consideration of the appellant paying the landlord compensation of £597,220.

  Lloyds contended there had been no taxable supply by the landlord and that the payment was by way of liquidated damages or compensation and thus *outside the scope* of VAT. It maintained that the effect of the deed was to vary the original lease by inserting a clause entitling the appellant to terminate and there had been no surrender as such. When the appellant gave notice in writing that it was exercising the right nothing had to be done by the landlord to trigger the payment of compensation and there was therefore no supply by the landlord.

  Against this, HMRC argued that, in substance and reality, what was paid by Lloyds to achieve a release from its obligations amounted to consideration for a supply by the landlord. The matter was governed by the decision of the ECJ in *Lubbock Fine & Co v C & E Commrs* (Case C-63/92) [1993] BVC 287 such that a change in the contractual relationship between the landlord and tenant, such as a 'termination of the lease for consideration', had to bear the same liability as the letting of the property. The Tribunal, on appeal, agreed.

- *Financial and General Print Ltd* [1996] BVC 2,623 also dealt with a compensation payment. This time, the payment was in respect of the cessation of a plant lease, which was terminable on the appointment of a receiver over the assets of the lessee. When this happened there was a default requiring possession of the plant to be given back to the lessor and the payment of compensation by the lessee. The Tribunal found the termination was not a supply of services effected for consideration in the sense contemplated by art. 2(1) of the Sixth VAT Directive (Directive 77/388), considered in the light of the judgment of the ECJ in *Apple and Pear Development Council v C & E Commrs* (Case 102/86) (1988) 3 BVC 274. There the Court took art. 2(1) to mean *against payment*. The lessor's termination of the lease was a unilateral act.

  In reaching its decision, the Tribunal, had clearly proceeded on the basis of making an objective determination of the entire transaction as revealed by the terms of the agreement. But see later in **Chapter 7** at 70-400.

- In *Holiday Inns (UK) Ltd* [1994] BVC 543, HMRC stated their position on payments which were *outside the scope of VAT* in the following way:

'... [where] payments made under out-of-court settlements ... such payments are in essence compensatory and do not relate directly to supplies of goods or services, they are outside the scope of VAT. This will be so even if the settlement is expressed in terms that the payment is consideration for the plaintiff's agreement to abandon his rights to bring legal proceedings. But payments will remain taxable if, and to the extent that, they are the consideration for specific taxable supplies by the plaintiff eg where the dispute concerns payment for an earlier supply, or where the plaintiff grants future rights to exploit copyright material under the settlement.

In general, liquidated damages are outside the scope of VAT. So if the damages had been fixed by the parties in the original agreement as liquidated damages they would not have been taxable. But if they are paid under a separate agreement ... they are taxable.'

This line seems subsequently to have been borne out in the appeal in *Themis FTSE Fledgling Index Trust plc* [2001] BVC 4,093, where compensation on a unilateral repudiation of a contract was held to be *outside the scope*.

(5) Free supplies

Goods or services genuinely made available free or gratuitously are a different matter and will often not result in a supply or supplies being made at all. There are, however, a number of important exceptions, such as:

- the disposal of goods forming part of the assets of a business free of charge will not be treated as a supply of goods if it is a business gift, or one of several business gifts, to the same person in the same year, costing less than £50 (VATA 1994, Sch. 4, para. 5(1)(a) and (2) – art. 16 of Council Directive 2006/112/EC (art. 5(6) of the Sixth VAT Directive (Directive 77/388));

  The disposal of goods forming part of the asset of a business free of charge will not be treated as a supply of goods if it is the provision to a person, for no consideration, of a sample of goods, distributed either by the taxable person or by a third party (VATA 1994, Sch. 4, para. 5(2)(b)). There is no longer a restriction which used to prevent VAT relief applying to a sample where more than one sample was given and those other samples were identical or did not differ in any material respect from the first sample. This restriction was removed by the *Finance (No. 3) Act* 2011. HMRC practice in relation to samples is as follows Samples, part-exchanges, barters, contras and VAT at www.hmrc.gov.uk (2011): 'You might decide to give free samples to advertise your products to members of the public. You could do this by engaging a third party, such as a business promotions company, to distribute them. Or you could give the samples to a client so that they can give one to each of their customers. An example would be a sweet manufacturer that gives retailers samples of a new chocolate bar to give to customers so they can try it. You won't have to account for VAT on any samples distributed to the general public by a third party if you meet all of the following conditions: - neither you nor the third party charge for them, - you supply them for genuine business reasons and they're a typical example of your products, - the final customer receives only one example of each product, - the samples remain your property until they're given to the final customer, - any samples that aren't used are returned to you or destroyed';

- the private use of business assets (VATA 1994, Sch. 4, para. 5(4) – art. 14 of Council Directive 2006/112/EC) but subject to certain exceptions for any interest in land, any building or part of a building, any ship, boat or aircraft (VATA 1994, Sch. 4, para. 5(4A));

3 Outputs and Output VAT

- the free provision of road fuel (i.e. petrol and diesel oil) provided for the private use of employees, which is taxed by way of a scale charge (VATA 1994, s. 56 and 57);
- the private use of business services (*Value Added Tax (Supply of Services) Order* 1993 (SI 1993/1507) – art. 26 of Council Directive 2006/112/EC);
- the deemed supply of goods sold in satisfaction of a debt (VATA 1994, Sch. 4, para. 7); and
- the deemed supply of chargeable goods remaining as part of the assets of a business when the owner ceases to be a taxable person (VATA 1994, Sch. 4, para. 8).

The rule on gifts of goods is, these days, less often triggered, as the £50 limit is more generous than the earlier limit of £10, and the extension of the £50 exemption from October 2003 to a series of gifts made to the same person will take many common situations out of the equation. In cases where the limit for gifts is exceeded, however, there will be a potential output tax liability (based on cost), although this can often be dealt with in practice, and by agreement with HMRC, by simply not claiming the underlying input VAT.

> **Practice point**
>
> Not seeking to claim the VAT on gifts as input tax is often a useful alternative to accounting for the supplies involved as outputs. However, if output tax is accounted for, the underlying input tax should often be recovered in full, even by the VAT-exempt businesses at which this book is aimed, because of the principle of *direct attribution* (see **Chapter 4** at 40-200).

Where the cost of the free supplies is £50 or less, although there is no supply to be accounted for, the related input VAT can, however, be recovered as part of the residual calculation under the partial exemption rules discussed in **Chapter 4** at 40-200.

The free gift rules are not applied (VATA 1994, Sch. 4, para. 5(5)) where the business is unable to recover (not just has not recovered) all of the underlying input VAT. They also do not apply to promotional or other goods given away as a business incentive and, as noted earlier, where there is a suggestion of any obligation or anything done in return by the donee (see *Naturally Yours Cosmetics v C & E Commrs* (Case 230/87) (1988) 3 BVC 428 and *Empire Stores Ltd v C & E Commrs* (Case C-33/93) [1994] BVC 253 and *C & E Commrs v Euphony Communications Ltd* [2004] BVC 473). In this case, there will be a supply for non-monetary consideration on which tax has to be accounted for on cost.

The tax in respect of road fuel is levied by way of a scale charge linked to engine capacity of the vehicle. The rule in VATA 1994, s. 57 does not apply, however, where a payment is received from the employee which equals or exceeds the cost incurred by the employer.

The rules on the private use of business assets will, typically, apply to assets made available to members of staff (i.e. directors and employees). As with the rules on the gift of goods, however, the rules on private use are not applied (VATA 1994 Sch. 4, para. 5(5)) where the business is unable to recover all of any underlying input VAT.

In the case of cars, if input tax has been recovered (see **Chapter 4**), output tax will be due on the cost of any benefit provided to an employee (see Sections 4 to 6 of HMRC Notice 700/64). There is no similar charge, however:

- if input tax has not been recovered; or
- if, in the case of a leased car, it has been subject to the 50 per cent input tax block.

There will also be no VAT due on any contribution to private use made by the employee. Tax will, however, be due on any payment received from an employee towards maintenance and running costs.

> **Practice point**
>
> It is interesting, perhaps, that HMRC do not seem to view the provision of the car, or any other benefit for that matter, as in any way in return for the employee's services; nor, following the successful Tribunal appeal by the *Co-operative Insurance Society Ltd* [1992] BVC 694, do they seek to tax the supply on the basis of salary sacrifice where a cash alternative is available (see HMRC Press Release 13/92 and the *Value Added Tax (Treatment of Transactions) Order* 1992 (SI 1992/630).
>
> However, care may still need to be taken lest any arrangement with employees can be seen as amounting to a deduction from pay rather than the calculation of the remuneration package. In that case VAT could still be due and there could also be income tax implications from the decision in *Heaton (HMIT) v Bell* ((1969) 46 TC 211).

The rule on the private use of business services was introduced from 1 August 1993 by the *Value Added Tax (Supply of Services) Order* 1993 (SI 1993/1507). It covers the free use, for example by employees, of taxable services acquired by a business where, again, all or part of the related input tax is recoverable (not just where it has not been recovered). Typically, it can affect the free use of licenced computer software, the payment of telephone charges and the availability of professional services. Another obvious situation where the rule can be applied is in the case of mobile phones, the rules for which will be found in Section 12A of HMRC Notice 700.

The level below which there would be no deemed supply of goods on cessation of registration was increased from £250 to £1,000 by the *Value Added Tax (Deemed Supply of Goods) Order* 2000 (SI 2000/266) from 1 April 2000.

The self-supply provisions for building services are an anti-avoidance measure. Their impact arises essentially in the context of the partial exemption rules, where the corresponding input VAT is wholly or partly irrecoverable. These are discussed later in **Chapter 4** at 40-100 and are aimed at newly constructed buildings or certain significant alterations or reconstructions of existing buildings. The charge is intended to effectively tax the cost of the land when the building is to be put to an exempt or partly exempt use. This is discussed in detail in **Chapter 8** at 80-150.

(6) Value

Consideration will, in practice, always have to be *valuable* consideration (e.g. not just natural love and affection) and *future* (i.e. not past consideration where something has previously occurred without expectation of a subsequent supply). It need not, however, be paid or provided by the person to whom the supply is made. Indeed, if the supply is agreed to be made for a stated price, it can take place regardless of whether a payment is ever in fact made. The value will, though, take into account any taxes, duties, levies, charges and incidental costs (art. 78 of Council Directive 2006/112/EC (Sixth VAT Directive (Directive 77/388), art. 11(A)(2))) and any discounts or price reductions agreed to (art. 79). Where applicable, the value of a supply will also be taken to include any withholding tax.

The value of a supply can also be reduced after the event (art. 90). It may not necessarily involve an adjustment between the immediate parties in a chain of supply, so long as the person giving the rebate is itself within the supply chain at an earlier stage (as established in *Elida Gibbs Ltd v C & E Commrs* (Case C-317/94) [1997] BVC 80 and *EC Commission v Germany* (Case C-427/98)[2003] BVC 205).

HMRC's policy on the value of consideration in this area is set out in VAT Notice 700/7 (May 2012) *Business Promotion Schemes*.

The bad debt relief case of *C & E Commrs v General Motors Acceptance Corporation (UK) plc* [2004] BVC 611 (see later at 30-600) also concerned the adjustment of the taxable amount. GMAC supplied cars on HP terms and the dispute was over whether, on premature termination on the customer's default, it was entitled to bad debt relief (as argued by HMRC) or to an adjustment of its original taxable amount (as argued by GMAC).

(7) Connected-party transactions

In addition to the rules so far discussed, there are specific anti-avoidance provisions in VATA 1994, Sch. 6, para. 1. This provides that:

'(1) Where -
  (a) the value of a supply made by a taxable person for a consideration in money is (apart from this paragraph) less than its open market value, and
  (b) the person making the supply and the person to whom it is made are connected, and
  (c) if the supply is a taxable supply, the person to whom the supply is made is not entitled under section 25 and 26 to credit for all the VAT on the supply,

the Commissioners may direct that the value of the supply shall be taken to be its open market value.'

A direction to use open market value on this basis can be imposed up to three years after a supply has been made. A connected-party for this purpose is defined by reference to what is now CTA 2010, s. 1122 (see **Appendix 7**).

The EU provision on market value attribution is Art. 80 of the VAT Directive, which provides that:

'1. In order to prevent tax evasion or avoidance, Member States may in any of the following cases take measures to ensure that, in respect of the supply of goods or services involving family or other close personal ties, management, ownership, membership, financial or legal ties as defined by the Member State, the taxable amount is to be the open market value:

(a) where the consideration is lower than the open market value and the recipient of the supply does not have a full right of deduction under Articles 167 to 171 and Articles 173 to 177;

(b) where the consideration is lower than the open market value and the supplier does not have a full right of deduction under Articles 167 to 171 and Articles 173 to 177 and the supply is subject to an exemption under Articles 132, 135, 136, 371, 375, 376, 377, 378(2), 379(2) or Articles 380 to 390b;

(c) where the consideration is higher than the open market value and the supplier does not have a full right of deduction under Articles 167 to 171 and Articles 173 to 177.'

The scope of Art. 80 was recently considered by the CoJ in *Balkan and Sea Properties ADSITs (C-621/10), Provadinvest OOD (C-129/11) v Direktor na Direktsia 'Obzhalvane i upravlenie na izpalnenieto' – Varna pri Tsentralno upravlenie na Natsionalnata agentsia za prihodite* where the Court concluded that Art. 80(1) is exhaustive and the rules cannot be applied beyond the ambit of the article, for example to situations where the taxpayers have a full right of input tax deduction. The CoJ held that Art. 80(1) has direct effect so that if any open market value provisions of a Member State are incompatible with the terms of Art. 80(1) then a taxpayer has the right to rely on it directly to oppose the application of provisions of national legislation that are contrary to it.

The application of these provisions was highlighted in an appeal involving four subsidiaries of The Royal Bank of Scotland.

- The case, *RBS Leasing and Services (No. 1) Ltd; RBS Leasing and Services (No. 2) Ltd; RBS Leasing and Services (No. 3) Ltd; RBS Leasing and Services (No. 4) Ltd* [1998] BVC 4,141 concerned a dispute over whether supplies made between members of the group should be taken to be at open market value.
The Bank sold plant and machinery, IT equipment and other short-life office assets, at cost to the appellants, who bought assets using funds provided by the Bank by subscribing for three per cent preference shares in the companies concerned. The appellants then leased the assets back to the Bank on leases with, typically, *primary periods* of five years. The rents under these *internal* leases were determined on a *nil cost of finance* basis, which HMRC maintained was less than the open market rent. A direction followed.
The appellants objected, saying VATA 1994, Sch. 6, para. 1 was an unauthorised derogation from art. 11A of the Sixth VAT Directive (Directive 77/388); the directions were not validly issued because HMRC failed to take the proper considerations into account and, in any event, the rental payments were not less than open market value as the Bank was prepared to enter into similar leases with third parties on similar terms.
None of these arguments were accepted, however and the appellants lost on all counts.

- As noted elsewhere, the European Court in *Ministero dell'Economia e delle Finanze and Agenzia delle Entrate v FCE Bank plc* (Case C-210/04) [2009] BVC 692 has confirmed that there is no supply for VAT purposes between two parts of the same legal entity. The dispute in this case concerned supplies from a UK bank to its Italian branch and at issue was whether the branch had to account for Italian VAT. It had, in fact, done so in accordance with Italian law, but, on a Reference to the ECJ, the Court was asked if transactions between two establishments of a single legal entity can be regarded as supplies for VAT purposes.

In a Ruling in March 2006, the Court concluded that the branch of a non-resident company is not independent and therefore there is no legal relationship between them. They must be considered as one and the same taxable person within the meaning of art. 4(1) of the Sixth Directive (art. 9 of Directive 2006/112). FCE IT was therefore a part of FCE Bank. It followed that the Italian administrative practice of recognizing a supply in this situation was incompatible with the Sixth Directive.

30-550 Single or multiple supplies

Not all transactions invite a straightforward application of the rules, even when the amount given by way of consideration is not in dispute. Sometimes the real issue is over liability in the sense of whether something is wholly taxable or wholly exempt – or, put another way, apportionable to two or more supplies, rather than just attributable to one. The question of whether a transaction involves the provision of a single or multiple supplies is a question of law (see *David Baxendale Ltd v R & C Commrs* [2009] EWCA Civ 831; [2009] BVC 663). A summary of the principles applicable to determining whether there is more than one identifiable supply is provided at the end of this section. The determination of whether there is a single supply or multiple supplies must first be answered since if there is only a single standard rated supply then it is unnecessary to consider whether an activity is within the scope of an exemption (this is illustrated by the approach of the CoJ in *Everything Everywhere Ltd (formerly T-Mobile UK) v R & C Commrs* (C-276/09) [2011] BVC 44 (see below)). Additionally, if supplies are treated as single or separate supplies this classification may also go on to determine the availability of zero-rating and exemption of the supplies.

Perhaps the best illustration of this is the case of *Card Protection Plan*.

- In *Card Protection Plan Ltd v C & E Commrs* (Case C-349/96) [1999] BVC 155, a case which went as far as the ECJ, as Advocate General Fennelly put it:

    'Special difficulties arise, in the mystic twilight of VAT legislation, where there is what in modern jargon is called "a package" of services, some of which may, and others of which may not, be within a VAT exemption.'

    For a fee CPP offered holders of credit cards a plan intended to protect them against financial loss and inconvenience resulting from the loss or theft of their cards or of certain other items such as car keys, passports and insurance documents.

    So far as this provided for indemnification of the cardholder against financial loss in the event of loss or theft, CPP obtained block cover from an insurance company. The policy was arranged by an insurance broker instructed by CPP. CPP's customers were mentioned in the policy as the assured, their names being added to the schedule on the policy. CPP paid the premiums in advance at the beginning of the policy year, making any necessary adjustments at the year-end.

    The services offered by CPP, corresponding to the cover described in the policy, were, in broad terms, indemnities:

- against the fraudulent use of cards;
- for costs incurred by the cardholder in finding lost luggage, bags or items tagged with labels issued by CPP;
- for costs incurred in carrying out the formalities of making claims and assisting the police with respect to valuable articles and/or important documents whose serial numbers had been registered with CPP;
- in respect of an emergency cash advance following loss of cards; and
- for the purchase of a return air ticket from anywhere in the world following loss of cards.

There were also representatives of the insurers to provide 24-hour telephone advice on access to medical services, including the arrangement of appointments for medical care abroad.

The plan also included other services, such as:

- a computerised record of customers' credit cards;
- a 24-hour telephone line for receiving notifications of loss, so as to allow the necessary measures to be taken for passing on the information to credit card issuers, and the supply of adhesive labels bearing that telephone number;
- help in the event of loss to obtain replacement credit cards;
- help in the event of change of address for notifying card-issuing companies;
- pre-printed key tabs so that they may be found in the event of loss;
- an annual print-out to check;
- a medical card for the entry of personal medical details; and
- discounts on car hire.

In the event of a claim, the customer was required to give notice of the loss to CPP within 24 hours. Claims for less than £5,000 were dealt with by CPP; larger claims were handled by the insurer, unless CPP was given specific authority.

HMRC had initially treated what was supplied by CPP as exempt. However, they later changed their mind and said the annual membership fee was subject to VAT at the standard-rate:

- they saw the plan as a *package of services* concerning the registration of credit cards, all taxable;
- they also said the insurer could not be seen as supplying insurance to CPP's customers as 'there was no privity between it and those customers'.

This dispute went to the Tribunal, where CPP lost and from thence to the High Court, where the privity of contract point was rejected. The Court held, however, that some of CPP's services were exempt as *the making of arrangements for the provision of insurance*, but others, *services of convenience*, were not. CPP then appealed to the Court of Appeal against the ruling that there was not a single exempt supply of insurance. HMRC cross-appealed, maintaining there was a single supply of a taxable card-registration service.

CPP then sought leave to appeal to the House of Lords, who ended up referring the matter to the ECJ, asking the following questions:

'(1) Having regard to the provisions of the sixth VAT directive and in particular to art. 2(1) thereof, what is the proper test to be applied in deciding whether a transaction consists for VAT purposes of a single composite supply or of two or more independent supplies?

(2) Does the supply by an undertaking of a service or services of the kind provided by Card Protection Plan (CPP) through the card protection plan operated by them constitute for VAT purposes a single composite supply or two or more independent supplies? Are there any particular features of the present case, such as the payment of a single price by the customer or the involvement of Continental Assurance Company of London plc as well as CPP, that affect the answer to that question?

(3) Do such supply or supplies constitute or include "insurance ... transactions including related services performed by insurance ... agents" within the meaning of art. 13(B)(a) of the sixth VAT directive? In particular, for the purpose of answering that question:

   (a) does "insurance" within the meaning of art. 13(B)(a) of the sixth VAT directive include the classes of activity, in particular "assistance" activity, listed in the Annex to Council directive 73/239 (the first Council directive on Non-Life Insurance), as amended by Council directive 84/641?

   (b) do the "related services of ... insurance agents" in art. 13(B)(a) of the sixth VAT directive constitute or include the activities referred to in art. 2 of Council directive 77/92?

(4) Is it compatible with art. 13(B)(a) of the sixth VAT directive for a member state to restrict the scope of the exemption for "insurance ... transactions" to supplies made by persons permitted to carry on insurance business under the law of that member state?'

Advocate General concluded that the services provided by CPP could not be insurance so it was not necessary to express an opinion on the single/multiple supply point. However, the court did address this and, in answering Questions 1 and 2, what it said was:

'26 By its first two questions, which should be taken together, the national court essentially asks, with reference to a plan such as that offered by CPP to its customers, what the appropriate criteria are for deciding, for VAT purposes, whether a transaction which comprises several elements is to be regarded as a single supply or as two or more distinct supplies to be assessed separately.

27 It must be borne in mind that the question of the extent of a transaction is of particular importance, for VAT purposes, both for identifying the place where the services are provided and for applying the rate of tax or, as in the present case, the exemption provisions in the sixth directive. In addition, having regard to the diversity of commercial operations, it is not possible to give exhaustive guidance on how to approach the problem correctly in all cases.

28 However, as the court held in *Faaborg-Gelting Linien v Finanzamt Flensburg* (Case C-231/94) [1996] BVC 436;[1996] ECR I-2395, para. 12-14, concerning the classification of restaurant transactions, where the transaction in question comprises a bundle of features and acts, regard must first be had to all the circumstances in which that transaction takes place.

29 In this respect, taking into account, first, that it follows from art. 2(1) of the sixth directive that every supply of a service must normally be regarded as distinct and independent and,

second, that a supply which comprises a single service from an economic point of view should not be artificially split, so as not to distort the functioning of the VAT system, the essential features of the transaction must be ascertained in order to determine whether the taxable person is supplying the customer, being a typical consumer, with several distinct principal services or with a single service.

30   There is a single supply in particular in cases where one or more elements are to be regarded as constituting the principal service, whilst one or more elements are to be regarded, by contrast, as ancillary services which share the tax treatment of the principal service. A service must be regarded as ancillary to a principal service if it does not constitute for customers an aim in itself, but a means of better enjoying the principal service supplied *C & E Commrs v Madgett & Anor (t/a Howden Court Hotel)* (Joined Cases C-308/96 and C-94/97) [1998] BVC 458, para. 24).

31   In those circumstances, the fact that a single price is charged is not decisive. Admittedly, if the service provided to customers consists of several elements for a single price, the single price may suggest that there is a single service. However, notwithstanding the single price, if circumstances such as those described in para. 7 to 10 above indicated that the customers intended to purchase two distinct services, namely an insurance supply and a card registration service, then it would be necessary to identify the part of the single price which related to the insurance supply, which would remain exempt in any event. The simplest possible method of calculation or assessment should be used for this (see, to that effect, *Madgett*, para. 45 and 46).

32   The answer to the first two questions must therefore be that it is for the national court to determine, in the light of the above criteria, whether transactions such as those performed by CPP are to be regarded for VAT purposes as comprising two independent supplies, namely an exempt insurance supply and a taxable card registration service, or whether one of those two supplies is the principal supply to which the other is ancillary, so that it receives the same tax treatment as the principal supply.'

The House of Lords, when the appeal before it resumed ([2001] BVC 158), decided on 31 January 2001 that there was, in the event, a single, overall exempt supply. This was followed on 15 February by HMRC *Business Brief* 2/2001 setting out their policy. Usefully, they cite the tests set out by the court, which can be briefly summarised as meaning that:

(1)   You must first look at all the circumstances surrounding a transaction.

(2)   At the same time:

    (a)   every supply must be regarded as distinct and independent; and
    (b)   something that is, economically, a single supply should not be artificially split.

(3)   You must also then fix on the essential features of the transaction to determine whether the recipient is being provided with several distinct supplies or with a single overall supply.

There is a single supply where one or more elements comprise the principal service, with other elements being *ancillary* – i.e. not an aim in itself, but a means of better enjoying the principal service. Charging a single price is not decisive, but may suggest there is a single service. However, indications that a recipient intended to buy two distinct services, with different VAT liabilities, could mean the single price should be apportioned.

HMRC said at the time they considered these would be appropriate in the great majority of cases, but went on to remark that they believed their application might produce a different result than that resulting from some earlier decided cases. The implication, perhaps, is that they considered some taxpayers might be getting too good a deal. However, whether companies should be worse off remains to be seen and many outsourcing situations might arguably benefit from the ruling in CPP and other subsequent cases.

- In *Laurentian Management Services Ltd; Lincoln Assurance Ltd* [2000] BVC 2,210 there was a similar issue, whether data processing and other services supplied from Canada to the UK constituted a single supply which fell to be treated as *supplied where received* or multiple supplies, some of which would be treated as supplied where received and others of which would be treated as supplied where the supplier belonged.

The appellants were representative members of two VAT groups one of which succeeded the other. The services were imported from an affiliate with which Laurentian Life plc had entered into two contracts. The first recited that:

'It being the intention of LL to concentrate on its life assurance business and to outsource all of its computer operations function, desires to contract for the supply of certain computer services.'

The second that:

'It being the intention of the client to outsource its mainframe processing function the client desires to contract for the supply of certain services.'

The relevant services, together with ancillary services, consisted of data processing, data storage, telecommunications and transmission and disaster recovery. The latter consisted of being able to provide an alternative supply if the normal telecommunication services broke down. On the basis of submissions made by the appellants, not challenged by HMRC, the split was approximately 60 per cent for services subject to the reverse charge as having been supplied in the UK and 40 per cent for other items which the appellants contended were outside the scope of UK VAT.

The appellants maintained they imported a number of different services, the nature of which determined the place of supply. HMRC argued that, on the basis of the test laid down for such cases by the ECJ, data processing was the *aim in itself* and the other services were simply the *means of better enjoying* it.

Deciding for the appellants, the Tribunal held that the services varied widely in nature and in taxability and it could not be right to cast over them a blanket label *computer services* and to equate that with data processing. Further, deciding the case in this way had the merit of avoiding a distortion of competition.

- Other cases in a similar vein and of particular interest to the finance and insurance sectors are those of *Continuum (Europe) Ltd* or *CSC Financial Services Ltd* (as it is now known) [2002] BVC 253. *Continuum* is discussed later in **Chapter 8** at 80-100(1) and *FDR and Lloyds TSB* in **Chapter 7** at 70-200.
- Another case, on single or multiple supplies, was that of *Primback Ltd v C & E Commrs* [2001] BVC 315. This was a dispute involving a retail furniture company using the standard method of accounting for VAT under Retail Scheme A.. As a promotional ploy, it offered

extended credit on terms described as *interest free*. The customer paid the advertised price by instalments to a finance company and the latter paid Primback a smaller sum than the price of the goods.

HMRC argued it was not necessary to make an apportionment of the price between the two elements, goods and finance, as the credit arrangements were not a supply within the exemption for the provision of instalment credit in VATA 1983, Sch. 6, Grp. 5, item 3 because the finance house, not Primback, made that supply.

When the matter reached the Court of Appeal, the matter was decided in Primback's favour, but essentially as a result of the mechanics of its retail scheme. HMRC, however, appealed to the House of Lords and, in April 1999, the matter was referred to the ECJ, where on 15 May 2001 the Court ultimately decided in HMRC's favour. The taxable amount for Primback (i.e. the amount on which it was to calculate the tax payable on its sales) was the full amount payable by the purchaser. The rationale for the judgment was that:

- The fact that the supply of services by the finance house was, in principle, VAT-exempt had no bearing on the basis for charging VAT on the transaction between Primback and the purchaser.
- Primback could not validly claim to apportion the price received between the goods and the cost of the credit because the price was the same, irrespective of the means by which the purchase of the goods was financed.
- Even if it were possible to distinguish the supply of credit, from the supply of goods, the former would have to be construed as, in any event, *ancillary* to the sale of the goods.
- Finally, even assuming that a reduction in the sales price could be permitted, a discount for cash was not volunteered but had to be requested by the customer, so that, in many cases, the customer simply paid the advertised price. Either because he was unaware that he could ask for a discount or because he did not want to ask for one.

In short, the commission charged to Primback for the provision of the finance was a cost and not a reduction in the value of its sales.

As remarked in *Laurentian*, the question is one of fact and degree, taking account of all the circumstances. One must look at the commercial reality of the whole situation and must neither artificially separate what ought to be joined nor simplistically join what ought to be separated. Charging a single price is not decisive and complicated charging arrangements are even less so.

Of far greater importance is the *aim in itself/means of better enjoying* distinction. The Tribunal in that case had initially looked at this in the context of whether data processing was an aim in itself or itself *ancillary* to the group's basic aim of selling more life assurance and related products. However, arguably, this is an incorrect approach, the better question being to consider what was the principal service that the affiliate performed and whether the data processing was ancillary to that. The Tribunal, to some extent, went along that line in citing Advocate General Léger in the *Madgett* case and ultimately decided the dispute on the basis that the services appeared to vary widely both in nature and in taxability.

Primback was later followed by several further cases involving free insurance and/or finance.

- *Peugeot Motor Co Plc & Anor v C & E Commrs* [2004] BVC 269 and *Ford Motor Co Ltd* [2007] BVC 479 were both concerned with free insurance offered as an incentive on the purchase of cars. Both were decided against the taxpayer on the basis of what the companies and their customers had *subjectively* agreed.
- However in a separate appeal by *Ford Motor Company Ltd v R & C Commrs* [2007] BVC 2,146 there was a different end-result. The case was about a bonus incentive offered by Ford to customers buying on credit from FCE Bank plc, a company in the Ford VAT group. The bonuses were paid by Ford to FCE to offset the capital payments due from the customer. Ford argued that the principles in *Elida Gibbs Ltd v C & E Commrs* (Case C-317/94) [1997] BVC 80 applied to, viewed *objectively*, reduce their taxable amount. HMRC cited Primback, saying that the deal was, in substance free finance, but this was not accepted and Ford won.
- *C & E Commrs v British Telecommunications plc* [1999] BVC 306 concerned car delivery charges and the input tax block – see **Chapter 4** at 40-050). As a large purchaser of motor vehicles, BT had entered into arrangements, whereby it bought its cars directly from the manufacturers, rather than through authorised dealers. The manufacturers used third-party transport companies to deliver the cars to BT and a separate charge for this was specified in the contracts and shown separately on invoices. BT sought to recover the tax on these charges on the basis that they represented separate supplies to the cars themselves. Ultimately, the House of Lords decided against them and to the effect that the delivery was part and parcel of a single supply of the cars, regardless of whether it was itemised separately, finding that:

  - Whether the delivery was *ancillary* or *incidental* to the supply of the car or whether it was a distinct supply, the fact that one *package price* was charged without separate charge for individual supplies being specified did not prevent there being two separate supplies for VAT purposes. The fact that separate charges were identified in a contract or on an invoice did not, on a consideration of all the circumstances, necessarily prevent the various supplies from constituting one composite transaction. Nor did the fact that delivery could have been arranged differently under a separate contract between BT and the transporter, or by BT collecting the car itself, mean that there were two supplies.
  - The contracts with manufacturers varied, but the result was the same in the case of all the supplies. In all the contracts one *package price* was charged whether the separate delivery charge was identified or not, and property in the cars passed to BT either on delivery or when payment was made later. As a matter of commercial reality, there was one contract for a delivered car and it would be artificial to split the various parts of the transaction into different supplies for VAT purposes.

Another indication that the delivery charge should be regarded as part of the price of a delivered car was that it would put BT in the same position as companies buying a small number of cars from dealers at a price for a delivered car including delivery to the dealers' premises. Because BT bought such a large number of cars it was able to obtain them directly from the manufacturers. If it could recover VAT paid on delivery it would have a considerable advantage over other traders.

Other cases in the same vein include:

- *C & E Commrs v Plantiflor* [2002] BVC 572 (where the House of Lords reversed the decision of the Court of Appeal which had held that where a supplier of goods included a postal charge in the invoice, that charge did not form part of the consideration for the supply of arranging the delivery service, and was therefore not within the charge to VAT).
- *Telewest Communications plc v C & E Commrs* [2005] BVC 156 (where the taxpayer supplied a package consisting of television services and a listings magazine and it was held in the High Court that the taxpayer had failed to demonstrate that the magazine formed a separate supply).
- The value shifting case of *Courts Plc* [2005] BVC 2003, where, if a customer took out an insurance policy against fabric and structural defects for a premium of 19 per cent of the retail value of the goods, a corresponding discount was given against that price. At the same time, Courts received an insurance commission not far short of that amount. The Tribunal Chairman found in that case that the attribution of part of the price to the insurance premium and the consequential discount was not in good faith, was not commercial and was an *abuse of rights*.

An interesting case outside of the insurance and finance sectors is the Court of Appeal decision in *David Baxendale Ltd v R & C Commrs* [2009] EWCA Civ 831; [2009] BVC 663 which involved the court deciding that there was a single supply of weight loss counselling, and not a mixed supply of counselling and food packs. The Court of Appeal decided that there was a single supply. The question arose out of the sale to the public by the supplier of something called the 'LighterLife' weight loss programme. In essence, the material points were as follows:

- the weight loss programme involved the total replacement (in the initial months) of normal food with LighterLife food packs;
- the programme was accompanied by counselling and advice in weekly group sessions run by the supplier;
- the supplier argued that the programme consisted of the supply of zero-rated food packs, to which the counselling services supplied at the weekly meetings were ancillary. The company also argued that the only charge made was for the food packs themselves and that these therefore constituted the only taxable supply;
- HMRC argued that the supplier was making a supply of services in the form of the weight loss programme of which the provision of the food packs was but one element. HMRC considered that whilst the supplies were not ancillary to each other, the two elements constituted a single composite supply which was economically indivisible. Accordingly, as a supply of services, it was subject to VAT at the standard rate.

The Court of Appeal in giving judgment in favour of HMRC, made the following comments in relation to how separate identifiable supplies should be considered in the context of being treated as a single supply (at para. 21 to 224 of the judgment):

> 'Where the transaction under consideration prima facie involves more than one identifiable supply neither of which can be regarded merely as ancillary to the other the correct tax treatment will still depend on whether, from an objective view, they form a single indivisible economic supply which it would be artificial to split.
>
> The determination of this question will depend upon a global assessment of all facts relevant to the transaction under which the supply or supplies took place. That is the taxable event. This will

3 Outputs and Output VAT

obviously include a consideration of the terms upon which the supply or supplies were made; how they were invoiced for; and what the consumer in fact acquired under the contract ...

What also emerges from this analysis is that the court's inquiry as to whether a composite transaction is a single indivisible economic supply must be both fact and transaction specific. The fact that the same or similar goods or services could be provided separately from different sources is irrelevant ... to the question whether, in the particular transaction under consideration, their combination produced a different economic result.'

Applying these principles to the evidence, the Court of Appeal agreed that the only conclusion was that there was a single composite supply. In this regard, the court noted (at para. 43 of the judgment):

'... on the facts found by the Tribunal, the proper conclusion is that what the typical customer purchases is a single package of food packs and support services which he wishes to use in combination with each other and which, in the context of the transaction, are not economically divisible. ... They are, so to speak, to be taken together and are purchased on that basis. The evidence is that the typical consumer regards them as complementing each other and values them both. The product is promoted on the basis that the customer will be supported in his or her slimming endeavours through the counselling services provided and, as mentioned earlier, these are an essential aid in re-enforcing the diet. In these circumstances it would ... be artificial to split up what anyone wishing to use the programme would regard as a single economic supply.'

The determination of whether there is a single supply or multiple supplies must first be answered since if there is only a single standard rated supply then it is unnecessary to consider whether an activity is within the scope of an exemption.

- In *Everything Everywhere Ltd (formerly T-Mobile UK) v R & C Commrs* (C-276/09) [2011] BVC 44 the Court of Justice were asked to consider the VAT treatment of charges invoiced by Everything Everywhere to its customers when they chose certain methods by which to settle their monthly mobile telephone phone bills. Customers had a choice of payment methods, including direct debit, transfer via Bankers' Automated Clearing System (BACS), debit or credit card (via the telephone or internet), cheque, over the counter at a branch of Everything Everywhere's bank or of another bank. The payment of bills by direct debit or BACS were not subject to any additional charges. However a payment by one of the other payment methods gave rise to an additional charge of £3, which was described as a 'separate payment handling charge' (SPHC). Broadly, the SPHC was invoiced to a customer who, e.g., paid by debit or credit card, with the result that the sum payable would then be transferred to Everything Everywhere's account by the bank which issued the card. The taxpayer argued that the SPHC should be treated as consideration for a payment handling service effected for consideration, and that such a supply was exempt from VAT under Article 13B(d) of the Sixth Directive (now art. 135(1)(d) of Council Directice 2006/112/EC). The CoJ held that the payment handling services was not separate from the supply of mobile phone services, and accordingly the SPHC should receive the same VAT treatment as the sums payable for the mobile phone services, which were standard rated. The court considered that the payment options provided by the supplier were designed to enable customers to pay by the most convenient method for them, and that it was inherent in the supply of telecom services that the supplier should seek payment and 'make appropriate efforts to ensure that the customer can make effective payment in consideration for the service supplied' (see para 28 of the judgment). The court commented that when a supply is not independent of another supply it will take its VAT treatment from the primary supply, noting that (at para. 23 to 25 of the judgment):

> 'Moreover, in certain circumstances, several formally distinct services, which could be supplied separately and thus give rise, in turn, to taxation or exemption, must be considered to be a single transaction when they are not independent (see Case C-425/06 *Part Service* [2008] ECR I-897, paragraph 51; Case C-572/07 *RLRE Tellmer Property* [2009] ECR I-4983, paragraph 18; and *Don Bosco Onroerend Goed*, paragraph 36).
>
> That is so in particular in cases where one or more elements are to be regarded as constituting the principal service, whilst one or more elements are to be regarded, by contrast, as ancillary services which share the tax treatment of the principal service (see, inter alia, CPP, paragraph 30; Case C-34/99 *Primback* [2001] ECR I-3833, paragraph 45; *RLRE Tellmer Property*, paragraph 18; and order of 14 May 2008 in Joined Cases C-231/07 and C-232/07 *Tiercé Ladbroke and Derby*, paragraph 21).
>
> In particular, a service must be regarded as ancillary to a principal service if it does not constitute for customers an aim in itself, but a means of better enjoying the principal service supplied (see, inter alia, CPP, paragraph 30; *Primback*, paragraph 45; *RLRE Tellmer Property*, paragraph 18; and order in *Tiercé Ladbroke and Derby*, paragraph 21).'

The CoJ also emphasised that the principle of fiscal neutrality was not undermined by the point that the supplies of payment handling made by Everything Everywhere would be treated differently if made by a financial services provider, since the position of the suppliers would be completely different. In this regard, the court stated (at para. 31 of the judgment):

> 'That conclusion cannot be undermined by the principle of fiscal neutrality inherent in the common system of VAT, which precludes treating similar supplies of services, which are thus in competition with each other, differently for VAT purposes (see, inter alia, Case C-94/09 *Commission v France* [2010] ECR I-0000, paragraph 40, and Case C-58/09 *Leo-Libera* [2010] ECR I-0000, paragraph 34), since Everything Everywhere's situation is entirely different from that of an economic operator which provides financial services to its clients as the principle supply.'

Since the court determined that the charges invoiced for payment handling did not constitute consideration for a supply of services distinct and independent from the principal supply of telecommunication services, it was unnecessary to consider the scope of the VAT exemption for payment handling.

- Another recent decision of the CoJ on single and multiple supplies is *Purple Parking Ltd, Airparks Services Ltd v R & C Commrs* (Case C-117/11: 19 January 2012). In this case the taxpayers supplies were treated as as a single composite standard rated supply. The taxpayers provided 'off-airport' parking and 'off-airport park-and-ride' services. The car parks had various benefits such as secure fencing, being floodlit at night, CCTV surveillance, and they were patrolled by security staff 24 hours per day and 7 days per week. Customers would leave their cars in an arrivals area and then board a bus or minibus provided by the car park operator to be transported, with their luggage, to the airport terminal. Their vehicles were then parked by the employees of that operator. On their return, the customers used the means of transport provided by the car park operator between the airport terminal and the car park, where their vehicle was made available in a departure area. The transport service was designed to be available at all times and in a sufficiently frequent and reliable manner, the buses leaving either at regular intervals or on demand. The price charged to their customers was entirely by reference to the time, calculated per day, that the vehicles were parked. The transport was not charged separately. The taxpayers had paid VAT on the basis of the standard rate for all the services supplied to their customers (due to Note 4A(b) to Group 8 of Annex 8 to the Value Added Tax Act 1994, which excludes transport services such as those provided by the taxpayers from the zero-rating prescribed, in principle, for transport in any vehicle designed or adapted to carry not less than 10 passengers). The taxpayers claimed that the exclusion infringed the principle of fiscal neutrality and that, therefore, their supplies of transport services should have been regarded as zero-rated supplies. HMRC refused their claim on the basis that the taxpayers provided a single supply, of parking services taxable at the standard rate, in relation to which the transport service was only an ancillary, incidental or closely linked supply. In delivering judgment the CoJ stated on the nature of the composite supplies (at para. 31 of the judgment):

'... the fact that, in other circumstances, the elements in issue can be or are supplied separately is of no importance, given that that possibility is inherent in the concept of a single composite transaction ... it is apparent that the parking and transport services supplied, in the circumstances described by the Upper Tribunal (Tax and Chancery Chamber), by the appellants to their customers form, for the purposes of VAT, a complex single supply in which the parking element is predominant ... In that respect, it is appropriate, in particular, to take into consideration the pricing of the services in issue ... The appellants charge their customers a single price, which may be an indication, without being decisive, that there is a single supply ... Furthermore, and above all, the amount of the price to be paid is exclusively calculated on the basis of the period for which the vehicle is parked, whereas the number of passengers and, therefore, the extent of use of the transport are irrelevant ... That pricing concept reflects the interests of the parties concerned. The customer seeks, first and foremost, parking at an advantageous price. By contrast, the transport service is only the inevitable consequence of the fact that the car park is located at a certain distance from the airport, a location accepted by the customer given that that distance allows him to pay less for the parking service. Secondly, the car park operator offers the transport service in order to be capable, in spite of that distance, of competing with the parking within the airport.'

The CoJ considered that the VAT treatment of the services did not infringe the principle of fiscal neutrality, since the composite supply by its very nature was different in character from that which would be represented by the supplies being provided separately. The court commented (at para. 39 of the judgment):

'... the treatment of several services as a single supply for the purposes of VAT necessarily leads to tax treatment different from that that those services would have received if they had been supplied separately ... Accordingly, a complex supply of services consisting of several elements is not automatically similar to the supply of those elements separately.'

Practice point

A summary of the material principles relevant to whether there is a single supply or multiple supplies is helpfully provided by the Upper Tribunal in *R & C Commrs v Bryce (t/a The Barn)* [2010] UKUT 26 (TCC); [2011] BVC 1,589. The case provides a summary of the relevant principles which are derived from leading European and UK case law. The facts of the case involved the use of premises called 'The Barn' which was used to run a business for the purpose of holding children's parties. Separately, the taxpayer operated another business called 'Birch Farm' which related to the operation of a day-care nursery. The businesses were carried on at distinct premises, but within the same complex. Additionally, there was the provision of play equipment and refreshments supplied in the course of catering. The taxpayer argued that there was a single supply, which was a licence to occupy land, and as such was exempt within Sch. 9, Group 1, Item 1 of VATA 1994. The provision of other elements, namely the play equipment and catering were purely ancillary supplies. HMRC argued that the supplies constituted a single supply, which should be characterised as the supply of a children's party and thus not exempt but subject to VAT at the standard rate. The Upper Tribunal concluded that once all of the elements of the transaction are brought into account, then from the perspective of the customer, what was supplied was a group of facilities for a children's party, provided as a single supply (due to the fact that the customer would receive a combination of facilities that enabled them to hold a party, as advertised on the taxpayer's website). The relevant principles were summarised as follows (at para. 22 to 23 of the judgment):

'The relevant principles are summarised in *Baxendale* by Patten LJ in his judgment (with which the Master of the Rolls and Goldring LJ agreed) as follows (at [21]-[22]):

"Where the transaction under consideration prima facie involves more than one identifiable supply neither of which can be regarded merely as ancillary to the other the correct tax treatment will still depend on whether, from an objective view, they form a single indivisible economic supply which it would be artificial to split. The determination of this question will depend upon a global assessment of all facts relevant to the transaction under which the supply or supplies took place. That is the taxable event. This will obviously include a consideration of the terms upon which the supply or supplies were made; how they were invoiced for; and what the consumer in fact acquired under the contract."

... that summary can be amplified by the following propositions derived from those authorities and, indeed, from *Baxendale* itself:

(a) Every supply of a service must normally be regarded as distinct and independent. However, a transaction which forms a single supply from an economic point of view should not artificially be split into separate supplies: Case C-349/96 *Card Protection Plan Ltd v Customs and Excise Comrs* [1999] ECR I-973, para. 29.

(b) For this purpose, regard must be had to all the circumstances in which the transaction takes place: *Card Protection Plan*, para 28.

(c) There is a single supply where one or more elements are to be regarded as constituting the principal supply, whilst one or more elements are to be regarded by contrast as ancillary to that principal supply: *Card Protection Plan*, para 30.

(d) However, the fact that one element in a package supplied cannot be described as ancillary to another element does not mean that it is to be regarded as a separate supply for tax purposes. The question is whether those separate elements are to be treated as separate supplies or merely as elements in some over-arching single supply: *College of Estates Management v Customs & Excise Commrs* [2005] UKHL 62, [2005] 1 WLR 3351, per Lord Rodger of Earlsferry at [12].

(e) In that regard, the test is whether the various elements supplied to the customer are so closely linked that they form, objectively, a single indivisible economic supply, which it would be artificial to split: Case C- 41/04 *Levob Verzekeringen BV v Staatssecretaris van Financiën* [2005] ECR I-9433, para 22.

(f) It is important to take an overall view at the level of generality that corresponds with social and economic reality, without over-zealous dissection: *Dr Beynon* per Lord Hoffmann at [31]; *Card Protection Plan [2001] UKHL 4, [2002] 1 AC 202*, per Lord Slynn at [22].

(g) The assessment should be made from the perspective of the customer, as a typical consumer, not the supplier: *Levob*, para 22; *Weight Watchers* at [17].

(h) The fact that a single price is charged for two or more elements is a relevant factor pointing to single supply but it is not decisive: *Card Protection Plan* (in ECJ), para 31. Similarly, the fact that separate prices are stipulated for various elements is not decisive where the two elements have an objective close link such that they form part of a single economic transaction: *Levob*, para 25.

(i) The fact that the same or similar goods or services could be supplied separately from different sources is irrelevant to the question whether in the particular transaction under consideration their combination produces a different economic result: *Baxendale* at [24], following Case C-425/06 *Ministero dell'Economia e delle Finanze v Part Service Srl* [2008] ECR I- 897, [2008] STC 3132.

(j) The test is not whether the different elements in the services provided by the taxpayer to its customers have value and utility in their own right: *Baxendale* at [39].'

30-600   Invoicing

Invoices, or rather tax invoices, are a key feature of VAT and one of the more important records. They are the means for many businesses of recognising output VAT and, for purchases, provide the necessary evidence for input VAT relief. The detailed requirements are found in Pt. III of the *Value Added Tax Regulations* 1995 (SI 1995/2518). Tax invoices are mandatory for taxable supplies to other taxable persons and, following the Single Market changes, for any supply other than an exempt supply to persons from other Member States.

Historically, the Regulations have been intended for use only for positive-rated taxable supplies and, with the exception of supplies to persons in other Member States for the purposes of acquisitions, do not apply to zero-rated supplies as such. They also do not apply to exempt supplies, supplies for no consideration or to supplies made under, say, the second-hand goods scheme. However, following the commencement of formal infraction proceedings by the European Commission (on the grounds that the UK had not fully implemented the VAT Directive), certain changes have now been made by the *VAT (Amendment) (No 5) Regulations* 2007 (SI 2007/2085), to impose invoicing requirements for certain intra-EC exempt or reverse-charge supplies (see **Chapter 5**).

The rules on what is to be shown are fairly detailed. They must, for example:

- be sequentially numbered (based on one or more series which uniquely identifies the document);
- identify the supplier;
- give his VAT registration number;
- identify the customer;
- give the type of supply;
- state the value of the supply in sterling; and
- show the amount of VAT due.

The tax on the invoice must be shown in sterling. There are further requirements where a tax invoice is provided to a person in other Member States and for credit notes.

When an invoice involves Intra-EC an exempt or zero-rated supply – then there must be an indication that the supply is exempt or zero-rated, as appropriate. The suggestions by HMRC in VAT Information Sheet 10/07 as to what these references should be are:

- 'exempt supply';
- 'exempt supply for VAT purposes';
- 'this supply is exempt for VAT'.

There are corresponding requirement for reverse-charge supplies, for which the HMRC suggestions are:

- 'reverse charge supply';
- 'this supply is subject to the reverse charge';
- 'subject to reverse charge in the country of receipt';
- 'subject to reverse charge in another member state';
- 'this is a UK exempt supply which may be chargeable in the country of receipt';
- 'this is a UK exempt supply which may be chargeable in another member state'.

However, these requirements only arise when the supply is business-to-business, across an EU border and an invoice is required by the Member State of receipt. Because custom and practice varies widely even in Member States whose legislation ostensibly requires an invoice, HMRC suggest that the supplier should always be guided by the customer about the need for an invoice.

The VAT Information Sheet also refers to intra EC zero-rated supplies of goods (dispatches) and the need to include one of three references – a reference to the relevant article in the EC Directive, a reference to the relevant UK legislation, or any other indication that the supply is a zero rate intra EC supply. The suggestions offered as to what might be included are:

- 'zero rated intra-EC supply';
- 'this is an intra-Community supply';
- 'intra-Community supply subject to VAT in the country of acquisition'.

The EC VAT Invoicing Directive (2001/115/EC) came into force on 1st January 2004, amending what was art. 22 of the EC Sixth VAT Directive. It was implemented into UK law by FA 2002, s. 24. The aim was to simplify and harmonise the rules on invoicing across the EU and remove barriers to electronic transmission and storage of invoices.

3 Outputs and Output VAT

A second VAT invoicing Directive (Council Directive 2010/45/EU) was adopted on 13 July 2010, and it will take effect in Member States from 1 January 2013 (a copy of the Directive is provided at **Appendix 23**). For HMRC's notice on the changes see HMRC Technical Note 31 May 2012. The purpose of the second EU VAT Directive is to promote and further simplify invoicing rules by removing existing burdens and barriers, including by ensuring equal treatment between paper and electronic invoices. Additionally, its provisions are designed to promote the uptake of electronic invoicing by allowing freedom of choice regarding the invoicing method. One of the key aims is to ensure that invoices accurately reflect actual supplies of goods and services and therefore requires that the authenticity of the origin, the integrity of the content and the legibility of invoices are insured from their issue until the end of the period of storage. The principles underlying the Directive recognise that this can be achieved through business controls that provide a reliable audit trail between the invoice and the supply, and that assure the identity of the supplier or issuer of the invoice (authenticity of origin), that the VAT details (the invoice content required by the VAT Directive) on the invoice are unchanged (integrity of content) and that the invoice is legible (see recitals (8) to (11) of the Directive). In this regard, the key principles are (which are further expanded upon in the Explanatory Notes: available at www.europa.eu):

- the taxable person can fulfil his obligation to ensure the authenticity of the origin and integrity of the content, for example, by using technologies mentioned in Article 233(2) of the VAT Directive (as amended by 2010/45/EU): an advanced electronic signature or electronic data interchange (EDI),
- the choice of methods to enable a taxable person to fulfil its obligations is for that person to decide by using business controls which create a reliable audit trail between an invoice and a supply of goods or services (Art. 233 as amended by 2010/45/EU),
- for the purposes of the VAT Directive "electronic invoice" will mean an invoice that contains the information required in the Directive, and which has been issued and received in any electronic format (Art. 217 as amended by 2010/45/EU). The choice of format is determined by the taxable person, and this would include invoices as structured messages (such as XML) or other types of electronic format (such as an email with a PDF attachment or a fax received in electronic not paper format); invoices created in paper form, that are scanned, sent and received via e-mail can be considered as electronic invoices (see the Explanatory Notes),
- the use of an electronic invoice will be subject to acceptance by the recipient (Art. 232 as amended by 2010/45/EU),
- the authenticity of the origin, the integrity of the content and the legibility of an invoice is an obligation for the taxable person receiving the supply of goods or services as well as for the taxable person making the supply (Art. 233 as amended by 2010/45/EU),
- the issue of invoices is subject to further rules under Art. 219a (covering which Member State's rules are applicable), Art. 221(3) (applicable Member State's invoicing rules for exempt supplies), Art. 220(2) and 221(2) (invoicing rules for exempt financial supplies (within Art. 135(1)(a) to (g) of the VAT Directive), and Art. 224(1) (self-billed invoices). Broadly, the scope of these provisions are as set out below.

Which Member State's rules are applicable?

Art. 219a provides:

'Without prejudice to Articles 244 to 248 [obligations relating to the storage of all invoices], the following shall apply:

(1) Invoicing shall be subject to the rules applying in the Member State in which the supply of goods or services is deemed to be made, in accordance with the provisions of Title V [Place of Taxable Transactions under the VAT Directive].

(2) By way of derogation from point (1), invoicing shall be subject to the rules applying in the Member State in which the supplier has established his business or has a fixed establishment from which the supply is made or, in the absence of such place of establishment or fixed establishment, the Member State where the supplier has his permanent address or usually resides, where: (a) the supplier is not established in the Member State in which the supply of goods or services is deemed to be made, in accordance with the provisions of Title V, or his establishment in that Member State does not intervene in the supply within the meaning of Article 192a, and the person liable for the payment of the VAT is the person to whom the goods or services are supplied. However where the customer issues the invoice (self-billing), point (1) shall apply. (b) the supply of goods or services is deemed not to be made within the Community, in accordance with the provisions of Title V.'

Put another way (as expressed in the Explanatory Notes):

'The basic rule is that the Member State where the supply takes place sets the invoicing rules. However, there are two exceptions to the basic rule which are contained in art. 219a(2)(a) and (2)(b). These are for cross-border supplies subject to the reverse charge and for supplies taxable outside the EU. In these cases the invoicing rules of the Member State where the supplier is established or has a fixed establishment from which the supply is made or has his permanent address or usually resides shall apply. For suppliers not established in the EU making taxable supplies of goods or services in the EU, the exceptions do not apply and the basic invoicing rule always applies, that being the Member State where the supply takes place. '

Invoicing rules for exempt insurance and financial supplies (Article 135(1)(a) to (g) of the VAT Directive)

Article 220(2) provides:

'By way of derogation from paragraph 1, and without prejudice to Article 221(2), the issue of an invoice shall not be required in respect of supplies of services exempted under points (a) to (g) of Article 135(1).'

Article 221(2) provides:

'Member States may impose on taxable persons who have established their business in their territory or who have a fixed establishment in their territory from which the supply is made, an obligation to issue an invoice in accordance with the details required in Article 226 or 226b [content of invoices] in respect of supplies of services exempted under points (a) to (g) of Article 135(1) which those taxable persons have made in their territory or outside the Community.'

Put another way (as expressed in the Explanatory Notes):

'Member States may not require an invoice for supplies exempt under points (a) to (g) of Article 135(1) of the VAT Directive when the supplier – established in their territory or who has a fixed establishment in their territory from which the supply is made – makes such a supply taxable in another Member State. When the place of taxation and the establishment of the supplier making the supply are in the same Member Sate then for B2B and B2C supplies that Member State may require an invoice. '

Self-billed invoices

Article 224(1) provides:

> 'Invoices may be drawn up by the customer in respect of the supply to him, by a taxable person, of goods or services, where there is a prior agreement between the two parties and provided that a procedure exists for the acceptance of each invoice by the taxable person supplying the goods or services. Member States may require that such invoices be issued in the name and on behalf of the taxable person.'

Various provisions under Council Directive 2010/45/EU, amending the VAT Directive, relate to the contents of an invoice, in connection with: sequential numbering (Art. 226(2)), cash accounting (Art. 226(7a)), Exempt supplies (Art. 226(11)), Conversion of the VAT amount into the national currency (Art. 91 and 230), Simplified invoices (Art. 226b). In connection with Art. 226(11) and exempt supplies this requires the following details of the reference to the applicable provision of the VAT Directive, or to the corresponding national provision, or any other reference indicating that the supply of goods or services is exempt.

Various provisions under Council Directive 2010/45/EU, amending the VAT Directive, relate to the storage of invoices in connection with: Storage period (Art. 247), Translation and languages used on invoices (Art. 248a) and Medium of storage (Art. 247).

30-650   Bad debt relief

Although, the responsibility for accounting for VAT rests generally with the supplier of any goods or services, the burden of the tax is meant to fall on the customer or final consumer. The taxpayer (i.e. the business) is no more than an agent collecting tax on behalf of the government. If the recipient of the supply does not pay, however, the economic burden can easily revert to the supplier.

Recognising this, there is a system of VAT bad debt relief.. The rules do not rely on the insolvency of the customer as the basis for relief, but look simply at non-payment. They also allow relief to businesses who supply goods on hire purchase and other reservation of title agreements.

The rules, to be found in VATA 1994, s. 36 and Pt. XIX of the *Value Added Tax Regulations* 1995 (SI 1995/2518), allow the taxpayer to claim a refund of the VAT element of an outstanding debt where:

- the original taxable supply took place on or after 1 April 1989;
- was for a consideration in money, the VAT on which has been accounted for;
- the whole or part of the consideration has been written off in the accounts of the business; and
- a period of six months has passed since the supply was made.

Claims must be made within four years and six months of when the consideration for the supply was due or the date of supply, whichever is the later.

For the purpose of this relief, the normal taxpoint rules apply (see 30-300 earlier). Where part of a debt has been paid, relief will only be given by reference to the balance outstanding. In no case, however, will a refund be given where the consideration for a supply was above open market value.

Where a business is transferred as a going concern and the purchaser takes over the VAT registration of the seller (using the 'VAT 68 procedure') the purchaser will acquire the seller's entitlement to bad debt relief on supplies made and also the obligations to make any repayments of input tax on unpaid supplies received.

All payments, or part payments, of consideration for a supply must be taken into account in making an initial bad debt claim, including those made to a person to whom a debt may have been assigned. Once a claim has been made, any payments received by an assignee, will not oblige the original claimant to repay bad debt relief previously claimed.

Following announcements in the 2002 Budget *The VAT (Amendment) (No. 4) Regulations*, (SI 2002/3027) provide that businesses claiming bad debt relief will no longer need to write to the debtor advising that a claim for bad debt relief has been made. However, to balance this, from 1 January 2003, VATA 1994, s. 26A has the effect that any business that has made a claim for input tax on a supply, but has not paid the supplier of the goods or services within six months of the date of that supply (or the date on which payment is due, if later), must repay any such input tax claimed. This is to be achieved by making an adjustment to the input tax claimed on the VAT return for the accounting period in which the end of the six months falls.

Goods supplied by hire purchase or conditional sale

A change in policy was announced on 6 December 2001 in *Business Brief* 19/2001 and confirmed in *Business Brief* 23/2002 of 20 August 2002. This was directed at goods supplied by HP or conditional sale agreements. Suppliers can now allocate each payment received from defaulting customers to goods and to finance in the same ratio as the total cost of goods and the total cost of finance to the customer. Where goods are repossessed, and the disposal of the repossessed goods will be subject to VAT, suppliers no longer have to deduct the proceeds of the disposal from the outstanding debt of their customer, when claiming bad debt relief. Only the payments made by the customer have to be deducted.

Two cases will be of particular interest,

- In *Abbey National plc v C & E Commrs* [2005] BVC 348 Abbey National objected to this HMRC approach, which seemed to fly in the face of commercial reality. Unfortunately, neither the Tribunal nor the Court shared their view.

    Wagon Finance Ltd, one of Abbey National's subsidiaries, carried on business primarily in providing finance for the purchase of vehicles by private individuals. When customers defaulted, it had to allocate the instalments received between taxable goods and exempt credit. HMRC argued that, where there was a mixed supply of this kind, the allocation should be made in accordance with the rules prescribed in the VAT Regulations (reg. 170A of the *VAT Regulations* 1995 (SI 1995/2518)) on the basis of a straight-line apportionment with each instalment being allocated in the proportions of the total cost of the goods and the total credit. Against this, Abbey maintained this did not apply in the particular circumstances of Wagon and that, in any event, it was inconsistent with the Sixth Directive.

Essentially, Abbey said the allocation should be determined by reference to:

- the terms of the instalment credit finance agreements; and
- the accounting entries it was required to make under relevant accounting standards.

This should be carried out on an amortisation basis, where the constant rate of interest implicit in the agreement is applied to a reducing balance of principal so that the principal is reduced to zero at the end of the agreed term.

The Tribunal had dismissed the appeal on the basis that the terms of Wagon Finance's conditional sale agreements didn't provide, expressly or impliedly, for an allocation of consideration by the parties between the two supplies made pursuant to those agreements. Had they done so, the right to bad debt relief should follow from that allocation. However, in the absence of such provision, the law determined the method of apportionment. The method chosen by HMRC wasn't the only method, and might not be the method which most closely accorded with the taxpayer's accounting requirements. However, it wasn't contrary to Community law.

On appeal, the Court concluded that nothing in Community law required that the parties' own arrangements as to apportionment should oust domestic law – or had to be taken into account. As it was, the Court did not feel able to say that the time basis used in reg. 170(2), qualified as it was by the ability of the consumer to make a specific allocation, was irrational and any contractual arrangements between the parties as to apportionment, if there were any, couldn't stand in the way of an apportionment on the statutory basis.

- In *C & E Commrs v General Motors Acceptance Corporation (UK) plc* [2004] BVC 611, the taxpayer supplied cars on HP and the initial dispute was over whether, on premature termination, it was entitled to bad debt relief or to an adjustment of its original taxable amount.

The VAT payable on the supply of goods under the agreement was calculated by reference to the total sum payable over its term, net of credit charges and that supply of goods was seen as taking place when the hirer took possession (VATA 1994, s. 6(2)(a) and Sch. 4, para. 1(2)(b)). Tax thus became due at that point. In the event of early termination:

- it was common ground that, where the agreement was ended by the hirer pursuant to a contractual or statutory right, if the documents satisfied the requirements of reg. 24 of the *VAT Regulations* 1995 (SI 1995/2518), GMAC could adjust its VAT account by making a negative entry for the reduction in the consideration for the original supply;
- when terminated following a breach by the hirer, GMAC claimed clause 9 of its standard Conditions applied, with the same result.

HMRC disagreed with the latter argument and contended that the situation was one of non-payment, not one of a reduced price, with the result that the relief GMAC was entitled to was bad debt relief under VATA 1994 s. 36, not a price adjustment under reg. 38.

In the event, GMAC won on appeal to the High Court, where it was held that art. 11(C)(1) of the Sixth Directive (art. 90(1) of Council Directive 2006/112/EC) was applicable both to a price reduction occurring by operation of the terms of the original agreement under which the supply was made and to a price reduction resulting from a subsequent variation of those agreements. The effect of clause 9 was that the consideration for the supply of goods was reduced by agreement from the cash price to the cash price less any outstanding instalments and the resale proceeds. Bad debt relief was not, therefore, in point.

GMAC also, incidentally, raised a further argument over the treatment of the cars it took back. Whether the termination was the result of a breach by the hirer or not, it maintained the resale of the car was covered by art. 4(1)(a) of the *Value Added Tax (Cars) Order* 1992 (SI 1992/3122). As such, it was not a VATable supply. GMAC was thus not liable for tax on that resale. HMRC, didn't accept this as, in its view, art. 4(1)(a) only applied where the termination was brought about by the hirer's default. Again the Court decided for GMAC. Article 4(1)(a) plainly applied, but, even if it were ambiguous, it could still apply where there had been a consensual termination since its purpose was to preclude a second charge to VAT on the resale of a used car which had already borne VAT when first bought.

Receiverships

As will be seen later in **Chapter 4**, there can be difficulties sometimes in the financial sector, where, for example, a borrower may be asked to pay the legal and other costs of the lender. The costs involved may be seen as representing supplies to, i.e. inputs of, the lender, who may not be entitled to claim input tax relief as the VAT will normally then be attributable to an exempt supply (see **Chapter 4** at 40-150). Fortunately, there is an HMRC easement which can be used in some insolvency situations to help with this.

When it applies, this allows lenders to be seen as agents of the borrower. A lender may, for example, incur VAT on the costs of selling property which has been repossessed. On the face of it, the VAT will fall to be disallowed in the lender's hands. However, if the costs involved can be seen as representing supplies to the borrower, not the lender, it opens up the possibility of steps being taken to obtain relief in the hands of the borrower (if a VAT-registered business) by recharging the costs (and a reduction in costs overall). The easement, which addresses problems with the right of set-off in insolvency law, helps with VAT bad debt relief for the lender and was first publicised in Business Brief 24/94. It is now found in HMRC Guidance Manuals at VATSC95500 to VATSC95900. What this says is:

'**Recovery of VAT on costs incurred by mortgage lenders in respect of a sale of property under a power of sale**

20.1.1 Background

Business Brief 20/93 indicated that Customs (now HMRC) were prepared to see lenders as agents of the borrower in arranging the sale of repossessed property, and hence allow them to claim bad debt relief (BDR), where appropriate, on the VAT incurred on selling costs. However, Customs subsequently became aware that the order of attribution of the proceeds of sale under s. 105 of the Law of Property Act 1925 might override the Bad Debt Relief Regulations. This is because under s105 the proceeds of sale are allocated first to costs such as those incurred in selling the property, which threw some considerable doubt over whether a bad debt was created on which relief could be claimed.

Doubts arose also about the status of lenders as agents and there was concern that some claims had included costs which went beyond the terms of the Business Brief. Customs therefore issued a further Business Brief 5/94 suspending the processing of claims, until such time as they could take legal advice and examine more fully the issues involved.

20.1.2 VATSC95600 Current position

Having taken Counsel's advice, Customs are of the view that there is a good argument that in arranging the sale of repossessed property, mortgagees act under rights conferred by the mortgage agreement, and not as agents of the borrower. However, Customs believe they can rely on the wider interpretation of "agent" contained in the Sixth VAT Directive in maintaining their current view on agency, as laid out in Business Brief 20/93. They face more difficulty with s. 105 LPA, as it may override the order of attribution in the BDR Regulations, but again the matter is not free from doubt.

In the circumstances, Customs believe that the finely balanced nature of the legal advice allows some freedom of choice and they re-introduced a form of easement.

20.1.3 VATSC95700 New arrangements

(a) General

The easement is strictly for the purposes of allowing a measure of relief for VAT on bad debts and depends crucially on Customs taking a relaxed view of the supply position. Lenders must not extend this treatment more widely in accounting for VAT within their businesses.

The arrangements apply to BDR claims relating to supplies made on or after 1 July 1994. The overall aim is to provide relief to lenders where they suffer sticking tax on the costs of selling property in circumstances where borrowers have defaulted – in effect where the net proceeds of sale are reduced because the VAT element of the costs has not been recovered.

In principle, the easement covers costs incurred by lenders in arranging the sale of repossessed property and also to selling costs incurred when property is sold through an LPA receiver. It is emphasised that, with the single exception of build-out costs, the arrangements apply only to sale costs, and not to any incurred in relation to letting.

Although the Law of Property Act does not apply in Scotland, there are analogous provisions in Section 27 of the Conveyancing and Feudal Reform (Scotland) Act 1970. The arrangements therefore apply equally in Scotland.

(b) Basic principle

Under the arrangements, lenders can be seen as agents of the borrower in relation to the costs of sale whether or not the mortgage deed specifies such a relationship. As an agent, the lender may treat the selling costs incurred as supplies made to them and by them under s47(3) of the VAT Act 1994. The order of attribution of the sale proceeds in the BDR regulations can then be applied and bad debt relief claimed as appropriate in accordance with normal rules.

These arrangements apply only to costs relating directly to the sale of property, which would ordinarily have been incurred by the borrower had he arranged the sale himself. Examples of such costs include charges for professional services connected with the sale eg legal and estate agency fees. The easement does not include costs incurred on services provided to, and used by, the lender as principal, even though they may be charged on to the borrower under the mortgage deed. Examples of such costs include legal fees associated with taking possession, and locksmith's fees for securing the property. Costs incurred in pursuing claims against a valuer for negligence are also excluded.

(c) Other expenses

The position of certain other expenses incurred by lenders was discussed at meetings with trade representatives. Treatment of these under the arrangements is as follows:

(i) LPA Receivers' charges

LPA receivers' charges which relate specifically to the sale (not letting) of the property and any costs incurred by them in respect of the sale can be regarded as falling within the scope of the arrangements, but only where the proceeds of sale received by lenders have been reduced by the VAT element of the charges. Where this happens, lenders may be regarded as acting as agents for the borrower in paying the costs.

This means that Customs are not prepared to apply this arrangement where the LPA receiver recovers the VAT incurred on behalf of a VAT registered borrower and this is reflected in the proceeds passed to the lender. This may occur, for example, where the LPA receiver has control of the borrower's VAT returns.

(ii) Build-out costs (expenses incurred on completion of a partly-built building or major refurbishment of the property, before sale)

Customs legal advice is that lenders incur such costs as principals and do not make any onward supplies to the borrower even though the costs are charged on under the terms of the mortgage deed. It was argued at the meetings with trade representatives that strict application of this line would create a hidden VAT charge in respect of buildings whose sale is zero-rated. Customs are sympathetic to this view and are therefore prepared, very exceptionally, to treat the onward charge of the build-out costs as a supply by the lender as principal to the borrower, where the sale of the building by the borrower is the subject of a taxable supply or the transfer of a going concern for VAT purposes. In the case of build-out costs only, Customs are also prepared to see a supply where the property is the subject of a taxable let and output tax on the rents has been accounted for to Customs.

Customs are not prepared to see an onward supply (creating an entitlement to bad debt relief) when the sale of the building is exempt, where the VAT incurred on building costs would be sticking tax. Customs believe it would be quite wrong to allow recovery of tax by lenders in these circumstances. As at (i) above, the arrangements will also not apply if the proceeds of sale or rent received by lenders reflect any input tax on build-out costs recovered by the borrower.

(iii) Other building works (repairs and maintenance)

Lenders can be seen as agents of the borrower in incurring these expenses and may use the s.47(3) VATA 1994 invoicing procedure to qualify for bad debt relief.

(iv) If lenders use their own in-house estate agencies or solicitors to deal with the sale, they may, exceptionally, be regarded as making a supply of those services as principal to the borrower under the new arrangements. However lenders may adopt this treatment in order to claim bad debt relief only where output tax has been accounted for on the supply to the borrower in accordance with normal rules.'

For the position generally on an insolvency see HMRC's Notice 700/56 (October 2012).

3 Outputs and Output VAT

> **Summary**
>
> This Chapter has aimed to outline the basic rules on supplies or outputs for VAT purposes. VAT is a tax on supplies and, although many of the industries covered by this book are VAT-exempt, there will be many situations where this does not apply. Being aware of what these are is, important both in terms of ensuring that tax is properly accounted for and of maximising the opportunities for recovering input tax.
>
> Later Chapters will deal with the more specialist areas of VAT liability.

4 Input VAT and Partial Exemption

> **Overview**
>
> This Chapter considers:
>
> (1) The meaning of inputs and input VAT:
>
>   (a) the importance of the recipient;
>   (b) the significance of business;
>   (c) avoidance and abuse of rights.
>
> (2) Exclusions: blocked input VAT.
>
> (3) Self-supplies.
>
> (4) The right to recover:
>
>   (a) the general idea;
>   (b) tax paid abroad.
>
> (5) Partial exemption:
>
>   (a) direct attribution;
>   (b) residual input tax;
>   (c) the Standard Method, including the Standard Method Override;
>   (d) Special Methods;
>   (e) non-UK supplies, warehoused goods and other specified supplies;
>   (f) capital goods.
>
> (6) Special situations:
>
>   (a) new registrations and pre-incorporation/pre-registration VAT;
>   (b) adjustments after the event;
>   (c) holding companies.
>
> (7) Accounting generally and records.

40-000 The meaning of inputs and input VAT

The basic concept of VAT is that it should be a tax on *value added*. Tax is charged by each supplier in the chain and on the full value of the supplies made. To ensure VAT is borne only by the ultimate consumer and, to avoid a cascade effect, relief is given for any tax paid at the intermediate stages. But this is only to the extent it is incurred in the making of *taxable* and certain other *specified* supplies (art. 167 onwards of Council Directive 2006/112/EC ('the VAT Directive') (previously art. 17 of the Sixth Directive (Directive 77/388)), something important in the context of finance and insurance. This relief, for what is known as input VAT, is usually by way of deduction or repayment through VAT returns. The right to deduction arises at the time the deductible input VAT becomes chargeable (art. 167 of the VAT Directive).

Input VAT, in broad terms, represents tax paid on business costs. Article 168 of the VAT Directive opens with the provision that:

> 'In so far as the goods and services are used for the purposes of the taxed transactions of a taxable person, the taxable person shall be entitled, in the Member State in which he carries out these transactions, to deduct the following from the VAT which he is liable to pay:
>
> (a) the VAT due or paid in that Member State in respect of supplies to him of goods or services, carried out or to be carried out by another taxable person.'

and goes on to extend that right to deduct to tax relating to intra-Community acquisitions of goods and imports.

Article 169 then confers that same right of deduction in respect of tax incurred in making supplies outside the taxpayer's Member State, where the VAT would otherwise be deductible (if they had been carried out within that Member State), for transactions not subject to VAT because, say, they relate to exports or international transport, and for underlying transactions which are basically VAT-exempt but supplied to persons outside the Community or relating to exports. The European Court of Justice (CoJ) has emphasised that the deduction mechanism for input VAT is 'intended to relieve the trader entirely of the burden of the VAT payable or paid in the course of all his economic activities' (see *R & C Commrs v RBS Deutschland Holdings GmbH* (Case C-277/09) [2011] BVC 138 at para. 38 of the judgment). The right to deduct input VAT is a fundamental principle underlying the common system of VAT which applies throughout the EU, and in principle may not be limited with the consequence that any taxable person is entitled to deduct VAT imposed on goods and services acquired for taxable activities (see generally *Abbey National v C & E Commrs* (Case C-408/98) [2001] ECR I-1361; [2001] BVC 581 , paragraph 24; *Investrand BV v Staatsecretaris van Financien* (Case C-435/05) [2007] ECR I-1315; [2009] BVC 733 , paragraph 22; and *NCC Construction Danmark A/S v Skatteministeriet* (Case C-174/08) [2009] ECR I-10567; [2010] BVC 1,093 , paragraph 27, *Gabalfrisa & Ors v Agencia Estatel de Administracion Tributaria (AEAT)* (Joined Cases C-110/98 to C-147/98) [2000] ECR I-1577; [2002] BVC 333 , paragraph 43, and Case C-74/08 *PARAT Automotive Cabrio* [2009] ECR I-3459, paragraph 15). The right to deduct input VAT is not dependent on the output transaction giving rise to the actual payment of output VAT (see *R & C Commrs v RBS Deutschland Holdings GmbH* (Case C-277/09) [2011] BVC 138 at para. 41 of the judgment).

More specifically in the UK, input VAT is defined by VATA 1994, s. 24(1) to mean (emphasis added) in relation to a given taxable person:

> (a) VAT on the supply *to him* of any goods or services;
> (b) VAT on the acquisition *by him* from another member State of any goods; and
> (c) VAT paid or payable *by him* on the importation of any goods from a place outside the member states,
> being (in each case) goods or services used or to be used *for the purpose of any business carried on or to be carried on by him.*'

Put another way, the input VAT must be incurred on an actual supply (or acquisition or import, each taking place in the UK):

- made to the recipient; and
- for the purpose of his business.

See also the general principles listed by HMRC in the VAT Input Tax Guidance Manual at VIT20500 on the meaning of input tax.

The distinctions referred to above are especially relevant in the context of certain situations common to the sectors covered by this book (which are considered in paragraphs (1) to (4) below). This is because input VAT does not become an automatic deduction merely because it has been incurred by a VAT registered person.

In some circumstances input VAT can be deducted where a person makes an exempt supply of finance within Group 5, Sch. 9 of VATA 1994 to a person outside the EU. The right to deduct input VAT in these circumstances in the UK is provided by the *Value Added Tax (Input Tax) (Specified Supplies) Order* 1999 (SI 1999/3121) (see 40-200(3)(b)). However, in other circumstances, recovery of input tax will be blocked if the supply received is subject to a specific input tax restriction by order of the Treasury (see 40-050).

Value added tax on private costs or incurred in relation to non-business activities is not input VAT; it cannot be relieved. Similarly, VAT on items supplied to someone else will not be input VAT for a person who is merely paying a cost under, say, an indemnity arrangement. Where real estate forms part of the business assets of a taxable person, and it is used for both the purposes of the business and private use then VAT on expenditure relating to the property is only deductible up to the proportion of the property's use for the purposes of the taxable person's business (Art. 168a of the VAT Directive).

The evidence required for deduction of input VAT is governed under UK domestic law by the *Value Added Tax Regulations 1995*, reg 29(2), which provides:

"At the time of claiming deduction of input tax ... a person shall, if the claim is in respect of-

(a) a supply from another taxable person, hold the document which is required to be provided under regulation 13 [obligation to provide a VAT invoice];

(b) a supply under section 8(1) of the Act, hold the relative invoice from the supplier [reverse charge on supplies received from abroad];

(c) an importation of goods, hold a document authenticated or issued by the proper officer, showing the claimant as importer, consignee or owner and showing the amount of VAT charged on the goods;

(d) goods which have been removed from warehouse, hold a document authenticated or issued by the proper officer showing the claimant's particulars and the amount of VAT charged on the goods;

(e) an acquisition by him from another member State of any goods other than a new means of transport, hold a document required by the authority in that other member State to be issued showing his registration number including the prefix "GB", the registration number of the supplier including the alphabetical code of the member State in which the supplier is registered, the consideration for the supply exclusive of VAT, the date of issue of the document and description sufficient to identify the goods supplied; or

(f) an acquisition by him from another member State of a new means of transport, hold a document required by the authority in that other member State to be issued showing his registration number including the prefix "GB", the registration number of the supplier including the alphabetical code of the member State in which the supplier is registered, the consideration for the supply exclusive of VAT, the date of issue of the document and description sufficient to identify the acquisition as a new means of transport as specified in section 95 of the Act [namely any of the following: ship exceeding 7.5 metres in length, aircraft the take-off weight of which exceeds 1550 kilograms and certain motorised land vehicles, each of which is intended for the transport of persons or goods];

provided that where the Commissioners so direct, either generally or in relation to particular cases or classes of cases, a claimant shall hold or provide such other evidence of the charge to VAT as the Commissioners may direct.'

(1) The importance of the recipient of the supply

The first of the two preconditions for input VAT relief is that the relevant supply has been *to the claimant* and to nobody else. As it happens, this is not always straightforward. What is certain is that it does not depend on who has been invoiced for a supply, who has paid for it or, for that matter, necessarily who has ordered or commissioned it.

The following paragraphs discuss the issues which arise in the context of indemnity situations, and the requirement for there to be a direct link between input VAT costs and supplies to create a right to an input tax deduction. However, the general approach to identifying the recipient of a supply of services for the purposes of input tax deduction were stated by Lord Millet in *C & E Commrs v Redrow Group plc* [1999] BVC 96 as set out below (but in applying this approach it is necessary to bear in mind the economic realities in identifying the person to whom goods and services are supplied: *R & C Commrs v Loyalty Management (UK) Ltd and Baxi Group Ltd* (Cases C-53/09 and C-56/09) [2011] BVC 1: see **Chapter 1**):

> "The first is that anything done for a consideration which is not a supply of goods constitutes a supply of services. This makes it unnecessary to define the services in question. The second is that unless the services are rendered for a consideration they cannot constitute the subject matter of a supply. In fact, of course, there can be no question of deducting input tax unless the taxpayer has incurred a liability to pay it as part of the consideration payable by him for a supply of goods or services.
>
> In my opinion, these two factors compel the conclusion that one should start with the taxpayer's claim to deduct tax. He must identify the payment of which the tax to be deducted formed part; if the goods or services are to be paid for by someone else he has no claim to deduction. Once the taxpayer has identified the payment the question to be asked is: did he obtain anything – anything at all – used or to be used for the purposes of his business in return for that payment? This will normally consist of the supply of goods or services to the taxpayer. But it may equally well consist of the right to have goods delivered or services rendered to a third party. The grant of such a right is itself a supply of services.'

In *WHA Ltd v C & E Commrs* [2004] BVC 485 (CA), Neuberger LJ (after considering Redrow in detail) commented at [53]:

"Although it is plainly dangerous to generalise, it seems to me that to justify a claim for input tax in principle, it would normally be sufficient for the person presented with the relevant invoice to establish that he had authorised and paid for the work the subject of the invoice, and that he received a genuine benefit in the course of his business from the carrying out of the work.'

(a) Indemnity situations

In the financial sector, for example, it is not uncommon for a borrower to be asked to pay the legal and other costs of the lender in securing a charge on mortgaged property. As such, these costs will involve supplies to, i.e. inputs of, the lender. Any VAT recovery, if available, would accordingly be a matter solely for him and not the borrower. The cost to the borrower will thus tend to be the gross amount as, on this analysis, the VAT will normally then be an expense of the lender (as attributable to an exempt supply (see ¶40-150)).

This treatment of input VAT on cost indemnity payments, i.e. the payment of another party's costs, was confirmed in a note from the Law Society and reproduced in the *Law Society's Gazette* of 24 October 1990. Another statement agreed between the Law Society and Customs was issued on 11 July 1990 covering fees payable for the registration of Notices of Assignment of leases. The general tenor of the Law Society notes was that:

> 'For registration fees, the obligation contained in a lease for the lessee to pay a fee in respect of a Notice of Assignment is a contract of indemnity between the lessee and the lessor; it is not a contract for the supply of goods or services. Thus, if the fee for the registration of an assignment is payable to the lessor direct, it does not appear that any service has been rendered. The fee will not be liable to VAT. However, where the registration is undertaken by services done on the lessor's behalf (for example by the lessor's solicitor), a service is being supplied – by the solicitor to his client, the lessor. [The recovery of the VAT as such will only be a matter for the lessor, the payment by the lessee being treated as for any other indemnity payment.]'

A further article was published in the *Law Society's Gazette* on 28 October 1992 which supersedes the earlier articles and HMRC refer to this in their Guidance Manuals at VATSC92100. This guidance comments that a payment of another party's costs will only be regarded as made on an indemnity basis and therefore outside the scope of VAT in certain circumstances (e.g. upon an order following completion of litigation/arbitration, or where the other party's costs have become abortive), and notes that there are other circumstances (particularly for lease transactions) where the payment of another party's costs can constitute part of the consideration for the supply by that other party for VAT purposes, such that VAT may be chargeable. The guidance also incorporates a change of HMRC practice regarding the VAT treatment of a tenant's payment of a landlord's costs incurred in respect of the tenant's exercise of an existing right under a lease or licence.

- In *Heritage Venture Enterprises Ltd* [1994] BVC 1,357 it was held that the borrower was not entitled to claim input tax on a surveyor's fee charged to the lender as instructing party, even though the cost was eventually passed on.
- In *Telent Plc v R & C Commrs* [2007] BVC 2,262, the appellant, the representative member of the former Marconi group, tried to get round this disallowance by raising an argument based on the *Redrow* decision (see later under *Direct Link*). The company had been involved in a major corporate restructuring and sought to argue that it was a joint recipient of the services of the lawyers acting for the banks. However, this was not

contractually the position and there was no other legal basis on which the claim could be allowed.

The implications of this have also arisen in the context of viability studies undertaken when a bank or other financial institution needs to investigate clients to assess the long-term prospects of a borrower. They are usually prepared by a third-party if either a borrower requires a new loan or extension to an existing loan, or if the borrower has gone into receivership and the bank needs to know if it can be saved. The borrower often has to pay the cost of the report which can cause difficulty in determining the direction of supply. HMRC's view, as initially recorded in *Business Brief* 6/95, is that the supply can only be seen as made to the person who contracted the study (as confirmed in *Eagle Trust plc* [1996] BVC 2,085). This view is reproduced in HMRC Guidance Manuals, VATSC93200 - Direction of supplies: Viability studies.

HMRC's Guidance Manual discusses the various situations that may apply in practice and, amongst other things, the circumstances when a supply can be seen to be made to both of the parties involved. In particular, it states:

> 'Where the company commissions the study but does not receive any report, the accountant's supply is made to the company, but it is not used for the purpose of its business. Therefore, neither the bank nor the company can recover input tax.'

Whether this is necessarily correct, however, seems debateable.

On the other hand, there can be a different result in some insolvency situations due to an HMRC relaxation that allows lenders to be seen as agents of the borrower. A lender may, for example, incur VAT on the costs of selling a property which has been repossessed under a power of sale. On the face of it, the VAT will again fall to be disallowed in the lender's hands, as attributable to an exempt supply. However, if, subject to the decision in the *Redrow* case (see later under *Direct Link*) the costs involved can be seen as representing supplies to the borrower, not the lender, this can have a number of benefits:

- first, it opens up the possibility of steps being taken to obtain relief in the hands of the borrower (if a VAT-registered business) by the lender recharging the costs (and a reduction in costs overall); and
- second, and this is where the relaxation or easement comes in, it helps with VAT bad debt relief for the lender, (see **Chapter 3** at ¶30-650).

In their *Business Brief* 20/93 of 30 June 1993, HMRC initially suggested the selling costs might be seen as incurred by the lender as agent of the borrower and effectively on-charged by him as a taxable supply. This allowed the VAT to be recovered by the lender using direct attribution. To the extent the output VAT accounted for by him remained unpaid, this could then be eventually recouped, if necessary, by means of a VAT bad debt relief claim. This practice assumed that the rules on set off under insolvency law allowed sale costs to be recouped last out of the sale proceeds received. However, doubts arose about the status of lenders as agents and the practice in relation to bad debts did not appear to be supported by the *Law of Property Act* 1925, s. 105 on the order of attribution of sale proceeds. The present position is now recorded in HMRC Guidance Manuals at VATSC95500 to VATSC95900, which, in summary, states that lenders can still be seen as agents and qualify for bad debt relief in respect of certain selling and other costs covered by HMRC's easement in circumstances where borrowers have defaulted and where, in effect, the net proceeds of sale recovered by the lender have been reduced by the VAT element of those costs.

(b) Direct link

As noted earlier, art. 168 of the VAT Directive provides that:

> 'In so far as the goods and services are used for the purposes of the taxed transactions of a taxable person, the taxable person shall be entitled, in the Member State in which he carries out these transactions, to deduct the following from the VAT which he is liable to pay:
>
> (a) the VAT due or paid in that Member State in respect of supplies to him of goods or services, carried out or to be carried out by another taxable person;'

This establishes, therefore, the need for a clear and *direct link* between the costs on which VAT is borne and the taxable transactions/supplies for which the expense is incurred. The cost must be an expense of the business, but it is not simply a matter of paying for something, or even contracting for the purchased supply. What is often more important is establishing who it is that the purchased supply is made to.

- *C & E Commrs v Redrow Group plc* [1999] BVC 96 referred to in previous paragraphs provided an interesting and potentially important clarification on this issue. Ending-up before the House of Lords, it was an appeal over whether Redrow, the representative member of a group of house-building companies, could recover input tax in respect of certain fees paid to estate agents. Most of its prospective buyers could not proceed until they had sold their existing homes. To overcome this, Redrow operated an incentive scheme whereby the company would instruct an agent of its choice to value and sell the properties. The agents' fees were then paid by Redrow, but only if the prospective buyer of one of its houses completed the purchase. If he or she did not, the liability to pay the fees was that of the prospective buyers. At issue was whether the supply by the estate agents whose fees were paid by Redrow were actually made to the prospective buyers or to Redrow.

HMRC had argued:

- the VAT on those fees was not Redrow's input tax;
- it was not enough to entitle Redrow to deduct input tax to say that it had to pay for the agent's services, nor that it benefited from them;
- it was the prospective buyers who were consumers of the services, and, as final consumers, they had to bear the burden of the tax;
- the *direct and immediate link* (see later at 40-200) with the services was between the estate agents and the prospective purchasers.

The Court of Appeal had largely gone along with this.

However, when the matter came before the House of Lords, the position was reversed. The estate agents were doing what Redrow instructed them to do for a fee. It was not necessarily helpful to ask who benefited from the service. The answer would differ according to the interest, which various people might have in the transaction. The matter was to be looked at from the standpoint of the person claiming the input tax. The fact that the prospective purchaser also received a service as part of the same transaction did not deprive the person who instructed the service, and who had to pay for it, of the benefit of the deduction and did not preclude a finding that there had been a concurrent supply to the payor.

The Court also held that, once the taxpayer had identified the payment, it had to be asked whether he obtained anything for it to be used for the purposes of the business. Normally, a supply of goods or services would have been obtained. But a right to have goods delivered or services rendered to a third party might equally have been obtained. Such a right would itself be a supply of services, which Redrow obtained and paid for. That was a separate service from that rendered to the prospective purchaser who did not pay for it. It was sufficient that Redrow obtained something for value in return for the payment of the agents' fees in those cases where it became liable to pay them, and that what it obtained was obtained for the purposes of its business. Lord Millet considered that the supply to a person may consist of the right to have goods delivered or services rendered to a third party, and that in particular, the grant of such a right is itself a supply of services ([1999] 1 WLR 408 at 418). In *Redrow* the estate agents were supplying normal agency services to person 'X'. However, they were also making a supply to Redrow of something of value to Redrow that was to be used in its own business. The right was a contractual right to have the householders' homes valued and marketed, to monitor the agent's performance and maintain pressure for a quick sale, and to override any alteration in the agents' instructions which the householders might be minded to give.

In *Business Brief* 27/99 in December 1999, HMRC expressed the view that the decision only applied where the circumstances are similar to the *Redrow* case. That is, where there is a claim to input tax credit by a taxable person who has commissioned (and paid for) the goods or services and contracted with the supplier for them that albeit, on the face of it, have been supplied to someone else. The claim would then be allowed to the extent that the goods or services provided by the supplier on which input tax is incurred are used by the taxable person in making taxable supplies for their business purposes.

Specifically, they did not consider that the *Redrow* decision supports a broad principle of 'anyone that pays for a supply is its recipient and can deduct the tax on it' or, alternatively, that 'anyone who pays must always be receiving a supply of something in return for the payment'. For example, it had no relevance to circumstances where a third party is simply meeting the costs of another or that a taxable person must have paid for a supply in order to be entitled to recover the input tax.

- In *C& E Commrs v Plantiflor Ltd* [2002] UKUL 33, the House of Lords applied *Redrow* and held that when Parcelforce made deliveries of goods on behalf of Plantiflor to its customers, it made two supplies; one to Plantiflor's customers of the deliveries (for no payment so not VATable) and the other to Plantiflor in securing that the goods were properly delivered (a VATable supply), both of which were supplied pursuant to a contract for delivery between Plantiflor and Parcelforce.
- *R & C Commrs v Airtours Holidays Transport Ltd* ([2010] UKUT 404 (TCC)); [2010] BVC 1,587 is a more recent example of the approach to be taken in the application of the decision in *Redrow*. The dispute related to input VAT on the fees of PriceWaterhouseCoopers

(PwC) which had been paid by Airtours under a tripartite agreement ('the Agreement') between Airtours, PwC and several financial institutions relating to Airtours' financial position in 2002. The financial institutions were described in the Agreement as the 'Engaging Institutions'. Airtours was in financial difficulties, owing some £2bn and it was seeking to renew lending facilities with these banks. PwC was approached by the financial institutions to provide advisory work which was necessary in order to provide an insight into Airtours' business. The Agreement between the parties identified the services to be provided by PwC, and it stipulated that the fees for those services were to be paid by Airtours. The taxpayer paid the fees and sought to recover the input VAT. HMRC opposed the deduction, and the First-tier Tribunal allowed Airtours appeal on the basis that on a proper construction of the Agreement, Airtours had wanted PwC's services for the purposes of its own business (i.e. to obtain a refinancing), and it was immaterial that the services were supplied to the financial institutions. In other words, the First-tier Tribunal considered that the advisory services were provided to Airtours, rather than in a Redrow style service of Airtours having the right to have PwC's services supplied to the financial institutions. However, the Upper Tribunal allowed HMRC's appeal.

HMRC had argued:

- the Agreement required PwC to provide services to the financial institutions for their own business purposes and not to Airtours;
- in *Redrow* there were two supplies, namely, (a) the right supplied to Redrow, and (b) the estate agents' service supplied to the prospective purchaser; and
- in the present case, there was no supply of the same service to both Airtours and the financial institutions.

Airtours had argued:

- that as a matter of contract law, references in the Agreement to 'You' included Airtours, who had also approved the scope of the work and authorised the work;
- receipt of a copy of PwC's report was a benefit to Airtours;
- the benefits to Airtours of having the PwC report were that it required it to place before the financial institutions, and it received a third party review of its strategic business plans;
- the First-tier tribunal had decided that Airtours was the recipient of PwC's services, and it did not matter that the financial institutions were also the recipients of it; and
- Airtours in any event obtained the continuation of the revolving credit facility.

The Upper Tier Tribunal concluded that Airtours could not claim the input VAT deduction. The tribunal decision was based on the following material points (it should be noted that this decision was reached (as agreed by the parties) without taking into account the CoJ's decision in *Loyalty Management UK Limited* (CoJ, C-53/09) which may have altered or limited the scope of *Redrow*, focussing on the 'economic reality' of 'to whom' a supply has been made, rather than on a contractual and payment analysis/review. For further detail on Loyalty Management, see the discussion at 10-100. It is also understood at the time of print that *Airtours* is on appeal to the Court of Appeal but it is not clear when the appeal will be heard):

(1) For Airtours to qualify for the input VAT deduction the crucial factor was whether, as in Redrow, Airtours received something from PwC in exchange for the payment of their

4 Input VAT and Partial Exemption

fees. However, it was not sufficient that Airtours received an indirect benefit, namely the commercial benefit of the hope that PwC's advice would result in the financial institutions continuing to provide finance to Airtours (para. 19 of the judgment). The Upper Tribunal emphasised that the key question was to whom PwC supplied their services, and it was therefore immaterial that any benefit flowed from the financial institutions to Airtours, and neither was it relevant that the continued finance of Airtours was the indirect benefit to Airtours following/derived from PwC's services since the Agreement was made for the purpose of determining whether there would be any continued finance (para. 19 of the judgment).

(2) The Upper Tribunal considered that the appeal turned on the construction of the Agreement, and in particular whether (a) Airtours was contracting for PwC's services to be supplied to it to be used for the purposes of its business (enabling Airtours to claim input VAT); (b) the financial institutions were contracting for PwC's services for themselves on terms that Airtours paid for them without Airtours receiving any benefit from PwC to be used for the purpose of its business (no input VAT entitlement for Airtours); or (c) Airtours was contracting for the right to have PwC's services supplied to the financial institutions (which was something of value) to be used for the purposes of its business, on the lines of Redrow (enabling Airtours to claim input VAT). The Tribunal concluded that the position was governed by point (b) since PwC's work did not discharge any business obligations of Airtours, or provide it with something to be used in its business; and neither did Airtours receive any Redrow-type benefit (para. 21 and 22 of the judgment). In this respect, the Upper Tribunal also commented that the position agreed between the parties had to be analysed based on what Airtours contracted for under the Agreement at the time of entering the Agreement and not to take into account benefits for Airtours which could only be identified with hindsight.

(3) The Upper Tribunal in construing the Agreement examined the substance of what was agreed, including taking into account that the initial approach to PwC was made by the financial institutions, that the letter of engagement issued by PwC was addressed to the 'Engaging Institutions', and that the flavour of the Agreement was that PwC was doing something that the financial institutions wanted done for the purposes of their own businesses in order to determine whether to continue supporting Airtours. The tribunal considered that the following parts of the Agreement provided the basis for this conclusion (para. 20 of the judgment):

'""PwC have been retained by the institutions" (clause 1); 'Our report and letters are for the sole use of the Institutions who have expressly agreed to this Letter of Engagement ("the Engaging Institutions") by countersigning below' (clause 4); "To enable the institutions to develop views on the Group's current financial position and financing needs, you have requested that we assist in providing information to the institutions providing facilities to the Group" (clause 6); "The first phase of it is to assist the institutions providing banking, bonding and other facilities to the Group to gain a more detailed understanding of the present financial position of the Group. During this phase our role is to obtain and comment on this information to enable the institutions to better consider the Group's likely requests for facility extensions" (clause 7); "Information and advice produced from this engagement is to be addressed to the Engaging Institutions with a copy to the directors of the Group" (clause 8); "You have requested us to undertake a review of the Group as set out below. Our work is required by the Institutions in considering the level of facilities to the Group" (clause 12).'

(4) The Upper Tribunal construed the Agreement as being one whereby the Engaging Institutions were contracting with PwC for its services which they needed, and that Airtours was a party to the Agreement solely to pay PwC for supplying the services to the financial institutions, rather than for receiving something of value from PwC to be used for the purposes of its business in return for its payment (para. 20 of the judgment).

(5) The approach of the Upper Tribunal emphasises the necessity to examine the precise nature of the contractual arrangements between the parties for the purposes of determining their VAT position and the direction of benefit of the respective supplies, and also the importance of ensuring that contracts are appropriately drafted in order to maximise input VAT recoverability while reflecting the economic substance of the facts. The Tribunal commented on the nature of the Agreement as follows (at para. 22):

"Having the work done did not discharge any business obligation of Airtours, or provide it with something to be used in its business. We do not consider that Airtours received any Redrow-type benefit in accordance with interpretation (c). Unlike Redrow (which used the estate agent's services supplied to X because that enabled Redrow to sell a new house to X simultaneously with the sale of X's house) ... there was no business use made by Airtours of having PwC's services supplied to the Engaging Institutions. It did not start by needing PwC's report to place before the Institutions; the Institutions started by wanting the report for themselves, as the Agreement states. The benefit to Airtours was that PwC's report might lead to continued finance from the Institutions for which Airtours was willing (or was forced) to pay. The choice between interpretations (a) and (b) is whether in reality Airtours received PwC's services to be used for the purpose of its business, or received nothing from PwC's services because they were supplied to the engaging Institutions to be used for the purpose of their business. In substance we decide it was (b) because, as the Agreement makes clear, the Engaging Institutions needed PwC's services for the purposes of their own businesses and the fact that Airtours received a copy of the report was more of a courtesy than the receipt of the supply of PwC's services. We consider that the substance is that the Engaging Institutions (and not Airtours) were contracting with PwC for the provision of services, and that PwC supplied those services to the Engaging Institutions (and not to Airtours) and that interpretation (b) is the correct one. In deciding otherwise the First-tier Tribunal made an error of law.'

- Finally, the Upper Tribunal held that it was not sufficient that Airtours had paid for the services provided by PwC to the financial institutions in order to be regarded as having authorised PwC to do the work. In this regard, it was again necessary to consider the substance of the Agreement. The Tribunal considered on this point that (para. 23 of the judgment):

"The First-tier Tribunal was also wrong in law in its construction of the Agreement that Airtours "authorised PwC to do the work" by paying for it. It was the Engaging Institutions that first approached PwC, and contracted for the work and therefore authorised it. Nor do we agree with the Tribunal's conclusion that it is clear from the terms of the Agreement that "The work of PwC was needed by [Airtours] and it is our holding that [Airtours] authorised it and secured it for its own purposes". We consider that the terms of the Agreement, particularly the ones summarised in paragraph 20 above, all point in the opposite direction, that it was the Engaging Institutions that wanted PwC's report for the purpose of their own business. This is not affected by the fact that Airtours had an input into the Agreement by influencing the appointment of PwC, and by agreeing the scope of the work for which they were paying.'

4 Input VAT and Partial Exemption

As regards *Redrow*, the present HMRC view is set out in further detail in their Guidance Manuals at VATSC91000, where they stress that the decision in *Redrow*, as discussed above, is not seen to support a culture of 'he who pays, deducts'.

- *Rushcombe Ltd* [1997] BVC 4,066 also concerned the need for a *direct and immediate link* but in another context. This was about a claim for input tax on legal costs following the acquisition of the benefit of a right of action by another company in liquidation. The agreement enabled the appellant to pursue an action against a bank for damages. If successful, Rushcombe would pay the liquidator sufficient to settle the claims of the other company's creditors, with any surplus being retained by it.

HMRC rejected the claim for input tax on the grounds that tax was only deductible if the services were to be used by the claimant in making taxable supplies. The Tribunal, in effect, agreed, holding it was not possible to identify the services concerned as the *cost-component* (see later at 40-300) of any taxable transaction of Rushcombe and in no way could it be sensibly said that the legal services were to be regarded as just general overheads of its taxable business.

(c) Insurance

There may be more fundamental problems in relation to insurance, for instance, with claims under a motor insurance policy. Accident reinstatement costs and other types of claims-related expenditure will often represent supplies to the policyholder, not the insurer. If registered for VAT, the policyholder may be able to recover the tax involved, something the insurer could not usually do, even were the supply to be to him. If the policyholder can recover the VAT, the claim under the policy need then only be for the reduced, net of VAT amount, which is clearly an important consideration.

The implications of this are considered in more detail later in **Chapter 9**.

> **Practice point**
>
> As general observations, these must be correct.
>
> For companies like insurers, however, the case law clearly has quite wide implications. Lawyers, for example, may be instructed by insurers:
> - to limit the liability of their insured in an accident or dispute; or
> - to help their insured pursue a claim against someone else,
>
> thereby limiting their own potential exposure. How this is treated is important as, if the insured is a business (and potentially able to recover the tax on the lawyers fees as input VAT), it could be better that *Redrow* did not apply (see later in **Chapter 9**).

(2) The significance of business

The second precondition for input VAT relief is more general concern as to whether the cost has been incurred for the purposes of a *business*, and specifically a business of the claimant. VAT is applied to supplies by *taxable persons*, Art. 9.1 of the VAT Directive providing, emphasis added:

'Taxable person shall mean any person who, independently, carries out in any place any *economic activity*, whatever the purpose or results of that activity. Any activity of producers, traders or persons supplying services, including mining and agricultural activities and activities of the professions, shall be regarded as "economic activity". The exploitation of tangible or intangible property for the purposes of obtaining income therefrom on a continuing basis shall in particular be regarded as an economic activity.'

In broad terms, this is taken to mean most activities undertaken in a commercial sense, with no distinction being made between capital and revenue. It is not the same, therefore, as trading and can, in certain situations, include investment. The issues are not always, however, clear-cut. A person who carries on an economic activity under a contract of employment, does not carry on the activity independently (Art. 10 of VAT Directive).

The question of whether expenditure is incurred for the purposes of a business where there is ambiguity turns on the subjective purpose of the taxpayer. In *Ian Flockton Developments Ltd v C & E Commrs* (1987) 3 BVC 23 at 28 the High Court provided the following guidance on the correct way to approach the question of whether expenditure is incurred for business purposes:

"The test is were the goods or services which were supplied to the taxpayer used or to be used for the purpose of any business carried on by him? The test is a subjective one: that is to say, the fact-finding tribunal must look into the taxpayer's mind as it was at the relevant time to discover his object. Where the taxpayer is a company, the relevant mind or minds are those of the person or persons who control the company or are entitled to and do act for the company. In a case such as this, where there is no obvious and clear association between the taxpayer company's business and the expenditure concerned, the tribunal should approach any assertion that it is for the taxpayer company's business with circumspection and care, and must bear in mind that it is for the taxpayer company to establish its case and the tribunal should not simply accept the word of the witness, however respectable. It is both permissible and essential to test such evidence against the standards and thinking of the ordinary business man in the position of the applicant. If they consider that no ordinary business man would have incurred such an expenditure for business purposes that may be grounds for rejecting the taxpayer company's evidence, but they must not substitute that as the test. It is only a guide or factor to take into account when considering the credibility of the witness, and no doubt there will be many other factors which bear on that question which the tribunal should well understand. The tribunal must look at all the circumstances of the case and draw such inferences as they think fit. In the end it is a question of fact for them whether they were satisfied on the balance of probability that the object in the taxpayer company's mind at the time the expenditure was incurred was that the goods and services in question were to be used for the purposes of the business.'

The burden of proof is on the taxpayer to show that the goods or services were used for the purposes of the business carried on, or to be carried on, by that person.

(a) Investment

One of the problems that can arise in this area was highlighted by the CoJ ruling in *Polysar*:

- *Polysar Investments Netherlands BV v Inspecteur der Invoerrechten en Accijnzen, Arnhem* (Case C-60/90) [1993] BVC 88 concerned an intermediate holding company with no commercial activity other than the holding of shares in subsidiaries. Polysar had, seemingly, been installed in the group for purely fiscal reasons and in its judgment the Court concluded that:

"Article 4 of the Sixth Council Directive 77/388 of 17 May 1977, on the harmonisation of the laws of the member states relating to turnover taxes – common system of VAT: uniform basis of assessment (art. 9(1) of Council Directive 2006/112/EC), must be interpreted as meaning that a holding company whose sole purpose is to acquire holdings in other undertakings, without involving itself directly or indirectly in the management of those undertakings, without prejudice to its rights as shareholder, does not have the status of a taxable person for the purposes of VAT…'

The Advocate General's opinion was that:

'The position would be different only where a company engages in share transitions which go beyond the activities of a normal investor in connection with the usual management of his assets, for instance where a company regularly buys and sells shares as profit-making transactions. In such a case, repeated transactions which involve buying and selling may be regarded as economic activities. That situation does not arise, however, in the case of a holding company such as Polysar, which forms a "link" in a group of companies and which has acquired shares in its subsidiaries with a view to retaining them.'

Other cases have also illustrated the difficulty there can be in determining an investment activity as a taxable activity for VAT purposes.

- The *National Society for the Prevention of Cruelty to Children* [1993] BVC 701 illustrates another aspect of this problem. The dispute was over whether investment transactions were *business activities*. The Tribunal decided they were not, essentially because they were tied up with the Society's charitable role.
- Interestingly, the decision in the case of *Wellcome Trust Ltd* [1995] BVC 1,011 took the same approach in a later appeal, where the Tribunal again found it hard to see the investment activities of a company acting as sole trustee of a charitable trust as an *economic activity*. The problem in this case was with the *predominant concern* test propounded by Gibson J in *C & E Commrs v Morrison's Academy Boarding Houses Association* (1977) 1 BVC 108 (see **Chapter 1** at ¶10-300).

> **Practice point**
>
> It is now generally accepted that the *Polysar* problem is, in practice, likely to be restricted to pure holding companies (see HMRC's VAT Input Tax Manual at VIT40100).
>
> It should not necessarily be assumed, however, that other holding companies will automatically be able to recover the input VAT involved merely on the basis of making, say, taxable management charges to operating subsidiaries. This could depend on how the partial exemption rules are applied in a particular case (see ¶¶40-150 and 40-250 later) or on whether the company is part of a VAT group (see **Chapter 2** at ¶20-250).

(3) Corporate issues

More generally, there is the position of holding companies and matters relating to the issue of shares and raising of capital, a subject considered in detail later at ¶40-250 under (3) **Holding Companies**.

Briefly, the problem with the issue of shares is that, historically, HMRC have seen this as a VAT-exempt activity, with little scope for the recovery of related input tax (see *Trinity Mirror* plc v C & E Commrs [2001] BVC 167, *Southampton Leisure Holdings plc* [2003] BVC 4,010, *Actinic plc v C & E Commrs* [2003] BVC 4,096 and *Halladale Group plc* [2003] BVC 4,140. However, this has now been effectively overturned by rulings of the CoJ, which have indicated that the issue, as opposed to the sale, of shares is not a supply at all. The first of these decisions was that of *KapHag Renditefonds v Finanzamt Charlottenburg* (Case C-442/01) [2005] BVC 566. This was later followed by *Kretztechnik AG v Finanzamt Linz* (Case C-465/03) [2006] BVC 66.

- *KapHag*, decided in June 2003, concerned the concepts of *economic activity* and whether there was a supply of services for consideration from a partnership to an incoming partner, when the partnership admitted the new partner in return for a contribution in cash. The CoJ ruled that there was a supply from the partnership to the new partner on granting admission and a consequent share in partnership profits. In particular, the finding of the Court was that the mere acquisition of financial holdings in other undertakings did not amount to the exploitation of property for the purpose of obtaining income therefrom on a continuing basis because any dividend yielded by that holding was merely the result of ownership of the property.
- *Kretztechnik*, decided in May 2005, involved a company which increased its capital by the issue of bearer shares. Adopting the same approach, the CoJ concluded that a company that issued new shares was increasing its assets by acquiring additional capital, whilst granting the new shareholders a right of ownership of part of the capital thus increased. From the issuing company's point of view, the aim was to raise capital; not to provide services such that the issue of shares was not a supply. The company was still entitled to recover input VAT on the listing and other related share issue costs to the extent of its taxable supplies activity.

Practice point

Although issuing shares and other securities does not, itself, amount to a supply of services for VAT, it is, however, accepted that it can form part of the *economic activities* of the issuer. The underlying VAT qualifies as input VAT of the business as a whole. See also HMRC's VAT Supply and Consideration Manual at VATSC97600.

(a) Shareholder-related costs

Shareholder-related costs have been a further contentious area as highlighted by the Shell case.

- *Shell International Petroleum Co Ltd* [2006] BVC 2,325 concerned a dispute over the treatment of investor relations expenses of two listed companies holding 40 per cent and 60 per cent respectively of its share capital. The dispute was over whether the services received were rendered to Shell and were to be used by it for the purposes of its business or whether it satisfied those tests only in part.

Shell conceded that, since the services were not *directly attributable* to any of its taxable activities, it was not entitled to deduct the whole of the VAT as input tax. Though, it contended that, the VAT should be deducted in part as residual input tax in accordance with the group's Partial Exemption Special Method. HMRC, however, claimed the disputed costs did not qualify as input tax for four reasons, arguing that:

- the expenditure was directed at maintaining relations with investors in two companies outside the Shell VAT group, namely Shell Transport and Trading Company plc; and Royal Dutch Petroleum Company;
- there was no real connection between the Shell VAT group's business or trading activities and the investor relations expenditure;
- the expenditure did not form a cost component of the Shell VAT group's taxable transactions; and
- the expenditure was not *for the purpose of* the Shell VAT group's business.

In reaching their decision, the Tribunal asked itself whether:

- the services received from third parties were rendered to Shell;
- the services (or at least some of them) had the required nexus with the business of the companies in Shell's;
- whether that nexus was merely a peripheral benefit from services primarily incurred for others not in the Shell VAT group; and
- whether the services were wholly used for the business purposes of companies in the Shell VAT group or partly for something else.

Allowing the company's appeal, the Tribunal felt that, with the exception of services that appeared to be for Shell Transport and Trading, the relevant services were provided to Shell. Except for three areas of services benefiting Shell Transport and Trading, Royal Dutch Petroleum and companies outside the group, there was a necessary nexus with the Shell VAT group's business. It also regarded the function of investor relations as being fundamentally for the purposes of Shell's business.

(4) Employee-related issues

A common area of difficulty is the recovery of VAT on employee- and director-related costs particularly as they may involve an element of private or mixed, non-business use. Whether they can be seen as costs of the business is not always therefore the same thing as whether they are business inputs for VAT purposes. However, costs incurred by an employee can often, for example, be incurred on the employer's behalf or in a business context and something paid for, for an employee's benefit can be part of his employment package and a legitimate business cost. Absent private use issues (see 40-000(5)), broadly, a business can recover VAT on various expenses incurred by an employee that are fully reimbursed by the employer and on the provision of certain employee benefits as if it were its input VAT, provided they can be regarded as legitimately paid for the purposes of the employer's business, e.g. to motivate or reward staff. However, despite this, there are some particular issues to note which can impact an employer's input VAT recovery.

(a) Benefits

The treatment of the provision of a company car has long been agreed (see **Chapter 3** at ¶30-450) and has tended to be relatively unproblematic. The incidence of the input tax block on the purchase or leasing of a car (see ¶40-050(1) later) means any disallowance is automatically taken into account, regardless of the extent of private use by an employee.

- However, in *BMW Financial Services (GB) Ltd* [2003] BVC 4,061 the issue went wider. In addition to the provision of a car, the company also paid for driver training for the employee and for their nominated second driver (who was not an employee). HMRC had accepted that the VAT on courses for the employee was deductible (attendance was mandatory for employees), but didn't allow this for the VAT on the nominated drivers' courses. BMW argued that these courses were aimed at:

- protecting their brand and reputation;
- reducing accidents (and the insurance costs); and
- maintaining the condition of the vehicles.

In short, they weren't intended as an employee benefit as most of the recipients regarded them as a burden rather, as BMW argued, the expenditure on the courses was incurred for the above aims and that they were therefore for the purposes of its business.

Unfortunately, the training was not compulsory for nominated drivers. This broke the causal link between the expenditure and the business. Accordingly, on the facts, the Tribunal concluded that any advantage BMW gained from the expenditure was a commercial benefit but there was no real connection between the expenditure and the purpose of BMW's business which was to sell motor cars. The Tribunal reluctantly agreed that the driving courses were not an employee benefit in relation to the nominated drivers – if it had been, the Tribunal stated it would have concluded that it was for the purpose of the business.

There are also special rules for certain costs incurred by or for staff. VATA 1994, s. 24(5A) and (5B) treats any relevant asset held for the purposes of a business carried on or to be carried on by a taxable person as not being used or to be used for the purposes of the business if, and to the extent that, it is used or to be used for the person's private use or for the private use of that person's staff. For this purpose, 'relevant asset' means (a) any interest in land, (b) any building or part of a building, (c) any civil engineering work or part of such a work, (d) any goods incorporated or to be incorporated in a building or civil engineering work (whether by being installed as fixtures or fittings or otherwise), (e) any ship, boat or other vessel, or (f) any aircraft.

It is also worth noting the CoJ's decision in *Astra Zeneca UK Limited v R & C Commrs* C-40/09. HMRC's policy was to make a distinction between the VAT treatment of supplies of goods and services to employees by a deduction from salary (VATable), and those provided under a salary sacrifice arrangement (no VAT due as the reduction in the salary did not constitute consideration for the benefits received). The CoJ's concluded that the employer's part payment of salary in vouchers was a supply for consideration for VAT purposes. The resulting changes to the VAT treatment of certain supplies by employers under salary sacrifice arrangements are noted by HMRC in Business Brief 28/11. Where the benefit is subject to VAT, output tax will be due from, and input VAT recoverable by the employer in accordance with the normal rules. Therefore, the amount of salary foregone is consideration for supplies of the benefits whether provided under a salary sacrifice or by a deduction from salary. The judgment only applies where an employee provides consideration in exchange for benefits. Where an employer provides, for example, a workplace gym which all employees may use for no deduction or reduction from their salary that will not fall within the scope of the judgment. Businesses may continue to recover VAT incurred on providing such facilities as a business overhead subject to the normal rules. Separate charges to use facilities, etc. remain within the scope of VAT. The judgment does not impact car benefits for which VAT recovery is restricted – when cars are made available to employees and where VAT recovery is restricted, output VAT is not due.

(b) Legal and removal costs

Where an employee is asked to relocate, HMRC will often, by concession, allow the employer to claim input VAT incurred on the employee's removal expenses. This will include the legal and sale costs associated with moving house and the cost of temporary accommodation, even though the supply is not, strictly, to the employer. This concession does not, however, extend to furnishings and other similar items.

Tax on other legal costs, such as defending an employee against criminal charges, will usually never be accepted as relating to a supply to the employer. This remains so, even if the employer arranges for the legal assistance and/or is invoiced direct. There will inevitably be exceptions to this rule. However, in practice, these are likely to be limited.

- In *P & O European Ferries (Dover) Ltd* [1992] BVC 955, for example, the company did manage to secure input VAT relief when it instructed and paid solicitors to act on behalf of its employees. But this was only achieved because of its own close involvement in the underlying problem. Following the *Herald of Free Enterprise* disaster at Zebrugge P & O, the employer, itself faced a charge of corporate manslaughter and ensuring its employees were properly represented was ultimately, therefore, its own best defence.
- In *R & C Commrs v Jeancharm Ltd (t/a Beaver International)* [2005] EWHC 839; [2005] BVC 316 the decision went the other way. An employee had been involved in an accident whilst driving a company car, killing two people. He was not on business at the time and pleaded guilty to causing death by dangerous driving. The employee was covered by the company's insurance, which included the costs of legal defence and at issue was whether the company was entitled to credit for the input tax incurred on those costs.

  Jeancharm initially won before the Tribunal, but lost on appeal. The Court decided the Tribunal had erred in law in deciding the correct question was whether the purchase of the policy had been for the purpose of the company's business. The important issue was *was the employee's legal representation properly to be seen as supplied to the company?* As it happened, there was no evidence that Jeancharm had paid for the lawyers' services, although it did pay for the policy. It did not follow, therefore, that it was the company that paid for and received the lawyers' services. The most simple and natural view was that the lawyers' services were provided to the employee, but if that was wrong, they were supplied to the insurer. *C & E Commrs v Redrow Group plc* [1999] BVC 96 was distinguished.

(c) Luxuries

Whether something is justified as a business expense can sometimes be a matter of judgment and, for expenditure that can be classed as a luxury, amusement or entertainment, a taxpayer can be effectively prevented from appealing a decision by HMRC to disallow any related input tax (VATA 1994, s. 84(4)).

The grounds for challenge are limited and, initially, HMRC seemed to feel this allowed them to arbitrarily refuse or restrict input VAT relief on staff entertainment costs, notwithstanding that this is specifically excluded from the input tax block on business entertainment (see ¶40-050). The disallowance originally suggested was 50 per cent (on the basis that the goods and services are used partly for private purposes) and could affect expenditure on, for example, an annual Christmas party. The net result, given that HMRC also expected a further disallowance to reflect non-employee guests, could be that only 25 per cent of the VAT might be recovered.

Whether this approach was or is correct seemed doubtful and HMRC have since accepted that VAT incurred on staff entertainment (staff parties, team building, staff outings/events) would be VAT recoverable. See later at 40-050(2) and (3) in the context of the input VAT block rules on business entertainment.

(d) Pension costs

In a sense related, is the treatment of tax on costs arising in the context of an employee pension fund.

- In *The Plessey Company Ltd* [1996] BVC 2,074, the company sought to recover tax on solicitors' costs it incurred on the occasion of the merger of a number of group pension funds. These were for advice necessarily provided to a number of groups of beneficiaries in order to see their interests were protected. They were borne out of the assets of the funds and Plessey argued that the services should be seen as supplied to it through the trustees. The problem with this was that the advice was given to the beneficiaries, not to the trustees. In that respect, the case was clearly distinguishable from *P & O* earlier and it was for this reason the appeal failed.
- *Ultimate Advisory Services Ltd* [1993] BVC 743 showed how important this can be. Here, the trustees of a pension fund had commenced Court proceedings against the joint owners of the company (the appellant). Under the trust deed the costs of administration and management of the scheme were payable by the appellant and the Tribunal accepted that the costs incurred by employers in providing pension schemes for their employees were properly regarded as being incurred in the course of their business. The appellant had contracted with the solicitors as a principal and benefited from the legal services by its own defence of the counterclaim and by preservation of its employees' pension fund. The input tax incurred on legal costs for services provided to the appellant and the trustees was therefore deductible.

A further point of interest is the extent of the deduction allowed for tax on pension fund administration costs. This is considered in **Chapter 8** at ¶80-400. HMRC have long allowed a 30/70 administration (deductible)/investment (not deductible) split, but, in August 2005 in *Business Brief* 15/05, they expressed concerns that businesses were applying this more generously than was intended. However, the position, as yet, remains unchanged.

(e) Subsistence and travel

For normal subsistence costs the position is relatively straightforward. The employee is usually seen as agent of the employer. Input VAT relief should thus generally be available, even though invoices may be made out in the employee's name. Hotel accounts can, however, often be unsatisfactory as they frequently fail to meet the requirements for tax invoices. Relief may,

4 Input VAT and Partial Exemption

in any event, be refused if the employee is given a round sum/fixed allowance as opposed to being reimbursed for the exact amount of the expenditure incurred (*British Broadcasting Corporation v C & E Commrs* (1974) VATTR 100).

Tax on road fuel was, until December 2005, specifically covered by the *Value Added Tax (Input Tax) (Person Supplied) Order* 1991 (SI 1991/2306). An employee's fuel costs relating to business use by an employee could be recovered by an employer. However, the justification for this was questioned by the infraction proceedings brought against the UK (*EC Commission v United Kingdom* (Case C-33/03) [2005] ECR I-1865; [2007] BVC 863. The Commission had argued that:

- the fuel purchases are supplied to the employees as individuals, not to the employers – so the employers have no right to deduct under the terms of former art. 17(2)(a) of the Sixth Directive (now art. 168 of the VAT Directive); and
- even if there were a right to deduct, employers cannot exercise that right because they do not hold a VAT invoice as required by art. 18(1)(a) of the Sixth Directive (art. 178 of the VAT Directive).

As announced in *Business Brief* 22/05, this has now been remedied by the *VAT Tax (Input Tax) (Reimbursement by Employers of Employees' Business Use of Road Fuel) Regulations* 2005 (SI 2005/3290). Under this, the existing arrangements remain largely unchanged, except that businesses must now retain VAT invoices to support their claims. The invoice can be a full VAT invoice or a less detailed VAT invoice, as appropriate.

As noted earlier, the recovery of input tax is an important right enshrined in the VAT Directive and of potentially significant benefit to many of the businesses in the sectors covered by this book. Article 168 opens, it will be remembered, with the provision that:

> "In so far as the goods and services are used for the purposes of the taxed transactions of a taxable person, the taxable person shall be entitled, in the Member State in which he carries out these transactions, to deduct the following from the VAT which he is liable to pay:
>
> (a) the VAT due or paid in that Member State in respect of supplies to him of goods or services, carried out or to be carried out by another taxable person;
> (b) ...'

going on to include tax relating to intra-Community acquisitions of goods and imports, with Art. 169 then conferring that same right of deduction in respect of tax incurred in making certain other supplies (such as transactions which are exempt under points (a) to (f) of Art. 135(1) (various finance activities) where the customer is established outside the EU or where those transactions relate directly to goods to be exported out of the EU). For businesses where this benefit is, in practice limited, there is a clear incentive to maximise whatever opportunity is available and, on occasion, this has been taken to the extreme.

(5) Business and private use

As mentioned above, VAT on private costs or incurred in relation to non-business activities is not input VAT; it cannot be relieved. However, where mixed use expenditure occurs, then subject to certain exceptions, a taxable person is entitled to a full and immediate input tax deduction (subject to any partial exemption restriction) on goods that are to be used (a) partly for business, and (b) partly for private use, but has to account for output tax on the private use as it takes place (this is the effect of the CoJ's decision in *Lennartz v Finanzamt München III* (Case C-97/90). But its application is limited by the decision of the CoJ in *Vereniging Noordelijke Land- en Tuinbouw Organisatie v Staatssecretaris van Financiën* (Case C-515/07). The *Lennartz* principle is now only available for goods that are put to mixed business and private use; and it cannot be used for immovable property, ships, boats or other vessels and aircraft. Neither can the *Lennartz* approach be used where the mixed use does not include private use, but instead non-business (rather than private) use of the goods that is normally undertaken by the business. See HMRC VAT Input Tax Manual at VIT25000 and VIT25900. The activity of providing something for free is likely to be non-business as opposed to private, for example, if part of the business' normal objectives.

Broadly, this means that for Lennartz to apply, the use of goods must be used in part for business supplies that confer the rights of input VAT recovery, i.e. taxable supplies, supplies that would be taxable if made in the UK, or certain financial and insurance supplies to non-EC customers; and the goods are also used in part for the private purposes of the business or its staff, or, exceptionally, for other uses which are wholly outside the purposes of the taxpayer's enterprise or undertaking. Where the *Lennartz* mechanism is not available due to goods being used for both business and non-business activities that are normally undertaken by the business then the taxable person must apportion any VAT incurred between the different activities on the basis of use or intended use (see generally HMRC's VAT Input Tax Manual at VIT25550: *Is it input tax: current Lennartz users*). This input VAT normally needs to be identified and split out between business and non-business use before any partial exemption calculation is made. Broadly, this requires two sets of calculations to determine the recoverable input tax, the first being the fair and reasonable business/non-business apportionment, and then the second, to determine the recoverable VAT attributable to taxable business use subject to the partial exemption method, assuming the business is partly exempt (see 40-200(5)). In effect, the purchase of a mixed use good is normally treated as if it is effectively two assets at the time of acquisition; one brought partly within the business (the included part) and one outside it. VAT on the included part relating to taxable business use is input tax which can be recovered. VAT relating to its non-business use is not input tax and is initially irrecoverable but this may be subject to adjustment under e.g. the Capital Goods Scheme (as from 1 January 2011) or if there is a change in intended use before any actual use happens. Accordingly, for goods other than capital items it is important to distinguish private use, including private use by the business' staff, from other non-business use, given that the *Lennartz* approach to VAT accounting may be available in respect of part private use (albeit with a output VAT charge to reflect private use).

At the time of acquisition of an asset, a business can alternatively decide not to include a mixed use asset within its business and treat it as wholly private or non-business, with no related input VAT recovery incurred on its acquisition or future disposal. In addition, the situation is generally different for mixed use of services – as noted by HMRC, the UK has relied on EU legislation that allows a more general input tax adjustment/apportionment as regards the mixed use of services. See as explained in HMRC's Input VAT manual at VIT25300. Special rules apply so that certain services which create new goods can be treated as if they were the

4 Input VAT and Partial Exemption

costs of acquiring the goods for *Lennartz* accounting purposes, or the VAT recovery of certain services creating or refurbishing capital goods may be adjusted under the Capital Goods Scheme (see 40-200(8)).

Where real estate forms part of the business assets of a taxable person, and it is used for both the purposes of the business and private use then VAT on expenditure related to the property is only deductible up to the proportion of the property's use for the purposes of the taxable person's business (Art. 168a of the VAT Directive). See further on the Capital Goods Scheme at 40-200(8).

(6) Avoidance and abuse of rights

This approach was originally highlighted in *Halifax plc, Leeds Permanent Development Services Ltd, County Wide Property Investments Ltd v C & E Commrs* (Case C-255/02) [2006] BVC 377, a case involving a VAT avoidance scheme. Initially, Halifax lost on the basis that the strategy adopted did not amount to a business, although, this was not followed by later Courts.

- Briefly, the Halifax, a bank, wanted to develop certain of its sites as call centres. However, as it made mostly exempt supplies, in the normal course of events, it stood to recover little of the input VAT likely to arise on the construction costs involved. With this in mind, it embarked on a plan with three of its wholly-owned subsidiaries. Two were separately registered for VAT and were the other parties joined in the appeal; the third was a property company, which was not VAT-registered.
- The way the scheme worked was that:
  - firstly, the Halifax granted an interest in the development sites to the first of the VAT-registered subsidiaries;
  - next, that company engaged the second VAT-registered subsidiary to carry out the construction works, using subcontracted builders;
  - the first company then paid for these works shortly before the end of its own partial exemption year, making in that year to Halifax a low-value standard-rated supply of minor construction services. Since that taxable supply was the only supply made in that year by the first company, all the VAT it paid to the second company on the construction works was recovered;
  - in its next partial exemption year, the first subsidiary transferred its leasehold interests in the sites to the third, non VAT-registered, subsidiary as exempt supplies; and
  - lastly, this third subsidiary, in turn, leased the sites as exempt supplies back to the Halifax.

It was also important that the property interests in the sites vested in the first VAT-registered subsidiary did not rank as capital items in order to avoid an adjustment to that company's input tax when the interests were eventually transferred to the third, non-VAT registered, subsidiary. Halifax had funded these transactions and had novated to the second VAT registered subsidiary one of the construction contracts that had already been entered into.

HMRC refused the input tax claims of the two VAT registered subsidiaries on the basis that, on a proper analysis of the transactions as a whole, the building services were supplied to the Halifax. The VAT Tribunal ([2002] BVC 370) upheld this view, finding that there was no business or commercial rationale for any of the transactions forming part of the scheme. If it worked it would cause distortions of competition at national and Community level. It went on to say the scheme had clearly the hallmarks of avoidance and, looking at all the relevant considerations, the construction services were, in reality, supplied to the Halifax itself.

When the ECJ ruled in February 2006, it was in a joint decision covering other, related, appeals, including that of *BUPA* (see earlier at 30-360). The non-business approach of the Tribunal was not accepted, but Halifax lost, largely because there was an *abuse of rights*.

As the Court put it, the Directive must be interpreted as precluding any right of a taxable person to deduct input VAT where the transactions from which that right derives constitute an abusive practice, i.e. where:

- the transactions concerned, notwithstanding compliance with the conditions laid down by the relevant provisions of the Directive and of national law, result in the accrual of a tax advantage the grant of which would be contrary to the purpose of those provisions;
- it is also apparent from a number of objective factors that the essential aim of the transactions is to obtain a tax advantage.

Where an abusive practice has been found to exist, the Court said the transactions involved must be redefined so as to re-establish the situation that would otherwise have prevailed.

Although, the principle of *abuse of rights*, rather than the *non-business* argument prevailed, this was not ruled out in *Halifax* and the Tribunal in the *BUPA* case gave a useful indication of what the objective criteria referred to were. Citing the *Rompelmann, Wellcome Trust* and *Breitsohl* cases, what it said was:

> 'Those cases illustrate a self-evident feature of business. Its character as such will be determined as much by objective characteristics such as its categorisation and its object clause as by subjective characteristics such as the particular motive or purpose of its decision makers. The same goes for the character of a particular transaction or activity of a person who is admittedly carrying on a business. Thus motive or purpose of a person effecting a transaction will be relevant to the question of whether that transaction is disqualified from ranking as an economic activity on the grounds that, on a proper analysis of the evidence, there was no motive or purpose other than the avoidance of tax. Thus when determining whether a person is carrying on an economic activity, his motive or purpose cannot be ignored.
>
> So, bearing in mind that the person seeking to deduct input tax has the burden of showing that he is carrying on an economic activity, it will be incumbent on the Appellants to demonstrate that they are not excluded on the grounds that tax avoidance was the motive or purpose for which the transactions in question were effected.
>
> If the transaction in question is carried out for avoidance of tax and, viewed alone or as part of a wider arrangement, has no demonstrable commercial or business purpose, those features will disqualify it from ranking as an economic activity or as a supply (as the case may be).'

This concept of *abuse of rights* can, in the present climate, be expected to figure increasingly in the challenges mounted by HMRC, especially where there is any suspicion of avoidance. As an argument, it will not always succeed, however, as illustrated in the decision in the *RBS* case.

- *RBS Property Developments Ltd; The Royal Bank of Scotland Group plc* [2003] BVC 2,074 concerned a company, RBS Property Developments Ltd (Developments), which was formed to act primarily as a property development contractor. Initially, one of its developments was to be sold or let to third parties, but, subsequently, it was decided it should be occupied by RBS itself. In the meantime, a scheme was put into effect whereby RBS would sell the land at South Gyle to Developments for the latter to construct the buildings. Upon completion, the buildings would be sold back to RBS on a payment-instalment basis. The intended effect was that Developments would reclaim the VAT incurred on the construction and RBS would only incur an irrecoverable proportion of the charge from developments for three years while the buildings were regarded as *new* for VAT purposes. The expected result would be a tax saving of 80 per cent. Construction was carried out in accordance with the scheme and, having decided that this was an improper tax avoidance scheme, the Commissioners issued the disputed assessments.

On appeal, it was held that:

(1) The transactions entered into by RBS were not carried out with the sole intention of obtaining a tax advantage; there were real and understandable business purposes.
(2) There was a substantial element of tax mitigation, but that was irrelevant and the Commissioners were unable to establish a sufficient measure of artificiality.
(3) A taxpayer is entitled to construct his activities so as to obtain favourable taxation consequences and not to conduct his business with a view to providing finance to the authorities.

Any concept of *abuse of rights* thus had no application and there was nothing improper, illegal or artificial.

- There has also been a successful appeal in the case of *Weald Leasing Ltd v R & C Commrs* [2007] BVC 2,321, where a company purchased assets in order to lease them to a separate company to lease-on to an exempt associate outside its VAT group. The insertion of the separate third party company avoided an open market value direction for the sublease rentals under VATA 1994, Sch. 6, para. 1 (valuation) and the purpose of the transaction was to spread or defer the irrecoverable VAT of the exempt associate. The case demonstrates the concept of the scope of abusive practice.

The materials facts were as follows:

- The Churchill Group of Companies had entered into VAT planning. The Group mainly provided supplies of insurance services that were exempt from VAT.
- Churchill Management Limited ('CML') and its subsidiaries, Churchill Accident Repair Centre ('CARC') and Weald Leasing were members of the Churchill Group.
- CML and CARC had an input VAT recovery rate of 1 per cent; which meant that when they purchased assets/equipment they could only deduct 1 per cent of the VAT on the purchase of those assets/equipment.
- Weald Leasing's sole trading activity was the purchasing of the assets/equipment, and then leasing them to Suas Limited ('Suas').
- Weald Leasing was independently registered for VAT.
- Suas was a company owned by a VAT consultant to the Churchill Group, but Suas was not part of that group and it was separately registered for VAT.
- Suas' only significant trading activity was leasing assets from Weald Leasing and then subleasing them to CML and CARC.
- The purpose of the series of transactions was to enable CML and CARC to avoid having to purchase directly the equipment they needed or pay the total amount of non-

deductible VAT on those purchases. It was anticipated that the aim of the transactions was to divide and spread the payment in order to defer the Churchill Group's VAT liability. CML and CARC were not immediately liable for the non-deductible VAT on the total cost of the equipment purchased, but on the amount of rent relating to that equipment, spread over the term of the leasing agreements.
- HMRC sought to disallow the deduction by Weald Leasing of the input VAT paid on the assets on the basis that the transaction were not economic activities and constituted an abuse of rights.
- The taxpayer appealed against the HMRC assessments.

The Tribunal allowed the appeal for a number of reasons. They thought, for example, the original footing for the assessments, that Weald was not engaged in an *economic activity* was clearly wrong in the light of *Halifax*. They also said the mere fact of Weald leasing through an independent entity (instead of the exempt associate buying assets outright) was not contrary to the purpose of the Directive and a redefinition of the transactions to remove an abusive practice of the rentals being at an undervalue would involve increased output tax. The High Court upheld the decision of the Tribunal ([2008] EWHC 30 (Ch)) on the basis that despite the fact that the transactions at issue were not carried out in the context of normal commercial transactions, this was not sufficient to conclude that they were an abusive practice due to the fact that the tax advantage obtained by the group was not contrary to the principle of fiscal neutrality or to any other provision of the former Sixth Directive (now recast as the VAT Directive). The case was referred to the Court of Justice by the Court of Appeal. The CoJ issued its judgment on 22 December 2010 (Case C-103/09), and provided the following guidance on the scope of choice available to a trader under the VAT Directive without that choice being treated as an abusive practice. The Court said (at para. 27 to 35):

"... a trader's choice between exempt transactions and taxable transactions may be based on a range of factors, including tax considerations relating to the VAT system. Where the taxable person chooses one of two transactions, the Sixth Directive does not require him to choose the one which involves paying the higher amount of VAT. On the contrary, taxpayers may choose to structure their business so as to limit their tax liability (see Halifax and Others , paragraph 73, and Part Service , paragraph 47).

In that context, *the Court has held that, in the sphere of VAT, finding that an abusive practice exists requires that two conditions be met.*

First, notwithstanding formal application of the conditions laid down in the relevant provisions of the Sixth Directive and in the national legislation transposing it, the transactions concerned must result in the accrual of a tax advantage the grant of which would be contrary to the purpose of those provisions (see Halifax and Others , paragraph 74, and Part Service , paragraph 42).

Second, it must also be apparent from a number of objective factors that the essential aim of the transactions concerned is to obtain a tax advantage. The prohibition of abuse is not relevant where the economic activity carried out may have some explanation other than the mere attainment of tax advantages (see Halifax and Others, paragraph 75, and Part Service , paragraph 42).

As regards the main proceedings, the decision making the reference states that the essential aim of the leasing transactions at issue in the main proceedings was to obtain a tax advantage, namely spreading the payment of the VAT on the purchases in question, so as to defer the Churchill Group's VAT liability.

However, before it can be concluded that there was an abusive practice, it must also be the case that, notwithstanding formal application of the conditions laid down in the relevant provisions of the Sixth Directive and the national legislation transposing it, that tax advantage is contrary to the purpose of those provisions.

In that regard, it should be pointed out that the leasing transactions come within the scope of the Sixth Directive and that the tax advantage that could arise through recourse to such transactions does not, in itself, constitute a tax advantage the grant of which would be contrary to the purpose of the relevant provisions of that directive and the national legislation transposing it.

A taxable person cannot be criticised for choosing a leasing transaction which procures him an advantage consisting, as is apparent from the decision making the reference, in spreading the payment of his tax liability, rather than a purchase transaction which does not procure him any such advantage, provided that the VAT on that leasing transaction is duly and fully paid.

It is not disputed that that is the position as regards the VAT on the leasing transactions at issue in the main proceedings and that, for each of those transactions, the companies concerned have paid the correct amount of output VAT and deducted, when they could, the correct amount of input VAT.' (emphasis added)

The Court concluded (at para. 34) that:

'The use of a leasing structure involving an unrelated third party or a wholly owned subsidiary which is independently registered for VAT by an exempt trader instead of purchasing assets outright in order to defer the payment of irrecoverable tax did not in itself give rise to a tax advantage contrary to the VAT Directive.

The use of a purely artificial structure essentially designed in order to gain a tax advantage by preventing tax authorities from directing in accordance with the provisions of national law adopted in full compliance with Sixth Directive (now the VAT Directive) that the value of leasing arrangements between connected persons be taken to be their open market value is an abusive practice.

Where an abusive practice is found to exist, the transactions involved must be redefined so as to re-establish the situation that would have prevailed in the absence of the transactions constituting that abusive practice. Where a purely artificial structure is adopted in leasing arrangements essentially in order to prevent tax authorities from directing that the value of those arrangements between connected persons be taken to be their open market value, those arrangements should be redefined by ignoring the presence of that structure.

The concept of 'normal commercial operations' in the context of VAT abuse is unrelated to the operations a taxpayer typically or habitually engages in. An assessment of whether a transaction is carried out in the context of 'normal commercial operations' refers to the nature of the transaction or scheme in question and whether it is a purely artificial construct established essentially in order to obtain a tax advantage rather than for other commercial reasons. The links of a legal, economic and/or personal nature between the operators involved in the scheme for reduction of the tax burden and thus whether the parties to the transaction operate at arm's length, the question whether a transaction gives rise to commercial burdens and risks typically associated with such transactions are relevant for the purpose of assessing the nature of the transaction.'

At the time of writing, the case of *Weald Leasing Ltd v R & C Commrs* is awaiting rehearing by the Court of Appeal.

Another recent example of abuse of rights is in the case of *RBS Deutschland GmbH*.

- *R & C Commrs v RBS Deutschland Holdings GmbH* (Case C-277/09)[2011] BVC 138 concerned a German car leasing company (a subsidiary of RBS) and the interaction of German and UK law. In the UK, leasing is a supply of services, which, under the place of supply of services rules prior to the implementation of Council Directive 2008/8/EC art. 2 (effective from 1 January 2010) (see **Chapter 3** at ¶30-250(3)), took place where the supplier belonged or was established. Under German VAT law at the time of the case, the supply was classified as one of goods other than services.

The transactions in dispute involved the leasing of cars bought, used and eventually sold in the UK, but which were leased to an unconnected person in the UK. RBS Deutschland did not belong in the UK for VAT, but was registered for UK VAT as a non-established taxable person because of the eventual sales of the cars. No UK VAT was accounted for on the lease rentals, though, as UK VAT law considered the leasing to be a supply of services made by RBS Deutschland in Germany. No German VAT was accounted for on the lease rentals either, as German VAT law considered the leasing to be a supply of goods made in the UK. Accordingly, no output VAT was accounted for in either the UK or Germany in respect of the supplies.

The disputed matter was over the company's entitlement to deduct the input VAT on the purchase of the cars through its UK VAT return. HMRC's position was that, as no output tax was accounted for at all on the rental payments, there was no corresponding right to deduct. Alternatively, they claimed the transactions were an *abuse of rights*.

Before the Tribunal (No 20,267: 24 July 2007), RBS Deutschland won, the Tribunal agreeing that the transactions had substance and were not artificial. However, HMRC appealed to the Court of Session, which in turn referred the case to the CoJ. The Court of Justice in its decision (C-277/09: 22 December 2010) concluded that under the VAT Directive a Member State cannot refuse to allow a taxable person to deduct input VAT on the acquisition of goods in a Member State, where those goods have been used for the purposes of leasing transactions carried out in another Member State, solely on the ground that the output transactions have not created any output VAT liability in the other Member State. Further, the CoJ held that the principle of abusive practices does not apply in circumstances where a parent company elects to have its subsidiary established in another Member State, carry out transactions for the leasing of goods to a third company established in the same Member State as the parent company, so as to avoid VAT being payable on the consideration arising under that supply. In relation to the concept of abusive practice, the Court of Justice emphasised that it can only be found to exist if (at para. 49 of the judgment):

"1. the transactions concerned, notwithstanding formal application of the conditions laid down by the relevant provisions of the directive and the national legislation transposing it, result in the accrual of a tax advantage the grant of which would be contrary to the purpose of the relevant provisions of the directive; and

2. it is apparent from a number of objective factors that the essential aim of the transactions concerned is solely to obtain that tax advantage.'

4 Input VAT and Partial Exemption

The CoJ concluded that there was not any abusive practice since the aim of the transactions was not to obtain a tax advantage contrary to EU law. The Court referred to the following principle points in reaching its conclusion in favour of the taxpayer:

- the transactions took place between two parties which were legally unconnected, the transactions were not artificial in nature and they were carried out at arm's length (unlike in *Weald*) in the context of normal commercial operations of the parties (para. 50 of the judgment), in particular, the transactions and the nature of the relations between the companies that carried out the transactions did not suggest an artificial arrangement, which did not reflect economic reality: RBS Deutschland was a company established in Germany carrying on business providing banking and leasing services (para. 51 of the judgment);
- against these circumstances, the fact that services were supplied to a company established in one Member State by a company established in another Member State, and that the terms of the transactions carried out were chosen on the basis of factors specific to the economic operators concerned, could not be regarded as constituting an abuse of rights (para. 52 of the judgment) and did not therefore preclude the right to deduct VAT (i.e. despite differences in the categorisation of the supplies in the UK and Germany;
- the Court re-emphasised prior decisions that 'a trader's choice between exempt transactions and taxable transactions may be based on a range of factors, including tax considerations relating to the neutral system of VAT (see Case C-108/99 *Cantor Fitzgerald International* [2001] ECR I-7257, paragraph 33). In that connection, the Court has made clear that, where it is possible for the taxable person to choose from among a number of transactions, he may choose to structure his business in such a way as to limit his tax liability (see *Halifax and Others*, paragraph 73)' (at para. 54 of the judgment).

The type of arrangements in issue in *RBS Deutschland Holdings GmbH* were stopped as of 1 January 2010 due to the place of supply rules being changed (see Chapter 3). The decision is of importance since it reaffirms the scope of the principle in *Halifax*; but also emphasises that if there are differences in the treatment of supplies between Member States it is open to parties in those Member States to structure transactions so as to achieve non-taxation. Accordingly, appropriate VAT planning is acceptable, provided it does not stray into the concept of abuse of rights.

40-050   Exclusions: blocked input VAT

Value added tax on certain types of costs must always be borne as an expense or capitalised. The main areas of concern in the present context will be those covering cars and business entertainment.

Following the CoJ's ruling in *EC Commission v Italy* (Case C-45/95) [1997] BVC 536, there is a now a VAT exemption for sales of goods on which input tax recovery was blocked, or was wholly irrecoverable because of exempt use. This is found in VATA 1994, Grp. 14, Sch. 9 and will only apply for those assets, where the seller has paid VAT on the full price on buying the goods concerned. Purchases under the margin schemes for second-hand goods, works of art, antiques and collectors' items are not affected.

(1) Cars

The recovery of input VAT on motor cars is covered by the *Value Added Tax (Input Tax) Order 1992* (SI 1992/3222) (as amended). Initially, this denied relief for all VAT on the purchase, but not the leasing, of a car. However, from August 1995 the rules were radically amended and, as now drafted the block applies to 100 per cent of the VAT paid on all cars purchased and to the input VAT on all cars leased (reg. 7(2G) of SI 1992/3222):

- for letting on hire free or at undervalue; or
- to be made available for free or subsidised private use.

A taxpayer is however allowed input VAT relief on the purchase of a qualifying car (e.g. one which will not be or made available to be used for any private use) used for a relevant purpose, and the scope of this relief is the subject of the 1992 Order (see generally HMRC Notice 700/64 (July 2012)). In order to support a claim for relief it is of critical importance to show adequate evidence (see e.g. *Ravenfield Ltd* [2010] UKFTT 359; [2011] TC 00641, where a claim for input tax relief on a Bentley GT Continental car used for self-drive hire failed due to lack of adequate evidence showing that the car had been acquired for the purposes of the business). Cars purchased for in-house leasing can be the subject of input VAT recovery. However, the amounts charged to the lessee must not be less than those for a commercial arm's length letting (i.e. an open market fee must be paid) (see reg. 7(2G) SI 1992/3222). Where a business leases a qualifying car it can normally recover 50 per cent of the VAT charged (the remaining 50 per cent is blocked to reflect private use of the car). A detailed review of the scope of the 1992 Order is beyond the scope of this chapter (although see the end of this chapter on the definition of motor car).

The validity of this input VAT block has not been without challenge.

Three separate appeals were taken at the same time in June 1995 (*RoyScot Leasing Ltd* [1996] BVC 2,388, *Allied Lyons plc* [1996] BVC 2,399 and *TC Harrison Group Ltd* [1996] BVC 2,404).

(1) The *RoyScot* appeal concerned cars purchased for use in long-term leasing.

(2) The *Allied Lyons* appeal was about cars for use by employees either by reason of *need* or as a perquisite of employment.

(3) The *Harrison Group* involved demonstrator cars and cars for both short-and long-term leasing.

It was argued that the disallowance of input VAT was incompatible with EC law principles, including art. 11 of the Second VAT Directive (Directive 67/228), and, inter alia, was not an authorised exclusion within art. 17(6) of the Sixth Directive (Directive 77/388) (now art. 176 of the VAT Directive).

Briefly, art. 11(1) of the Second VAT Directive provided for the right of deduction of input tax paid on goods supplied to a taxable person for the purposes of his undertaking. That was subject, however, to a general derogation in art. 11(4) to the effect that:

> 'Certain goods and services may be excluded from the deduction system, in particular those capable of being exclusively or partially used for the private needs of the taxable person or his staff.'

The corresponding rule in the Sixth Directive to that in art. 11(4), art. 17(6), made provision for a more qualified derogation:

> 'Before a period of four years at the latest has elapsed from the date of entry into force of this directive [1 January 1978], the Council, acting unanimously on a proposal from the Commission, shall decide what expenditure shall not be eligible for a deduction of value added tax. Value added tax shall in no circumstances be deductible on expenditure which is not strictly business expenditure, such as that on luxuries, amusements or entertainment.
>
> Until the above rules come into force, member states may retain all the exclusions provided for under their national laws when this directive comes into force.'

and the current wording in art. 176 of the VAT Directive, although slightly different, has the same effect.

Essentially, the issues in all three appeals were the same. In broad terms, it was argued that the blocking order was invalid. It was a blanket exclusion not distinguishing between cars that could and cars that could not be used for private purposes.

In the event, the case ended up before the ECJ, (Case C-305/97) [1999] BVC 419), where the Court followed the same line as the Tribunal. The clear and unambiguous wording of art. 11(4) of the Second VAT Directive authorised Member States to exclude from the right of deduction even expenditure not strictly business-related, and to introduce and retain the exclusion of cars from the system of deduction. Article 17(6) authorised the retention of exclusions on the purchase of cars used by a taxable person for the purpose of taxable transactions even though the cars were essential tools in his business and made it clear that the authorised exclusions from deduction could be retained in force until such time as the Council of the EU adopted the provisions envisaged by the article.

- *C & E Commrs v British Telecommunications plc* presented a rather more restricted challenge. This concerned just car delivery charges. As a large purchaser of motor vehicles BT bought its cars direct from the manufacturers, rather than through authorised dealers. The manufacturers used third-party transport companies to deliver the cars and made a separate charge for this, which was shown separately on their invoices. BT sought to recover the tax on these charges on the basis that they were not affected by the input tax block. They won before the Tribunal, but, ultimately, lost before the House of Lords essentially because the delivery charges were *ancillary* or *incidental* to the principal supplies of the cars (see the commentary on the CPP decision in **Chapter 3** at ¶30-500).

(2) Business entertainment

The rules on *business entertainment* are found in art. 5 of the *Value Added Tax (Input Tax) Order* 1992 (SI 1992/3222)). Article 5(1) provides that:

'Tax charged on any goods or services supplied to a taxable person, or on any goods acquired by a taxable person, or on any goods imported by a taxable person, is to be excluded from any credit under section 25 of the Act, where the goods or services in question are used or to be used by the taxable person for the purposes of business entertainment unless the entertainment is provided for an overseas customer of the taxable person and is of a kind and on a scale which is reasonable, having regard to all the circumstances.'

with *business entertainment* being defined in art. 5(3) to mean:

'entertainment including hospitality of any kind provided by a taxable person in connection with a business carried on by him, but does not include the provision of any such entertainment for either or both-

(a) employees of the taxable person;
(b) the taxable person is a body corporate, its directors or persons otherwise engaged in its management,

unless the provision of entertainment for persons such as are mentioned in sub-paragraph (a) and (b) above is incidental to its provision for others.'

Hospitality can include anything from the provision of meals and refreshments, accommodation or entertainment in the artistic sense to the use of yachts and aircraft for the purpose of entertaining, so that:

- meals provided at conferences or meetings are caught (*C & E Commrs v Shaklee International* (1981) 1 BVC 444);
- to be hospitality it must, however, be gratuitous (*Celtic Football and Athletic Co Ltd v C & E Commrs* (1983) 1 BVC 554);
- if it is not gratuitous (because, say, it is provided as part of a mutual contract arrangement) then input VAT can be relieved. But there may then be an onward supply on which output VAT will be due.

Input tax on the entertainment of customers, suppliers or advisers is thus disallowed under the restriction. The concept of employees will exclude (and therefore the restriction will apply in respect thereof) interviewees, former employees and shareholders (unless employees) (see further at HMRC Notice 700/65 on Business Entertainment (February 2012)).

However, as referred to above, the restriction does not apply to an overseas customer (this exception was introduced by the *VAT (Input Tax) (Amendment) Order* 2011 (SI 2011/1071, with effect from 1 May 2011). For this purpose an 'overseas customer' is defined to mean, by art. 5(4) as:

"... in relation to a taxable person, means— (a) any person who is not ordinarily resident nor carrying on a business in the United Kingdom or the Isle of Man and avails himself or herself, or may be expected to avail himself or herself, in the course of a business carried on by that person outside the United Kingdom and the Isle of Man, of any goods or services the supply of which forms part of the taxable person's business; and (b) any person who is not ordinarily resident in the United Kingdom or the Isle of Man and is acting, in relation to such goods or services, on behalf of an overseas customer as defined in paragraph (a) above or on behalf of any government or public authority outside the United Kingdom and the Isle of Man.'

The exception for an overseas customer was introduced due to HMRC deciding that the cases of *Danfoss A/S and AstraZeneca A/S v Skatteministeriet* (Case C-371/07) [2009] BVC 781 made the prior restriction on such a person inconsistent with EU law (the cases related to the Court holding that where meals were provided for a strict business purpose no private use charge should arise). In Revenue and Customs Brief 44/10 (3 November 2010) the following guidance is provided on a number of scenarios, as follows:

"Meetings in your office

HMRC considers that where you entertain overseas customers in your staff canteen or similar, and the entertainment is provided to facilitate a business meeting, then the VAT on such expenditure will be recoverable and no charge to reflect the private use will arise; we take the view that any private benefit derived by your overseas customer is accessory to the needs of your business. This approach satisfies the basic input tax recovery test by establishing a link between the expense and the taxable supplies that your business makes. It is also consistent with the approach adopted by the ECJ in assessing the applicability of any private use charge in that this expense has a strict business purpose.

External meetings/events

Where you cannot host meetings in the office because, for example, you have a large number of attendees or you have no in-house facilities, then you can still use the principles set out above to determine if your input tax is recoverable or there is a charge to output tax under the private use charge. The provision of basic refreshments at, for example, a training event or a meeting will be treated as if it were supplied by your own in-house canteen. However, where the provision goes beyond merely providing basic food and refreshment to facilitate the smooth running of the event, then you should not recover any input tax or, failing that, account for output tax under the private use charge. If the entertainment provided causes a private use charge to arise the business can treat the VAT incurred as non-deductible rather than deducting the input tax and offsetting with an output tax charge.

Corporate hospitality events

Many businesses offer their customers or potential customers general entertainment and hospitality, for example, golf days, track days, trips to sporting events, evening meals, trips to night clubs. HMRC will generally not allow deduction of VAT in respect of these events or will require you to account for output tax, as such events are unlikely to have a strict business purpose and be necessary for the business to make its supplies.'

Accordingly, an output tax charge to reflect private use may be due, cancelling out any recoverable input tax. Further guidance is provided by HMRC in Notice 700/65 (February 2012) on Business Entertainment, which provides at section 2.6:

"Meetings:

If normal basic food and refreshments such as sandwiches and soft drinks are provided in your office during a meeting to enable the meeting to proceed without interruption, then a private use charge will not apply. If there is no other alternative than to hold a meeting outside the office, only similar basic provisions would be allowable. Hospitality provided following a meeting will not meet the strict business purpose test and neither will hospitality involving the provision of alcohol. Taking a customer to a restaurant is very likely to lead to a private use charge.'

At one time there has been some question as to whether there can be any general right to apportionment. If the expenditure is on business entertainment, is the VAT wholly disallowable? Is it a matter of all or nothing?

The traditional HMRC approach has been that it is, indeed, on an all or nothing basis.

- *Plant Repair & Services (South Wales) Ltd* [1991] BVC 834 was the first case to test this. It concerned the recovery of tax on the costs of a box at Cardiff Arms Park. This was used partly for business entertainment and partly as an office. Although succeeding on apportionment before the Tribunal, the company lost before the High Court ([1994] BVC 52). The Court decided that, where goods and services are obtained for the purpose of business entertainment, and that use is not de minimis, the law provides that the whole of the input tax is not deductible.
- *Thorn EMI plc* [1992] BVC 867 raised a similar point, but with a different result. This was in the context of a hospitality chalet at the Farnborough Airshow. The chalet was largely used as a place in which to conduct business meetings during the show. It was also, however, used at various times during the the day to provide meals and other forms of hospitality. The company argued for an allowance of a substantial part of the tax involved. It lost before the Tribunal, but won before the High Court ([1994] BVC 133), and again before the Court of Appeal ([1995] BVC 282).
- However, *BMW (GB) Ltd v C & E Commrs* [1997] BVC 400 seems to have modified this in the case of other promotional events where dealers could order, and pay for, guest tickets. The Court upheld the ruling of the Tribunal that the dealers were paying for the right to invite customers to the events rather than paying for or on behalf of their customers with the result that there was a gratuitous provision of goods and services in the form of business entertainment to those customers, with no related input VAT recovery. There was nothing artificial about splitting the single event into the supply of a right to invite guests and the provision of the facilities in a case where there were three parties and three distinguishable transactions relationships: between BMW and the dealer; BMW and the customer; and the dealer and the customer. That analysis was supported by the fact that the amount paid by the dealers was not related to the cost of the event. The Court noted that a crucial characteristic of business entertainment was that it was provided to participants free of charge

HMRC has confirmed in Notice 700/65 (February 2012) on Business Entertainment (at section 2.7) that a taxable person is only blocked from recovering that element of input tax that relates to business entertainment. The portion of the input tax that relates to non-entertainment business use (subject to the rules on partial exemption) can be recovered.

(3) Staff

Where an employer provides entertainment for the benefit of employees (e.g. as a reward for their work, support staff morale) then HMRC treat this as being for business purposes. Any VAT incurred on such entertainment is input tax, and its recovery is not blocked under the rules (see generally Notice 700/65 on Business Entertainment (February 2012)). For a time, in the case of staff entertainment, HMRC's basic rule of thumb was to treat only 50 per cent of VAT incurred on providing entertainment to staff as input tax in order to reflect the personal benefit derived. However, an appeal by *Ernst & Young* [1997] BVC 2,541, found that, where they provided entertainment to their employees, they did so for wholly business purposes and all of the VAT incurred was input tax and recoverable. This did not apply, though to entertainment solely for the benefit of partners, which was not incurred for business purposes and where the VAT was not input tax. See further at HMRC's VAT Input Tax Manual at VITM3000.

The position has been further clarified in relation to staff functions in a second appeal in *KPMG (a firm)* [1997] BVC 2,469. Input tax incurred on entertaining staff is allowed, whereas tax on that part of the cost relating to guests is not.

HMRC permit by concession where directors and partners of the business attend staff parties together with other employees that the tax is input tax and is not blocked from recovery (Notice 700/65 on Business Entertainment (February 2012) at section 3.2).

> *Practice point*
>
> It is worth bearing in mind that, in the absence of a VAT group, the relief for the entertainment of employees will only apply to people who are employees of the company incurring the cost. It will not extend, for example, to employees of:
>
> - associated companies; or
> - contractors,
>
> whose *entertainment* will potentially be caught.
>
> The most obvious way to avoid this, and the corresponding disallowance for direct tax purposes, would be for the company incurring the cost to make a charge to the associate or contractor by ensuring what is provided is no longer gratuitous.
>
> If the intention is that the company incurring the cost should eventually bear the expense, this can usually be arranged by an appropriate increase in a management or contractor's fee.

40-100 Self-supplies

If a business cannot recover all its input VAT, it may be prompted to try, if possible, to reduce the amount of tax incurred. One way of doing this is for it to undertake certain VATable activities for itself, i.e. avoiding or limiting the taxable services normally provided independently by others. This is particularly attractive for the exempt or partly exempt businesses covered by this book. However, distortion of competition or, from HMRC's viewpoint, loss of revenue can then result. To counter this, VATA 1994, s. 5(5) allows the Treasury, by Order, to create deemed self-supplies in certain limited circumstances. To date only three such Orders have been made. These cover:

- self-supplied stationery (abolished from 1 June 2002);
- self-supplied construction services (*Value Added Tax (Self-supply of Construction Services) Order* 1989 (SI 1989/472); and
- certain appropriations of new cars by motor dealers (art. 5 of the *Value Added Tax (Cars) Order* 1992 (SI 1992/3122)).

There is also a developers' self-supply charge in respect of newly constructed buildings under VATA 1994, Sch. 10, Part 2.

Construction services

The self-supply of construction services under the *Value Added Tax (Self-supply of Construction Services) Order* 1989 (SI 1989/472) will be the only real concern in the context of this book.

These can require someone constructing, extending or altering for himself any building or civil engineering work to account for output VAT where the open market value of such services is not less than £100,000. Any corresponding input VAT is then recovered or not according to the position of the person concerned under the partial exemption rules. The deemed output is not included in any figure for outputs that is used to arrive at the amount of recoverable residual input VAT in a partial exemption calculation. If the value of the self-supply is £250,000 or more, and if the building is used to make exempt supplies it may be necessary to make subsequent adjustments to the amount of input tax deducted in accordance with the capital goods scheme. See further at section 24 of HMRC's Notice 708 Buildings and Construction (November 2011), and Notice 406/2 for the Capital Goods Scheme (October 2011).

40-150 The right to recover

(1) The general idea

As explained, The recovery of input tax is central to VAT. It is what stops it being cumulative or having a cascade effect, and makes it a tax on *value added*. In the VAT Directive, the authority for this derives from art. 167 onwards (formerly art. 17 of Sixth Directive (Directive 77/388)). In particular, art. 168 provides that:

> 'In so far as the goods and services are used for the purposes of the taxed transactions of a taxable person, the taxable person shall be entitled, in the Member State in which he carries out these transactions, to deduct the following from the VAT which he is liable to pay:
>
> (a) the VAT due or paid in that Member State in respect of supplies to him of goods or services, carried out or to be carried out by another taxable person;
> (b) the VAT due in respect of transactions treated as supplies of goods or services pursuant to Article 18(a) and Article 27;
> (c) the VAT due in respect of intra-Community acquisitions of goods pursuant to Article 2(1)(b)(i);
> (d) the VAT due on transactions treated as intra-Community acquisitions in accordance with Articles 21 and 22;
> (e) the VAT due or paid in respect of the importation of goods into that Member State.'

and art. 169 (previously art. 17(3)) provides for a similar deduction in so far as the goods and services are used for the purposes of:

- taxable transactions carried out in another country;
- certain exempt, or in UK terms zero-rated, transactions connected with imports, exports and international goods traffic; and
- certain basically exempt insurance and financial transactions, when the recipient is established outside the EU or they are directly linked to exports from the EU.

In UK terms, the equivalent rules are found in VATA 1994, s. 26 and Pt. XIV and XV of the *Value Added Tax Regulations* 1995 (SI 1995/2518). These are reproduced at **Appendix 8**.

VATA 1994, s. 26, so far as it is relevant at this point, provides that:

> (1) The amount of input tax for which a taxable person is entitled to credit at the end of any period shall be so much of the input tax for the period (that is input tax on supplies,

acquisitions and importations in the period) as is allowable by or under regulations as being attributable to supplies within subsection (2) below.

(2) The supplies within this subsection are the following supplies made or to be made by the taxable person in the course or furtherance of his business-

    (a) taxable supplies;
    (b) supplies outside the United Kingdom which would be taxable supplies if made in the United Kingdom;
    (c) such other supplies outside the United Kingdom and such exempt supplies as the Treasury may by order specify for the purposes of this subsection.'

To the extent that input tax is incurred *exclusively* or *wholly* for the purposes of making either taxable or exempt supplies, there is generally a process of *direct attribution*. This results in tax relating just to taxable supplies being recovered in full; tax relating just to exempt supplies is not recovered at all. What this means is discussed at ¶40-200.

Where tax is attributable to both taxable and exempt supplies, some means of apportionment or allocation of the input tax is required. The recovery of residual input VAT is considered further at ¶40-200.

(2) What is to be included as taxable supplies

Since the recovery of input tax depends on relating it to or establishing a link with *taxable supplies*, it is important to decide exactly what you include as taxable supplies and what you do not, a subject that has been before the Courts on a number of occasions.

- In *Floridienne SA and Berginvest SA v Belgian State* (Case C-142/99) [2001] BVC 76 the issue was over the treatment of dividends and interest received by a holding company from its subsidiaries. Briefly, Floridienne was a holding company at the head of an essentially taxable chemicals group. Berginvest was an intermediate holding company in that Group heading up the plastics division. Both were, directly or indirectly, involved in the management of their respective subsidiaries, to which they made taxable supplies of administrative, accounting and IT services. They also provided inter-company loans on which interest was received and, from time-to-time, received dividends on their shares.

  Both companies habitually recovered input tax in full. However, the Belgian authorities took the view that both the dividends and interest represented exempt supplies and were to be taken into account in the standard pro-rata partial exemption calculation in the Sixth Directive (Directive 77/388), art. 17. When the matter was referred to the ECJ, however, the Court considered that the effect of art. 19(2) of the Sixth Directive (art. 174(2) of the VAT Directive) (dealing with the exclusion of the value of certain *incidental* supplies) was that:

  - dividends paid by a subsidiary to a holding company in this situation were to be excluded for total income in partial exemption calculations (see 40-200), and also that;
  - interest paid by those subsidiaries to the holding company on loans made to them could likewise be excluded, where the loan transactions did not constitute an *economic activity*.

On the face of it, the reference by the CoJ to art. 19(2) seems largely irrelevant if what was received did not represent an *economic activity*. The ruling on dividends followed the line adopted in earlier cases (*Sofitam*, for example), and the CoJ said these were *outside the scope* of VAT as they were not consideration for any supply. This reflects, of course, what has long been the view in the UK. In *Floridienne SA and Berginvest SA* the companies reinvested the dividends back in their subsidiaries as loans. There were no taxable management services. The interest on the loans was received merely as the result of ownership of an asset. VAT on related costs was accordingly non-deductible. Loans that were made merely on an occasional basis, and in a way that was akin to managing an investment portfolio by a private investor (rather than to maximise returns) were not within the scope of VAT for recovery purposes.

> ### Practice point
>
> The position with interest, is that it is normally seen as an *economic activity* (and within the scope of VAT).
>
> Generally, HMRC do not regard interest received by holding companies as *incidental*, where they provide a Group treasury function and are not grouped for VAT with their subsidiaries. In appropriate cases, therefore, it may be worth considering whether this decision in *Floridienne* can be used so as to enable intra-group interest to be disregarded in the case of a separately registered company, in order to potentially increase input VAT recovery for the VAT group, i.e. on the basis this may help to prevent non-economic activities from affecting the group's ability to recover input VAT.

- In *Trinity Mirror plc v C & E Commrs* [2001] BVC 167 the Court of Appeal held that the issue by a company of its own shares is a supply of services by that company and accordingly the input tax attributable to shares issued to EU residents was attributable to an exempt supply and thus irrecoverable. However, this has now been effectively overturned by rulings of the CoJ, which indicated that the issue, as opposed to the sale, of shares is not a supply at all. As referred to briefly at 40-000(3), the first of these decisions was that of *KapHag Renditefonds v Finanzamt Charlottenburg* (Case C-442/01) [2005] BVC 566. This was later followed by *Kretztechnik AG v Finanzamt Linz* (Case C-465/03) [2006] BVC 66. For a more detailed commentary on this see later under **Holding Companies** and also **Chapter 3**.

- In *Empresa de Desenvolvimento Mineiro SGPS SA (EDM) v Fazenda Pública (Ministério Público, intervener)* (Case C-77/01) [2006] BVC 140, the CoJ decided that transactions which were *outside the scope* of VAT because they did not represent consideration for any supply or were not economic activities (such as the issue of shares) were to be excluded from the calculation of the deductible proportion. HMRC helpfully summarises this case in its Guidance Manuals as follows:

"EDM was a holding company that provided taxable supplies to businesses in the finance sector. It also carried on treasury activities. These activities included: dividends arising from shareholdings; interest on loans; disposal of shares; and other negotiable securities and other treasury operations. The Court held that the simple acquisition and the mere sale of shares or other negotiable securities could not amount to exploitation of an asset intended to produce revenue on a continuing basis (economic activity). This was because the only consideration for those transactions consisted of a possible profit on the sale of those securities. This also applied to EDM's income from placements in investment funds. However, in this case, interest received on bank deposits or placements in securities (such as Treasury notes or certificates of deposit) was within the scope of VAT. This is because the interest arose from making capital available to third parties (an economic activity). The annual granting of interest-bearing loans by EDM to its subsidiaries was also seen as part of its economic activities [and were exempt from VAT]'

- In *Ministero dell'Economia e delle Finanze and Agenzia delle Entrate v FCE Bank plc* (Case C-210/04) [2009] BVC 692 the CoJ confirmed that:

'a fixed establishment, which is not a legal entity distinct from the company of which it forms part, established in another Member State and to which the company supplies services, should not be treated as a taxable person by reason of the costs imputed to it in respect of those supplies.'

Accordingly, any apparent inter-branch supplies are, on this basis, generally ignored. That debit notes or adjustments may be made for management accounting or tax purposes is irrelevant. This can be important, for example, for many international banks, like FCE, operating on a branch basis. There is, however, a deemed supply for intra-EU acquisitions or dispatches of goods by branches (VATA 1994, Sch. 4, para. 6 (see **Chapter 3** at ¶30-300)).

It is also worth remembering that there is a further exception for VAT groups. Transactions between members of the group (see **Chapter 2** at ¶20-250) are also not usually recognised. The VAT group is effectively treated as a single person trading through the representative member so that intra-group supplies can be disregarded as any such supply is considered to be made/ received by the representative member. This can be an important planning point, where services or facilities are provided on a group basis, but is something that needs to be accommodated when it comes to partial exemption and the calculation of the recovery of *residual* input tax (see ¶40-200 later and generally in HMRC's Notice 706 Partial Exemption (June 2011) at para. 15.1).

(3) Tax paid abroad by persons not established in the Member State

Council Directive 2006/112/EC, art. 171 (the Sixth Directive (Directive 77/388), art. 17(4)) envisages the repayment, in certain circumstances, of tax charged to persons from outside the territory of supply.

(1) In the case of businesses established within the Community, the claim is made under an electronic cross-border refund scheme under Directive 2008/9/EC: known as the European Refund Scheme (previously the refund was obtained under the Eighth VAT Directive (Directive 79/1072), which was a paper based system). This Directive has effect from 1 January 2010 and was introduced on 12 February 2008. The relevant provisions in UK law are VATA 1994, s. 39 and the *Value Added Tax Regulations* 1995 (SI 1995/2518), reg. 173–184.

(2) For businesses established outside the Community, there is the Thirteenth VAT Directive (Directive 86/560), introduced in November 1986. The relevant provisions in UK law are, again, VATA 1994, s. 39 and the *Value Added Tax Regulations* 1995 (SI 1995/2518), in this case, reg. 185–197.

For both procedures see generally HMRC's Notice 732A, Refunds of VAT in the European Community for EC and non-EC businesses (October 2011).

There are general limitations as to what may be reclaimed and, in no case, can tax be recovered on:

- exported goods (including, from 1 January 1993, goods despatched to another Member State);
- certain expenditure by tour operators for the direct benefit of travellers (e.g. block booking of hotel accommodation); or
- personal expenditure (i.e. non-business expenses).

There is also a general block on the recovery of VAT by traders with an establishment registered in the territory of refund (see below), and the possibility of some restriction on partial exemption grounds.

- In this connection, the ECJ has ruled in *Debouche v Inspecteur der Invoerrechten en Accijnzen* (Case C-302/93) [1997] BVC 332 that, if a person's activity is exempt in the state in which he is established, he cannot recover tax paid in another Member State in connection with that activity.
- *WHA Ltd; Viscount Reinsurance* was initially heard by the Tribunal in October and November 2001 ([2002] BVC 4,061), ending up in the Court of Appeal (*WHA Ltd & Anor v C & E Commrs* [2004] BVC 485) in May 2004. It concerned an unusual arrangement designed to save the cost of VAT on motor vehicle repair costs arising under MBI policies. The policies were issued by a UK insurer, which reinsured 100 per cent with one of two re-insurers based outside the EC, in Gibraltar. WHA was appointed to act as claims handler, recharging the costs, plus a fee, to the re-insurer.

WHA would instruct a garage to carry out the repairs, and the garage's services were invoiced to and paid by WHA, which was a company registered for UK VAT. The latter supplied services to the re-insurer that were exempt, but with the right to recover input tax (being within VATA 1994, Sch. 9, Grp. 2, item 4 and what is now the *Value Added Tax (Input Tax) (Specified Supplies) Order 1999* (SI 1999/3140), art. 3). This, so it was maintained, enabled the VAT on the repair costs to be recovered.

Ultimately, the Court of Appeal decided there was a supply of services by the garages to WHA (rather than to policyholders, as the Commissioners had argued), which therefore paid input tax which was, at least in principle, recoverable. However, WHA's claim against HMRC could not succeed, because it made a taxable supply of services to Viscount, the re-insurer, and had to charge output tax.

HMRC only won in part, though, because Viscount, as a re-insurer based outside the EU claimed that it was a *taxable person* in art. 4.1 of the Sixth Directive (art. 9(1) of Council Directive 2006/112/EC) and was entitled to a refund by virtue of art. 17(3)(a) and/or (c) of the Sixth Directive (art. 171 of Council Directive 2006/112/EC, and Directive 86/560, the Thirteenth Directive). The Court of Appeal agreed, allowing Viscount's claim, on the basis that reg. 186 effectively required one to assume that the foreign-based, non-taxable trader claiming repayment *was a taxable person in the UK*, when considering its claim for repayment of VAT. Accordingly, Viscount was entitled to seek a refund of the VAT which, in light of the conclusion on the second issue, it had to pay WHA. However, HMRC had also challenged the structure on the basis that it was an artificial scheme, and amounted to an abuse of rights. The Court of Appeal decided in *WHA Ltd v C & E Commrs* [2007] EWCA Civ 728; [2007] BVC 695 that, in relation to the further elements of HMRC's appeal, the scheme should be redefined due to it being abusive (in accordance with *Halifax* principles), and accordingly that the VAT repayment would not be allowed. (It is understood at the time of writing that the taxpayer's appeal in *WHA* is scheduled to be heard by the UK Supreme Court in spring 2013.)

In December 2004 the UK amended the relevant part of the VAT Regulations by the *VAT (Amendment) (No. 4) Regulations 2004* (SI 2004/3140). These altered reg. 190 by excluding in 190(c) the right to recover VAT paid or due in the UK on goods or services in so far as they are used for the purpose of insurance or financial transactions supplied to customers established outside the EU. The European Commission formally requested the UK to reverse the change, and argued that a change was necessary due to the requirements of art. 169 to 171 of the VAT Directive, and art. 2(1) of the Thirteenth Directive. The matter was referred to the CoJ, where the Court decided that the UK legislation complies with art. 2(1) of the Thirteenth Directive (and accordingly the Commission's action was dismissed) (see *European Commission v United Kingdom* (Case C-582/08) [2010] ECR I-7195).

For the purposes of the European Union Refund scheme, the claim year is based on calendar years, with a nine-month period of grace, which ends, therefore, on 30 September in the year following. For Thirteenth Directive purposes the claim year runs to 30 June, with a six-month period of grace in which claims must be made, ending on the following 31 December.

To recover VAT under these provisions, the claimant must not be registered, or liable to be registered, or have a business establishment or fixed establishment in the Member State of refund, i.e. must not *belong* in the country concerned and must also not be regarded as supplying goods or services there, other than services which are regarded as *supplied where received* (see **Chapter 3**), certain international transport services and supplies of goods where tax is accounted for by the customer under special simplification rules (see **Chapter 5**).

More recently, the ECJ has decided in *Daimler AG and Widex A/S v Skatteverket* (Cases C-318/11 and C-319/11) that, to block a refund of input tax under the European Refund Scheme, a fixed establishment must actually carry out taxable transactions in the member state in which the refund is sought and that a mere ability to carry out such transactions is insufficient. The company concerned was established in one member state and carrying out technical testing or research work in the other but not active taxable transactions. The Court's conclusion was that there needed to be active VATable transactions in the refund state to exclude input VAT recovery claims. It made no difference that each taxable person had in the refund state a wholly-owned subsidiary whose purpose was mainly to supply it with services for its testing activity.

Details of how to claim and what is involved are to be found in HMRC Notice 723A (October 2011). Copies of this Notice and the claim form, VAT 65A, for applications for refunds of VAT under the Thirteenth Directive, can be obtained from the HMRC website at www.hmrc.gov.uk.

40-200 Recovering input tax – partial exemption

It will have been seen from ¶40-150 earlier that, whilst the recovery of input tax is central to VAT, it is meant to be available *only* to the extent that it relates to taxable supplies, or to certain other supplies *specified* in the regulations. Few, if any, businesses make *only* supplies that are subject to VAT; in the industries covered by this book, it is probably safe to say that the majority of supplies are not taxable at all, but are VAT-exempt. This situation, commonly referred to as *partial exemption*, calls for some formula or arrangement for recovering the correct amount that relates to taxable supplies and other supplies that carry the right to deduct. The attribution of input VAT costs between supplies arises only when an item is a *cost component* of two supplies, namely, one taxable and one exempt.

As described in HMRC's VAT Input Guidance Manuals, the concept of a cost component as referred to in art. 1(2) of the VAT Directive is in reference to supplies which are cost components of transactions which carry the right to deduct input tax, determined by reference to commercial reality, and includes general overheads of a business. Where the costs can be matched under normal accrual principles of accountancy to output transactions (for example, written off under the amortisation policy), this can confer cost component/direct and immediate link status. General overheads are cost components of the price of the goods or services supplied by the business and therefore have a direct and immediate link with the taxable person's economic activity as a whole. Direct costs such as goods for resale, transport of those goods and selling expenses (e.g. salesmen's commissions) are generally set against the sales they relate to in a trading account leading to a gross profit. The concept of a *direct and immediate* link covers the level of connection needed between a supply received and a supply made for the former to be a cost component of the latter. It prevents any 'look through' being applied to intervening or 'chain' breaking transactions stops VAT flowing through the chain in favour of the ultimate purpose of the business involved. VAT is a transaction based tax so it is only the immediate supply to which any input is a cost component that matters rather than the ultimate purpose of a business or what the business then does with revenues generated by those supplies (*BLP Group Plc v C & E Commrs* (Case C-4/94) [1995] BVC 159). See later at 40-250(3) for a further discussion on issues in the *BAA Ltd* case concerning the existence of a *direct and immediate* link.

In general there will be a temporal link between a particular input and output to have a direct and immediate link but HMRC recognise that this will not always be the case. It is also possible for costs incurred to have a direct and immediate link with more than one supply or with one or more supplies and with the business as a whole. However, unless the supplies that the costs have a direct and immediate link with are either taxable or exempt, the costs will not be *directly attributable*.

(1) Direct attribution

Direct attribution is generally a necessary first step in any partial exemption calculation to identify the input VAT incurred. It will apply to both the Standard Method and any Special Method agreed or directed by HMRC as set out in the VAT Regulations, reg. 101 and 102 (see later). In practice, most input tax incurred by businesses is general in nature, but, before this is apportioned or divided-up, wherever possible it is expected that there will be identified:

- any VAT incurred *exclusively* in making taxable supplies or supplies covered by the *VAT (Input Tax) (Specified Supplies) Order* 1999: this can be recovered in full; and
- any incurred *exclusively* in making exempt supplies or supplies not covered by the Order; this can not be recovered at all.

For many financial or insurance sector businesses, this will not be a major issue; indeed many will find direct attribution difficult to identify and operate; and the scope for recovering VAT in full can be limited. Whether a supply received can be directly attributed is ultimately a question of fact, using the above-mentioned concepts of *direct and immediate link/cost components*.

> **Practice point**
>
> It is not uncommon to find that some Special Methods express direct attribution in terms of attributing tax *to the greatest extent possible*.
>
> This is clearly not quite the same as *exclusively*, or even *wholly*, and could arguably allow apportionment on the basis of, say, cost or management accounts and a greater potential recovery in some cases.

- *C & E Commrs v Deutsche Ruck UK Reinsurance Co Ltd* [1995] BVC 175, for instance was an example of where it can be important to be able to attribute input VAT to taxable supplies. The taxpayer was able to successfully relate tax to what were then zero-rated premiums. The tax arose on the cost of legal services relating to disputes as to the amounts payable by it as re-insurer under reinsurance contracts with persons established outside the EU. It did not matter that the contracts in this case were void.
- A more recent case where the taxpayer attempted to follow the same line as Deutsche Ruck is that of *C & E Commrs v Midland Bank plc* (Case C-98/98) [2000] BVC 229. This was over the recovery of input tax by a subsidiary of Midland and a member of its VAT group. The subsidiary, a merchant bank, had acted for an American company in a take-over of a UK quoted company. The client was really interested in the target's wholesale broking business, and, when another company expressed interest in the target, it entered into an agreement with the seller. It came to an arrangement with that company to buy just the division. The takeover went ahead, but, the purchase of the division fell through due to lack of funds.

Legal proceedings ensued, including action against Midland's subsidiary for damages for alleged negligent misrepresentation. The matter was finally settled out of Court. The same firm of lawyers had acted for Midland throughout and its argument was that the full amount of input tax was deductible, following the line in *Deutsche Ruck* given that the subsidiary was, throughout the relevant period, supplying banking and financial services to its client, a person *belonging* outside the EU. HMRC disagreed, taking the view that the tax related to the business as a whole and was *residual*.

The Tribunal agreed with Midland, but, when the matter was later referred to the CoJ by the High Court, the ruling that was given was to the effect that:

'In principle, the existence of a direct and immediate link between a particular input transaction and a particular output transaction or transactions giving rise to entitlement to deduct is necessary before the taxable person is entitled to deduct input value added tax and in order to determine the extent of such entitlement.

It is for the national court to apply the direct and immediate link test to the facts of each case before it. A taxable person who makes transactions in respect of which VAT is deductible and transactions in respect of which it is not may deduct the value added tax in respect of the goods or services acquired by him, provided that such goods or services have a direct and immediate link with the output transactions in respect of which value added tax is deductible, without it being necessary to make a distinction depending on whether the sixth VAT directive, art. 17(2), (3) or (5) is applied. However, such a taxable person cannot deduct in its entirety the value added tax charged on input services where they have been utilised not for the purpose of carrying out a deductible transaction but in the context of activities which are no more than the consequence of making such a transaction, unless that person can show by means of objective evidence that the expenditure involved in the acquisition of such services is part of the various cost components of the output transaction.'

- Direct attribution was also not required or appropriate in *Edgemond Group Ltd* [1995] BVC 627. Legal and accounting services incurred in a management buy-out were found to relate to more than just the (then, pre-*Kretztechnik*) exempt issue of shares or securities. But here the outcome depended very much on the facts and the way in which it was agreed that the services would be provided and the fees billed.
- A further example where direct attribution was important arose in *C & E Commrs v UBAF Bank Ltd* [1995] BVC 69. This concerned the recovery of VAT on the cost of acquiring shares in three other companies. Normally, one might expect the input tax in this case to be treated as *residual* or overhead input VAT. However, the companies acquired were lessors, whose businesses were immediately transferred to the bank to extend its own taxable leasing activities. On this basis, the High Court found the VAT on the related professional fees should be recovered in full, attributing the VAT to the ongoing taxable leasing.

As it happens, HMRC officially accepted they were wrong in this, following a subsequent appeal to the Court of Appeal (see *Business Brief* 7/96 of 3 May 1996).

According to HMRC's *Business Brief*, this treatment only applied to the purchaser. Any tax incurred by the seller was always to be seen as VAT on general business overheads, because the costs incurred are not used to make any supply. However, this latter statement contrasts with *Abbey National plc*.

Practice point

Input VAT incurred on the legal and other associated costs of acquiring assets as part of a going concern can sometimes be attributed to the future taxable supplies of that business and not simply included in the *residual* calculation. In other words:

- tax relating to a fully taxable business can be recovered in full;
- tax relating to a fully exempt business is not recoverable; and
- apportionment will, potentially, be required if both taxable and exempt supplies are to be made.

4 Input VAT and Partial Exemption

> Where, as in *UBAF*, there is a share acquisition and a transfer of business it could be important to ensure that all the companies concerned in the buying group are registered together for VAT, preferably from the time of acquisition. But see further on this in relation to the BAA case (at 40-250(3)).

- In *Abbey National plc v C & E Commrs* (Case C-408/98) [2001] BVC 581, the issue was whether the appellant, which was partly exempt, could reclaim all or any of the input tax incurred on the sale of a tenanted commercial property. Abbey, the representative member of a partly exempt financial services group, also had a property letting business. One of the companies in the group had a portfolio of about 75 properties, amongst which was a long lease on a property and on which the company had opted to tax (see **Chapter 8** at ¶80-150). When the property was sold as a going concern (see **Chapter 3** at ¶30-450), Abbey sought to reclaim all the input tax on related lawyers' fees on the basis that it was *directly attributed* to the sale of (or a part of) a taxable business. The sale itself was not actually a supply, of course, due to art. 5 of the *Value Added Tax (Special Provisions) Order* 1995 (SI 1995/1268).

Following their stated practice, HMRC said the input tax was *residual* and also argued that, as the sale of the property was not a taxable supply (or a supply), no input tax at all could be deducted!

The Tribunal agreed with HMRC, but the matter was subsequently referred to the CoJ, where Advocate General Jacobs came down in favour of Abbey, remarking:

> 'However, in the light of the conclusion which I have reached with regard to the transfer of a totality of assets, I think those apparent complexities may be seen to dissipate. To the extent that the VAT on services related to the transfer is deductible, it is because it is attributable to – because there is a direct and immediate link with – supplies made by the part of the business whose assets are transferred. Thus, if those supplies are all taxable, it will be deductible in full, and there will be no need to look any further. Apportionment will come into play if the supplies are partly taxable and partly exempt.'

This view was eventually confirmed by the CoJ when it issued its judgment on 22 February 2001.

- In *C & E Commrs v Trustees for R & R Pension Fund* [1996] BVC 348, the issue was whether the appellants were entitled to a revised initial input tax credit on the development of property where the option to tax was exercised after the grant of a lease. HMRC maintained they could not because the land was within the capital goods scheme (see ¶40-200(7)). If the land had not been within this scheme they would have agreed some revised initial attribution of input tax. Initially the Tribunal, ([1996] BVC 2,578), decided there was no reason why the Commissioners should not agree a revised initial attribution of input tax in lieu of the capital goods scheme. However, the High Court later reversed this. HMRC were obliged to apply the capital goods scheme and were entitled to grant the option subject to its application. It was not open to HMRC to approve arrangements, which overrode the scheme. It was also not open to them to accept as fair and reasonable a result different from that which the law had provided in introducing the scheme, which was binding on the taxpayer.
- Another appeal in relation to property, *AA Insurance Services Ltd* [1999] BVC 2,330, concerned a claim for the direct attribution of input tax to a taxable supply on the

surrender of a lease. The AA, as tenant of the property, could only surrender on payment of £120,000, plus VAT. It wasn't paid for the surrender, but the AA claimed, notwithstanding, that there were two supplies on the surrender:

- the first by the landlord in agreeing to give up its rights;
- the second by them in supplying the legal surrender of their interest.

The AA argued that both were taxable and that the VAT on the £120,000 was attributable to the supply by them.

Unfortunately, in the absence of any indication of consideration passing from the landlord to the AA, the Tribunal saw no supply to which the VAT could be attributed other than those arising in the ordinary course of the company's insurance business and for which the building had been occupied.

- The *Dial-a-Phone Ltd v C & E Commrs* [2004] BVC 640 appeal was an attempt by a company selling mobile phones and accessories and arranging related insurance to argue the input tax incurred by it on certain marketing and advertising costs was attributable just to its taxable supplies of airtime and network commissions; not, in part, to the commission received for selling the insurance.

The case went to the Court of Appeal, Dial-a-phone losing at each stage. The words *attributable* and *attributed* in reg. 101 of the *VAT Regulations* 1995 fell to be interpreted by reference to art. 2 of the First Directive and art. 17 of the Sixth Directive (art. 173 of the VAT Directive). The appropriate test of attributability in this context was the *direct and immediate link/cost component* test and the quest for that link was not for the *closest* but for a *sufficient* link and it mattered not that the insurance commissions might be, in a sense, secondary.

- A further example is provided by the Court of Justice decision in *Skatteverket v AB SKF* (Case C-29/08: 29 October 2009) [2011] BVC 359 which involved SKF, a parent of an industrial group, which carried on activities in several countries. SKF had an active role in the management of its subsidiaries and made supplies to them in respect of management, administration and marketing services. SKF intended to restructure its group, and also to dispose of the business of one of its subsidiaries (to be effected by a share sale). The purpose of the disposals was to fund activities of the wider group. SKF sought to deduct input VAT on the supplies of services acquired as part of the disposal of shares in the subsidiary (and another controlled company which was also being sold). The question arose as to whether there can be a right to deduct for expenditure directly attributable to the disposal transaction in the same way as there is for general costs. The CoJ held that it is for the referring court of the Member State to take account of all the circumstances surrounding the transactions in issue and to determine whether the costs incurred are likely to be incorporated in the price of the shares sold or whether they are among only the cost components of transactions within the scope of the taxable person's economic activities. The Court provided the following guidance (at para. 57):

"According to settled case-law, the existence of a direct and immediate link between a particular input transaction and a particular output transaction or transactions giving rise to entitlement to deduct is, in principle, necessary before the taxable person is entitled to deduct input VAT and in order to determine the extent of such entitlement (see Case C-98/98 Midland Bank [2000]

ECR I-4177, paragraph 24; Abbey National , paragraph 26; and Investrand , paragraph 23). The right to deduct VAT charged on the acquisition of input goods or services presupposes that the expenditure incurred in acquiring them was a component of the cost of the output transactions that gave rise to the right to deduct (see Cibo Participations , paragraph 31; Kretztechnik , paragraph 35; Investrand , paragraph 23; and Securenta , paragraph 27).

It is, however, also accepted that a taxable person has a right to deduct even where there is no direct and immediate link between a particular input transaction and an output transaction or transactions giving rise to the right to deduct, where the costs of the services in question are part of his general costs and are, as such, components of the price of the goods or services which he supplies. Such costs do have a direct and immediate link with the taxable person's economic activity as a whole (see, inter alia, Midland Bank , paragraphs 23 and 31; Abbey National , paragraph 35; Kretztechnik , paragraph 36; and Investrand , paragraph 24).

On the other hand, where goods or services acquired by a taxable person are used for purposes of transactions that are exempt or do not fall within the scope of VAT, no output tax can be collected or input tax deducted (see, to that effect, Case C-184/04 Uudenkaupungin kaupunki [2006] ECR I-3039, paragraph 24; Case C-72/05 Wollny [2006] ECR I-8297, paragraph 20; and Case C-515/07 Vereniging Noordelijke Land- en Tuinbouw Organisatie [2009] ECR I-0000, paragraph 28).

It follows that whether there is a right to deduct is determined by the nature of the output transactions to which the input transactions are assigned. Accordingly, there is a right to deduct when the input transaction subject to VAT has a direct and immediate link with one or more output transactions giving rise to the right to deduct. If that is not the case, it is necessary to examine whether the costs incurred to acquire the input goods or services are part of the general costs linked to the taxable person's overall economic activity. In either case, whether there is a direct and immediate link will depend on whether the cost of the input services is incorporated either in the cost of particular output transactions or in the cost of goods or services supplied by the taxable person as part of his economic activities.

In the present case, the referring court describes the costs linked to the services acquired by SKF, first, as "directly attributable" to the disposal of shares and, second, as forming part of the general costs associated with SKF's overall economic activities.

In that regard, it must be held that it is not possible from the case-file submitted to the Court to determine whether those costs have a direct and immediate link, within the meaning of the case-law cited in paragraphs 57 and 58 of this judgment, with the envisaged share disposals or with SKF's overall economic activity, given that, according to the referring court, the purpose of those transactions was to secure funds to finance other activities of the group. In order to establish whether there is such a direct and immediate link, it is necessary to ascertain whether the costs incurred are likely to be incorporated in the prices of the shares which SKF intends to sell or whether they are only among the cost components of SKF's products.'

HMRC's policy in relation to *SKF* is that transfers of existing shares for a consideration are exempt supplies within Sch. 9 of VATA 1994 provided that the supplies occur in the course of business activity, i.e. more than a mere sale of services as in *Empresa* (see HMRC's VAT Input Tax Manual at VIT 64050). However, in such cases, the input VAT that relates to the transfer will be exempt input tax and only recoverable to the extent that the shares have been sold to purchasers outside the European Union (see 40-200(3)(6)). There is no recovery of VAT in respect of transfers of existing shares which are not part of an economic activity.

- In *Skipton Building Society* [2009] UKFTT 191; [2010] TC 00146 the Tribunal decided that input VAT attributable to advertising costs was not directly attributable to the sale of houses since the advertising referred to mortgage services (exempt for VAT purposes). The facts of the case were that the Skipton Building Society, was the representative member of a VAT group of which its subsidiaries were also members. The VAT group made both taxable and exempt supplies, with the result that it was treated as a partially exempt trader. One of the activities carried on by the subsidiaries was residential estate agency. The issue arose as to whether the VAT incurred by Skipton's estate agency subsidiaries on the cost of advertisements placed in local newspapers was wholly attributable to the sales of the properties advertised and therefore recoverable in full. HMRC argued that the VAT costs were partially attributable to the exempt services which the group supplied so that it had to be treated as residual input tax for the purposes of the special method agreed with the taxpayer under reg. 102 of the *Value Added Tax Regulations 1995*. The tribunal decided that input tax was not fully recoverable to the extent that advertisements mentioned the availability of mortgage services. The tribunal commented 'in those cases in which the "strap line", even if briefly, mentioned mortgage services the input tax incurred must be regarded as a cost component of both taxable and exempt supplies, and was therefore residual' (at para. 26 of the judgment).

Direct attribution does not, of course, just apply to taxable supplies. However difficult or inconvenient it may sometimes be, it is still something that is expected to be done to the extent that input tax is incurred on costs relating specifically to exempt supplies. Where, for example, a lender incurs legal fees in establishing a charge over assets to secure an advance the tax will generally be expected by HMRC to be irrecoverable. But whether this is ultimately borne as an expense is another matter. Often, the expense will be charged to the borrower (see *Indemnity situations* at ¶40-000), so that the VAT cost can then be recouped by ensuring the reimbursement is for the full VAT-inclusive amount.

Other cases where direct attribution has featured are referred to under *Residual input tax* below. See also further in HMRC's Partial Exemption Guidance Manual, particularly pages PE1250 and PE1300, on the meaning of attribution and on attribution of case law.

(2) Residual input tax – the general idea

Residual input tax, i.e. VAT attributable to both transactions on which it is deductible and to transactions on which it is not will, in practice, make up most of the input tax businesses incur. Residual input tax represents VAT incurred on business overheads, which support both exempt and taxable supplies (such as information technology, rent, service charges, heat, light, etc.). How the recoverable amount is calculated or arrived at is discussed at (3) later. In the meantime, going on from direct attribution earlier at (1), it is useful to look further at what should, or should not, be included.

- *Capital One Bank (Europe) plc* [2006] BVC 2,148 and *MBNA Europe Bank Ltd v R & C Commrs* [2006] EWHC; [2007] BVC 3 were two interesting cases on very similar points, Both concerned the securitisation of credit card receivables, involving their assignment to a company outside the EU. If this amounted to a supply, for VAT, potentially, it would be *outside the scope with recovery* as a result of the *VAT (Input Tax)(Specified Supplies) Order* (see below) and, if it could be included in the numerator and denominator of the calculation of residual input tax, the recovery percentage would significantly increase. There were subsidiary issues of the valuation of any supply, whether any such supply was *incidental* (and to be disregarded) and of the effect of other, related, income from cardholders.

In both appeals at the Tribunal stage, the assignment of the receivables was held not to constitute a supply within the meaning of art. 4(2) of the Sixth Directive (art. 9.1 of the VAT Directive) or VATA 1994, s. 5(2), but to amount to no more than the granting of security for a loan. As such, there was nothing on that account to include. The other income, could not, however, be ignored.

Later, in *MBNA*, the High Court also decided there was no supply on the assignment, but for a different reason. However, it also held that, where a single business activity constituted the supply of a service to two different persons who each paid separately for what they had received, there was no reason why the inputs incurred in the carrying out of that single activity should have been solely attributable to the supply to the one of them.

The matter was therefore remitted to the Tribunal for reconsideration.

- In *Britannia Building Society* [1997] BVC 4,106 the case concerned the input tax incurred on four advertisements produced as part of a corporate plan to increase market share and establish a new corporate identity. They featured discussions of Britannia's services including mortgages, investment products, saving and domestic products appropriate to first time buyers, but no reference was made to any specific type of product or service. HMRC maintained the tax should be treated as wholly attributable to the making of exempt supplies, i.e. the advertising of financial products and that the correct test was to establish whether there was a *direct and immediate link*, viewed from an objective standpoint, between the input tax incurred and the making of taxable supplies. Without such a link, there was no right of deduction at all: it was not sufficient to show that the appellant's business, taken as a whole, benefited from the supplies if the cost components of the commercials were *direct cost components* of the exempt supplies.

  Britannia argued there was no specific supply for which the services were used; it was continually making both taxable and exempt supplies and it was permissible to look at the *long-term* purpose of the supply, where there was some intervening activity, which was not a supply, to which the tax should be attributed. The cost of making the advertisements had been a cost-component for all its divisions, including one making taxable supplies and others making a mixture of taxable and exempt supplies. The Tribunal agreed and the input tax was accordingly *residual* and recoverable in accordance with the appellant's agreed Special Method.

- The *Dial-a-Phone Ltd v C & E Commrs* appeal (*see* **Direct Attribution** above) came to essentially the same conclusions over the recovery by a mobile phone supplier of the input tax incurred by it on certain marketing and advertising costs, which it argued should not be attributed, even in part, to insurance commissions received.
- Another case where the input tax was residual was that of *Halifax plc* [2001] BVC 2,029, although this was not what the taxpayer wanted. Halifax incurred considerable expenditure on stationery from third-party suppliers. Initially, this was treated in its partial exemption calculations as *residual*. However, some of what it bought became obsolete or out-of-date

and was scrapped, being sold to scrap-paper merchants in return for an undertaking that it would be destroyed.

This disposal constituted a taxable supply of goods and, prompted by the earlier *Nationwide Building Society* case (an appeal over the self-supply of stationery rules), Halifax tried to argue that the proportion of the original VAT incurred should, at that stage, be attributed to that taxable supply and allowed in full, using the change-of-use rules in the *Value Added Tax Regulations* 1995 (SI 1995/2518), reg. 109.

Unfortunately, HMRC disagreed, as did the Tribunal.

The starting point was the initial purchase of the stationery. The example given at the hearing was a quantity of 150,000 identical forms. In VAT terms, this was a single supply, which was then put to exempt or partly exempt use. It was not 150,000 separate supplies some of which were not so put. As noted earlier at ¶40-100, the rules for self-supplied stationery were abolished from 1 June 2002.

- *Svenska International plc v C & E Commrs* [1999] BVC 221, referred to earlier in **Chapter 3** at ¶30-350, was a further case where a change in intention arose. This was about continuous supplies of management services supplied by a UK subsidiary of a Swedish bank to the London branch of its parent. The branch, which was partly exempt, later became part of a VAT group with the bank, but in the meantime, the bank provisionally attributed the VAT on the underlying costs directly to the intended taxable management charges. These, in the event, never materialised as payment was received after grouping occurred, with the result that the House of Lords dismissed *Svenska's* appeal.
- In *Garsington Opera Ltd* (LON/2008/0449); [2009] TC 00045 the First-Tier Tribunal was asked to consider whether VAT incurred by Garsington Opera on the production costs of its operatic performances could be recovered. The issue was whether the input VAT due on the productions costs were attributable exclusively to Garsington Opera's exempt supplies of tickets giving admission to the performances (such supplies falling within VATA 1994, Sch 9, Group 13). Garsington Opera argued that the goods and services used by it, which incurred input VAT, were attributable to making both exempt supplies of tickets and taxable supplies in the form of grants of sponsorship rights to sponsors (e.g. an agreement with the Barbican required Garsington Opera to deliver a Mozart opera production, semi-staged on an agreed date). The Tribunal agreed with Garsington Opera that the input VAT was partly deductible (residual) because the production costs had a direct and immediate link not only to exempt admissions, but also to taxable supplies such as the corporate sponsorship and touring (supplies of the production to an outside concert hall), programmes, CDs, intellectual property rights and the occasional supplies of production props and equipment. In relation to the specific facts, the Tribunal commented (at para. 29) that:

"Without recourse to the authorities, domestic and ECJ, our reaction to HMRC's case is that it must be wrong. The goods and services on which VAT was charged were obtained and used in the creation of the three opera productions for public performance. The grants of sponsorship rights were one means by which Garsington Opera exploited those productions for reward; other means of exploitation included the sales of tickets and the agreements to present the semi-staged performances at the Barbican. Each of those means of exploitation involved supplies by Garsington Opera. The relevant goods and services supplied to Garsington Opera, ie the production inputs, are essential ingredients in each onward supply; they are costs components of such supplies. No other use made by Garsington Opera of those supplies and no other supply of Garsington Opera has severed the connection between the production inputs and Garsington Opera's onward supplies to sponsors of their guaranteed priority rights to purchase tickets.'

The Tribunal commented (at para. 31) that 'Where that partially exempt taxpayer makes use of the input both for his taxable and his exempt transactions (as Garsington Opera have in the present circumstances) the tax on the input falls to be apportioned. An input is, according to the CoJ's jurisprudence, used for the purposes of a trader's taxable transactions if there is a "direct and immediate link between the input and the output". The test is sometimes expressed as an inquiry into whether the input is a "cost component" of the output. See *BLP Group Plc v C & E Commrs* (Case C-4/94) [1995] BVC 159' (on this case see later in **Chapter 11** at ¶110-100 and ¶110-200). The Tribunal's approach in applying the law to the factual circumstances is illustrative of the degree of connection which should exist in order to ensure that input VAT costs will not be attributed exclusively to exempt supplies (see para. 33 to 34 of the judgment):

> "Here the inputs in question are the production inputs. The inference is, we think, irresistible that these were sufficiently linked to the relevant outputs. The evidence from Garsington Opera's budgets and management accounts which formed the basis of its board decisions demonstrates a business objective to assemble the three operas for the season in question and to meet the costs by sales of sponsorship rights and of tickets. Then, as we have already observed, Garsington Opera gives a commitment to each sponsor to stage the three operas for the season and in doing so to bear the costs of the production inputs. Every production input is obtained by Garsington Opera for the purpose of making it an ingredient in an opera production that, as a component part of a summer season, becomes the subject of exploitation by Garsington Opera in the course of its business. Another linking factor is that the sponsors obtain the first of their benefits derived from Garsington Opera's expenditure on production inputs (most of which has yet to incurred) at the point of time when they buy the right to acquire tickets for the season's productions. Those factors show that the production inputs and the grants of sponsorship rights are two inseverable parts of a single business process. The link between them is sufficient to satisfy the direct and immediate test.
>
> It will then be seen that no transaction breaks the chain between Garsington Opera's receipt of the supplies of production inputs and its onward supplies of rights to purchase tickets to the sponsors. The production inputs are put together by the opera's director and others into the season's operas. The first transactions that operate as onward supplies are, as we have just observed, the grants of sponsorship rights. In the run up to the 2006 season those were completed at or shortly after the end of 2005. The sponsors then exercised their rights to buy tickets. Only after that were the unsold tickets put on sale and made the subject-matter of exempt supplies. It follows that the chains starting with the supplies to Garsington Opera of the production inputs were not broken by any exempt supplies. Nor, to use the expressions of Advocate General Saggio in paragraph 29 of his opinion in *Midland Bank Plc v C & E Commrs* (C-98/98) [2001] BVC 229, will any third transaction have broken the "causal chain" so as to sever the "particularly close link" of a "direct" and "immediate" nature between production input and the supply of sponsorship rights. Even if the sequence of events had been different, the unbroken causal chain between production inputs and taxable supplies of sponsorship rights would still exist because the exploitation of the season's operas through sales of sponsorship rights and sales of tickets was Garsington Opera's business objective.'

HMRC did not appeal the Tribunal's decision, and issued Business Brief 65/09 (VAT deduction by theatres on production costs) to reflect their change in policy following the decision.

(3) Residual input tax – the Standard Method

This is what, intentionally, is the default Method and the one which will, in practice apply to most businesses, although not, as it happens, necessarily to the businesses in the sectors covered by this book. For HMRC's application of the standard method see generally their Partial Exemption manual (PE1000).

(a) The Directive

In Community law, the recovery of *residual input tax*, i.e. VAT that is attributable to both taxable and exempt supplies, is found in art. 173 and 174 of the VAT Directive. Article 173 (previously art. 17(5) of the Sixth Directive) provides:

(1) In the case of goods or services used by a taxable person both for transactions in respect of which VAT is deductible pursuant to Articles 168, 169 and 170, and for transactions in respect of which VAT is not deductible, only such proportion of the VAT as is attributable to the former transactions shall be deductible.

The deductible proportion shall be determined, in accordance with Articles 174 and 175, for all the transactions carried out by the taxable person.'

and art. 174:

(1) The deductible proportion shall be made up of a fraction comprising the following amounts:

   (a) as numerator, the total amount, exclusive of VAT, of turnover per year attributable to transactions in respect of which VAT is deductible pursuant to Articles 168 and 169;
   (b) as denominator, the total amount, exclusive of VAT, of turnover per year attributable to transactions included in the numerator and to transactions in respect of which VAT is not deductible.

Member States may include in the denominator the amount of subsidies, other than those directly linked to the price of supplies of goods or services referred to in Article 73.'

Thus, you have a simple arithmetic formula to determine a recoverable percentage of residual input VAT:

$$\frac{\text{value of taxable supplies (excluding VAT)}}{\text{value of total supplies (excluding VAT)}} \times 100$$

with art. 174(2) going on to provide a derogation from para. 1, by excluding from the calculation the value of certain incidental financial and property supplies (see later at 40-200(3)(c)).

Article 173(2) permits Member States to adopt alternative arrangements, discussed later in the context of Special Methods.

(b) The VAT Regulations

The Standard Method in the UK (introduced by s. 26(3) of VATA 1994) does not specifically follow that in the Directive, however. The rules in this case (*Value Added Tax Regulations* 1995 (SI 1995/2518), reg. 101) require the input VAT that a person is entitled to deduct (i.e. other

4 Input VAT and Partial Exemption

than that which is blocked, see ¶40-050) to be attributed to taxable supplies in a particular way though the scope of the Standard Method has been widened by HMRC as from 1 April 2009 (see HMRC's Partial Exemption Manual at PE1355 for further details of these changes). Specifically, reg. 101(2) (as amended) provides, subject to certain exceptions discussed below (attribution of input VAT to investment gold is dealt with separately under reg. 103A):

'... in respect of any prescribed accounting period [e.g. VAT quarter or month] -

(a) goods imported or acquired by and goods or services supplied to, the taxable person in the period shall be identified,
(b) there shall be attributed to taxable supplies the whole of the input tax on such of those goods or services as are used or to be used by him exclusively in making taxable supplies,
(c) no part of the input tax on such of those goods or services as are used or to be used by him *exclusively* in making exempt supplies, or in carrying on any activity other than the making of taxable supplies, shall be attributed to taxable supplies,
(d) where a taxable person does not have an immediately preceding longer period and subject to paragraph (e) below, there shall be attributed to taxable supplies such proportion of the residual input tax as bears the same ratio to the total of such input tax as the value of taxable supplies made by him bears to the value of all supplies made by him in the period,
(e) the attribution required by subparagraph (d) above may be made on the basis of the extent to which the goods or services are used or to be used by him in making taxable supplies,
(f) where a taxable person has an immediately preceding longer period and subject to subparagraph (g) below, his residual input tax shall be attributed to taxable supplies by reference to the percentage recovery rate for that immediately preceding longer period, and
(g) the attribution required by subparagraph (f) above may be made using the calculation specified in subparagraph (d) above provided that that calculation is used for all the prescribed accounting periods which fall within any longer period applicable to a taxable person.'

In other words you:

- identify sources of taxable and exempt outputs;
- quantify any input tax *exclusively* used in making taxable supplies; this can be recovered in full;
- quantify any input tax again, *exclusively* used in making exempt supplies or in any activity which does not result in the making of taxable supplies; this cannot be recovered at all;
- quantify any residual input tax as bears the same ratio to the total of such input tax as the value of taxable supplies made by him bears to the value of all supplies made by him in the period so that a proportion of the input VAT can be attributed to taxable supplies. For this purpose 'residual input tax' means input tax incurred by a taxable person on goods or services which are used or to be used by him in making both taxable and exempt supplies: (*Value Added Tax Regulations* 1995 (SI 1995/2518), reg. 101(10)). The requirement of reg. 101(2)(d) is that the Standard Method for deduction of input tax must reflect the use of a relevant asset in making a supply. In *R & C Commrs v London Clubs Management Ltd* [2011] EWCA Civ 1323; [2011] BVC 406 the Court of Appeal commented in the context of the standard method and the necessity to assess the use of an asset in making a supply that '[t]he assessment must be of the real economic use of the asset, that is to say having regard to economic reality, in the light of the observable terms and features of the taxpayer's business' (see para. 34 of the judgment).

The recovery percentages determined by reg. 101(2)(d), (e) or (g) must be expressed as a percentage and, if that percentage is not a whole number it must be rounded up in accordance with the requirements of reg. 101(5), which provides:

"The percentage shall be rounded up-

(a) where in any prescribed accounting period or longer period which is applied the amount of input tax which is available for attribution under paragraph 2(d), (e) or (g) above prior to any such attribution being made does not amount to more than £400,000 per month on average, to the next whole number, and (b) in any other case, to two decimal places.'

The effect of reg. 101(2)(f) and (g) above is to provide an in-year recovery rate, which is optional. The affect is that a taxable person uses its previous year's recovery percentage to determine their provisional recovery of residual input tax in each period. This is then finalised by way of an annual adjustment. The finalised annual recovery percentage is then used as the provisional recovery percentage for the next year and so on, saving the need to calculate separate recovery percentages for each period. However, to use this option the taxable person must have been required to carry out an annual adjustment in a previous year (otherwise the taxable person will not have an annual adjustment recovery percentage). A taxable person may continue to operate without adopting the approach permitted under (f) and so calculate separate recovery percentages for each of its VAT returns. There is no need to notify HMRC. However, the only condition is that a business must consistently apply either the new rules or the old rules in any given tax year.

The Standard Method calculation looks much like the corresponding VAT Directive provisions. As from 1 April 2009, taxable supplies in the context of reg. 101 are taken to mean not only supplies where the place of supply for VAT is in the UK, but also supplies of a description falling within reg. 103 (reg. 101(7)). The type of supplies mentioned in reg. 103 are (a) supplies outside the UK which would be taxable supplies if made in the UK, or (b) supplies specified in an Order under s. 26(2)(c) of VATA 1994, other than supplies of a description falling within reg. 103A (i.e. supplies of investment gold). The Order made under s. 26(2)(c) of VATA 1994 is the *VAT (Input Tax) (Specified Supplies) Order* 1999 (SI 1999/3121), and the services specified are those (i) which are supplied to a person who belongs outside the member States; (ii) which are directly linked to the export of goods to a place outside the member States; or (iii) which consist of the provision of intermediary services within the meaning of item 4 of Group 2, or item 5 of Group 5, of Schedule 9 to the VATA 1994; and in relation to any transaction specified in paragraph (i) or (ii) above, provided the supply is exempt, or would have been exempt if made in the United Kingdom, by virtue of any item of Group 2, or any of items 1 to 6 and item 8 of Group 5, of Sch. 9 to VATA 1994 (broadly, certain financial and insurance transactions to non-EC customers).

For non-UK supplies, to the extent they are not included under reg. 101, the recovery of related input VAT is dealt with separately by provisions in the special rules in reg. 103.

Initially, as has been seen, there is an emphasis in the Standard Method on direct attribution discussed at (1) earlier. In most businesses, however, the majority of input VAT is on overheads or administration. This is clearly not capable of being *directly* or *exclusively* attributed to

4 Input VAT and Partial Exemption

any particular supplies. This residue, commonly referred to as the *pot*, must then be divided between:

- taxable activities; and
- exempt activities and non-supplies if relating to an economic activity (unless to be excluded, e.g. TOGC transactions or issue of new shares to raise capital).

Only that attributable to taxable supplies is then recovered (*Value Added Tax Regulations* 1995 (SI 1995/2518) reg. 101(2)(d)). In the present regulations this is achieved by a pro rata calculation based on the respective values (see **Chapter 3** at ¶30-500) of taxable and exempt supplies. In other words, by the formula:

$$\frac{\text{value of taxable supplies in the period (excluding VAT)}}{\text{value of all supplies in the period (excluding VAT)}} \times 100$$

This gives the claimable percentage of non-attributable input tax.

The following supplies are excluded from the values-based calculation (see 40-200(5)(c) below) (reg. 101(3)(e)) but the realted input tax for these supplies is otherwise recovered on a 'use' basis (reg. 101(8)):

(i) Supplies falling within either item 1 or item 6 of Group 5 of Schedule 9 to the Act (i.e. mainly supplies of financial instruments, such as shares and bonds); or

(ii) supplies made from an establishment situated outside the United Kingdom.

In relation to these particular supplies, reg. 101(8) provides that input tax on goods or services acquired by or supplied to a taxable person which are used or to be used by him in whole or in part in making such supplies shall, whether the supply in question is made within or outside the United Kingdom, be attributed to taxable supplies on the basis of the extent to which the goods or services are used or to be used by him in making taxable supplies (including those *foreign* and *specified* supplies which carry the right to deduct). In other words, input tax relating to such supplies within reg. 101(8) are ring-fenced and subject to recovery on the basis of their use. All remaining input VAT is recovered by reference to the values-based calculation, unless the taxpayer opts to use a 'use-based' approach.

The standard method under paragraph (e) of reg. 102(2) allows the taxable person to adopt a use-based approach in the calculation of input VAT available for deduction. HMRC Notice 706 (Partial Exemption: June 2011) provides the following guidance in the application of sub-paragraph (e):

> "Sometimes the standard method will not produce a fair and reasonable result for new businesses in the early periods although it will when the businesses are fully up and running. Those businesses are able to use an alternative calculation without permission from HMRC, saving the need for a new partly exempt business to seek approval of a special method. This calculation can be adopted:
>
> During your "registration period"'. This is the period running from the date you were first registered for VAT to the day before the start of your first tax year (normally 31 March, 30 April or 31 May depending on the periods covered by your VAT returns).

During your first tax year (normally the first period of 12 months commencing on 1 April, 1 May or 1 June following the end of your registration period) provided you did not incur input tax relating to exempt supplies during your registration period.

During any tax year, provided you did not incur input tax relating to exempt supplies in your previous tax year.

Once this period has expired, you must revert to using the normal "standard method" calculation based on the values of your supplies.

This change is optional and you may still recover input tax using the normal "standard method"calculation based on the values of your supplies (unless you have incurred input tax relating to supplies of financial instruments or make supplies from an establishment located outside the UK ...) or seek approval of a special method if you prefer.'

The input tax which is initially claimed is done on a provisional basis (reg. 101(1)). The amount claimed is reviewed, typically at the end of each year (known as the annual adjustment) in order to reflect any seasonal variations in supplies (e.g. a change in the value of supplies or the amount of input VAT incurred). The adjustment is made under reg. 107. See generally on annual adjustments in Notice 706 Partial Exemption (June 2011), at section 12

(c) The exclusion for certain categories of supplies

For the purpose of the Standard Method certain supplies are normally disregarded where they are *incidental* to the business concerned so not a separate supply in their own right and would distort this simple pro-rata calculation. In the VAT Directive, the authority is in art. 174(2) and, in the UK, reg. 101(3) of the *VAT Regulations* 1995. This requires the exclusion of:

(1) Any sum receivable by the taxable person in respect of any supply of capital goods (not restricted to those within the Capital Goods Scheme) used by him for the purposes of the business, e.g. the sale proceeds of fixed assets such as plant and machinery, or a painting in the boardroom.

(2) Any sum receivable by the taxable person which is *incidental* to business activities (i.e. the receipt is a minor or subordinate activity that is not a part of the normal business activity, with only slight use of residual input tax), and which is in respect of:

   (a) any supply of a description falling within either item 1 or item 6 of Group 5, Sch 9 VATA (such as interest received on a bank account);

   (b) any other financial transaction;

   (c) any real estate transaction (see **Chapter 8** at ¶80-350(8)): for this purpose a 'real estate transaction' includes any grant, assignment (including any transfer, disposition or sale), surrender or reverse surrender of any interest in, right over or licence to occupy land (reg. 101(7)).

   For further details on the meaning of *incidental supplies* and relevant case law see HMRC's Partial Exemption Guidance Manual at PE1400.

(3) That part of the value of certain supplies of goods on which output tax is not chargeable unless the taxable person has imported, acquired or been supplied with the goods for the purpose of selling them. This will generally exclude, for example, the selling price of any motor car used in the business where the input VAT has been blocked (see ¶40-050). This will only be included to the extent that the car is sold at a profit over original cost.

(4) The value of any deemed self-supplies. This will include, for example:
   (a) a supply resulting from the acquisition of a going concern by a partly exempt VAT group (see **Chapter 3** at ¶30-450);
   (b) the value of any imported services to which the reverse charge applies (see **Chapter 5**); and
   (c) certain self-supplied construction and development services (see ¶40-100).

(5) Supplies falling within reg.101(8), which provides as follows:

"input tax incurred on goods or services acquired by or supplied to a taxable person which are used or to be used by him in whole or in part in making:

   (a) supplies falling within either item 1 or item 6 of Group 5 of Schedule 9 to the Act; or
   (b) supplies made from an establishment situated outside the United Kingdom,

shall, whether the supply in question is made within or outside the United Kingdom, be attributed to taxable supplies on the basis of the extent to which the goods or services are used or to be used by him in making taxable supplies.'

Prior to 1 April 2009, all 'foreign' and 'specified' supplies were dealt with outside the standard method. However, from 1 April 2009 the only supplies dealt with outside of the Standard Method are supplies of financial instruments and supplies from establishments located outside the UK (and in relation to which, the input VAT on such supplies is recovered on the basis of use, as discussed earlier and later at 40-200(6)).

Also left out on general principles are:

(1) The value of any goods or services not supplied in the course of business.
(2) The value of any goods or services provided as a business transaction which is neither a taxable nor an exempt supply, e.g.:
   (a) the transfer of goods by a UK head office or branch to a place of business of the same legal entity abroad or a corresponding charge for services;
   (b) the transfer of business assets as a going concern satisfying the requirements of art. 5 of the *Value Added Tax (Special Provisions) Order* 1992 (SI 1992/3129) (see **Chapter 3** at ¶30-450).

As already mentioned, any input VAT, which is never recoverable (e.g. on certain car transactions and business entertainment) (see ¶40-050), must be excluded altogether. So too must any VAT incurred wholly for non-business purposes, which is, by definition not input VAT in the first place (VATA 1994, s. 24(1)). This will include, if necessary, any VAT disallowed as attributable to luxuries, amusements or entertainments (see ¶40-000).

There is also the *Standard Method Override*.

(4) The Standard Method Override

From 18 April 2002, there have been special rules targeted primarily on aggressive VAT avoidance by large businesses that use the Standard Method. Fully taxable businesses and partly exempt businesses using a Special Method are not affected; nor are the vast majority of businesses for whom the Standard Method produces a fair and reasonable result. HMRC said at the time that, other than avoiders, very few businesses were required to make an adjustment, and those that were would be as likely to benefit as to lose. They were covered in a special VAT Information Sheet 04/02. Businesses are only subject to the override rule if (reg. 107A of the *VAT Regulations* 1995):

- they are partly exempt and use the Standard Method; *and*
- their residual input tax is more than £50,000 per year (£25,000 per year for group undertakings not members of the same VAT group) or pro rata for periods of less than a year; and
- the Standard Method does not give a fair and reasonable reflection of use.

Even then, they only have to make an adjustment if there is a *substantial* difference between the input tax deducted and the amount deductible, given the extent to which their purchases are used in making taxable supplies. *Substantial* in this context means more than (reg. 107C):

- £50,000; or
- 50 per cent of the residual input tax incurred and £25,000.

The adjustment, based on the use, or intended use, of the purchases on which the input tax is incurred, is made only once a year, and not in each VAT period. There are special provisions governing companies, which are members of a group.

> ### Practice point
> A values-basis for apportioning residual input VAT has its attractions, for example:
> - it is generally simple to operate; and
> - it can allow certain *incidental* exempt supplies to be disregarded.
>
> However;
> - it is often distortive and a Special Method based on transaction numbers can often give a fairer result.

(5) Residual input tax – partial exemption special methods (PESM)

For the businesses covered by this book, the Standard Method is not, as it happens, the norm.

(a) The Directive

In Community law, art. 173 of the VAT Directive, in dealing with input tax that is only partly deductible, provides, in art. 173(2) (previously Art. 17(5) of the Sixth Directive):

(2) Member States may take the following measures:

(a) authorise the taxable person to determine a proportion for each sector of his business, provided that separate accounts are kept for each sector;

(b) require the taxable person to determine a proportion for each sector of his business and to keep separate accounts for each sector;

(c) authorise or require the taxable person to make the deduction on the basis of the use made of all or part of the goods and services;

(d) authorise or require the taxable person to make the deduction in accordance with the rule laid down in the first subparagraph of paragraph 1, in respect of all goods and services used for all transactions referred to therein;

(e) provide that, where the VAT which is not deductible by the taxable person is insignificant, it is to be treated as nil.'

The nature of the provisions in Art. 173(2) were the subject of comment by the CoJ in *Portugal Telecom SGPS SA v Fazenda Pública* (C-496/11). In this case, Portugal Telecom provided technical and management services to companies in which it held a shareholding. The claimant had incurred VAT on services from consultants. It then invoiced its subsidiaries for services at the same price as that for which it had acquired them, plus VAT. The Portuguese tax authority considered that the claimant could not deduct all the VAT on the input services, but that it should use a pro rata method of deduction, which was set at approximately 25 per cent. The claimant argued that instead in so far as the taxable transactions made by it in connection with its shareholdings were supplies of services having a direct and immediate link with the services acquired with a view to their supply, then it should be entitled to deduct all the VAT paid when the acquisitions were made using the method of deduction based on actual use.

The Court held that a holding company, carrying on the activities of the claimant, which, in addition to its main activity of managing shares in companies in which it holds all or part of the share capital, acquires goods and services which it subsequently invoices to those companies is authorised to deduct the amount of input VAT provided that the input services acquired have a direct and immediate link with the output economic transactions giving rise to a right to deduct. The following points were emphasised by the Court:

- Where goods and services are used by a holding company in order to perform both economic transactions giving rise to a right to deduct and economic transactions which do not, the deduction is allowed only in respect of the part of the VAT which is proportional to the amount relating to the former transactions and the national tax authorities are authorised to provide for one of the methods for determining the right to deduct in Art. 173(2) of the VAT Directive (previously Art. 17(5) of the Sixth Directive).
- Where goods and services are used both for economic and non-economic activities, Art. 17(5) (now Art. 173(2) of the VAT Directive) is not applicable and the methods of deduction and apportionment are to be defined by the Member States which, in exercising that power, must take account of the purpose and general scheme of the VAT Directive and, on that basis, lay down a method of calculation which objectively reflects the input expenditure actually attributed to each of those two activities.

In relation to the facts of the case, the Court commented as follows (para. 43 to 47 of the judgment):

"Portugal Telecom submits that the national tax authorities maintain that, having regard to their character as ancillary to the main activity, the supplies of technical administration and management services are indissociable from the management of shares. Therefore, the services acquired by SGPS and provided to their subsidiaries are regarded as mixed transactions for the purposes of the right to deduct VAT and those authorities impose the pro rata method of deduction.

If the position of the tax authorities is indeed as described in the previous paragraph, which is for the referring court to ascertain, it should be observed that the deduction system is meant to relieve the trader entirely of the burden of the VAT payable or paid in the course of all his economic activities. The common system of VAT consequently ensures complete neutrality of taxation of all economic activities, whatever their purpose or results, provided that they are themselves subject in principle to VAT ...

If the input services were to be regarded, overall, as having a direct and immediate link with the output economic transactions giving rise to a right to deduction, the taxable person concerned would be entitled ... to deduct all the VAT chargeable on the relevant input services acquired. That right to deduct cannot be limited simply because, on account of the purpose or general activity of those companies, the national legislation treats the taxed transactions as ancillary to their main activity.

When those services are used in order to perform both transactions in respect of which VAT is deductible and transactions in respect of which VAT is not deductible, the deduction is allowed only for the part of the VAT which is proportionate to the amount attributable to the former transactions and Member States are authorised to provide for one of the methods of determining the right to deduction set out in Article 17(5) of the Sixth Directive [now Art. 173(2)].

Finally, where the services are used both for economic and non-economic activities, Article 17(5) of the Sixth Directive is not applicable and the methods of deduction and apportionment are defined by the Member States ...'

The matter has been referred to the National court. However, the views of the CoJ helpfully clarify the scope and nature of when Art. 173(2) is applicable, and the requirements on a Member State to apply a method outside of Art. 173 which takes account of the purpose and general scheme of the VAT Directive and, specifically lays down a method of calculation which objectively reflects the input expenditure actually attributed to activities.

(b) The VAT Regulations

Under UK law, a partial exemption special method (PESM) may be agreed provided it produces a fair and reasonable result (*VAT Regulations* 1995 (SI 1995/2518), reg. 102). The onus is on the taxpayer to show that the proposed PESM is more fair and reasonable than the standard method (*Royal Bank of Scotland Group plc v R & C Commrs* (Case C-488/07) [2009] BVC 248 at para. 24 of the judgment). HMRC may even direct the use of a Special Method in appropriate cases. The considerations affecting the special arrangements which commonly apply in particular sectors are discussed in later Chapters. Almost invariably, there will be a requirement for *direct attribution*, i.e. as in reg. 101. However, what is generally more important is how *residual input tax* is dealt with. This is discussed in detail at 40-200(6) later. For HMRC's approach to special methods see their Partial Exemption manual at PE3000. As an indication of what is possible, and subject to 40-200(6) later (Non-UK supplies, warehoused goods and other *specified* supplies) businesses may wish to consider approaches such as:

- The use of numbers of taxable and exempt transactions, rather than values, to apportion the *pot* of *residual* input tax. This may be useful to avoid distortion when transactions are undertaken both as agent and as principal. In fact anywhere where the cost of executing individual transactions tends to be fairly uniform regardless of the amounts involved. Stockbrokers/dealers earning commissions and also making sales of securities are particular cases in point. The differences in the respective values can easily influence the extent of input VAT recovered under the simple pro-rata formula used in the Standard

Method, for example, where relief could be significantly depressed if, say, the majority of high value-principals transactions involved recipients in the UK or in other Member States. Insurance broking is another area, where a similar approach can be attractive.

> **Practice point**
>
> As noted above, a values-basis for apportioning residual input VAT has its attractions but a transaction count, on the other hand, will generally give a fairer result. It may even be the only practical way of dealing with certain activities such as foreign exchange.
>
> In a purely brokerage situation, it may well be that there is little difference between a values-based apportionment and one based on transaction numbers. However:
>
> - it is often worth comparing the relative results over time;
> - it is also important, in this context, to carefully define what the transactions to be counted represent – and, following cases like *MBNA Europe Bank* and *Capital One Bank (Europe) Plc* (see later in **Chapter 7** at ¶70-100 under *Securitisation*), what are not supplies at all;
> - it could also be important to see that the *incidental* finance and property supplies can still be left out of account or their impact on the restriction in input VAT minimised.

- The use of cost/income or profit-centres. This will generally require allocations or apportionments to be made at several levels, from cost-centres to income or profit-centres (and possibly even between income and profit-centres). The result may then be wholly taxable or wholly exempt income or profit-centres. More often, though, the income or profit centres will themselves be partially exempt. The recovery of input VAT may then be achieved according to, say, usage, values or numbers of transactions, depending on the income or profit-centre concerned and what is accepted by HMRC as reasonable.

This approach can potentially recognise with greater accuracy those areas where input VAT arises and can thus, again, avoid distortion. An existing management accounting system, for example, could well form the basis of such an approach, although it can be important to recognise that an income or expense item is not always allocated for management accounts purposes on an *actual* basis but on a basis dictated by other management considerations.

- Distinguishing between categories of income where input tax is incurred disproportionately. This has been useful in the past, for example, for banks to differentiate between:
    - service charge income;
    - interest income; and
    - income from securities.

An insurer might wish to distinguish insurance from re-insurance or life from general insurance business. Investment income also tends to be dealt with separately and recognising this could be an important first step in improving the level of recovery achieved.

Again, within each category of income, there may then be a choice as to how the recoverable proportion is arrived at, numbers or values.

- Even a Method disregarding direct attribution and allocating all input VAT on the basis of either values or numbers of transactions can be an option. In other words, the Standard

Method, referred to earlier, minus direct attribution. This is not now generally in favour, though, but could sometimes offer an acceptable compromise between accuracy and administrative effort and cost.

Special Methods need not, however, necessarily be precise. They need not, for example, require the analysis of VAT and VATable costs as and when incurred. With the agreement of HMRC, a fair allocation can sometimes be arrived at pragmatically by using existing available information. It may even be possible to do this retrospectively at a year end, with interim calculations for the first three-quarters during a VAT year being estimated or based on the previous year's figures.

From 1 January 2011, it is possible for businesses to take account of non-business expenditure (excluding private use apportionments) as well as any exempt supplies in a single combined special method calculation (reg. 102ZA of the *VAT Regulations* 1995) (mainly to benefit charities and educational bodies) in order to save the cost of seeking approval of two separate calculations/methods and to help ensure a fair recovery of VAT overall as the calculations can be considered in their entirety. No de minimis limit (40-200(7)) applies for the use of a combined method or for non-business VAT.

Whatever Special Method is used, what HMRC will look for is that:

- no more input tax should be reclaimed other than as is incurred in making taxable supplies; and
- the accuracy of the Method must be easy to check.

HMRC give the following guidance as to the information which they will often require in order to determine whether a special method should be accepted or rejected (Partial Exemption Manual at PE3055):

> "You are likely to need the following core information to enable you to consider fully a new PESM proposal:
>
> - A brief explanation of why the current method is no longer suitable or the new proposal is better (or, for a new business, why the standard method is not suitable). It may be helpful to consider why a business considered and rejected other options;
> - Details of the business structure. This may include VAT group or division details or separate accounting functions within a single business (e.g. a self-accounting branch) …;
> - Brief details of all the business activities which the business undertakes or intends to undertake and their approximate values;
> - The VAT liabilities of their main supplies and their place of supply;
> - Details of the main costs they incur which bear input tax and the activities to which those costs relate;
> - A worked example of the proposed method using actual figures. You should only consider proposals which use projected figures where this is not possible, for example a new business or a totally new activity by an existing business;
> - A copy of the most recent annual accounts;
> - Copies of management accounts or other management information where relevant.
>
> In addition, the following information, where relevant, will assist you in making your decision. Each item is covered in more detail below [see PE3055]:

- Details of all non-business activities and other income sources/streams
- Foreign ('out of country') and specified supplies
- Incidental and distorting income
- Values-based methods
- Unused input tax
- Land and computers subject to the Capital Goods Scheme (CGS)
- Items subject to 'Lennartz' accounting
- Sectors
- Cost accounting
- Group Registrations
- Corporate Groups with separate VAT registrations
- Non accounting-based methods'

Any such Method must also generally be used for at least two years.

Even if a Special Method can be agreed, things are not always straightforward as there can still be disputes over how it is to be applied.

- *The Governor and Company of the Bank of Scotland* [1996] BVC 2,664, for example, was about the correct way to calculate the Bank's entitlement to deduct residual input tax, i.e. VAT which could not be *directly* attributed to either taxable or exempt supplies in the recovery percentage calculations used in the Special Method.

  Briefly, the Bank was the representative member of a VAT group and calculated its input tax recovery using an agreed Special Method. Until the start of 1990 the bank used a Method under which *residual* input tax was apportioned in the ratio of taxable supplies to total supplies. However, before making such an apportionment, it divided its income by making a *services* and *lending* split. HMRC had agreed the basis for the Bank's recovery percentage, but later discovered that, in some periods, costs allocated to the service activity exceeded the related income. They put this down to what they described as *free services*, e.g. *free banking*, *deposit accounts*, which did not amount to supplies within the definition of *service charge income*, with the result that the recovery was neither fair nor reasonable. However, the Tribunal disagreed. (For a discussion of the type of Method used by the Bank see **Chapter 7** at ¶70-250.)

- In *Sovereign Finance plc* [2000] BVC 4,023, the dispute arose because of a VAT voluntary disclosure. Sovereign was a finance company, lending money, leasing vehicles, plant and machinery and providing hire-purchase (HP). In April 1993, HMRC approved a Special Method, subsequently altered by letter in October 1994. This required Sovereign to treat its HP transactions as wholly exempt from VAT on account of its interpretation of the word *deals*, the term used in the numbers count of the residual input tax calculation. Later, Sovereign realised its HP transactions included a taxable element and made a voluntary disclosure to recover for under-claimed input tax. HMRC argued Sovereign was seeking a retrospective change of Method, not just correcting a mistake. They also said Sovereign's action in going along with treating HP as wholly exempt precluded them from now arguing the opposite.

  On appeal, the Tribunal sided with Sovereign as HP transactions had a substantial element attributable to a supply of goods and HMRC's assertion that the predominant element in hire-purchase transactions was finance could not be accepted. Also, Sovereign could not be precluded from advancing their interpretation, which produced a fairer result.

- The appeal by *Pearl Assurance plc* [1999] BVC 2,176 was about whether a Special Method had been agreed (or directed) at all. There had been lengthy correspondence between Pearl and HMRC, culminating in an approval letter, which was not, as it happened, signed and returned. Pearl did, however, complete its VAT returns in a manner that excluded, for the purposes of apportionment, its investment activities, which were not *incidental*. Later Pearl sought to argue that nothing had been agreed so that the Standard Method applied, in which supplies from the investment activities were included. They also contended that, whether or not a Special Method had been directed or approved was a matter of considerable significance and therefore any approval or direction must be clear and unambiguously communicated to the trader. The Tribunal did not accept this, however and the fact that Pearl had excluded the values of part of its supplies meant it was adopting in its VAT returns a Special Method. It did not use the Standard Method in the *VAT Regulations* 1995 (SI 1995/2518), reg. 101(2)(d) based on the value of all its supplies.

- In *Kwik-Fit (GB) Ltd v C & E Commrs* [1998] BVC 48, the Court of Session (Inner House) considered the question of a direction by HMRC that a Special Method be used. Kwik-Fit was the representative member of a VAT group, which, from November 1993, included a company providing insurance services. At the time, the Standard Method was being used, which HMRC felt was unfair. They accordingly issued a direction to use a Special Method based on direct attribution, with residual input tax being dealt with separately for each member of the group. However, part of the wording was ambiguous, with the result that the Court considered the direction not fair and reasonable, and was therefore void.

- In a similar vein, an appeal in *Merchant Navy Officers Pension Fund Trustees Ltd; Merchant Navy Ratings Pension Fund Trustees Ltd* [1996] BVC 2,924, succeeded in preventing HMRC upsetting existing agreed Special Methods. The Methods were themselves inherently unsatisfactory, but the direction simply to cease using them was unfair. This was because, in the absence of any alternative agreed Method, the Standard Method applied. The Standard Method was even more unfair and likely to lead to greater distortions than what had been previously agreed. The proper course was to direct that the existing schemes be terminated and replaced by other specific schemes, which were fairer and more reasonable.

- An appeal, which failed on this score, was *BMW (GB) Ltd* [1997] BVC 4,090. The appellant was a representative member of a VAT group, which was the concessionaire for BMW cars and motor cycles, which it imported and sold to a network of independent dealers. Within the appellant's group were two companies, one of which provided finance and the other leasing. Both joined the VAT group in December 1993, which, from then onwards, ceased to be fully taxable.

Recognising that the VAT group was now partly exempt, the appellant proposed a Special Method whereby:

- the companies in the group making only taxable supplies recovered all their input tax; and
- the finance subsidiary apportioned its residual input tax by reference to the values of its taxable supplies (included cars sold under HP and contract purchase agreements) and the value of exempt supplies.

4 Input VAT and Partial Exemption

No formal approval was given for this Method, which was used until May 1996, and in 1994 HMRC rejected the proposed Method and directed the appellant to use the Special Method agreed for the *Finance Houses Association Ltd* (see **Appendix 9**), a Method that has now effectively been abandoned by the FHA (see in **Chapter 7** at ¶70-300). On appeal, the Tribunal held that following *C & E Commrs v John Dee Ltd* [1995] BVC 361 its jurisdiction was limited to deciding whether the decision of HMRC to issue the direction was reasonable, which it did. The appeal was therefore dismissed.

The approach to determining a special method that produces a fair and reasonable result has been considered recently in several cases. In *Volkswagen Financial Services (UK) Ltd* [2011] UKFTT 556; [2011] TC 01401 the First Tier Tax Tribunal decided that a fair and reasonable method of attribution of residual input VAT in respect of the taxpayer's hire purchase business was to attribute part of the residual input VAT to the taxable business of the supply of the vehicle, as well as to the exempt supply of finance. However, the decision of the FTT is under appeal by HMRC, and is expected to be heard in the Autumn of 2012.

The material facts of the case were as follows:

Volkswagen Financial Services Ltd (VWFS) in relation to its retail business of hire purchase ('HP') transactions sought to agree a method with HMRC for recovery of residual input tax, as part of an approved partial exemption special method (PESM). VWFS was a partially exempt trader. The PESM provided that residual input tax was to be recovered to the extent that it was incurred on goods or services which were used to make taxable supplies, expressed as a proportion of the whole use or intended use. VWFS claimed that a fair and reasonable method of use was to quantify the ratio of taxable transactions to total transactions, counting every HP agreement as two transactions (one taxable, one exempt), every leasing transaction as two transactions (both taxable) and every fixed price service and maintenance contract as one (taxable) transaction. This methodology would produce a recoverable position for 50 per cent of the residual input tax referable to HP transactions. The purpose of the methodology was to accurately reflect through weighting the extent to which the transactions used the overheads of the business to which the residual input VAT related. Accordingly, the residual input tax attributable to the businesses activities would then be multiplied by the proportion by which the number of taxable transactions bore to the total number of transactions (the number of transactions being calculated by reference to the payments made under the HP contracts). In contrast, HMRC's approach was to allocate input tax between HP transactions, leasing transactions, service and maintenance contracts on a contracts-count basis and then to apportion the tax using the value of taxable and exempt outputs in each sub-sector. In relation to HP transactions, no account was taken of the value of the car. The effect of HMRC's approach was to substantially eliminate the taxable value of the HP transactions, with the result that most of the residual input tax was apportioned to the exempt interest in those transactions so that the VAT was irrecoverable. Further details of the case are as follows

- VWFS incurred input tax directly attributable to the making of either taxable or exempt supplies, and some of which were not directly attributable to the making of taxable or exempt supplies (ie is residual input tax). VWFS entered into the following principal transactions: HP agreements in respect of VW brand cars; leasing agreements with customers in respect of VW brand cars; and fixed price service and maintenance contracts on VW cars. It also carried on a variety of other activities relating to providing funding to dealers for the purchase of demonstrator cars, the arrangement of insurance for owners of VW cars, servicing (and reporting on) securitised hire purchase contracts, and the disposal of previously leased and/or repossessed VW cars. Broadly, the HP transactions involved VWFS buying the car from the retailer and supplying it to the customer on deferred payment terms under an HP agreement. Under an HP contract, title does not pass to the customer until all payments have been paid. VWFS was deemed to be the supplier under the HP agreement. Accordingly, the service provided by VWFS was not limited to the provision of funding, but extended to the provision of support in terms of the vehicle itself, such as dealing with complaints regarding quality (since as a matter of law it was supplying a car required to be of satisfactory quality).

- The HP agreements specified the cash price of the car, which was equal to the price paid by VWFS to the retailer, with no profit element. From this amount VWFS deducted any advance payment (such as a deposit), leaving an amount of credit to be financed over the HP period. The HP agreement identified the difference between the cash price and the total amount payable as the total charge for credit, which would be broken down in the agreement between interest charges, an acceptance fee and an option to purchase fee. The option to purchase and the acceptance fee were set at market rates. The market or advertised rate of interest was determined by VWFS. It did this by applying a margin for overheads, a profit margin and an allowance for bad debts to its own cost of financing the vehicle. The overheads were built into the interest rate, the option to purchase fee and the acceptance fee.

VWFS did not charge any separate fee to cover overheads. Overheads did not form part of the cash price for the vehicle, as that solely reflected the price paid by VWFS to the retailer. The residual input tax related to overhead expenditure, e.g.: (i) temporary staff, staff training and recruitment; (ii) hotel accommodation, staff meals and drinks; (iii) travel, parking, road tolls and car hire, service and repairs; (iv) marketing and corporate hospitality; (v) IT maintenance and enhancement; (vi) heating, lighting, cleaning, security and other premises costs; (vii) furniture leasing; (viii) couriers, stationary, printing, photocopying and archiving; and (ix) legal, tax and accounting expenses.

- VWFS had agreed a PESM with HMRC which distinguished the HP part of VWFS's business from the rest of its business. The recoverable proportion of the residual input tax allocated to the HP part of the business was restricted to 15 per cent in accordance with an agreement between HMRC and the FLA (see Chapter 7 for further discussion on this aspect) and an additional 5.4 per cent was allowed to reflect services provided to VWFS's securitisation sector activities. The recoverable proportion of the remainder of the residual input tax was established by a values-based formula similar to the standard method, namely by reference to the ratio of taxable income to total income.

Following the FLA's withdrawal from the trade sector agreement with HMRC (as discussed in Chapter 7) the parties sought to agree a PESM. However, as discussed above, each party had different methodologies for determining a PESM. The Tribunal concluded that VWFS's proposed special method was 'fair and reasonable' in determining the amount of input VAT it incurred on its overhead expenses, which were attributable to taxable supplies under the HP agreements. HMRC had argued that the method was not fair and reasonable on the basis that the cost of overheads was not normally built into the price of the supply of the car sold at cost/no profit, but would usually be built solely into the price charged for the supply of credit (para. 40 of the judgment). On this basis the overheads were cost components of the exempt supply according to HMRC, so that the input tax therefore was irrecoverable. From HMRC's perspective if recovery for input VAT were allowed a business would continually enjoy net VAT refunds despite charging a total consideration under the HP agreement that fully recovers its costs and a mark-up (para. 40 of the judgment). However, during the hearing HMRC did not challenge the 50/50 weighting in respect of VWFS's methodology for taxable supplies (cars) and exempt supplies (finance under the HP agreements) (para. 41 of the judgment). The weighting was accepted as realistic by HMRC's expert witness. The Tribunal accordingly made the following comments in reaching its conclusion:

"Following a review of the case law on input VAT recovery for overhead costs, that such costs are overhead or general costs, they are, by virtue of the fact, cost components of the price of a taxable person's products. Accordingly, "[t]here is no separate test or hurdle of incorporation into price that has to be met or overcome. Those costs are then directly and immediately linked with the taxable person's economic activity as a whole"(para. 64 of the judgment). '

The Tribunal rejected any approach of treating overhead costs as solely cost components of a particular element to the exclusion of another element of a transaction as not being fair and reasonable (see para. 60 of the judgment). In relation to HMRC's published policy, the Tribunal disapproved of their approach (at para. 71 of the judgment):

"What HMRC's argument amounts to, in essence, is that there is a limit to the amount of cost that can be a cost component of a supply, and that because the supply of the vehicle is at cost, and so reflects only the price paid by VWFS to the dealer, and input tax on the acquisition of the vehicle by VWFS is directly attributable to that supply, the cost component capacity of the vehicle supply has been exhausted, with the result that no other costs can be cost components of that supply. We consider that to be wrong in principle. The mere fact that only particular costs are recovered by a supplier in the price he charges for the making of a particular supply does not lead to the conclusion that no other costs are cost components of that supply. Unrecovered costs not directly attributable to a particular supply, or such costs recovered in other ways, for example by marking up other supplies, are nonetheless cost components of transactions of the business in general, and to the extent that those transactions include taxable supplies, the input tax incurred on those costs is deductible.'

Another example of the approach to deciding whether a partial exemption special method (PESM) is fair and reasonable is provided by the decision of the Court of Appeal in *R & C Commrs v London Clubs Management Ltd* [2011] EWCA Civ 1323; [2011] BVC 406 . The facts of this case were as follows:

- The taxpayer was the representative member of the VAT group of several companies operating in the UK, Egypt and South Africa. The business of the group was operating casinos (of which there were 11 in the UK).
- The taxpayer was a tenant of substantial premises which had been acquired in anticipation of a greater floor area being available for slot machines. However, the taxpayer found itself in a position where not all of the additional floor space was required due to a limitation on the number of slot machines which would be allowed in a casino. Against this background the taxpayer adopted a new business strategy to enable it to make the best use of the available space it had acquired under the lease, which involved the addition of restaurants,

Recovering input tax – partial exemption 40-200

- bars, carrying on of an entertainment business (such as providing entertainment for corporate events, providing dedicated space for poker, etc.).
- The taxpayer provided the following services for VAT purposes: gaming, such as roulette and blackjack, which is exempt from VAT but is subject to gaming duty; slot machines, which are VAT standard rated; dedicated poker facilities, which were VAT standard rated until 27 April 2009, and were then exempt from VAT but subject to gaming duty; bar sales, catering, entertainment and venue hire, all of which are VAT standard rated.

The following further findings of fact were made by the First-Tier Tribunal (see para. 12 to 14 of the judgment):

- The premises in each case had a mixed use of gaming, restaurants, bars and entertainment, all within a casino context
- Some areas of the premises were physically separated, e.g the restaurant area was separated from the main gaming floor by being on a separate floor of the premises, and was separated from the poker room by a curtain. In the case of other areas, such as the bars, there was less physical separation. In all areas separate and identifiable floor space was occupied by the different parts of the business.
- Full restaurant dining facilities were provided, in defined restaurant areas, with extensive menus and table service. The type of restaurant differed from venue to venue.
- Customers were able to move easily between the different areas, from the restaurant to the gaming areas and from the gaming areas to the bar. Customers could consume drinks in the gaming area, and could be served light snacks, such as sandwiches, at the gaming tables.
- Use of a particular area of floor space for a particular activity was liable to change; for example, in order to increase profitability the space formerly occupied by a bar could be changed to use for gaming. Substantial areas of floor space were designated for use other than gaming, food, beverages and entertainment. Those areas included reception, toilets, staff rooms, management offices, corridors, lifts and the space occupied by the cashiers. Evidence was given that cash for all elements of the business was dealt with by the cashier function.
- Not all of the food and drink consumed was charged for: a significant percentage was supplied free of charge to certain gaming customers. The percentage of non-charge food and beverage differed substantially between different casinos. For example, the non-charge percentage of total food and beverage sales for the period April 2008 to March 2009 varied from as little as 14.6 per cent to 94 per cent.
- The food and beverage element of the business, comprising the restaurants and bars, was not profitable in its own right. It did, however, generate a positive return in each of the casino venues for the period in question in the proceedings (after deduction of direct costs). It made a contribution to overheads in management accounting terms, except for The Sportsman casino, which achieved a break even result.

In view of the above, the First-Tier Tribunal found as a matter of fact that the catering activities, whilst not profitable at the time, were nonetheless businesses in their own right and were not merely ancillary to the gaming business (at para. 48 of the judgment). In other words, the catering activity was a potential source of profit and was carried on as such, independently of the taxpayer's gaming activity.

4 Input VAT and Partial Exemption

As regards the PESM:

- The taxpayer sought to change its original PESM, which involved residual input tax being apportioned by applying a fraction comprising taxable turnover over total turnover, with an adjustment to take account of the fact that residual input tax attributable to food and drink for which customers had not been charged was not deductible.
- The taxpayer's proposed PESM involved a move away from their turnover based method to a floor space method. The fraction to be applied to the residual input tax under the proposed PESM was, in essence, the area of floor within the taxpayer's premises occupied to make taxable supplies over the area of floor occupied to make taxable and exempt supplies, with an adjustment to take account of residual costs associated with non-charged food and drink.

The First-Tier Tribunal and the Upper Tribunal each upheld the taxpayer's approach to the PESM. The Court of Appeal in upholding their decisions, approached the issue on the following basis by identifying three points of principle, following a detailed review of the relevant case law (at para. 41 of the judgment):

> "... First, it shows the importance in these cases of close attention to the facts in order to understand the economic or commercial reality underlying the use of the relevant VAT inputs. Secondly, identification of the source or potential source of profit in a business may be an important feature of a business throwing light on whether or not the standard method or a PESM is a more fair, reasonable and accurate method of attribution. It all depends on the facts of each case ... Thirdly, depending again on the precise factual situation under consideration, the approach of the Tribunal in Aspinall's Club at [49] may well be appropriate in a case where the taxable supplies are not, in themselves, a source of profit:

> "'Those costs are funded by the gaming. That in itself does not make them cost components of those exempt supplies. But in this case it is additional proof, if any is needed, that gaming is the foundation of the business and it is the furtherance of that gaming which causes and is seen as justifying commercially the decisions to incur the expenditure.'"

The First-Tier Tribunal concluded that the floor space PESM was fair and reasonable, and in this regard observed in connection with the operation of the taxpayer's business that (at para. 38 of the tribunals decision, and referred to at para. 45 of the Court of Appeal's decision):

> "The residual costs with which we are here concerned are not one-off costs [...], but are ongoing costs, such as rent, in running the business as a whole. Taking premises costs, such costs are incurred in order to provide premises for the carrying on of the whole of the Appellant's business. We have found that the food and beverage supplies made by the Appellant are made from defined and measurable parts of the Appellant's premises and accordingly we find that part of the purpose of the Appellant in incurring that expenditure is to provide space for the provision of those supplies. Although it is accepted that gaming is able to generate a higher turnover and profit for each square foot of the premises that it occupies as compared with the restaurants and bars, that does not, in our view, lead to the conclusion that gaming is the principal user or consumer of the premises costs incurred and that, as a result, a partial exemption method must reflect that in assuming greater use by the gaming part of the business. It seems to us that the proposed floor space method does provide a fair and reasonable allocation of such costs, as it reflects directly the use of those costs.'

The First-Tier Tribunal further commented on the proportion of the residual costs that were property-related and those that were not property-related in the context of the PESM as follows (at para. 43 to 44 of the Tribunal's decision, and referred to at para. 49 of the Court of Appeal's decision):

> "43. We have found that a substantial proportion of the residual costs of the Appellant's business are property-related. Although this proportion may fluctuate from quarter to quarter, we accept that the figures presented to us, which showed property-related costs at 71% of total residual costs, are a fair representation of the position. A floor space method is, in our view, appropriate for providing a reasonable proxy for such costs. It assumes that costs that cannot be directly-attributed are used or consumed by the separate parts of the business by reference to the amount of floor space those separate parts occupy. The greater the space so occupied, the more consumption of those inward supplies is assumed.
>
> 44. For costs that are not property-related, the floor space method does not provide such a close approximation to use. The consumption of such costs is likely to depend on a number of factors, of which the area of the floor space occupied by a particular part of the business is only one. We had no evidence that in this case the use of a floor space method for non-property related costs would be so distortive as to render the proposed method, as it would operate in relation to costs in the aggregate, unfair or unreasonable. A substantial proportion of the costs in this case are property-related, for which we consider the proposed method to be fair and reasonable, and it is not prevented from being fair and reasonable by the fact that it also operates in respect of the minority of non-property related costs.'

Finally, in relation to the issue of whether the PESM was fair and reasonable compared to the original method, the First-Tier Tribunal concluded that (at para. 52 of the Tribunal's decision, and referred to at para. 51 of the Court of Appeal's decision):

> "... What we regard as the essential question is: which of the methods, the existing or the proposed method, is the more fair and reasonable approximation for the use of costs? [...] In our view, in the case of a business whose residual costs are predominantly property-related, the existing method does not, in our view, provide as coherent a proxy for the use of those costs as does the floor space method proposed by the Appellant. That method, as we have found, takes account of the economic use of the floor space (including the effect of the non-chargeable catering supplies) and thus the use and consumption of property-related costs, in a way that the existing method fails to do. The treatment of non-property related costs we regard as neutral as between the two methods. Accordingly, we conclude that the proposed method is more fair and reasonable than the existing method.'

Based on the principles identified above, and the findings of fact made by the First-Tier Tribunal the Court of Appeal upheld the taxpayer's proposed PESM as mentioned above.

Following the 2007 Budget, it is now a prerequisite for the agreement of a Partial Exemption Special Method that the applicant must give a declaration that the Method produces a fair and reasonable result (with the sanction that the Method, or the offending part of it, will become void if HMRC subsequently form the view that the Method did not produce a fair and reasonable result).

This is now provided for in reg. 102(9) to (16) of the *VAT Regulations* 1995 (SI 1995/2518). Also from 1 April 2007, businesses can seek approval of a combined (special) method under reg. 102(1A)(b). This gives businesses the legal right to seek approval of a single special method that caters for calculations of input tax on non-UK supplies that confer the right of recovery (i.e. foreign and specified supplies under reg. 103, such as supplies of finance and insurance to customers outside the EU – see later at 40-200(6)) as well as input tax attributable to UK taxable supplies. The 'combined' method will attribute all of the input tax except for input tax wholly or partly relating to incidental financial supplies and investment gold (see 40-200(6)(b) and (c)).

Particular considerations affecting businesses in the different sectors in this book are discussed later in **Chapters 7** to **10**.

> *Practice point*
> With Special Methods:
> (1) It is generally worth exploring a cost or income-centre approach to enable an initial apportionment of input tax. This can be especially useful if management accounts are available and can be fairer than a rough-and-ready calculation based just on, say, values of supplies:
>
> (a) often, the level of recovery can vary for different categories within the same broad service classification and with the same basic unit of valuation. With insurance, for example, the position can easily differ according to the type of VAT risk involved. Motor insurance and life and pensions business tend to be almost exclusively domestic, with consequently little scope for recovery. This is often the opposite for other risks, such as MAT, or for reinsurance;
>
> (b) different levels of input tax may be incurred for different activities – as recognised, for instance, in the services/lending split once common within the banking sector;
>
> (c) especially following *LIPA* (see ¶40-200(6)) and the latest references to a *combined method* in the guidance provided by HMRC in their Question and Answer leaflet *Changes to the VAT partial exemption special method regime* following the 2007 Budget changes, it can be important to ensure that services supplied to persons outside the UK can be part of a single calculation and not dealt with separately.
>
> (2) There is nothing to say that the recovery of residual input tax should necessarily be calculated in the same way for different income centres or classes of supply.
>
> (3) There is also no reason why there should not effectively be a combination of Special Methods within a VAT group.
>
> Deciding on the Method to be used is, clearly, something over which considerable care needs to be taken. It also especially important to be absolutely sure of what is agreed, since what may appear to be subtle differences in wording can have a material impact at times on what can, or cannot, be recovered.

(6) Non-UK supplies, warehoused goods and other specified supplies

The special rules in reg. 103 of the *Value Added Tax Regulations* 1995 (SI 1995/2518) require non-UK supplies, warehoused goods and other *specified* supplies to be treated differently from other supplies in determining recoverable input tax to the extent that they are not attributed under reg. 101 or a special method agreed with HMRC. They were introduced initially by HMRC in 1994 as an anti-avoidance measure in an attempt to counter a perceived manipulation of the Standard Method to achieve what they believed was an unfair recovery of input tax. The rules are not, however, restricted in application to the Standard Method, as such, and can apply equally to Special Methods. Whether they can be strictly justified in terms of European Community law as a standard approach is, perhaps, open to doubt.

(a) The general idea

As now drafted, reg. 103 reads:

'Other than where it falls to be attributed under regulation 101 or a method approved or determined by the Commissioners under regulation 102 ... Input tax incurred by a taxable person in any prescribed accounting period on goods imported or acquired by, or goods or services supplied to, him which are used or to be used by him in whole or in part in making-

(a) supplies outside the United Kingdom which would be taxable supplies if made in the United Kingdom, or
(b) supplies specified in an Order under section 26(2)(c) of the Act other than supplies of a description falling within regulation 103A below,

shall be attributed to taxable supplies to the extent that the goods or services are so used or to be used expressed as a proportion of the whole use or intended use.'

The Order referred to in (b) above is the *Value Added Tax (Input Tax) (Specified Supplies) Order* 1999 (SI 1999/3121). It covers exempt financial and insurance services supplied to persons outside the EU (where the place of supply is *where received*) or similar services *directly linked to exports* to places outside the EU (see **Chapters 7** and **9**). As noted earlier, prior to April 2009, all foreign and specified supplies were dealt with outside the Standard Method, with residual input tax being recoverable according to the use of the relevant costs/inputs in making those supplies as a proportion of the whole use of such inputs

The Regulation clearly contemplates:

- a separate exercise from the basic partial exemption calculation; and
- an allocation or division based on *use*, rather than a pro-rata apportionment based on the values of supplies.

This was given judicial approval from the House of Lords in the *Liverpool Institute for Performing Arts* case, described as follows, but this is for reference only given the changes to reg. 101 in April 2009 (see also HMRC's Partial Exemption Guidance Manual at PE3900 and Notice 706 Partial Exemption (June 2011) at section 9).

- *C & E Commrs v Liverpool Institute for Performing Arts* [2001] BVC 333 was a long-running appeal about the recovery of input tax under the Standard Method. LIPA had been established to provide exempt educational services in the field of the performing arts and started to do so in 1995. However, from March to May 1993, it provided advertising and publicity services to a German company, supplies which were *outside the scope* of UK VAT, being services within VATA 1994, (former) Sch. 5, para. 2 and treated as *supplied where received* by reason of the *Value Added Tax (Place of Supply of Services) Order* 1992 (SI 1992/3121), art. 16 (see **Chapter 3** at ¶30-250).

4 Input VAT and Partial Exemption

The dispute was over whether these *outside the scope* supplies were to be included in the calculation under the Standard Method or were to be looked at separately for input tax recovery purposes.

Initially, before the Tribunal, the taxpayer won, on the basis that:

(1) The supplies made to the German company were supplies, which would have been taxable supplies if treated as made in the UK.

(2) Regulations 30 and 32 (of the *Value Added Tax (General) Regulations* 1985 (SI 1985/886), reg. 101 (prior to the amendments made in 2009) and 103 of the *Value Added Tax Regulations* 1995 (SI 1995/2518)) had to be read together and set out the correct approach to be adopted for securing a fair and reasonable attribution of input tax to taxable supplies and supplies made outside the UK, which would be taxable supplies if made in the UK. This was to attribute input tax to taxable supplies wherever possible and thereafter apportion according to the use or intended use.

(3) On that basis, the input tax attributable to the supplies made to the German company fell to be included in the input tax attributable to taxable supplies for the purposes of reg. 30(2)(b).

This view was subsequently upheld on HMRC's appeal to the High Court, with the further finding that the scheme of the relevant regulations paralleled art. 17 and 19 of the Sixth Directive (now art. 173 and 174 of the VAT Directive), which corresponded more closely to the view that reg. 30 and reg. 32 should be read together. The rule in art. 17(1)–(3) was that *out of country supplies* were to be treated in precisely the same way as taxable supplies. *Out of country supplies* were, therefore, to be included in the term *all supplies* in reg. 30(1)(d).

Unfortunately, on HMRC's further appeal, the Court of Appeal came to a different view (i.e. that the Standard Method only applied to apportion input tax relating to taxable supplies made in the UK). HMRC's appeal was allowed and the House of Lords later agreed.

As seen above, the legislative position has now changed following LIPA as the Standard Method has been widened as from 1 April 2009 so that it deals with input VAT on all supplies, unless dealt with separately under reg. 103A (see next section). HMRC notes the impact of the changes in its Partial Exemption Guidance manual at PE1375; under the old rules, businesses that made foreign and specified supplies were required to carry out an additional calculation (known as a regulation 103 calculation) to determine the recoverable input tax on these supplies on the basis of use, or they could seek approval of a combined special method that catered for these types of supply. (According to HMRC, the reason that foreign and specified supplies were excluded from the Standard Method was because they could sometimes distort the values-based calculation). A separate calculation is no longer required and a few examples as to how the new rules now operate are given by HMRC at PE1375, as below. Where a business provisionally recovers input tax on the basis of use in accordance with the Standard Method, this would need to be finalised by way of an annual adjustment:

- 'Example 1: A business provides consultancy services to customers within the UK and outside the UK. Under the current rules the business is required to calculate a recoverable amount of input tax relating to its services to customers outside the UK by way of a separate regulation 103 calculation or alternatively seek approval of a special method. The new rules

simplify this by requiring residual input tax to be recovered by reference to the values-based calculation which includes the consultancy services irrespective of their place of supply.
- Example 2: A business makes supplies of insurance, shares and bonds to customers located inside and outside the EU. Under the current rules, the business would be required to calculate input tax recoverable as attributable to these supplies to customers located outside the EU by way of a separate regulation 103 calculation. The new rules simplify this so that while input tax relating to shares and bonds [see reg. 101(8)], irrespective of their place of supply, must be recovered on the basis of use (for example on a transactions count basis), input tax relating to insurance can be recovered by reference to the values-based calculation which includes the supplies of insurance irrespective of their place of supply.
- Example 3: A business makes supplies of management services from an establishment located within the UK and outside the UK. Under the current rules the business would be required to recover input tax relating to its supplies to customers outside the UK using a regulation 103 calculation. The remaining input tax would be recovered using the values-based calculation including supplies made to customers in the UK from the establishment located outside the UK, which could be distortive. To reduce this risk of distortion, the new rules require input tax relating to supplies made from establishments located outside the UK to be recovered on the basis of use. The remaining input tax is recovered using the values-based calculation (excluding supplies made from the establishment located outside the UK).'

(b) Special rules on investment gold

Regulation 103A is a special measure to cover transactions in *investment gold* (see **Chapter 10** at ¶100-450). This applies to a taxable person who makes supplies of a description falling within VATA 1994, Sch. 9, Grp. 15, item 1 or 2 and allows input tax incurred to be allowable as being attributable to those supplies only where it is incurred on the following:

(1) On purchases of investment gold in respect of which the option to tax has been exercised.

(2) On a purchase, an acquisition or an importation of gold other than investment gold which is to be transformed by the business or on its behalf into investment gold.

(3) On services supplied to the business changing the form, weight or purity of gold.

Someone producing investment gold or transforming gold into investment gold is also entitled to credit for input tax incurred on any supplies of goods or services or any acquisitions or imports of goods if linked to the production or transformation of that gold into investment gold.

Relief under these provisions is meant to be assessed according to the use or intended use of the services or goods concerned expressed as a proportion of their whole use or intended use.

(c) Services and related goods used to make financial supplies

From 3 December 2004, the treatment of *incidental* financial transactions within reg. 103 is now found in reg. 103B, other than where it falls to be attributed under reg. 101.

Where residual input tax has been incurred by a taxable person in any prescribed accounting period on services supplied by:

4 Input VAT and Partial Exemption

- accountants;
- advertising agencies;
- bodies which provide listing and registration services;
- financial advisers;
- lawyers;
- marketing consultants;
- persons who prepare and design documentation;
- any person or body which provides similar services to those listed above,

and those services (and any related goods) are used or are to be used by the person concerned in making both:

- any financial supplies within item 1 or 6 of Group 5 of Sch 9 of VATA (for example, intergroup loans, sales of subsidiaries and, before *Kretztechnik* (see **Chapter 3** at ¶30-200) the issue of shares and stocks) that are *incidental* to the business; and
- any other supply,

the input tax is to be apportioned to taxable supplies to the extent of that proportion of the whole use or intended use. See generally HMRC's Notice 706 Partial Exemption (July 2011) at section 10.

(7) De minimis rules

The de minimis rules tend not to be especially important in the context of this book. However, the present rules, in the *VAT Regulations* 1995, reg. 106(1) treat all input tax as attributable to taxable supplies where, in any prescribed accounting period or in any longer period (see (10) below), the exempt input tax:

- does not amount to more than £625 per month on average; and
- does not exceed one half of all input tax for the period concerned.

For this purpose, the reliefs discussed earlier are disregarded. In other words, exempt input tax is treated as attributable to taxable supplies (e.g. under the rule at ¶40-150(3) earlier). Also no account is taken of adjustments under the capital goods rules (see ¶40-200(8) below). Additionally, there are simplified tests and an annual test which make it easier for a taxable person to determine whether a taxable person satisfies the de minimis status (see generally HMRC Notice 706: Partial Exemption at para. 11 (June 2011)).

(8) Capital goods

Article 187(1) of the VAT Directive (formerly Art. 20(2) of the Sixth Directive (Directive 77/388) requires adjustments to the recovery of input VAT on capital goods over a period of time. Generally, this is to be spread over a five-year period, including the year of purchase or manufacture (or first use); though, in the case of immovable property (i.e. land and buildings) this adjustment period is generally extended from five to up to ten years. Adjustments are made under the scheme to reflect changes in the business use of capital items, and if during the adjustment period there is any change in the proportion of taxable use then an adjustment is made to the input VAT to reflect this change. The scheme is of no application where assets are purchased by a taxable person for the purposes of resale. For the scheme to apply a person does not have to be carrying on partly exempt or non-business activities for it to be relevant. For example, where a building is purchased for the purposes of a wholly taxable business, and there is a subsequent diversification into an exempt activity (e.g. insurance) and use of the building changes to accommodate a team of insurance personnel then the capital goods scheme may require adjustments to be made to input VAT recovery on the building. Adjustments can be required to reflect changes in levels of non-business use, including private use, of the asset over the adjustment period. This is as a result of legislative changes to the rules having effect from January 2011. Prior to the changes the rules required adjustments for changes in taxable or exempt use of a capital item, and only VAT on business-related expenditure fell within the scheme.

The relevant UK provisions are in Pt. XV of the *Value Added Tax Regulations* 1995 (SI 1995/2518), reg. 112 to 116 (which in their current form apply to input VAT incurred by a taxable person on goods imported or acquired by, or goods or services supplied to, that taxable person on or after 1 January 2011). For further details of the changes in the UK to the Capital Goods Scheme as from 1 January 2011 and example adjustments, see HMRC's VAT Information Sheet 06/11: March 2011, and generally in HMRC Notice 706/2 Capital Goods Scheme (October 2011). These do not apply to all capital assets, only to:

(1) computers and individual items of computer equipment of a value of not less than £50,000 (the reference to computer means a single item of equipment and not a complete network). HMRC have stated that computer software and computerised equipment such as a phone exchange is not included (HMRC Notice 706/2 Capital Goods Scheme (October 2011);

(2) an aircraft, a ship, boat or other vessel of a value of not less than £50,000;

(3) land;

(4) buildings (or parts of a building); and

(5) civil engineering works (or part of a civil engineering work) (e.g. works on roads, bridges, installation of pipes for connection to mains services).

And then the expenditure must be of the following types:

(1) in the case of an item falling within (1) or (3) the expenditure must relate to its acquisition;

(2) in the case of an item falling within (2), (4) or (5) the expenditure must relate to its (a) acquisition, (b) construction (including where appropriate manufacture), (c) refurbishment, (iv) fitting out, (v) alteration, or (vi) extension (including the construction of an annex).

The value of the expenditure must not be less than the following:

(1) not less than £250,000 (exclusive of VAT) where the item falls within (3), (4) or (5) of the items listed above;

(2) not less than £50,000 (exclusive of VAT) where the item falls within (1) or (2) of the items listed above.

As to whether something is *capital* or not, there may be occasions HMRC will not be able to accept a business' accounting treatment, either because of avoidance or because the accounting treatment does not reflect their understanding of the every day meaning of *capital expenditure* i.e. of enduring benefit to the business. Examples are:

- where costs are not treated as *capital* because the effect would not be *material*. For large companies, *materiality* may be much more than the £250,000 limit for the capital goods scheme;
- a building, which is leased with the intention of disposing of it as a transfer of a going concern, may not be treated as capital because the business would consider it to be developed solely for resale. However, HMRC would consider that such a building would fall within the definition of *capital expenditure* because the costs would be of enduring benefit to the business, albeit that the business (and benefit) is transferred.

There was an Extra-Statutory Concession allowing businesses to use an alternative means of valuing refurbishment or fitting-out work for the purposes of the capital goods scheme. The concession became obsolete and was withdrawn with effect from 1 January 2011.

Under the capital goods scheme, input VAT is initially recovered on the full asset cost in the longer accounting period or VAT year in which the asset was acquired or constructed. The proportion of input tax deducted on a capital item is adjusted over a period of time comprising ten successive intervals (for land, buildings or civil engineering works), or five successive intervals (for computers, aircraft and ships). The amount actually recovered in that year will depend on the partial exemption position at that time. In each subsequent longer accounting period or VAT year (four years for computers; usually nine for land and buildings) one-fifth or one-tenth of the original input VAT is adjusted to reflect the corresponding partial exemption position in that later period.

For each asset, the adjustment is calculated by the formula:

$$\frac{\text{Total input VAT incurred}}{5 \text{ or } 10} \times \text{the adjustment percentage}$$

The adjustment percentage is the percentage change in use compared with that of the first longer accounting period or VAT year. This results in an addition to or deduction from the input VAT to be recovered in the later period concerned.

Special rules apply where an asset is disposed of within the five or ten year adjustment period, other than the final year. If the disposal involves a taxable supply, the owner is treated as using the asset for each of the remaining complete years wholly in making taxable supplies; if the disposal is exempt, there will be a corresponding deemed exempt use. In either case, a single adjustment is made for the last longer accounting period or VAT year in which the asset is actually used.

Where the owner of a capital item disposes of it and the *total input tax* deducted is greater than the output tax due on its sale, he can be required to make an adjustment to repay the excess. For this purpose, the input tax recoverable is the aggregate of:

- the initial deduction of input tax incurred on the purchase or development of the item;
- any adjustments made previously in respect of the item under the scheme; and
- any final adjustment otherwise required due to the disposal.

This *disposal* test was part of a package of anti-avoidance measures. It was meant to ensure partly exempt businesses, such as banks and insurance companies, did not obtain an unjustified tax advantage by being able to recover the VAT incurred on land or property intended to be used for exempt purposes (see further below). It was not meant to affect bona fide commercial transactions and will not be applied (see HMRC Notice 706/2 Capital Goods Scheme: October 2011, at para. 11.2):

- to sales of computer equipment;
- where an owner disposes of an item at a loss due to market conditions (such as a general downturn in property prices);
- where the value of the item has depreciated;
- where the value of the item is reduced for other legitimate reasons (such as accepting a lower price to effect a quick sale);
- where the amount of output tax on disposal is less than the total input tax claimed only due to a reduction in the VAT rate;
- where the item is used only for taxable (including zero-rated) purposes throughout the adjustment period (which includes the final disposal).

In practice, it will only operate where the owner of a capital item would otherwise gain an unjustified tax advantage. Even then, the tax charge will be limited to the unjustified amount. Where there is no unjustified tax advantage, a business should not apply the disposal test and it is not necessary to apply to HMRC for a specific ruling. This is only needed where arrangements for tax mitigation have been entered into affecting the particular capital item or its disposal.

There are further special provisions covering businesses transferred on a going concern basis (see **Chapter 3** at ¶30-450). In this case, the special self-supply charge in VATA 1994, s. 44 for VAT groups will not apply to any relevant capital goods, if the transfer is to a partly exempt VAT group (see VATA 1994, s. 44(4)). Also, and more generally, there is no final adjustment on the transfer of the asset. The scheme interval then applying for the transferor will end, but the transferee will, thereafter, continue to adjust the original VAT for the remainder of the five or ten year adjustments period – although by reference to his own VAT periods. The new owner also becomes responsible for any payback or clawback adjustments of input VAT that may become necessary upon a change of intended use (see HMRC Notice 700/9 Transfer of Business as a Going Concern: April 2008 at para. 3.2, and 40-250(2)).

Practice point

For those affected, the rules greatly extend the requirements on record-keeping. Details can now need to be kept for up to 16 years.

From a practical point of view, it is as well also to bear in mind that the intention is not necessarily to see a single overall calculation for all of the capital assets affected.

However, many taxpayers, particularly in the finance and insurance sectors, will be operating Partial Exemption Special Methods. Often these will be based on direct attribution or cost centre lines. Depending on what is agreed with HMRC, therefore, it may well be necessary to consider separately the actual use of each asset. Calculations could thus be fairly complex, and this may dictate the form and extent of the records to be kept.

HMRC's policy concerning the recovery of input tax in cases where an option to tax is made and the land or property in question has already been the subject of an exempt grant was set out in *Business Brief* 17/96 of 16 August 1996 following the decision in *C & E Commrs v Trustees for R & R Pension Fund* [1996] BVC 348. What they said was:

> 'The High Court decision (CO/103/96) in the case of R & R Pension Fund gave clear support to Custom's policy concerning the recovery of input tax in cases where an option to tax is made and the property in question has already been the subject of an exempt grant.
>
> In such cases, where input tax has been incurred on the acquisition of a capital item, legislation introduced on 1 January 1992 removes what was a block on input tax recovery and allows the Capital Goods Scheme to run its course.
>
> Thus, where a building is a capital item falling within the scope of the Capital Goods Scheme and an election to waive exemption (option to tax) is allowed after an exempt grant has been made, any adjustment to the input tax initially incurred must be made on an annual basis for the remaining intervals of the ten year adjustment period of the Capital Goods Scheme. Adjustments should start on the date when the building was first brought into use, in accordance with the normal operation of that scheme.'

- *Centralan Property Ltd* (MAN/00/88) was a case over the application of the capital goods rules that ended up before the ECJ in 2005 (Case C-63/04) [2007] BVC 341. The dispute concerned a subsidiary of a university, which entered into a tax planning scheme designed to enable the university to recover VAT incurred on construction work in respect of a new building. The property was let to the university at a rent that was subject to VAT, Centralan having exercised the option to tax (see later in **Chapter 8** at ¶80-150).

The aspect with which the appeal was concerned involved an exempt grant some two years later of a 999-year lease at a substantial premium (in excess of £6 million) to a fellow subsidiary, which was not VAT-registered. The supply, in this case, was not subject to VAT, because the option to tax had, by then, been disapplied for grants made on or after 30 November 1994 to a connected person by what was then VATA 1994, Sch. 10, para. 3A. Three days later, however, the company sold the freehold reversion to the university for £1,000, which, like the rents, was subject to VAT (this time because this freehold sale took place within three years of the completion of construction (VATA 1994, Sch. 9, Grp. 1, Item 1(a)(ii) (see **Chapter 8** at ¶80-150)).

The point of the dispute was how these transactions fitted into the capital goods rules. Centralan maintained there were two distinct supplies, and that there was only three days exempt use in the adjustment period ending on the date of the freehold sale. This gave a required adjustment under reg. 115(2) of only around £900 and there was no further, final, adjustment under reg. 115(3) when the freehold sale took place. HMRC, however, saw the two supplies, taken together, as the disposal of the building to which reg. 115(3) applied. Initially, they suggested the taxable element should be disregarded as de minimis in making this final adjustment. This gave a somewhat larger figure of £796,250 on which Centralan were assessed. HMRC later advanced an alternative argument, namely that the total consideration for what amounted, in reality, to the disposal of the property should be apportioned in making the final adjustment between exempt and taxable supplies. The difference between HMRC's two positions was under £200.

In the event, the Tribunal had concluded that HMRC's alternative argument was to be preferred. This was eventually followed by the ECJ in December 2005, ruling to the effect that:

> 'Article 20(3) of Sixth Council Directive 77/388/EEC of 17 May 1977 on the harmonisation of the laws of the Member States relating to turnover taxes - Common system of value added tax: uniform basis of assessment, as amended by Council Directive 95/7/EC of 10 April 1995, is to be interpreted as meaning that, where a 999-year lease over capital goods is granted to a person against the payment of a substantial premium and the freehold reversion in that property is transferred three days later to another person at a much lower price, and where those two transactions
>
> - are inextricably linked, and
> - consist of a first transaction which is exempt and a second transaction which is taxable,
> - and if those transactions, owing to the transfer of the right to dispose of those capital goods as owner, constitute supplies within the meaning of Article 5(1) of that directive,
>
> the goods in question are regarded, until the expiry of the period of adjustment, as having been used in business activities which are presumed to be partly taxable and partly exempt in proportion to the respective values of the two transactions.'

The VAT planning scheme thus failed in its objective.

Practice point

The capital goods scheme can also impact on the taxpayer's direct tax position.

Changes were made, for example, to the *Capital Allowances Act* 1990 by the *Finance Act* 1991, s. 59 and Sch. 14 (see now Capital Allowances Act 2001, Ch.18). The effect, in the case of plant and machinery (e.g. computers) was, broadly, to treat any adjustment in favour of HMRC as additional expenditure eligible for writing-down allowances in the chargeable period in which the adjustment is made. Any increase in recoverable VAT is taken as disposal proceeds and deducted from the pool.

(9) Rounding-up

In any residual input tax calculation based on percentages or respective values of supplies, the question arises as to the extent to which an element of rounding-up is appropriate.

Article 175 of the VAT Directive provides that:

> (1) The deductible proportion shall be determined on an annual basis, fixed as a percentage and rounded up to a figure not exceeding the next whole number.'

and, in the UK, in the VAT Regulations 1995, reg. 101(5) (the Standard Method) as:

> 'The percentage shall be rounded up-
>
> (a) where in any prescribed accounting period or longer period which is applied the amount of input tax which is available for attribution ... prior to any such attribution being made does not amount to more than £400,000 per month on average, to the next whole number, and
> (b) in any other case, to two decimal places.'

- In *The Royal Bank of Scotland Group plc* [2006] BVC 4,057, one of the issues was whether, when calculating the proportion of residual input tax deductible in respect of each sector of its business under a Partial Exemption Special Method, the Bank was entitled to round-up the proportion to the next whole number. In an agreement in May 2002 between HMRC and a number of banks, (the Bank included), a rounding-up was envisaged to two decimal places. The Bank later decided that the rounding in each of its sectors should be to the nearest whole number (as per art. 19 of Directive 77/388, the Sixth Directive (art. 175 of the VAT Directive)). The Tribunal, however, held that art. 19(1) specifically dealt with Partial Exemption Standard Methods and allowed rounding-up to the next unit. No restriction was placed on the Special Methods and no mention was made of rounding and, since by definition a Special Method derogated from the prescribed Standard Method, there was no objection to an agreement allowing for a different form of rounding than to the next whole unit. The matter was eventually referred to the European Court of Justice (Case C-488/07) which held that the rounding up rule was not applicable where a particular type of case was subject to a special set of rules laid down under one of the special methods (now within art. 173(2)(a), (b), (c), (d) of the VAT Directive, the purpose of which was to permit Member States to achieve greater accuracy by taking into account the specific characteristics of the taxable activities.

(10) Accounting for partial exemption and VAT periods

It will be seen from what has been said that, at its simplest, the calculation of recoverable input VAT can be open to distortion. Seasonal fluctuations, abnormal transactions (or simply timing differences) may affect the amount of VAT recovered in one period as compared with another. For this reason the rules (*VAT Regulations* 1995 (SI 1995/2518), reg. 107) look beyond the single VAT period for which a return is submitted:

(1) Initially, the partial exemption calculations are made for each normal VAT period – i.e. the normal prescribed accounting periods for which returns are submitted.

(2) The exercise is then repeated for a longer period, which for most businesses will correspond with their tax year.

(3) Any under-or over-recovery highlighted as a result of the annual review is then adjusted in the next following VAT return (reg. 107(2)).

Any adjustments needed under the *Capital Goods Scheme* are usually made in the next, subsequent return.

The *tax year* for this purpose is defined (reg. 99(1)(d)) to be normally a period of 12 months commencing 1 April, 1 May, or 1 June, according to the VAT periods originally allocated. For many businesses in the sectors covered by this book, the VAT year will, in practice, correspond with the year to 31 March. It is also possible to agree a different VAT year – for example, one coinciding with that for statutory accounts purposes. HMRC can also agree that a longer period shall apply which need not correspond with a tax year (reg. 99(7)). However, this is purely discretionary and, as seen in *Yorkhurst Ltd* [1997] BVC 4,004, HMRC are likely to refuse where the request is felt to be unreasonable.

Any adjustments under the partial exemption rules are subject to the normal four-year capping provisions. HMRC policy about how the four-year cap affects businesses' partial exemption position is illustrated in HMRC Notice 706 Partial Exemption (June 2011), at section 14.

40-250 Recovering input tax – special situations

(1) New registrations and pre-incorporation/pre-registration VAT

Most input VAT claims are straightforward. The tax is included in the return for the period in which the supply or import arises. For new registrations, however, there is further relief in reg. 111 of the *VAT Regulations* 1995 (SI 1995/2518). This falls under two basic headings:

(1) Tax on goods or services supplied to or imported by the person concerned before he was registered or liable to be registered and which were for the purposes of the business.

(2) In the case of a company, tax on goods or services acquired for its benefit or in connection with its incorporation and before incorporation by someone who:

   (a) became a member, officer or employee and was or was to be reimbursed by the company for the whole amount;
   (b) was not at the time of the supply or importation registered for VAT; and
   (c) acquired the goods or services for the company and has not used them for any other purpose.

To recover the input tax, goods must normally still be on hand at the date of registration or when the liability to be registered first arose and must have been incurred within four years before registration (reg. 111(2)(b)). The deduction of input tax on services is limited to services brought in within the six months before registration. The rule in (2) above will often not apply, of course, to companies acquired off-the-shelf (reg. 111(2)(d)). As from 1 January 2011, the ability to recover input tax under reg. 111 does not apply to items within the capital goods scheme (see reg 111(2)(e)). This is because the VAT may from that date be adjusted under the scheme. Where the person initially incurring the expenditure is VAT-registered, obtaining relief may simply be a matter of re-invoicing the costs as taxable supplies after registration, with the underlying VAT being claimed as input VAT in the meantime. Otherwise, businesses are required to claim any pre-registration input VAT on the first VAT return they are required to make. If this is not done, the claim to input tax is subject to time restrictions, so that it cannot be claimed more than four years after the date by which the return for the first period in which the input tax could be claimed (see *VAT Regulations* 1995, SI 1995/2518, reg. 29(1A)). See further HMRC's VAT Input VAT Manual at VIT 32000 and HMRC's Notice 700 The VAT Guide (May 2012), at section 11.

- As emerged from *Jolly Tots Ltd* [1996] BVC 4,068, however, the above rules are special arrangements. The normal partial exemption rules do not apply and the apportionment between taxable and exempt supplies is to be made on the basis of actual use without any of the de-minimis or other reliefs applying.
- The case of *Haugh* [1997] BVC 2,525 showed there can also be other problems. The appellant had previously been registered under another VAT number and had accounted for VAT on machinery he retained after de-registration. When he subsequently re-registered

he tried to claim back this VAT on machinery he still owned. This was denied as reg. 111 did not cover VAT on the deemed supply by the appellant on de-registration to himself.
- On a somewhat different tack, in *Gulland Properties* [1996] BVC 2,722, a case on pre-registration input tax, a property developer, who became registered when there was a change in the law to zero-rate sales of certain types of residential conversions, could not recover VAT on costs previously incurred, when such transactions were exempt.
- A further case involving property development was that of *The Trustees of Park Avenue Methodist Church* [2002] BVC 4,021, when the Tribunal concluded that the right to deduct input tax was not inviolate and the actions or inactions of the taxpayer himself may result in the right being lost.
- In *Finanzamt Offenbach am Main-Land v Faxworld Vorgründungsgesellschaft Peter Hünninghausen und Wolfgang Klein* GbR (Case C-137/02) the ECJ held that a partnership established for the sole purpose of founding a capital company is entitled to deduct the input tax paid on supplies of goods and services where its only output transaction in the performance of its object was to effect by formal act the transfer (for consideration) of the supplies obtained to that company once founded. The partnership in this case had acquired the premises and other assets of a business and incurred other expenditure preparatory to the formation of a company into which it was to be transferred. It then transferred all those assets to the company and ceased its own activities. Its claim to deduct input tax had been refused on the ground that, under German law, the transfer to the company would not have been a supply for VAT purposes. Under UK law, the corresponding provisions in the TOGC rules (art. 5 of the *VAT (Special Provisions) Order* 1995 (SI 1995/1268) would not have resulted in no supply treatment in the absence of any intention by the partnership to itself carry on the business concerned (see **Chapter 3** at ¶30-450).
- See also HMRC's VAT Input Tax Manual ay VIT63200

(2) Other adjustments after the event

In addition, the *VAT Regulations* 1995 (SI 1995/2518), reg. 108 and 109 can require or allow further adjustments of input VAT. They apply if goods or services acquired for the making of taxable supplies or exempt supplies are not so used, but are diverted to another use within six years. In the case of reg. 108, the result will be that all, or a proportion of, the input tax originally recovered must be repaid. In similar circumstances, reg. 109 can result in a corresponding repayment often previously unrecovered. See generally in HMRC's Notice 706 Partial Exemption (July 2011) at section 13. These rules have been extended as of 1 January 2011 to include (and allow adjustments in non-business (including private)) use other than VAT initially allocated entirely for non-business purposes (reg. 110(5)).

- *Tremerton Ltd v C & E Commrs* [2000] BVC 3 was a case over whether there should be an adjustment after the event under reg. 108. Tremerton was a property developer which had entered into an agreement to acquire part of a former hospital for redevelopment. The idea was to demolish the existing building and construct residential apartments in its place. Various fees were incurred and, as the intended development was within the zero-rating provisions (see **Chapter 8** at ¶80-100), the related input tax was recovered in full.

In the event, finance was not forthcoming and the site was sold, with the benefit of the consents obtained, as an exempt supply. HMRC sought to recover the tax refunded. The

Tribunal, and ultimately, the High Court agreed. Permission to appeal to the Court of Appeal was refused.

- *Wiggett Construction Ltd* [2001] BVC 2,159 provided another example. The appellant was, again a property developer, whose stock-in-trade was housebuilding. The issue was whether input tax incurred by it on the purchase of property, and subsequently recovered as input tax, should be repaid to HMRC as being attributable to the exempt disposal of the property to a housing association or should be apportioned to reflect the improvements arising from the subsequent construction of buildings on that land by the appellant.

  HMRC said there was no connection between the appellant's sale of the land and the building works. The input tax incurred on the purchase of the land was attributable to its subsequent exempt sale and was, therefore, non-deductible.

  The appellant argued the exempt sale was dependent upon agreement by the housing association that it would carry out the building works. The Tribunal agreed. It was necessary to consider the relationship between reg. 108 and art. 185(2) of the VAT Directive (formerly art. 20(1)(b) of the Sixth Directive (Directive 77/388)). The latter provides for adjustment to the initial deduction of VAT where, after the return is made, some change occurs in the factors used to determine the amount to be deducted. One of those factors is the extent to which inputs are attributable to taxable or exempt supplies. The only real change in the factors was the exempt supply of property to the housing association. The appellant never had the intention of disposing of the property undeveloped: the intention at the time of purchase was to make taxable supplies and that intention was fulfilled when the property was disposed of. If the property was sold for a consideration that contemplated the construction works being carried out, then the time of construction was a matter of mechanics rather than substance.

- *Royal and Sun Alliance Insurance Group plc v C & E Commrs* [2003] BVC 341, considered adjustments under reg. 109. It concerned a number of surplus leasehold properties, all of which had been occupied by the Group in its insurance business at one time or another. Attempts were made to sublet and, in the meantime, as the superior landlords had opted to tax the properties, VAT was incurred during the vacant periods on the rents and service charges paid. None of this tax was claimed at first. Royal had not itself opted to tax the properties as it wished to retain some flexibility in case a potential occupier were found for which VAT on property costs was unattractive. It eventually, in November 1995, did opt to tax the properties, however, and, at that stage, relied on reg. 109 (which applies, where there is a change in intention) to give retrospective relief.

  HMRC had allowed the recovery of input tax from November 1995 onwards, but said anything incurred before then could only be attributed to exempt supplies. The sale or letting of property was essentially VAT-exempt and, in the absence of an option to tax by Royal in this intervening period, this was all the input tax could be related to. The Tribunal agreed and, although this was overturned by the High Court on appeal, Royal ultimately lost before the House of Lords.

  As the House saw it, each lease was intended to be used in supplying either an exempt sublease or (after an election) a taxable sublease; one or the other, but not both. To come within reg. 109, Royal must have:

  - first had an intention to use the inputs in supplying exempt subleases; and
  - then used them, or formed an intention to use them, in supplying taxable subleases.

4 Input VAT and Partial Exemption

The claim under reg. 109 was made on the basis that, during the vacant unelected period Royal was carrying on an *economic activity* for the purpose of making exempt outputs. In such a case, there was no right to deduction. (*Belgium v Ghent Coal Terminal NV* (Case C-37/95) [1998] BVC 139 ECR I-1 considered.)

In deciding to elect and make taxable supplies, Royal was in no different position from someone who decided to change from an activity which involved making exempt supplies to a different activity making taxable supplies. If there were still inputs around from the previous activity which could be used in the new taxable activity, like a building which had been constructed for exempt letting and was then used, after an election, for taxable letting, the taxpayer would be entitled to an adjustment. But he could not form a new intention about the services supplied for the purposes of the old business. They were different services which had already been used.

Practice point

It is notable, perhaps, that two of their Lordships dissented. The position was, therefore, hardly clear-cut and many might feel that Royal should have succeeded. However, a better example of how reg. 109 is expected to work might be hard to find.

The case serves as a reminder to watch for the potential consequences of a change in intent, which can have the effect of allowing full, as opposed to a partial, or even nil, recovery, of input tax and, especially where property is concerned, to keep an eye on the implications of opting to tax (or not).

It also, of course, serves as a reminder of the possible reduction in the recovery of input tax under the corresponding reg. 108, where input tax is provisionally attributed to taxable supplies, or to both taxable and exempt supplies, and, within six years, it turns out that the VAT is, in the event, only used to make supplies that are exempt.

(3) Holding companies

One area that has given particular difficulties is that of holding companies. On the face of it, this may be of a less obvious concern in the finance and insurance sectors. Recovery rates tend in any event to be low so that any further restriction is likely to be marginal. However, this will not always be the case.

(a) The general situation

The problem stems largely from the *Value Added Tax Regulations* 1995 (SI 1995/2518), reg. 101. Input tax on costs incurred in making exempt supplies or in carrying on any activity other than the making of taxable supplies may not be deducted. Putting this into context:

- taxable supplies, other than perhaps management charges to a subsidiary, may be limited, or not made at all;
- the emphasis will often be on acquiring and owning subsidiaries, receiving dividends (outside the scope), interest (exempt) and ultimately, perhaps, sale proceeds (also exempt);
- the company may, in addition, carry out a group treasury function, looking after group borrowing, the investment of surplus funds and the hedging of currency risk (again largely exempt); and

- it may also provide the main Board function, which may directly generate no supplies at all.

The scope for recovering input VAT can thus be clearly limited and, for some time, HMRC adopted a rather narrow approach. Input VAT relief was denied on a wide front and holding companies could generally expect little, if anything, back. It mattered little whether they were registered on their own or as part of a VAT group. However, the position as it is at present is that:

- tax on general holding company expenses is eligible for deduction in the same way as VAT incurred on other expenses, unless the company is a pure holding company and not VAT-registered;
- direct attribution is expected wherever possible.
- VAT on non-supply economic activities and VAT of a general overhead nature is treated as part of residual input VAT;
- full relief will only be given if the taxpayer is fully taxable. Exempt input VAT may thus need to be below the de minimis limits (i.e. £625 per month on average (or less than 50 per cent of total input VAT) see ¶40-150(5)), if partial exemption calculations are not to be made.
- A holding company may be entitled to input tax recovery to the extent it/or its subsidiaries make taxable supplies outside the group or in accordance with any partial exemption method, but this may be in doubt for share acquisition costs (see later).

In addition, from a Community law perspective, the CoJ has recently helpfully clarified VAT deductibility rules for holding companies in *Portugal Telecom* (see ¶40-200(5)(a)).

(b) Acquisition costs

A particular problem with holding companies can be the recovery of input VAT on acquisition costs. As cases like *Polysar Investments Netherlands BV v Inspecteur der Invoerrechten en Accijnzen, Arnhem* (Case C-60/90) [1993] BVC 88 have shown, the ECJ has consistently held that art. 4 of the Sixth Council Directive (art. 9 of Council Directive 2006/112/EC) must be interpreted as meaning that a holding company, whose sole purpose is to acquire holdings in other undertakings, and which does not involve itself directly or indirectly in their management does not have the status of taxable person for VAT. Consequently, there is no inherent right to deduct input tax (see also *Floridienne SA v Belgium* (Case C-142/99) [2001] BVC 76). There has to be a *direct and immediate link* with the acquirer's business activities as a whole and the making of taxable supplies.

In this context, therefore, the making of management charges may clearly sometimes be the key to input VAT recovery, although not surprisingly, perhaps, HMRC do not tend to accept that the VAT on, say, acquisition costs or the cost of defending against a take-over bid can be directly attributable under reg. 101(2)(b) to taxable management charges made to subsidiary companies. However, the decision of the ECJ in the *Cibo* case seems to have put this in perspective.

- *Cibo Participations SA v Directeur régional des impôts du Nord-Pas-de-Calais* (Case C-16/00) [2001] ECR I-6663[2002] BVC 605 concerned a taxpayer who had sought to deduct input VAT on expenditure on services rendered to it in connection with the purchase of shares in subsidiary companies, on the basis that it subsequently provided management and other services to those companies for which it charged a fee. The French VAT authorities took the view, however, that the deduction should be disallowed as the expenditure related simply to the ownership of shares and receipt of dividends, which were *outside the scope* (see **Chapter 3** at ¶30-200). The Court, however, held that:

(1) The involvement of a holding company in the management of companies in which it has acquired a shareholding constitutes an economic activity within the meaning of Article 4(2) of the Sixth Council Directive 77/388/EEC of 17 May 1977 (art 10 of Council Directive 2006/112/EC) on the harmonisation of the laws of the Member States relating to turnover taxes – Common system of value added tax: uniform basis of assessment, where it entails carrying out transactions which are subject to value added tax by virtue of Article 2 of that directive, such as the supply by a holding company to its subsidiaries of administrative, financial, commercial and technical services.

(2) Expenditure incurred by a holding company in respect of the various services which it purchases in connection with the acquisition of a shareholding in a subsidiary forms part of its general costs and therefore has, in principle, a direct and immediate link with its business as a whole. Thus, if the holding company carries out both transactions in respect of which value added tax is deductible and transactions in respect of which it is not, it follows from the first subparagraph of Article 17(2) of the Sixth Directive 77/388 (art 168 of Council Directive 2006/112/EC) that it may deduct only that proportion of the value added tax which is attributable to the former.

(3) The receipt of dividends does not fall within the scope of value added tax.'

thus effectively going against the HMRC view.

There is recent litigation as to whether input tax can be claimed on certain acquisition costs (see generally Chapter 11). In *R & C Commrs v BAA Ltd* [2011] UKUT 258; [2011] BVC 1,664 the Upper Tribunal decided that BAA was not in a position to recover the VAT it incurred on fees related to a successful takeover bid. The case is under appeal to the Court of Appeal. The material facts of this case were that:

- BAA incurred VAT on fees paid by it in connection with a successful takeover bid of a target company. The taxpayer was previously called Airport Development and Investments Limited (ADIL) which was formed as a company to bid for the target, which was BAA. Against this background, following the takeover, ADIL joined the same VAT group as BAA. The representative member of that VAT group claimed recovery of the VAT as input tax as part of the group's general overheads. At the time of the bid for BAA, ADIL was not registered for VAT.
- HMRC argued that no recovery was available for the VAT costs incurred on fees, and sought to recover £6.7 million. ADIL appealed against the assessment.
- The First-Tier Tribunal allowed ADIL's appeal on the basis that it was carrying on an economic activity. However, the Tribunal's decision was subsequently reversed by the Upper Tribunal.

The reasons for the Upper Tribunal's decision were as follows:

- ADIL carried on an economic activity at the time the services were received.. The purpose of ADIL's acquisition of BAA was not an end in itself but was the first step of an onwards investment, which involved management of BAA (see para. 71 of the judgment). The nature of the management included the provision of services by ADIL to the BAA group.

- However, the Tribunal decided that there was no *direct and immediate* link between the costs and any onward taxable supplies made by ADIL. Referring to the finding of fact by the First-Tier Tribunal, the Court said (at para. 72 of the judgment):

"... ADIL was found by the Tribunal to have an intention to provide taxable services to BAA only from the time of completion of the BAA takeover (not before, when the VAT was incurred). ADIL was not found to have any such intention prior to then.'

- In relation to the costs incurred by ADIL, the largest fee was £30 million paid to Macquarie Bank Limited for its services as co-financial adviser in connection with the acquisition of BAA. In this regard, the Upper Tribunal commented that there was no link between the costs incurred by ADIL and the services it was to supply to BAA (at para. 73 to 74 of the judgment):

"The Macquarie fee was, as we have observed, expressly found by the Tribunal to be mainly concerned with the takeover and not for any services to be provided for ADIL to BAA (or any other company in the BAA group) post- takeover albeit the Macquarie services had a continued beneficial effect on the ADIL/BAA group after the takeover. The First-tier Tribunal was silent about the other fees as to any allocation between the takeover itself and post-takeover activities and we do not make any observation in relation to the other fees. Any continuing indirect benefit (for example, "being open to strategic management": see paragraph 84 of the First-tier Tribunal decision) is too remote to provide a direct and immediate link to taxable supplies by ADIL, even if it were established (as it has not been) that those management services had been intended taxable supplies before the takeover.

Thus we cannot attribute any of the fees (or the VAT incurred by ADIL) to any post-completion activity or supply made by ADIL at all. In other words none of the costs incurred by ADIL can be considered to be cost components of a taxable supply by ADIL itself or attributed to ADIL by reason of the VAT grouping provisions which means there is no direct or immediate link between ADIL's VAT and any onward taxable supply.'

The decision of the Upper Tribunal is the subject of appeal, but as yet the decision of the Court of Appeal has not been released.

In contrast to *BAA*, in *Cloud Electronics Holdings Limited v R & C Commrs* [2012] UKFTT 699 (TC), released on 11 November 2012, the First-Tier Tribunal has held that a newly formed company established to acquire and manage a target company in a management buyout was entitled to recover input tax on professional fees incurred during the acquisition process. On the facts, it was regarded as carrying on a genuine economic activity (management services) and there was a direct and immediate link between the supply of services to the new company and the onward supply by it of management services to the target company (there was e.g. evidence of management charges). This case illustrates that steps should be taken as early as possible in an acquisition process to minimise the risk of challenge (e.g. registering the new company for VAT, ensuring suppliers' letters of engagement clarify that services will be provided to the new entity, receipt of invoices post-incorporation of the new entity, clearly documenting the entity's intention before completion to carry out economic activities, e.g. taxable management services, and/or to join a VAT group, and charging for the management services immediately upon the acquisition, etc).

> **Practice point**
>
> Whilst, on this basis, the making of management charges may well be important, it should not, perhaps, be relied upon as the key to input VAT relief. It could still be vital to consider the overall context and a degree of synergy with the business of the company or group as a whole could be necessary.

A holding company may also still need to consider what exempt supplies are made, especially if it arranges finance for the group or looks after the group's property interests. Some of these may or may not be disregarded (HMRC have been known to suggest that they may well not be prepared to ignore as *incidental*, for example, exempt supplies, such as interest or the sale of shares in subsidiaries) and holding companies with a substantial trade or which are VAT grouped with trading subsidiaries will generally be in the best position to obtain relief.

In the case of acquisition costs, VAT grouping with the target company from the outset would seem generally to give the best prospect of relief on technical grounds.

- The decision of the ECJ in *Empresa de Desenvolvimento Mineiro SGPS SA (EDM) v Fazenda Publica* (Case C-77/01) ECJ [2006] BVC 140 may, however, put the sale of subsidiaries into perspective. As noted earlier, it was held in this case that activities which consist in the simple sale of shares and other securities, such as holdings in investment funds, do not constitute *economic activities* within the meaning of art. 4(2) of Sixth Directive and that turnover relating to these transactions was to be excluded from the calculation of deductible input tax.

  Conversely, cases like *Securenta* (see also below) and *Portugal Telecom* (see 40-200(5)(a)) have clarified that companies which carry on some non-economic activities outside the scope of VAT (e.g. the acquisition, holding or sale of shares as an investment activity) may suffer irrecoverable input VAT that flows through to those activities, as only the proportion of the input VAT which is attributable to the business' economic activity should be recoverable within (and subject to) the partial exemption calculation. However, this should mean that where proceeds raised are solely used to acquire or fund a fully taxable activity/business, the input tax associated with that should be recoverable (in full or subject to any partial exemption rate). Therefore, in appropriate cases, holding companies within VAT groups may be able to retain further VAT recovery because VAT inputs associated with raising capital for acquiring or funding a subsidiary within the VAT group to generate taxable supplies may be regarded as incurred for a business purpose (subject to cases like *BAA* above). The internal arrangement within a group whereby one company raises money in order to invest it in a separate group company can be disregarded because companies within a group are treated as a 'single taxable person' (Art. 11 of the VAT Directive).

  Finally, it is, however, also worth noting here that there are scheduled hearings at the CoJ with regard to the European Commission's infringement proceedings against a number of member states, including the UK and Ireland, for allowing the inclusion of non-taxable persons (e.g. passive holding companies) in VAT groups. The proceedings were announced by the European Commission in 2009 and it referred several countries to the CoJ in June 2010. Most recently on 27 November 2012, Advocate General Jääskinen delivered his opinion to the proceedings against Ireland, opining that the VAT Directive does permit non-taxable persons to be members of a VAT group. If the CoJ follows the Advocate

General's opinion, the UK's current VAT grouping rules will be compliant with the VAT Directive.

(c) Issuing shares or securities

The position of share issue costs has now, of course, been radically altered following the decisions of the ECJ in the *KapHag* and *Kretztechnik* cases mentioned earlier at ¶40-000 and in **Chapter 1** where an issue as such was held not to be a supply for VAT. As noted earlier, if the share issue is made for the purposes of an economic activity (e.g. raising capital, then any related input VAT may be recoverable in full or subject to an d in accordance with any partial exemption method being used. To recap *Kretztechnik*, the VAT incurred on associated costs was residual input tax because the share issue was carried out by Kretztechnik in order to increase its capital for the benefit of its economic activity in general. As Kretztechnik only made taxable supplies, the input tax was fully recoverable. However, the subsequent CoJ case of *Securenta Göttinger Immobilienanlagen und Vermögensmanagement AG v Finanzamt Göttingen* (Case C-437/06) indicated that a share issue was not automatically connected with taxable supplies, but could also be made to fund a non-economic purpose as well, and in that case a business/non-business apportionment was also needed. Where the business was partly exempt then a proportion, as determined by the partial exemption method in place at the time, could be recovered.

Accordingly, to ensure recovery of input VAT incurred in connection with a share issue, a group with non-economic activity will need to carefully consider what action (supported by evidence) it can take to ensure that share issue proceeds are used solely for economic activities. For example, before deciding upon a share issue, it could be prudent to ensure that professional advice on general funding options can be clearly identified and separate (and billed separately) (in order to be treated as overhead expenditure) from advice relating to a share issue itself.

One other point that should also be mentioned is that, prior to *Kretztechnik*, where a company issued shares to non-EU investors, the related input tax on any professional fees was recoverable (*Value Added Tax (Input Tax) (Specified Supplies) Order* 1999 (SI 1999/3121)). HMRC however confirmed post-*Kretztechnik* in *Business Briefs* 21/05 (23 November 2005) and 22/05 (1 December 2005) that, from 29 November 2005, input tax on costs related to shares/securities issued to non-EU investors should be treated as residual as such issues are no longer supplies for VAT purposes. According to HMRC, the residual input tax will still be recoverable in full if the issue was made for the purposes of a fully taxable business, or restricted if made for the purposes of a partly-exempt business.

40-300   Accounting generally and records

The timing of claims

Article 167 of Council Directive 2006/112/EC provides that:

> 'A right of deduction shall arise at the time the deductible tax becomes chargeable.'

4 Input VAT and Partial Exemption

As a general rule, this means input VAT is reclaimable in the return made for the prescribed accounting periods in which the tax points (see **Chapter 3** at ¶30-300) for the VAT inputs arise (*Value Added Tax Regulations* 1995 (SI 1995/2518), reg. 29).

Before making any claim, however, the taxpayer must usually hold (although satisfactory alternative evidence may be considered by HMRC under reg. 29 to allow a claim (see HMRC's Input VAT Manual at VIT31200)):

- a VAT invoice made out to him by the supplier of any standard-rated goods or services (see **Chapter 3** at ¶30-600);
- a supplier's invoice in the case of imported services within VATA 1994, Sch. 5 and s. 8 (see **Chapter 5**); or
- Customs import documents showing VAT in the case of imported goods.

Where input VAT exceeds output VAT, as will be the case for many businesses in the sectors covered by this book, a net repayment is made.

In the event that there are errors in accounting for output or input VAT or in any return submitted, these are to be corrected as and when HMRC require and in accordance with the particular rules in reg. 35 and 36. With the introduction of the present simplified VAT return, they are to be separately notified unless the net value of errors arising in a given VAT period is less than £50,000, except where the then VAT turnover is less than £5,000,000 when the limit only increases to 1 per cent of that turnover (unless the net error is less than £10,000) (*Value Added Tax Regulations* 1995 (SI 1995/2518), reg. 34(3)).

In short, as shown in *Terra Baubedarf-Handel GmbH v Finanzamt Osterholz-Scharmbeck* (Case C-152/02) [2006] BVC 672, in order to claim input tax relief, the claimant must be able to show that the goods or services must have been delivered and must hold an invoice. The claim must also, strictly, be exercised in respect of the tax period in which these two conditions are satisfied.

In addition, following the ruling of the ECJ in *Finanzamt Gummersbach v Bockemühl* (Case C-90/02) [2006] BVC 95 a person who, as the recipient of services, is liable to account for VAT under the reverse-charge (see **Chapter 5**) is not obliged, in order to exercise his right to deduct, to be in possession of an invoice.

An accommodation has been reached with HMRC over the treatment of transactions paid for by the use of the corporate purchasing cards developed by several banks and card companies. Sometimes known as *procurement cards*, they are designed to eliminate much of the paperwork traditionally surrounding the purchasing process, and also to be fully compatible with VAT accounting requirements. One of the main features of purchasing cards is that, under normal circumstances, suppliers are not required to issue invoices to their customers. The invoicing is carried out by the customer's card company or bank, on their behalf, using transaction information that has been transmitted through the purchasing card system. Details of what this accommodation entails are to be found in Notice 701/48 (March 2002). This deals, amongst other things, with the special considerations that arise in relation to tax points, invoicing and the evidence required to support an input tax claim.

> **Summary**
>
> This Chapter has attempted to cover the essential elements affecting the recovery of input tax, something which is often one of the main concerns for the VAT-exempt sectors at which this book is aimed.
>
> How partial exemption is approached will, however, depend very much on the nature of the business concerned and of the types of transactions undertaken. A frequent cause of difficulty can be the failure to properly appreciate what particular activities or products actually involve, both legally and from a practical point of view, and to put this into context.
>
> Hopefully, the commentary in later Chapters, especially Chapters 7 to 10 will help put this into perspective.

Further commentary on the exclusions in the recovery of input VAT on cars under the Value Added Tax (Input Tax) Order 1992 (SI 1992/3222) (see Chapter 4 at ¶40-050).

The definition of a motor car will be of interest to finance companies providing such vehicles on lease or contract hire.

More specifically, the wording of art. 7(2) of the 1992 Order, as now amended, reads (emphasis added), so far as is relevant in the present context:

'Paragraph (1) above [the exclusions from credit] does not apply where -

(a) the motorcar is -
   (i) a *qualifying* motor car;
   (ii) supplied (including on a letting on hire) to, or acquired from another Member State or imported by, a taxable person; and
   (iii) the *relevant condition* is satisfied;

(aa) (aa) the motor car forms part of the stock in trade of a motor manufacturer or a motor dealer;

(b) the supply is a letting on hire of a motor car which is not a qualifying motor car (other than a supply on a letting on hire of a motor car which is not a qualifying motor car by virtue only of the application of paragraph (2C) below, to a person whose supply on a letting on hire prior to 1st August 1995 resulted in the application of that paragraph);

(c) the motor car is unused and is supplied to a taxable person whose only taxable supplies are concerned with the letting of motor cars on hire to another taxable person whose business consists predominantly of making supplies of a description falling within item 14 of Group 12 of Schedule 8 to the Act [hiring to other lessors for onward hire to disabled persons in receipt of a mobility allowance or mobility supplement]; or

(d) the motor car is unused and is supplied on a letting on hire to a taxable person whose business consists predominantly of making supplies of a description falling within item 14 of Group 12 of Schedule 8 to the Act by a taxable person whose only taxable supplies are concerned with the letting on hire of motor cars to such a taxable person.'

Article 7(2A) then defines a motor car as a *qualifying* motor car if:

(a) it has never been supplied, acquired from another member State, or imported in circumstances in which the VAT on that supply, acquisition or importation was wholly excluded from credit as input tax by virtue of paragraph (1) above; or
(b) a taxable person has elected for it to be treated as such.'

Article 7(2B), (2C) and (2D) contain further provisions on *qualifying* motor cars and art. 7(2E) defines the *relevant condition* in art. 7(2)(a)(iii) in terms of the car being intended for use either:

(a) exclusively for the purposes of a business carried on by him, but this is subject to paragraph (2G) below [i.e. a qualification]; or
(b) primarily for a relevant purpose.'

The *relevant purposes* (art. 7(2F)) are:

(a) to provide it on hire with the services of a driver for the purpose of carrying passengers;
(b) provided it for self-drive hire; or
(c) use it as a vehicle in which instruction in the driving of a motor car is to be given by him.'

In this context, self-drive hire (art. 7(3)(b)) means hire where the hirer is the person normally expected to drive the car and where the period of hire to each hirer, together with the period of hire of any other motor car expected to be hired to him by the taxable person will normally be less than:

- 30 consecutive days; and
- 90 days in any 12-month period.

The qualification in art. 7(2G) alluded to in art. 7(2E)(a) applies where the car is let or made available either:

- for no consideration or for a consideration of below market value; or
- whether or not for a consideration (otherwise than by letting it on hire), to any person for private use.

Where these rules apply the effect (art. 7(2H)) is, as noted earlier, that one half of the tax remains blocked. The block does not apply where the motor car is used, i.e. is not new.

A 'motor car' for the purposes of these provisions means any motor vehicle of a kind normally used on public roads which has three or more wheels and either:

- constructed or adapted solely or mainly for the carriage of passengers; or
- having to the rear of the driver's seat roofed accommodation fitted with side windows or constructed or adapted for the fitting of side windows;

but does not include vehicles:

- capable of accommodating only one person;
- meeting the requirements of the *Road Vehicles (Construction and Use) Regulations* 1986 (SI 1986/1078) and capable of carrying 12 or more seated persons;
- of not less than three tonnes unladen weight;
- constructed to carry a payload of one tonne or more;
- constructed for a special purpose other than the carriage of persons and having no other accommodation for carrying persons than such as is incidental to that purpose;

- or caravans, ambulances and prison vans;
- vehicles constructed for a special purpose other than the carriage of persons and having no other accommodation for carrying persons other than as incidental to that purpose.

London type taxis were included from 1 December 1999, as were 12-seater vehicles not meeting road safety regulations.

5 Services from Abroad – The Reverse-Charge

Overview

This Chapter considers:

(1) The general concept for imported services, including some limitations in their scope.

(2) The types of services covered.

(3) Some points affecting particular supplies, including:

    (a) seconded staff; and
    (b) management charges.

(4) Implementation and accounting issues.

50-000 The general concept for imported services

A principal feature of VAT is that it is territorial. Each Member State is meant to tax only consumption within its own jurisdiction (see **Chapter 1**). Looking at this simplistically, the obvious inference, perhaps, is that acquiring a service from abroad can be cheaper. Were this to be true, the result would potentially, therefore, be a loss of revenue and distortion of competition.

To counter this, for most types of services, the importer who is a business recipient is subject to a *reverse-charge*; what this means is that the onus for accounting for any resulting VAT is placed on any taxable person to whom those services are supplied (art. 196 of Council Directive 2006/112/EC). In the UK, the corresponding statutory rules are found in VATA 1994, s. 8.

The principal services to which these rules are applied are those in art. 44 of Council Directive 2006/112/EC (previously the reverse charge was focused on the services referred to in art. 56 of Council Directive 2006/112/EC, prior to its amendment by Council Directive 2008/8/EC, with effect from 1 January 2010). This provides for certain services to be treated as *supplied where received*, where the customer is in a different country to the supplier. In the UK, the services used to be those listed in VATA 1994, Sch. 5, but are now all services where the recipient of the services is a relevant business person who belongs in the UK, and the place of supply of services is in the UK; and to all services to which any paragraph of Part 1 or Part 2 of Sch. 4A to VATA 1994 applies, and the recipient is registered as a taxable person under VATA 1994 (s. 8(2), VATA 1994) (see **Appendix 4** for details of the services subject to Sch. 4A). However, the reverse charge does not apply to services of any of the descriptions specified in Sch. 9 of VATA, such as Group 5 finance (see generally Chapters 7 to 10) (s. 8(4A)). Where the reverse-charge applies, the potential loss of revenue is countered by the recipient charging itself VAT in what amounts to a self-supply process;

- output VAT is accounted for by reference to what is paid; and
- at the same time, corresponding input VAT relief is given (subject, in the case of many of the businesses covered by this book, to a potential restriction under the partial exemption rules (see **Chapter 4** at 40-200)).

In its practical effect, this is not dissimilar, therefore, to the rules for acquisitions of goods from other Member States (see **Chapter 3** at 30-300), or the provisions on the self-supply of building services (see 40-100 and 80-150).

How the reverse-charge works is explained later at 50-050.

(1) Limitations

The imported services provisions do not apply to services imported by private individuals or otherwise for non-business purposes, and they do not apply to any services which are exempt supplies within any of the descriptions of Sch 9 to VATA (s. 8(4A)), such as the finance exemption for services referred to in Group 5. They only apply to importations by businesses.

The reverse charge does not apply to supplies of services where both the supplier and customer belong in the UK.

Equally, because they relate to *supplies*, they do not operate for transfers within the same legal entity, e.g. on a secondment of staff from head office to branch (this is expressly recognised by HMRC in their manuals at VATFIN1560). In such circumstances there can, of course, be no supply in the real sense:

- one cannot provide the services to oneself;
- by the same token, there can also never be consideration.

In contrast if the same services are acquired from a third party, e.g. under an outsourcing arrangement, then the services will be subject to the reverse charge.

To that extent, therefore, the rules will differ from those for acquisitions (see **Chapter 3** at 30-300) and also from the rules for imported goods (VATA 1994, s. 1(4)).

The position on self-supplies stems from basic principles, as now confirmed in the *FCE Bank plc* case.

- The ECJ Ruling in *Ministero dell'Economia e delle Finanze and Agenzia delle Entrate v FCE Bank plc* (Case C-210/04) [2009] BVC 692 concerned the supply of management, consulting, data processing, employees' training, and the supply and management of software, from the Head Office of a UK bank, FCE Bank plc, to its branch in Italy. Under Italian VAT law, these services were liable to Italian VAT, which the branch could not fully recover. FCE disputed the charge to tax and, on a Reference to the ECJ, the Court ruled that:

'a fixed establishment, which is not a legal entity distinct from the company of which it forms part, established in another Member State and to which the company supplies services, should not be treated as a taxable person by reason of the costs imputed to it in respect of those supplies.'

(2) Groups

It may be thought that a similar position to that in *FCE* would apply in the case of companies, which are members of a VAT group in as much as VATA 1994, s. 43 creates the fiction of a single taxable person in the form of the representative member. However, although not strictly a reverse-charge issue as such, there has, since 1996, been a tax charge for the representative member of a VAT group, where certain supplies are purchased by an overseas member of that group and on-supplied to another, UK member. These measures are to be found in VATA 1994, s. 43(2A) to (2E). The supplies affected are also those to which the reverse charge applies (see (1) above), and the provisions were introduced as an anti-avoidance measure to prevent services being routed tax-free via an overseas branch of one of the companies forming the VAT group, which, as a non-UK establishment, belongs outside the UK and can thus acquire those services VAT-free.

- Briefly, *Shamrock Leasing Ltd* [1999] BVC 2,032 was a case involving the alleged interaction of the rules on the place of supply of services and the grouping provisions in VATA 1994, s. 43 (prior to the amendment of the place of supply rules in what is now Council Directive 2006/112/EC). Equipment leased to a contractual customer within the VAT group, but belonging outside the EC was then leased back to a UK end-user within the same VAT group under a sub-lease. The idea was that the first lease, a head lease to a US-based company with no presence in the UK, was not subject to VAT by reason of the rules on services supplied where received in art. 16 of the *Value Added Tax (Place of Supply of Services) Order* 1992 (SI 1992/3121) (see **Chapter 3** at 30-250). The subsequent underlease, being within the VAT group, was disregarded under the rules in VATA 1994, s. 43(1) so that, in theory, the end-user, a partly exempt bank (see **Chapter 4**) effectively enjoyed the equipment VAT-free instead of incurring a substantial amount of irrecoverable input tax.

HMRC issued an assessment in respect of the period ending 31 August 1996, on the basis that the initial supply under the head-lease was within the scope of UK VAT, as it was to be treated as made to the representative member of the VAT group, a company having a business establishment in the UK. In the event, they lost the appeal, not because their point was incorrect, but because the inclusion in the VAT group of the US company was invalid. The initial supply was thus correctly outside the scope, but not for quite the reason the taxpayer anticipated. The subsequent intra-group supply was, by the same token, not relieved by VATA 1994, s. 43(1) and was, in theory, taxable under the reverse charge. Unfortunately, it seems, by the time the decision was given, HMRC were too late to issue an amending assessment.

In short, the appeal succeeded because of what the Tribunal held was an invalid approach to membership of a VAT group. In a sense, therefore, *Shamrock* appear to have won by accident rather than design.

Whilst only a few schemes had been found in operation, the measure was particularly intended to prevent attempts to circumvent the rules introduced from 1997 for the treatment of telecommunications services provided by non-UK service providers.

(3) Imports by fully exempt businesses

The reverse-charge does not just apply to businesses carried on by *taxable* persons in the sense of traders who are both making taxable supplies and are registered for VAT (or required to be registered see **Chapter 2**). It also affects otherwise fully exempt businesses, which can be required to become registered, where the value of any of the specified imported services, together with any other taxable supplies made or deemed to be made, exceeds the registration limits.

50-050 What is covered?

Almost any service can be imported, and the principal reverse-charge rules apply to the full scope of services which are supplied to a recipient who is a relevant business person who belongs in the UK, and in respect of which the place of supply of services is in the UK (VATA 1994, s 8(2)). Additionally, the reverse charge applies to the services to which any of the paragraphs of Part 1 or 2 of Sch 4A to VATA 1994 apply and the recipient is registered as a taxable person under VATA. Briefly, the range of services within this Schedule are (see Appendix 4):

General Exceptions

- services relating to land;
- passenger transport;
- hiring means of transport;
- restaurant and catering services;
- EC on-board restaurant and catering services;
- hiring of goods (other than transport);
- telecommunication and broadcasting services;
- exceptions relating to supplies made to relevant business person;
- electronically supplied services; and
- admission to cultural, educational and entertainment activities.

The reverse charge provisions are clearly important – especially for an exempt or partly exempt business, for which they can represent the prospect of an additional VAT cost. However, the provisions do not apply to any services which are exempt supplies within any of the descriptions of Sch 9 to VATA 1994 (s. 8(4A)).

Deciding what is, and what is not affected, is not always straightforward, because a number of different factors can come into play, ranging from defining what it is that is actually being supplied, something that is not always apparent from the descriptions and documentation used, to deciding the appropriate VAT liability – e.g. whether something is standard-rated, zero-rated or exempt. Specifically:

- what the rules do not cover is any service which is exempt from VAT, e.g. monetary financial services or insurance (see **Chapters 7 and 9**); and
- there will also be no effective charge where the service is zero-rated.

What is covered? 50-050

As noted earlier at 50-000, the rules will also not apply to facilities provided within the same legal entity (e.g. branch/branch or branch/head office) this is true even where debit notes or adjustments are made for internal accounting purposes, because, as confirmed in *Ministero dell'Economia e delle Finanze and Agenzia delle Entrate v FCE Bank plc* (Case C-210/04), there can, from basic principles, be no actual supply in this situation.

The types of service the rules will apply to within the banking, financial and insurance sectors will include most forms of service other than any services which are exempt supplies within any of the descriptions of Sch 9 to VATA 1994 (s. 8(4)).

Type of service	Commentary	Legislation
(a) General		
Services which are supplied to a recipient who is a relevant business person who belongs in the UK, and in respect of which the place of supply of services is in the UK		VATA 1994, s 8(2)
Illustrative services	Standard-rated	
Actuarial, auditing, accountancy and data processing services	Standard-rated	
Advertising services	Standard-rated	
Legal services	Standard-rated	
Management services	Standard-rated	
Supply of staff	Standard-rated	
Surveys and appraisal services (e.g. surveyors, architects, engineers, etc.)	Standard-rated	
(b) Part 1 services (General Exceptions)		Sch 4A VATA 1994
Services relating to land (to the extent not within Sch. 9 of VATA 1994)	Standard-rated	
Passenger transport	Standard-rated	
hiring means of transport	Standard-rated	
restaurant and catering services	Standard-rated	
EC on-board restaurant and catering services	Standard-rated	
hiring of goods (other than transport)	Standard-rated	
telecommunication and broadcasting services;	Standard-rated	
(c) Part 2 services (exceptions relating to supplies made to relevant business person)		Sch 4A VATA 1994
electronically-supplied services	Standard-rated	
admission to cultural, educational and entertainment activities	Standard-rated	

5 Services from Abroad – The Reverse-Charge

Type of service	Commentary	Legislation
(d) Investment expenses	Standard-rated	
Euroclear charges	Euroclear is seen as providing a single supply of services. However, the service comprises the delivery of stock against payment, stock lending and the associated custody and money transfer services. As such the supply is treated as essentially exempt. The reverse charge does not, therefore, apply	VATA 1994, Sch. 9, Grp. 5
Investment advice	Standard-rated	
Stockbrokers' services on the purchase and sale of investments	Exempt and not subject to the reverse charge	
Trustee services	Normally standard-rated	
(e) Insurance and related costs		
Claims handling services by insurers, ILU agents, overseas agents and insurance brokers	Exempt and hence not subject to the reverse charge provisions	VATA 1994, Sch. 9, Grp. 2, item 4
Consultant engineers' services	See Loss adjusters', etc. below	
Engineering inspection services	See Loss adjusters', etc. below	
Lloyd's agents' services	If the services are of claims handling, as under Claims handling, etc. above. Otherwise, treatment is as for loss adjusters' services	
Loss adjusters' or others' services supplied in connection with the assessment of any claim	Normally standard-rated. However, the supply will not be within the reverse charge if it is a service relating to land outside the UK or comprises valuing goods where the goods are situated and the services are performed outside the UK and the Isle of Man. This is because different place of supply rules apply (see Chapter 3)	
Marine surveyors' and aviation engineers' services	Normally these are standard-rated. However, they will be zero-rated if a service is for or in connection with the survey of a ship or aircraft described by Sch. 8, Grp. 8, item 9. The reverse charge will not then apply	
Motor assessors' services	See Loss adjusters', etc. above	
The service of loss adjusters when handling the complete settlement of a claim (including payment) as agent of the insurer	Exempt as for Claims handling services above - thus not subject to the reverse charge	VATA 1994, Sch. 9, Grp. 2

The further simplification

As a *simplification* measure the reverse charge was, broadly, further extended to a number of other supplies. Those affected were, and are services, where the supplier is *established* outside the UK but for which the place of supply is the UK for reasons other than the status or location of the recipient. In other words, to things like:

- services related to UK land, *Value Added Tax (Place of Supply of Services) Order* 1992 (SI 1992/3121), art. 5 (art. 45 of Council Directive 2006/112/EC), see Part 1 Sch 4A VATA 1994;
- the hiring of a means of transport for use in the UK, *Value Added Tax (Place of Supply of Services) Order* 1992 (SI 1992/3121), art. 17 and 18 (art. 58 of the Sixth VAT Directive (Directive 77/388)), see Part 1, Sch 4A, VATA 1994.

These are the services referred to in Part 1 and Part 2 of Sch 4A VATA (as discussed above).

The measure was introduced in order to make things easier for overseas suppliers not established in the UK, by imposing a reverse-charge in place of a requirement for the supplier to be registered here. Registration can still be due, however, if UK supplies to non-VAT registered recipients exceed the current VAT registration threshold (see **Chapter 2**). The supplier may also still request to be registered, in which case the relaxation does not operate.

Where the overseas supplier makes use of this simplification and is not registered for VAT in the UK, any VAT incurred on costs arising in the UK will be recoverable under the European Refund Scheme or Thirteenth VAT Directive (Directive 86/560) refund rules in the *Value Added Tax Regulations* 1995 (SI 1995/2518), Pt. XX and XXI (see **Chapter 4** at 40-150).

50-100 Points affecting particular supplies

In practice, the most commonly imported services will often be those involving staff secondment and management charges. This will be especially so for international groups. The control exercised by a foreign holding company or parent, for example, will result in varying degrees of management involvement and this will usually mean charges of one kind or another.

(1) Seconded staff

A simple charge from an overseas parent/associate for the use of expatriate personnel will clearly be caught. However, the reverse-charge can be avoided if either:

- the individuals concerned become, temporarily at least, actual employees of the host company. So long as there is then no charge from the original employer no supply will arise (i.e. due to employed persons not being treated as carrying on an economic activity, and accordingly being outside the scope of VAT: Art. 10 of the VAT Directive); or, alternatively,
- they retain their legal employer/employee relationships with the overseas company but the UK host pays any salaries or other employment costs direct to the employee, and the UK host exercises exclusive control over the allocation and performance of the employee's

duties during the period of secondment, and/or discharges the employer's obligations to pay any third party PAYE, NICs, pension contributions and similar payments relating to the employee.

The second of these situations can be especially useful but only applies so long as the amounts paid are:

- not recharged to the overseas employer, who then raises a management fee; and
- are expressed to be borne by the UK business *in consideration of* the secondment.

Where both conditions are satisfied, the reverse-charge should disregard the amounts so paid. No further amounts should be paid to the employer seconding its employee. The individuals are in essence regarded as de facto employees of the UK business (see HMRC Notice 700/34 Statement of Practice B (May 2012)).

For either to be effective, however, care needs to be taken over the form and wording of any contractual arrangements. There can also be a number of commercial, income tax and National Insurance implications to be considered.

> ### Practice point
>
> A point to watch is where the secondment is arranged or accounted for via a member of a VAT group with establishments both in the UK and abroad. In this situation, unless the employee is legally employed by the VAT group member concerned, there can be a problem from the anti-avoidance provisions found in VATA 1994, s. 43(2A) to (2E) and referred to earlier.
>
> What can easily happen, in practice, is that the actual Group employer is a holding company or affiliate not connected with, or part of, the VAT group. The salary costs of the seconded expatriate staff are billed intra-group abroad to the non-UK establishment of the VAT group member. When these are then recharged through to the UK, it is easy to miss the fact that another non-UK company is involved and the fact that this may be a purely related-party transaction will not prevent s. 43(2A) to (2E) from applying.

(2) Management charges

Management services are within the scope of the reverse charge. Administration or secretarial services are also within the scope of the provisions.

> ### Practice point
>
> M*anagement charge* is a ubiquitous term that tends to be used indiscriminately, and because of this, it can be important to examine exactly what is being provided:
>
> - management, as such, is often not provided, but, instead the service may be one of consultancy, advice, legal services or accountancy;
> - on occasions, the service may be better described as marketing or sales; or

> - alternatively, perhaps, it may be better classified as the provision of finance – a disguised interest charge.
>
> Identifying the true nature of what is being provided can be important in ensuring the correct result. It can also be important to consider any knock-on implications for direct tax, because, to cite just one possibility, a different treatment could be required within the direct tax system, with the prospect, in some cases, that tax might need to be withheld. With HMRC now dealing with both direct and indirect tax issues a comparison by both branches of the Department could have unfortunate consequences.
>
> It can be equally important to see that the charge is afforded the correct treatment in the Statutory Accounts.

(3) Services relating to land

Services relating to land are subject to the reverse charge provisions (VATA 1994, Sch. 4A, para. 1), but only to the extent they are not services within any of the descriptions specified in Sch. 9 of VATA 1994.

Land for this purpose includes walls, fences, landscaping, growing crops and buildings or other structures fixed permanently to the land. It also includes plant, machinery or equipment, which is an installation or edifice in its own right (e.g. a refinery). It will not normally, however, extend to machinery, which is merely installed in buildings and is capable of being removed. This is regarded as goods unless incorporated into the structure of the building as such.

Architects' or other design fees are also subject to the reverse charge provisions since they will fall within the general scope of services supplied to a relevant business person.

As observed earlier, the reverse-charge can also be extended to land-related services if the supplier is not established in the UK and the recipient is not VAT-registered but in consequence of receiving the supply breaches the threshold for registration (see **Chapter 2**).

(4) Insurance

For insurance services, it is necessary to distinguish between claims-handling and claims-assessment. The former, which includes the payment of claims as agent for the insured, is basically exempt (VATA 1994, Sch. 9, Grp. 2, item 4). Claims adjustment or assessment, on its own, is basically standard-rated.

(5) Telecommunications

In the case of telecommunications, there are special rules in VATA 1994, Sch. 4A, para. 8 governing the treatment of rights to relevant telecommunications services. However, these are subject to the reverse charge.

(6) Accounting

In accounting terms, services within s. 8 VATA 1994 acquired from abroad must be included in the return for the VAT period in which the supply occurs. Output tax is accounted for in the

5 Services from Abroad – The Reverse-Charge

VAT period in which the tax-point arises, at the same time, corresponding input VAT relief is given by including the VAT accounted for along with any other input VAT incurred by the business in that period. However, businesses which are partly exempt will then potentially suffer restriction in the amount that can be claimed (see **Chapter 4** at 40-150). The tax point in this context is deemed to take place (*Value Added Tax Regulations* 1995 (SI 1995/2518), reg. 82) as follows:

(i) such services (excluding those supplied for a period for a consideration the whole or part of which is determined or payable periodically or from time to time) are treated as made when the services are performed;

(ii) such services that are supplied for a period for a consideration the whole or part of which is determined or payable periodically or from time to time are treated as separately and successively made at the end of the periods in respect of which payments are made or invoices issued, and to the extent covered by the relevant payment or invoice;

(iii) when in the case of a service to which (i) applies, a payment is made in respect of the supply before the time specified in (i) the time of supply is treated as made at the time the payment is made;

(iv) where in the case of services to which (ii) applies, and either (a) a payment is made at a time that is earlier than the end of the period to which it relates or (b) a payment is made which is not made in respect of any identified period the time of supply is treated as made at the time the payment is made;

(v) where the supply of services to which (iii) applies (a) commences before 1 January and continues after 31 December of any year, and during that year no invoice is issued that has effect for the purposes of (iii) above and no payment is made in respect of that supply then the services supplied during that year are treated as being supplied on the 31 December of that year to the extent that the recipient has received the benefit of them.

Payment for this purpose will not, however, be limited to a simple remittance of cash. In many cases, there will also be *constructive payment*, for example, where amounts due are subject to set-off on inter-company account. The value (i.e. the amount on which tax is due) is determined for this purpose by VATA 1994, Sch. 6, para. 8:

- where the consideration is in money, the value is equal to the consideration actually paid;
- where the consideration is not money or is not wholly money, it is such an amount in money as is equivalent to the consideration. In other words, it equates with the value or cost to the recipient of the supply of what is given in return.

50-150 Implementation

Where a business has a *fixed establishment* or *place of belonging* in more than one Member State, there can clearly be a conflict, when there is a choice as to in which Member State the rules are to be applied. This was an issue that arose in the *Zurich Insurance* case (a case prior to the *EU Implementing Regulations*, which are discussed below).

- *R & C Commrs v Zurich Insurance Co* [2007] BVC 283 involved a taxpayer, a Swiss company, with its headquarters in Zurich and subsidiaries and branches in a number of other countries, including a branch in the UK. New software was introduced in the UK with the help of consultants, PwC. PwC were hired by Zurich's head office in Switzerland, but subcontracted the work to their UK office, most of the services being physically provided at Zurich's offices in the UK.

The invoices submitted by PwC did not include VAT, but, had Zurich obtained the same or similar services from a supplier based in the UK, it would have suffered tax at 17.5 per cent, which, given the nature of Zurich's business, would have been largely irrecoverable. HMRC considered Zurich was liable to account for tax under the reverse-charge. However, the company maintained the services were supplied in Switzerland, where it was established, not, as HMRC argued, in the UK where it had a fixed establishment.

The Tribunal allowed the taxpayer's appeal but Park J, in the High Court ([2006] BVC 458), decided differently:

(1) Article 9(2)(e) of the Sixth Directive (art. 56 of Council Directive 2006/112/EC, but repealed by Council Directive 2008/8/EC art 2 with effect from 1 January 2010, and replaced by art. 59 by Council Directive 2008/8/EC art 2) provided that the place where services of consultants were supplied when performed for customers established outside the European Community, such as Switzerland, was the place where the customer had established his business or had a fixed establishment to which the services were supplied.

(2) On the facts, the only tenable conclusion was that the consultancy services in question were supplied to the taxpayer at its UK establishment. The Tribunal had erred in viewing the most important consideration as the place at which the contract for the services to be supplied was made. VAT was not charged on the supply of the service making a contract for services. It was charged on the supply of the services, which had been contracted to be supplied.

(3) When a work order was signed, the taxpayer contracted with the consultants for them to provide services to its UK establishment. It was a contract made in Switzerland of a kind that, for commercial reasons, the head office would want to be involved. However, the consultants were not providing or supplying their services to the taxpayer at its head office by making a contract to do so. They provided or supplied the services after they had made the contract, performing them entirely in the UK through a subcontractor. The actual provision of the services to the taxpayer in the UK far outweighed in importance the feature that the contract which the consultants performed in the UK had been made in Switzerland. In reality, the fixed establishment of the taxpayer to which the services were supplied was its establishment in the UK and not its head office in Switzerland.

(4) The conclusion that the consultancy services were supplied to the taxpayer's fixed establishment in the UK was not just the only tenable conclusion on the facts. It was also the conclusion which produced a rational result which avoided non-taxation in a case where there ought to be taxation and which avoided distortion of competition.

Accordingly the Tribunal's decision could not stand.

The following EU VAT principles apply to determine in which country a supply is taxable where a taxable person is established in more than one country (EU Implementing Regulation, art. 21, see further at HMRC'S guidance at www.hmrc.gov.uk/mauals/vatprossmanual/VATPOSS05000. htm; Place of supply of sercices: Establishment making or receiving the supply: Contents. See also HMRC Notice 741A (January 2010), in particular at para 3.6 and 3.7):

- the supply is taxable in the country where that taxable person has established his business (i.e. the head office is the preferred establishment, unless that leads to an inappropriate or irrational result for tax purposes);
- where the service is provided to a fixed establishment of the taxable person located in a place other than that where the customer has established his business, that supply is taxable at the place of the fixed establishment receiving that service and using it for its own needs;
- where the taxable person does not have a business establishment or a fixed establishment, the supply is taxable at his permanent address or usual residence.

The following principles are applied to determine the identity of the fixed establishment to which a service is supplied (EU Implementing Regulation, Art 22):

- the supplier is required to examine the nature and use of the service provided to the taxable person;
- where the nature and use of the service provided do not enable the supplier to identify the fixed establishment to which the service is provided, the supplier, in identifying that fixed establishment, is required to pay particular attention to whether:
  - the contract;
  - the order form; and
  - the VAT identification number attributed by the Member State of the customer and communicated to the supplier by the customer, identify the fixed establishment as the customer of the service, and whether the fixed establishment is the entity paying for the service.

Where the customer's fixed establishment to which the service is provided cannot be determined in accordance with the above principles or where services are supplied to a taxable person under a contract covering one or more services used in an unidentifiable and non-quantifiable manner (e.g. under a global contract whereby a business could enter into a contract for a single supply of consultancy services to analyse the global set-up and e-commerce practices at the head office and overseas branches), the supplier is entitled to consider that the services have been supplied at the place where the customer has established its business (EU Implementing Regulation, art 22). HMRC should regard services under a global contract with a clear direct benefit to the business as a whole, including a number of establishments, as supplied to the main business establishment. However, this approach should be distinguished from a global framework agreement which sets the terms for a number of individual supplies. HMRC considers that it is important to look at the individual transactions which, as separate supplies, will have separate VAT consequences. HMRC's example is that of a head office which enters into a framework agreement with a supplier pursuant to which individual branches draw up and purchase work from local brances of the Supplier. According to HMRC, the services will be viewed as supplied to the branches even if the head office dictates the terms and receives an indirect benefit. There are also further rules on who accounts for VAT where a taxable person has a fixed establishment. These are that where a taxable person (supplier) has a fixed establishment in the territory of a Member State where VAT is due, the supplier is treated as a taxable person who is not established within that Member State when it makes a taxable supply in that Member State and any fixed establishment of the supplier 'does not intervene in that supply' (VAT Directive, art 192a).

In other words, VAT is not due from a supplier's fixed establishment within the same Members State as their customer, unless that establishment intervenes in the supply. In the application of this Article, a fixed establishment of a taxable person will only be taken into consideration when it is characterised by a sufficient degree of permanence and a suitable structure in terms of human and technical resources to enable it to make the supply of goods or services in which it intervenes (EU Implementing Regulation, art 53(1)). Where a taxable person has a fixed establishment within the territory of the EU where the VAT is due, that establishment shall be considered as not intervening in the supply of goods or services, unless the technical and human resources of that fixed establishment are used by that person for transactions inherent in the fulfilment of the taxable supply of those goods or services made within that Member State, before or during this fulfilment: art 53(2). Where the resources of the fixed establishment are only used for administrative support tasks such as accounting, invoicing and collection of debt-claims, they shall not be regarded as being used for the fulfilment of the supply of goods or services: art 53(2). However, if an invoice is issued under the VAT identification number attributed by the Member State of the fixed establishment, that fixed establishment shall be regarded as having intervened in the supply of goods or services made in that Member State unless there is proof to the contrary: art 53(2). In the UK, HMRC states that the UK position is that the establishment making the supply is the one most closely connected to it. Therefore, minimal involvement in making the supply will not be viewed as 'intervening' for UK VAT purposes. However, where a taxable person has established its place of business within the territory of the Member State where the VAT is due, this does not apply, irrespective of whether or not that place of business intervenes in the supply of goods or services which are made in that Member State (EU Implementing Regulation, art 54).

> ### *Practice point*
>
> Not surprisingly, given how they generally arise, the impact of imported services is often overlooked. For example:
>
> - it may simply be that VAT is not expected, especially if the supplier is outside the EU, although, as noted in **Chapter 3** at 30-550, the present requirements for intra EU supplies between businesses do require invoices with an indication of the applicability of the reverse-charge;
> - the absence of a VAT invoice can cause the point to be missed;
> - many occur in the context of groups and the relationships between those involved will then cause charges for services of this kind to be viewed as merely *internal adjustments*.
>
> Unfortunately, VAT law makes no allowance for this and it can be important to ensure that proper procedures are put in place so that any VAT is correctly identified and accounted for.
>
> Imported services can also arise in situations where there are reciprocal arrangements between the two parties involved. As with ordinary supplies, the rules do not permit any *netting-off*. Services paid for *in kind* must still be grossed-up to the value to the supplier (VATA 1994, s. 19(3)) (see 30-400).

5 Services from Abroad – The Reverse-Charge

> **Summary**
>
> This Chapter addresses some of the more common issues with imported services, something that is frequently overlooked and which, as a result, can be the cause of unexpected and unwelcome expense.
>
> Many of the issues arise in the context of connected-party arrangements, especially with international groups, a topic explored in Chapter 6. The issues are also becoming increasingly relevant in relation to outsourcing, a topic also covered in later Chapters in this book.

60-050

6 Groups and Connected Parties

> **Overview**
>
> This Chapter considers:
>
> (1) Some problems and planning opportunities for connected parties.
>
> (2) Central administration issues and cost-sharing.
>
> (3) Employment and secondments.
>
> (4) Consortiums and joint ventures.
>
> (5) VAT groups.
>
> (6) Cost sharing arrangements.

60-000 Introduction

Many of the problems (or, for that matter, planning opportunities) occur in situations where there are close structural or organisational ties, for example, in the context of groups or connected parties.

(1) Often this results from the holding of shares:

    (a) in the case of a group, more than 50 per cent of the equity;

    (b) in other cases, say, on a 50:50 basis, as a membership of a consortium or as a minority associated shareholder.

(2) Alternatively, the link may be via a partnership or joint venture.

(3) There may simply be common organisational needs.

In any of these situations, matters can arise on a day-to-day basis, which can be important from a VAT point of view, but which are not always recognised. The result can then be potentially avoidable problems or planning opportunities that may be missed.

60-050 Central administration: cost-sharing

Cost-sharing is a common situation. A major advantage in groups, for example, is the ability to rationalise overheads: having one centre for administration, a central accounting function, and, often, sharing premises. Costs may initially be paid, or incurred, by one company, perhaps the holding company, a service company or, as often happens, the largest trading company in the group. Once paid, these may or may not then be re-charged or shared. Whether and how this is done then becomes an issue.

Charges, if made, can be assumed to be for a variety of things:

- just *cost re-allocations* and of little consequence;
- agency payments;
- justified as a *management charge*; or
- attributed to the provision of a service of one kind or another.

Just as often, perhaps, the matter may be viewed simply as an *internal arrangement*, with little thought being given to what is really involved and, in many cases, without much to show in the form of documentation.

All of these, though, can have quite different VAT implications, quite apart from how much is to be charged. Not making charges at all may also sometimes be considered, but, often, that will itself not be without risk.

(1) Cost-sharing

Cost-sharing should, in theory, create no greater VAT burden than arises on the underlying expense. If two or more people agree to split the cost of doing something, and that cost is shared without uplift, there is no value-added, merely the passing on of part of the expense in its original form.

In practice, however, arrangements for actually contracting jointly with third-party suppliers are rare. Most cost-sharing situations tend to start out with one party incurring the expense in the first instance as principal, often before any question of cost-sharing arises. In consequence, what the *cost-sharing* then results in is the provision of a service of some kind to the others involved.

Recharges of salaries, rent and rates, lighting, heating and insurance, computer time and overheads may then simply be elements of an overall service charge. Non-VATable costs such as salaries and rent (*outside the scope* and *exempt*) may thus become taxable as part of an overall *management charge*. The issue then is to decide what that service represents.

Whether it is possible to improve the position by separately itemising the constituents is debatable. It is necessary, as a starting point to be able to justify looking at the different elements as distinct and separate supplies in their own right. Subject to this:

- rent, for example, can only be on-charged as exempt (VATA 1994, Sch. 9, Grp. 1) if the person charged is genuinely occupying identifiable accommodation. However, this will not generally be possible if the space is shared, is supplied on a flexible hot-desk basis or is occupied by staff who are, themselves, shared or jointly employed. In such circumstances it can be hard to see the necessary exclusivity that occupation implies;
- a charge for salaries or wages can only be VAT-free if the staff are employed from the outset under joint contracts of employment. Recharges for either must generally be standard-rated.

In any event, a charge for property costs may attract VAT, even if there is an actual right of occupation, where the party making the charge has opted to tax (see **Chapter 8** at 80-150).

Whether and to what extent it ultimately matters that VAT is due may depend, of course, on the status of the recipient:

- if exempt or partly exempt, the result can be an internally created VAT cost;
- if taxable, however, the addition of VAT will not be a problem, but there may then be an improvement in the position of the charging company if the way it applies the partial exemption rules (see **Chapter 4**) means its ability to recover input VAT is enhanced.

Cost sharing is subject to an exemption in art. 132(1) of Council Directive 2006/112/EC. The measure allows groups to exempt from VAT, supplies made to their members, provided that certain conditions are met. Article 132(1) provides:

> '(f) the supply of services by independent groups of persons, who are carrying on an activity which is exempt from VAT or in relation to which they are not taxable persons, for the purpose of rendering their members the services directly necessary for the exercise of that activity, where those groups merely claim from their members exact reimbursement of their share of the joint expenses, provided that such exemption is not likely to cause distortion of competition;'

The exemption provided in the Directive is implemented in UK law by Group 16, Sch. 9 of VATA 1994 (introduced by the FA 2012), which provides:

> 'The supply of services by an independent group of persons where each of the following conditions is satisfied: (a) each of those persons is a person who is carrying on an activity ("the relevant activity") which is exempt from VAT or in relation to which the person is not a taxable person within the meaning of Article 9 of Council Directive 2006/112/EC, (b) the supply of services is made for the purpose of rendering the members of the group the services directly necessary for the exercise of the relevant activity, (c) the group merely claims from its members exact reimbursement of their share of the joint expenses, and (d) the exemption of the supply is not likely to cause distortion of competition.'

The application of this exemption is governed by detailed secondary legislation, which is discussed at 60-300.

Practice point

It can be important to remember that if a service is being provided, this will not necessarily equate with the underlying costs and VAT liabilities.

(1) A charge for a share of VAT-exempt rent could remain VAT-exempt, if that is all the charge represented; and

    (a) the party incurring the original cost has not opted to tax; and
    (b) the person charged is in actual occupation of a distinct part of the property; but

(2) a charge for salaries and wages, which are non-VATable when paid to an employee, becomes taxable as a secondment fee or a fee for a share of the employee's time when part of the cost is on-billed to the extent not within the scope of the Secondment Concession in Notice 700/34 (May 2012); and

(3) a charge that is simply itemised between a series of administration or overhead costs tends to be for an overall management service of some kind – often taxable.

(2) Agency

Genuine agency arrangements tend to be equally rare, even in a group context. Again, what usually happens is that expenditure is incurred first; consensus on who bears what is reached later.

- Certainly, as demonstrated in *C & E Commrs v Tarmac Roadstone Holdings Ltd* (1987) 3 BVC 91, it is difficult to argue otherwise, where contracts are already in place (for example, for telephones, leases or staff) before some of the participants join the group or share in the administration arrangements.

To an extent, perhaps, this may be qualified as a result of the decision in *Durham Aged Mineworkers' Homes Association v C & E Commrs* [1994] BVC 145. The appellant provided leasehold housing for aged miners, typically residential care accommodation. Durham Mineworkers' Homes Association also provided leasehold accommodation to miners, the two entities sharing headquarters, office accommodation and staff. The appellant, Aged, held the freehold of the office accommodation, and Mineworkers employed and paid all the staff. Aged paid all the bills for the office accommodation and other administrative overheads, and charged 50 per cent of those costs to Mineworkers. Mineworkers charged 50 per cent of all the headquarters' staff's, and 100 per cent of all residential care staff's, salaries and associated costs to Aged. Two staff items were paid for directly by Aged, namely staff training and travel, and it charged 50 per cent of such costs to Mineworkers.

There was no express contract between the two entities covering this sharing of costs, and they did not invoice each other in respect of them. HMRC saw this as giving rise to taxable supplies. However, the view of the Court was that the only reasonable conclusion on the evidence showed an implied agreement between the parties to share expenses and that the appellant, Aged, would pay for them as principal in respect of its agreed share and as agent for Mineworkers in respect of the remainder.

Whether this would be followed, though, in a more commercial context is, possibly debateable.

Practice point

As a general rule, if real joint contracting or agency is to be effective, establishing that the appropriate relationships are actually agreed, and in place, at the material times will be vital, as will be the documentation. Seldom is it possible to rely on either being accepted by implication. Careful drafting of the contracts and associated documentation is necessary to achieve certainty of VAT treatment of supplies. For further discussion see Chapter 1 at 10-100.

(3) Management charges

The real problem with *management charges* is that this is a fairly ubiquitous term and can mean anything or nothing. Often, they are not well documented or the documents do not properly reflect what is being provided. In order to reach the correct answer from a VAT perspective, it can be necessary, therefore, to analyse exactly what it is that is involved, and, sometimes, the motivation behind the charge.

(1) Some of the problems with itemised costs (as in *Cost sharing* above), which are frequently necessary for things like transfer pricing issues, for example, can be in deciding whether they are supplies in themselves or are simply functions in the context of an overall service. This, in turn, raises the question of *single or multiple supplies* as in the *Card Protection Plan* case (see **Chapter 3**) and of defining the VAT liabilities.

(2) In terms of defining the supply, *management*, as such, is a service within the reverse charge, so there are obvious potential implications for charges to and from overseas affiliates. It may be that a more appropriate description is required in order to properly fix the VAT treatment.

(3) Consultancy, advice, legal services or accountancy, or the provision of information, for example, would be within the reverse charge provisions, and the place of supply and the VAT treatment would then depend on the place where the recipient of the service belonged.

(4) Marketing or sales assistance, on the other hand, would, potentially, be an agency service, where the place of supply would follow that of the underlying transaction that is arranged.

(5) Sometimes, a *management charge* really represents finance or interest, in which case, its treatment would be basically VAT-exempt, rather than taxable.

(6) As shown in *C & E Commrs v Tilling Management Services Ltd* (1978) 1 BVC 185, something like the surrender of group relief, which, on its own, would be *outside the scope*, can be taxable if expressed to be *in return* for the procurement of a service of some kind.

And occasions do arise where management charges are simply made in order to move profit from one part of a group to another and, in reality, do not represent supplies at all – something that can give potential problems from both a VAT and direct tax standpoint.

(4) Exemption

Charges are not, of course, always VATable. Sometimes they are exempt – a particular advantage if the recipient is unable to recover all or part of its input VAT.

- For an insurance company, for example, charges representing the underlying costs of administration might represent an insurance or reinsurance transaction within VATA 1994, Sch. 9, Grp. 2 (art. 135(1)(a) of Directive 2006/112/EC (art. 13B(a) of the Sixth Directive, Directive 77/388)).

  An underwriting manager or an underwriting agency may charge separately for salaries and other administration costs on an itemised bill. VAT can easily be expected, if this type of charge is taken at face-value. However, recognising instead that the service is really a single composite supply of underwriting management or the arrangement of insurance could give it a quite different complexion. The salaries and other costs could then simply be elements of the calculation of the overall fee. This will then be exempt if the supplier can import a sufficient insurance flavour by showing it requires particular insurance expertise. It may then be accepted as falling within VATA 1994, Sch. 9, Grp. 2, item 1 or be an *insurance related* service within art. 135(1)(a) of Directive 2006/112/EC (art. 13(B)(a) of the Sixth VAT Directive (Directive 77/388)). This now needs to be considered, though, in the light of the potential implications of *Staatssecretaris van Financiën v Arthur Andersen & Co. Accountants c.s.* (Case C-472/03) [2006] BVC 228 discussed later in **Chapter 9**.

In the financial sector, a similar charge representing the management of a company providing, say, consumer credit might amount to the arrangement of exempt finance.

To secure exemption, however, it is even more important to decide exactly what is being supplied and how; also to see it is properly described in any inter-company agreements. It is often also now necessary in this context to consider the implications of single or multiple supplies and the decision in *Card Protection Plan Ltd v C & E Commrs* (Case C-349/96) [1999] BVC 155 (see **Chapter 3** at 30-550).

Depending on the circumstances, it may also be possible, as hinted earlier, to reduce an otherwise VATable supply by highlighting individual exempt elements in the overall amount billed.

- A specific charge might, for example, be made for rent. To justify this, though, it must be possible to show that identifiable accommodation is being separately occupied. This would be hard to justify, of course, if the employees using the accommodation were jointly employed or were employed by the company making the charge. But isolating a charge for a supply of accommodation would, potentially, then raise other implications. It might, for example cause the party being charged to have a presence (a fixed establishment, say) at the location concerned, which might, in turn, if that person is normally based overseas, mean that it also *belonged* here for VAT.

A charge for exempt interest is another possibility. However, it must be possible to show there is a subsisting loan on which the interest can be based. The interest charge should also be reasonable.

Practice point

With both rents and interest there are, of course, direct tax and accounting aspects to consider as well:

- rents, for example, may need to be treated for tax purposes as property income, rather than trading income and the possibility that the person charged, if non-UK resident, might have a permanent establishment here for corporation tax purposes;
- with interest, there is the requirement, perhaps, to deduct income tax in the absence of being able to pay on a gross basis between UK corporates (see ITA 2007, Part 15, Chapter 11).

For both, rents and interest, the accounting treatment may also be quite different from that for a management charge and a consistent approach will clearly be important.

---

(5) Not charging for something

If no charges are made, because the party incurring a particular cost is normally able to recover input tax, whilst the person benefiting could not, or would suffer some restriction, there is a risk of a total disallowance. To qualify as input tax of the claimant the expense would need to be for something supplied to the claimant and for the purposes of the claimant's business. The absence of any charge might lead to the conclusion that either:

- the expense was not incurred for the purposes of a business, since *business* implies the making of taxable supplies; or
- there was an *abuse of right*.

If charges are made below full-value, other problems can arise. If the person paying the costs ends up bearing an expense, which is only partly for its own benefit:

- there is the risk of a partial disallowance of input VAT. This could be either under VATA 1994, s. 24(5) or under s. 25 and reg. 101 of the *Value Added Tax Regulations* 1995 (SI 1995/2518);
- there is also, now, perhaps the possibility of a deemed onward-supply as a result of the *Value Added Tax (Supply of Services) Order* 1993 (SI 1993/1507) in the case of the free supply of business services – or under VATA 1994, Sch. 4, para. 5 in the case of the free use of business assets.

Making a charge at a less than fair price to a connected party gives HMRC the power of directing tax to be accounted for as if a market value charge had been made. VAT law contains express anti-avoidance provisions where the parties are connected within the terms of CTA 2010, s. 1122 (see **Appendix 7**). Under VATA 1994, Sch. 6, para. 1, HMRC may direct that VAT will be accounted for as if market values had been charged. These cannot, however, be applied retrospectively.

The EU provision on market value attribution is Art. 80 of the VAT Directive, which provides that:

> '1. In order to prevent tax evasion or avoidance, Member States may in any of the following cases take measures to ensure that, in respect of the supply of goods or services involving family or other close personal ties, management, ownership, membership, financial or legal ties as defined by the Member State, the taxable amount is to be the open market value:
>
> (a) where the consideration is lower than the open market value and the recipient of the supply does not have a full right of deduction under Articles 167 to 171 and Articles 173 to 177;
>
> (b) where the consideration is lower than the open market value and the supplier does not have a full right of deduction under Articles 167 to 171 and Articles 173 to 177 and the supply is subject to an exemption under Articles 132, 135, 136, 371, 375, 376, 377, 378(2), 379(2) or Articles 380 to 390b;
>
> (c) where the consideration is higher than the open market value and the supplier does not have a full right of deduction under Articles 167 to 171 and Articles 173 to 177.'

The scope of Art. 80 was recently considered by the CoJ in *Balkan and Sea Properties ADSITs* (C-621/10), *Provadinvest OOD (C-129/11) v Direktor na Direktsia 'Obzhalvane i upravlenie na izpalnenieto' – Varna pri Tsentralno upravlenie na Natsionalnata agentsia za prihodite* where the Court concluded that Art. 80(1) is exhaustive and the rules cannot be applied beyond the ambit of the article, for example to situations where the taxpayers have a full right of input tax deduction. The CoJ held that Art. 80(1) has direct effect so that if any open market value provisions of a Member State are incompatible with the terms of Art. 80(1) then a taxpayer has the right to rely on it directly to oppose the application of provisions of national legislation that are contrary to it.

There are also further anti-avoidance measures to prevent the option to tax in relation to property being effective for supplies between connected persons where one of the parties is partly exempt. These are discussed later in **Chapter 8** at 80-150.

60-100   Employment

Similar problems arise from employment arrangements. In a group context, it is not uncommon for one company to act as paymaster. A single staff department may be used for administrative convenience and to ensure a common approach to contracts and other employee issues. There may even be a group payroll. Whatever the arrangement, charges will be made to the other companies concerned. In some cases, these will be linked to the salary and other costs of specific employees; in others, there will be a different allocation, perhaps on the basis of work done.

Paying and recharging salary costs VAT-free is not, however, always easy to achieve. Salaries and wages are *outside the scope* – but only between employee and employer i.e. if the companies charged are the true employers. But this usually requires evidence, something that can sometimes be difficult to identify. What is needed can include corroboration from employment contracts, hiring and firing practice and belief on the part of employees. Then, and often only then, can the recharge be simply a disbursement and not chargeable.

The position is especially difficult where costs are shared, as the recharge almost invariably means a taxable supply of services (see *C & E Commrs v Tarmac Roadstone Holdings Ltd* (1987) 3 BVC 91, *British Airways Board and British Airways Housing Trust Ltd* (LON/78/191) No. 663, *PHH Europe plc* [1995] BVC 889 and *WJ Marston & Son Ltd* [1998] BVC 4,025).

But avoiding VAT is possible. For example:

- one company may employ individuals as agent for another, possibly even for itself and others jointly; or
- there may even be joint employment contracts.

Either would enable costs to be recharged or shared without VAT. Substantiating them can, again, be difficult, though, given the tendency towards inadequate documentation in a group context. Both, however, are rarely met and it can be hard to justify if employment by one company is already in place.

Nonetheless, the HMRC Statement of Practice now found in an Appendix to HMRC Notice 700/34 (May 2012) will often eliminate, or significantly reduce, any exposure to a VAT charge or cost. What it says, in particular, in part B (emphasis added), is:

> 'B Secondment of staff by businesses other than employment businesses
>
> (1)   The arrangements described in paragraph 2 below apply from 1 April 1997.

(2) The secondment by an employer (other than an employment business within the meaning of the Employment Agencies Act 1973) of a member of its staff (the employee) to another business which –

   (a) exercises exclusive control over the allocation and performance of the employee's duties during the period of secondment;
   (b) is responsible for paying the employee's remuneration directly to the employee; and/or
   (c) discharges the employer's obligations to pay to any third party PAYE, NICs, pension contributions and similar payments relating to the employee, then, to the extent that any such payments as are mentioned in paragraphs (b) and (c) above form the consideration or part of the consideration for the secondment of the employee to the other business, they shall be disregarded in determining the value of seconding the employee.

(3) For the purposes of paragraph 2 above, an employer shall not be treated as seconding an employee to another business, if the placing of the employee with that other business is done with a view to the employer's (or any other person associated with him) *deriving any financial gain* from –

   (a) the placing of the employee with the other business, or
   (b) any other arrangements or understandings (whether or not contractually binding and whether or not for any consideration) between the employer (or any other person associated with him) and the other business (or any person associated with it) with which the employee is placed.'

Practice point

It can be as well to remember that restructuring employment or payment arrangements can involve considerations other than just VAT.

(1) Employing seconded individuals direct avoids the VAT but can bring an extra cost in terms of National Insurance, where the extra employer's contributions alone may exceed the potential net VAT saving. Businesses also sometimes need to consider the effect on matters such as pension plans and benefit packages.

(2) Simply paying seconded employees direct often achieves much the same result as if there were a change in employer. (See para. 3 of HMRC Leaflet 700/34 (May 2012), and the scope of the conditions). The National Insurance issue may still, though, remain. Businesses also need to avoid cross-charging the costs between the host and an overseas employer, as this can easily reinstate the reverse charge on the resultant management fee.

60-150 Consortia and joint ventures

Consortia and joint ventures are also fairly common. How they are treated for VAT purposes depends, however, on what precisely is involved.

(1) Companies

Consortia and joint ventures can be found in a variety of corporate structures. The distinctions, if there are any, usually come down to differing degrees of share-ownership:

- the shares in a consortium company will tend to be owned by a number of other companies, usually more than two, but with no single company having control;
- those in a joint venture will be limited to two, often on a 50:50 or deadlock basis.

In the financial sector, where these occur, there tends often to be a high degree of inter-company trading and support and as with groups, the consequences of separate legal identity are often overlooked. With a support function, there can easily then be the risk of a VAT cost being generated internally on underlying VAT-free expenses. As many consortium companies are partly, if not wholly foreign-owned, there is also the potential difficulty of the reverse charge (see **Chapter 5**) especially for seconded expatriate personnel.

When it comes to inter-company trading, there may clearly be benefits as well as possible disadvantages. A consortium bank, for example, may be used by its overseas shareholders to access the UK financial markets. Where the shareholders are based outside the EU, any charges made abroad for arrangement or interest will confer the right to recover underlying input VAT (see **Chapter 4** at 40-100(3)).

(2) Other situations

Outside of a corporate structure, the concepts can vary enormously.

(a) Consortia

In its simplest form, a consortium may just mean a joint arrangement for sharing costs. Several companies with common interests, but trading independently, may decide, for example, to finance expenditure on research and development collectively. One of their number may then arrange to contract on behalf of them all; any recharges of costs will then be seen as the provision of what is then a taxable service to the others. Where this creates a problem, from the loss or restriction of input VAT, for example, it may be possible to argue that the costs are genuinely contracted for on an agency basis. But this can be difficult to sustain without proof.

A consortium may also arise in the case, say, of an agreement to the financing of a loan. A number of banks may participate in an overall facility with one of their number as manager. Just as for direct tax (especially double tax relief), the form of the relationship is important.

- If, contractually, each of the consortium members is lending direct to the overseas borrower (i.e. is a co-participator), each makes an appropriate part of the overall supply. If the borrower is outside the EU, each will stand to benefit from input VAT recovery.
- Where, however, the lead manager is the initial lender and belongs in the EU, with the other consortium members contributing on a back-to-back basis for their respective shares (i.e. sub-participation), only the manager will gain.

(b) Joint ventures/co-ownerships

These tend to involve quite different relationships.

(1) At times they will be synonymous with partnerships. They may thus need to be registered as such under VATA 1994, s. 45. Supplies to and by the partnership or joint venture, including supplies to or by the joint venturers or partners, will then have to be accounted for in the normal way.

(2) Alternatively, the venture may simply be two or more parties with a common aim, making and receiving supplies separately but agreeing to pool the resulting profits and losses. Here, HMRC sometimes agree that each party will be responsible for the VAT consequences of its own transactions and any settlement between the parties will then generally be *outside the scope*.

(3) The treatment will have been given some support by the decision in *Empresa de Desenvolvimento Mineiro SGPS SA (EDM) v Fazenda Pública (Ministério Público, intervener)* (Case C-77/01) [2006] BVC 140, where the ECJ observed that operations carried out by members of a consortium were generally not paid for, and thus not taxable transactions – even for the member which managed the consortium. This may, however, need to be specifically agreed. In some respects, therefore, this situation is not dissimilar to the cost-sharing arrangement described earlier.

(4) In other situations, particularly with property development, for example, the joint venture may really be an arrangement where one of the parties provides goods or services in return for a results-based fee. The service in this case might, perhaps, be the provision of finance or the development or marketing of a product.

Whatever the arrangement, profit-sharing in the accepted sense will not attract VAT (not being consideration for any supplies). However:

- where the *profit share* is not a true share of profits but a fee, it will be consideration for a supply and generally chargeable to VAT unless it is exempt as, say, the equivalent of interest or for the procurement of finance;
- a profit share may also sometimes be inflated by the value of facilities provided but not charged for. This might apply, for example, where one of the parties contributes the use of business assets in return for a greater share of profits. Again it is possible that a taxable, or even an exempt, supply will have arisen.

Practice point

Anything to do with consortia or joint ventures can call for careful consideration to establish the true nature of the relationships involved and the VAT consequences that follow.

It is sometimes assumed that these are simply administrative arrangements and that transactions between the participants, for example, are VAT-free. However, this very much depends on the circumstances and it is often wise to be prepared for the possibilities and, where necessary, to obtain appropriate HMRC clearances.

60-250 VAT groups

Most taxable persons register individually. There are exceptions, however, for organisations such as clubs, unincorporated associations and partnerships (and at some stage those for the joint ownership of property). In the context of the businesses covered by this book, however, the only other situation in which there may be a joint registration is in practice in the case of VAT groups. This applies, however, only to companies, and then only when certain conditions are met, including, in particular, requirements as to common control and being established or having an established place of business in the UK. The particular provisions that apply, VATA 1994, s. 43, are explored earlier in **Chapter 2** at 20-250 and, in terms of VAT planning, have a number of important consequences.

Opting for a VAT group effectively creates, for example, a single registrable unit of all the companies concerned (*C & E Commrs v Kingfisher plc* [1994] BVC 3). Used as a practical planning tool, it can thus overcome a number of the problems associated with the more common connected-party arrangements.

Where one company pays or incurs costs centrally, the economic burden can be borne anywhere in the VAT group without the risk of creating an artificial VAT cost. This makes it possible for employment (see **Chapter 6** at 60-100), accommodation or administration to be organised without any of the complications referred to elsewhere in this Chapter.

It also avoids the problems that may arise where third-party suppliers invoice the incorrect company. The *Value Added Tax Act* 1994, s. 24, for example, requires the claimant to show that the relevant input tax relates to his own business; not that of someone else. Regulation 29 of the *Value Added Tax Regulations* 1995 (SI 1995/2518) can also call for the holding of a VAT invoice made out in the claimants name. None of this matters if the potential recipient companies are in the same VAT group.

What a VAT group does not do, however, is create a single business or mean that a single overall calculation is made for partial exemption purposes (*Joseph Nelson Investment Planning Ltd* [1994] BVC 657).

Equally important, grouping is extremely flexible. Which companies are or are not included is generally the taxpayer's choice; a corporate group can even establish more than one combined registration on this basis and HMRC have only limited powers to object.

> ### Practice point
> VAT groups are often the most useful means of avoiding or minimising VAT costs for associated companies. They will often, for example:
> - help avoid the internally generated VAT cost on, say, staff secondment or administration, something that is even possible where the VAT group as a whole is fully exempt;
> - help in the recovery of residual input VAT by bringing a much wider range of taxable activities into what is then a single registered unit; and

- offer a greater chance of disregarding potentially distortive transactions as *incidental* in a residual input tax calculation (see **Chapter 4** at 40-200) (e.g. the sale of centrally-owned group premises or subsidiary companies).

If the criteria are met, the sensible approach is generally always to assume that an application for grouping should be made.

Most companies using the VAT grouping rules do not do so for aggressive avoidance, but to prevent an artificial VAT cost arising from the way the various activities are organised within the group. There is much to be said for this approach. Generally, the advantages will outweigh the possible disadvantages and the question to be asked should not be *whether to group*, but *why not*.

There may, for example, be benefits from not including certain companies in a VAT group. Cash-flow, say, may dictate that repayment businesses should account monthly, leaving the net VAT payers to submit returns on a quarterly basis. When this occurs, the considerations discussed earlier in this Chapter then become important. Having staff employed by or equipment owned by a company, which is separately registered and accounts for tax quarterly, can immediately create a positive cash-flow benefit, if taxable charges are then made to a company which accounts monthly. The timing of the charges will, of course, be important.

Practice point

A possible disadvantage of having a VAT group is the complication of compliance and penalties. For example:

- preparing the group VAT return is often more time-consuming than preparing returns for individual companies;
- there may inevitably be duplication of effort and the added time can easily cause returns to be submitted late;
- the aggregation of the results of several companies can also sometimes increase the amount of penalty and interest in the event there is a serious misdeclaration. (But, by the same token, the risk may be less if the effect of intra-group supplies is removed.)

On balance, however, being able to create a VAT group is the ideal solution for avoiding many of the pitfalls from related-party transactions, where the consequences of not grouping are all too easily overlooked.

Whatever decision is taken, though, it should be taken consciously and in good time.

60-300 Cost sharing arrangements

Article 132(1)(f) of the VAT Directive exempts from VAT supplies made under cost sharing arrangements. Article 132(1) states that the following is exempt:

> '(f) the supply of services by independent groups of persons, who are carrying on an activity which is exempt from VAT or in relation to which they are not taxable persons, for the purpose of rendering their members the services directly necessary for the exercise of their activity, where

those groups merely claim from their members exact reimbursement of their share of the joint expenses, provided that such exemption is not likely to cause distortion of competition;'

The UK has implemented the exemption by s. 197 of the *Finance Act* 2012. The measure will have effect on or after the date of Royal Assent, which was 17 July 2012. The effect of s. 197 is to add a new Group 16 to Sch. 9 of VATA 1994 dealing with the supplies of services by groups involving cost sharing. The effect of it is to exempt from VAT the supply of services by a group which consists of persons engaged in exempt or non-taxable activities so long as the services are supplied to group members at cost and for the purposes of those activities. Group 16 provides that the following supplies are exempt:

'1. The supply of services by an independent group of persons where each of the following conditions is satisfied–

(a) each of those persons is a person who is carrying on an activity ("the relevant activity") which is exempt from VAT or in relation to which the person is not a taxable person within the meaning of Article 9 of Council Directive 2006/112/EC,
(b) the supply of services is made for the purpose of rendering the members of the group the services directly necessary for the exercise of the relevant activity,
(c) the group merely claims from its members exact reimbursement of their share of the joint expenses, and
(d) the exemption of the supply is not likely to cause distortion of competition.'

The Treasury have power to impose conditions in connection with the application of the exemption (VATA 1994, s. 31(3) to (5), as introduced by the *Finance Act* 2012, s. 197). HMRC have released detailed guidance as to the framework of the exemption, a copy of the guidance is provided at Appendix 24.

The purpose of the exemption is to enable businesses and organisations that make exempt and/or non-business supplies who incur irrecoverable VAT costs on their purchases to co-operate by forming a group to provide them with services which are exempt from VAT. Obviously, the more members involved in a cost sharing group (CSG) should mean that there are greater savings and lower costs per member of operating the relevant CSG, thus reducing the costs attributable to irrecoverable VAT. However, the cost sharing exemption is only available where the services are necessary to their exempt/non-business activity. The exemption ensures that such services are exempt only to the extent that the services are supplied by the group to group members at cost and only if relief does not distort competition.

HMRC issued a consultation document on the Cost Sharing arrangements on 28th June 2011, entitled *VAT: Cost Sharing Exemption*, and they stated that whilst it was not possible to determine precisely how a cost-sharing group (CSG) should operate, HMRC would expect it to have some or all of the following characteristics (at para. 3.26):

- A common valuation basis for services supplied.
- Members have access to contracts for the supply of goods and services by and to the CSG.
- The benefits of the CSG's operations flow to the members and not a third party.
- Strategic decisions are taken by the members.
- The majority of the Executive body managing the CSG comprises individuals appointed by the members.

- Minutes of executive meetings are made available to members.
- The CSG acts independently in appointing and discharging suppliers.'

Particular points to note in connection with the exemption, include:

- The exemption does not apply to the supply of goods,
- The exemption does not apply to supplies made by members of the group who supply services directly to other CSG members,
- The exemption applies to any supplies falling within Sch. 9 of VATA 1994,
- Supplies of services where the place of supply is outside the EU are outside the scope of VAT, and as such are not exempt supplies,
- If the CSG makes supplies outside the scope of the exemption such supplies will be subject to the VAT rules with the consequence that the CSG may have to register for VAT if it exceeds the VAT registration limits,
- Supplies of goods and services to a CSG are subject to the VAT rules, and in consequence of its supplies being exempt it will not be able to claim any input VAT in relation to any onward supply made by it,
- Exemption does not apply to CSG's established outside the EU or to CSG members established outside of the EU,
- CSG must be a separate taxable person from its members (in other words, it must be capable of being a taxable person that can be registered for VAT),
- All members of the CSG must receive supplies within the scope of the exemption,
- All members of the CSG must have exempt and/or non-business activities. In this regard, HMRC comment in their guidance (reproduced in Appendix 24):

'36. Do all members have to have exempt and/or non-business activities?

Yes.

The EU Commission accept that it is legitimate, in order to facilitate the correct and straightforward application of the exemption for Member States, under Article 131 of the Principal VAT Directive, to require that the exempt and/or non-business activities of members be carried on in a regular and consistent manner rather than merely sporadically. The relevant activities need to represent a significant (not a de minimis) part of the taxpayer's business.

HMRC consider that an entity would be eligible for membership if:

- 5 per cent or more of its total supplies were exempt and/or non-business supplies in the immediate 12 months prior to joining the CSG
- or 5 per cent or more of its total supplies were exempt and/or non-business supplies in its last completed partial exemption, business/non-business year prior to its membership of a CSG
- or at the time of joining a CSG, although it does not fulfil the first two tests it:
    (i) has an intention to receive and does receive, qualifying services which are 'directly necessary' from the CSG, in the 12 month period starting from the date of joining and
    (ii) those services are directly utilised within 12 months of receipt by the member to make 5 per cent or more exempt and/or non-business onward supplies.

If a member ceases to be eligible for membership of the CSG, going forward, there have to be at least two remaining eligible members for the CSG itself to continue to be a CSG falling within the terms of Group 16 of Schedule 9 to the VAT Act 1994 and therefore to continue to be able to make exempt supplies.

If a body is wholly taxable but has a clear intention to make exempt and/or non-business supplies within the next 12 months HMRC would accept it is eligible to join a CSG.'

- The exemption requires that supplies made by a CSG to its members must be 'directly necessary' for their exempt and/or non-business activities. If they are not, the exemption does not apply and the supplies are subject to normal VAT rules. The word 'necessary' used alone could be interpretive that any supplies used for a CSG member's exempt and/or non-business activity would be entitled to exemption. However, the word 'necessary' is, in this case, qualified by the use of the word 'directly' meaning that the supplies received from the CSG must relate 'directly' to the exempt and/or non-business supplies made by the CSG member in their own right (see para. 39 of the HMRC guidance). For further details on how HMRC will apply this in practice see para. 40 to 45 of HMRC's guidance.
- In relation to HMRC's position on the interpretation of the concept of 'direct reimbursement of costs' it states at para. 46 of the guidance:

    'What is meant by "direct reimbursement of costs"?

    For the exemption to apply the consideration for supplies made by the CSG to its members has to be an "exact reimbursement" of the members' share of the joint expenses, this includes any general overheads incurred by the CSG in providing services to its members as well as any discounts received or input tax recovered by the CSG. Therefore there should be no profit element in the charges made by the group to its members, i.e. no margin or mark-up must be factored into the cost of providing the services. So, for example, if the CSG receives discounts from its suppliers they have to be passed to on to members by computing them into the CSGs charges to its members. If supplies to members of the CSG by the CSG do include a profit element the exemption will NOT apply and those supplies will be subject to the normal VAT rules.

    CSGs can make supplies to non-members and in these circumstances the normal VAT rules apply and profit element may be included.

    An expense can normally be defined as a cost incurred to generate revenue and would include for example:

    - Cash payments or liabilities
    - Costs incurred but not yet invoiced (accruals)
    - Amounts required to meet anticipated future expenditure
    - Depreciation in the value of the CSG's assets.

    How such costs are calculated and charged is a matter for the CSG members to agree. However HMRC expect CSGs to have a clear audit trail that can be checked if necessary.'

- In relation to HMRC's position on the interpretation of the concept of 'distortion of competition' it states at para. 51 of the guidance:

    'A CSG is a cooperative self-supply arrangement. It is not a commercial outsourcing arrangement therefore it does not exist or compete in a market. As long as all the conditions of the exemption are met, particularly that it can only supply its members on a "direct reimbursement" basis, that is, itself supplies at cost, there should be little question of the exemption distorting a market and therefore little question of failing to meet this condition.'

- A CSG can be a member of a VAT group provided all the conditions for grouping are satisfied.

- A member of a VAT group can be a member of a CSG. Supplies received by a member of a VAT group will be treated as being supplied to the representative member of the VAT group (VATA 1994, s. 43(1)).

> ## Summary
>
> This Chapter has attempted to highlight some of the more common issues with connected parties. Close relationships can easily cause the reality of a situation to be overlooked, with potentially unfortunate consequences.
>
> To address these properly, it is often important to ensure things are well documented and to be aware of exactly what different situations and structures entail. That, together with a proper degree of forethought, will often help avoid unnecessary complications. Circumstances permitting, the use of VAT groups, (see Chapter 2) can also often offer the opportunity of simplifying things where sufficient common ownership is involved. The formation of a cost sharing group may also provide assistance in appropriate circumstances.

7 Banks and Financial Institutions

> **Overview**
>
> This Chapter considers:
>
> (1) The typical types of transactions encountered in the financial sector, including:
>
>   (a) what they involve;
>   (b) their general VAT liabilities; and
>   (c) how they should be treated for VAT in different situations.
>
> (2) The particular considerations affecting banks and other financial institutions, including some partial exemption considerations.
>
> (3) Special issues affecting certain supplies.
>
> (4) Outsourcing.

70-000 What is involved?

All the businesses covered by this Chapter provide, or are in one way or another involved in, finance. Most of what they do is directly related to money. At its simplest, this will mean dealings in money or its equivalent (including foreign exchange) and the provision of credit (i.e. lending). It also extends to providing current account facilities, letters of credit and other more specialist types of finance, including hire-purchase or instalment credit finance, the discounting of commercial bills of exchange and debt factoring. More permanent or long-term finance may involve securities such as shares or loan stock.

However, by no means all financial services have this direct link with money. Equipment leasing, for example, is a popular means of financing the acquisition of capital equipment without resorting to borrowing. There is also a wide range of associated services and facilities to which the monetary link is peripheral: investment or other financial advice, trustee and executorship services and debt collection.

For example: also investment brokerage and the underwriting/arranging of the issue of securities. In addition, Islamic Finance is designed to provide Sharia'a compliant products for Muslims unable or unwilling to obtain conventional credit finance in order to purchase goods and/or services.

As discussed in **Chapter 1**, the European Commission issued a proposal for a Directive to the Council of The European Union, the purpose of which was to amend Directive 2006/112/EC (i.e. the VAT Directive) in regards the VAT treatment of insurance and financial services. The aim of the proposal is:

- clarification and updating of the definitions of exempt insurance and financial services to ensure consistent treatment throughout the EU;
- broadening the existing option for taxation by transferring the right to opt from the Member States to financial and insurance institutions;
- introduction of a cost-sharing group to allow re-distribution of costs; but the Council decided in 2010 that no further work was required on the cost-sharing arrangements (as to the nature of the exemption see Chapter 6).

To date work continues to be undertaken in exploring a way forward on these matters, but there are no actual proposals which are the subject of implementation. The nature of the European Commission proposals are outlined below, to the extent relevant. A copy of the current draft of proposals are provided in **Appendix 3**.

70-050 General VAT liability issues

The VAT liability of these various activities to some extent follows this broad monetary: non-monetary split.

Monetary financial services, which will be the main area of concern, will be almost exclusively exempt. This, as seen elsewhere (**Chapter 4**), implies loss or restriction in input VAT relief but, for the end consumer, will mean a lower overall cost – even if the supplier's irrecoverable input tax is passed on. Few supplies, if any, will now be taxed at the standard-rate.

With many businesses, however, a number of supplies will be *outside the scope* and, depending on the circumstances and what these involve, this may mean input VAT is not inevitably an expense. This will apply particularly to certain international, as opposed to purely domestic, transactions.

Although non-monetary services are still, in some cases, VAT-exempt, most will be taxed at the standard-rate. This will apply, in particular, to areas such as leasing and debt collection, but will also extend to many services of a professional or broadly administrative nature. Again, depending on what is involved, a number of supplies will be *outside the scope* and zero-rating is still available in some situations. Where it occurs, zero-rating will always override standard-rating, and even exemption (VATA 1994, s. 30(1)).

With exemption the norm, recovering input VAT rather than accounting for output VAT is clearly likely to be the main concern. How much is recovered depends, however, on the individual business and, in many cases, the extent to which it is internationally based rather than domestic. It may also depend on the nature of any agreement made with HMRC in relation to, say, partial exemption, either on an industry basis or company-by-company. Sometimes equally important can be the extent to which individual accounting systems can accommodate some of the more sophisticated approaches.

The principles involved as they apply in the present context are discussed in more detail below. Tables are provided in **Appendix 10**, indicating the types of VAT treatment which would normally be afforded to typical banking and financial activities.

70-100 Monetary financial services

Most supplies in what will tend to be the main areas of interest are VAT-exempt. Being aware of how they arise and the particular implications of different types of supply can have a material impact on the eventual overall VAT position of the business concerned.

(1) Exemption

Exemption as its name implies, effectively removes transactions from the charge to tax altogether. It applies to what are generally economically and socially important services, the *quid pro quo* being the restriction in underlying input VAT. The scope of the finance exemptions is subject to the interpretation of the CoJ and domestic courts, which is currently in a constant state of refinement. Accordingly, it is important to be mindful of current case law in construing the scope of the exemptions. The exemption provisions of most concern in the context of this Chapter follow from art. 135(1) of Council Directive 2006/112/EC (Art. 13(B)(d) of the Sixth VAT Directive (Directive 77/388)):

'(b)　the granting and the negotiation of credit and the management of credit by the person granting it;

(c)　the negotiation of or any dealings in credit guarantees or any other security for money and the management of credit guarantees by the person who is granting the credit;

(d)　transactions, including negotiation, concerning deposit and current accounts, payments, transfers, debts, cheques and other negotiable instruments, but excluding debt collection;

(e)　transactions, including negotiation, concerning currency, bank notes and coins used as legal tender, with the exception of collectors' items; that is to say, gold, silver or other metal coins or bank notes which are not normally used as legal tender or coins of numismatic interest;

(f)　transactions, including negotiation, but not management or safekeeping, in shares, interests in companies or associations, debentures and other securities, but excluding documents establishing title to goods and the rights or securities referred to in article 15(2));

(g)　the management of special investment funds as defined by Member States.'

Interestingly, the reference in Art. 135(1)(d) to the exclusion for debt collection no longer makes any reference to factoring (see also 70-200(15) and 70-450). Whether anything can be read into this is, perhaps, doubtful. Whilst the exemptions are imposed by the VAT Directive in each Member State, the way in which they are implemented is subject to the interpretation of each Member State. Sometimes Member States take divergent views on how to interpret the scope of the exemptions, and it is important to be mindful of the guidance provided by the tax authorities of any particular State in which a transaction is being contemplated.

These exemptions in Art. 135(1) are translated into UK law by VATA 1994, Sch. 9, Grp. 5, which is reproduced in full at **Appendix 12**. However, for the purposes of the present Chapter, the main items of interest are:

'Item No.:

1　The issue, transfer or receipt of, or any dealing with, money, any security for money or any note or order for the payment of money.

2	The making of any advance or the granting of any credit.
2A	The management of credit by the person granting it.
3	The provision of the facility of instalment credit finance in a hire-purchase, conditional sale or credit sale agreement for which facility a separate charge is made and disclosed to the recipient of the supply of goods.
4	The provision of administrative arrangements and documentation and the transfer of title to the goods in connection with the supply described in item 3 if the total consideration therefore is specified in the agreement and does not exceed £10.
5	The provision of intermediary services in relation to any transaction comprised in item 1, 2, 3, 4 or 6 (whether or not any such transaction is finally concluded) by a person acting in an intermediary capacity.
5A	The underwriting of an issue within item 1 or any transaction within item 6.
6	…
7	…
8	The operation of any current, deposit or savings account.
9	…
10	…'

In considering these exemptions, it is important also to look at a number of the Statutory Notes.

'*Notes:*

(1) Item 1 does not include anything included in item 6.

(1A) Item 1 does not include a supply of services which is preparatory to the carrying out of a transaction falling within that item.

(2) This Group does not include the supply of a coin or a banknote as a collectors' piece or as an investment article.

(3) Item 2 includes the supply of credit by a person, in connection with a supply of goods or services by him, for which a separate charge is made and disclosed to the recipient of the supply of goods or services.

(4) This Group includes any supply by a person carrying on a credit card, charge card or similar payment card operation made in connection with that operation to a person who accepts the card used in the operation when presented to him in payment for goods or services.

(5) For the purposes of item 5 "intermediary services" consist of bringing together, with a view to the provision of financial services-

(a) persons who are or may be seeking to receive financial services, and
(b) persons who provide financial services,

together with (in the case of financial services falling within item 1, 2, 3 or 4) the performance of work preparatory to the conclusion of contracts for the provision of those financial services, but do not include the supply of any market research, product design, advertising, promotional or similar services or the collection, collation and provision of information in connection with such activities.

(5A) For the purposes of item 5 a person is "acting in an intermediary capacity" wherever he is acting as an intermediary, or one of the intermediaries, between—

   (a) a person who provides financial services, and
   (b) a person who is or may be seeking to receive financial services.

(5B) For the purposes of Notes (5) and (5A) "financial services" means the carrying out of any transaction falling within item 1, 2, 3, 4 or 6.'

Notes (1A), (5A), and (5B) represented three of a number of major changes made to Grp. 5 by the *Value Added Tax (Finance) Order* 1999 (SI 1999/594) from 10 March 1999. What they mean in practice is dealt with below and elsewhere in this Chapter. The Order also introduced two further Notes, 2A and 2B, which were subsequently removed from 1 August 2003 by the *Value Added Tax (Finance) (No. 2) Order* 2003 – (SI 2003/1569). These read:

'(2A) This Group does not include a supply of services comprising the management of credit, other than such a supply made by the person granting the credit.

(2B) For the purposes of this Group a person makes "a supply of services comprising the management of credit" if he performs any one or more of the following in relation to a credit, a credit card, a chargecard or a similar payment card, operation-

   (a) credit checking;
   (b) valuation;
   (c) authorisation services;
   (d) taking decisions relating to a grant or an application for a grant of credit;
   (e) creating and maintaining records relating to a grant or an application for a grant of credit on behalf of the credit provider; and
   (f) monitoring a creditor's payment record or dealing with overdue payments.'

As HMRC would probably have put it, the changes in 1999 were designed to *put the clock back* to where it was before the cases of *CSMA, Continuum/CSC Financial Services and Lloyds TSB*, which they had previously lost before the VAT Tribunal and the Courts, and which are also discussed later at 70-200. The trouble is, they (i.e. HMRC) seemed also to want to put the clock back before *Sparekassernes Datacenter* (also discussed later at 70-200) as well.

When it comes to interpretation, there is often room for differences of opinion and the principles emerging from judicial decisions are not always the easiest to discern. However, many commentators believe the changes were unnecessary and/or had gone too far. Following the later decision in July 2000 by the Court of Appeal in the case of *C & E Commrs v FDR Ltd* [2000] BVC 311, which is discussed later at 70-200(10) under *Credit and charge card companies*, HMRC now seem to accept this and the amendment from 1 August 2003 brought UK law much more into line with the Directive.

Where exemption is concerned, a line has, of course, to be drawn between what is covered and what is not. The exemption must be construed narrowly but Notes 2A and 2B were arguably inappropriate. Credit management, for example, as it is found in art. 135(1)(b) (art. 13(B)(d)(1)), is probably not the same thing as the idea HMRC had of it when these Notes were introduced. Arguably, before you can have the *management of credit*, you first have to have the credit to manage. In other words, management comes *after* the credit has been created. Much of what HMRC had put in their definition was, however, *preparatory* and either part of, or ancillary to *negotiation* – or perhaps covered elsewhere in art. 135(1). What HMRC seemed to want was to exclude *everything* within their definition of credit management from being exempt, something the Sixth VAT Directive itself did not do.

Following the refusal of the House of Lords to grant HMRC leave to appeal the Court of Appeal's judgment in the case of *First Data Resources* case, a dispute over the treatment of services provided to the issuers of credit and charge card companies (see later at 70-200(9) below), HMRC accepted that the borderline between what was an exempt and taxable supply needed to be redrawn.

In a Consultation prior to the changes in 2003, HMRC said they believed that Note (1A) was still relevant, because it was consistent with the judgments in both *Sparekassernes Datacenter*, and *CSC Financial Services*, but were aware of concerns over whether it was wholly consistent with *Card Protection Plan*. With that in mind, they felt that, by including the word *separate* before *supply of services*, the Note had a much better read across to the CPP tests. Equally, they considered there should be no contradiction with the decisions in the cases of *Sparekassernes Datacenter* and *FDR*, because, in both cases, the businesses were making the legal and financial changes and, therefore, the *essence* of their supply was an exempt financial activity.

However, in the event, this suggested amendment to the wording was not taken up and the removal of Notes 2A and 2B resolved many of the objections to the wording of the Group.

The Commission proposals

As noted earlier in this book, a number of factors have caused a wide-ranging review of the treatment of finance and insurance services within the Community, with consultations with the Member States and with representatives of the various industries. A draft proposal for a new Directive (amending Council Directive 2006/112/EC as regards financial and insurance services) was published on 28 November 2007 (which is reproduced in **Appendix 3**). In addition, the Commission also published extensive draft Regulations, which were issued with the version of the draft directive that was published on 16 July 2007 (not reproduced here), which can be found on the Commission website at http://ec.europa.eu/taxation_customs/resources/documents/common/consultations/tax/working_paper_definitions_en.pdf. For details of the current status of the proposed directive published on 28 November 2007 information is available on the European Parliament website at: www.europarl.europa.eu.

The effect of the proposals is to replace points (a) to (g) in art. 135(1) by the following compromise text (published on 30 September 2011 as FISC 122 (see **Appendix 3**)):

- '(a) Insurance and reinsurance [and transfer of insurance and reinsurance contracts];
- (b) Granting of credit and management of credit by the creditor;
- (c) guaranteeing of debt and provision of any other surety bonds;
- (d) transfer of a credit position and assumption of a debt position and excluding debt collection;
- (e) financial transfer;

(f) financial deposit taking and account operation;
(g) currency exchange and provision of cash;
(ga) transactions in securities, excluding their safekeeping and management;
(gaa) transactions in interests in companies and associations other than securities, excluding their safekeeping and management;
(gb) transactions in financial derivatives, excluding their safekeeping and management;
(gc) management of investment funds and pension funds established within the territory of the Community;
(gd) intermediation in insurance and financial transactions as referred to in points (a) to (gb)'

A new art. 135a will then qualify how the exemption in points (a) to (g) is to be applied and, in particular, provides that:

'(7) Intermediation in insurance and financial transactions shall mean the supply of services rendered to, and remunerated by, a contractual party as a distinct act of mediation in relation to the insurance or financial transactions referred to in points (a) to (e) of Article 135(1), by a third party intermediary;'

A related service distinct in character is to be regarded as the main service to which it relates, where it is specific to and essential for the transaction exempted under art. 135(1) (a) to (e).

How these will affect the present treatment remains to be seen, particularly as these proposals are still officially draft. However, for the moment, it seems likely that the effect of cases like *Sparekassernes Datacenter*, *Card Protection Plan* and *FDR* may still hold good.

The Council of the European Union have been consulting on amendments to the proposals as regards insurance and financial services, and the current status of these discussions can be accessed on the European Council Register Consilium website (http://register.consilium.europa.eu). Appendix 3 also contains a compromise text proposed by the Council of the European Union on the VAT treatment of insurance and financial services, which reflects proposed amendments to the text published on 28 November 2007 (the text is sourced from Interinstitutional File 2007/0267 (CNS): LIMITE FISC 11 (1 February 2011)). FISC 11 discloses proposals relating to the scope of the original concepts, and provides further clarification on key terms contained in the draft proposed amendments. LIMITE FISC 127 (Interinstitutional File 2007/0267 (CNS)) (7 October 2011) provides an update on progress in connection with the Draft Directive, and identifies four major oustanding issues of political importance, namely the treatment of 1) transfer of insurance and reinsurance contract portfolios, 2) outsourcing, 3) management of investment funds and 4) derivatives. The nature of these issues are referred to in FISC 127, which is reproduced in Appendix 3. Since there are no final draft proposals, this edition will not comment on the amendments due to the developing nature of the draft provisions. However, it is possible for the reader to track the progress of evolving discussions by referring to LIMITE FISC 100 (11 July 2011), LIMITE FISC 124 (30 September 2011), LIMITE 141 (14 November 2011) and additional papers as they are released onto the Council website.

The Items and Notes within Group 5

Item 1 essentially deals with anything to do with money or settlements. The term 'money' relates to coins or banknotes (whether in Sterling or foreign currency) where supplied as legal tender. The term does not apply to numismatic or gold coins (but these may be covered by the investment gold exemption (VAT Notice 701/21 Gold and VAT Notice 701/21A Investment gold coins) or coins and banknotes, which are not legal tender. In addition, platinum nobles are excluded (Council Regulation No 1777/2005, with effect from 1 July 2006; and EU Implementing Regulation (art. 45)). In addition to cash and foreign exchange, it covers bills of exchange and promissory notes, Sterling Commercial Paper and Euronotes or Euro Commercial Paper, in fact the types of negotiable instrument to which the *Bills of Exchange Act* 1882 applies. A number of these give problems in terms of whether, and to what extent, they should be recognised for VAT purposes. For example:

- to take matters to the extreme, should you record as the value of an exempt supply the cash or cheque you give in return for goods or services? After all, *supply* includes all forms of supply (VATA 1994, s. 5(2)(a)). However, following the ruling of the ECJ in *Kretztechnik AG v Finanzamt Linz* (Case C-465/03) ECJ [2006] BVC 66 (see earlier in **Chapter 1** at 10-300 and **Chapter 4** at 40-200), this is now resolved and the *issue*, as opposed to a subsequent *secondary supply*, of financial instruments of this kind will not be a supply for VAT purposes;
- until the successful appeals in *Republic National Bank of New York* and *The First National Bank of Chicago* (discussed at 70-200(5) and (11) below, foreign exchange had also generally not been acknowledged by HMRC as capable of being the subject of a supply, except to the extent of any fee or handling charge. To many outside HMRC, this had long been felt incorrect. The fact that the value might be distortive and/or difficult to record was no basis for denying the existence of any supply. To ignore altogether these transactions has often been to distort the level of input VAT recovery that should be achieved, although, as shown in the decision of *Willis Pension Trustees Ltd* [2006] BVC 2,045 (see **Chapter 1** at 10-300) a supply will still not be recognised in all situations.

The complications that some of these items create is discussed in more detail at 70-200.

The scope of Grp. 5, item 1 has been considered in a number of Tribunal cases.

- In *The British Hardware Federation* (1975) VATTR 172, for example, the exemption was held to apply to a clearing house payment scheme operated by a trade association.
- In *Williams & Glyn's Bank Ltd* (1974) 1 BVC 1,021 *dealing with money* was not found to extend to the carriage of *secured packages* by Securicor. In the view of the Tribunal (at p. 1,023):

  '... these words, in the context, require the relevant services to have sufficient of the characteristics of a financial transaction or operation so as to be capable of being fairly so described. The words appear in a Group dealing with financial transactions. They appear in item 1 and item 4 in relation to money, and also in relation to securities for money, such as charges and guarantees, and notes and orders for the payment of money. This explains why the words "dealing with" and not "dealing in" were used by the draughtsman; a financial institution does not, for example, "deal in" guarantees. We hold that, in the context, the words were not intended to, and do not, extend to the services of safe carriage supplied by Securicor to the Bank in the present case.'

- A different view, however, was reached in *Barclays Bank plc* (1988) VATTR 23; (1988) 3 BVC 692. This resulted in a successful appeal over credit-checking and change services. Both went well beyond the transportation and safe keeping of non-specific amounts of cash. In the words of the Tribunal (at p. 694), on this occasion:

'... Securicor did, in providing the credit checking service and the change service, perform services which were normally performed by the Bank as an integral part of its banking activities.'

HMRC contended this was not the right conclusion since Securicor took no part in the wider ramifications of financial transactions. In the unanimous judgment of the Tribunal, however, this was too narrow an interpretation of the provisions of Grp. 5. The Tribunal, moreover, went on to add that they concluded that both the credit-checking service and the change service constituted transactions concerning currency, banknotes and coins used as legal tender within the context of the Sixth VAT Directive, art. 13(B)(d)(4) (art. 135(1)(e) of Council Directive 2006/112/EC).

- In *Concept Direct Ltd* [2007] BVC 4,013, there was a different slant, in that the taxpayer found suitable sites for the placement of cash machines, negotiating with the site owner for the installation but taking no part in the agreement, with the bank by whom the machines were operated. However, in addition to being paid a lump-sum finder's fee, Concept Direct was also paid a fee per transaction, presumably reflecting the value of its judgment in choosing the site. VAT was accounted for on the lump-sum fee but, on the instigation of one of the banks, had claimed the fee per transaction was VAT-exempt as a financial intermediary service in arranging a supply within Item 1 of Group 5. The Tribunal, however, disagreed finding the fees were simply for finding sites, a decision that was hardly surprising in the light of the line taken in cases like *Sparekassernes Datacenter* and *FDR*.

Item 2 deals with short-or long-term advances, indebtedness or deposits. Examples will include bank and local authority loans and mortgages and building society deposits.

- However, as *MBNA Europe Bank Ltd v R & C Commrs* [2007] BVC 3 has shown the assignment of receivables as part of a securitisation exercise may not itself be a supply for VAT, even if, contrary to what was previously held by the Tribunal in *Capital One Bank (Europe) plc* [2006] BVC 2,148, it did not just represent the provision of security for a loan.

Items 3 and 4 concern hire-purchase, conditional sale and credit sale agreements and *Item 5* covers most arrangement and brokerage transactions involving supplies of monetary financial services.

- In *Smarter Money Ltd v R & C Commrs* [2006] BVC 4,098 there was a dispute over the applicaton of *Item 5* and the treatment of services provided via the internet of introducing customers to potential lenders. The taxpayer had no input into any actual contract concluded but made use of the internet to bring together customers who required mortgage advice with professional advisors authorised to provide it. Its function involved the capture and supply to brokers of a significant part of the data required by them to find the client a mortgage and also removed the need for brokers to source new business.

HMRC argued the supplies made by the company were standard-rated. It wasn't carrying out a distinct act of mediation or negotiating the terms of contracts but was merely providing information. Smarter Money, however, claimed what it did was provide services of *negotiation of credit* and that was sufficient for the exemption under both Community and domestic law to apply. It brought together persons seeking financial services and persons providing such services, and since it was not contracting on its own account it must be providing exempt intermediary services. The Tribunal agreed. What was required for the exemption to apply were negotiations, which did not have to result in the actual conclusion of the contract and could be carried out electronically.

7 Banks and Financial Institutions

> **Practice point**
>
> With HP and instalment credit finance, the exempt supply of finance will only be recognised *if and to the extent that* the credit element is separately identified and charged. If it is not, and there is a single overall price, the supply ceases to be a mixed supply of goods and credit; it is simply one of goods. A source of exempt supplies is thus removed, and with it a potential restriction of input VAT, improving the overall position of the finance house.
>
> - This could be of particular interest where the customer for a large item of equipment is fully taxable and thus able to recover any input VAT in full.
> - It would clearly be less attractive, however, where the customer is a private individual or an exempt business. Both would be unable to recover the VAT involved so that the commercial price would increase. However, in situations where the offer to the customer is of interest-free credit, as in *Primback*, this would not be an issue.
>
> For transactions with individuals, there is also the constraint that the *Consumer Credit Act 1974* requires the amount charged for finance to be disclosed. Attention to the contractual wording is likely also to be important as shown in the Tribunal appeal by *Freight Transport Leasing Ltd* [1991] BVC 536.

Item 8 applies to the operation of customer accounts. Particular issues arising from supplies under these headings are again discussed at 70-200 later.

Statutory Note (4) was originally introduced from, 1 May 1985, to exempt the merchant discounts charged by the card companies to participating retailers. Essentially, the discount is now treated as the consideration for the service of settlement. Prior to that date, it was seen as a taxable charge for business promotion, an argument still perceived as valid in some parts of the industry.

The exemption does not tend to apply, however, to certain of the fuel cards operated by many of the major oil companies and by independent groups such as Harpur (Overdrive and Dial) and PHH (Allstar), although in *Auto Lease Holland BV v Bundesant fur Finanzen* (Case C-185/01) [2005] BVC 182, the taxpayer, which leased motor vehicles and also offered the facility of a fuel management agreement, was unable to persuade the ECJ that the fuel management agreement was not a contract for the supply of fuel, but a contract to finance its purchase (see later at 70-500 below).

The position of charges to the cardholder will be covered by the normal exemptions in *Items 1* and *2*. Again, some of the more interesting aspects are discussed at 70-200.

Items 6, 7 and 9 relate to securities and are dealt with in **Chapter 8**.

Broadly, therefore, the exemption, so far as concerns matters covered by this Chapter, applies to:

- transfers of and dealings in money; loans or credit;
- credit brokerage and administration; and
- current, deposit or savings account operations; and credit cards.

From 1 January 2000, there is also now a new exemption for investment gold. This is discussed later in **Chapter 10** (Commodities, Financial Futures and Derivatives).

(2) Standard-rating

As noted earlier, monetary finance is almost exclusively VAT-exempt. The more important of the standard-rated exceptions will be for:

- dealings in numismatic items and precious metal coins;
- hire-purchase; and
- fuel cards.

Subject to the special rules on the exemption of investment gold (discussed elsewhere in **Chapter 10**) the supply of coins and banknotes is standard-rated, whether or not they are legal tender, when sold as collectors' items, for investment or as items with numismatic interest. If over 100 years old, they may be sold under the special margin scheme available for works of art, antiques and collectors' pieces.

The standard-rating of gold coins follows from the statutory system introduced in November 1983 and is found in what is now VATA 1994, s. 55. The rules are essentially designed to combat serious fraud and are also discussed in **Chapter 10**.

In the case of hire-purchase, there is a mixed supply. There is the supply of credit, which is exempt, and the supply of the underlying goods, which are taxable (usually at the standard-rate). How this is dealt with is explored later at 70-300.

With fuel cards, mentioned briefly at (1) above, any exempt supply is limited to just the finance element of the charge to the customer. In other respects the transactions are usually structured as successive sales and purchases of standard-rated product (via the card company to the customer) rather than as a payment or settlement mechanism. In some cases, there is also a charge for fleet management information. What these can involve is discussed, in more detail later at 70-200.

(3) Outside the scope, exemption with the right of recovery and zero-rating

Exemption, as such, is clearly attractive because of the absence of any need to charge VAT. However, as seen in **Chapters 3** and **4**, this tends to come at a price – a restriction in the recovery of underlying input tax, with the consequence that the supplier bears the economic cost unless it is passed on to the ultimate purchaser through higher prices.

Equally important for many banks and financial institutions, therefore, is the fact that VAT will also *not* need to be charged if a supply is *outside the scope* – because, for example, the place of supply is abroad, (see **Chapter 3** at 30-250), when the recovery of input tax can then become a possibility. This is becoming increasingly an issue with the tendency in recent years for more and more costs to bear VAT.

7 Banks and Financial Institutions

Whether or not something is *outside the scope* depends, generally, on the rules on the place of supply (see **Chapter 3** at 30-250(2)), on the type of service provided and on the circumstances in which it occurs. The same can be said in many respects of the ability to recover input VAT. There are, for example, particular reliefs afforded by Council Directive 2006/112/EC to encourage international trade with non-EU countries. This is allowed in a specific and limited range of circumstances by art. 169(b) and (c) of Council Directive 2006/112/EC) (art. 17(3) (b) and (c) of the Sixth VAT Directive (Directive 77/388)). This is mirrored in UK terms in the partial exemption rules by reg. 103 of the *Value Added Tax Regulations* 1995 (SI 1995/2518) (see **Chapter 4** at 40-200(5)). On top of this, there are certain situations in which a supply may be zero-rated, i.e. taxed at a nil rate.

> ### *Practice point*
>
> Foreign banks sometimes have a presence in the UK to access the UK money markets in order to finance lending to customers elsewhere. However, money-market dealings for head office may often not be a separate activity from other dealings at the UK branch or office. Identifying any underlying input VAT specifically incurred can therefore be impractical: it may not, in any event, be significant as much of the costs will be indirect and part of general overheads.
>
> In principle, however, relief under art. 3 of the *VAT (Input Tax) (Specified Supplies) Order 1999* is often justified, but:
>
> - HMRC usually refuse to allow any actual overseas income to be recognised in a normal partial exemption calculation; and
> - inter-branch transactions are also not supplies for VAT.
>
> Nonetheless, it can sometimes be possible to agree that the inter-branch transaction is treated as a *notional* supply in a numbers count within a Special Method (see **Chapter 4** at 40-200(5)), which can be beneficial especially if the head office is outside the EU. Alternatively, it can be worth considering interposing a suitable non-EU affiliate between the branch and head office.

(a) Services supplied where received by a relevant business person and other non-EU recipients

Services *supplied where received* are, perhaps, the most important category of supply to consider. The services concerned used to be solely those listed in art. 56 of Council Directive 2006/112/EC) (art. 9(2)(e) of the Sixth VAT Directive (Directive 77/388)); and in UK law these were to be found in VATA 1994, Sch. 5, para. 5, in particular, which covered banking, finance and insurance. As discussed in **Chapter 5**, VATA 1994, Sch. 5 was repealed and now all services are treated as supplied where received where the recipient of the services is a relevant business person (VATA 1994, s. 7A); and also to those services referred to in Part 1 or 2 of Sch. 4A of VATA 1994. Additionally, services specified in VATA 1994, Sch. 4A para. 16 are treated as supplied where the recipient belongs where provided to a person who is not a relevant business person and who belongs in a non-EU country. Paragraph 16(2)(e), in particular, applies to banking, financial and insurance services (including reinsurance), other than the provision of safe deposit facilities.

As a result of these provisions, any service within their scope will be treated as supplied in the place where the recipient *belongs*. Putting this in context, what this means in practice is that a supply will be outside the scope of UK VAT if made:

- to someone in business and who is established in another EU country or non-EU country; or
- to anyone belonging or established outside the EU.

Relief for input VAT then depends on whether the supply is basically taxable or exempt. Regulation 103 of the *Value Added Tax Regulations* 1995 (SI 1995/2518) and, in the case of supplies that are basically exempt, art. 3 of the *Value Added Tax (Input Tax) (Specified Supplies) Order* 1999 (SI 1999/3121) have the effect of allowing relief for:

- any basically taxable service supplied to a business outside the UK or to anyone else outside the EU; and
- any basically exempt service supplied to anyone outside the EU.

The result for banks, therefore, is that they can potentially recover input VAT on costs relating to loans and advances provided to non-EU customers; also for other monetary services, including normal account transactions, money transfers and financial guarantees, where the recipient is established outside the EU.

The relief extends to debt or loan assignments, including both normal customer accounts and the rebooking of major international borrowings (see *Barclays Bank plc (No. 2)* [1991] BVC 585. It will apply, in short, to all those supplies listed in (1) above, and which qualify as banking and financial services under VATA 1994, Sch. 4A, para. 16.

This enhancement of input tax was not, however, achieved in the two cases mentioned earlier that concerned the assignment of receivables to trustees outside the EU as part of a securitisation exercise (*MBNA* and *Capital One*).

- In *MBNA Europe Bank Ltd v R & C Commrs* [2007] BVC 3, it was held that the assignments, viewed separately from the rest of the scheme, were in theory, capable of constituting supplies. However, because they were no more than the necessary pre-condition to the supply of a securitisation service to the bank by the special purpose company to whom they were assigned, they were thereby deprived of the character of a supply.
- A similar conclusion (on there being no supply) was earlier taken by the Tribunal in *Capital One Bank (Europe) plc* [2006] BVC 2,148, (and followed by the Tribunal in *MBNA*) although, in both cases, the reason then given was that the assignments were simply security for a loan. For a fuller discussion of these cases see later under *Securitisation* at 70-200).

The rules so far outlined do not just apply to principal's transactions. They will also cover appropriate agency services where the agent makes arrangements for or negotiates a qualifying supply of financial services for a client belonging outside the EU. There tends, however, to be more scope for relief where brokers and agents are concerned. The various possibilities for this are considered in more detail at (c) below.

7 Banks and Financial Institutions

The crucial factor, of course, is showing where the customer or client *belongs*. In many situations, this will be far from easy and, to achieve an equitable result, some accommodation may be called for – a balance of probabilities approach, perhaps. As an illustration of what can be achieved, there is an easement available for dealings in securities, details of which are found in **Chapter 8** at 80-100(3)(a).

(b) Finance for exports

Services in the first five categories of VATA 1994, Sch. 9, Grp. 5 are given further relief when connected with exports. In this case, the relevant provisions are to be found in art. 2 and 3(b) and (c) of the *Value Added Tax (Input Tax) (Specified Supplies) Order* 1999 (SI 1999/3121), i.e. services:

> 'which are directly linked to the export of goods to a place outside the member States.'

This clearly requires a specific, rather than a general, association with what is being exported. When the rule applies, any underlying input VAT is recoverable regardless of the status of the recipient or of where the supply is to take place. In terms of the place of supply, this may be:

- inside the UK, where the recipient *belongs* in the UK or, if not in business, belongs in another Member State (in this case the supply is exempt); or
- outside the UK, where the recipient is a business *belonging* in another Member State or otherwise belongs outside the EU (in which event the supply is *outside the scope*).

As with services supplied where received, the rules here apply, not just to principal's transactions, but also, in appropriate cases, to brokerage or agency services. Again, this is explored further below.

Practice point

With export-related finance, the possibility of recovering underlying input VAT is sometimes simply overlooked.

The supply may be a loan to someone established in the UK. As such, it will be exempt and the assumption easily made that that is the end of the matter.

However, if the loan can be identified, and specifically related to exports or other non-EU shipments, relief under art. 3(b) of the *VAT (Input Tax) (Specified Supplies) Order* 1999 may simply be a matter of documentation or putting the right procedures in place.

(c) Agency, brokerage and the services of an intermediary

Relief for financial brokerage or agency services is possible under three main headings:

(1) *The general rule*

> The general rule is simply to follow the principles discussed earlier for services *supplied to a relevant business person or services supplied to a person outside the EU in respect of services specified in para. 16 Sch 4A of VATA 1994*. Agency, or the services of most financial intermediaries are within either the general B2B rule or para. 16 Sch. 4A of

VATA 1994. Where the underlying supply is basically exempt, the agency service will be *outside the scope* with the right to recover underlying input VAT where the client or the recipient of the service is outside the EU.

(2) *Exemption with the right of recovery*

This is a further possibility. It results from art. 3(c) of the *Value Added Tax (Input Tax) (Specified Supplies) Order* 1999 (SI 1999/3121). It applies where a supply is not outside the scope, i.e. is made to someone in the UK or to someone in another Member State, who is not in business. Relief for underlying input VAT is given where the service is one of arranging:

(a) the supply of a basically exempt financial service to someone from outside the EU – i.e. under the rules in (a) above; or

(b) the supply of export finance – under the rules in (b) above or export insurance.

The critical factor is that the *buying counterparty* of the underlying client trade is outside the EU.

This rule will similarly apply where the supply is technically *outside the scope* because the person to whom the agency service is provided is in business in another Member State.

(3) *The zero-rate option*

Zero-rating, although important, is of limited interest for the sectors covered here because it does not apply to anything within VATA 1994, Sch. 9, Grp 2 or 5. Where available, it arises under VATA 1994, Sch. 8, Grp. 7. Item 2 zero-rates a supply of brokerage or agency services where the place of supply, adopting the rules referred to earlier, is in the UK. The services covered are those of *arrangement* where there is a named principal. The relief applies where what is arranged is:

(a) an export of goods to a place outside the Member States;

(b) a supply of services of the description specified in item 1 of the Group (not relevant in the context of this book); or

(c) any supply of services which is made outside the Member States.

Where this applies, the main focus will be on category (c). In other words, the arrangement for a client belonging in the UK (or, if a private individual, in another Member State) of a basically taxable service provided by that client to someone established or *belonging* outside the EU. Because the supply in this case will be zero-rated, the effect is that any normal exemption (or standard-rating) is overridden (VATA 1994, s. 30(1)) and related input VAT becomes automatically recoverable.

Whether or not the agency rules apply (or how they apply in particular cases) has raised a number of interesting issues and these are discussed later at 70-200.

(d) Other zero-rating

Apart from what has been said previously, there may sometimes be other situations where monetary financial supplies are zero-rated, rather than being exempt or standard-rated. These will include especially:

- the supply, by a Central Bank to another Central Bank or between a Central Bank and a member of the London Gold Market, of gold (which includes gold coins) (VATA 1994, Sch. 8, Grp. 10);
- the issue or re-issue by a bank of Bank of England, Scottish and Northern Irish banknotes (VATA 1994, Sch. 8, Grp. 11); and
- certain supplies of gold coin covered by the *Value Added Tax (Terminal Markets) Order* 1973 (SI 1973/173).

Supplies of coins will also be *outside the scope* of UK VAT if held abroad. The treatment of coins is considered in more detail at **Chapter 10**.

70-150 Non-monetary services

Many banks and financial institutions also offer a range of services not directly concerned with the provision of monetary finance or financial assistance. As a general rule, these will be taxable in VAT terms, for the most part, at the standard-rate.

(1) Standard-rating

The more typical standard-rated services found in the banking and financial sector will in practice include:

- accounting services;
- bullion;
- commodities;
- debt collection, credit control and sales ledger accounting services;
- depository and trustee services;
- equipment leasing;
- executor and trustee services and the administration of estates;
- factoring;
- financial advice;
- investment advice;
- investment management;
- management consultancy;
- merger and takeover advice;
- monitoring and recording interest payments;
- nominee services;
- paying agents services;
- portfolio management;
- registration services;
- research, information and communications services;
- safe custody charges;
- service company activities, including payroll administration and the payment of wages;
- telecommunications;
- taxation advice and compliance;
- trustee and executorship services;

- underwriting or arranging issues or sales of securities; and
- valuation of shares and other securities.

In the case of bullion and commodities, standard-rating is often, however, replaced by zero-rating. This applies particularly for transactions involving contracts on one of the UK commodity exchanges and covered by the *Value Added Tax (Terminal Markets) Order* 1973 (SI 1973/173). This affects both principals' and brokerage transactions when a member of the appropriate market is involved and is discussed in some detail later at **Chapter 10**. For some contracts, however (notably financial futures and options and contracts based on indices) the standard-rating is replaced by exemption. Again, this is explored at **Chapter 10**.

The standard-rating for debt collection follows from the specific exclusion from the exemption in art. 135(1)(d) of Council Directive 2006/112/EC) (art. 13(B)(d)(3) of the Sixth VAT Directive) for debt collection (see earlier at 70-100). It applies, however, to debt collection in its simplest form, i.e. the collection of debts on an agency basis.

HMRC's current views on debt collection are to be found in Section 5.10 of Notice 701/49 (Finance) (November 2011), where they consider, for example, that although supplies by a debt collection agency, or by someone involved in debt collection may involve some negotiation of the repayment of a debt, this will tend to be ancillary to the principal service of debt collection, and taxable at the standard rate. So far as factoring is concerned there is a rather different treatment in as much as the contracts usually involve the acquisition of debts by the factor, which are then collected by him on his own account. The *discount* is, to that extent, seen as *outside the scope* and not consideration for any supply of services to the client. There is also often an exempt interest charge for money advanced. Standard-rating is confined, in this case, to just the factoring charge, although this can often result in a significant recovery of input VAT. This is discussed in more detail at 70-400.

The standard-rating for investment management is also regarded by HMRC as applying to commissions earned in relation to broker managed funds (see **Chapters 8** and **9**). It does not, however, extend to the management of special investment funds, such as an authorised unit trust (art. 135(1)(g) of Council Directive 2006/112/EC) (art. 13(B)(d)(6) of the Sixth VAT Directive) and VATA 1994, Sch. 9, Grp. 5, item 9). The standard-rating in this case has now, however, been considered by the ECJ in references in the cases of *Abbey National plc v C & E Commrs (No 2)* (Case C-169/04) [2006] ECR I-4027 and *JP Morgan Fleming Claverhouse Investment Trust v HMRC* been given a more restricted meaning than had hitherto generally been thought. This is considered in more detail in **Chapter 8** at 80-150.

(2) Exemption

The main exemptions for non-monetary financial services are:

- investment brokerage (VATA 1994, Sch. 9, Grp. 5, item 5);
- share and security underwriting (VATA 1994, Sch. 9, Grp. 5, item 5A);
- dealings in shares and other securities (VATA 1994, Sch. 9, Grp. 5, item 6);
- the management of special investment funds (VATA 1994, Sch. 9, Grp. 5, item 9); and
- the management of a close-ended collective investment undertaking (VATA 1994, Sch. 9, Grp. 5, item 10).

The scope of these exemptions is considered further in **Chapter 8**.

As noted at (1) above, exemption will also apply to some of the services of debt factors and companies providing invoice discounting. In this case, the exemption arises as dealings in money or debts and the provision of credit under VATA 1994, Sch. 9, Grp. 5, items 1 and 2.

(3) Outside the scope, exemption with the right of recovery and zero-rating

As with the monetary financial services discussed earlier at 70-100, non-monetary services are often given special relief when provided in an international context. The place of supply rules again take many of the services under this heading outside the scope of UK VAT. In terms of both Council Directive 2006/112/EC (previously the Sixth VAT Directive) and UK law, however, there can be the same ability to recover input tax, albeit often more extensively since the supplies made tend to be inherently taxable rather than exempt. Zero-rating is more widely available.

Again, therefore, it is necessary to look at a combination of factors as they apply to each of the various types of supply that can arise.

(a) Services supplied where received

The main interest for services under this heading is again with the *services, supplied where received*, i.e. those within VATA 1994, s. 7A and Sch. 4A (see the discussion in **Chapter 3**), which are principally services received by a relevant business person (subject to certain overriding place of supply rules in connection with supplies outside the EU as discussed in **Chapter 3**). As noted earlier, the effect of the place of supply rules is that a supply is *outside the scope* of UK VAT if made:

- to someone in business and who is established in another EU country; or
- to anyone belonging or established outside the EU.

This, coupled with what is provided for in reg. 103 of the *Value Added Tax Regulations* 1995 (SI 1995/2518) and art. 3 of the *Value Added Tax (Input Tax) (Specified Supplies) Order* 1999 (SI 1999/3121), has the effect that underlying input VAT can be recovered for:

- any basically taxable service supplied to a business outside the UK or to anyone else outside the EU; and
- any basically exempt service supplied to anyone outside the EU.

This general heading thus covers most of the types of services listed at the start of this section. Many will be banking or financial services . Where provided to a non business person outside the EU most services will be banking or financial services within Sch. 4A, para. 16(2)(e). Some will be within para. 16(2)(d) (services of consultants etc.) of Sch. 4A. It specifically does not, however, cover the provision of safe deposit facilities (para. 16(2)(d) where supplies are made outside the EU to a non-business person). But this latter point is subject to an exception for the storage of gold bullion by a bank or a dealer in gold who is a subsidiary of a bank (see the illustrations at Section 15.6.1 of HMRC Notice 741A (January 2010)).

In practice, the heading in relation to supplies within para. 16(2)(d) (services of consultants etc.) will often also not cover management services as such or administration/secretarial services, unless that is, on a correct analysis, they represent something else altogether (see Section 15.5.3 of Notice 741A (January 2010)). Situations where this might apply might include charges which are really for advice, consultancy or investment management (see Section 15.5.3 of the same HMRC Notice).

(b) Leasing – means of transport and freight containers

Leasing is an essentially VATable activity, except in relation to property, i.e. land and buildings, which will be considered later in **Chapter 8**. The precise VAT treatment will, however, differ according to what assets are involved, where they are located and to whom the supply is made. There is no distinction drawn, through, between finance and operating leases, even if, for accounting purposes these are not recognised in the same way. For the specific nature of the place of supply rules see generally the discussion in **Chapter 3**, and the Table summarising the supply of services rules.

(i) Means of transport

The term *means of transport* will include ships, boats, yachts, barges, cars, trailers, trucks, railway rolling stock and aircraft. It will not extend to freight containers or any vehicle used on a closed circuit, such as a racing car or fairground rides.

The reference to leasing in the list of para. 16(2)(h) of Sch 4A services (i.e. those services supplied to a person who is not a relevant business person, and is outside the EU) in **Appendix 4** specifically does not include the leasing of any means of transport so that a supply will not be outside the scope of UK VAT merely because the recipient of the supply is based or belongs outside the UK. A supply may, nonetheless, still be *outside the scope*, but on a quite different basis. The normal place of supply rule for a means of transport (not being short-term hiring) looks to where the recipient belongs, provided the recipient is a relevant business person; otherwise it is where the supplier belongs (VATA 1994, s. 7A). However, Sch. 4A, para. 3 fixes the place of supply of a short-term hiring of a means of transport as being in the country in which the means of transport is actually put at the disposal of the person by whom it is hired; but if the place of effective use and enjoyment would be outside the EU, there will not be a UK supply and VAT will not need to be applied (VATA Sch 4A, para. 3(3)); and equally a VAT charge will arise if the place of effective use and enjoyment is in the UK, but would otherwise be treated as being made in a country outside the EU (VATA Sch 4A, para. 3(4)).

Other than services of short-term hiring of a means of transport and hiring of goods which are governed by specific rules, with cross-border leases between one Member State to another, however, there is instead, the basic rule in art. 44 of Council Directive 2006/112/EC, i.e. looking to where the recipient is *established* or *belongs* where the recipient is a relevant business person. In the case of *ARO Lease BV v Inspecteur der Belastingdienst Grote Ondernemingen, Amsterdam* (Case C-190/95) [1997] BVC 547, and in *Lease Plan Luxembourg SA v Belgium State* (Case C-390/96) [1998] BVC 412, the question was posed as to whether an asset can itself constitute a sufficient presence for this purpose. The ECJ held it could not.

As seen earlier in **Chapter 4** at 40-000, there were prior to the change in the place of supply rules differences in the treatment of leases, which invited arbitrage. This has been highlighted by the appeal in *RBS Deutschland GmbH*, which concerned a German car leasing company supplying cars bought, used and eventually sold in the UK. RBS Deutschland does not belong in the UK for VAT. No UK VAT is accounted for on the lease rentals, as UK law considers the leasing to be a supply of services made in Germany: no German VAT is accounted for either, as German VAT law considers the leasing to be a supply of goods, which takes place in the UK. The dispute was over the company's entitlement to recover the input VAT on the purchase of the cars. HMRC's position is that, as no output tax is accounted for at all on the rental payments, there is no corresponding right to deduct. Alternatively, they claimed the transactions were an abuse of right. Before the Tribunal, RBS Deutschland won, but HMRC believe the case was wrongly decided and expressed their intention to appeal to the Court of Session. On appeal the Court of Session in turn referred the case to the Court of Justice. The Court of Justice in its decision (C-277/09: 22 December 2010) concluded that under the VAT Directive a Member State cannot refuse to allow a taxable person to deduct input VAT on the acquisition of goods in a Member State, where those goods have been used for the purposes of leasing transactions carried out in another Member State, solely on the ground that the output transactions have not created any output VAT liability in the other Member State. Further, the Court of Justice held that the principle of abusive practices does not apply in circumstances where a parent company elects to have its subsidiary established in another Member State, carry out transactions for the leasing of goods to a third company established in the same Member State as the parent company, so as to avoid VAT being payable on the consideration arising under that supply.

For large ships not designed nor adapted for use solely for recreation or pleasure; and for qualifying aircraft, relief may also be available, where the place of supply is in the UK. This is under the normal zero-rating rules for transport in item 1 and 2 of Grp. 8 (VATA 1994, Sch. 8, Grp. 8). In the case of ships, the vessels must be of a gross tonnage of not less than 15 tons; for aircraft, they should be used by an airline operating for reward chiefly on international routes, or used by a State institution and be of a weight of not less than 8,000 kilogrammes and which is neither adapted for use for recreation or pleasure. The supply, in either case, will include, not just sales, but also supplies under charter or lettings on hire (Grp. 8, Note (2); VATA 1994, Sch. 8, Grp. 8, Note (2)).

(ii) Other assets

Other items of moveable equipment or plant fall within the general rules of s. 7A of VATA 1994, so that a supply to a relevant business person is treated as made where the recipient belongs (B2B), and as being made where the supplier belongs where the supply is to a non-business recipient (B2C), but in all cases subject to the specific rules on overriding places of supply in Sch. 4A of VATA 1994. The Schedule provides that for the hiring of goods if the place of effective use and enjoyment would be outside the EU, there will not be a UK supply and VAT will not need to be applied (VATA Sch 4A, para. 7(1)); and equally a VAT charge will arise if the place of effective use and enjoyment is in the UK, but would otherwise be treated as being made in a country outside the EU (VATA Sch 4A, para. 7(2)). Further, the hiring of goods to a non-relevant business person is treated as being outside the UK if the recipient belongs in a country which is outside the Member States (Sch 4A, para. 16(2)(h) of

VATA 1994). para. 7 in the list of services in **Appendix 4** as the *letting on hire of goods*, for which the treatment is generally as in (a) above.

In the case of containers, leasing or hiring may, additionally, qualify for relief under the rules for export of goods (VATA 1994, s. 30 and *Value Added Tax Regulations* 1995 (SI 1995/2518), reg. 129), when exported to persons outside the Member States. In this case, however, there can be detailed requirements as to proof of movement. This is discussed further at 70-350.

In relation to plant permanently affixed to a building or structure, the supply is generally of an interest in or right over land, which tends to be basically VAT-exempt, unless an option to tax has been made. Different rules altogether then apply in this case, and these are discussed later in **Chapter 8** at 80-150.

As with the services covered by the general rule in (a) above, input VAT relief is given for non-UK supplies by reg. 103 of the *Value Added Tax Regulations* 1995 (SI 1995/2518).

(c) Agency and the services of an intermediary

As discussed earlier, relief for agency services provided to a relevant business person is possible under three main headings:

(1) *The general rule*

The general rule is that the procurement of any service when supplied to a relevant business person, is itself subject to the same rules as apply to the primary service. Thus:

(a) where the underlying supply is basically taxable, the agency service will be *outside the scope* with the right to recover underlying input VAT, where the client or the recipient of the service is a business outside the UK;

(b) where the underlying supply is basically exempt, the agency service will also be *outside the scope* with the right to recover underlying input VAT, where the client or the recipient of the service is outside the EU.

(2) *Exemption with the right of recovery*

As before, this is a further possibility. Following from art. 3(c) of the *Value Added Tax (Input Tax) (Specified Supplies) Order* 1999 (SI 1999/3121), a basically exempt service, such as security brokerage, and which is within the scope of UK VAT, i.e. is made to someone in the UK or to someone in another Member State who is not in business, will confer the right to relief for underlying input VAT, where the sale or other supply being arranged is to someone from outside the EU.

This rule will similarly apply where the supply is technically *outside the scope* because the person to whom the agency service is provided is in business in another Member State.

(3) *The zero-rate option*

Again, this arises under VATA 1994, Sch. 8, Grp. 7. Item 2 zero-rates a supply of brokerage or agency services where the place of supply, adopting the rules referred to earlier, is in the UK. The services covered are those of arrangements where there is a named principal. The relief applies where what is arranged is:

(a) an export of goods to a place outside the Member States;
(b) a supply of services of the description specified in item 1 of the Group (not relevant in the context of this book); or
(c) any supply of services which is made outside the Member States.

The only real interest for most businesses in the sectors covered here will again be in category (c), where the underlying client transaction is outside the EU, for example by being made to someone established or belonging outside the EU. Relief from VAT under this head is specifically not, however, available for any service that is itself VAT-exempt.

70-200 Points affecting particular supplies

(1) Agency and the services of an intermediary

Whether or not a fee is exempt as the provision of an intermediary service within VATA 1994, Sch. 9, Grp. 5, item 5 depends on the particular circumstances involved.

- The decision in *Wright Manley Ltd* and *Wright & Partners* [1993] BVC 1,595, heard in January 1993, threw light on this often difficult issue. The appellants were auctioneers, estate agents and valuers. For some years they held agency appointments with a number of building societies at various offices. Following restrictions in the *Financial Services Act* 1986, they entered into arrangements with Hill Samuel Investment Services Ltd and later with Steggles & Mather (a firm of solicitors) to provide financial advice to persons they introduced as part of the arrangements. They provided accommodation for the use of the financial advisers and office facilities for interviews. None of the appellants' staff were, however, involved in offering financial advice.

  The question at issue was whether what was provided in return for the commissions amounted to what was then 'the making of arrangements' within VATA 1983, Sch. 6, Grp. 2, item 3. The Tribunal concluded it did not. What the appellants did was simply to provide facilities to be used by financial consultants, arrange a meeting or pass on the name and addresses of possible clients. The *Donald Ford* and *BISCO* cases (see **Chapter 9** at 90-350) were easily distinguished. The same situations would equally not qualify for exemption under the present wording in item 5 as qualified by the new statutory Note (5).

- *Devoti t/a Belmont Associates* [1995] BVC 1,421, raised a similar point, where the taxpayer made exempt supplies as a corporate financier. He also prepared, and submitted to lending institutions, financial reports and profiles with a view to obtaining loans for the clients concerned. The appeal followed the cancellation of the taxpayer's VAT registration, with HMRC maintaining that the fees for the preparation and submission of the reports were not taxable, but were exempt. Deciding for HMRC, the Tribunal found the fees were clearly within VATA 1983, Sch. 6, Grp. 5, item 5. In all probability, they would equally qualify as exempt under the corresponding provisions in VATA 1994, as presently drafted.

- In *Lindum Resources Ltd* [1995] BVC 1,118 the issue was, again, whether a fee was exempt within Grp. 5, item 5. In this case, there was a contract to endeavour to procure finance. Two fees were charged, one, the application fee, at the commencement and the other, the funding fee, at the successful conclusion of the negotiations. The question to be decided was whether, as the taxpayer maintained, the application fee was standard-rated, thus enabling part of its input VAT to be recovered. Again, finding for HMRC, the Tribunal held the fees were exempt, this time on the basis that there was a single overall supply. It was specious to say that it covered a separate part of the contract and it appeared not to matter that the application might not prove successful.

In many respects, the outcome of these decisions was understandable, as were the reasons for the HMRC approach.

Also of interest in this context were the written answers to questions in the House of Commons on 3 February 1993 by Sir John Cope, the Paymaster General. In relation to arrangement fees, the response given was that:

– 'arrangement fees charged by banks for loans or other forms of credit form part of the consideration for the loan, which is an exempt supply;
– where a borrower issues shares in return for loan capital, any arrangement fee would also be exempt from VAT;
– in either of the above cases, any associated VAT incurred by the bank is irrecoverable.'

He then went on to deal with a further aspect, which some financial sector businesses may need to consider, namely the treatment of non-executive directors. Charges are often made by investing institutions to investee companies for the services of such directors. Whilst there had been no specific agreement on this, the position taken was very much similar in that:

– 'any charges for a director appointed as a condition of a loan are part of the consideration for the exempt supply of the loan;
– where the investor acquires shares and exercises the right to appoint a director, Customs take the view that there is no supply for VAT purposes, as any shares are supplied to the investing institution by the investor company;
– in neither of the above circumstances is any associated VAT incurred by the investing institution recoverable.'

This would be subject always to the proviso that in some cases (e.g. where the borrower is established outside the EU) exemption carries the right to input VAT relief.

The particular issues raised by the new (post FA 1999) provisions on agency or *intermediary* services in VATA 1994, Sch. 9, Grp. 5, were specifically addressed in the *BAA* case.

- In *BAA plc* [2001] BVC 2,405, the Tribunal followed essentially the same line as that in *C & E Commrs v Civil Service Motoring Association* [1998] BVC 21 (see later under *Outsourcing* at 70-500)). They held, that services provided in relation to a Bank of Scotland affinity credit card were VAT-exempt. The Sixth VAT Directive (Directive 77/388), art. 13(B) (art. 135(1) of Council Directive 2006/112/EC) was not intended to be restrictive and art. 13(B)(d)(1) (art. 135(1)(b)) did not require the credit to be granted to the person who arranges it.
  The work performed by BAA Enterprises under the agreement amounted to:
  - *Pre-selection*: identifying potential WorldCard applicants, principally from BAA databases.

- *Communication with potential applicants*: writing to potential applicants and sending them an application form.
- *Endorsement*: endorsement of the WorldCard and operation of the WorldPoints scheme in tandem with it.
- *Processing applications*: performing clerical checks to ensure application forms have been correctly and fully completed. Communication with Bank of Scotland. Sending completed application forms to Bank of Scotland.

BAA Enterprises did not perform credit checking, which was the responsibility of the Bank, or valuation. On the facts, the services fell within the terms of VATA 1994, Sch. 9, Grp. 5, item 5 namely the *provision of intermediary services in relation to any transaction comprised in item 1, 2, 3, 4 or 6 ... by a person acting in an intermediate capacity*. The exclusions at the end of Grp. 5, Note (5) did not apply; nor did the Tribunal consider that the words in the present Note (5A) affect the issue. In particular the service was not one of the management of credit as defined.

In addition the Tribunal did not consider that the issue sufficiently uncertain so as to require a reference to the ECJ.

The Tribunal's decision was upheld on appeal by the High Court in February 2002 (*C & E Commrs v BAA plc* [2002] BVC 463) where it was decided that the *negotiation of credit* within art. 13(B)(d)(1) (art. 135(1)(a) of Council Directive 2006/112/EC) was not restricted to the brokering of an actual exempt transaction by an intermediary who had power to affect the transaction itself. The activities carried out by the taxpayer satisfied the requirements for *negotiation of credit* in art. 13(B)(d)(1) (art. 135(1)(a)). They amounted to *a distinct act of mediation* and without the company's services, the individual contracts for the issue of World Cards would not take place. The activities could not be fairly characterised as mere clerical formalities; nor could they merely be seen as the carrying out of promotional or marketing activities for the bank. Furthermore, the activities fell within the exemption for *intermediary services* in relation to any transaction comprised in VATA 1994, Sch. 9, Grp. 5, item 2.

This was later confirmed by the Court of Appeal in *C & E Commrs v BAA plc; Institute of Directors v C & E Commrs* [2003] BVC 112, who also held that the Tribunal in the similar *IoD* case had been wrong to hold that the services did not come within the exemption because to do so the IoD would have to be in a position to negotiate the rates or to be otherwise involved in the actual transaction binding the other party to the credit card agreement as an agent. There was no material difference between the two cases. HMRC did not appeal and now accept it is no longer necessary for the introducer to be capable of affecting the terms of the principal financial service for the exemption to apply.

Exemption thus applies where an intermediary:

- stands between the parties to a contract in the performance of a distinct act of mediation;
- brings the two parties to the contract together; and
- undertakes 'work preparatory' such as completing or assisting with the completion of application forms, forwarding forms to the credit card company, and making representations on behalf of either party.

However, HMRC do not view marketing and promotional services supplied in isolation, nor the performing of clerical functions (such as providing a list of names or access to a database) as exempt intermediary services.

- The same line was subsequently followed by the Tribunal in 2005 in *Prudential Assurance Co Ltd* [2006] BVC 2,340 where Boots Plc entered into an arrangement with Egg, a member of the Prudential Group, for a co-branded card scheme under which payment to Boots was based on the use of the card. The co-branded *Egg* credit card was offered to all Boots' *Advantage Card*-holders, who were able to earn Advantage points in the normal way but also earn points at a lower rate when using the Prudential Group's Egg card to make purchases elsewhere than at Boots.

Many of the issues that arise in this context are particularly apparent in relation to outsourcing. There have been a number of important cases, which illustrate the principles that need to be adopted in deciding how the relevant provisions of EC law are to be applied in particular situations. Many appear to indicate that the present exemptions in the VATA 1994, Sch. 9, Grp. 5 from 10 March 1999 may be too restricted. The subject of outsourcing is discussed at 70-200.

- Interestingly, in relation to outsourcing, the Tribunal in *TeleTech UK Ltd* [2003] BVC 2,514 considered intermediary services in a different context, the use of call centres to effect sales by *cold-call* telephone calls. The arrangements in this case involved insurance. Teletech's staff *cold called* individuals by telephone to try to sell them two types of insurance policies for the insurer, American Life Insurance Company, ALICO. Once a customer was persuaded and a Direct Debit Authorisation obtained, ALICO were immediately on risk, with no input, at that stage on their part. This was subject, of course, to the usual 30-day cooling-off period and the like. The way Teletech was remunerated was somewhat unusual in that, after being paid start-up costs, they got a fixed sum per employee, each of whom were expected to sell half of one policy per hour.
- HMRC argued exemption was prevented by Note 7 to Exemption Group 2 (see **Chapter 9** at 90-350) as advertising and promotional services, but this was rejected by the Tribunal as semantics. The Tribunal also rejected the suggestion that Teletech were not proper insurance agents because of the way they were paid.

Practice point

HMRC have now acknowledged the correctness of *Teletech* in Business Brief 07/03 of 30 June 2003 (and their policy is reflected in HMRC's manual at VATINS5330). However, due to the unique nature of the insurance exemption, they see this as applying only to call-centre services supplied in connection with insurance and not having any implications for cases concerning the VAT liability of call centre services supplied to other sectors.

Teletech rightly won because the substance of what they did amounted to the provision of *insurance-related services* in the capacity of an *agent or broker*.

Not all outsourced marketing will be able to be brought within the exemption, of course. At the end of the day, it all comes down to what is actually being done and how. Whether HMRC are right in saying *TeleTech* only applies in the context of the rules on insurance, and not also to finance, seems questionable. To achieve exemption, under Group 2 for insurance or Group 5 for Finance, it is important that what is done is sufficiently integral to the underlying exempt activity and the danger is that often what is done will not go quite far enough. But there seems no reason why the sort of call-centre services exempted in *TeleTech* could not equally be exempt for financial services if the right conditions prevailed.

However, what this means, if the particular supply is to be exempt, is not just that it is an important function for the client, but that it is, in a sense, part of the underlying exempt activity. This was essentially the problem in *Morpheus 2002 Ltd*.

- In *Morpheus 2002 Ltd* [2007] BVC 2,224, the taxpayer provided outsourced services to a number of mortgage lenders requiring the services of a solicitor or licensed conveyancer in order to effect remortgaging arrangements. Only solicitors are allowed to prepare the documents necessary to transfer or charge property in this situation and, if lenders don't have the professional staff in-house, they must use outside firms. Morpheus, who were paid a fixed fee per transaction, maintained a panel of solicitors willing to do this work, was responsible for allocating cases and negotiated the fees those solicitors were, in turn, to receive.

Before the Tribunal, Morpheus argued the critical events within what it did were the making of the lending contract and the movement of money, which were part of an exempt supply of credit pursuant to art. 13B(d)(3) of the Sixth Directive. However, this was rejected as the making of payments to panel firms was only one element of the service provided and did not predominate over the other elements. What Morpheus did was really to provide management, administrative and IT support. It clearly cannot have helped that the underlying loan arrangements were already agreed to when the matter was put in Morpheus's hands and that any negotiation on their part was only over the level of the solicitor's fees, a matter that concerned just Morpheus as it affected the profit they made.

In short, the case is probably a good example of the mere physical or technical supplies alluded to in the *Sparekassernes Datacenter (SDC) v Skatteministeriet* (Case C-2/95) [1997] BVC 509 discussed later under *Outsourcing* at 70-500.

A further recent example of the principles involves is found in the *Ludwig* case.

- *Ludwig v Finanzamt Luckenwalde* (Case C-453/05) was a German case, that concerned a self-employed agent marketing financial services. Ludwig was a sub-agent for another agent. The services provided involved analysing the financial situation of potential clients and then putting forward appropriate financial products, such as credit facilities. If the client wanted to proceed, Ludwig prepared the contractual offer, which was sent to the principal agent for submission to the lender, which could accept, reject or amend the offer. If a contract was concluded, the principal agent received a commission and, in turn, paid a commission to Ludwig.

  There were two issues:
  - whether Ludwig made a single supply of services; and
  - whether the fact that he had no contractual link with any of the parties to a credit agreement prevented the supply being exempt under art. 13(B)(d)(1).

  The Court held that the fact that a taxable person analysed the financial situation of clients did not prevent the service supplied being an exempt negotiation of and it was for the National Court to determine whether there was a single supply of which the advisory aspects were ancillary. There was also no reason why someone who had no contractual link with any of the parties to a credit agreement to the conclusion of which he had contributed, could not be exempt.

HMRC provide a summary of the key factors as to when they regard an intermediary is falling within the scope of the exemption. HMRC say (VATFIN7210):

> 'An intermediary for the purposes of the finance exemption must: be providing an intermediary service in relation to an exempt financial transaction (that is, the transaction of one of the parties must itself fall within items 1, 2, 3, 4 or 6 of Group 5; be acting in an intermediary capacity (i.e. bringing together someone seeking a financial service with someone providing a financial service); and if the transaction falls with items 1, 2, 3 or 4, be carrying out work preparatory to the conclusion of contracts for the provision of those services. Therefore, in deciding whether something is an intermediary service, the key factors are those set out above rather than, for example, how the person is paid (e.g. by commission or fee) or by their professional status.'

HMRC provide a flow chart for helping to decide whether a person is acting as an intermediary for the purposes of Group 5 item 5, and this is reproduced in Appendix 25.

(2) Arbitration services

Prior to the change in the place of supply rules under Council Directive (2006/112/EC, art 43 to art. 45), the services of a member of an arbitration Tribunal were liable to VAT in the country where the arbitrator was established. This was because they were not services *supplied where received*, i.e. within art. 56 of the Sixth VAT Directive (Directive 77/388) (the Sixth VAT Directive (Directive 77/388), art. 9(2)(e)). This was confirmed by the ECJ in *Von Hoffman v Finanzamt Trier* (Case C-145/96) [1997] BVC 562. However, such arbitration services are now subject to the general business to business, and business to consumer rules (see Chapter 3). But where arbitration services are supplied to a non-relevant business person who belongs outside the EU the services will be treated as being made where the supplier belongs. This is because arbitration services do not fall within VATA 1994, Sch 4A, para. 16(2)(d) as 'similar services' (see *Von Hoffman v Finanzamt Trier* (Case C-145/96) [1997] BVC 562).

(3) Automated Teller Machines (ATMs)

ATMs provide a convenient way for customers of banks and building societies to obtain immediate funds and account services. Within the UK, this is made possible by accessing the service via machines operated by the customer's own bank or building society or by independent ATM deployers, such as retail stores through the Link Interchange Network Ltd ('LINK'). Under the LINK rules each member can charge either the customer or the counter-party bank, although banks and building societies generally only charge the counter-party bank.

The provision of money through ATMs, or cash-point machines and the settlement services provided by LINK, are basically exempt supplies within art. 135(1)(d) or (e) of Council Directive 2006/112/EC of 28 November 2006 as:

> '(d) transactions, including negotiation, concerning deposit and current accounts, payments, transfers, debts, cheques and other negotiable instruments, but excluding debt collection;'

or

> '(e) transactions, including negotiation, concerning currency, bank notes and coins used as legal tender, with the exception of collectors' items, that is to say, gold, silver or other metal coins or bank notes which are not normally used as legal tender or coins of numismatic interest;'

the exemption covering any *convenience* fees charged to card-holders or any interchange and reciprocity fees charged between banks and other providers where the fees relate to one of the following: the facility to obtain money, the provision of money, transaction processing or the operation of accounts (HMRC Notice 701/49 VAT: Finance (November 2011) at para. 2.9).

This exemption does not, however, extend to the provision of an ATM or software required to run the ATM, cash point machine replenishment (see later at (8)) or to the provision of suitable sites. The granting of a right to permanently attach an ATM to the ground, or for its incorporation into the fabric of a building, is an exempt supply of an interest in or right over land (see **Chapter 8**) unless the grantor has opted to tax. As shown in the decision in *Concept Direct*, any fees charged for the procurement of suitable sites for the placement of machines, including negotiating with the site owner, are taxable.

- In *Concept Direct Ltd* (MAN/05/071), the company, in addition to being paid a lump-sum finder's fee, was also paid a fee per transaction, presumably reflecting the value of its judgment in choosing the site. However, the Tribunal, found these fees were simply part and parcel of its reward for finding sites, a decision hardly surprising in the light of the line taken in cases like *Sparekassernes Datacenter* and *FDR*.

(4) Banknotes

The issue of banknotes is zero-rated under VATA 1994, Sch. 8, Grp. 11. An appeal in February 2001 by the Royal Bank of Scotland highlighted one of the fundamental issues with this, and with VAT generally, namely the importance of defining exactly what it is that is being supplied.

Whether the Tribunal has got it quite right, however, is perhaps debatable.

- The dispute in *Royal Bank of Scotland Group plc* [2001] BVC 2,275, the dispute centred round the use of ATMs and the reciprocity fees charged by the Bank to other banks and financial organisations, whenever its machines were used by people who were not its customers. The Bank, one of three Scottish banks still able to issue bank notes, was used to stocking all its ATMs in Scotland with its own new bank notes, but those in England and elsewhere with notes issued by the Bank of England.

    There was no question of VAT being chargeable on the fees. What was in dispute was whether:

    - as the Bank argued, the fees relating to ATMs in Scotland were zero-rated; or
    - as HMRC maintained, they were exempt under Sch. 9, Grp. 5 (as simply payments for the facility to obtain money).

    If the Bank were correct, the result would have meant an improvement in its input tax recovery.

    Unfortunately, the Tribunal decided for HMRC. It considered itself bound by the test propounded in *Ivory and Sime Trustlink* to determine what specifically and essentially was supplied in consideration of the payment received. It seemed artificial to attempt to subdivide the service, which the reciprocity agreements envisaged, into differing categories depending on whether particular ATMs were situated in Edinburgh or London.

The matter was taken to the Court of Session on appeal (*Royal Bank of Scotland plc v C & E Commrs* [2002] BVC 389, where the decision given by the Tribunal was confirmed.

(1) The fee was payable in consideration of the Bank providing a facility to withdraw cash, in whatever form it was dispensed.
(2) The contractual agreements emphasised the reciprocal nature of the system and, whatever the benefits for individual customers, the system was established for the mutual benefit of the participating banks.
(3) The agreements did not oblige the Bank to dispense its own notes in Scotland and the nature of the supply for VAT could not depend on a voluntary decision of the Bank to dispense one type of note rather than another.
(4) Dispensing the Bank's own bank notes through ATMs did not constitute the issuing by the bank of notes payable to bearer on demand.

Practice point

Whilst one can see some attractions in this approach, the fees were clearly transaction-based and not for a single, overall supply.

It seems not unreasonable, therefore, to make a distinction on geographical lines based on which machines were being used. Since VATA 1994, s. 30 specifically provides for zero-rating to override exemption (or the standard-rate), it is difficult to see why such a distinction should not be made in this case.

It is also worth observing, that the decision in *Kretztechnik AG v Finanzamt Linz* (Case C-465/03) ECJ [2006] BVC 66 (see earlier in **Chapter 1** at 10-300 and **Chapter 4** at 40-200), decided that the issue of shares, and presumably other financial instruments will not be a supply for VAT purposes. On this basis, possibly Sch. 8, Grp. 11 may have no effect, so that all supplies by the Bank would be VAT-exempt, regardless.

(5) Bills of exchange and notes or orders for the payment of money

Bills of exchange and promissory notes (as defined in the *Bills of Exchange Act* 1882) are also within VATA 1994, Sch. 9, Grp. 5, item 1 (art. 135(1)(a) of Council Directive 2006/112/EC)). As with money, no consideration (and no supply) was, historically, recognised by HMRC unless, and to the extent that, proceeds exceed face value. On this basis, they did not see a supply on disposal of a bill, e.g. by a customer to a discount house or on delivery up for redemption. Equally, if a discount house rediscounted a bill for no more than the total amount receivable, this will again not have given rise to a supply.

This view changed, however, with the issue in November 1995 of Business Brief 25/95. This covered bills of exchange, trading coupons, eurocurrency paper, instruments and paper negotiable for cash, local authority bills and certain promissory notes. HMRC accepted that the actual price paid is the consideration for a supply by the drawer or the seller so that, where the recipient of the supply belongs outside the EU, there is now the prospect of input VAT relief.

In Section 3.1 of HMRC Notice 701/49 (November 2011) on Finance, they say, however, (under the heading of Securities for money) that the issue itself, as opposed to a subsequent onward-supply, is exempt. Whether this is still valid must now be doubtful following the Ruling of the ECJ in *Kretztechnik AG v Finanzamt Linz* (Case C-465/03) ECJ [2006] BVC 66 (see earlier in **Chapter 1** at 10-300 and **Chapter 4** at 40-200), where it was decided that the issue, as opposed to a subsequent, secondary, supply, of financial instruments of this kind will not be a supply for VAT purposes.

Amounts payable on redemption will always, however, be *outside the scope*. A discount house will also not make a supply in providing finance for a customer merely by discounting a bill of exchange. The *discount* is simply the reduction in the purchase price paid for the bill and is thus *outside the scope*. A supply will in fact tend to occur only if a separate interest charge is made for the ready availability of funds or is to be added to the sums payable on redemption.

This original failure by HMRC to recognise a supply appears to have been largely a matter of historical convention. They remain concerned, however, at the potential for distortion and will normally require the exclusion of values of supplies from any outputs-based proportional partial exemption calculation. The treatment is thus very much in line with that expected for commercial paper following the previous change in August 1992.

(6) Block discounting

Block discounting is, in many respects, like factoring (see 70-450 later), being a form of finance which releases the value of future receivables under equipment leases or rental agreements. Often, the rental streams will remain collected by the original owner on behalf of the discounter, but the VAT treatment depends on whether or not the legal title to the assets is transferred:

- if it is, there is a potentially taxable transfer of the assets from the owner to the discounter and subsequent supplies under the leases or rental agreements by discounter to the lessees or hirers.
- if it is not, the subsequent supplies under the leases or rental agreements remain made by the owner and there is then an exempt supply of credit by the discounter.

Whether there is a supply of the debts/receivables by the owner to the discounter in the latter situation would depend on whether the transaction amounted to a sale (see (17) later) or an assignment in a situation akin to factoring.

(7) Cash collection and checking and change services

The processing of money involving the collection by a security organisation of bulk cash and its subsequent checking and safe delivery are regarded as exempt financial services within VATA 1994, Sch. 9, Grp. 5, item 1 (*Barclays Bank plc* (1988) VATTR 23; (1988) 3 BVC 692). However, HMRC consider that where the core supply is simply collection, counting and sorting money the supply is taxable. HMRC state in their guidance (at VATFIN2420):

> 'Where supplies include collection, counting, sorting and holding, as well as notifying a bank of the amounts collected, the service is seen as a single composite supply, the counting, sorting and holding of money being the predominate element, or core, of the supply. This

core is taxable. All other elements are ancillary and thus follow the liability of the main supply. In essence, the bank is paying for independent verification of the money, which includes counting and sorting of it.'

HMRC consider the decision in *Barclays Bank plc* to now be incorrect. This is on the basis that following the decision of the ECJ in the *SDC* case simply doing something that a bank would otherwise do is not sufficient for exemption. Any supply must be exempt in its own right.

(8) Cash-point machine replenishment

A somewhat different line to that in (7) above was taken by the Tribunal on cash-point machine replenishment

- In *Nationwide Anglia Building Society* [1995] BVC 1,413, the appeal related to the treatment of services supplied by Securicor in keeping the ATMs restocked and included a cash-checking service and the transport of money to and from the various sites. Nationwide maintained these were exempt under VATA 1983, Sch. 6, Grp. 5, with the possible exception of the transport element. HMRC disagreed, maintaining everything was taxable at the standard-rate.

  Deciding for HMRC, the Tribunal distinguished the present situation from that of Barclays Bank (see (3) above). Securicor was not dealing with money as money in the same way that a bank would do. Nor did it think the services could come within VATA 1994, Sch. 9, Grp. 5, item 5 as the *making of arrangements*. As in *Williams & Glyn's Bank Ltd* ((1974) VATTR 262; (1974) 1 BVC 1,021), the services assisted Nationwide in making its supplies, but Securicor did not arrange the supply itself as it had no involvement with the supply to Nationwide's customers. The services also did not come within item 8 of the Group as the operation of a current, deposit or savings account.

Following *Nationwide*, HMRC announced that they considered the same principles should apply to the services of supermarket operators and other retailers restocking ATMs in shops (see also *Banknotes* at (4) above).

(9) Coins and banknotes

VATA 1994, Sch. 9, Grp. 5, item 1 also covers coins and banknotes when supplied as legal tender in a financial transaction and the services of sorting and counting money and the giving of change. The exemption does not, however, apply to:

- dealings with numismatic and investment items;
- gold coins, which are standard-rated whether or not they are legal tender (unless exempt as a supply of investment gold: See Notices 701/21 (Gold) and 701/21A (Investment gold coins);
- certain supplies of banknotes, which can be zero-rated on issue or reissue by the bank of issue, i.e. the Bank of England, or the appropriate banks in Scotland and Northern Ireland; and
- coins and banknotes, which are not legal tender. These are taxable at the standard-rate on the full selling price unless eligible under the special arrangements for antiques.

The exemption under item 1 will also not cover supplies of banknotes or coins as collectors' pieces, investments or articles of numismatic interest (e.g. proof coins or maundy money). These are taxable on the full selling price unless they are over 100 years old and covered by the special scheme for antiques (art. 4 of the *Value Added Tax (Special Provisions) Order* 1995 (SI 1995/1268) and Customs Notice 718 (April 2011).

As with bills of exchange, HMRC historically saw no consideration (and no supply) if and to the extent that dealings are at or below face value. However, the successful Tribunal appeal by the *Republic National Bank of New York* [1992] BVC 968 showed this to be incorrect. However, the matter was further put beyond doubt by the decision in *First National Bank of Chicago v C & E Commrs* (Case C-172/96) [1998] BVC 389.

(10) Confirming houses

The function of a confirming house is essentially to provide a service to importers of goods by, in one way or another, effectively guaranteeing payments. It may also on occasion provide credit.

Some arrangements involve the confirming house effectively taking over the purchase of the goods from the original supplier. The goods will then be on-sold as taxable supplies by the confirming house to the client. Any credit provided will either be incorporated into the price for the goods (and reflected in the payment terms) or result in a separate financial charge. In the former case the *credit* will be taxable as part of the price for the goods (see, for example, the principles in *Muys' en De Winter's Bouw-en Aannemingsbedrijf BV v Staatsecretaris van Financiën* (Case C-281/91) [1993] ECR I-5405); in the latter it will be exempt under VATA 1994, Sch. 9, Grp. 5, item 2.

Other confirming agreements are obviously financial. A *confirming commission* will be charged for the financial guarantee provided to the supplier on behalf of the importer. Also frequently provided will be an extended credit by way of loan on which interest is charged. In both cases, the supply is exempt. In the case of commissions, this will be under Grp. 5, item 1; in the case of credit, under item 2. Both confirming commissions and interest attract input VAT relief when charged to persons belonging outside the EU or where the destination of the goods is outside the EU.

(11) Consortium or syndicated loans

A consortium or syndicated loan is where a number of banks agree to participate in an overall facility with one of their number as manager. Just as for direct tax (especially double tax relief), the form of the relationship is important.

(1) If, contractually, each of the consortium members is lending direct to the overseas borrower (i.e. is a co-participator), then each makes an appropriate part of the overall supply.

(2) If the borrower is outside the EU, each will stand to benefit from input VAT recovery.

(3) Where, however, the lead manager is the initial lender and belongs in the EU, with the other consortium members contributing on a back-to-back basis for their respective shares (i.e. sub-participation), only the manager will gain.

In terms of agents' fees, the treatment depends on the identity of the person to whom the agent's services are provided and on whether that supply falls within the scope of the exemptions in VATA 1994, Sch. 9, Grp. 5. Based upon the terms of the standard facility arrangement, HMRC are prepared to see the supply as made by the agent to the borrower. They also accept that the supply is primarily of the collection and distribution of loan payments and, as such is exempt under VATA 1994, Sch. 9, Grp. 5, item 1, regardless of by whom it is paid and would not be affected where the agent bank ceases to be a lender. This will also apply, where the contract specifies the agency fee is for a service to the borrower, but not where the contract is not specific about what the agency fee is for.

HMRC say that exemption will not apply, however, if the agent's fees are consideration for the service provided to the lenders of managing loan payments, adjusting interest rates, managing late payments/defaults, ensuring that each party gets its due, etc. They see such services as the supply as standard-rated credit management. However, whether this is strictly correct or is to apply in all cases may be arguable.

In contrast, the service provided to the borrower entails primarily receiving and passing on payments. Therefore, if the agent's fee is consideration for this service to the borrower, HMRC see the supply as a payment service, exempt under Grp. 5, item 1.

> *Practice point*
>
> Syndicated/consortium loans can be undertaken in broadly one of two ways:
>
> - each member of the syndicate/consortium can lend direct to the ultimate borrower (co-participation); or, alternatively,
> - only one party may make the actual advance to the client, with the others contributing on a back-to-back basis (sub-participation).
>
> If the borrower *belongs* outside the EU and the Isle of Man, the supply will be potentially exempt with the right to input VAT recovery.
>
> However:
>
> - in the case of co-participation, where each member participates directly, each will potentially benefit from relief; but
> - with sub-participation, only the principal lender, the lead manager, will gain.
>
> This distinction is not unlike that for corporation tax, when it comes to claiming double taxation relief and is something it can be worth planning for.

(12) Credit, debit and charge cards

See 70-300 later.

(13) Credit management

In February 2002, HMRC embarked on a Consultation over the wording of Group 5 following the taxpayer's successful appeal in *FDR Limited*. The real problem with the Group as it stood had been the references to the *management of credit*. In the corresponding rules in art. 13B(d) of the Sixth Directive, this only appeared in the context of exempting the management of credit by the person granting it. Article 13 said nothing about what may, or may not, be provided by anyone else, and which could easily be exempt under another head. Following the changes to the Group in 1999, however, UK law had put the emphasis the other way round, excluding entirely from exemption anything, which fell within HMRC's definition of that term, unless it was provided by the actual grantor of the credit itself. What the law then said, in Note (2B) to Grp. 5, was that:

> 'For the purposes of this Group a person makes "a supply of services comprising the management of credit" if he performs *any one or more of the following* in relation to a credit, a credit card, a chargecard or a similar payment card, operation-
>
> (a) credit checking;
> (b) valuation;
> (c) authorisation services;
> (d) taking decisions relating to a grant or an application for a grant of credit;
> (e) creating and maintaining records relating to a grant or an application for a grant of credit on behalf of the credit provider; and
> (f) monitoring a creditor's payment record or dealing with overdue payments.'

What this seemed to mean, therefore, was that, in UK law at least, exemption was prevented for a number of activities to which many in the financial sector believed it should be available, if not necessarily as the *management of credit*.

The proposals then put forward by HMRC recognised this and appeared nicely to deal with most of the objections and the *management of credit* is now put in proper context. From August 2003, a new item 2A reads simply:

> 'The management of credit by the person granting it.'

and the offending definition has been removed.

However, what HMRC continue to say in Section 4.10 of Notice 701/49 (November 2011) is

> 'If you provide credit management, and you do **not grant** the credit, your supply is taxable. If, on the other hand, you grant the credit **and also** manage that credit, your supply will be exempt.
>
> A supply by a third party of taxable credit management could typically include the following features:
>
> - credit checking, this includes debt profiling, assessing credit worthiness, electoral roll checks and obtaining references
> - valuation of assets such as property, land, vehicles
> - authorisation services (including those that go beyond just checking the applicant's signature or agreeing credit or payment within limits set by the person providing the credit)
> - taking decisions on credit applications on behalf of the credit provider
> - creating and maintaining records on behalf of the credit provider in order to enable them to fulfil their legal obligations, such as those relating to credit applications, payments and credit transactions
> - monitoring a payment record or dealing with overdue payments (although read section 5 on debts and related services).'

They go on to add the list is not exhaustive.

> **Practice point**
>
> Significantly perhaps, HMRC no longer say that, if someone performs *any one or more* of these activities, what is done is not VAT-exempt. This could well leave it open for something in the list (authorisation or taking decisions on credit applications, say) to still be exempt as *part of the provision of intermediary services* within Item 5 or, under the corresponding provisions in art. 135(1)(c), (d) or (e) of Council Directive 2006/112/EC of 28 November 2006.
>
> It may be important, therefore, to avoid taking what is said in Notice 701/49 entirely at face-value.

Of interest, perhaps, is an exchange in the House of Commons in November 2002. Mr David Curry, Conservative MP for Skipton & Ripon had asked the Chancellor of the Exchequer:

- whether all suppliers of mortgage administration services in the UK are subject to VAT; whether joint venture companies between UK mortgage lenders and US service providers have been granted exemptions from VAT; and if he will make a statement
- which Member States of the EU impose VAT on outsourced mortgage administration services; and at what rates.

In a written answer, Mr John Healey, Economic Secretary to the Treasury, replied that:

> 'Mortgage administration services are VAT exempt when supplied by the mortgage provider but are liable to VAT when provided by a third party. Supplies between two companies in a joint venture will be disregarded for VAT purposes if the companies are part of the same VAT group. Customs & Excise are currently taking action to prevent artificial structures involving joint ventures being used to bring third party companies within VAT groups. Little information is available on the VAT treatment of outsourced mortgage administration services in other member states, although the French advise that they would also charge VAT on outsourced loan administration services.'

As a matter of interest, in this context, there has now been a judgment of the ECJ relating to a preliminary ruling on the meaning of negotiation in art. 13B(d)(1) of the Sixth Directive (art. 135(1)(b)) in the case of *Volker Ludwig v Finanzamt Luckenwalde* (Case C-453/05). The following questions were put:

> '(1) Is there negotiation within the meaning of Article 13B(d)(1) of Directive 77/388/EEC, when a taxable person, in some circumstances represented by a subagent, negotiates credit for clients canvassed by it from various providers, with which it has previously negotiated general terms and conditions for its clients and from which it receives a commission for the negotiation of a product, even if, in the process, it investigates and analyses the financial situation of clients and their personal and financial needs, or is that service a dependent service ancillary to the principal service, which is a financial service not covered by Article 13B(1)(d)?
>
> (2) Is it a precondition of the turnover tax exemption in respect of negotiation of credit under Article 13B(d)(1) of Directive 77/388/EEC that
>
>   (a) there is a direct contractual relationship between the negotiator, on the one hand, and the borrower and/or the lender on the other, and

(b) the negotiator establishes contact not only with the borrower, but also with the lender, and himself negotiates the details of the contract with the latter,'

'or does the tax exemption also cover commission payments received by a taxable person from a main agent (for which he works as a subagent and in whose name he acts vis-à-vis its clients) in return for those clients entering into credit agreements with providers indicated by him, but without the subagent establishing contact with the lender?'

The taxpayer (Mr Ludwig) was a financial adviser, and he brought proceedings against the German tax authorities in relation to their refusal to exempt from turnover tax a net commission received by him. The taxpayer was self-employed and acted under a commercial agency agreement with a business called Deutsche Vermögensberatung AG (DVAG). DVAG provided financial products to individuals, which would be canvassed to them by financial advisers (such as Mr Ludwig), in the name of DVAG. The financial advisers would review the financial situation of an individual and would then determine their possible investment requirements. The assessment would be carried out using software provided by DVAG. For example, if the individual decided to take credit then the financial adviser would prepare a contractual offer which, after signing by the client, would be sent to DVAG (which in turn would check conformity with any legal requirements), and in turn would send the offer to a lender (who could decide whether to accept, reject or amend the offer). If any contract was concluded then the lender would pay a commission to DVAG, which would then pay to their sub-agent (i.e. the financial adviser), a sub-commission reflecting the role of the financial adviser in the conclusion of the contract. Mr. Ludwig claimed that the payment of the commission was exempt and not subject to German VAT.

The CoJ held that the services rendered by DVAG and its subagent were remunerated by the lenders only on condition that the clients approached and advised by the financial adviser entered into a credit agreement, which suggested that the negotiation of the financial product should be regarded as the principal service and the giving of advice was merely ancillary (see para. 19 of the judgment). Further, the negotiation of credit appeared to the CoJ to be the decisive service both for the borrowers and for the lenders, in so far as the activity of giving financial advice occurred only in a preliminary phase and was limited to helping the client choose, from among the various financial products, which were best adapted to his situation and to his needs (para. 19 of the judgment). In essence, in this situation the CoJ held that where a taxable person analyses the financial position of a client which is canvassed by a financial adviser with a view to obtaining credit for their client then this does not prevent recognition of the service supplied as being a negotiation of credit which is exempt for the purposes of the VAT Directive if 'in the light of the foregoing interpretative criteria, the negotiation of credit offered by that taxable person falls to be considered as the principal service to which the provision of financial advice is ancillary, in such a way that the latter shares the same tax treatment as the former. It is for the national court to determine whether that is the case in the proceedings before it' (at para. 20 of the judgment).

In relation to the concept of 'negotiation' the CoJ emphasised that (at para. 28 of the judgment):

'the Court has held that negotiation is an act of mediation, which may consist, amongst other things, in pointing out to one of the parties to the contract suitable opportunities for the conclusion of such a contract, in making contact with another party or negotiating, in the name and on behalf of a client, the detail of the payments to be made by either side, the purpose of such an activity being to do all that is necessary in order for two parties to enter into a contract, without the negotiator having any interest of his own in the terms of that contract (see, to that effect, with regard to Article 13B(d)(5) of the Sixth Directive, CSC Financial Services , paragraph 39).'

There is no requirement for a direct contractual link to exist between the negotiator and one party to the credit agreement (at para. 33of the judgment):

> 'the application of the exemption provided for in Article 13B(d)(1) of the Sixth Directive cannot depend on the existence of a contractual link between the provider of the service of negotiation and one of the parties to the credit agreement, but must be assessed with regard to the very nature of the service rendered and its purpose, as referred to in ... the present judgment'

There is no requirement for a direct contractual link between the negotiator and any of the parties to a credit agreement in order to qualify for a service being a negotiation of credit. The CoJ commented (at para. 36 to 39):

> '... in order to be classed as exempt transactions for the purposes of Article 13B(d)(1) of the Sixth Directive, the service provided must, viewed broadly, form a distinct whole, fulfilling in effect the specific and essential functions of the service of negotiation. It is not, therefore, inconsistent with Article 13B(d)(1) of the Sixth Directive for the service of negotiation of credit to be divided, as in the case before the referring court, into two services, the first provided by the main agent DVAG, in the context of the negotiation with the lenders, and the second by its subagent, Mr Ludwig, in his capacity as financial adviser, in the context of the negotiation with the borrowers. ... negotiation is an act of mediation which may consist, amongst other things, in pointing out to one party to the contract suitable opportunities for the conclusion of such a contract, the purpose of such an activity being to do all that is necessary in order for two parties to enter into a contract, without the negotiator having any interest of his own in the terms of that contract. The concept of negotiation does not, therefore, necessarily presuppose that the negotiator, as subagent of the main agent, enters into direct contact with both parties to the contract, in order to negotiate its terms, provided, however, that his activity is not limited to dealing with some of the clerical formalities related to the contract. In addition, the very fact that the terms of the credit agreement have been fixed in advance by one of the parties to the contract cannot, as such, preclude the supply of a negotiation service for the purposes of Article 13B(d)(1) of the Sixth Directive, given that, as stated in the previous paragraph, the activity of negotiation may be limited to pointing out to one party to the contract suitable opportunities for the conclusion of such a contract.'

(See also *Debt (re)negotiation* at (16) later.)

(14) Current accounts

The operation of a current account is exempt, along with the operation of deposit or savings accounts, under VATA 1994, Sch. 9, Grp. 5, item 8 (art. 135(1)(d) of Council Directive 2006/112/EC of 28 November 2006). The exemption covers bank charges and the supply of chequebooks, credit slip books and bank statements when ancillary to the operation of an account and so exempt under item 8. It does not, however, cover the supply of special cheques and credit slip books, as shown in *National Westminster Bank Plc* [2003] BVC 2,003, which are treated as separate taxable supplies of goods.

The existence of an exempt supply can arise even in the case of so-called *free* banking services as shown in *The Governor and Company of the Bank of Scotland* [1996] BVC 2,664. This can be important for partial exemption purposes and is something that will generally need to be taken into account. In such a situation the supply is an exempt item 8 supply for a consideration. For HMRC's discussion on this point see VATFIN2970.

(15) Debt collection and factoring

Debt collection and factoring were specifically excluded from the exemption in art. 13B(d)(3) of the EC Sixth Directive (Directive 77/388 EEC) and are probably similarly excluded by art. 135(1)(d) of Council Directive 2006/112/EC, albeit that factoring is not actually referred to.

On 26 June 2003, the ECJ confirmed the line taken by Advocate General Jacobs in the *MKG* case. This was all about the treatment under the EC Sixth Directive of factoring, a term that, at one level, can mean just the collection of debts and the undertaking of sales ledger accounting. However, *mainline* factoring (or *true* factoring as referred to in *MKG-Kraftfahrzeuge-Factoring*) is, essentially, a specialist form of *off-balance sheet* finance involving the sale of trade debts by the client to the factor, with:

- in full, or non-recourse, factoring, the factor assuming all the risk of non-payment; but
- in recourse factoring, with the debts being re-assigned to the client should the debtor default.

Both types, however, involve the factor assuming responsibility for any sales ledger accounting.

Generally, contracts envisage the acquisition of these debts by the factor at face-value, but with the client not being paid this at the outset. Instead, the client will usually be made cash advances of up to 80 per cent of that sum, with the full price being settled at, say, the end of the client's normal period of credit or when the factor is himself paid. The service thus involves three elements:

- finance;
- risk control; and
- sales ledger administration.

in return for which the factor charges the client interest and a factoring fee or discount.

- In *Finanzamt Groß-Gerau v MKG-Kraftfahrzeuge-Factory GmbH* (Case C-305/01) [2003] BVC 616, MKG took the view that the services it provided were taxable, but the German tax authorities argued that *true* factoring did not result in an *economic activity* by the factor at all – much like the situation in *Polysar* with the acquisition of shares. There was not so much a service provided to the client, as a sale of a debt by the client to the factor. They also went on to argue that the service, if there was one, was VAT-exempt under art. 13B(d)3 as a 'transaction concerning debts'. In other words, if the debts were acquired by the factor, he would be collecting them for himself and not providing a service to the client.

The Court, however, felt it would ignore economic reality if true factoring were *outside the scope*. In purchasing trade debts, the factor provided a service by relieving the client of debt-recovery operations and the risk of non-payment of debts, in return for a consideration which comprised not merely debts included in the factor's assets, but payment by way of commission and a *del credere* fee. There was a direct link between the factor's activity and the amount received by him in payment therefore. True factoring was therefore an economic activity within art. 2 and 4 and fell within the scope of VAT. Also, the proviso at the end of art. 13(B)(d)(3) of the Sixth Directive referring to factoring (which was found in the English and Swedish versions (but not the other language versions) and which is now omitted) was to be interpreted in the light of the spirit and scheme of the Sixth Directive. As an exception to derogation from the general application of VAT, it was to be interpreted broadly as simply a variant of the general concept of 'debt collection'.

This decision was essentially in line with the existing UK treatment of factoring, which is discussed later at 70-450. See also Debt sales and assignment of debt at a discount at (17) later.

In *R & C Commrs v Axa UK plc (C-175/09)* [2011] BVC 35 the Court of Justice emphasised that the term 'debt collection and factoring" in art. 13B(d)(3) of the Sixth Directive (now art. 135(1)(d)) referred to financial transactions designed to obtain payment of a pecuniary debt. The case related to a payment plan operated by Denplan, which was part of Axa, and the issue arose as to whether collecting payments was within the scope of the exemption in, what is now, art. 135(1)(d) of the VAT Directive. Ultimately the court decided that the service fell within the exception to the payment exemption as being one of debt collection. The material facts were as follows:

- Denplan provided services for dental practices, and the principal service related to the operation of payment plans between dentists and their patients. Under the terms of the plans, dentists provided regular check ups and/or any necessary treatment, on a continuing basis against payment by those patients of a fixed monthly charge. The collection of payments formed part of several services provided by Denplan.
- Broadly, each payment plan would be entered into by a patient signing a contract with the dentist (which would be in a standard form produced by Denplan).
- The monthly charge would be paid by the patient to Denplan, as the dentist's agent, in receiving payments due to that dentist. Patients would complete a bank 'mandate'in favour of Denplan.
- Denplan would process the material financial information provided by a patient (including recording it to computer systems), Denplan collected the payments due from patients (via the Bankers' Automated Clearing System (BACS), which involved sending the patient's bank account number and the amount which Denplan was to collect from that account). This would result in BACS posting a corresponding credit to Denplan's bank for the credit of Denplan's account. Denplan would also provides payment advices to dentists and contact the patients whose payments it has not received.
- Denplan on receipt of payment from patients would then account to each dentist for the payments it was entitled to from patients subject to agreed deductions for fees. Part of the fees deducted from the patients' payments represented consideration for Denplan's services in collecting payment for the dentists (namely, services of seeking payments from patients' bank accounts via BACS).

The Court of Justice approached the issue of the VAT treatment of the fees for the payment collection services by asking these three questions:

(1) Does Denplan supply its clients with several distinct and independent services requiring separate VAT assessment or a single complex service comprising several elements?

(2) Does the service come within the exemption from VAT under Art. 13B(d)(3) (now Art. 135(1)(d)) of the Sixth Directive relating to transactions concerning payments or transfers?

(3) If in principle within the scope of the exemption, was the service one of 'debt collection or factoring' and so subject to VAT?

In answering these questions the Court adopted the following reasoning:

As to (1), does Denplan supply its clients with several distinct and independent services requiring separate VAT assessment or a single complex service comprising several elements?

The Court decided that Denplan provided a single service.

The Court commented that distinct services which could be supplied in isolation give rise, separately, to taxation or exemption, must be considered to be a single transaction when they are not independent (para. 21 of the judgment). The Court considered that '[t]his is particularly true where two or more elements or acts supplied by the taxable person to the customer are so closely linked that they form, objectively, a single, indivisible economic supply, which it would be artificial to split' (para. 21 of the judgment).

Where a transaction comprises a bundle of features and acts, regard must be had to all the circumstances in which the transaction in question takes place in order to determine whether there are two or more distinct supplies or one single supply (para. 22 of the judgment).

The Court decided that the actions performed by Denplan were a single transaction due to the fact that '[t]he economic purpose of those actions is the transfer of the sum due each month from the patient to the dentist. The transfer of the sum due to the service supplier's bank account is of no use to its client unless that sum, less the service supplier's remuneration, is then paid to the client and the service supplier accounts to that client for the sums received' (para. 23 of the judgment).

As to (2), does the Denplan service come within the exemption from VAT under Art 13B(d)(3) (now Art. 135(1)(d)) of the Sixth Directive relating to transactions concerning payments or transfers?

The Court concluded that in principle the service was in the scope of the exemption concerning payments, unless it was a service of debt collection or factoring (see point (3), below). The court considered that the service was within the scope of the exemption in principle because:

> 'As regards the service in question in the main proceedings, it is appropriate to point out that its purpose is to benefit Denplan's clients, namely dentists, by the payment of the sums of money due to them from their patients. Denplan is, in return for remuneration, responsible for the recovery of those debts and provides a service of managing those debts for the account of those entitled to them'

(para. 28).

The Court emphasised that the terms used in the exemptions are to be interpreted strictly, since they constitute exceptions to the general principle that VAT is to be levied on all goods and services supplied for consideration by a taxable person. However, the interpretation of those terms must not deprive the exemption in question of its intended effect (para. 24 of the judgment). The transactions exempted under art 13B(d)(3) (now art. 135(1)(d) of the Sixth Directive) are defined in terms of the nature of the services provided and not in terms of the person supplying or receiving the service. The exemption is not subject to the condition that the transactions be effected by a certain type of institution or legal person, where the transactions in question relate to the sphere of financial transactions (para. 26 of the judgment).

To be regarded as exempt transactions the services must, viewed broadly, form a distinct whole, fulfilling the specific, essential functions of a service described in that provision (para. 27 of the judgment).

As to (3), if in principle within the scope of the exemption, was the service one of 'debt collection or factoring' and so subject to VAT?

The Court concluded that the Denplan services fell within the scope of debt collection and were subject to standard rating.

The Court emphasised that derogations from the general application of VAT, are to be interpreted strictly, but that the term 'debt collection and factoring' is to be interpreted broadly as it is an exception to such derogation (para. 29 of the judgment).

The term 'debt collection and factoring' refers to financial transactions designed to obtain payment of a pecuniary debt (the Court citing *Finanzamt Groß-Gerau v MKG-Kraftfahrzeuge-Factoring* [2003] BVC 616 (at para 78): see para. 31 of the judgment). Specifically the court commented: 'In fact, the object of that service is to benefit Denplan's clients, namely dentists, by payment of the sums of money due to them from their patients. That service is therefore intended to obtain the payment of debts. By undertaking the recovery of debts for the account of those entitled to them, Denplan frees its clients of tasks which, without its intervention, those clients, as creditors, would have to perform themselves, tasks consisting in requesting the transfer of the sums due to them, via the direct debit system' (para. 33 of the judgment).

The Court also commented that the exception covers the collection of debts of any nature, without limiting its application to debts which are not paid on their due date, and it is not limited to debts in respect of which the debtor has already defaulted. Specifically it can also have as its object debts which have not yet become due and which will be paid on the due date (para. 34 of the judgment).

The Court also noted that in the application of the exception it is irrelevant to the treatment of the service that it does not provide for coercive measures for the effective payment of the debts concerned (para. 35 of the judgment).

HMRC have sought to emphasise certain comments made by the CoJ in connection with debt collection. In particular, HMRC at VATFIN3250 has commented that the concept of debt collection has wide application:

> 'Following the AXA judgment, therefore, 'debt collection' cannot be seen as applying solely to the service of chasing and recovering overdue payments on behalf of the creditor. All services principally concerned with collecting payments from the person owing them for the benefit of the entity to which those payments are owed (regardless of whether those payments are received before, on, or after their due date) fall within the exclusion and are consequently liable to VAT at the standard rate.'

Following the decision of the CoJ (as discussed above) the Court of Appeal has followed the decision of that Court (see *R & C Commrs v Axa UK plc* [2011] EWCA Civ 1607; [2012] BVC 1). Lady Justice Arden delivered the unanimous decision of the Court, and concluded that Group 5, item 1 of Sch. 9 of VATA 1994 implements the whole of the relevant EU legislation. However, the Court acknowledged that the scope of the exemption is ambiguous, noting that 'the precise scope of the exemption and carve out is unclear, and will require further definition in the future. However, the authoritative determination of what falls within the exemption and the carve out is within the jurisdiction of the Court of Justice. If there is any ambiguity, therefore, it can be cured by a further reference to the Court of Justice in a future case. Therefore, this lack of clarity is not a reason for not giving the finance exemption a conforming interpretation in the present case' (at para. 49 of the judgment). As to the effect of the CoJ's ruling, Lady Justice Arden commented (at para. 49 of the judgment):

> 'As to the effect of the ruling in the present case, in my judgment, it is clear that the Court of Justice concluded that the words "debt collection" in the carve out have a meaning capable of being applied to "transactions concerning payments" within the exemption in article 13B(d)(3) (judgment, paragraph 28, last sentence). It then has to be decided whether the actual transaction in question falls within the exemption or the carve out, and this will depend on its precise facts. If it falls within the exemption it will fall outside the carve out, and vice-versa (see final sentence of paragraph 28). The Court of Justice does not define the purpose of the exemption. It is unnecessary to decide on this appeal what the full scope of the exemption might be. However, for the purposes of this judgment it may hypothetically be taken to be normal retail banking activities (and indeed that is one way of reading paragraphs 24 to 27 of the judgment of the Court of Justice in Nordea). On that hypothesis, the carve out takes out of the scope of the exemption any separate supply of services which is more properly regarded as a service of debt collection.'

Obviously, everything depends on the particular circumstances of a supply in order to determine whether it's properly construed as a debt collection service with the consequence of it being standard rated. It is possible that on a proper consideration of the nature of the supply that it will be treated as an exempt supply.

A further example of the VAT treatment of debt collection services is provided by the Court of Session decision in *HBOS plc v R & C Commrs* [2008] CSIH 69; [2009] BVC 48. This case involved HBOS using agents to obtain payment of some of the sums then due under credit facilities which had been advanced to their customers. HBOS used agents where they were unable or not equipped to recover such sums themselves. HBOS had argued that the VAT status of these arrangements involved the agents acting as intermediaries within art. 13B(d)(3) of the Sixth Directive (now art. 135(1)(d) of the VAT Directive), and VATA 1994, Sch. 9, Group 5, item 5. HMRC considered that the supply made by the agents was debt collection with any other activities being ancillary to it. There was a single supply of services by the agent to HBOS. In this context, the court considered that its main task was to decide what was the objective character of the supply, having regard to its essential aim or features. The material features of what the agent did were as follows (at para. 46 of the judgment):

- the services provided by the agents were described as 'debt negotiation services' in the contract with HBOS;
- HBOS' principal objective, using their agents' skills, was to recover as much of a crystallised debt as possible;
- an agent might adopt various techniques to induce a debtor to pay, varying from the threat of litigation to the offer of inducements, such as offering the debtor the opportunity to pay less than the amount due, or to pay it over a longer period of time, or both;
- the sole measure of the agent's remuneration was an agreed percentage of the amount recovered: the agent was paid by the results achieved in pursuance of the objective of maximising recoveries.

The Court held that on the evidence that 'the essential features of the arrangement between HBOS and the agent ... point towards the essential aim or dominant purpose of the service supplied being debt recovery' (at para. 46 of the judgment). Accordingly, the service supplied by the agent was debt collection. The Court went on to state that where there is an element of negotiation that it does not prevent a service being characterised as debt collection. In this regard, the Court commented:

> 'While the agent and the customer may agree upon a reduced amount or an extended period for payment, or both, and thus innovate upon the original contract, this is always in a situation where there is a debt which has crystallised. What the agent is doing is recovering some at least of the debt; and any negotiation concerning the debt is no more than incidental to its recovery. Moreover, the agent is not "acting in an intermediary capacity" within the meaning of item 5, as that term is properly understood. The agent acts on behalf of and is answerable to HBOS as its principal, and from the customer's point of view stands in for HBOS rather than acts as a go-between (at para. 47 of the judgment).'

Court and legal fees

In December 1997 HMRC announced changes to the treatment of Court and legal fees paid by debt collectors. From 1 April 1988, distinction is drawn between collectors acting as agent and those acting as principal. The emphasis is over the extent to which the retention by the collector of an award of Court fees and solicitors' scale charges is *outside the scope* or is consideration for a supply of services by him.

Moneys received from the collection of the debts themselves remain *outside the scope*.

More information on this is to be found in HMRC Notice 700 The VAT Guide (April 2002) at section 25.6.

(16) Debt (re)negotiation

In line with its treatment of credit management, until the decision in the *Debt Management Associates* case, HMRC had seen debt renegotiation services as essentially taxable. It is now accepted that they are exempt under VATA 1994, Sch 5, Grp. 9, item 5 (art. 135(1)(d) of Directive 2006/112/EC of 28 November 2006).

- In *Debt Management Associates Ltd v C & E Commrs* [2003] BVC 4,055, the company's clients typically had debt problems and the company provided a service of negotiating a repayment plan with the creditor and, thereafter, collecting monthly instalments. For this, it received a flat-rate negotiation fee and further fees for collecting and handling the payments, the income from the latter being around 17 times the income from negotiation fees. Before the Tribunal, DMS argued these were two separate exempt supplies or, alternatively, there was a single exempt supply, with payment-handling the dominant part. HMRC had maintained there was a single, composite supply, with negotiation being the dominant part, making the whole supply standard-rated.

Deciding for DMS, the Tribunal held there was no support for HMRC's contention that to qualify for exemption, negotiations must lead to a contract similarly, there was no merit in the argument that Note (5) to Grp. 5 of VATA 1994, Sch. 9 was to be read as if the bringing together of the parties and the conclusion of a contract were cumulative conditions. Article 13(B)(d)(3) of Directive 77/388, the Sixth VAT Directive (now art. 135(1)(d) of Directive 2006/112/EC of 28 November 2006), referred to negotiations concerning debts and, while the word *debt* did not feature at all in Grp. 5, debt and credit were merely opposite sides of the same coin and there was no difference of substance between the two. On the basis of both UK and EC law, therefore, DMS' negotiation service was exempt.

This was subsequently acknowledged by HMRC in Business Brief 30/03 of 30 December 2003 and this is currently found in Section 5.9 of Notice 701/4.

Since the Debt Management Associates case, there has been a further appeal by HBOS Plc.

- *HBOS plc* [2007] BVC 2,394 was about debt collection. As a provider of credit, the Bank, for the most part, uses its own collections department, but also employs agents where there are complications. These agents could vary the terms of the contract with the customer by allowing extra time to pay, or reducing the amount if expedient to secure payment of the outstanding amounts and the Bank argued these services were exempt as the granting or negotiation of credit. However, HMRC saw the supply as simply a debt collection service, with any element of credit negotiation being ancillary. The Tribunal agreed. Following from Card Protection Plan, the dominant purpose of the entire economic arrangement was the recovery of money due to the Bank, despite the skill of the negotiators and the discretion they were given. They were unable to find that the negotiation involved was an aim in itself, but was just ancillary.

(17) Debt sales and sale of debt at a discount

The sale of a debt, as opposed to the assignment of a debt under a factoring agreement, is a basically exempt supply, probably under VATA 1994, Sch. 9, Grp. 5, item 1 (art. 135(1)(d) of Council Directive 2006/112/EC). The term the 'sale' of debt is used by HMRC to describe the situation where all legal and beneficial or equitable interest in the debt passes to the buyer to whom full title and risk is transferred; whilst in contrast an assignment of debt is treated as an assignment of the equitable interest in the debt which is passed to the assignee and the assignor retains the legal interest in the debt and any liability to obligations arising from the original contract (see HMRC manual VATFIN3215).

In the case of assignments under a factoring agreement, the assignment is likely not to be regarded as a supply, following the lines taken in *MBNA Europe Bank Ltd v R & C Commrs* [2007] BVC 3 and in *Capital One Bank (Europe) plc* [2006] BVC 2,148 (see under *Securitisation* at (36) later and *Factoring* in 70-450). However, see *MKG-Kraftfahrzeuge-Factoring* (at point 15, above where there was a supply for VAT purposes).

Where a trade debt is sold by a supplier of goods or services, the exempt supply will generally be accepted by HMRC as *incidental* for the purposes of a residual input VAT calculation under the partial exemption rules (see earlier in **Chapter 4** at 40-200).

The sale (and assignment) of debt at a discount on a non-recourse basis should not be subject to VAT provided that the discount (i.e. the difference between the face value of the debts and their purchase price) is a reflection of the actual economic value of the debt at the time of their assignment. The position is governed by the decision of the CoJ in *Finanzamt Essen-NorOst v GFKL Financial Services AG* (Case C-93/10) 27 October 2011, which also provided clarification on the scope of the Court's decision in *Finanzamt Groß-Gerau v MKG-Kraftfahrzeuge-Factory GmbH* [2003] BVC 616 (as discussed in point 15, above).

The material facts in *Finanzamt Essen-NorOst v GFKL Financial Services AG* were as follows:

- GFKL, a German company, owned a subsidiary that purchased mortgages on immovable property and debts relating to 70 loan agreements. The mortgages and debts were acquired from a bank. The face value of the debts was €15,500,915.16, but the purchase price of the debts was €8,034,883 (reflecting the realisable value of the debts and the period of recovery being over three years).
- Under the terms of the sale agreement the purchaser was treated as being at risk on the mortgages and debts, the assets were treated as being held for the sole benefit of the purchaser, the purchaser was entitled to the payments attributable to the mortgages and debts and liability of the seller for the recovery of the debts was excluded.
- The parties to the sale agreement decided that the debts were not subject to VAT, since the purchaser was not providing a service to the seller. However, the German tax authority required VAT to be account for on the discount. The VAT treatment was the subject of a tax appeal. The German Court referred the following questions to the CoJ concerning the VAT treatment of the mortgages and debts:

> '(1) For the interpretation of art 2(1) and art 4 of the Sixth Directive: Does the sale (purchase) of defaulted debts constitute, on account of the assumption of responsibility for debt recovery and the risk of loss, a service for consideration and an economic activity on the part of the purchaser of the debts even if the purchase price is not based on the face value of the debts, with a flat-rate reduction agreed for the assumption of responsibility for debt recovery and the risk of loss, but is set by reference to the risk of loss estimated for the debt concerned, with only secondary importance attached to the recovery of the debt compared to the reduction for the risk of loss? (2) If the answer to Question 1 is in the affirmative, for the interpretation of art 13B(d)(2) and (3) of the Sixth & Directive (a) Is the assumption of the risk of loss by the purchaser of defaulted debts at a purchase price significantly lower than their face value exempt from tax, as being the provision of a different security or guarantee? (b) If the assumption of the risk is exempt from tax, is the recovery of the debts exempt from tax, as part of a single service or as an ancillary service, or taxable as a separate service? (3) If the answer to Question 1 is in the affirmative and no exempt service has been supplied,

for the interpretation of art 11A[1](a) of the Sixth & Directive ; Is the consideration for the taxable service determined by the recovery costs presumed by the parties or by the actual recovery costs?'

The CoJ reached its conclusion that the supply was not subject to VAT for the following reasons:

- Question 1: In essence the question was whether an operator, who at its own risk, purchases defaulted debts at a discount effects a supply of services for consideration and carries out an economic activity. The CoJ decided that the purchaser did not carry on an economic activity or supply services (para. 22 and 26 of the judgment). This case was in contrast to the position in *MKG-Kraftfahrzeuge-Factoring*, so that in GFKL the assignee of the debts received no consideration from the assignor. The CoJ considered that unlike the factoring commission and the del credere fee which were retained by the factor in *MKG*, in this case the discount was not intended to provide direct remuneration for a service supplied by the purchaser of the assigned debts (para. 24 of the judgment). In this regard, the court commented that the critical feature as to why the discount did not constitute a supply subject to VAT was because (para. 25 of the judgment): 'The difference between the face value of the assigned debts and the purchase price of those debts constitutes not the consideration for such a service, but a reflection of the actual economic value of the debts at the time of their assignment, which results from the fact that they are doubtful and from the increased risk of default of the debtors.'
- Questions 2 and 3: These issues were not considered due to the decision of the court on Question 1.

Practice point

The assignment of a debt is not subject to VAT since there is no supply, unless the assignee provides consideration, such as the provision of a debt collection service. In determining how to structure the sale of debt at a discount it is important to ensure that there is no consideration which can be construed as being in exchange for the provision of any service by the assignee. If the discount is calculated on the basis of its net present value (e.g. by reference to rates of default and interest rates) then there should be no consideration. In other words, it is critical to ensure that the transfer value only reflects the actual economic value of the debt.

(18) Deferred payments

The supply of goods or services on deferred payment terms will involve an exempt supply of credit under VATA 1994, Sch 9, Grp. 5, item 2 (art. 135(1)(b) of Council Directive 2006/112/EC of 28 November 2006), but only where: this is for an additional charge, and covers periods after the delivery of the goods or services has taken place. (See *Muys' en De Winter's Bouw-en Aannemingsbedrijf BV v Staatssecretaris van Financiën* (Case C-281/92).)

(19) Deposits, loans, overdrafts and mortgages

These are all covered by VATA 1994, Sch. 9, Grp. 5, item 2. The measure of the supply will, in most cases, be the amount of interest received. Where applicable, it will also cover any front-end fees required. Any commitment fees payable (and which are due irrespective of whether or not the facility is taken up) and any commission paid on the introduction of a loan will fall to be treated within Grp. 5, item 5.

A lender who advances money to enable the borrower to purchase a property makes an exempt supply of credit within item 2. The security (namely a mortgage) over the property does not take the supply out of item 2.

(20) Face-value vouchers

Face-value vouchers that give a right to goods or services are not seen by HMRC as securities for money (see Section 3.2 of HMRC Notice 701/49). What they say, though, is

> 'However, if the voucher is issued on credit and the presentation/redemption of the voucher establishes the issuer's obligation to pay the face value voucher then at the point the voucher can be exchanged for money it is a security for money and any consideration for it is exempt. For example, where the voucher is presented to a retailer as payment for goods or services it is not a security for money, but when the retailer presents the voucher to a third party to be exchanged for money, it becomes a security for money at that point if the voucher had been issued to the redeemer under a credit arrangement/initial grant of credit. You can find further information on face value vouchers in VAT Information Sheets 03/2003 and 12/2003 and Notice 700/7 Business promotion schemes.'

Arguably, though, this view is incorrect as it is based (see VATA 1994. Sch. 10A, para. 1.1) on the premise that a 'face-value voucher':

> 'means a token, stamp or voucher (whether in physical or electronic form) that represents a right to receive goods or services to the value of an amount stated on it or recorded in it.'

With most, if not all, vouchers of this kind, there is no inalienable right to be supplied with goods or services, but simply a right to require that the voucher is accepted in full or part-payment. The issue or supply of such a voucher would seem, therefore, to be basically exempt from VAT as, for example, a transaction concerning payments within art. 135(1)(d) of Council Directive 2006/112/EC, i.e. within the heading of:

> 'transactions, including negotiation, concerning deposit and current accounts, payments, transfers, debts, cheques and other negotiable instruments, but excluding debt collection.'

For the purposes of VATA 1994 Sch 10A there are two principal types of face value vouchers, namely (i) retailer vouchers and (ii) credit vouchers. As discussed in Revenue & Customs Brief 12/12:

> '• A retailer voucher is a voucher issued by the same person who will redeem it. This includes, for example, gift tokens sold by a retailer for use in its own shops
> • A credit voucher is any type of face value voucher that is issued by one person but which can be exchanged for goods and services from another person. This includes, for example, gift tokens sold by one company that can be exchanged for goods or services in a variety of high street shops.'

Under Sch 10A the consideration for all supplies of credit vouchers is disregarded with VAT being brought into account by the redeemer when the vouchers are exchanged for goods or services. With retailer vouchers the initial consideration on issue is disregarded but the vouchers are then taxed for subsequent supplies. The issuer is required to account for VAT on the supply when the voucher is redeemed.

Following the decision of the CoJ in *Lebara Ltd v R & C Commrs* (C-520/10)[2012] BVC 219, HMRC have removed single purpose face value vouchers from VATA 1994, Sch 10A with the consequence that they are taxed when they are issued (the changes apply with effect from 10 May 2012) (see section 201 of FA 2012). In other words, where such a voucher is sold both initially and by retailers or distributors, it is treated as a supply of the goods or services for which it can be redeemed. A single purpose face value voucher is one that carries the right to receive only one type of goods or services which are all subject to a single rate of VAT. The rules apply to all single purpose vouchers, whether credit, retailer or other types of voucher. HMRC give as an example of such a voucher one that can be redeemed only for electronically supplied services will be a single purpose voucher even if the electronic service can have slightly different forms (e.g. streamed movies, music or games) (see generally Revenue & Customs Brief 12/12).

The VAT treatment of voucher transactions, particularly through cross border supply chains, has been fraught with difficulties in the absence of EU legislation clearly defining a common EU VAT treatment, with the consequence of various Member States applying their own national practices on an inconsistent basis leading to VAT inefficiencies or avoidance.

The case of *Lebara* involved UK based telecoms operator, Lebara, who sold phone cards to distributors in other Member States who then resold them to end-consumers directly or through other distributors. An end-consumer's use of the phone cards was routed through a UK sited telephone exchange. HMRC considered there were two supplies by Lebara, one to distributors which was outside the scope of UK VAT, and the other to users of the cards at the time of redemption, which HMRC considered to be taxable in the UK.

The CoJ was asked to consider the nature of the phone card transactions and when they should be taxed. It ruled against HMRC, finding that there was a single supply by Lebara to distributors and not a second supply to end users on redemption.

In a press release published 10 May, the EU Commission proposed new VAT rules to create a genuine single market for vouchers, noting that there is no justification for the market to be held back because of uncertainty and complications in the tax rules.

The EU Commission proposes a uniform set of rules, to be adopted at a national level by 1 January 2014 and to have effect from 1 January 2015. These rules cover:

- a new definition of different categories of vouchers
- the time of transaction for voucher transactions – at the point-of-sale and/or redemption, depending on the nature of the voucher
- distinguishing vouchers from other means of payment (including mobile payment services)

- clarifying the VAT treatment of free discount vouchers
- introduction of common rules for supply chains involving the distribution of certain vouchers through intermediaries
- technical measures to deal with input VAT recovery, redemption and reimbursement procedures, determining the person liable for payment of the VAT and other obligations for businesses

Further details can be found at: http://europa.eu/rapid/pressReleasesAction.do?reference=IP/1 2/464&format=HTML&aged=0&language=EN&guiLanguage=en.

(21) Financial guarantees and bonds

The exemption under VATA 1994, Sch. 9, Grp. 5, item 1 extends also to financial guarantees. Exemption here only applies where the guarantee, etc. is secondary to a primary contract, and is a contract of security issued by a guarantor or surety obliging him to indemnify a party to the primary contract for any loss arising from the failure or default of the other party to fulfil his obligations. Where the guarantor is a permitted insurer, the supply may equally be exempted under Sch. 9, Grp. 2 (see **Chapter 9**).

(22) Foreign exchange (FOREX)

Although within VATA 1994, Sch. 9, Grp. 5, item 1, in practice foreign exchange was, for many years, regarded by HMRC as *outside the scope*. No supply was recognised unless and to the extent that any proceeds exceeded face value. This will normally only, of course, occur where currency is exchanged *over-the-counter* and a fee is charged; otherwise all dealings will be at normal exchange rates and effectively par. The position on FOREX will depend on the circumstances of the transaction. Broadly, if the FOREX transaction involves a spread position that is adopted over a period of time then it will be a supply for VAT purposes. In this situation the consideration for VAT purposes will be the net position of all the supplier's FOREX transactions, which would be exempt within item 1 of Group 5. Additionally, any fee or commission would also be exempt within item 1 of Group 5.

However, this view was long felt by many commentators to be incorrect. A foreign exchange transaction must involve a basically exempt supply of one currency for another. A barter, if nothing else. If the buyer is outside the EU and the Isle of Man, there should then be the possibility of input VAT relief under reg. 103 of the *Value Added Tax Regulations* 1995 (SI 1995/2518). With some reluctance, the HMRC view changed following two important appeals by the Republic National Bank of New York and by the First National Bank of Chicago.

- In *Republic National Bank of New York* [1992] BVC 968, the issue was over whether sales of banknotes were *supplies for consideration*. Sales of notes were to other banks and to travel companies, not to retail customers. The Bank provided good, clean notes and made its profit by charging a price higher than the prevailing market or *screen* rate. It sold currency received in exchange more or less immediately, aiming to avoid any risk of loss (or profit).
  The Tribunal agreed with the Bank. The provision of notes in one currency in return for payment in another was a supply for consideration in the EU sense of that word, as was the disposal of the currency received. In doing either, the Bank was carrying out the terms of a contract to exchange. There was nothing special about an exchange of currency. It is just

as much a contract for consideration as an exchange of a certificate of deposit. HMRC's wider argument was not sustainable in law. The narrower ground favoured by the Bank, i.e. that the excess of the deal price over the screen price was itself consideration, was also accepted.

The circumstances in *First National Bank of Chicago v C & E Commrs* (Case C-172/96) [1998] BVC 389 were somewhat different. The Bank was a market maker and here the concern was simply over the treatment of its normal currency exchanges. The Tribunal had some difficulty in simply endorsing the earlier decision in the *Republic National Bank of New York* case as the conclusions on the alternative arguments were hard to reconcile. Ultimately, however, it reached the same conclusion, namely there was a supply for consideration. The case then proceeded to the High Court, from whence a reference was made to the ECJ, where, in July 1998, the decision was again given in favour of the Bank.

The Court had little difficulty in reaching its main conclusion, that there was, indeed, a supply for consideration. Its reasoning in reaching this conclusion, it observed that:

'33 To hold that currency transactions are taxable only when effected in return for payment of a commission or specific fees, which would thus allow a trader to avoid taxation if he sought to be remunerated for his services by providing for a spread between the proposed transaction rates rather than by charging such sums, would be a solution incompatible with the system put in place by the sixth directive and would be liable to place traders on an unequal footing for purposes of taxation.

34 It must therefore be held that foreign exchange transactions, performed even without commission or direct fees, are supplies of services provided in return for consideration, that is to say supplies of services effected for consideration within the meaning of art. 2(1) of the sixth directive (art 2(1)a of Council Directive 2006/112/EC).

35 The answer to be given to the first question must therefore be that transactions between parties for the purchase by one party of an agreed amount in one currency against the sale by it to the other party of an agreed amount in another currency, both such amounts being deliverable on the same value date, and in respect of which transactions the parties have agreed (whether orally, electronically or in writing) the currencies involved, the amounts of such currencies to be purchased and sold, which party will purchase which currency and the value date, constitute supplies of services effected for consideration within the meaning of art. 2(1) of the sixth directive (art 2(1)a of Council Directive 2006/112/EC).'

However, what gave it more of a problem was assessing the amount of the taxable value, the consideration. What it said on this was:

'42 It should be borne in mind that art. 11A(1)(a) of the sixth directive (art 73 of Council Directive 2006/112/EC) provides that the taxable amount is, in respect of supplies of services, that which constitutes the consideration which has been or is to be obtained by the supplier from the purchaser for such supplies.

43 While they are the subject of a supply, the currencies transferred to a trader by his counterparty in the course of a foreign exchange transaction cannot be regarded as constituting remuneration for the service of exchanging currencies for other currencies or consequently as constituting consideration for that service.

44 Determining the consideration therefore comes down to determining what the Bank receives for foreign exchange transactions, that is to say the remuneration on foreign exchange transactions which it can actually take for itself (see, in this regard, *HJ Glawe Spiel-und Unterhaltungsgeräte Aufstellungsgesellschaft mbH & Co KG v Finanzamt Hamburg-Barmbek-Uhlenhorst* (Case C-38/93) [1994] BVC 242; [1994] ECR I-1679, para. 9).

45 In this regard, the spread representing the difference between the bid price and the offer price is only the notional price which the bank would obtain if it were to conclude, at the same instant and on similar conditions, two corresponding purchase and sale transactions for the same amounts and the same currencies.

46 However, these are simply theoretical considerations, since the bank carries out a large number of transactions relating to different amounts and involving different currencies, the rates of which are in constant fluctuation. A trader cannot normally foresee, when concluding one particular transaction, at what moment and at what price he may subsequently effect one or more transactions enabling him to eliminate or fix, at a specific amount, the risk of a change in rate to which he is exposed following the first transaction.

47 So, the consideration, that is to say the amount which the bank can actually apply to its own use, must be regarded as consisting of the net result of its transactions over a given period of time.

48 It should be borne in mind in this regard that, in the case of transactions which are effected for consideration but the actual consideration for which depends on future factors such as passage of time, the court has already ruled that the taxable amount must be defined on the basis of, in particular, the interest accrued over a deferred payment period, which was not yet known when the taxable transaction was concluded (*Muys' en De Winter's Bouw-en Aannemingsbedrijf BV v Staatssecretaris van Financiën* (Case C-281/91) [1993] ECR I-5405, para. 18).

49 Nor is it necessary for either the taxable person supplying the goods or performing the service or the other party to the transaction to know the exact amount of the consideration serving as the taxable amount in order for it to be possible to tax a particular type of transaction (*Argos Distributors Ltd v C & E Commrs* (Case C-288/94) [1997] BVC 64; [1996] ECR I-5311, para. 21 and 22). Consequently, it does not matter that when the transaction is concluded the parties do not know the basis on which VAT will be charged and that it remains unknown, even afterwards, to the recipient of the service.

50 The answer to be given to the second question must therefore be that art. 11A(1)(a) of the sixth directive (art 73 of Council Directive 2006/112/EC) is to be construed as meaning that, in foreign exchange transactions in which no fees or commission are calculated with regard to certain specific transactions, the taxable amount is the net result of the transactions of the supplier of the services over a given period of time.'

In some ways, one can appreciate the difficulty faced by the Court in accepting that the value of the supply in each case was the contract value, generally the market value of the currency at the time. However, to fix the taxable amount under (art. 73 of Council Directive 2006/112/EC) (art. 11(A)(1) of the Sixth VAT Directive (Directive 77/388)) by reference to the *profit* or *turn* made, arguably ignores the fact that there could well be losses over time. To say then there is no supply (absent consideration), seems illogical, a comment with which many commentators would agree. The problem with recognising the contract value, as it were, is the distortion that would produce in recovering input tax under a standard or values-based partial exemption calculation. However, the practice adopted in the UK of looking at things such as the numbers of transactions undertaken, rather than their monetary amounts easily overcomes this difficulty.

These two decisions are especially valuable for money brokers, whose scope for input VAT recovery often depends on the underlying client transaction being a supply. Their effect has, however, now been somewhat tempered by the decision of the Tribunal given in July 2005 in the *Willis Pension Trustees Ltd* case.

- In *Willis Pension Trustees Ltd* [2006] BVC 2,045, the company was the Trustee of the Willis Pension Fund, a scheme which held various investments, including a number of overseas. To hedge or minimise the risk of exchange-rate fluctuations, Willis entered into forex deals with various UK banks. It didn't offer a spread or charge a separate fee or commission, but relied on the movements in rates to minimise losses and, where possible, make a profit. The issue was whether, in entering these transactions, Willis made a supply for VAT and the conclusion reached by the Tribunal was that it did not. The only supply in this situation was made by the bank. The Tribunal, incidentally, expressed the view that similar principles applied to transactions such as interest rates swap contracts (where, for example, a manufacturer who has borrowed at a floating rate of interest but wishes to fix in advance at the effective rate of interest, agrees with the bank that he will pay to the bank a fixed rate of interest on a notional amount of, say, £100m, and in return for that payment receive a floating rate of interest on a notional amount of £100m from the bank).

This decision in Willis Pension Trustees Ltd was not appealed and HMRC have since reviewed their policy in this respect, culminating in Revenue & Customs Brief 05/07, issued on 26 January 2007. The Tribunal decision in *Willis* applied to a very specific set of circumstances and, whilst some general principles can be drawn, care needs to be taken when seeking to give it wider application. In *Willis*, forex deals were entered into for the purposes of *hedging*, which is not, in itself, a test for determining whether or not there is a supply for VAT purposes. They go on to add that (see HMRC Manuals at VATFIN2740):

> 'In general, forex transactions are supplies for VAT purposes if you adopt a spread position over a period of time when buying and selling currency. This applies whether this is being done for your own account, in support of other areas of your business, or to reduce any exposure position in forex that you hold. A spread position means a difference between a bid price and a sell price from which you would expect to derive a profit. These forex transactions would include both "spot" and "forward" transactions, as envisaged by the FNBC judgment.
>
> Most businesses actively involved in forex trading should readily be able to identify whether their forex transactions fall under the FNBC principle of adopting a spread position. If uncertainties remain, you should consider whether, in selling a currency, you are in a position to set the selling price. If so, you are able to determine the consideration you receive by setting a spread, even if only mimicking market movements, and your forex transactions are likely to be supplies for VAT purposes.
>
> Where your forex transactions are supplies, the consideration will be the net result of all your forex transactions over a period of time and would be exempt under VATA 1994, Sch. 9, Group 5, Item 1. Any forex transactions, for which you charge an attributable fee or commission, would also be exempt supplies under Item 1.'

Points affecting particular supplies 70-200

and later:

> 'Businesses with a corporate treasury operation active in the financial markets may need to look carefully at their forex transactions. If no spread position is being taken and no profit being actively sought, it is unlikely that any forex transactions would be regarded as supplies. However, a number of larger businesses have corporate treasury operations that are much more pro-active, either externally or internally, within their commercial groups. For example, a business might typically run a "forex desk" in a similar manner to any other financial institution or market maker more traditionally associated with forex dealing. Such businesses are likely to be taking a spread position and would be making supplies. All their forex transactions, whether spot or forward and whether proprietary or in support of other activities or areas of the business, should be treated as forex supplies.
>
> Intermediaries acting in relation to a forex transaction can exempt their intermediary services under item 5, Group 5 of Schedule 9. This applies whether or not the underlying forex transaction is a supply for VAT purposes.'

Although the Tribunal had made reference in its decision to interest rate swaps, the view taken by HMRC is that there would appear to be nothing arising directly out of that case that indicates a shortfall in their current approach to other financial instruments. It is not, therefore, intended to revise existing published policy, although they recognise that there may be particular circumstances where *Willis* principles could apply to transactions in other financial instruments.

(23) Forfaiting

Forfaiting is a form of trade finance under which unconditional debts from the supply of goods or services are sold *without recourse* to a bank. Typically it will arise in the context of exports, with the exporter agreeing to sell its rights to the payment for a discounted sum. The supply, by the exporter, in this case, is exempt under VATA 1994, Sch. 9, Grp 5, item 1 (art. 135(1) (d) of Council Directive 2006/112/EC). The on-sale of the debt by the bank will, likewise be exempt, but collection on maturity is *outside the scope*.

See also *Factoring* at 70-450.

(24) Forward rate agreements

Forward rate agreements are a useful off-balance sheet means of reducing or hedging interest risk. They involve an agreement fixing an interest rate for a specified future period by reference to a notional principal sum. Depending on how the interest rate moves, they can result in payments being made by either party to the other of the difference between the actual and agreed rate.

As with interest rate swaps (see (8) earlier), the HMRC practice is to see these as basically exempt supplies by the party receiving payment: i.e. supplies only to the extent that money changes hands. They do not see mutual supplies by both.

As noted at (17) earlier in relation to *Foreign exchange*, although the Tribunal in *Willis Pension Trustees Ltd* had made reference in its decision to interest rate swaps and similar contracts, the view taken by HMRC is that there is no need for them to revise existing published policy.

(25) Imported services (see Chapter 5)

Apart from importing services on their own account, banks sometimes incur charges in respect of customer securities held to their order. The bank will then either act as principal or as agent, depending on the circumstances. Many customer accounts will be dealt with on sub-dossiers and, where these are clearly identifiable to a particular customer, the bank will be regarded as agent and will not apply the imported services rules. A bank may also be regarded as agent in relation to a global dossier provided:

- it divides such charges between the customers involved and charges to each customer the exact expenditure incurred in respect of his security;
- the total amount charged to various customers is the same as the charge received from abroad; and
- there is evidence that the bank has agreed with each of the customers involved to be an agent on his behalf.

Documentary proof usually has to be kept and customers should be advised of their own need to account for VAT, if appropriate.

Where services from abroad cannot be identified specifically to individual customers, banks will generally make their own apportionment, which will be reflected in their own onward charges to their customers. In such circumstances, the bank will account for VAT on the imported service and recover the underlying input VAT in full if the onward supply to the customer is taxable. It will not recover the input VAT where the onward supply is exempt, e.g. where the service relates to charges concerning the holding, completing and perfecting of securities held as collateral for a loan.

(26) Instalment credit finance and credit provided free

If, in the case of hire-purchase, conditional sale or credit sale agreements, charges made for the *credit* element are separately disclosed, the result is that there are two supplies, the credit and the underlying supply of the goods. The former will be exempt under VATA 1994, Sch. 9, Grp. 5, item 3 and the latter taxable at the appropriate rate. Administration and documentation fees on hire-purchase, conditional and credit sale agreements are similarly exempt, provided again that they are specified and do not exceed £10. If a separate charge for the credit element is not made and separately disclosed to the customer, then there is a single composite supply just of the goods, which is again taxable at the appropriate rate.

- The treatment of HP administration fees in HP and conditional sale agreements was at issue in the case of *Wagon Finance Ltd* [2000] BVC 2,125. The agreements in this case were for the purchase of cars and the fees, originally set at £50 (later £65), were charged to the customer at the time the agreement was entered into. The payments were clearly in excess of the £10 limit in VATA 1994, Sch. 9, Grp. 5, item 4 and HMRC maintained that the supplies they represented were taxable at the standard-rate. The taxpayer, however, argued they were part and parcel of the consideration for the provision of instalment credit finance, which was exempt within item 3. The Tribunal agreed.
- HMRC summarise the treatment of such supplies with credit in the following way (VATFIN3120):

Type of agreement	Comments
Conditional sale	Consideration is payable by instalments and the goods remain the property of the seller until the full price is paid and/or any other conditions are met by the customer. The full amount of VAT on the goods is normally payable with the first instalment; any charge for credit finance will be exempt provided the disclosure conditions have been met.
Credit sale	The sale of goods which immediately become the property of the customer, but where the price is payable by instalments. Again, the charge for credit finance will be exempt if the disclosure conditions have been met.
Hire purchase (other than conditional sale)	Legally, such goods are hired for periodic payments and the hirer has the option to purchase. However, the VAT supply position is the same as for conditional sale because ownership is intended to transfer.

> *Practice point*
>
> HMRC subsequently announced their decision not to appeal *Wagon Finance*. However, at the time of writing, the provisions of Grp. 5 remain unchanged.
>
> Finance houses providing credit in the motor, furniture and electrical, etc. sectors will be primarily affected by this decision and, in some cases, this may have an impact on the overall partial exemption position.
>
> The decision in *Wagon Finance* turned on the nature of the agreements entered into. The evidence showed the fees had nothing to do with the supply of the cars and were simply for the facility of instalment credit finance. This clearly underlines the need for care in the way agreements are drafted.

Fees relating to the goods, such as option fees or fees for transfer of title, do not fall within the exemption, but are taxable, since they represent the right to secure ownership of the goods.

- In *General Motors Acceptance Corp (UK) plc* [1999] BVC 2,347. The taxpayer had argued the fee was exempt as part of the consideration for a supply of credit under VATA 1994, Sch. 9, Grp. 5, items 2-4 or art. 135(1)(b) and (d) of Council Directive 2006/112/EC (the Sixth VAT Directive (Directive 77/388), art. 13(B)(d)(1) and (3)). However, HMRC maintained that Grp. 5, item 4 (provision of administrative arrangements and documentation *and the transfer of title to the goods*) was not derived from any provision in art. 13(B)(d) but was a simplification. The fees, in any event, were over the £10 provided for in that item.
  The Tribunal concluded that the *option fee* payable in a hire-purchase agreement was subject to VAT and not exempt. It took the view that the proper test to apply was '*what specifically does GMAC supply in consideration for the payment?*' The answer it came up with was the right to secure, if the necessary conditions are fulfilled, ownership of the car. This, throughout, was the ultimate object of the agreement.
- In *C & E Commrs v Lloyds TSB Group Ltd* [1998] BVC 173, Lloyds TSB and Volkswagen Financial Services successfully argued before Tribunal that the outsourcing of the vetting and approval of HP proposals for the sale of cars on behalf of a finance company was also exempt.

In the event that a supply of credit is recognised the value of the exempt supply will be the amount of any initial charge, together with the interest effectively paid with each instalment. The taxpoint, or time of supply, for the interest element will be when the instalments are paid (see 30-350). The taxpoint for the supply of goods, whether in a single composite supply or not, occurs at the commencement of the contract or when the goods are made available to the hirer. It is at that stage that the VAT must be accounted for by the finance house or may be claimed by the customer.

- In the appeal by *Freight Transport Leasing Ltd* [1991] BVC 536, the issue was whether exemption applied to the finance element included in monthly instalments but not separately disclosed. This was considered in conjunction with Art. 13(B) of the Sixth VAT Directive (Art. 135(1)(l) of Council Directive 2006/112/EC). As the customers were provided with information from which they could easily calculate the amounts of finance charged, the Tribunal held that the conditions for exemption were satisfied.

(27) Interest-free finance

A number of attempts have been made, primarily in the retail sector, to attribute part of the otherwise taxable consideration for goods or services to an exempt supply within the overall price, thus reducing the VAT to be accounted for. Generally, these have arisen in the context of business promotion schemes. Customers have been induced to purchase by the offer of, say, interest-free credit, frequently provided by a third-party finance company at the expense of the retailer concerned.

Most of these situations seem to fail because, looked at *subjectively*, the bargain between the retailer and the customer is for the sale of the goods or services at the advertised price. It can be difficult for the retailer to argue otherwise. The contribution made by the retailer to the cost of providing the finance is a cost-component of the retailer's business and covered by the principles in *Chaussures Bally SA v Belgian State* (Case C-18/92) [1993] ECR I-2871. A good example of the issues involved arose in the *Primback* case.

- *C & E Commrs v Primback Ltd* (Case C-34/99) [2001] BVC 315 involved a company which made retail sales of furniture on terms, which involved interest-free credit being provided by a separate finance company. To compensate the finance company, Primback allowed a *discount* to the finance company from the amount invoiced to the customer. Initially, the Tribunal, as with Provident Financial, declined to accept that tax was to be accounted for only on the reduced amounts. The *discount* reflected the finance company's agreement to provide interest-free loans to Primback's customers the *payment received* by Primback in respect of the sale of the goods was the gross amount payable by the customer and not the discounted sum.

    On appeal, the High Court, also decided, for HMRC (*Primback Ltd v C & E Commrs* [1994] BVC 268). Although a subsequent appeal to the Court of Appeal produced a different result ([1996] BVC 260) a reference in 1999 to the ECJ came down, again, in HMRC's favour. The taxable amount for Primback (i.e. the amount on which it was to calculate the tax payable on its sales) was the full amount payable by the purchaser. The rationale for the judgment was that:

- the fact that the supply of services by the finance house was, in principle, VAT-exempt had no bearing on the basis for charging VAT on the transaction between Primback and the purchaser;

- Primback could not validly claim to apportion the price received between the goods and the cost of the credit because the price was the same, irrespective of the means by which the purchase of the goods was financed;
- even if it were possible to distinguish the supply of credit, from the supply of goods, the former would have to be construed as, in any event, *ancillary* to the sale of the goods.
- finally, even assuming that a reduction in the sales price could be permitted, a discount for cash was not volunteered but had to be requested by the customer. In many cases, the customer simply paid the advertised price, either because he was unaware that he could ask for a discount or because he did not want to ask for one.

In short, the commission charged to Primback for the provision of the finance was a cost and not a reduction in the value of its sales.

- *Provident Financial plc* [1993] BVC 884 provided a variation of this theme. It involved two companies, Provident Home Shopping Ltd (PHS) and Provident Personal Credit Ltd (PPC), which together sold goods to retail customers on credit. Although members of a group, they were not registered together for VAT purposes. The contractual documents indicated that PHS sold the goods to the customer, whilst PPC supplied credit and collected payments. Visits to customers were arranged by the local PPC branch and made jointly by the PPC agent and the PHS representative in a PHS van. After the initial sale, customers continued to deal with the PPC agent, the goods being returned to PPC in the event they were rejected. PPC were recompensed by PHS for their efforts by what purported to be a *discount* on the retail price of an intra-group sale of the goods from PHS to PPC. PHS thus sought to account for tax only on the lower, *discounted* price. Alternatively, it was argued that the *discount* was effectively a sales commission from PPC to PHS. Unfortunately, the contractual arrangements supported neither view. The Tribunal found the amount allowed by PHS to PPC was further consideration for the provision of exempt finance to the customer. A different form of contractual arrangements could well, however, have produced a different result.

For similar situations involving postal charges see *C & E Commrs v Plantiflor Ltd* [2002] BVC 572 and insurance *Peugeot Motor Co plc & Anor v C & E Commrs* [2004] BVC 269.

(28) Interest rate caps

Interest rate caps are essentially guarantees provided to the holders that interest rates will not exceed a stated amount. The facility is a basically exempt supply within VATA 1994, Sch. 9, Grp. 5, item 1. The value is the premium charged.

- The case of *Iliffe* [1994] BVC 625 produced an interesting exception to this, however. The appeal concerned a mortgage interest capping agreement allegedly given as an inducement to enter into a long lease at a premium and a peppercorn rent. HMRC argued that the payments received by the partnership were taxable under the general principles in the *Gleneagles Hotel plc* and *Neville Russell* (a firm) reverse premium cases (1986) VATTR 196; (1985) 2 BVC 208,108 and (1987) VATTR 194; (1987) 3 BVC 611. The Tribunal, however, disagreed. On the facts, the mortgage capping was not in any way an inducement to enter into the agreement for lease. There was no apparent need for such an inducement; nothing was done by the partnership in the form of recognisable commercial services that could be directly, or even indirectly, linked to the mortgage capping agreement other than the payment of the purchase price, i.e. the premium. The Tribunal also felt it would be incorrect in any event to recognise the actual payments made as the value of any supplies.

The upshot was that, in this particular case, mortgage capping gave rise to neither exempt nor taxable supplies. The outcome will, however, have depended very much on the facts of the case and on the form of the actual agreements entered into.

(29) Interest rate and currency rate swaps

Interest rate and currency rate swaps are essentially hedging mechanisms. In the case of interest rate swaps, they effectively involve the exchange of the servicing obligations of *notional* fixed and floating interest debts. Usually, but not always, settlement is by netting the notional fixed and floating rates of interest; occasionally it may involve *gross* payments with perhaps one party paying at intervals over the period of the facility and having a single compensating receipt at the end. Currency swaps operate on the same principles with the contract amounts being established initially at an agreed rate.

For VAT purposes, the practice in either case is to recognise a basically exempt supply within VATA 1994, Sch. 9, Grp. 5, item 1, but only when and to the extent that money changes hands. Thus, a supply will usually be seen by HMRC only as made by the party receiving any net amount due in cases where gross settlements are not made. Whether this is correct, however, is debatable. It may be arguable that both parties make mutual supplies equal to the grossed up or fixed or floating rate interest in the case of interest rate swaps, and perhaps no supplies at all in the case of currency (see (9) earlier). However, supplies may be recognised in both directions in cases where the arrangement does not simply involve a *netting-off*.

What is recognised and how, will, of course, have an effect on the partial exemption calculation.

(1)   A *netting-off* arrangement will involve just one supply by the recipient.

(2)   Where gross payments are made each party makes supplies.

(3)   If numbers of transactions rather than values are used, the recipient of the periodic payments could end up with considerably more supplies being recognised than would otherwise be the case.

Indeed, with a netting-off basis, one of the parties might not be regarded as making any supplies at all. If the counterpart is either outside the EU, there could, therefore, be a significant impact on input VAT relief.

As noted earlier at (22) in relation to foreign exchange, although the Tribunal in *Willis Pension Trustees Ltd*. had made reference in its decision to interest rate swaps, the view taken by HMRC is that there is no need for them to revise existing published policy.

(30) Islamic finance

The basis for all Islamic finance lies in the principles of the Shariah, or Islamic Law, taken from the Koran and from the example of Prophet Muhammad. A central theme is that money itself has no intrinsic value so Muslims cannot lend or receive money and expect to benefit.

Wealth can only be generated through legitimate trade and any gains relating to that trade are to be shared between the person providing the capital and the person providing the expertise. The basic Shariah prohibitions relate to:

- the charging or receipt of interest (*riba*);
- uncertainty or deception, for example an ambiguity or lack of clarity in the terms of a contract that can give rise to speculation (*gharar*);
- gambling or speculation, for example any transaction undertaken for purely speculative purposes (*maisir*);
- unethical investments, for example dealing in activities or commodities that include pork, pornography, arms or munitions, conventional financial services, cinema, tobacco, gambling or alcohol.

With the result that many Muslims have been unable or unwilling to obtain conventional credit finance.

Various Shariah products have therefore evolved to provide investment opportunities and meet the financing needs of people and businesses in the Islamic community. These include:

- *Murabaha* (a basic price plus *profit* concept);
- *Ijara* (based on the leasing of an asset); and
- *Musharaka* (an equity investment/profit and loss sharing concept),

the VAT effects of which are different from those for the more traditional financial products as they can involve supplies of goods, property and commodities, for example, rather than VAT-exempt interest. The principles of what these Shariah compliant products involve and how they are agreed to be treated for VAT has been set out in a special HMRC VAT Information Sheet – *VAT: Guidance on the VAT treatment of certain Islamic products* (VAT Infomation Sheet 11/06), which whilst not available, it is to be found at **Appendix 20**.

For further commentary see the HMRC Internal Guidance Manuals at VATFIN8000 (which in substance reproduces VAT Information Sheet 11/06).

(31) Money brokerage

Acting as an intermediary for a loan or mortgage (see 70-100(1)) or for a transaction in foreign exchange (see (22) earlier) is a basically exempt financial service act within VATA 1994, Sch. 9, Grp. 5, item 5, provided, usually, that there is a direct rather than a tenuous link with what is provided to the client. Anything short of this (such as a general introduction to a money broker) tends to be taxable at the standard-rate. The value of the supply is the brokerage or commission earned.

As with other financial services, exemption is linked with the right of input VAT recovery where the client belongs outside the EU and the Isle of Man. The position of brokerage for currency transactions is further illustrated at **Appendix 13**. Following the decision of the ECJ in *First National Bank of Chicago v C & E Commrs* (Case C-172/96) [1998] BVC 389 (see earlier at (17)), this recovery of input tax has been largely based on the assumption that the underlying client transaction involves a supply by both client counter-parties. However, this has now been somewhat tempered by the decision of the Tribunal given in July 2005 in *Willis*

Pension Trustees Ltd [2006] BVC 2,045 (see earlier at 70-200), where Willis, the Trustee of a Pension Fund, has been held not to be making a supply when entering into a transaction purely as a financial hedge. The only supply in this situation was made by the bank with whom the hedge was undertaken. This could potentially affect the matrix in the illustration at **Appendix 13**.

The present HMRC position is found in Revenue & Customs Brief 05/07, issued on 26 January 2007, where guidance is given as to when the principles in the decision will apply. Most brokers acting as intermediaries between banks and other financial institutions or major corporate groups may well find they are not affected or affected only to a minor degree, but, in appropriate cases, it will be as well to agree this with HMRC.

As mentioned earlier, although the Tribunal had made reference in its decision to interest rate swaps, the view taken by HMRC is that there would appear to be nothing arising directly out of that case that indicates a shortfall in their current approach to other financial instruments. It is not, therefore, intended to revise existing published policy, although they recognise that there may be particular circumstances where *Willis* principles could apply to transactions in other financial instruments.

See also *Foreign exchange* at (22) above.

(32) Pawnbroking

Pawnbroking is essentially the supply of credit against the security of goods and is exempt under VATA 1994, Sch. 9, Grp 5, item 2 (art. 135(1)(d) of Council Directive 2006/112/EC). The exemption applies to the interest charged and to any charge for valuation or for cleaning or repair when part and parcel of the supply of credit provided.

The redemption of the goods by the borrower will not give rise to a supply of goods by the pawnbroker when this takes place within the agreed redemption period. Under the *Consumer Credit Act* 1974, the redemption period is always a minimum of six months.

For loans under £75, if the goods are redeemed within three months after the end of the redemption period, there may still be no VAT due if the redemption period is less than six months: otherwise, if the pawnbroker obtains title to the goods, he must account for VAT as appropriate on any sale.

For loans over £75, ownership of the goods will not pass to the pawnbroker who will not be liable to account for VAT on any sale.

For further guidance see generally HMRC's VAT Finance manual (VATFIN3180 – Credit, debts and related services: Credit and related services: Pawn broking).

(33) Pension fund management

In November 2002, HMRC consulted on the VAT Treatment of Pension Fund Management. The 'Sandler review of medium and long-term savings in the UK' was published in July 2002

Points affecting particular supplies 70-200

and made a number of tax recommendations. Two of the recommendations related to indirect tax are outlined below.

(1) The Government should consider in particular the difference between insurers and others for the VAT treatment of pension fund management with a view to making the playing field level wherever possible.

(2) Consideration should also be given to the inconsistency in the VAT treatment between the management of investment trusts and the management of open-ended investment companies (OEICs)/authorised unit trusts (AUTs).

HMRC sought views on a number of options in response to the Sandler recommendations including:

- making all pension fund management exempt regardless of the provider;
- applying VAT to all pension fund management;
- what should be exempt if, on evaluating the consultation responses, redrawing the borderline is a favoured option?
- Should the management of investment trusts and/or common investment funds be included within the scope of VAT exemption?

It was, however, stressed that the Government was not attracted to the option of taxing all pension fund management.

Predictably, there was no clear consensus in respect of the main options raised, although there was agreement between the relevant parties for the exemption of common investment fund management.

In the event, the Government decided not to make any immediate changes to the VAT treatment of fund management, but to keep the issue under review.

(34) Search agencies

HMRC regard the fiche or document obtained from Companies House as a piece of information rather than a tangible object. Consequently, search fees recharged to clients:

(1) may be treated as disbursements and outside the scope:

    (a) if the information is passed on unaltered; or
    (b) if a process is carried out on the fiche or document so long as the data therein is not used to form an opinion or report; and

(2) will be treated as part of the consideration for the agency's services if the agency analyses, comments on or produces a report from the fiche or document concerned.

(35) Secured loans, securities for money (including credit guarantees)

Loans and advances may be secured or unsecured. However, at first glance, the issue of a security in connection with an advance (e.g. a certificate of deposit or a debenture) potentially takes the advance from VATA 1994, Sch. 9, Grp. 5, item 2-6. In *C & E Commrs v Guy Butler (International) Ltd* (1976) 1 BVC 84 it was held (at p. 94) that:

> 'The issue of a certificate of deposit is not in the ordinary sense security for a loan of money; it is really only a transferable receipt, which may of course at some later stage be used as a security for a loan.'

and later (at p. 96):

> 'So far as certificates of deposit are concerned, there was no suggestion in argument that they are ever issued except in connection with a loan (and in that sense "incidental" to a loan), so that unless items 2 and 4 [the present item 6] are mutually exclusive there would be no scope for item 4 in relation to certificates of deposit, nor in relation to other "securities" covered by item 4 when used as security for a loan.'

However, following the ruling of the ECJ in *Kretztechnik AG v Finanzamt Linz* (Case C-465/03) ECJ [2006] BVC 66 (see earlier in **Chapter 1** at 10-300 and **Chapter 4** at 40-200) the issue, as opposed to a subsequent secondary supply, of financial instruments of this kind will not be a supply for VAT purposes.

- What is a *security for money* in the wider sense was considered in *Dyrham Park Country Club Ltd* (1978) VATTR 244; (1978) 1 BVC 1,099. This concerned the treatment of a bond required to be subscribed for by a member of a golf club and which was repayable on the winding up of the club or on the cessation of membership after five years. In the event, the point at issue was whether the payment for the bond was for a wholly exempt supply or was part of the taxable consideration for the facilities of membership. Finding against the club, the Tribunal agreed the bond was capable of being a security within what is now VATA 1994, Sch. 9, Grp. 5, item 6 (see **Chapter 8**). However, it was not a bond in the sense of a credit guarantee. Commenting on the possibility of the bond being a security for money, the Tribunal remarked (at p. 1,100) that:

> 'These words appear with "any note or order for the payment of money". In such context it appears to us that the words "security for money" as used as a generic term, having no special or exclusive reference to a document which gives a charge upon specific property, in other words, in the same sense as the words "security for money" appear in s. 1(3)(c) of the *Moneylenders Act* 1927 (see the judgment of Atkin L.J. in *Sterling v John* [1923] K.B. 557 at p. 561). In our view "security for money" in such item 1 means a document under seal or under hand at a consideration containing a covenant, promise or undertaking to pay a sum of money. In our view, a document to be such a "security for money" does not have to be either "marketable" or "transferable" or "negotiable" as submitted ...'

In short, a security for money neither needs to give a charge on a specific property in the sense contemplated in the *Moneylenders Act* 1927, nor to be marketable, transferable or negotiable. Securities for money include, euro currency paper, bills of exchange and promissory notes (see HMRC's manual at VATFIN2820).

A security for money also includes a credit guarantee. A credit guarantee is a financial instrument under which the guarantor continues the repayments of a particular debt in the event that a third party is unable to do so because of a specified cause. HMRC's Finance Manual gives as an example, a financial institution issuing a credit guarantee to an exporter of goods or services against non-payment by the importer (see HMRC's Manual at VATFIN2830).

A security for money may also include a surety bond, which is a bond providing for monetary compensation in the event of failure, often by a third party contractor, to perform specified acts within a stated period. Such a bond will be within item 1 of Group 5 of Sch. 9 if the bond guarantees the payment of money where the debtor defaults. In contrast a surety bond will not be within item 1 of Group 5 where it does not guarantee payment of money where the debtor defaults.

The value of the supply for VAT purposes is the total price paid for the service of providing the guarantee or if it is transferred the total price paid for it (see HMRC at VATFIN2840).

(36) Securities dealing

Securities for this purpose include shares, stock, bonds, notes, debentures, debenture stock, units under a unit trust scheme, letters of allotment, letters of rights, option warrants, certificates of deposit and government bills. Securities in this sense must be distinguished from securities for money. Securities for money were stated in *Dyrham Park Country Club Ltd* (see (28) earlier) to mean 'a document under seal or under hand at a consideration containing a covenant, promise or undertaking to pay a sum of money'. In the view of the Tribunal in that case, for a document to be a security for money it did not have to be marketable or transferable or negotiable.

The exemption for securities under VATA 1994, Sch. 9, Grp. 5, item 6 applies only to dealings as principal; agency services fall within the concept of *the provision of intermediary services* in item 5. Item 5 does not, however, cover fund management. The value of the supply in the case of a transaction as principal is the total consideration received (before commission) for a sale; otherwise it is the gross interest received (i.e. before withholding tax, if any). The receipt of dividends is *outside the scope*. For agency or brokerage transactions, the value of the supply is the gross commission earned.

This is dealt with more fully in **Chapter 8**. Securities for money are exempt under VATA 1994, Sch. 9, Grp. 5, item 1.

(37) Securitisation

Securitisation is the packaging of designated pools of loans or receivables with an appropriate level of credit enhancement and the redistribution of these packages to investors. Investors buy the repackaged assets in the form of securities or loans, which are collateralized (secured) on the underlying pool and its associated income stream.

- In *MBNA Europe Bank Ltd v R & C Commrs* [2007] BVC 3 the securitisation process involved the assignment of credit card receivables to trustees outside the EU, the points at issue being whether these assignments constituted supplies for VAT purposes, and, if so, the effect on the companies ability to recover the input tax they incurred.
- MBNA provided credit card facilities for customers in the UK, for which it continually required working capital. To obtain this more cheaply than it could achieve by borrowing directly, it used a scheme, the essence of which was that its receivables were transferred, for a set consideration and by way of *equitable assignment*, to a bare trustee established in Jersey. The beneficiaries under the trust included MBNA itself and a special purpose vehicle, which, directly or indirectly through further entities, borrowed in capital markets,

using the assigned receivables as security. These borrowings were at more favourable rates of interest than could have been achieved by MBNA directly, a financial institution, secured on its interest in the receivables. As part of the arrangement, MBNA retained a continuing obligation to service the receivables for the special purpose vehicle and the dispute centred round the extent to which the recovery of input tax incurred by MBNA could take into account the assignments to the Jersey Trust and the obligation to the special purpose vehicle to service the receivables.

- The Tribunal, following the line in *Capital One Bank (Europe) plc* [2006] BVC 2,148 (where the circumstances were broadly similar), found the arrangements for securitising the credit card debts did not constitute the making of supplies, but amounted to no more than the granting of security for a loan. However, in the High Court in *MBNA*, Briggs J, whilst still holding there was no supply, disagreed with this analysis. The whole point of the securitisation structure was that the banks should not be borrowers, and their receivables should not be charged by them as security. That was exactly what it achieved and was why the Tribunal had got it wrong in finding that the arrangements involved MBNA providing security for a loan, rather than making a supply by reason of the sale of debts. The assignments, if viewed on their own, were, in theory, capable of constituting supplies for VAT. However, because they were no more than the necessary pre-condition to the supply of a securitisation service to MBNA by the SPV, they were thereby deprived of the character of a supply by MBNA itself. They were thus an addition to the exceptional class of transactions which looked, prima facie, like a supply, but which lost that character when viewed in their context.
- In terms of the effect on MBNA's input tax (see **Chapter 4**), the administration of the receivables had been paid for by the card-holders and, in a sense, by the special purpose vehicle. Where, in such a situation, a single business activity arguably represented the supply of a service to two different persons, there was no reason why the underlying input tax should be solely attributed just to the supply to one and not to the other. They thus had to be remitted to the Tribunal for reconsideration.

(38) Sterling commercial paper and Euronotes

Sterling commercial paper and Euronotes are also regarded as forms of promissory note within the *Bills of Exchange Act* 1882 and falling within VATA 1994, Sch. 9, Grp. 5, item 1. The particular implications of these instruments are discussed later in 80-100 (see also (5) earlier).

(39) Travellers cheques

Exemption under VATA 1994, Sch. 9, Grp. 5, item 1 also covers the issue or encashment of travellers cheques. Unissued or unsigned cheques, however, are neither securities for money nor orders for the payment of money. Their supply or importation is taxable at the standard-rate.

(40) Clearing and settlement

The services supplied by a clearing-house for settling indebtedness between members is an exempt supply within art. 135(1) of Council Directive 2006/112/EC of 28 November 2006. See also HMRC Notice 701/49 on VAT and Finance (November 2011) at para. 2.8.

(41) Multi-currency loans and management of currency exposure

A supplier who manages multi-currency loans for the purpose of managing the foreign currency exposure makes an exempt supply within item 1 of Group 5 of Sch. 9 of the VATA 1994. In applying the exemption under UK law it is necessary to interpret it in the context of the VAT Directive. In this context, the exemption applies not only to those suppliers that actually effect transfers but also to those who provide services which have directly 'brought about' or caused a money transaction. In *ECU Group plc* [2010] UKFTT 297; [2010] TC 00585 the First Tier Tribunal held that the taxpayer, who was involved in managing foreign currency exposure of a multi-currency loan, was making an exempt supply within item 1 of Group 5. The material facts of the case were:

- The taxpayer manages the foreign currency exposure of a loan which is provided to its client by a lender. There were two aspects to the service: (1) the taxpayer would predict the direction of movements in foreign exchange rates, looking for currencies which would weaken against the base currency in which the loan was made; and (2) the taxpayer gave instructions on behalf of its client to various execution banks to carry out a series of foreign exchange trades over a period of time, which would alter the currency denomination of a client's loan facility.
- The management of the foreign currency exposure of the loan was conducted by the taxpayer with the following objectives:
    (a) monitoring the major deliverable international currencies on a spot basis and seeking to denominate the loan on a spot basis in the currency or currencies, permitted by the lender;
    (b) notifying which currencies in the opinion of the taxpayer are considered to be appropriate and likely to provide benefit to the client by way of debt reduction and/or interest saving;
    (c) the taxpayer would use its reasonable endeavours to instruct the lender, or any prime broker or counterparty with whom the taxpayer effects foreign exchange transactions, to change the currency exposure and denomination of the loan as and when the taxpayer considered it appropriate or desirable to do so.
- Each client agreed to execute a power of attorney in a standard form in favour of the taxpayer to enable it to change the exposure and denomination of the loan at any time.
- Each client agreed to pay the taxpayer a monthly management fee, which was not refundable. The fee was calculated on the amount of the loan and at a rate declining from 1 per cent per annum to 0.65 per cent per annum depending on the size of the loan. The monthly management fee could not be at a rate less than £2,500 per annum (exclusive of any VAT).
- A performance fee could also be payable to the taxpayer. This was 20 per cent of any 'Net Profit' achieved during the course of the agreement.
- The taxpayer did not physically move any money itself. It would execute all the trades, but as agent for the prime broker or lender, and the taxpayer would issue instructions for the movement of money between the various banking counterparties on behalf of its clients (the particular nature of how the trades were executed is provided at para. 17 of the judgment).

The First-Tier Tax Tribunal held that the taxpayer was making an exempt supply of services within item 1, Group 5 of the VATA 1994. In essence the reasons for the decision were as follows:

- The essential aim and essential features of the services supplied by the taxpayer were for it to use its best endeavours in the procurement for the client by means of foreign exchange transactions of the reduction in the capital value of a loan. The Tribunal commented that 'the exchange of one currency for another is of the essence of the services provided by the Appellant even though it does not actually make any such exchanges. The essence of its services informs their essential aims and features and, thus, the objective character of the supplies made by the Appellant'(at para. 58 of the judgment).
- The services provided by the taxpayer 'form a distinct whole' which fulfilled 'the specific, essential functions' of adopting the art. 135(1)(d) and (e) formulations – 'transactions concerning currency' and/or 'transactions concerning payments, transfers' and/or 'negotiations concerning currency, payments or transfers'. The Tribunal commented (at para. 61 to 62 of the judgment):

> 'Even applying the correct strict interpretation to exemption provisions, it is right to recognise that 'transactions concerning' currency, transfers or payments is a wider concept than transactions which themselves constitute currency transactions, transfers or payments. In the legal and factual context in which the Appellant's services are provided, we are satisfied that the only realistic answer to the question posed by that test is that they do indeed bring about currency transactions and, more generally, payments or transfers.'

70-250   Banks

The VAT treatment of banks depends on a variety of different factors. From what has been seen earlier, the services provided will be, for the most part, basically exempt. However, income may arise from a number of different sources and the extent and effect of this will differ from one bank to another.

(1) Retail banking, for example, will inevitably invite low levels of input VAT recovery as suppliers to customers with accounts with banks operating in the UK (see **Chapter 4** at 40-000).

(2) Foreign banks, on the other hand (and this will include branches or subsidiaries of overseas banks), may be established in the UK largely to access the UK money markets or facilitate trade. As such, there will often be much greater scope for the reliefs described earlier at 70-100(3) above. If the home country is outside the EU and the Isle of Man, the level of interest income from non-EU borrowers or from loans to finance exports may thus be that much higher than for a bank whose customer base leans more heavily towards the UK domestic market, and this will be reflected in the levels of input VAT recovered.

(3) Merchant banks may be different again. In this case, there may be proportionately more taxable supplies in the form of non-monetary services such as merger and take-over advice and investment services.

Banks may also be involved in other taxable activities such as equipment leasing.

(1) The approach to partial exemption

The overriding concern, whatever the type of bank, is with the recovery of input VAT (see **Chapter 4**). Seldom, though, will tax be incurred in a uniform manner. Not only will there be variations between banks, but input VAT will arise differently in the different areas of operation within the same bank. Some activities, foreign exchange for example, will typically involve high levels of VATable expenditure on dealing desks and telecommunications. Others, like inter-bank lending, will involve very much less and there will be many possible variations in between.

It is not just a matter of how and where the input VAT is incurred. There are also areas where the pattern of outputs (or rather their relative values) can be widely unequal, with a potentially distortive impact on the VAT that can ultimately be recovered. In the case of securities, for example, the same amount of input VAT will generally be incurred per transaction whether they are sold as principal or on an agency basis. This may be compounded, moreover, by the fact that dealings in certain types of securities, such as eurobonds, will usually give much less scope for input VAT recovery than, say, US equities. To some extent this will be a product of the markets involved, but, either way, the effect will often need to be taken into account.

Given these conflicts, it is perhaps hardly surprising that a simple pro rata apportionment on the lines of the residual input VAT calculation in the Standard Partial Exemption Method (see **Chapter 4** at (40-200)), i.e.:

$$\frac{\text{Value of taxable supplies}}{\text{Value of total supplies}} \quad \frac{(SR + Z) \times \text{input VAT}}{(E + SR + Z)}$$

is rarely acceptable. Most banks have either adopted or been directed to use something else. Special Methods are the norm. The emphasis is also on *direct attribution*, often coupled with a more scientific cost/profit centre approach.

(a) The services: lending split

A good illustration of what might be considered is the Special Method which, for many years, had been agreed for the clearing banks by the British Bankers' Association. This is not now in general use.

Given their large branch networks, a means of apportionment was devised in the early days of VAT based on a services: lending split. It works by recognising that, as a basic proposition, a greater amount of input VAT tends to be incurred on service activities as opposed to lending. For this purpose:

- service charge income broadly includes all normal banking income, including rents received – but excluding income where underlying input VAT is blocked (e.g. on cars see **Chapter 4**), income which is treated separately or to which direct attribution applies, outputs arising from the imported services rules (see **Chapter 5**) and interest;

- interest income, on the other hand, includes only interest on advances and loans, discounts and the gross interest on investments other than investments involving securities.

In outline, the method calculates the overall recovery of *residual* or non-attributable input VAT by applying the formula:

$$\frac{\text{taxable service charge income}}{\text{taxable and exempt service charge income}} \times \text{percentage of costs relating to service income} = X\%$$

$$\frac{\text{taxable interest income}}{\text{taxable and exempt interest income}} \times \text{percentage of costs relating to interest income} = Y\%$$

To the residual input tax recoverable under the formula, i.e. X plus Y is added any input VAT recoverable in full under direct attribution principles. In calculating this, relief is specifically allowed in full on the following:

(1) Certain goods which are purchased for onward taxable supply in the same state, e.g.:
   (a) coin trays/coin cases;
   (b) positive-rated gold bullion and coin;
   (c) savings boxes and globes;
   (d) goods provided for leasing, hire-purchase and credit sale.

(2) Costs incurred in equipping and running a staff canteen, except where fully subsidised.

(3) Costs incurred in the manufacture, but not the subsequent use of, self-supplied stationery (see **Chapter 4**).

Special adjustments are made for activities such as hire-purchase, leasing, new issues and trustee and executorship services. Supplies, which are likely to be distortive, are also expected to be treated separately.

(b) Other methods

As a result, amongst other things, of a number of cases (including *Barclays Bank plc (No. 2)* [1991] BVC 585 and *The Governor and Company of the Bank of Scotland* [1996] BVC 2,664) banks generally now have to consider other acceptable alternatives. Usually, this means an expectation that methods will treat separately the different areas of activity on cost-or income-centre lines as discussed earlier in **Chapter 4**. How far this can be taken or how detailed such a Method can, or should be, clearly varies. Different banks have different structures or systems and much may depend on the records available. Subject to this, a Method on these lines will generally follow normal management accounting principles. Expenditure will be allocated in the first instance to:

- cost-centres (such as administration, property management and accounting/IT); and
- income-centres (such as account transactions, customer lending, inter-bank lending, foreign exchange and money market, corporate finance, leasing, hire-purchase, securities and advisory/trustee services).

The input VAT allocated to the cost-centres will then be further allocated to the income-centres on an appropriate basis. How any initial and subsequent allocation will be made can, however, vary. The type of expense is sometimes a factor. Accommodation may be spread on the basis of floor space; communications and information technology according to the number of telephone calls, receivers or computer terminals. In other cases, the allocation may be based on staff numbers, salary and wage costs, or the volume of business transacted.

Once directly or indirectly allocated to income/profit centres, the VAT will be split within each between taxable and exempt supplies. The overall amount of input VAT recoverable will then be the aggregate of the amounts for each income or profit centre together with any tax that is directly attributed to taxable supplies.

Methods usually also now require distortive transactions to be segregated, with HMRC paying especial attention to foreign debt supplies, as in the *Barclays* case, and bullion, as in *Union Bank of Switzerland* (1987) VATTR 221; (1987) 3 BVC 654.

Special Methods can obviously invite complications. How far this is desirable or appropriate is then often a subjective matter. Much depends on the degree of sophistication of the particular bank concerned and its mix of business. How diverse are its activities and does the accounting system lend itself to a detailed analysis of the VAT? The amount of input VAT involved can also be a factor. If this is not significant, a much simpler approach may be justified. This may, perhaps, just involve the separation of more obviously distortive activities such as securities, leasing and hire-purchase. Subject to direct attribution, which will generally be easier for the latter categories than elsewhere, any remaining input VAT may then be recovered by a simple formula based on, say, output values or numbers of transactions.

> ### *Practice point*
>
> Whatever Partial Exemption Method is agreed, it will generally be important to agree the treatment of foreign exchange (see (70-200(22)). Following *First National Bank of Chicago v C & E Commrs* (Case C-172/96) [1998] BVC 389 and *Willis Pension Trustees* [2006] BVC 2,045, consensus as to how these are to be recognised for the purposes of recovering underlying input tax could be material to the recovery of input tax in the areas affected.
>
> In the case of foreign-based banks, it can also be important to see how far inter-branch and branch/head office transactions can or should be accommodated in the input tax recovery calculations.

70-300 Credit and charge card companies

Credit and charge cards provide an important ingredient of consumer credit. As such, there is a general inference that the transactions involved are exempt, thus implying restrictions in input VAT. This, as with other areas discussed in this book, can be an oversimplification: some card company services are taxable, as, indeed, are some types of card operation.

Typically, a card operation will involve a number of different legal agreements between the company and, for example:

- the cardholder for the use of the card (specifying the membership fees, interest and penalties, etc. and monthly settlement terms);
- the retailers or merchants for the acceptance of the cards (specifying the merchant charges and any other fees and the settlement arrangements);
- other card companies for the mutual/reciprocal acceptance of each others cards and use of each others retailer or merchant outlets (specifying interchange and other fees);
- clearers like FDR, MasterCard and VISA; and
- third-party suppliers for point of sale equipment and other services.

(1) Membership fees and charges

The charges card companies make to members or cardholders vary. Some, but by no means all, make an annual membership charge, usually irrespective of usage. Credit card companies make, in addition, an interest charge to cover amounts remaining unpaid. Charge card companies, where credit is not intended to be available, impose penalties.

(1) Membership charges to cardholders are, as might be expected, treated as exempt. If nothing else, they are seen as the provision of *intermediary services* in relation to payments or credit (VATA 1994, Sch. 9, Grp. 5, item 5 and art. 135(1)(b) and (d) of Council Directive 2006/112/EC).

(2) Interest charges will similarly be exempt, this time under item 2.

(3) In the case of charge cards, where interest is not seen as the appropriate sanction, there is generally a penalty for late payment. In practice penalties in the accepted sense are not, of course, consideration for anything supplied. Despite this, the general treatment seems to be the same as for interest, i.e. contributing to a corresponding loss of input VAT.

(2) Merchant charges and retailer discounts

As between the card company and the retailer, there are also retailer/merchant discounts or commissions. These are charges of, generally, around one to two per cent of the transaction value payable by the merchant to the card company. At one time, they were seen in the UK as consideration for a taxable supply of business promotion. However, they are now treated as exempt by reason of Note (4) to what is now VATA 1994, Sch. 9, Grp. 5.

Since most discounts or commissions are charged to businesses within the same territory as the card company, companies, as a result, are generally able to recover little of the input VAT they incur.

Imprinter/terminal rental

The exemption also covers charges to retailers or merchants by way of imprinter/terminal rental charges, when provided as an ancillary part of other exempt card services (see HMRC Notice 701/49 VAT: Finance (November 2011) at para. 4.8).

Imprinter/terminal rental charges are taxable, however, when they represent an optional or additional service by the card company to the retailer. Also taxable is any consideration received for a sale of goods such as imprinters or terminals even if in connection with a credit, debit or charge card scheme.

- The exemption for merchant discounts was, however, challenged in *C & E Commrs v Diners Club Ltd* (1989) 4 BVC 74. Before the VAT Tribunal Diners Club sought to distinguish their position on the grounds of the underlying contractual relationship. Charge cards, as opposed to credit cards, had, it was argued, the effect of creating an assignment of the customer debt from the retailers to the card company at a discount on face value. Thus, it was maintained, there was no supply of services by the card company to the retailer as such, but vice versa, much the same, therefore, as in the case of discount in bills of exchange (see (2) earlier) and, arguably, not dissimilar from many of the factoring agreements discussed later.

Diners Club won before the Tribunal. Unfortunately, they lost before the High Court and again on appeal to the Court of Appeal. The Courts were unable to accept that there was an assignment of debts; the liability to the retailer was simply extinguished on the acceptance of a card. It was also held that the discount was consideration for services provided to the retailer, including in particular the assurance of payment which was exempt.

(3) Interchange and other fees

A number of other supplies will typically arise relating to the authorisation, settlement and interchange arrangements. Some are between the card companies and organisations such as VISA or MasterCard and FDR.

- Base 1 fees are essentially for the authorisation of individual card transactions;
- Base 2, for the arrangement of settlements; and
- interchange fees are fees both received and paid by the card-issuing companies.

They arise where one card company's cardholder effects a transaction at another's retail outlet, thus making use of the latter's merchant agreements. They effectively represent, therefore, a sharing of the merchant discount and are treated as VAT-exempt.

Historically, HMRC had regarded Base 1 fees as taxable at the standard-rate and the remainder as exempt. The treatment of Base 1 fees had seemed, arguably, incorrect. However, the matter has now been put finally to a test in a dispute over a VAT assessment raised on FDR on the basis that the fees were all subject to VAT.

- On appeal, FDR won before the Tribunal and, again, by a unanimous verdict before the Court of Appeal, *C & E Commrs v FDR Ltd* [2000] BVC 311. Leave to appeal to the House of Lords was refused.

    FDR's business consisted, essentially, of providing services to banks issuing credit or debit cards to cardholders and to banks (acquirers) contracting with merchants (normally retailers) to acquire vouchers accepted by those merchants in payment for goods and services. The facts of the case were extremely complex. However, in essence, FDR acted as a clearing house for credit and debit card transactions involving its clients, whether issuers or acquirers or both, effecting settlement of the net positions of its clients and supplying related services to them.

Fees were charged at various levels, depending on the degree of service required in a particular case. Both FDR and HMRC accepted there was a core supply, but differed as to what it comprised and how it should be treated for VAT purposes. HMRC contended that the core service provided by FDR was predominantly a service of bookkeeping, accountancy and reporting and that it was not within the exemption in art. 13(B)(d)(3) (now art. 135(1)(d) of the Sixth VAT Directive (Directive 77/388)), i.e.:

> 'transactions, including negotiation, concerning deposit and current accounts, payments, transfers, debts, cheques and other negotiable instruments, but excluding debt collection and factoring'

as no money was paid, nor liabilities discharged.

The Tribunal had held that the taxpayer made an exempt core supply, to which various other services were *ancillary*, in relation to both issuers and acquirers. This core supply consisted of 'processing all their card transactions and settling their liabilities and claims under these transactions in accordance with the obligations of the issuers and acquirers.' When it came before the Court of Appeal, the decision was the same:

- FDR's functions were identical to functions which would have been exempt if carried out by the banks themselves. In settling the Card transactions for cardholders' accounts and between banks, transfers were effected within the meaning of the Sixth VAT Directive, art. 13(B)(d)(3) (art. 135(1)(d) of Council Directive 2006/112/EC of 28 November 2006) in the same way as if, as between all the acquirers, issuers and payment systems, each debt had been the subject of individual credit and debit entries in each account. The decision in *Sparekassernes Datacenter (SDC) v Skatteministeriet* (Case C-2/95) [1997] BVC 509 (see earlier at 70-100) was followed.
- The Tribunal's identification of FDR's core supply as the processing of card transactions and settling liabilities and claims was justified. *Card Protection Plan Ltd v C & E Commrs* (Case C-349/96) [1999] BVC 155 (see 30-150), *C & E Commrs v Madgett (t/a Howden Court Hotel* (Joined Cases C-308/96 and C-94/97) [1998] BVC 458) and *C & E Commrs v Wellington Private Hospital Ltd* [1997] BVC 251 were considered.
- The core supply, as identified, consisting in the movement of money between cardholder, merchant, issuer and acquirer for the convenience of the cardholder and the profit of the other three parties. It amounted to an 'outsourced' banking function and was to be regarded as falling within art. 13(B)(d)(3) of the Sixth VAT Directive (art. 135(1)(d) of Council Directive 2006/112/EC of 28 November 2006).

The upshot, therefore, is that these charges, as many commentators anticipated, are properly treated as exempt. And, like the cases of *CSMA, Lloyds TSB and Continuum/CSC Financial Services*, discussed later at 70-500 on *Outsourcing*, this is not on the basis of the wording in VATA 1994, Sch. 9, Grp. 5 (as it was before 10 March 1999), but on the basis of the corresponding Sixth VAT Directive (now Council Directive 2006/112/EC of 28 November 2006) provisions, as clarified in cases like *Sparekassernes Datacenter* and *Card Protection Plan Ltd*. The inference, therefore, is that HMRC had been placing a too restricted view on the available exemptions (see the observations at 70-100 earlier), something it remains important to watch out for and which seems to have been borne out in *Smarter Money Ltd v R & C Commrs* [2006] BVC 4,098.

Following *FDR*, HMRC entered into consultations with the financial sector and the professions over the way in which the UK exemptions have been drafted. These eventually culminated in changes to Exemption Group 5 from 16 June 2003 by the *VAT (Finance) Order* 2003 (SI2003/1568). This removed the former Statutory Note 2B, and has meant that a relevant supply of financial services will be taxed or exempted according to its overall character instead of by reference to the presence or absence of a service listed in Note 2B. Whether that means they have got the balance right elsewhere remains, however, open to debate.

> *Practice point*
>
> In many cases, it will be a matter of fact and degree as to on which side of the line a particular situation falls. However, looking at the context in which something is provided can be vital and it could well pay to adopt a constructive approach as to how things are presented and documented.
>
> In appropriate cases, any of these supplies may be outside the scope if the recipient is established outside the UK, with input VAT relief being available where the recipient is based outside the EU.
>
> HMRC's VATFIN manual provides the following summary of liabilities associated with credit, debit and payment cards (VATFIN3160):
>
> **'General liability table**
>
> | Service | Customer belonging in UK | Customer belonging in EU (non-business) | Customer belonging in EU (business) | Customer belonging in non EU |
> |---|---|---|---|---|
> | Membership/joining fees and annual subscriptions (cardholder) | exempt | exempt | O/S | O/S-R |
> | Credit charges (interest) | exempt | exempt | O/S | O/S-R |
> | Joining fees/service charges (merchants) | exempt | exempt | O/S | O/S-R |
> | Merchant fees (discounts) | exempt | exempt | O/S | O/S-R |
> | Interchange fees inc. issuer's reimbursement fees | exempt | exempt | O/S | O/S-R |
> | Rental of imprinter/terminal | S/R | S/R | O/S-R | O/S-R |
> | Rental of imprinter/terminal rental when provided as an integral part of other **exempt** card services | exempt | exempt | O/S | O/S-R |
> | Sales of imprinters/terminals or other related goods) | S/R | S/R | O/S-R | O/S-R |
>
> O/S-R = outside the scope with recovery of input tax
> S/R = standard rate of VAT
> O/S = outside the scope without recovery of input tax'

(4) Fuel cards

In addition to the normal credit and charge cards, a number of other card arrangements, in particular fuel cards, can lend themselves to a quite different treatment. The cards in this case are often structured so as to involve the successive purchase and sale of the underlying goods rather than offering a payment or credit mechanism. They, typically, involve a series of supplies from the retail outlet to the card company, and from the latter to the cardholder. The merchant discount is thus, in reality, a discount in the purchase price of goods, not the payment for an exempt supply.

The cards involved will include the Overdrive, Dial and OFIS cards of the Harpur Group, the Allstar petrol card and the agency cards operated by most of the major oil companies. The concept in itself is fairly simple. However, the agreements and procedures under which these cards operate are very different from those used by the more traditional card companies.

- The difficulty this can entail was illustrated by the appeal in November 1993 by *The Harpur Group Ltd* [1995] BVC 841 which was the culmination of what appears to have been a drawn-out dispute. Briefly, the standard Overdrive scheme relied on the cardholder being treated as the agent of Overdrive in procuring the *supply of fuel* from the garage. It also anticipated that title in the fuel passed from the garage to Overdrive when the parties intended it to pass, i.e. on the signing of the supply voucher, the merchant slip. Unfortunately for Harpur, this analysis was not accepted by the Tribunal, largely on the basis that title has passed much earlier on delivery into the tank at the pump. At that stage, the cardholder had a personal obligation to pay for the fuel, property in which had passed to him. Whilst it might be possible to treat the subsequent signing of the supply voucher as superseding and discharging the pre-existing obligation to pay, this did not alter the fact that the supply had already been made to the cardholder, which could not then be changed. The decision largely followed, therefore, the principles in the earlier income tax case of *Richardson (HMIT) v Worrall* ([1985] BTC 508). This same difficulty was not, however, experienced with the OFIS card which was used for vehicle-related goods and services and where the card was required to be produced and the transaction authorised as an OFIS purchase before the supply took place at all.

Practice point

Initially, HMRC were more concerned with the independently operated cards like Overdrive and Allstar than with the agency cards of the major oil companies. It was, after all, the latter's primary purpose to sell fuel and in many cases the problems over the passage of title just did not arise. However, following *Harpur*, this position was reviewed and a common approach adopted. As stressed in the *Business Brief* 25/94 of 16 December 1994, the treatment depends crucially on the precise terms of the contractual arrangements between the parties to the transactions. See also HMRC's VAT: Supply and Consideration Manual at VATSC96600.

It may also, of course, depend on the procedures adopted at the time the transactions are carried out. If carefully executed things can still be structured as a series of taxable supplies of goods in much the same way as some of the confirming house arrangements referred to above.

One of the advantages of the fuel card arrangement is the ability of the customer to control employee purchases and to more effectively manage its vehicle fleet. This is partly manifest in the fact that the card company may be able to issue a composite VAT invoice for all relevant purchases in the period, something other card companies cannot do. In addition, the companies can also often offer a range of other information and control facilities for which separate charges are made. These are accepted as taxable at the standard-rate. Where credit is provided interest is due, which is exempt under the normal rules in Grp. 5.

(5) Corporate purchasing or procurement cards

A relatively new phenomenon are corporate purchasing or procurement cards for use by companies to pay for high-volume, low-value purchases by employees. These work in much the same way as normal credit cards (with the same liability considerations). However, the attraction is that, for single purchases of a value of less than £5,000, the card company, rather than the retailer, can issue a single composite VAT invoice covering all purchases in a given period, and will do this on behalf of all the suppliers concerned. At the same time, HMRC have agreed to waive the normal taxpoint requirements in favour of an *accommodation taxpoint* to be agreed with the corporate cardholder concerned, with the result that companies can potentially achieve material savings in accounting and administration costs. For further guidance see HMRC Notice 701/48 (March 2002) Corporate purchasing cards.

(6) Differential prices and card handling fees

Following legislation introduced in 1991, retailers are allowed to charge differential prices to customers using credit cards. Initially, there was a suggestion that the price differential was exempt as consideration for credit or a payment facility. In the event, this was not accepted. The total value is taken as a payment for the goods. This was later confirmed in *Business Brief* 17/98 of 7 August 1998, where HMRC said that:

> 'If the charge for payment by credit card is made by the supplier of the goods/services being bought, Customs view this as a further payment for the purchase. VAT would be payable on the charge at the same rate as on the goods/services.
>
> However, if the charge is made by an agent acting for the supplier of the goods/services, for example a travel agent acting on behalf of a tour company, then HMRC consider that the charge is for a separate supply of exempt services. i.e. accepting payment in the form of a credit card.'

Interestingly, they didn't take quite that line in the *Bookit Ltd* and *Scottish Exhibition Centre Ltd* cases.

- *Bookit Ltd v R & C Commrs* [2006] BVC 605 concerned the supply of Odeon cinema tickets. Customers wishing to purchase cinema tickets remotely, e.g. by phone or internet, were redirected to Odeon's agent, Bookit, who charged the customer an additional fee over and above the price of the ticket for their service. Bookit contended this fee was for credit or debit card handling services and was VAT-exempt as a transaction concerning payments or transfers.

  The Tribunal found for HMRC and held that that Bookit was providing a taxable card handling service to the customer in return for the additional fee and was not performing intermediary services within VATA 1994, Sch. 9, Grp. 5, item 5. However, this was overturned on appeal and the Court of Appeal later agreed, holding that the supply by Bookit to the customer included the following components:

(1) Obtaining the card information with the necessary security information from the customer.
(2) Transmitting that information to the card issuers.
(3) Receiving the authorisation codes from the card issuers.
(4) Transmitting the card information with the necessary security information and the card issuers' authorisation codes to Girobank.

The Tribunal had been correct in finding components (1) to (3) were taxable. However, as the fourth component was part of Bookit's service to the customer, and had the effect that funds were transferred to its account with Girobank, and what was charged by Bookit was exempt. In the present case the exemption provided for in art. 13(B)(d)(3) (now art. 135(1)(d) of Council Directive 2006/112/EC of 28 November 2006) applied on the basis that the fourth component of the service supplied by the taxpayer to the customer had the effect that funds were transferred to the taxpayer's account with Girobank. (*Sparekassernes Datacenter v Skatteministeriet* (Case C-2/95) [1997] BVC 509; [1997] ECR I-3017 applied.) Leave to appeal to the House of Lords was refused.

- *Scottish Exhibition Centre Ltd* [2005] BVC 2,529 was about the supply of tickets to events held in the Scottish Exhibition and Conference Centre in Glasgow. SEC acted as agent of the promoter in the selling of tickets and charged an additional fee to customers on tickets paid for by credit and debit card. SEC contended this fee was for card handling services and was VAT exempt.

  The Tribunal and, again, the Court of Session, following the line taken by the Court of Appeal in *Bookit*, found SEC was carrying out an exempt card-handling service.

  HMRC subsequently issued Business Brief 18/06 (VAT-Liability of agents' credit and debit card handling services) on 30 October 2006 to announce their *revised policy* on the VAT liability of credit and debit card handling services supplied by agents, making the observation that:

  > 'Charges levied on the cardholder for payment by credit and debit card in any other circumstances will not fall within the exemption for financial services and the normal VAT treatment will apply.

  > The judgments do not alter the general principle that the taxable amount for a supply of goods or services includes all payments which the supplier requires the customer to make as a condition of receiving the supply. If, for example, a supplier of goods or services requires a customer to pay an additional charge, above that of the price of the actual goods or services, for payment by credit or debit card, that charge is further consideration for the purchase of those goods or services and VAT is payable on that amount in accordance with the VAT treatment of the goods or services.'

- The ECJ Ruling in *Chaussures Bally (SA) v Belgium* (Case C-18/92) [1993] ECR I-2871 showed the other side of the coin, as it were. Here it was argued by the taxpayer that the taxable amount in a card transaction was the sum received net of commission (i.e. merchant/retailer discount). However, the Court disagreed, holding that the commission was the consideration for a service offered by the credit card company to the supplier which resulted in an independent transaction to which the purchaser was not a party. If anything, this underlines the need for care in structuring any arrangements along the lines of the fuel cards discussed earlier.

HMRC's policy on the implication of these cases for card handling is stated as follows (VATFIN2320):

> 'The judgments have provided further guidance on when a service of credit or debit card handling by an agent is VAT exempt. If an agent, acting for the supplier of the goods or services, makes a charge to the customer for a separately identifiable service of handling payment by credit or debit card, over and above that of the cost of the actual goods or services, and is providing the four components listed above [referring to *Bookit Ltd* as discussed above], the additional charge will be exempt under item 1. Charges levied on the cardholder for payment by credit and debit card in any other circumstances will not fall within the exemption for financial services and the normal VAT treatment will apply. Where a business provides some or all of the first three of these components without providing the fourth component, the charge is taxable at the standard rate of VAT. The judgments do not alter the general principle that the taxable amount for a supply of goods or services includes all payments made by the customer. If, for example, a supplier of ticket booking services, or any other goods or services, requires a customer to pay an additional charge where payment is by credit or debit card, above that of the cost of the actual goods or services, the charge is further consideration for the purchase of those goods or services and VAT is payable on that amount according to the correct VAT treatment of the goods or services.'

However, the effect of the EU Implementing Regulation must also be taken into account which provides (in art. 42) that where a supply of either goods or services, as a condition of accepting payment by credit or debit card, requires the customer to pay an amount either to the supplier or another undertaking, and where the total price payable by that customer is unaffected, irrespective of how payment is accepted, that amount shall constitute an integral part of the taxable amount for the supply of goods or services (for the purposes of art. 73 to 80 of the VAT Directive).

(7) Affinity cards

Following the decision in *C & E Commrs v Civil Service Motoring Association* [1998] BVC 21 and *C & E Commrs v BAA plc; Institute of Directors v C & E Commrs* [2003] BVC 112 cases (see 70-200) it is possible that, depending on the documentation and circumstances of individual cases, the commissions paid by card companies to charities and other organisations for the introduction and use by members of affinity credit cards can be treated as exempt, rather than subject to VAT at the standard-rate.

- Incidentally the same line was subsequently followed by the Tribunal in 2005 in *Prudential Assurance Co Ltd* [2006] BVC 2,340, where Boots Plc entered into an arrangement with Egg, a member of the Prudential Group, for a co-branded card scheme under which payment to Boots was based on the use of the card. The co-branded *Egg* credit card was offered to all Boots' *Advantage Card*-holders, who were able to earn Advantage points in the normal way but also earn points at a lower rate when using the Prudential Group's Egg card to make purchases elsewhere than at Boots.

This is a potentially important issue as the amounts paid by way of commissions will generally need to include VAT, where appropriate, which many such organisations may be hard pressed to recover.

(8) Avoidance

At the time of writing the fifth edition, a number of major high street stores were in dispute with HMRC over a tax avoidance scheme involving credit and debit card handling fees, which the companies insist are exempt from VAT. This proceeded as far as the Court of Appeal, but, ultimately, proved unsuccessful.

- The case, *R & C Commrs v Debenhams Retail plc* [2005] BVC 425, concerned a scheme, put together by a major accounting firm, aimed to achieve a VAT saving of around £4m a year. It set out to do this by causing less VAT to be accounted for in the case of sales paid for by credit or debit card. The arrangements were structured on the basis that, for goods with a ticket price of, say, £100 a customer paying by card will have entered into two purported contracts at the point of sale. One was with Debenhams Retail (Debenhams) for the sale of the goods for £97.50; the other with another company in the Group, Debenhams Card Handling Services Ltd (DCHS) for VAT-exempt card-handling services.

    HMRC challenged the scheme on the following grounds.

(1) There was no contract for a supply of card-handling services between the customer and DCHS.

(2) Even if there were such a contract, it was commercial reality that determined the VAT consequences. The fact of the matter was that DCHS provided no such services to the customer and the customer provided no consideration (in VAT terms) for them.

(3) Even if there were a contract between DCHS and the customer for card-handling services, that supply formed part of a single supply by Debenhams to the customer, and subject to VAT at the same rate.

(4) The sole or predominant purpose of the scheme was avoidance, rendering it ineffective either:

    (a) on the principle in *Halifax Plc* (at the Tribunal) (that, as a matter of economic reality, DCHS was not a *taxable person acting as such*); or
    (b) that the arrangements constitute an 'abuse of rights' satisfying the tests in the *Emsland-Starke* case,

    and won decisively on virtually all counts.

- Debenhams lost the contract argument mainly because customers were largely kept in the dark and the wording on the till slip the customer had to sign:

    'I agree that 2.5% of the above value is payable to DCHS for card handling services. The total payment I make remains the same.'

    wasn't enough to show Debenhams' own supply was for just 97.5 per cent of the ticket price.

(1) On commercial reality, DCHS really had no capacity to contract independently, but merely facilitated Debenhams' own supplies.

(2) The single supply point was a possibility, but commercial reality meant any supplies by DCHS were *ancillary* to those of Debenhams.

(3) In terms of the *Halifax* approach, the evidence showed no reason or purpose for the scheme other than avoidance and what DCHS did were not *economic activities*. (Interestingly, though this was not later supported at the Court of Appeal.)

(4) There was also an *abuse of rights* following the doctrine in *Emsland-Starke*.

The High Court allowed the taxpayer's appeal ([2004] BVC 554), but the Court of Appeal decided firmly against Debenhams and the matter went no further. What the Court decided was:

(1) The proper approach under Community law to the identification of any supply and consideration depended, save in exceptional cases, upon the *objective* character of the transaction. When the ordinary customer shopped in a retail store, he or she expected to pay the ticket price. That was a matter of potential significance when assessing what the ordinary customer would regard as the bargain being made but it was not an essential factor in the conclusions reached by the Court under either domestic or European law. Payment by card was not conditional upon anything in the chain of separate contracts between the buyer, the card-issuing company and the store. The general understanding of the public was that, when a customer signed the voucher, he had discharged his obligations to the supplier and that he paid for the goods or services he had obtained when he paid the card-issuing company. Any services performed in relation to settlement or card handling were on that basis services performed, by the card issuer, for the supplier and normally paid for by the supplier by deduction or other charge. In this case the contractual position under domestic law was the starting and finishing point for the VAT analysis.

(2) In the present case, there was nothing in the till slips, read against the background of the notification words, which showed sufficiently clearly that the customer was required to enter into some separate contract with DCHS. The till slip words were consistent with the taxpayer having to engage DCHS to undertake card handling services, and either informing the customer that 2.5 per cent of the price would go to DCHS for DCHS's services or requiring the customer to pay 2.5 per cent of the price to DCHS for DCHS's services. Thus there was only one contract between the taxpayer and the customer whereby at most the customer was required and agreed to pay 2.5 per cent of the total consideration to a third party, DCHS. The taxpayer was deemed to have made a taxable supply of goods for a consideration consisting of 100 per cent of the total paid by the customer.

(3) Even if there were a separate contract between the customer and DCHS, the taxpayer should be regarded as stipulating for and obtaining consideration consisting both of the 97.5 per cent of the price paid to it directly and the 2.5 per cent paid at its insistence to DCHS to cover the cost of services which the taxpayer had required to be rendered to it by DCHS.

(4) On that analysis, the question of abuse did not arise since the taxpayer fell manifestly within the scope of the VAT regime in relation to 100 per cent of the total paid by any customer paying by card. However, if, on the facts, DCHS were regarded as having contracted with the taxpayer's customers to supply either the taxpayer or its customers

with card handling services in return for payment by customers of 2.5 per cent of the total paid, it was clear that there was no other economic justification for interposing DCHS or for causing it to contract as it did other than that of creating a tax advantage.

> **Practice point**
>
> In short, the reason Debenhams, and the other high street stores, lost was because they had got it wrong.
>
> The robust *non-economic activity* argument advanced, and approved, at the Tribunal was not accepted. However, the doctrine of *abuse of rights* will always have made the objective hard to achieve.
>
> The result can also hardly be surprising in view of what was said by the ECJ in *Chaussures Bally (SA) v Belgium* (Case C-18/92) [1993] ECR I-2871 where it was argued unsuccessfully by the taxpayer that the taxable amount in a card transaction was the sum received net of commission (i.e. merchant/retailer discount).
>
> Any proposal on these lines should, therefore, be viewed with caution, especially if there is any suggestion that success may depend on aspects being not entirely clear.

70-350 Finance houses

Finance houses, in broad terms, facilitate the acquisition of plant and equipment, vehicles or consumer durables. In many cases, this will be by way of instalment credit finance in a hire-purchase, conditional sale or credit sale agreement; in other cases by various forms of equipment leasing. Sometimes different classes of business may be undertaken by the same company; in others by separate companies within a group.

The essence of a hire-purchase or credit sale agreement is that it involves the supply of goods (VATA 1994, Sch. 4, para. 1(2)(b)). This applies where the possession of goods is transferred:

> 'under agreements which expressly contemplate that the property also will pass at some time in the future (determined by, or ascertainable from, the agreements but in any case not later than when the goods are fully paid for).'

There will also generally be a charge for credit.

(1) The approach to partial exemption

This clearly gives rise to a number of problems, especially in terms of the recovery of input VAT.

(a) The old FLA Agreement

There have been a number of agreements between HMRC and what is now the Finance and Leasing Association (FLA), the latest of which was in September 1994. The FLA withdrew from this at the beginning of the year 2000, however. The agreement was withdrawn on

31 January 2000, but several finance houses have continued to use the agreement in formulating proposals for special methods on partial exemption. The essence of these agreements entered into under the original agreement with the FLA was that finance houses undertaking only hire-purchase transactions could adopt a method whereby they could deduct:

- the whole of the input tax directly attributable to goods bought and sold in the same state (e.g. goods sold under the hire-purchase contracts); plus
- 15 per cent of the remaining input tax,

in the case of a contract involving a motor car, full recovery of input VAT being allowed as tax on *same state goods* for which the block under art. 7 of the *Value Added Tax (Input Tax) Order* 1992 (SI 1992/3222) does not apply.

Where companies undertook a variety of supplies, the non-attributable VAT was apportioned.

(b) The present position

The withdrawal by the FLA to the agreement followed a growing perception amongst a number of the major finance houses that they were moving away from mainly just providing credit and were becoming increasingly involved in the actual sale of the underlying asset to the customer. Consequently, they felt the 15 per cent of residual input tax previously acknowledged as applicable to their taxable supplies had become unrealistically low.

As it is, companies now need to agree an appropriate allocation of input tax more applicable to their own individual businesses. Some companies have continued to use a method akin to that in the FLA agreement, whilst others have argued for a higher percentage, with HMRC increasingly taking the view that businesses of this kind should not recover any input tax, because they are wholly concerned with making exempt supplies of credit. This was initially brought to a head with an appeal by *The Royal Bank of Scotland Plc* and an HMRC Revenue and Customs Brief.

- The appeal by *The Royal Bank of Scotland Group Plc v R & C Commrs* [2007] BVC 2,295 concerned the recoverable proportion of input tax paid by companies within the Lombard Finance Group (Lombard) which is part of the RBS VAT Group, on general overheads allocated to instalment credit business.

RBS claimed Lombard's interests differed from those of a bank. It didn't just provide money but had an interest in the assets and, amongst other things, needed:
- to be satisfied as to their durability, identity and saleability;
- to understand the customers' business to be in a position to advise;
- to be able to advise on the best machine, the deals available and any tax advantages.

Lombard also had to be in contact with the supplier, looking after viability, quality, guarantees, insurance and sometimes maintenance.

Neither RBS, which had earlier used the FLA method, nor HMRC, believed the method produced a fair result. The Tribunal agreed and, given that RBS' proposed special method on a transaction based approach (which treated 50 per cent of the related overhead input tax as attributable to exempt supplies) seemed fair and reasonable – and that no other method was suggested to replace the unfair and unreasonable method currently operated, the appeal was allowed.

The case was appealed to the Court of Session in Scotland, which allowed HMRC's appeal on the basis that there were no material findings of fact that were capable of supporting the tribunal's decision (see [2008] CSIH49).

In the meantime, HMRC took the step, on 30 March 2007 of issuing *Revenue & Customs Brief* 31/07 which was then re-issued by Revenue & Customs Brief 82/09 (January 2010). In it, they place emphasis on the extent to which costs are *used* for making taxable supplies, citing ECJ principles highlighted in the Court of Appeal in *Dial-a-phone* [2004] BVC 640. Costs are *used*, they say, to make taxable supplies of goods or services if they:

- have a *direct and immediate link* with the taxable transaction (see *BLP Group plc v C & E Commrs* (C-4/94) [1995] BVC 159);
- are borne directly by the *cost components* of a taxable transaction (see *C & E Commrs v Midland Bank plc* (Case C-98/98) [2000] BVC 229);
- are costs of the various components of the price (see *DA and EA Rompelman* (Case C-268/83) (1985) 2 BVC 200,157).

In applying these ECJ principles, HMRC's view is that a cost-component of a taxable supply should normally be reflected in the selling price and that normally it is clear when VAT on costs is recoverable. As, in most HP transactions, the goods are resold at cost, without any margin to cover overheads, the overheads are purely, therefore, cost-components of the exempt supply.

HMRC's policy was disapproved by the First-Tier Tax Tribunal in the decision of *Volkswagen Financial Services Ltd* [2011] UKFTT 556; [2011] TC 01401. However, the decision of the FTT was reversed by the Upper Tier Tribunal [2012] UKUT 394 (see 40-200).

Practice point

With HP and instalment credit finance, the exempt supply of finance will only be recognised if and to the extent that the credit element is separately identified and charged. If it is not, and there is a single overall price, the supply ceases to be a mixed supply of goods and credit; it is simply one of goods. A source of exempt supplies is thus removed, and with it a potential restriction of input VAT, improving the overall position of the finance house.

- This could be of particular interest where the customer for a large item of equipment is fully taxable and thus able to recover any input VAT in full.
- It would clearly be less attractive, however, where the customer is a private individual or an exempt business. Both would be unable to recover the VAT involved so that the commercial price would increase. However, in situations where the offer to the customer is of interest-free credit, as in *Primback*, this would not be an issue.

For transactions with individuals, there is also the constraint that the *Consumer Credit Act 1974* requires the amount charged for finance to be disclosed. Attention to the contractual wording is likely also to be important as shown in the Tribunal appeal by *Freight Transport Leasing Ltd* [1991] BVC 536.

> **Practice point**
>
> Companies could also possibly improve their overall input VAT recovery by examining the basis on which input tax is recovered under their partial exemption arrangements, especially now that the long-standing agreement between the FLA and HMRC has been suspended.

(2) The sale of repossessed goods

In the event the goods are subsequently repossessed, the finance house can adjust the VAT on the original supply by applying the VAT bad debt relief rules (see 30-500). There can, however, be an alternative treatment, following the *Motors Acceptance Corporation* case.

- In *C & E Commrs v General Motors Acceptance Corporation (UK) plc* [2004] BVC 611, GMAC sold cars to the public under credit agreements that included HP. Ownership of the cars transferred only when all required payments had been made, at which point, customers had the option of not having to make the final instalment. Instead the car could be returned to GMAC, and, provided it was in acceptable condition, the customer was liable for nothing more. GMAC could require the customer to pay the cost of repairs if the car was not in acceptable condition. Customers could also, under the Consumer Credit Act, similarly return the car and end any further liability once they had made 50 per cent of the total payments due. GMAC, for its part, could, if the customer defaulted, repossess the car and resell it. In this situation the customer remained liable for any outstanding balance.

What the Court decided was that:

(1) When a car was returned voluntarily or was subject to a default repossession, and the price actually required to be paid by the customer was reduced then there was a consequent decrease in consideration, which would give rise to an adjustment under VAT Regulation 38.

(2) Irrespective of how the car came back into the possession of GMAC, the return of the car constituted a repossession for the purposes of art. 4(1)(a) of the Cars Order 1992. The sale of the repossessed car accordingly fell to be de-supplied, subject to all of the other conditions in the Order.

(3) For unregistered customers, or for customers unable to recover the VAT charged as input tax, the level of documentation presented in the GMAC case was satisfactory for the purposes of VAT Regulation 24.

In other words, depending on the wording of the contractual documentation used, the more appropriate way to deal with the VAT effect of a hire-purchase repossession may be as a price adjustment.

70-400 Equipment leasing and rental

The hiring of equipment under operational or finance leases (and also under rental agreements) is a supply of services for VAT purposes, being the transfer of the possession of goods within

VATA 1994, Sch. 4, para. 1(1)(b). The supply in this case is essentially taxable, usually at the standard-rate. As such, it entitles the lessor to recover, not only the input VAT directly incurred on the acquisition of the asset, but also the tax on related overhead costs. Only those leases which contemplate the transfer of title to underlying equipment (such as hire purchase agreements) will be treated as a supply of goods (see VATA, Sch. 4, para. 1(2)).

The position on leasing of equipment will need to be watched in light of any developments following from the CoJ decision in *Eon Aset Menidjmunt OOD v Direktor na Direktsia Obzhalvane i upravlenie na izpalnenieto* (C-118/11) which related to the application of Bulgarian VAT. The UK treats a lease of equipment as the supply of services due to the feature that there will not be contemplated any title transfer to the equipment. In *Eon Aset Menidjmunt OOD* the Court considered an issue on the deductibility of VAT paid in relation to leases for cars used to transport employees. In the course of its judgment the CoJ suggested that finance leases of equipment should be regarded as a supply of goods, even in circumstances where it is not envisaged that title to the equipment will pass to the lessee. The CoJ commented (at para. 40) that:

> 'Accordingly, where a financial leasing contract relating to a motor vehicle provides either that ownership of that vehicle is to be transferred to the lessee on the expiry of that contract or that the lessee is to possess all the essential powers attaching to ownership of that vehicle and, in particular, that substantially all the rewards and risks incidental to legal ownership of that vehicle are transferred to the lessee and that the present value of the amount of the lease payments is practically identical to the market value of the property, the transaction must be treated as the acquisition of capital goods.'

However, the CoJ then noted that it is for the national court to determine whether the criteria (referred to above) are applicable. If the case is followed in Member States which treat a finance lease as the supply of services it will have an immense impact on such leases for equipment, e.g. the application of different rules on place of supply, time for payment of VAT, exemption for finance charges etc. The approach of the CoJ was to consider the broad economic realities of the finance lease arrangement; whereas in contrast the UK examines whether legal title is expected to be transferred in respect of the equipment in order to determine whether it is a supply of goods or services. Any change in approach is unlikely to be done on a retrospective basis, but would have material ramifications for any new leases entered into following any change of law.

In *Rudolf Maierhofer v Finanzamt Augsburg-Land* (Case C-315/00) [2003] BVC 325 the ECJ has concluded that exemption for the *letting of immovable property* within Art. 13(B)(b) of Sixth VAT Directive (Art. 135(1) of Council Directive 2006/112/EC) covers the letting of buildings constructed from prefabricated materials if they are firmly fixed to or in the ground. This would, on the face of it, equally apply to large fixed structures such as lifts and elevators were it not for the fact that Art. 135(2)(c) of Council Directive 2006/112/EC specifically excludes the letting of permanently installed equipment and machinery.

An illustrative UK case on the VAT treatment concerning the hire of plant which was incorporated into UK real estate is *Queen Mary, University of London v R & C Commrs* [2011] UKFTT 229. In this case the First-Tier Tribunal were asked to decide whether a supply, of plant and machinery incorporated on land, by a subsidiary of a bank was a single or multiple supply; and whether VAT at the standard rate should apply, due to it being the provision of equipment. The material facts were as follows:

- Queen Mary College (QMC) conducts medical teaching and research;
- a subsidiary company of QMC, Queen Mary Developments Ltd (QMD) procured work, materials and plant to build a teaching and research facility site;
- the facility required a material amount of plant and equipment (e.g. laboratory equipment and lifts); of the total cost of £44m, some £16m was expected to be on plant and equipment;
- the equipment was to be permanently installed in, and substantial majority of it was to be fixed to, the site;
- QMC entered into a financing arrangement with a subsidiary of a bank (Lloyds Property Investment Company No. 5 Ltd (LPIC)). The purpose of the arrangement was to permit LPIC to claim capital allowances on the plant and equipment in the building, and for it to pass some of the benefit of those allowances on to QMC by funding the acquisition of the equipment and making charges to QMC which were lower than the costs it would have borne if it had borrowed the money by a simple loan;
- to give effect to the financing arrangement QMC granted LPIC a lease of the site, LPIC agreed to the grant, and then granted QMC an underlease. QMD agreed to supply plant for incorporation in the facility to LPIC and LPIC agreed to pay for the plant. The rent payable by QMC was determined by reference to the cost of the plant (apart from a fixed £10,000 p.a.);
- the lease and underlease were part of the same bargain between the parties; and on the same day as the real estate leases were entered into by the parties, they entered into a Plant Agreement 'to record the agreement between [LPIC] and [QMC] under which [LPIC] has agreed to incur capital expenditure on the provision of plant and equipment to be incorporated' into the site;
- the foregoing arrangements were designed to ensure that LPIC could claim capital allowances in respect of the plant under the *Capital Allowances Act* 2001;
- on completion of the site, rents became due under the real estate leases (so that a fixed £10,000 p.a. payable to LPIC under the underlease was matched by the £10,000 p.a. payable by LPIC to QMC under the lease). The net cost of the arrangement to QMC was the payment of the variable rental reflecting the costs (including funding costs) of the plant and equipment;
- the parties also entered into a financial agreement, which determined the variable rent that would be payable under the underlease (i.e. by QMC) when it was granted. The agreement provided for the construction of a cashflow model under which QMC made equal quarterly rent payments, which reduced LPIC's net investment in the project. LPIC's net investment at any time was for these purposes the amount it has expended under the Plant Agreement, plus interest costs on its investment, less the tax benefit of capital allowances (plus tax on rental profits), less the payments received from QMC;
- payments under the leases were made with applicable VAT. The parties opted to waive exemption under para. 2, Sch. 10 to VATA 1994 in respect of supplies of land made in connection with the site;
- the issue was whether the whole of the supply reflected in each rental payment was subject to VAT at the standard rate or only part of it (due to the possible application of zero-rating under VATA 1994, Sch. 8, Group 15 (supply of medical or other equipment)).

The First-Tier Tax Tribunal held that there was a single supply received by QMC which was a supply of credit linked to its use of the plant and machinery, provided as a package through QMD. The Tribunal reached this decision by reference to the CoJ principles established in *Card Protection Plan Ltd v C & E and Levob Verzerkeringen BV and Another v Staatssecretaris van Financien* (for discussion on these cases see **Chapter 3** at 30-550). The Tribunal identified the following essential features of the financing arrangements, and in consequence why there was a single supply (at para. 32 to 33 of the judgment):

> 'What then were the essential features of the provision made by LPIC? It seems to us that they were the following:-
>
> (i) in broad economic terms QMC received a single package of financing for the plant and machinery in the Blizard Building. Its interest in the land was in substance unaffected by the transactions. The transactions did not affect the costs it bore on the structure of the building (excluding the plant and machinery). It was in economic substance paying LPIC for the plant and machinery;
>
> (ii) the monetary consideration for each rental supply was determined as £10,000 p.a. plus a single amount computed by reference to the totality of the expenditure on plant and machinery without differentiation between the specific pieces of plant and machinery;
>
> (iii) it was clearly important to QMC to obtain and retain the use of the Blizard Building as a whole including the equipment installed in it;
>
> (iv) the pieces of plant and machinery were for the most part fixtures in the building and thus used in the context of the use of the building as a whole;
>
> (v) the nature of the equipment supplied was determined by the agreement between QMD and QMC. LPIC took title to whatever QMD supplied and provided it as a whole to QMC.
>
> It seems to us that the elements received by QMC were so closely linked that they formed a single economic supply which it would be artificial to split. The elements of the supply were received together and used together. The provision of each bit of equipment (or bit of land to which it was affixed) would have had little practical benefit. QMC was acquiring not the benefit of lots of little bits of the site, or separate bits of equipment, but the whole package: what QMC (the only and thus the typical customer) wanted and got was the facility as a whole, not separate parts of it. The leasing to QMC was part of a single transaction. The undifferentiated consideration, although decisive, reinforces the close connection between the elements of the supply. If viewed as the provision only of plant and machinery rather than land, what QMC got and wanted was all the plant and machinery in place in the building, not separate parts of it. In broad economic terms QMC received a single supply of credit linked to its use of the plant and machinery, provided as a package through QMD, and dressed up as a lease of the land.'

The Tribunal then decided that the supply was of the use of permanently installed plant and machinery. The reasoning of the Tribunal identifies the key reasons for the classification of the supply in this way, which will in practice be relevant to many equipment leasing arrangements (at para. 38 to 43):

> 'First the Directive, by exempting from Art 135(1) the supply in Art 135(2)(c), makes clear that merely because English land law would treat a supply of land and fixtures as a supply of land, the same concept is not to be read into the exemption. If a supply of land with fixtures can properly be described as a supply of permanently installed plant and machinery, it falls outside the exemption ...

Second, as a matter of the mechanics of the agreements, the plant and machinery is sold to LPIC and then let, as part of the land to QMC.

Third, the vast bulk of the consideration payable by QMC is directly linked only to the cost of the plant and machinery.

Fourth, the economic effect of the arrangements as a whole was the leasing or financing of the plant and machinery to QMC.

Fifth the plant and machinery was (for the most part) permanently installed.

Although in legal form LPIC made periodic supplies of land to QMC under the Underlease, that Underlease was part of a composite transaction which encompassed the granting of the lease to LPIC. The effect of that composite was that QMC's interest in the land was in substance unaffected and that it acquired the use of, and paid rent for, the plant and machinery. Although VAT is a tax determined by reference to individual transactions, it seems to us that the transaction to which it is to be applied in this case is the composite transaction, and not the individual transactions evidenced only by separate documents.'

The Tribunal considered that zero-rating could not apply by reference to Sch. 8 to VATA 1994, due to there being a single supply which was fully taxable.

(1) Movable property generally

With the exception of supplies involving any means of transport, the treatment of leasing will depend on the particular place of supply rules for services. In other words, the leasing of assets such as plant and equipment is one of those services within Art. 44 and 45 of Council Directive 2006/112/EC and listed in UK terms in VATA 1994, s. 7A and Sch. 4A (see generally Chapter 3). Accordingly, the default B2B and B2C rules apply subject to any modification by overriding rules specified in VATA 1994, Sch. 4A (as discussed below).

To some extent, the test is a physical one – the basic rule is fixed by where the supplier of the service is located in relation to supplies to non-business customers; and where the recipient, if a relevant taxable business person, of the supply of services is located. However, this is just the starting point. Other rules place greater emphasis on exactly what is provided, to whom it is provided, and where. If the recipient of services is a relevant business person then the place of supply is where the recipient belongs (unless overriding place of supply rules apply in Sch. 4A to VATA 1994). However, there are a number of special rules found in VATA 1994, s. 7A and Sch. 4A (as discussed in **Chapter 3**).

A supply of services consisting of the hiring of any goods (Sch. 4A, para. 7(1) of VATA 1994) other than a means of transport (as discussed in (2) below) which would otherwise be treated as made in the United Kingdom, and the services are to any extent effectively used and enjoyed in a country which is not a Member State is treated as made in the non-EU country to the extent it is effectively used and enjoyed in that country. A supply of services consisting of the hiring of any goods (Sch. 4A, para. 7(2) of VATA 1994) other than a means of transport which would otherwise be treated as made in a country which is not a Member State, and the services are to any extent effectively used and enjoyed in the United Kingdom will be treated as made in the UK to the extent it is effectively used and enjoyed in the UK. However, from 1 January 2013 (without prejudice to the use and enjoyment rule), the supply is not subject to VAT if the supplier demonstrates that the place of supply is outside the EU in accordance with the EU Implementing Regulations (art. 3). Where the place of supply is outside the UK, VAT is nonetheless potentially recoverable under reg. 103 of the *Value Added Tax Regulations* 1995 (SI 1995/2518).

> ### Practice point
>
> Equipment leasing is a financial service, mostly taxable at the standard rate, a potential disincentive to a lessee unable to recover all or part of any VAT involved.
>
> - If the lessor had no presence here (VATA 1994, s. 7A and 9) and in the EU, it could also avoid charging VAT, but could use the refund Directives to recover VAT paid, perhaps on the purchase of the equipment, leaving no VAT cost.
>
> However:
>
> - a lessee in business will need to apply the reverse-charge, even if not otherwise registrable for VAT; and
> - if the lessor operated through a UK representative, it could potentially *belong* in the UK, making its supply taxable in the normal way.

(2) Means of transport

In short, the rule to be applied is that for UK VAT purposes.

For a supply consisting of the short-term hiring of a means of transport (para. 3, Sch. 4A of VATA 1994) the supply is treated as made in the country in which the means of transport is actually put at the disposal of the person by whom it is hired; but this rule is modified as follows: (a) if the hiring of a means of transport would otherwise be treated as being made in the UK, and the services are to any extent effectively used and enjoyed in a country which is not a Member State then the supply is to be treated to that extent as being made in that country; and (b) where a supply consists of the hiring of a means of transport which would otherwise be treated as made in a country which is not a Member State, and the services are to any extent effectively used and enjoyed in the UK the supply is to be treated to that extent as made in the UK. The place where the means of transport is put at the disposal of the customer is the place where the customer or a third party acting on his behalf takes physical possession of it (EU Implementing Directive, Art 40). A hiring of a means of transport is 'short-term' if it is hired for a continuous period not exceeding (a) if it is a vessel, 90 days, and (b) otherwise, 30 days (VATA 1994, Sch 4A, para. 3(1)). For this purpose, a 'means of transport' includes vehicles, whether motorised or not, and other equipment and devices designed to transport persons or objects from one place to another, which might be pulled, drawn or pushed by vehicles and which are normally designed to be used and actually capable of being used for transport. The means of transport includes, in particular, the following vehicles: (a) land vehicles, such as cars, motor cycles, bicycles, tricycles and caravans; (b) trailers and semi-trailers; (c) railway wagons; (d) vessels; (e) aircraft; (f) vehicles specifically designed for the transport of sick or injured persons; (g) agricultural tractors and other agricultural vehicles; (h) mechanically or electronically propelled invalid carriages. But vehicles which are permanently immobilised and containers will not be considered to be means of transport (EU Implementing Directive,

Art. 38). In practice, this heading will cover most means of transport and will include ships, boats, yachts, barges, aircraft, cars, trucks, lorries, motorcycles, cycles, touring caravans and trailers, railway wagons. It will not include freight containers, static caravans, racing cars (where forming part of a supply of sporting activities).

As discussed in Chapter 3, other rules apply to short-term hiring, and long-term hiring to non-business recipients. See generally the summary Table.

A UK supply will not always, however, attract VAT at the standard-rate. There are further special conditions, which apply to ships and aircraft.

(3) Ships or aircraft

There is a variation to the normal rule in the case of ships or aircraft. If the supply is in the UK, the normal standard-rating is replaced by zero-rating if the asset is a ship or aircraft that meets certain requirements in VATA 1994, Sch. 8, Grp. 8, items 1 and 2 . This provides:

'Item No.

(1) The *supply*, repair or maintenance of a qualifying ship or the modification or conversion of any such ship provided that when so modified or converted it will remain a qualifying ship.

(2) The *supply*, repair or maintenance of a qualifying aircraft or the modification or conversion of any such aircraft provided that when so modified or converted it will remain a qualifying aircraft.'

Supply in this case extends beyond the sale of a ship or aircraft to supplies on certain types of charter as well as by way of normal hire or lease. The zero-rating, rather than standard-rating, will thus potentially apply to all such supplies by UK lessors or charterers to lessees or users of qualifying ships or aircraft and whose use and enjoyment is in the UK or in any other Member State. Where the use and enjoyment is outside the EU, the supply will be outside the scope.

Zero-rating is only available for a 'qualifying ship' and 'qualifying aircraft', which is defined as (VATA 1994, Sch 8, Notes, (A1)):

(a) a 'qualifying ship' is any ship of a gross tonnage of not less than 15 tons which is neither designed nor adapted for use for recreation or pleasure; and
(b) a 'qualifying aircraft' is any aircraft which: (i) is used by an airline operating for reward chiefly on international routes, or (ii) is used by a State institution and meets the condition in Note (B1). The condition in Note (B1) is that the aircraft: (a) is of a weight of not less than 8,000 kilograms, and (b) is neither designed nor adapted for use for recreation or pleasure. The term 'airline' means an undertaking which provides services for the carriage by air of passengers or cargo (or both) (Note (C1)). The term 'State institution' has the same meaning as in Part B of Annex X to the Council Directive 2006/112/EC on the common system of value added tax (transactions which member States may continue to exempt).

The supply of a qualifying aircraft or ship, as the case may be, includes the supply of services under a charter of that aircraft or ship except where the services supplied under such a charter consist wholly of any one or more of the following:

(a) transport of passengers;
(b) accommodation;
(c) entertainment;
(d) education;

in each case being services wholly performed in the United Kingdom (VATA 1994, Sch 8, Note (1)). For general guidance on HMRC's position see Notice 744C (July 2011).

A key issue for aviation lessors is whether supplies of aircraft (e.g. disposals or leases) can be 'zero-rated' for VAT purposes. As discussed above, in the context of aircraft, zero-rating applies to supplies/imports/acquisitions of a 'qualifying aircraft', which effectively means any aircraft which is used by an 'airline operating for reward chiefly on international routes'.

Zero-rating also includes (i) the 'letting on hire' of a qualifying aircraft, (ii) the modification/conversion of any such aircraft provided that it will remain a qualifying aircraft, and (iii) any incidental supplies of services under a charter of a qualifying aircraft, subject to exceptions (e.g. passenger transport). Sales of parts and equipment will also qualify for zero-rating if they are to be installed in or incorporated in a 'qualifying aircraft'.

For the purposes of zero-rating it does not matter if the recipient of a supply (e.g. a lessor purchasing an aircraft) is not itself an airline so long as the ultimate user of the aircraft (i.e. lessee) is an 'airline operating for reward'. Sellers/lessors of aircraft looking to apply zero rating on this 'look through' basis will require contractual protection such as warranties/certificates from purchasers/lessees as to the entitlement to apply zero rating in these circumstances. HMRC permit this practice, in very narrow circumstances, so that suppliers 'look through' the supply to an immediate customer that is not an airline and on to the ultimate consumer of the supply. The critical point being that the ultimate consumer of the supply of either goods or services must be an airline (or a State institution) operating qualifying aircraft and that the entities in the supply chain are fully taxable for the purposes of the transaction so that no input tax restriction would occur anywhere in the chain were the zero-rating not to be permitted.

The Court of Justice in *Re A Oy* C-33/11 (19 July 2012) has decided that supplies of aircraft can be VAT zero-rated by intermediaries (such as operating/finance lessors) where the end user is an airline operating for reward chiefly on international routes, and that international routes includes not just regular flights but also charter flights. The decision will apply across the EU. The Court also decided that zero-rating can apply where an operator operates chiefly international charter flights.

What does the case mean for the aviation sector within the EU?

1 Zero-rating on the sale of aircraft to an intermediary non-airline (such as a finance/operating lessor) where the aircraft is purchased for exclusive use by an airline operating for reward chiefly on international routes.

2 Zero-rating on supplies to an airline operating for reward chiefly on international routes (which includes either regular or charter flights).

3. Appropriate evidence should be obtained that the ultimate end-user is a qualifying airline. In terms of the type of evidence which would be required by an intermediary in order to obtain zero-rating, the Court alludes to this in its judgment (at para. 59) stating:

> 'Making the exemption in such circumstances subject to the intended use being known and duly established as of the time of acquisition of the aircraft and to subsequent verification of the actual use of the aircraft by such an undertaking does not seem, in the light of the type of object at issue here and, inter alia, the registration and authorisation mechanisms in place for its use, to be liable to give rise to constraints for the Member States and the economic agents concerned which would be irreconcilable with the correct and straightforward application of the exemptions prescribed by the Sixth Directive.'

The practice of tax authorities in Member States is likely to vary in terms of the nature of the evidence which should be obtained. But clearly it will be important to obtain evidence from the end-user that it will use the aircraft for relevant purposes.

To enable zero rating to be available the airline must operate chiefly on international routes. There is no condition that needs to be met that any particular aircraft is used on a particular international route. However, aircraft that are used wholly or partly for purposes other than for the supply of passenger or freight transportation cannot be considered qualifying aircraft. HMRC's interpretation is as follows (Notice 744C (July 2011) para 3.5):

'**What is an airline?**

An airline is defined in the law as "an undertaking which provides services for the carriage by air of passengers or cargo". The undertaking can be a sole proprietor, partnership, corporate body or any other entity, but is not necessarily confined to a single entity. A VAT or corporate group of companies may also be airlines and HMRC will consider other arrangements and business structures on a case by case basis, this treatment does not affect the normal accounting arrangements between the entities or within and by VAT groups.

An airline will need to operate at least one aircraft which it may own, lease or hire for the purpose above. If the business does not have an Air Operators Certificate (AOC) it is an indicator that it is unlikely to be allowed to operate as an "airline" for the purposes of using Qualifying Aircraft.

What is "operating for reward"?

The airline must be providing either passenger or freight transportation (or both) on scheduled or unscheduled flights (or a mixture of both) in return for a consideration for that supply. There is no need for the airline to be operating for profit, but it must be a business operation in nature.

What is an "international" route?

An international route is any route that is not a domestic route within UK airspace, UK airspace boundary is normally twelve nautical miles from the coast. However, routes wholly within the VAT Fiscal territory of the UK and Isle of Man are also to be treated as UK domestic flights.

Routes between the UK to the Channel Islands and oil rigs outside the twelve mile limit are international routes.

Routes which leave UK airspace in the course of a UK domestic route are not international routes, for example, Northern Ireland to Wales crossing the Irish Republic.

What does "chiefly" mean?

"Chiefly" means that the international route operations of an airline must exceed its UK domestic route operations. While turnover from the respective operations will be particularly significant, other information may also be taken into account that indicates the relative importance of the type of operations undertaken. Whatever method is adopted, the result must be fair and reasonable and capable of verification by HMRC.

However, where pertinent to a method, HMRC consider that:
- non-operational use, for example, testing flights are not counted either way
- normal positioning flights should be counted by reference to the next flight for which the aircraft is being positioned, but positioning flights as a result of an emergency diversion should be counted by reference to the original routing of the diverted flight.'

As well as supplies of qualifying aircraft being zero-rated, certain supplies of passenger or freight transportation are also zero-rated. In the case of passenger transport, the aircraft must be designed or adapted to carry not less than 10 passengers (see Sch. 8, Group 8, Item 4 of VATA). Where aircraft are leased there can be a thin dividing line between a supply of an aircraft and a supply of passenger transport:

- a 'dry' charter (i.e. without crew) should be a 'letting on hire' of the aircraft which will be zero-rated, if it is a "qualifying aircraft" and standard-rated otherwise
- a 'wet' charter (i.e. with crew) will not be treated as a 'letting on hire' unless there is a true written charter (in which case it should be zero-rated if it is a qualifying aircraft but not otherwise). If there is no charter, the supply will be subject to VAT unless it can be shown that there is a supply of zero-rated passenger/freight transport.

(4) Freight containers

The leasing (or hire) of freight containers will be a supply of services, and the VAT liability of such a supply will depend on the place of belonging of the supplier and customer (as to which see the discussion in Chapter 3).

(5) The input tax block

Historically, the main exception to the recovery of VAT on the asset has been in the case of motor cars (see 40-050(1)). This was specifically blocked by art. 7 of the *Value Added Tax (Input Tax) Order* 1992 (SI 1992/3222).

For cars purchased on or after 1 August 1995, the VAT can now generally be recovered by the lessor where acquired for the purposes of leasing, unless the purpose is:

- for letting on hire free or at undervalue; or
- for the cars to be made available for free or subsidised private use.

A *motor car* for the purposes of these provisions (see art. 2) means any motor vehicle of a kind normally used on public roads which has three or more wheels and either:

- constructed or adapted solely or mainly for the carriage of passengers; or
- having to the rear of the driver's seat roofed accommodation fitted with side windows or constructed or adapted for the fitting of side windows;

but does not include vehicles:

- capable of accommodating only one person;
- meeting the requirements of the *Road Vehicles (Construction and Use) Regulations* 1986 (SI 1986/1078), Sch. 6 and capable of carrying 12 or more seated persons;
- of not less than three tonnes unladen weight;
- constructed to carry a payload of one tonne or more;
- constructed for a special purpose other than the carriage of persons and having no other accommodation for carrying persons than such as is incidental to that purpose,
- caravans, ambulances and prison vans; or
- vehicles constructed for a special purpose other than the carriage of persons and having no other accomodation for carrying persons than such as is incidental to that purpose.

London-type taxis were included from 1 December 1999, as were 12-seater vehicles not meeting road safety regulations.

The change in the definition of a motor car will be of interest to finance companies providing such vehicles on lease or contract hire. It will also affect finance companies and insurers, whose sale of second-hand goods following a finance repossession or an insurance claim is usually disregarded so long as they are resold in the same state.

Whilst there is a common thread with other types of equipment leasing to the effect that supplies will generally be taxable, there are differences in the place of supply (and even in the VAT liability) depending on the type of asset concerned. There are also a number of special situations that can need to be recognised.

A lessee will be restricted to recovery of 50 per cent of the input tax where it leases a qualifying car (see **Chapter 4**).

(6) Lease termination payments

Frequently, a lessee may be required to make a payment to the lessor to secure agreement to the early termination of an equipment lease. How this is treated for VAT purposes depends on the circumstances and, in particular, the legal nature of the payment. This is not always easy to decide. However, following agreement between HMRC and what is now the Finance and Leasing Association, it is generally accepted that any such payment by a lessee to a lessor may be treated as consideration for a supply of services by the lessor to the lessee (see HMRC's VAT Supply and Consideration Manual at 35600). VAT will thus be charged as appropriate according to the nature of the goods. If, following or at the time of early termination, the equipment is sold, VAT will also be due on the sale of the asset by the lessor.

- However, a different treatment was afforded in *Financial and General Print Ltd* [1996] BVC 2,623, where an insolvent taxpayer sought to recover tax on a substantial termination payment made on cancelling a finance lease. Its main argument was effectively that the payment was tied up with the supply under the lease and was part of the consideration for that supply. Alternatively, it was consideration for the lessor's service of terminating the lease.

    Unfortunately, the Tribunal disagreed, so no relief was available. The lessor's termination was not a supply of services but simply a unilateral act and there was no relevant service to which the compensation payment could be directly linked. With slightly different facts, however, and more explicit agreement between the parties, it is possible that a different conclusion might have been reached.

(7) Rebates of rental

In the case of certain types of lease, particularly finance leases, it is common for equipment to be sold at the end of the lease period. Depending on the terms of the agreement, the lessee may then receive a payment from the lessor calculated by reference to the sale proceeds. This may be described as a rebate of rental or as a commission payable to the lessee for procuring the sale; alternatively, it may be given no description at all. How the payment is treated for VAT purposes can again vary according to its precise legal nature. However, in practice, by agreement with Customs (see VATSC 37400):

- no VAT need be accounted for by the lessee provided VAT is not identified on any invoice or other document issued by him or on his behalf;
- no adjustment shall be made to any VAT previously charged or accounted for by the lessor, and any statement or other document stating the amount to be paid or credited shall not identify an amount of VAT and shall be endorsed 'this is not a credit note for VAT purposes'.

VAT has to be charged and accounted for on the sale of the equipment in the normal way.

(8) Transfers/disposals of leasing agreements

The transfer of all or part of a leasing company's portfolio involves the effective disposal of the underlying chargeable assets. On the face of it, VAT may then be due at the standard or zero-rate according to the nature of the asset concerned or its location. In practice, however, this is usually seen as the transfer of the assets of a business or part of a business as a going concern within art. 5 of the *Value Added Tax (Special Provisions) Order* 1995 (SI 1995/1268). As such, it does not give rise to a supply for VAT purposes, for example, see the VAT and Duties Tribunal decision in the case of *Baltic Leasing Ltd* (1986) VATTR 98; (1986) 2 BVC 208,097.

Where the acquisition of a business is by a partly exempt VAT group, the deemed self-supply rules in VATA 1994, s. 44 (see 30-350(3)) will apply. However, direct attribution should in most cases ensure full relief for any related input VAT.

(9) Non-UK lessors

For years there had been a quirk in the law that, on the face of it, gave non-UK lessors of equipment a distinct advantage over their UK counterparts. The leasing of equipment, being within VATA 1994, s 7A and Sch. 4A, is one of those services supplied where the business recipient is located, or made in the UK to the extent effective use and enjoyment is in the UK. Where the supplier belongs outside the UK, rental charges for equipment leased for use in the UK and made to a business here will usually be subject to tax under the reverse-charge. However, when it comes to a sale at the end of the lease, the way the registration provisions in VATA 1994 had worked meant the lessor was not required to join the club. There was a let-out in the rules in Sch. 1, para. 1(7) of VATA 1994 that said you could ignore the sale of capital assets for the purposes of the turnover criteria.

This was especially attractive bearing in mind that companies in this position could in practice recover, under the Eighth or Thirteenth VAT Directives (Directives 79/1072 and 86/560), any VAT incurred on the import into the UK or purchase here of those assets, whilst, at the same time, ultimately sell them on VAT-free.

This position changed which the *Finance Act* 2000, s. 132(8) and Sch. 36 which introduced, from 22 March, a new Sch. 3A, which effectively requires foreign companies leasing equipment to persons in the UK to register for UK VAT when there is an intention to sell the equipment here at the end of the lease. There is no exclusion for capital items.

70-450 Factoring

The factoring of debts is a specialist form of *off-balance sheet* finance. The form it takes will vary according to the service required by the client, the options falling into two broad categories, mainline factoring and invoice discounting. Mainline factoring can be broken down into:

- full factoring (non-recourse) (i.e. the factor bear the loss if the debtor defaults);
- recourse factoring (the factor does not bear the loss if the debtor defaults and has the right to assign the debt back to the original lender);
- agency factoring (involving the factor taking over the debt and extending credit to the debtor but does not bear any loss: the factor's client operates its own sales ledger and debt recovery system as agent of the factor);
- bulk factoring (also known as 'agency factoring'); and
- undisclosed factoring.

All forms of factoring essentially involve the transfer by way of equitable assignment of trade debts by the client to the factoring company. In the case of recourse factoring, the debts will be reassigned to the client in the event that the debtor defaults.

Both full and recourse factoring also involve the factoring company assuming responsibility for any sales ledger accounting. Other forms of factoring, including in particular invoice discounting, leave the sales ledger and collection of debts to be undertaken by the client.

Factoring is thus seen as involving potentially three elements:

- finance;
- risk control; and
- sales ledger administration.

How these are incorporated into the factoring contract and the way in which they are expressed will depend on the particular company concerned.

(1) Finance

Generally, factoring contracts envisage the acquisition of debts by the factoring company at face-value. The client is not paid this at the outset, but only at the end of an agreed period (either the client's normal period of credit or when the factor is himself paid by the debtor). In the meantime, cash advances will generally be made to the client of up to 80 per cent of the face value of the debts. For this facility, the factor will charge the client interest or factoring discount at a rate, which will vary from two to three per cent above bank rate on the amounts outstanding from time to time.

In VAT terms the acquisition of the debts by the factor is, arguably, outside *the scope* of VAT as simply being by way of security for a monetary loan, following the decisions in *MBNA Europe Bank Ltd v R & C Commrs* [2007] BVC 3 and in *Capital One Bank (Europe) plc* [2006] BVC 2,148. *MBNA* and *Capital One* (see earlier under *Securitisation* at 70-200). However, previously, it had been seen as an exempt supply by the client within VATA 1994, Sch. 9, Grp. 5, item 1, although HMRC accepted that, as a general rule, this could generally be ignored as *incidental* in the context of a pro-rata calculation under the Standard Partial Exemption Method.

The interest or discount charged by the factoring company for the provision of finance is, however, treated as consideration for an exempt supply under VATA 1994, Sch. 9, Grp. 5, item 2 (art. 135(1)(b) of Council Directive 2006/112/EC).

For the client, any related input VAT will be treated as residual input tax and will not be regarded as exempt input VAT (see **Chapter 4**). However, when debts are factored, they may no longer be dealt with under the cash accounting scheme. The trader concerned must account for tax on the original supplies under the normal rules.

(2) Risk control and other services

Apart from providing finance, the factor may also offer various other facilities, particularly in the context of mainline factoring. These are reflected in the factoring or service charge.

The first of these elements is risk control. Non-recourse factoring, by implication, minimises the client risk by the factor effectively assuming liability for bad debts. Factors can also provide credit advice, appraising the client of a particular debtor's credit worthiness before sales are made. Another service is sales ledger administration. Apart from relieving the client of the need to maintain its own sales ledger, this also does away with the need for the client to maintain its own credit control department and can lessen the risk of damage to the customer relationship from sales staff and management requesting payment.

The level of service charge will vary from client-to-client and according to the type of factoring undertaken. In the case of non-recourse factoring, it will take into account the likelihood of bad debts and otherwise will reflect a degree of administration required by the factor in accounting for and collecting what are in effect at that stage its own debts. Charges will represent a percentage of the face value of the debts in the case of invoice discounting (where there is generally a lower level of service provided) and a higher percentage for full or recourse factoring. This element of the factoring service is regarded by HMRC as taxable at the standard-rate.

(3) Partial exemption for the factor

Given that factoring companies make both exempt supplies of credit and taxable supplies of risk management and sales ledger administration, there will inevitably be some restriction of input VAT under the partial exemption rules (see **Chapter 4**). Agreement has been reached with HMRC that, except for invoice discounting, the input VAT incurred by a factoring company may be treated as recoverable in proportion to the respective numbers of taxable, as opposed to exempt, transactions processed through the sales ledgers maintained by the factors (and not according to the actual amounts of taxable service charge and exempt interest or factoring discount received). For this purpose, the taxable transactions are taken to be represented by the entries on the sales ledger accounts to record invoices, credit notes, and customers' and clients' payments; the exempt transactions will be represented by the interest/factoring discount entries and advances.

Invoice discounting is treated differently. The principal charge in this case is likely to be a discount charge linked to established base rates so that the range of services will be predominantly, if not totally, exempt. The customer, in this case, usually undertakes most of the sales ledger functions itself, as well as credit control and other dealings with customers.

The present partial exemption agreement between HMRC and the Association of British Factors and Discounters is set out at **Appendix 9**.

70-500   Outsourcing

Outsourcing is, arguably, the most important single issue at present for many in the finance and insurance sectors. Today's commercial pressures mean businesses are continually looking for ways to cut costs and/or do things more efficiently and sharing functions or farming-out all or part of day-to-day administration is a common option that is explored. Unfortunately, this can come at a price. Something that is done VAT-free, or relatively so, in-house (e.g. between members of the same VAT group or within a single entity) may suddenly due to outsourcing attract a tax charge:

- accounting and administration;
- the supply or sharing of staff;
- operating accounts;
- customer services and call-centres; and
- other back-office functions,

tend to be VATable and, if outsourced abroad, will still be subject to VAT under the reverse-charge.

For the position on the VAT exemption for cost sharing arrangements see **Chapter 6** at 60-300.

For sectors that, typically, recover little input VAT, this is unwelcome, to say the least.

7 Banks and Financial Institutions

Whilst, however, much of what is outsourced may have the outward appearance of something that is taxable in VAT terms, it will be important always to view things in context and decide exactly:

- what it is that is being supplied;
- and to whom.

HMRC expressly acknowledge that outsourcing arrangements are capable of falling within the ambit of the Group 5 finance exemption, subject to the specific nature of the arrangements. They state that (at VATFIN1600):

> 'There is no reason in principle why a sub-contracted service should not fall within the scope of the financial exemption. But many outsourced services may be administrative in nature, rather than services of a financial nature, and will therefore be taxable at the standard rate.'

For example, many of the *services* involved are often, in reality, functions in a much broader, single supply, to which the principles in *Card Protection Plan Ltd v C & E Commrs* (Case C-349/96) [1999] BVC 15 (see **Chapter 3** at 30-550) might apply. Looking at this *single* supply critically and applying the principles for assessing VAT liability described in this and other Chapters of this book, the conclusion might then be reasonably reached that what is being outsourced is, in reality, VAT-exempt. However, the key for a service falling within the Group 5 Sch. 9 VATA 1994 exemption is that the service, as a distinct whole, fulfills in effect the essential function of a service described in the exemption, the service must have the effect of altering the legal and financial situation between the parties, and the supply must therefore not be a mere physical, technical or administrative service which does not alter the legal or financial position of the parties.

As observed earlier at 70-100(1), where the exemptions are concerned, a line has to be drawn between what is covered and what is not and a cardinal principle is that they must be construed narrowly. Needless to say, this has led to a number of disputes, both in the UK and elsewhere, and, as far as the UK is concerned, in radical amendments to the exemptions for finance in VATA 1994, Sch. 9, Grp. 5.

Whether these have been wholly justified is often a matter for debate. However, a number of important cases have highlighted many of the important issues to look for in an area which is likely to see change and developments for some time to come.

(1) The bench-mark case of Sparekassernes Datacenter: services comprising an exempt activity in their own right

The *Sparekassernes Datacenter* case was an important milestone in the treatment of outsourcing because it marked the turning-point. Before then, outsourced services were almost invariably taxed. What the case has done is lay some vital ground rules by which the situation may be judged.

- *Sparekassernes Datacenter (SDC) v Skatteministeriet* (Case C-2/95) [1997] BVC 509 is a bench-mark case and at the heart of many of the current disputes, largely because of the way the ECJ has interpreted EU law. To understand the issues involved, it is useful to look at what exactly it was that SDC provided and the questions that were put to the Court.

SDC was an association registered for Danish VAT. Most of its members were savings banks and it provided to its members, and to certain other customers connected to its data-handling network:

- services relating to transfers;
- advice on, and trade in, securities; and
- management of deposits, purchase contracts and loans.

SDC also offered services relating to its members' administrative affairs.

Before 1993 SDC provided the banks with services performed wholly or partly by electronic means. Those supplies of services were analogous to those, which the biggest financial institutions carry out themselves using their own data-handling centres. A typical SDC supply was described by the Danish Court as consisting of a number of components, which, added together, made up the service, which a bank, or its customers, wished to have performed. A price was quoted for each service component appearing in SDC's products catalogue, but SDC did not receive this from the customers but from the banks.

The services were performed only at the request of a bank, a customer or other persons authorised, under a contract with the customer, to require transactions such as payments to be effected. A customer could give information to SDC only after having been authorised to do so by a bank, in particular by the issue of a payment or credit card. SDC's name was not used vis-à-vis customers and SDC had not undertaken any legal obligation in regard to them. The documentation produced by SDC was sent out in the name of the bank.

In 1993, that is to say after the main proceedings had been initiated, most of SDC's activities and assets were transferred to newly formed companies which, at the time of the Hearing, were controlled by SDC's members. One of those companies performed all the services in question. For organisational reasons, that company invoiced SDC, which in turn invoiced its members.

Initially, the Danish Authorities took the view that the services were exempt. However, in February 1992, the Danish VAT Tribunal decided otherwise and after an appeal to a higher court in Denmark, questions were referred to the ECJ for a preliminary ruling, producing the answer that what SDC had been providing was, indeed, VAT-exempt.

Looking closer at the detail

The questions referred to the Court were:

'(1) Should art. 13(B)(d) 3, 4 and 5 of the sixth VAT directive (art 135(1)(d)(e) and (f) of Council Directive 2006/112/EC) be interpreted as meaning that VAT exemption should be granted for services of a type described in para. 3 and 5 of the order for reference [; essentially, these are supplies of data-handling services to SDC members and to other financial institutions]?

In that connection, is the granting of exemption from VAT under art. 13(B)(d) 3, 4 and 5 (art 135(1)(d)(e) and (f)) precluded where a transaction within the meaning of that provision is performed, wholly or in part, electronically?

(2) The wording used in art. 13(B)(d) 1 and 2 of the VAT directive (art 135(1)(b)(c) of Council Directive 2006/112/EC) is "by the person granting [the credit]" (ved den person, som har ydet lånene) and "by the person who is granting the credit" (ved den person, der har ydet kreditten). That description is not employed in art. 13(B)(d) 3, 4 and 5 (art 135(1)(d)(e) and (f)).

Should any importance be attached to that difference in the interpretation of art. 13(B)(d) 3, 4 and 5 (art 135(1)(d)(e) and (f))?

(3) A. Is it significant, as far as the application of art. 13(B)(d) 3, 4 and 5 (art 135(1)(d)(e) and (f)) is concerned, whether transactions are performed by financial institutions or by others?

  (A) Is it significant, as far as the application of art. 13(B)(d) 3, 4 and 5 (art 135(1)(d)(e) and (f)) is concerned, whether the entire financial service is performed by a financial institution which has links with a customer?
  (B) If it is unnecessary for the application of art. 13(B)(d) 3, 4 and 5 (art 135(1)(d)(e) and (f)) that the financial institution itself should perform the entire service, can the financial institution buy in transactions wholly or in part from another person with the effect that the services performed by that other person are covered by art. 13(B)(d) 3, 4 and 5, or may particular requirements be made of that other person?

(4) How is the wording used in art. 13(B)(d) 3 and 4 (art 135(1)(d) and (e)) "transactions concerning" to be interpreted?

This question seeks to ascertain whether the words "transactions concerning" are to be understood as meaning that VAT exemption should also be granted in cases where a person either performs only a part of the service or performs only some of the transactions within the meaning of the directive which are necessary for supplying the complete financial service.

(5) In interpreting art. 13(B)(d) 3, 4 and 5 (art 135(1)(d)(e) and (f)) should significance be attached to the fact that the taxable person who requests tax exemption for transactions within the meaning of the provision effects those transactions on behalf of the financial institution in whose name the service is performed?

(6) After the plaintiff's reorganisation, is it significant, as far as application of art. 13(B)(d) 3, 4 and 5 (art 135(1)(d)(e) and (f)) is concerned, that the services in question are now provided by a company which supplies the services to the associated financial institutions?

It will be noted that the said services are invoiced by the company to the plaintiff which in turn invoices its financial institution members [reference is made here to the explanations given in the first paragraph of the order for reference].'

The judgment was delivered on 5 June 1997 in the following terms:

'(1) Points (3) and (5) of art. 13(B)(d) of the Sixth Council Directive 77/388 of 17 May 1977, on the harmonisation of the laws of the member states relating to turnover taxes - common system of VAT: uniform basis of assessment (art 135(1)(d) and (f) of Council Directive 2006/112/EC), are to be interpreted as meaning that the exemption is not subject to the condition that the transactions be effected by a certain type of institution, by a certain type of legal person or wholly or partly by certain electronic means or manually.

(2) The exemption provided for in points (3) and (5) of art. 13(B)(d) of the sixth directive (art 135(1)(d) and (f) of Council Directive 2006/112/EC) is not subject to the condition that the service be provided by an institution which has a legal relationship with the end customer. The fact that a transaction covered by those provisions is effected by a third party but appears to the end customer to be a service provided by the bank does not preclude exemption for the transaction.

(3) Point (3) of art. 13(B)(d) of the sixth directive (art 135(1)(d) of Council Directive 2006/112/EC) is to be interpreted as meaning that transactions concerning transfers and payments include operations carried out by a data-handling centre if those operations are distinct in character and are specific to, and essential for, the exempt transactions.

(4) Services consisting in making financial information available to banks and other users are not covered by points (3) and (5) of art. 13(B)(d) of the sixth directive (art 135(1)(d) and (f) of Council Directive 2006/112/EC).

(5) The mere fact that operations concerning the management of deposits, purchase contracts and loans are carried out by a data-handling centre does not prevent them from constituting services covered by points (13) and (15) of annex F to the sixth directive [no longer extant]. It is for the national court to determine whether, [p. 535] before 1 January 1991, those operations were separate in character and specific to, and essential for, those services.

(6) The mere fact that a service is invoiced by a third party does not prevent the transaction to which it relates from being exempt under points (3) and (5) of art. 13(B)(d) of the sixth directive (art 135(1)(d) and (f) of Council Directive 2006/112/EC).'

The HMRC reaction

Shortly after this Ruling, HMRC issued *Business Brief* 13/97, in which they set out their reaction. The judgment, they said, gave rise to no change in policy in the UK and they would continue to accept that services provided by persons who themselves directly effect payments and transfers of funds qualified for exemption. Outsourced activities generally, however, remained liable to VAT at the standard-rate.

As HMRC summarised the position, the Advocate-General, in his Opinion delivered on 4 July 1996, drew a clear distinction between the legal transaction between the bank and its customers, and the means of carrying out that transaction. Only the legal transaction between the financial institution and its customer would qualify for the financial exemption. Instrumental, technical or ancillary services supplied by third parties for the performance of the legal transaction would not be covered. The full Court decided that, to qualify for exemption, a service did not have to be supplied by a person who stood in a *direct legal relationship* with a bank's final customer, but subcontracted services must, to qualify, be exempt in their own right. The judgment did not follow the Advocate-General's Opinion, but was in accordance with the observations made to the Court by the UK during the proceedings.

This analysis explains the line HMRC took in subsequent cases and the changes made from 10 March 1999 to the provisions in VATA 1994, Sch. 9, Grp. 5.

However, in looking at this, it is necessary to consider what the Court actually said. The crucial issue is whether, in the context in which they are provided, the services supplied by

SDC are themselves exempt. The rationale for the Court's conclusions on this point emerges from paras. 60 to 66:

'60. By its fourth question the national court seeks to ascertain whether the VAT exemption must be granted where a person either performs only part of a complete service or carries out only certain operations necessary for the supply of a complete exempt financial service. Given that the first question concerns the exemption of the data-handling element in the services envisaged by points (3) and (5) of art. 13(B)(d), these questions can be examined together.

Transfers and payments

61. It is necessary to consider first of all whether the operations carried out by a data-handling centre such as SDC in the effecting of a transfer can in themselves be described as transactions concerning transfers within the meaning of point (3) of art. 13(B)(d) of the sixth directive (art 135(1)(d) of Council Directive 2006/112/EC).

62. The Danish Ministry for Fiscal Affairs argues that the services provided by SDC are in fact composed of various administrative or technical components which are invoiced individually. No price is fixed in advance for the transfer, the transfer of funds or the services in their entirety. Consequently, the services provided by SDC are different from those covered by point (3) of art. 13(B)(d) of the sixth directive (art 135(1)(d)).

63. SDC, on the other hand, states that, in order for the exemption to apply, it is not necessary for the services supplied to be complete services but it is sufficient that the supply in question should be an element of a financial service in which various operators participate and which, taken as a whole, constitutes a complete financial service.

64. Given this difference of view, it must be noted first of all that the wording of point (3) of art. 13(B)(d) of the sixth directive (art 135(1)(d)) does not in principle preclude a transfer from being broken down into separate services which then constitute "transactions concerning transfers" within the meaning of that provision and which are invoiced by specifying the elements of those services. The invoicing is irrelevant for the application of the exemption in question, provided that the actions necessary for effecting the exempt transaction can be identified in relation to the other services.

65. However, since point (3) of art. 13(B)(d) of the sixth directive (art 135(1)(d)) must be interpreted strictly, the mere fact that a constituent element is essential for completing an exempt transaction does not warrant the conclusion that the service which that element represents is exempt. The interpretation put forward by SDC cannot therefore be accepted.

66. In order to be characterised as exempt transactions for the purposes of points (3) and (5) of art. 13(B), (art 135(1)(d) and (f)) the services provided by a data-handling centre must, viewed broadly, form a distinct whole, fulfilling in effect the specific, essential functions of a service described in those two points. For "a transaction concerning transfers", the services provided must therefore have the effect of transferring funds and entail changes in the legal and financial situation. A service exempt under the directive must be distinguished from a mere physical or technical supply, such as making a data-handling system available to a bank. In this regard, the national court must examine in particular the extent of the data-handling centre's responsibility vis-à-vis the banks, in particular the question whether its responsibility is restricted to technical aspects or whether it extends to the specific, essential aspects of the transactions.'

The Court then went on to remark that it was for the national court to determine whether the operations carried out by SDC had such a distinct character and whether they were specific and essential.

The essential points

In short, what the Court was saying (para. 66) was that, to be exempt:

(1) The services of the data-handling centre had, viewed broadly, to form a distinct whole, fulfilling in effect the specific, essential functions of a service described in that part of what is now art. 135(1)(d) of Council Directive 2006/112/EC (art. 13(B)(d)(3) of the Sixth Directive).

(2) Accordingly, they had to have the effect of:
 (a) transferring funds; and
 (b) *entail changes in the legal and financial situation* of the parties to the underlying transaction.

(3) Such a situation was to be distinguished from a *mere physical or technical supply*, such as data-handling.

(4) To reach a conclusion in a particular case, you had to look at the facts and responsibilities undertaken to see whether what was provided was just mechanical or if it extended to the specific, essential aspects of the underlying transactions.

As the Court put it in para. 68 of its judgment:

'In view of all foregoing considerations the reply to be given to the first and fourth questions concerning point (3) of art. 13(B)(d) of the sixth directive (art 135(1)(d)) must be that this provision is to be interpreted as meaning that transactions concerning transfers and [p. 533] payments include operations carried out by a data-handling centre if those operations are distinct in character and are specific to, and essential for, the exempt transactions.'

> ### *Practice point*
>
> Some crucial points to focus on appear to be to see how far what is done:
>
> - *entails making changes in the legal and financial situation* of the parties to the underlying transaction;
> - is specific to, and essential for, the exempt transactions; or
> - is a *mere mechanical or technical* supply, which is not *ancillary* to the main supply.
>
> Three cases then followed, *Civil Service Motoring Association, Lloyds TSB Group Ltd* and *Continuum (Europe) Ltd* (or CSC Financial Services Ltd, as it later came to be known), which triggered the change in the law.

HMRC give the following example of how it is necessary to accurately identify the nature of the supplies made by the party to whom an activity is outsourced. Simply administrative services will be standard rated supplies (VATFIN2950):

'You should always ensure that there is a supply for VAT purposes in the first instance.

For example, an authorised deposit taker sending out account statements, and charging the account holder a fee, would exempt its services because it is part of the operation of the account. However, if this service is outsourced to a third-party, and that third party sends out the statements and charges the authorised deposit taker, whilst the fee charged to the customer by the authorised deposit taker would remain exempt, the service provided by the third party to the authorised deposit taker would be taxable. This is because it is not the operation of an account by the third party but is administrative assistance to the authorised deposit taker.'

(2) Other back-office situations: negotiation of credit and payments

Most outsourcing issues seem to arise in the context of administration, where the benefits of shared facilities and economies of scale are often more readily apparent.

- *C & E Commrs v Lloyds TSB Group Ltd* [1998] BVC 173 was an appeal by a company that supplied support functions for Volkswagen Financial Services (UK) Ltd. Volkswagen Financial Services (VFS) provided finance under HP agreements and Lloyds TSB handled the HP and leasing applications and enquiries from dealers and distributors. It also vetted applications, obtained credit references and decided whether or not to accept or reject applications, as well as maintaining records and provided administrative services after credit was arranged.

Vehicles sold under HP arrangements were first sold by dealers to VFS, which provided the finance.

The various elements in the service provided by Lloyds TSB could be divided into two categories:

- dealing with new business; and
- post acceptance functions,

with the greater part of what it did relating to the former.

HMRC decided the supplies by Lloyds TSB to Volkswagen were not exempt as the *making arrangements for the granting of credit* in Grp. 5, item 5 (as it then was). They also, said item 5 had to be construed consistently with art. 13(B)(d)(1) (art. 135(1)(b)) and that the services provided were not predominantly *negotiations* but *management of credit*. It was not disputed that the supply of services was a single composite supply.

The Court, however, dismissing the HMRC appeal, found the predominant nature of the single supply was as Lloyds TSB maintained the following.

(1) Although there was some management of credit, the main character of the package was in the fundamental functions of arranging deals, checking creditworthiness and settling the precise terms.

(2) Merely adding up the defined elements in the package and seeing how many fell within the exemption and how many did not would not take account of the relative importance of the individual elements in the total package.

(3) Nor should one look solely at the cost of the individual ingredients or the staff time devoted to them, although that should be taken into account.

(4) The package of supplies considered as a whole and taking account of all the relevant circumstances, the predominant character of Lloyds TSB's business was negotiation of credit within the exemption.

Leave to appeal to the Court of Appeal was refused.

(a) Credit and charge cards companies

As one might imagine, credit and charge card operations, which tend to be heavily reliant on communications, data processing and shared support, are a prime example of the sort of arrangements that might be seen as *mere physical or technical supplies* such as data-handling. A number of other supplies will typically also arise relating to the authorisation, settlement and interchange arrangements. Some are between the card companies and organisations such as VISA or Mastercard and FDR.

- Base 1 fees are essentially for the authorisation of individual card transactions;
- Base 2, for the arrangement of settlements; and
- interchange fees are fees both received and paid by the card-issuing companies.

They arise where one card company's cardholder effects a transaction at another's retail outlet, thus making use of the latter's merchant agreements. They effectively represent, therefore, a sharing of the merchant discount and are treated as VAT-exempt.

Historically, HMRC had regarded Base 1 fees as taxable at the standard-rate and the remainder as exempt. The treatment of Base 1 fees had seemed to many, arguably, incorrect. However, a successful appeal by FDR following the line taken in *Sparekassernes Datacenter* has shown this to be incorrect.

- In *C & E Commrs v FDR Ltd* [2000] BVC 311, the appellant's business consisted of providing services to banks, which fell into two categories:
    - services to banks issuing credit or debit cards to cardholders; and
    - services to banks (acquirers) contracting with merchants (normally retailers) to acquire vouchers accepted by those merchants in payment for goods and services.

  The facts of the case were complex. However, in essence, FDR acted as a clearing house for credit and debit card transactions involving its clients, card issuers or acquirers, effecting settlement of their net positions and supplying related services.

  Fees were charged at various levels, depending on the degree of service required. Both FDR and HMRC accepted there was a core supply, but differed as to what it was and how it should be treated for VAT. HMRC contended the core service was predominantly bookkeeping, accountancy and reporting and not within the exemption in art. 13(B)(d)(3) (now art. 135(1)(d) of the Council Directive (Directive 2006/112/EC)), i.e.:

  > 'transactions, including negotiation, concerning deposit and current accounts, payments, transfers, debts, cheques and other negotiable instruments, but excluding debt collection and factoring'

  as no money was paid, nor liabilities discharged.

The Tribunal had held the taxpayer made an exempt core supply, to which various other services were *ancillary*, to both issuers and acquirers. This *core supply* consisted of 'processing all their card transactions and settling their liabilities and claims under these transactions in accordance with the obligations of the issuers and acquirers'. The Court of Appeal agreed:

- FDR's functions were identical to functions, which would have been exempt if carried out by the banks themselves. In settling the card transactions for cardholders' accounts and between banks, transfers were effected within the meaning of the Sixth VAT Directive, art. 13(B)(d)(3) (art. 135(1)(d) of Council Directive 2006/112/EC of 28 November 2006) in the same way as if, as between all the acquirers, issuers and payment systems, each debt had been the subject of individual credit and debit entries in each account. The decision in *Sparekassernes Datacenter (SDC) v Skatteministeriet* (Case C-2/95) [1997] BVC 509 (see earlier at 70-100) was followed.
- The Tribunal's identification of FDR's core supply as the processing of card transactions and settling liabilities and claims was justified. *Card Protection Plan Ltd v C & E Commrs* (Case C-349/96) [1999] BVC 155 (see 30-150), *C & E Commrs v Madgett (t/a Howden Court Hotel)* (Joined Cases 96 and C-94/97) [1998] BVC 458 and *C & E Commrs v Wellington Private Hospital Ltd* [1997] BVC 251 were considered.
- The core supply, as identified, consisting in the movement of money between cardholder, merchant, issuer and acquirer for the convenience of the cardholder and the profit of the other three parties. It amounted to an *outsourced* banking function and was to be regarded as falling within art. 13(B)(d)(3) of the Sixth VAT Directive (art. 135(1)(d) of Council Directive 2006/112/EC of 28 November 2006).

In short, the key, as in *Lloyds TSB*, was the application of the tests in *Sparekassernes Datacenter*. The clear inference is that HMRC had been placing too restricted a view on the available exemptions (see the observations at 70-100 earlier), something it remains important to watch out for and which seems to have been borne out in the *Smarter Money Ltd v R & C Commrs* [2006] BVC 4,098.

Following *FDR*, HMRC entered into consultations with the financial sector and the professions over the way in which the UK exemptions have been drafted. These eventually culminated in changes to Exemption Group 5 from 16 June 2003 by the *VAT (Finance) Order* 2003 (SI 2003/1568). This removed the former Statutory Note 2B, and has meant that a relevant supply of financial services will be taxed or exempted according to its overall character instead of by reference to the presence or absence of a service listed in Note 2B.

Back-office functions often entail more mundane computer-based administration systems and customer service centres that, again, have frequently been seen as taxable and failing the *mere physical or technical* test. However, that can be a superficial approach, as the appeal in the *EDS* case has also shown.

- The appeal in *C & E Commrs v Electronic Data Systems Ltd* [2003] BVC 451 concerned a company supplying outsourced services to Lloyds Bank plc. Before 1997, the bank had granted loans to its customers through its network of branches. However, the computer system it had at the time could only enable it to offer one loan product, a fixed rate, fixed term loan. Wanting to expand its range, it decided to outsource this to someone, who could provide a central lending platform and a dedicated loan centre running, and being responsible for, the complete operation from initial contacts with borrowers to the eventual redemption and repayment of the loans. The Bank was to retain things like sales and marketing, setting credit policy and collecting loans and other legal and compliance issues.

HMRC saw what EDS supplied the Bank as taxable. They maintained the supplies of the grant or negotiation of credit were made by the Bank, not by EDS, whose services were those of a call centre. They accepted loan protection insurance sold by EDS when dealing with loan applications was exempt. However, they argued those supplies were *ancillary* to the main standard-rated supplies and were thus wrapped up in a single composite taxable supply.

EDS, on the other hand, maintained its supplies to the Bank were exempt because:

- it granted or negotiated credit within the meaning of art. 13(B)(d)(1) of the Sixth VAT Directive (art. 135(1)(b) of Council Directive 2006/112/EC); or, alternatively
- it entered into transactions, including negotiation, concerning deposit and current accounts, payments, transfers and debts within the meaning of art. 13(B)(d)(3) (art. 135(1)(d));

EDS also argued its supplies under the insurance agreement were exempt under art. 13(B)(a) (art. 135(1)(a)) as *related services performed by insurance brokers and insurance agents*.

EDS won at the Tribunal on all counts.

- Its principal supplies to the Bank were the granting of credit within the meaning of art. 13(B)(d)(1) (art. 135(1)(b)), notwithstanding that the Bank itself was the actual lender.
- Were they to be wrong in that, however; what EDS did was still exempt as the *negotiation of credit* within art. 13(B)(d)(1) (art. 135(1)(b)) or, alternatively, as *transactions, including negotiation, concerning deposit and current accounts, payments, transfers and debts* within art. 13(B)(d)(3) (art. 135(1)(d)).
- The insurance amounted to separately exempt supplies of insurance under art. 13(B)(a) (art. 135(1)(a)) and was not ancillary to a main supply of standard-rated services.

This was later confirmed, on appeal, by the Court of Appeal.

What was done by EDS, again, clearly had the crucial effect of altering the legal and financial situation of both the bank and its customers and satisfied the requirements established by the ECJ in *Sparekassernes Data Center* and *FDR*. A petition by HMRC to the House of Lords for permission for a further appeal was refused. HMRC guidance following the decision in EDS is that supplies by a business of the nature made by EDS are accepted as payment transfer services. However, to qualify for exemption the following conditions must be satisfied (HMRC VATFIN3135):

> 'To qualify for exemption, a business making a supply that consists of services to a loan provider prior to and after the granting of a loan must be undertaking all of the following functions as a central part of that supply:
>
> - the operation of bank accounts on behalf of the credit provider and
> - arranging the transfer of funds to the borrower and
> - the processing of loan repayments (and any additional charges or fees) received by direct debit or cheque.'

However, the outsourcing of the administration and collection of payments due under a closed loan book portfolio will be taxable debt collection services regardless of whether the loan is in default (see (b) below).

> **Practice point**
>
> In many cases, it will be a matter of fact and degree as to on which side of the line a particular situation falls.
>
> However, looking carefully at the context in which something is provided can be vital and it could well pay to adopt a constructive approach as to how things are presented and documented.
>
> Looking at a service in the round is important, rather than necessarily focussing on the component functions.
>
> It can also pay to ensure that what is outsourced goes far enough to take what is provided beyond being a mere physical or technical supply.

(b) Payments

The nature of the outsourcing arrangements in *R & C Commrs v Axa UK plc* (Case C-175/09) [2011] BVC 35 were sought to be structured so as to enable the services to fall within the finance exemption from VAT. However, in this case the outsourced services were considered to fall within the exception of 'debt collection and factoring' in art. 13B(d)(3) of the Sixth Directive (now art. 135(1)(d)) with the consequence that they were standard rated. The case is considered in detail at 70-200 (15). The outsourcing related to a payment plan operated by Denplan, which was part of Axa, and the issue arose as to whether collecting payments was within the scope of the exemption in, what is now, art. 135(1)(d) of the VAT Directive. The material facts were as follows:

- Denplan provided services for dental practices, and the principal service related to the operation of payment plans between dentists and their patients. Under the terms of the plans, dentists provided regular check ups and/or any necessary treatment, on a continuing basis against payment by those patients of a fixed monthly charge. The collection of payments formed part of several services provided by Denplan.
- Broadly, each payment plan would be entered into by a patient signing a contract with the dentist (which would be in a standard form produced by Denplan).
- The monthly charge would be paid by the patient to Denplan, as the dentist's agent, in receiving payments due to that dentist. Patients would complete a bank 'mandate' in favour of Denplan.
- Denplan would process the material financial information provided by a patient (including recording it to computer systems), Denplan collected the payments due from patients (via the Bankers' Automated Clearing System (BACS'), which involved sending the patient's bank account number and the amount which Denplan was to collect from that account). This would result in BACS posting a corresponding credit to Denplan's bank for the credit of Denplan's account. Denplan would also provides payment advices to dentists and contact the patients whose payments it has not received.
- Denplan on receipt of payment from patients would then account to each dentist for the payments it was entitled to from patients subject to agreed deductions for fees. Part of the fees deducted from the patients' payments represented consideration for Denplan's

services in collecting payment for the dentists (namely, services of seeking payments from patients' bank accounts via BACS).

The Court decided that Denplan provided a single service, and that in principle the service was in the scope of the exemption concerning payments, unless it was a service of debt collection. The Court considered that the service was within the scope of the exemption in principle because:

> 'As regards the service in question in the main proceedings, it is appropriate to point out that its purpose is to benefit Denplan's clients, namely dentists, by the payment of the sums of money due to them from their patients. Denplan is, in return for remuneration, responsible for the recovery of those debts and provides a service of managing those debts for the account of those entitled to them (para.28 of the judgment).'

However, the Court concluded that the Denplan services fell within the scope of debt collection and were subject to standard rating. Specifically the Court commented:

> 'In fact, the object of that service is to benefit Denplan's clients, namely dentists, by payment of the sums of money due to them from their patients. That service is therefore intended to obtain the payment of debts. By undertaking the recovery of debts for the account of those entitled to them, Denplan frees its clients of tasks which, without its intervention, those clients, as creditors, would have to perform themselves, tasks consisting in requesting the transfer of the sums due to them, via the direct debit system (para. 33 of the judgment).'

(3) Sales and call-centres

Sales and call-centres are a particular problem area, because they are often seen just as communications, information and customer relations; not as something integral to a larger activity. As such, they have the appearance of being taxable when supplied by a third-party provider. Whilst that can certainly be true, it is always worth looking at the supply in context and seeing if, taken as a whole, the tests in *Sparekassernes Data Center* and *Lloyds TSB* enable the apparent *taxable* elements to be treated as *ancillary* to something that might arguably fall within one or other of the VAT exemptions.

- The case of *Electronic Data Systems Ltd* discussed earlier provides a good illustration of what this entails. *EDS had* provided a dedicated call-centre, but this was just a means to an end, because what it really did was assume, for the Bank, complete responsibility for its loan operations, from initial contacts with borrowers to the eventual redemption and repayment. In terms of the *Sparekassernes Data Center* tests this entailed effecting changes in the legal and financial situation of the bank and its customers and went beyond a mere physical or technical supply.
- *Continuum (Europe) Ltd* [1998] BVC 2,131 (or CSC Financial Services Ltd, as it later came to be known) was another case in point. Continuum provided services to the Sun Alliance group by taking over its dealings with the public in connection with the issue of its Daisy PEP. It dealt with telephone enquiries, sent out application forms, checked them on return and then sent them to the PEP host administrator, which issued the units in the unit trust held within the PEP. The general public were unaware that what Continuum did had been outsourced by Sun Alliance.

> Continuum argued its services were exempt under Grp. 5, item 7 as *the making of arrangements for any transaction within item 6* and that its services were intrinsically linked with the supply

of securities; without them, there would be no supply of securities and, even they were too far removed from the issue of the securities, they were, nonetheless introduction services.

HMRC, however, said the services were standard-rated supplies of administration. Article 13(B)(d)(5) (art. 135(1)(f) of Council Directive 2006/112/EC) exempted 'transactions, *including negotiation, excluding management* and safekeeping, in shares, interests in companies and associations, debentures and other securities …' and Continuum did not negotiate any of the terms, introduce the investors or make arrangements for the issue of securities. All it did was arrange the marketing and administration of the PEP.

HMRC initially lost and the case ended up being referred to the ECJ, which considered the same analysis applied, mutatis mutandis, as in *Sparekassernes Data Center*. It went on to add that the words *including negotiation* in art. 13(B)(d)(5) (art 135(1)(f)) were clearly not intended to define the principal object of the exemption laid down in the provision, but to extend the scope of the exemption to negotiation. However, whilst it was not necessary to consider the precise meaning of the word *negotiation* (the purpose of which is to do all that is necessary in order for two parties to enter into a contract, without the negotiator having any interest of his own in the terms of the contract) it is not *negotiation* where, as in the case of CSC/Continuum, one of the parties entrusts to a sub-contractor some of the clerical formalities related to the contract, such as providing information to the other party and receiving and processing applications for subscription to the securities which form the subject-matter of the contract. In other words, as the Court put it in answer to the questions submitted to it:

- transactions in securities means transactions liable to create, alter or extinguish parties' rights and obligations in respect of securities;
- negotiation in securities does not cover services limited to providing information about a financial product and, as the case may be, receiving and processing applications for subscription, without issuing them.

At first glance, this Ruling of the Court may appear altogether bad news – and it was for CSC/Continuum. But, if viewed constructively, it may serve as a useful pointer for making the achievement of exemption easier to secure.

Practice point

Sparekassernes Datacenter succeeded because what it did was to alter the legal and financial situation as between the parties to the underlying transactions.

There was much the same situation in *FDR*.

But the reason CSC/Continuum failed, may have been because its services to Sun Alliance didn't go quite far enough.

- As noted by the Court, they were not authorised to provide advice, merely information.
- They also processed application forms submitted by prospective investors, checking that they had been properly filled in, and so forth.
- But what CSC/Continuum *did not* undertake were the formalities for issuing and transferring the securities, i.e. the units in the unit trust. These were carried out by another company altogether and one which was unconnected with CSC/Continuum, the PEP host administrator.

Had these latter functions been also contracted for with CSC/Continuum, it might have been hard for the Court to deny that the effect of what the company provided was to alter the legal and financial situation as between the parties to the underlying transactions.

Interestingly, HMRC have expressed the view that the *Teletech UK Ltd* decision on insurance, which went in favour of the taxpayer, has no implications for call centre services supplied to other sectors due to the unique nature of the insurance exemption. The implications for insurance will be touched on briefly below and explored more fully in **Chapter 9** at 90-350. Whether this is correct seems debatable.

- *Teletech UK Ltd* [2003] BVC 2,514 concerned fees received for insurance sold by *cold-call* telephone and, in particular, whether they were exempt (under art. 13(b)(a) of the Sixth Directive and VATA 1994, Sch. 9, Grp. 2, item 4) as the *services of an insurance agent* relative to provision of insurance (as Teletech maintained) or were taxable as promotion.

Teletech did work for a number of companies, amongst which was American Life Insurance Company (ALICO). Its staff *cold-called* individuals by telephone to try to sell them two types of insurance policies. Once a customer was persuaded and a Direct Debit Authorisation obtained, ALICO were immediately on risk, with no input, at that stage on their part. This was subject, of course, to the usual 30-day cooling-off period.

The way Teletech was remunerated was somewhat unusual in that, after being paid start-up costs, they got a fixed sum per employee, each of whom were expected to sell half of one policy per hour.

HMRC argued exemption was prevented by Note 7 to Exemption Group 2 (as advertising and promotional services), but this was rejected by the Tribunal as semantics. The Tribunal also rejected the suggestion that Teletech were not proper insurance agents because of the way they were paid. Teletech rightly won because the substance of what they did amounted to the provision of insurance-related services in the capacity of an agent or broker. *Sparekassernes Datacenter* does not appear to have been mentioned as HMRC's case was clearly flawed. However, the similarities with *Lloyds TSB* and *EDS* seem obvious.

Practice point

Not all outsourced marketing will be able to be brought within the exemption, of course.

At the end of the day, it all comes down to what is actually being done and how. As the CoJ decision in *R & C Commrs v Axa UK plc* (C-175/09) illustrates it is particularly important to review the nature of contractual arrangements to ensure that services fall within the scope of an exemption.

To achieve exemption, under Group 2 for insurance or Group 5 for Finance, it is important that what is done is sufficiently integral to the underlying exempt activity and the danger is that often what is done will not go quite far enough. If a service does not fall within the scope of an exemption, it is particularly important for the outsourcing contract to permit the supplier to charge VAT to its customer. If the contract does not permit VAT to be charged in addition to the agreed price for the services, then the supplier will have to account for VAT out of the consideration received from the customer.

(4) Joint Employment Contracts

One option for structuring outsourcing arrangements is for the services to be provided under a joint employment contract so that the service provider is not treated as making a supply. This form of structuring depends on the point that an economic activity must be conducted 'independently' with the result that employed persons are excluded since they are bound to an employer by a contract of employment (art. 10 of Council Directive 2006/112/EC). Additionally, the exclusion applies to 'other legal ties creating the relationship of employer and employee as regards working conditions, remuneration and the employer's liability' (art. 10 Council Directive 2006/112/EC).

Outsourcing arrangements involving information technology were sought to be structured as a joint employment contract in the case of *CGI Group (Europe) Ltd* [2010] UKFTT 396 (TC); [2011] TC 00678 . HMRC successfully challenged the arrangements so that VAT was due on the amounts paid by the customer to the service provider. The matter was not appealed to the Upper Tier Tribunal. In this case part of the payment to the service provider was designed as a recharge of salary and other employment costs. The Tribunal held that the payment made by Cox was for the provision of services under the control and direction of CGI.

The material facts were as follows:

- Cox Services Limited (renamed Equity Insurance Group Limited) (Cox) outsourced the operation of its information technology department to CGI Group (Europe) Limited (CGI).
- Cox's principal business was insurance, and prior to entering into the outsourcing arrangements with CGI it operated an IT department with 200 employees. In order to focus on their core business, Cox transferred all the IT employees to CGI, which was subject to the Transfer of Undertakings (Protection of Employment) Regulations 1981. CGI offered the employees joint employment with itself and Cox and they accepted by signing a contract.
- Cox entered into a master services agreement with CGI for a 10 year term, whereby Cox, as supplier, agreed to provide the following services (summarised at para. 3 of the judgment):

    '2.1 Common server services [followed by these bullet points:] Operations; Production control and scheduling; General technical support; Capacity planning; Data base management and support; Online storage management; External storage media management; Off-site media storage management; Centralised printing; Centralised printing fulfilment; Distributed printing; Backup and recovery services 2.2 End user computing [followed by these bullet points:] End user support infrastructure support at agreed locations; Remote user support; Installs, Moves, Adds, Changes (IMACs). 2.3 Telecommunications [followed by these bullet points:] Technical support – voice; Technical support – LAN; Network operations; Mobile phone services. 2.4 Application services [followed by these bullet points:] Application emergency, corrective and preventative maintenance; Application development; Application maintenance for third party applications retained by the Customer; Practices and procedures. 2.5 Cross functional services [followed by these bullet points:] Project Management; Service desk support; Incident management; Problem

management; Configuration planning; Release management; Request management (request for service); System change management; Facilities management and support; Physical security management; System security management; Enterprise systems management; Disaster recovery; Yearly planning; Procurement; Equipment maintenance; Administration; 3rd party contract administration/ management; Asset management of defined assets.'
- The charge for these arrangements was determined in accordance with a pricing schedule to the agreement. The charging reflected an annual base charge plus several further components. An invoice would show separate staff salary re-charges (outside the scope of VAT), and other charges (liable to VAT). The additional components would show matters for specific charges, e.g. maintaining a specific number of desktop computers at a set charge for each, with adjustment for volume changes with a different additional charge for volume changes up to 15 per cent and between 15 per cent and 30 per cent (see generally para. 3(h) of the judgment).
- In relation to the remuneration of the employees, the master agreement specified that (see para. 3(m) of the judgment):

> '11.12 To the extent that payments made under this Agreement by the Customer to the Supplier are referable to services provided by a Joint Employee, such payments shall be made to the Supplier in its capacity as agent for the Customer in remuneration of such Joint Employee and not to the Supplier acting as principal on its own behalf.'

- Under the letter contract entered into by all former employees of Cox with CGI, the letter stated:

> 'You are employed by CGI Group (Europe) Limited (CGI) and Cox Services Limited (Cox) as your employers jointly and severally ("the employers"). In the event that the performance of your duties under your contract of employment requires you to work wholly on clients other than Cox, then on notice from CGI, Cox will cease to be your employer jointly with CGI and your employer from that date will be CGI solely (para. 2(5) of the judgment). '

The First-Tier Tax Tribunal decided in favour of HMRC. The Tribunal reached its decision on the basis of the following reasons:

- The Tribunal considered that a joint employment contract existed, so that both Cox and CGI were the employers of the employees. Indeed, they considered that it was irrelevant as to how the employers agreed that the obligations were split between them (para. 10 of the judgment).
- The correct approach to determining the VAT treatment is to:'start with the contractual position and then test whether this really reflects "the precise way in which performance satisfies the interests of the parties' (para. 14 of the judgment).
- The Tribunal identified the following material facts arising out of the arrangements between Cox and CGI in connection with the employees (para. 14 of the judgment): The Master Services Agreement is an agreement for providing the Services in accordance with service levels. So far as the staff are concerned the following provisions are relevant:

> '(1) At the start the employees working on the services supplied under the Master Services Agreement were Cox's former employees who became the Appellant's employees by TUPE and then Cox's employees jointly by agreement. The Appellant must not change their terms of service in the first six months without Cox's consent. The Appellant could not dismiss Key Employees (as defined) in the first 12 months. (2) By agreement between the

two employers, new employees spending a regular amount of time each month on Cox's business are to be made joint employees. And on ceasing to spend a regular amount of time each month on Cox's business there is provision for discussions leading to their becoming the Appellant's sole employees or being made redundant. By agreement with the employee if the performance of the duties requires a joint employee to work wholly on clients other than Cox then on notice from the Appellant, Cox ceases to be his employer jointly with CGI and the employer becomes the Appellant solely. (3) The Appellant has control over all aspects of the employment of joint employees. (4) The Services are provided through Supplier Personnel defined as any person in respect of whom the Supplier [the Appellant] exercises control including, but not limited to the Supplier's directors, employees and agents and the Sub-Contractors of the Supplier, in any such case who are assigned or engaged by the Supplier from time to time to perform the Supplier's obligations under this Agreement. While not mentioning the joint employees specifically they are included because they are the Appellant's employees and the Appellant exercises control over them. Presumably it also includes the Appellant's sole employees who spend less than a regular amount of time each month on Cox's business. The appointment of Supplier Personnel and the nature and duration of their assignment is at the Appellant's discretion. Cox could only request the Appellant to replace any Supplier Personnel who has shown evidence of incompetence. (5) The employment costs of joint staff are paid by the Appellant as agent which re-charges an amount that is calculated to reflect the staff time used for Cox's benefit. (6) There is no agreement with Cox to manage the joint staff as such; it is merely a consequence of the staff being under the Appellant's control.'

- The Tribunal considered that the 'substance and reality' of the arrangements were that CGI was doing far more than supervising Cox's employees. In particular, the Tribunal noted that (at para. 16 of the judgment):

  'one starts with the Appellant agreeing to provide the Services in accordance with the specified service levels, this implies that when doing so the staff are effectively working solely for the Appellant and not for Cox (even though for the benefit of Cox). The staff are a major ingredient in making this supply. The Appellant needs to have control over whether a particular member of the staff will work on Cox business or something else, which is consistent with the contractual position of its appointing Supplier Personnel and determining the nature and duration of their assignment. This goes much further than managing Cox's staff and demonstrates that whether they are working for the benefit of Cox or someone else, they are working for the Appellant. We consider that this is the substance and reality of the arrangement and paying the staff as agent is not consistent with it.'

- The Tribunal decided that the essential aspect of the arrangements was a single supply of the services, for which the human resources element provided by CGI was an essential element. This was with the consequence that CGI was providing the services solely as principal, and not as Cox's agent when paying the employees. Accordingly, VAT was payable on the consideration paid by Cox to CGI.

The use of contracts of employment to eliminate unnecessary VAT costs is an acceptable form of planning. However, it is necessary to ensure that the arrangements reflect the true economic position of an employer and employee relationship. For example, in the CGI Group (Europe) Limited case the First Tier Tribunal accepted that Cox could have retained its employees, and entered into an agreement with a third party to manage the employees (with the consent of the employees, if required) so that VAT would only be payable on the fees attributable to the service of managing the employees, and the payment by Cox of its employees' salaries would be outside the scope of VAT (see para. 12 of the judgment).

(5) Affinity

Mention was made earlier of three cases following *Sparekassernes Datacenter*. Two have been referred to already, the third, that of *Civil Service Motoring Association*, was not, strictly, outsourcing, but related to affinity cards.

- *C & E Commrs v Civil Service Motoring Association* [1998] BVC 21 concerned a non-profit making non-charitable voluntary association providing motoring and other services to its members. In 1990 CSMA negotiated an agreement with a banking group, FBS, to provide its members with a credit card scheme on favourable terms. The banking group paid CSMA a commission for introducing its members to the banking group's credit card scheme and was granted the right to develop, market and issue an affinity card bearing the CSMA logo, with the object of encouraging the CSMA members to take up the card.

CSMA also worked with FBS under what was described as a *partnership agreement* in the areas of customer handling, marketing, setting prices, discussing interest rates, negotiating the provision of benefits, providing an arbitration service and holding joint discussions on operational and market issues for the protection of its members.

At issue was whether CSMA was liable for VAT on the commission received or whether it fell within the exemption for credit transactions in Grp. 5 of what was then VATA 1983, Sch. 6, provisions intended to implement art. 13(B)(d)(1) of the Sixth VAT Directive (art. 135(1)(b) of Council Directive 2006/112/EC), namely:

> 'the granting and the negotiation of credit and the management of credit by the person granting it;'

HMRC said the exemption should be narrowly construed and limited to intermediaries bringing together the principals to a transaction and arranging particular exempt transactions between them for the specific grant of credit. It did not extend to the supply of a general preparatory marketing arrangement to develop credit products. Alternatively, they said there was sufficient ambiguity in the term *negotiation of credit* in art. 13(B) of the Sixth VAT Directive (art. 135(1) of Council Directive 2006/112/EC), to justify a reference to the ECJ.

It was held, dismissing the HMRC appeal that:

(1) Neither the purpose, nor the context of the exemption justified a restricted meaning for the wide general language of the Sixth VAT Directive and of VATA 1983. The expressions *negotiation of credit* and *making of arrangements* for any transaction for granting of any credit were not to be construed as implicitly limited to particular transactions for a specific grant of credit. Both referred to activities leading directly to the granting of credit.

(2) What CSMA did in return for the commission could reasonably and sensibly be described as negotiation of, or making arrangements for the granting of credit. There was no distinction between the negotiation, or making arrangements for particular transactions for the specific grant of any credit and these negotiations or arrangements designed for the specific purpose of leading directly to the grant of credit CSMA members.

(3) Although the ECJ had not given a ruling on the particular point, the Sixth VAT Directive was accurately reflected in the provisions of VATA 1983 and was sufficiently clear to enable this appeal to be determined without a further Reference.

Leave to appeal to the House of Lords was refused.

The line in CSMA was also, incidentally, later followed in *BAA plc* [2001] BVC 2,405, where the Tribunal held, that services provided in relation to a Bank of Scotland affinity credit card were VAT-exempt. The Sixth VAT Directive (Directive 77/388), art. 13(B) (art. 135(1) of Council Directive 2006/112/EC) was not intended to be restrictive and art. 13(B)(d)(1) (art. 135(1)(b)) did not require the credit to be granted to the person who arranges it. This was subsequently upheld on appeal by the High Court in February 2002 (*C & E Commrs v BAA plc* [2002] BVC 463 and the Court of Appeal in December 2005 (*C & E Commrs v BAA plc; Institute of Directors v C & E Commrs* [2003] BVC 112) (see 70-200(1) above).

(6) Insurance

The question of outsourcing is equally, if not more, important for insurance, where input tax recovery rates tend to be especially low. In theory, although the wording of the insurance exemptions in both EU and UK law are different to the corresponding rules on finance, it seems reasonable to suppose that, ultimately, whether an outsourced service is taxable or exempt should still depend on the nature and context of what is supplied. In this respect, the principles that emerged from cases like *Sparekassernes Datacenter*, *Lloyds TSB*, *FDR* and *EDS* must arguably be persuasive.

To date, however, there have been two cases, *Försäkringsaktiebolaget Skandia (publ)* (Case C-240/99) [2001] BVC 281 and *Staatssecretaris van Financiën v Arthur Andersen & Co. Accountants c.s.* (Case C-472/03) [2006] BVC 228 that have, significantly, gone against the taxpayer. Quite possibly, in the *Skandia* case this may have been because of the questions that were asked of the Court, rather than what was being supplied. In the case of *Arthur Andersen & Co*, it may not have helped that the consulting arm of a firm of accountants was involved; perhaps also it was a matter of not enough being assumed by the supplier of the service.

There is more commentary on outsourcing as it affects insurance in **Chapter 9** at 90-350.

(7) The Commission proposals on finance and insurance

A draft proposal for a new Directive (amending Council Directive 2006/112/EC as regards financial and insurance services) was published on 28 November 2007 (which is reproduced in **Appendix 3**). In addition, the Commission also published extensive draft Regulations, which were issued with the version of the draft directive that was published on 16 July 2007 (not reproduced here), which can be found on the Commission website at http://ec.europa.eu/taxation_customs/resources/documents/common/consultations/tax/working_paper_definitions_en.pdf. For details of the current status of the proposed directive published on 28 November 2007 information is available on the European Parliament website at: www.europarl.europa.eu.

The effect of the proposals is to replace points (a) to (g) in art. 135(1) by the following compromise text (published on 30 September 2011 as FISC 122 (see **Appendix 3**)):

'(a) insurance and reinsurance [and transfer of insurance and reinsurance contracts];
(b) granting of credit and management of credit by the creditor;
(c) guaranteeing of debt and provision of any other surety bonds;
(d) transfer of a credit position and assumption of a debt position and excluding debt collection;
(e) financial transfer;
(f) financial deposit taking and account operation;;
(g) currency exchange and provision of cash;
(ga) transactions in securities, excluding their safekeeping and management;
(gaa) transactions in interests in companies and associations other than securities, excluding their safekeeping and management;
(gb) transactions in financial derivatives, excluding their safekeeping and management;
(gc) management of investment funds and pension funds established within the territory of the Community;
(gd) intermediation in insurance and financial transactions as referred to in points (a) to (gb)'

A new art. 135a will then qualify how the exemption in points (a) to (g) is to be applied and, in particular, provides that:

'(8) "Intermediation in insurance and financial transactions" shall mean the supply of services rendered to, and remunerated by, a contractual party as a distinct act of mediation in relation to the insurance or financial transactions referred to in points (a) to (e) of Article 135(1), by a third party intermediary; .'

How these will affect the present treatment remains to be seen, particularly as these proposals are still officially draft. However, for the moment, it seems likely that the effect of cases like *Sparekassernes Datacenter, Card Protection Plan* and *FDR* may still hold good.

The Council of the European Union have been consulting on amendments to the proposals as regards insurance and financial services, and the current status of these discussions can be accessed on the European Council Register Consilium website (http://register.consilium.europa.eu). Appendix 3 also contains a compromise text proposed by the Council of the European Union on the VAT treatment of insurance and financial services, which reflects proposed amendments to the text published on 28 November 2007 (the text is sourced from Interinstitutional File 2007/0267 (CNS): LIMITE FISC 11 (1 February 2011)). FISC 11 discloses proposals relating to the scope of the original concepts, and provides further clarification on key terms contained in the draft proposed amendments. LIMITE FISC 127 (Interinstitutional File 2007/0267 (CNS)) (7 October 2011) provides an update on progress in

7 Banks and Financial Institutions

connection with the Draft Directive, and identifies four major outstanding issues of political importance, namely the treatment of 1) transfer of insurance and reinsurance contract portfolios, 2) outsourcing, 3) management of investment funds and 4) derivatives. The nature of these issues are referred to in FISC 127, which is reproduced in Appendix 3. Since there are no final draft proposals, this edition will not comment on the amendments due to the developing nature of the draft provisions. However, it is possible for the reader to track the progress of evolving discussions by referring to LIMITE FISC 100 (11 July 2011), LIMITE FISC 124 (30 September 2011), LIMITE 141 (14 November 2011) and additional papers as they are released onto the Council website.

Summary

This Chapter has considered the principal VAT issues affecting banks and other financial institutions, apart from those relating to investment, which are dealt with in Chapter 8, insurance in Chapter 9 and commodities and financial derivatives in Chapter 10.

As with other areas in this book, the important thing is often to establish precisely what a particular transaction or activity involves and what the legal and commercial relationships really entail. Only then is it possible to establish the correct VAT position.

8 Securities, Property and Investment

> **Overview**
>
> **This Chapter considers:**
>
> (1) The nature of investment.
>
> (2) The application of EU and UK law to:
>
> (a) financial investments; and
> (b) property.
>
> (3) Issues affecting particular supplies.
>
> (4) Some particular issues for:
>
> (a) brokers and dealers;
> (b) investment managers;
> (c) investment and unit trusts.
>
> (5) Pension funds.

80-000 What is involved?

Capital and investment are vital to the function of the City. The security markets, in particular, are an important focus for those either seeking or providing finance. Apart from the International Stock Exchange, there is also an Alternative Investment Market, each catering for the differing needs of different types and sizes of business requiring capital. Some securities, Eurobonds for example, are also actively traded directly by telephone or by computer-based services such as Reuters.

But investment is not just about shares and securities. It is also about property and development and all that that entails.

The major investors are, as might be expected, the large institutional investors: insurance companies, pension funds and investment and unit trusts. At the other extreme, there are a large number of private investors.

Facilitating all of this are brokers, market-makers, investment banks, merchant banks and issuing houses who, in their various capacities, promote and underwrite flotations and new issues and operate the primary and secondary markets.

80-050 General VAT liability issues

Investment, for the most part, falls broadly into two main categories:

- financial investments; and
- property.

Each is inherently exempt, with the result that any input VAT incurred on related costs is often largely irrecoverable. Property, however, is very much a mixed situation, zero-rating, which was once an important feature to be reckoned with, has now largely disappeared except in certain limited situations discussed later at 80-150(3).

Investment can also extend to commodities and financial contracts, many of which will be taxable in VAT terms. This, however, tends to be a highly specialised area and is considered later in **Chapter 10**.

80-100 Financial investments

The supplies falling under the first of the two main headings in 80-050 will mainly involve loans and long-term advances and securities. For the most part, these will be basically exempt from VAT, regardless of the capacity in which they are made. As with many of the other areas covered by this book, however, the ultimate VAT position can depend very much on what precisely any given transaction amounts to and on the circumstances of the parties concerned.

(1) Exemption

In common with many of the areas covered in the previous chapter, the exemption provisions of most concern originate in Art. 135(1) of Directive 2006/112/EC (formerly, Art. 13(B)(d) of the Sixth VAT Directive (Directive 77/388)). In particular Art. 135(1)(b)(d)(f) and (g) (formerly, Art. 13(B)(d)(1), (3), (5) and (6)) applies to:

- '(b) the granting and the negotiation of credit and the management of credit by the person granting it; ...
- (d) transactions, including negotiation, concerning deposit and current accounts, payments, transfers, debts, cheques and other negotiable instruments, but excluding debt collection; ...
- (f) transactions, including negotiation, but not management or safekeeping, in shares, interests in companies or associations, debentures and other securities, but excluding documents establishing title to goods and the rights or securities referred to in article 15(2);
- (g) management of special investment funds as defined by Member States.'

The EU Implementing Regulation provides that the sale of an option as a financial instrument, which is within the scope of Art. 135(1)(f), is a supply of services (Art. 9), and that the supply of services is distinct from the underlying transactions to which the services relate.

In applying the exemption it is important to bear in mind the following points:

- the exemptions mentioned in Art. 135 of the VAT Directive (previously Art. 13 of the Sixth Directive) represent independent concepts of EU law, whose purpose is to avoid divergences in the application of the VAT system between one Member State and another (Case C-259/11 *DTZ Zadelhoff vof v Staatssecretaris van Financiën*, para. 19, Case C-349/96 CPP [1999] ECR I-973, para. 15, and Case C-540/09 *Skandinaviska Enskilda Banken* [2011] ECR I-0000, para. 19);
- the exemption must be interpreted strictly because they are exceptions to the general principle that VAT is to be levied on all services supplied for consideration by a taxable person (Case C-259/11 *DTZ Zadelhoff vof v Staatssecretaris van Financiën*, para. 20, Case C-472/03 *Staatssecretaris van Financiën v Arthur Andersen & Co* [2005] ECR I-1719, para 24);
- their interpretation must be consistent with the objectives pursued by the exemptions provided for in Art. 135 of the VAT Directive, and comply with the requirements of the principle of fiscal neutrality inherent in the common system of VAT. As stated in Case C-259/11 *DTZ Zadelhoff vof v Staatssecretaris van Financiën* at para. 21: '... the requirement of strict interpretation does not mean that the terms used to specify the exemptions referred to in Article 13 [now Art. 135] should be construed in such a way as to deprive the exemptions of their intended effect'.

(a) The Commission proposals and scope of UK provisions

A draft proposal for a new Directive (amending Council Directive 2006/112/EC as regards financial and insurance services) was published on 28 November 2007 (which is reproduced in **Appendix 3**). In addition, the Commission also published extensive draft Regulations, which were issued with the version of the draft directive that was published on 16 July 2007 (not reproduced here), which can be found on the Commission website at http://ec.europa.eu/taxation_customs/resources/documents/common/consultations/tax/working_paper_definitions_en.pdf. For details of the current status of the proposed directive published on 28 November 2007 information is available on the European Parliament website at: www.europarl.europa.eu.

The effect of the proposals is to replace points (a) to (g) in art. 135(1) by the following compromise text (published on 30 September 2011 as FISC 122):

'(a) Insurance and reinsurance [and transfer of insurance and reinsurance contracts];
(b) granting of credit and management of credit by the creditor;
(c) guaranteeing of debt and provision of any other surety bonds;
(d) transfer of a credit position and assumption of a debt position and excluding debt collection;
(e) financial transfer;
(f) financial deposit taking and account operation;;
(g) currency exchange and provision of cash;
(ga) transactions in securities, excluding their safekeeping and management;
(gaa) transactions in interests in companies and associations other than securities, excluding their safekeeping and management;
(gb) transactions in financial derivatives, excluding their safekeeping and management;
(gc) management of investment funds and pension funds established within the territory of the Community;
(gd) intermediation in insurance and financial transactions as referred to in points (a) to (gb)'

8 Securities, Property and Investment

The draft art. 135 1(a) to (c) then goes on to specify when the exemption will apply to supplies which involve an insurance or financial service:

'1a The exemption provided for in points (a) to (e) of paragraph 1 shall apply to the supply of any constituent element of an insurance or financial service, which constitutes a distinct whole and has the specific and essential character of the exempt service.

1b Where a complex transaction includes an element of insurance which is set out separately, the insurance shall be a distinct service exempted under point (a) of paragraph 1.

1c Where the supply of goods or services includes the granting of credit which is not set out separately, the grant of credit shall not be a distinct service exempted under point (b) of paragraph 1.'

A new art. 135a will then qualify how the exemption in points (a) to (g) is to be applied and, in particular, provides that:

'8 "supply of securities" means the supply of tradable instruments other than an instrument establishing title to goods or to the rights referred to in Article 15(2), representing financial value and reflecting any one or more of the following: (a) an equity ownership position in a company or other association; (b) a creditor's position for debts; (c) unit ownership in undertakings for collective investment in the securities referred to in points (a) or (b), in other exempted financial instruments referred to in points (a) to (d) of Article 135(1) or in other undertakings for collective investment;

9 "intermediation in insurance and financial transactions" means the supply of services rendered to, and remunerated by, a contractual party as a distinct act of mediation in relation to the insurance or financial transactions referred to in points (a) to (e) of Article 135(1), by a third party intermediary;

10 "investment funds" means undertakings for collective investment in the exempted financial instruments referred to in points (a) to (e) of Article 135(1) and in real estate;

11 "management of investment funds" means activities aimed at realising the investment objectives of the investment fund concerned.'

The Council of the European Union have been consulting on amendments to the proposals as regards insurance and financial services, and the current status of these discussions can be accessed on the European Council Register Consilium website (http://register.consilium.europa.eu). Appendix 3 also contains a compromise text proposed by the Council of the European Union on the VAT treatment of insurance and financial services, which reflects proposed amendments to the text published on 28 November 2007 (the text is sourced from Interinstitutional File 2007/0267 (CNS): LIMITE FISC 11 (1 February 2011)). FISC 11 discloses proposals relating to the scope of the original concepts, and provides further clarification on key terms contained in the draft proposed amendments. LIMITE FISC 127 (Interinstitutional File 2007/0267 (CNS)) (7 October 2011) provides an update on progress in connection with the Draft Directive, and identifies four major outstanding issues of political importance, namely the treatment of (1) transfer of insurance and reinsurance contract portfolios, (2) outsourcing, (3) management of investment funds and (4) derivatives. The nature of these issues is referred to in FISC 127, which is reproduced in **Appendix 3**. Since there are no final draft proposals, this edition will not comment on the amendments due to the developing nature of the draft provisions. However, it is possible for the reader to track the progress of evolving discussions by referring to LIMITE FISC 100 (11 July 2011), LIMITE

FISC 124 (30 September 2011), LIMITE 141 (14 November 2011) and additional papers as they are released onto the Council website.

The provisions in UK law corresponding to art. 135(1)(b), (d), (f) and (g) of Council Directive 2006/112/EC are to be found in VATA 1994, Sch. 9, Grp. 5 (the nature of the provisions relating to debt securities were considered in detail in **Chapter 7**). So far as it relates to investment, this provides:

(i) In relation to short-or long-term advances or deposits (items 1, 2, 2A, 5 and 5A)

'1   1 The issue, transfer or receipt of, or any dealing with, money, any security for money or any note or order for the payment of money.

2   2 The making of any advance or the granting of any credit... .

5   5 The provision of intermediary services in relation to any transaction comprised in item 1, 2, 3, 4 or 6 (whether or not any such transaction is finally concluded) by a person acting in an intermediary capacity.

5A   5A The underwriting of an issue within item 1 or any transaction within item 6.'

Item 1 covers bills of exchange and promissory notes, sterling commercial paper and Euronotes or Euro commercial paper and will apply both to new issues for the purposes of raising capital and to sales on the secondary markets.

Item 2 deals with short-or long-term advances, indebtedness or deposits.

Examples will include local authority loans, mortgages and building society deposits.

Although following the *Kretztechnik AG v Finanzamt Linz* case anything of this kind is, itself, not a supply. HMRC's guidance on the case is as follows (VATSC97600):

'Following the European Court of Justice ruling in *Kretztechnik*, where a business has issued another type of security, such as bonds, debentures or loan notes, to raise capital for its business activities these issues are also no longer to be treated as supplies. The VAT treatment to be applied to such issues is exactly the same as that to be applied to issues of shares.'

(ii) In relation to securities (items 5A, 6, 7, 9 and 10)

'5A   The underwriting of an issue within item 1 or any transaction within item 6.

6   The issue, transfer or receipt of, or any dealing with, any security or secondary security being

   (a) shares, stocks, bonds, notes (other than promissory notes), debentures, debenture stock or shares in an oil royalty; or
   (b) any document relating to money, in any currency, which has been deposited with the issuer or some other person, being a document which recognises an obligation to pay a stated amount to bearer or to order, with or without interest, and being a document by the delivery of which, with or without endorsement, the right to receive that stated amount, with or without interest, is transferable; or
   (c) any bill, note or other obligation of the Treasury or of a Government in any part of the world, being a document by the delivery of which, with or without endorsement, title is transferable, and not being an obligation which is or has been legal tender in any part of the world; or

(d) any letter of allotment or rights, any warrant conferring an option to acquire a security included in this item, any renounceable or scrip certificates, rights coupons, coupons representing dividends or interest on such a security, bond mandates or other documents conferring or containing evidence of title to or rights in respect of such a security; or

(e) units or other documents conferring rights under any trust established for the purpose, or having the effect of providing, for persons having funds available for investment, facilities for the participation by them as beneficiaries under the trust, in any profits or income arising from the acquisition, holding, management or disposal of any property whatsoever.

7 [Omitted by SI 1999/594, art. 4, operative in respect of supplies made on or after 10 March 1999.]

9 The management of

(a) an authorised open-ended investment company; or
(b) an authorised unit trust scheme; or
(c) a Gibraltar collective investment scheme that is not an umbrella scheme; or
(d) a sub-fund of any other Gibraltar collective investment scheme; or
(e) an individually recognised overseas scheme that is not an umbrella scheme; or
(f) a sub-fund of any other individually recognised overseas scheme; or
(g) a recognised collective investment scheme authorised in a designated country or territory that is not an umbrella scheme; or
(h) a sub-fund of any other recognised collective investment scheme authorised in a designated country or territory; or
(i) a recognised collective investment scheme constituted in another EEA state that is not an umbrella scheme; or
(j) a sub-fund of any other recognised collective investment scheme constituted in another EEA state.

10 The management of a close-ended collective investment undertaking.'

It is intended that Item 9, Group 5 of Sch. 9 to VATA will be amended to include the management of an authorised contractual scheme (ACS), and this will take effect by the *Value Added Tax (Finance) Order* 2012 once the *Collective Investment in Transferable Securities (Contractual Scheme) Regulations* 2012 are brought into force. An ACS is a form of collective investment scheme.

Underwriting in the context of of item 5A includes sub-underwriting. The exemption applies to services provided in relation to both the traditional form of equity underwriting where the underwriter, or sub-underwriter, guarantees that an agreed proportion of the issue will be subscribed for and also to the bought deal arrangements more commonly used in the case of bonds. Some of the considerations that can arise in this area are considered later at 80-200(24).

The exemption in item 6 is limited to supplies of securities undertaken as principal, i.e. on one's own behalf rather than as agent. It will thus cover:

- the raising of capital by the issue of shares, stocks or bonds;
- the sale of such instruments on the secondary markets or otherwise; and
- transactions such as securities lending,

and not brokers' services in such contexts.

In the context of item 9 *authorised open-ended* and *investment company* and *authorised unit trust scheme* have the same meanings as in s. 237(3) of the *Financial Services and Markets Act* 2000. Similarly, *collective investment scheme* has the same meaning as in s. 235 of the *Financial Services and Markets Act* 2000. Other definitions used for item 9, such as 'recognised collective investment scheme' are provided by Note (6) to Group 5.

In terms of the issue of shares or securities it is clear from the Rulings of the ECJ in *KapHag Renditefonds v Finanzamt Charlottenburg* (Case C-442/01) [2005] BVC 566 and *Kretztechnik AG v Finanzamt Linz* (Case C-465/03) [2006] BVC 66 that this is not, itself a supply where the purpose of the issue is to raise finance.

- In *KapHag*, decided in June 2003, the issues concerned the concepts of *economic activity* and whether there was a supply of services for consideration when a partnership admitted a new partner in return for a contribution in cash. The finding of the Court was that the mere acquisition of financial holdings in other undertakings did not amount to the exploitation of property for the purpose of obtaining income therefrom on a continuing basis, because any dividend yielded by that holding was merely the result of ownership of the property. It followed that the entry of a new partner into a partnership in consideration for a contribution in cash, in circumstances such as those of the main case, did not constitute an economic activity within the meaning of the Sixth Directive, on the part of the partner.

    If the taking of shares did not in itself constitute an *economic activity* within the meaning of the Sixth Directive, the same had to be true of activities consisting in the transfer of such shares. The admission of a new partner into a partnership did not therefore constitute a supply of services to him. In that context, it was irrelevant whether the admission of the new partner was regarded as the act of the partnership itself or as that of the other partners, since the admission of a new partner did not in any event constitute a supply of services for consideration for the purposes of the Directive.

- The later Reference in *Kretztechnik,* decided in May 2005, involved a case where a company increased its capital by the issue of bearer shares, the dispute being over whether there was a right to deduct input tax under art. 17(1) and (2) of the Sixth VAT Directive (now art. 168 of Directive 2006/112) (see **Chapter 4**) in respect of the associated costs of advertising, agent's fees, and legal and technical advice.

    Adopting the same approach, the Court concluded that a company that issued new shares was increasing its assets by acquiring additional capital, whilst granting the new shareholders a right of ownership of part of the capital thus increased. From the issuing company's point of view, the aim was to raise capital and not to provide services.

    As far as the shareholder was concerned, payment of the sums necessary for the increase of capital was not a payment of consideration but an investment or an employment of capital. It followed that a share issue did not constitute a supply of goods or of services for consideration within the meaning of art. 2(1) of the Sixth Directive (art. 4(1) of Directive 77/388). That being the case, it followed that the costs of the supplies acquired in connection with the issue formed part of the company's overheads and had a direct and immediate link with the whole of its economic activities.

Although this has not been explicitly decided on, the same general principles will apply to other issues, such as those involving bonds, debentures and loan stock, as well as other financial instruments.

- The same general conclusion was also reached in the Ruling of the Court in *Empresa de Desenvolvimento Mineiro SGPS SA (EDM) v Fazenda Pública* (Case C-77/01) [2006] BVC 140, where it was held that the mere sale of shares, or securities (or the receipt of interest on securities) may not, in itself, constitute an economic activity or supply for VAT and may thus be *outside the scope* of VAT.

The exception, in the case of brokerage services, is where a broker, or perhaps an investment manager, contracts for a client on a back-to-back or matched basis, something which is probably less common now since the enactment of the Financial Services Act. Where this does occur, the distinction between agency and principals trading will be important, although usually the contractual terms of trade with the client will make this clear. In considering these exemptions, it is important to also take into account the Statutory Notes. These were added to in March 1997 and also radically changed from 10 March 1999. They were also further amended from 1 December 2001 following the enactment of the *Financial Services and Markets Act* 2000 by art. 347 of the *Financial Services and Markets Act 2000 (Consequential Amendments and Repeals) Order* 2001 (SI 2001/3649). The detailed Notes are set out in full in **Appendix 12**. Note (5) provides that:

> 'For the purposes of item 5 "intermediary services" consist of bringing together, with a view to the provision of financial services –
>
> (a) persons who are or may be seeking to receive financial services, and
> (b) persons who provide financial services,'

together with (in the case of financial services falling within item 1, 2, 3 or 4) the performance of work preparatory to the conclusion of contracts for the provision of those financial services, but do not include the supply of any market research, product design, advertising, promotional or similar services or the collection, collation and provision of information in connection with such activities. Note (5A) and (5B) state that:

> '(5A) For the purposes of item 5 a person is "acting in an intermediary capacity" wherever he is acting as an intermediary, or one of the intermediaries, between –
>
> (a) a person who provides financial services, and
> (b) a person who is or may be seeking to receive financial services.
>
> (5B) For the purposes of Notes (5) and (5A) "financial services" means the carrying out of any transaction falling within item 1, 2, 3, 4 or 6.'

(b) Transactions as principal

The measure of the supply for transactions within item 6 will be the gross proceeds and, in the exceptional cases where a broker acts as principal, any commission or transaction will simply be part of an overall price.

The CoJ has concluded in relation to art. 135 (1)(f) of the VAT Directive (formerly art. 13B(d) (f) of the Sixth Directive) that transactions in shares and other securities are transactions on the market in marketable securities, and that trade in securities involves acts which alter the legal and financial situation between the parties (see *DTZ Zadelhoff vof v. Staatssecretaris van Financiën* Case C-259/11 at para. 22.) In *Skatteverket v AB SKF* (Case C-29/08) [2009] ECR

I-10413 [2011] BVC 359 (discussed in **Chapter 1** at 10-300) the CoJ commented as follows on the scope of the exemption (para. 48 to 50):

> 'With regard to the scope of that exemption, the Court has held that transactions in shares and other securities are transactions on the market in marketable securities and that trade in securities involves acts which alter the legal and financial situation as between the parties (see, to that effect, Case C 2/95 SDC [1997] ECR I 3017, paragraphs 72 and 73). The words 'transactions ... in securities' within the meaning of Article 13B(d)(5) of the Sixth Directive refer, therefore, to transactions which are liable to create, alter or extinguish parties' rights and obligations in respect of securities (Case C 235/00 CSC Financial Services [2001] ECR I 10237, paragraph 33).
>
> It follows that administrative, material or technical services and activities involving the supply of financial information which do not alter the legal and financial position of the parties are not covered by the exemption laid down in Article 13B(d)(5) of the Sixth Directive (see SDC, paragraph 66, and CSC Financial Services, paragraphs 28 and 30).
>
> By contrast, it is clear that a sale of shares changes the legal and financial position of the parties to the transaction.'

Any supplies do still, however, have to be made *in the course or furtherance of a business*. This has given particular difficulties in two cases, where many would have assumed this was not an issue.

- In *National Society for the Prevention of Cruelty to Children* [1993] BVC 701, the Tribunal considered this did not extend to the ordinary investment managing function undertaken in support of its charitable role.
- *Wellcome Trust Ltd v C & E Commrs* (Case C-155/94) [1996] BVC 377, where the disposal of shares owned by a charitable foundation was held not to amount to a transaction in the course of a business. As the Advocate General in that case put it:

> '"Economic activities" did not cover sales of shares and securities by a person who is not a dealer in shares and securities but is acting in the management of his own assets.'

Other cases include:

- *Harnas & Helm v Staatssecretaris van Finaciën* (Case C-80/95) [1997] BVC 358, where the same rule applied in the case of the acquisition and holding of bonds.
- *Floridienne SA and Berginvest SA v Belgium*(Case C-142/99) [2001] BVC 76, where share dividends were said not to be consideration for any supplies and interest on loan to subsidiaries from funds derived from dividend income were not the result of an *economic activity*.
- *Empresa de Desenvolvimento Mineiro SGPS SA (EDM) v Fazenda Pública* (Case C-77/01) [2006] BVC 140 where it was held that the mere sale of shares, or securities (or the receipt of interest on securities) may not, in itself, constitute an *economic activity* or supply for VAT and may thus be outside the scope of VAT.

However, in *Business Brief* 21/96 of 17 October 1996 HMRC referred to the decision of the ECJ in the *Wellcome Trust* case and allayed the concerns being expressed by tax advisers and some financial organisations that this would have wider implications for financial trading. What it said was:

'However, the Court made it clear that its decision applies to charitable trusts. There will, therefore, be no changes affecting organisations other than charitable trusts as a result of this case.'

The same problem is unlikely to occur in the context of the issue of unit and investment trusts or, for that matter, for insurers. It may be that at some stage HMRC will seek to adopt a similar approach in regard to the investments made by the trustees of a funded pension scheme (see 80-400), although there was some suggestion in the Advocate General's Opinion in *Wellcome Trust* that the actions of the trustees of a pension fund might be distinguished. It could be that the link with the employer will be sufficient to impart the necessary *business* flavour.

- Certainly, this line had not been taken in *Willis Pension Trustees Ltd* [2006] BVC 2,045 (see earlier in **Chapter 7** at 70-200). Willis was the Trustee of the Willis Pension Fund, a scheme which held various investments some of which were overseas. To hedge or minimise the risk of exchange-rate fluctuations, Willis entered into forex deals with various UK banks. It did not offer a spread or charge a separate fee or commission, but relied on the movements in rates to minimise losses and, where possible, make a profit. The issue was whether in entering these transactions, Willis made a supply for VAT, something that will have been important for the Fund's recovery of input tax. The conclusion reached by the Tribunal was that it did not – not because the trustees were not carrying on a business, but because the Tribunal felt the only supply in this situation was made by the bank.

(c) Intermediary services

The term *intermediary services* (item 5), covers normal stockbroking services as agent and also the introduction of clients to persons acting in that capacity. In addition, it can cover many of the activities within the ambit of corporate finance, including the promotion and arrangement of issues or flotations of shares and other securities. Corporate finance is considered in some detail at 80-200(3). However, it is worth noting at this juncture that, in *Hargreaves Landsdown Asset Management Ltd* [1995] BVC 896, the Tribunal effectively considered that, to qualify for exemption, the service had to amount to a direct involvement in the transaction being arranged, rather than be simply a matter of promotion and marketing.

This principle is, in fact, not dissimilar to that adopted in the *Sparekassernes Datacenter* case referred to earlier in the sense of the provision of the assumption of control over the acquisition, disposal and administration of an investment portfolio – and indeed in *CSMA and Lloyds TSB*.

Recently the CoJ has concluded that brokerage and consultancy activities of an intermediary which resulted in the sale of shares in a company are within the scope of art. 135(1)(f) (formerly art. 13B(d)(5) of the Sixth Directive). The case is *DTZ Zadelhoff vof v Staatssecretaris van Financiën* (Case C-259/11/5 July 2012) which related to the services of DTZ in the negotiation of a transaction involving the transfer of shares in company, which owned immovable property. As discussed below, the CoJ emphasised that intermediary services are those which have as their purpose to do all that is necessary in order for two parties to enter into a contract. The material facts were as follows:

- DTZ Zadelhoff (DTZ) carried on a real estate brokerage and consultancy business in The Netherlands;

- DTZ was instructed by a Swedish company, for a fee, to find prospective purchasers for the World Fashion Centre Complex (WFC) in The Netherlands. The Swedish company owned the WFC indirectly via a subsidiary, and it intended to transfer the WFC by a sale of the shares in a company which owned it. The asking price of the shares reflected almost entirely the market value of the WFC as real estate. DTZ found a purchaser to whom the shares were sold;
- DTZ was also instructed by a company established in The Netherlands, for a fee, to find prospective purchasers for an office complex. The Dutch company was open at the time of instructing DTZ as to whether the legal ownership of the complex or the ownership of the shares in the property holding company were to be sold. DTZ found a purchaser, and subsequently the shares in the property owning company were sold to the purchaser; and
- DTZ did not charge VAT in respect of its services on the basis that they were considered to be within the scope of what is now Art. 135(1)(f).

The CoJ concluded that DTZ's services represented the negotiation of a transaction in securities for the purposes of art. 135(1)(f). The Court's reasons were, in essence as follows, with particular reference to the nature of the concept of 'negotiation':

- the words 'transactions ... in securities' within the meaning of Art. 13B(d)(5) of the Sixth Directive (now Art. 135(1)(f)) refers to transactions which are liable to create, alter or extinguish parties' rights and obligations in respect of securities (para. 23 of the judgment, referring to *C & E Commrs v CSC Financial Services*(Case C-235/00); [2001] ECR I-10237[2002] BVC 253, para. 33, and *SKF*, para. 48);
- following the engagement of DTZ, its services enabled the Swedish and Dutch companies to sell immovable property via a sale of shares in the respective property owning companies;
- the fact that the Dutch company had failed to indicate whether it was the ownership of the office complex or the ownership of the shares in the company, which was to be transferred to the purchasers is irrelevant. The reason being that '... it is necessary, in accordance with the VAT system's objectives of ensuring legal certainty and facilitating application of the tax, to have regard, save in exceptional cases, to the objective character of the transaction in question (see, to that effect, Case C-4/94 BLP Group [1995] ECR I-983, paragraph 24, and SKF, paragraph 47). Thus, irrespective of any original intention on the part of [the Dutch company], the transaction which ultimately took place was, from an objective standpoint, a transaction in shares and must therefore, subject to any exceptions, be regarded as such' (para. 25 of the judgment);
- the CoJ rejected the argument of the Dutch tax authorities that Art. 135(1)(f) did not apply due to the fact that there was an exception to the exemption provided in the then Art. 5(3)(c) (now Art. 15(2)(c)) which enabled Member States to consider that shares giving the holder de jure or de facto ownership over immovable property could be treated as tangible property. The Netherlands had not made use of the exception, with the Court commenting (at para. 36): '... it would hardly be consistent with the general scheme of the Sixth Directive to accept that the reference in the second indent of Article 13B(d)(5) of the Directive to Article 5(3) applies to all the transactions set out in the latter provision irrespective of whether the Member State concerned has exercised the choice afforded it by that provision'.
- The Court gave detailed consideration to the nature of the concept of 'negotiation' and stated that its scope should be considered as follows (at para. 26 to 28 of the judgment):

'... with regard in particular to whether the services provided by DTZ Zadelhoff at issue in the main proceedings are covered by the word "negotiation" in Article 13B(d)(5) of the Sixth Directive, it should be noted that the Court has already held that it is clear from that provision that the words "including negotiation" are not intended to define the principal object of the exemption laid down in the provision, but to extend the scope of the exemption to negotiation (*CSC Financial Services*, paragraph 38).

Accordingly, it is not necessary to consider the precise meaning of the word "negotiation", which also appears in other provisions of the Sixth Directive, including Article 13B(d)(1) to (4), in order to hold that, *in the context of Article 13B(d)(5), it refers to the activity of an intermediary who does not occupy the position of any party to a contract relating to a financial product, and whose activity amounts to something other than the provision of contractual services typically undertaken by the parties to such contracts. Negotiation is a service rendered to, and remunerated by, a contractual party as a distinct act of mediation. It may consist, amongst other things, in pointing out suitable opportunities for the conclusion of such a contract, making contact with another party or negotiating, in the name of and on behalf of a client, the detail of the payments to be made by either side. The purpose of negotiation is therefore to do all that is necessary in order for two parties to enter into a contract, without the negotiator having any interest of his own in the terms of the contract* (*CSC Financial Services*, paragraph 39).

The purpose of the brokerage and consultancy activities undertaken by DTZ Zadelhoff in the main proceedings, which consisted in finding, for a fee, buyers for immovable property that was subsequently sold and transferred by means of a share transfer, was to ensure that Fabege and the buyer and Stienstra and the buyer, respectively, concluded a contract, without DTZ Zadelhoff having any interest of its own in the terms of the contracts. Those activities therefore correspond to the word 'negotiation' in shares within the meaning of Article 13B(d)(5) of the Sixth Directive.'
(emphasis added)

As is evident the UK has not adopted the concept of 'negotiation' as referred to in Art. 135 of the VAT Directive, but has instead sought to implement the Directive through using the concept of 'intermediary services' as referred to in Item 5, Sch 9 of VATA. Nonetheless it is clear that UK law must be construed in accordance with the decisions of the CoJ in relation to the comparable European provisions in the VAT Directive.

- In the context of investment, there is also *Ivory & Sime Trustlink Ltd v C & E Commrs* [1998] BVC 191, which HMRC also lost. This reached the Scottish Court of Session and concerned a ruling by HMRC that the initial charge made by a personal equity plan (PEP) manager for the purchase of investments was not exempt from VAT.

Ivory & Sime offered investments in PEPs, whereby shares in investment trusts managed by it were purchased for an investor and held in the name of a nominee company. The investor had a choice. He might choose a *self-selection* option, under which he would be offered a range of investment trusts from which to make a choice. Otherwise an investor might choose the *managed portfolio* option, under which the selection of investments was made by the taxpayer. Ivory & Sime were prohibited from advising potential investors on whether to invest in one of their PEPs and, if so, in what plan or security to invest.

Ivory & Sime made two charges:

- an initial dealing charge of four per cent of the amount invested was made in the case of both types of PEP; and

- a smaller, six-monthly, administration charge, being less in the case of the self-select PEP.

The initial charge was described as *consideration for the service of buying securities for the investor*, while the six-monthly administration charge was described as *consideration for providing the necessary administrative services*.

The question was whether the initial dealing charge on a managed portfolio PEP was exempt from VAT under VATA 1994, Sch. 9, Grp. 5, item 6, which exempted the issue, transfer or receipt of, or any dealing with, any security, including shares and, by item 7 (as it then was) as *the making of arrangements for any transaction within item 6*. That provision derived from art. 13(B)(d)(5) of the Sixth VAT Directive which provided that 'transactions, including negotiation, excluding management and safe-keeping, in shares …' should be exempt.

It was conceded before the Tribunal that the initial charge on a self-select PEP was not taxable (as agreed between HMRC and the Association of Unit Trust and Investment Managers). However, the Tribunal did agree with HMRC and held that the initial charge related to what was primarily and essentially a management service and was accordingly not exempt. As the Tribunal put it:

> 'When making an investment into a managed PEP the investor was purchasing the benefit of the manager's expertise in selecting appropriate investment trusts to achieve the investment philosophy of the particular portfolio. The investor's only choice was to invest or not to invest. He had no input whatsoever into the decision about which trust shares to hold in the portfolio or the proportions in which to hold them.'

The Court, however, found there was no difference between the two types of PEPs and there were no grounds for holding that the initial dealing charge was for anything other than the purchase of securities and exempt.

What is interesting, and potentially important in the context of how the changes to Grp. 5 are viewed, is that this decision was given in the full knowledge of what was said in the *Sparekassernes* case and in the light of the corresponding provisions in the Sixth VAT Directive itself.

- In the later *Prudential Assurance Co Ltd* [2001] BVC 2,201 case, the Edinburgh Tribunal considered the exemption extended to sub-contracted management services provided to the operator of an authorised unit trust. The Tribunal also said the exemption in Grp. 5, item 9 was too narrowly drawn.
- In January 2002, the Tribunal similarly decided for the taxpayer in *Winterthur Life UK Ltd* [2002] BVC 2,136. A subsidiary of Winterthur Life, Personal Pension Management Ltd, undertook the management of a self-administered pension scheme for Scottish Equitable plc. Following the decision of the ECJ in the *Forsakrinsaktiebolaget Skandia* case, it was clear that the term *related services* could be services which did not necessarily place the provider of them, the agent or broker, in the position of having a direct insurance relationship with the insured. The services of PPM were characterised by permanent authority, by being within the normal scope of insurance business and the entry into commitment, although not of insurance commitments. It was closely concerned with the administration of the part of the insurance transaction, which was the self-administered scheme. PPM was providing *related* services and, although the exemption in art. 135(1)

(a) of Council Directive 2006/112/EC (art. 13(B)(a) of the Sixth VAT Directive (Directive 77/388)) must be narrowly construed, what PPM did clearly came within it.

In terms of UK law, Note (2) to VATA 1994, Sch. 9, Grp. 2 stated that an insurance agent is acting in an intermediary capacity whenever he is acting as an intermediary between a person who provides insurance and a person who is seeking insurance. The Tribunal could not interpret this as meaning that an insurance agent, when he is not acting in an intermediary capacity, is any the less an insurance agent.

HMRC provide a summary of the key factors as to when they regard an intermediary as falling within the scope of the exemption. HMRC say (VATFIN7210):

'An intermediary for the purposes of the finance exemption must:

- be providing an intermediary service in relation to an exempt financial transaction (that is, the transaction of one of the parties must itself fall within items 1, 2, 3, 4 or 6 of Group 5);
- be acting in an intermediary capacity (i.e. bringing together someone seeking a financial service with someone providing a financial service); and
- if the transaction falls with items 1, 2, 3 or 4, be carrying out work preparatory to the conclusion of contracts for the provision of those services.

Therefore, in deciding whether something is an intermediary service, the key factors are those set out above rather than, for example, how the person is paid (e.g. by commission or fee) or by their professional status.'

HMRC provide a flow chart for helping to decide whether a person is acting as an intermediary for the purposes of Group 5 item 5, and this is reproduced in **Appendix 25**.

The First Tier Tribunal decision in *Bloomsbury Wealth Management LLP* [2012] UKFTT 379 [2012] TC 02063 illustrates the application of the intermediaries exemption applying in the context of items 5 and 6 of Grp 5, Sch 9 of VATA 1994. The material facts were as follows:

- Bloomsbury Wealth Management LLP ('Bloomsbury') supplied services in the nature of introducing its clients to providers who issue securities to them. Bloomsbury considered that such services were exempt intermediary services within item 5 of Group 5 of Sch 9 of VATA,
- Bloomsbury provided high level advice to clients on asset allocation, types of assets and choice of fund managers. Bloomsbury did not provide portfolio management services,
- If the individual decides to become a client, Bloomsbury would arrange for the client's financial assets to be transferred to a third party nominee unconnected with Bloomsbury,
- Bloomsbury was given authority to communicate purchase instructions to the nominee. When the money is received by the nominee, it sends an electronic message to Bloomsbury and Bloomsbury then sends electronic instructions to the nominee to purchase units in a fund or funds appropriate to the client's circumstances and aims. The nominee then acquires the investment products and holds them on behalf of the client.
- The investment products into which the client's money is transferred were collective investment funds in which the client receives units in Exchange Traded Funds, Open Ended Investment Companies or Unit Trusts. These products are provided by a small range of third party fund managers.

- Bloomsbury did not make use of discretionary fund managers and used only passively managed, i.e. index tracking, investment vehicles.
- After the investments have been acquired, Bloomsbury conducts a quarterly 'rebalancing' of the portfolio to ensure that it meets the client's original stated wishes. The rebalancing exercise involved buying and selling units in the client's investment portfolio to achieve the appropriate balance of different investments. This was an automatic process which owed nothing to discretion but simply gave effect to the plan agreed as part of the initial discussion. The rebalancing did not involve the provision of any advice by Bloomsbury to the client.
- If a client wished to sell any investments then Bloomsbury would send an electronic instruction to the nominee to sell units.
- Bloomsbury charged its clients an initial fee and an annual fee, both of which were based on a percentage of the value of the assets transferred. The initial fee covered Bloomsbury's costs of buying the investments in the funds. Bloomsbury did not accept commission from the fund managers and any received was offset against the annual fee due from the client.

The Tribunal concluded that the services were exempt due to being intermediary services in connection with item 6 of Sch 9. This was for the following reasons:

- On the facts, Bloomsbury's services were not predominantly the introduction of clients to fund managers with a view to the clients receiving fund management services.
- Bloomsbury's clients sought and were provided with, initially, advice on the most appropriate investments for the client and, thereafter, implementation of that advice.
- Bloomsbury introduced clients to the fund managers and acted as an intermediary between the clients and the fund managers for the purpose of acquiring and maintaining the portfolio of investments on behalf of the clients.
- The fund managers provided fund management services to Bloomsbury's clients but that was a necessary consequence of the fact that the clients held units in the funds.
- The Tribunal rejected on the facts HMRC's argument that Bloomsbury supplied services of wealth management and advice as well as intermediary services but that the intermediary services were ancillary to the principal supply of wealth management and advice. The Tribunal noted that there was no fee for that advice if the client decided not to invest and this showed that it was not the most important part of the service to Bloomsbury or its clients.

(2) Standard-rating

In a few cases, however, VAT is chargeable at the standard-rate of 20 per cent (2012). This mainly covers investment management, investment advice and corporate finance and research, information and communication services.

(a) Investment management

Investment management is essentially a management service, in the sense of the provision of the assumption of control over the acquisition, disposal and administration of an investment portfolio. Usually, it involves the manager being given authority to make portfolio investments on behalf of clients. In some cases the authority will be absolute; in others it may be discretionary within certain parameters or require certain decisions to be discussed with the client. Fees may be at a flat rate, a fixed percentage of the funds or, occasionally, on a per-transaction basis.

Exemption, in this case, is specifically precluded by art. 135(1)(f) of Council Directive 2006/112/EC (art. 13(B)(d)(5) of the Sixth VAT Directive). Standard-rating does not, however, apply to the management of *special investment funds* (i.e. Unit Trusts and Single Property Trusts) (exempt by art. 135(1)(g) of Council Directive 2006/112/EC); nor to fees based on the number and value of purchases and sales (see (1) earlier).

As noted earlier, however, in the Appeal by *Prudential Assurance Co Ltd* [2001] BVC 2,201, the Edinburgh Tribunal considered that the exemption extended to sub-contracted management services provided to the operator of an authorised unit trust and that the exemption in Grp. 5, item 9 was too narrowly drawn. HMRC now accept this is the case and that exemptions should be extended to sub-contracted fund management services. This followed the decision of the Tribunal in favour of the taxpayer in December 2001 in *Abbey National plc* [2002] BVC 2,077 on the sub-contracted management of an Open-ended Investment Company, a decision that has now been approved by the ECJ (*Abbey National plc and Inscape Investment Fund v C & E Commrs* (Case C-169/04) [2008] BVC 488). As the eventual Ruling of the ECJ in *JP Morgan Fleming Claverhouse Investment Trust plc and The Association of Investment Trust Companies v R & C Commrs* (Case C-363/05) [2010] BVC 337 has now followed the Opinion of the Advocate General, this exemption also applies to the management of *closed-ended investment funds*, such as investment trust companies. The principle of *fiscal neutrality* requires all similar and therefore competing, special investment funds to be treated equally as regards the levying of VAT. The effect of the decision in *Claverhouse Investment Trust plc* was to cause the exemption in UK law to be redefined. Until 30 September 2008, items 9 and 10 of Group 5, Sch. 9 defined only the following funds as exempt for VAT purposes: (a) authorised unit trust schemes, (b) open-ended investment companies, and (c) trust-based schemes. The list of exemptions is now far more extensive (as discussed in (1) above). The purpose of the extension to the exemption was to ensure that there is a level playing field for all similar collective investment undertakings in the UK retail market. It should be noted that trust-based schemes are not included in the recast exemption.

However, in *Revenue & Customs Brief* 58/07 in August 2007, HMRC referred to a number of claims that had been made for overpaid VAT in respect of the management of other funds not at issue in the litigation. The view taken, though, is that this case does not concern the management of funds other than investment trust companies (ITCs) and that the ECJ judgment is clear in that it does not address the issues that arise concerning such other funds.

The effect of the decision in *JP Morgan Claverhouse* is illustrated by the circumstances of the decision in *Investment Trust Companies (in liquidation) v HMRC* [2012] EWHC 458 ('ITC'). In *ITC* the claimants paid consideration to managers in respect of supplies of investment management services; and the supplies were treated as being standard-rated for VAT purposes. Following the decision of the ECJ in *JP Morgan Claverhouse* it became clear that the managers' supplies to ITC should have been treated as VAT exempt. A claim for repayment was made by the managers (who had accounted to HMRC for the VAT) under s. 80 of VATA. HMRC repaid to the managers the over-declared output tax, less the over-claimed input tax. The managers paid these sums to the claimants. The claimants then brought mistake-based restitution claims against HMRC in respect of which the High Court held that ITC had a direct remedy against HMRC to recover the irrecoverable VAT element in specified circumstances.

As also mentioned earlier, in *Ivory & Sime Trustlink Ltd v C & E Commrs* [1998] BVC 191, it was concluded that the initial charge made for the purchase of investments in the case of a PEP is exempt, whereas the annual management fee was not.

(b) Investment advice and corporate finance

Investment advice and corporate finance is, again, often just that, a professional service. Historically, this has often been the province of the merchant banks but increasingly, also now is something offered by many of the larger accounting or management consultancy firms. In many cases, it will simply amount to consultancy and advice. On occasions, however, it can go beyond that to the stage when the adviser plays a much more direct part in the negotiation or arrangement of the sale or acquisition of a company or of the issue of shares or other securities. When this happens, what may start out as an essentially taxable activity can easily become exempt as an intermediary service.

- In *Nightfreight plc* [1998] BVC 2,232 there was an attempt to argue that the services of reporting accountants to a share flotation were exempt as being part of a transaction in shares, or were merely the standard-rated provision of financial information. In other words, were the words *transactions in shares* in (art. 135(1)(f) of Council Directive 2006/112/EC (art. 13(B)(d)(5) of the Sixth VAT Directive) to be read in the light of the French, German, Italian and Portuguese versions, which intended exemption to extend to *transactions relating to shares*.

HMRC argued, whichever language version was used, the services of the reporting accountants consisted of nothing more than the provision of financial information and those services could have been part of any supply, and were therefore not exempt from VAT. The Tribunal agreed, holding that:

(1) What was exempted was the *making of arrangements* for the transaction in securities, but not every element of the making of such arrangements was exempt.
(2) A distinction must be drawn between (a) supplies which were a discrete part of the larger exempt transaction and (b) supplies which happened to be part of an exempt transaction but which could equally have been part of any transaction. Even essential elements of an exempt transaction had to be analysed in this way.

There were two stages to every flotation. In the first stage, information was obtained from a variety of sources and from it a prospectus was prepared. When the prospectus was ready, and all the decisions as to the terms and marketing of the shares had been made, the second stage was the flotation itself. Only this second stage was exempt.

As the Tribunal observed:

'Nightfreight was attempting to expand the scope of activities attracting exemption by reference to a linguistic analysis of different language versions of the sixth Directive. In addition to that being an incorrect approach to the problem, it was directly at odds with the purposive approach to art. 13(B)(d)(5) adopted by the ECJ in *Sparekassernes Datacenter (SDC) v Skatteministeriet* (Case C-2/95) [1997] BVC 509 ("Datacenter"), an approach endorsed by the Courts of the UK.'

The case is a useful reminder, therefore, of the limits beyond which the decision in *Sparekassernes* cannot be taken.

The implications of what can be involved in this area are considered in more detail later at 80-200(5).

(c) Research, information and communication services

Research, information and communication services generally represent supplies of the provision of or transmission of information.

(3) Outside the scope, exemption with the right of recovery and zero-rating

As mentioned elsewhere, the benefit of exemption normally comes at a price. Not having to charge VAT usually means a restriction in the recovery of input VAT. There are, however, other situations where UK VAT is not accounted for, some of which allow input tax to be reclaimed. Tax is not due, for example, if a supply is *outside the scope* – because, say, the place of supply is abroad.

Whether or not something is *outside the scope* depends generally on the rules on the place of supply (see **Chapter 3** at 30-250(2)), on the type of service provided and on the circumstances in which it occurs. The same can be said in many respects of the ability to recover input VAT. EU law contains, for example, a number of reliefs aimed at encouraging international trade with non-EU countries. This is allowed in a specific and limited range of circumstances by art. 169(b) and (c) of Council Directive 2006/112/EC (art. 17(3)(b) and (c)), which is mirrored in UK terms in the partial exemption rules in respect of input VAT recovery by reg. 103 of the *Value Added Tax Regulations* 1995 (SI 1995/2518) and the *VAT (Input Tax) (Specified Supplies) Order* 1999 (SI 1999/3121) (see **Chapter 4** at 40-200(5)). On top of this, there are certain situations in which a supply may be zero-rated, i.e. taxed at a nil rate.

As noted earlier, the Ruling of the ECJ, in *Kretztechnik AG v Finanzamt Linz* (Case C-465/03) [2006] BVC 66 has meant the issue of shares (and in consequence also of other securities) does not constitute a supply for VAT. The consequence of this is that, generally, any underlying input tax will now be treated as *residual* and recovered according to the position of the business overall, rather than with regard to the persons to whom the issue is made.

(a) Services supplied with right of recovery to input tax

The main area of interest in the context of this Chapter will be with the services that are supplied and carry a right to recovery of input tax. The services which permit recovery are those which are outside the scope of UK VAT, and which are supplied in certain prescribed circumstances.

Any service will be treated as supplied outside the UK where the recipient is a 'relevant business person' (as discussed in Chapter 3). Where a service is supplied to a non-relevant business person the place of supply is where the supplier belongs, unless overriding place of supply rules apply in Sch. 4A to VATA 1994. In this context, the supply of banking, financial and insurance services (including reinsurance), other than the provision of safe deposit facilities, to a person who is not a relevant business person and belongs in a country which is not a Member State of the EU will be treated as supplied where the recipient belongs (Sch. 4A, para. 16(2)). Putting this in context, what this means in practice is that a supply will be outside the scope of UK VAT if made:

- to *someone in business* and who is established in another EU country; or
- to *anyone* belonging or established outside the EU.

This, coupled with what is provided for in reg. 103 of the *Value Added Tax Regulations* 1995 (SI 1995/2518) and art. 3 of the *Value Added Tax (Input Tax) (Specified Supplies) Order* 1999 (SI 1999/3121), has the effect that underlying input VAT can be recovered for:

- any *basically taxable* service supplied to a business outside the UK or to anyone else outside the EU; and
- any *basically exempt* service supplied to anyone outside the EU.

The interest in terms of investment will, clearly, be over the sale or issue of securities or the receipt of interest. In the main, these will be *outside the scope*, and not simply exempt, where the recipient of the supply is outside the UK. There will be a particular benefit, however, where the person concerned is someone who is established or resident outside the EU since it opens the possibility of input tax recovery. In the case of securities, there is also the slightly odd phenomenon that underlying input VAT can be recovered when *any* shares or stock are sold to someone outside the EU and also when interest is received by someone in the UK on a bond or other interest-bearing security issued by someone outside the EU. In other words, it is not simply a matter of looking, in the case of securities, at sales, something that is easily overlooked.

What is meant by *belonging* is discussed earlier in **Chapter 3** at 30-250. This is not always easy to determine and, in the case of securities, a special rule or easement applies. This easement is to be found in Section 6.16 of HMRC Notice 701/49 (November 2011) and reads:

> 'If
>
> - your place of belonging is the UK;
> - you sell securities to a customer; and
> - you cannot identify your customer, or their place of belonging;
>
> you may
>
> - treat the supply as being in the UK and exempt; or
> - use the place of belonging of a nominee account for the purchaser to determine the place of supply; or
> - use a special rule known as "the easement". This works by using the following tests in sequential order:
>
>   (a) **Where the place of transaction, that is the relevant security exchange, is known then a sale transacted:**
>   - in the UK is treated as made to a person belong in the UK and exempt;
>   - in any other EU Member State is treated as made to a taxable person belonging in that Member State, and is outside the scope of UK VAT, but without recovery of your related input tax;
>   - outside the EU is treated as made to a person belonging outside the EU and is outside the scope of UK VAT. You can recover related input tax subject to normal rules.

(b) **Where the place of the transaction is not known**, then the place of supply is deemed to be a place where the security is listed.
(c) **Where the place of transaction is not known and the security is not listed or is listed on both an EU and non-EU exchange,** then the place of supply is deemed to be the place where the last known broker in the transaction "belongs".'

In the case of underwriting services, the position is addressed according to the circumstances of the immediate recipient of the supply (as determined by the terms of the contract). Thus, the lead underwriter will look to the position of the issuing client; a sub-underwriter will look just to the position of the underwriter, unless the terms of the underwriting agreement is such that both are supplying underwriting services to the issuer.

- *Water Hall Group plc v C & E Commrs* [2003] BVC 4,085 raised an interesting point in this connection on the issue, or sale, of shares where there are nominees. The appellant had incurred VAT on costs associated with an issue of shares, which it sought to recover in proportion to the number of shares issued to non-EU persons. Unfortunately, many had been issued to UK nominees for the non-EU beneficial owners. The appellant's claim that you had to look-through the nominees to the underlying beneficial owners was, unfortunately not accepted, something the Tribunal itself admitted was anomalous.

Following *Kretztechnik AG v Finanzamt Linz* (Case C-465/03) [2006] BVC 66 this is now not really a problem with the issue of shares or securities, although it can remain a concern where the transaction involves a sale.

Practice point
- As the sale of securities is VAT-exempt, relief for underlying input VAT can be limited. However, relief is afforded where the buyer is outside the EU (art. 3 of the *VAT (Input Tax) (Specified Supplies) Order* 1999 (SI 1999/3121)). Reviewing where the client *belongs* can often be worthwhile as the billing address, for example, may not always reflect the location to which a supply is made.
- Routing sales via a suitable non-EU associate as an intermediate step in an overall transaction may sometimes be worth considering. However, it will be important to pay attention to detail and to be able to show that the sale is, in itself, a real transaction and not a sham.
- Monitoring the use of UK dealing desks for non-EU associates could also be important to avoid any possibility that this creates a presence for the associate (see perhaps *C & E Commrs v DFDS A/S* (Case C-260/95) [1997] BVC 279).

(b) Agency and brokerage and the services of intermediaries

In the case of agency or brokerage, there are three further reliefs:

(i) The general rule

The general rule is simply to follow the principles discussed earlier (see particularly Chapter 3 for a detailed discussion on the nature of the place of supply rules). Following, therefore, the rules for services, the supply of brokerage will be outside the scope of UK VAT when supplied to a business in another EU Member State or to anyone belonging outside the UK

(s. 7A of VATA 1994 (supplies to a relevant business person)). Underlying input tax will then be recoverable to the extent that the recipient of the service belongs outside the EU as a result of art. 3(a) of the *Value Added Tax (Input Tax) (Specified Supplies) Order* 1999 (SI 1999/3121).

(ii) Exemption with the right of recovery

A further possibility follows from art. 3(c) of the *Value Added Tax (Input Tax) (Specified Supplies) Order* 1999, which enables input tax to also be recoverable where what the broker or agent arranges is:

(a) the supply of a basically exempt financial service to someone outside the EU, i.e. under the rules in (i) above; or
(b) the supply of export finance above or export insurance.

> **Practice point**
>
> The critical factor in (ii) above is that the *buying counterparty* of the underlying client trade is outside the EU.
>
> This rule will similarly apply where the underlying client supply is itself technically *outside the scope* because the selling counterparty to whom the agency service is provided is outside the EU.

(iii) The zero-rate option

Zero-rating, although important, is of limited interest for the sectors covered here because it does not apply to anything within VATA 1994, Sch. 9, Grp. 2 or 5. Where available, it arises under VATA 1994, Sch. 8, Grp. 7. Item 2 zero-rates a supply of brokerage or agency services where the place of supply, adopting the rules referred to earlier, is in the UK. The services covered are those of arrangement where there is a *named principal*. The relief applies where what is arranged is:

(1) An export of goods to a place outside the Member States.
(2) A supply of services of the description specified in item 1 of the Group (not relevant in the context of this book).
(3) Any supply of services which is made outside the Member States.

The only real interest for most businesses in the sectors covered by this last category will be in paragraph (3). However, this Group does not include any services of a description specified in Grp. 2 or Sch. 9, Grp. 5 (Insurance or Finance) so that, in practice, for the most part, this will be confined to the arrangement for someone belonging in the UK (or, if a private individual, in another Member State) of a basically taxable financial service provided by that person to someone *established* or *belonging* outside the EU.

80-150 Property

Property is one of the more complex areas of VAT and seems set to be increasingly so. Most supplies of property itself are inherently VAT-exempt. The costs, however, (construction, reinstatement, maintenance and management) are not. VAT is likely, therefore, to be a major expense and one which many property owners will wish to avoid. At one time, zero-rating offered the best means of achieving this. The circumstances where this is possible are, however, now very much more limited.

More importantly, many supplies are currently subject to tax at the standard-rate and VAT is more of an issue than it ever was. Companies, particularly investors, are finding the consequences of getting things wrong can be costly.

(1) Exemption

The exemption in Council Directive 2006/112/EC (Art. 135(1)(j)(k) and (l) (the Sixth VAT Directive Art. 13(B)(b))) covers:

'(j) the supply of a building or parts thereof, and of the land on which it stands, other than the supply referred to in point (a) of Article 12(1);

(k) the supply of land which has not been built on other than the supply of building land as referred to in point (b) of Article 12(1);

(l) the leasing or letting of immovable property.'

But not (Art. 135(2)), in the case of (l) above:

'(a) the provision of accommodation, as defined in the laws of the Member States, in the hotel sector or in sectors with a similar function, including the provision of accommodation in holiday camps or on sites developed for use as camping sites;

(b) the letting of premises and sites for the parking of vehicles;

(c) the letting of permanently installed equipment and machinery;

(d) the hire of safes.'

Member States are also free to apply further exclusions, which the UK has duly done.

These exemptions are reflected in UK law in VATA 1994, s. 8 and Sch. 9, Grp. 1, which is reproduced in full at **Appendix 14**. Item 1 of Sch. 9 Group 1 (the only item, as it happens) is couched in relatively simple and outwardly comprehensive terms:

'The grant of any interest in or right over land or of any licence to occupy land, or, in relation to land in Scotland, any personal right to call for or be granted any such interest or right ...'

Land, in this context, includes buildings and other structures, land covered with water, and any estate, interest, easement, servitude or right in or over land (*Interpretation Act* 1978, Sch. 1). It will also be taken to include trees, plants and other natural objects so long as they remain attached to it. However, as noted earlier, art. 135(2)(c) of Council Directive 2006/112/EC specifically excludes from exemption the letting of permanently installed equipment and machinery. The exemption is clearly widely drawn. It can apply to most sales, assignments, lettings and licences, and also to informal arrangements such as tenancies at will. As established in *Stichting 'Goed Wonen v Staatssecretaris van Financiën* (Case C-326/99) [2002] BVC 46, it also covers *usufructory rights* – the legal right to use and derive profit or benefit from property that belongs to another person, so long as the property is not damaged.

The fact that land is widely interpreted can raise questions in itself.

- In *Aquarium Entertainments Ltd* [1995] BVC 728, for example, the taxpayer sought to recover input VAT on the installation of fire equipment in a building. The building was let and the lease was drafted so as to create separate rent charges for the premises itself and for the equipment, the latter being treated as standard-rated. HMRC, however, saw the supply as a single supply of exempt accommodation. On appeal, the Tribunal found in favour of the taxpayer. Although English law made the equipment part of the premises, art. 13 of the Directive (now art. 135(2)(c)) allowed this to be discounted but, following the ruling of the ECJ in *Skatteministeriet v Henriksen* (1990) 5 BVC 140, not if there is a single economic transaction. The Tribunal decided there was not, in fact, a single supply in this case, so the appeal succeeded.

- In *Blandy* [1996] BVC 4,075, the position was, if anything, the reverse. This was an input VAT dispute taken by owners of a nursing home. The appellant had incurred expenditure on property owned jointly with her husband on trust for sale. The expenditure involved an extension, fixtures and fittings, which she then purported to lease as a taxable supply to the partnership with her husband. Unfortunately, the extension, fixtures and fittings were affixed to the land. As the freehold was jointly owned, this meant she had no interest in the land in her personal capacity and was thus unable to grant any right to any of the items of expenditure she had paid for. In short, she could not make any supply at all under the lease agreement, which was null and void.

Practice point

Both *Aquarium Entertainments* and *Blandy* highlight the same issue faced on corporate tax some years earlier in *Costain Property Investments Ltd v Stokes (HMIT)* [1984] BTC 92.

Structures and fixtures attached to the land become part of it and, on the face of it, belong to the freeholder.

The problem, though, may not be insuperable as it is possible legally to separate the plant from the land. However, this must really be done *before* the expenditure is incurred.

As with the Directive, however, there are a number of specific exceptions to the exemption, which, by implication, are taxable at the standard-rate. In the main, these will involve supplies of a generally transitory nature as in the exceptions in art. 13. These exceptions are explored further at (2) later.

As observed in **Chapter 7** in the section on *Equipment leasing* (70-400), it is, perhaps, interesting in this connection that in a Ruling, delivered on 16 January 2003 in *Rudolf Maierhofer v Finanzamt Augsburg-Land* (Case C-315/00) [2003] BVC 325, the ECJ has concluded that the exemption for the letting of immovable property within art. 13(B)(b) of Sixth VAT Directive (art. 135(1) of Council Directive 2006/112/EC) covers the letting of buildings constructed from prefabricated materials if they are firmly fixed to or in the ground. It was also, according to the Court, irrelevant whether the lessor makes available to the lessee both the building and the land on which it is erected or merely the building which he has erected on the lessee's land. This would, on the face of it, equally apply to large fixed structures, such as lifts and elevators were it not for the fact that art. 135(2)(c) of Council Directive 2006/112/EC specifically excludes the letting of permanently installed equipment and machinery.

Grant is defined in statutory Note (1) of VATA 1994 Sch 9., Group 1, which, as now drafted, reads:

"'Grant" includes an assignment or surrender and the supply made by the person to whom an interest is surrendered when there is a reverse surrender.'

Reverse surrender is defined by Note (1A) as one in which the person to whom the interest is surrendered is paid by the person by whom the interest is being surrendered to accept the surrender.

The term *grant* does, as it happens, have particular connotations in relation to land law and has raised a number of concerns, particularly in relation to the option to tax (see (2) later). It is possible that at some stage the reference may need to be changed in the interests of clarity to, for example, the more familiar VAT term of *supply*.

Statutory Note (1) was originally drafted so as to:

> 'include an assignment, other than an assignment to the person to whom a surrender of the interest could be made.'

The exemption thus specifically excluded the surrender of any such interest. This exception was, however, successfully challenged by the accountancy firm Lubbock Fine in an appeal that ultimately came before the European Court ([1993] BVC 287). Ruling for the taxpayer, the Court held that surrenders fell within art. 13(B)(b) of the Sixth VAT Directive (art. 135(1)(l) of Council Directive 2006/112/EC) and were exempt. Specifically, the ECJ said:

> '9 Where a given transaction, such as the letting of immovable property, which would be taxed on the basis of the rents paid, falls within the scope of an exemption provided for by the sixth Directive, a change in the contractual relationship, such as termination of the lease for consideration must also be regarded as falling within the scope of that exemption.
>
> 10 Consequently, the reply to be given to the national Court is that the term "letting of immovable property" used in art. 13(B)(b) of the sixth Directive (art 135(1)(l)) to define an exempt transaction covers the case where a tenant surrenders his lease and returns the immovable property to his immediate landlord ...
>
> 11 The essence of the second question put by the national Court is whether art. 13(B)(b) (art. 135(1)(l)), which allows Member States to apply further exclusions to the scope of the exemption for the letting of immovable property, authorises them to tax the consideration paid by one party to the other in connection with the surrender of the lease where the rent paid under the lease was exempt from VAT.
>
> 12 Article 13(B) (art 135) allows Member States to exclude certain types of letting from the scope of the exemption and hence to subject them to tax. However, it cannot be construed as allowing them to tax a transaction terminating a lease where the grant of that lease was compulsorily exempt. The relations created by a lease cannot be broken up in this way.'

This judgment was acknowledged by HMRC in *Business Brief* 35/93 of 20 December 1993 when the terms of the ruling were first known. In March 1995 formal effect was given to this by an amendment to the law as a result of the *Value Added Tax (Land) Order* 1995 (SI 1995/282).

(a) Inducements

At the same time, the Order also amended Grp. 1 to extend the exemption to what are colloquially known as *reverse surrenders* – i.e. cases where the consideration passes to the person to whom the surrender is made rather than vice versa. This view has now been accepted by HMRC to have always applied following the successful appeal by *Central Capital Corporation Ltd* [1996] BVC 2,336. The supply had previously been regarded by HMRC as taxable, being the agreement to accept the surrender as opposed to the grant of any interest as such in the land or building concerned.

Since then, the extent to which the principles in *Lubbock Fine* can be extended has been further explored in the appeals in the *Mirror Group plc* and *Cantor Fitzgerald International* cases, the former relating to the grant of a lease, the latter to an assignment of a lease. The two appeals were ultimately referred to the ECJ, where they were heard together. The Opinion of Advocate General Tizzano, when it emerged in January 2001, came down in favour of both taxpayers on essentially the same argument, namely that the exemption under art. 13(B)(b) of the Sixth VAT Directive (art. 135(1)(l) of Council Directive 2006/112/EC) in its reference to *the leasing or letting of immovable property*, covered supplies represented by reverse premiums or inducements paid to prospective tenants for entering into, or assuming, obligations under a lease. However, the Court, when it gave judgment on 9 October 2001 ([2001] BVC 9) took quite the opposite view and decided for HMRC.

- *C & E Commrs v Mirror Group plc* (Case C-409/98) [2002] BVC 16 was all about inducements received to take on a new lease on moving to new premises. Given its high profile, *Mirror Group* commanded *anchor tenant* status and could expect particularly favourable terms. As a result, it entered into a series of agreements with Olympia and York in three separate documents comprising:

(1) An Agreement for Lease (the principal agreement) relating to five floors of a building in Canary Wharf in London.

(2) A lease of those five floors.

(3) A further agreement giving it the option, exercisable within six months, to take a lease or leases of up to four more floors of the same building.

In return for entering into these agreements the Mirror Group received inducements of approximately £12m (plus VAT), being approximately £6.5m (exclusive of VAT) for the Agreement for Lease and £5.5m (exclusive of VAT) to take up the option. These sums, together with a further amount to cover the VAT, were paid into escrow. The lease of the five floors was for 25 years, with no rent being payable for the first five years and a below market rent being due for the remainder.

The Mirror Group had paid over VAT on the sums it received, but sought to reclaim this on the basis that its supplies to Olympia and York were not taxable, but were covered by the exemption. The Tribunal ([1998] BVC 2,188) had allowed the company's appeal on the first payment, but not on the second, which it said related solely to the options and not directly to the lease.

- *C & E Commrs v Cantor Fitzgerald International* (Case C-108/99) [2002] BVC 9 concerned a similar inducement, but, this time, for an assignment of an existing lease, rather than the grant of a new one. The subject matter was the remaining eight years of a 15-year lease originally granted by Prudential Assurance to a company by the name of Wako International (Europe) Limited. The lease could not be assigned without the Prudential's consent and the transaction again resulted in three agreements:

    (1) An agreement for assignment between Wako and Cantor Fitzgerald (guaranteed by another Cantor company), under which, in return for £1.5m Cantor Fitzgerald agreed to take over the lease.

(2) A licence to assign between the Prudential, Wako and Cantor Fitzgerald, again with Cantor Fitzgerald Securities as guarantor.
(3) A formal assignment of the lease from Wako to Cantor Fitzgerald.

Cantor Fitzgerald duly received the £1.5m, on which it accounted for VAT, which it later sought to claim back.

The essence of the HMRC approach in both cases was that the Ruling in *Lubbock Fine* could only apply where there was a variation of contractual relations based on an existing lease. The Tribunals in both cases had disagreed, but the High Court had experienced doubts.

In the Advocate General's opinion, however, whilst what can be gleaned from *Lubbock Fine* could not be conclusive, one had to look at the transactions as a whole. As the purpose of the whole of the transactions in both cases was to transfer the right of enjoying the immovable property from the owner to the tenant, it had to follow that the transactions fell, in their entirety, within the meaning of the phrase *the leasing or letting of immovable property* in Art. 13(B)(b) of the Sixth VAT Directive (Art. 135(1)(l) of Council Directive 2006/112/EC).

In reaching their contrary view, the ECJ itself made what seems a crucial observation. This is that:

'it is necessary, in every case, to consider which party supplied the goods or services and which party provided the consideration. It is supplies of goods or services, which are subject to VAT, rather than payments made by way of consideration for such supplies.'

In other words, it is important, in a case of this kind, to ascertain which of the assignor and the assignee (or landlord and tenant) makes the payment to the other and which of them makes the supply of services. It does not always follow that a payment is made for a supply of services.

In the *Mirror Group* and *Cantor Fitzgerald* cases, the supplies were provided by the incoming tenants in exchange for inducement payments. Mirror's supply, by acting as an anchor tenant, was a supply of advertising services while Cantor Fitzgerald made a supply by agreeing to take on a liability (the lease) via assignment. In both cases the ECJ held that such supplies do not fall within the art 13B(b) exemption and are subject to VAT at the standard rate.

Following the Ruling in the *Mirror Group*, HMRC now generally accept that entering into a new lease does not constitute a supply for which inducement payments on entering leases are considered. The majority of such payments are thus likely to be *outside the scope of VAT* being no more than *inducements* to tenants to take leases and to observe the obligations in them. There will be a taxable supply only where a payment is linked to benefits a tenant provides outside normal lease terms. However, merely putting such a benefit as an obligation in a lease will not mean it ceases to be a taxable transaction. Inducement payments on the grant of a lease are thus on a similar VAT footing to rent-free periods.

Examples of taxable benefits by tenants that may be supplied in return for such inducements include (see HMRC's VAT Manual: Supply and Consideration at VATSC46800)

- carrying out building works to improve the property by undertaking necessary repairs or upgrading the property;

- carrying out fitting-out or refurbishment works for which the landlord has responsibility and is paying the tenant to undertake;
- acting as anchor tenant.

HMRC accept this is a difficult area where the undertakings of landlords and tenants can change and will therefore seek as much documentation as possible before reaching a decision. They will not assume there has been a supply and agree that less specific indicators do not determine the issue. For example:

- publicity indicating that Company X is to take a lease in a development does not, in itself, determine that the company is an anchor tenant.
- equally, undertakings to use improved materials as part of continuous repairs under a tenant repairing lease would not constitute a taxable benefit to the landlord under the first example above.

However, HMRC are very clear that payments to an 'anchor tenant' will always be a standard rated supply. In HMRC Notice 741A (June 2012) at para. 10.1 it is stated that:

> 'Where the tenant acts as an anchor tenant (in order to attract other tenants) their supply will always be a standard rated supply. In such cases, the input tax you incur on the payment to the tenant is attributable to your lettings of the building and will generally be recoverable where you have opted to tax.'

Unfortunately though, HMRC do not define who will be an 'anchor tenant', or indicate any factors as to how this is to be determined.

Since the *Cantor Fitzgerald* ruling the First Tier Tax Tribunal's decision in *British Eventing Ltd* [2010] UKFTT 382, [2011] TC 00664 has served as a timely reminder that while VAT is generally not chargeable (subject to the exceptions set out above) on an inducement paid by a landlord to a tenant on the grant of a lease, in an assignment context the courts will treat incoming tenants as making a supply of taking on an onerous lease where inducements are paid by the outgoing tenants. In *British Eventing* the Tribunal found that a £340,000 inducement payment in exchange for the supply was subject to VAT at the standard rate whilst also ruling that a nominal £10 paid by the incoming tenant was not sufficient to constitute consideration. The outgoing tenant was thus left without any outbound supply to allow it to reclaim the VAT charged on the supply made by the incoming tenant.

All three cases, *Cantor Fitzgerald*, the *Mirror Group* and *Lubbock Fine*, involved payments to a tenant or prospective tenant by a landlord, or owner of a property or outgoing tenant. However, the difference between the *Cantor Fitzgerald* and *Mirror Group* cases, on the one hand, and *Lubbock Fine,* on the other was that Lubbock Fine started out with an interest in land, namely the lease it was giving up; the other two appellants did not. This led the Court to the inevitable conclusion that, ultimately, someone, who does not initially have any interest in a property and who enters into an agreement for an assignment or lease with an existing tenant or a landlord, cannot make an exempt supply of that property within art. 13(B)(b) (art 135(1)(l)).

In other words, *you can't supply what you don't have in the first place*. The supplies which were made in *Mirror Group* and *Cantor Fitzgerald* are supplies of services and are thus fundamentally different from the supply of property in *Lubbock Fine*, namely the surrender of the lease.

There was also a third principle that emerged from *Cantor Fitzgerald*. One of the assertions, made on Cantor's behalf by the European Commission, was that the principle of the *neutrality* of VAT, which must be applied in interpreting the Sixth VAT Directive required Art. 13(B)(b) (Art. 135(1)) to be broadly interpreted so that *the leasing or letting of immovable property* covers a transaction like the one Cantor carried out. The company making the assignment could have remained a tenant and sub-let the property to Cantor for a lower rent than that which it had to pay the landlord. Equally, it could have paid compensation to the landlord so that the latter would accept early termination of the lease. In both instances, the *economic* impact would have been comparable to that of the transaction at issue. In both these situations, no VAT would be due, which was clearly in contrast to the assertions of HMRC that the supplies, which Cantor made, were subject to VAT.

The Court's answer to that was that it did not justify interpreting Art. 13(B)(b) (Art. 135(1)(l)) so as to mean that it also applies to a supply of services that does not include the assignment of a right to occupy property.

The Court stated at para. 33 of its judgment that:

> 'An approach of that kind would be contrary to the VAT system's objectives of ensuring legal certainty and a correct and coherent application of the exemptions provided for in art. 13 of the sixth Directive (arts 131 to 137). The Court observes in that connection that, to facilitate the application of VAT, it is necessary to have regard, save in exceptional cases, to the objective character of the transaction in question (see *BLP Group* (Case C-4/94) [1995] BVC 159; [1995] ECR I-983, para. 24). A taxable person who, for the purposes of achieving a particular economic goal, has a choice between exempt transactions and taxable transactions must therefore, in his own interest, duly take his decision while bearing in mind the neutral system of VAT (see, to that effect, *BLP Group*, above, para. 25 and 26). The principle of the neutrality of VAT does not mean that a taxable person with a choice between two transactions may choose one of them and avail himself of the effects of the other.'

In short (the author's words not the Court's), *you pay your money and make your choice*.

(b) Virtual assignments

As shown in an appeal by *Abbey National plc*, the exemption does not cover *virtual assignments*.

- In *C & E Commrs v Abbey National plc* [2006] BVC 645, Abbey National, the high street bank, made predominantly exempt supplies and decided to transfer its interest in a large number of freehold and leasehold properties to an independent third-party, leasing back those properties which it wished to occupy. There was no difficulty in transferring or assigning the freehold or long leasehold properties. However, landlord's consent was required for the assignment of most of the short-term leases. Since it was felt that such consent would not be given a concept of *virtual assignment* was devised under which:
    - Abbey transferred the benefits and burdens of the leases to the third-party, whilst remaining in occupation; and
    - the third-party was paid a fee equivalent to the rent it would have paid had a formal leaseback occurred.

    HMRC took the view that, under the *virtual assignment*, the supply by the third-party to Abbey was not an exempt supply of the leasing or letting of immovable property within the meaning of art. 13(B)(b) of the Sixth Directive (art. 135(1)(l) of Council Directive 2006/112/EC). The Tribunal agreed ([2004] BVC 2,367. This was reversed on appeal by the High Court, ([2005] BVC 331) but subsequently confirmed by the Court of Appeal.

It was clear that the expression *leasing or letting,* when used in the article, had a wider meaning than it did under English law, although the exemptions in art. 13(B)(b) were to be interpreted strictly. A right of occupation was an essential and fundamental element of a transaction of leasing or letting for the purposes of art. 13(B)(b). It followed that, as the third-party had acquired no such right in the case of the properties subject to the virtual assignment, it was never able to transfer such a right back to Abbey. HMRC were right, therefore, in seeing the supply by the third-party as a taxable supply of agency and property management.

Following a Reference from the House of Lords in *Sinclair Collis Ltd v C & E Commrs* (Case C-275/01) [2003] BVC 374, it is now decided that the exemption for the letting of immovable property does not extend to a grant of a right to install and operate cigarette vending machines where no rights of possession or control are granted.

(c) Service charges

In the case of leases, the exemption will cover not just the rent, but also many elements of a service charge, when made by the landlord and relating to common areas or facilities enjoyed by tenants of the property generally.

(1) Property insurance and rates, for example, when paid by the landlord are usually passed on as additional rent (see *Globe Equities Ltd* [1996] BVC 2,209).

(2) Cleaning, maintenance and heating and the provision of a reception will also be treated in this way.

(3) But surrenders are not the only special situation that needs to be considered.

In other words, unless the charges relates specifically to separate facilities provided separately to the tenant's particular demised premises, there will be a single composite supply of the accommodation. This is, however, subject to an exception in the case of certain service charges due from occupants of residential property.

The CoJ in *Field Fisher Waterhouse LLP v HMRC* (C-392/11) has confirmed the UK's VAT treatment of service charges under the VAT Directive. The VAT treatment under a lease will depend on whether the landlord has opted to tax the property since the services will usually be treated as being part of a single supply linked to the leasing of the land. Where a landlord has not opted to tax the property, and wishes to charge VAT then it would need to use a management company to supply the services on an independent basis. The material facts of *Field Fisher Waterhouse LLP* ('FFW') were as follows:

- FFW's lease from its landlord provided that premises were let in consideration of the payment of three 'rents', covering:
  - occupation of a building,
  - FFW's share of the cost of insuring the building, and

- the provision of services which the landlord was obliged to provide under the lease. This rent covered service charges for, among other things, the supply of water, heating throughout the building, repair of the structure and machinery of the building (including the lifts), cleaning of the common parts, and the security of the building.
- The lease provided that if the tenant failed to pay these three rents then the landlord could terminate the lease.
- The landlord had not exercised the right to opt for taxation of the leasing of the premises within the meaning of Art. 137(1)(d) of the VAT Directive.
- The lease of the immovable property was exempt from VAT.
- The landlord had not invoiced VAT on the supplies of services to FFW, as it considered that they were exempt from VAT.
- FFW regarded the supplies of services by the landlord as being subject to VAT. FFW made an application to reclaim the VAT paid in respect of those supplies. HMRC rejected the application on the basis that the lease and the supplies of services constituted a single supply which was exempt from VAT.

The CoJ concluded that (para. 29 of the judgment):

- The leasing of immovable property and the supplies of services linked to such leasing may constitute a single supply under the VAT Directive.
- The fact that a lease gives the landlord the right to terminate it if the tenant fails to pay the service charges supports the view that there is a single supply, but does not necessarily constitute the decisive element for the purpose of assessing whether there is such a supply.
- The fact that services could in principle be supplied by a third party does not allow the conclusion that they cannot constitute a single supply.
- The referring Court must determine whether having regard to the particular circumstances of the case the transactions are so closely linked to each other that they must be regarded as constituting a single supply of the leasing of immovable property.

By concession (see *Business Brief* 3/94 of 15 February 1994 and ESC 3.18 in Notice 48 (March 2012)), do not seek to tax charges for the upkeep of common areas of an estate or dwellings or a block of flats, for the provision of a warden, superintendants or caretakers, etc. and for the general maintenance of the exterior when these are something the tenant cannot refuse.

The exemption will not, however, apply where the service charges are paid to someone other than the landlord (see *Trustees of the Nell Gwynn House Maintenance Fund* [1995] BVC 1,100).

(d) Licences to occupy

Whilst the wording of Grp. 1, item 1 is couched in terms of *the grant of any interest or right over land or of any licence to occupy land ...*, it is interesting that these words do not appear in the Directive itself. Article 135(1)(l)) (art. 13(B)(b) of the Sixth Directive), for example, talks of *the leasing or the letting of immovable property*, art. 135(1)(j) (art. 13(B)(g)) of *the supply of buildings or parts thereof and of the land on which they stand* and art. 135(1)(k) (art. 13(B)(h)) of *the supply of land which has not been built on other than building land*.

As to what constitutes a *licence to occupy*, HMRC say in Section 2.5 of Notice 742 (June 2012) that a licence must have the characteristics of a 'leasing or letting of immovable property'. They go on to state that:

'A licence to occupy is a written or oral agreement which falls within the European concept of 'leasing or letting of immovable property' but falls short of being a formal lease for the purpose of UK land law.

For a licence to occupy to exist, the agreement has to have all characteristics of a "leasing or letting of immovable property". This is the case if the licensee is granted right of occupation of:

- a defined area of land (land includes buildings ...)
- for an agreed duration
- in return for payment, and
- has the right to occupy that area as owner and to exclude others from enjoying that right.

All of these characteristics must be present.

Where a licence to occupy is granted together with other goods and services as part of a single supply, the nature of the overarching supply will determine how it should be categorised for VAT purposes.'

Since, therefore, *supply* includes all forms of supply it may be worth, in some cases, looking to the Directive rather than relying on the wording of Grp. 1, if the possibility of exemption is being challenged.

(2) Standard-rating

As noted earlier, there are specific exceptions to the exemption, both under the Directive and under VATA 1994, Sch. 9, Grp. 1. As permitted by the Directive, the list of what is standard-rated (see **Appendix 14**) has been extended in the UK, although the common thread, perhaps, is that this has always tended to apply to the more transitory enjoyment of land and buildings rather than anything that can extend long-term. Following the types of supply referred to in (Art. 135(2) (Art. 13(B)(b)), the exclusions from exemption will include, in particular:

- the provision of hotel or holiday accommodation;
- camping and car parking facilities or facilities for housing or mooring aircraft or boats;
- shooting or fishing rights;
- the granting of any right to fell and remove standing timber; and
- the letting of permanently installed equipment and machinery (although this is not specifically mentioned in Sch. 9, Grp. 1).
- In *C & E Commrs v Venuebest Ltd* [2003] BVC 444, it was confirmed that this exclusion for car parking extended to the lease of a site laid out for car parking and not just to the supply of parking by the lessee.

Standard-rating also extends, as a separate matter, to:

(1) The freehold sale of:

    (a) a completed or partly completed new building (except a dwelling or certain buildings intended for use solely for *relevant* residential or *relevant* charitable purposes);

    (b) a completed or partly completed new civil engineering work.

(2) Supplies under a developmental tenancy, lease or licence (but this exception will be repealed with effect in relation to supplies made on or after 1 June 2020 (see art 4 of the *Value Added Tax (Buildings and Land) Order* 2008 (SI 2008/1146)).

(3) The granting of any right (e.g. equitable rights, options and, in Scotland, personal rights) to call for any of the taxable exceptions specified in the Group.

In addition, there are also a number of further standard-rated exceptions now found in VATA 1994, Sch. 10. These include:

- a supply under an otherwise zero-rated lease of a *relevant* residential building or a building intended for use for *relevant* charitable purposes, where the building ceases to be used for the intended purpose (Sch. 10., Part 2);
- an election to exercise the option to tax (Sch. 10., Part 1).

(a) New freehold buildings and civil engineering works

The exemption in Sch. 9, Grp. 1 is expressly overridden for (exclusion (a) to item 1):

'(a) the grant of the fee simple in –

(i) a building which has not been completed and which is neither designed as a dwelling or number of dwellings nor intended for use solely for a relevant residential purpose or a relevant charitable purpose;
(ii) a new building which is neither designed as a dwelling or number of dwellings nor intended for use solely for a relevant residential purpose or a relevant charitable purpose after the grant;
(iii) a civil engineering work which has not been completed;
(iv) a new civil engineering work.'

For this purpose, a building is new for three years from completion. This is defined (Note (2) to Grp.1) to mean *practical completion* (or when first fully occupied, whichever happens first). Standard-rating is, moreover, not limited to the first such grant; it can also apply to successive grants within that three-year period.

HMRC consider that the sale of land containing 'minor' civil engineering works is the supply of exempt land (unless an option to tax has been made) (see Notice 742 Land and Property (June 2012 at para. 3.3)).

(b) Opting to tax

An option to tax (formerly, 'waiving the exemption') can be exercised by each owner separately for each interest in land or buildings, which he holds. The rules, which are found in VATA 1994, Sch. 10, Part 1–, do not, however, apply to all types of property, and particularly do not cover:

- dwellings;
- *buildings designed, adapted, intended for use solely for a relevant* residential purpose; and
- buildings used for *relevant* charitable purposes.

They thus apply effectively only to commercial land and buildings.

The option, once exercised, was originally irrevocable. However, as a result of para. 25 of Sch. 10 the option can be rescinded after a period of 20 years on application to HMRC, and subject to specified conditions being met. It may also be withdrawn during a 'cooling off' period if, it having been exercised, the taxpayer satisfies the following conditions (para. 23, Sch 10 of VATA 1994):

- less than six months have elapsed from the time the option had effect; and
- the option has not taken practical effect, i.e. VAT has not been charged; and
- the property has not been disposed of as part of a going concern to which the rules in art. 5 of the *Value Added Tax (Special Provisions) Order* 1995 (SI 1995/1268) apply (see **Chapter 3** at 30-450); and
- notice of the revocation is given to HMRC.

However, things like cleaning, maintenance and heating to the tenant's demised premises outside the terms of the lease are separate supplies, not taking the character and VAT liability of the rents, but looked at on their own merits.

An option to tax is also only exercisable from a current date (not retrospectively), with a requirement to notify HMRC in writing within 30 days (para. 20, Sch. 10 of VATA 1994). If notification is not made in this time, the option is ineffective. The actual timing of an option to tax and the evidence needed to show that an option has been validly made are clearly, therefore, important. In this regard, HMRC issued a special reminder in August 1999 in *Business Brief* 17/99, following the *Blythe Limited Partnership* case.

- The issue in *Blythe Ltd Partnership* [1999] BVC 2,224 was how many properties the partnership had opted on and whether they were bound by the written notification made by their solicitors. The solicitors had sent in the rectification and attached a list of 16 properties. Blythe subsequently sold one of these, without charging VAT. They argued that, of the 16 properties, they had in fact only opted on four, and the property sold was not one of these. On the basis of documentary evidence available at the hearing, the Tribunal found that Blythe had indeed only opted on four buildings. Consequently, it was not bound by the incorrect notification with regard the other 12 properties.

Other cases also show how significant the timing is.

- That of *Higher Education Statistics Agency Ltd* [2000] BVC 150, for example, concerned the purchaser of an investment property at auction. The property was being sold as a going concern and the option to tax had been exercised by the vendor. In order for the transfer of the property to be entirely VAT-free under the transfer of business rules in art. 5 of the *Value Added Tax (Special Provisions) Order* 1995 (SI 1995/1268) (see **Chapter 3** at 30-250), HESA was also required to elect to tax. Unfortunately, it only did so after the payment of the deposit, which was held to be too late.
- In *Fforestfach Medical Centre* [2000] BVC 410, in November 1999, it was held that, although the appellant had supposedly expressed the intention to elect to tax a property from the time it had been acquired from the developer, the letter notifying HMRC had been sent some six months after the event and the election could not be given retrospective effect.

Following *HESA* and the later case of *Chalegrove Properties Ltd* [2001] BVC 2,279 in March 2001, HMRC reported, in *Business Brief* 11/2001 of 21 August 2001, a change in their approach where a property is acquired as part of the assets of a going concern.

HMRC had originally argued that this notification had to be actually *received* by them by the relevant time. However, in the *Chalegrove Properties* case, the Tribunal held it was sufficient to show that, on or by the relevant date, the transferee had properly addressed, pre-paid and posted the letter.

This was accepted by HMRC and acknowledged on 21 August 2001 in *Business Brief* 11/01, which is now referred to in section 11.2.1 of Notice 742A on Opting to tax land and buildings (June 2010).

In certain circumstances it is possible to make a real estate election (REE) under para. 21 Sch.10 of VATA 1994. Once a REE has been made each property subsequently acquired by a person (subject to exceptions) will be treated as subject to an option with effect from the start of the day it is acquired.

> **Practice point**
>
> Timing can clearly be vital.
>
> - Completion under an agreement for the transfer or sale is not necessarily the date to go by, for example, if an earlier payment has been received. Leaving things until then could easily, therefore, be too late.
> - There is no particular reason why opting to tax and notifying HMRC cannot be done well before anything like a time of supply occurs. This can always be conditional on Completion eventually taking place and at least one major potential problem will be out of the way.
>
> Timing can also be important as:
>
> - The option cannot be exercised retrospectively and will only have effect from the date on which it is made – or from such later date as is specified in the election. In short, you can opt in advance, but not in arrears.
> - To have effect at all, the decision must be formally notified. Usually, HMRC must be told within 30 days. Unless this is done, the option is ineffective.

The notification of the option to tax is not the end of the matter, because HMRC must also give their written permission if the taxpayer has made any exempt supply of the property before the date of its intended effect unless any of the following four conditions are met (para. 28 of Sch 10, VATA 1994 and para. 5.2 of Notice 742A *Opting to tax land and buildings* (June 2010)):

(1) The property is a mixed-use development and the only exempt supplies have been in relation to dwellings.

(2) The taxpayer does not wish to recover input tax incurred before the option is to have effect; *and*

   (a) the consideration for the earlier exempt supplies has only been by way of rent; and
   (b) the only input tax to be recovered subsequently is on building works and day-to-day overheads.

(3) The taxpayer satisfies the first (outputs) requirement and (if applicable) the second (inputs) requirement, namely:

(a) the taxpayer does not intend or expect that any supply which will be taxable as a result of making the option to tax will either: (1) be made to a person connected with the taxpayer; or (2) arise from an agreement under which the taxpayer or another person has made or will make an exempt supply in respect of a right to occupy the property, where the right begins or continues after the date on which the option takes effect ; and

(b) this condition applies if the taxpayer has been or expects to be entitled to credit for any part of the input tax incurred on its capital expenditure on the property as being wholly or partly attributable to supplies that are taxable supplies by virtue of its option to tax. Where this requirement applies the taxpayer must not intend or expect to use any part of the capital expenditure for either of the following purposes: (a) making exempt supplies which do not confer a right to credit for input tax pursuant to s. 26(2)(c) of VATA 1994; or (b) for private or non-business purposes, other than purposes giving rise to a right to a refund of VAT on the supplies under s. 33, 33A or 41(3) of VATA 1994.

(4) The exempt supplies have been *incidental* to the main use of the property.

- In *C & E Commrs v R & R Pension Fund* [1996] BVC 348, the question was *how much input tax can be recovered after an election to tax had been made*? The trustees had suffered a developer's self-supply charge (now abolished) on the completion of a new building and tried to recover the tax involved by electing to tax future rents due under a 150 year lease. For the first 16 months, until the election was made, exempt rents had been received and, based on the length of the lease, the trustees proposed that 99.1 per cent of the input tax on the self-supply should be allowed. However, whilst HMRC were happy to permit the election to be made, since the property was within the capital goods scheme, they said the relief should be spread over a ten-year period instead.

On appeal, the Court agreed. HMRC were obliged to apply the capital goods scheme and were entitled to grant the option subject to its application. It was not open to them to approve arrangements, which overrode the scheme and accept as fair and reasonable a result different from that which the law had provided.

(i) The extent of the option

The option applies to the whole of the interest concerned, e.g. to the whole of an office block or to a building and all of the land within its curtilage, when owned by the same person. For this purpose, buildings linked internally or by a covered walkway are treated as parts of a single building, as are buildings making up a complex, such as a purpose-built shopping centre, if they are grouped around a fully enclosed concourse.

It does not, however, automatically bind successors in title, who are free to make their own decisions as to whether to opt to tax.

However, an option exercised by a company, which is a member of a VAT group, *will* bind any other company which was also a member of the VAT group at the time the option was exercised, and any other company which becomes a member of the VAT group when the opter still has an interest in the opted property.

> **Practice point**
>
> The attractions of opting and recovering input VAT are obvious. However, whether and to what extent it is beneficial to do so can need careful consideration.
>
> Many tenants will be fully, or at least substantially, able to recover input VAT. An option exercised by the landlord may well then be an attraction. Costs are likely to be lower as there will be no unrecovered VAT built into the rents or service charges.
>
> Exempt occupiers, however (e.g. financial or insurance sector businesses or schools or those providing healthcare) will be in a different position. They will be generally unable to recover any VAT charged, so that an exempt rent or sale price could then be considerably more attractive. Unless, therefore, the amount of tax is large, it may not be in the landlord's best interests to opt. By not doing so he may well be able to negotiate a higher rent or price.
>
> Subject to this, whether to opt is a decision solely for the owner or landlord concerned.
>
> It does not require the consent of the buyer or tenant, something that was shown in *R Walia Opticians Ltd* [1997] BVC 2,511.
>
> However, it is generally sensible not to opt to tax unilaterally across a property portfolio without each property being looked at on its own merits.

(ii) Restrictions and avoidance

For some time, there have been restrictions on the use of the option for VAT avoidance, especially where lease-and-leaseback arrangements are involved.

Some of the present rules were introduced with effect from 19 March 1997 by the *Finance Act* 1997 and were further amended from 10 March 1999 by the *Value Added Tax (Buildings and Land) Order* 1999 (SI 1999/593), and from 1 June 2008 by the *Value Added Tax (Buildings and Land) Order* 2008 (SI 2008/1146). They focus on:

(1) Land and buildings within the scope of the capital items scheme (see **Chapter 4** at 40-200(8)).

(2) The intention at the time of any grant of the developer or of the person financing the purchase, construction or reconstruction, etc. of the land or buildings as to:

   (a) their being treated as capital items by the developer or by any person to whom the land or buildings are transferred; and
   (b) the use to which the land or buildings will be put.

The aim, overall, is for an option to tax not to apply where a person funding the capital cost of a building (either directly or using an associate) intends to occupy the building itself for exempt or non-business purposes. It is not intended to dis-apply an option to tax for ordinary arms-length leasing or speculative development by commercial property developers or where commercial property developers have obtained funding from a source such as a bank, and later the bank happens to take a lease of part of the development. The provisions also apply to a building that has been refurbished or fitted out. However, Sch. 10 of VATA 1994 is subject to exceptions in the disapplication of the option to tax, which were introduced by the *Value Added Tax (Buildings and Land) Order* 2011 (SI 2011/86) the effect of which is that the option to tax will not be disapplied where a development financier or a person connected to the development financier occupies 10 per cent or less of any building included in the grant. Further, it will not be disapplied where a grantor or a person connected to the grantor occupies 2 per cent or less of any building included the grant. It will also not be disapplied in either scenario where the only occupation of the person concerned ('P') is in relation to an automatic teller machine of P. Broadly, the effect of the provisions is as follows:

- where a person ('P') is in occupation of the land at any time before the end of the relevant adjustment period as defined in Sch. 10 (essentially the period provided in *VAT Regulations* 1995 for the making of adjustments relating to the deduction of input tax as respect the land), P is treated as not in occupation of the land for the purposes of the anti-avoidance provisions at that time if certain building occupation conditions are met, or if the occupation arises solely by reference to any automatic teller machine of P (para. 15, Sch. 10 of VATA 1994);
- the anti-avoidance provisions provide that occupation by a person connected with P is treated as occupation by P unless that occupation is wholly, or substantially wholly, for eligible purposes. However, the building occupation conditions are subject to a 'maximum allowable percentage' that P may occupy in order to be treated as not in occupation of the land (para. 15A,Sch. 10 VATA 1994). If P is a grantor or a person connected to the grantor, the maximum allowable percentage is 2 per cent (para 15A(4)(a), Sch. 10 of VATA 1994). If P is a development financier or person connected to a development financier, the maximum allowable percentage is 10 per cent (para 15A(4)(b), Sch. 10 of VATA 1994). A 'relevant building' is defined as excluding any building that P occupies solely by reference to any automatic teller machine of P (para 15A(4), Sch. 10 of VATA 1994).
- Whether an option should be disapplied was tested in *Winterthur Life UK Ltd* [1999] BVC 2,093, where the issue was whether the contributions of members of a personal pension scheme were to be regarded as funds provided *for meeting the whole or any part of the cost of the grantor's development of the land*, with the effect that the election to tax the grant of the lease to them of a building, which they then occupied was not to be treated as a taxable supply by virtue of the election. It was held, dismissing the company's appeal, that the conditions for disapplying the election were present and it was hard to understand how the wide terms of the definition of *providing finance* had not been met. It was also felt immaterial whether the direct or indirect provision of the funds was solely or mainly for meeting any part of the cost of acquisition and that the transactions were not for the avoidance of tax.

(c) Developmental leases and tenancies

Since 1 January 1992, a landlord has had to apply VAT to any rents, etc. charged to the tenant under a *developmental* tenancy, lease or licence (VATA 1994, Sch. 9, Grp. 1, item 1 exception (b)). A tenancy, lease or licence is treated as a *developmental* tenancy, lease or licence where:

- construction, reconstruction, etc. has begun on or after 1 January 1992; and
- the property is subject to a developer's self-supply.

This is independent of the option to tax. The need to charge VAT under these rules ceases on the termination of the tenancy, etc. but not on an assignment.

(d) Taxable self-supplies

There is a taxable self-supply under the *Value Added Tax (Self-supply of Construction Services) Order* 1989 (SI 1989/472), which can require someone constructing, extending or altering a building or civil engineering work for himself to treat those services as supplied to and supplied by him for the purposes of the business. There is a de minimis limit of £100,000 and members of a VAT group are treated as a single person for this purpose.

There is presently no plan for this charge to be phased out, unlike the self-supply charge for building land, which affected newly constructed buildings or civil engineering works and which was phased out from 1 March 1995 and abolished from 1 March 1997.

(e) Surrenders

Following the successful appeal to the ECJ by the accountants, Lubbock Fine in *Lubbock Fine & Co v C & E Commrs* (Case C-63/92) [1993] BVC 287, all surrenders are now accepted as exempt except where the tenant has opted to tax.

Reverse surrenders, which occur where, say, a tenant agrees to pay the landlord to accept a surrender of an onerous lease, involve a supply by the landlord to the tenant. The position historically taken by HMRC has been to see these as taxable, being the supply of the agreement of the landlord to accept the surrender, rather than the grant, of any interest in or right over land. However, as a result of the *Value Added Tax (Land) Order* 1995 (SI 1995/282), from 1 March 1995 the supply is now to be treated as exempt, a position supported by the successful appeal by *Central Capital Corporation Ltd* [1996] BVC 2,336. Where the landlord has opted to tax, such a supply will be standard rated.

- In a similar vein, the Tribunal in *Lloyds Bank plc* [1996] BVC 2,875 looked at a termination payment from a tenant, which was argued by the taxpayer as being in the nature of *liquidated damages* and *outside the scope*. However, the payment arose in the context of a clause incorporated into the original lease by a deed of variation. The variation had taken place immediately before the termination and the suggestion by the taxpayer was that the payment was thus outside the scope. The Tribunal, however, was inclined to look at the entire transaction and the substance of the deal. The payment was thus, in effect, consideration for a reverse surrender and, as the landlord had opted to tax, was subject to VAT.

The idea of looking at the entire transaction seems like a *Furniss v Dawson* approach that has not, of course, so far really succeeded in the realms of VAT. However, here the parties to the transaction were the same throughout, which may limit the taxpayer's ability to argue the two aspects should be treated separately.

(3) Zero-rating

Zero-rating, which was once probably the single most important planning opportunity for those involved in property development/investment, now applies just to buildings which are dwellings or for use for certain residential or charitable purposes. As now enacted, VATA 1994, Sch. 8, Grp. 5, item 1 applies (emphasis added) only to:

'The *first* grant by a person –

(a) constructing a building –
  (i) designed as a dwelling or a number of dwellings; or
  (ii) intended for use solely for a *relevant* residential purpose or a *relevant* charitable purpose; or
(b) converting a non-residential building or a non-residential part of a building into a building designed as a dwelling or a number of dwellings or a building intended for use solely for a relevant residential purpose,

of a major interest in, or in any part of, the building or its site.'

Grant, for this purpose, includes an assignment or surrender. It will be noted that the zero-rating only applies to the first such grant. In the case of a tenancy or lease, it also only applies to the initial premium, or, if there is no such premium, to the first payment of rent.

An institutional investor will, in fact, fall within these provisions if it:

- commissions the construction of such a building on land which it owns (or in which it has an interest);
- supplies of construction services are made to it; and
- exercises some measure of control over the construction of the building, e.g. control over design or planning.

In appropriate cases, the concept can extend to someone who, at the time of construction, has entered into a development agreement/agreement for lease with a freeholder for a major interest lease to be obtained on completion of the development. There is, however, the requirement for the onward supply to itself be a *major interest*. This is defined in VATA 1994, s. 96(1) to effectively mean the freehold or a long lease, i.e. one for *a term certain exceeding 21 years*. Short leases are thus not enough and will always give rise to exempt supplies.

Practice point

Before zero-rating is available, the supplier must qualify as a *person constructing a building* or someone who is carrying out the appropriate conversion or substantial reconstruction.

It is sometimes assumed this means just someone who acts as a building contractor or who physically carries out the works of construction or reconstruction. However, it can include someone, such as:

- a bank;
- an investment company;
- an insurer;
- a pension fund; or a
- a property company,

provided there is sufficient involvement in commissioning the construction or other works and exercising control over or planning and development.

Sometimes this may simply be a matter of recognising that this is what is actually happening; in other cases, it may be necessary to amend the agreements or structures used. However, any such amendments can often be made without any major impact on the overall commercial position.

Similar zero-rating (i.e. for major interests in dwellings or *relevant* residential or commercial buildings) is also afforded for protected (e.g. listed) buildings (see Group 6, Sch. 8 of VATA 1994). However, zero-rating is not permitted for supplies from 1 October 2012 in respect of Items 2 and 3 of Group 6 which zero rate construction services and building materials in the course of an approved alteration (see FA 2012, s. 196, Sch. 26, para. 1, 3). Additionally changes have been made to remove the test in Note (4) of Sch. 8 which zero rates the first sale or long lease of a substantial reconstruction where 60 per cent by value is an approved alteration. Instead, a new Note (4) (see Sch. 26 to FA 2012) has been inserted ('the shell test') which provides that a protected building is not regarded as substantially reconstructed unless, when the reconstruction is completed, the reconstructed building incorporates no more of the original building (that is to say, the building as it was before the reconstruction began) than the external walls, together with other external features of architectural or historic interest, hence the shell test. Accordingly, major interests must again be granted, this time by persons who have reconstructed a building from a shell. Previously zero rating was granted to persons undertaking a *substantial reconstruction*, which had meant that the work had first to constitute a *reconstruction* so that:

- at least three-fifths of the work, measured by reference to cost, must be on, *approved alterations*; or
- the reconstructed building must incorporate no more of the original building than the external walls, together with any external features of architectural or historic interest.

Certain transitional provisions apply to maintain zero-rating in circumstances where a contract was entered into or where planning consent was applied for before 21 March 2012 (see the *Value Added Tax (Zero-rating) Order* 2012 and para. 7, Sch. 26 to FA 2012). For guidance on the position generally see HMRC VAT Information Sheet 10/12 (August 2012).

An *approved alteration* means, broadly, an alteration which cannot be carried out without prior consent under the *Planning (Listed Buildings and Conservation Areas) Act* 1990 (or its equivalent in Scotland or Northern Ireland) and for which such consent has been obtained. As with the rules prior to 1 April 1989, zero-rating is also available under item 2 and 3 of Grp. 5 for the services of constructing a new dwelling or *intended for use solely for a relevant residential purpose* , and under Grp. 6 for approved alterations (but not for professional costs or other services of a supervisory nature).

Knowing which buildings continue to qualify for zero-rating is clearly also important. A *dwelling* is perhaps self-explanatory. It will, though, only include buildings, which can lawfully be occupied throughout the year by the persons to whom the grant is made. It will thus not include holiday or timeshare accommodation. Use for a relevant residential purposes means use as:

- home or other institution providing residential accommodation for children;
- home or other institution providing residential accommodation with personal care ;
- a hospice;
- residential accommodation for students or school pupils;
- residential accommodation for members of any of the armed forces;
- monasteries, nunneries or similar establishments; and
- an institution which is the sole or main residence of at least 90 per cent of its residents,

but in no case including hospitals, prisons or other penal institutions or hotels, inns or similar establishments.

A building intended for use solely for a relevant charitable purposes also qualifies for zero-rating on first grant by a person constructing such a building. Use for a relevant charitable purpose means use by a charity in either or both the following namely: (a) otherwise than in the course or furtherance of a business, (b) as a village hall or similarly in providing social or recreational facilities for a local community.

If the major interest granted is a tenancy or lease, zero-rating only applies to (Note (14) to Group 5, Sch. 8, VATA 1994):

- the premium, if the consideration for the grant is or includes a premium;
- where there is no premium, the first payment of rent.

The significance of zero-rating is the potential for recovering input VAT without the need to charge tax at the standard-rate. Subject, however, to certain transitional arrangements in 1989 for commercial buildings, the present zero-rating, although useful, is now of much less interest than it was previously.

> **Practice point**
>
> The *person constructing* (e.g. the institutional investor) must grant a major interest. This requires, in the case of a lease, that it be for a *term certain exceeding 21 years*.
>
> Sometimes leases of over 21 years are neither practicable nor sensible in the prevailing economic climate. However, this need not prevent zero-rating. It may still be possible to achieve the desired result, namely the recovery of related input VAT by:
>
> - granting a lease for a stated term of, say 25 years, with a mutual break clause at a more convenient intermediate date; or
> - granting a suitable major interest lease to a connected entity but which was not treated as part of a VAT group with the grantor. This might achieve a zero-rated intra-group lease, with the lessee company then being able to grant exempt sub-leases at will with little or no VAT expense.
>
> It is not possible to grant a short lease with an option to extend. This would involve two exempt supplies.
>
> It should be emphasised that zero-rating under VATA 1994, Sch. 8, Grp. 5 is limited to the first such grant. If the major interest is a tenancy or lease, it will thus generally only apply to the premium, or if no premium is payable, to the first payment of rent.

(a) Change of use

There is a qualification, however, where any zero-rated services described above have been supplied in the construction of a relevant residential building or a building used or intended for relevant charitable purposes if (para. 36, Sch. 10, VATA 1994):

- within ten years of the completion, a VAT charge will arise (i) on each occasion that there is an increase in the use of the premises for a non-relevant purpose; (ii) where a person disposes of the entire interest in the premises or in a part of the premises; (iii) where an identifiable area of the premises, or of a part of the premises, is used by a person in occupation of the premises (or part) for a non-relevant purpose.

(b) Commercial buildings

Following legislative changes, since 1989 zero-rating only applies to commercial buildings where:

- steps were taken to pre-empt the imposition of the standard-rate on new building work by the pre-payment of building contracts prior to 1 April 1989. How far this will have succeeded in particular cases depends, of course, on the steps actually taken and the degree to which they individually or collectively may be susceptible to challenge; or
- prior to 21 June 1988, when the proposals for change were first announced, there was either a pre-existing contract to let or sell a building or a pre-existing contract or obligation to construct. This was subject to a number of conditions (including appropriate evidence) being satisfied, and in some cases planning permission also having been obtained prior to 21 June 1988.

(4) Outside the scope transfers

Where property is concerned, it is also necessary to consider the special rules for the acquisition or disposal of the assets of a business as a going concern (art. 19 and 29 of Council Directive 2006/112/EC). In the UK, these are found in art. 5(1) of the *Value Added Tax (Special Provisions) Order* 1995 (SI 1995/1268), which is discussed in detail in **Chapter 3** at 30-450.

Article 5(1) provides that, subject to para. 2, a person shall be treated as making neither a supply of goods nor a supply of services on the supply of the assets of a business where:

'(a) their supply to a person to whom he transfers his business as a going concern where -

    (i) the assets are to be used by the transferee in carrying on the same kind of business, whether or not as part of an existing business, as that carried on by the transferor, and

    (ii) in a case where the transferor is a taxable person, the transferee is already, or immediately becomes as a result of the transfer, a taxable person or a person defined as such in section 3(1) of the Manx Act'

Similar rules, art. 5(1)(b), apply in the case of the transfer of part of a business, with the further proviso that the part transferred is capable of separate operation.

The rules are further modified (art. 5(2)) to the extent that one or more of the assets transferred which is either:

- a new freehold building or civil engineering work, the disposal of which would otherwise be subject to VAT (VATA 1994, Sch. 9, Grp, 1, item 1 – exception (a)). This covers, in particular, commercial, non-residential, non-charitable buildings (see 80-350);
- any other commercial, non-residential, non-charitable land or building where the transferor has opted to tax rather than treat any supplies as exempt (VATA 1994, Sch. 10, para. 2–4) (see 80-350).

In either case, the transferor will be required to account for VAT on the land or building concerned, unless certain conditions are satisfied. These are that the transferee has, no later than the relevant date.

(1) Exercised an option to tax in relation to the land which has effect on the relevant date and has given any necessary written notification of the election to HMRC.

(2) Notified the transferor that the following does not apply:
   (a) the supply of the asset to be transferred would become, in relation to him, a capital item as described in reg. 113 of the *Value Added Tax Regulations* 1995 (see **Chapter 4**) if the supply of that asset to him;
      (i) were to be treated as neither a supply of goods nor a supply of services; or
      (ii) were not so treated; and
   (b) his own supplies of that asset will be, or would fall to be, exempt by virtue of para. 12, Sch. 10 of VATA 1994 (i.e. as a result of the occupation of the property not wholly or substantially wholly, for eligible purposes (namely, not being a taxable person and not in occupation for the purposes of making creditable supplies) (being supplies which entitle the person to a credit for any input tax wholly attributable to those supplies): para. 16, Sch. 10 of VATA 1994.

This is an anti-avoidance measure to prevent input tax on a new development or refurbishment by the transferor with the property subsequently being let VAT-free by the transferee. It will apply, for example, to transfers of pre-let buildings, such as office blocks, but also covers other commercial and industrial premises.

In short, for a sale of a business, where the assets include property in respect of which an option to tax had been made , to qualify as a VAT-free TOGC, the transferee must now opt to tax the property and notify HMRC *before*:

- the transaction occurred. Failure to do this means the transferor is required to charge VAT on the sale; and
- notify the transferor, before the transfer takes place, that the transferee's option to tax will not be disapplied.

If the transferee cannot make this latter notification, the transaction cannot be VAT-free.

What HMRC say in relation to transfers involving let property, is set out in Section 6 of Notice 700/9 (April 2008), which is discussed in **Chapter 3**. Section 2.4 of that Notice contains guidance on the anti-avoidance rules and the option to tax, which is also covered separately in Notice 742A.

> *Practice point*
>
> It can be important to remember that, if the transferor has made an option to tax, before the transfer can be disregarded, for VAT purposes as a transfer of a going concern, the transferee must also opt and must do so before the transfer takes place, something underlined only too well in *Higher Education Statistics Agency Ltd*. If the transferee does not, the relief will not apply and

- the seller may then face a VAT liability for which provision has not been made; alternatively,
- the purchaser may be charged VAT he will not then be able to recover.

Timing in this situation can clearly be critical.

It can also be important for either or both of the parties to seek warranties and/or indemnities over the extent to which the option has, in fact, been exercised.

80-200 Points affecting particular supplies

(1) Advisory and other professional services

Advisory and professional services are generally taxable for VAT at the standard-rate. On occasions, however, the supply goes beyond mere advice, for example, where an accountant or a merchant/investment bank is wholly responsible for arranging and negotiating a management buy-out. In this case, the nature of the supply can be quite different. To the extent it relates to the procurement or arrangement of finance (by loan or by the issue of shares or debentures), it will then be basically exempt under VATA 1994, Sch. 9, Grp. 5, item 5 or 5A. What this can then entail is considered later at (5) under *Corporate finance*. Where a broker provides advisory services in addition to buying and selling securities, there will be a taxable supply of the advice if made as a separate supply for an identifiable charge, and an exempt supply if the contract with the client is for arranging transactions in securities and the broker raises charges only in relation to the transactions executed, and his advice is incidental to that service.

(2) Bonds

Often issued at a discount, bonds are essentially promises, in return for an immediate loan, a borrower will repay the principal, plus interest at an agreed rate, on or by a set date. The bond represents a security within VATA 1994, item 6. Interest paid to the holder of the bond is exempt within Group 5, Item 2. The redemption of a bond (e.g. on maturity) and the resulting payment is outside the scope of VAT since there is no supply of goods or services by the holder. This is in contrast to the position where a bond is sold.

The heading does not include performance bonds or guarantees.

(3) Clearing services

The provision of clearing or settlement services by a member of the International Stock Exchange are accepted as basically VAT-exempt. The exemption covers clearance and settlement services of CREST and other International Stock Exchange central services, including clearance and settlement services relating to futures and options in shares. Equally, settlement clearing services purchased from overseas will not be liable to the reverse charge (see **Chapter 5**). However, where a charge is made for a supply of safe custody services, it remains basically taxable at the standard-rate, although not subject to the imported service rules. Additionally, any electronic messaging system which underlies the financial system, such as SWIFT, will be treated as a supply taxable at the standard-rate (*Re Nordea Pankki Suomi Oyj* (C-350/10) 28 July 2011: see **Chapter 12**).

(4) Commission sharing

Under FSA rules in PS 05/09, it is no longer possible for more than one broker to receive commission for the execution of the same deal; nor is it possible for commission payments to cover third-party services other than research. On the face of it, this limits the availability of the exemption. However, investment banks have entered into *commission sharing* arrangements under which the main broker supplies execution services to a fund manager client in return for a commission, an element of which the broker has agreed to pay away to a third broker on the fund manager's instructions.

This is in recognition of services supplied by the third broker to the fund manager and is accepted as exempt on the basis that it represents consideration for a financial intermediary service that was not finally concluded. For this to apply, however (see HMRC's VATFIN at 7590):

- the intention at all times must have been to secure execution business;
- the services provided must be sales-orientated i.e. provided by sales traders dealing directly with clients;
- the research information provided to the client must not be generic trend and stock analysis but specific to the execution of potential transactions that the provider is capable of seeing through;
- the services must go further than just the provision of information and include an element of *intermediation* i.e. discussion of pricing, volumes etc. with a view to a potential sale.

Any fees or commission not meeting these tests will be liable to VAT at the standard-rate.

(5) Corporate finance

Corporate finance is one of those difficult areas of VAT, where things are not always what they may seem. Traditionally the province of merchant/investment banks and stockbrokers, it is now increasingly common to find this work being undertaken by the consultancy arms of the larger accounting firms. For many it will be a sector affording a high level of input VAT recovery, a result which often follows from the fact that the service is perceived as being one of advice. To a large extent this may be true. However, to the extent that the adviser becomes closely involved in the procurement or facilitation of finance, there is then the possibility that the service might in reality be exempt, with all that that entails. Only those businesses which make a Group 5, item 5 (intermediary) supply can treat their supplies as exempt intermediary services.

Whatever the basic liability position, corporate finance is still always a service, subject to the place of supply rules discussed in Chapter 3. Depending on what is involved and where the client belongs, therefore, there will be times when the supply is outside the scope of UK VAT or exempt with the right of input VAT recovery – or, if acquired from abroad, subject to the imported services rules.

In an attempt to clarify the position, in February 2003, HMRC issued guidance in the form of VAT Information Sheet 02/03, which expanded on the advice already set out in Notice 701/49. However, VAT Information Sheet 02/03 has been superseded by HMRC's discussion in their VAT and Finance Manual.

8 Securities, Property and Investment

Briefly, HMRC give the following examples of services provided by a corporate finance business (CFB), which may involve exempt supplies as an intermediary (within Group 5, item 5) (VATFIN at 7460):

'Clear or specific mandate agreements

The CFB's client may choose to issue, sell or purchase securities (e.g. shares) or take out a loan. The CFB is engaged to negotiate the transaction. If the CFB meets all the criteria for exemption (bearing in mind that for transaction in securities there need be no preparatory work) and you are satisfied there is a single supply, this is an exempt intermediary service. You may find that other companies are sub-contracted for their advisory services in the sale of the securities. Unless they themselves are responsible for bringing together the parties, their supply will be taxable. Where the agreement is aborted and the services provided would have been exempt had the transaction gone through, the services remain exempt.

Open mandates

An open mandate arises when an organisation is engaged for its specialist skills, but it is not known at the time of engagement if there will be any specific exempt transaction. For example, a merchant bank could be asked to evaluate methods of refinancing the business and eventually decide that the best way to do so is by issuing shares in the company (an exempt item 6 transaction). The merchant bank offers advisory services under the agreement to evaluate methods of finance and these will be supplies for VAT purposes only when supplied for a consideration. These will be liable to VAT at the standard rate up until any such time as an exempt transaction is actually envisaged. This is a complex area and open to some debate because the point at which the services change from being advisory to intermediary in nature is often unclear. If the business subsequently decides to effect a transaction that is exempt (e.g. share issue), then the intermediary's services will be exempt except to the extent that any specific charge for the advisory element may be identified (see VATFIN7220). It is important to look at how the services are supplied: there may be a new agreement with the bank outlining a change in engagement terms (in which case the advisory services supplied under the first agreement will be liable to VAT) or an exempt transaction will be envisaged from the outset, albeit that it is not known exactly which exempt transaction (with the advisory services seen as part of this single exempt supply). You should always check the agreements etc to confirm the terms on which the CFB or any other organisation has been engaged. Where the agreement is aborted, the liability depends on the nature of the service supplied. Exemption is not permitted for advisory services - only where work has specifically been undertaken in relation to an exempt supply (and provided all the criteria are met). If an exempt transaction was envisaged, and you can see that the work already carried out reflects this, the fee will be exempt regardless of whether or not the contract was concluded.

Services to a target company

A company may need to defend itself against a hostile take-over bid and engage another party to help deal with this. Such services are often advisory and will be taxable. However, as with the situation above, their services may involve raising capital (perhaps by issuing shares) or arranging a de-merger or sale of a subsidiary in order to defend the take-over. It is again important to examine precisely what is being supplied and contracts will help you do this. Where such services are supplied to a company in connection with an agreed bid, these may involve only advice (liable to VAT at the standard rate). However, it could be that the adviser eventually becomes involved as an intermediary for the take-over, for example, by setting up the terms and conditions for the final deal. Provided the criteria are met, such services would fall within the exemption.'

Following the Ruling of the ECJ in *Kretztechnik AG v Finanzamt Linz* (Case C-465/03) ECJ [2006] BVC 66 (see earlier in **Chapter 1** at 10-300 and **Chapter 4** at 40-000) the issue, as opposed to a subsequent secondary supply, of shares or financial instruments will not be a supply for VAT purposes. This can clearly now have a potential bearing on the VAT treatment of the corporate advisory services provided, particularly where the consideration for the purchase of assets takes the form of the issue of shares or other securities.

Each contract must, of course, be viewed on its own. The scope of what is provided will vary from situation to situation and from client to client; it may also change during the course of an assignment. At the one extreme, there is the simple provision of advice, a professional service which is generally taxable at the standard-rate. At the other, there is the more *hands on* involvement, with the adviser putting together a capital-raising operation, share placement, merger or acquisition or sale to an extent that the advice is more appropriately described as *intermediary services*. Unless the transaction amounts to just the acquisition or disposal of assets, the likelihood is that some or all of the service will fall within item 5 or 6 of exemption Group. 5. And, in between, you can have an assets deal which ends up as a share-for-share exchange or vice versa. Where in this situation does taxability end and exemption begin?

For something to be exempt, there must clearly be a direct involvement in the arrangement or provision of finance or the issue or sale of shares or other securities.

Exemption will not, however, cover the normal services of reporting accountants, lawyers, printers and public relations firms, although these may all be involved to varying degrees.

- An illustration of the potential issues is provided by *Hargreaves Lansdown Asset Management Ltd* [1995] BVC 896. The taxpayer, one of the largest independent financial advisers, was engaged by Lloyds Merchant Bank to co-ordinate an offer for subscription of package units on behalf of Lloyds Smaller Companies Investment Trust. The company had been responsible for providing potential investors with the mini-prospectus and, without its services, the issue would not have taken place. Various elements of this service were described, but what decided the matter, at the end of the day, was the fact that much of the issue proceeded through other FIMBRA members. In that respect, what the company had provided had amounted to marketing assistance, not the *making of arrangements* (as the exemption was then expressed). On this basis, the Tribunal considered the exemption could only apply to transactions involving the taxpayer's own clients, not to services related to other FIMBRA members or their clients. As a side issue, and something that underlines the uncertainties there can be, the taxpayer had originally charged VAT prior to receiving advice on the matter from Lloyds.

(a) The possible conflict of interest

The issue is not just of interest to the adviser. Clients will often be equally concerned that the VAT treatment should be correct or that the effect of the tax should be limited. VAT on fees will by no means always be recoverable (see **Chapter 4** at 40-150), although, in the case of costs related to the issue of shares or securities, this should not now be concern following the Ruling of the ECJ in the *Kretztechnik AG v Finanzamt Linz* case.

- In *Nightfreight plc* [1998] BVC 2,232, for example, the client sought to argue that the services of reporting accountants to a share flotation were exempt and not merely the provision of financial information. The contention was that the words *transactions in shares* in art. 13(B)(d)(5) of the Sixth VAT Directive (Directive 77/388) (art. 135(1)(f) of Council Directive 2006/112/EC) should be read in the light of the French, German, Italian and Portuguese versions, which intended exemption to extend to *transactions relating to shares*. However, the Tribunal disagreed, holding that a distinction must be drawn between:
  - supplies which were a discrete part of the larger exempt transaction; and
  - supplies which happened to be part of an exempt transaction but which could equally have been part of any transaction.

There were two stages to every flotation. In the first stage, information was obtained from a variety of sources and from it a prospectus was prepared. When the prospectus was ready, and all the decisions as to the terms and marketing of the shares had been made, the second stage was the flotation itself. Only this second stage was exempt – and this should now only be a concern in cases where, following *Kretztechnik*, the flotation is made at some point subsequent to the issue itself.

In short, there can easily be a conflict of interests. The adviser may wish the supply to be taxable because this improves his own VAT position. The client, on the other hand, may prefer it to be exempt as this means no irrecoverable VAT and consequently less cost. But in between there can be a halfway house. There may be a point up to which the service can be said to be of general benefit to the business of the client as a whole rather than specifically directed at, say, the issue or sale of shares or the raising of finance.

The client will also be affected differently to the extent that the service relates to an acquisition of shares, as opposed to a sale. In this case, any input tax incurred on the related professional and other costs will generally be treated as *residual* input tax of the business and recoverable on the same basis as tax on normal overhead costs, unless the acquisition itself is seen as a pure investment as in cases like *Polysar* (see **Chapter 1** at 10-300) and not an *economic activity* for VAT.

(b) Defences against hostile takeovers

Sometimes, services will involve assistance in defending a company against a hostile take-over. Whilst the VAT treatment will, again, depend on what is supplied, the service in this case will tend to be taxable rather than exempt. Equally, services supplied in connection with an agreed bid will often mean only standard-rated advice is provided.

(c) Abortive assignments

There is no automatic presumption, however, that in the event that a project becomes aborted the service provided will be taxable. In essence, the VAT liability will ultimately depend on the intentions of the parties and on what would have happened had the matter proceeded as planned. In the case of an open mandate agreement, the liability of the services provided up to the time the decision is taken to abort depends on the nature of the service provided (see (a) above).

(6) Dealing services

The provision of dealing systems, enabling the user to deal in securities or interfacing between market makers or between market makers and their clients, were regarded as taxable, prior to January 1990, but are now often exempt. This is because once trades have taken place there is a need to settle indebtedness between the parties. This service would typically include: identifying payments for transactions, balancing accounts for the principals and notifying final liabilities to the parties for settlement purposes. This service may be exempt under item 5 of Group 5 as intermediary services in connection with transactions in securities. It might also be exempt under item 1 of Group 5. However, for systems similar to SWIFT (a secure global financial messaging service used between financial institutions for interbank money and security transactions) the service is treated as taxable: *Nordea Pankki Suomi Oyj* (C-350/10).

(7) Depositaries or trustees

Under the EU and UK law regulating undertakings for collective investment there is a requirement for separately appointed depositaries (under UK law in the case of an authorised unit trust scheme, *trustees*). Their functions are essentially supervisory, with the aim of protecting the interests of consumers and investors. Under Art. 22 of Directive 2009/65/EC, the EU Directive on the co-ordination of laws, regulations and administrative provisions relating to undertakings for collective investment in transferable securities (UCITS), the assets of a common fund (which includes a unit trust) must be entrusted to a depositary for safe-keeping, and in this regard a depositary must:

'(a) ensure that the sale, issue, repurchase, redemption and cancellation of units effected on behalf of a common fund or by a management company are carried out in accordance with the applicable national law and the fund rules;
(b) ensure that the value of units is calculated in accordance with the applicable national law and the fund rules;
(c) carry out the instructions of the management company, unless they conflict with the applicable national law or the fund rules;
(d) ensure that in transactions involving a common fund's assets any consideration is remitted to it within the usual time-limits; and
(e) ensure that a unit trust's income is applied in accordance with the applicable national law and the fund rules.'

In the case of investment companies, Art. 32 of the same Directive provides that apart from safe-keeping the assets, the depositary must ensure:

'(a) that the sale, issue, repurchase, redemption and cancellation of units effected by or on behalf of an investment company are carried out in accordance with the law and with the investment company's instruments of incorporation;
(b) that in transactions involving an investment company's assets any consideration is remitted to it within the usual time-limits; and
(c) that a company's income is applied in accordance with the law and its instruments of incorporation.'

How these services are treated for VAT was considered in Abbey National plc and Inscape Investment Fund v C & E Commrs, (Case C-169/04) [2008] BVC 488 (see later at 80-300), where the ECJ felt they did not come within the scope of the exemption for in art. 13B(d)(6) of the Sixth Directive (art. 135(1)(g) of Council Directive 2006/112/EC of 28 November 2006). They did not rank as the management of undertakings for collective investment but amounted to the control and supervision of their activities, the aim being to ensure they are managed in accordance with the law. The services are, therefore, taxable.

(8) Dividends

Although the supply of securities is exempt from VAT, the dividends received from the holding of shares are *outside the scope*. Unlike interest, they are not consideration for any supply of goods or services (for example, of finance) but are simply the sharing-out of profits (see, for example, the comments on the *Floridienne* case at 80-100(1)).

(9) Euronotes

As with Sterling Commercial Paper, Euronotes will in most cases take the form of promissory notes. They are generally used for short-term borrowings – in this case, borrowing by financial institutions rather than other commercial or industrial organisations. On occasions, however, the terms of the documents may fall outside the Bills of Exchange Act, leaving the notes to be treated as securities or secondary securities within VATA 1994, Sch. 9, Grp. 5, item 6. Subject to this, Euronotes take a variety of forms, depending on the requirement of the particular circumstances. Notes which are underwritten may include:

- note issuance facilities (NIFS);
- revolving underwriting facilities (RUFS);
- short-term note issuance facilities (SNIFS); and
- global revolving underwriting facilities (GRUFS),

and, where not underwritten, are referred to as Euro Commercial Paper.

Arranging or undertaking an issue of these types of instrument is again basically exempt under item 5, although, following the *Kretztechnik AG v Finanzamt Linz* case, the issue itself will not now be a supply.

(10) Exchange bargain charges

These were at one time subject to VAT but are now basically exempt. There is, however, the right to input VAT relief where the supply is to a broker *belonging* outside the EU and the Isle of Man. The place of supply in that case is outside the UK.

(11) Face-value vouchers

Face-value vouchers that give a right to goods or services are not seen by HMRC as securities for money (see Section 3.2 of HMRC Notice 701/49 (November 2011)). What they say, though, is

'However, if the voucher is issued on credit and the presentation/redemption of the voucher establishes the issuer's obligation to pay the face value voucher then at the point the voucher can be exchanged for money it is a security for money and any consideration for it is exempt. For example, where the voucher is presented to a retailer as payment for goods or services it is not a security for money, but when the retailer presents the voucher to a third party to be exchanged for money, it becomes a security for money at that point if the voucher had been issued to the redeemer under a credit management/initial grant of credit. You can find further information on face value vouchers in VAT Information Sheets 03/2003 and 12/2003 and Notice 700/7 Business promotion schemes.'

Arguably, this view is incorrect as it is based (see VATA 1994, Sch. 10A, para. 1.1) on the premise that a *face-value voucher*:

'means a token, stamp or voucher (whether in physical or electronic form) that represents a right to receive goods or services to the value of an amount stated on it or recorded in it.'

With most, if not all, vouchers of this kind, there is no inalienable right to be supplied with goods or services, but simply a right to require that the voucher is accepted in full or part-payment. The issue or supply of such a voucher would seem, therefore, to be basically exempt from VAT as, for example, a *transaction concerning payments* within art. 135(1)(d) of Council Directive 2006/112/EC, i.e. within the heading of:

'transactions, including negotiation, concerning deposit and current accounts, payments, transfers, debts, cheques and other negotiable instruments, but excluding debt collection;'

For the purposes of VATA 1994 Sch 10A there are two principal types of face value vouchers, namely (i) retailer vouchers and (ii) credit vouchers. As discussed in Revenue & Customs Brief 12/12:

- '• A retailer voucher is a voucher issued by the same person who will redeem it. This includes, for example, gift tokens sold by a retailer for use in its own shops
- A credit voucher is any type of face value voucher that is issued by one person but which can be exchanged for goods and services from another person. This includes, for example, gift tokens sold by one company that can be exchanged for goods or services in a variety of high street shops.'

Under Sch. 10A the consideration for all supplies of credit vouchers is disregarded with VAT being brought into account by the redeemer when the vouchers are exchanged for goods or services (but for the position on single purpose vouchers see the following paragraph). With retailer vouchers the initial consideration on issue is disregarded but the vouchers are then taxed for subsequent supplies. The issuer is required to account for VAT on the supply when the voucher is redeemed.

Following the decision of the CoJ in *Lebara Ltd v R & C Commrs* (C-520/10) [2012] BVC 219, HMRC have removed single purpose face value vouchers from VATA Sch 10A with the consequence that they are taxed when they are issued (the changes apply with effect from 10 May 2012) (see section 201 of FA 2012). In other words, where such a voucher is sold both initially and by retailers or distributors, it is treated as a supply of the goods or services for which it can be redeemed. A single purpose face value voucher is one that carries the right to receive only one type of goods or services which are all subject to a single rate of VAT. The rules apply to all single purpose vouchers, whether credit, retailer or other types of voucher.

HMRC give as an example of such a voucher one that can be redeemed only for electronically supplied services will be a single purpose voucher even if the electronic service can have slightly different forms (e.g. streamed movies, music or games) (see generally Revenue & Customs Brief 12/12).

The VAT treatment of voucher transactions, particularly through cross border supply chains, has been fraught with difficulties in the absence of EU legislation clearly defining a common EU VAT treatment, with the consequence of various Member States applying their own national practices on an inconsistent basis leading to VAT inefficiencies or avoidance.

The case of *Lebara* involved UK based telecoms operator, Lebara, who sold phone cards to distributors in other Member States who then resold them to end-consumers directly or through other distributors. An end-consumer's use of the phone cards was routed through a UK sited telephone exchange. HMRC considered there were two supplies by Lebara, one to distributors which was outside the scope of UK VAT, and the other to users of the cards at the time of redemption, which HMRC considered to be taxable in the UK.

The CoJ was asked to consider the nature of the phone card transactions and when they should be taxed. It ruled against HMRC, finding that there was a single supply by Lebara to distributors and not a second supply to end users on redemption.

In a press release published 10 May, the EU Commission proposed new VAT rules to create a genuine single market for vouchers, noting that there is no justification for the market to be held back because of uncertainty and complications in the tax rules.

The EU Commission proposes a uniform set of rules, to be adopted at a national level by 1 January 2014 and to have effect from 1 January 2015. These rules cover:

- a new definition of different categories of vouchers
- the time of transaction for voucher transactions – at the point-of-sale and/or redemption, depending on the nature of the voucher
- distinguishing vouchers from other means of payment (including mobile payment services)
- clarifying the VAT treatment of free discount vouchers
- introduction of common rules for supply chains involving the distribution of certain vouchers through intermediaries
- technical measures to deal with input VAT recovery, redemption and reimbursement procedures, determining the person liable for payment of the VAT and other obligations for businesses

Further details can be found at: http://europa.eu/rapid/pressReleasesAction.do?reference=IP/1 2/464&format=HTML&aged=0&language=EN&guiLanguage=en.

(12) Individual savings accounts (ISAs) and related services

Individual savings accounts are a type of tax-free personal savings scheme, which started from 6 April 1999. There are three ways, *components* in which money can be invested – cash savings, stocks and shares, and some specially designed life insurance policies:

- cash ISAs may be suitable for short-term savings, and can enable easy access to the money saved;
- stocks and shares ISAs are more appropriate for savers intending to leave funds untouched for longer than, say, five years; and
- life insurance ISAs, which are meant for long-term saving and which also offer some built-in life cover.

There are two main types of ISA, maxi and mini ISAs:

- a maxi ISA can include cash, stocks and shares and life insurance in a single ISA with one manager;
- mini ISAs mean you can have separate ISAs, from different managers, for cash, stocks and shares and life insurance.

Most services connected with ISAs are exempt, but a few will be standard-rated. The exempt supplies will include:

- operating a savings account;
- providing insurance and insurance intermediaries' services;
- selling securities (stocks/shares, etc.);
- providing securities intermediaries/brokers' services; and
- effecting cash transfers and payments.

The standard-rated services will include:

- tax management;
- marketing and advertising;
- administration services, unless for insurance;
- discretionary fund management of securities; and
- advice.

Commentary is offered in Section 7.8 of HMRC Notice 701/49.

(13) Investment management

Investment management is generally treated differently to other, broadly, intermediary services. The wider role of investment managers usually extends beyond just the acquisition and disposal of investments and into more administrative areas. As such, this can take managers outside the exemption rules that normally apply to financial services. Exactly how managers are affected depends, though, on precisely what they do and for whom and there are special provisions in art. 135 (1)(g) of Council Directive 2006/112/EC (art. 13(B)(d)(65) of the Sixth VAT Directive), which allow exemption in certain situations for special investment funds as defined by Member States (see 80-300 for a discussion).

The extent of the exemption and the effect of cases like *Abbey National plc and Inscape Investment Fund v C & E Commrs*, (Case C-169/04)[2008] BVC 488 , and *JP Morgan Fleming Claverhouse Investment Trust plc and The Association of Investment Trust Companies v R & C Commrs* (Case C-363/05) [2010] BVC 337 is considered later at 80-300.

(14) Nominee services

HMRC regard the service of a nominee, i.e. acting as nominal holder of securities on behalf of the beneficial owner, as basically exempt. There is no input VAT relief if supplied to a UK or EU client *belonging* in the UK or the Isle of Man or another Member State.

For the treatment of supplies to nominee holders and the relationship with the beneficial owners (see the commentary on the *Water Hall* case earlier at 80-100).

(15) Open-ended investment companies (OEICs)

The *Finance Act* 1995 gave the Treasury power to legislate for open-ended investment companies (OEICs). The present rules governing these are contained in the *Open-Ended Investment Companies Regulations* 2001 (SI 2001/1228).

In March 1997, in *Business Brief* 12/97, HMRC accepted that the management of OEICs by their corporate directors was exempt, but expressed the view that this did not extend to services that were sub-contracted. This treatment of sub-contracted services has now been shown to be potentially incorrect by the ECJ in their Ruling in in *Abbey National plc and Inscape Investment Fund v C & E Commrs* (Case C-169/04) (see later at 80-300). However, just because a particular service is a requirement of regulations, being within a list of what is covered within the definition of *management* does not necessarily mean that it is exempt if provided in isolation. To be exempt, it must, viewed broadly, form a distinct service of fund administration fulfilling in effect the specific essential functions of fund management. Exemption will not apply, for example to legal services, such as advice or drafting required to ensure that certain documents, e.g. a trust deed or fund prospectus, are valid and comply with the regulations.

The introduction of someone to a manager of either an AUT or an OEIC will also not, be exempt, but will be taxable.

(16) Outsourcing

As discussed in **Chapter 7** at 70-500, outsourcing is arguably the most important single issue at the present time for those in the financial and insurance sectors. Farming-out all or part of the day-to-day administration, accounting or back-office function of a business to someone else is increasingly common and the addition of VAT to the charges made is an unwelcome extra burden for companies whose recovery of input tax is almost invariably low.

Attempts have been made to argue against this by maintaining that the delegation to others of a function, which a finance or insurance sector company would normally do for itself, have unfortunately met with resistance from HMRC, despite the success of a number of appeals through the Tribunal and the Courts, in *CSMA and Lloyds TSB* and, initially *Continuum/CSC Financial Services Ltd*, in particular. It is a cardinal principle, of course, that the exemptions must be construed narrowly and that a line has to be drawn between what is covered and what is not. However, the changes in the exemptions for finance in VATA 1994, Sch. 9, Grp. 5 referred to earlier are felt by many to have taken the matter too far.

A fuller discussion of the issues involved is to be found in **Chapter 7** at 70-500. See also the commentaries on depositaries/trustees and on investment management above and on Investment Management at 80-300, especially following *Abbey National plc and Inscape Investment Fund v C & E Commrs*, (Case C-169/04), and *JP Morgan Fleming Claverhouse Investment Trust plc and The Association of Investment Trust Companies v R & C Commrs* – (Case C-363/05).

Practice point

Cutting costs by shedding staff and outsourcing can easily have the opposite effect by increasing irrecoverable input tax.

- non-VATable employee costs can be replaced by a taxable supply of staff;
- administration which would not be an issue were it carried out in-house, where it can be subsumed into an overall exempt activity, can become a taxable management service;
- outsourcing abroad is also no solution because of the reverse-charge.

However, sometimes it is possible to argue that what is outsourced is not taxable at all, but is exempt. Generally, though, this can require ensuring that:

- what is supplied is more than a mere physical or technical supply (para. 66 of the decision in *Sparekassernes Datacenter (SDC) v Skatteministeriet* (Case C-2/95) [1997] BVC 509);
- the conditions for the exemption sought are satisfied (see *Staatssecretaris van Financiën v Arthur Andersen & Co Accountants c.s.* (Case C-472/03) [2006] BVC 228);
- what is outsourced goes far enough. In *Continuum/CSC* the conclusion seems to have been that the company's services to Sun Alliance did not go quite far enough. They were not authorised to provide advice, merely information. They also processed application forms submitted by prospective investors, checking that they had been properly filled in, and so forth. But what CSC/Continuum *did not* undertake were the formalities for issuing and transferring the securities, i.e. the units in the unit trust;
- what is claimed as the exempt supply is predominantly what is supplied as part of a single supply and is not *incidental* or *ancillary* (see *Card Protection Plan Ltd v C & E Commrs* [2001] BVC 158).

In short, outsourcing more, rather than less, may well make it easier to achieve the desired result. It is important that the factors that are at the heart of the exemption remain an essential part of the service bought-in. But equally important will be how what is outsourced is approached and, in particular, is described in any agreements or contracts. Referring to underlying cost-components (such as data processing and staff) as if they were services in their own right invites difficulties.

---

(17) PEP management and introductory fees

A PEP was treated in the same as a share ISA for VAT purposes, and the PEP was replaced by the ISA from 6 April 1999. As at 6 April 2008, all remaining PEPs became stocks and shares ISAs (see above).

(18) Portfolio or fund management services

The nature of these services is discussed below in the context of the CoJ's decision in *Deutsche Bank AG*. It is anticipated that HMRC will issue a Revenue and Customs Brief in due course to explain their view of the treatment of portfolio management services.

A periodic charge, invoiced as such, for portfolio management will be exempt if it is within the scope of either item 9 or 10 of Group 5 of Sch. 9 to VATA 1994, but this only applies to special investment funds (see 80-300). Article 135(1)(g) of the VAT Directive exempts 'the management of special investment funds as defined by Member States', and this was enacted into UK law by items 9 and 10 of Group 5. Otherwise, the supply will be standard-rated, and this will usually be the case where the funds are not marketed to the retail market. Accordingly, in such circumstances where the fund is not within the exemption then the supply by a manager to a fund (the customer) established in the UK will be subject to VAT; whilst if the fund is established outside the UK, the supply will be outside the scope of UK VAT and the supply will carry a right to deduct input tax.

Item 9 is an exemption for open-ended funds (namely, collective investment schemes which are: all UK-established authorised unit trust schemes and authorised OEICs, or recognised overseas schemes). Item 10 exempts the management of 'closed-ended collective investment undertakings' which have the sole objective of investing capital raised from the public wholly or mainly in securities.

Services which are exempt under items 9 or 10 of Group 5 are not included in the *VAT (Input Tax) (Specified Supplies) Order* (SI 1999/3121) which means there is no right to deduct input tax, even if the customer is established outside the EU.

A recent decision of the CoJ has considered the VAT position of portfolio management services. Broadly, the decision supports the UK's current application of VAT to portfolio investment management services. The case is *Finanzamt Frankfurt am Main V-Höchst v Deutsche Bank AG* Case C 44/11 (19 July 2012), which concerned the extent to which Art. 135(1) of the VAT Directive applies to portfolio management services. It follows from the CoJ decision that the VAT treatment applied by the UK is in conformity with EU law on this point. The relevant parts of the VAT Directive considered by the CoJ were Art. 135(1) (f) and (g), which provide that the following are exempt:

> '(f) transactions, including negotiation but not management or safekeeping, in shares, interests in companies or associations, debentures and other securities, but excluding documents establishing title to goods, and the rights or securities referred to in Article 15(2) [namely, certain rights and interests in immovable property];
>
> (g) the management of special investment funds as defined by Member States [see later discussion at 80-300];'

The material facts of the case can be summarised as follows:

- Deutsche Bank provided services whereby investors instructed it to manage security holdings for them, at its own discretion and without obtaining prior instruction, but in accordance with a strategy chosen by the investor, and to take all appropriate measures in managing those holdings.

- Deutsche Bank was permitted to sell securities in the name and on behalf of the investor. The investor paid an annual fee equivalent to 1.8% of the value of the assets managed, comprising a share for management equivalent to 1.2% of that value and a share for buying and selling securities equivalent to 0.6%.
- Deutsche Bank's fee also covered account and portfolio administration and commission on the acquisition of investment fund units.
- Investors received regular progress reports and could terminate the instruction at any time with immediate effect.
- Deutsche Bank treated its services in connection with the management of security holdings to be VAT-exempt when supplied to investors in Germany and the EU and not taxable when provided to investors elsewhere. The German tax authority treated the services as taxable.
- The parties accepted that the services did not constitute 'management of special investment funds' within the meaning of Art. 135(1)(g) of the VAT Directive.
- The reference to the CoJ included the following terms:

'1. Is the management of security holdings (portfolio management), where a taxable person determines for remuneration the purchase and sale of securities and implements that determination by buying and selling the securities, exempt from tax

– only in so far as it consists in the management of investment funds for a number of investors collectively within the meaning of Article 135(1)(g) of Directive 2006/112/EC or also

– in so far as it consists in individual portfolio management for individual investors within the meaning of Article 135(1)(f) of Directive 2006/112/EC (transactions in securities or the negotiation of such transactions)?

2. For the purposes of defining principal and ancillary services, what significance is to be attached to the criterion that the ancillary service does not constitute for customers an aim in itself, but a means of better enjoying the principal service supplied, in the context of separate reckoning for the ancillary service and the fact that the ancillary service can be provided by third parties?'

The CoJ concluded that the portfolio management services:
- represented a single supply for VAT purposes, and
- did not come within the scope of the exemption provided by Art 135(1)(g) of Directive 2006/112/EC.

The Court's decision contains the following statements, which are of particular interest:
Was there a single supply?
- The CoJ stated (para. 23 to 28):

'...it is apparent that the service basically consists of a combination of a service of analysing and monitoring the assets of client investors, on the one hand, and of a service of actually purchasing and selling securities on the other.

It is true that those two elements of the portfolio management service may be provided separately. A client investor may wish only for an advisory service and prefer to decide on and make the investments himself. Conversely, a client investor who prefers to take the decisions on investments in securities and, more generally, to structure and monitor his assets himself, without making purchases or sales, may call on an intermediary for the latter type of transaction.

However, the average client investor, in the context of a portfolio management service such as that performed by Deutsche Bank in the main proceedings, seeks precisely a combination of those two elements.

As the Advocate General stated at point 30 of her Opinion, to decide on the best approach to the purchase, sale or retention of securities would be pointless for investors within the context of a portfolio management service if no effect were given to that approach. Likewise, to make – or not, as the case may be – sales and purchases without expertise and without a prior analysis of the market would also be pointless.

In the context of the portfolio management service at issue in the main proceedings, those two elements are therefore not only inseparable, but must also be placed on the same footing. They are both indispensable in carrying out the service as a whole, with the result that it is not possible to take the view that one must be regarded as the principal service and the other as the ancillary service.

Consequently, those elements must be considered to be so closely linked that they form, objectively, a single economic supply, which it would be artificial to split.'

Was the service an exempt supply?

- The Court concluded that the services provided by Deutsche Bank were not supplies within either Art. 135(1)(f) or (g).
- the services provided were not within Art. 135(1)(g) due to the fact that they did not correspond to the concept of 'management of special investment funds'. The Court stated that (para. 31 to 35):

> 'As regards the exemption provided for in Article 135(1)(g) of Directive 2006/112, it must be pointed out that the concept of 'management of special investment funds' is not defined in Directive 2006/112. The Court has however stated that the transactions covered by that exemption are those which are specific to the business of undertakings for collective investment (Case C-169/04 Abbey National [2006] ECR I 4027, paragraph 63).
>
> In that regard, it is apparent from Article 1(2) of Council Directive 85/611/EEC of 20 December 1985 on the coordination of laws, regulations and administrative provisions relating to undertakings for collective investment in transferable securities (UCITS) (OJ 1985 L 375, p. 3), as amended by Directive 2001/108/EC of the European Parliament and of the Council of 21 January 2002 (OJ 2002 L 41, p. 35), that they are undertakings the sole object of which is the collective investment in transferable securities and/or in other liquid financial assets of capital raised from the public, which operate on the principle of risk-spreading and the units of which are, at the request of holders, re-purchased or redeemed, directly or indirectly, out of those undertakings' assets.
>
> In specific terms, as the Advocate General stated in points 14 and 15 of her Opinion, what are involved are joint funds, in which many investments are pooled and spread over a range of securities which can be managed effectively in order to optimise results, and in which individual investments may be relatively modest. Such funds manage their investments in their own name and on their own behalf, while each investor owns a share of the fund but not the fund's investments as such.
>
> By contrast, services such as those performed by Deutsche Bank in the main proceedings concern generally the assets of a single person, which must be of relatively high overall value in order to be dealt with profitably in such a way. The portfolio manager buys and sells investments in the name and on behalf of the client investor, who retains ownership of the individual securities throughout, and on termination of, the contract.
>
> Consequently, the portfolio management activity carried out by Deutsche Bank, at issue in the main proceedings, does not correspond to the concept of "management of special investment funds" within the meaning of Article 135(1)(g) of Directive 2006/112.'

— the crux of the Court's decision as to why the portfolio management services were not within the scope of the Art. 135(1)(f) exemption was given as follows (para. 39 to 43):

> 'Although services of purchasing and selling securities may be covered by Article 135(1)(f) of Directive 2006/112, the same is not, by contrast, true of services of analysing and monitoring assets as the latter services do not necessarily involve transactions which are liable to create, alter or extinguish parties' rights and obligations in respect of securities.
>
> Deutsche Bank and the European Commission are of the opinion that the essence of the portfolio management service at issue in the main proceedings is the active buying and selling of securities and, for that reason, that that service must be exempt from VAT under Article 135(1)(f) of Directive 2006/112. The Finanzamt and the German, Netherlands and United Kingdom Governments take the view that that service must be regarded as a service of analysing and monitoring, to which the exemption provided for in that provision cannot apply.
>
> However, it is apparent from ... this judgment that it is not possible to regard the elements of which that service consists as constituting a principal service on the one hand and an ancillary service on the other. Those elements must be placed on the same footing.
>
> In that regard, it is established case-law that the terms used to specify the exemptions referred to in Article 135(1) of Directive 2006/112 are to be interpreted strictly, since they constitute exceptions to the general principle that VAT is to be levied on all services supplied for consideration by a taxable person (see, inter alia, Case C 8/01 Taksatorringen [2003] ECR I-13711, paragraph 36, and DTZ Zadelhoff, paragraph 20).
>
> Consequently, since that service may be taken into account for VAT purposes only as a whole, it cannot be covered by Article 135(1)(f) of Directive 2006/112.'

The Court's decision illustrates that it is important to consider the scope of any mandate for portfolio management services, since if any services are regarded as a single indivisible supply then they are likely to be treated as standard rated. Portfolio management services, which are discretionary, are not likely to be treated as exempt services. However, where there are introductory services with exempt execution this may not be subject to standard rating (see *Bloomsbury Wealth Management LLP* at 80-100(1)(c)).

See also Investment Management at (13) above and later at 80-300.

(19) Redemption of securities

Unlike the sale of securities, money paid on redemption is not consideration for a supply of goods or services but is *outside the scope* of VAT altogether. This is not the case, however, with the proceeds received from the purchase by a company of any of its own securities, which may subsequently be cancelled. This will particularly apply to stocks such as debentures and debenture stock, but can also apply in the case of shares.

(20) Rent-free periods

Where someone grants a lease on a property and receives rental income, he is seen by HMRC as carrying on a property rental business. At one time they expressed some doubt as to whether such a business can be said to be carried on at a time when a lease is subject to an initial rent-free period. However, they accept that a building which is sold during such a period may, nonetheless, be treated as a going concern for the purposes of art. 5 of the *Value Added Tax*

(Special Provisions) Order 1995 (SI 1995/1268) (see Notice 700/9 Transfer of business as a going concern at 6.2 (April 2008)).

(21) Repurchases of securities (repos)

Whilst outwardly perhaps similar to stock lending (see (29) below), repos have a quite different function. They are more obviously contracts for the sale and repurchase of the securities and are frequently used to raise cash finance by the immediate proceeds of sale. In some cases they may be used to achieve a *bed and breakfast* arrangement.

As they amount to dealings in the underlying securities, they are basically exempt under Sch. 9. Grp 5, item 6. Supplies will be made by both parties one on the initial sale and one on the repurchase.

When the person to whom the supply is made *belongs* outside the EU and Isle of Man reg. 103 of what is now the *Value Added Tax Regulations* 1995 (SI 1995/2518) and art. 2 and 3 of the *Value Added Tax (Input Tax) (Specified Supplies) Order* 1999 (SI 1999/3121) allows related input VAT to be recovered.

(22) Safe custody services

Safe custody services can involve different supplies:

(1) The purely physical service of, say, safe-keeping, is standard-rated irrespective of where the recipient belongs. The supply is specifically excluded from exemption under Art. 13(B)(d)(5) of the Sixth VAT Directive (Art. 135(1)(f) of Council Directive 2006/112/EC) and is not regarded as a financial service to which VATA 1994, Sch. 5, para. 5 applies.

(2) Other services may be provided as part of an overall service of safe-keeping. These will, typically, include dividend collection and dealing with scrip/bonus issues. Here the service (including any element of physical safe-keeping) is exempt, but with the right to input VAT recovery if supplied to a client outside the EU.

(23) Securitisation

Securitisation is an arrangement, which creates a type of financial instrument linked to assets, particularly assets such as mortgages or property, which are normally less marketable in their own right. What it involves is the creation by a company of securities in the form of debenture stock, for example, which are then *secured* on the underlying assets by a way of a legal charge. Usually, the return on the securities will be linked to the performance of and income derived from the underlying investments. The holders of the securities thus have an effective equity interest in what is produced.

Following *Kretztechnik AG v Finanzamt Linz* (see earlier at 80-200), the creation by a company of securities for a securitisation will not be a supply. Also, as *MBNA Europe Bank Ltd v R & C Commrs* [2007] BVC 3 has shown (see **Chapter 7** at 70-200) the assignment of receivables as part of a securitisation exercise may equally not be a supply for VAT, even if, contrary to what was previously held by the Tribunal in *Capital One Bank (Europe) plc* [2006] BVC 2,148, it did not just represent the provision of security for a loan.

(24) Share registration

The services of a share registrar are regarded as taxable and this will apply to things such as:

- operating a company's share register;
- designating certificates;
- processing proxy forms;
- registering grants of probate; and
- administering share options and dividend schemes.

The statutory fees charged for inspection of the register and for production of shareholders lists in accordance with company law are not, however, subject to VAT and, when on-charged to a client, should normally be treated as disbursements. The services of a share registrar are not regarded by HMRC as financial services. The services of a share registrar are supplied where the recipient belongs when supplied to a business customer (see generally the discussion on place of supply in Chapter 3).

(25) Soft commissions

Soft commissions can refer to a situation where one business may fund part of the cost of research or other services provided by a third-party direct to a client in the expectation that the client meets target levels of commission business.

This type of soft commissions do not represent consideration for a supply by the intermediary, but may be consideration for a supply of research.

See also, though, **Chapter 3**.

(26) Sterling Commercial Paper

Sterling Commercial Paper is essentially a form of promissory note issued by companies to raise short-term capital. As such, any dealings in these notes, are basically exempt within VATA 1994, Sch. 9, Grp. 5, item 1. Being a form of promissory note, HMRC historically saw no supply except and to the extent that issue or sale proceeds exceeded face value. However, since 1991, they have accepted that, in the case of commercial paper (see HMRC *Business Brief* 11/91 of 9 August 1991), the consideration is the price paid, including interest.

Following the Ruling in the *Kretztechnik AG v Finanzamt Linz* case (see earlier at 80-200), the issue itself, as opposed to dealings on the secondary market, is not now a supply.

Arranging or underwriting an issue of Sterling Commercial Paper are both basically exempt under item 5 of Grp. 5. In appropriate cases input VAT relief is available under reg. 103 of what is now the *Value Added Tax Regulations* 1995 (SI 1995/2518) and art. 2 and 3 of the *Value Added Tax (Input Tax) (Specified Supplies) Order* 1999 (SI 1999/3121).

(27) Stock Exchange and FSA listing fees

Fees charged by institutions, such as the London Stock Exchange, for admission to join are taxable at the standard-rate. The place of supply is where the recipient belongs where provided to a relevant business person under the VATA 1994, s. 7A.

Before 1 January 2004, this treatment was also applied to the listing fee charged by the FSA. The fee was also seen as falling within the VAT Act 1994, Sch. 5, and thus the place of supply was where the recipient belonged, under the then place of supply rules. Following a review undertaken after the House of Lords decision in the case of *Institute of Chartered Accountants in England and Wales* [1999] BVC 215, it was decided that the correct VAT treatment of the fee should be that it is non-business, and *outside the scope (see Notice 701/49 Finance November 2011 at 6.8)*

(28) Stock Exchange membership fees

Stock Exchange membership fees are taxable at the standard-rate.

(29) Stock lending

Stock lending is fairly common in relation to Eurobonds but can also be used for most other types of security. In its simplest form:

- a dealer in securities may be *short* in a particular stock at a given point in time;
- to square his position and deliver to those with whom he has entered into sale contracts, he may agree with, say, a bank, an investment trust or an insurance company to *borrow* a given amount of that stock for a specified term and consideration;
- at the end of the term the borrower will re-deliver securities to the lender, paying an agreed fee;
- during the term of the facility the borrower will be entitled to deal in the securities, although the lender may be stated as retaining beneficial ownership.

Usually, the lender also reserves rights to any dividends, interest or warrants falling due or arising to the holder or the securities whilst lent.

As the aim is to obtain securities (rather than an advance of money), it will often be accompanied by some form of collateral given by the borrower to the lender. This may take the form either of cash or of securities:

- with cash collateral, the lender will have full use of the money but will pay the borrower interest at a rate calculated to give the lender an overall return equivalent to the facility fee, which may not in that event be charged as such;
- for collateral other than cash, the normal facility fee will be retained and the coupon and rights will accrue to the borrower as owner of the securities pledged. The lender will not be entitled to deal in the securities tendered as collateral.

The effect of the transaction is that, prima facie, the party providing the facility will have made a disposal of securities since the exact same securities will not be *paid back* (despite the inference that beneficial ownership of the original securities could be retained by the lender). However, outwardly, this is similar to an advance of money within VATA 1994, Sch. 9, Grp. 5, item 2 and, whilst the transaction is a transaction in securities, the effect is generally much the same.

- In an appeal to the VAT Tribunal in Edinburgh by the *Scottish Eastern Investment Trust plc* [2001] BVC 4,058, it has been held that the value of the consideration for the supply in the case of stock-lending is limited to the fee paid. It was wholly artificial and unreal to attempt to attribute a consideration based upon the whole value of shares which were transferred for a temporary purpose in what HMRC's own notice described as a non-monetary transaction.

A stock lending transaction is essentially within VATA 1994, Sch. 9, Grp. 5, item 6 as:

> 'The issue, transfer or receipt of, or any dealing with, any security or secondary security ...'

or, in Council Directive 2006/112/EC terms, within 135(1)(f) (Sixth VAT Directive, art. 13(B)(d)(5)) as a:

> 'transaction, including negotiation, excluding management and safekeeping, in shares, interests in companies or associations, debentures and other securities...'

Where the borrower is a VAT-registered person from another Member State or is from outside the EU and the Isle of Man the supply is *outside the scope*. Regulation 103 of what is now the *Value Added Tax Regulations* 1995 (SI 1995/2518) and art. 2 and 3 of the *Value Added Tax (Input Tax) (Specified Supplies) Order* 1999 (SI 1999/3121) then allow related input VAT to be recovered where the supply is to someone outside the EU.

(30) Underwriting commissions/arrangement fees

The underwriting and arrangement of issues or sales of new or existing securities are both basically exempt from VAT, even though, so far as an issuer is concerned, following *Kretztechnik AG v Finanzamt Linz* (see earlier at 80-100), the issue itself may not be a supply.

(1) With the traditional form of equity underwriting, the issue is made to the subscribers directly by the issuing company and the underwriter, or sub-underwriter, guarantees, for a fee, that a given proportion of the issue will be subscribed for.

(2) A typical bond underwriting, however, will take the form of a bought deal with the underwriter or issuing house agreeing to take securities on allotment and then on-sell on the secondary markets or by placement.

This distinction between the different forms of underwriting can sometimes have a material impact on the VAT position of both the issuer and the issuing house.

Where an issuing house incurs, as principal, the costs of:

- Stock Exchange listing fees;
- advertising;
- printing;
- receiving bank charges;
- accountants' fees (unless covered by the exemptions or zero-ratings referred to above);
- legal fees;
- additional advisers' fees; and
- services provided by accountants or others in checking multiple applications before allotment of shares,

any recharge is part of the issuing house fee, and basically VAT-exempt.

The underwriting service is exempt under Sch. 9, Grp 5, item 5A, which implies it is not the provision of *intermediary services* within item 5. Whether such a distinction should be made, however, may well depend on the facts of a particular situation. If there is a distinction, the scope for the recovery of input tax by the underwriter is somewhat less than that afforded for brokerage or other intermediary services. Relief will only be available when the client is established outside the EU. Where a fee is charged for a service, which guarantees that: a securities issue or sale will be subscribed for or purchased and the issuer shall receive a certain amount of capital that underwriting service is exempt under item 5A of Group 5. This point was confirmed by the ECJ in *Skandinaviska Enskilda Banken AB Momsgrupp v Skatteverket* (Case C-540/09) 10 March 2011where the court ruled that an underwriting guarantee was exempt as a transaction in shares. This was regardless of whether the share issue was ultimately entirely covered by market investors; as the underwriting agreement was liable to create, alter or extinguish rights in ownership of shares, this possibility alone is sufficient to treat the underwriting service as exempt.

The position of sub-underwriting is similarly affected. In this case, it is necessary to determine whether the sub-underwriter is providing a service to the underwriter or to the client. If the former applies and the underwriter is in the UK, the commission or fee is exempt, even if the issuer is from outside the EU. If the service can be argued as an intermediary service, however, the position is more flexible with that much greater scope for relief.

> **Practice point**
>
> It can pay to be aware of the distinctions between the different forms of underwriting.
>
> (1) Traditional equity underwriting amounts to a straightforward guarantee that the issue will be subscribed for.
>
> (2) The underwriting of bond issues, on the other hand, tends to be structured as bought deals.
>
> The latter involve the underwriter effecting the guarantee by agreeing to subscribe at the outset for a given percentage of the issue, with the shares then being on-sold on the secondary market. A vendor placing gives much the same result.
>
> What this means is that there could be advantages if a non-EU issuing house is used rather than one based in the UK or in another Member State:
>
> - the issuer could benefit as its supply is arguably made to the issuing house;
> - many of the costs charged to the issuing house will be VAT-free; and
> - even where tax is charged, this could be recovered under the Thirteenth VAT Directive (Directive 86/560).

(31) Valuation services

Valuation services are standard-rated if supplied as such to any clients belonging in the UK or the Isle of Man, or to clients belonging in other Member States and who are not VAT-registered. In other cases they are *outside the scope* but with the right to recover underlying input VAT.

(32) Automated Teller Machine (ATM) services

Supplies relating to ATMs are treated as either taxable or exempt, depending on the nature of the supply (see generally Notice 701/49 VAT: Finance (November) 2011 at 2.9).

The supply of an ATM or the software which is necessary to operate the ATM is a taxable supply, irrespective of whether the consideration is based on the level of use of the ATM.

The following supplies are exempt, where a charge (i.e. convenience fees, interchange fees, reciprocity fees) is made by ATM suppliers for:

- the facility to obtain money
- the provision of money
- transaction processing
- the operation of accounts

The granting of a right to permanently attach an ATM to land, or for its incorporation into a building, is an exempt supply within Group 1 of Sch 9 of VATA 1994, unless the grantor has elected to exercise the option to waive exemption.

80-250 Brokers and dealers

Traditionally, the term *broker* in the context of securities has implied someone who acts in an agency or intermediary capacity. However, many brokers now act as principal or perform a dual capacity function, i.e. entering into agency or principal's transactions according to the needs or wishes of the particular client or situation.

Some brokers are also market makers or interbroker dealers.

Whatever capacity applies in any given situation should be clear from the agreed terms of trade between the broker and the particular client concerned, and the agreement should be clear as to whether the services are execution only or advisory. The FSA are introducing new regulatory rules which come into force on 31 December 2012 following a Retail Distribution Review, which will change the way in way certain advisers are remunerated so that they will move from receiving commission to fees agree with customers in respect of all Retail Investment Products (the impact of this is discussed below at (3)).

(1) Outputs

Both agency services and principals trading are basically exempt within VATA 1994, Sch. 9, Grp. 5 (art. 135(1)(f) of Council Directive 2006/112/EC). Principals transactions fall under item 6 and agency or brokerage under item 5 as *the provision of intermediary services*. The differences in treatment can, however, be significant.

(1) An agent or broker acting purely as an intermediary will make a supply represented only by the fee or commission earned. As a matter of agency and regulatory law, if nothing else, this will usually require to be disclosed and will be a relatively small part of the overall bargain price.

(2) Someone trading as principal, on the other hand, will make (or receive) a supply for the full amount payable by or to the client. On those occasions where a *commission* is separately stated, unless this is clearly an agency disbursement, this will be simply part of that overall price. Often what the broker makes is hidden merely forming an undisclosed *turn*.

The values of supplies can thus be vastly different. This becomes especially significant when it comes to how you calculate the recovery of input VAT (see (2) below) – as is the general distinction between agency and principals trades.

> **Practice point**
> The purchase and sale of securities is VAT-exempt, so relief for underlying input VAT can be limited. However, this restriction does not apply where the buyer is outside the EU (art. 3 of the *VAT (Input Tax) (Specified Supplies) Order* 1999 (SI 1999/3121), something easily overlooked.
> (1) Just reviewing where the client belongs can be worthwhile.
> (2) It may also sometimes be possible to route sales via a suitable non-EU associate as an intermediate step in an overall transaction.
>
> As always, though, it will be important to pay attention to detail and to be able to show that the sale is, in itself, a real transaction and not a sham.

(2) Input VAT implications

The fact that supplies will be basically exempt means brokers will invariably face some restriction in the amount of input tax they can recover. However, to the extent that supplies are to clients *belonging* outside the EU, specific relief is afforded by art. 2 of the *Value Added Tax (Input Tax) (Specified Supplies) Order* 1992 (SI 1992/3123). With agency transactions, the extent of relief may not just depend on the location of the client or immediate recipient of the supply, but also on whether the recipient of the supply in the underlying client transaction also belongs outside the EU.

The nature and treatment of the supply (e.g. the different basis of valuation, commissions or sale proceeds) also has a more immediately practical effect on input VAT recovery under the partial exemption rules. How partial exemption (**Chapter 4** at 40-200) is approached is, clearly, important. A simple method based on values, on the lines of:

$$\frac{\text{Value of exempt or outside the scope supplies conferring input VAT relief}}{\text{Value of total supplies}} \times \text{input VAT}$$

gives a rough and ready answer and is easy to use, but will be a Special Method to be agreed. It is easily subject, however, to distortion, especially where both agency and principal's transactions occur and is not generally in favour for this reason.

The preferred approach is often to use the same basic formula, but this time with numbers of transactions rather than values, i.e.:

$$\frac{\text{Numbers of transactions conferring input VAT relief}}{\text{Numbers of total transactions}} \times \text{input VAT}$$

the premise being that overheads/operating costs will be broadly the same, regardless of the capacity in which the broker acts.

The present partial exemption rules (see **Chapter 4** at 40-200) also expect direct attribution where possible. The position of security brokers' commissions, i.e. when acting in an agency capacity, is illustrated in **Appendix 13**.

(3) Retail Investment Products

The FSA has undertaken a Retail Distribution Review (RDR) which has the aim of ensuring that consumers are offered a transparent and fair charging system for the advice, consumers are clear about the service they receive, and consumers receive advice from highly respected professionals. In order to achieve these objectives the FSA have issued new rules that will require, as of 31 December 2012:

- advisory firms to explicitly disclose and separately charge clients for their services;
- advisory firms to clearly describe their services as either independent or restricted; and
- individual advisers to adhere to consistent professional standards, including a code of ethics.

For details on the nature of the rules is provided on the FSA website (www.fsa.gov.uk/rdr).

The rules will apply to all advisers in the retail investment market, irrespective of the type of firm they work for (such as banks, product providers, independent financial advisers, wealth managers and stockbrokers). The impact of the new rules will be relevant for VAT purposes due tot the fact that where they apply advisers are required to move from receiving commissions to fees agreed with customers in respect of all retail investment products (RIPs). The VAT treatment is of importance since the provision of advice is subject to VAT at the standard rate, whilst the receipt of commission from a product provider for intermediary services is VAT exempt (within Group 5 of Sch. 9 of VATA 1994). HMRC has published guidance on how they will apply the VAT rules to the new approach required under the FSA rules. The new rules apply to RIPS, as defined by the FSA which are (a copy of the guidance is provided in **Appendix 22**):

(a) a life policy; or
(b) a unit; or
(c) a stakeholder pension scheme; or
(d) a personal pension scheme;
(e) an interest in an investment trust savings scheme;
(f) a security in an investment trust;
(g) any other designated investment which offers exposure to underlying financial assets, in a packaged form which modifies that exposure when compared with a direct holding in the financial asset; or
(h) a structured capital-at-risk product;

whether or not any of (a) to (h) are held within an ISA or CTF.

8 Securities, Property and Investment

The definition of RIPs does not include protection-only insurance or charges for trading in securities. The FSA rules do not apply to investment management under a discretionary mandate or to execution only transactions.

The HMRC guidance acknowledges that the term 'advice' under the RDR covers a broad range of functions including providing recommendations, referrals, and intermediary work in connection with product distribution. In this regard, HMRC acknowledge that such matters would continue to be VAT exempt under general principles, whilst general financial advice will be a standard-rated supply.

A summary of HMRC's approach to the VAT treatment of such supplies is set out below (their detailed guidance is provided at **Appendix 22**, which is derived from HMRC's VAT Finance Manual).

Services of an adviser

If the adviser performs an arrangement which involves acting between the product provider and the customer with a view to arranging the sale of the RIP agreed with the customer (regardless of whether the sale of the product is finally concluded), and if the adviser is able to evidence that they have acted on this basis, then the supply will be exempt provided that any of the following services are within the agreement concluded with the customer:

(1) gathering fact-finding information in relation to the customer

(2) carrying out research to find suitable investment options

(3) providing the customer with reports, forecasts

(4) recommending specific investment products to the customer

(5) acting between the provider and customer with a view to arranging the sale of RIPs agreed with the customer

(6) where applicable, i.e. where the customer agrees to an ongoing review service, monitor the customer's ongoing position to ensure that the products continue to meet the requirements of the customer.

HMRC correctly observe in their guidance that the VAT liability depends on what is done by the adviser, and it is irrelevant whether a fee is levied up front or over the life of a product (see VATFIN 7665).

Ongoing services

The VAT liability of ongoing services will turn on the nature of the services that the customer has agreed the adviser should perform.

Evidence for VAT treatment

HMRC emphasise in their guidance (at VATFIN 7675) that an adviser must keep sufficient evidence of support the VAT treatment applied to the services which are supplied. HMRC say that:

> 'This evidence will need to be specific to the services performed for the customer and demonstrate that the adviser acted between the customer and the product provider with a view to arranging the sale of Retail Investment Products. If an adviser is unable to provide evidence that an exempt supply has taken place, VAT will be due on that supply.'

80-300 Investment managers

Investment management tends to be treated differently from most other areas in the financial sector. Managers can often carry out a wider role than simply acting as an intermediary in respect of client transactions, something which can take them outside the exemption rules that normally apply. Exactly how they are affected depends, on precisely what they do and for whom – and the relationships that exist.

- *Cornhill Management Ltd* (1990) 5 BVC 901 considered, for example, a commodity fund and the point at issue was whether the manager was dealing on its own account, being financed by advances from the clients, or whether the clients jointly owned the investments with the manager who bought and sold as agent. Each of these possibilities had different consequences and the Tribunal eventually decided in favour of the taxpayer, upholding the agency argument. How things were documented was, however, important.

(1) The general position

Investment management, as such, is an essentially taxable, non-monetary financial service. Exemption is specifically precluded in this case by art. 135(1)(f) of Council Directive 2006/112/EC (art. 13(B)(d)(5) of the Sixth VAT Directive).

(2) Special investment funds

Article 135(1)(g) of Council Directive 2006/112/EC (art. 13(B)(d)(5) of the Sixth VAT Directive) exempts the management of *special investment* funds as defined by Member States. In UK law, this is expressed in items (9) and (10) of VATA 1994, Sch. 9, Grp. 5 as:

'9   The management of

   (a) an authorised open-ended investment company; or
   (b) an authorised unit trust scheme; or
   (c) a Gibraltar collective investment scheme that is not an umbrella scheme; or
   (d) a sub-fund of any other Gibraltar collective investment scheme; or
   (e) an individually recognised overseas scheme that is not an umbrella scheme; or
   (f) a sub-fund of any other individually recognised overseas scheme; or
   (g) a recognised collective investment scheme authorised in a designated country or territory that is not an umbrella scheme; or
   (h) a sub-fund of any other recognised collective investment scheme authorised in a designated country or territory; or

8 Securities, Property and Investment

    (i) a recognised collective investment scheme constituted in another EEA state that is not an umbrella scheme; or

    (j) a sub-fund of any other recognised collective investment scheme constituted in another EEA state.

10   The management of a close-ended collective investment undertaking.'

with Statutory Note (6) to Group 5 providing that:

'For the purposes of this Group—

"authorised open-ended investment company" and "authorised unit trust scheme" have the meaning given in section 237(3) of the Financial Services and Markets Act 2000;

"closed-ended collective investment undertaking" means an undertaking in relation to which the following conditions are satisfied—

(a) its sole object is the investment of capital, raised from the public, wholly or mainly in securities; and
(b) it manages its assets on the principle of spreading investment risk; and
(c) all of its ordinary shares (of each class if there is more than one) or equivalent units are included in the official list maintained by the Financial Services Authority pursuant to section 74(1) of the Financial Services and Markets Act 2000; and
(d) all of its ordinary shares (of each class if there is more than one) or equivalent units are admitted to trading on a regulated market situated or operating in the United Kingdom;

"collective investment scheme" has the meaning given in section 235 of the Financial Services and Markets Act 2000;

"Gibraltar collective investment scheme" means—

(a) a collective investment scheme to which section 264 of the Financial Services and Markets Act 2000 applies pursuant to an order made under section 409(1)(d) of that Act; or
(b) a collective investment scheme to which the Financial Services and Markets Act 2000 applies pursuant to an order made under section 409(1)(f) of that Act;

"individually recognised overseas scheme" means a collective investment scheme declared by the Financial Services Authority to be a recognised scheme pursuant to section 272 of the Financial Services and Markets Act 2000;

"recognised collective investment scheme authorised in a designated country or territory" means a collective investment scheme recognised pursuant to section 270 of the Financial Services and Markets Act 2000;

"recognised collective investment scheme constituted in another EEA state" means a collective investment scheme which is recognised pursuant to section 264 of the Financial Services and Markets Act 2000;

"regulated market" has the meaning given in section 103(1) of the Financial Services and Markets Act 2000;

"sub-fund" means a separate part of the property of an umbrella scheme that is pooled separately;

"umbrella scheme" means a collective investment scheme under which the contributions of the participants in the scheme and the profits or income out of which payments are to be made to them are pooled separately in relation to separate parts of the scheme property.'

Statutory Note (6A) goes on to deal with de minimis provisions which say that:

'A collective investment scheme, or sub-fund, that is not for the time being marketed in the United Kingdom is to be treated as not falling within item 9(c) to (j) if—
(a) it has never been marketed in the United Kingdom, or
(b) less than 5% of its shares or units are held by, or on behalf of, investors who are in the United Kingdom.'

HMRC comment in their guidance manual (VATFIN at 5220) that recognised overseas schemes fall into three basic categories: (a) Collective investment schemes established elsewhere in the EEA, which are authorised as UCITS-compliant in their own Member State and where notification has been given to the FSA of the intention to market the units to UK retail investors. This category will also cover schemes established in Gibraltar; (b) Collective investment schemes established in Guernsey, Jersey, the Isle of Man and Bermuda, which have similar regulation to UK CIS and have been recognised by the FSA so that their units can be marketed to UK retail investors; and (c) Collective investment schemes established elsewhere, which have similar regulation to UK CIS and have been given an individual recognition order by the FSA so that their units can be marketed to UK retail investors.

In relation to the de minimis provisions HMRC give the following guidance (VATFIN5280):

'If at the time that active marketing ceases more than 5% of the shares or units in the fund/sub-fund are held by UK retail investors, the management of the fund/sub-fund falls within the exemption. If at any future point the level of investment by UK retail investors falls below 5%, the management of the fund/sub-fund will be deemed to fall outside the exemption from then on, unless and until a decision is taken to resume active marketing.'

Since investment is a basically exempt activity, charging VAT on management fees is unattractive as it inevitably leads to increased costs. This has caused a number of disputes over liability issues, as illustrated by the *Abbey National* and *JP Morgan Fleming Claverhouse* cases which related to the law as it then existed where until 30 September 2008 the management exemption in Items 9 and 10 of Group 5, Sch. 9 only applied to authorised unit trust schemes (AUTS), Open-ended investment companies (OEIC) and Trust-based schemes (TBS). The latter were single property schemes, which have not been authorised in recent years with the result that they are no longer referred to in the new exemption.

- *Abbey National plc and Inscape Investment Fund v C & E Commrs* (Case C-169/04) concerned a number of companies in the Abbey National VAT group, Abbey National Unit Trust Managers Ltd, Scottish Mutual Investment Managers Ltd, Inscape Investments Ltd, Inscape Investment Fund and Abbey National Asset Managers Ltd. Between them, they managed a number of authorised unit trusts, and acted as Authorised Corporate Director (ACD), of a number of OEICs. The dispute was over the VAT treatment of the fees that were charged and also the fees that were charged by separately appointed depositaries (under UK law in the case of an authorised unit trust, *trustees*). The latter were a requirement of the EU and UK law regulating undertakings for collective investment and their functions were essentially supervisory nature with the aim of protecting the interests of consumers and investors. Unit trusts, not being legal persons, had, of necessity to appoint outside managers and EU and UK law also allowed investment companies, in certain circumstances, to delegate one or more of their own functions to a third party.

The issues were:

(1) Whether the exemption for *management of special investment funds* (as defined by Member States), meant Member States had the power to define:

    (a) what was meant by the *management* of the special investment funds, as well as
    (b) what special investment funds could benefit from the exemption.

(2) Whether, if the answer to this was *no* and *management* had an independent Community law meaning, in the light of Directive 85/611 the EU Directive on the coordination of laws, regulations and administrative provisions relating to undertakings for collective investment in transferable securities (UCITS), the charges by a depositary or were also covered by that exemption.

(3) Whether, again, if the answer to the first question was *no*, the exemption applied to services performed by a third-party manager in respect of the administrative management of the funds.

What the Court decided was that the concept of *management* of special investment funds in art. 13(B)(d)(6) had its own independent meaning in Community law, which Member States could not alter. Since this was not defined in the Directive, it had to be interpreted in the light of the aims and scheme of the article, the purpose of which was to facilitate investment in securities for small investors through collective investment undertakings. What was covered by the exemption were transactions or activities specific to those businesses collective investment, such as those set out in Directive 85/611 (as amended), the Community Directive on the co-ordination of laws, regulations and administrative provisions relating to undertakings for collective investment in transferable securities. Annex II to that Directive contains a non-exhaustive list of the functions included in the activity of management, mentioning in particular:

(1) Investment management.

(2) Administration, which comprised:

    (a) legal and fund management accounting services;
    (b) customer inquiries;
    (c) valuation and pricing (including tax returns);
    (d) regulatory compliance monitoring;
    (e) maintenance of unit-holder register;
    (f) distribution of income;
    (g) unit issues and redemptions;
    (h) contract settlements (including certificate dispatch); and
    (i) record keeping.

(3) Marketing.

The functions of depositaries, which were supervisory rather than management, did not fall within this category, but the services of a third-party manager could be exempt within art. 13(B)(d)(6), depending on the nature of what was provided, rather than that of the supplier. The principle of *fiscal neutrality* required that businesses should be free to choose how best they should organise things commercially without losing the benefit of a VAT exemption.

However, for the exemption to apply, what was provided had to form a distinct whole and involve specific essential elements of the management function and not be *mere material or technical supplies*.

Article 13(B)(d)(6) covered all special investment funds, whether they were constituted under contract law, trust law or statute.

- In the subsequent case of *JP Morgan Fleming Claverhouse Investment Trust plc and The Association of Investment Trust Companies v R & C Commrs* (Case C-363/05), the Court decided that the exemption should also apply to the management of *closed-ended investment funds*, such as investment trust companies. The principle of *fiscal neutrality* requires all similar, and therefore competing special investment funds to be treated equally as regards the levying of VAT. The material points of the judgment were that: (a) the concept of 'special investment funds' applies to close-ended investment funds, (b) Member States have a discretion to define 'special investment funds' for the VAT exemption but, in doing so, must pay due regard to: (i) the purpose of the exemption, and (ii) the principle of fiscal neutrality. The CoJ considered that the purpose of the exemption is to facilitate investment in securities for investors through investment undertakings. Accordingly, there must be VAT neutrality between the choice of direct investment in securities and investment through collective investment undertakings (since such undertakings incur management charges). Further, there has to be equality of VAT treatment for funds which are similar to, and in competition with, funds within the scope of the exemption, such as those covered by the UCITS Directive. As a result of the court's decision the exemption in item 9 of Group 5 applies to all similar collective investment undertakings which compete in the UK retail market under comparable conditions.

As observed earlier, in *Revenue & Customs Brief* 58/07 in August 2007, HMRC referred to a number of claims that had been made for overpaid VAT in respect of the management of other funds not at issue in the litigation. The view taken, is that this case does not concern the management of funds other than ITCs and that the ECJ judgment is clear in that it does not address the issues that arise concerning such other funds.

The position on overseas collective investment schemes is that the exemption should only apply to funds actively marketed to UK retail investors. In this regard, HMRC comment that (VATFIN5240): 'The aim of the law is to capture only those sub-funds in which units are, or have been, actively marketed to UK retail investors and so the FSA register is not necessarily definitive in identifying them.'

For overseas CIS the exemption is aimed at the marketing of funds/sub-funds to the general public. Therefore, any active marketing of funds/sub-funds exclusively to institutional investors does not fall within the exemption. Where, however, a fund/sub-fund is actively marketed to both UK retail investors and institutional investors, the management of that fund/sub-fund will fall within the exemption. HMRC provide considerable practical guidance on when they will treat a fund/sub-fund as being 'actively marketed', and this is reproduced in **Appendix 26**.

- The VAT analysis of services provided by a third-party manager to an investment fund management company in connection with the 'management of special investment funds' will be considered by the CoJ in C-275/11 *GfBk v Finanzamt Bayreuth*. The question in issue is whether a service provided by the third-party manager of a special investment fund is sufficiently specific to secure exemption only if:

(a) the manager performs a management function and not only an advisory function; or if
(b) the service differs in nature from other services by reason of a characteristic feature that qualifies for tax exemption under this provision; or if
(c) the manager operates on the basis of a delegation of functions under Article 5g of Directive 85/611/EEC,* as amended?

The issue arises in the context of Art. 13B(d)(6) of the Sixth Directive (now Art. 135(1)(g) of the VAT Directive). Hopefully the views of the CoJ in this area will create certainty on third-party services throughout Member States.

* Directive 2001/107/EC of the European Parliament and of the Council of 21 January 2002 amending Council Directive 85/611/EEC on the coordination of laws, regulations and administrative provisions relating to undertakings for collective investment in transferable securities (UCITS) with a view to regulating management companies and simplified prospectuses (OJ 2002 L 41, p. 20).

The material facts of the case were as follows:

- GfBk was a German undertaking the objects of which were the dissemination of information and advice relating to the stock market and the provision of advice and marketing in connection with financial assets.
- GfBk was engaged by an investment fund management company ('the IMC') to advise the IMC 'in the management of the fund' and 'constantly to monitor the fund and to make recommendations for the purchase or sale of fund assets'. GfBk was also required 'to pay heed to the principle of risk diversification, to statutory investment restrictions ... and to investment conditions'.
- GfBk's fee was determined as a percentage of the value of the special investment fund.
- GfBk made recommendations concerning the purchase and sale of securities to the IMC by telephone, fax and web server. Once processed, the recommendations were analysed in order to check whether they contravened any statutory limits. At the end of the verification, the IMC would implement the recommendations (which sometimes occurred very quickly).
- The German tax authorities considered that the services provided by GfBk did not constitute the 'management of special investment funds'.

The Advocate General delivered an Opinion (8 November 2012) in this case, and concluded as follows (at para. 58 of the Opinion):

- Art. 13B(d)(6) (now Art. 135(1)(g)) must be interpreted as meaning that an advisory and information service provided by a third party, relating to the management of a special investment fund and the purchase and sale of assets, constitutes an activity of 'management' specific and distinct in nature, provided that the service is found to be autonomous and continuous in respect of the activities actually performed by the recipient of the service, a matter which it is for the national court to verify.
- Article 13B(d)(6) must be interpreted as meaning that, in so far as the term 'management' includes services that do not entail the alteration of legal positions, the fact that there was no authorisation allowing for the delegation to GfBk did not place conditions on the application of the exemption.

A reference has also been made to the CoJ in *Wheels Common Investment Fund Trustees Ltd* [2011] UKFTT 534 [2011] TC 01381 as to whether a defined-benefit occupational pension scheme (or a common investment fund in which the assets of several such schemes are pooled) constitutes a 'special investment fund' for the purposes of the exemption in Art. 135(1)(g) of the VAT Directive.

(3) Unit trusts

The managers of unit trusts essentially perform two functions:

- the management of the trust itself; and
- the creation, buying, selling and liquidation of units.

(a) Management

In terms of the management of the trust, the position is much as described earlier at (2) above in the context of *Special investment funds*. Fees are charged to the trustees, often monthly and a per cent per annum of the funds invested and are exempt under VATA 1994, Sch. 9, Grp. 5, item 9.

Taxable outputs tend now to be limited. In the main, they will be confined to fees for acting as registrar or as manager of an unauthorised unit trust.

- In January 2001 the Tribunal gave a decision in *Prudential Assurance Co Ltd* [2001] BVC 2,201 on the subject of outsourcing. Scottish Amicable Unit Trust Managers Ltd (SAUTML) was a member of the Prudential VAT group and the manager of 25 unit trusts. For the purpose of the *Financial Services Act* 1986, SAUTML was the manager and operator of the trusts and, under reg. 7.15 of the *Financial Services (Regulated Schemes) Regulations* 1991, could delegate any of its functions. Having few resources, it delegated both its investment management and its administration, initially to another member of the VAT group but, later, to other investment managers.

Prudential argued the outsourced services were exempt, whether or not this function was carried out by the operator or by a delegated or subcontracted manager. They were thus within VATA 1994, Sch. 9, Grp. 5, item 9. HMRC, however, maintained they were not. Although the manager was allowed to delegate any function, he remained responsible for the management. The Sixth VAT Directive specified management of funds and not delegated services.

The Tribunal found that, whilst the supplies were not exempt under UK law, they were under the Directive, which was unambiguous in exempting subcontracted management of special investment funds. Since the service supplied was distinct in character, specific to, and essential for, the management of a special investment fund, it was entitled to exemption since UK VAT law failed to accurately enact EC VAT law.

(b) Creating, buying, selling and liquidating units

The basic position is, in this respect, much the same as for any other investment dealer. Sales are exempt as dealings in securities under VATA 1994, Sch. 9, Grp. 5, item 6.

In addition to selling existing units, however, the managers also create new units. This is either as a reaction to demand (where sales cannot be met from existing units already held in the manager's *book*) or in anticipation of future sales (when, for example, a fund is being actively promoted). When demand falls, the managers also liquidate (i.e. cancel) units, reducing the size of the fund and the numbers of units otherwise held in their book.

On the creation of new units, cash will be invested by the managers on behalf of the trustees. In doing this, the managers retain a preliminary or initial charge, representing a specified per cent and a rounding of up to one per cent. Neither is treated as consideration for a supply.

(4) Input VAT implications

The investment manager's ability to recover input VAT is clearly an important issue and the decisions in the *Abbey National* and *JP Morgan Fleming Claverhouse* cases, whilst improving the position overall in terms of charges to clients, have faced managers with the need to review the way in which they address partial exemption. Managers will also need to review the terms of their management agreements to reflect the additional costs in terms of irrecoverable input tax that will, in future, potentially need to be passed on to clients if profitability is to be maintained.

More generally, in the case of basically taxable supplies of management services, there will be relief for any underlying input VAT where the client is a business established in another Member State or is anyone who belongs outside the EU. This is given under VATA 1994, s. 25 and reg. 103 of the *Value Added Tax Regulations* 1995 (SI 1995/2518).

For basically exempt supplies, where there is a supply of fund management within item 9 or 10 of Group 5 of VATA 1994 the normal partial exemption rules apply. Input tax incurred on costs which are used exclusively to make exempt supplies are not deductible. Any services which are exempt under items 9 or 10 are not included under the *Value Added Tax (Input Tax) (Specified Supplies)* Order 1999 (SI 1999/3121) which means there is no right to deduct input tax, even if the customer is established outside the EU. In other words, fund management services made to a CIS or sub-fund established in the Channel Islands, which is recognised under s. 270 of FSMA 2000, and so defined in item 9 does not give rise to a recovery of input tax on related costs.

80-350 Investment and unit trusts

Investment trusts are usually companies, whose activities largely comprise buying and holding securities as principal for the purposes of deriving income and/or capital growth, but who can also be involved in other investments, particularly property.

Unit trusts are investment arrangements established under a deed of trust. As such, they are not legal entities or persons separate from the trustees. The functions and activities of a unit trust are, however, essentially the same as for investment trusts, but with the day-to-day administration of the trust, being the responsibility of third-party managers.

In the case of unit trusts, the person or persons to be registered for VAT, if at all, will be the trustees (usually banks) rather than the trust. Generally, however, authorised unit trusts tend not to be registered due to the high proportion of exempt supplies and low or negligible input VAT.

(1) Outputs

The purchase and sale of securities is an essentially exempt activity. In terms of EU law, the supply falls within art. 135(1)(f) of Council Directive 2006/112/EC (art. 13(B)(d)(5)) as:

> 'transactions ... in shares, interests in companies or associations, debentures and other securities.'

In VATA 1994, the equivalent rule is in Sch. 9, Grp. 5, item 6.

Investment trusts will also from time-to-time receive underwriting or sub-underwriting commissions. These are again basically exempt, this time under Grp. 5, item 5A (see earlier at 80-200(31)). The place of supply, in either case, will follow the rules discussed in Chapter 3.

Receipts from property can be an important area with some funds and is discussed in detail at 80-150. Although property is basically VAT-exempt, commercial developments and lettings are now generally subject to VAT and the zero-rating for new buildings and for construction and alteration services is now greatly reduced.

(2) Input VAT implications

Ultimately, how investment trusts are affected can depend largely on the type of investments and the markets on which they are dealt in. In the case of basically exempt supplies, there will normally be relief for any underlying input VAT only where the client *belongs* outside the EU. This is given under reg. 103 of what is now the *Value Added Tax Regulations* 1995 (SI 1995/2518) and art. 2 and 3 of the *Value Added Tax (Input Tax) (Specified Supplies) Order* 1999 (SI 1999/3121) (art. 169(c) of Council Directive 2006/112/EC). However, relief will not be given where management is within the scope of items 9 or 10 of Group 5 of VATA 1994.

However, the distinction between exempt income as such and exempt income with the right to input VAT relief not only affects the level of input VAT recovered, it can also indicate, if not decide, the actual amount of input VAT that is incurred. For a UK portfolio, the position will be relatively straightforward. Input VAT will be incurred on many of the day-to-day costs, including accounting, administration, communications and data processing and even on occupancy costs such as rent. A North American or Far East portfolio, however, may be in a quite different position altogether. It may, for example, be managed abroad. Charges may not, therefore attract VAT, except perhaps under the reverse charge (see **Chapter 5**).

80-400 Funded pension schemes

Funded pension schemes are major institutional investors. In contrast to *insured* schemes, which essentially involve the payment of premiums and are more within the scope of *Insurance* in **Chapter 9**, *funded* schemes are directly concerned with investment itself. The range of investments will, of course, differ from fund to fund; in the case of the larger funds, it may even extend to overseas securities, property and works of art.

For VAT purposes, therefore, funded pensions schemes needed to be considered in broadly the same way as investment and unit trusts and, indeed, as for any other commercial investment organisation. The VAT implications, though, can be easily overlooked as they may not be seen in that light, as businesses. Being generally the responsibility of trustees and often distanced from the business of the employer, the possibility of registration and the recovery of VAT (and even the prospect of output VAT liability) can sometimes be missed. It should be noted that a reference has been made to the CoJ as to whether fund management services provided to and for the benefit of defined occupational pension schemes are liable to VAT (see 80-300)

To address these issues, HMRC have provided guidance in their Notice on Funded Pension Schemes (Notice 700/17, November 2011). This attempts to simplify the position and, for some schemes, does just that.

(1) Registration

As with investment and unit trusts, the first thing to consider is VAT registration. A funded pension scheme, being a fund, not a legal person (or even a collection of persons) but merely a collection of assets, cannot be registered, as such. Registration under VATA 1994, s. 3 is possible, however, but will need to be in the names of the trustees – those charged by the Trust Deed to receive the contributions, administer the scheme generally, pay pensions and make any necessary investments. Normally, this will mean that they will be treated in much the same way as for partnerships.

The trustees may or may not include the employer. In some cases, however, the employer will be the sole trustee or there will be a sole trustee company which is a subsidiary of the employer allowing the possibility of registering as a group under VATA 1994, s. 43. Those individuals such as employee representatives, who would usually act as trustees, are directors.

This, in theory, gives precisely the same result as where the employer alone is the sole trustee. Either situation can, however, then blur the distinction between the two categories of activity or responsibility referred to earlier at (2), as shown by the *British Rail* case discussed later.

In the case of VAT groups, there is also, of course, the matter of HMRC's possible recourse against fund assets, something highlighted by the joint and several liability under s. 43. At one time, this was a real concern. However, HMRC have now been advised that this liability does not extend to the assets of any trust except to the extent that the group VAT debt is in whole or part attributable to the management of the trust (see Funded Pension Schemes (Notice 700/17, November 2011) at 4.3).

(2) The activities

The matter is not simply, though, one of registering the trustees, because the activities of a pension fund are seen as falling into two broad categories:

(1) **Administration** – comprising the receipt of contributions, the payment of pensions and the discharge of general administration costs. All of these are undertaken as an obligation of the Trust Deed rather than as a commercial activity.

(2) **Investment** – including the purchase and sale of investments, the receipt of interest and income therefrom, and the payment of costs such as obtaining advice and management and the service of trustees. All of these are generally regarded as matters undertaken in the course of economic activities despite what was said in the Wellcome Trust case *Wellcome Trust Ltd v C & E Commrs* (Case C-155/94) [1996] BVC 377 (see earlier at 80-100 and **Chapter 1** at 10-300). The circumstances of the trustees of a pension fund are somewhat different from those of a charity and it may well be that the association with the employer's business, for example, would, if necessary, be sufficient to impart the required *business* flavour.

These are considered separately below, since, so far as the expenses are concerned, there is also the question of what, if any, of the tax paid is input VAT, and for whom.

Input VAT, it will be remembered, has a special meaning (VATA 1994, s. 25) being, broadly, VAT incurred by the claimant on goods or services acquired by him for the purposes of his business. It is not the same as simply paying or bearing an expense as many as the Tribunal decisions have shown (e.g. *Linotype and Machinery Ltd* (1978) VATTR 123).

The circumstances of the trustees and the manner in which costs are incurred can have an important bearing on the eventual outcome.

(3) Administration

As noted earlier, the receipt of contributions, the payment of pensions and the discharge of general administration costs are generally seen as an obligation of the Trust Deed, rather than as a commercial activity. As such, input VAT relief will not be available to the trustees or the fund. However, in practice, administration is often undertaken and paid for by the employer and this can radically affect the VAT position.

Despite the fact that the costs may be for supplies to the trustees, HMRC in practice allow the employer input VAT relief (see Section 2.3 of HMRC Notice 700/17) on services in connection with:

- making the arrangements to set up a pension fund;
- managing the scheme, i.e. collecting contributions and paying pensions;
- advice on review of the scheme, and implementing any changes to the scheme;
- accountancy and auditing, so far as they relate to the management of the scheme, e.g. preparation of annual accounts;
- actuarial valuations of the assets of a fund;
- general actuarial advice to do with fund administration;
- providing general statistics on the performance of investments, properties, etc;
- legal instructions and general legal advice, including drafting trust deeds so far as they relate to the management of the scheme.

Provided the employer has a VAT invoice made out in its name, input VAT may be recovered by it, subject only to the constraints of its own partial exemption position. It does not, in fact, seem to matter to HMRC who pays, or whether in fact the supply is to the employer at all (the cost can even be recharged to the fund). The principle here seems, in fact, to be in conflict with the decision in the *Linotype and Machinery Ltd* case and to draw more from the High Court decision in *Manchester Ship Canal Co v C & E Commrs* (1982) 1 BVC 471), when certain specific actuarial costs were more clearly the result of supplies to the employer. However, to the extent that it gives relief which otherwise would not be available, then it is only to be welcomed.

However, as illustrated in the British Railways Board case, the issue can also be affected by the role the employer has to play.

- In *C & E Commrs v British Railways Board* [1976] 1 BVC 103, the taxpayer, which operated railway services in the UK, also operated a pension scheme for the benefit of its employees and acted as trustee. In its capacity as trustee it employed staff and received professional advice on the investment of pension funds, claiming input tax relief on the costs incurred. This was denied by HMRC, but the Tribunal, and later the Court sided with British Railways. The management of the pension funds was a part of the Board's function as an employer and it was not possible to separate its functions as railway operator from its administration of the funds. Both were part of its general undertaking and it followed that the costs were supplies for the purpose of its business on which it was entitled to deduct the VAT.

In appropriate circumstances, this principle would seem equally relevant to situations where the trustee is not the employer, but a subsidiary of the employer with which it is grouped under VATA 1994, s. 43.

(a) Professional management fees

With professional management fees, it is common for managers to apportion their charges between administration and investment, generally on a 30:70 basis. The former category includes the accounting/reporting function and, where this is invoiced separately to the employer, the latter may recover the related input VAT, leaving tax on the investment activities to be recovered by the trustees or the fund.

(b) Recharges of costs

Not all employers pay the day-to-day administration costs. Even if they do, they will frequently seek reimbursement, sometimes for administration costs but more often for the costs of looking after the investments. Many costs will be VAT-free (e.g. salaries, rents and other overheads) but this does not necessarily apply to the recharge (see *British Airways Board and British Airways Housing Trust Ltd* (LON/78/191) No. 663).

In Notice 700/17, HMRC draw a distinction between administration/management and investment:

- the employer can recharge the fund *VAT free* any costs on day-to-day administration (see para. 2.6); but
- recharges of investment costs are seen as consideration for taxable supplies of services.

However, this may not be strictly correct.

- The *British Rail* decision referred to earlier showed that providing a pension fund and acting as trustee can be part and parcel of an employer's business. In that case the Board was sole trustee so that the question of recharges to the fund was irrelevant. It did, however, lay the basis for the idea that costs can, in certain circumstances, rank as VAT inputs of the employer.
- In the case of the *National Coal Board*, however (*The National Coal Board v C & E Commrs* (1982) 1 BVC 515), the issue did arise. The employer was not sole trustee and HMRC were seeking to argue that what they saw as recharges of costs were consideration for supplies, the emphasis being on administration. HMRC lost, because under the Trust Deed the *recharges* were part of the calculation of contributions. They were not simply a *netting off* of a charge for services against the contributions, i.e. a deduction therefrom. There was thus no consideration for what was provided to the trustees and, consequently, no supply of services for VAT purposes.

What HMRC have done, however, is to take the matter one stage further. Applying the idea *across the board* they allow the principle for administration costs to be followed regardless of how a particular fund is organised – although not for investment expenses. But the *National Coal Board* case did in fact involve investment related services as well. On this basis, and relying also on the *British Rail* decision, the employer can arguably, in appropriate cases, justify input VAT relief for investment management/advisory services to the same extent as for administration. How the Trust Deed is worded will, though, be important, especially if the ultimate cost is to be borne by the fund. What the *National Coal Board* decision showed is just how important this wording can be.

HMRC also say that, where there are two or more employers who are not grouped for VAT purposes, the principal employer cannot recover all of the input VAT unless appropriate recharges are made to the others (para. 2.8).

(4) Investment

In contrast to administration, investment is generally not a matter for the employer, but solely for the trustees. Unless the employer is sole trustee, as in the *British Rail* case (or there is a sole trustee, which is a subsidiary of the employer with which it is grouped under VATA 1994. s. 43), there is then normally no question of using the employer's VAT returns either for recovering input VAT or, for that matter, for accounting for any outputs that occur. Indeed, most employers these days wish quite the reverse. Since investments cannot generally be ignored for partial exemption purposes, the prospect, therefore, is of a negative impact on the employer's input VAT recovery position.

The trustees are, as a result, in much the same position as investment and unit trusts. Typical outputs will comprise:

- sale proceeds and interest from securities;
- interest on loans and deposits;
- share underwriting commissions;
- sale proceeds, premiums and rents of properties; and
- works of art.

8 Securities, Property and Investment

Costs will also be incurred on a variety of fronts, including investment advice, brokerage and agents' charges, investment management, property management and the services of a professional trustee.

How the income and expenses will be dealt with for VAT purposes depends again on what is involved and the circumstances in which it is undertaken.

(a) Financial investments

Financial investments are basically exempt from VAT – sale proceeds and interest from securities under VATA 1994, Sch. 9, Grp. 5, item 6; interest on loans and deposits under item 2. Exemption does, however, confer the right to input VAT recovery where:

- securities are sold to persons *belonging* outside the EU and the Isle of Man;
- interest is received from securities issued by persons also *belonging* outside the EU and the Isle of Man;
- interest is received on loans and deposits made to persons *belonging* outside the EU and the Isle of Man.

This will be especially relevant for investment in Japanese and North American stocks.

In practice, with the current emphasis on direct attribution, relief tends to be concentrated on the more general costs, such as investment management, investment advice and trustees' services.

- Following the decision of the VAT Tribunal in *Willis Pension Trustees Ltd* [2006] BVC 2,045 it is now decided that foreign exchange transactions will not always constitute supplies by both parties, but may only rank as a supply of financial services by the bank. Willis Pension Trustees had entered into a foreign exchange transaction as a financial hedge. The Tribunal, in finding the Trustee company made no supply, also indicated that the same principle would equally apply to other hedge transactions, such as interest rate swaps. Although HMRC have accepted this decision in relation to foreign exchange, they are not proposing to alter their policy in recognising supplies by boh parties in the case of the other financial products.

(b) Share underwriting

Share underwriting is discussed in detail earlier at 80-200 and is also basically VAT-exempt.

(c) Property

Property investment can be an important area with some funds and is discussed in detail earlier at 80-150. Although property is basically VAT-exempt, commercial developments and lettings are now generally subject to VAT and the zero-rating for new buildings and for construction and alteration services is now greatly reduced.

(d) Other assets

Other assets, such as works of art or antiques are generally taxable at the standard-rate. However, usually, the purchase and sale will be subject to the special scheme for second-hand goods.

(e) Partial exemption

How a fund approaches partial exemption and the recovery of input tax will be a matter for individual discussion and negotiation with HMRC. At one time, the residual input VAT calculation was often made on the basis of the respective values of taxable and exempt income or receipts. However, in the present climate, a more structured approach, taking into account the different types of investment and cost is likely to be more appropriate and acceptable.

> **Summary**
>
> **Investment plays a vital part in the working of the City and financial institutions and is important to the long-term growth and stability of the economy.**
>
> **Many investments are VAT-exempt, as are a number of investment-related services. However, the financial services exemptions do not always apply and, with VAT currently at 20 per cent then being a possibility on both outputs or investment supplies and on a seemingly ever-increasing level of costs, it can be important to be alert to the potential implications.**
>
> **This Chapter has attempted to give some pointers in that direction.**

9 Insurance

> **Overview**
>
> This Chapter considers:
>
> (1) The general nature of insurance.
>
>   (a) the typical types of transactions encountered in the insurance sector, including:
>
>   (i) what they involve:
>   (ii) their general VAT liabilities; and
>   (iii) how they should be treated for VAT in different situations.
>
> (2) The particular considerations affecting:
>
>   (a) insurance companies;
>   (b) Members of Lloyds; and
>   (c) brokers and other intermediaries.
>
> (3) Outsourcing.

90-000 What is involved?

This Chapter addresses, in more detail, some of the concerns of insurers, insurance agents, brokers and underwriting managers. Income, in the case of insurers or reinsurers, will mainly be from premiums. There will also always be significant receipts from investment, both in financial instruments and in property. Insurance intermediaries will largely receive consideration in the form of commission, brokerage or fees and, again, may derive income from the short-term investment of funds.

90-050 General VAT liability issues

By far the majority of supplies by businesses in this sector do not attract VAT. Insurance is, with rare exceptions, exempt. So too are the financial investments which are a fundamental part of any insurance operation, whether they involve securities or monetary loans or other financial products. Property, where insurance companies are major institutional investors, is also inherently exempt, though as landlords of commercial property insurance companies will in most cases exercise the option to tax under VATA 1994, Sch. 10. Financial investments and property are largely covered in **Chapters 7** and **8**.

The exemption for insurance and insurance-related supplies is broad and unspecific. What matters for VAT purposes both for the finance exemption and the insurance exemption is the nature of what is supplied (*natura negotii*), not the label attached to the supply or the regulatory status of the supplier. In defining the scope of the finance and insurance exemptions in art. 135 of the VAT Directive (2006/112/EC) the European Court (ECJ) has adopted a dynamic interpretation. In relation to the finance exemption (art. 135(1)(d)) *Sparekassernes Datacenter (SDC) v Skatteministeriet* (Case C-2/95) [1997] BVC 509 the ECJ held at p. 516 (para. 32–35 of judgment) that a business did not have to be a bank to operate bank accounts. In *Card Protection Plan Ltd v C & E Commrs* (Case C-349/96) [1999] BVC 155 the ECJ held at para. 22 of the judgment that a business did not need to be an insurance company to provide insurance. In both cases it was the substance of what was done that mattered.

The relevant concept of art. 135(1)(a)–(f) is 'negotiation' ('intermediation'). Again, in defining the nature and scope of negotiation the ECJ has adopted a functional approach.

In an industry where most of the outputs or supplies do not attract VAT, the emphasis is often on minimising the levels of input VAT as recovery rates tend to be low. Avoiding VAT on external management or outsourcing costs for example, is an area of growing concern, where attempts have been made to argue that these services are within the exemption for insurance as insurance-related services. Such services require 'a distinct act of mediation': *C & E Commrs v CSC Financial Services Ltd* (Case C-235/00) [2002] BVC 253 at para. 39 of the judgment. This requirement will not be fulfilled where the supply is of back-office services in the form of administrative and clerical support, as was held to be the case by the ECJ in *Staatssecretaris van Financiën v Arthur Andersen & Co Accountants c.s.* (Case C-472/03) [2006] BVC 228.

The case has prompted a broader debate over the scope of the insurance exemption, which has been part of an ongoing EU review, together with exemption for financial services, a review which has, to date, culminated in the draft Commission proposals discussed later at 90-100. The effect of this decision on existing UK law is considered later in this Chapter, particularly in the context of *Intermediaries and Outsourcing* in 90-350.

Whilst most outputs or supplies are VAT-exempt, there are still occasions when income or receipts are taxed. This is especially true of commercial property, where there is an increasing tendency for proceeds or rents from commercial property to be subject to VAT at the standard-rate and where exemption is now almost a thing of the past. Taxable supplies clearly open up the prospect of input VAT relief, something which, although available for some otherwise VAT-exempt insurance or investment supplies, tends to be limited.

There are also a number of other situations, primarily in the retail sector, where insurance is offered as part of a package to generate increased sales. The ability to split the *price* between the different elements could (in the case of consumers) effectively reduce the overall amount of output tax charged, or (in the case of exempt supplies) enable HMRC to secure additional output tax. In such cases the VAT treatment will depend upon whether the supply is analysed as a mixed or a composite supply.

In *Birkdale School, Sheffield v R & C Commrs* [2008] BVC 397 a fee-paying school arranged, for an additional charge, school fees remission insurance, which entitled the parent to a refund of fees in specified circumstances, such as absence from school through illness. The school fees were exempt from VAT but HMRC claimed that the additional payment should be standard-rated. The High Court held that there was a composite supply of education, to which the arrangement for fees remission was ancillary.

90-100 Providing or arranging cover

Supplies under this heading are largely represented by premiums, brokerage or fees. What is or is not insurance is clearly important.

In the absence of any statutory definition, either in Council Directive 2006/112/EC (before 1 January 2007, the Sixth VAT Directive (Directive 77/388)), VATA 1994 or the *Financial Services and Markets Act* 2000, the matter falls to be construed according to the principles of general law. In *Medical Defence Union Ltd v Department of Trade* [1979] 2 All ER 421 at p. 424, Megarry VC identified three elements, which had to be present.

(1) The contract must provide that the assured will become entitled to something on the occurrence of some event.

(2) The event must be one which involves some element of uncertainty.

(3) The assured must have an insurable interest in the subject-matter of the contract.

There has also been some interesting commentary on the nature of insurance in the decision in *Winterthur Life UK Ltd (formerly Provident Life Association Ltd)* [1997] BVC 2,433, where the Tribunal remarked that:

> '6.1 The nature of "insurance", more specifically of "life insurance", was recently considered by the Court of Appeal in *Fuji Finance Inc v Aetna Life Assurance Co Ltd* [1997] Ch 173. Morritt LJ, giving the lead judgment, expressed the following conclusions on the issues relevant to this appeal at pp. 883-884 of the report:
>
>> "The essence of life assurance, as emphasised in all cases is that the right to the benefits is related to life or death. The obvious case ... is where the benefit is payable on death or its notifications. But over the years other less obviously life-or death-related events have been recognised as sufficient. Thus survival to a given date, as in *Joseph v Law Integrity Insurance Co Ltd* (1912) 2 Ch 581, ... being alive and therefore able to retire or leave a specified employment, as in *NM Superannuation Pty Ltd v Young* 113 ALR 39, have all been recognised as being sufficiently related to life or death ..."
>
> If the event on which a benefit is payable is sufficiently life-or death-related then I can see no reason in principle why it should matter if that benefit is the same as that payable on another life-or death-related event. That is a matter for the insurer and it is well established that it is not necessary that the insurer should be exposed to any risk at all: *Flood v Irish Provident Assurance Co Ltd (Note)* (1912) 2 Ch 597; *N M Superannuation Pty Ltd v Young* 113 ALR 39. This was evidently the view of Hill J in the last mentioned case, as demonstrated earlier, and I agree with him.'

Earlier in his judgment (pp. 880-881), Morritt J referred to *Marac Life Assurance Ltd v IR Commrs* [1986] 1 NZLR 694 stating (at p. 881G) that:

> 'this case recognised that the investment element of a policy, which has become such a feature of modern insurance, is consistent with its characterisation as a life policy.'

In terms of the general law of contract, this usually means:

(1) *Offer and acceptance* – there must be an offer by one party, which is unequivocally accepted by the other party. In insurance the proposer makes an offer to the insurer,

which the latter either accepts or rejects. The parties must be in agreement as to the intention of the contract.

(2) *Intention* – there must be an intention to enter into a legal relationship under which both parties have a legal obligation to perform the contract.

(3) *Consideration* – there must be some payment, right or benefit granted by the parties to a contract. The premium forms the policyholder's consideration in return for the insurer's promise to pay accordingly to the terms of the policy.

The risks covered can be very wide and will include, for example, fire, accident, motor, loss of profits and general indemnity, as well as permanent health and life and endowment business.

The regulation of insurance in the UK is now governed by the *Financial Services and Markets Act* 2000. HMRC say, in Notice 701/36 that, generally, something is insurance for VAT purposes if it is an activity that requires the provider to be *authorised* as an insurer under the provisions of that Act. However, they accept that certain funeral plan contracts are insurance (and therefore exempt from VAT) even though they are not regulated as such under the Act. Similarly, vehicle breakdown insurance can be seen as insurance even though providers are given a specific exclusion under the Act from the requirement to be authorised. Likewise, it is acknowledged that following the Ruling of the ECJ in the case of *Card Protection Plan Ltd (CPP)* [2001] BVC 158 the UK cannot restrict the exemption under VATA 1994 to persons who are *authorised insurers* (see **Chapter 3** at 30-500).

It is worth, perhaps, just noting that the *Financial Services and Markets Act* 2000 makes it illegal for UK businesses to effect contracts of insurance without being authorised to do so (with the exception of those bodies that are specifically exempted from this requirement). Also, under *Financial Services and Markets Act* 2000, s. 19, an insurance company is not permitted to carry out activities in the UK or elsewhere, otherwise than in connection with or for the purposes of its insurance business.

(1) Exemption

Exemption, which applies to the majority of supplies in this sector, clearly has its advantages. Many final consumers are private individuals or otherwise not registered for VAT. Not having to charge VAT thus makes it possible for insurers to reduce the cost of what is provided.

Whether or not supplies are exempt, with generally no input VAT recovery, *outside the scope* or taxable depends, however, on a number of factors. These can differ according to the nature of the risk, whether it is insurance or reinsurance, and on the position of the insured – or even, sometimes, of the insurer.

The basis for the exemption for insurance and insurance-related activities derives from art. 135(1)(a) of Council Directive 2006/112/EC (art. 13(B)(a) of the Sixth VAT Directive). This is fairly brief and to the point. It refers simply to:

> 'insurance and reinsurance transactions, including related services performed by insurance brokers and insurance agents.'

In the UK, the corresponding provisions are found in VATA 1994, Sch. 9, Grp. 2. As now drafted the Group reads:

'Item No.

(1) Insurance transactions and reinsurance transactions.

(2) ...

(3) ...

(4) The provision by an insurance broker or insurance agent of any of the services of an insurance intermediary in a case in which those services-

    (a) are related (whether or not a contract of insurance or reinsurance is finally concluded) to an insurance transaction or a reinsurance transaction; and

    (b) are provided by that broker or agent in the course of his acting in an intermediary capacity.'

The law was changed to give effect to the ruling of the ECJ in *Card Protection Plan* ((Case C-349/96) [1999] BVC 155) (see **Chapter 3** at 30-500), which held that a Member State may not restrict the scope of the exemption for insurance transactions to supplies by insurers, who are authorised by national law to pursue the activity of insurer. In other words, what is important is the nature of what is supplied, not the identity of the supplier and the fact that something may, as a result, be being carried on illegally is irrelevant.

(2) The Commission proposals

The draft proposal for the new Directive (amending Council Directive 2006/112/EC as regards financial and insurance services) was published on 16 July 2007. In addition, the Commission also published extensive draft Regulations (not reproduced here), which can be found on the Commission website at http://ec.europa.eu/taxation_customs/resources/documents/common/consultations/tax/working_paper_definitions_en.pdf.

The effect of the proposals is to replace points (a) to (g) in art. 135(1) by the following:

'(a) Insurance services;
(b) Granting of credit and the financial safeguarding of credits;
(c) Deposit services and account operation services;
(d) Currency exchange and cash services;
(e) Supplies of securities;
(f) Management services for investment funds;
(g) Intermediation in insurance and financial services;'.

A new art. 135a will then qualify how the exemption in points (a) to (g) is to be applied and, in particular, provides that:

'(1) "Insurance services" shall mean commitments whereby a person is obliged, in return for payment of a premium, to provide in the event of materialisation of a significant risk, with a service as determined by the commitment.'

and

'(8) "Intermediation in insurance and financial services" shall mean related services distinct in character and specific to and essential for the conclusion, amendment or prolongation of an agreement whereby a person engages to supply one of the exempt main services listed in Article 135(1)(a) to (e).'

'(2) A related service distinct in character shall be regarded as the main service to which it relates, where it is specific to and essential for the transaction exempted under art. 135(1)(a) to (e).'

It is especially interesting that the Fifth Recital to the draft Directive makes the following observation:

'Intermediation in insurance services and intermediation in financial services are treated equally because the market of insurance services increasingly overlaps with the market for financial services, requiring the same or similar forms of intermediation. Services which are related to intermediation do not benefit from an exemption because intermediation services are themselves already related services. However, subcontracting of intermediation services is covered by the exemption.'

(a) Insurers and reinsurers – Item 1

Article 131 of Directive 2006/112/EC provides that the exemptions are to apply without prejudice to other Community provisions and in accordance with conditions which the Member States shall lay down for the purposes of ensuring the correct and straightforward application of those exemptions and of preventing any possible evasion, avoidance or abuse. At one time, this was taken to mean that, in terms of UK law, it was only available to someone who had permission under Pt. IV of the *Financial Services and Markets Act* 2000 to effect or carry out contracts of insurance, (or previously was authorised to carry out insurance business under the corresponding provisions in the *Insurance Companies Act* 1982). However, as already noted, this was in conflict with rulings of the ECJ in a number of cases, notably *Card Protection Plan Ltd v C & E Commrs* (Case C-349/96) [1999] BVC 155 and *Fischer v Finanzamt Donaueschingen* (Case C-283/95) [1998] BVC 431; and it is now accepted that exemption can apply so long as what is being provided is, in fact, insurance.

The *Card Protection Plan* and *Fischer* cases are discussed in **Chapter 3** at 30-550.

An alternative exemption for financial guarantees or bonds is available under VATA 1994, Sch. 9, Grp. 5, item 1 (see **Chapter 7** at 70-200).

(b) Insurance intermediaries – Item 4

As now drafted, this covers both the normal broking or introductory services as well as things like the handling and settlement of claims, but is qualified by the Statutory Notes.

Subject to their being provided by an insurance broker or insurance agent, services are exempt as those of an *insurance intermediary* are exempt if they amount to:

'(a) the bringing together, with a view to the insurance or reinsurance of risks, of–
    (i)   persons who are or may be seeking insurance or reinsurance, and
    (ii) persons who provide insurance or reinsurance;
(b) the carrying out of work preparatory to the conclusion of contracts of insurance or reinsurance;

(c) the provision of assistance in the administration and performance of such contracts, including the handling of claims; or
(d) the collection of premiums.'

According to Note (2) an insurance broker or insurance agent is acting *in an intermediary capacity* when acting as an intermediary between:
'(a) a person who provides any insurance or reinsurance and
(b) a person who is or may be seeking insurance or reinsurance or is an insured person.'

Under Note (7) item 4 specifically does not include:

(1) Market research, product design, advertising, promotional or similar services or the collection, collation and provision of information for use in connection therewith.

(2) Valuation or inspection services.

(3) The services of loss adjusters, average adjusters, motor assessors, surveyors or other experts except where:

(a) they services consist in the handling of a claim under a contract of insurance or reinsurance;
(b) the person handling the claim is authorised, when doing so to act on behalf of the insurer or reinsurer; and
(c) that person's authority so to act includes written authority to determine whether to accept or reject the claim and, where accepting it in whole or in part, to settle the amount to be paid on the claim.

It also excludes any services that are supplied as part of the actual indemnity under a contract of insurance or reinsurance.

On the face of it, whilst the exemption, as expressed in terms of *related services* in the context of *services performed by insurance brokers and insurance agents*, seems to borrow much from the descriptions of services covered by the *Intermediaries Directive* (Directive 92/77), art. 2:

'(1) This Directive shall apply to the following activities falling within ex ISIC Group 630 in Annex III to the General Programme for the abolition of restrictions on freedom of establishment:

(a) professional activities of persons who, acting with complete freedom as to their choice of undertaking, bring together, with a view to the insurance or reinsurance of risks, persons seeking insurance or reinsurance and insurance or reinsurance undertakings, carry out work preparatory to the conclusion of contracts of insurance or reinsurance and, where appropriate, assist in the administration and performance of such contracts, in particular in the event of a claim;

(b) professional activities of persons instructed under one or more contracts or empowered to act in the name and on behalf of, or solely on behalf of, one or more insurance undertakings in introducing, proposing and carrying out work preparatory to the conclusion of, or in concluding, contracts of insurance, or in assisting in the administration and performance of such contracts, in particular in the event of a claim;

(c) activities of persons other than those referred to in (a) and (b) who, acting on behalf of such persons, among other things carry out introductory work, introduce insurance contracts or collect premiums, provided that no insurance commitments towards or on the part of the public are given as part of these operations.'

The ruling in the *Arthur Andersen* case has expressed the view that the *Intermediaries Directive* definitions do not determine the status of a business as insurance agent or broker for the purposes of the VAT exemption. The Court also found, in relation to insurance brokers or agents, that:

- the essential characteristic of brokers is their complete freedom as to choice of insurer for their clients;
- the essential characteristic of agents is that, although they may be tied to one or more insurers, their role is to find and introduce prospective customers; and
- an insurance agent or broker must not be carrying out only subcontracted activities on the insurer's behalf and which the insurer would normally perform for itself. It must be carrying out the independent function of bringing the parties to the insurance or reinsurance contract together.

The Court also held that, as Advocate General Poiares Maduro pointed out in his Opinion, it cannot be inferred from that case-law that the existence of a power to render the insurer liable is the determining criterion for recognition of an insurance agent within the meaning of art. 13B(a) of the Sixth Directive. Recognition of a person as *an insurance agent* presupposes an examination of what the activities in question comprise.

Directive 92/77 has now been replaced by the *EC Insurance Mediation Directive* (Council Directive 2002/92), where the corresponding provisions in art. 3 state that:

'3. "insurance mediation" means the activities of introducing, proposing or carrying out other work preparatory to the conclusion of contracts of insurance, or of concluding such contracts, or of assisting in the administration and performance of such contracts, in particular in the event of a claim.

These activities when undertaken by an insurance undertaking or an employee of an insurance undertaking who is acting under the responsibility of the insurance undertaking shall not be considered as insurance mediation.

The provision of information on an incidental basis in the context of another professional activity provided that the purpose of that activity is not to assist the customer in concluding or performing an insurance contract, the management of claims of an insurance undertaking on a professional basis, and loss adjusting and expert appraisal of claims shall also not be considered as insurance mediation.'

Article 4 has similar wording for 'reinsurance mediation'.

The *Arthur Andersen* case was about the treatment of *outsourcing*. As *Card Protection Plan Ltd v C & E Commrs* (C-349/96) [1999] BVC 155 has shown, a Member State may not restrict the scope of the exemption for insurance transactions exclusively to supplies by insurers who are authorised by national law to pursue that activity.

In a sense, perhaps, and as discussed in later at 90-350, this ruling of the ECJ in the *Arthur Andersen* case has gone against the trend of similar cases relating to intermediary services for finance, such as *Sparekassernes Datacenter (SDC) v Skatteministeriet* (Case C-2/95) [1997] BVC 509 and *C & E Commrs v FDR Ltd* [2000] BVC 311 (see earlier in **Chapter 7**). The Court had, admittedly, followed a similar line in *Försäkringsaktiebolaget Skandia (publ)* (Case C-240/99) [2001] BVC 281 (also discussed later at 90-350), but there may be reasons why that decision was not quite right.

However, as cases like *Card Protection Plan* have shown, an examination of what particular activities comprise is always important in this sort of context.

Recent cases have emphasised the scope of the insurance exemption and in particular the exemption for the provision of insurance-related services by an insurance agent or broker acting in an intermediary capacity.

In *Ludwig v Finanzamt Luckenwalde*(Case C-453/05) [2009] BVC 967, in a case involving a sub-agent of a financial services company, the ECJ made it clear that the requirement of negotiation could be satisfied without a contractual link with either of the parties to the concluded contract (para. 29 of judgment).

In *JCM Beheer BV v Staatssecretaris van Financiën* (Case C-124/07) [2011] BVC 287 the Court reached the same conclusion in relation to a sub-agent of an insurance, namely, that an indirect link with the insurers sufficed (para. 23 of judgment).

All these authorities have now been extensively reviewed in *R & C Commrs v InsuranceWide. com Services Ltd*[2010] BVC 606. This involved the provider of a website which offered a 'click through' facility to insurance services, including quotations for policies and policies. The Court of Appeal held that constituted an insurance-related provision of services by a person acting in an intermediary capacity. At p. 634, [85], Etherton LJ put forward a series of propositions about the scope of the insurance exemption:

> '(1) The insurance intermediary exemption should be interpreted so far as possible, consistently with its terms, in a way that reflects the jurisprudence of the ECJ and the United Kingdom's obligations under the Sixth Directive and the 2006 VAT Directive ...
>
> (2) The exemption in art. 13(B)(a) [art. 135(1)(a)] must be interpreted strictly, since it constitutes an exception to the general principle that VAT is to be levied on all services supplied by a taxable person. This does not mean, however, that the words and expression in art. 13(B)(a) and the insurance intermediary exemption are to be given a particularly narrow or restricted interpretation. It is for the supplier to establish that it and its activities come within the interpretation of the words of the exemption.
>
> (3) The exemption for "related services" under art. 13(B)(a) only applies to services performed by a person acting as an insurance broker or an insurance agent. Although those expressions are not defined by EU legislation, they are independent concepts of Community law which have to be placed in the general context of the common system of VAT.
>
> (4) Whether or not a person is an insurance broker or an insurance agent, within art. 13(B) (a) depends on what they do. How they choose to describe themselves or their activities is not determinative.

(5) The definitions of "insurance broker" and "insurance agent" in the Insurance Directive are relevant to the meaning of the same expressions in art. 13(B)(a) to the extent, but only to the extent, that they should be taken into consideration as reflecting legal reality and practice in the area of insurance law. it is not necessary, in order to invoke the exemption in art. 13(B)(a), for the taxpayer to perform precisely the description of activities in art. 2(1)(a) or (b) of the Insurance Directive.

(6) On the other hand, the mere fact that a person is performing one of the activities described in art. 2(1)(a) or (b) of the Insurance Directive or the definition of "insurance mediation" in the Insurance Mediation Directive does not automatically characterise that person as an insurance agent or an insurance broker for the purposes of art. 13(B)(a).

(7) It is an essential characteristic of an insurance broker or an insurance agent or an insurance agent within art. 13(B)(a), that they are engaged in the business of putting insurance companies in touch with potential clients or, more generally, acting as intermediaries between insurance companies and clients or potential clients.

(8) It is not necessary in order to claim the benefit of the exemption in art. 13B(a) for a person to be carrying out all the functions of a insurance agent or broker. It is sufficient if a person is one of a chain of persons bringing together an insurance company and a potential insured and carrying out intermediary functions, provided that the services which that person is rendering are in themselves characteristic of the services of an insurance agent or broker.

(9) All the above principles are capable of being applied, and must be applied, to the insurance intermediary exemption in Sch. 9 to VATA 1994.'

A business operated a website which enabled users to obtain quotations for and buy a wide range of insurance products from a number of providers. Applying these principles, the Court of Appeal had no doubt that the activities of business constituted insurance intermediation within the exemption.

Following the Court of Appeal's decision in *InsuranceWide.com* HMRC Brief 31/10, sought to limit the scope of the decision. According to HMRC's interpretation of the decision, for the insurance intermediary exemption to be available, four conditions must be fulfilled:

(1) The person claiming the exemption must put insurance companies in touch with persons requiring insurance.

(2) The business must provide the means of introduction in a chain leading to an insurance provider.

(3) That introduction takes place at the time the customer is seeking to enter into an insurance contract.

(4) The introducer plays a proactive part in putting in place the arrangements under which that introduction is effected.

This approach goes back to and seeks to revive the long-discredited interpretation attempted but decisively rejected in *C & E Commrs v Civil Service Motoring Association* [1998] BVC 21, namely, that to come within the exemption it is not enough to operate generic arrangements, one must also broker individual transactions.

More generally in relation to intermediary services:

- *C & V (Advice Line) Services Ltd* [2001] BVC 2,369 concerned a company providing services to Direct Line in relation to its FLP policy. This offered a legal expenses indemnity as an addition to a home or a motor policy and C & V provided a 24-hour, 7-day-a-week telephone helpline service on any private legal matter exclusively to policyholders.
  C & V argued that, in providing the interface with the policyholder and filtering out problems that did not lead to formal claims, its activities assisted in the performance of the policy, including claims. It was, accordingly, an *insurance agent* within art. 13(B)(a) of the Sixth VAT Directive (art. 135(1)(a)), as interpreted in accordance with the Insurance Intermediaries Directive. Its services (as described) were also those of an *insurance intermediary* as defined in VATA 1994, Sch. 9, Grp. 2, Note (1)(c), because they involved the provision of assistance in the administration and performance of [insurance] contracts, including the handling of claims and those services were *related services* as that expression is used in art. 13(B)(a) (art. 135(1)(a)) in that they were intimately related to the FLP policy. It made a single supply of exempt insurance services as the insurance intermediary elements were sufficiently dominant. The Tribunal agreed.
  In terms of art. 13(B)(a) (art. 135(1)(a)), the service provided must be *related to insurance and reinsurance transactions* and, on the evidence, in the light of the Court of Appeal's decision in *Century Life*, C & V's services were well within the *close nexus* test established in that case.
  To be exempt, C & V's services had still to be services of *an insurance intermediary*, acting as such. C & V was not an insurance broker and could not properly be described as an insurance agent as that expression is used, at least in England and Wales (as the services had nothing to do with the making of the FLP policy contracts with the policyholders). For C & V to succeed, therefore, *insurance agent*, as used in art. 13(B)(b), had to have a wider connotation. This was where the *Insurance Intermediaries Directive* became important in the absence of any definition in the Sixth VAT Directive. The Tribunal was satisfied that this was the case and that the services were within VATA 1994, Sch. 9, Grp. 2.
  On the single or multiple supply point, the insurance intermediary elements of C & V's services were sufficiently dominant to create a single exempt supply.

- The *Century Life* appeal, *C & E Commrs v Century Life plc* [2001] BVC 116, concerned the treatment of the outsourcing of the review of personal pension policies. This is considered later at 90-200, but the Court of Appeal concluded there was no purpose in the qualification in the VAT Act of the phrase *services performed by insurance brokers* as the language of the Directive had already defined the nature of the services to be supplied if they were to be *related to* insurance transactions and exempt. Applying the general principle of interpretation of Community law, if a service was only remotely or *incidentally* connected with an insurance transaction, it was not *related to* it; there had to be a *close nexus* between the service and the insurance transaction concerned. Ensuring that a policy complied with regulations was intimately related to it.

Looking at just the domestic legislation, what Century did was more than merely *ancillary* to the provision of insurance. It fell within VATA 1994, Sch. 9, Grp. 2, item 4, Note (1) (c) and was a vital part of the administration of the contracts.

> **Practice point**
>
> HMRC, in *Business Brief* 2/2001 of 15 February 2001 on *CPP*, said they accept that and would continue to regard the transactions involved in that case as exempt, subject to the usual conditions for the exemption for insurance intermediaries.
>
> However, the implications of the *Century Life* appeal indicate that the interpretation of the exemption may not be as narrow as HMRC would like to suggest. Having regard to the Court of Appeal's analysis in *InsuranceWide.com* many of the services arising in outsourcing situations could fall within the scope of the exemption.

The principles behind the present rules are also explored in other cases.

- In *Countrywide Insurance Marketing Ltd* [1995] BVC 580, the appellant was part of a group of mutually-owned companies formed to provide services to independent insurance brokers and intermediaries throughout the UK. Recognising the collective potential purchasing power of the group's members could enable them to compete with the banks, building societies, motor organisations and national chains, they set out, not just to regulate and represent members, but also to devise new insurance products with advantageous terms and to negotiate the underwriting with suitable insurers. These products were then made available for sale only by those independent insurance brokers and intermediaries who were members of Countrywide. Countrywide was remunerated by passing on a share of the commissions earned on the policies they sold. Countrywide itself, however, took little or no part in the arrangement of these individual policies and had no direct contact with clients. HMRC argued the commissions earned by Countrywide were VATable and not exempt, either under VATA 1994, Sch. 9, Grp. 2, item 3 or under the Sixth VAT Directive, art. 13(B)(a) (art. 135(1)(a) of Council Directive 2006/112/EC). They also maintained that, in any event, art. 13 (art. 135) did not have a direct effect.
- The Tribunal looked at this in terms of the following six questions and answered each in favour of Countrywide:
  (1) Did the wording of VATA 1994, Sch. 9, Grp. 2, item 3 (as it then was) mean that activities are only exempt if the taxpayer negotiates a specific insurance contract or policy with the insured?
  (2) In considering whether services come within VATA 1994, Sch. 9, Grp. 2, item 3 (as it then was), should a distinction be drawn between services which are integral to the provision of the insurance itself and services which are external to it?
  (3) To come within VATA 1994, Sch. 9, Grp. 2, item 3 (as it then was) must the activities be similar to insurance broking and 'something that a broker might do'?
  (4) Were the services supplied by the appellant company 'services related to insurance transactions' within the meaning of the Sixth VAT Directive, art. 13(B)(a)?
  (5) Did the appellant company perform services related to insurance transactions 'as an insurance agent' within the meaning of the Sixth VAT Directive, art. 13(B)(a)?
  (6) Are the provisions of the Sixth VAT Directive, art. 13(B)(a) of direct effect?
- In *Curtis Edington & Say Ltd* [1995] BVC 1,389, the taxpayer was an advertising agent acting for a ferry operator. It devised a form of travellers' insurance, the terms of which it negotiated with an insurer. In practice, this was the limit of its involvement as the policies

were then marketed by the ferry company alongside its inclusive holidays. Curtis Edington & Say received a commission from the insurer for each of the policies taken out.
- HMRC maintained this was taxable, given that the company took no direct part in any of the individual arrangements. The Tribunal, however, disagreed, following the line adopted in Countrywide.

- *Barclays Bank plc (No. 3)* [1991] BVC 893 concerned an insurance broking subsidiary of Barclays, Barclays Insurance Services Co Ltd (BISCO), which was grouped with the bank for VAT purposes. BISCO, in addition to acting as an insurance broker in the accepted sense, had developed an activity referred to as *the mail shot activity* or *direct marketing*. This involved BISCO in considerable research with customers being specifically targeted with details of those products likely to be particularly attractive to them, as opposed to the public generally. Typical of mailshots, the level of response was small. Also, most who replied did so direct to the insurer, not via BISCO, although the company's helpline was available. For its involvement BISCO got a commission, which Barclays successfully maintained was exempt. The services were more than just publicity and were insurance-related in the sense implied in the Sixth VAT Directive, art. 13(B)(a) (art. 135(1)(a) of Council Directive 2006/112/EC).

> **Practice point**
>
> In the event, HMRC decided against appealing any of these cases and opted instead to change the law – much as they later did for finance – (see earlier in **Chapters 7** and **8**).
>
> Although, at the time, the indications were that HMRC wanted to restrict the scope of the exemption, the effect overall was probably not to negate *BISCO*, *Countrywide* or *Curtis Edington & Say*.

Brokers or agents

As noted earlier, in its ruling in the *Arthur Andersen* case, the ECJ has expressed the view that the activity of an insurance broker or an insurance agent must have 'an independent substance distinct from the business of the insurer' (Advocate General at para. 33). Accordingly 'a pure sub-contracting of activities usually performed by the insurance company', i.e. doing what the insurer could have done for himself, was not an intermediary activity (para. 34). It was 'not negotiation, but simply sub-contracting' (para. 36). The court observed in para. 36 of the judgment that 'essential aspects of the work of an insurance agent' include 'the finding of prospects and their introduction to the insurer'.

- In *Donald Ford (Financial Services)* [1987] 3 BVC 609, the appellant, a chartered accountant, carried on a business as a financial adviser. He formed a close association with another business, which had special knowledge of pensions insurance. The principal director of the latter business, S, co-operated with the appellant to expand their mutual business, the appellant provided tax expertise and S his knowledge of the pension market. When a client entered into a pension arrangement the appellant received a share of the commission from S. HMRC contended the commission was taxable because it did not fall within VATA 1983, Sch. 6, Grp. 2, item 3 (as it then was) as the *making of arrangement for the provision of insurance*. The Tribunal disagreed, holding that the commission was exempt. It was not just the case of a bare introduction but one where the appellant was fully involved in the marking of the arrangements.

The *Donald Ford* case subsequently prompted the Institute of Chartered Accountants in England and Wales (ICAEW) to seek clarification from HMRC in view of the potential impact on its members. The result was an agreed statement released by the Institute in March 1990 as TR 787 and now appearing as Tax Guide 1/02 issued in February 2002.

In some ways, what was provided in the *Donald Ford* case is easier to argue as VAT-exempt under the pre-2001 wording in UK law of *the making of arrangements* than it would be today. However, to the extent that someone like an accountant maintains the sort of direct involvement with the taking out of insurance as mentioned in Tax Guide 1/02, the commissions received should be capable of coming within the spirit of intermediary services on which the exemption currently focuses.

- More recently, in *Morganash Ltd* [2007] BVC 2,184 the Tribunal found that a service supplied to life insurance companies of carrying out telephone interviews of persons who have submitted life insurance cover proposals, as to their medical history and condition is not exempt under European law but is exempt under the corresponding provisions in UK law. The interviews lasted between 20 and 40 minutes and were conducted by qualified nurses, with a written report being given to the life insurance company. Morganash made no recommendation as to whether the proposal should be accepted or declined. as an insurance-related service carried out by an insurance agent and a service with sufficient nexus to the contract of insurance provided by the insurer.

Claims settlement

Claims settlement services will also not be exempt, unless carried out by insurance brokers, insurance agents and insurers. Exemption also specifically does not include the provision, on its own, of the services of loss adjusters, average adjusters, motor assessors, surveyors and other experts; nor of legal services in connection with the assessment of claims. For these to be exempt, they must go beyond mere assessment and must involve authority to settle. If these conditions are not met, the supply is automatically taxable at the standard-rate.

- It is interesting in this connection that the Court of Appeal in *WHA Ltd v C & E Commrs* [2004] BVC 485 upheld the Tribunal's decision on the question of whether the re-charge to a Guernsey re-insurer of motor vehicle repair costs arising under MBI policies was part of an exempt supply of claims handling. The appellant had maintained the charging of its fee, together with the costs concerned, amounted to a single exempt supply, but with the right to recover input tax (being within VATA 1994, Sch. 9, Grp. 2, item 4 and former *Value Added Tax (Input Tax) (Specified Supplies) Order* 1992 (SI 1992/3123), art. 3). The Tribunal, however, considered the costs were a separate matter altogether and were subject to VAT at the standard-rate.

As it happens, the taxpayers had a fall-back position, in that they then claimed that the Guernsey re-insurer, Viscount Reinsurance, could recover the tax charged by WHA under the EC Thirteenth Directive (see **Chapter 4** at 40-150(3)). In disagreement with the Tribunal, the Court of Appeal felt Viscount was entitled to recover the tax charged by WHA under the Thirteenth Directive. However, this was subject to further arguments by HMRC, on which judgment was deferred. These were the subject of a subsequent hearing before the Court of Appeal, *WHA Ltd v R & C Commrs* [2007] BVC 695 where the Court accepted HMRC's contention that fiscal neutrality required that an insurer who provided insurance services, which were exempt from VAT in the EU, could not recover input tax attributable to those services. Thus, in transactions in the context of *normal commercial operations* of an insurer and a claims handler, such as that embodied in the arrangements which were replaced by the scheme, the input tax attributable to the cost of repairs and parts was not recoverable. On the evidence, this was the sole purpose of the scheme and amounted to an *abuse of rights* (see **Chapter 4** at 40-000(4)).

- In *Assurandor-Societetet (acting on behalf of Taksatorringen) v Skatteministeriet* (Case C-8/01) [2006] BVC 199 there was a reference by an association whose members were small or medium-sized insurance companies writing motor-vehicle insurance in Denmark. The purpose of Taksatorringen was to assess damage to motor vehicles in Denmark on behalf of its members and Taksatorringen's cost were apportioned among them so that payments corresponded exactly to that member's share of the joint expenses. Taksatorringen argued its services were exempt, within art. 13B(a) of the Sixth Directive. However, the ECJ concluded that the services it provided were neither insurance transactions nor services related to insurance transactions that were performed by insurance brokers or insurance agents.

Valuations for insurance purposes are also normally taxable. However, on occasions they may be exempt if structured as an integral part of the premium (see later at 90-200).

Outside the scope, exemption with the right of recovery and zero-rating

Exemption is, in itself, generally welcome, particularly as it avoids having to charge VAT to those customers or clients (private individuals, for example) by whom it might not be recovered.

Although not quite as important as in some of the other sectors covered by this book, VAT will also not need to be charged if a supply is *outside the scope* because, for example, the place of supply is abroad. This is probably less important for the insurance sector because insurance tends often to be provided predominantly to domestic customers within the territory of the insurer. Some risks will, however, be insured, or services supplied internationally, which, in some situations, then makes the recovery input VAT a possibility.

Whether or not something is *outside the scope* depends generally:

- on the rules on the place of supply (see **Chapter 3** at 30-250(2));
- on what it is that is provided; and
- on the circumstances in which it occurs.

The ability to recover input VAT comes from particular reliefs designed to encourage international trade with non-EU countries. This is allowed in a specific and limited range of circumstances by art. 169(b) and (c) of Council Directive 2006/112/EC (art. 17(3)(b) and (c)), which is mirrored in UK terms in the partial exemption rules by reg. 103 of the *Value Added Tax Regulations* 1995 (SI 1995/2518) (see **Chapter 4** at 40-200(4)) and the *Value Added Tax (Input Tax) (Specified Supplies) Order* 1999 (SI 1999/3121).

9 Insurance

On top of this there are certain situations in which a supply may be zero-rated, i.e. taxed at the nil rate.

(a) Services supplied where received

Business to business supplies of services will be supplied where the customer is established: Directive 2006/112/EC, art. 44. Supplies of services to non-business customers will be supplied where the supplier is established, unless the customer is a non-business customer established outside the EU and the service falls within the 'supplied where received' categories listed in art. 59. These are to be found in VATA 1994, Sch. 4A (see **Appendix 4**). Paragraph 16 covers banking, finance and insurance.

Any Sch. 4A service will be treated as supplied *in the place where the recipient belongs*. Putting this in context, what this means in practice is that a supply of financial services or insurance will be *outside the scope* of UK VAT if made:

- to *someone in business* and who is established in another EU country; or
- to a non-business person belonging or established outside the EU.

Coupled with what is provided for in reg. 103 of the *Value Added Tax Regulations* 1995 (SI 1995/2518) and art. 3 of the *Value Added Tax (Input Tax) (Specified Supplies) Order* 1999 (SI 1999/3121), this has the effect that underlying input VAT can be recovered for:

- any *basically taxable* Sch. 4A service supplied to a business outside the UK or to anyone else outside the EU; and
- any *basically exempt* Sch. 4A service supplied to anyone outside the EU,

but otherwise remains restricted, subject to the further reliefs discussed below.

In short, where the recipient is a business in another Member State, a supply of insurance or insurance-related services is *outside the scope* of VAT, but generally still has the same consequences as if it were exempt. However, where the recipient of the service *belongs* outside the EU and Isle of Man, the supply is not just *outside the scope*. The supplier can then recover underlying input VAT. This applies, moreover, for supplies to all clients, whether in business or not. Deciding where someone belongs is not always easy, though especially where that person is a private individual.

- How difficult this is was illustrated by *USAA Ltd* [1993] BVC 1,612. USAA Ltd, an insurance subsidiary of a US corporation, provided motor insurance to officers in the US forces. Specifically in terms of the appeal, this was to officers, who were about to serve in the UK, were so serving, or had retired from service, but who continued to reside in the UK. It was agreed that the supply took place at the moment the insurance contract was made. The issue was whether it was outside the scope with tax recovery on the basis that the persons to whom it was supplied did not *belong* in the EU.

    HMRC argued the supplies were exempt. In each case the insured did, in effect, *belong* in the EU. They were either stationed here for terms of duty of three years or more or were retired personnel permanently residing here. The UK was thus their *usual place of residence*.

The Tribunal largely agreed. They did not rule out the possibility that a taxpayer may, in some cases, have more than one *usual place of residence*. However, they felt that an officer serving a three-year term in the UK, whose family was living here in a house or apartment, whose home in the US was let and who may, if he goes back to the US for training, leave his wife and family here has a usual place of residence in the UK and has no *usual place of residence* in the USA. The Tribunal took a similar view in the case of an unmarried officer occupying quarters here. One had to concentrate on a point in time and not, as in *Levene v IR Commrs* [1928] AC 217 and *IR Commrs v Lysaght* [1928] AC 234, on a year of assessment basis. The Chairman also concluded, amongst other things, that a retired officer, who sets up house here and does not keep a house in the US, is plainly usually resident here but going on to add that an officer, being in the US and about to move to the UK, had in his view a *usual place of residence* in the US.

In short, the concept is not necessarily on all fours with the *resident and ordinarily resident* tests as applied for income tax purposes.

Deciding where the recipient *belongs* is not the only problem. Sometimes, the first question to address is precisely who the recipient is. In the case of a broker, for example, there is clearly a choice. Is it the insured or is it the insurer? Either or both may *belong* in a country other than the UK or the EU, so that deciding which it is can have a material bearing on the broker's ability to recover input VAT. In practice, however, most brokers will see their client as being the insured, notwithstanding that any commissions may actually be paid by the insurer. But this is not necessarily going to be the correct or the best answer.

(b) Insurance for exports

Where the supply is *directly linked* to the export of goods to a place outside the Member States, services within either of the categories of VATA 1994, Sch. 9, Grp. 2 and which are supplied:

- in the UK (i.e. the insured belongs in the UK or Isle of Man or belongs in another Member State but is not VAT-registered); or
- outside the UK (i.e. to a VAT-registered business in another Member State),

will attract input VAT relief (art. 3 of the *Value Added Tax (Input Tax) (Specified Supplies) Order* 1999 (SI 1999/3121)).

(c) Agency and the services of intermediaries

In the case of agency or brokerage, there are three further reliefs:

(i) The general rule
The general rule is simply to follow those for the underlying supply described earlier. Under art. 46 of Council Directive 2006/112/EC:

> 'The place of supply of services rendered to a non-taxable person by an intermediary acting in the name and on behalf of another person, other than those referred to in Articles 50 and 54 and in Article 56(1), shall be the place where the underlying transaction is supplied in accordance with this Directive'

9 Insurance

Following, therefore, the rules for business to business supplies, the supply of brokerage will be *outside the scope* of UK VAT when supplied to a business in another EU Member State or to anyone *belonging* outside the UK. Underlying input tax will then be recoverable to the extent that the recipient of the service belongs outside the EU as a result of art. 3(a) of the *Value Added Tax (Input Tax) (Specified Supplies) Order* 1999 (SI 1999/3121).

(ii) Exemption with the right of recovery

A further possibility also follows from art. 3(c) of the *Value Added Tax (Input Tax) (Specified Supplies) Order* 1999, which enables input tax to also be recoverable, where what the broker or agent arranges is a supply to someone belonging in the UK and amounts to:

(a) the supply of a basically exempt insurance service to someone from outside the EU, i.e. under the rules in (a) above; or
(b) the supply of export insurance (under (b) above).

> **Practice point**
>
> The critical factor in (ii)(a) above is that the *buying counterparty* of the underlying client trade is outside the EU.
>
> This rule will similarly apply where the underlying client supply supply is itself technically *outside the scope* because the selling counterparty to whom the agency service is provided is outside the EU.

(iii) The zero-rate option

Zero-rating, although important, is of limited interest for the sectors covered here because it does not apply to anything within VATA 1994, Sch. 9, Grp. 2 or 5. Where available, it arises under VATA 1994, Sch. 8, Grp. 7. Item 2 zero-rates a supply of brokerage or agency services where the place of supply, adopting the rules referred to earlier, is in the UK. The services covered are those of arrangement where there is a *named principal*. The relief applies where what is arranged is:

(1) An export of goods to a place outside the Member States.
(2) A supply of services of the description specified in item 1 of the Group (not relevant in the context of this book).
(3) Any supply of services which is made outside the Member States.

The only real interest for most businesses in the sectors covered by this last category will be in paragraph (c). However, this Group does not include any services of a description specified in Sch. 9, Grp. 2 or 5.

(3) Standard-rating

Although exemption is the norm, there are some situations where the supply will, at first sight, be taxed.

(a) Charges for insurance made in conjunction with something else

The possibility of taxable, rather than exempt, supplies also arises, where a charge for *insurance* is made in conjunction with something else. To the extent that part of the overall price can be attributed to insurance, the VATable amount remaining is reduced.

In effecting changes to Grp. 2 in 1996, HMRC took the opportunity to make it harder to avoid VAT in this situation by introducing a stipulation that the service of arranging such insurance will qualify for exemption only if the full charge for the insurance premium and any additional charge are disclosed to the customer.

The disclosure requirement (which reflects the insurance industry code of practice) is not, however, the primary anti-avoidance measure, since insurance premium tax (IPT) is now charged at the equivalent of the standard rate of VAT on the insurance element of most packages, which consist of insurance and other goods and services e.g. mechanical breakdown insurance with secondhand cars.

The statutory authority for this is now found in Notes (3) to (6) to VATA 1994, Sch. 9, Grp. 2, and is described more fully in HMRC Notice 701/36/2012, section 11.3.

(i) Insurance provided with vehicle hire
Until the change in treatment of block policies following *Card Protection Plan Ltd*, this was a common issue, for example, for charges for insurance made by persons such as car hire companies. Charges for *Road Traffic Act* insurance and *Collision Damage Waiver* tended to be seen as part of the calculation of the overall taxable hire charge and not as a separate supply of exempt insurance by the hire company to the customer.

Similar problems can, potentially, arise for charges for goods-in-transit cover, but the issues can now largely be avoided if there is separate disclosure and care is taken over the use of the rules on block policies (see later at 90-200).

(ii) Breakdown and warranty cover
Charges for warranty cover or mechanical breakdown on the sale or rental of cars or consumer durables can also sometimes be subsumed into the calculation of the price of an overall taxable supply, depending on the circumstances, including:

- the way the cover is sold;
- whether it is self-insured;
- the amount charged; and
- the way in which the insurance is disclosed.

This is considered later at 90-200(9)).

- In *CR Smith Glaziers (Dunfermline) Ltd* [2003] BVC 249, the taxpayer supplied and installed double glazing, providing a warranty in relation to workmanship and materials. It decided to include warranty insurance to satisfy customers that the product warranty would be honoured were the company to become insolvent. It wanted to treat the insurance element as exempt. However, it showed the premium as a percentage of total cost in its contract with customers.

VATA 1994, Sch. 9, Grp. 2 contained a number of detailed requirements on disclosure so that each customer, and HMRC, could know what sum related to exempt supplies. In the circumstances, HMRC felt the disclosure of a percentage of total cost did not go far enough. The Court of Session in Scotland agreed, but, on appeal this was reversed in a majority ruling in the House of Lords.

It was the duty of a Court in the UK to construe a statute, so far as possible, in conformity with European law. HMRC's construction did not conform to the terms of the Sixth Directive and it was, therefore, necessary to adopt the alternative construction which did. The construction of Note (5)(b) for which HMRC contended would have the effect of denying the exemption to the taxpayer.

(See later at 90-200(11)).

(b) Charges where the insurance element is really ancillary or incidental

Arguing that a charge as an *insurance* commission will not be enough if what is done falls short of insurance intermediary services, with the inevitable conclusion that the income is taxable, not exempt.

- In *Dogbreeders Associates* (1989) 4 BVC 777, for example, the appellants were the canine equivalent of an estate agent, acting as a go-between for reputable dog breeders and purchasers of puppies. They had an arrangement or contract with an insurance broker, by whom they were paid a commission. This was a substantial sideline, but their attempt to secure exemption failed because they did little more than offer publicity. Also, although this was not specifically remarked upon, there did not seem to be a sufficiently *insurance* flavour to the taxpayer's overall business.
- In *Wright Manley Ltd and Wright & Partners* [1993] BVC 1,595, the appellants were auctioneers, estate agents and valuers. For some years they held agency appointments with a number of building societies at various offices. Following restrictions in the *Financial Services Act* 1986, they arranged with Hill Samuel Investment Services Ltd, and later with Steggles & Mather (a firm of solicitors), to provide financial advice to persons they introduced. They provided accommodation for the use of the financial advisers and office facilities for interviews. None of the appellants' staff were, however, involved in offering financial advice.

The issue was whether what was provided in return for the commissions amounted to *the making of arrangements* within what was then VATA 1983, Sch. 6, Grp. 2. The Tribunal concluded it did not. What the appellants did was simply to provide facilities to be used by financial consultants, arrange a meeting or pass on the name and addresses of possible clients.

- Likewise in *British Horse Society Ltd* [2000] BVC 2,062, the appellant, a charity, provided members with various benefits, including free equestrian-related insurance, personal accident cover and personal liability cover, which it arranged through its brokers. It also offered significant discounts on other insurance products on items ranging from trailers and saddlery to household and private medical insurance, all provided through the same brokers. The arrangement with the brokers allowed for what was termed a *contingent discount* to be paid to the Society on all brokers' business in the UK. However, an analysis of the facts showed this was not a discount; nor was it an exempt insurance commission. What the Society did in providing its customer base to the broker was to promote its business under the terms of the agreement. This had no nexus with the provision of insurance and was therefore standard-rated.

90-200 Other insurance-related activities

The heading 'Other insurance-related activities' covers those activities which are not directly involved in the provision of insurance, but which are nonetheless an important feature of the industry. Apart from investment, few, if any, will be exempt.

(1) Standard-rating

As noted earlier standard-rating tends to be the exception for the insurance industry. It does, however, arise in a number of particular areas – especially in the context of property investment.

(a) General

Standard-rating will apply to a variety of supplies, largely of services peripheral or incidental to insurance. Common examples will include:

- average adjustment;
- engineering inspection or survey (unless provided by an underwriter as a condition of a policy of insurance);
- investment advice (unless provided by a broker or underwriting agency/ manager without a separate charge);
- legal and other professional assistance in the settlement of claims;
- loss adjustment;
- motor assessment services;
- salvage; and
- trustee fees.

Also covered will be charges for:

- computer time;
- data processing;
- management and administration (other than by an underwriting manager or agency to an insurance company or syndicate);
- secondments or the sharing of staff;
- staff canteens; and
- certain free supplies of business assets or bought-in VATable services.

As noted earlier, standard-rating will also potentially extend to introductory fees or commissions earned by persons other than insurance brokers, where the recipient is not directly instrumental in specific insurance being provided. It will include, in particular, payments made to persons such as accountants or solicitors for any essentially advisory or general introductory services, but not where they are party to the actual arrangements for the provision of insurance.

Valuations for insurance purposes are normally taxable under this heading. However, on occasions they may be exempt if structured as an integral part of the premium (see 90-200(21) later).

(b) Property investment

Standard-rating can also often arise with supplies of land and buildings. This can be especially important for insurers in terms of their role as funding institutions. At one time, most supplies by way of the sale, assignment or rent of accommodation will have been either exempt from VAT under VATA 1994, Sch. 9, Grp. 1 or zero-rated. Standard-rating will have tended to be limited to generally transitory rights such as:

- the provision of car parking facilities or facilities for housing or mooring aircraft or boats;
- shooting or fishing rights; and
- the granting of any right to remove standing timber.

However, standard-rating also applies to:

- the freehold sale of new or partly completed new commercial buildings (e.g. buildings which are neither dwellings nor in use for relevant residential or relevant charitable purposes) (VATA 1994, Sch. 9, Grp. 1, item 1(a)). This is irrespective of whether or not the person concerned was initially involved as developer;
- the sale, assignment or letting, etc. of any interest in or right over land not otherwise standard-rated and where the person concerned has exercised the option to tax (VATA 1994, Sch. 10, para. 2 to 4); and
- rents received under certain developmental tenancies (VATA 1994, Sch. 9, Grp. 1, item 1(b)).

These are considered earlier in the context of *Property* in **Chapter 8** at 80-150.

(2) Exemption

The interest here will principally relate to investment. This can be divided into two broad categories: financial investments and property.

(a) Financial investments

Loans and advances, including loans to local authorities, bank deposits and money market operations, are generally exempt under VATA 1994, Sch. 9, Grp. 5, item 2 (art. 135(1)(b) of Council Directive 2006/112/EC); investments in securities, which will generally be as important if not more so, under item 6 (art. 135(1)(f)). The latter will, in broad terms, cover investments in:

- shares, stock, bonds, notes (other than promissory notes), debentures, debenture stock, and shares in an oil royalty;
- certificates of deposit;
- Treasury or Government bills;
- letters of allotment, options, rights to shares; and
- units in a unit trust.

Exemption also covers fees for underwriting or arranging issues of shares or securities or underwriting or agency for certain negotiable instruments, such as bills of exchange and Sterling Commercial Paper (VATA 1994, Sch. 9, Grp. 5, item 5A).

Financial investments are discussed in more detail in **Chapters 7** and **8**.

(b) Property

Historically, supplies involving land and buildings have been largely exempt. In VATA 1994 the relevant provisions are to be found in Sch. 9, Grp. 1. This covers, succinctly:

> 'The grant of any interest in or right over land or of any licence to occupy land, or, in relation to land in Scotland, any personal right to call for or be granted any such interest or right ...'

Exemption is thus extremely wide. Potentially, it applies to most types of supply other than the type of specific exceptions referred to in 90-150(1)(b) and to certain limited situations in the case of dwellings and relevant residential or relevant charitable buildings, where zero-rating is available.

An important point to bear in mind is that, for leases, the supply will not just be related to the rent or premiums received; it will also potentially cover service charges made by the landlord, where they relate to common parts.

- In a landlord's repairing lease, for example, this would apply to the upkeep of the building as a whole.
- In the case of an office building, it will apply to the maintenance of the reception area, corridors and lifts.

The VAT treatment essentially, therefore, follows that of the rent. Thus, if the rent is exempt, the service charge is also exempt, being simply part of a single overall supply by the landlord to the tenant. Only where a service charge relates to separate supplies to the tenant (e.g. cleaning, lighting, heating or electricity specifically supplied to the demised premises) will the supply be taxable.

Having said this, there is an extra-statutory concession that exempts various mandatory service charges paid by the occupants of residential property, including charges for the upkeep of common areas of the estate or flats, the provision of a caretaker or warden and the general maintenance of the exterior of the dwelling. (see Section 3.18 of HMRC Notice 48 (2012 edn)).

The extent of exemption is explained in more detail in **Chapter 8** at 80-150.

In practice, exemption is now increasingly likely to be confined to supplies of dwellings and relevant residential or relevant charitable buildings. Supplies involving commercial buildings may also be exempt. However, the combination of the standard-rating for new commercial buildings and the option to tax, together with some of the other measures affecting property and construction, will tend to make this less common even for established property.

(3) Outside the scope, exemption with the right of recovery and zero-rating

Just as for the supplies concerned with the actual provision of cover, exemption or being able to treat a supply as *outside the scope* can be an advantage (see 90-100). Tax does not have to be charged, which can be important for customers unable, for one reason or another, to recover input VAT. However, at the same time, it can be equally attractive to an insurer or broker to save the tax he himself incurs. The basis on which this may be achieved is explained at 90-100(2) above but, briefly, is found in the partial exemption rules in reg. 103 of the *Value Added Tax Regulations* 1995 (SI 1995/2518). This affords relief for tax incurred on goods or services which are used or to be used by the person concerned in whole or in part in making:

- supplies made abroad, which would be taxable supplies if made in the UK; or
- certain basically exempt supplies specified in the *Value Added Tax (Input Tax) (Specified Supplies) Order* 1999 (SI 1999/3121):

  '(a) which are supplied to a person who belongs outside the member States;
  (b) which are directly linked to the export of goods to a place outside the member States; or
  (c) which consist of the provision of intermediary services within the meaning of item 4 of Group 2, or item 5 of Group 5, of Schedule 9 to the Value Added Tax Act 1994 in relation to any transaction specified in paragraph (a) or (b) above.'

Basically exempt supplies which are *outside the scope* but which are provided to persons belonging elsewhere in the EU do not, therefore, qualify unless they come within (b) or (c) above. Subject to this, you need to look at the type of service supplied and the circumstances in which it occurs.

(a) Services supplied where received

As elsewhere, this is perhaps the most important category to address. Most of the services which will be of interest to the insurance sector will be within VATA 1994, Sch. 4A (art. 59 of Council Directive 2006/112/EC) (see **Appendix 4**). Following from art. 16 of the *Value Added Tax (Place of Supply of Services) Order* 1992 (SI 1992/3121), any Sch. 4A service will be treated as supplied *in the place where the recipient* belongs, so that, in practice, a supply will be *outside the scope* of UK VAT if made:

- to *someone in business* and who is established in another EU country; or
- to *anyone* belonging or established outside the EU.

This, coupled with the effect of reg. 103 of the *Value Added Tax Regulations* 1995 and art. 3 of the *Value Added Tax (Input Tax) (Specified Supplies) Order* 1999, means underlying input VAT can be recovered for:

- any *basically taxable* Sch. 4A service supplied to a business outside the UK or to anyone else outside the EU; and
- any *basically exempt* Sch. 4A service supplied to anyone outside the EU.

Of the various categories within Sch. 4A:

Paragraph 3 will cover, for example:

- advisory, consultancy, legal or accountancy services;
- arbitration services;
- computer timesharing;
- information;
- training when performed outside the UK; and
- valuations performed in the UK,

but not anything which relates to land. It thus excludes legal or survey work which might occur, for example, in the case of collision damage to piers or jetties occasioned by foreign-owned vessels.

Paragraph 5 will be of interest in connection with matters such as:

- finance provided for non-EU and Isle of Man borrowers;
- the issue and/or sale of securities to non-EU or Isle of Man customers;
- the receipt of interest from non-EU securities;
- share underwriting;
- the provision of certain insurance-related services such as those of loss and average adjusters;
- the services of motor assessors, surveyors or other experts and legal services in connection with the assessment of any insurance claim; and
- the collection of debts or other amounts owing to non-UK or Isle of Man insurers.

Supplies in the first four categories are essentially financial in nature. They are thus generally only eligible for input VAT relief if the person to whom the supply is made *belongs* outside the EU and the Isle of Man. Determining the *belonging* status of the recipient of a supply is not, however, always easy and, in the case of securities, a special rule applies if, and only if, this is not otherwise known:

- sales which are traded in the EU are treated as made to persons belonging in the EU;
- sales which are traded in any other country (except the Isle of Man) are treated as made to persons outside the EU;
- if, in turn, it is not known where the sale is transacted this can be deemed to be where the security is listed or, as a last resort, where the final broker belongs.

Paragraph 6 will also be of interest, which will apply particularly to staff secondments.

(b) Services relating to land

Also important in the context of the supplies covered here are the categories of services, which are connected with or relate to land. Under art. 47 of Council Directive 2006/112/EC (art. 9(2) of the Sixth VAT Directive), these are taken to be supplied where the property is situated. The corresponding provisions in UK law are now found in VATA 1994, Sch. 4A, para. 1.

9 Insurance

Thus, where the land is outside the UK, the supply is not within the scope of UK VAT, even if the service is physically performed in the UK. Instead, it is seen as taking place in whichever country the land itself is. In implementing this rule, the general principles of land law usually mean land is taken to include anything permanently attached to and forming part of it. It thus normally covers growing crops, buildings and other fixed structures.

The rule for supplies under this heading will cover, for example:

- engineering inspection and survey fees in connection with land abroad;
- similar work in relation to offshore oil rigs and drilling platforms outside UK territorial waters; and
- legal costs in the settlement of claims in respect of damage to property but not where the association with the land is more tenuous, e.g. where related to machinery sited in a building but not part of the fabric.

It will not, however, extend to:

- the actual insurance of property outside the UK;
- advertising; or
- anything listed in VATA 1994, Sch. 4A (see **Appendix 4**) for which there is the alternative treatment described earlier at (a).

Unlike some of the other provisions, relief under this heading does not depend on the identity or belonging status of the recipient. As most *outside the scope* supplies under this heading will be essentially taxable, input VAT will thus tend to be recoverable under reg. 103 of the *Value Added Tax Regulations* 1995.

It is interesting, perhaps, to note that art. 47 of Council Directive 2006/112/EC (art. 9(2)(a) of the Sixth VAT Directive) is expressed in terms of *services connected with* the land. This seems to imply a somewhat different meaning to that of a service which is a *supply of* the land itself. Paragraph 1(2)(c) of VATA 1994, Sch. 4A includes the granting, etc. of interests in, rights over or licences to occupy land. Whether this is correct appears, therefore, to perhaps be debatable.

(c) Zero-rating for property

Zero-rating is a relief which has been especially important in relation to property investment. The rules, in this case, arise under VATA 1994, Sch. 8, Grp. 5 and 6. In particular, item 1 of Grp. 5 zero-rates:

> 'The first grant by a person–
>
> (a) constructing a building–
>
> (i) designed as a dwelling or number of dwellings; or
> (ii) intended for use solely for a relevant residential or a relevant charitable purpose; ...
>
> of a major interest in, or in any part of, the building, dwelling or its site.'

> **Practice point**
>
> Often confused with exemption, zero-rating is particularly important because, being taxable albeit at a nil rate, it confers the right to recover input VAT. Although now less important than once was the case, it may still be usefully considered for flats and other dwellings and for buildings to be used for relevant residential or relevant charitable purposes. In this connection:
>
> - a person constructing a building will include a person who commissions construction. It can thus cover an insurance company or any other institutional investor so long as, generally, it owns an interest in the land and is the recipient of building services;
> - a major interest for this purpose means, broadly, the freehold or a lease for a term certain exceeding 21 years (VATA 1994, s. 96(1)).

What can be involved in terms of zero-rating is again explained more fully in **Chapter 8** at 80-150.

90-220 Points affecting particular supplies and claims costs (other than points specific to Lloyd's – see also 90-300)

(1) Block policies

The decision of the ECJ in *Card Protection Plan* [2001] BVC 158 (see **Chapter 3** at 30-500(6)) caused HMRC to re-think their treatment of charges for insurance made in certain situations in conjunction with other supplies. They now accept that such charges made by block policy-holders can be seen as exempt insurance transactions, even though they would not be seen as insurance for regulatory purposes. Block policy-holders are acting as principals in this situation and not as insurance intermediaries.

The key characteristics of a block policy are that there is a contract between the block policyholder and the insurer which allows the block policyholder to effect insurance cover, subject to certain conditions, namely that:

- the block policyholder, acting in its own name, procures insurance cover for third parties from the insurer;
- there is a contractual relationship between the block policyholder and third parties under which the insurance is procured; and
- the block policyholder stands in place of the insurer in effecting the supply of insurance to the third parties.

The policy holder will normally be the business taking out the policy and the persons insured will be, or include, its customers, who may or may not be individually named.

Such policies are often taken out by suppliers of goods or services to cover a number of small transactions over a set period. A removal company, for example, may take out a block policy to provide its customers with insurance against the risk of damage to their belongings during a house move. Block (or *master*) policies are also used by some clubs and associations to effect insurance cover on behalf of their members.

Sometimes a block policy will cover the risks of the block policyholder as well as those of their customers. In the example of the removal company, this might, say, cover its own risk of damaging its customers' property as well as its customers' risk of damage to their property for which the removal company is not liable.

Block policies do not include delegated authority arrangements between insurers and brokers or other professional insurance agents under which the agent is allowed by the insurer to enter into contracts on its behalf.

Businesses taking out policies of this kind and making charges for insurance are likely to need to consider their position under the partial exemption rules (see **Chapter 4**).

Examples of situations where this type of insurance occurs will include:

- mechanical breakdown insurance (MBI) with cars and domestic appliances (see later at (9));
- travel insurance with holidays;
- insurance with removal services;
- insurance with rented property; and
- insurance with car hire.

In other, outwardly similar, situations not involving block policies, for example:

- There will be a separate supply of exempt insurance (by the actual supplier of the insurance (the insurance company) to the customer buying the goods or services), where the cover being supplied is genuine insurance and the risk covered is that of the customer and not the risk of the supplier of those goods or services.

What has to be decided in this situation is whether, if the insurer is paid by the supplier of the goods or services, this payment can reduce his taxable amount for those goods or services (see, for example, cases like *Primback* and *Ford*).

- Where there is an uninsured guarantee or warranty, any charge for this, even if it represents part of the cost of third-party cover for the supplier of the goods or services, will form part of the overall taxable price.
- Where a landlord takes out insurance on a building he is renting out under a landlord's repairing lease, any charge made to the tenant to cover the cost will not represent a separate supply of insurance, but will have the same VAT treatment as the rent.
- In *Global Self Drive Ltd* [2006] BVC 2,020, the Tribunal decided against HMRC in a case where an insurance charge made by vehicle hire company renting motor vehicles to business and private customers. The insurance cover was arranged through a policy taken out by GSD with a third-party insurer and the terms and conditions incorporated into the standard form rental agreement and invoice used provided for a customer either:
    - to elect to adopt the insurance cover provided; or
    - to undertake to keep the hired vehicle insured.

GSD had been told by HMRC to charge VAT on the insurance from 1 April 1993 but had queried this in July 2003 following the ECJ Ruling in *Card Protection Plan*.

HMRC argued *Card Protection Plan* did not apply as the policy was not a *block policy* but one allowing it to supply insured vehicles to customers. The Tribunal disagreed and, interestingly, went on to add that HMRC placed too much emphasis on the need for a *block policy*.

(2) Brokerage

The question sometimes arises as to whom the services of the broker are supplied.

Notwithstanding that it is the insurers, rather than the insured, who generally pay commissions, HMRC accept that this is simply a reflection of how the insurance industry generally is organised. It does not imply that a broker will be providing a service to the insured for no consideration

The recipient of the supply, on this basis, is thus the insured. Where the contrary is to apply (i.e. where the recipient of the supply is the insurer) should normally be clear from the terms of the specific contracts involved.

This distinction will potentially have an effect on the amount of input VAT a broker can recover under the partial exemption rules (see **Chapter 4**). This might be important where, for example, the insurers are based in the UK or in other Member States but risks placed are on behalf of clients worldwide. It does not, however, affect the value of the supply by the insurer, which is normally the gross premium without deduction of brokerage.

The value of the brokers supply is the full gross commission, flat-rate fee or re-charge of costs incurred. No deduction is given for any commission allowable to other intermediaries employed.

(3) Call-centres

The position of call-centres arises quite frequently in the context of outsourcing, where the concern is that charges incurred will be subject to VAT, which may then prove largely irrecoverable. In *Teletech UK Ltd* [2003] BVC 2,514, the Tribunal held that these charges could, in certain situations though, be VAT-exempt, especially where they resulted in the insurer being put on risk. However, this ruling was given before that of the ECJ in the *Arthur Andersen* case. Although the availability of exemption following the Tribunal's decision was acknowledged, HMRC subsequently indicated that it no longer applied.

This is considered further under *Intermediaries and Outsourcing* later at 90-350.

(4) Claims

The actual payment or settlement of an insurance claim as such is *outside the scope* of VAT. The settlement is simply made under an indemnity contract and is not itself consideration for a supply.

(a) Tax on the costs of re-instatement

A consequence of this is that it tends to mean, inter alia, that any VAT on the costs incurred on re-instatement is not generally input VAT (VATA 1994, s. 25 – see **Chapter 4**) of the insurer, because it will represent a supply to the insured.

- The tax could then be input VAT of the insured. The latter, if VAT-registered, should thus seek appropriate input VAT relief and claim only for the net sum.
- If no input tax claim can be made by the insured, the claims cost is increased and under-insurance can then result if there has been a failure to take VAT fully into account. It may then be necessary for an underwriter to consider averaging.

This latter aspect is especially important for property insurance. Re-instatement costs can at times be zero-rated where a domestic or relevant residential or relevant charitable building is completely destroyed – for example, by fire (VATA 1994, Sch. 8, Grp. 5, items 2 and 3 – see **Chapter 8** at 80-350). However, as noted elsewhere, zero-rating is a strictly limited relief. Most reinstatement/repair costs will bear VAT at the standard rate, as will the complete construction of new commercial property. Even in the case of a dwelling, etc., if a part, however small, of the original building remains, the costs of reinstatement will be standard-rated. Failure to allow for this and undue reliance on restitution on a total loss basis may mean that costs exceed the cover provided.

(b) Legal costs

By agreement between HMRC and the Association of British Insurers (the ABI) and other insurance bodies, policyholders, who are registered for VAT, can treat as input VAT tax incurred on legal services supplied to them in connection with an insurance claim relating to their business. This applies whether the solicitor is instructed by the policyholder or by the insurer on his behalf and whether or not in practice the proceedings are controlled by the insurer. Normally such legal services will be supplied to the policyholder, in any event, and not to the insurer – even when the insurer exercises his right of segregation to pursue or defend a claim in the name of the policyholder.

(c) Motor policies

A particular issue can potentially arise in relation to claims under a motor insurance policy. As noted earlier, accident re-instatement costs and other types of claims-related expenditure will often represent supplies to the policyholder, not the insurer.

- If registered for VAT, the policyholder may be able to recover the tax involved, something the insurer could not usually do, even were the supply to be to him.
- If the policyholder can recover the VAT, however, the claim under the policy need then only be for the reduced, net of VAT amount, which is clearly an important consideration.

Motor insurers, understandably, take steps to control the level of costs, incurred, with some going to the extent of having their own repair shops to which customers cars are taken in the event of an accident or of taking full control over the nomination of the garage at which the work will be carried out and over the scope of what will be done.

What this type of arrangement can result in is a structure whereby:

- the contract is not a financial indemnity for the cost of replacement/repair but an agreement to actually replace or repair; and
- the costs are inputs of the insurer and *cost-components* of the insurer in the provision of cover.

This will, potentially, work well in the case of cover provided to private customers, However, for cover provided to businesses, it could prevent the business recovering any VAT, so that claims costs might increase as a result. To avoid this, different contractual arrangements could be needed for business customers to emphasise that, for example, any instructions for repair were being given as agent for the insured.

> ### Practice point
>
> Particularly, following the decision in *Redrow Group plc*, it may well pay companies to take particular care over how policies are worded. It could be important, for example, to draw distinctions between:
>
> - policies to, say, private individuals; and
> - policies to companies and others able, generally, to recover input VAT on their business costs.
>
> This could be essential if claims costs are to be reduced by allowing business customers to recover input tax.

(5) Claims-handling

The exemption under VATA 1994, Sch. 9, Grp. 2, item 4 includes any service, such as claims checking, necessary before final settlement of a claim can be made, when provided by an insurance broker or insurance agent acting in an intermediary capacity

Following agreement between HMRC and bodies representing the insurance industry, the exemption is accepted as covering the services of loss adjusters, motor assessors and similar experts where it is provided under a written delegated authority from the insurer. It is not necessary for the loss adjuster, etc. to actually pay the claim; merely that they have exercised an authority to bind the insurer as to settlement. The text of this agreement, in March 1994, is reproduced in full at **Appendix 9**.

However, the exemption does not cover specialist and professional services such as assessment, valuation and advice.

(6) Direct MAT

This is insurance, but not reinsurance, for any marine, aviation and transport (MAT) risks relating to hull and cargo and identifiable with journeys involving the carriage of passengers or goods. The classes of risk covered are those defined in para. 1, 4–7, 11 and 12 of Pt. 1 of

Sch. 1 to the *Financial Services and Markets Act 2000 (Regulated Activities) Order* 2001 (SI 2001/544). These are:

- accident (in connection with MAT risks only);
- railway rolling stock;
- aircraft;
- ships;
- goods in transit;
- aircraft liability; and
- liability of ships,

but not risks relating to:

- motor and land vehicles;
- oil and gas rigs permanently fixed to the sea bed;
- specific policies for ships laid-up or aircraft grounded;
- specific policies for ships and aircraft under repair; or
- port and airport owners and operators' liability and manufacturers' liability.

Some MAT premiums cover risks arising both inside and outside the EU, e.g. premiums covering the transport of goods insured on a *world-wide* basis. Following discussions between HMRC and the Industry for the treatment of direct MAT business, guidelines were agreed, which have been operative since 5 July 1993. The terms of this agreement are set out at **Appendix 9**. The coding agreed for this purpose was that business should be classified:

z 'right to deduct'	if either the insurance is provided to a person belonging outside the EU; *or*
	it is insurance directly linked to the export of goods to a place outside the EU;
x 'no right to deduct'	if the insurance is provided to a person belonging within the EU, and it is not insurance directly linked to the export of goods to a place outside the EU;
m 'mixed'	only if the insurance does not directly relate to the export of goods from inside to outside the EC and the policy has no clear principal insured and at least one, but not all, of the insured parties belongs outside the EC. The m (mixed) code brings with it an entitlement to treat 50 per cent of input tax incurred on related goods and services as recoverable and 50 per cent as non-recoverable.

Where only one party is insured, the address shown on the broker's slip (or equivalent document) is to be used to determine where the insured *belongs*. If no address is shown, where the insured belongs should be determined by reference to the broker or other intermediary involved. If the insured has more than one address, the one on the slip (or equivalent document) should be used unless it is clear that this is simply there for administrative reasons.

Where more than one party is insured, which is often the case, the principal parties should be identified where possible and their place of belonging used to determine the VAT code. Where the identities of the insured parties are known but a principal insured cannot be identified, the places where all of the insured parties *belong* should be ascertained (if practicable) and the business coded accordingly. The *m* code should only be used as a last resort.

(7) Engineering insurance and inspection services

Engineering insurance amounts to cover for large items of plant and machinery or industrial structures like boilers, cranes and lifts and is intended to afford financial protection against the risk of failure or damage. Often the insurer will also provide inspection services. As separate supplies, the latter will be taxable and insurers are required to tax the inspection element, when provided as part of an engineering insurance policy.

Such policies should now be considered in the light of the criteria in *Card Protection Plan* (see 90-200) to see if there are separate supplies of exempt engineering insurance and taxable inspection services or a single composite supply of either exempt insurance (to which the inspection services are ancillary) or taxable inspection services (to which the insurance is *ancillary*).

(8) Insurance-related services

The exemption for services other than the actual provision of insurance is not just directed at agency or brokerage. It is expressed in art. 135(1)(a) of the VAT Directive (2006/112/EC) in terms as insurance and reinsurance *related* services performed by an insurance broker or agent (or an insurance intermediary as other language versions of the Directive have it). What is meant by *related services* is not defined, but, subject to the observations in the *Arthur Andersen* case, a useful indication of what is involved is contained in art. 2 of the *Intermediaries Directive*.

To be *insurance-related*, a service must be closely connected to insurance. It must have an insurance flavour to it and not just be something that is *incidental*. Examples of what is included will include:

- introductory services, including work preparatory to the conclusion of a contract;
- assisting in the administration and performance of contracts;
- claims handling; and
- collecting premiums.

Not included are things like:

- mere secretarial and office administration services;
- computer services, data processing and accounting;
- market research;
- product design;
- advertising and promotion;
- valuation or inspection services;
- loss and average adjustment, motor claims assessment; and
- surveyors and other experts.

But this tends to apply most where what is provided is stand-alone. If something in one or other of these latter categories is really part of a larger composite supply that can properly be regarded as exempt, VAT will not need to be applied. How these matters are expressed in the related contracts and other documentation can clearly help in this and often it may be better to refer to them, not as services, but as necessary functions in the performance of a more obviously insurance-related supply.

Who qualifies as an insurance intermediary for this purpose is an important consideration and, whilst this is not an exclusive indication, HMRC accept that the term will apply to people, who are members of the General Insurance Standards Council. This is an industry-run body established to regulate the sale of general insurance within the UK, membership beings open to businesses such as retailers, car dealers and solicitors and accountants, as well as insurers and traditional brokers and agents.

For further commentary on this see 90-350 later.

(9) Mechanical breakdown

Because of the circumstances in which mechanical breakdown insurance is sometimes marketed, the charges borne by the ultimate customer may easily end up being taxed. When provided under a block insurance policy (see earlier at (1)) with the supplier of the goods or services being the policyholder, the treatment as VAT-exempt is relatively straightforward. In other cases, there will be a separate supply of exempt insurance by the supplier of the insurance (the insurer) to the customer buying the goods or services to which the warranty relates, where:

- the cover supplied is genuine insurance and not, for example, an uninsured guarantee or warranty; and
- the risk is that of the customer, and not of the supplier.

In this case, it may be possible to treat the insurance premium element as a disbursement (provided this is limited to the actual premium charged), and, at the same time, recognise a further part of what is paid by the customer as consideration for an exempt supply of arrangement, i.e. an insurance-related service. However, to achieve this, it is necessary to meet the disclosure requirements referred to in 90-100(3) earlier and as set out in Section 11.3 of HMRC Notice 701/36.

- *Centurions* [1993] BVC 1,346 illustrated how this can be a problem. Centurions sold second-hand classic sports cars and accounted for VAT under the special margin scheme in the *Value Added Tax (Input Tax) Order* 1992 (SI 1992/3222). Cars were advertised for a composite price, including a 12-month warranty, which was insured under a policy with an insurance company and arranged through a company acting as Centurions' agent. Centurions allocated the price on the invoice between the car and the warranty and argued the *insurance* amount was exempt. However, they failed in their appeal, broadly, because the warranty was not optional. The amount allocated to *insurance* was also considerably in excess of what Centurions paid the insurer and there was no disclosure of the purported *commission* earned as the customer's agent.

    The Tribunal felt that, if this really had been the arrangement of insurance, this might well constitute a secret profit Centurions were not entitled to make.

HMRC have since provided guidance on this subject, the present position being set out in Section 20 of Notice 718 (margin schemes for second-hand goods) (2011 edn). The guidance given for dealers is, inter alia, to the effect that:

'If you provide your customer with a "free" warranty or MBI against mechanical defect or breakdown, then the selling price of the item includes the cost to you of providing such a warranty or MBI. The price of the item shown on the invoice to the customer must be the same as that entered in your stock book. Any mention of the warranty or MBI on your invoice must show that no separate charge is being made.' (para. 20.2)

'If you make a separate charge to your customer for a warranty or MBI, then the VAT treatment of this charge depends on whether any risk covered by the insurance policy is yours or your customer's.

(a) *MBIs.* If you arrange Mechanical Breakdown Insurance for your customer, the supply is exempt subject to satisfying the conditions outlined in paragraph 20.4. If the insurance contract is between you and the insurer and only your risk of having to repair defective items is covered, then the charge you show on your invoice for insurance will be standard-rated.
(b) *Warranties*. If you provide a warranty the charge you show on your invoice will be standard-rated.' (para. 20.3)

'You may treat the price charged for MBI as exempt if:

- it is supplied under a contract between an insurer and your customer;
- it is your customer's risks which are insured;
- your customer is entirely free to purchase the item at the price advertised without the MBI; and
- you disclose to the customer the premium and any other amount (fees or commission) being charged

This is because there are separate supplies of the item and the MBI, each with its own consideration.' (para. 20.4)

Practice point

What is important, therefore, is how the MBI is sold, the contractual relationships that are created as a result and also the amount actually charged for the MBI element. This raises, of course, a potential problem for the dealer under the partial exemption rules.

In short, for the insurance element to be exempt:

- it must be clear that it is the customer's own risk which is being insured, i.e. the individual customer's risk must be referred to in the policy; and
- where the supplier is selling goods or services liable to VAT, the amount of the premium, and any fee charged over and above that premium, must be disclosed in writing in a document issued to the customer at or before the time when the insurance transaction is entered into.

It is not necessary for an individual customer to be specifically named in a policy, but, where goods or services are supplied under one of the VAT margin schemes, the VAT invoice issued by the supplier must make the necessary disclosures before the exemption may apply.

(10) Other breakdown situations

In a slightly different context, two further Tribunal appeals have concerned arrangements for the insurance of consumer durables. Both were successful and resulted in significant savings due to the fact that, somewhat unusually, the services of re-instatement were seen as a supply to the insurer rather than to the insured. The end result in each case was, however, arrived at by quite different routes.

- The first was a joint appeal, *Thorn EMI plc* [1993] BVC 792 and *Granada plc* [1993] BVC 792. Both appellants were involved in TV rental arrangements under which customers were required to contract separately for the hire and for the maintenance of the equipment. The maintenance aspect took the form of an insurance agreement with an in-house captive insurance company, which undertook to procure any necessary repairs. The repairs were, in practice, carried out for the insurer by other subsidiaries in each group, all the relevant companies in those respective groups being registered together for VAT.

  HMRC argued the separate contracts should be disregarded. There was, in reality, just a single composite supply, albeit by two companies; also, the supply by the insurer was integral to the hire and that this should determine the character of the supply for VAT.

  Thorn and Granada maintained the customer's payment under the insurance contract was exempt, reducing the effective retail cost; further, the charges to the insurer for carrying out the work effectively bore VAT only to the extent of the underlying materials, not on the non-VATable costs such as labour; nor on the service company profit.

  HMRC's argument was, in a sense, attractive in as much as the effect of what is now VATA 1994, s. 43 is to treat all third-party supplies as being made by the representative member. However, the Tribunal looked at the factual position. There were clearly two agreements and two supplies. A supply could not be characterised without reference to the supplier, and the fact that the companies were related was not relevant.

- The second appeal, *Dixons Group plc* [1993] BVC 752, concerned an extended warranty under a five-year *cover plan*. Customers of Dixons or its associated company Currys, contracted with a third-party insurer, Cornhill Insurance, for the repair/replacement of their goods. Cornhill, in turn, contracted with a company called Mastercare Ltd, a member of the Dixons group having a succession of agreements with Cornhill or with its agents, Dixons Finance.

  The arrangement was, thus in many respects, similar to that in *Thorn EMI/Granada*, again, involving companies in a VAT group – but with the insurer being independent and not included. Payments by Cornhill to Mastercare were at agreed rates, often less than the normal service charge, settlement, in some cases, involving initial payment of the full retail price, followed by adjustments.

  The benefit derived from the fact that the VAT cost of the repair/replacement was confined, so it was argued, to the price agreed between Dixons and Cornhill. Predictably, HMRC, however, saw the supply of the repair/replacement as being to the customer, with tax being due on the open market value, not on the much lower settlements received from Cornhill. However, following the line of the actual agreements involved, the Tribunal held the supply was, in reality, to Cornhill.

> **Practice point**
>
> The two appeals are unusual for several reasons.
>
> (1) Most insurance seems to imply a financial indemnity with the repair/reinstatement being a supply to the insured. Where the latter is a business, this is important as it enables the insured to recover the tax on the supply as input VAT, thus reducing substantially the cost of the claim. In both appeals, the insured had no choice as to who was to carry out the work, which is generally the case, in any event.
>
> (2) In the *Thorn EMI/Granada* appeal, the cost of the claim will have been reduced by the repair service being carried out as between two companies in the same VAT group.
>
> In both appeals, the form of the contractual documentation was clearly vital. Companies wishing to follow this approach will, for that reason, need to take special care.

(11) Medico-legal and other medical services

Revenue & Customs Brief 06/07 announced changes from 1 May 2007 to the exemption for medical services following the ECJ Ruling in the case of *Dr Peter d'Ambrumenil and Dispute Resolution Services* (Case C-307/01) [2005] BVC 741. The Court held that this exemption was restricted to *medical care*, which it defined as those services intended principally to protect (including maintain or restore) the health of an individual. Medical services primarily to enable a third-party, such as an insurer, to take a decision (many of which are currently exempt from VAT under UK law) are taxable.

The services most affected are:

- witness testimony/reports for litigation, compensation or benefit purposes;
- reports/medicals for the purpose of providing certain fitness certificates; and
- some occupational health services.

In *Morganash Ltd* [2007] BVC 2,184 the Tribunal decided that medical services undertaken for the purpose of enabling a provider of life assurance to decide whether to accept a proposal for a policy fall within the scope of the UK exemption for insurance-related services.

Medical services provided for the purpose of valuing insurance policies for tax purposes, such as inheritance tax, are liable to VAT at the standard rate.

(12) Mixed or composite supplies

An area frequently causing problems of definition and interpretation is where several services or facilities are provided at the same time and for a single price. The questions to be answered are:

- does what is provided represent a single overall, supply; and if so
- is that supply is taxable or exempt?

If the answer is that there is no single, overall supply, but a range of different supplies, the issue then is one of apportionment and the allocation of the correct VAT liability to the respective parts.

The best illustration of this is *Card Protection Plan Ltd v C & E Commrs* (Case C-349/96) [1999] BVC 155, a case which went as far as the ECJ. As Advocate General Fennelly put it:

> 'Special difficulties arise, in the mystic twilight of VAT legislation, where there is what in modern jargon is called "a package" of services, some of which may, and others of which may not, be within a VAT exemption.'

This is discussed in detail in **Chapter 3** at 30-500. However, briefly, CPP offered holders of credit cards, on payment of a certain sum, a plan intended to protect against financial loss and inconvenience resulting from the loss or theft of cards or of certain other items, such as car keys, passports and insurance documents.

So far as the plan provided for indemnification of the cardholder against financial loss, CPP obtained block cover from an insurance company. The policy was arranged by a broker instructed by CPP and it was CPP's customers who were mentioned in the policy as the assured, their names being added to the schedule of the assured covered by that policy. CPP paid the premiums to the insurer in advance at the beginning of the policy year, with any necessary adjustments being made at the year-end.

HMRC had initially treated what was supplied by CPP as exempt. However, they later changed their mind and said the annual membership fee was subject to VAT at the standard-rate. Essentially, they saw the Plan as a *package of services* concerning the registration of credit cards, all taxable. They also said the insurer could not be seen as supplying insurance to CPP's customers as 'there was no privity between it and those customers'.

This dispute ultimately went to the ECJ, which took the view that CPP held a block insurance policy (see 90-200(1)) with a third-party insurer, under which its customers were the insured. Going on to consider whether there was a single supply or multiple supplies, the Court set out a number of criteria by which this was to be judged. It concluded by saying that it was for the National Court to determine, in the light of those criteria, whether transactions such as those performed by CPP were to be regarded for VAT purposes as comprising two independent supplies, namely an exempt insurance supply and a taxable card registration service, or whether one of those two supplies is the principal supply to which the other is *ancillary*, so that it receives the same tax treatment as the principal supply. On this basis, the House of Lords decided there was a single exempt supply.

Other cases have concerned situations where something has, initially been offered free alongside the sale of goods or services on which tax has been charged, but it has subsequently been argued that the price paid should be split so as to reduce the taxable amount of the VATable element.

- The joint appeal *Peugeot Motor Co plc; Citroën UK Ltd* [1999] BVC 2,314, for example, concerned free insurance offered by a motor manufacturer (or wholesaler) as an inducement for the purchase of a new car. It was initially accepted by the Tribunal that this could be recognised as a separate supply, notwithstanding that purchasers could not know how much had been paid by the appellants to third-party insurers. However, this was later reversed by the High Court on appeal *Peugeot Motor Co plc v C & E Commrs* [2004]

BVC 269. The High Court held that there was a composite supply. The principal element was the supply of the car, to which the supply of insurance was ancillary.

Much the same conclusion was reached in the *Ford Motor Company Ltd* case in the High Court in March 2007 ([2007] BVC 479).

(13) Overseas claims costs

Special administrative arrangements have been agreed in relation to the treatment of overseas claims costs by marine, aviation and transport insurance underwriters who are members of the Institute of London Underwriters (ILU). This covers, in particular, the position of underwriters in respect of claims-related input tax and associated imported services. The text of the arrangement is set out at **Appendix 9**.

(14) Pension funds

Pension fund administration services (such as, the administration of investments, dealing with queries, maintaining records and the processing of forms) are exempt as insurance when supplied as part of a single supply.

- In *Winterthur Life UK Ltd* [2002] BVC 2,136, it was decided in January 2002 that services provided to an authorised insurer in the administration of its pension scheme were exempt as agency services. A subsidiary of Winterthur Life, Personal Pension Management Ltd, undertook the management of a self-administered pension scheme for Scottish Equitable plc. Following the decision of the ECJ in *Forsakrinsaktiebolaget Skandia*, it was clear that *related services* could include services which did not place the provider of them, the agent or broker, in the position of having a direct insurance relationship with the insured. The services of PPM were characterised by permanent authority, by being within the normal scope of insurance business and the entry into commitment, although not of insurance commitments. It was closely concerned with the administration of the part of the insurance transaction, which was the self-administered scheme. PPM was providing *related* services and, although the exemption in art. 135(1)(a) of Council Directive 2006/112/EC (art. 13(B)(a) of the Sixth VAT Directive (Directive 77/388)) must be narrowly construed, what PPM did clearly came within it.

In terms of UK law, Note (2) to VATA 1994, Sch. 9, Grp. 2 stated that an insurance agent is acting in an intermediary capacity whenever he is acting as an intermediary between a person who provides insurance and a person who is seeking insurance. The Tribunal could not interpret this as meaning that an insurance agent, when he is not acting in an intermediary capacity, is any-the-less an insurance agent.

In 2003, following *Winterthur Life*, HMRC conducted a consultation on the VAT treatment of pension fund management generally but the result was inconclusive and it was decided that no changes would be made for the time being.

(15) Premiums

Generally, with the exception of direct MAT insurance, the value of any supply is on a gross basis, i.e. before brokerage, claims and reinsurance premiums or local taxes, but after discounts. However:

(1) In the case of direct MAT it is often hard to establish the true premium figure. It has therefore been agreed with the ABI and the AIOA (the Aviation Insurance Offices Association) that, where actual figures are not available, insurers may add five per cent to the net premium to arrive at the equivalent *gross*. This uplift does not apply to reinsurance. Individual insurers may negotiate different uplifts if these can be substantiated.

(2) For reinsurance, the output is the gross premium, after deduction of:

   (a) reinsurance commission (known as treaty, flat, ceding or overriding commission), which is agreed between the re-insurer and the insurer to cover the costs of the insurer in obtaining the business. This is regarded as a discount; and/or

   (b) profit commission (payable by the re-insurer to the reinsured if the business proves to be profitable). This is regarded as a contingent discount and reduces the amount which the insurer pays for the reinsurance.

(16) Protection and Indemnity (P & I) insurance

Protection and indemnity insurance is essentially cover for all liabilities likely to be incurred by a shipowner relating to the ship and cargo, except for actual damage to the hull. It covers, therefore, damage caused by the ship or by or to the passengers, crew or cargo. Underwriting is by P & I clubs, which are non-profit making associations of shipowners and which are located outside the UK. Business is handled by representatives, who are not paid brokerage in the normal sense. Instead, they act on a *net premium* basis, with the intermediary *grossing-up* the premiums charged to the insured.

The clubs are deemed to be making a supply of insurance within VATA 1994, Sch. 9, Grp. 2, item 1 or 2. If established in the UK, they may, nonetheless be required to be registered for VAT if the value of any taxable supplies they make, together with any taxable imported services, exceed the registration threshold.

P & I club managers are required to be separately registered from any clubs they manage. If empowered to accept risks on behalf of the club, they are deemed to be providing the services of an insurance intermediary within VATA 1994, Sch. 9, Grp. 2, item 4. Usually, the partial exemption recovery rate of the managers will follow that of the P & I club they manage unless other supplies are made.

P & I club agents, on the other hand, are seen by HMRC to be supplying taxable management services to the manager, but which are generally accepted as falling within VATA 1994, Sch. 5.

(17) Reviewing pension policies

Services provided by an insurer in administering a review of the sale by an insurance company of pension policies are exempt and not subject to VAT.

- *C & E Commrs v Century Life plc* [2001] BVC 116 concerned work undertaken to comply with a requirement of the Securities Investment Board and Personal Investment Authority in October 1994 to check for indications of mis-selling. HMRC argued the company was not acting as an *insurance agent* or *intermediary* as its function arose from the statutory regulation of insurance business, not the contractual relationship between insurer and insured. The Tribunal had agreed, but the High Court, and later the Court of Appeal, reversed this on appeal. The Tribunal had erred in taking into account the frequency with which this type of service was performed. It had accepted that the company was an insurance agent in the context of the Insurance Intermediaries Directive, but was wrong in concluding that a distinction could be drawn between services identified in art. 13(B)(a) of the Sixth VAT Directive (art. 135(1)(a) of Council Directive 2006/112/EC) and services arising from regulatory requirements.

The appeal did not turn on the question whether Century was an insurance agent or not. It was clear that it had such a capacity. There was no distinction between commercial insurance activities falling within art. 13(B)(a) of the Sixth VAT Directive (art. 135(1)(a)) and services intended to ensure compliance with the regulatory requirements: compliance was a commercial necessity. If the activities of review and ensuring compliance had been undertaken by the insurance company itself, they would have been part of its insurance business. Century was merely doing on behalf of the insurer what should have been done in the first place and would have formed part of the insurer's exempt insurance business. It was necessary for there to be a *close nexus* between the service supplied and insurance transactions.

(18) Roadside assistance

The provision of car accident or breakdown services by an automobile touring club in return for the payment of a fixed annual subscription is a form of insurance. This has long been the accepted treatment in the UK and has now been confirmed by the ECJ in *EC Commission v Greece* (Case C-13/06) [2009] BVC 729.

(19) Run-off situations

A run-off situation arises when an insurer or re-insurer ceases to underwrite insurance, or a particular class of insurance, but a liability remains for claims for business already written. Additional or return premiums may still be receivable or payable for various reasons, because the business is long-term, for example. They will usually, however, be treated in the same manner as the original premiums received, and with the same impact on the recovery of input VAT by the insurer or re-insurer concerned. Return premiums are generally, however, not to be included with those received in respect of on-going business for the purposes of calculating normal recoverable input tax, although alternative special arrangements may be agreed.

Third-party services provided to the insurer or re-insurer in the run-off period will generally be accepted as a single composite supply and exempt within VATA 1994, Sch. 9, Grp. 2. This will particularly apply where the person concerned takes over responsibility for accountancy and legal work in connection with the management of the business in the run-off period and provides services of handling and settling claims and dealing with premium adjustments. The services supplied will not be exempt as insurance transactions as the third-party (even though possibly an insurer) will not have a contractual relationship with the insured and will not assume any risk. Instead, the third-party may be regarded as acting as an *intermediary* so that the liability of the services, will follow that of the insurance or reinsurance itself.

Other services not part of this composite supply may not qualify for exemption and may need to be treated separately. In this connection, it may be useful to consider the comments elsewhere in this book on *Outsourcing* (see 90-350 later).

(20) Salvage

Sometimes a claim will be settled on the basis of total loss instead of a repair. What is damaged then becomes the property of the insurer and its subsequent disposal generally represents a supply subject to VAT. Tax may then be due on the full proceeds realised. This is subject, however, to an exception where the goods in question are works of art, antiques and collectors' items or second-hand goods. In this case, the supply is covered by a special second-hand scheme in art. 4 of the *Value Added Tax (Special Provisions) Order* 1995 (SI 1995/1268). VAT need not then be accounted for provided:

- the goods are sold in the same condition as acquired;
- if the goods had been supplied in the UK by the person from whom they were obtained, the supply would not have been subject to VAT or would have been chargeable at less than full value (e.g. acquisition from a private individual or from a dealer himself operating one of the special schemes for second-hand goods); or
- if imported into the UK, the goods must have borne VAT, which has not been reclaimed or refunded.

If these conditions are not met, the supply may nonetheless be zero-rated for certain large boats and aircraft (VATA 1994, Sch. 8, Grp. 8) or *outside the scope* of VAT if the goods are salvaged or sold while outside the UK and the Isle of Man.

Any VAT incurred on repairs prior to sale (or indeed in making a sale) will be potentially recoverable.

(21) Soft commissions

Soft commissions can refer to a situation where one business may fund part of the cost of research or other services provided by a third-party direct to a client in the expectation that the client meets target levels of commission business.

This type of soft commissions do not represent consideration for a supply by the intermediary, but may be consideration for a supply of research.

See also, though, **Chapter 3** at 30-500.

(22) Valuation

The service of valuation for insurance purposes is normally taxable, but on occasions may be exempt if structured as an integral part of the premium.

- In the case of *Lancaster Insurance Services Ltd* (1990) 5 BVC 928, the amount of insurance cover was decided by the valuation of the cars insured for members of the MG Owners Club; it was a term of the insurance policy that the agreed value should be determined by the appellant. The premium included a valuation fee of £8 (currently £15) which HMRC said was taxable. The Tribunal, however, found the charge to be exempt.

As noted earlier, medical services provided for the purpose of valuing insurance policies for tax purposes, such as inheritance tax, are now liable to VAT at the standard rate. following the ECJ Ruling in *Dr Peter d'Ambrumenil and Dispute Resolution Services* (Case C-307/01). The ECJ held that the healthcare exemption was restricted to *medical care*, which it defined as those services intended principally to protect (including maintain or restore) the health of an individual.

90-250   Insurance and reinsurance companies

The main focus under this heading will be on companies underwriting risks as insurers or re-insurers and who are persons who have permission under Pt. IV of the *Financial Services and Markets Act* 2000 to effect or carry out contracts of insurance. The heading also applies to certain insurers who are specifically exempted by an order under FSMA 2000, s. 38 and certain other specified types of person.

(1) Input tax

In common with other businesses operating in this sector, few, if any, supplies will attract VAT. Most will be exempt, so that the concern of most insurers will tend to be on the recovery of input tax, rather than with calculating and accounting for any output tax that may be due. Indeed, because of the nature of insurance (as opposed to reinsurance), inasmuch as it is tends to be provided principally to a domestic market rather than cross-border, the rates of recovery achieved will tend to be generally much lower than those experienced in the financial sectors dealt with earlier in **Chapters 7** and **8** or later in **Chapter 10**. Rates of ten per cent or lower are common, but the high incidence of VAT on many areas of expense makes this an important issue.

Partial exemption and the issues affecting the recovery of input tax are explored in detail in **Chapter 4**. However, there are a number of issues that tend to be more to the forefront with insurers than for other exempt or partly exempt sectors.

(a) Direct attribution

Direct attribution is a requirement of the Standard Partial Exemption Method under reg. 101 of the *Value Added Tax Regulations* 1995 (SI 1995/2518), which few insurers will tend, in practice, to be allowed to use.

It is also invariably a feature of the Special Methods most companies agree.

In practice, however, most input VAT incurred will not fall within this description, but when it does, being alert to the possibility of full input tax relief can be important. The *Deutsche Ruck* case discussed earlier (see **Chapter 4** at 40-150(5)) is a particular example of a situation

9 Insurance

where tax on foreign legal costs, caught by the reverse-charge (see **Chapter 5**), may not always give rise to an expense.

Direct attribution to taxable supplies can also be useful at times in the context of a staff canteen, a small matter perhaps, but one which many companies find worthwhile.

(b) Residual input tax

Residual input tax is where the vast majority of input tax will arise. As with other areas covered by this book, the correct classification of supplies and the identity and location of the recipient will be important. Generally, the greatest scope for recovering underlying input tax may be recovered will be with reinsurance, where the incidence of cross-border supplies is that much greater. For insurers, risks such as life and motor insurance tend to be very heavily exempt, rather than *outside the scope* with recovery.

More importantly, there is usually a requirement to split activities between insurance proper (i.e. insurance or reinsurance) and investment, which, although commercially and economically integral to any area of insurance, is invariably seen as a separate business activity. Separate calculations are expected, although, unlike in other areas, it is not uncommon to find that the recoverable amounts are calculated by the simple formula:

$$\frac{\text{value of taxable supplies}}{\text{value of total supplies}} \times \text{input VAT}$$

or expressed another way:

$$\frac{\text{value of all supplies in respect of which input tax is recoverable}}{\text{value of total supplies}} \times \text{input VAT}$$

as taxable in this context is generally defined under the Special Methods agreed by companies so as to encompass all supplies (whether subject to VAT at the standard rate, zero-rated, exempt or *outside the scope*), where underlying input VAT may be recovered. In practice, therefore, there is generally no need for separating *out of country* supplies as in the *LIPA* case discussed in **Chapter 4** at 40-150. This constitutes *a composite method*.

(i) Investment
So far as investment is concerned, the main areas of interest will be the treatment and classification of financial investments as insurers represent probably the greatest part of institutional investors alongside pension funds and unit and investment trusts.

Property is also a significant area of interest for many insurers, where a different approach to the recovery of input tax (possibly on a property-by-property basis may be more appropriate, especially given the incidence and importance of the option to tax under VATA 1994, Sch. 10, para. 2). The separation of activities will be especially relevant where they are substantial and involve different people undertaking the investment/treasury functions. Whether this is an altogether reasonable approach, however, could be open to doubt in some cases.

(ii) Other factors, including the mix of business

Beyond this, it may be useful to look at the mix of business, the degree to which individual divisions within a company specialise in particular types of risk, e.g. direct MAT, motor, or life and pensions or reinsurance and the extent to which costs can be identified and allocated. Depending on what is involved, a number of options may then be available to produce differing levels of input VAT relief.

- With motor and life, for example, business tends to be rather more domestic in nature so that premiums will usually be predominantly exempt without the right to input VAT relief.
- In other cases, for example direct MAT or reinsurance, business can, in practice, often be more international with the prospect that relief may be significantly higher.

The amount of input VAT actually incurred in generating different types of insurance business may also not necessarily be incurred uniformly.

In terms of what might be considered, it could be worth looking at an initial division of input tax such as:

- a simple allocation between divisions based on staff. If employees engaged in generating particular categories of premium income can be identified, an initial allocation of input VAT might be agreed on the basis just of the relative staff numbers or salary costs; or
- a more complicated, but often more accurate, cost/income centre approach. Under this arrangement expenditure and related VAT is first allocated specifically where possible to particular cost or income centres.

Where neither is possible, e.g. where tax arises on general overheads or group costs, the allocation may need to be done indirectly on an appropriate basis.

VAT allocated to cost or overhead centres might then be re-allocated to the appropriate income centres, again on a reasonable basis according to use or contribution, perhaps according to the relative volumes of business or the numbers of staff employed in each section. Often a method on these lines will follow the general format of internal management accounts:

- general overheads, for example, might be allocated according to staff numbers or the volume of business generated;
- telecommunications might be apportioned on the basis of metered calls, the number of telephone extensions or on the estimated use of direct lines;
- for premises/occupancy costs, the allocation could be by reference to the space occupied;
- computer and other accounting costs will often be shared according to the numbers of terminals or numbers of transactions processed.

Input VAT, once allocated to a particular profit or income centre, might then be recovered either according to a values-based formula using premiums or income/receipts, or, perhaps, on the relative numbers of transactions, e.g. policies or premiums received.

Where costs cannot be allocated specifically or a detailed cost/income centre approach is impractical, the apportionment of input VAT between different classes of income might be made on a more pragmatic basis by reference to the relative levels of premium income or,

9 Insurance

alternatively, according to the relative numbers of transactions, e.g. policies or premiums received.

Clearly, no single rule will apply to all companies and the approach decided upon may, in the end depend as much on the amounts of tax at stake and the complexity of the various options as on the desire for an accurate result.

> **Practice point**
>
> Mistakes are sometimes made on basic issues like identifying where a customer or client belongs or is resident. This can affect an insurer's ability to recover input tax.
>
> Most life business, for example, is domestic and exempt with no recovery. However, cover provided for a UK citizen could potentially qualify for input tax recovery if, say:
>
> - he is due to go abroad, outside the EU, for an extended tour of duty;
> - he has accommodation arranged abroad; or
> - he is due to emigrate.

> **Practice point**
>
> In looking at a Special Partial Exemption Method, it could be worth considering how far it is necessarily correct, or appropriate, to look at different activities in isolation. Investment, for example, is fundamental to insurance:
>
> - premiums come under the insurance exemption;
> - the receipt of interest and the proceeds of sale of investments are within the rules on finance;
> - rents and the proceeds of sale of property are within the rules on land; and
> - dividends are outside the scope,
>
> but none of the investment function is possible without the generation of funds by the collection of premiums.
>
> Is it always entirely reasonable, therefore, to use different methods of calculating recoverable input tax without recognising that some of the initial costs have a dual purpose?

(c) Captives and non-permitted/authorised insurers

(i) Captives

The use of captive insurance companies by commercial and industrial groups is increasingly popular. Generally, this involves companies established offshore in places like Bermuda or the Channel Islands, where the normal VAT rules do not apply.

For captives established in the Isle of Man, however, the effect of the Common Purse arrangement with the UK means that these companies are subject to the normal VAT regime. Any premium income is exempt under Sch. 2, Grp. 2 of the *Value Added Tax and Other Taxes Act* 1973 (the equivalent legislation in the Isle of Man). In appropriate cases, however, such companies may be grouped with a UK associate under VATA 1994, s. 43.

(ii) Other situations

As an alternative to exemption under the insurance rules, there is also a possible exemption for financial guarantees or sureties under what is now VATA 1994, Sch. 9, Grp. 5.

(d) The sale of an insurance business

In *Winterthur Swiss Insurance Co* [2006] BVC 2,376 the question arose as to whether the supply of a UK insurance business to a Swiss insurer not itself intending to carry on insurance business in the UK was the transfer of a going concern within art. 5 of the *Value Added Tax (Special Provisions) Order* 1995 (SI 1995/1268). Winterthur, a Swiss insurer with branches in the EU and a UK subsidiary, Churchill Management Ltd (CML), entered into an agreement with Prudential Assurance Co Ltd for the acquisition of Prudential's reinsurance business. The day-to-day administration was to be handled by CML, which took over the assets and employees involved; Winterthur took over the actual business, paying £350m for goodwill, including renewal rights. Subsequently, the company found that Swiss regulatory problems made it difficult to operate the business in Switzerland, so decided to transfer it to a group company based in Bermuda.

There were three issues:

(1) Was the transfer of Prudential's general insurance the transfer of a going concern for VAT?

(2) If it wasn't, where was the place of supply?

(3) If the supply was taxable, could Winterthur recover the VAT under the EC Eighth Directive (Directive 79/1072 (replaced by Directive 2008/9))?

Winterthur ultimately failed on the first point as, although the transfer from Prudential involved an identifiable part of the Prudential's business and was capable of separate operation, the assets were not, in the event, used by Winterthur in carrying on the same kind of business as Prudential and, anyway, Winterthur was not a taxable person for UK VAT. On the second and third points taken together, however, they succeeded. The supply of goodwill by Prudential was not within art. 9(2)(e) of the Sixth Directive (VATA 1994, Sch. 5 and art. 56 of Council Directive 2006/112/EC). However, Winterthur, being VAT-registered in other EU Member States was able to claim back the VAT charged by Prudential because nothing in the Directive prevented this.

90-300 Lloyd's

In essence, the same rules apply for Lloyd's of London (Lloyd's) as for insurance and reinsurance companies. However, the structure of the market is such that special arrangements are needed to accommodate the VAT position. A summary of how the market operates is in the HMRC Insurance Manual at para. VATINS 4000.

Briefly, Lloyd's does not itself write insurance business but provides and regulates a market for others in which almost anything can be insured. Business is written by the underwriting members (names), whose personal obligations provide the capacity, receiving premiums and being liable to pay claims. Members can be either individuals having unlimited liability or companies. Although, underwriting members carry on the business, in practice, this has to be organised through what are known as syndicates – unincorporated associations recognised by Lloyd's but not having a separate legal identity. Each syndicate member is only liable for his stated proportion of the risk, the liability being several (and not joint).

Each syndicate is managed by a managing agent, who employs, pays and supervises the leading underwriter and provides the necessary administrative facilities. The managing agent also arranges the reinsurance of the contracts of insurance and pays claims on behalf of members. Underwriting members must also generally appoint a members' agent who arranges for them to join or leave the syndicates in which they participate, bids on their behalf at the auctions of syndicate underwriting capacity; contracts with the managing agent of each syndicate, analyses syndicate trends, prepares and transmits information to Lloyd's and to managing agents, sees that members comply with Lloyd's regulatory requirements and assists with the reinsurance of the members' exposure at Lloyd's.

Lloyd's publishes a *Blue Book* which contains the number of each syndicate, the name of its managing agent, the names of the members' agents who have underwriting members in the syndicate and the names of the underwriting members in the syndicate.

Having individual names registered for VAT, would clearly cause enormous practical difficulties, especially where they are members of more than one syndicate. For many years up to the end of 1999 the special arrangements adopted were focussed on the managing agents. Individual members did not register for VAT; nor did the syndicates they belonged to. Instead, any VAT accounting was mostly achieved through the VAT registration of the managing agents.

Developments in EC VAT law and several VAT cases on the concept of *establishment* have, however, caused this to have to be changed as the existing Lloyd's VAT arrangements were no longer tenable. From 1 January 2000, therefore, there has been a new regime, the text of the current Lloyd's VAT Agreement, revised in January 2004, is found at **Appendix 15**.

The essence of what this entails is that, whilst individual names will continue, generally, not to be expected to register, the position has changed as regards the syndicates. Notwithstanding that they are not, in law, in the nature of partnerships, they are now to be seen as the principal registrable unit.

(1) Syndicates

The VAT year remains from 1 January to 31 December and, unlike with most other businesses, the annual adjustment for partial exemption purposes is made in the last period in the VAT year, the December quarter, rather than in the period immediately following. (This treatment of the annual adjustment does not apply to other Lloyd's VAT registrations, where the adjustments are made in the return following the end of the VAT year.)

In terms of the approach to partial exemption, the arrangements are, however, fairly simple and follow the sort of principles adopted elsewhere in the industry. Direct attribution is, as elsewhere, expected where appropriate and, for the recovery of residual input tax, underwriting and investment are seen as distinctly separate business areas.

(a) Underwriting

This part of the calculation is based on premiums processed, both through the Lloyd's Policy Signing Office (LPSO) and elsewhere. Those processed by the LPSO are notified quarterly in arrears, with the Global Market Rate being generally allowed to be used for the first VAT period of a new registration, subject to the agreement of HMRC being obtained. Premiums are coded by LPSO as:

- X = exempt;
- Z = outside the scope (O/S) with input tax (I/T) credit;
- M = mixed, this will be split 50/50 to X and Z,

and the sector recovery calculation is on the basis of:

$$\frac{\text{value of premiums O/S with I/T credit}}{\text{value of total premiums}} = \text{recoverable \% to 2 decimal places}$$

(b) Investments

Investments are treated, again, in much the same way as elsewhere, the calculation of recoverable input tax being based on either the number or the value of securities sales, i.e:

$$\frac{\text{number or value of O/S with I/T credit sales of securities}}{\text{number or value of total sales of securities}} = \text{recoverable \% to 2 decimal places}$$

Similar calculations are expected for other Lloyd's entities.

Syndicates, which only have EU business will not, on that account, be entitled to register, although it is possible that the operation of the reverse-charge procedure on certain services received from outside the UK may trigger an obligation to register where their value exceeds the VAT registration threshold (see **Chapter 2**). Investment activities that generate supplies treated and made outside the UK, but which carry the right to underlying input tax recovery, can also affect this entitlement to be registered.

Syndicates wholly owned by a corporate member or by a Scottish limited partnership, will not be allowed to register as such. In this situation, syndicate-level items are expected to be accounted for via the VAT registration of the corporate member, or Scottish limited partnership, itself.

(2) Managing agents

HMRC accept that the fees or profit commission charged to members are basically exempt as insurance intermediary services under VATA 1994, Sch. 9, Grp. 2, item 4. The outputs to be declared are the values of charges made by the managing agents to the syndicates that they are authorised to manage, plus any other supplies made by the agent. The partial exemption calculation relating to insurance and investment activities is essentially made on the same lines

9 Insurance

as that for syndicates, with the ability to recover input tax generally following the treatment of the premiums and investment income of the syndicates to which the members' fees are charged.

(3) Members' agents and Lloyd's advisers

At one point, HMRC were disputing whether services supplied by members' agents and by Lloyd's advisers, who negotiate syndicate participations, are exempt. This has now been resolved, however, as a result of the decision in *SOC Private Capital Ltd*.

- *SOC Private Capital Ltd* [2003] BVC 2,038, concerned a Lloyd's members' agent acting for a number of underwriting members, who were members of one or more syndicates. The main issue was whether supplies made by SOC, as a members' agent at Lloyd's, were exempt under art. 13(B)(a) of the Sixth Directive (art. 135(1)(a) of Council Directive 2006/112/EC) – in the UK, VATA 1994, Sch. 9, Grp. 2, item 4, as:

    '(a) insurance and reinsurance transactions, including related services performed by insurance brokers and insurance agents; …'

or were standard-rated, as argued by HMRC.

There was also a dispute over whether, alternatively, the services were exempt as financial services under art. 13(B)(d)(3) of the Sixth Directive (art. 135(1)(d) of Council Directive 2006/112/EC) as:

'(3) transactions, including negotiation, concerning deposit and current accounts, payments, transfers, debts, cheques and other negotiable instruments, but excluding debt collection and factoring …'

SOC maintained the supplies of insurance were made by the underwriting members and that they, as members' agents, were *insurance agents*, performing *services related to insurance transactions*; alternatively, what they supplied was *insurance and reinsurance transactions* or *financial services*. HMRC, on the other hand maintained the insurance was not supplied by the underwriting members but by the syndicates and that members' agents were not insurance agents. The services were insufficiently related to insurance or reinsurance and SOC did not carry out insurance or reinsurance transactions. They also said any supplies of financial services were *ancillary* (see the discussion earlier at 90-200 on the *CPP* case).

Deciding for SOC, the Tribunal held that:

(1) The insurer was the underwriting member, not the syndicate.

(2) Members' agents were insurance agents within the meaning of art. 13(B)(a), their activities falling within the definition of art. 2(1)(b) of Directive 77/9, the insurance Directive. They were persons instructed by the underwriting members and empowered to act in their name and on their behalf, introducing members to the syndicates, proposing to members the syndicates in which they should participate, and carrying out work preparatory to the conclusion of contracts of insurance.

(3) Members' agents supplied services related to insurance transactions within the meaning of art. 13(B)(a), there being a very close nexus between what was provided and the

insurance transactions entered into by the member. As such, the services were more than merely ancillary; and, without them, the insurance would not take place.

(4) Members' agents also supplied insurance or reinsurance transactions within the meaning of art. 13(B)(a) as they participated in insurance transactions by being part of the chain of events between the member and the insured.

HMRC were right, though, in relation to any financial services being *ancillary*. In substance and reality, what the members' agent supplied was not financial services but the ability to enter into insurance transactions.

Members' agents and those Lloyd's advisors who negotiate syndicate participations must use the Members' Agents Rate for the year ended 31 December 2001 to determine input tax recovery for the year ended 31 December 2002, when preparing VAT returns

(4) Mixed agents

Recovery of input tax will be based on a combination of the value of the members' agent services (for the members' agent activities) and the value of the managing agent services (for the managing agent activities).

(5) Other registrations

Natural members, corporate members and Scottish Limited Partnerships may be able to register in their own right to account for VAT on activities other than insurance underwriting and to account for and recover input tax on insurance-related costs (such as those incurred on members' agents and Lloyd's advisors and other professionals), that are incurred by the member directly and not at syndicate level.

Subject to what was said earlier at (1) above in relation to syndicates wholly owned by corporate members and Scottish Limited Partnerships, no outputs will be declared in these separate registrations from the underwriting of insurance in the Lloyd's market as these are to be declared by the syndicates themselves. The only outputs to be declared will be those from other activities. The recovery of input tax on insurance-related members costs will, however, be recovered by a formula based on the corresponding premium or investment calculation of the syndicate(s) to which the member belongs. A special accommodation is needed, though, for the recovery of input tax by members, particularly corporate members and Scottish Limited Partnerships, who participate in a number of syndicates. If this makes the calculation relative to the underwriting activities difficult, subject to agreement with HMRC, the Global Market Rate may be used in its place to calculate the recovery of input tax incurred on insurance activities. Input tax incurred on investment activities is recovered on a basis similar to that for syndicates.

(6) Other issues affecting Lloyd's

(a) Global Market Rate

The Global Market Rate is a fixed rate calculated by Lloyd's, which may be used for the recovery of input tax in certain situations, but only with the agreement of HMRC. It is arrived at by a calculation based on the VAT status of all premiums processed through the LPSO in the previous quarter.

The Global Market Rate is only calculated once in the year, at the end of the year, and input VAT recovery during the year will be based on the Global Market Rate for the previous year.

(b) Members' status

Active members are treated as being in business for VAT; inactive or non-working members are not. A natural member who usually resides outside the UK does not have any business or other fixed establishment is deemed to *belong* where he resides. A corporate member with no business or fixed establishment is deemed to belong where it is incorporated.

(c) Lloyd's entrance fees and subscriptions

HMRC accept that entrance fees and subscriptions charged to members are regarded as payment for mixed supplies. Part is regarded as attributable to the general facility of Lloyd's membership and is taxable at the standard-rate; the balance represents an insurance service which is accordingly exempt or *outside the scope*, with part conferring the right of input VAT recovery.

(d) Imported services

It has been agreed with HMRC that the fees charged by LeBoeuf Lamb Green & Macrae are to be subject to VAT under the reverse-charge provisions in VATA 1994, s. 81 (see **Chapter 5**). They are paid centrally by Lloyd's and recharged to the syndicates. The fees cannot be directly attributed to specific supplies of insurance and are thus regarded as *residual* for partial exemption purposes.

Following *Deutsche Ruck* (see **Chapter 4** at 40-150(5)), HMRC initially agreed that US legal fees recharged to the Market could be regarded as being directly related to US insurance policies (where premiums were *outside the scope* but conferred the right to recover underlying input tax). However, they are now of the view that the services are of a more general nature.

90-350 Insurance intermediaries (other than Lloyd's) and outsourcing

The treatment of insurance intermediaries needs to be looked at under three broad headings:

- brokers;
- underwriting managers; and
- outsourcing

For each, the underlying issues tend to be much the same, the extent to which the VAT exemptions apply and the recovery of input VAT is restricted.

(1) The general pattern of the exemption

The basis for the exemption for insurance intermediaries derives from art. 135(1)(a) of Council Directive 2006/112/EC (art. 13(B)(a) of the Sixth VAT Directive):

> 'insurance and reinsurance transactions, including related services performed by insurance brokers and insurance agents.'

and, in the UK, in VATA 1994, Sch. 9, Grp. 2, item 4:

> '4 The provision by an insurance broker or insurance agent of any of the services of an insurance intermediary in a case in which those services-
>
> (a) are related (whether or not a contract of insurance or reinsurance is finally concluded) to an insurance transaction or a reinsurance transaction; and
> (b) are provided by that broker or agent in the course of his acting in an intermediary capacity.'

Subject to their being provided by an insurance broker or insurance agent, services are exempt as those of an *insurance intermediary* are exempt if they amount to:

> '(a) the bringing together, with a view to the insurance or reinsurance of risks, of–
>
> (i) persons who are or may be seeking insurance or reinsurance, and
> (ii) persons who provide insurance or reinsurance;
>
> (b) the carrying out of work preparatory to the conclusion of contracts of insurance or reinsurance;
> (c) the provision of assistance in the administration and performance of such contracts, including the handling of claims; or
> (d) the collection of premiums.'

and an insurance broker or insurance agent is acting *in an intermediary capacity* when acting as an intermediary between:

> '(a) a person who provides any insurance or reinsurance and
> (b) a person who is or may be seeking insurance or reinsurance or is an insured person.'

Item 4 specifically does not include:

(1) Market research, product design, advertising, promotional or similar services or the collection, collation and provision of information for use in connection therewith.

(2) Valuation or inspection services.

(3) The services of loss adjusters, average adjusters, motor assessors, surveyors or other experts except where:

(a) the services consist in the handling of a claim under a contract of insurance or reinsurance;
(b) the person handling the claim is authorised when doing so to act on behalf of the insurer or reinsurer; and
(c) that person's authority so to act includes written authority to determine whether to accept or reject the claim and, where accepting it in whole or in part, to settle the amount to be paid on the claim.

It also excludes any services that are supplied as part of the actual indemnity under a contract of insurance or reinsurance.

(a) The Intermediaries Directive

Whilst the same words used in different Directives may have different meanings, the wording of art. 135(1)(a) of Council Directive 2006/112/EC (art. 13(B)(a) of the Sixth VAT Directive) which defines the exemption in terms of *related services* in the context of *services performed by insurance brokers and insurance agents*, seems to borrow much from the descriptions of services covered by the *Intermediaries Directive* (Directive 92/77), art. 2:

'(1) This Directive shall apply to the following activities falling within ex ISIC Group 630 in Annex III to the General Programme for the abolition of restrictions on freedom of establishment:

(a) professional activities of persons who, acting with complete freedom as to their choice of undertaking, bring together, with a view to the insurance or reinsurance of risks, persons seeking insurance or reinsurance and insurance or reinsurance undertakings, carry out work preparatory to the conclusion of contracts of insurance or reinsurance and, where appropriate, assist in the administration and performance of such contracts, in particular in the event of a claim;

(b) professional activities of persons instructed under one or more contracts or empowered to act in the name and on behalf of, or solely on behalf of, one or more insurance undertakings in introducing, proposing and carrying out work preparatory to the conclusion of, or in concluding, contracts of insurance, or in assisting in the administration and performance of such contracts, in particular in the event of a claim;

(c) activities of persons other than those referred to in (a) and (b) who, acting on behalf of such persons, among other things carry out introductory work, introduce insurance contracts or collect premiums, provided that no insurance commitments towards or on the part of the public are given as part of these operations.'

The ruling in the *Arthur Andersen* case (see *Outsourcing* later at (4)) expressed the view that the *Intermediaries Directive* definitions do not determine the status of a business as insurance agent or broker for the purposes of the VAT exemption. The Court also found, in relation to insurance brokers or agents, that:

- the essential characteristic of brokers is their complete freedom as to choice of insurer for their clients;
- the essential characteristic of agents is that, although they may be tied to one or more insurers, their role is to find and introduce prospective customers; and
- an insurance agent or broker must not be carrying out only subcontracted activities on the insurer's behalf and which the insurer would normally perform for itself. It must be carrying out the independent function of bringing the parties to the insurance or reinsurance contract together.

The Court also held that, as Advocate General Poiares Maduro pointed out in his Opinion, it cannot be inferred from that case-law that the existence of a power to render the insurer liable is the determining criterion for recognition of an insurance agent within the meaning of art. 13B(a) of the Sixth Directive. Recognition of a person as *an insurance agent* presupposes an examination of what the activities in question comprise.

Directive 92/77 has now been replaced by the *EC Insurance Mediation Directive* (Council Directive 2002/92), where the corresponding provisions, art. 3, provide that:

'3. "insurance mediation" means the activities of introducing, proposing or carrying out other work preparatory to the conclusion of contracts of insurance, or of concluding such contracts, or of assisting in the administration and performance of such contracts, in particular in the event of a claim.

These activities when undertaken by an insurance undertaking or an employee of an insurance undertaking who is acting under the responsibility of the insurance undertaking shall not be considered as insurance mediation.

The provision of information on an incidental basis in the context of another professional activity provided that the purpose of that activity is not to assist the customer in concluding or performing an insurance contract, the management of claims of an insurance undertaking on a professional basis, and loss adjusting and expert appraisal of claims shall also not be considered as insurance mediation;'

with art. 4 having similar wording for *reinsurance mediation*.

(b) The Commission proposals

The draft proposal for the new Directive (amending Council Directive 2006/112/EC as regards financial and insurance services) was, as it happens, published on 16 July 2007. In addition, the Commission also published extensive draft Regulations (not reproduced here), which can be found on the Commission website.

The effect of the proposals is to replace points (a) to (g) in art. 135(1)by the following:

'(a) Insurance services;
 (b) Granting of credit and the financial safeguarding of credits;
 (c) Deposit services and account operation services;
 (d) Currency exchange and cash services;
 (e) Supplies of securities;
 (f) Management services for investment funds;
 (g) Intermediation in insurance and financial services;'.

A new art. 135a will then qualify how the exemption in points (a) to (g) is to be applied and, in particular, provides that:

'(1) "Insurance services" shall mean commitments whereby a person is obliged, in return for payment of a premium, to provide in the event of materialisation of a significant risk, with a service as determined by the commitment.'

and

'8 "Intermediation in insurance and financial services" shall mean related services distinct in character and specific to and essential for the conclusion, amendment or prolongation of an agreement whereby a person engages to supply one of the exempt main services listed in Article 135(1)(a) to (e).'

A *related service distinct in character* is to be regarded as the main service to which it relates, where it is specific to and essential for the transaction exempted under art. 135(1) (a) to (e).

It is especially interesting that the Fifth Recital to the draft Directive makes the following observation:

> 'Intermediation in insurance services and intermediation in financial services are treated equally because the market of insurance services increasingly overlaps with the market for financial services, requiring the same or similar forms of intermediation. Services which are related to intermediation do not benefit from an exemption because intermediation services are themselves already related services. However, subcontracting of intermediation services is covered by the exemption.'

Given that it is an accepted principle of VAT that the exemptions must be narrowly construed, it is not surprising that these provisions have given rise to a number of disputes, notably those of *Barclays Bank plc (No. 3)* [1991] BVC 893, *Countrywide Insurance Marketing Ltd* [1995] BVC 580 and *Curtis Edington & Say Ltd* [1995] BVC 1,389 all of which were concerned with item 3 (as it then was) – *the making of arrangements*. These are discussed at 90-100 earlier and, whilst they may still have some relevance today, must be looked at in the light of the comments in the *Arthur Andersen* case and the proposed changes in EU law.

(2) Brokers

As with insurers, the concern of most brokers will be over the recovery of input VAT.

Determining the extent to which commissions confer the right to input VAT relief, as opposed to simply being exempt, will again be the crucial factor, rather than the need to account for output tax. Generally, this will follow the treatment of the underlying premiums arranged – i.e. according to the risk and the nature and status of the insured. Brokerage in the case of engineering inspection will usually require apportionment to identify the inspection element on the issue or renewal of an unendorsed combined policy. VAT at the standard-rate will then need to be applied to the inspection element. In the case of inspection-only contracts, no apportionment is needed and the entire brokerage is standard-rated.

(a) Partial exemption

Also important will be the way a particular broker is treated for partial exemption purposes.

As with most businesses, there will usually be an initial requirement to apply direct attribution. Tax incurred exclusively in making taxable or exempt or *outside the scope* supplies with the right of recovery will be recouped in full; tax incurred exclusively in making exempt or *outside the scope* supplies without the right of recovery will be lost. The recovery of what remains will then normally be arrived at on a pro-rata basis by applying the formula:

$$\frac{\text{value of supplies with the right of input tax recovery}}{\text{value of all supplies}} \times \text{residual input VAT}$$

or a similar formula using numbers of transactions rather than values.

Supplies in this context will mainly comprise commission and brokerage, but there will also generally be a variety of other fees and supplies, including interest and other investment income. In many cases, especially as regards investment and other potentially distortive transactions the method adopted will require a measure of segregation, with separate calculations being made as appropriate for each part of the overall business. How this is arrived at will be open to negotiation.

(3) Underwriting managers

Underwriting managers, like Lloyd's underwriting agencies, accept insurance or reinsurance in the name of the insurer. As such they are treated as supplying a basically exempt insurance service of the services of an *insurance intermediary* (VATA 1994, Sch. 9, Grp. 2, item 4). The supply is treated as a single composite supply embracing usually the provision of underwriting expertise, together with the collection of premiums, claims handling and settlement, investment and investment management, accounting and the provision of any necessary administration in order to meet DTI, etc. requirements. This applies regardless of how the underwriting manager is remunerated, whether by commission, flat-rate fee or recharge of costs – or by a combination of one or more of these. In appropriate cases, however, depending on the nature of the risk and/or the status of the insured, exemption may be coupled with the right to input VAT relief where, for example, the cover is provided to persons belonging outside the EU.

In the event of that other non-insurance services are provided, these will need to be accounted for separately in the normal way.

This treatment seems to remain accepted by HMRC and does not appear to have been undermined by the *Skandia* case (see later under *Outsourcing* at (4)).

How underwriting managers achieve input VAT relief will generally depend on the circumstances of the individual company concerned. There is no single agreement corresponding to that adopted for Lloyds. Underwriting managers will also not account for the premium and other income/expenses of the companies for which they act. In most cases, a formula based on a simple ratio of the values of supplies will be a reasonable approach, with investment and other insurance activities being dealt with separately. It may also be worth considering an approach on cost- or income-centre lines where an underwriting manager acts simultaneously for two or more insurance or reinsurance companies, whose individual ranges of business produce different mixes of supplies on which underlying input VAT can or cannot be recovered.

Whether and how far this treatment is ultimately affected by the Commission proposals and the review of finance and insurance or by the *Arthur Andersen* case remains to be seen.

(4) Outsourcing

As observed earlier in **Chapter 7** at 70-500, outsourcing is, arguably, the most important single issue at present for many in the finance and insurance sectors. Modern-day commercial pressures mean businesses are ever looking for ways to cut costs and/or do things more efficiently and sharing functions or farming-out all or part of day-to-day administration is a common option that is explored. Unfortunately, this can come at a price. Something that is done VAT-free, or relatively so, in-house may suddenly attract a tax charge:

- accounting and administration;
- the supply or sharing of staff;
- customer services and call-centres; and
- other back-office functions,

tend to be VATable and, if outsourced abroad, will still be subject to VAT under the reverse-charge.

For sectors that, typically, recover little input VAT, this is unwelcome, to say the least.

In **Chapter 7** there was commentary on the bench-mark case of *Sparekassernes Datacenter (SDC) v Skatteministeriet* (Case C-2/95) [1997] BVC 509 and a number of other important cases in this area. Most have involved the financial sector, rather than insurance. However, whilst the provisions in EU and UK VAT law that apply to each are undoubtedly different, it seems certainly arguable that many of the principles that have emerged could apply equally to both.

For example, whilst much of what is outsourced may have the outward appearance of something that is taxable in VAT terms, it will be important always to view things in context and decide exactly what it is that is being supplied *and to whom*. Many of the so-called *services* involved are often, in reality, functions in a much broader, single supply, to which the principles in *Card Protection Plan Ltd v C & E Commrs* (Case C-349/96) [1999] BVC 15 (see **Chapter 3** at 30-550) might apply. Looking at this *single* supply critically and applying the principles for assessing VAT liability described in this and other Chapters of this book, the conclusion might then be reasonably reached that what is being outsourced is, in reality, VAT-exempt.

(a) The Sparekassernes Datacenter benchmark tests

The details of the *Sparekassernes Datacenter* and other financial-sector cases are set out earlier so that repeating them here is unnecessary. However, because of the potentially wider application, it is useful, before looking at the specifically insurance-related cases, to summarise the general conclusions that appear to have emerged.

- *Sparekassernes Datacenter (SDC) v Skatteministeriet* (Case C-2/95) [1997] BVC 509 concerned an association registered for Danish VAT. Most of its members were savings banks and it provided to its members, and to certain other customers connected to its data-handling network:
    - services relating to transfers;
    - advice on, and trade in, securities; and
    - management of deposits, purchase contracts and loans.

SDC also offered services relating to its members' administrative affairs.

Before 1993 SDC provided the banks with services performed wholly or partly by electronic means. Those supplies of services were analogous to those, which the biggest financial institutions carry out themselves using their own data-handling centres. A typical

SDC supply was described by the Danish court as consisting of a number of components, which, added together, made up the service, which a bank, or its customers, wished to have performed. A price was quoted for each service component appearing in SDC's products catalogue, but SDC did not receive this from the customers but from the banks.

The services were performed only at the request of a bank, a customer or other persons authorised, under a contract with the customer, to require transactions such as payments to be effected. A customer could give information to SDC only after having been authorised to do so by a bank, in particular by the issue of a payment or credit card. SDC's name was not used vis-à-vis customers and SDC had not undertaken any legal obligation in regard to them. The documentation produced by SDC was sent out in the name of the bank.

In 1993, that is to say after the main proceedings had been initiated, most of SDC's activities and assets were transferred to newly formed companies, which, at the time of the hearing, were controlled by SDC's members. One of those companies performed all the services in question. For organisational reasons, that company invoiced SDC, which in turn invoiced its members.

Initially, the Danish Authorities took the view that the services were exempt. However, in February 1992, the Danish VAT Tribunal decided otherwise and after an appeal to a higher court in Denmark, questions were referred to the ECJ for a preliminary ruling. This produced the answer that what SDC had been providing was, indeed, VAT-exempt.

Briefly, what the Court seemed to be saying (para. 66 of its judgment) was that, to be exempt:

(1)   The services of the data-handling centre had, viewed broadly, to form a distinct whole, fulfilling in effect the specific, essential functions of a service described in that part of what is now art. 135(1)(d) of Council Directive 2006/112/EC (art. 13(B)(d)(3) of the Sixth Directive).

(2)   Accordingly, they had to have the effect of:
  (a)   transferring funds; and
  (b)   entailing changes *in the legal and financial situation* of the parties to the underlying transaction.

(3)   Such a situation was to be distinguished from a *mere physical or technical supply*, such as data-handling.

(4)   To reach a conclusion in a particular case, it was important to look at the facts and responsibilities undertaken to see whether what was provided was just mechanical or if it extended to the specific, essential aspects of the underlying transactions.

As the Court put it in para. 68 of its judgment:

'In view of all foregoing considerations the reply to be given to the first and fourth questions concerning point (3) of art. 13(B)(d) of the sixth directive (art 135(1)(d)). must be that this provision is to be interpreted as meaning that transactions concerning transfers and [p. 533] payments include operations carried out by a data-handling centre if those operations are distinct in character and are specific to, and essential for, the exempt transactions.'

> **Practice point**
>
> Some crucial points to focus on appear to be to see how far what is done:
>
> - *entails making changes in the legal and financial situation* of the parties to the underlying transaction;
> - is specific to, and essential for, the exempt transactions; or
> - is a *mere mechanical or technical* supply, which is not *ancillary* to the main supply.

(b) The Skandia and Arthur Anderson cases on insurance

This raises a possible question, though, about a further potentially important judgment in the context of outsourcing, that of the *Skandia* case, which was delivered by the ECJ in March 2001.

- *Försäkringsaktiebolaget Skandia (publ)* (Case C-240/99) [2001] BVC 281, concerned an insurance company with a wholly-owned subsidiary, Livbolaget, which carried on the business of life assurance, particularly in the sector of capital insurance and insurance provision for old age. Skandia and Livbolaget considered transferring Livbolaget's staff and operations to Skandia so that, in effect, Skandia would be conducting all Livbolaget's business, whether this consisted of the sale of insurance, the settlement of claims, the calculation of actuarial forecasts or capital management. In return, Skandia would receive remuneration from Livbolaget at market rates. Skandia would assume no liability in respect of those insurance activities. All risks would devolve wholly upon Livbolaget, preserving its status of insurer for the purposes of Swedish civil law.

The Reference asked whether an insurance company's commitment, of the kind which Skandia planned to assume, to run the business of a wholly-owned subsidiary constituted an insurance transaction or insurance transactions within the meaning of art. 135(1)(a) of Council Directive 2006/112/EC (art. 13(B)(a) of the Sixth VAT Directive).

The answer, was not altogether surprising. The Court ultimately held that what was provided did not constitute an *insurance transaction* within the meaning of art. 13(B)(a) of the Sixth VAT Directive (art. 135(1)(a)). However, interestingly, the Court went on to remark that the fact that art. 13(B)(a) of the Sixth VAT Directive (art. 135(1)(a)) mentions transactions other than insurance transactions, *namely related services performed by insurance brokers and insurance agents*, supported the conclusion it had reached.

But this last point begs the question as to why Skandia had previously conceded that its services to Livbolaget were not the services of an insurance intermediary and had not seen to it that the Court was also asked whether the services it provided to its subsidiary were exempt under that alternative head. It is likely that underwriting managers, for example, would still be exempt on that account. One can see, perhaps, some limitation of the exemption, to the extent possibly of things like the preparation of the statutory accounts. But, overall, it is hard to see that Skandia can have acted otherwise than as an *insurance intermediary*, in the context of which *Sparekassernes Datacenter* would arguably be much more in point.

One reason why the concession had been made and the question had not been put to the Court may have been that Skandia was not permitted under the Swedish regulatory rules to act as an insurance intermediary. However, as cases like *Card Protection Plan* ((Case C-349/96) ECJ [1999] BVC 155) have shown, a Member State may not restrict the scope of the exemption for insurance transactions exclusively to supplies by insurers who are authorised by national law to pursue that activity.

The *Skandia* case has been followed by the *Arthur Andersen* case, also involving a reference to the ECJ.

- *Staatssecretaris van Financiën v Arthur Andersen & Co. Accountants c.s.* (Case C-472/03) [2006] BVC 228 concerned a firm of accountants, which included a private company established under Netherlands law called Andersen Consulting Management Consultants (ACMC). ACMC and a Dutch life assurance company, Universal Leven N (UL), entered into a collaboration agreement, under which ACMC was to perform for UL various *back office* activities. ACMC, in turn, delegated those activities to one of its divisions.

These *back office* activities consisted of:

- accepting applications for insurance;
- handling amendments to contracts and premiums;
- issuing, managing and rescinding policies;
- managing claims;
- setting and paying commission to insurance agents;
- organising and managing information technology;
- supplying information to UL and to insurance agents; and
- drafting reports for insured and third parties.

When the information supplied by an applicant for insurance showed that a medical examination was necessary, the decision as to whether to accept the risk was made by UL, but, otherwise, any decision was made by ACMC and bound UL. ACMC was in charge of almost all contact with the insurance agents.

Arthur Andersen had initially charged VAT, but subsequently claimed reimbursement on the basis that the services it provided for UL were exempt as *services related to insurance transactions performed by an insurance agent* within art. 13(B)(a) of the Sixth Directive. The Court, however, disagreed.

The Intermediaries Directive definitions do not, as claimed by Arthur Andersen, determine the status of a business as insurance agent or broker for the purposes of the VAT exemption. The Court also found, in relation to insurance brokers or agents, that:

- the essential characteristic of brokers is their complete freedom as to choice of insurer for their clients;
- the essential characteristic of agents is that, although they may be tied to one or more insurers, their role is to find and introduce prospective customers; and
- an insurance agent or broker must not be carrying out only subcontracted activities on the insurer's behalf and which the insurer would normally perform for itself. It must be carrying out the independent function of bringing the parties to the insurance or reinsurance contract together.

The Court also held that, as Advocate General Poiares Maduro pointed out in his Opinion, it cannot be inferred from that case-law that the existence of a power to render the insurer liable is the determining criterion for recognition of an insurance agent within the meaning of art. 13B(a) of the Sixth Directive. Recognition of a person as *an insurance agent* pre-supposes an examination of what the activities in question comprise.

(c) The Century Life appeal

The *Century Life* appeal, *C & E Commrs v Century Life plc* [2001] BVC 116, also concerned outsourcing in this case on the review of personal pension policies, but was decided in favour of the taxpayer. The *Century Life* decision is considered earlier at 90-100.

(d) The end-result?

In a sense, perhaps, the ruling of the ECJ in the *Arthur Andersen* case has gone against the trend of similar cases relating to intermediary services for finance, such as *Sparekassernes Datacenter (SDC) v Skatteministeriet* (Case C-2/95) [1997] BVC 509 and *C & E Commrs v FDR Ltd* [2000] BVC 311 (see earlier in **Chapter 7** at 70-500).

It is clear from those cases that a mere technical or administrative function cannot qualify for the exemption for financial services in what was art. 13(B)(d) (art. 135(1)(b) to (g) of Council Directive 2006/112/EC). However, the role of ACMC did seem to extend to actions that had the effect of making changes of a legal and financial character in the relationship between the insurer and the insured. The wording of the insurance exemptions is, of course, different from that on finance.

Insurance, though, is essentially part of the wider financial sector and this raises, perhaps, a question of whether the ruling is entirely in accordance with the neutrality principle enshrined in the Directives, to the effect that, as observed by the Advocate General in *JP Morgan Fleming Claverhouse Investment Trust plc, The Association of Investment Trust Companies v R & C Commrs* (Case C-363/05) [2010] BVC 337,

'(1) In a number of decisions it [the Court] has stated: "The principle of fiscal neutrality precludes … economic operators carrying on the same activities from being treated differently as far as the levying of VAT is concerned."'

Regard will need to be had to the proposals following from the recent EU review of finance and insurance services.

Article 2 of the draft proposed Directive provides, as part of a new art. 135a to Council Directive 2006/112/EC, that points (a) to (g) in art. 135(1) will be replaced by the following:

'(a) Insurance services; and …
(b) …; and
(c) Intermediation in insurance and financial services;'.

A new art. 135a will then qualify how the exemption in points (a) to (g) is to be applied and, in particular, provides that:

'(1) "Insurance services" shall mean commitments whereby a person is obliged, in return for payment of a premium, to provide in the event of materialisation of a significant risk, with a service as determined by the commitment.

and

(8) "Intermediation in insurance and financial services" shall mean related services distinct in character and specific to and essential for the conclusion, amendment or prolongation of an agreement whereby a person engages to supply one of the exempt main services listed in Article 135(1)(a) to (e).

(2) A related service distinct in character shall be regarded as the main service to which it relates, where it is specific to and essential for the transaction exempted under Article 135(1) (a) to (e).'

On the face of it, this offers some prospect of exemption being accepted on a reasonably wide front if one looks at the predominant nature of what is being supplied, applying the principles in *Card Protection Plan*. However, at the same time, it is noted that Regulations 22 and 23 of the draft Regulations, published on 13 July 2007, seem somewhat less helpful.

'(22) Insurance Company Administration services should not be covered by the exemption for insurances. Such services ensure inter alia that regulatory and other legal requirements for carrying out insurance business such as solvency requirements are complied with. Although they are essential, they are not specific to the transactions of supplying exempt insurance services. In fact, many business sectors operate in a legal and regulatory environment of rules they must respect. These rules may be essential and specific to the type of business carried out and even a pre-condition for doing business in insurances but they are not specific to and essential for the supply of an exempt insurance service. The supply itself can be made without these administrative services. Other administrative services involving handling activities such as the acceptance of applications for insurance, the setting and paying of commission to insurance agents, the organisation and management of information technology, the supply of information and the drafting of reports for insured parties and third parties are also not specific to the supply of exempt insurance services and should therefore be excluded.

(23) Policy Administration consists of reviewing procedures, putting policyholders on risk, checking that sales procedures including regulatory requirements have been carried out, sending out of documentation to policyholder, record policy details in insurers systems and dealing with policyholder queries; such services should not be covered by the exemption for insurances. They are typically general administrative tasks and therefore not specific to and essential for the supply of exempt insurance services.'

although recital (4) to the draft Directive seems to make this less of a problem than might first appear in that it provides that:

'4 Related services which are distinct in character and specific to and essential for the exempt transactions are covered by the specific exemptions, resolving some of the problems which economic operators encounter when they outsource activities to independent persons or pool activities between operators to increase the efficiency of their investments. Services which are related to the management of investment funds do not benefit from an exemption because management services are themselves already related services and the services listed by the Directive as exempt management services, is exclusive. However, sub-contracting of these exclusive services is covered by the exemption.'

It will be interesting to see how things develop in the next few years and, in particular, if the proposals in the draft Directive and Regulations are modified.

It is also interesting that art. 4 of the draft proposed Directive provides for a new art. 137b, which would, potentially, seem to allow limited outsourcing to be provided VAT-free on a cross-border basis. As drafted, this reads:

'*Article 137b*

(1) Member States shall authorise independent groups of persons and exempt services supplied by such a group to members of the group where the following conditions are fulfilled:

   (a) The group itself and all its members are established or domiciled in a fiscal territory to which this Directive applies;
   (b) The group carries out an autonomous activity and acts as an independent entity towards its members;
   (c) Members of the group are carrying out an activity of supplying services which are exempt under Article 135(1) (a)-(f), or other services in respect of which they are not considered taxable persons or where the annual turnover of supplies of each member generating a right to deduct does not exceed 30% of the entire business activity of the member concerned;
   (d) The services are exclusively supplied by the group to members of the group and are necessary for members' capability of supplying services which are exempt in accordance with Article 135(1) (a)-(f);
   (e) The group claims only from its members the exact reimbursement of their share of the joint expenses; eventual mark-ups required for direct tax purposes are excluded from the calculation of expenses.
   (f) The exemption does not cause distortion of competition and is not used in conjunction with single taxable persons referred to in Article 11;

(2) Where one or more members of the group are established in another Member State than that granting the exemption for the group, this later Member State shall notify the fiscal administrations of the Member States, where these members of the group are established or domiciled.'

How useful this will prove in the light of the ruling in the *Taksatorringen* case remains to be seen.

- *Assurandør-Societetet (acting on behalf of Taksatorringen) v Skatteministeriet* (Case C-8/01) [2006] BVC 199 concerned an association whose members were small or medium-sized insurance companies authorised to underwrite motor-vehicle insurance policies in Denmark. The purpose of Taksatorringen was to assess damage and members paid according to an apportioned share of costs. One of the arguments was that the services provided were exempt under art. 13(A)(1)(f) of the Sixth Directive. However, the Court held this could not be applied if there was a genuine risk that the exemption might by itself, immediately or in the future, give rise to distortions of competition.

> **Practice point**
>
> Cutting costs by shedding staff and outsourcing can easily have the opposite effect by increasing irrecoverable input tax:
>
> - non-VATable employee costs can be replaced by a taxable supply of staff;
> - administration which would not be an issue were it carried out in-house, where it can be subsumed into an overall exempt activity, can become a taxable management service;
> - outsourcing abroad is also no solution because of the reverse-charge.
>
> Although, sometimes, it is possible to argue that what is outsourced is not taxable, but exempt, generally this can be hard to achieve:
>
> (1) What is supplied must be more than a *mere physical or technical supply* (para. 66 of the decision in *Sparekassernes Datacenter (SDC) v Skatteministeriet* (Case C-2/95) [1997] BVC 509).
>
> (2) The conditions for the exemption must be satisfied (see *Staatssecretaris van Financiën v Arthur Andersen & Co Accountants c.s.* (Case C-472/03) [2006] BVC 228).
>
> (3) What is outsourced must go far enough. In *Continuum/CSC* the conclusion seems to have been that the company's services to Sun Alliance did not do this as Continuum were not authorised to do anything more than provide information and process application forms. What it did not undertake were the formalities for issuing and transferring the securities, i.e. the units in the unit trust.
>
> (4) What is claimed as the exempt supply needs to be what is predominantly supplied as part of a single supply and not *incidental* or *ancillary* (see *Card Protection Plan Ltd v C & E Commrs* [2001] BVC 158).
>
> In short, outsourcing more, rather than less, may well make it easier to achieve the desired result. It is important that the factors that are at the heart of the exemption remain an essential part of the service bought-in. But equally important will be how what is outsourced is approached and, in particular, is described in any agreements or contracts. Referring to underlying cost-components (such as data processing and staff) as if they were services in their own right invites difficulties.

(e) Sales and call-centres

Sales and call-centres are a particular problem area because they are often seen just as communications, information and customer relations; not as something integral to a larger activity. As such, they have the appearance of being taxable when supplied by a third-party provider. Whilst that can certainly be true, it is always worth looking at the supply in context and seeing if, taken as a whole, the tests in *Sparekassernes Data Center* and *Lloyds TSB* enable the apparent *taxable* elements to be treated as *ancillary* to something that might arguably fall within one or other of the VAT exemptions.

There have been a number of useful cases in this area, including, in particular:

- *Electronic Data Systems Ltd* [2003] BVC 451, which involved a dedicated call-centre for the loan operations of a bank, and

- *Continuum (Europe) Ltd* [1998] BVC 2,131 (or *CSC Financial Services Ltd*, as it later came to be known), where services were provided to the Sun Alliance group in connection with the issue of its Daisy PEP.

These are considered in **Chapter 7** at 70-500.

More especially, in relation to insurance:

- *Teletech UK Ltd* [2003] BVC 2,514 concerned fees received for insurance sold by *cold-call* telephone and, in particular, whether they were exempt (under art. 13(b)(a) of EC Sixth Directive and VATA 1994, Sch. 9, Grp. 2, item 4) as the *services of an insurance agent* relative to provision of insurance (as Teletech maintained) or were taxable as promotion. Teletech did work for a number of companies, amongst which was American Life Insurance Company (ALICO). Its staff *cold-called* individuals by telephone to try to sell them two types of insurance policies. Once a customer was persuaded and a Direct Debit Authorisation obtained, ALICO were immediately on risk, with no input, at that stage on their part. This was subject, of course, to the usual 30-day cooling-off period and the like. The way Teletech was remunerated was somewhat unusual in that, after being paid start-up costs, they got a fixed sum per employee, each of whom were expected to sell half of one policy per hour.
HMRC argued exemption was prevented by Note (7) to exemption Grp 2 (as advertising and promotional services), but this was rejected by the Tribunal as semantics. The Tribunal also rejected the suggestion that Teletech were not proper insurance agents because of the way they were paid. Teletech rightly won because the substance of what they did amounted to the provision of insurance-related services in the capacity of an agent or broker. *Sparekassernes Datacenter* does not appear to have been mentioned as HMRC's case was clearly flawed. However, the similarities with *Lloyds TSB* and *EDS* seem obvious.
- In *Morganash Ltd* [2007] BVC 2,184 the Tribunal found that a service supplied to life insurance companies of carrying out telephone interviews of persons who have submitted life insurance cover proposals, as to their medical history and condition is not exempt under European law but is exempt under the corresponding provisions in UK law.
The interviews lasted between 20 and 40 minutes and were conducted by qualified nurses, with a written report being given to the life insurance company. Morganash made no recommendation as to whether the proposal should be accepted or declined as an insurance-related service carried out by an insurance agent and a service with sufficient nexus to the contract of insurance provided by the insurer. The case, interestingly, was heard after the *Arthur Andersen* decision. However, although the decision was not appealed and was accepted for the time being, the benefit of what the Tribunal concluded may well not be available indefinitely.

> *Practice point*
>
> Not all outsourced marketing will be able to be brought within the exemption.
>
> At the end of the day, it all comes down to what is actually being done and how.
>
> To achieve exemption, under Grp. 2 for insurance or Grp. 5 for finance, it is important that what is done is sufficiently integral to the underlying exempt activity. The danger is that often what is done will not go quite far enough.

Summary

This Chapter has considered what is involved with insurance and re-insurance transactions and the different implications for insurers, for Members of Lloyds and for brokers and other intermediaries.

The Chapter also considers the potential implications for outsourcing, an increasingly important issue in the present economic climate.

As insurance is also very much tied up with finance and other forms of investment, reference should also be made to the commentaries in Chapters 7 and 8.

10 Commodity Derivatives and Financial Derivatives

> **Overview**
>
> This Chapter considers:
>
> (1) The nature of the different contracts for physical commodities.
>
> (2) What is involved in similar contracts for financial products and derivatives.
>
> (3) The application of EU and UK law to:
>
>   (a) spot, futures, forward and options contracts for physical commodities;
>   (b) the special *Black Box* arrangements for UK terminal markets;
>   (c) the corresponding treatment for financial futures and derivatives; and
>   (d) the implications of both for brokers.
>
> (4) The new EU rules on the place of supply of electricity and gas.

100-000 What is involved?

A derivative is :

(a) the sale of a promise solely to deliver a commodity at a date in the future for an agreed price, i.e. a forward contract;. This is a commodity derivative;

(b) the sale of a promise either to deliver a commodity or to pay its value in the future for an agreed price, i.e. a futures contract. This may be either a commodity derivative or a financial derivative;

(c) the sale of a promise solely to pay at a future date a sum of money, calculated by reference to a fixed amount (K) and a variable amount (ST), i.e. a contract for differences. This is a financial derivative.

The subject-matter of a contract may be physically deliverable or not capable of physical delivery (a non-deliverable). In the case of a financial derivative the subject-matter of the contract is (K – ST), the sum of money represented by ST being calculated by reference to changes in the underlying measure of value or payment.

The underlying means the subject-matter by reference to which the amounts payable under the contract are calculated. A derivative is thus a contract which is to be performed at a future date whose value depends upon (derives from) the value of an underlying subject-matter whose value fluctuates between the date of the contract and the date of its performance. Derivatives are always at one remove from their underlying subject-matter. The underlying may be deliverable (aviation fuel, wheat, electricity supplies, foreign currency, shares) or non-deliverable (interest rates, the return on an index). Where the underlying subject-matter is deliverable, the parties may intend that the contract should run to delivery or that it should be cash-settled.

Forwards are expected to run to delivery (e.g. an airline which bases ticket prices on the futre cost of aviation fuel, and buys aviation fuel forward both to fix costs and to have fuel for its airliners). Even in these cases, however, the contract can be settled for cash, by closing out the contract, i.e. entering into an equal and opposite contract. This will happen if the airline decides it has over-estimated its future requirements for aviation fuel, or the price has moved in such a way as to make the contract uneconomic.

Thus all commodity derivatives are potentially financial derivatives.

The VAT issue is which derivatives to treat as financial instruments and which to treat as commodity derivatives, whether to regard all derivatives as contracts for differences or whether to focus on the underlying. This gives rise to three groups:

(1) contracts where the underlying is capable of physical delivery and the parties intend the contract to be completed by delivery;

(2) contracts where the underlying is not capable of delivery or the parties intend the contract to be cash-settled;

(3) contracts where there is a physical deliverable and the contract may either run ot delivery or be cash-settled.

Group (1) is for VAT purposes a supply of the underlying subject-matter. Group (2) is purely a financial transaction. The problem is whether to assimilate Group (3) to (1) or (2). The answer depends upon: (a) the expectations of the parties; and (b) whether or not the derivative is in its nature purely a financial transaction. The broad principles are:

(a) if a contract can be completed by delivery of the underlying, and the parties intend or contemplate that the contract will be so performed, the nature of the VAT treatment depends upon the nature of the underlying which is to be supplied. The contract is a commodity derivative or treated as such.

(b) in all other cases it is a financial derivative and so exempt or outside the scope.

Supplies of power are regarded as supplies of goods, and so assimilated to commodity forwards: VATA 1994, Sch. 4, para. 3.

Unlike the case of direct taxes, there is minimal VAT legislation dealing specifically with derivatives. The accounting rules which play such a large role for direct tax purposes have no importance for VAT purposes. The reason is simple. Under a cash-settled derivaitive A agrees to pay B $(K - ST)$ if at the date of maturity ($K > ST$), in consideration of B's promise to pay A $(ST - K)$ if at the date of maturity $ST > K$. Money is consideration for a supply, but not a supply in itself. VAT only becomes applicable if a contract can only or might be performed by the delivery of the underlying, and the supply of the underlying in a non-derivative contract would give rise to a charge to VAT.

In practice this gives rise to four possible VAT treatments:

- Such transactions are outside the scope of VAT
- Such transactions are exempt financial services
- Such contracts are contracts for the supply of the underlying goods or services
- Such contracts are zero-rated on pragmatic grounds if made in the UK.

Commodity derivatives are derivatives of commodities traded in commodity markets. 'Terminal market' is defined as 'a commodity market in a place such as London'. A commodity is defined as 'a raw material such as grain, coffee, metal or oil' that is traded on a commodity market. The word 'terminal' in this connection simply means that the market deals in contracts run to a fixed future date, i.e. have a terminal.

The only specific UK legislation dealing with commodity derivativesis the *Value Added Tax (Terminal Markets) Order* 1973, SI 1973/173. Remarkably (considering the changes which have occurred since 1973) it is also the oldest UK VAT legislation which is still in force. This is supplemented by:

- VAT Notice 701/9 Commodities and Terminal Markets
- VAT Notice 701/49 Finance
- VAT Notice 702/1 Gold.

The common system of EU and UK VAT has undergone fundamental transformation since 1973. In 1977, when the Sixth VAT Directive was introduced, derivatives markets scarcely existed outside commodity and foreign exchange trading. The almost complete absence of EU law had left national law to go its own way. The limited scope of UK law has left practice king. In practice, the VAT treatment of derivatives has been loosely assimilated to that of other financial services, while commodity derivatives have been largely zero-rated. Compared with the other areas dealt with in this book, the VAT-treatment of derivatives is largely law-free.

The one major case in this area is *First National Bank of Chicago v C & E Commrs (Case C-172/96)* [1998] BVC 389. This illustrated many of the difficulties in this area. The bank exchanged foreign currency for its customers. No commission was charged, but the bank was remunerated by the spread between the bid and offer prices for the currencies in which it dealt. The bank was registered for VAT. The bank was able to recover input tax incurred in respect of exempt supplies to non-EC customers. It had a special partial exemption method, the rate of recovery for input tax between the number of transactions with non-EC customers divided by the total number of transactions. HMRC excluded foreign exchange transactions from the calculation, on the grounds that these were solely money contracts which did not constitute a supply for VAT purposes. The ECJ held that the bank was making a supply of services for consideration, namely the spread. There did not need to be a specific charge for each transaction to constitute consideration. A global link between the amount received and the transactions as a whole over a period was sufficient to make the transactions into a supply. As the Court said at para. 47:

> 'So, the consideration, that is to say the amount which the bank can actually apply to its own use, must be regarded as consisting of the net result of the transactions over a given period of time.'

Accordingly the foreign exchange transactions should enter into the partial exemption calculation.

Derivatives are over the counter (OTC, i.e. bespoke contracts) or exchange-traded in the form of standardised contracts. Exchange traded contracts can only be settled in cash, and the solvency risk of parties is reduced by making the exchange a party to each contract.

The scheme of the legislation, as expanded by the VAT Notices, is as follows:

(1) The 1973 Order applies to the commodity markets listed in art. 2: London Metal Exchange, London Rubber Market, London Cocoa Terminal Market, London Coffee Terminal Market, International Petroleum Exchange of London etc.

(2) The 1973 Order only applies to contracts intended to be performed by delivery. It does not apply to cash-settled transactions.

(3) Dealings between members of the enumerated commodity markets and their agents, whether in futures, options or actuals, and whether or not leading to delivery.

(4) There are special rules for gold.

(5) OTC trades in commodities are taxable, including fuures and whether or not leading to delivery.

(6) Supplies in relation to commodity derivatives by agents and other intermediaries to principals are zero-rated.

(7) Foreign exchange transactions are exempt supplies.

(8) Dealings in cash-settled financial derivatives and derivatives which have no physical deliverable are exempt.

(9) Where as financial derivatives relates to a deliverable security, the supply of the derivative will be exempt.

This Chapter is concerned mainly with the position of brokers and others dealing in financial futures and derivatives, often directly or indirectly through one or more of the commodity or terminal markets. Even with products not based on financial instruments, many of the contracts entered into are still outwardly *financial*. Some contracts will be entered into with a view to delivery of the underlying subject matter, e.g. an airline which buys aviation fuel forward. Many will be undertaken as a financial hedge (to guard against movements in price, for example) rather than with any intention to acquire the underlying commodity. Others will be undertaken purely for speculative purposes. However, it is in the nature of derivative contracts that they can be closed out at any time for cash. Hence the purpose for which a contract is entered into is likely to change during the term of the contract, and does not provide any guidance on the financial outcome.

Derivatives accordingly have two aspects from the point of view of VAT. On one hand, all derivatives are financial instruments, i.e. promises to pay a sum of money in the future by reference to the difference between two sums of money, i.e. a contract for differences. . In that regard they are exempt or outside the scope of VAT. Many derivatives are also promises to supply goods, such as oil, wheat or copper. The contract reference point will often be tangible, in other words, one of the hard or soft commodities or, increasingly, something like electricity or gas. To that extent, the normal rules for VAT exemption described elsewhere in this book may clearly not apply. There are, though, exceptions. Sometimes contracts can only be cash-settled or are based on indices and, more importantly, they are for financial futures and options, for which rules similar to those described in **Chapters** 7 and **8** can operate. There are also contracts for environmental products, such as emissions allowances. Moreover, all contracts relating to commodies can be cash-settled.

Derivatives are conventionally classified for VAT purposes as:

(1) commodity derivatives (supply of goods); and

(2) financial derivatives (exempt supply of services)

How a given supply is to be dealt with will depend on a variety of factors, for example:

- what the subject matter/reference point of the contract is;
- whether the supply is regarded as goods or services;
- whether delivery occurs, and if so where;
- the intention of the parties;
- to what extent the parties involved are members of a relevant commodity exchange;
- in the case of a broker or intermediary, in what capacity he acts; and, on occasions
- where the buyer or seller *belongs* and how they are in business; and possibly
- whether, following the decision in *Willis Pension Trustees Ltd* [2006] BVC 2,045, someone effecting a hedge is doing so as an *economic activity* (see earlier in **Chapter 1** at 10-300 and **Chapter 3** at 30-000).

Increasingly, it is also now important to look at how the VAT rules in other Member States apply.

100-050 The commodities, products and markets

In theory, almost any commodity or product can be dealt in on a terminal market or exchange, provided it is possible to fix an acceptable standard quality and specification, and provided, also, there are sufficient buyers and sellers. In practice, however, certain commodities, such as tin, are unsuitable and others may be traded for short periods of time or only in certain locations. Commodities and derivatives may be traded over the counter, i.e. on a bespoke basis, or more commonly through an exchange, which provides a clearing process, requires the payment of margin and provides protection against counterpary insolvency.

(1) The products

As a broad indication, and especially for the purposes of this Chapter, trades in:

- *hard commodities* will mean largely metals and will include: aluminium, nickel, copper, tin, lead, zinc, and also precious metals such as gold, silver and platinum;
- *soft commodities* will often involve foodstuffs, and will include: cocoa, sugar, coffee, potatoes, pig meat, barley and wheat, soybean meal, vegetable oil, rubber (including synthetic rubber) and oil;

- *intangibles* will be mainly financial futures and options and will include: interest rates, foreign currencies, securities (especially UK and other Government stocks) and forward freight agreements and other contracts based on indices such as those produced by the Baltic Exchange.

There are also now markets in energy and related products, such as electricity and gas and emissions, i.e permits to emit CO_2 and other green house gases.

(2) The markets

The main UK markets in which these contracts will be traded will be those operating in London, such as:

(1) The London Metal Exchange, LME, the world's premier non-ferrous metals market, offering futures and options contracts for aluminium, copper, tin, nickel, zinc and lead plus two regional aluminium alloy contracts.

(2) EDX London, formed in 2003 to combine the strength and liquidity of the London Stock Exchange with the advanced derivatives technology of OMHEX. More than 150 contracts are offered, including standardised and flexible futures and options contracts on indices and single stocks, with trading services on three linked derivatives exchanges in Stockholm, Copenhagen and Oslo.

(3) IntercontinentalExchange, ICE, operates the leading global, electronic marketplace for trading both futures and OTC energy contracts and the leading soft commodities exchange. In June 2001, it acquired the IPE, subsequently renamed ICE Futures. ICE offers trades in contracts based on crude oil and refined products, natural gas, power and emissions, as well as soft commodities including cocoa, coffee, cotton, ethanol, orange juice, wood pulp and sugar, as well as currency, index futures and options.

(4) Euronext.liffe, formed in January 2002 by the takeover by Euronext of the London International Financial Futures and Options Exchange, LIFFE. As well as the traditional financial futures, options and derivatives traded on LIFFE, contracts on offer include cocoa, coffee, sugar, corn, wheat and rapeseed oil. Euronext.liffe also owns the exchanges of Euronext (Amsterdam, Brussels, Lisbon and Paris).

Outside the UK, the main centres of interest will include:

(1) Eurex, a major futures and options exchange jointly operated by Deutsche Börse AG and SWX Swiss Exchange and offering a broad range of financial derivatives and an electronic trading and clearing platform.

(2) Chicago Board of Trade, CBOT, the world's oldest futures and options exchange. It merged in July 2007 with the Chicago Mercantile Exchange, CME, which trades several types of financial instruments: interest rates, equities, currencies, and commodities. It also offers trading in exotic instruments such as weather and real estate derivatives.

(3) The New York Mercantile Exchange, NYMEX, is the world's largest physical commodity futures exchange.

(4) The Multi Commodity Exchange, MCX, is an independent commodity exchange based in India established in 2003 and offering futures trading in agricultural commodities,

bullion, ferrous and non-ferrous metals, pulses, oils and oilseeds, energy, plantations, spices and other soft commodities.

100-100 The parties and the capacities in which they act

Commodity transactions are undertaken by a wide range of different people for a number of different reasons. How and why they go about this, and the capacities in which they act, can have material bearing on their ultimate VAT position.

(1) Market members

Market members will generally be involved as brokers but can also, in some cases, be market-makers, dealers, primary producers or manufacturers/end users.

(a) Brokers

How brokers transact their business can depend partly on the rules of the particular exchange concerned and partly on their own circumstances and terms of trade.

(1) A number of exchanges, the LME and LIFFE for example, specify that contracts are on a principal-to-principal basis. This is done largely for reasons associated with the clearing function and the guarantees and assurances necessary for market stability. Any *brokerage* or *commission* thus, strictly speaking, forms part of the price; it is not itself consideration for any service, as such. Trading on behalf of clients will be on a *back-to-back* basis.

(2) Where the market does not have this stipulation, the broker's own particular terms of trade will decide the issue, so that the service provided may simply be one of agency as represented by the commission.

Historically, this distinction between agency and principals trading has been somewhat blurred. Conceptually and legally, the relationship between broker and client has often been seen as a mixture of both.

(b) Clearing members

Both exchange and over-the-counter trades can be subject to a clearing process, either through the exchange itself or via an organisation such as LCH.Clearnet, a group formed following the merger of the London Clearing House and Clearnet SA in 2003.

Briefly, clearing works by a central counterparty, the clearing house, acting as a go-between between two parties to a trade. Any monetary risk involved is borne by the clearing-house, as guarantor. The way this is achieved is that, once the trade is registered with the clearing-house, the clearing-house itself becomes a party to that trade by interposing itself between the buying and selling members by a legal process known as *novation* or *open offer*.

Central to this process is the requirement that the clearing member acts as a principal rather than in an agency capacity. The clearing-house has risk management protection against the default of a clearing member by the collection of an initial margin and daily variation margins.

(c) Market-makers and dealers

In addition to acting as brokers, intermediaries or clearers, members may also take a position in a particular commodity or be market-makers.

(2) Non-market member brokers

Often the position of brokers who are not market members (and the type of contract adopted) will mirror that of the market members through whom they deal. Unlike market members, however, they will not be bound by the rules of the relevant exchange and will have more flexibility as to whether they deal as principals or as agents.

(3) Clients

The range of clients involved in commodity transactions can vary enormously. At one end of the scale, there will be the primary producers, manufacturers or end-users:

- some will wish to secure the delivery or sale of the commodity with which they are concerned;
- others will be aiming to safeguard their businesses against undue fluctuations in price.

At the other end, there will be investors and speculators, some of whom will be individuals but all of whom are important to the operation of the terminal markets in providing liquidity and volume.

It is possible, following the decision in *Willis Pension Trustees Ltd* [2006] BVC 2,045, that a client taking part in a commodity transaction, especially a hedge involving a financial product like an interest rate swap, may not be regarded as doing so as an *economic activity* for VAT (see earlier in **Chapters 1** and **3**).

100-150 The contracts and their place of supply

In terms of their basic VAT liabilities:

- contracts based on tangible commodities, including electricity and gas, will be essentially taxable (except where they are purely cash-settled contracts);
- contracts for intangibles, such as currency, securities, interest rate swaps and other contracts for differences will be basically exempt; and
- contracts for other intangibles, such as CO_2 emissions allowances and renewables obligations certificates will be basically taxable and regarded as within VATA 1994, Sch. 4A (art. 59 of Council Directive 2006/112/EC) but will be exempt if purely cash-settled.

Certain of the contracts in either case, are regarded as *financial*, something which, as will be seen later, will potentially affect both the place of supply and the ability to recover underlying input tax.

In the case of tangible commodities, a distinction may also need to be drawn between whether a commodity is *allocated* (which may include ascertained or unascertained goods) or *unallocated*. This distinction is important as it can determine whether a particular supply is to be treated under the rules for goods or under the rules for services. The terms 'fungible' (allocated) and 'non-fungible' (unallocated) may also be used.

(1) Allocated goods

Contracts for allocated goods are contracts that anticipate the delivery of specific goods, immediately or at a future date and are treated for VAT purposes under the rules appropriate to supplies of goods. Futures contracts on a recognised commodity exchange involve sales of *unascertained goods* within the *Sale of Goods Act* 1979. Although no property passes until maturity, the goods are ascertained or identified when that occurs, which is sufficient to bring futures contracts within the general heading of *allocated goods*. Whether or not a supply of *allocated goods* is subject to VAT or not (i.e. is *outside the scope*) thus depends, as on where the goods are physically located rather than where the contract is made or the supplier *belongs*.

The concept of the supply of *allocated goods* comes within art. 14(1) of Council Directive 2006/112/EC:

'"Supply of goods" shall mean the transfer of the right to dispose of tangible property as owner.'

and VATA 1994, Sch. 4, para. 1(1):

'Any transfer of the whole property in goods is a supply of goods; ...'

(2) Unallocated or unascertained goods

Contracts for hard and soft commodities may also be *unallocated* (or unascertained). This means that, whilst the buyer acquires title, a right to a given quantity of goods, he does not acquire title to those goods as such, since the actual goods are not identified. In the case of unallocated goods, they remain as an unidentified part of a larger stock held by the supplier. Until delivery, the seller has a certain amount of freedom to deal in the goods and the buyer's title is merely recorded as a series of book entries.

In the VAT Act, this idea of goods being unallocated is expressed in terms of an undivided share (VATA 1994, Sch. 4, para. 1(1)(a)) and a supply of services. In Directive terms the corresponding provision is art. 24(1).

In the *Sale of Goods Act* 1979, the corresponding reference to unascertained goods, whilst clearly embracing unallocated goods in this sense, is not necessarily always going to be synonymous. Under that Act, the buyer of unascertained goods will not acquire title until they are ascertained. But the term can be used to cover goods, which, at the point of contract, may not exist, but which, in the case of a forward or futures sale, for example, will exist and will be ascertained at the point of delivery. Forward and futures contracts are discussed later at (3) (b) and (c).

This concept of an *undivided share* presupposes that the whole property of which it is part can be determined. For VAT purposes, the supply is, as noted, of services and not goods (VATA 1994, Sch. 4, para. 1(1)(a) and art. 14 of Council Directive 2006/112/EC). The place of supply rules are thus different from those for physicals or futures. The treatment tends to depend:

- more on the identity of the supplier and recipient and where both *belong*;
- than the nature or location of the commodity itself.

In some cases, the supply will be seen as a financial service within what is now VATA 1994, Sch. 4A, para. 16 (art. 59 of Council Directive 2006/112/EC). This applies particularly to precious metals such as gold, silver, platinum and palladium, a list extended from 1 December 1994 to include rhodium, ruthenium, osmium, and iridium (HMRC *Business Brief* 20/94).

The place of supply of services depends upon (a) the location of the supplier, (b) the type of services supplied, (c) the location of the customer, and (d) whether the customer receives the supply in a business or non-business capacity.

For these purposes customers are divided into three categories (art. 44–45, 49 of Council Directive 2006/112/EC):

(a) a taxable person, i.e. a person carrying on a business (whether in the UK, another Member State or anywhere in the world);
(b) an EU resident non-taxable person, i.e. a person not registered for VAT, who is established or resident in the EU;
(c) a non-EU non-taxable person, i.e. a person not carrying on a business, who is established or resident outside the EU.

In the case of a supply of services to a taxable person a supply of any type of service is made where the customer has established his business or has a fixed establishment ('supplied where received rule', art. 44 of Council Directive 2006/112/EC).

In the case of a supply of services to a non-taxable person, wherever established or resident, the general rule is that the place of supply is where the supplier is established or has a fixed establishment (art. 45 of Council Directive 2006/112/EC).

In the case of a supply of services of a particular description, including financial services ('supplied where received services') a special rule applies for supplies to non-EU non-taxable persons. A supply of these services to a non-taxable person established or resident outside the EU is made where that person is established or has his permanent address or usually resides art. 59 of Council Directive 2006/112/EC).

As a result of these rules art. 16 of the *Value Added Tax (Place of Supply of Services) Order 1992* (SI 1992/3121) financial services are treated as supplied where the recipient belongs (see **Chapter 3**) if the recipient:

'(a) belongs in a country, other than the Isle of Man, which is not a member State; or
(b) is a person who belongs in a member State, but in a country other than that in which the supplier belongs, and who–

   (i) receives the supply for the purpose of a business carried on by him;
   (ii) has been assigned a registration number by the member State in which he belongs; and
   (iii) is not treated as having himself supplied the services by virtue of section 78 of the Act [the reverse charge – see **Chapter 5**].'

Where the place of supply is outside the UK, the supply will be, strictly speaking, *outside the scope* of UK VAT. Related input VAT nonetheless remains recoverable as a result of the rules in reg. 103 of the *Value Added Tax Regulations* 1995 (SI 1995/2518).

For other unallocated contracts (in other commodities or, say, where the arrangement is not seen or undertaken as a financial hedge), the basic place of supply operates. The transaction will take place where the supplier belongs.

This distinction could be important for determining the liability, not only of the underlying commodity contract, but also that of any related brokerage or commissions.

To the extent that the supply is one of financial services, there are further implications if the supplier, but not the recipient, is based or *established* outside the UK. In this case, the imported services rules (see **Chapter 5**) will apply, causing tax to be potentially due under the reverse-charge rules in VATA 1994, s. 8. The net effect, however, should generally be nil as the associated input VAT will, in most instances, be fully recoverable as a result of the rules on direct attribution.

(3) The contracts themselves

The contracts fall into the following main categories:

- physicals/actuals;
- futures;
- forward contracts;
- options;
- swaps;
- contracts for differences;
- commodity loans; and
- contracts for brokerage.

There will also be other derivative contracts.

(a) Physicals/actuals

Physicals/actuals involve contracts for the purchase or sale of the actual commodity concerned. Contracts will often, but by no means necessarily, involve dealings on one or other of the commodity exchanges. They may either be *spot*, i.e. for immediate delivery, or *forward*, i.e. for delivery at some future date. Either way, the contract may call for immediate payment of the contract price and will generally relate to a specific, and often identified, quantity and grade.

Contracts may also specify the location of the goods and the place and time of delivery. In the case of hard and soft commodities dealt in on one or other of the exchanges, this will often be in approved warehouses or locations in the territory in which the exchange itself is situated.

Contracts involve supplies of goods so that the place of supply is determined, broadly, by their location (see **Chapter 3**).

A physicals contract will not necessarily be an investment within *Financial Services and Markets Act* 2000, Pt II, Sch. 2.

(b) Futures

Futures, even where they involve physical commodities, are investments within *Financial Services and Markets Act* 2000, Pt II, Sch. 2. They are a hedging or trading mechanism, with standardised contracts being traded on one or other of the markets or commodity exchanges. Contracts are for lots, i.e. standard quantities and grades of a particular commodity or financial instrument or product and are subject to the rules of the relevant exchange. They lock both buyers and sellers in to predetermined prices but the buyer does not obtain title unless and until delivery occurs, and they do not require payment of the full contract price at the outset. Instead, buyers are only required to pay margins or deposits:

- initially these tend to be between five per cent and ten per cent of the contract price;
- daily margin calls are then made during the currency of an open contract to cover losses in the price and to maintain the position.

Margin payments are made in respect of profits with the balance only being settled on the contract being *closed-out* or on maturity, when delivery takes place.

In the case of physical commodities, on the spot or maturity date, any sellers with *short* positions tender warrants via the appropriate commodity exchange to back the outstanding contracts, and which buyers with *long* positions are required to receive. There are similar delivery arrangements for securities and other financial contracts.

In practice, however, whilst nearly all contracts for hard and soft commodities, and those for some security-based futures, will expressly contemplate delivery, few in fact ever reach that stage. The vast majority are *closed-out* – a process by which the open positions are settled by entering into equal and opposite *bought* or *sold* contracts, which are netted-off in clearing. The fact that a contract may be closed-out does not, however, prevent the supply being regarded as one of goods.

Only at the maturity date, therefore, will actual goods (or securities) and their location be identified.

For any of the relevant commodity exchanges, the approved warehouses or other places of storage for physical commodities may be either inside or outside the country in which the exchange is located. Oil traded on the IPE/ICE, for example, will often be held in Rotterdam.

A futures contract will not, in itself, however, specify the place of delivery or supply. The matter is thus, to that extent, left open. Where this happens, it may, nonetheless, be possible for the parties to a contract to agree, as between themselves, where delivery would take place were the contract to run to maturity. Failing that, in practice, HMRC seem generally prepared to regard the location of the goods, in the case of physical commodities, and consequently the place of supply, as being in the same country as the exchange on which the futures contract is traded:

- if this is in the UK, a supply will be taxable;
- if it is abroad, the supply will be *outside the scope*.

(c) Forward contracts

Forward contracts have essentially the same aims as futures. They are a means of hedging or securing a particular price for an agreed quantity of a given commodity, product or derivative at a future date. The difference is that they are *over-the-counter* and are not subject to the rules of any exchange. As with futures, they will lock both buyers and sellers into pre-determined prices. However, whether payment of the full contract price is required at the outset is often a matter of agreement between the parties.

(1) Non cash-settled contracts may or may not involve sales of *unascertained goods* within the *Sale of Goods Act* 1979, s. 16, but are regarded as involving supplies of goods for VAT purposes. As noted earlier at (2), the fact that goods may be unascertained at the time a contract is made does not, ultimately, prevent the supply being one of the whole property in goods. Whether or not a supply is potentially subject to VAT or not (i.e. is *outside the scope*) thus depends, as in (1) earlier, on where the goods are physically located rather than where the contract is made or the supplier *belongs*.

(2) Cash-settled contracts, such as Forward Freight Agreements (FFAs) are basically VAT-exempt financial services, with the place of supply potentially depending on where the recipient *belongs*.

(d) Options

An option, in this context, is essentially the right to acquire either goods or a futures contract and can be an investment within the *Financial Services and Markets Act* 2000, Pt. II, Sch. 2. It may be either a straight or a traded option.

- *Straight options* – straight options need not involve a member of an exchange and are specific as between the buyer and seller. If the buyer wishes to dispose of the option, before maturity, the way this is done is usually by the grant of an option, which is equal and opposite.
- *Traded options* – traded options, on the other hand, are non-specific and may relate to the actual commodity or to futures contracts. They are dealt on the commodity exchanges and may be disposed of before maturity simply by sale.

An option may also fall into one of the following three further broad categories.

(1) *Call options*, which give the buyer the right to buy at a stated price at any time between the date of purchase and the expiry date.

(2) *Put options*, which give the buyer the right to sell at the stated price at any time between the date of purchase and the expiry date.

(3) *Double options*, which give the buyer the right either to buy or to sell.

Like futures, with which they are sometimes confused, options also provide a means of hedge against possible price fluctuations. They will not, however, lock the buyer into anything. A call option, for example, will not commit the purchaser to exercise it and buy. It will simply confer the right to buy a specified type and quantity of a commodity at a given future date. The buyer will pay a *premium* for the option, and can either hold and eventually exercise it or dispose of it at any time prior to maturity, or even allow it to lapse. All that is at risk, therefore, is the premium.

Options, being rights to acquire either the underlying commodity or futures contracts, are supplies of services. HMRC again regard the supply in the case of options as *financial* in nature. Within VATA 1994, Sch. 4A, para. 16(2)(e) (art. 59(e) of Council Directive 2006/112/EC), on the basis that they are used as a means of hedging price.

As a financial service, the treatment in terms of the place of supply follows the rules described earlier in *Unallocated goods*. It will only be deemed to take place in the UK if the recipient of the service *belongs* here or belongs in another Member State and is not VAT-registered (see **Chapter 3**).

Again, as with supplies of unallocated commodities, the imported services rules in VATA 1994, s. 8 will apply as the option is within Sch. 5, para. 5. Tax will need, strictly, to be accounted for in respect of all contracts for options involving deliverable tangible commodities, or for futures options contracts for deliverable tangible commodities, where the person making the supply, the broker perhaps, is established outside the UK. This could be an issue, for example, where the contract is one involving a traded option on one of the non-UK exchanges. Overall, however, the net end result should, in most cases, be a nil VAT cost, in that the rules in reg. 103 of the *Value Added Tax Regulations* 1995 should allow the associated input VAT to be recovered in full.

(e) Swaps

Commodity swaps can be either physical or financial:

- Physical swaps, as the term implies, are actual exchanges of a commodity and will involve reciprocal supplies by each of the parties to the other. Each party will account for its own supply within the whole transaction and will apply the treatment appropriate to that supply as discussed elsewhere in this Chapter.
- Price swaps are contracts for differences and are merely related to differences in price, say between a fixed and floating rate. Contracts for differences are discussed later at (f).

It can be important to distinguish between the two because the consequences in VAT terms are not the same.

It is possible that swaps which, in the context of this Chapter, involve securities or financial instruments may only be seen as a service by one of the parties to the transaction, following the decision in *Willis Pension Trustees Ltd* [2006] BVC 2,045.

(f) Contracts for differences

Contracts for differences are, in a sense, similar to physical swaps (see (e) above), but with the essential difference that they are always cash-settled. The contracts were initially purely hedging instruments but are now often used speculatively. Typically, they will involve a contract in which one party will *notionally* agree to supply a given quantity and quality of a given commodity at a future date and at a fixed price in return for the agreement of the other party to *notionally* supply the same quantity and quality of the same commodity at the same future date, but at the then market price. At the settlement date, the difference between the two prices is paid by one party to the other, depending on how the prices move in relative to each other over the duration of the contract. One party may also charge a fee to the other for agreeing to participate.

Being purely cash-settlement contracts, contracts for differences are essentially financial and VAT-exempt and fall within VATA 1994, Sch. 9, Grp. 5, item 1.

Following the decision in *Willis Pension Trustees Ltd* [2006] BVC 2,045, it may be necessary to consider whether the person using contract is doing so as an *economic activity* (see earlier in **Chapters 1** and **3**). However, in *Revenue & Customs Brief* 05/07, issued 26 January 2007 HMRC said that:

> 'The Willis Tribunal made reference in its decision to interest rate swaps. It suggested that, in its view, there would only be a supply when it was possible to identify the consideration being obtained by a party entering into the contract.
>
> There would appear to be nothing arising directly out of *Willis* that indicates a shortfall in HMRC's current approach to the VAT treatment of other financial instruments and it is, therefore, not intended to revise existing published policy. HMRC do, however, recognise that there may be particular circumstances where *Willis* principles could apply to transactions in other financial instrument transactions and HMRC would consider such cases on an individual basis.'

Forms of contracts for differences include, price swaps, currency swaps, Forward Freight Agreements and other contracts based on indices.

Like interest rate swaps (which are also a form of contract for differences – see **Chapter 7** at 70-200(29)), there seems to be no hard and fast rule as to how they are to be treated. Generally, however, a supply is recognised only when and to the extent that a settlement payment is received. Netting-off usually occurs when the money flows are denominated in the same currency. The ISDA standard documentation provides for netting, but this can be deleted if the parties agree. In practice, netting may be done on a portfolio basis, so that a single relatively small payment can represent settlement of a very large number of high-value transactions. It is arguable, therefore, that, where both parties have payment obligations (albeit they may, in practice, be netted-off) there will be supplies by each party to the contract. The value of the supply by each is then what each party is entitled to receive (ignoring netting).

For transaction-count Partial Exemption Special Methods (see **Chapter 4** at 40-200), the question of what is recognised as a transaction will depend upon the specific terms of the method agreed. Sometimes this can be based on the number of contracts entered into, with the recovery of input tax being dependent on the proportion that involve counterparties outside the EU. Clearly, it is potentially important in this respect whether it is accepted that the contract is a bilateral agreement with supplies being made by both parties in each period, rather than just by the party to whom a net settlement payment is made.

(g) Commodity loans

Commodity loans, like security loans discussed earlier in **Chapter 8** at 80-200(21), typically arise where someone, such as a manufacturer, is temporarily in need of a commodity *borrowing* from someone with sufficient stock. The terms of the loan will be for a specific quantity and quality of the commodity to be borrowed or lent and will be for a specific period and at a stated rate of interest. In some cases, however, the loans may simply amount to a financial arrangement with a client or customer.

Outwardly the appearance is similar to an advance of money within VATA 1994, Sch. 9, Grp. 5, item 2. However, as with securities lending, the effect is, generally, that the lender will make a disposal of the asset concerned, since the exact same goods will not be *paid back*. The *interest* is to that extent not itself strictly consideration for an advance but is part of the value of a much larger transaction. Similarly, the borrower will, on redemption, make a further supply of the goods.

With the lending of securities, the Tribunal in *Scottish Eastern Investment Trust Plc* [2001] BVC 4,058 (see earlier in **Chapter 8** at 80-200) concluded that there was only a supply by the lender to the borrower. However, this position is not taken in relation to tangible commodities. When outside the *Black Box* (see later at 100-200), VAT will tend to be due at the standard-rate, unless the goods are already outside the UK.

Commodity loans are a particular feature of the market in gold bullion and are discussed in detail later at 100-400(4).

(h) Brokers' or agency services

Brokerage or agency transactions (where the broker or agent is not dealing on a principal-to-principal basis) are also supplies of services for VAT purposes.

Where they involve contracts on a terminal market they are arguably always financial services, the underlying contracts and their arrangement being in the nature of *investments* and *regulated activities* within *Financial Services and Markets Act* 2000, s. 22 and Pt I and II of Sch. 2. This would, arguably, apply regardless of the underlying commodity. HMRC do not always seem to accept this, though, for futures brokerage involving physical commodities other than precious metals.

To the extent that the broker's services, as such, are accepted as financial services, the rules on the place of supply will, again, follow those for taxable financial services described in *Unallocated or unascertained goods* previously.

For other contracts, where this is not accepted, the position is likely to depend on the circumstances and nature of the underlying client transactions.

If these are essentially financial, because, say, they are undertaken as a hedge or are intended to be cash-settled, the brokerage will also, arguably, be financial. As a financial service, VATA 1994, Sch. 4A, para. 16(2)(e) applies (art. 59 of Council Directive 2006/112/EC) to determine the place of supply. Such supplies are treated as taking place where the recipient belongs (see **Chapter 3**).

In terms of relief for underlying input tax, in the case of essentially taxable brokerage, this follows, where the place of supply is outside the UK, from the rules in reg. 103 of the *Value Added Tax Regulations* 1995 (SI 1995/2518). Where the brokerage is essentially VAT-exempt, there is a specific, but limited relief for input VAT for certain supplies involving transactions with persons outside the EU. This arises as a result of a combination of the rules in reg. 103 and of art. 2 and 3 of the *Value Added Tax (Input Tax) (Specified Supplies) Order* 1999 (SI 1999/3121). These are discussed earlier in **Chapter 4** at 40-200. The effect, briefly, is that underlying input VAT will be recoverable where the recipient is either:

- established outside the EU and Isle of Man; or
- is a business established in the UK or in another Member State and the service is one of agency involving the arrangement of a basically exempt financial supply by that client to someone outside the EU.

The distinction between financial and non-financial services will again be important in the context of the imported services rules in VATA 1994, s. 8 if supply is basically taxable output, the broker is established outside the UK. This could be an issue, for example, where the contract is one involving a traded option on one of the non-UK exchanges. The net end result should, in most cases, be that there is a nil VAT cost in that the rules on direct attribution are likely again to allow the associated input VAT to be recovered in full.

The inter-relation of these factors on the liability of contracts for hard and soft commodities is illustrated in **Appendix 17**. The detailed liability position is considered below.

100-200 Zero-rating and the Black Box

On the introduction of VAT, the importance of the London Commodity Markets was recognised by the specific relief afforded in the *Value Added Tax (Terminal Markets) Order* 1973 (SI 1973/173) and what is now VATA 1994, s. 50. From 25 July 1997, the *Terminal Markets Order* was extended by the *Value Added Tax (Terminal Markets) (Amendment) Order* 1997 (SI 1997/1836) to include supplies in the course of dealings on the London Securities and Derivatives Exchange (OMLX), now part of EDX, involving contracts relating to paper pulp, for which terminal market VAT treatment was required. The Order was further amended from 1 January 2000 to cater for investment gold by the *Value Added Tax (Terminal Markets) (Amendment) Order* 1999 (SI 1999/3117). As observed later, the benefit of the Order has also been extended, by concession, to certain other supplies on ICE and APX.

The text of the *Terminal Markets Order* is reproduced at **Appendix 18**. Its effect is to zero-rate a range of contracts undertaken in certain specified circumstances. The relief, which only applies to commodities ordinarily dealt on the exchanges, means that:

(1) **Transactions in physicals/actuals** which result in delivery can be zero-rated, but only when between two market members, and:

(a) if the market is the LME, the transaction is between members entitled to deal in the *ring*;
(b) if the market is the London Rubber Market or the London Bullion Market, the transaction is between members of the respective market;
(c) if the market is the London Grain Futures Market, the transaction is a sale registered at the Clearing House of the Grain and Feed Trade Association (in practice now LCH.Clearnet);
(d) if the market is any of the others listed in the Terminal Markets Order, the transaction is a sale registered with LCH.Clearnet.

(2) **Futures or sales of unallocated commodities** may be zero-rated provided they are between:

(a) two market members (in which case delivery may or may not take place); or
(b) a market member and a non-member so long as the transaction does not result in physical delivery.

In the case of supplies within this latter category, delivery will normally take place when instructions are given for the goods to be physically removed from the warehouse or vault in which they are held. Should this occur, the supplies are effectively reinstated. HMRC also take the view that sales in vault removed from the sellers' to the buyers' cage involve delivery and are thus potentially outside the *Terminal Markets Order* (but see later at 100-350(4)). In either case, VAT is then charged according to the liability which would have applied were it not for the *Terminal Markets Order*. On this basis, if the supply is a UK supply, the standard-rate of VAT will apply unless the goods may be zero-rated as foodstuffs, are in a customs duty or VAT warehouse (see 100-250(2) later), or happen to be situated in a warehouse or other location abroad, in which event the supply will be outside the scope of VAT (see **Chapter 3** and (3) later).

(3) **Options,** which are rights to acquire goods or futures contracts, can be zero-rated if the supply is by or to a member of the relevant market and is:

(a) exercisable at some future date; or
(b) would involve a sale which would otherwise be covered by the rules on physicals, futures and unallocated commodities discussed above.

Further supplies will arise in the event that an option is exercised.

(4) **Brokers' or agents' commission** may be zero-rated if, but only if:

(a) the broker is a member of the relevant market; and
(b) the supply of services is to another market member.

Whether, as regards the second of these conditions, commissions can be zero-rated to both clients, so long as at least one of them is a market member seems to be an open issue.

As for futures contracts and contracts in unallocated commodities earlier, any zero-rating may need to be reversed should the necessary conditions cease to be satisfied, for example, in the event of delivery to a non-market member.

In short, the *Terminal Markets Order* will thus not apply to:

- supplies of goods between a market member and a non-market member which lead to physical delivery;
- supplies between two non-members (e.g. a non-member broker and his client) *even if delivery does not result*; and
- any brokerage/commission earned by someone who is not himself a market member.

These will all need to be dealt with under the normal rules, which are discussed below. Whilst some may be zero-rated or *outside the scope*, many will be potentially liable to VAT at the standard-rate.

> **Practice point**
>
> Zero-rating under the *Black Box* is strictly limited. It only applies to certain transactions in hard and soft commodities and at least one of the parties must be a member of the relevant UK exchange. Brokers who are not market-members can find that:
>
> - supplies are liable to VAT; and
> - if dealing on a principals basis, tax is due on the full contract value.
>
> This may be acceptable if the client is a VAT-registered business. But this will not always be the case and, if tax is not anticipated, there can be a real cost to the broker concerned.
>
> The answer may be to either:
>
> - act as agent rather than as principal, leaving VAT to be due, if at all, only on the broker's commission; or, alternatively
> - agree with HMRC that the underlying place of supply is, or would be, abroad, putting the supply offshore and effectively *outside the scope* of VAT.

100-250 Other supplies involving deliverable hard and soft commodities

(1) The general position

(a) Physicals/actuals and forward sales

For physicals/actuals and forward sales contracts the VAT liability is determined partly by the nature of the commodity and partly by the place where they are located. For goods which are located in the UK, this means that the general rule is that they will be subject to VAT at the standard-rate unless the goods are either:

- zero-rated as exports (VATA 1994, s. 30(6) and (7));
- zero-rated as foodstuffs (VATA 1994, Sch. 8, Grp. 1) – e.g. cocoa, coffee, grain, meat, sugar, vegetable oil and soya bean meal; or

- treated as outside the UK by reason of being in a customs duty, excise duty or VAT warehouse (VATA 1994, s. 18, 18A and 18B – see (2));
- *outside the scope* of UK VAT altogether by reason of being located or warehoused outside the UK at the time of delivery.

In this latter case, consideration may well need to be given, where appropriate, as to whether foreign VAT is chargeable – especially if the commodities are located in another Member State. This is considered further at (c).

(b) Futures contracts

Since futures contracts also involve the supply of goods, the VAT liability will, again, depend on the type of commodity and the location. The position is broadly as in (a) above, subject to the general inference referred to in 100-150(3) above to the effect that the goods will be located in the territory in which the particular commodity exchange is situated.

(c) Unallocated goods

As noted at 100-150(2) earlier (and subject to what is said later at (2)), unallocated goods involve supplies of services rather than goods. The place of supply will not, therefore, depend on where the commodity is located but according to whether or not the supply is seen as an essentially financial service. The latter will apply, in principle, to all contracts involving precious metals or undertaken as a financial hedge. In this event, the place of supply is generally where the recipient, the buyer, is located, the supply being *outside the scope* if made to:

- a VAT-registered business *belonging* in another Member State; or
- anyone, including a business or a private investor, *belonging* outside the EU and the Isle of Man.

In other cases: i.e. where the supply is not a financial service, the place of supply will be where the supplier is established.

A sale which, on this basis, is made in the UK will be subject to tax at the standard-rate, unless, for example, this is replaced by zero-rating where the underlying commodity is food (VATA 1994, Sch. 8, Grp. 1). Where the supply is treated as made outside the UK, any input VAT continues to be recoverable by reason of reg. 103 of the *Value Added Tax Regulations* 1995 (SI 1995/2518).

(d) Options

As noted earlier, options are also supplies of services (see 100-150(4) earlier). The general VAT treatment is thus broadly as in (c) above, subject to the proviso that traded options are, in principle, always accepted as representing financial services.

In this case, however, the supply is of a right to acquire goods or a futures contract, rather than goods as such. If made in the UK, therefore, the supply will always be taxable at the standard-rate.

(e) Brokers' or agency services

The treatment of brokers' or agency services will depend, as with supplies of unallocated goods, on the view taken of the nature of the supply in the particular context in which it is found.

The arrangement of contracts, including futures and options, traded on a recognised commodity exchange should generally be seen as a financial service. This should also apply where the underlying client transaction is a financial hedge. The place of supply is thus usually where the recipient or client is located (VATA 1994, s. 7A and Sch. 4A, para. 16) and will be outside the UK when the supply is to:

- a business belonging in another Member State; or
- anyone, including a business or private investor, belonging outside the EU and the Isle of Man.

In other cases, it will tend to depend on the place of supply of the underlying client transaction itself – in general, on the location of the goods themselves except where the client is registered for VAT in another Member State.

In either event, however, where the supply is outside the UK and no VAT is due, related input VAT again continues to be recoverable by reason of reg. 103 of the *Value Added Tax Regulations* 1995.

Where the place of supply, on this basis, is in the UK, tax will usually be chargeable at the standard-rate. However, this is replaced by zero-rating where:

(1) The broker arranges an export of goods from the EU (VATA 1994, Sch. 8, Grp. 7, item 2(a)). This applies irrespective of the status of the client.

(2) The broker (often, but not always, a buying broker) arranges a supply of goods or services for which the place of supply is outside the EU and Isle of Man (Grp. 7, item 2(c)). Again, who the client is or where he belongs is unimportant. In practice, this will apply to:

   (a) sales or purchases for a EU client of physicals/actuals or futures (whether or not resulting in delivery), when conducted on an appropriate non-EU commodity exchange; and

   (b) the sale for a UK client of an unallocated commodity on a non-EU exchange.

(2) Foreign and warehoused supplies

Where a transaction takes place is clearly a key factor in deciding VAT liability. Many of the tangible or physical commodities dealt in are not, or not always, warehoused in the UK. Oil traded on the IPE/ICE, for example, will frequently be held in Rotterdam and metals on the LME will be in a variety of locations, including warehouses in Belgium and the Netherlands.

If the place of supply is outside the UK, the special rules under the *Value Added Tax (Terminal Markets) Order* 1973 (SI 1973/173) will not operate. This does not necessarily mean that tax

10 Commodity Derivatives and Financial Derivatives

will be chargeable. Usually it will not, especially if the commodities are held in a warehousing regime. However, this should not be taken for granted and the possibility of a VAT liability elsewhere should always be borne in mind.

(a) The Second Simplification Directive

As physicals and futures contracts involve supplies of goods, the place of supply will, in broad terms, be where the goods are at the time they are made available or appropriated. On this basis, many of the contracts will, strictly speaking, be *outside the scope* of UK VAT – but within the scope of VAT in other Member States. Historically, this does not seem to have been a major problem in practice, largely due to the particular VAT regimes available in the more important countries concerned. The existence of fiscal or VAT warehouses, for example, has meant that often the liability to VAT only arises on removal from the warehousing regime, so that intermediate dealings in the goods are not taxed.

The position was not uniform throughout the Community, however. To remedy this potential uncertainty and disparity in treatment, the Second Simplification Directive (Directive 95/7 of 10 April 1995) was introduced providing a scheme whereby Member States may adopt special measures to exempt supplies of certain raw materials and other goods negotiated on international forward markets. This is subject, broadly, to the provisos that:

- transactions are not aimed at the final use and/or consumption; and
- the tax payable when the rules cease to apply shall correspond to the VAT that would otherwise be due.

The scheme was achieved by amendments to art. 16 of the Sixth VAT Directive (now art. 157 of Council Directive 2006/112/EC), which allow the goods concerned to be placed under a warehousing regime similar to that for customs and excise duties, which are covered in the UK by VATA 1994, s. 18 (see (i) below). In the UK, the scheme was implemented by the *Finance Act* 1996, which extended the rules in s. 18 by introducing a new s. 18A–18F. The goods which may be warehoused under these arrangements are set out in VATA 1994, Sch. 5A. They will in all cases be goods which are in free circulation within the EU and on which excise duty (where appropriate) or customs duty and VAT (in the case of imports) has either been paid or deferred.

There are also regulations in Pt. XVIA of the *Value Added Tax Regulations* 1995 (SI 1995/2518).

(i) The basic position

The acquisition from another Member State or the supply in the UK of *eligible goods* is treated as supplied outside the UK if either:

- the acquisition or supply takes place while the goods are subject to a fiscal warehousing regime; *or*
- after the acquisition or supply of the goods but before the next supply of those goods, the person making the acquisition or to whom the supply is made causes the goods to be placed in a fiscal warehousing regime; *and, in either case*:
- the supply is not a retail transaction.

With goods acquired from another Member State, the acquirer must prepare and keep a certificate that the goods are subject to a fiscal warehousing regime or that he will cause the goods to be placed in such a warehouse. For goods which have been the subject of a supply, the person to whom the supply has been made must give the supplier a similar certificate that the goods will be placed in such a warehouse. In either case, the certificate must be prepared, and given, at or before the time the supply or acquisition takes place. For goods which are supplied, the supply itself must also not be a supply by retail.

Where this does not apply (e.g. where the next supply is not within the fiscal warehousing regime) the tax due on the relevant acquisition or supply is accounted for on removal from the warehouse. Where the person required to pay the tax is registered for VAT, this is simply achieved through the VAT return. In the case of someone who is not VAT-registered, the VAT must be accounted for on a removal document and actually be paid in cash. The value on which tax is then due is the value of the acquisition or supply immediately preceding the removal, but increased, where zero-rated services (see below) have been provided in relation to those goods between the time of the transaction concerned and removal, by the value of those services.

In short, eligible goods may be placed VAT-free into a fiscal warehouse and supplied VAT-free while warehoused but so that a tax charge arises on exit by reference to the immediately preceding event – i.e. acquisition or supply.

(ii) Services

In conjunction with the relief in s. 18B, there is further relief by way of zero-rating for a number of services carried out within the warehouse and which are wholly performed on or in relation to the goods concerned (s. 18C). These are essentially the storage and handling charges made by the keeper of the warehouse and physical services, such as preservation and repackaging or the carrying out on the goods of operations or processes permitted by the customs and excise duty regimes.

(iii) Interaction with the Terminal Markets Order

On the face of it, the fiscal warehousing rules potentially overlap with those under the *Value Added Tax (Terminal Markets) Order* 1973 (SI 1973/173). Many of the goods to which the latter applies will be, or will potentially be, held in the warehousing regime and businesses may well, at times, be uncertain as to which rules are to be applied. This may clearly need to be reviewed at some stage. In the meantime, those involved may need to exercise particular care lest unforseen liabilities are to arise. The fiscal warehousing rules are also unlikely, for the time being, to be extended to the services of someone acting as a broker.

It was initially put to HMRC that traders in the relevant commodities should be able, while the goods remain fiscally warehoused, to opt for supplies of those goods to be made under either regime. HMRC were not prepared to agree to this, however. Supplies which involved goods which were within the fiscal warehousing regime had, they said, to legally be treated under the warehousing rules. Anyone wishing to use the *Terminal Markets Order* procedures for supplies of goods which are held under fiscal warehousing arrangements should first remove the goods from that regime (and pay any tax then due) *before* making a supply under the provisions of the *Terminal Markets Order*. It may in many cases be arguable, however, that any supply immediately preceding removal should, in any event be zero-rated under the Order, especially if made between two members of the market concerned.

Fiscal warehousing does not appear to be something that is widely used by the trade.

(b) Goods in a customs duty or excise duty warehouse

The fiscal warehouses discussed at (a) above are in addition to the more established customs duty and excise duty warehouses (VATA 1994, s. 18). These operate in much the same way, with the exception that customs duty warehouses are used only for imported goods not *released for free circulation* within the EU. Excise duty warehouses will be of particular interest in the context of hydrocarbon oil, where much of the trading involves goods in a bonded refinery or storage.

Supplies may again be made VAT-free on the basis that they are treated as supplied outside the UK. In the case of imported goods, the VAT suspended, and payable on removal, is the tax otherwise due on importation; for home-produced goods, it is tax on the last supply within the warehouse.

(c) Other outside the scope supplies

There are, in addition, other situations where supplies will be *outside the scope*. Physicals or futures transactions involving goods traded outside the UK on exchanges such as NYMEX, for example, will usually be presumed to relate to goods held abroad (i.e. outside the UK). For some commodities, oil for example, there is also the possibility of trading in respect of cargoes on the high seas.

> **Practice point**
>
> With international commodity trading, it can be important to establish:
>
> - what particular trades involve; and
> - what the local VAT treatment and requirements are.
>
> Local VAT registration may need to attend to if accounting and compliance problems are to be avoided. Being in a position, contractually, to charge VAT where needed could also be vital (see also the spread rules on electricity and gas later at 100-350).

100-300 Financial futures and options and other intangibles

The VAT treatment of contracts involving currency, interest rates, securities or indices will be different from that for hard and soft commodities. The *Black Box* arrangements (see 100-200 earlier) are not available. Also, most transactions will be exempt rather than taxable. In particular:

- currency contracts are basically exempt transactions involving money (VATA 1994, Sch. 9, Grp. 5, item 1 and (art. 135(1)(d) of Council Directive 2006/112/EC));
- long and short interest rate contracts are similarly exempt, essentially as transactions involving credit (item 2 of Grp. 5 and art. 135(1)(b));

- contracts based on gilt edged securities, treasury bonds or other similar instruments are exempt as dealings in securities (item 6 of Grp. 5 and art. 135(1)(f));
- index-based contracts, such as the FTSE 100 index and the index of freight rates on the Baltic Exchange are again exempt as involving money or payments (item 1 of Grp. 5 and art. 135(1)(d));
- brokerage or agency transactions are intermediary services (within item 5 of Grp. 5).

However, as a result of VATA 1994, s. 7A(2), these are not treated as supplied in the UK if the recipient is a relevant business person in another country (see **Chapter 5**).

Although, the supply in all cases will be basically exempt, there is, however, a specific, but limited relief for input VAT for certain supplies involving transactions with persons outside the EU. This arises as a result of the rules in reg. 103 of the *Value Added Tax Regulations* 1995 (SI 1995/2518) and art. 2 and 3 of the *Value Added Tax (Input Tax) (Specified Supplies) Order* 1999 (SI 1999/3121). These are discussed earlier in **Chapter 4** at 40-150(4). The effect, briefly, is that underlying input VAT will be recoverable where the recipient is either:

- established outside the EU and Isle of Man; or
- is a business established in the UK or in another Member State and the service is one of agency involving the arrangement of a basically exempt financial supply by that client to someone outside the EU.

(1) LIFFE

In the absence of zero-rating under the *Black Box*, the treatment of transactions on LIFFE has been the subject of specific agreement between the Exchange, now Euronext.liffe, and HMRC, the essence of which is set out in para. 8 of HMRC Notice 701/49/2011.

(a) The general position

As with the tangible commodities, the VAT treatment is, to some extent, determined by the rules of the Exchange. In the case of LIFFE, members are required to deal with one another and with clients on a principal-to-principal basis. This, as with certain other exchanges, stems from the need to effectively guarantee payment as part, inter alia, of the clearing mechanism. This rule does not, however, necessarily apply to intermediaries, who are not LIFFE members and who may thus deal on an agency basis.

(b) Futures

The VAT treatment also depends on the circumstances in which a futures contract is traded.

Contracts may be transacted in the pit, either on the market floor or on the APT system. In either case, the parties will both be members of the Exchange dealing in the particular contract concerned. No turn or *commission* arises in this situation. As a result, HMRC see no supply. There is also no supply recognised when a position is *closed-out*.

In the case of transactions with clients, including members not dealing in the pit, contracts will typically involve a dealing profit, turn or *commission*. This is seen by HMRC (see para. 8.3

of Notice 701/49/2011 – Finance) as the measure of the supply by the member to the client, whether charged separately for each leg or for a *round trip* in a *closed-out* transaction. HMRC also do not see a supply by the client to the member in a closed-out situation. Any cash settlements, including deposits, margins and balances between members or between members and clients, are *outside the scope* of VAT.

This view of things dates from the time when LIFFE came into being as an attempt to start operations with the minimum negative effect from exemption, given that it was not possible to include the new exchange in the zero-rating regime of the *Terminal Markets Order*. Whether it is always, strictly, justifiable seems open to debate. Whilst there may be some argument that there is a supply only by the market member to the client in the case of contracts such as interest rate futures (which are only ever cash-settled), this may be much less tenable where, as with contracts for bonds, the subject matter is deliverable. However, the line taken by the Tribunal in *Willis Pension Trustees Ltd* [2006] BVC 2,045 (see earlier in **Chapter 8** at 80-100) may give some support to the proposition that there is a supply only by the member in certain situations.

The view that there is no supply by a client to a market member in a *closed-out* financial futures transaction reflects the fact that it is the member that issues the *sold* contract, not the client and also the fact that the market member will charge a commission or turn for both *bought* and *sold* contracts. However, this is really only a selection of the mechanics and would be equally true of any normal stock exchange transaction.

> **Practice point**
>
> From an accounting viewpoint, the approach adopted by most companies to bond contracts reflects commercial reality.
>
> (1) The trades are undertaken on a *principal-to-principal* basis, with the client accounting in its books for the gross contract values of both *bought* and *sold* contracts.
>
> (2) Any *commission* or *turn* charged by the market member is accounted for separately, but is, in reality, an adjustment of the price.
>
> (3) Where a client is *short* at the maturity date, it will be required to deliver to the market member the bonds contracted for, exactly as it would in a corresponding *actuals* contract.
>
> (4) If the client is *long* at the maturity date, it will be required to take delivery of the bonds contracted for – again just as it would in a corresponding *actuals* contract.
>
> (5) *Closing-out* in a futures situation is no more than the client, having first entered into a *bought* or *sold* contract, entering into an equal and opposite *sold* or *bought* contract, allowing the two to be matched-off. There is still, however, an underlying purchase or sale by each of the two parties, with ultimately a settlement as between themselves of any difference in the price.
>
> Recognising that there is, in fact, a supply by the client acknowledges commercial reality. The fact that a sold contract is obtained from the broker is no different to the situation where

> there is a simple sale of shares and can arguably be seen as much as a matter of mechanics as anything else. Acknowledging this may produce a fairer, and less distortive, result in terms of the partial exemption positions of both the member and the client, especially if trades are undertaken on similar exchanges outside the EU (such as the CME or NYMEX – see later), where the recovery of underlying input tax would normally be expected (art. 3 of the *Value Added Tax (Input Tax) (Specified Supplies) Order* 1999 (SI 1999/3121)) if there is a supply.

In terms of what the contracts represent:

- *Currency, short interest rate and FTSE 100 and other index-based contracts* – these are effectively regarded as dealings in money or securities for money. They are accordingly basically exempt under VATA 1994, Sch. 9, Grp. 5, item 1. Where the contracts run to maturity, there is no further supply. Any cash settlements are *outside the scope* and are disregarded for VAT purposes.
- *Long gilts, Treasury Bonds, Bonds and other securities-based contracts* – contracts based on securities where the subject matter is deliverable are basically exempt under VATA 1994, Sch. 9, Grp. 5, item 6. Where contracts are not deliverable, the treatment is as for the currency and index-based contracts above. Where deliverable contracts run to maturity, there is a further supply, the value of which is the price fixed in the underlying futures contract.

To sum up, therefore, HMRC's view is that:

(1) For item 1 contracts, there is only ever a supply by the member to the client. There is no supply by a client to a broker in a closed-out contract.

(2) For brokers, the measure of supply is initially the turn or commission charged. In the absence of a turn, no supply is recognised in a transaction between members dealing in the pit – the value is taken as nil.

(3) For deliverable securities-based contracts running to maturity (delivery) there will be further exempt supplies or series of exempt supplies:

   (a) by a selling client (including a non-member);
   (b) by a non-clearing member to a clearing member; and
   (c) by a selling member to a buyer.

In all cases the value of the supply is the total consideration payable under the contract.

(c) Options

Options have a different treatment as they represent, in effect, the granting of rights. The value, in this case, is the premium charged and, unlike with futures contracts, there is a supply in member/member trades. There are basically three types of option contract.

(i) Futures options

Futures options are again basically exempt under VATA 1994, Sch. 9, Grp. 5. The treatment essentially follows that for the underlying contract. Securities-based options, where the security is deliverable, are themselves securities and are thus within item 6. Other options fall within item 1. There is no further supply in relation to the option itself in the event it is exercised.

(ii) Equity options

Equity options are based on equities rather than on any related futures contract. They are again securities and, as such, within item 6. In this case, however, there will be a further supply, of the securities, in the event the option is exercised (apart from eventually, perhaps, under the futures contract itself).

(iii) Index options

Index options are always cash-settled and are thus within item 1.

In short:

- currency, short interest rate, FTSE 100 and other index contracts are treated as dealings in money within VATA 1994, Sch. 9, Grp. 5, item 1 (art. 135(1)(d) of Directive 2006/112/EC);
- Gilt and Treasury Bond contracts are supplies of secondary securities as defined in VATA 1994, Sch. 9, Grp. 5, item 6 (art. 135(1)(f) of Directive 2006/112/EC).

The value of the supply, in either case, is the premium paid or payable under the terms of the option contract (plus, where appropriate, the commission charged).

(iv) Locals

Locals are traders registered to members of LIFFE but who act to some extent independently. When trading in the pit the local represents the member to whom he is registered.

Employees

Being on the member's payroll, there is no supply between the member and the local in this situation.

Self-employed locals

This type of local may trade on his own account. When dealing in the pit, it is the member, rather than the local, that is party to the contract. When the trade is completed, however, there is then a back-to-back contract between the member and the local, who is now treated as a third-party client. When pit broking as agent for the member, the local's supply is of the services of an intermediary within item 5 of Grp. 5.

Joint ventures and partnerships

In this case, every trade executed in the pit is a trade by the member. The remuneration of the local will then depend on the precise nature of the agreement entered into.

(2) Freight derivatives

Freight derivatives provide a means of hedging exposure to freight market risk through the trading of specified time charter and voyage rates for forward positions. Settlement is against a relevant route assessment, often one published by the Baltic Exchange.

Forward Freight Agreements (FFAs) are *over-the-counter* products made on a principal-to-principal basis. As such, they are flexible and not traded on any exchange.

Contracts traded will normally be based on the terms and conditions of the FFABA standard contracts amended, as agreed between the principals. The main terms of such an agreement cover:

- the agreed route;
- the day, month and year of settlement;
- the contract quantity; and
- the contract rate at which differences will be settled.

Settlement is between counter-parties in cash within five days following the settlement date. Commissions will be agreed between principal and broker. The broker, acting as intermediary only, is not responsible for the performance of the contract.

Cleared contracts are settled on a daily basis through a clearing-house and settlements are based on a close-of-play trading price. At the end of each day, traders pay or receive the difference between the price of the paper contract and the market index.

As the contracts invariably involve an index of freight rates rather than actual affreightment, delivery does not occur and they are cash-settled. Contracts are thus always seen as essentially relating to money or payments, and basically exempt within VATA 1994, Sch. 9, Grp. 5, item 1 (art. 135(1)(d) of Council Directive 2006/112/EC).

(3) Other markets and situations

Whether and to what extent the rules described earlier apply to other situations will clearly depend on the circumstances.

Over-the-counter trading, for example, may involve non-standard contracts and, whilst the general principles on liability will still hold good, the value of the supply will depend on the precise contractual relationships and whether, for example, the broker trades as principal or as agent.

The same will be true of dealings outside the UK on exchanges such as Eurex, the Chicago Board of Trade (CBOT), and the New York Mercantile Exchange (NYMEX). The basic VAT position may well be as in (1) and (2) above. However, ultimately, the rules of the exchange and local law could be important.

To the extent that the contracts involve services for VAT purposes, the place of supply may well not be determined by the location of the particular exchange involved (as in the case of futures contracts in hard and soft commodities). Instead it will be decided by where the recipient, e.g. the client or the buyer of a contract, belongs. The location of the exchange may, however, be an indication of where this should be taken to be, which, as explained earlier, can be important in terms of the ability to recover underlying input VAT.

Unlike with contracts in hard and soft commodities, transactions involving:

- financial futures; or
- options relating to financial products or derivatives,

on any of the non-UK exchanges will not give rise to any liability under the imported services rules, which do not apply to anything that is VAT-exempt.

100-350 Electricity and gas trading

Derivatives of power supplies are extensively traded nationally and internationally.

Recognising the complications from international trade, 1 January 2005 saw the implementation of the *Gas and Electricity Directive* – Council Directive 2003/92/EC of 7 October 2003, which made important changes to the rules on the place of supply of gas and electricity. The implications of this are separately considered later at (3).

(1) Electricity

Buyers and sellers of electricity will largely be generators and suppliers producing or consuming actual quantities of electrical energy. However, there are also non-physical traders – i.e. people who wish to buy or sell electricity or derivatives without either taking physical delivery or delivering electricity to final consumers.

Supplies by electricity generators are traded through New Electricity Trading Arrangements (NETA). These are based on the idea of freely negotiated contracts, which may be traded *over-the-counter* through a variety of bilateral and multilateral agreements or on one or more exchanges. NETA provides the required mechanisms for near real-time clearing and settlement of the imbalances between contractual and physical positions:

- traders may buy more or less energy than they have sold;
- generators may physically generate more or less than they have sold; and
- customers may use more or less energy that their supplier has purchased on their behalf.

The central NETA systems, managed by Elexon Ltd, are designed to measure these surpluses and deficits (or *imbalances*). These result in *imbalance settlements*, which are set at prices determined by Elexon Ltd, a non-profit-making company, which is the Balancing and Settlement Code Company. Elexon Ltd calculates the prices at which imbalances are to be settled, sends out, on behalf of Elexon Clear, invoices for the amounts due and collects the payments that result. Because metered data for generation and wholesale demand is available half-hourly, imbalance settlements are also half-hourly under NETA. Volumes and imbalance prices are calculated on a half-hourly basis, and settlement is daily, approximately 29 days in arrears.

Balancing is on the basis of notifications to the System Operator, the National Grid Company, by generators and suppliers. An initial physical notification relating to expected operating levels throughout the whole day must be submitted by 11.00am on the previous day and there can be a final physical notification relating to proposed operating levels in a particular half-hour, with the traded quantities being notified in respect of each half-hour.

With futures and forward contracts, trades may, in some cases, be made a year or more in advance of the half-hour segment to which they relate. However, whilst trades may be notified some time in advance, they cannot be notified after the event (i.e. after the half-hour to which they relate has passed) or after the deadline, called a *Gate Closure*, one hour prior to the start of that half-hour segment.

All products traded on APX Power UK will be automatically notified by them before *Gate Closure*. For over-the-counter (OTC transactions), notification is achieved by parties reporting positions through an authorised Energy Contract Volume Notification Agent (ECVNA).

(a) Trading

The basic treatment of the contracts and supplies for trades in electricity follows that for similar contracts discussed elsewhere in this Chapter. Trading in the UK may also be over-the-counter or anonymously on an exchange, such as APX Power UK (formerly UKPX).

- Ordinary over-the-counter spot or forward trades involve supplies of goods. They will be potentially liable to VAT at the standard rate, subject to the implications of the Gas and Electricity Directive (see (3) below), where trading is with businesses *belonging* or *established* in other countries.
- Trading on APX Power UK is treated differently as it is an exchange. APX Power UK part of the Anglo-Dutch APX Group and offers integrated trading, clearing and notification for spot and prompt power contracts and a trading platform for cleared forwards contracts. These have, as a practical matter, been accepted by HMRC as eligible for treatment under the *Value Added Tax (Terminal Markets) Order* 1973, notwithstanding that APX Power is not one of the exchanges mentioned. Any supplies, and related brokerage charged by members of that exchange, will thus be capable of being zero-rated under the *Black Box* arrangements described earlier at 100-200.

APX is, in common with other exchanges, a counterparty to the underlying trades, its position being secured by guarantees and cash-collateral from members, who are required to trade as principal.

Base load and peak load forwards contracts can be traded over APX Power UK with clearing services offered by LCH.Clearnet. The contracts are then notified through services provided by APX Group to LCH.Clearnet before going to delivery.

(b) Other issues

(i) Energy lending

Energy lending can arise when, for example, a company has entered into a contract to supply electricity, but does not have the necessary resources at the time delivery required. The contract will take the form of an agreement to borrow electricity from the lender, possibly for a fee, in return for an undertaking to deliver back the same amount of energy at a future date. In the

UK, such a contract is treated as being for reciprocal supplies of goods. In Belgium the same view is taken, but it understood that in the Netherlands and Germany energy lending is seen as a supply of services.

(ii) Elexon Ltd charges

Charges levied by Elexon Ltd on Trading Parties to cover its costs are subject to VAT. They are taxable at the standard-rate, but are *outside the scope* when made to companies belonging or established outside the UK, being services within the list in VATA 1994, Sch. 4A (art. 59 of Directive 2006/112/EC (art. 9(2)(e) of the Sixth Directive, 77/388/EC)).

(iii) Imbalance settlements

Payments made to or received from Elexon Clear in respect of Imbalance Settlements represent consideration for standard-rated supplies of electricity under the balancing process. Elexon Clear is a separate body from Elexon Ltd, by which it is administered. As clearer, it is legally a contracting party to the settled trades, but is not itself treated as making any supplies for VAT purposes, and is not VAT-registered. However, whilst it cannot, itself, issue VAT invoices or enter into conventional self-billing arrangements where necessary the Confirmation Notices issued by Elexon Ltd on its behalf are accepted by HMRC as constituting the equivalent of VAT invoices for the parties concerned, who account for the output and input tax thereon in the normal way. The settlement is made through a special clearing bank account maintained by Elexon Ltd specifically for this purpose.

Any netting-off of elements in the settlement process for BM Unit Cash-flow, Non-delivery charges, Energy Imbalance Cash-flow and Residual Settlement Cash-flow, is simply part of the calculation of a single amount that each trading party either owes or is owed in respect of each day, and is treated as the consideration for a single standard-rated supply. Any netting-off amount is accordingly, as such, *outside the scope*.

(iv) Information imbalance charges

These are charges made by Elexon Clear for the failure to provide information and are in the nature of fines. As such, they may not be subject to VAT, although the treatment of these charges, which are currently set to zero under the Code, has not been finally agreed with HMRC.

(v) Options

Options, which are contracts to buy (or sell) a supply of electricity at a future date represent a supply of services for VAT, rather than goods. In the UK, an option is seen as a financial hedge, albeit that, in the case of an option to buy or sell electricity, it is basically taxable, rather than exempt under any of the heads in VATA 1994, Sch. 9, Grp. 5. As a financial service, it will fall within VATA 1994, Sch. 4A, para. 16 (or art. 59 of Council Directive 2006/112/EC (art. 9(2)(e) of the Sixth VAT Directive)), so that the place of supply is where the non-business buyer or recipient is located. In some other Member States, such as the Netherlands, options are considered to be exempt.

(vi) Swaps

Electricity swaps are, as the term implies, exchanges of physical electricity and will involve reciprocal supplies by each of the parties to the other. Frequently, with electricity, swaps will be undertaken to avoid transmission costs. This is common practice in the Netherlands, Belgium and Germany triangle. Such transactions are normally treated as two supplies of goods. This contrasts with the treatment of gas, where it is more difficult to see the supply as other than one of unallocated goods, and thus of services for VAT.

(vii) Transmission charges

Transmission charges represent consideration for the movement of electricity, although there appears to be a divergence of views between Member States as to how they should be treated in terms of the place of supply.

(2) Gas

New gas trading arrangements (NGTA) meet the requirements for balancing the gas distribution system. Under the Uniform Network Code (UNC) the on-the-day gas commodity market (OCM) is managed by an independent market operator, APX Gas Ltd, under the brand of APX Gas UK (formerly EnMO Ltd). This meets the National Grid's needs in keeping the gas transportation system constantly in balance as well as to facilitate trade in within-day and day-ahead gas at the National Balancing Point (NBP).

Buyers and sellers are not just limited to producers and gas utilities and others delivering gas to consumers, but also include banks or other financial institutions.

Upon completion of a trade, the trader receives electronic notification on-screen. In addition, confirmation is sent instantly by fax to each of the buyer's and seller's offices. The terms of the completed transaction appear on the completed historical transactions screen for the benefit of all market participants. All companies who participate have to subscribe to the UNC and trading is fully cleared by the market operator, with statements being issued monthly, by calendar month, by the 23rd business day following the month-end. Settlement is due 12 calendar days after the issue of the monthly statement.

The monthly statements detail separately the amounts due to and from each subscriber in respect of each NBP trade and also the APX charges for that month. For VAT purposes, the monthly statements are not treated as VAT invoices. Rather, VAT invoices are produced on payment date following the issuing of the monthly statements. The only exception to the invoicing arrangements is that National Grid self-bill APX for the gas trades they have incurred.

(a) Trading

As with electricity, the basic treatment of the contracts and supplies for trades in gas follows that for similar contracts discussed elsewhere in this Chapter. Trading in the UK may also be over-the-counter or via APX Gas.

Ordinary over-the-counter spot or forward trades, again, involve supplies of goods. They will be potentially liable to VAT at the standard-rate, subject to the implications of the Gas and Electricity Directive (see (3) below), where trading is with businesses *belonging* or *established* in other countries.

Trading on APX Gas UK is treated differently as the *day ahead* and OCM *within the day* APX contracts have, as a practical matter, been accepted by HMRC as eligible for treatment under the *Value Added Tax (Terminal Markets) Order* 1973, notwithstanding that APX Gas UK is not one of the exchanges mentioned. Any supplies, and related brokerage charged by members of that exchange, will thus be capable of being zero-rated under the *Black Box* arrangements described earlier at 100-200.

APX is, in common with other exchanges, a counter-party to the underlying trades, its position being secured by guarantees and cash-collateral from members, who are required to trade as principal.

(b) Other issues

(i) Charges and fees

The amounts appearing on the monthly statements for trades and transmission charges and by way of APX's fees and other costs are subject to VAT at the standard rate.

(ii) Options

Options, which are contracts to buy (or sell) a supply of gas at a future date represent a supply of services for VAT, rather than goods. In the UK, an option is seen as a financial hedge, albeit that, in the case of an option to buy or sell gas, it is basically taxable, rather than exempt under any of the heads in VATA 1994, Sch. 9, Grp. 5. As a financial service, it will fall within VATA 1994, Sch. 5, para. 5 (or art. 59 of Council Directive 2006/112/EC, art. 9(2)(e) of the Sixth VAT Directive), so that the place of supply is where the buyer or recipient is located. In some other Member States, such as the Netherlands, options are considered to be exempt.

(3) Special rules for the place of supply of gas and electricity

In addition to trading within the domestic market, there is also extensive international trade in energy and energy products. With the growth in business, it became increasingly apparent that there were considerable practical difficulties due to the nature of the commodities involved and the differing treatment afforded between Member States.

The basic problem stemmed from the fact that supplies of both electricity and gas were treated under the Sixth Directive as supplies of goods for VAT purposes. Consequently, within the Community, cross-border deliveries were dealt with under the rules for dispatches and acquisitions (see **Chapter 3** at 30-300), rather than under any of the rules for services. Given the nature and extent of the trade, the rules on the place of supply also meant that companies actively trading electricity and gas internationally had, historically, often needed to become VAT-registered and account for tax in more than one country.

To address these issues, Council Directive 2003/92/EC of 7 October 2003 amended the Sixth Directive rules 77/388/EEC, the Sixth Directive, as regards the rules on the place of supply of gas and electricity.

(a) Place of supply

These rules now appear in art. 38 of Council Directive 2006/112/EC. The place of supply for wholesale supplies (i.e. purchases for resale) of both natural gas and of electricity is treated as being where the customer's business is established. Supplies to final consumers are taxed where the natural gas or electricity is consumed.

The need for suppliers to have multiple VAT registrations is generally now removed. How the Directive puts, this, in art. 38(1), is that:

> '... in the case of the supply of gas through a natural gas system situated within the territory of the Community or any network connected to such a system, the supply of electricity, or the supply of heat or cooling energy through heating or cooling networks to a taxable dealer: the place of supply shall be deemed to be the place where that taxable dealer has established his business or has a fixed establishment or, in the absence of such a place of business or fixed establishment, the place where he has his permanent address or usually resides.'

A *taxable dealer* for this purpose means a taxable person whose principal activity in respect of purchases of gas and electricity is reselling such products and whose own consumption of these products is negligible.

The concept of where a business is *established* for this purpose is much the same as for the *belonging* rules in the case of the place of supply of services (see **Chapter 3** at 30-250).

(1) A *business establishment* is the principal place of business and is usually the head office, headquarters or *seat* from which the business is run.

(2) A *fixed establishment* is an establishment other than the business establishment, to which the natural gas and electricity is supplied. A business may have several fixed establishments, and, if the customer has establishments in more than one country, the supply will take place at whichever establishment is most directly connected with that particular supply.

Where the supplier belongs outside the customer's Member State, there is a *reverse-charge* mechanism, which enables VAT-registered customers to account for the VAT due as output tax on their VAT returns, rather than the supplier, thus removing the requirement for the supplier to register for VAT in that Member State for the supplies involved.

There is a corresponding impact on the time of supply. The normal rule is that this occurs each time a payment is received by the supplier, or a VAT invoice is issued, whichever is the earlier. However, in the case of supplies covered by the new reverse-charge, the recipient accounts for the VAT due in the VAT accounting period when the goods are paid for or, if payment is not in money, on the last day of the accounting period in which the gas or electricity is removed or made available.

Gas or electricity distribution systems for this purpose are the transmission networks of pipelines, cables and inter-connectors, which enable the national and international transport of gas and electricity to be carried out (in the UK, the National Grid or the network of pipelines owned by National Grid/Transco). It will also, in practice, include the Interconnector between the UK and Belgium and, at the present time, some of the dry gas pipelines between offshore production platforms and the UK, such as including the Langaled pipeline into Easington. It will not include separately-owned storage facilities where the gas needs to be treated to bring it up to the correct specification for transmission to consumers before injection into the transmission system itself.

The treatment as part of the gas distribution system of dry gas pipelines between offshore production platforms and shore terminals is not at present, however, followed in all Member States, so that imports into some countries may be subject to VAT.

(b) Services

The rules also apply in a similar manner to services in the form of allowing access to, and actual use of, the distribution networks and other *directly linked* services such as:

- the provision of data on network usage;
- the storage of gas within the natural gas distribution system; and
- services involving injection of gas into the system,

which have been added to the list of services in VATA 1994, Sch. 4A, para. 16 (art. 59 of Directive 2006/112/EC (art. 9(2)(e) of the Sixth Directive 77/388/EC)). Not included in Sch. 4A, however, are:

- balancing and imbalance charges;
- contract termination payments;
- fees/subscriptions for membership of regulatory or trade bodies; and
- brokerage.

(c) Third-country imports

Natural gas imported via the natural gas distribution system and electricity are not chargeable on import but are zero-rated. In the case of gas, this only applies, however, to dry gas. Wet gas cannot, as such, be released into the natural gas distribution system.

(d) Brokerage

Brokerage earned on transactions relating to electricity and natural gas can be treated differently from that on currency and financial products. This is because:

(1) The commissions will usually be taxable for VAT, and not VAT-exempt, especially if the reference point for the commissions is the arrangement of a supply of a deliverable tangible commodity, and not something that is cash-settled.

(2) The basic rules on the place of supply of the brokers' services (which determine, for example, whether UK VAT or the VAT of another EU Member State is to be accounted for) follow the place of supply of the underlying client transactions. Since gas and electricity are goods, the basic place of supply of the goods, and of the brokers' services, may thus be where the gas or electricity is located at the time it is appropriated to the supply, unless the rules in (a) above apply.

The importance of (1) above is that the commissions will potentially improve the broker's overall VAT position, if other commissions earned are VAT-exempt.

In the UK, Directive 2003/92/EC has been implemented by a new VATA 1994, s. 9A introducing the reverse charge mechanism for natural gas and electricity and secondary legislation in the form of the following five statutory instruments:

(1) The *Value Added Tax (Place of Supply of Goods) Order* 2004 – which contains the new place of supply provisions (SI 2004/3148).

(2) The *Value Added Tax (Imported Gas, Electricity, Heat and Cooling) Relief Order* 2010 – which relieves natural gas and electricity from VAT at importation (SI 2010/2924).

(3) The *Value Added Tax (Reverse Charge) (Amendment) Order* 2004 – which changes the place of supply of services in the form of access to, and transport or transmission through, natural gas and electricity distribution systems to the place where the customer belongs. This also includes other directly related services (SI 2004/3149).

(4) The *Value Added Tax (Removal of Gas, Electricity, Heat and Cooling) Order* 2010 – which excludes removals of natural gas and electricity from one Member State to another as a deemed supply in the form of a transfer of own goods (SI 2010/2925).

(5) The *Value Added Tax (Amendment) (No. 4) Regulations* 2004 – which creates a new time of supply rule for supplies subject to the reverse-charge mechanism and makes other consequential amendments to the *Value Added Tax Regulations* 1995 (SI 2004/3140).

More commentary on this can be found in VAT Information Sheet 10/04 – Changes to the place of supply of natural gas and electricity.

100-400 Emissions allowances and other environmental products

With the growing awareness of the effects of global warming and climate change a similar market is also now developing in permits relating to CO_2 and greenhouse gas emissions.

(1) Greenhouse Gas Emissions Trading Scheme

Emissions trading is becoming a key part of the move to reduce greenhouse gas emissions, the rationale being to ensure that emission reductions take place where the cost of the reduction is lowest, thus lowering the overall costs of combating climate change.

The EU Emissions Trading Scheme (EU ETS) introduced by Directive 2003/87/EC embodies Europe-wide policies to reduce emissions and combat climate change. In the UK, the Regulations implementing this are the *Greenhouse Gas Emissions Trading Scheme Regulations* 2005 (SI 2005/925).

Emissions Trading allows governments to regulate the amount of emissions produced in aggregate by setting the overall cap for the scheme but gives companies the flexibility of determining how and where the emissions reductions will be achieved. By allowing participants the flexibility to trade allowances the overall emissions reductions are achieved in the most cost-effective way possible.

Participating companies are allocated allowances, each representing a tonne of the relevant emission, in this case, CO_2 equivalent, the idea being that:

- companies that emit in excess of their allocation of allowances can purchase allowances from the market; and, similarly,
- companies emitting less than their allocation can sell any surplus allowances.

In contrast to regulation, which imposes limits on particular factories and installations, emissions, trading thus gives companies the flexibility to meet targets according in their own way.

APX Power UK, as part of the Climex Alliance, offers clearing services for the APX Power UK Spot Carbon contract.

In VAT terms, allowance/permit trading and transfers represent supplies of taxable services rather than of goods. It has now been agreed, in accordance with what is now the general rule for business to business supplies, that for cross-border supplies of allowances, the place of supply should be the place where the customer belongs.

This approach aligns the UK treatment with that of other Member States and therefore avoids instances of double taxation. It only, however, affects supplies of allowances when traded across borders; there is no change to the place of supply of supplies within a country (which continue to be taxed where the supplier is based, subject to the normal rules).

As Business Brief 28/04 of 23 October 2004 observes, the place of supply of brokers' services needs to be determined separately. As the place of supply for cross-border transactions in allowances is where they are received, the broker's supply will take place where that broker's customer belongs, regardless of where the actual emissions allowances are sold. According to the normal rules, a broker is regarded as such when sufficient intermediation is performed. Introduction is not sufficient – where the service is one of mere introduction, the supply will be seen in accordance with the basic rule i.e. where the introducer *belongs*.

(2) Renewable energy

There is also a UK renewable electricity market, based on Renewables Obligation Certificates (ROCs). Regulations under the *Utilities Act* 2000 requires power suppliers to derive a specified proportion of the electricity they supply from renewable sources. This started at three per cent in 2003, and is to rise gradually to 10.4 per cent by 2010, and 15.4 per cent by 2015. Eligible renewable generators receive ROCs for each MWh of electricity generated. These certificates can then be sold to suppliers, in order to fulfil their obligation. Suppliers can either present enough certificates to cover the required percentage of their output, or they can pay a *buyout* price for any shortfall. All proceeds from buyout payments are recycled to suppliers in proportion to the number of ROCs they present. The buyout price is set each year by Ofgem.

A *qualifying renewable source* is any source of energy *other than* fossil fuel or nuclear fuel used at a generating station not excluded by the RO Orders.

Trading in ROCs is considered to be a taxable supply of services, with a place of supply under the basic rule – i.e. they are taxed in the country where the customer is based.

In *Revenue and Customs Brief* 52/2007 of 22 August 2007 (*VAT – place of supply of trading allowances in greenhouse gas emissions (update)*) HMRC further clarified their position, having considered the nature and purpose of the various instruments available under the different Schemes in use and which that are currently being, or will be in future, traded cross-border.

The Brief covers instruments representing emission reductions, carbon credits, and certificates that identify that the production of energy has been generated from renewable sources. These include, but are not limited to, Certified Emission Reductions (CERs), Renewal Obligation Certificates (ROCs), Emission Reduction Units (ERUs), Levy Exemption Certificates (LECs), Assigned Amount Units (AAUs), EU Allowances (EUAs) and Renewable Energy Certificates (RECs).

In the case of supplies of Verified Emission Reductions (VERs) the place of supply will be the same as for emissions allowances.

> '*Place of supply rules*
>
> The place of supply of cross border trading in greenhouse gas emissions instruments is the place where the recipient belongs (falling within VATA 1994[, s. 7A(2) and Sch. 4A, para. 16] and art. 56 of the VAT Directive). Transactions that take place between parties established in the UK will continue to be taxed where the supplier belongs, under section 7(10) of the Act (art. 43 of the VAT Directive).
>
> This will not affect certificates or instruments that are sold with goods or services. In these circumstances the certificates will usually be viewed as incidental or ancillary to the main supply. An example of this is where a guarantee of origin is issued to customers purchasing electricity that certifies the electricity was generated from renewable sources.'

100-450 Points affecting particular supplies

(1) Arbitration services

Arbitration services are essentially taxable services which are, arguably, provided jointly to each of the parties concerned. Because of this, the whole of the fee should, on the face of it be standard-rated where one of the parties is in the UK.

Nonetheless, by concession HMRC are prepared to allow apportionment but this depends on the award of costs. Thus, if party W is required to pay 70 per cent of the costs and party B 30 per cent, the supply will be regarded as split between them in that proportion. Only in the exceptional cases, where there is no award of costs, will HMRC treat the consideration as split 50:50 between the two parties in dispute.

Under this arrangement it makes no difference which of the parties decides to take up, and initially pay for, the award.

(2) Commodity fund management

Fees charged by managers of individual portfolios, commodity funds or syndicates are usually based on a percentage of the funds. They will tend to be taxable for VAT purposes, usually at the standard-rate.

- In *Cornhill Management Ltd* (1990) 5 BVC 901 HMRC sought to argue that the company was, in reality, acting as principal in its dealings with a financial futures fund. The agreement, however, pointed to agency and the ownership of the assets by the clients.

(3) Fees and clearing house charges

Fees and clearing house charges involve supplies of services, which, in the case of UK exchanges, will be largely taxable at the standard-rate.

The clearing house registration charge is fixed at a set amount per lot bought and sold, with a rebate according to aggregate monthly turnover. It is regarded by HMRC as payment for an administration service, which is taxed at the standard-rate for exchanges other than those involved with financial products (e.g. LIFFE). In the latter cases, the charge is exempt.

The accommodation charge is made where a member's liability is covered by approved securities other than cash in the case of:

- margins;
- deposits; and
- cover account debit balances.

The charge is regarded as payment for a financial service. It is basically standard-rated in the case of exchange dealing in hard and soft commodities; otherwise exempt.

The Euronext.liffe, LME and IPE/ICE levies are always standard-rated.

Interest paid by LCH to members on deposits or liabilities covered by cash or on balances is essentially exempt (VATA 1994, Sch. 9, Grp. 5, item 2).

(4) Gold

Transactions in gold and gold coins invite a number of special considerations. The high values often involved mean standard-rating can be both a burden and an opportunity for large scale fraud and evasion. Zero-rating, by the same token, is important but the circumstances in which this is available are not always easily understood, a factor which lead to the agreement reached in June 1991 between HMRC and the London Bullion Market Association (the LBMA) and which is reproduced at **Appendix 9**. The specialist HMRC publication on gold is Notice 701/21.

(a) Central Banks

The supply of gold or gold coins is given a special, but limited, zero-rating under VATA 1994, Sch. 8, Grp. 10. This applies for any supply between Central Banks or between a Central Bank and a member of the London Gold Market, where the supply involves:

- gold or gold coins held in the UK;
- the right to acquire gold or gold coins held in the UK; or
- unallocated gold or gold coins, again held in the UK.

The value of the supply, in all cases, is the full amount of consideration received, although, for gold coins which are legal tender, this is reduced by their face value.

Apart from this, other supplies of gold coins are standard-rated, whether legal tender or not except where they come within the special scheme for investment gold (see (f) below and HMRC Notice 701/21A Investment Gold Coins).

An investment gold coin is:

(1) a gold coin minted after 1800 that:

    (a) is of a purity of not less than 900 thousandths;
    (b) is, or has been, legal tender in its country of origin; and
    (c) is of a description of coin that is normally sold at a price that does not exceed 180 per cent of the open market value of the gold contained in the coin; or

(2) a gold coin included on a list published by the European Commission.

A coin not on the lists can still be exempt from VAT if it falls within the description at (1) above, but the business records must show that any such coin meets the criteria.

Coins that do not fall within (1) or (2) above are subject to VAT at the standard rate.

(b) The Black Box

In addition to the relief under Grp. 10, there is also the wider zero-rating available for transactions in gold and gold bullion under the *Value Added Tax (Terminal Markets) Order 1973* (SI 1973/173) (see 100-200 earlier). This can apply to most transactions involving gold between members of the London Gold Market or between members and non-members. As with the other markets to which the Order applies, however, relief is limited to transactions in items ordinarily dealt with in the market, which is taken by HMRC to exclude coins when transacted between members and non-members (para. 3.3.6 of HMRC Notice 701/9/2011).

The LBMA agreement is particularly important in this respect as it in many ways confirms what had previously often been market practice. Briefly, with certain exceptions, all supplies of bullion, including loans, will be treated as zero-rated provided bullion is not physically removed from the *Black Box*. This applies to all supplies irrespective of the counterparties (whether LBMA members or not, or whether the bullion is allocated or unallocated). Bullion is regarded as having been removed when effective physical control is transferred from an LBMA member to a non-member. When bullion leaves the physical control of an LBMA member, the market agreement considers the member to have supplied the bullion to the person taking delivery, tax generally being chargeable at the standard rate on the value of the gold at the time.

However, the *supply* deemed to be made by the LBMA member may well not in law be a supply by him. In this situation, there would appear also to be no contractual 'right' on the part of the member to demand VAT from the person taking delivery. This clearly raises a number of potential difficulties, which may need to be watched.

In the case of an LBMA member providing only safe carriage from another LBMA member, the supply on delivery will be regarded as made by the latter. Similarly, the rules are modified where an LBMA member merely holds bullion in safe custody for a customer, the arrangements in that case not resulting in a supply by the member concerned.

A number of other aspects of the agreement affect the position of bullion transferred for refining purposes.

(c) Bullion loans

Typically, bullion loans will involve someone who is temporarily in need of actual gold *borrowing* what is required from someone with sufficient stock. The terms of the loan will be for a specific quantity and quality of gold to be borrowed or lent for a specific period and at a stated rate of interest. Borrowers may be manufacturers/end-users whose normal supplies, although contracted for, have not yet been delivered or brokers who for some reason are *short* at a given point in time. Alternatively, the loans may simply amount to a financial arrangement with a client or customer.

Outwardly the appearance is similar to an advance of money within VATA 1994, Sch. 9, Grp. 5, item 2 (art. 135(1)(b) of Council Directive 2006/112/EC). However, as with securities lending (see **Chapter 8** at 80-200(29)), the effect seems to be that the lender will make a disposal of the asset concerned, since the exact same gold will not be *paid back*. The *interest* is to that extent not itself strictly consideration for an advance but is part of the value of a much larger transaction. Similarly, the borrower will, on redemption, make a further supply of the physical gold. When outside the *Black Box* (see 100-200(1)) VAT will tend to be due at the standard rate unless:

- the goods are already outside the UK; or
- the gold is unallocated and the supply is to someone outside the UK.

Having said this, the matter of bullion loans is specifically addressed in the LBMA agreement, which seems to ascribe a quite different treatment. Distinction is drawn between *paper transactions* and *consignments*.

Paper transactions involve loans which are purely book transfers not involving physical delivery. Interest is normally calculated at an agreed rate expressed in ounces of the metal concerned. This is then converted into sterling or US dollars and is treated as the measure of a basically exempt supply within VATA 1994, Sch. 9, Grp. 5, item 2. This exemption is replaced by zero-rating when a loan could be regarded as taking place within the *Black Box*. It is also perhaps worth noting that the basis for exemption in art. 135 of Council Directive 2006/112/EC (art. 13(B)(d) of the Sixth VAT Directive) seems to contemplate credit in terms just of a purely monetary transaction.

Consignments are loans where bullion is physically made available to the customer to work on, payment not being required until a later date. VAT is charged in this case at the standard-rate on the market value of the bullion. Any financing charge is seen as further consideration for that standard-rated supply.

Where loans are unallocated rather than specifically identified gold, the rules are somewhat different. The supplies will still involve disposals of gold rather than loans in the monetary sense and will thus, subject to the LMBA agreement, arguably be taxable rather than exempt. When either lender or borrower is a member of the London Gold Market, zero-rating is available under the *Black Box*. However, being supplies of services for VAT purposes (see 100-150(3) earlier), the supply will be *outside the scope* of UK VAT when made to a VAT-registered business belonging in another Member State or to anyone outside the EU. Related input tax is recoverable under reg. 103 of the *Value Added Tax Regulations* 1995 (SI 1995/2518).

(d) The special scheme

There is also a compulsory scheme which applies for VAT accounting on certain supplies of gold (VATA 1994, s. 55). It is aimed at combating cases of serious VAT fraud and covers all standard-rated supplies of fine gold and gold coins – but not dental fine gold, gold targets and gold slugs. It also applies to supplies of goods containing gold – but not to certain manufactured or part-manufactured goods.

The scheme operates where both parties are registered or liable to be registered for VAT. The seller issues a VAT invoice to the buyer in the normal way, but does not account for the tax. This is included by the buyer as output VAT in his VAT return, with input VAT being claimed at the same time. The seller, whose invoice is to be endorsed to that effect, is then paid only the net of the VAT amount. Unlike the previous scheme, the VAT is accounted for in the buyer's next VAT return; it is not paid to HMRC immediately. The cash-flow disadvantage to the buyer is thus largely removed.

Full details of the scheme are set out in Pt. 11 of HMRC Notice 701/21 reproduced at **Appendix 17**.

(e) Unallocated gold

Transactions in unallocated gold are supplies of services for VAT purposes (VATA 1994, Sch. 4, para. 1) and not goods. Being regarded by HMRC as financial services, the VAT treatment can also depend on where the buyer belongs (see 100-200(3)).

(f) Investment gold

A special scheme for *investment gold* was introduced from 1 January 2000. This came about as a result of the *Gold Directive* (Directive 98/80), and was put in place in the UK by FA 1999, s. 13 and the *Value Added Tax (Investment Gold) Order* 1999 (SI 1999/3116). The scheme is based on an exemption in VATA 1994, Sch. 9, Grp. 15. The text of Grp. 15 will be found at **Appendix 19**. A detailed explanation of the scheme is to be found in HMRC Notice 701/21.

Before 1 January 2000, gold was taxable in the UK, regardless of purity or use. This differed from the treatment afforded in a number of other Member States and the exemption puts investment in gold on a similar footing to financial investments. However, gold continues to be supplied by the industrial market to the investment market and this still bears tax. The *Value Added Tax (Terminal Markets) Order* 1973 (SI 1973/173) (see earlier at 100-400(4)) also still applies to certain transactions.

Investment gold is defined as:

(1) Gold of a purity not less than 995 thousandths and in the form of a bar, or a wafer, and of a weight accepted by the bullion markets.

(2) Gold coins minted after 1800 that are:
   (a) of a purity of not less than 900 thousandths;
   (b) or have been, legal tender in its country of origin; and
   (c) of a description of coin that is normally sold at a price that does not exceed 180 per cent of the open market value of the gold contained in the coin.

(3) Gold coins of a description specified in Notice 701/21A.

The European Commission have published a list, usually updated annually, of those gold coins that must be treated as investment gold in all Member States. Supplies or importations of coins not included in Notice 701/21A are generally subject to VAT at the standard-rate. Gold coins, which are investment gold are not eligible to be sold under the margin scheme for second-hand goods, works of art, antiques and collectors' items.

Although based around an exemption, the scheme has three special features:

(1) There is an option to tax (an election to waive exemption), for certain transactions, enabling the recovery of underlying input tax (subject to the normal rules).

(2) Input tax can also be recovered on purchases of gold and on the costs of transforming gold into investment gold.

(3) Producers and transformers of investment gold can recover input tax on certain costs linked to the production or transformation process.

The option to tax is conferred by art. 3 of the *Value Added Tax (Investment Gold) Order* 1999 (SI 1999/3116) and, unlike the option to tax in the case of property under VATA 1994, Sch. 10, para. 2 (see **Chapter 8** at 80-150), is exercised in respect of individual supplies of investment gold. The relief for input tax is given in the *Value Added Tax (Input Tax) Order* 1999 (SI 1999/3222) and the *Value Added Tax (Input Tax) (Specified Supplies) Order* 1999 (SI 1999/3121). The scheme also allows special procedures for transactions on the London Bullion Market.

The exemption applies to:

- supplies of investment gold;

- supplies conferring rights to take possession of investment gold, including unallocated investment gold, loans, swaps, forward and future contracts, but not options;
- supplies of agents attempting to bring about supplies within either of the above, even if abortive.

As with certain of the other transactions in gold, there are special accounting arrangements for supplies covered by the option to tax, which are accounted for under a *reverse charge* procedure by the buyer, rather than by the seller. In many respects, this is similar, therefore, to that applying for other supplies of gold and discussed earlier at 100-400(4).

Those dealing in investment gold must also notify HMRC the first time an exempt supply is made of a value of more than £5,000, or when the value of supplies to any one customer exceeds £10,000 in any 12-month period. HMRC also have to be notified when the option to tax is exercised and there are other special rules governing accounting, invoicing and record keeping.

There are also special rules on partial exemption in reg. 103A of the *Value Added Tax Regulations* 1995, which are discussed earlier in **Chapter 4** at 40-200(b).

(5) The IPE/ICE Brent Crude contract

One of the conditions of zero-rating under the *Value Added Tax (Terminal Markets) Order* 1973 (SI 1973/173) is that the underlying subject matter of the futures contract should be deliverable. The Brent Crude contract, however, is expressed in terms of quantities that, on their own, are generally commercially too small for delivery. This means that the contract would, on the face of it, be cash-settled and VAT-exempt. However, in practice, this is overcome by a device known as an *exchange for physicals*, the exchange of a futures position for a physical (swap) position between two agreeing parties through the Exchange.

(6) Spread betting

Financial spread betting is betting on financial instruments and works in the same way as sports spread betting. It involves speculating by placing a bet on a financial index such as those for commodity prices or the FTSE 100 index. In the same way as sports betting, financial spread betting is liable to General Betting Duty and is exempt from VAT under VATA 1994, Sch. 9, Grp. 4. Duty is calculated on the total amount due from customers less any winnings paid out. The duty rate is three per cent of the gross margin.

10 Commodity Derivatives and Financial Derivatives

> **Summary**
>
> Commodity derivatives and financial derivatives play a vital part in the working of the City and of many commercial and industrial sectors.
>
> As will have been seen, many commodity transactions will be taxable. Some will be zero-rated under Terminal Markets Order or the *Black Box* or even *outside the scope of VAT*, so that no tax is, in the event, chargeable. However, financial products and derivatives will be VAT-exempt with the prospect that underlying input tax may be liable to be restricted.
>
> This, coupled with the possibility that some of the markets on which trading is done impose requirements for members to act as principal, rather than in an agency capacity, can make arriving at the correct VAT interpretation potentially more difficult than for other sectors covered by this book.

11 Mergers and Acquisitions

> **Overview**
>
> **This Chapter considers:**
>
> (1) **VAT on corporate transactions.**
>
> (2) **The ability to recover input VAT incurred on mergers and acquisitions.**
>
> (3) **Maximising VAT recovery.**

110-000 Mergers and acquisitions: general

Introduction

The great rule in business as in life is that, like the stars turning in their motions, we fall down if we try and stand still. Mergers and acquisitions are accordingly normal and integral features of the life of most businesses.

The only specific VAT concepts that exist in relation to such transactions are:

(a) the transfer of a going concern (TOGC), and
(b) intra-group transactions where a grouping election has been made.

These are both options available to Member States under the VAT Directive. Other than these two concepts, there are no special VAT rules for mergers and acquisitions.

VAT on expenses is at best a cashflow cost and at worst an absolute cost. The particular matters which need to be addressed are:

- economic activity;
- activities of holding companies;
- share purchases/acquisition of a business;
- share sales/disposal of a business;
- business combinations – impact of grouping;
- business continuity;
- share purchases – use of special purpose vehicles (SPVs);
- direct and immediate link;
- share issues;
- abortive supplies;
- TOGCs;
- supplies to third parties;
- maximising VAT recovery.

Company law and tax law

The *Companies Act* 2006 and *Insolvency Act* 1986 provide for three methods of reconstruction and amalgamation:

(1) a transfer of assets to another company in a members' voluntary liquidation under *Insolvency Act* 1986, s. 110 and 111;

(2) arrangements and reconstructions under *Companies Act* 2006, s. 895–901;

(3) acquisition of dissenting or minority shareholders under Pt. 28 of the *Companies Act* 2006.

FRS 6 and FRS 7 contain a series of definitions of corporate transactions, including:

- acquisition;
- business combination;
- group reconstruction;
- merger.

For VAT purposes, five principal questions arise:

(1) Is an entity engaged in an economic activity?

(2) Is input tax chargeable on expenses attributable to a particular transaction or to the business of the undertaking as a whole?

(3) Is VAT incurred on the costs of transactions incurred for the purpose of making taxable supplies?

(4) Do the TOGC rules or grouping rules impact on the transaction?

(5) How can the fundamental principle of the common system of VAT that wholly taxable traders should be able to recover input tax in full be implemented?

As regards issue (3), for input tax to be recoverable:

- the entity seeking to recover VAT must be carrying on an economic activity or intending to carry on an economic activity;
- in relation to a given taxable person, the supply must be made to him for the purpose of his business;
- there must be a direct and immediate link between the input tax incurred and the taxable outputs of the business;
- that direct and indirect link must take the form of either (a) direct attribution of input tax to specific supplies or (b) attribution of overheads VAT to the activities of the business as a whole.

As regards issue (4), TOGCs are dealt with in detail at: **Chapter 2**, 20-250(5); **Chapter 3**, 30-450; **Chapter 4**, 40-150(9). Accordingly, TOGCs are only mentioned briefly at the end of this Chapter.

As regards issue (5) in applying the law in this area, the ECJ consistently emphasises the importance of giving effect to the policy of the law, that a fully taxable person should recover his input tax. As the Court says in *Skatteverket v AB SKF* (Case C-29/08) [2011] BVC 359, at para. 55:

> 'it should be recalled that the right of deduction provided for in arts 17 to 20 of the Sixth Directive is an integral part of the VAT system and in principle may not be limited.'

110-050 Economic activity

In order to be within the scope of VAT, i.e. a taxable person, that person must be carrying on an 'economic activity' within art. 9(1) of the VAT Directive (2006/112/EC). He must be a taxable person acting as such. The concept of economic activity in VAT law is a very wide one. It is translated into UK legislation as being engaged in 'business' (VATA 1994, s. 4(1)). It is defined both positively and negatively. Economic activity means making supplies of goods and services to third parties for payment. The key concept is consumption in return for consideration within the framework of a bilateral legal relationship. Economic activity must be carried on 'independently'. Hence the services of employees do not constitute economic activity for VAT purposes: art. 10.

The Advocate General in *Banque Bruxelles Lambert SA v Belgium* (Case C-8/03) [2007] BVC 101 observed at para. 10 of his Opinion that two criteria had to be fulfilled for an economic activity to be established – a functional criterion and a structural criterion:

> 'the concept of economic activity is based on a double criterion, not only a functional criterion relating to activity but also and above all a structural criterion relating to organisation ...'

This is not unlike the requirement in relation to direct taxation that for a trade to exist an activity must be pursued in an organised and on a planned basis, with a view to profit. However, in VAT the profit requirement is absent.

Economic activity requires an active rather than a passive role. It is the opposite of being a final consumer. Passive activity, i.e. consuming goods and services without making supplies of goods and services, is not economic activity. The parameters of 'economic activity' within art. 9(1) are set down in *Wellcome Trust Ltd v C & E Commrs* (Case C-155/94) [1996] BVC 377. The Advocate General said at para. 28 (p. 385):

> 'The Sixth Directive ... is intended to apply only to persons who are economically active within the meaning of that directive, not to those whose activity is analogous to that of a private investor.'

The Court said at para. 32 (p. 391):

> '... mere exercise of the right of ownership by its holder cannot, in itself, be regarded as constituting an economic activity.'

Ownership per se and the mere acquisition of financial holdings in other undertakings are not an economic activity, unless some additional element is present. The European Court has referred to this extra element as 'activities which go beyond the compass' of an exempt transaction or non-supply, *Skatteverket v AB SKF* at p. 381 (para. 33 of judgment). That additional element is that the exercise of rights of ownership or transaction in securities must be what the ECJ has called 'the direct, permanent and necessary extension of taxable activity': *Regie Dauphinoise - Cabinet a Forest SARL v Ministre du Budget* (Case C-306/94) [1996] BVC 447 at p. 462 (para. 18 of judgment). In other words, the activity which in isolation would be an exempt supply or outside the scope of VAT must be a subordinate part of or subservient to or an integral part of an overall taxable activity.

Hence in *Wellcome Trust* the disposal of shares in order to diversify a trust's investments did not by itself constitute or form part of a wider economic activity because the trust was doing no more than a private investor would do with his investments, be it on a grand scale. The trust was not making taxable outputs.

The issue of shares is not a supply, so money subscribed to acquire new shares is not consideration for VAT purposes. By the same token, assets contributed in return for shares will not give rise to a supply for VAT purposes. The same principle applies to the contributions of assets or cash to a partnership in return for a share in the partnership's assets and profits. In all these cases the person paying the cash or contributing the assets is simply regarded as transferring money from his right hand trouser pocket to his left hand trouser pocket.

The raising of capital by admitting partners or issuing new shares is not an economic activity and so does not involve a supply to or by the investor. In *KapHag Renditefonds v Finanzamt Charlottenburg* (Case C-442/01) [2005] BVC 566 a joint venture property partnership was formed. A share in the partnership could be acquired by subscribing capital to the partnership. The question was referred to the ECJ, whether the admission of a partner in return for a capital contribution was a supply of services.

As regards the concept of 'economic activity', the Advocate General said at para. 26:

> 'The concept is a very wide one ... The decisive factor is that the purpose is to obtain income on an ongoing basis ...'

The court held at para. 38–39 that the admission of a new partner for a capital contribution was not an economic activity, because it was the mere acquisition of a financial holding in an undertaking.

The receipt of dividends is not the obtaining of income on an ongoing basis, because the payment is not obtained from third parties. The same applies to the receipt of interest by an investor who acquires or is holding bonds: *Harnas & Helm CV v Staatssecretaris van Financien* (Case C-80/95) [1997] BVC 358 at p. 376 (para. 19 of judgment).

Acts preparatory to the carrying on of an economic activity constitute economic activity. In *Rompelman v Minister van Financien* (Case 268/83) (1985) 2 BVC 200,157 couple incurred expenditure prior to the making of taxable supplies (letting). The ECJ held that a person undertaking acts preparatory to the carrying on of an economic activity qualified as a taxable person within art. 4(1) of the Sixth Directive:

> 'the economic activities referred to in Article 4(1) may consist in several consecutive transactions ... the preparatory acts, such as the acquisition of assets and therefore the purchase of immovable property, which form part of those transactions, must themselves be treated as constituting economic activity.'

Economic activity is an objective concept. It does not depend upon subjective intention, except in so far as that is manifested in concrete acts.

In *Rompelman* the ECJ said that whether or not a person was carrying on an economic activity was a matter of objective evidence. The court said at p. 200,157 (para. 12 of judgment):

> 'exploitation must not be considered to exist until there is more objective evidence of the investor's intention. A declaration of intention must be confirmed by other facts and circumstances.'

In *BLP Group plc v C & E Commrs* (Case C-4/94) [1995] BVC 159 the question was (as explained above) whether the input VAT should be linked with the sale of the shares or with the company's general economic activity. The court said at p. 173 (para. 24 of judgment) that, for VAT purposes, regard must be had to what happened, not some underlying subjective intention:

> 'Moreover, if BLP's interpretation were accepted, the authorities, when confronted with supplies which, as in the present case, are not objectively linked to taxable transactions, would have to carry out inquiries to determine the intention of the taxable person. Such an obligation would be contrary to the VAT system's objectives of ensuring legal certainty and facilitating application of the tax by having regard, save in exceptional cases, to the objective character of the transaction in question.'

110-100 Activities of holding companies

It follows that a passive holding company, i.e. a holding company which simply holds investments and receives dividends, will not be engaged in economic activity.

In *Polysar Investments Netherlands BV v Inspecteur der Invoerrechten en Accijnzxeb, Arnhem* (Case C-60/90) [1993] BVC 88 a company which was simply inserted as a conduit company in a chain of shareholdings in order to take advantage of the Netherlands' network of double taxation agreements was held not to be carrying on an economic activity.

The Advocate General summed up the position as regards holding companies in *KapHag* at para. 30:

> '... a holding company which restricts its activity to acquiring shares in other undertakings is not entitled to deduct input VAT, since it is not a taxable person in the sense that in the absence of consideration, it does not carry out an economic activity within the meaning of the Sixth Directive, nor is it a taxable person when it receives dividends ... In such a situation the only activity consists in the administration of an asset.'

However, the ECJ indicated that, given the expansive nature of the concept of economic activity, it would only require very modest activity on the part of a parent undertaking to shift it from passive holding company to active holding company status. As the Court said at paras. 13–14 of the judgment:

> '13. The mere acquisition of financial holdings in other undertakings does not amount to the exploitation of property for the purposes of obtaining income therefrom on a continuing basis because any dividend yielded by that holding is merely the result of ownership of the property.

14. It is otherwise where the holding is accompanied by direct or indirect involvement in the management of the holdings in which the holding has been acquired, without prejudice to the rights held by the holding company as shareholder.'

This established a distinction between passive holding companies (which are not carrying on economic activity) and active holding companies (which are).

A company will characteristically become an active holding company by making supplies for consideration to subsidiaries. A mixed holding company will both hold shares in subsidiaries and provide taxable services to the companies in which they hold shares, such as management, technical assistance, accounting, legal and IT services. Provision of services by a holding company is an alternative to outsourcing.

Floridienne SA v Belgium(Case C-142/99) [2001] BVC 76 concerned a mixed holding company which (a) received dividends from subsidiaries, (b) lent back the dividends paid and (c) was paid interest by them. The question was, whether in the partial exemption recovery formula, interest and dividends should be included in the denominator, so restricting the amount recovered. The ECJ held that:

'(a) only income which was within the scope of VAT could be included in the denominator [para. 12];

(b) dividends should always be excluded from the denominator of the partial exemption calculation because there was no direct link between the dividends and the management services supplied [para. 21];

(c) the making of capital available to subsidiaries with a view to obtaining interest may be considered an economic activity in its own right [para. 28]. '

The right to deduct VAT incurred in effecting a takeover carries over post-acquisition. In *Cibo Participations SA v Directeur régional des impôts du Nord-Pas-de-Calais* (Case C-16/00) [2002] BVC 605 an active holding company was held to be entitled to recover VAT on costs incurred in connection with the acquisition of shares in subsidiaries. After the take-over it had provided management and other services to those companies on a fee-paying basis. The Advocate General argued that if a company was acquiring a majority or 100 per cent shareholding, the ability to exercise substantial influence on the management of the subsidiaries indicated that this was an economic activity:

'8 A holding company does not carry out any economic activity and is therefore not a taxable person unless it involves itself in the management of the subsidiary ... In both cases [majority shareholding and 100% shareholding], the acquisition the acquisition of shares is an economic activity within the scope of the Sixth Directive, because it is possible, in fact or in law, for the holding company to involve itself in the management of its subsidiary undertaking to a greater extent than usual shareholder rights would permit.'

The Court held that expenditure on acquisition costs was an overhead with a direct and immediate link to its business as a whole (AG para. 37, Court para. 33). The Court held:

'33. the costs of those services [acquisition costs] are part of the taxable person's general costs and are, as such, cost components of an undertaking's products. Such services therefore do, in principle, have a direct and immediate link with the taxable person's business as a whole ...

35. ... expenditure incurred by a holding company in respect of the various services which it purchased in connection with the acquisition of a subsidiary forms part of its general costs and therefore has, in principle, a direct and immediate link with its business as a whole ...'

A share purchase is an input, not an output. In *Cibo Participations* the VAT incurred on professional costs incurred in purchasing three companies was held to be recoverable, as being the direct, permanent and necessary extension of a taxable activity, which the holding company continued after takeover of the subsidiaries by providing management services on a fee-paying basis.

Cibo Participations brings out the importance of linking inputs to outputs in order to be able to obtain credit for input tax. However, the need for a specific attribution has been largely removed by the ability – which the Court recognised in that case, so anticipating *Abbey National* (Case C-169/04) [2008] BVC 488 and *Kretztechnik* (Case C-465/03) [2006] BVC 66 – to relate inputs to the business of an undertaking as a whole, in other words to treat VAT which is not specifically attributable to taxable supplies as overheads VAT attributable to the supplies of the business in general.

110-150 Share purchases – acquisition of a business

As *Cibo* demonstrates, to recover VAT on professional costs incurred on the purchase of shares or a business, it has to be shown that the activity takes place in the course of furtherance of a business, which in the case of a group may be demonstrated by provision of group management services on a chargeable basis. Trading in securities is exempt: VAT Directive, art. 135(1)(f). Accordingly, transactions in shares or securities may be:

(a) commercial share-dealing and securities trading; or
(b) undertaken in order to secure direct or indirect involvement in the management of the company in which the shareholding is acquired; or
(c) a direct, permanent and necessary extension of taxable activity; or
(d) an acquisition of property to secure rights of ownership rather than exploitation of property to produce income on a continuing basis.

Transactions (a)–(c) are within the scope of VAT; transaction (d) is not: *Harnas & Helm CV v Staatssecretaris van Financien* (Case C-80/95) [1997] BVC 358 at p. 376 (para. 15 of judgment); *Skatteverket v AB SKF* (Case C-29/08) [2011] BVC 359 at p. 381 (para. 31 of judgment).

If share purchases come within the scope of VAT, then it follows that the disposal of the shares will also form part of an economic activity: *Skatteverket v AB SKF* at p. 381 (para. 34 of judgment).

110-200 Share sales – disposal of a business

In *BLP* the input tax incurred on professional expenses incurred in order to make a share sale was not recoverable because it was consumed in making a directly attributable sale of shares, which was an exempt supply.

Hence, if on an objective basis VAT is directly attributable, there is no scope for treating it as overheads VAT. On the other hand, raising funds from external creditors can constitute an economic activity, because it involves a supply by the lender to the debtor.

> '25. It is true that an undertaking whose activity is subject to VAT is entitled to deduct the tax on the services supplied by accountants or legal advisers for the taxable person's taxable transactions and that if BLP had decided to take out a bank loan for the purpose of meeting the same requirements, it would have been entitled to deduct the VAT on the accountant's services required for that purpose.'

The right to deduct was lost in *BLP* because the share sale brought the chain of supply to an end in an exempt supply. If a taxable person makes exempt supplies, he cannot recover input tax attributable to those supplies, either in whole or in part, because the direct and immediate link is to an exempt supply. The exempt supply is a 'chain-breaking transaction'. On the concept of 'chain-breaking transaction': *BLP Group plc v C & E Commrs* (Case C-4/94) [1995] BVC 159 at p. 165 (para. 30); *Abbey National* [2001] BVC 581 (para. 35, 38 of Advocate General).

A more nuanced analysis was adopted by the European Court in *SKF*. The facts were:

(1) SKF was a mixed holding company, being the parent company of an international industrial group, owning shares in and making taxable supplies to subsidiaries.

(2) As part of a group restructuring SKF wanted to sell shares in certain subsidiaries which were or had been wholly owned, and to which taxable management supplies had been made.

(3) SKF sought an advanced ruling from the Swedish tax authorities, whether as such the input VAT on the costs of the share sale and group reorganisation would be recoverable.

The ECJ (departing from the opinion of the Advocate General) held that the input tax would deductible if the costs of the share sale were cost components of SKF's taxable activities. The costs will have such a link where they are attributable to the seller's downstream economic activity. The Court applied the 'direct, permanent and necessary extension of taxable activity' test (*Regie Dauphinoise*):

> '33. By the disposal of all its shares in the subsidiary and in the controlled company, SKF brought to an end its holdings in those companies. The disposal ... can be regarded as a transaction that consists in obtaining income on a continuing basis from activities which go beyond the compass of the simple sale of shares ... That transaction has a direct link with the organisation of the activity carried out by the group and constitutes accordingly the direct, permanent and necessary extension of the taxable activity of the taxable person ...'

The Court also accepted that the transfer of shares could in some circumstances constitute a transfer of a business, so as to be a TOGC: *SKF* [2011] BVC 359 at p. 382 (para. 41 of judgment).

110-250 Business combinations – impact of grouping

A business acquisition or merger will often be accompanied by the formation of a VAT group embracing the acquiring and the acquired businesses. As grouping is intended to provide administrative simplification for both the taxpayer and the tax authority, this is a routine and normal step.

The UK has adopted the option of allowing VAT groups. VATA 1994, s. 43 provides for grouping.

> '(1) Where under sections 43A to 43D any bodies corporate are treated as members of a group, any business carried on by a member of the group shall be treated as carried on by the representative member, and –
>
> (a) any supply of goods or services by a member of the group to another member shall be disregarded, and
>
> (b) any supply which is a supply to which paragraph (a) above does not apply shall be treated as a supply to the representative member, and
>
> (c) ...
>
> and all members of the group shall be liable jointly and severally for any VAT due from the representative member.'

The effect of grouping under VATA 1994, s. 43 is to create for VAT purposes a single taxable person: *C & E Commrs v Kingfisher plc* [1994] BVC 3 at p. 10, cited with approval in *C & E Commrs v Thorn Materials Supply Ltd* [1998] BVC 270 at p. 274.

Within a VAT group it is accordingly impossible to make taxable supplies.

In deciding whether or not input VAT is recoverable, acts of a successor body can be taken into account in cases where the input VAT was incurred by a predecessor body. In a grouping context, this can be seen from *C & E Commrs v Svenska International plc* [1999] BVC 221. A Swedish bank has both a UK subsidiary and a UK branch. The subsidiary incurred inputs with the intention of making taxable supplies to the branch. Before the tax point for the on-supplies, the subsidiary grouped with the branch, which made predominantly exempt supplies. HMRC successfully argued that reg. 108 of the *Value Added Tax Regulations* 1995 then applied, so that the purpose of the subsidiary's input had to be re-evaluated by reference to the new group situation. This led to the supplies being regarded as used for the branch's exempt supplies and so the subsidiary was assessed to tax in respect of part of the input tax previously recovered. A corollary must be that if at the time it incurred the input VAT the subsidiary had intended to group, input tax recovery would not have been permitted. Conversely, had the group made predominantly taxable supplies, recovery would have remained permissible. The conclusion is that, if a company intends to group and use the supplies for group purposes, then the recovery of those supplies must be judged by that future group purpose.

Grouping was further considered in *Royal & Sun Alliance Insurance Group plc v C & E Commrs* [2003] BVC 341, where Lord Hoffmann explained *Svenska* as follows:

'[50] ... The decision in the Svenska case turned on the special effect of the grouping provisions, which, as the House decided, made it necessary to treat the inputs to Svenska as having been inputs to the group and used by the group to make exempt supplies at the time that Branch so used them. This appears most clearly from the speech of Lord Hope of Craighead ([1999] 1 WLR 769 at 778):

"The question raised by reg 34(1)(b) [now reg 108(1)(b)] as to whether, after the group registration, [the supplies to Svenska] [current Section 43] were used or appropriated for use in making an exempt supply must be answered by applying the rule which s 29(1) [of the 1983 Act] lays down, that any business carried on by any member of the group must be treated as carried on by the representative member. For the purposes of this exercise the business carried on by [Branch] must be treated as carried on by Svenska ... As that business involved the making of exempt supplies outside the group to customers of [Branch], Svenska ... must be treated as having used ... the supplies which were attributed to an intended taxable supply ... in making exempt supplies ... I think that the tribunal put the point correctly when it said that this reconstruction of the transactions for VAT purposes, so that inward supplies from outside actually made to Svenska may be looked at with regard to the outward supplies actually made by [Branch], follows from the effect of s 29 ..."

[51] Thus the effect of s 29 of the 1983 Act [current Section 43] was that Svenska was treated as never having carried on the economic activity of making supplies of services. It was the group which was treated as having acquired the input services supplied to Svenska and the group which was treated as having used them for the economic activity of making exempt services supplied by Branch ...'

110-300 Business continuity

In deciding whether VAT incurred by a predecessor body can be attributable to taxable supplies made by a successor body so as to be recoverable, the ECJ has applied a business continuity test. Is the same business being carried on, be it under different formal ownership?

If the same business is being carried on, VAT incurred by the predecessor body can be attributed to taxable supplies made by the successor body.

What needs to be demonstrated is:

'the continuity of the business from preparatory to operational stages – the continuity of its identity as a business'

Finanzamt Offenbach am Main-Land v Faxworld Vorgrundungsgesellschaft (Case C-137/02) [2004] ECR I-554 at para. 37 of Advocate General.

In *Faxworld* the facts were as follows:

(1) A partnership ('Faxworld GbR') was formed in order to set up a limited company ('Faxworld AG').

(2) The partnership incurred input tax but did not make any taxable supplies and so could not recover any input tax.

(3) The partnership transferred its business to the company by way of TOGC.

(4) The partnership sought to recover the input tax incurred but not recovered by the limited company.

The ECJ upheld the recovery claim and stated at para. 41–42:

> '41 ... The taxable person ... Faxworld [i.e. the partnership] ... did not even intend to effect itself taxable operations, its sole object being to prepare the activities of the ... limited company. None the less, the VAT which Faxworld GbR wishes to deduct relates to supplies acquired for the purpose of effecting taxable transactions, even though those transactions were only the planned transactions of Faxworld AG.
>
> 42. In those precise circumstances, and in order to ensure the neutrality of the taxation ... the transferor must be entitled to take account of the taxable transactions of the recipient ... so as to be entitled to deduct the VAT paid on input services which have been procured for the purposes of the recipient's taxable operations.'

The same principle was applied in *Koplania Odkrywkowa Polski Trawertyn v Dyrector Izby Skarbowej w Poznaniu* (Case C-280/10) (1 March 2012). In that case two individuals ('future partners') incurred input VAT in December 2006 in respect of the acquisition of an opencast stone quarry. VAT was payable on the purchase price. They also incurred VAT in April 2007 on legal fees on the formation of a partnership. The invoice for the quarry was addressed to the two individuals, and the invoice for the legal fees was addressed to the partnership. The future partners contributed the quarry in kind to their partnership. The partners did not possess their own VAT registration and did not make any taxable supplies to any person (the contribution of the quarry to the partnership was an exempt transaction). The partnership registered for VAT and sought to recover the input tax both on the quarry purchase and the legal fees. The Polish tax authorities denied the recovery of VAT.

The ECJ was asked to consider whether national legislation which precluded both the future partners and the partnership from exercise of the right to deduct in respect of investment costs incurred by the future partners before the partnership was established and registered for VAT was contrary to EU law. The Court considered the decisions in *Rompelman* and in *INZO*, and applied the principle, citing *Rompelman* that anyone who carries out preparatory acts which are closely connected with and necessary for the making of future taxable supplies must be regarded as a taxable person, even in circumstances where those future taxable supplies were to be carried out by a different person. The Court therefore held that at [31]–[33]:

> '31. Accordingly in a situation such as that at issue... in which the partners of a partnership incurred, before registration and identification of the partnership for the purposes of VAT, investments necessary for the future exploitation of immovable property by the partnership, those partners may be considered to be taxable persons for the purposes of VAT, and are therefore, in principle, entitled to exercise the right to deduct input tax.
>
> 32. Therefore, the fact that the contribution of an immovable property to a partnership by its partners is a transaction exempted from VAT and the fact that those partners do not pay VAT upon the transactions cannot have the consequence of burdening them with the cost of the VAT in the context of their economic activity without any possibility of their deducting it or of obtaining a refund (see, to that effect, *Rompelman* (para. 23)).

33. Second, it should be noted that the court has held that, in applying the principle of neutrality of VAT, a taxable person whose sole object is to prepare the economic activity of another taxable person and who has not effected any taxable transaction may exercise a right to deduct in relation to taxable transactions carried out by the other taxable person (see, to that effect, ... Faxworld ... paras 41 and 42). That interpretation of the Sixth Directive concerned a situation where the VAT which the first taxable person wished to deduct related to supplies acquired by it for the purpose of carrying out taxable transactions planned by the second taxable person.'

In reaching that conclusion the Court confirmed that a series of acts which culminate in the establishment of a taxable business constitute economic activity. The Court said at [28] (p. 1108):

'according to the case law of the court, the economic activities referred to in art 4(1) of the EC Council Directive 77/388 of 17 May 1977 ... may consist in several consecutive transactions and that preparatory acts, such as the acquisition of business assets ... must themselves be treated as constituting economic activity ...'

The words in para. 42 of the judgment in *Faxworld*, 'in those precise circumstances' are designed to confine the circumstances in which B can recover input tax incurred by A as 'his' input tax to cases where there is business continuity (whatever form it may take) between A and B. The governing principle is stated by the ECJ in para. 28 (p. 1207) of *Faxworld*:

'28. According to settled case law, a person who acquires goods for the purposes of an economic activity within the meaning of art 4 does so as a taxable person ... even if the goods are not used immediately for such economic activities ... the validity of those findings is in no way limited by the identity of the person whose economic activity is in question.'

110-350 Share purchases – use of an SPV

Acquisitions will often be implemented by companies specially established for the purpose (special purpose vehicles, SPVs). A newly established SPV will only be a taxable person if it is carrying on an economic activity. As *Rompelman* shows, that may be a question of future intention, to be determined as a matter of objective fact. A person intending to carry on an economic activity is a taxable person from Day One. If the SPV has an objectively demonstrable intention to make taxable supplies (e.g. by making intra-group supplies of management and technical services as in *Cibo*), VAT on professional costs of the acquisition will be recoverable because made in the course of an economic activity involving the making of taxable supplies.

R & C Commrs v BAA Ltd [2011] BVC 1,664 concerned an SPV which acquired all the shares in a target company so becoming the new holding company of the group, but then made an election to join the target's existing VAT group, which made wholly taxable supplies. Membership of the VAT group precluded the making of intra-group taxable supplies of management and technical services. The question which arose was whether the VAT costs of the acquisition could be attributed to taxable supplies of the group constituted post-acquisition.

The facts were:

(1) On 27 March 2006 a company ADIL was formed, financed by three major investors. The purpose for which the company was established was to acquire all the shares in a listed holding company, BAA plc, and take over the management of the BAA group.

(2) ADIL raised finance by equity of debt of £13.1 billion to effect this transaction, and also carry though capital investment post-acquisition.

(3) Immediately after its formation ADIL entered into contracts with investment bankers, solicitors and other professionals, in order to carry out this intention.

(4) On 26 June 2006 the agreed offer for all the BAA plc shares became unconditional.

(5) On 22 September 2006 ADIL joined the BAA VAT group, and became the representative member of the group.

(6) ADIL assumed strategic direction of the group, including responsibility for its ongoing financing.

(7) ADIL (by then renamed 'BAA Ltd') sought as representative member of the group to recover the input VAT incurred by ADIL on the professional costs incurred in acquiring the BAA shares.

Crucially, both the First-tier Tribunal and the Upper Tribunal found that the acquisition by ADIL of the shares in BAA plc did not constitute a cessation, but formed part of a continuum of economic activity (FTT Decision, para. 151; UT Decision, para. 71). As the Upper Tribunal put it:

> 'ADIL's acquisition of BAA was not an end in itself ... but was expressly recorded by the Tribunal as being the first step of an onwards investment, which involved management (para 71).'

Accordingly, ADIL was engaged in economic activity and was a taxable person from inception.

Applying the business continuity principle in *Faxworld*, the First-tier Tribunal allowed recovery. The Upper Tribunal, however, held that there was not a 'sufficiently' direct and immediate contract between the inputs and the outputs to enable recovery of input tax to be made. The Upper Tribunal observed at para. 75:

> 'That preparatory acts of a taxable person may attract VAT recoverability does not affect that conclusion, since those preparatory acts must, at the time at which they attract the payment of VAT, have a direct and immediate link, of sufficient strength, to an onward taxable supply.'

In the Upper Tribunal's view it followed therefore that 'there is no direct and immediate link between the supplies made to ADIL on which the relevant VAT was incurred by ADIL and any onward taxable supplies either made to ADIL or attributed to ADIL' (para. 86).

It would be curious, and difficult to reconcile with the neutrality principle, if an SPV which became a holding company and made taxable supplies to subsidiaries could recover VAT on acquisition costs (Cibo) but an SPV which became a holding company and exercised the option of becoming a member of the acquired VAT group could not recover VAT on acquisition costs. The Upper Tribunal's decision has been appealed to the Court of Appeal.

110-400 Direct and immediate link

It follows from the *BAA* decision that it is essential to show a direct and immediate link between inputs incurred in the course of the corporate transaction and taxable outputs. As the European Court puts it (*SKF* [2011] BVC 359 at p. 384 (para. 60 of judgment)):

> '60. ... whether there is a right to deduct is governed by the nature of the output transactions to which the input transactions are assigned. Accordingly, there is a right to deduct when the input transactions subject to VAT has a direct and immediate link with one or more output transactions giving rise to the right to deduct.'

As Lord Millett has put it (*C & E Commrs v Redrow Group plc* [1999] BVC 96 at p. 103):

> 'It is the acquisition of goods or services by a taxable person acting as such that gives rise to the application of the VAT system and consequently of the deduction mechanism.'

'Direct and immediate link' is a judicial gloss on the statutory words in art. 168 of the VAT Directive, 'used for the purposes of the taxed transactions of a taxable person'. The expression 'direct link' first appears in a VAT case in the *Dutch Potato Co-operative* case in the context of charging VAT, namely, 'there must therefore be a direct link between the service provided and the consideration received': *Staatssecretaris van Financien v 'Cooperatieve Aardappelenbewaarplaats'* [1981] ECR 445 at p. 454 (para. 12 of ECJ).

The phrase was thus originally used in a quite different context to that in which it is found when used to describe the necessary relationship between inputs and outputs. The concept of 'direct and immediate link' applied to inputs first occurred in *BLP Group plc v C & E Commrs* (Case C-4/94) [1995] BVC 159 at p. 17 (para. 19):

> 'Paragraph 5 [of art. 17] lays down the rules applicable to the right to deduct VAT where the VAT relates to goods and services used "both for transactions covered by paragraphs 2 and 3, in respect of which value added tax is deductible, and for transactions in respect of which value added tax is not deductible". The use is that provision of the words "for transactions" shows that to give the right to deduct under para. 2, the goods or services must have a direct and immediate link with the taxable transactions, and that the ultimate aim pursued by the taxable person is irrelevant in this regard.'

The question which the ECJ had to decide in that case was not whether there was a link between inputs and outputs as such, but to which of two possible output transactions the inputs should be attributed. HMRC said that the inputs were attributable to a sale of shares (exempt supply). The taxpayer argued that the inputs were attributable to the activities of the business as a whole (taxable supply). The 'direct and immediate link' test was the means of deciding between two possible attributions. It is not relevant to the question, whether a link as such exists. In any case, the ability to link inputs to the outputs of the business as a whole ('overheads VAT') has in most cases rendered otiose the need to demonstrate a more specific linkage.

The same question fell to be decided in *Midland Bank plc v C & E Commrs* (Case C-98/98) [2000] BVC 229 at p. 247. The ECJ had to decide to which of two possible supplies the link was direct and immediate, i.e. whether input tax should be attributed to a particular supply (a planned sale of shares in a US company, which had already occurred) or to the general business of the bank. In the former case, all the VAT was recoverable. In the latter case, only a small proportion was recoverable.

In its judgment the ECJ distinguished at para. 31 between specific linkage (as in *BLP*) and a more general connection. The ECJ said at para. 29–31 (pp. 246–247) of its judgment:

> '29. It should be borne in mind that, according to the fundamental principle which underlies the VAT system, and which follows from art 2 of the First and Sixth Directives, VAT applies to each transaction by way of production or distribution after deduction of the VAT directly borne by the various cost components …
>
> 30. It follows from this principle as well as the rule enshrined in the judgment in of BLP … according to which, in order to give rise to the right to deduct, the goods or services acquired must have a direct and immediate link with the taxable transactions, that the right to deduct the VAT charged on such goods or services presupposes that the expenditure incurred in obtaining them was part of the cost components of the taxable transactions. Such expenditure must therefore be part of the costs of the output transactions which utilise the goods and services acquired. That is why those cost components must generally have arisen before the taxable person carried out the taxable transactions to which they relate …
>
> 31. it follows that … there is no direct and immediate link in the sense intended in the BLP Group, between an output transaction and services used by a taxable person as a consequence of and following completion of the said transaction … On the other hand, the costs of those services are part of the taxable person's general costs and are, as such, components of the price of an undertaking's products. Such services, therefore, do have a direct and immediate link with the taxable person's business as a whole, so that the right to deduct VAT falls within art. 17(5) of the Sixth Directive and the VAT is, according to that provision, deductible only in part.'

In *Abbey National plc v C & E Commrs* (Case C-408/98) [2005] BVC 348 a double application of the direct and immediate link test arose:

(a) were inputs attributable to a transfer of a going concern (a non-supply) or to the transferor's business (a partly exempt supply);
(b) if the latter, was the attribution to the part of the business transferred (wholly taxable) or the business as a whole (partly exempt)?

The Advocate General said at para. 35 and para. 40:

> 'Thus, what matters is whether the taxed input is a cost component of a taxable output, not whether the most closely-linked transaction is itself taxable … As the Commission submitted at the hearing, the conclusion to be drawn from BLP … is that the question to be asked is not what is the transaction with which the cost component has the most direct and immediate link but whether there is a sufficiently direct and immediate link with a taxable economic activity … The need for a "direct and immediate link" thus does not refer exclusively to the very next link in the chain but services to exclude situations where the chain has been broken by an exempt supply.
>
> 42. Clearly not all goods and services consumed by a taxable person will be incorporated directly into an identifiable output. Some will be of the nature of general overheads and, to the extent that those overheads are cost components of taxable supplies, VAT levied on them must be deducted.'

What the Advocate General was saying was that, where there is more than one possible attribution, so it is necessary to decide to which of two outputs the inputs have the direct and immediate link, regard must be had to the relevant output rather than to 'the very next link in the chain'. In other words, the BLP test has to be applied flexibly. Here 'sufficiently direct and immediate link' means 'the most relevant link'.

In *Dial-a-Phone Ltd v C & E Commrs* [2004] BVC 640 the question was (as in *Midland Bank*) were inputs to be attributed to:

(a) supply of general intermediary services (taxable, so input tax fully recoverable); or
(b) the activities of the company as a whole, the other activity of which was insurance intermediary services (exempt, so input tax only recoverable at company's partial exemption rate). The company sought to attribute its inputs to its taxable supplies alone. Having reviewed the cases cited above, the Court of Appeal concluded at [75]–[77] that the direct and immediate link ('the sufficient link') was to both the taxable and the exempt supplies, so that the input VAT was residual (overheads) VAT.

The absence of any need for a specific link in the case of overheads VAT was expressly stated in *Skatteverket v SKF AB* (Case C-29/08) [2011] BVC 359. The choice of attribution was again between (a) a disposal of shares, and (b) the company's economic activity as a whole. The ECJ said at para. 58 (p. 384):

> 'It is, however, also accepted that a taxable person has a right to deduct even where there is no direct and immediate link between a particular input transaction and an output transaction or transactions giving rise to the right to deduct, where the costs of the services in question are part of his general costs and are as such, components of the price of goods or services which he supplies. Such costs do have a direct and immediate link with the taxable person's economic activity as a whole.'

Accordingly, there are five stages in the application of the direct and immediate link test:

(1) Is the person incurring the input tax carrying on an economic activity as such?

(2) If so, are there taxable activities to which the inputs may be attributed?

(3) Has any link between inputs and outputs been severed by a chain-breaking transaction?

(4) If not, are the inputs specifically attributable?

(5) Or should the inputs be classified as overheads VAT, attributable to the person's economic activity as a whole?

110-450 Share issues

In *Kretztechnik AG v Finanzamt Linz* (Case C-465/03) [2006] BVC 66 a company sought to recover input tax on professional fees incurred in obtaining a listing for new shares on the Frankfurt Neues Markt exchange. Issuing shares is a non-supply. As the Advocate General said (para. 60, p. 74):

> 'Such a step defies categorisation as a supply of services by the company … there is an acquisition of capital, not a supply.'

The two possible attributions of input tax were either to a share issue (which was not a supply, so did not give rise to a right to deduct) or to the activities of the business as a whole (full recovery). The Advocate General said at para. 76:

> 'It seems likely that the use of the capital – and the services connected with the capital – cannot be linked to any specific output transactions, but must rather be attributed to the company's economic activity as a whole.'

To be recoverable input VAT must be either (Advocate General at para 76):

'(1) a specifically attributable a cost component of a transaction giving rise to a right of deduction ("directly attributable"); or

(2) part of a taxable person's general costs ("overheads VAT").'

See *Abbey National* [2008] BVC 488 at p. 514 (para. 42); *Investrand BV v Staatssecretaris van Financien* (Case C-435/05) [2009] BVC 733 at p. 733 (para. 24 of judgment).

Accordingly, though the share issue in *Kretztechnik* did not involve any supply, it did not follow that the input tax was irrecoverable. As in *Abbey National*, because there was no transaction to which it could be attributed, it fell back within the company's residual VAT, and was as such part of its general costs. As the court said at para. 36 (p. 80):

> 'it must be considered that the costs of the supplies acquired by the company in connection with the operation concerned form part of its overheads and are therefore, as such, component parts of the price of its products. Those supplies have a direct and immediate link with the whole economic activity of the taxable person.'

'Overheads' were defined in *C & E Commrs v Redrow Group plc* [1999] BVC 96 at p. 103 as being:

> 'the costs of goods and services which are properly incurred in the course of his business but cannot be linked with any goods or services supplied by the taxpayer to his customers.'

110-500 Abortive supplies

Belgium v Ghent Coal Terminal NV (Case C-37/95) [1998] BVC 139 shows that once an economic activity is carried on, the right of deduction of VAT is acquired. Nor is the right of recovery lost if the intending trader never makes taxable supplies.

In 1980, the taxpayer, GCT, bought land for development. It intended to use this for taxable transactions and so recovered its input VAT as an intending trader. However, part of the land was compulsorily purchased, and so the development became impossible and so was not carried out. The tax authorities sought to make GCT repay the input VAT. The Court disagreed. It said that the fact that the investment purpose was not achieved did not affect the recoverability of the input tax (para. 17). See also *Abbey National plc v C & E Commrs* (Case C-408/98) [2001] BVC 348 para. 43.

Hence, once an economic activity is commenced (absent exempt or private consumption) the right of deduction of VAT is acquired. Once the entitlement to deduct has arisen, it is retained and can be exercised, even if the trader never makes taxable supplies (*Ghent Coal* (para. 17, p. 152); *Intercommunale voor Zeewaterontzilting INZO v Belgium* (Case C-110/94) [1996] BVC 326 at p. 336 (para. 20 of judgment).

110-550 TOGCs

A sale or transfer of a business or part of a business which is capable of functioning as a distinct business, and which is transferred direct to a person who will carry on a business, without passing through any intermediate purchasers, is likely to be a TOGC and so outside the scope of VAT. Input VAT incurred on the costs of making the TOGC are recoverable as overheads VAT, either in their entirety or in the proportion given by a person's partial exemption formula. This was established in *Abbey National plc v C & E Commrs* (Case C-408/98) [2001] BVC 348 (see above).

110-600 Supplies to third parties

In reconstructions it is a common scenario for a company seeking additional finance to instruct its advisers to provide services direct to a bank or other financing institution, with the cost being borne by the company seeking the financial support. The question then arises whether the input VAT on the costs borne by the company is recoverable.

In *R & C Commrs v Airtours Holidays Transport Ltd* [2010] BVC 1,587 a company (AHT) in financial difficulties instructed accountants to prepare at its expense reports for financial institutions which were considering offering financial support to the company, to assist those institutions in their decision. The Upper Tribunal held that there was no identifiable benefit to AHT from the accountants' work, and accordingly it did not incur the VAT in the course of furtherance of its business. The services were supplied exclusively to the financial institutions.

This decision is surprising, in that the accountants' work was necessary, if AHT was going to stay in business at all.

110-650 Maximising VAT recovery

In order to maximise VAT recovery on mergers and acquisitions, the following points need to be borne in mind.

(1) The person incurring the VAT must from the start of the transaction be carrying on an economic activity. That suggests that, notwithstanding *Rompelman*, the person concerned should be registered for VAT from the start. In particular, he must intend to exercise direct or indirect influence in the acquired business.

(2) The person incurring the VAT must be able to demonstrate a clear connection between the inputs and taxable supplies made either by himself or by someone else carrying on the same business.

(3) In the case of a holding company that can be demonstrated by the making of or intention to make taxable supplies of management and technical services to new subsidiaries, or supplies which would have been taxable supplies in the absence of a group election.

(4) A subsidiary to which a holding company makes such supplies will be regarded as a business rather than as an investment asset.

(5) In the case of an acquisition it is important to avoid any break or caesura in the process.

(6) Engagement letters should expressly cover both pre- and post-acquisition services.

(7) A decision or intention to make intra-group supplies should be documented, most conveniently by board minutes, in both holding company and subsidiary.

12 Electronic Banking, Finance, Insurance and Related Services

> **Overview**
>
> This Chapter considers:
>
> (1) The VAT treatment of electronic banking, finance and insurance services.
>
> (2) The VAT treatment of related electronic services (such as payment and electronic messaging services and intermediary services on websites providing 'click through' services).
>
> (3) The VAT treatment of electronically provided services under the place of supply rules.

120-000 Introduction

Many of the banking, finance and insurance services which are supplied to customers are capable of being provided electronically between computers, and portable electronic devices (such as mobile phones etc.). In other words, the business sectors discussed in this book are using e-commerce as a way of carrying on their activities. Additionally, any of the businesses discussed in this book are likely to be using electronic services to support their activities, such as advertising, payment management services.

120-050 Electronic banking and associated services: the e-commerce context

The Organisation for Economic Co-operation and Development (OECD) developed a narrow and broad definition of e-commerce, which was supplemented by proposed guidelines (OECD Working Party on Indicators for the Information Society (WPIIS): see the Statistics Newsletter, OECD, Issue 2, June 2001, and ICT Use by Businesses: Revised OECD Model Survey (DSTI/ICCP/IIS(2005)2/FINAL), at p. 14). The OECD definitions set out below, and are helpful in illustrating the extent of what can be included within e-commerce activities (see the Statistics Newsletter, OECD, Issue 2, June 2001):

> 'Narrow definition
>
> An Internet transaction is the sale or purchase of goods or services, whether between businesses, households, individuals, governments, and other public or private organisations, conducted over the Internet. The goods and services are ordered over the Internet, but the payment and the ultimate delivery of the good or service may be conducted on or off-line.

Guidelines for the Interpretation of the Definitions (WPIIS proposal April 2001)

Include: orders received or placed on any online application used in automated transactions such as Internet applications, EDI, Minitel or interactive telephone systems

Broad definition

An electronic transaction is the sale or purchase of goods or services, whether between businesses, households, individuals, governments, and other public or private organisations, conducted over computer-mediated networks. The goods and services are ordered over those networks, but the payment and the ultimate delivery of the good or service may be conducted on or off-line.

Guidelines for the Interpretation of the Definitions (WPIIS proposal April 2001)

Include: orders received or placed on any Internet application used in automated transactions such as Web pages, Extranets and other applications that run over the Internet, such as EDI over the Internet, Minitel over the Internet, or over any other Web enabled application regardless of how the Web is accessed (eg, through a mobile or a TV set, etc.)

Exclude: orders received or placed by telephone, facsimile, or conventional e-mail.'

As these definitions show there are extensive possibilities for how e-commerce can be utilised for the purposes of delivering banking, finance and insurance services. The VAT points which arise in relation to these services in the context of e-commerce are considered in this chapter.

120-100 Electronic services related to banking, finance and insurance

The provision of electronic banking services will cover a variety of matters, such as account management, provision of financial information, access to financial markets for the purposes of buying shares, traded options, buying insurance products etc. The provision of electronic services to either businesses or individual customers, may be as an addition or alternative to conventional banking, finance and insurance services.

For VAT purposes it is necessary to identify the specific factual circumstances of a supply chain and/or transaction to determine the correct VAT treatment (these matters were discussed in **Chapters 1** and **3**).

Some businesses may use computer equipment, which might be leased or purchased from a bank (the nature of the VAT consequences of leasing activities is discussed in **Chapter 3**). The computer equipment might be used for the general purposes of a customer's business or for specific finance related purposes.

HMRC and the British Bankers' Association (BBA) entered into an administrative agreement on the VAT liability of electronic banking and cash management services (which is reproduced in **Appendix 9**). The substance of the agreement with the BBA is provided in HMRC's Notice 701/49 on Finance (November 2011) at section 2.12. In essence, the approach of HMRC on electronic banking services is to establish whether the service is provided as a supply in its own right, or as part of a package of services. As discussed in **Chapter 3**, the determination of whether there is a single supply or multiple supplies must first be answered since if there is only a single standard rated supply then it is unnecessary to consider whether an activity is within the scope of an exemption (this is illustrated by the approach of the CoJ in *Everything Everywhere Ltd (formerly T-Mobile UK)* (C-276/09)). Additionally, if supplies are treated as single or separate supplies this classification may also go on to determine the availability of zero-rating and exemption of the supplies.

Once the supplies are classified then in principle, services which would have been treated as exempt under Sch. 9, Group 5 of VATA 1994 (as discussed in **Chapter 7**) if they had been provided by a supplier (such as a bank) by conventional means should be treated as exempt when provided within the framework of electronic banking services (see HMRC Notice 701/49 on Finance (November 2011) at section 2.12). However, any finance related services which are not within the scope of Sch. 9 Group 5 will be treated as standard rated supplies.

HMRC Notice 701/49 on Finance (November 2011) at section 2.12 provides the following summary of how charges for the supplies identified below should be treated for VAT purposes.

Supply	Liability
Provision of information on share prices, foreign exchange rates, balances on accounts with other financial institutions	Taxable at the standard rate
Provision of information on the state of the client's accounts by the bank providing the electronic banking services, bank statements, the transfer of funds and the debiting and crediting of accounts	Exempt
Hire of equipment and related charges, such as training, if supplied and shown as a separate item on the invoice	Taxable at the standard rate
Hire of equipment and related charges, such as training, if not shown as a separate item on the invoice	Dependent on predominant or intended use when absorbed with other charges
Hire of equipment which can be used for other purposes (e.g. where the link gives access to Bloomberg etc.)	Taxable at the standard rate
Sale of equipment	Taxable at the standard rate
Service charges/overall service charges	Dependent on predominant use

The exemption provided by VATA 1994, Sch. 9, Group 5 does not apply to electronic data services. HMRC give the following examples of what will fall to be treated as standard rated supplies (VATFIN 4600):

> 'Exemption does not apply to electronic data services that simply provide subscribers with a message facility or an information service (e.g. on share price movements or financial news); these services are liable to VAT at the standard rate. The capturing of share data, investor information, etc is also a standard rated service, as it has no part in the exempt transaction. However, if the system executes the buying and selling of shares by allowing a user to insert bids and offer quotes for securities, and another user to insert acceptance and the system to match "buy" and "sell" deals, this will be exempt under item 5 as an intermediary service …
> It is important to be clear about whether the service being provided is one of intermediary services or data processing, hire of software etc.'

120-150 Classification of exempt and standard rated supplies: electronic messaging and payment services

Many suppliers of financial services outsource the services necessary to support the infrastructure of their activities (e.g. data messaging services for money transfers). The VAT issues arising out of outsourcing arrangements are discussed in **Chapter 7**. A substantial number of these outsourcing activities will not fall within the exempt classification of the supplies made by the primary banking, finance and insurance suppliers.

The CoJ's decision in *Proceedings brought by Nordea Pankki Suomi Oyj* (C-350/10) illustrates how outsourced activities are unlikely to be treated as being exempt supplies in the context of electronic messaging and payment services. The case concerned the use of electronic messaging services delivered by the Society for Worldwide Interbank Financial Telecommunication (SWIFT), and whether the provision of these services should be exempt under (what is now) art. 135(1)(d) of the VAT Directive (namely, 'transactions ...concerning deposit and current accounts'). The material facts of this case were as follows (see generally para. 9 to 16 of the judgment):

- SWIFT is a co-operative society owned by more than 2,000 financial institutions in more than 200 countries throughout the world.
- The taxpayer, Nordea, is the Finnish subsidiary of Nordea Bank AB (based in Sweden). Nordea purchased services from SWIFT. Nordea's expenses on services provided by SWIFT, including the connection and maintenance of that connection to those services were €1,999,559.96 (2001). Due to the operation of the VAT reverse charge procedure it had incurred VAT of €439,903.19. The tax authority in Finland refused Nordea's claim for a VAT refund in respect of the reverse charge.
- The taxpayer had both retail and corporate banking businesses. Its banking activities included purchase and brokerage of securities and currency. It also offered investment and fiduciary services.
- The taxpayer was the representative of a VAT group.
- The business of SWIFT involves managing a worldwide electronic messaging service for financial institutions, which enables thousands of banks, financial and securities management institutions and other corporate clients to exchange standardised financial messages between them. The provision of the electronic messaging services is achieved by software developed by SWIFT and an international secure data exchange network.
- In addition, to the messaging service, SWIFT processes messages relating to interbank payments (either domestic and international) and transactions in securities.
- Financial institutions affiliated to SWIFT are connected to the network by their own computer systems through a special gateway. In order to access its services SWIFT requires its clients to use computer hardware it has approved in advance.
- The mechanism for transmission of messages concerning interbank payments involved:
  - When a message is sent via the SWIFT network the issuing bank receives a first acknowledgement that the message was received for processing by SWIFT (this formality marks the start of SWIFT's financial responsibility for the transmission of the message concerned and for the performance of the transaction in accordance with that message).

- After the arrival of the first acknowledgement, the transaction described in the relevant message becomes binding.
- From the moment the receiving bank informs the system that it has received the message, SWIFT's responsibility for the performance of the transaction ends. At the same time, SWIFT sends the bank which gave the order an acknowledgement that the message has been received.
• Additionally, SWIFT provides services to carry out cross-border securities transactions. On the evidence before the CoJ from the referring court only the registration of shares in the client's securities account made via SWIFT services provides protection against third parties, although the ownership of the securities has already been transferred at the time the transaction on the stock exchange is made. SWIFT's responsibility for the messages connected with transactions in securities is similar to that described above for interbank payments.
• To maintain banking secrecy, SWIFT may and must open only the message fields which are necessary in order to establish their conformity with message transmission standards.

Whilst the CoJ recognised that the services provided by SWIFT were within the scope of the Sixth Directive (representing a supply of services for consideration), the Court decided that the services provided by SWIFT did not fall within the finance exemption (points 3 and 5 of art. 13B(d) of the Sixth Directive). The reasoning of the COJ was as follows:

• For the services provided by SWIFT to be VAT exempt supplies of finance, it was necessary for two conditions to be satisfied (para. 28 of the judgment):
    - First, the provision of the services had to be capable of giving rise to changes of a legal and financial character similar to those resulting from interbank payments or transactions in securities themselves;
    - Second, SWIFT's responsibility towards its clients could not be limited to technical aspects, but had to extend to specific, essential aspects of the financial transactions.
• In relation to the first condition, the services provided by SWIFT were solely electronic messaging services by means of which payment orders and orders concerning transactions in securities were transmitted from one financial institution. SWIFT did not have access to the actual content of the messages transmitted. Although the services were, on a number of markets, essential and the only services available, the mere fact that a constituent element was essential for completing an exempt transaction did not make that service element exempt (see para. 29 to 31 of the judgment). Additionally, legal ownership rights in relation to funds/securities were transferred only by the financial institutions (para. 32 of the judgment).
• In relation to the second condition, the CoJ decided that the financial consequences of SWIFT's responsibility could not be relevant to determine whether that responsibility extended to specific, essential elements of the financial transactions (para. 36 of the judgment). Specifically, SWIFT's contractual obligations were limited to the technical aspects of the messaging service, in particular, implementation, activation, connection, maintenance and software licences, and SWIFT was only responsible for the proper transmission of financial messages via the approved computer system (para. 37 of the judgment).

12 Electronic Banking, Finance, Insurance and Related Services

The CoJ provided the following legal principles in relation to the scope of the VAT exemptions, relevant to deciding whether the SWIFT services were within their scope:

- For the SWIFT services to be exempt transactions (within points 3 and 5 of art. 13B(d) of the Sixth Directive) (now art. 135(1)(f) of the VAT Directive) 'the services provided must, viewed broadly, form a distinct whole, fulfilling in effect the specific, essential functions of a service described in those points'. The CoJ emphasised that (at para. 24 of the judgment): 'As regards transactions concerning transfers, within the meaning of art 13B(d)(3) of that directive, the services provided must have the effect of transferring funds and entail changes of a legal and financial character. A service exempt under the directive must be distinguished from a mere physical or technical supply, such as making a data-handling system available to a bank. To that end, the national court must examine in particular the extent of the responsibility of the supplier of services vis-à-vis the banks, in particular the question whether that responsibility is restricted to technical aspects or whether it extends to the specific, essential aspects of the transactions…'
- The CoJ noted that based on prior court case law (at para. 25 of the judgment) 'a transfer is a transaction consisting of the execution of an order for the transfer of a sum of money from one bank account to another. It is characterised in particular by the fact that it involves a change in the legal and financial situation existing between the person giving the order and the recipient and between those parties and their respective banks and, in some cases, between the banks. Moreover, the transaction which produces this change is solely the transfer of funds between accounts, irrespective of its cause…'
- The foregoing analysis relating to transactions concerning transfers or payments within the meaning of art. 13B(d)(3) of the Sixth Directive applies, in principle to transactions in securities within the meaning of art. 13B(d)(5) (para. 26 of the judgment).
- CoJ noted that suppliers of services external to financial institutions which do not have a direct link with the clients of those institutions may still provide exempt services provided that the services 'viewed broadly, form a distinct whole, fulfilling in effect the specific, essential functions of the financial transactions described in art 13B(d)(3) and (5) of the Sixth Directive' (para. 27 of the judgment).

Another case that illustrates the difficulties of an electronic service being treated as the provision of an exempt finance service is *Bookit Ltd v R & C Commrs* (2006) which concerned the supply of Odeon cinema tickets. However, in this instance the supply was treated as the provision of intermediary services for the purposes of Sch. 9, Group 5 of VATA 1994. Customers wishing to purchase cinema tickets remotely, e.g. by phone or internet, were redirected to Odeon's agent, Bookit, who charged the customer an additional fee over and above the price of the ticket for their service. Bookit contended this fee was for credit or debit card handling services and was VAT-exempt as a transaction concerning payments or transfers. The Tribunal found for HMRC and held that Bookit was providing a taxable card handling service to the customer in return for the additional fee and was not performing intermediary services within VATA 1994, Sch. 9, Grp. 5, item 5. However, this was overturned on appeal and the Court of Appeal later agreed, holding that the supply by Bookit to the customer included the following components:

(1) Obtaining the card information with the necessary security information from the customer.

(2) Transmitting that information to the card issuers.

(3) Receiving the authorisation codes from the card issuers.

(4) Transmitting the card information with the necessary security information and the card issuers' authorisation codes to Girobank.

The Tribunal had been correct in finding components (1) to (3) were taxable. However, as the fourth component was part of Bookit's service to the customer, and had the effect that funds were transferred to its account with Girobank, what was charged by Bookit was exempt. In the present case the exemption provided for in art. 13(B)(d)(3) (now art. 135(1)(d) of Council Directive 2006/112/EC of 28 November 2006) applied on the basis that the fourth component of the service supplied by the taxpayer to the customer had the effect that funds were transferred to the taxpayer's account with Girobank (*Sparekassernes Datacenter v Skatteministeriet (Case C-2/95)* ECR I-3017; [1997] BVC 509 applied). Leave to appeal to the House of Lords was refused.

> ### Practice point
>
> Whilst the decision of the CoJ in *Proceedings brought by Nordea Pankki Suomi Oyj* (C-350/10) makes it clear that the threshold for achieving exempt status is high, it is nonetheless clear that supplies should be capable of achieving such a status provided that they go further than the services mentioned in the case and satisfy the two key conditions identified by the CoJ (see discussion above).

The provision of internet payment services (IPS) is another example of a service which is not viewed as an exempt supply but a standard rated supply. HMRC regard an IPS as providing debt collection services. HMRC's guidance in their *Finance Manual* (at 2440) provides as follows:

> 'An IPS provider will typically supply its service to the Internet retailer ("e-retailer"). Usually its sole aim is to offer a payment service and deal with the collection and distribution of customers' payments, never taking title to the goods or services provided by the e-retailer to its customer. Therefore, where it:
>
> - requests payment from the merchant acquirer to the total value of the goods ordered by the customer (this might include postage and packing)
> - has the payment transferred into its bank account by the e-retailer's customer's merchant acquirer, where it will remain for a specified time and
> - transfers the money, less commission, via BACS or a similar agency, to the e-retailer,
>
> we would see the core of the supply as being that of the collection of debt and thus taxable.
>
> The liability of these types of services, which involve the collection of payments on behalf of the party to whom they are owed, was the subject of the ECJ decision in AXA ... and, in some instances services previously treated as exempt have become taxable as a result.'

120-200 Classification of exempt and standard rated supplies: internet based services of an intermediary/comparison web sites

The nature of the internet enables intermediaries to provide prospective customers with access to a variety of insurance and finance based services. The supply of actual insurance and finance services will be exempt supplies to the extent that they are within Sch. 9 Group 2 (insurance) or Group 5 (finance). However, the question arises as to how the services of the intermediary using the internet to bring a customer and finance/insurance provider together should be classified for VAT purposes. The type of services which an intermediary of insurance/finance may provide over the internet, include comparison website services that provide a 'click through' facility to insurer or broker websites.

The nature of the exemptions for insurance and finance intermediary services are different, in that they provide as follows:

- Insurance, Sch. 9, Group 2, item 4 (see art. 135(1)(a) of Council Directive 2006/112/EC):

   'The provision by an insurance broker or insurance agent of any of the services of an insurance intermediary in a case in which those services–

   (a) are related (whether or not a contract of insurance or reinsurance is finally concluded) to an insurance transaction or a reinsurance transaction; and

   (b) are provided by that broker or agent in the course of his acting in an intermediary capacity.'

- For the position generally on insurance related supplies see **Chapter 9**.
- Finance, Sch. 9, Group 5, item 5:

   'The provision of intermediary services in relation to any transaction comprised in item 1, 2, 3, 4 or 6 (whether or not any such transaction is finally concluded) by a person acting in an intermediary capacity.'

- For the position generally on insurance related supplies see **Chapter 9**.

To be within the finance exemption for intermediary services UK law usually requires businesses to be both bringing together a prospective customer with a product provider with a view to entering a contract for the provision of financial services and carrying out work preparatory to the conclusion of those contracts.

The nature of insurance 'click through' websites was considered by the Court of Appeal in *R & C Commrs v Insurancewide.com Services Ltd & Anor* [2010] EWCA Civ 422; [2010] BVC 606 in the context of insurance intermediary services. The judgment provides some guidance on the application of the finance intermediary services exemption, but the difference in nature between the exemptions must be remembered. The Court of Appeal decided that both taxpayers were making supplies that were within the scope of the insurance intermediary exemption (Sch. 9, Group 2, Item 4). The material facts of the case were as follows:

- Insurancewide.com (IW) was a comparison website providing 'click through' services to insurer or broker websites.

- Trader Media Group (TMG) provided 'click through' services from its Auto Trader car auction site to a third party co-branded broker website.
- IW and TMG were paid commission on successful take-up by customers of insurance products.

The Court of Appeal's reasons for their decision in favour of IW and TMG were as follows:

- It was not necessary for there to be intermediation of the insurance contracts and the introductory services provided by IW and TMG. The Court of Appeal stated that (at para. 87 of the judgment):

    'It is sufficient that they were providing services characteristic of an insurance broker or agent, and which were vital to the process of introducing those seeking insurance with insurers, even if they were only part of a chain of such persons. In any event, they did have direct relations with the customers who used their website ... and they did have collaborative arrangements with intermediaries who did have legal relations with insurers. It would therefore also be immaterial that neither InsuranceWide nor Trader Media had anything to do with the negotiation of the terms of the insurance contract or its preparation or the collection of premiums or the handling of claims.'

- The services were exempt because they were doing much more than providing a mere 'click through' facility to a broker or insurer (that is, they were not acting as a 'mere conduit'). In particular, the companies concerned were also fulfilling the following functions (see para. 86 of the judgment):

    – they identified those looking for insurance and provided them with access to insurers who provided a range of competitive products;
    – they appraised and selected those insurers according to the competitiveness of their pricing and products and their level of consumer service.

- IW (in certain instances) also provided those seeking insurance with a means of directing them effectively and efficiently to the most appropriate insurers (whether directly or through an intermediary).
- TMG had input into the format of the co-branded broker website to which the customer was directed and into the composition of the insurer panel based on its understanding of the consumers using its website.
- IW and TMG were not acting as subcontractors and overall, their relevant activities could be described as the business of bringing together insurers and those seeking insurance.
- An insurance agent or broker is defined for the purposes of the VAT exemption by:

    – what they do and not by how they choose to describe themselves;
    – whether or not they fall within the definition of an insurance intermediary for regulatory purposes.

Following the decision of the Court of Appeal, HMRC issued Brief 31/10 whereby they stated that if the following conditions are all met then they would accept that a supplier was providing intermediary services within the scope of Sch. 9, Group 2, Item 2:

'1. The services are provided by someone engaged in the business of putting insurance companies in touch with potential clients or more generally acting as intermediaries between the two parties (although this may not necessarily be their principal business activity).

2. The business provides the means (that is, by way of an internet "click through" or some other form of introduction) by which a person seeking insurance is introduced to a provider of insurance or to another intermediary in a chain leading to an insurance provider.

3. That introduction takes place at the time a customer is seeking to enter into an insurance contract (although in some instances an insurance contract may not actually go on to be finally concluded).

4. The introducer also plays a proactive part in putting in place the arrangements under which that introduction is effected.'

In connection with item 4, above, HMRC consider that all or some of the following will be sufficient to enable the condition to be met:

- '• active endorsement of the insurer or the insurance product
- involvement in the selection of the insurance products and/or providers
- involvement in the process under which the insurance contract is entered into, even though the intermediation of the contact itself is undertaken by a 3rd party (for example, by having input into what questions should be asked of the prospective insured or the design of the 3rd party's website)
- negotiating a special rate for the insurance product/s on behalf of its customers or membership base
- some form of assessment of the customer's requirements so that they are directed to the most appropriate insurer for them.'

120-250 Electronically supplied services

(1) Introduction

Electronically supplied services can relate to a wide and exceptionally diverse subject-matter. For VAT purposes it is necessary to identify as a matter of fact what is being supplied, by whom and to whom in order to determine the relevant VAT treatment. Examples of services that are defined in VATA 1994 as being representative of electronically supplied services, and which are the subject of special place of supply rules (see discussion in (2) below) are (VATA 1994, Sch 4A, Part 2, paras 9 and 15 and Council Implementing Regulation 282/2011/EU laying down implementing measures for Directive 2006/112/EC ('the VAT Directive') on the common system of value added tax (recast), OJ L77/1, 15/03/2011 pp. 1–22 ('the EU Implementing Regulation'):

- website supply, web-hosting and distance maintenance of programs and equipment;
- the supply of software and the updating of software;
- the supply of images, text and information, and the making available of databases;
- the supply of music, films and games (including games of chance and gambling games);
- the supply of political, cultural, artistic, sporting, scientific, educational and entertainment broadcasts (including broadcasts of events); and
- the supply of distance teaching.

However, where the supplier of a service and that person's customer communicate via e-mail, that does not of itself mean the service performed is an electronically supplied service (VATA

1994, Sch 4A, para. 9(4)). The table summary of the place of supply rules in (2) below provides illustrations of what is regarded as electronically supplied services as defined by VATA 1994 and the EU Implementing Regulations.

An illustration of what constitutes electronically supplied services is provided by the First-Tier Tax Tribunal decision in *Smart Voucher Ltd* [2009] UKFTT 169; [2009] TC 00131. The case related to the place of supply of 'Ukash' services which were provided by a UK supplier to merchants in consideration for the payment of commission. The First-Tier Tribunal decided that the supplies were 'electronically supplied services' for the purposes of Sch. 5, as it was then in force, of VATA 1994, with the consequence that the services were supplied where they were received (as provided for in para. 7C of Sch. 5, as it was then in force). The material facts were as follows:

- The taxpayer was based in the UK, and acted as an issuer of electronic money (e-money), being registered with and regulated by the Financial Services Authority as an electronic money institution (ELMI). For this purpose electronic money is defined by art. 3 of the *Financial Services and Markets Act 2000 (Regulated Activities) Order* 2001 as:

    '"electronic money" means monetary value, as represented by a claim on the issuer, which is-
    (a) stored on an electronic device;
    (b) issued on receipt of funds; and
    (c) accepted as a means of payment by persons other than the issuer'

- The taxpayer provided access to e-money under a system known by the name 'Ukash'. The system could only be received electronically and was set around a patented system of process and technology. The taxpayer made a single supply of services.
- The function of the e-money services was to 'digitise cash'.
- The taxpayer issued e-money in three ways: through particular merchants who branded the product as their own; to provide a form of pre-payment for credit and debit cards; and as Ukash, which could be purchased by members of the public from participating retailers. The VAT issues under consideration in the Tribunal's decision related solely to Ukash.
- The target market for Ukash were consumers who did not possess a credit or debit card.
- The taxpayer would enter into a contract with an issuing merchant network provider that could provide access to individual retail stores. Retailers belonging to a particular network were then able to offer the Ukash facility.
- A consumer wishing to purchase Ukash would pay the retailer a sum of money and receive a piece of paper (described as a 'voucher') which set out a unique 19 digit number.
- The issuing network contracted separately with each retailer that issued Ukash and collected the takings, consolidated them, and paid the taxpayer net of the issuing commission. The issuing network connected and integrated directly with the taxpayer's system.
- There was no contractual relationship between the taxpayer and the ultimate consumer who purchases Ukash.
- A Ukash 'voucher' expired after one year, but was usually redeemed within two hours of purchase.
- The taxpayer would contract with merchants both in and outside the UK; which was done both directly and indirectly, through payment service providers (PSPs). Under these arrangements merchants would accept Ukash as online payment for their products and services.

- Any consumer having purchased Ukash and wishing to use it to buy a product or service from a participating merchant's website would input the 19 digit number when prompted on-screen by the merchant's website to do so. This would then perform validity checks and other requisite tasks.
- The taxpayer would then settle any monies owed to merchants for all Ukash spent on merchants' websites, less commission. The sale and purchase relationship was between the merchant and the consumer. Ukash was always a payment method used for a transaction.
- The contract between the taxpayer and the merchant provided for the following key points (para. 4 of the judgment):
  - Merchant offers goods and services to its customers via its website and uses the Ukash payment service as a means of enabling payment for goods and services to its customers.
  - Ukash payment service consists of an electronic voucher issuing and redemption system whereby customers can purchase Ukash vouchers via the Ukash issuing network or online via a Merchant or Ukash website, for defined values, and redeem Ukash vouchers on Merchant websites.
  - Ukash will process payment amounts due to Merchant and effect settlement to Merchant. Ukash will keep all monies received from voucher redemptions on behalf of Merchant separately from the assets of Ukash. Ukash will provide Merchant with on-line reporting of all monies processed by Ukash on behalf of Merchant.
  - Ukash to provide to merchants a messaging interface to Ukash to provide Ukash Voucher Issuance and Redemption services, provision of a messaging interface from the merchant website to Ukash to provide Ukash Voucher Issuance and Redemption services to customers accessing the Merchant website, provision of a Help Desk to support the Merchant Customer Service Desk.

The First-Tier Tax Tribunal decided that the Ukash services were electronically provided services, and the tribunal's reasoning was as follows:

- the Ukash services that the taxpayer supplied to merchants were supplied only by electronic means. The system operated online, was automatic, and performed its functions in real time (para. 12 of the judgment).
- The Tribunals conclusion was not affected by the fact that some elements of the Ukash system involved human intervention (which were confined to the Help Desk and the accounting function through which cash settlement was made to the merchants). These elements were purely ancillary to the core verification service and did not therefore affect the characterisation of the main supply as an electronically supplied service (para. 13 of the judgment).
- The taxpayer was not making a supply of the right to participate in the Ukash scheme or of the benefit of access to a wider market of potential customers; but was solely providing the services referred to in the contract with merchants (para. 23 of the judgment).

- The Tribunal rejected HMRC's argument that to be within the scope of the concept of electronically supplied services that it was necessary for the services of have the key feature of being digitised products. In this regard, the Tribunal commented (at para. 28 to 29 of the judgment) in relation to the then law (but now see art. 7 of the EU Implementing Regulations (summarised in the table below)):

> 'In our view the important point is not the description or analysis of the nature of the service, but the manner in which it is supplied. A supply of music, or of films or games, for example, though included in the illustrative or indicative lists in the Directives and in para 7C itself, is not inherently an electronically supplied service. It may be rendered such, not by its nature, but by the manner in which it is delivered. We consider that the expression "electronically supplied services" should be construed according to its natural meaning. This seems to us to be supported by the fact that communication by a supplier of a service with his customer via electronic mail is specifically excluded from qualifying as an "electronically supplied service". The perceived need to make this exclusion to our minds also demonstrates that the expression is capable of having broad application.
>
> In this case, apart from in respect of those matters which we have found to be ancillary, the only means of providing the services of the Appellant to the merchants – however they might be characterised – was electronically. The service of participation in the scheme, or in providing the benefit of access to a wider market of consumers, if those would indeed contrary to our view be recognised as separate supplies, would not in our view properly be regarded as supplied on the entry into the contractual arrangements with the merchants, but would be ongoing services throughout the relationship. The means of providing those services and benefits would, along with the other core services, be through the electronic medium created by the Appellant. Accordingly, in our judgment, all such services would be electronically supplied services.'

(2) Place of supply of electronically supplied services

As discussed in **Chapter 3** the place of supply is determined by reference to a number of specific rules. A summary of the place of supply rules relevant for electronically supplied services is provided below.

Type of supply	Place of supply	VATA 1994/EU
General rules		
Business to consumer (B2C)		
Supply of services by a supplier who belongs in the UK to a non-relevant business person (i.e. a private individual, charity, government department or other body that has no business activities) (VATA 1994, s 7A(4))	Service supplied in the country in which the supplier belongs (unless overriding place of supply rules apply in Sch 4A to VATA 1994, which includes electronically supplied services) (VATA 1994, s 7A(5))	s 7A(2)(b) Art 44 VAT Directive

Business to business (B2B)		
Supply of services to a 'relevant business person'	Service supplied in the country in which the recipient/customer belongs (unless overriding place of supply rules apply in Sch 4A to VATA 1994, which includes electronically supplied services) (VATA 1994, s. 7A(5))	s. 7A(2)(a) Art 45 VAT Directive
	If the customer is outside the UK then the supply is outside the scope of UK VAT; if the customer is outside the EU then there will be no VAT.	
	If the customer belongs in another Member State (and is VAT registered) the supply is subject to VAT in that Member State under the reverse charge. Supplier may need to complete and submit an EC Sales List, which must now be completed by suppliers for supplies of taxable services subject to the reverse charge in the customer's Member State.	
Exceptions to place of supply of services relating to supplies made to a relevant business person (B2B)		
Electronically supplied services		
Provision of electronically supplied services to a relevant business person. Examples: <ul><li>website supply, web-hosting and distance maintenance of programmes and equipment;</li><li>the supply of software and the updating of software;</li><li>the supply of images, text and information, and the making available of databases;</li><li>the supply of music, films and games (including games of chance and gambling games);</li><li>the supply of political, cultural, artistic, sporting, scientific, educational or entertainment broadcasts (including broadcasts of events); and</li><li>the supply of distance teaching.</li></ul>	Covered by the B2B general rule so the place of supply is where the business customer belongs, but this is subject to the use and enjoyment rule. If there is a supply of services consisting of the provision of electronically supplied services to a relevant business person which would otherwise be treated as made in the UK, but the services are to any extent effectively used and enjoyed in a country which is not a Member State, then the supply is to be treated to that extent as made in that country. If there is a supply of services consisting of the provision of electronically supplied services to a relevant business person which would otherwise be treated as made in a country which is not a Member State, but the services are to any extent effectively used and enjoyed in the UK, then the supply is to be treated to that extent as made in the UK. NB. The use and enjoyment rule does not apply in the UK to B2C supplies of these services. Changes being introduced in 2015 for the place of supply of cross border B2C supplies of these services (see the Table in **Chapter 3**).	Sch 4A, para 9 Art 58 VAT Directive
NB: Under the EU Implementing Regulation the concept of 'electronically supplied services' includes services which are delivered over the internet or an electronic network and the nature of which renders their supply essentially automated and involving minimal human intervention, and impossible to ensure in the absence of information technology.		

The concept includes all of the following matters:
(a) the supply of digitised products generally, including software and changes to or upgrades of software;
(b) services providing or supporting a business or personal presence on an electronic network such as a website or a webpage;
(c) services automatically generated from a computer via the internet or an electronic network, in response to specif c data input by the recipient;
(d) the transfer for consideration of the right to put goods or services up for sale on an internet site operating as an online market on which potential buyers make their bids by an automated procedure and on which the parties are notified of a sale by electronic mail automatically generated from a computer;
(e) internet service packages of information in which the telecommunications component forms an ancillary and subordinate part (i.e. packages going beyond mere internet access and including other elements such as content pages giving access to news, weather or travel reports, playgrounds, website hosting, access to online debates etc);
(f) the services listed:
  (1) Point (1) of Annex II to Directive 2006/112/EC (website supply, web-hosting, distance maintenance of programs and equipment):
    (a) website hosting and webpage hosting;
    (b) automated, online and distance maintenance of programs;
    (c) remote systems administration;
    (d) online data warehousing where specific data is stored and retrieved electronically;
    (e) online supply of on-demand disc space.
  (2) Point (2) of Annex II to Directive 2006/112/EC (supply of software and updating thereof):
    (a) accessing or downloading software (including procurement/accountancy programs and anti-virus software) plus updates;
    (b) software to block banner adverts showing, otherwise known as Bannerblockers;
    (c) download drivers, such as software that interfaces computers with peripheral equipment (such as printers);
    (d) online automated installation of filters on websites; (e) online automated installation of firewalls.
  (3) Point (3) of Annex II to Directive 2006/112/EC (supply of images, text and information and making available of databases):
    (a) accessing or downloading desktop themes;
    (b) accessing or downloading photographic or pictorial images or screensavers; (c) the digitised content of books and other electronic publications;
    (d) subscription to online newspapers and journals;
    (e) weblogs and website statistics;
    (f) online news, traffic information and weather reports;
    (g) online information generated automatically by software from specific data input by the customer, such as legal and financial data (in particular such data as continually updated stock market data, in real time);
    (h) the provision of advertising space including banner ads on a website/web page;
    (i) use of search engines and internet directories.

(4) Point (4) of Annex II to Directive 2006/112/EC (supply of music, films and games of chance and gambling games, and of political, cultural, artistic, sporting, scientific and entertainment broadcasts and events):

    (a) accessing or downloading of music on to computers and mobile phones;

    (b) accessing or downloading of jingles, excerpts, ringtones, or other sounds;

    (c) accessing or downloading of films;

    (d) downloading of games on to computers and mobile phones;

    (e) accessing automated online games which are dependent on the internet, or other similar electronic networks, where players are geographically remote from one another.

(5) Point (5) of Annex II to Directive 2006/112/EC (supply of distance learning):

    (a) automated distance teaching dependent on the internet or similar electronic network to function and the supply of which requires limited or no human intervention, including virtual classrooms, except where the internet or similar electronic network is used as a tool simply for communication between the teacher and student;

    (b) workbooks completed by pupils online and marked automatically, without human intervention.

In particular, the concept excludes all of the following matters:

(a) radio and television broadcasting services;

(b) telecommunications services;

(c) goods, where the order and processing is done electronically;

(d) CD-ROMs, floppy disks and similar tangible media;

(e) printed matter, such as books, newsletters, newspapers or journals;

(f) CD-ROMs and audio cassettes;

(g) video cassettes and DVDs;

(h) games on a CD-ROM;

(i) services of professionals such as lawyers and financial consultants, who advise clients by e-mail;

(j) teaching services, where the course content is delivered by a teacher over the internet or an electronic network (namely via a remote link);

(k) offline physical repair services of computer equipment;

(l) offline data warehousing services;

(m) advertising services, in particular as in newspapers, on posters and on television;

(n) telephone helpdesk services;

(o) teaching services purely involving correspondence courses, such as postal courses;

(p) conventional auctioneers' services reliant on direct human intervention, irrespective of how bids are made;

(q) telephone services with a video component, otherwise known as videophone services;

(r) access to the internet and world wide web;

(s) telephone services provided through the internet.

Exceptions relating to supplies not made to a relevant business person (B2C)		
Electronic services		
A supply consisting of the provision by a person who belongs in a country which is not a Member State (other than the Isle of Man) of electronically supplied services (see above for meaning) to a person ('the recipient') who: (a) is not a relevant business person and (b) belongs in a Member State.	Made in the country in which the recipient belongs. From 1 January 2015 (without prejudice to the use and enjoyment rule where applicable), the supply is not subject to VAT if the supplier demonstrates that the place of supply is outside the EU in accordance with the EU Implementing Regulation (Art 3) – see further **Chapter 3**, and section (3) of this chapter below.	Sch 4A, para 15 EU Implementing Regulation, Art 24(2)
Other services provided to a recipient belonging outside EC		
A supply consisting of the provision to a person ('the recipient') who: (a) is not a relevant business person and (b) belongs in a country which is not a Member State (other than the Isle of Man) of electronically supplied services (until January 2015).	Made in the country in which the recipient belongs. Without prejudice to the use and enjoyment rule (if applicable), the supply is not subject to VAT if the supplier demonstrates that the place of supply is outside the EU in accordance with the EU Implementing Regulation (Art 3) – see further **Chapter 3**, and section (3) of this chapter below.	Sch 4A, para 16

(3) VAT registration and supplies to non-business customers: the 'One Stop Shop'

The place of supply rules discussed in (2) above, will result in some supplies being made in the UK/European Union by non-EU suppliers. This may cause a non-EU supplier to register for VAT in particular Member States. However, EU rules allow such a supplier to register under a single scheme for the whole of the EU. A person may request registration for VAT purposes in the UK (which would then be effective throughout the EU in respect of 'qualifying supplies') if five conditions mentioned below are met; and if met then HMRC must permit registration (VATA 1994, Sch. 3B, para. 4; see also HMRC's Notice 741A Place of Supply of Services (January 2010), Section 20). Upon registration, a supplier is given a registration number (which is notified electronically) (VATA 1994, Sch. 3B, para. 6). The effect of registration is that a supplier must pay VAT in respect of qualifying supplies. If the supply is treated as made in the UK, the amount is the amount of VAT that would have been charged on the supply under VATA 1994 if the person had been registered under the VAT rules when the supply was made (VATA 1994, Sch. 3B, para. 10(3)). However, if the supply is treated as made in another EU Member State under the place of supply rules, then the amount of VAT due is the amount of VAT that would have been charged on the supply in accordance with the law of that Member State if the person had been treated as a taxable person in that Member State when the supply was made (VATA 1994, Sch. 3B, para. 10(4)).

For purposes of registration, 'qualifying supplies' refers to a supply of 'electronically supplied services' (i.e. those set out in the Table above) to a person who (a) belongs in the UK or another EU Member State and (b) receives those services otherwise than for the purposes of a business carried on by that person (i.e. B2C supplies) (VATA 1994, Sch. 3B, para. 3). HMRC states that a non-EU supplier can use the special scheme for B2C supplies to consumers in the EU even if they also make B2B supplies, but they are not entitled to use the special scheme for those B2B supplies. This should not generally be problematic, however, since, as noted earlier, the non-EU supplier should not be required to charge and account for VAT on B2B cross-border supplies of electronically supplied services supplied in the EU because their business customers will account for the VAT due in their Member State under the reverse charge procedure (see **Chapter 5**).

The five conditions identified in VATA 1994 for registration are (VATA 1994, Sch. 3B, para. 2):

- Condition 1: the person makes or intends to make 'qualifying supplies' in the course of business carried on by that person.
- Condition 2: the person has neither a business establishment nor a fixed establishment in the UK or in another Member State in relation to any supply of goods or services.
- Condition 3: the person is not (a) registered under VATA 1994, (b) identified for the purposes of VAT in accordance with the law of another Member State or (c) registered under an Act of Tynwald (the laws of the Isle of Man) for the purposes of any tax imposed by or under an Act of Tynwald which corresponds to VAT.
- Condition 4: the person (a) is not required to be registered or indentified as mentioned in Condition 3 or (b) is required to be so registered or identified, but solely by virtue of the fact that he makes or intends to make qualifying supplies.
- Condition 5: the person is not identified under any provision of the law of another Member State which corresponds to the registration which is permitted under UK law in respect of qualifying supplies (i.e. which implements the VAT Directive) (see arts 359–369 of the Directive).

Future developments

From 1 January 2015, B2C supplies of telecommunication and broadcasting services will move from the current general rule (location of supplier) to where the customer is established, has their permanent address, or usually resides. The 'one stop shop' or OSS registration scheme (as discussed above) is available to non-EU suppliers in respect of electronically supplied services to EU private consumers, will be extended to both EU and non-EU businesses, and be widened to include telecommunications and broadcasting services.

The European Commission is committed to ensuring that, in a VAT system based on taxation at destination, a OSS is a crucial instrument to facilitate access to the single market, in particular for SMEs (see generally the European Commission Communication COM(2011) 851 *On the future of VAT Towards a simpler, more robust and efficient VAT system tailored to the single market*). In particular, from 2015 onwards the Commission will envisage a managed broadening of the OSS concept over time to other categories of supply. The current OSS will be amended to accommodate the changes necessary to extend the scheme to other services.

The Council Regulation No 967/2012 amending Implementing Regulation (EU) No 282/2011 as regards the special schemes for non-established taxable persons supplying telecommunication services, broadcasting services or electronic services to non-taxable persons is provided at **Appendix 27**. Progress on any further developments can be accessed at www.europa.eu.

> *Summary*
>
> **This chapter has aimed to outline the basic rules on supplies which are made electronically. It is important to first identify the nature of the supply and secondly determine whether due to the nature of the supply it is subject to any particular place of supply rules, e.g. due to the supply being treated as electronically supplied services. The nature of the electronic supply will often be treated as standard rated other than where it is within a specific exemption for VAT.**

Appendix 1: Important HM Revenue & Customs Notices and Leaflets

700	The VAT guide
700/2	VAT group treatment
700/9	Transfer of a business as a going concern
700/17	Funded pension schemes
700/34	Staff
700/57	VAT: administrative agreements entered into with trade bodies
701/9	Commodities and terminal markets
701/21	Gold
701/36	Insurance
706	Partial exemption
706/2	Capital goods scheme
708	Buildings and construction
718	Margin scheme for second-hand goods, works of art, antiques and collectors' items
723A	Refunds of VAT in the European Community for EC and non-EC business
741A	Place of supply of services
742	Land and property

Appendix 1: Important HM Revenue & Customs Notices and Leaflets

Appendix 2: VATA 1994, s. 43

43 Groups of companies

43(1) Where under sections 43A to 43D any bodies corporate are treated as members of a group, any business carried on by a member of the group shall be treated as carried on by the representative member, and–
(a) any supply of goods or services by a member of the group to another member of the group shall be disregarded; and
(b) any supply which is a supply to which paragraph (a) above does not apply and is a supply of goods or services by or to a member of the group shall be treated as a supply by or to the representative member; and
(c) any VAT paid or payable by a member of the group on the acquisition of goods from another member State or on the importation of goods from a place outside the member States shall be treated as paid or payable by the representative member and the goods shall be treated–
 (i) in the case of goods acquired from another member State, for the purposes of section 73(7); and
 (ii) in the case of goods imported from a place outside the member States, for those purposes and the purposes of section 38,
 as acquired or, as the case may be, imported by the representative member;
and all members of the group shall be liable jointly and severally for any VAT due from the representative member.

43(1AA) Where–
(a) it is material, for the purposes of any provision made by or under this Act (**'the relevant provision'**), whether the person by or to whom a supply is made, or the person by whom goods are acquired or imported, is a person of a particular description,
(b) paragraph (b) or (c) of subsection (1) above applies to any supply, acquisition or importation, and
(c) there is a difference that would be material for the purposes of the relevant provision between–
 (i) the description applicable to the representative member, and
 (ii) the description applicable to the body which (apart from this section) would be regarded for the purposes of this Act as making the supply, acquisition or importation or, as the case may be, as being the person to whom the supply is made,
the relevant provision shall have effect in relation to that supply, acquisition or importation as if the only description applicable to the representative member were the description in fact applicable to that body.

43(1AB) Subsection (1AA) above does not apply to the extent that what is material for the purposes of the relevant provision is whether a person is a taxable person.

43(1A) [Repealed by FA 1996, s. 31(5) and 205 and Sch. 41, Pt. IV(5).]

43(2) An order under section 5(5) or (6) may make provision for securing that any goods or services which, if all the members of the group were one person, would fall to be treated under that section as supplied to and by that person, are treated as supplied to and by the representative member and may provide for that purpose that the representative member is to be treated as a person of such description as may be determined under the order.

43(2A) A supply made by a member of a group (**'the supplier'**) to another member of the group (**'the UK member'**) shall not be disregarded under subsection (1)(a) above if–
(a) it would (if there were no group) be a supply of services to which section 7A(2)(a) applies made to a person belonging in the United Kingdom;
(b) those services are not within any of the descriptions specified in Schedule 9;
(c) the supplier has been supplied (whether or not by a person belonging in the United Kingdom) with any services which do not fall within any of the descriptions specified in Schedule 9 and section 7A(2)(a) applied to the supply;

(d) the supplier belonged outside the United Kingdom when it was supplied with the services mentioned in paragraph (c) above; and
(e) the services so mentioned have been used by the supplier for making the supply to the UK member.

43(2B) Subject to subsection (2C) below, where a supply is excluded by virtue of subsection (2A) above from the supplies that are disregarded in pursuance of subsection (1)(a) above, all the same consequences shall follow under this Act as if that supply–
(a) were a taxable supply in the United Kingdom by the representative member to itself, and
(b) without prejudice to that, were made by the representative member in the course or furtherance of its business.

43(2C) Except in so far as the Commissioners may by regulations otherwise provide, a supply which is deemed by virtue of subsection (2B) above to be a supply by the representative member to itself–
(a) shall not be taken into account as a supply made by the representative member when determining any allowance of input tax under section 26(1) in the case of the representative member;
(b) shall be deemed for the purposes of paragraph 1 of Schedule 6 to be a supply in the case of which the person making the supply and the person supplied are connected within the meaning of section 1122 of the Corporation Tax Act 2010 (connected persons); and
(c) subject to paragraph (b) above, shall be taken to be a supply the value and time of which are determined as if it were a supply of services which is treated by virtue of section 8 as made by the person by whom the services are received.

43(2D) For the purposes of subsection (2A) above where–
(a) there has been a supply of the assets of a business of a person (**'the transferor'**) to a person to whom the whole or any part of that business was transferred as a going concern (**'the transferee'**),
(b) that supply is either–
 (i) a supply falling to be treated, in accordance with an order under section 5(3), as being neither a supply of goods nor a supply of services, or
 (ii) a supply that would have fallen to be so treated if it had taken place in the United Kingdom, and
(c) the transferor was supplied with services at a time before the transfer when the transferor belonged outside the United Kingdom and section 7A(2)(a) applied to the supply,

those services, so far as they are used by the transferee for making any supply to which section 7A(2)(a) applies, shall be deemed to have been supplied to the transferee at a time when the transferee belonged outside the United Kingdom.

43(2E) Where, in the case of a supply of assets falling within paragraphs (a) and (b) of subsection (2D) above–
(a) the transferor himself acquired any of the assets in question by way of a previous supply of assets falling within those paragraphs, and
(b) there is a supply to which section 7A(2)(a) applies of services which, if used by the transferor for making such a supply, would be deemed by virtue of that subsection to have been supplied to the transferor at a time when he belonged outside the United Kingdom,

that subsection shall have effect, notwithstanding that the services have not been so used by the transferor, as if the transferor were a person to whom those services were supplied and as if he were a person belonging outside the United Kingdom at the time of their deemed supply to him; and this subsection shall apply accordingly through any number of successive supplies of assets falling within paragraphs (a) and (b) of that subsection.

43(3) [Repealed by FA 1999, s. 16 and Sch. 2, para. 1(3) and s. 139(1) and Sch. 20, Pt. II(1).]
43(4) [Repealed by FA 1999, s. 16 and Sch. 2, para. 1(3) and s. 139(1) and Sch. 20, Pt. II(1).]
43(5) [Repealed by FA 1999, s. 16 and Sch. 2, para. 1(3) and s. 139(1) and Sch. 20, Pt. II(1).]
43(5A) [Repealed by FA 1999, s. 16 and Sch. 2, para. 1(3) and s. 139(1) and Sch. 20, Pt. II(1).]

43(6) [Repealed by FA 1999, s. 16 and Sch. 2, para. 1(3) and s. 139(1) and Sch. 20, Pt. II(1).]
43(7) [Repealed by FA 1999, s. 16 and Sch. 2, para. 1(3) and s. 139(1) and Sch. 20, Pt. II(1).]
43(8) [Repealed by FA 1999, s. 16 and Sch. 2, para. 1(3) and s. 139(1) and Sch. 20, Pt. II(1).]
43(9) Schedule 9A (which makes provision for ensuring that this section is not used for tax avoidance) shall have effect.

Appendix 3: EU Proposals

COMMISSION OF THE EUROPEAN COMMUNITIES

Brussels, 28.11.2007
COM(2007) 747 final

2007/0267 (CNS)

Proposal for a

COUNCIL DIRECTIVE

amending Directive 2006/112/EC on the common system of value added tax, as regards the treatment of insurance and financial services

(presented by the Commission)

{SEC(2007) 1554}
{SEC(2007) 1555}

Appendix 3: EU Proposals

EXPLANATORY MEMORANDUM

1. **CONTEXT OF THE PROPOSAL**

- **Grounds for and objectives of the proposal**

The objectives of the proposal are twofold:

- increasing legal certainty for economic operators and national tax administrations, reducing their administrative burden for correctly applying the rules for the VAT exemption of insurance and financial services;

- reducing the impact of hidden VAT in costs of insurance and financial services providers.

These objectives are achieved by the three measures contained in the proposal:

- clarification of the rules governing the exemption from VAT for insurance and financial services;

- broadening of the existing option for taxation by transferring the right to opt from the Member States to the economic operators;

- introduction of a cost-sharing group which allows economic operators to pool investments and re-distribute the costs for these investments exempt from VAT from the group to its members.

Clarification of rules

The clarification of the rules governing the exemption from VAT for insurance and financial services has the objective to provide a more uniform application of the VAT exemption, creating more legal certainty for economic operators and reducing the administrative burden for economic operators to comply with the rules. This clarification consists of the following elements:

- the conditions for applying the VAT exemption are based on objective economic criteria decoupling them from an interpretation based on national private law concepts which is one of the main reasons for different interpretation and application in the Member States (e.g. an insurance must address a risk and provide for an indemnity or a benefit); these objective economic criteria ensure that also new services which will be developed in the future will be covered by the VAT exemption if they fulfil these criteria;

- the new rules introduce the concept that the exemption shall cover the supply of any constituent element of an insurance or financial service, which constitutes a distinct whole and has the specific and essential character of the exempt service concerned;

- a common harmonised concept of intermediation is introduced for insurance and financial services;

- where this was possible, the new definitions also create more consistency with internal market rules (e.g. investment funds).

The proposal for a Directive is accompanied by a proposal for a Regulation which enumerates in a non-exhaustive way cases which are covered by or excluded from the VAT exemption for insurance and financial services.

The option for taxation

Under the broadened option for taxation, it will be the economic operator who decides if he wants to be fully taxable; where he exercises this right, he will be able to deduct input VAT on his investments like any other economic operator. In this way a level playing field for the financial industry is created that was not achieved so far as only very few Member States have granted the option to business and this under differing conditions.

At the same time Member States are given the necessary flexibility to specify themselves the rules for applying that option, adapting it to their national tax supervision structures. Where the need arises implementing provisions could also be envisaged at Community level on the basis of Article 397 of the Directive.

Cost-sharing

Under the proposed cost-sharing model, in particular smaller economic operators can pool their investments (e.g.: computer technology of specialised staff) in groups which can buy these investments at better market conditions and re-distribute them exempt from VAT to the members of the group.

- **General context**

The definitions of exempt insurance and financial services are out of date and have led to an uneven interpretation and application of these exemptions by Member States. Stakeholders are confronted with a considerable legal complexity of varying administrative practices generating legal uncertainty for economic operators and fiscal authorities. This legal uncertainty has led to an increasing number of court cases and increased the administrative charges of operators and administrations for applying these exemptions. It is therefore necessary to clarify the rules governing the exemption from VAT for insurance and financial services with the objectives to create more legal certainty and to reduce the administrative charges for operators and administrations. A public consultation of stakeholders carried out in 2006 and an independent "Study to increase the Understanding of the Economic Effects of the VAT Exemption for Financial and Insurance Services" commissioned by the Commission confirmed this conclusion.

The second problem is that of hidden VAT in the cost structure of insurance and financial services. In financial services and insurance services all economic operators are striving to improve their competitiveness since they are increasingly exposed to competition both between themselves on account of the trend towards a single pan-European market place as well as from economic operators established outside the EU. Consolidation within the sector has been driven to a great extent by the need for efficiency but cost reduction strategies manifest themselves in various ways. These developments are accelerated by the emerging of a wider regulatory framework for an integrated European financial services market as set out in the Financial Services Action Plan. This regulatory framework increases the competition between suppliers of insurance and financial services through the steady move towards a level playing field. In this environment, economic operators have developed various techniques for improving their own competitiveness but some of the more common basic techniques include the following:

- outsourcing of activities (with the intention of lowering administrative and labour costs, e.g.: depository of shares, administrative tasks etc.);

- pooling of activities (with a cost-sharing intention, e.g.: the common development of computer systems and software for several banks, the creation of credit factories which may either be associated with consolidation or be undertaken on the basis of);

- sub-contracting (insertion of a supplementary distribution level for the financial products or insurances).

These techniques involve that less value in created in-house but supplied as services by independent third parties to the suppliers of insurance and financial products. This generates the problem that such services may no longer come under the exemption for financial and insurance services and are therefore invoiced with VAT. This VAT is often not deductible for the client because he has no right for deduction as he supplies himself exempt insurance and financial services. Such non-deductible VAT becomes part of the costs. The proposal contains elements which will reduce that impact on the costs.

- **Existing provisions in the area of the proposal**

Articles 135(1)(a) to (g) and 137(1)(a) and (2)

- **Consistency with the other policies and objectives of the Union**

Where this was possible, the new definitions also create more consistency with internal market rules (e.g. investment funds, credit rating, derivatives).

The proposal is part of the Commission's Strategy for the Simplification of the Regulatory Environment (Section 66 of COM(2006) 690). Both economic operators and Member States' tax authorities will benefit from these simplifications. However, it is not possible to quantify these benefits.

The proposal will improve legal certainty and reduce the administrative burden of operators and national tax authorities. As it would have a positive impact on costs, it should not have negative effects on the cost of retail consumer insurance and financial services.

2.   CONSULTATION OF INTERESTED PARTIES AND IMPACT ASSESSMENT

- **Consultation of interested parties**

Consultation methods, main sectors targeted and general profile of respondents

Fiscalis seminar, December 2004 in Dublin with representatives from the insurance and financial services industry and from the fiscal authorities of Member States

Tax Conference in Brussels on 11 May 2006 with representatives from the insurance and financial services industry and from the fiscal authorities of Member States

Public consultation of stakeholders in June 2006

Fiscalis seminar in March 2007

Publication of working documents containing first legal drafts on the Directorate General's website in June 2007

Roundtable with stakeholders in July 2007

Summary of responses and how they have been taken into account

The Fiscalis seminar in December 2004 in Dublin analysed the various problem areas for economic operators, in particular the outsourcing phenomenon and led to the conclusion by both, economic operators and Member States that a legislative initiative of the Commission services is required.

In the follow-up to this seminar DG TAXUD services commissioned a study with an independent expert to increase the understanding of the economic effects of the VAT exemption for Financial and Insurance services and undertook a series of bilateral consultations with Member States and DG MARKT which resulted in the elaborating of a basic document (Working Document Taxud 1802/06) outlining the basic problems which were identified as well as possible technical measures to address them. This document was discussed with stakeholders and Member States in the Tax Conference in Brussels in May 2006.

A second Fiscalis seminar was held in March 2007 with the objectives of familiarising concerned officials from the national tax administrations with the policies driving change in the regulatory framework, and the economic drivers for cross-border financial integration. The programme also covered practical implementation issues in the current legislation.

Draft legislations was extensively discussed with all stakeholders involved.

An open consultation was conducted over the internet from 9 May 2006 to 9 June 2006. The Commission received 82 responses. The results are available on http://ec.europa.eu/taxation_customs/common/consultations/tax/article_2447_en.htm

- **Collection and use of expertise**

Scientific/expertise domains concerned

Study to increase the understanding of the economic effects of the VAT exemption for Financial and Insurance services (Tender no taxud/2005/AO-006)

Methodology used

independent outside study

Main organisations/experts consulted

Price Waterhouse Coopers

Appendix 3: EU Proposals

Summary of advice received and used

The existence of potentially serious risks with irreversible consequences has not been mentioned.

There was broad consistency between the conclusions of the study, the Commission's own analysis in Working Document Taxud 1802/06 and the reactions from stakeholders in the public consultation, allowing Directorate General Taxation and Customs Union to impose the necessary priorities and focus its work on the most appropriate solutions.

Means used to make the expert advice publicly available

Publication on the Directorate General's website

http://ec.europa.eu/taxation_customs/common/publications/studies/index_en.htm

- **Impact assessment**

The options which were considered, are described extensively in the impact assessment

Zero rating on page 31

Extending the scope of exempted services on page 32

Uniform limited input tax deduction on page 33

Option to tax on page 34

Cross border VAT bodies on page 37

Single legal entities and cross-border transactions on page 37

VAT grouping on page 38

Cost sharing arrangements on page 41

Reduced VAT rate for bought-in service on page 44

Other options on page 44

The Commission carried out an impact assessment listed in the Work Programme, whose report is accessible on Document Taxud 15570.

3. **LEGAL ELEMENTS OF THE PROPOSAL**

- **Summary of the proposed action**

This proposal consists of three measures:

- clarification of the rules governing the exemption from VAT for insurance and financial services;

- broadening of the existing option for taxation by transferring the right to opt from the Member States to the economic operators;
- introduction of a cost-sharing group which allows economic operators to pool investments and re-distribute the costs for these investments exempt from VAT from the group to its members.

- **Legal basis**

Article 93 of the Treaty

- **Subsidiarity principle**

The proposal falls under the exclusive competence of the Community. The subsidiarity principle therefore does not apply.

- **Proportionality principle**

The proposal complies with the proportionality principle for the following reason(s).

The proposals are contained in a draft Directive; there can only be one correct interpretation of the rules governing the VAT exemption for insurance and financial services which apply throughout the Community; this objective can only be achieved by amending the old rules in Directive 2006/112/EC. Allowing suppliers of exempt insurance and financial services to group their investments and re-distribute these exempt from VAT from the group to its members requires an appropriate vehicle which works also in cross-border scenarios; the creation of such a vehicle can only be achieved by an amendment of Directive 2006/112/EC.

Clear rules based on economic criteria reduce the substance for possible litigation and therefore generate an environment of legal certainty within which the administrative charges for agreeing possibly with several Member States on how the rules are to be interpreted and applied are considerably reduced.

- **Choice of instruments**

Proposed instruments: directive.

Other means would not be adequate for the following reason(s).

The existing Council Directive 2006/112/EC can only be amended by another Directive.

4. **BUDGETARY IMPLICATION**

The proposal has no implication for the Community budget.

5. **ADDITIONAL INFORMATION**

- **Simplification**

The proposal provides for simplification of legislation.

The proposal includes the following elements of simplification:

– it bases the conditions for applying the VAT exemption on objective economic criteria which make the exemption from VAT more manageable;

– it clarifies that the exemption covers the supply of any constituent element of an insurance or financial service, which constitutes a distinct whole and has the specific and essential character of the exempt service concerned; this reduces the potential for litigation;

– it introduces a common harmonised concept of intermediation for insurance and financial services; the same principles apply to insurances and financial services.

- **Correlation table**

The Member States are required to communicate to the Commission the text of national provisions transposing the Directive as well as a correlation table between those provisions and this Directive.

2007/0267 (CNS)

Proposal for a

COUNCIL DIRECTIVE

amending Directive 2006/112/EC on the common system of value added tax, as regards the treatment of insurance and financial services

THE COUNCIL OF THE EUROPEAN UNION,

Having regard to the Treaty establishing the European Community, and in particular Article 93 thereof,

Having regard to the proposal from the Commission[1],

Having regard to the opinion of the European Parliament[2],

Having regard to the opinion of the European Economic and Social Committee[3],

Whereas:

(1) The financial service industry makes an important contribution to growth, competitiveness and job creation but can fulfil its role only under neutral conditions of competition in an internal market. It is necessary to provide a framework which provides legal certainty as to the value added tax (VAT) treatment of financial products and their marketing and management.

(2) The existing rules governing the exemptions from VAT for financial and insurance services laid down in Council Directive 2006/112/EC of 28 November 2006 on the common system of value added tax[4] are out of date and have led to uneven interpretation and application. The complexity of the rules and the variation in administrative practices generates legal uncertainty for economic operators and tax authorities. This uncertainty has led to considerable litigation and has increased the administrative burden. It is therefore necessary to clarify which insurance and financial services are exempt and thereby create greater legal certainty and reduce the administrative burden for operators and authorities.

(3) In order to ensure tax neutrality, the exemptions should be linked to the nature of the services concerned, on the basis of objective economic criteria, and not to the persons supplying them.

---

[1] OJ C , , p. .
[2] OJ C , , p. .
[3] OJ C , , p. .
[4] OJ L 347, 11.12.2006, p. 1. Directive as amended by Directive 2006/138/EC (OJ L 384, 29.12.2006, p. 92).

Appendix 3: EU Proposals

(4) Particular uncertainty arises where economic operators outsource activities to independent persons or pool activities between operators. To avoid such uncertainty, it is appropriate to make it clear that activities which form a constituent element of an insurance or financial service, constitute a distinct whole and have the specific and essential character of the exempt service fall within the exemption applying to the service concerned.

(5) Insurance services and financial services require similar forms of intermediation. It is therefore appropriate for intermediation in insurance and intermediation in financial services to be treated in the same way.

(6) The modernisation of the exemptions for insurance and financial services seeks also to ensure consistency with internal market provisions, in particular the Financial Services Action Plan[5] and the rules governing undertakings for collective investments in transferable securities. Nevertheless, in order to observe the requirement for strict interpretation of VAT exemptions, it is in some cases necessary for the definitions of exempt insurance and financial services to be narrower than the definitions provided for in the internal market rules.

(7) Suppliers of insurance and financial services are increasingly able to allocate input VAT on costs incurred by them precisely to the output to be taxed. Where the services they supply are fee-based, they can establish the taxable amount for these services easily. It is therefore appropriate to extend the possibility to opt for taxation for such operators.

(8) By strengthening cross-border co-operation, providers of insurance and financial services may increase their competitiveness and contribute to the realisation of the internal market. Subject to compliance with the principle of tax neutrality, the economic operators concerned should therefore be given the right to opt for taxation and to co-operate on a cost-sharing basis.

(9) Directive 2006/112/EC should therefore be amended accordingly,

HAS ADOPTED THIS DIRECTIVE:

Article 1

Directive 2006/112/EC is amended as follows:

(1) Article 135 is amended as follows:

    (a) In paragraph 1, points (a) to (g) are replaced by the following:

        "(a) insurance and reinsurance;

        (b) granting of credit and guaranteeing of debts resulting from the granting of credit;

---

[5] COM(1999) 232.

Appendix 3: EU Proposals

      (c)   transactions concerning financial deposits and account operation;

      (d)   exchange of currency and provision of cash;

      (e)   supply of securities;

      (f)   intermediation in insurance and financial transactions as referred to in points (a) to (e);

      (g)   management of investment funds;"

(b)   The following paragraphs 1a, 1b and 1c are inserted:

"1a.   The exemption provided for in points (a) to (e) of paragraph 1 shall apply to the supply of any constituent element of an insurance or financial service, which constitutes a distinct whole and has the specific and essential character of the exempt service.

1b.   Where a complex transaction includes an element of insurance which is set out separately, the insurance shall be a distinct service exempted under point (a) of paragraph 1.

1c.   Where the supply of goods or services includes the granting of credit which is not set out separately, the grant of credit shall not be a distinct service exempted under point (b) of paragraph 1."

(2)   The following Article 135a is inserted:

"Article 135a

For the purposes of applying the exemptions provided for in points (a) to (g) of Article 135(1), the following definitions shall apply:

(1)   "insurance and reinsurance" means a commitment whereby a person is obliged, in return for a payment, to provide another person, in the event of materialisation of a risk, with an indemnity or a benefit as determined by the commitment;

(2)   "granting of credit" means the lending of money or the promise to lend money;

(3)   "guaranteeing of debts" means the acceptance of liability for the debt of another person;

(4)   "financial deposit" means a deposit of money held on behalf of the depositor who retains rights to the deposits, which must be repaid under the legal and contractual conditions applicable;

(5)   "account operation" means the operation of a monetary account for a customer;

(6)   "exchange of currency" means the supply of services whereby a person changes the currency of bank notes or coins normally used as legal tender, of

deposits or of money in a monetary account on the basis of rates of exchange between currencies of countries;

(7) "cash" means bank notes and coins normally used as legal tender or negotiable means of payment;

(8) "supply of securities" means the supply of tradable instruments other than an instrument establishing title to goods or to the rights referred to in Article 15(2), representing financial value and reflecting any one or more of the following:

(a) an equity ownership position in a company or other association;

(b) a creditor's position for debts;

(c) unit ownership in undertakings for collective investment in the securities referred to in points (a) or (b), in other exempted financial instruments referred to in points (a) to (d) of Article 135(1) or in other undertakings for collective investment;

(9) "intermediation in insurance and financial transactions" means the supply of services rendered to, and remunerated by, a contractual party as a distinct act of mediation in relation to the insurance or financial transactions referred to in points (a) to (e) of Article 135(1), by a third party intermediary;

(10) "investment funds" means undertakings for collective investment in the exempted financial instruments referred to in points (a) to (e) of Article 135(1) and in real estate;

(11) "management of investment funds" means activities aimed at realising the investment objectives of the investment fund concerned."

(3) In Article 137(1), point (a) is deleted.

(4) The following Articles 137a and 137b are inserted:

"Article 137a

1. From 1 January 2012, Member States shall allow taxable persons a right of option for taxation in respect of the services referred to in points (a) to (g) of Article 135(1).

2. The Council shall adopt the measures necessary for the implementation of paragraph 1 pursuant to the procedure provided for in Article 397. So long as the Council has not adopted such measures, Member States may lay down the detailed rules governing exercise of the option under paragraph 1.

Article 137b

Member States shall exempt services supplied by a group of taxable persons to members of the group where the following conditions are fulfilled:

(1) the group itself and all its members are established or resident in the Community;

(2) the group carries out an autonomous activity and acts as an independent entity towards its members;

(3) members of the group are supplying services which are exempt under Article 135(1)(a) to (g) or other services in respect of which they are not taxable persons;

(4) the services are supplied by the group only to its members and are necessary to allow members to supply services which are exempt pursuant to Article 135(1)(a) to (g);

(5) the group claims from its members only the exact reimbursement of their share of the joint expenses, excluding any transfer-pricing adjustments made for the purposes of direct taxation."

(5) In Article 174(2), point (c) is replaced by the following:

"(c) the amount of turnover attributable to financial transactions as referred to in points (b) to (g) of Article 135(1) in so far as those transactions are incidental."

Article 2

Transposition

1. Member States shall bring into force the laws, regulations and administrative provisions necessary to comply with this Directive by 31 December 2009 at the latest. They shall forthwith communicate to the Commission the text of those provisions and a correlation table between those provisions and this Directive.

    When Member States adopt those provisions, they shall contain a reference to this Directive or be accompanied by such a reference on the occasion of their official publication. Member States shall determine how such reference is to be made.

2. Member States shall communicate to the Commission the text of the main provisions of national law which they adopt in the field covered by this Directive.

Article 3

This Directive shall enter into force on the [...] day following that of its publication in the *Official Journal of the European Union*.

Appendix 3: EU Proposals

Article 4

This Directive is addressed to the Member States.

Done at Brussels, […]

For the Council
The President

Appendix 3: EU Proposals

COUNCIL OF
THE EUROPEAN UNION

Brussels, 30 September 2011

14964/11

Interinstitutional File:
2007/0267 (CNS)

LIMITE

FISC 122

NOTE	
from:	Presidency
to:	Working Party on Tax Questions – Indirect taxation (VAT)
Subject:	Proposal for a Council Directive amending Directive 2006/112/EC on the common system of value added tax, as regards the treatment of insurance and financial services

Delegations will find attached a new compromise text for the Council Directive on the VAT treatment of insurance and financial services, which has been drawn up on the basis of the earlier compromise (doc. 12290/11 FISC 98).

<u>ANNEX</u>

Proposal for a

COUNCIL DIRECTIVE

amending Directive 2006/112/EC
on the common system of value added tax
as regards the treatment of insurance and financial services

Article 1

Directive 2006/112/EC is hereby amended as follows:

1) Article 135 is amended as follows:

    (a) In paragraph 1, points (a) to (g) shall be replaced by the following:

        (a) insurance and reinsurance [and transfer of insurance and reinsurance contracts];

"<u>Insurance and reinsurance</u>" means the acceptance of a commitment by a person to provide another person, in return for payment of a premium, in the event of materialisation of a risk covered, with an indemnity or a benefit as determined by the contract.

Appendix 3: EU Proposals

(b) granting of credit and management of credit by the ~~person granting it~~ **creditor**;

"Granting of credit" means the lending of money or the promise to lend money, as well as the granting of a deferment of payment of a debt [**, provided that the consideration for granting the credit and the grounds for determination the consideration are separately identified]**.

(c) guaranteeing of debt and provision of any other ~~securities for debt~~ **surety bonds**;

"Guaranteeing of debt and provision of any other ~~securities for debt~~ **surety bonds**" means the acceptance of a monetary obligation to pay a debt or any other financial commitment on behalf of the debtor in response to his default or to pay on behalf of a ~~contractor~~ **contracting party** in cases where he does not fulfil his contractual obligations.

(d) transfer of a credit position and assumption of a debt position **and excluding debt collection**;

"Transfer of a credit position" means the **definitive** cession of the right of receiving money excluding one constituting a supply of securities[~~and excluding debt collection~~].

"Assumption of a debt position" means the **definitive** assumption of an obligation to pay money, excluding one constituting a supply of securities.

Appendix 3: EU Proposals

(e) financial transfer;

"Financial transfer" means the execution following an order for transmission of funds.

(f) financial deposit taking and account operation;

"Financial deposit" means funds held for ~~the depositor~~ **a deposit holder** which must be repaid, transferred or which generate a return under the legal and contractual conditions applicable.

"Account operation" means the administration of monetary accounts for their holders.

(g) currency exchange and provision of cash;

"Currency exchange" means exchanges between currencies based on exchange rates between different currencies.

"Provision of cash" means the provision of bank notes and coins used as legal tender, with the exception of collectors' items, or the provision of negotiable or transferable means of payment.

Appendix 3: EU Proposals

(ga) transactions in securities, excluding their safekeeping and management;

"Securities" means transferable instruments other than those establishing title to goods or the rights referred to in Article 15 (2), representing a financial value or the right to acquire a financial value and reflecting one or more of the following:

    (a)   an equity ownership position in a company, association or other undertaking;
    (b)   a creditor's position for debts;
    (c)   unit ownership in undertakings for collective investment.

(gaa)   transactions in interests in companies and associations other than securities, excluding their safekeeping and management;

"Interests in companies and associations" means negotiable equity ownership positions in a company or association.

(gb)   transactions in financial derivatives, excluding their safekeeping and management;

"Financial derivatives" means instruments in the form of contracts relating to the value of securities, currencies, interest rates or yields, financial indices or measures, commodities, transfers of credit risk, climatic variables, freight or inflation rates, emission allowances or other official economic statistics in which at least one of the parties is committed, on a firm or optional basis, to such value provided that profits and losses are derived without any possibility of delivery or fulfilment of any underlying goods or services, other than exempt insurance or financial services.

Appendix 3: EU Proposals

(gc) management of investment funds and pension funds established within the territory of the Community;

"Management of investment funds and pension funds" means services of collective portfolio management necessary for achieving the investment objectives of the investment fund and pension fund concerned.

"Investment funds" means undertakings for collective investments the sole object of which is investment in securities, cash, other financial assets or in real estate of capital raised **directly or indirectly** from investors and which are subject to rules designed to protect investors and operate on the principle of risk spreading.

"Pension funds" means undertakings for collective investments operating similarly to investment funds and the ~~main~~ **basic** object of which is to provide retirement benefits in the context of an occupational activity.

(gd) intermediation in insurance and financial transactions as referred to in points (a) to (gb).

"Intermediation in insurance and financial transactions" means a distinct act of mediation rendered by a third party who [brings the parties together and] does what is necessary in order for the parties to enter into, **maintain,** renew or alter a contract in insurance or financial transactions as referred to in points (a) to (gb).

Appendix 3: EU Proposals

(b) The following paragraph 1a shall be inserted:

Article 135 (1a)

"1a. The exemption provided for in points (a) to (gc) of paragraph 1 shall apply to the supply of any constituent element of an exempt insurance or financial service, which itself constitutes a distinct whole and fulfils in effect the specific and essential [functions] of that exempt service."

2) Point (a) of Article 137(1) is amended as follows:

"(a) the financial transactions referred to in points (b) to (gd) of Article 135(1), excluding intermediation in insurance transactions;"

3) Point (c) of Article 169 is amended as follows:

"(c) transactions which are exempt pursuant to points (a) to (gb) and (gd) of Article 135(1), where the customer is established outside the Community or where those transactions relate directly to goods to be exported out of the Community."

4) Point (c) of Article 174 (2) shall be replaced by the following:

"(c) in so far as the transactions specified in points (b) to (gd) of Article 135(1), excluding intermediation in insurance transactions, are incidental, the amount of turnover attributable to these transactions."

Appendix 3: EU Proposals

5) Article 220(2) is amended as follows[*]:

"2. By way of derogation from paragraph 1, and without prejudice to Article 221 (2), the issue of an invoice shall not be required in respect of supplies of services exempted under points (a) to (gd) of Article 135(1)."

6) Article 221(2) is amended as follows[*]:

"2. Member States may impose on taxable persons who have established their business in their territory or who have a fixed establishment in their territory from which the supply is made, an obligation to issue an invoice in accordance with the details required in Article 226 or 226b in respect of supplies of services exempted under points (a) to (gd) of Article 135(1) which those taxable persons have made in their territory or outside the Community."

7) Article 288(4) is amended as follows:

"(4) the value of real estate transactions, insurance and financial transactions as referred to in points (a) to (gc) of Article 135(1), and intermediation in financial transactions as referred to in points (b) to (gb) of Article 135(1), unless those transactions are ancillary transactions."

---

[*] Changes to be made to the text as amended by Council Directive 2010/45/EU and applicable from 1 January 2013.
[*] Changes to be made to the text as amended by Council Directive 2010/45/EU and applicable from 1 January 2013.

8) New Chapter 5a is inserted:

"Chapter 5a

Special scheme for transactions on a regulated commodity market

Article 356a

Member States may, after consulting the VAT Committee, for purposes of simplification, authorise suspension of the tax to be collected on transactions between taxable persons who are members of a regulated commodities market, or between a taxable person who is a member of that market and the central counterparty of that market, **in respect of transactions on that market**."

Member States making use of the possibility provided for in the first subparagraph shall submit annually – by 31 March - information for the preceding calendar year to the VAT Committee concerning the operation of suspension of the tax, including in particular the revealed methods of tax avoidance and the impact of suspension of the tax on competition.

Article 356b

1. Member States making use of the possibility provided in Article 356a may dispense with some ~~or all~~ recording requirements of value added tax.

2. Without prejudice to paragraph 1, Member States shall, as a minimum, ensure that members of a regulated commodities market keep account of transactions and keep the documentation to allow identification of the customer in such transactions.

Members of a regulated commodities market shall keep this information for a period of at least five years, starting from the end of the year when the transaction took place.

Appendix 3: EU Proposals

3. Member States may accept equivalent obligations under measures adopted pursuant to other Community legislation, such as Council Directive 91/308/EEC of 10 June 1991 on prevention of the use of the financial system for the purpose of money laundering, to meet the requirements of paragraph 2."

[4. Member States may lay down obligations which are more stringent, in particular as regards the keeping of special records or special accounting requirements.]

Appendix 3: EU Proposals

COUNCIL OF
THE EUROPEAN UNION

Brussels, 6 June 2011

11092/11

LIMITE

Interinstitutional File:
2007/0267 (CNS)

FISC 84

NOTE
from: Presidency
to: COREPER/Council
Subject: Proposals for a Council Directive and Regulation as regards the VAT treatment of insurance and financial services
 - draft Presidency progress report

Delegations will find in the Annex the revised version of the draft Presidency progress report on the VAT treatment of insurance and financial services, which takes into account discussions at the Working Party on Tax Questions (Indirect Taxation) on 1 June 2011.

Appendix 3: EU Proposals

ANNEX

**PRESIDENCY PROGRESS REPORT
ON THE PROPOSALS FOR A COUNCIL DIRECTIVE AND REGULATION
AS REGARDS THE VAT TREATMENT OF INSURANCE AND FINANCIAL SERVICES**

I. BACKGROUND

1. In December 2007, the Commission submitted to the Council a proposal to amend Council Directive 2006/112/EC on the common system of value added tax, as regards the treatment of financial and insurance services, and a proposal for a Council Regulation laying down implementing measures for Council Directive 2006/112/EC, as regards the treatment of financial and insurance services.

2. The proposals are aimed at clarification and modernisation of the definitions of exempt financial and insurance services in order to ensure consistent interpretation across the European Union. In addition, a mechanism to establish cross-border cost sharing groups and an extension of the option to apply the normal VAT rules were also proposed by the Commission.

3. The proposals have been discussed extensively in the Council's Working Party on Tax Questions under the Slovenian, French, Czech, Swedish, Spanish and Belgian Presidencies, and progress was made.

4. At its meeting on 17 November 2010, the Council (ECOFIN) took stock of the situation and endorsed the orientations for future work as prepared by the Belgian Presidency (doc. 15578/10). The Hungarian Presidency draws attention to the Minutes of that Council (ECOFIN) meeting and the comments made by the German and French delegations (doc. 16455/10).

II. STATE OF PLAY OF THE DISCUSSIONS UNDER THE HUNGARIAN PRESIDENCY

5. The Hungarian Presidency continued the work on the two proposals in line with the orientations received from the Council focusing, as a priority, on the definitions of exempt financial and insurance services. In the context of harmonised and modernised definition of the exemption for the management of investment funds, and as specifically requested by the Council, the Working Party examined the overall effect, as far as VAT is concerned, of the changes in the regulatory climate for these funds.

6. The Hungarian Presidency organised six meetings of the Council Working Party on this subject, and prepared four sets of compromise proposals, accompanied by several discussion papers and explanatory notes.

7. At the meetings profound and detailed technical debates took place, and this enabled delegations to clarify their positions.

8. Progress has been made and a tentative agreement was reached on a number of issues including the definition of insurance and reinsurance services (except for the transfer of insurance and reinsurance contract portfolios and the processing of insurance and reinsurance claims), currency exchange, and provision of cash. There is also an emerging agreement among the delegations that the VAT Directive should not provide for separate rules as to the tax treatment of complex supplies with an element of credit or insurance service as these would be too rigid to reflect all possible business scenarios. Furthermore, the discussions on the positive and negative examples in the draft regulation concerning financial transfer, financial deposit taking, account operation, currency exchange, provision of cash, securities and financial derivatives are essentially drawing to a closure.

Appendix 3: EU Proposals

9. As a result of the work undertaken on the definitions the Presidency has improved the wording on guaranteeing of debt and thus included the acceptance of monetary obligations to pay in those cases where the original obligation of the contractor is not of a pecuniary nature. In order to take into consideration the differences in the civil laws of Member States as regards the concept of securities, and to make sure that the exemption as regards interests in companies and associations will continue to be applied in the same scope as currently, the Presidency has appropriately adjusted the definition of exemption. The Presidency made changes in the definition of transfer of debt position in order to reflect that the service is provided by the person assuming the debt.

10. The Presidency also added to the proposal the technical provisions needed to reflect the changes in the definitions of the Directive.

11. As a result of the detailed discussions, the differences in Member States' interpretation of the current rules were highlighted, but at the same time it was also revealed that delegations wished to achieve well-defined limits for the exemptions, which could pave the way for a future compromise.

12. On the basis of these discussions, at this stage the Hungarian Presidency identified, among others, *four major outstanding issues* of political importance: 1) transfer of insurance and reinsurance contract portfolios; 2) outsourcing; 3) management of investment funds; 4) derivatives.

Appendix 3: EU Proposals

1) According to the jurisprudence of the European Court of Justice the ***transfer of insurance and reinsurance contract portfolios*** is a taxed transaction, while under the current VAT Directive the transfer of a portfolio of <u>credit</u> contracts is interpreted by most Member States as being exempt. The majority of delegations are of the view that in order to avoid distortion of competition the transfer of insurance contract portfolios should also be exempt, while others point out that this would entail the widening of the scope of the current exemption, which would not be fully in line with the initial aim of the proposal.

2) Currently, the VAT Directive does not provide rules for the VAT treatment of ***services outsourced by suppliers of exempt financial and insurance services***. The legal uncertainties are reflected by the fact that the ECJ has ruled on several occasions in this respect, and those rulings are, to a certain extent, interpreted differently. Within the spectrum of views expressed, some delegations assert that the exemption for outsourcing should cover only those services which fulfil in effect all the specific and essential functions of an exempt financial or insurance service; other delegations would, however, exempt a wider range of services, to include those which have at least one of the core functions of financial and insurance services.

Appendix 3: EU Proposals

3) Regarding *management of investment funds*, the main issue concerns the conditions an investment fund must meet in order for its management to be exempt. In addition, there are outstanding questions as regards which management services are covered by the exemption. The relevant ECJ rulings state that the purpose of the exemption is, particularly, to facilitate investment for small investors by means of investment undertakings, and that VAT should be fiscally neutral as regards the choice between direct investment and investment through undertakings for collective investment. Against this background, a number of Member States are of the opinion that the exemption should be limited to investment funds collecting the savings of small investors. Others argue that fiscal neutrality and competitiveness of the European fund industry would point towards inclusion of other investment funds. It should also be taken into account that small investors may invest in funds which would then invest in other funds not covered by the exemption, which would result in the same negative impact for the small investor which the exemption is intended to avoid.

Since the management of pension funds could be considered as similar to management of investment funds, the VAT treatment of *management of pension funds* should also be addressed.

4) In the context of *derivatives*, work is still ongoing on the definition of exempt financial derivatives, on how to secure their continued exemption and on the possible introduction of a general optional tax suspension arrangement for commodity derivatives traded on regulated commodity markets.

III. GENERAL OBSERVATIONS

13. As outlined above, Member States interpret the current rules differently, and come to the discussions from different points of departure. In the opinion of the Hungarian Presidency, despite these differences there is a common understanding that a level playing field should be achieved through the modernisation of the definitions. Harmonised rules would require a careful balancing of several aspects of a complex situation (level playing field, competitiveness of the sector, budgetary implications), as these cannot always be achieved without some trade-off. A future agreement should also take into account the ongoing work on identifying the tax base for financial services. The Hungarian Presidency underlines the need to acknowledge the eventual evolution of the VAT Strategy and the initiatives on the taxation of the financial sector.

o

o   o

14. The Council is invited to take note of the progress achieved so far.

_____

COUNCIL OF THE EUROPEAN UNION	Brussels, 1 February 2011
	5906/11
Interinstitutional File: 2007/0267 (CNS)	LIMITE
	FISC 11

NOTE
from:	Presidency
to:	Working Party on Tax Questions – Indirect taxation (VAT)
Subject:	Proposal for a Council Directive amending Directive 2006/112/EC on the common system of value added tax, as regards the treatment of insurance and financial services

Delegations will find attached a new compromise text for the Council Directive on the VAT treatment of insurance and financial services, which has been drawn up on the basis of the earlier compromise (doc. 17919/10 FISC 158).

Appendix 3: EU Proposals

<u>ANNEX</u>

Proposal for a

COUNCIL DIRECTIVE

amending Directive 2006/112/EC
on the common system of value added tax
as regards the treatment of insurance and financial services

Article 1

Directive 2006/112/EC is hereby amended as follows:

1) Article 135 is amended as follows:

    (a) In paragraph 1, points (a) to (g) shall be replaced by the following:

    (a) insurance and reinsurance [and transfer of insurance and reinsurance contracts];

    "<u>Insurance and reinsurance</u>" means the acceptance of a commitment by a person to provide another person, in return for payment of a premium, **by organising a group of persons exposed to the same risk or to similar risks and** in the event of materialisation of a risk covered ~~and based on the pooling of risks~~, with an indemnity or a benefit as determined by the contract.

Appendix 3: EU Proposals

(b) granting of credit and credit management;

"Granting of credit" means the lending of money or the promise to lend money, as well as the granting of a deferment of payment of a debt.

(c) guaranteeing of debt;

"Guaranteeing of debt" means the acceptance of a monetary obligation to pay a debt or any other financial commitment on behalf of the debtor in response to his default.

(d) transfer of a credit **position** and **assumption of a** debt position;

"Transfer of a credit position" means the cession of the right of receiving money excluding the one constituting a supply of securities.

"~~Transfer~~ **Assumption** of a debt position" means the assumption of an obligation to pay money, excluding the one constituting a supply of securities.

(e) financial transfer;

"Financial transfer" means the execution of an order for transmission of funds.

(f) financial deposit taking and account operation;

"Financial deposit" means funds which must be repaid, transferred or which generate a return under the legal and contractual conditions applicable.

"Account operation" means the administration of monetary accounts for their holders.

Appendix 3: EU Proposals

(g) currency exchange and provision of cash;

"Currency exchange" means exchanges between currencies based on exchange rates between different currencies.

"Provision of cash" means the provision of bank notes and coins used as legal tender, with the exception of collectors' items, or the provision of negotiable or transferable means of payment.

(ga) transactions in securities, excluding their safekeeping and management;

"Securities" means transferable instruments other than those establishing title to goods or the rights referred to in Article 15 (2), representing a financial value or the right to acquire a financial value and reflecting one or more of the following:

    (a) an equity ownership position in a company or other undertaking;
    (b) a creditor's position for debts;
    (c) unit ownership in undertakings for collective investment.

(gb) transactions in financial derivatives, excluding their safekeeping and management;

"Financial derivatives" means instruments in the form of contracts relating to the value of securities, currencies, interest rates or yields, financial indices or measures, commodities, transfers of credit risk, climatic variables, freight or inflation rates, emission allowances or other official economic statistics in which at least one of the parties is committed, on a firm or optional basis, to such value provided that profits and losses are derived without any possibility of delivery or fulfillment of any underlying goods or services, other than exempt insurance or financial services.

(gc) management of investment funds;

"Management of investment funds" means services included within the ~~functions~~ tasks of portfolio management and administration aimed at achieving the investment objectives of the investment fund concerned.

"Investment funds" means undertakings for collective investments the sole object of which is investment in securities, other financial instruments and in real estate of capital raised from investors and which are subject to rules designed to protect investors and operate on the principle of risk spreading.

(gd) intermediation in insurance and financial transactions as referred to in points (a) to (gb).

"Intermediation in insurance and financial transactions" means a distinct act of mediation rendered by a third party whose purpose is to do what is necessary in order for the parties to enter into, renew, alter or terminate a contract in insurance or financial transactions as referred to in points (a) to (gb).

Appendix 3: EU Proposals

(b) The following paragraphs 1a, 1b and 1c shall be inserted:

Article 135 (1a)

"1a. The exemption provided for in point**s** (a) **to (gb)** of paragraph 1 shall apply to the supply of any constituent element of an exempt insurance **or financial** service, which itself constitutes a distinct whole and is specific to and essential for the supply **and fulfils in effect the specific and essential functions** of that exempt service.

The exemption provided for in points (b) to (gb) of paragraph 1 shall apply to the supply of any constituent element of an exempt financial service if the following conditions are met:

- the constituent element constitutes a distinct whole and is specific to and essential for the supply of that exempt service;

- the constituent element entails a change in the legal and financial relationship between the parties if the exempt financial service is characterized by such change.

The exemption provided for in point (gc) of paragraph 1 shall apply to the supply of **a** bundles of services making up the function of **included in the task of** portfolio management or administration concerning the given investment fund **referred to in that point, if that bundle of services constitutes a distinct whole and fulfils in effect the specific and essential functions of that task**."

Appendix 3: EU Proposals

Article 135 (1b)

"1b. Where a supply of goods or services comprises, in part, insurance or credit which constitutes an aim in itself, and whose price is thus set out separately, that part shall be considered a distinct supply of services exempted under points (a) or (b) of paragraph 1."

Article 135 (1c)

"1c. Where a supply of goods or services comprises, in part, insurance or credit which does not constitute an aim in itself, even if its price is set out separately, that part shall not be considered a distinct supply of services exempted under points (a) or (b) of paragraph 1."

COUNCIL OF
THE EUROPEAN UNION

Brussels, 7 October 2011

15265/11

Interinstitutional File:
2007/0267 (CNS)

LIMITE

FISC 127

NOTE

from:	Presidency
to:	High Level Working Party
Subject:	Proposals for a Council Directive and Regulation as regards the VAT treatment of insurance and financial services = Orientation debate

With a view to an orientation debate, the Presidency has prepared a note (Annex), which explains the state of play of the discussions on the VAT treatment of insurance and financial services and invites the High Level Working Party to pronounce itself on suggested orientations for future work in respect of those issues, which could not be agreed at the working party level.

ANNEX
NOTE
ON THE VAT TREATMENT OF INSURANCE AND FINANCIAL SERVICES

This note sets out the state of play of the discussions on the VAT treatment of insurance and financial services and proposals of directions for future work in respect of those issues, which could not be agreed at the working party level.

A. State of play

1. The provisions governing VAT treatment of insurance and financial services have not been changed for more than 30 years. Their interpretation and application by the Member States are however far from uniform. Furthermore, in the light of dynamic development of the EU insurance and financial services market and new complex products being offered in the market, it is also necessary to adjust the definitions to the current conditions of the common market. Therefore, the European Commission submitted to the Council in 2007 a proposal for a Council Directive amending Directive 2006/112/EC on the common system of value added tax, as regards the VAT treatment of insurance and financial services. The aim of the proposal was :

- clarification and updating definitions of the exempt insurance and financial services in order to ensure consistent interpretation throughout the European Union,

- broadening of the existing option for taxation by transferring the right to opt from the Member States to the financial and insurance institutions,

- introduction of a cost sharing group which allows re-distribution of costs.

The above mentioned proposal is accompanied by a proposal for a Regulation, in which the Commission enumerated in a non-exhaustive way the examples of insurance and financial services covered by or excluded from the VAT exemption in respect of definitions of insurance and financial services provided for in the directive.

Appendix 3: EU Proposals

2. At its meeting on 17 November 2010, the ECOFIN Council took note of the situation and endorsed guidelines for future work (docs. 15578/10 and 16455/10). According to the guidelines in question further work should be continued both with due consideration being given to ensure a level playing field between operators and between Member States, to strengthen the overall competitiveness of the financial and insurance sector of the European Union and to the budgetary implications. Furthermore the Council considered that there is no need for further work on cost sharing arrangements at the Council level. As regards option to tax, the Council invited the Commission to explore possible solutions allowing to depart from the existing VAT exemption. Further work on the definitions of exempt financial and insurance services should be pursued as a priority.

3. During more than 3-years of work in the Council's Working Party on Tax Questions, the proposals have been discussed extensively under the Slovenian, French, Czech, Swedish, Spanish, Belgian and Hungarian Presidencies, and visible progress was made.

4. According to the Hungarian Presidency's progress report (doc. 11092/11), of which the ECOFIN Council took note on 20 June 2011 (doc. 11271/11), further work on the taxation of the financial sector requires a careful balancing of several aspects which affect the Member States' perception of these issues, i.e. level playing field, competitiveness of the sector, budgetary implications; the future agreement should take into the ongoing work on identifying the tax base for financial services; and the evolution of the VAT Strategy and the initiatives on the taxation of the financial sector should also be acknowledged.

5. The Polish Presidency has been continuing work on the two proposals in the Council's Working Party on Tax Questions – Indirect Taxation (VAT), focusing on the definitions of exempt financial and insurance services and taking into consideration guidelines of the Council of 17 November 2010, i.e. necessity of ensuring a level playing field between operators and between Member States, strengthening the overall competitiveness of the financial and insurance sector of the European Union and budgetary implications. However, as mentioned in the Hungarian Presidency progress report there are four outstanding issues of political importance that can hardly be solved at the working party level: transfer of insurance and reinsurance contract portfolios, outsourcing, management of investment funds and derivatives.

a)   transfer of insurance and reinsurance contract portfolios

Pursuant to binding VAT provisions and according to the jurisprudence of the Court of Justice of the European Union (C-242/08 Swiss Re) the transfer of insurance and reinsurance contract portfolios is subject to VAT taxation, while under current VAT directive transfer of credit contract portfolios is interpreted by most Member States as being exempt. In view of some kind of discrimination of insurance and reinsurance sector (in respect to credit services) and distortion of competition, the majority of Member States opt for the exemption of the transfer of insurance and reinsurance contract portfolios, while a few Member States (pointing out the negative budgetary implications caused by widening the scope of the current exemption) opt for keeping them taxed.

b)   outsourcing

Currently, the VAT Directive does not provide rules for the VAT treatment of services outsourced by suppliers of exempt financial and insurance services. Despite of the several rulings in this respect by the Court of Justice of the European Union (e.g. C-2/95 SDC, C-472/03 Arthur Andersen), the issue is still dubious. In the course of discussions within the working party delegations expressed divergent opinions. In view of some delegations, the exemption for outsourcing should cover only those services which fulfill in effect all the specific and essential functions of an exempt financial or insurance service. Other delegations take the position that the exemption should cover a wider range of services, i.e. those services which as well have at least one of the core functions of financial and insurance services.

Appendix 3: EU Proposals

c) ***management of investment funds***

Currently, the VAT Directive confers some discretion to select the investment funds covered by the notion of 'special investment funds'. The provisions concerning the management of investment funds do not provide any visible reference which would limit the scope of exemption, e.g. to funds collecting the savings of "small investors". However, according to the case law of the Court of Justice of the European Union (C-169/04 Abbey National) the purpose of the exemption is, particularly, to facilitate investment in securities for small investors by means of investment undertakings. Furthermore, the Court stated that VAT should be fiscally neutral as regards the choice between direct investment and investment through undertakings for collective investment. Some Member States quoting the above mentioned judgment are of the opinion that the exemption should be limited to investment funds collecting the savings of small investors. Others - considering the fiscal neutrality and competitiveness of the European fund industry - take the position that the exemption should cover other investment funds, e.g. funds which invest in other funds.

d) ***derivatives***

In the course of works pursued at the working party level divergent views concerning the scope of exemption for transactions in financial derivatives have been revealed. Some delegations are of the opinion that transactions in financial derivatives, which are or may be settled by physical delivery of goods or services other than the exempt financial or insurance services, should be subject to taxation. Other Member States argue that taxation should apply only to transactions, which in practice are settled by physical delivery of goods or services other than the exempt financial or insurance services.

* * *

Appendix 3: EU Proposals

B.   Possible solutions :

Taking into account almost 4-years of work in the Council's Working Party on Tax Questions and particularly upcoming work in the Council on the VAT strategy and the financial sector taxation, the Polish Presidency identified at this stage two possible solutions :

I. To continue the work on the basis of the package of guidelines that would form a future compromise. The Polish Presidency sees the following guidelines for future work on definitions as a possible compromise:

- *exemption from VAT of transfer of insurance and reinsurance contract portfolios;*

- *narrow definition of the scope of exemption for outsourced financial and insurance services, so that only services of financial or insurance nature would be exempt;*

- *VAT exemption for the management of investment and pension funds that would be applicable for any funds, regardless of investor;*

- *taxation of only those transactions in financial derivatives, which are settled by physical delivery of goods or services.*

Q1: Delegations are invited to express their views on this package of guidelines;
Q2: Delegations are invited to indicate which guideline possibly is not acceptable for them and for what reasons, in particular to what extent it is influenced by the overarching issues of the level playing field, competitiveness or   budgetary concerns;

II. To postpone further work on the dossier until examination of the VAT strategy and proposals on the financial sector taxation, which may lead to a new impulse in this file.

Q3: Delegations are invited to indicate whether this would be an acceptable solution at this stage.

Appendix 4: VATA 1994, Sch. 4A & SI 2012/2787

SCH. 4A – PLACE OF SUPPLY OF SERVICES: SPECIAL RULES

Section 7A

Part 1 – General Exceptions

SERVICES RELATING TO LAND

1(1) A supply of services to which this paragraph applies is to be treated as made in the country in which the land in connection with which the supply is made is situated.

1(2) This paragraph applies to–

(a) the grant, assignment or surrender of any interest in or right over land,
(b) the grant, assignment or surrender of a personal right to call for or be granted any interest in or right over land,
(c) the grant, assignment or surrender of a licence to occupy land or any other contractual right exercisable over or in relation to land (including the provision of holiday accommodation, seasonal pitches for caravans and facilities at caravan parks for persons for whom such pitches are provided and pitches for tents and camping facilities),
(d) the provision in a hotel, inn, boarding house or similar establishment of sleeping accommodation or of accommodation in rooms which are provided in conjunction with sleeping accommodation or for the purpose of a supply of catering,
(e) any works of construction, demolition, conversion, reconstruction, alteration, enlargement, repair or maintenance of a building or civil engineering work, and
(f) services such as are supplied by estate agents, auctioneers, architects, surveyors, engineers and others involved in matters relating to land.

1(3) In sub-paragraph (2)(c) '**holiday accommodation**' includes any accommodation in a building, hut (including a beach hut or chalet), caravan, houseboat or tent which is advertised or held out as holiday accommodation or as suitable for holiday or leisure use.

1(4) In sub-paragraph (2)(d) '**similar establishment**' includes premises in which there is provided furnished sleeping accommodation, whether with or without the provision of board or facilities for the preparation of food, which are used by, or held out as being suitable for use by, visitors or travellers.

PASSENGER TRANSPORT

2(1) A supply of services consisting of the transportation of passengers (or of any luggage or motor vehicles accompanying passengers) is to be treated as made in the country in which the transportation takes place, and (in a case where it takes place in more than one country) in proportion to the distances covered in each.

2(2) For the purposes of sub-paragraph (1) transportation which takes place partly outside the territorial jurisdiction of a country is to be treated as taking place wholly in the country if–

(a) it takes place in the course of a journey between two points in the country (whether or not as part of a longer journey involving travel to or from another country), and
(b) the means of transport used does not (except in an emergency or involuntarily) stop, put in or land in another country in the course of the journey between those two points.

2(3) For the purposes of sub-paragraph (1) a pleasure cruise is to be regarded as the transportation of passengers (so that services provided as part of a pleasure cruise are to be treated as supplied in the same place as the transportation of the passengers).

2(4) In sub-paragraph (3) **'pleasure cruise'** includes a cruise wholly or partly for education or training.

HIRING OF MEANS OF TRANSPORT

3(1) A supply of services consisting of the short-term hiring of a means of transport is to be treated as made in the country in which the means of transport is actually put at the disposal of the person by whom it is hired.

But this is subject to sub-paragraphs (3) and (4).

3(2) For the purposes of this Schedule the hiring of a means of transport is **'short-term'** if it is hired for a continuous period not exceeding–

(a) if the means of transport is a vessel, 90 days, and
(b) otherwise, 30 days.

3(3) Where–

(a) a supply of services consisting of the hiring of a means of transport would otherwise be treated as made in the United Kingdom, and
(b) the services are to any extent effectively used and enjoyed in a country which is not a member State,

the supply is to be treated to that extent as made in that country.

3(4) Where–

(a) a supply of services consisting of the hiring of a means of transport would otherwise be treated as made in a country which is not a member State, and
(b) the services are to any extent effectively used and enjoyed in the United Kingdom,

the supply is to be treated to that extent as made in the United Kingdom.

CULTURAL, EDUCATIONAL AND ENTERTAINMENT SERVICES ETC

4 [Omitted by FA 2009, s. 76 and Sch. 36, para. 15(2), with effect in relation to supplies made on or after 1 January 2011.]

RESTAURANT AND CATERING SERVICES: GENERAL

5(1) A supply of services to which this paragraph applies is to be treated as made in the country in which the services are physically carried out.

5(2) This paragraph applies to the provision of restaurant services and the provision of catering services, other than the provision of services to which paragraph 6 applies.

EC ON-BOARD RESTAURANT AND CATERING SERVICES

6(1) A supply of services consisting of

(a) the provision of restaurant services, or
(b) the provision of catering services,

on board a ship, aircraft or train in connection with the transportation of passengers during an intra-EC passenger transport operation is to be treated as made in the country in which the relevant point of departure is located.

6(2) An intra-EC passenger transport operation is a passenger transport operation which, or so much of a passenger transport operation as,–

(a) has as the first place at which passengers can embark a place which is within the EC,
(b) has as the last place at which passengers who embarked in a member State can disembark a place which is within the EC, and

(c) does not include a stop at a place which is not within the EC and at which passengers can embark or passengers who embarked in a member State can disembark.

6(3) '**Relevant point of departure**', in relation to an intra-EC passenger transport operation, is the first place in the intra-EC passenger transport operation at which passengers can embark.

6(4) A place is within the EC if it is within any member State.

6(5) For the purposes of this paragraph the return stage of a return passenger transport operation is to be regarded as a separate passenger transport operation; and for this purpose–

(a) a return passenger transport operation is one which takes place in more than one country but is expected to end in the country in which it begins, and

(b) the return stage of a return passenger transport operation is the part of it which ends in the country in which it began and begins with the last stop at a place at which there has not been a previous stop during it.

HIRING OF GOODS

7(1) Where–

(a) a supply of services consisting of the hiring of any goods other than a means of transport would otherwise be treated as made in the United Kingdom, and

(b) the services are to any extent effectively used and enjoyed in a country which is not a member State,

the supply is to be treated to that extent as made in that country.

7(2) Where–

(a) a supply of services consisting of the hiring of any goods other than a means of transport would otherwise be treated as made in a country which is not a member State, and

(b) the services are to any extent effectively used and enjoyed in the United Kingdom,

the supply is to be treated to that extent as made in the United Kingdom.

TELECOMMUNICATION AND BROADCASTING SERVICES

8(1) This paragraph applies to a supply of services consisting of the provision of–

(a) telecommunication services, or

(b) radio or television broadcasting services.

8(2) In this Schedule '**telecommunication services**' means services relating to the transmission, emission or reception of signals, writing, images and sounds or information of any nature by wire, radio, optical or other electromagnetic systems, including–

(a) the related transfer or assignment of the right to use capacity for such transmission, emission or reception, and

(b) the provision of access to global information networks.

8(3) Where–

(a) a supply of services to which this paragraph applies would otherwise be treated as made in the United Kingdom, and

(b) the services are to any extent effectively used and enjoyed in a country which is not a member State,

the supply is to be treated to that extent as made in that country.

8(4) Where–

(a) a supply of services to which this paragraph applies would otherwise be treated as made in a country which is not a member State, and

(b) the services are to any extent effectively used and enjoyed in the United Kingdom,

the supply is to be treated to that extent as made in the United Kingdom.

Part 2 – Exceptions Relating to Supplies Made to Relevant Business Person

ELECTRONICALLY-SUPPLIED SERVICES

9(1) Where–
(a) a supply of services consisting of the provision of electronically supplied services to a relevant business person would otherwise be treated as made in the United Kingdom, and
(b) the services are to any extent effectively used and enjoyed in a country which is not a member State,

the supply is to be treated to that extent as made in that country.

9(2) Where–
(a) a supply of services consisting of the provision of electronically supplied services to a relevant business person would otherwise be treated as made in a country which is not a member State, and
(b) the services are to any extent effectively used and enjoyed in the United Kingdom,

the supply is to be treated to that extent as made in the United Kingdom.

9(3) Examples of what are electronically supplied services for the purposes of this Schedule include–
(a) website supply, web-hosting and distance maintenance of programmes and equipment,
(b) the supply of software and the updating of software,
(c) the supply of images, text and information, and the making available of databases,
(d) the supply of music, films and games (including games of chance and gambling games),
(e) the supply of political, cultural, artistic, sporting, scientific, educational or entertainment broadcasts (including broadcasts of events), and
(f) the supply of distance teaching.

9(4) But where the supplier of a service and the supplier's customer communicate via electronic mail, this does not of itself mean that the service provided is an electronically supplied service for the purposes of this Schedule.

ADMISSION TO CULTURAL, EDUCATIONAL AND ENTERTAINMENT ACTIVITIES ETC

9A(1) A supply to a relevant business person of services to which this paragraph applies is to be treated as made in the country in which the events in question actually take place.

9A(2) This paragraph applies to the provision of–
(a) services in respect of admission to cultural, artistic, sporting, scientific, educational, entertainment or similar events (including fairs and exhibitions), and
(b) ancillary services relating to admission to such events.

Part 3 – Exceptions Relating to Supplies not made to Relevant Business Person

INTERMEDIARIES

10(1) A supply of services to which this paragraph applies is to be treated as made in the same country as the supply to which it relates.

10(2) This paragraph applies to a supply to a person who is not a relevant business person consisting of the making of arrangements for a supply by or to another person or of any other activity intended to facilitate the making of such a supply.

TRANSPORT OF GOODS: GENERAL

11(1) A supply of services to a person who is not a relevant business person consisting of the transportation of goods is to be treated as made in the country in which the transportation takes place, and (in a case where it takes place in more than one country) in proportion to the distances covered in each.

11(2) For the purposes of sub-paragraph (1) transportation which takes place partly outside the territorial jurisdiction of a country is to be treated as taking place wholly in the country if–

(a) it takes place in the course of a journey between two points in the country (whether or not as part of a longer journey involving travel to or from another country), and

(b) the means of transport used does not (except in an emergency or involuntarily) stop, put in or land in another country in the course of the journey between those two points.

11(3) This paragraph does not apply to a transportation of goods beginning in one member State and ending in another (see paragraph 12).

INTRA-COMMUNITY TRANSPORT OF GOODS

12 A supply of services to a person who is not a relevant business person consisting of the transportation of goods which begins in one member State and ends in another is to be treated as made in the member State in which the transportation begins.

ANCILLARY TRANSPORT SERVICES

13(1) A supply to a person who is not a relevant business person of ancillary transport services is to be treated as made where the services are physically performed.

13(2) '**Ancillary transport services**' means loading, unloading handling and similar activities.

LONG-TERM HIRING OF MEANS OF TRANSPORT

13A [To be inserted by FA 2009, s. 76 and Sch. 36, para. 17.]

VALUATION SERVICES ETC

14 A supply to a person who is not a relevant business person of services consisting of the valuation of, or carrying out of work on, goods is to be treated as made where the services are physically performed.

CULTURAL, EDUCATIONAL AND ENTERTAINMENT SERVICES ETC

14A(1) A supply to a person who is not a relevant business person of services to which this paragraph applies is to be treated as made in the country in which the activities concerned actually take place.

14A(2) This paragraph applies to the provision of–

(a) services relating to cultural, artistic, sporting, scientific, educational, entertainment or similar activities (including fairs and exhibitions), and

(b) ancillary services relating to such activities, including services of organisers of such activities.

ELECTRONIC SERVICES

15 A supply consisting of the provision by a person who belongs in a country which is not a member State (other than the Isle of Man) of electronically supplied services (as to the meaning of which see paragraph 9(3) and (4)) to a person ('the recipient') who–

(a) is not a relevant business person, and

(b) belongs in a member State,

15 is to be treated as made in the country in which the recipient belongs.

OTHER SERVICES PROVIDED TO RECIPIENT BELONGING OUTSIDE EC

16(1) A supply consisting of the provision to a person ('the recipient') who–

(a) is not a relevant business person, and
(b) belongs in a country which is not a member State (other than the Isle of Man),

of services to which this paragraph applies is to be treated as made in the country in which the recipient belongs.

16(2) This paragraph applies to–

(a) transfers and assignments of copyright, patents, licences, trademarks and similar rights,
(b) the acceptance of any obligation to refrain from pursuing or exercising (in whole or in part) any business activity or any rights within paragraph (a),
(c) advertising services,
(d) services of consultants, engineers, consultancy bureaux, lawyers, accountants, and similar services, data processing and provision of information, other than any services relating to land,
(e) banking, financial and insurance services (including reinsurance), other than the provision of safe deposit facilities,
(f) the provision of access to, or transmission or distribution through–
   (i) a natural gas system situated within the territory of a member State or any network connected to such a system, or
   (ii) an electricity system, or
   (iii) a network through which heat or cooling is supplied,and the provision of other directly linked services,
(g) the supply of staff,
(h) the letting on hire of goods other than means of transport,
(i) telecommunication services (as to the meaning of which see paragraph 8(2)),
(j) radio and television broadcasting services, and
(k) electronically supplied services (as to the meaning of which see paragraph 9(3) and (4)).

SI 2012/2787 – Value Added Tax (Place of Supply of Services) (Transport of Goods) Order 2012

This order amends Part 2 of Schedule 4A of the Valued Added Tax Act 1994 to remove UK VAT from supplies of freight transport and associated services which take place wholly outside the EU. This Order comes into force on 20 December 2012.

(SI 2012/2787)

Made on 6 November 2012 by the Treasury in exercise of the powers conferred by s. 7A(6) of the Value Added Tax Act 1994. Operative from 20 December 2012.

Published 8 November 2012

Released 8 November 2012

Made on 6 November 2012 by the Treasury in exercise of the powers conferred by s. 7A(6) of the Value Added Tax Act 1994. Operative from 20 December 2012.

CITATION AND COMMENCEMENT

1(1) This Order may be cited as the Value Added Tax (Place of Supply of Services) (Transport of Goods) Order 2012 and comes into force on 20 December 2012.

1(2) The amendments made by this Order have effect in relation to supplies made on or after 20 December 2012.

AMENDMENT OF PART 2 OF SCHEDULE 4A TO THE VALUE ADDED TAX ACT 1994

2(1) Part 2 (exceptions relating to supplies made to relevant business person) of Schedule 4A (place of supply of services: special rules) to the Value Added Tax Act 1994 is amended as follows.

2(2) After paragraph 9A insert–

"Transport of goods

Where–a supply of services to a relevant business person consisting of the transportation of goods would otherwise be treated as made in the United Kingdom, and

the transportation takes place wholly outside the member States,

the supply is to be treated as made wholly outside the member States.

Ancillary transport services

Where–a supply of services to a relevant business person consisting of ancillary transport services would otherwise be treated as made in the United Kingdom, and

the services are physically performed wholly outside the member States,

the supply is to be treated as made wholly outside the member States.

In sub-paragraph (1)(a) **'ancillary transport services'** means loading, unloading, handling and similar activities".

EXPLANATORY NOTE

(This note is not part of the Order)

This Order amends Part 2 of Schedule 4A to the Value Added Tax Act 1994 to add two new categories into the list of exceptions relating to supplies of services made to a relevant business person. Article 2 inserts new paragraphs 9B and 9C into Part 2 of Schedule 4A to add the specified supplies to the list of supplies of services made to a relevant business person that are subject to special place of supply rules. As a result, the place of supply of the specified services will, in the circumstances specified, be where they take place (are used and enjoyed) rather than the place where the recipient belongs. A Tax Information and Impact Note covering this instrument was published on 28 May 2012 on the HMRC website at http://www.hmrc.gov.uk/thelibrary/tiins.htm.

Appendix 5: The EU Member States

These include:
  Austria;
  Belgium;
  Bulgaria (from 1 January 2007);
  Cyprus (from 1 May 2004);
  Czech Republic (from 1 May 2004);
  Denmark (excluding Greenland);
  Estonia (from 1 May 2004);
  Finland (excluding the Aland Islands);
  France (including Monaco, but excluding France's overseas departments: Martinique, French Guiana, Guadeloupe, Réunion and St Pierre and Miquelon);
  Germany (excluding the Island of Heligoland and the territory of Busingen);
  Greece (excluding Mount Athos, which is also known as Agion Poros);
  Hungary (from 1 May 2004);
  Ireland (the Republic of) (also known as Eire);
  Italy (excluding Livigno, Campione d'Italia and the Italian waters of Lake Lugano) San Marino and the Vatican City are not part of the territory of the EC for VAT purposes;
  Latvia (from 1 May 2004);
  Lithuania (from 1 May 2004);
  Luxembourg;
  Malta (from 1 May 2004);
  Netherlands (also known as Holland);
  Poland (from 1 May 2004);
  Portugal (from 1 May 2004);
  Romania (from 1 January 2007);
  Slovakia (from 1 May 2004);
  Slovenia (from 1 May 2004);
  Spain (including the Balearic Islands but excluding the Canaries, Ceuta and Melilla);
  Sweden;
  United Kingdom (including the Isle of Man) and (from 1 May 2004) the Sovereign base areas in Cyprus (Akrotiri and Dhekelia), but excluding the Channel Islands and Gibraltar.

The following territories are not part of the EU for VAT purposes:
  The Channel Islands;
  Andorra;
  San Marino;
  Lichtenstein;
  The Vatican City;
  Gibraltar.

Appendix 6: VATA 1994, Sch. 9

SCHEDULE 9 – EXEMPTIONS

Sections 8 and 31

GROUP 14 – SUPPLIES OF GOODS WHERE INPUT TAX CANNOT BE RECOVERED

Item No.
1 A supply of goods in relation to which each of the following conditions is satisfied, that is to say–
(a) there is input tax of the person making the supply ('**the relevant supplier**'), or of any predecessor of his, that has arisen or will arise on the supply to, or acquisition or importation by, the relevant supplier or any such predecessor of goods used for the supply made by the relevant supplier;
(b) the only such input tax is non-deductible input tax; and
(c) the supply made by the relevant supplier is not a supply which would be exempt under Item 1 of Group 1 of Schedule 9 but for an option to tax any land under Part 1 of Schedule 10.

Notes:
(1) Subject to Note (2) below, in relation to any supply of goods by the relevant supplier, the '**goods used**' for that supply are–
(a) the goods supplied; and
(b) any goods used in the process of producing the supplied goods so as to be comprised in them.
(2) In relation to a supply by any person consisting in or arising from the grant of a major interest in land ('**the relevant supply**')–
(a) any supply consisting in or arising from a previous grant of a major interest in the land is a supply of goods used for the relevant supply; and
(b) subject to paragraph (a) above, the goods used for the relevant supply are any goods used in the construction of a building or civil engineering work so as to become part of the land.
(3) Subject to Notes (7) to (10) below, '**non-deductible input tax**' is input tax to which Note (4) or (5) below applies.
(4) This Note applies to input tax which (disregarding this Group and regulation 106 of the Value Added Tax Regulations 1995 (de minimis rule)) is not, and will not become, attributable to supplies to which section 26(2) applies.
(5) This Note applies to input tax if–
(a) disregarding this Group and the provisions mentioned in Note (6) below, the relevant supplier or a predecessor of his has or will become entitled to credit for the whole or a part of the amount of that input tax; and
(b) the effect (disregarding this Group) of one or more of those provisions is that neither the relevant supplier nor any predecessor of his has or will become entitled to credit for any part of that amount.
(6) The provisions mentioned in Note (5) above are–
(a) Article 5 of the Value Added Tax (Input Tax) Order 1992 (no credit for input tax on goods or services used for business entertainment);
(b) Article 6 of that Order (no credit for input tax on non-building materials incorporated in building or site);
(c) Article 7 of that Order (no credit for input tax on motor cars);
(d) any provision directly or indirectly re-enacted (with or without modification) in a provision mentioned in paragraphs (a) to (c) above.
(7) For the purposes of this Group the '**input tax of a person**' shall be deemed to include any VAT which–

(a) has arisen or will arise on a supply to, or acquisition or importation by, that person; and
(b) would fall to be treated as input tax of that person but for its arising when that person is not a taxable person.

(8) Subject to Note (9) below, the input tax that is taken to be **'non-deductible input tax'** shall include any VAT which–
(a) is deemed to be input tax of any person by virtue of Note (7) above; and
(b) would be input tax to which Note (4) or (5) above would apply if it were input tax of that person and, in the case of a person to whom section 39 applies, if his business were carried on in the United Kingdom.

(9) **'Non-deductible input tax'** does not include any VAT that has arisen or will arise on a supply to, or acquisition or importation by, any person of any goods used for a supply of goods (**'the relevant supply'**) if–
(a) that VAT; or
(b) any other VAT arising on the supply to, or acquisition or importation by, that person or any predecessor of his of any goods used for the relevant supply,
has been or will be refunded under section 33, 33A, 33B, 39 or 41.

(10) Input tax arising on a supply, acquisition or importation of goods shall be disregarded for the purposes of determining whether the conditions in Item No 1(a) and (b) are satisfied if, at a time after that supply, acquisition or importation but before the supply by the relevant supplier, a supply of the goods or of anything in which they are comprised is treated under or by virtue of any provision of this Act as having been made by the relevant supplier or any predecessor of his to himself.

(11) In relation to any goods or anything comprised in any goods, a person is a predecessor of another (**'the putative successor'**) only if Note (12) or (13) below applies to him in relation to those goods or that thing; and references in this Group to a person's predecessors include references to the predecessors of his predecessors through any number of transfers and events such as are mentioned in Notes (12) and (13).

(12) This Note applies to a person in relation to any goods or thing if–
(a) the putative successor is a person to whom he has transferred assets of his business by a transfer of that business, or a part of it, as a going concern;
(b) those assets consisted of or included those goods or that thing; and
(c) the transfer of the assets is one falling by virtue of an order under section 5(3) (or under an enactment re-enacted in section 5(3)) to be treated as neither a supply of goods nor a supply of services.

(13) This Note applies to a body corporate in relation to any goods or thing if–
(a) those goods or that thing formed part of the assets of the business of that body at a time when it became a member of a group of which the putative successor was at that time the representative member;
(b) those goods or that thing formed part of the assets of the business of that body corporate, or of any other body corporate which was a member of the same group as that body, at a time when that body was succeeded as the representative member of the group by the putative successor; or
(c) those goods or that thing formed part of the assets of the putative successor at a time when it ceased to be a member of a group of which the body corporate in question was at the time the representative member.

(14) References in Note (13) above to a body corporate's being or becoming or ceasing to be a **'member of a group'** or the **'representative member'** of a group are references to its falling to be so treated for the purposes of section 43.

(15) In Notes (11) to (13) above the references to **'anything comprised in other goods'** shall be taken, in relation to any supply consisting in or arising from the grant of a major interest in land, to include anything the supply, acquisition or importation of which is, by virtue of Note (2) above, taken to be a supply, acquisition or importation of goods used for making the supply so consisting or arising.

(16) Notes (1) and (1A) to Group 1 shall apply for the purposes of this Group as they apply for the purposes of that Group.

Appendix 7: CTA 2010, s. 1122

1122 'Connected' persons

1122(1) This section has effect for the purposes of the provisions of the Corporation Tax Acts which apply this section (or to which this section is applied).

1122(2) A company is connected with another company if–
- (a) the same person has control of both companies,
- (b) a person ('A') has control of one company and persons connected with A have control of the other company,
- (c) A has control of one company and A together with persons connected with A have control of the other company, or
- (d) a group of two or more persons has control of both companies and the groups either consist of the same persons or could be so regarded if (in one or more cases) a member of either group were replaced by a person with whom the member is connected.

1122(3) A company is connected with another person ('A') if–
- (a) A has control of the company, or
- (b) A together with persons connected with A have control of the company.

1122(4) In relation to a company, any two or more persons acting together to secure or exercise control of the company are connected with–
- (a) one another, and
- (b) any person acting on the directions of any of them to secure or exercise control of the company.

1122(5) An individual ('A') is connected with another individual ('B') if–
- (a) A is B's spouse or civil partner,
- (b) A is a relative of B,
- (c) A is the spouse or civil partner of a relative of B,
- (d) A is a relative of B's spouse or civil partner, or
- (e) A is the spouse or civil partner of a relative of B's spouse or civil partner.

1122(6) A person, in the capacity as trustee of a settlement, is connected with–
- (a) any individual who is a settlor in relation to the settlement,
- (b) any person connected with such an individual,
- (c) any close company whose participators include the trustees of the settlement,
- (d) any non-UK resident company which, if it were UK resident, would be a close company whose participators include the trustees of the settlement,
- (e) any body corporate controlled (within the meaning of section 1124) by a company within paragraph (c) or (d),
- (f) if the settlement is the principal settlement in relation to one or more sub-fund settlements, a person in the capacity as trustee of such a sub-fund settlement, and
- (g) if the settlement is a sub-fund settlement in relation to a principal settlement, a person in the capacity as trustee of any other sub-fund settlements in relation to the principal settlement.

1122(7) A person who is a partner in a partnership is connected with–
- (a) any partner in the partnership,
- (b) the spouse or civil partner of any individual who is a partner in the partnership, and
- (c) a relative of any individual who is a partner in the partnership.

1122(8) But subsection (7) does not apply in relation to acquisitions or disposals of assets of the partnership pursuant to genuine commercial arrangements.

Appendix 8: Value Added Tax Regulations 1995, Pt. XIV and XV

(SI 1995/2518, as variously amended)

PART XIV – INPUT TAX AND PARTIAL EXEMPTION

INTERPRETATION OF PART XIV AND LONGER PERIODS

99(1) In this Part–
- (a) **'exempt input tax'** means input tax incurred by a taxable person on goods imported or acquired by, or goods or services supplied to, him in so far as they are used by him or are to be used by him, or a successor of his, in making exempt supplies, or supplies outside the United Kingdom which would be exempt if made in the United Kingdom, other than any input tax which is allowable under regulation 101, 102, 103, 103A or 103B; and 'successor' in this paragraph has the same meaning as in regulation 107D;
- (b) **'prescribed accounting period'** means–
  - (i) a prescribed accounting period such as is referred to in regulation 25, or
  - (ii) a special accounting period, where the first prescribed accounting period would otherwise be 6 months or longer, save that this paragraph shall not apply where the reference to the prescribed accounting period is used solely in order to identify a particular return;
- (c) **'special accounting period'** means each of a succession of periods of the same length as the next prescribed accounting period which does not exceed 3 months, and–
  - (i) the last such period shall end on the day before the commencement of that next prescribed accounting period, and
  - (ii) the first such period shall commence on the effective date of registration determined in accordance with Schedule 1, 2, 3 or 3A to the Act and end on the day before the commencement of the second such period;
- (d) the **'tax year'** of a taxable person means–
  - (i) the first period of 12 calendar months commencing on the first day of April, May or June, according to the prescribed accounting periods allocated to him, next following his effective date of registration determined in accordance with Schedule 1, 2, 3 or 3A to the Act, or
  - (ii) any subsequent period of 12 calendar months commencing on the day following the end of his first, or any subsequent, tax year,

  save that the Commissioners may approve or direct that a tax year shall be a period of other than 12 calendar months or that it shall commence on a date other than that determined in accordance with paragraph (i) or (ii) above;
- (e) the **'registration period'** of a taxable person means the period commencing on his effective date of registration determined in accordance with Schedule 1, 2, 3 or 3A to the Act and ending on the day before the commencement of his first tax year.

99(1A) In this Part **'non-business VAT'** has the meaning given in section 24(5)(b) of the Act.

99(2) In this Part, any reference to **goods** or **services** shall be construed as including a reference to anything which is supplied by way of a supply of goods or a supply of services respectively.

99(3) The provisions of paragraphs (4), (5), (6) and (7) below shall be used for determining the longer period applicable to taxable persons under this Part.

99(4) A taxable person who incurs exempt input tax during any tax year shall have applied to him a longer period which shall correspond with that tax year unless he did not incur exempt input tax during his immediately preceding tax year or registration period, in which case his longer period shall–
- (a) begin on the first day of the first prescribed accounting period in which he incurs exempt input tax, and

(b)   end on the last day of that tax year,

except where he incurs exempt input tax only in the last prescribed accounting period of his tax year, in which case no longer period shall be applied to him in respect of that tax year.

99(5)   A taxable person who incurs exempt input tax during his registration period shall have applied to him a longer period which shall begin on the first day on which he incurs exempt input tax and end on the day before the commencement of his first tax year.

99(6)   In the case of a taxable person ceasing to be taxable during a longer period applicable to him, that longer period shall end on the day when he ceases to be taxable.

99(7)   The Commissioners may approve in the case of a taxable person who incurs exempt input tax, or a class of such persons, that a longer period shall apply which need not correspond with a tax year.

100   Nothing in this Part shall be construed as allowing a taxable person to deduct the whole or any part of VAT on the importation or acquisition by him of goods or the supply to him of goods or services where those goods or services are not used or to be used by him in making supplies in the course or furtherance of a business carried on by him.

ATTRIBUTION OF INPUT TAX TO TAXABLE SUPPLIES

101(1)   Subject to regulations 102, 103A, 105A and 106ZA the amount of input tax which a taxable person shall be entitled to deduct provisionally shall be that amount which is attributable to taxable supplies in accordance with this regulation.

101(2)   Subject to paragraph (8) below and regulation 107(1)(g)(ii), in respect of each prescribed accounting period–
(a)   goods imported or acquired by and goods or services supplied to, the taxable person in the period shall be identified,
(b)   there shall be attributed to taxable supplies the whole of the input tax on such of those goods or services as are used or to be used by him exclusively in making taxable supplies,
(c)   no part of the input tax on such of those goods or services as are used or to be used by him exclusively in making exempt supplies, or in carrying on any activity other than the making of taxable supplies, shall be attributed to taxable supplies,
(d)   where a taxable person does not have an immediately preceding longer period and subject to subparagraph (e) below, there shall be attributed to taxable supplies such proportion of the residual input tax as bears the same ratio to the total of such input tax as the value of taxable supplies made by him bears to the value of all supplies made by him in the period,
(e)   the attribution required by subparagraph (d) above may be made on the basis of the extent to which the goods or services are used or to be used by him in making taxable supplies,
(f)   where a taxable person has an immediately preceding longer period and subject to subparagraph (g) below, his residual input tax shall be attributed to taxable supplies by reference to the percentage recovery rate for that immediately preceding longer period, and
(g)   the attribution required by subparagraph (f) above may be made using the calculation specified in subparagraph (d) above provided that that calculation is used for all the prescribed accounting periods which fall within any longer period applicable to a taxable person.

101(3)   In calculating the proportion under paragraph (2)(d) or (g) above, there shall be excluded–
(a)   any sum receivable by the taxable person in respect of any supply of capital goods used by him for the purposes of his business,
(b)   any sum receivable by the taxable person in respect of any of the following descriptions of supplies made by him, where such supplies are incidental to one or more of his business activities–
   (i)   any supply of a description falling within Group 5 of Schedule 9 to the Act,
   (ii)   any other financial transaction, and
   (iii)   any real estate transaction,
(c)   that part of the value of any supply of goods on which output tax is not chargeable by virtue of any order made by the Treasury under section 25(7) of the Act unless the taxable person has imported, acquired or been supplied with the goods for the purpose of selling them,

(d) the value of any supply which, under or by virtue of any provision of the Act, the taxable person makes to himself, and
(e) supplies of a description falling within paragraph (8) below.

101(4) The ratio calculated for the purpose of paragraph (2)(d), (e) or (g) above shall be expressed as a percentage and, if that percentage is not a whole number, it shall be rounded up as specified in paragraph (5) below.

101(5) The percentage shall be rounded up–
(a) where in any prescribed accounting period or longer period which is applied the amount of input tax which is available for attribution under paragraph 2(d), (e) or (g) above prior to any such attribution being made does not amount to more than £400,000 per month on average, to the next whole number, and
(b) in any other case, to two decimal places.

101(6) For the purposes of this regulation, a **'real estate transaction'** includes any grant, assignment (including any transfer, disposition or sale), surrender or reverse surrender of any interest in, right over or licence to occupy land.

101(7) In this regulation **'taxable supplies'** include supplies of a description falling within regulation 103.

101(8) Input tax incurred on goods or services acquired by or supplied to a taxable person which are used or to be used by him in whole or in part in making–
(a) supplies falling within either item 1 or item 6 of Group 5 of Schedule 9 to the Act; or
(b) supplies made from an establishment situated outside the United Kingdom,
shall, whether the supply in question is made within or outside the United Kingdom, be attributed to taxable supplies on the basis of the extent to which the goods or services are used or to be used by him in making taxable supplies.

101(9) For the purposes of this regulation in relation to a taxable person–
(a) **'immediately preceding longer period'** means the longer period applicable to him which ends immediately before the longer period in which the prescribed accounting period in respect of which he is making the attribution required by paragraph (2)(d) to (g) above falls;
(b) **'percentage recovery rate'** means the amount of relevant residual input tax which he was entitled to attribute to taxable supplies under regulation 107(1)(a) to (d), expressed as a percentage of the total amount of the residual input tax which fell to be so attributed and rounded up in accordance with paragraphs (4) and (5) above;
(c) **'relevant residual input tax'** means all residual input tax other than that which falls to be attributed under paragraph (8) above.

101(10) In this regulation **'residual input tax'** means input tax incurred by a taxable person on goods or services which are used or to be used by him in making both taxable and exempt supplies.

USE OF OTHER METHODS

102(1) Subject to paragraphs (2) and (9) below and regulations 103, 103A, 103B, 105A and 106ZA, the Commissioners may approve or direct the use by a taxable person of a method other than that specified in regulation 101.

102(1A) A method approved or directed under paragraph (1) above–
(a) shall be in writing,
(b) may attribute input tax which would otherwise fall to be attributed under regulation 103 provided that, where it attributes any such input tax, it shall attribute it all, and
(c) shall identify the supplies in respect of which it attributes input tax by reference to the relevant paragraph or paragraphs of section 26(2) of the Act.

102(2) Notwithstanding any provision of any method approved or directed to be used under this regulation which purports to have the contrary effect, in calculating the proportion of any input tax on goods or services used or to be used by the taxable person in making both taxable and exempt supplies which is to be treated as attributable to taxable supplies, the value of any supply of a description falling within regulation 101(3)(a) to (d) whether made within or outside the United Kingdom shall be excluded.

102(3) A taxable person using a method as approved or directed to be used by the Commissioners under paragraph (1) above shall continue to use that method unless the Commissioners approve or direct the termination of its use.

102(4) Any direction under paragraph (1) or (3) above shall take effect from the date upon which the Commissioners give such direction or from such later date as they may specify.

102(5) Any approval given or direction made under this regulation shall only have effect if it is in writing in the form of a document which identifies itself as being such an approval or direction.

102(6) Where a taxable person who is using a method which has been approved or directed under this regulation incurs input tax of the description in paragraph (7) below, that input tax shall be attributed to taxable supplies to the extent that the goods or services are used or to be used in making taxable supplies expressed as a proportion of the whole use or intended use.

102(7) The input tax referred to in paragraph (6) above is input tax–
(a) the attribution of which to taxable supplies is not prescribed in whole or in part by the method referred to in paragraph (6) above, and
(b) which does not fall to be attributed to taxable or other supplies as specified under regulations 103, 103A or 103B.

102(8) Where the input tax specified in paragraph (7)(a) above is input tax the attribution of which to taxable supplies is only in part not prescribed by the method, only that part the attribution of which is not so prescribed shall fall within that paragraph.

102(9) With effect from 1st April 2007 the Commissioners shall not approve the use of a method under this regulation unless the taxable person has made a declaration to the effect that to the best of his knowledge and belief the method fairly and reasonably represents the extent to which goods or services are used by or are to be used by him in making taxable supplies.

102(10) The declaration referred to in paragraph (9) above shall–
(a) be in writing,
(b) be signed by the taxable person or by a person authorised to sign it on his behalf, and
(c) include a statement that the person signing it has taken reasonable steps to ensure that he is in possession of all relevant information.

102(11) Where it appears to the Commissioners that a declaration made under this regulation is incorrect in that–
(a) the method does not fairly and reasonably represent the extent to which goods or services are used by or are to be used by the taxable person in making taxable supplies, and
(b) the person who signed the declaration knew or ought reasonably to have known this at the time when the declaration was made by the taxable person,

they may subject to paragraph (12) below serve on the taxable person a notice to that effect setting out their reasons in support of that notification and stating the effect of the notice.

102(12) The Commissioners shall not serve a notice under this regulation unless they are satisfied that the overall result of the application of the method is an over-deduction of input tax by the taxable person.

102(13) Subject to paragraph (14) below, the effect of a notice served under this regulation is that regulation 102B(1) shall apply to the person served with the notice in relation to–
(a) prescribed accounting periods commencing on or after the effective date of the method, and
(b) longer periods to the extent of that part of the longer period falling on or after the effective date of the method, save that no adjustment shall be required in relation to any part of any prescribed accounting period,

unless or until the method is terminated under regulation 102(3).

102(14) In relation to any past prescribed accounting periods, the Commissioners may assess the amount of VAT due to the best of their judgement and notify it to the taxable person unless they allow him to account for the difference in such manner and within such time as they may require.

102(15) The service of a notice on a taxable person under this regulation shall be without prejudice to the Commissioners' powers to serve a notice on him under regulation 102A and any notice served under regulation 102A shall take priority in relation to the periods which it covers.

102(16) In this regulation 'the **effective date of the method**' is the date when the method to which the declaration relates first takes effect and may predate the date when the declaration was made.

102(17) In this regulation and in regulations 102A, 102B, 102C and 107, where paragraph (1A)(b) above applies, **'taxable supplies'** includes supplies of a description falling within regulation 103.

102ZA(1) A taxable person who is required to make an apportionment under section 24(5) of the Act in relation to goods or services which are used or are to be used partly for business purposes and partly for other purposes may effect that apportionment using a method provided for in regulation 102(1).

102ZA(2) Where the taxable person referred to in paragraph (1) is not a fully taxable person, the method used shall be the only method used to calculate that person's deductible input tax.

102ZA(3) Where a person who was a fully taxable person at the time when the method was approved subsequently incurs exempt input tax, regulation 102B shall apply from the date on which that person first incurs such exempt input tax.

102ZA(4) Where a person effects the apportionment referred to in paragraph (1) using a method provided for in regulation 102(1)–
(a) regulations 102(1A) to (17) and 102A to 102C shall apply;
(b) regulations 105A, 106 and 106ZA shall not apply; and
(c) for the purposes of defining a longer period and determining an adjustment of attribution under regulation 107, **'exempt input tax'** shall include non-business VAT.

102ZA(5) In this regulation, a fully taxable person is a person who, disregarding paragraph (4)(c), has not incurred any exempt input tax in that person's current or immediately preceding (if any) tax year or registration period.

102A(1) Notwithstanding the Commissioners' powers to serve a notice under regulation 102, where a taxable person–
(a) is for the time being using a method approved or directed under regulation 102, and
(b) that method does not fairly and reasonably represent the extent to which goods or services are used by him or are to be used by him in making taxable supplies,

the Commissioners may serve on him a notice to that effect, setting out their reasons in support of that notification and stating the effect of the notice.

102A(2) The effect of a notice served under this regulation is that regulation 102B shall apply to the person served with the notice in relation to–
(a) prescribed accounting periods commencing on or after the date of the notice or such later date as may be specified in the notice, and
(b) longer periods to the extent of that part of the longer period falling on or after the date of the notice or such later date as may be specified in the notice.

102B(1) Where this regulation applies, a taxable person shall calculate the difference between–
(a) the attribution made by him in any prescribed accounting period or longer period, and
(b) an attribution which represents the extent to which the goods or services are used by him or are to be used by him in making taxable supplies,

and account for the difference on the return for that prescribed accounting period or on the return on which that longer period adjustment is required to be made, except where the Commissioners allow another return to be used for this purpose.

102B(2) This regulation shall apply from the date prescribed under regulation 102A(2) or 102C(2), unless or until the method referred to in regulation 102A(1)(a) or 102C(1)(a) is terminated under regulation 102(3).

102C(1) Subject to regulation 102A, where a taxable person–
(a) is for the time being using a method approved or directed under regulation 102, and
(b) that method does not fairly and reasonably represent the extent to which goods or services are used by him or are to be used by him in making taxable supplies,
the taxable person may serve on the Commissioners a notice to that effect, setting out his reasons in support of that notification.

102C(2) Where the Commissioners approve a notice served under this regulation, the effect is that regulation 102B shall apply to the person serving the notice in relation to–
(a) prescribed accounting periods commencing on or after the date of the notice or such later date as may be specified in the notice, and
(b) longer periods to the extent of that part of the longer period falling on or after the date of the notice or such later date as may be specified in the notice.

ATTRIBUTION OF INPUT TAX TO FOREIGN AND SPECIFIED SUPPLIES

103 Other than where it falls to be attributed under regulation 101 or a method approved or directed by the Commissioners under regulation 102, input tax incurred by a taxable person in any prescribed accounting period on goods imported or acquired by, or goods or services supplied to, him which are used or to be used by him in whole or in part in making–
(a) supplies outside the United Kingdom which would be taxable supplies if made in the United Kingdom, or
(b) supplies specified in an Order under section 26(2)(c) of the Act other than supplies of a description falling within regulation 103A below,
shall be attributed to taxable supplies to the extent that the goods or services are so used or to be used expressed as a proportion of the whole use or intended use.

ATTRIBUTION OF INPUT TAX TO INVESTMENT GOLD

103A(1) This regulation applies to a taxable person who makes supplies of a description falling within item 1 or 2 of Group 15 of Schedule 9 to the Act.

103A(2) Input tax incurred by him in any prescribed accounting period in respect of supplies by him of a description falling within paragraph (1) above shall be allowable as being attributable to those supplies only to the following extent, that is to say where it is incurred–
(a) on investment gold supplied to him which but for an election made under the Value Added Tax (Investment Gold) Order 1999, or but for Note 4(b) to Group 15 of Schedule 9 to the Act would have fallen within item 1 or 2 of that Group, or on investment gold acquired by him;
(b) on a supply to him, an acquisition by him, or on an importation by him of gold other than investment gold which is to be transformed by him or on his behalf into investment gold;
(c) on services supplied to him comprising a change of form, weight or purity of gold.

103A(3) Where a taxable person produces investment gold or transforms any gold into investment gold he shall also be entitled to credit for input tax incurred by him on any goods or services supplied to him, any acquisitions of goods by him or any importations of goods by him, but only to the extent that they are linked to the production or transformation of that gold into investment gold.

103A(4) Where input tax has been incurred on goods or services which are used or to be used in making supplies of a description falling within item 1 or 2 of Group 15 of Schedule 9 to the Act and any other supply, that input tax shall be attributed to the supplies falling within item 1 or 2 to the extent that the goods or services are so used or to be used, expressed as a proportion of the whole use or intended use.

103A(5) Where input tax is attributed to supplies of a description falling within item 1 or 2 of Group 15 of Schedule 9 to the Act under paragraph (4) above, the taxable person shall be entitled to credit for only so much input tax as is reasonably allowable under paragraph (2) or (3) above.

103A(6) For the purpose of attributing input tax to supplies of a description falling within item 1 or 2 of Group 15 of Schedule 9 to the Act under paragraph (4) above, any input tax of the description in that paragraph shall be deemed to be the only input tax incurred by the taxable person in the prescribed accounting period concerned.

ATTRIBUTION OF INPUT TAX INCURRED ON SERVICES AND RELATED GOODS USED TO MAKE FINANCIAL SUPPLIES

103B(1) This regulation applies to a taxable person who incurs input tax in the circumstances specified in paragraph (2) below.

103B(2) Other than where it falls to be attributed under regulation 101, where–
(a) input tax has been incurred by a taxable person in any prescribed accounting period on supplies to him of any of the services specified in paragraph (4) below and of any related goods, and
(b) those services and related goods are used or to be used by the taxable person in making both a relevant supply and any other supply, and
(c) the relevant supply is incidental to one or more of the taxable person's business activities,that input tax shall be attributed to taxable supplies to the extent that the services or related goods are so used or to be used expressed as a proportion of the whole use or intended use, notwithstanding any provision of any input tax attribution method that the taxable person is required or allowed to use which purports to have the contrary effect.

103B(3) In this regulation–
(a) **'relevant supply'** means a supply of a description falling within item 1 or 6 of Group 5 of Schedule 9 to the Act and any supply of the same description which is made in another member State; and
(b) **'taxable supplies'** includes supplies of a description falling within regulation 103.

103B(4) The services referred to in paragraph (2)(a) above are services supplied by–
(a) accountants;
(b) advertising agencies;
(c) bodies which provide listing and registration services;
(d) financial advisers;
(e) lawyers;
(f) marketing consultants;
(g) persons who prepare and design documentation; and
(h) any person or body which provides similar services to those specified in sub-paragraphs (a) to (g) above.

ATTRIBUTION OF INPUT TAX ON SELF-SUPPLIES

104 Where under or by virtue of any provision of the Act a person makes a supply to himself, the input tax on that supply shall not be allowable as attributable to that supply.

TREATMENT OF INPUT TAX ATTRIBUTABLE TO EXEMPT SUPPLIES AS BEING ATTRIBUTABLE TO TAXABLE SUPPLIES

105 [Omitted by SI 1999/599, reg. 4. In relation to a taxable person whose registration period (as defined by reg. 99(1)(e)) commenced before 10 March 1999 and ends after that day, the omission has effect from the commencement of his first tax year (as defined by reg. 99(1)(d)(i)). However, in relation to a taxable person who was registered before 10 March 1999, and whose registration period (as defined by reg. 99(1)(e)) did not commence before 10 March 1999 and end after that day, the omission has effect from the first day of the first of his tax years commencing after that day.]

105A(1) Subject to regulation 106ZA(1), where, in relation to a taxable person, total input tax incurred less any input tax incurred on goods or services used or to be used exclusively in making taxable supplies–
(a) in any prescribed accounting period, or
(b) in any applicable longer period,
does not amount to more than £625 per month on average, all input tax incurred in that period shall be treated as attributable to taxable supplies provided that the value of exempt supplies does not exceed one half of the value of all supplies.

105A(2) In the application of paragraph (1) above to a longer period–
(a) any treatment of input tax as attributable to taxable supplies in any prescribed accounting period shall be disregarded, and
(b) the amount of input tax incurred on goods or services used or to be used exclusively in making taxable supplies must reflect any changes in use or intention during that period.

105A(3) In this regulation–
(a) **'taxable supplies'** includes supplies of a description falling within regulation 103, and
(b) **'exempt supplies'** means any supplies that are not taxable supplies.

106(1) Where regulation 105A does not apply then, subject to regulations 106A and 106ZA(1), where relevant input tax–
(a) in any prescribed accounting period, or
(b) in the case of a longer period, taken together with the amount of any adjustment in respect of that period under regulation 107B–
   (i) does not amount to more than £625 per month on average, and
   (ii) does not exceed one half of all his input tax for the period concerned,
all such input tax in that period shall be treated as attributable to taxable supplies.

106(2) In the application of paragraph (1) above to a longer period–
(a) any treatment of relevant input tax as attributable to taxable supplies in any prescribed accounting period shall be disregarded, and
(b) no account shall be taken of any amount or amounts which may be deductible or payable under regulation 115.

106(3) For the purposes of this regulation, **relevant input tax** is input tax attributed under regulations 101, 102, 103, 103A, 103B and, where the case arises, regulation 107, to exempt supplies or to supplies outside the United Kingdom which would be exempt if made in the United Kingdom (not being supplies specified in an Order made under section 26(2)(c) of the Act).

106ZA(1) A taxable person who–
(a) was entitled to attribute his input tax to taxable supplies under regulation 105A(1)(b) or regulation 106(1)(b) in his immediately preceding longer period, and
(b) does not expect to incur more than £1,000,000 input tax in his current longer period,
may treat input tax incurred in each prescribed accounting period within his current longer period as attributable to taxable supplies, provided that he does so for all of the prescribed accounting periods that fall within that longer period.

106ZA(2) For the purposes of this regulation in relation to a taxable person, **'immediately preceding longer period.'** means the longer period applicable to that person which ends immediately before the longer period in which the prescribed accounting period in respect of which he is making the attribution under paragraph (1) above falls.

106A(1) This regulation applies where regulation 107A applies.

106A(2) Where, taken together with the amount of any adjustment under regulation 107A, input tax attributed under regulations 101, 103, 103A and 103B to exempt supplies, or to supplies outside the

United Kingdom which would be exempt if made in the United Kingdom (in each case not being supplies specified in an Order made under section 26(2)(c) of the Act)–
(a) does not amount to more than £625 per month on average, and
(b) does not exceed one half of all his input tax for the period concerned,

all such input tax in that period shall be treated as attributable to taxable supplies.

106A(3) Where, in accordance with regulations 101, 103, 103A and 103B, a taxable person has attributed an amount of input tax to exempt supplies, or to supplies outside the United Kingdom which would be exempt if made in the United Kingdom (in each case not being supplies specified in an Order made under section 26(2)(c) of the Act) and, after applying regulation 107A, he is entitled to treat all his input tax as attributable to taxable supplies under paragraph (2) above, he shall–
(a) calculate the difference between–
   (i) the total amount of input tax for that prescribed accounting period, and
   (ii) the amount of input tax deducted in that prescribed accounting period, taken together with the amount of any adjustment under regulation 107A, and
(b) include this difference as an under-deduction in a return for the first prescribed accounting period next following the prescribed accounting period referred to in regulation 107A(1), except where the Commissioners allow another return to be used for this purpose.

106A(4) Where in a prescribed accounting period a taxable person has treated input tax as attributable to taxable supplies under regulation 106(1) but is not entitled to do so because of the operation of paragraph (2) above, he shall include the amount so treated as an over-deduction in a return for the first prescribed accounting period next following the prescribed accounting period referred to in regulation 107A(1), except where the Commissioners allow another return to be used for this purpose.

106A(5) But where a registered person has his registration cancelled at or before the end of the prescribed accounting period referred to in regulation 107A(1), he shall account for any adjustment under this regulation on his final return.

ADJUSTMENT OF ATTRIBUTION

107(1) Subject to regulation 105A(1)(b), where a taxable person to whom a longer period is applicable has provisionally attributed an amount of input tax to taxable supplies in accordance with a method or treated an amount of input tax as attributable to taxable supplies under regulation 105A(1)(a) or regulation 106ZA(1) and save as the Commissioners may dispense with the following requirement to adjust, he–
(a) shall, subject to subparagraphs (b), (c), (d) and (da) below, determine for the longer period the amount of input tax which is attributable to taxable supplies according to the method used in the prescribed accounting periods,
(b) shall, where he has provisionally attributed input tax in accordance with regulation 101(2)(e) in any prescribed accounting period, determine for the longer period the amount of residual input tax which is attributable to taxable supplies on the basis of the extent to which the goods or services are used or to be used by him in making taxable supplies,
(c) may, where he has not provisionally attributed input tax in accordance with regulation 101(2)(e) but was nevertheless entitled to do so, determine for the longer period the amount of residual input tax which is attributable to taxable supplies on the basis of the extent to which the goods or services are used or to be used by him in making taxable supplies,
(d) shall, where he has provisionally attributed residual input tax under regulation 101(2)(f), determine for the longer period the amount of residual input tax which is attributable to taxable supplies using the calculation specified in regulation 101(2)(d) subject to the provisions of regulation 101(3) to (5),
(da) shall, where he has treated an amount of input tax as attributable to taxable supplies under regulation 105A(1)(a) or regulation 106ZA(1), determine for the longer period the amount of input tax that is attributable to taxable supplies in accordance with sub-paragraphs (a) to (d) above as appropriate,
(e) shall, except where a taxable person is using a method provided for in regulation 102(1) to make the apportionment referred to in regulation 102ZA(1), apply the tests set out in regulation 106 to

determine whether all input tax in the longer period in question shall be treated as attributable to taxable supplies,
(f) shall calculate the difference between the amount of input tax determined to be attributable to taxable supplies under subparagraphs (a) to (e) above and the amounts of input tax, if any, which were deducted in the returns for the prescribed accounting periods, and
(g) shall include any such amount of over-deduction or under-deduction in a return for–
   (i) the first prescribed accounting period next following the longer period, or
   (ii) the last prescribed accounting period in the longer period, except where the Commissioners allow another return to be used.

107(2) Where a taxable person makes no adjustment as required by paragraph (1) above, the requirement shall be that the adjustment is made in the return for the first prescribed accounting period next following the longer period.

107(3) But where a registered person has his registration cancelled at or before the end of a longer period, he shall account for any adjustment under this regulation on his final return.

107(4) In this regulation '**residual input tax**' has the same meaning as in regulation 101(10).

107A(1) This regulation applies where a taxable person has made an attribution under regulation 101(2)(b) and (d) and the prescribed accounting period does not form part of a longer period, and the attribution differs substantially from one which represents the extent to which the goods or services are used by him or are to be used by him, or a successor of his, in making taxable supplies.

107A(2) Where this regulation applies, the taxable person shall calculate the difference and account for it on the return for the first prescribed accounting period next following the prescribed accounting period referred to in paragraph (1) above, except where the Commissioners allow another return to be used for this purpose.

107A(3) But where a registered person has his registration cancelled at or before the end of the prescribed accounting period referred to in paragraph (1) above, he shall account for any adjustment under this regulation on his final return.

107B(1) Other than where input tax falls to be attributed under regulation 101(8) or regulation 107(1)(b) or (c), this regulation applies where a taxable person has made an attribution under regulation 107(1)(a) or (d) according to the method specified in regulation 101 and that attribution differs substantially from one which represents the extent to which the goods or services are used by him or are to be used by him, or a successor of his, in making taxable supplies.

107B(2) Where this regulation applies the taxable person shall–
(a) calculate the difference, and
(b) in addition to any amount required to be included under regulation 107(1)(g), account for the amount so calculated on the return for the first prescribed accounting period next following the longer period or the return for the last prescribed accounting period in the longer period if applicable, except where the Commissioners allow another return to be used for this purpose.

107B(3) But where a registered person has his registration cancelled at or before the end of a longer period, he shall account for any adjustment under this regulation on his final return.

107C For the purposes of regulations 107A and 107B, a difference is **substantial** if it exceeds–
(a) £50,000; or
(b) 50% of the amount of input tax falling to be apportioned under regulation 101(2)(d) within the prescribed accounting period referred to in regulation 107A(1), or longer period, as the case may be, but is not less than £25,000.

107D For the purposes of regulations 107A and 107B a person is the **successor** of another if he is a person to whom that other person has–
(a) transferred assets of his business by a transfer of that business, or part of it, as a going concern; and

(b) the transfer of the assets is one falling by virtue of an Order under section 5(3) of the Act to be treated as neither a supply of goods nor a supply of services;
and the reference in this regulation to a **person's successor** includes references to the successors of his successors through any number of transfers.

107E(1) Regulations 107A and 107B shall not apply where the amount of input tax falling to be apportioned under regulation 101(2)(d) within the prescribed accounting period referred to in regulation 107A(1), or longer period, as the case may be, does not exceed–
(a) in the case of a person who is a group undertaking in relation to one or more other undertakings (other than undertakings which are treated under sections 43A to 43C of the Act as members of the same group as the person), £25,000 per annum, adjusted in proportion for a period that is not 12 months; or
(b) in the case of any other person, £50,000 per annum, adjusted in proportion for a period that is not 12 months.

107E(2) For the purposes of paragraph (1) above, undertaking and group undertaking have the same meaning as in section 1161 of the Companies Act 2006.

107F The references in regulations 107C and 107E to an apportionment under regulation 101(2)(d) in relation to a longer period include cases where the apportionment is made under regulation 107(1)(a) or (d) using the calculation specified in regulation 101(2)(d).

108(1) This regulation applies where a taxable person has deducted an amount of input tax which has been attributed to taxable supplies because he intended to use the goods or services in making either–
(a) taxable supplies, or
(b) both taxable and exempt supplies,
and during a period of 6 years commencing on the first day of the prescribed accounting period in which the attribution was determined and before that intention is fulfilled, he uses or forms an intention to use the goods or services concerned in making exempt supplies or, in the case of an attribution within sub-paragraph (a) above, in making both taxable and exempt supplies.

108(2) Subject to regulation 110 and save as the Commissioners otherwise allow, where this regulation applies the taxable person shall on the return for the prescribed accounting period in which the use occurs or the intention is formed, as the case may be, account for an amount equal to the input tax which has ceased to be attributable to taxable supplies in accordance with the method which he was required to use when the input tax was first attributed and he shall repay the said amount to the Commissioners.

108(3) For the purposes of this regulation any question as to the nature of any supply shall be determined in accordance with the provisions of the Act and any Regulations or Orders made thereunder in force at the time when the input tax was first attributed.

109(1) This regulation applies where a taxable person has incurred an amount of input tax which has not been attributed to taxable supplies because he intended to use the goods or services in making either–
(a) exempt supplies, or
(b) both taxable and exempt supplies,
and during a period of 6 years commencing on the first day of the prescribed accounting period in which the attribution was determined and before that intention is fulfilled, he uses or forms an intention to use the goods or services concerned in making taxable supplies or, in the case of an attribution within sub-paragraph (a) above, in making both taxable and exempt supplies.

109(2) Subject to regulation 110 and where this regulation applies, the Commissioners shall, on receipt of an application made by the taxable person in such form and manner and containing such particulars as they may direct, pay to him an amount equal to the input tax which has become attributable to taxable supplies in accordance with the method which he was required to use when the input tax was first attributed.

109(3) For the purposes of this regulation any question as to the nature of any supply shall be determined in accordance with the provisions of the Act and any Regulations or Orders made thereunder in force at the time when the input tax was first attributed.

110(1) Subject to paragraph (2) below, in this regulation, in regulations 103B, 108 and 109 above and in Part XV of these Regulations–
(a) **'exempt supplies'** includes supplies outside the United Kingdom which would be exempt if made in the United Kingdom, other than supplies of a description falling within subparagraph (b) below; and
(b) **'taxable supplies'** includes supplies of a description falling within regulation 103 above.

110(2) Subject to paragraph (3) below, for the purposes of identifying the use, or intended use, of goods and services in regulations 108 and 109 above and in Part XV of these Regulations–
(a) **'exempt supplies'** shall be construed as including supplies of a description falling within regulation 103A(1) above, but only to the extent that there is, or would be, no credit for input tax on goods and services under that regulation; and
(b) **'taxable supplies'** shall be construed as including supplies of a description falling within regulation 103A(1) above, but only to the extent that there is, or would be, credit for input tax on goods and services under that regulation.

110(3) Any adjustment under regulations 108 and 109 above shall not cause any more or any less input tax to be credited, as the case may be, in respect of supplies of a description falling within regulation 103A(1) above than would be allowed or required under that regulation.

110(4) Subject to regulations 103 and 103B, where–
(a) regulation 108 or 109 applies,
(b) the use to which the goods or services concerned are put, or to which they are intended to be put, includes the making of any supplies outside the United Kingdom, and
(c) at the time when the taxable person was first required to attribute the input tax he was not required to use a method approved or directed under regulation 102 or that method did not provide expressly for the attribution of input tax attributable to supplies outside the United Kingdom,

the amount for which the taxable person shall be liable to account under regulation 108 or the amount which he is entitled to be paid under regulation 109, as the case may be, shall be calculated by reference to the extent to which the goods or services concerned are used or intended to be used in making taxable supplies, expressed as a proportion of the whole use or intended use.

110(5) In regulations 108 and 109 a reference to–
(a) **'exempt supplies'** includes a reference to non-business activities that give rise to an amount of non-business VAT;
(b) a method which a taxable person is required to use includes a reference to an apportionment which a taxable person is required to make under section 24(5) of the Act.

EXCEPTIONAL CLAIMS FOR VAT RELIEF

111(1) Subject to paragraphs (2) and (4) below, on a claim made in accordance with paragraph (3) below, the Commissioners may authorise a taxable person to treat as if it were input tax–
(a) VAT on the supply of goods or services to the taxable person before the date with effect from which he was, or was required to be, registered, or paid by him on the importation or acquisition of goods before that date, for the purpose of a business which either was carried on or was to be carried on by him at the time of such supply or payment, and
(b) in the case of a body corporate, VAT on goods obtained for it before its incorporation, or on the supply of services before that time for its benefit or in connection with its incorporation, provided that the person to whom the supply was made or who paid VAT on the importation or acquisition–
   (i) became a member, officer or employee of the body and was reimbursed, or has received an undertaking to be reimbursed, by the body for the whole amount of the price paid for the goods or services,
   (ii) was not at the time of the importation, acquisition or supply a taxable person, and
   (iii) imported, acquired or was supplied with the goods, or received the services, for the purpose of a business to be carried on by the body and has not used them for any purpose other than such a business.

111(2) No VAT may be treated as if it were input tax under paragraph (1) above–
(a) in respect of
  (i) goods or services which had been supplied, or
  (ii) save as the Commissioners may otherwise allow, goods which had been consumed, by the relevant person before the date with effect from which the taxable person was, or was required to be, registered;
(b) subject to paragraph (2A), (2C) and (2D) below, in respect of goods which had been supplied to, or imported or acquired by, the relevant person more than 4 years before the date with effect from which the taxable person was, or was required to be, registered,
(c) in respect of services performed upon goods to which sub-paragraph (a) or (b) above applies;
(d) in respect of services which had been supplied to the relevant person more than 6 months before the date with effect from which the taxable person was, or was required to be, registered; or
(e) in respect of capital items of a description falling within regulation 113.

111(2A) Paragraph (2)(b) above does not apply where–
(a) the taxable person was registered before 1st May 1997; and
(b) he did not make any return before that date.

111(2B) In paragraph (2) above references to the **relevant person** are references to-
(a) the taxable person; or
(b) in the case of paragraph (1)(b) above, the person to whom the supply had been made, or who had imported or acquired the goods, as the case may be.

111(2C) Where the relevant person was, or was required to be, registered on or before 1st April 2009, no VAT may be treated as if it were input tax under paragraph (1) above in respect of goods which were supplied to, or imported or acquired by the relevant person more than 3 years before the date with effect from which that person was, or was required to be, registered.

111(2D) Where the relevant person was or was required to be registered on or before 31st March 2010 and paragraph (2C) above does not apply, no VAT may be treated as if it were input tax under paragraph (1) above in respect of goods which were supplied to, or imported or acquired by, the relevant person on or before 31st March 2006.

111(3) Subject to paragraphs (3A) and (3B) below, a claim under paragraph (1) above shall, save as the Commissioners may otherwise allow, be made on the first return the taxable person is required to make and, as the Commissioners may require, be supported by invoices and other evidence.

111(3A) Where the taxable person was registered before 1st May 1997 and has not made any returns before that date paragraph (3) above shall have effect as if for the words 'the first return the taxable person is required to make' there were substituted the words 'the first return the taxable person makes'.

111(3B) Subject to paragraph (3C) the Commissioners shall not allow a person to make any claim under paragraph (3) above in terms such that the VAT concerned would fall to be claimed as if it were input tax more than 4 years after the date by which the first return he is required to make is required to be made.

111(3C) The Commissioners shall not allow a person to make any claim under paragraph (3) above in the circumstances where the first return the taxable person was required to make was required to be made on or before 31st March 2006.

111(4) A taxable person making a claim under paragraph (1) above shall compile and preserve for such period as the Commissioners may require–
(a) in respect of goods, a stock account showing separately quantities purchased, quantities used in the making of other goods, date of purchase and date and manner of subsequent disposals of both such quantities, and
(b) in respect of services, a list showing their description, date of purchase and date of disposal, if any.

111(5) Subject to paragraph (6) below, if a person who has been, but is no longer, a taxable person makes a claim in such manner and supported by such evidence as the Commissioners may require, they may pay to him the amount of any VAT on the supply of services to him after the date with effect from which he ceased to be, or to be required to be, registered and which was attributable to any taxable supply made by him in the course or furtherance of any business carried on by him when he was, or was required to be, registered.

111(6) Subject to paragraph (7) and (8) below, no claim under paragraph (5) above may be made more than 4 years after the date on which the supply of services was made.

111(7) Paragraph (6) above does not apply where–
(a) the person ceased to be, or ceased to be required to be, registered before 1st May 1997; and
(b) the supply was made before that date.

111(8) No claim may be made under paragraph (5) above in relation to a supply of services which was made on or before 31st March 2006.

PART XV – ADJUSTMENTS TO THE DEDUCTION OF INPUT TAX ON CAPITAL ITEMS

INTERPRETATION OF PART XV

112(1) Any expression used in this Part to which a meaning is given in Part XIV of these Regulations shall, unless the contrary intention appears, have the same meaning in this Part as it has in that Part and in particular, exempt supplies and taxable supplies shall be accorded the same meanings as defined in regulation 110 above.

112(2) Any reference in this Part to a **capital item** shall be construed as a reference to a capital item to which this Part applies by virtue of regulation 113, being an item which a person who has or acquires an interest in the item in question (hereinafter referred to as '**the owner**') uses in the course or furtherance of a business carried on by him, and for the purpose of that business, otherwise than solely for the purpose of selling the item.

112(3) In this regulation and in regulation 114, an interest includes an interest which is treated as being supplied to a person under paragraph 37(1) of Schedule 10 to the Act provided that the numerator of the fraction in paragraph 37(3) of that Schedule is 36 or more.

112(4) The reference to '**owner**' in paragraph (2) shall be taken to refer to–
(a) subject to sub-paragraph (b), the transferee where the whole or part of a capital item is transferred from one person to another and that transfer is not treated as a supply for the purposes of VAT; and
(b) the representative member of a group under section 43 of the Act if the capital item is owned by a member of the group.

112(5) Where the owner is a transferee or representative member, that person shall be treated as having done everything that the transferor or group member (as may be the case) has done in respect of the capital item.

CAPITAL ITEMS TO WHICH THIS PART APPLIES

113(1) The capital items to which this Part applies are any of the items specified in paragraph (2) on or in relation to which the owner incurs VAT bearing capital expenditure of a type specified in paragraph (3), the value of which is not less than that specified in paragraph (4).

113(2) The items are–
(a) land;
(b) a building or part of a building;
(c) a civil engineering work or part of a civil engineering work;
(d) a computer or an item of computer equipment;
(e) an aircraft;
(f) a ship, boat or other vessel.

113(3) The expenditure–
(a) in the case of an item falling within paragraph (2)(a) or (d), is the expenditure relating to its acquisition;
(b) in the case of an item falling within paragraph (2)(b), (c), (e) or (f), is the expenditure relating to its–
  (i) acquisition,
  (ii) construction (including where appropriate manufacture),
  (iii) refurbishment,
  (iv) fitting out,
  (v) alteration, or
  (vi) extension (including the construction of an annex).

113(4) The value for the purposes of paragraph (3) is–
(a) not less than £250,000 where the item falls within paragraph (2)(a), (b) or (c);
(b) not less than £50,000 where the item falls within paragraph (2)(d), (e) or (f).

PERIOD OF ADJUSTMENT

114(1) The proportion (if any) of the total input tax on a capital item which may be deducted under Part XIV shall be subject to adjustments in accordance with the provisions of this Part.

114(2) Adjustments shall be made over a period determined in accordance with the following paragraphs of this regulation.

114(3) Subject to paragraphs (3A) and (3B), the period of adjustment is–
(a) 10 successive intervals in the case of a capital item of a description falling within regulation 113(2)(a) to (c);
(b) 5 successive intervals in the case of a capital item of a description falling within regulation 113(2)(d) to (f),
determined in accordance with paragraphs (4) to (5B) and (7).

114(3A) If, at the time of the owner's first use, the number of intervals specified in paragraph (3)(a) or (b) (as may be the case) exceeds the number of complete years that the owner's interest in the capital item has to run by more than one, the number of intervals shall be reduced to one more than the number of complete years that the owner's interest has to run calculated from the date of the owner's first use of the item (but not to less than three intervals).

114(3B) Where the owner's interest falls within regulation 112(3), the number of intervals shall be the same as the numerator of the fraction in paragraph 37(3) of Schedule 10 to the Act divided by 12 and rounded up to the next whole number.

114(3C) Where paragraph (3A) or (3B) applies, the relevant denominator in regulation 115(1) shall be adjusted accordingly.

114(3D) Where a person who registers for VAT already owns an item of a description falling within regulation 113, for the purposes of calculating the period of adjustment–
(a) one complete interval shall be deducted for each complete year which has elapsed since the date of that person's first use of the capital item prior to the date of VAT registration, and
(b) the first interval applicable to the capital item which ends after the date of VAT registration shall be treated as a subsequent interval for the purposes of regulation 115(1).

114(4) Subject to paragraphs (5A), (5B) and (7), the first interval applicable to a capital item shall commence on the day on which the owner first uses the capital item and shall end on the day before the start of his next tax year whether or not this is his first tax year.

114(5) Subject to paragraphs (5A), (5B) and (7) below, each subsequent interval applicable to a capital item shall correspond with a longer period applicable to the owner, or if no longer period applies to him, a tax year of his.

114(5A) On the first occasion during the period of adjustment applicable to a capital item that the owner of the item–
(a) being a registered person subsequently becomes a member of a group under section 43 of the Act;
(b) being a member of a group under section 43 ceases to be a member of that group (whether or not he becomes a member of another such group immediately thereafter); or
(c) transfers the item in the course of the transfer of his business or part of his business as a going concern (the item therefore not being treated as supplied) in circumstances where the new owner is not, under regulation 6(1) above, registered with the registration number of and in substitution for the transferor,

the interval then applying shall end on the day before he becomes a member of a group or the day that he ceases to be a member of the group or transfers the business or part of the business (as the case may require) and thereafter each subsequent interval (if any) applicable to the capital item shall end on the successive anniversaries of that day.

114(5B) Where the extent to which a capital item is used in making taxable supplies does not change between what would, but for this paragraph, have been the first interval and the first subsequent interval applicable to it and the length of the two intervals taken together does not exceed 12 months the first interval applicable to the capital item shall end on what would have been the day that the first subsequent interval expired.

114(6) [Omitted by SI 1997/1614, reg. 11(e).]

114(7) Where the owner of a capital item transfers it during the period of adjustment applicable to it in the course of the transfer of his business or a part of his business as a going concern (the item therefore not being treated as supplied) and the new owner is, under regulation 6(1) above, registered with the registration number of, and in substitution for the transferor, the interval applying to the capital item at the time of the transfer shall end on the last day of the longer period applying to the new owner immediately after the transfer or, if no longer period then applies to him, shall end on the last day of his tax year following the day of transfer.

METHOD OF ADJUSTMENT

115(1) Where in a subsequent interval applicable to a capital item, the extent to which it is used in making taxable supplies increases from the extent to which it was so used or to be used at the time that the original entitlement to deduction of the input tax was determined, the owner may deduct for that subsequent interval an amount calculated as follows–
(a) where the capital item falls within regulation 114(3)(b)–

$$\frac{\text{the total input tax on the capital item}}{5} \times \text{the adjustment percentage};$$

(b) where the capital item falls within regulation 114(3)(a)–

$$\frac{\text{the total input tax on the capital item}}{10} \times \text{the adjustment percentage}.$$

115(2) Where in a subsequent interval applicable to a capital item, the extent to which it is used in making taxable supplies decreases from the extent to which it was so used or to be used at the time that the original entitlement to deduction of the input tax was determined, the owner shall pay to the Commissioners for that subsequent interval an amount calculated in the manner described in paragraph (1) above.

115(3) Paragraph (3ZA) applies where, during an interval other than the last interval applicable to a capital item, the owner–
(a) supplies the whole or part of his interest in the capital item, or
(b) is deemed to supply the whole or part of his interest in the capital item, or

(c) would have been deemed to supply the whole of his interest in the capital item but for the fact that the VAT on the deemed supply (whether by virtue of its value or because it is zero-rated or exempt) would not have exceeded the sum specified in paragraph 8(1)(c) of Schedule 4 to the Act.

115(3ZA) If the supply (or deemed supply) of the capital item referred to in paragraph (3) is–
(a) a taxable supply, the owner shall be treated as using the whole or part (as may be the case) of the capital item for each of the remaining complete intervals applicable to it wholly in making taxable supplies, or
(b) an exempt supply, the owner shall be treated as not using the whole or part (as may be the case) of the capital item for any of the remaining complete intervals applicable to it in making any taxable supplies,

and, in each case, the owner shall, except where paragraph (3A) applies, calculate for each of the remaining complete intervals applicable to the capital item, in accordance with paragraph (1) or (2) as the case may require, such amount as the owner may deduct or be liable to pay to the Commissioners.

115(3A) This paragraph applies if the total amount of input tax deducted or deductible by the owner of a capital item as a result of the initial deduction, any adjustments made under paragraph (1) or (2) above and the adjustment which would apart from this paragraph fall to be made under paragraph (3ZA) above would exceed the output tax chargeable by him on the supply of the whole or part of that capital item.

115(3B) Save as the Commissioners may otherwise allow, where paragraph (3A) above applies the owner may deduct, or as the case may require, shall pay to the Commissioners such amount as results in the total amount of input tax deducted or deductible being equal to the output tax chargeable by him on the supply of the whole or part of the capital item.

115(4) If a capital item is irretrievably lost or stolen or is totally destroyed, no further adjustment shall be made in respect of any remaining complete intervals applicable to it.

115(5) Subject to paragraph (5A), for the purposes of this Part–

'**the adjustment percentage**' means the difference (if any) between the extent, expressed as a percentage, to which the whole or part as appropriate of the capital item was used or to be used for the making of taxable supplies at the time the original entitlement to deduction of the input tax was determined and the extent to which the whole or part of it as appropriate is so used, or is treated under paragraph (3ZA) as being so used, in the subsequent interval in question;

'**the original entitlement to deduction**' means the entitlement to deduction under sections 24 to 26 of the Act and regulations made under those sections;

'**the total input tax on the capital item**' means–
in relation to any capital item, all VAT incurred by the owner on the capital expenditure on that item (whether or not the person incurring it is VAT registered at the time that it is incurred) including any non-business VAT; and
where a person is treated as making a supply to himself under paragraph 37(1) of Schedule 10 to the Act, the VAT charged on that supply;

'**VAT bearing capital expenditure**' means capital expenditure on which VAT is charged at the standard rate or at a reduced rate.

115(5A) Where paragraph (3ZA) applies in respect of part of a capital item, for the remaining complete intervals the total VAT incurred on the capital item as defined in paragraph (5) shall be reduced accordingly.

115(5B) The person responsible for making an adjustment under paragraph (1), (2) or (3ZA) shall be the person who is treated as the owner of the capital item under regulation 112 at the point immediately prior to the end of the interval in question or, in the case of an adjustment under paragraph (3ZA), the event specified in paragraph (3).

115(6) Subject to paragraphs (9) and (11) below, a taxable person claiming any amount pursuant to paragraph (1) above, or liable to pay any amount pursuant to paragraph (2) above, shall include such amount in a return for the second prescribed accounting period next following the interval to which that amount relates, except where the Commissioners allow another return to be used for this purpose.

115(7) Subject to paragraphs (9) and (11) below, a taxable person claiming any amount or amounts, or liable to pay any amount or amounts, pursuant to paragraph (3ZA) above, shall include such amount or amounts in a return for the second prescribed accounting period next following the interval in which the supply (or deemed supply) in question takes place except where the Commissioners allow another return to be used for this purpose.

115(8) For the purposes of paragraph (9), a **'specified return'** means a return specified in paragraph (6) or (7).

115(9) The Commissioners shall not allow the taxable person to use a return other than a specified return unless it is the return for a prescribed accounting period commencing within 4 years of the end of the prescribed accounting period to which the specified return relates.

115(10) [Omitted by SI 2010/3022, reg. 13(m).]

115(11) Where a person is required to make an adjustment under paragraph (1), (2) or (3ZA) at a time when he is no longer registered for VAT, he shall make the required adjustment in his final VAT return.

ASCERTAINMENT OF TAXABLE USE OF A CAPITAL ITEM

116(1) Subject to regulation 115(3) and (3B) and paragraphs (2), (A2) and (3) below, for the purposes of this Part, an attribution of the total input tax on the capital item shall be determined for each subsequent interval applicable to it in accordance with the provisions of sections 24 to 26 of the Act and regulations made under those sections as they apply to that interval and the proportion of the input tax thereby determined to be attributable to taxable supplies shall be treated as being the extent to which the capital item is used in making taxable supplies in that subsequent interval.

116(A2) Subject to paragraph (2) below, the attribution of the total input tax on a capital item for subsequent intervals determined in accordance with regulation 114(5A) above shall be determined by such method as is agreed with the Commissioners.

116(2) In any particular case the Commissioners may allow another method by which, or may direct the manner in which, the extent to which a capital item is used in making taxable supplies in any subsequent interval applicable to it is to be ascertained.

116(3) Where the owner of a building which is a capital item of his grants or assigns a tenancy or lease in the whole or any part of that building and that grant or assignment is a zero-rated supply to the extent only as provided by–
(a) note (14) to Group 5 of Schedule 8 to the Act, or
(b) that note as applied to Group 6 of that Schedule by note (3) to Group 6, or
(c) paragraph 8 of Schedule 13 to the Act,
any subsequent exempt supply of his arising directly from that grant or assignment shall be disregarded in determining the extent to which the capital item is used in making taxable supplies in any interval applicable to it.

Appendix 9: Customs Industry Agreements

Extracts from VAT Notice 700/57 Administrative agreements entered into with trade bodies (August 2004)

General

The agreements in this notice permit the members of trade bodies to use procedures which take into account their individual circumstances so they may meet their obligations under VAT law. The agreements apply only to areas where we can exercise discretion, and they convey no direct financial advantage or relief from the legal requirements of the tax.

However, the agreements can provide unique solutions to particular problems and reduce the burdens on business. Some of them might usefully be applied by other businesses, but please remember that you cannot adopt any special method based on these agreements unless Customs and Excise has given approval in advance. Nothing in any of these agreements can override any subsequent change in the law, and they can be terminated at any time by us.

Details of new agreements will be published in Business Briefs and will subsequently be included in the next revision of this notice.

Details of changes to March 2002 version:

- The agreement with the Association of British Insurers about engineering insurance business (formerly agreement no.2) which was reproduced for information has been removed.
- No.4 – The agreement with Finance Houses Association Ltd about finance houses and partial exemption (formerly agreement no.6) has been cancelled with effect from 31/1/2000 and is now reproduced for information only.
- No.10 – The agreement with the National Caravan Council Limited and the British Holiday and Home Park Association Limited about the method of valuing removable contents sold with zero-rated caravans (formerly agreement no.12) has been amended.
- No.11 – The agreement with the Association of Unit Trust and Investment Managers about the VAT liability of charges made in connection with Personal Equity Plans (formerly agreement no. 13) has been amended.
- No.15 – The agreement with Gaming Board for Great Britain and the British Casino Association about Competitions in Card Rooms (formerly agreement no.17) has been revised. A new agreement is now in force with effect from September 2001.

Appendix 9: Customs Industry Agreements

New agreements included are:

- No.22 – The agreement with the Meat and Livestock Commission Circulars about the VAT treatment of levies collected (invoiced) from 1 October 1990 by the Commission from operators of slaughterhouses and exporters of live animals.
- No.23 – The agreement with the Society of Motor Manufacturers and Traders Limited about how the one tonne payload test will be applied in practice to double cab pick-ups.
- No.24 – The agreement with the Society of Motor Manufacturers and Traders Limited about a simplified method by which motor manufacturers, importers and wholesale distributors may calculate the VAT due on the private use of stock in trade cars provided to directors and employees free of charge.
- No.25 – The agreement with the Retail Motor Industry Federation about a simplified method by which retail motor dealers may calculate the VAT due on the private use of demonstrator cars provided to directors and employees free of charge.
- No.26 – The agreement with the British Vehicle Rental and Leasing Association about a simplified method which daily rental companies may use to calculate the VAT due on the incidental private use of their hire fleets.

You can access details of any changes to this notice since August 2004 either on our Internet website at http://www.hmce.gov.uk or by telephoning the National Advice Service on 0845 010 9000.

This notice and others mentioned are available both on paper and on our website.

CONTENTS

Paragraph

1 Agreement with the London Bullion Market Association about supplies of bullion

2 Agreement with the Association of British Factors and Discounters (formerly the Association of British Factors) about partial exemption and factors (October 1995).

3 Agreement with the Finance Houses Association Ltd about finance houses and partial exemption (September 1984) (Cancelled in 2000).

4 Agreement negotiated with the Association of British Insurers (ABI) [formerly the British Insurance Association (BIA)] about recovery of input tax incurred in the UK in connection with supplies by branches outside the European Community (cancelled in 2006).

5 Agreement with the Association of Investment Trust Companies about partial exemption.

6 Arrangement allowed to marine, aviation and transport insurance underwriters who are members of a particular trade organisation in respect of claims related input tax and associated imported services.

7 Agreement with the Association of British Insurers, Lloyd's of London, the Institute of London Underwriters and the British Insurance and Investment Association about coding supplies of marine, aviation and transport (MAT) insurance services.

Appendix 9: Customs Industry Agreements

8   Agreement with the Association of Unit Trust and Investment Managers about the VAT liability of charges made in connection with Personal Equity Plans (PEPs).

9   Agreement with the British Bankers' Association about the VAT liability of electronic banking/cash management services.

1. Agreement with the London Bullion Market Association about supplies of bullion

1. The Commissioners of HM Customs and Excise have agreed with the London Bullion Market Association (LBMA) certain practical rules to govern the VAT treatment of supplies of bullion (gold and silver excluding coins) on the London Bullion Market. Supplies on or after the 1 July 1991 come within the terms of this agreement.

2. Under the terms of the Value Added Tax (Terminal Markets) Order 1973 there is provision for zero-rating supplies of bullion where both parties to the transaction are LBMA members. In addition, supplies to and from an LBMA member and a non-member are zero-rated provided the transaction does not lead to physical delivery. Supplies on the Market which are zero-rated can be regarded as taking place within a VAT-free ring or 'black box', the term used in this agreement.

3. It has been agreed, broadly in confirmation of existing working practices within the Market, that with certain exceptions all supplies of bullion, including loans, should be treated as being zero-rated, provided the bullion is not physically removed from the black box. This will apply to all supplies of bullion irrespective of the counterparties involved (whether LBMA members or non-members, or whether the bullion is allocated or unallocated). Bullion will be regarded as having been so removed when effective physical control is transferred from an LBMA member to a non-member. The term effective physical control includes cases where bullion leaves the possession of an LBMA member but remains under the member's control and responsibility. Where physical bullion leaves the black box because an LBMA member relinquishes effective physical control, VAT will be charged and accounted for by the LBMA member so relinquishing control. VAT will be charged at the standard-rate for domestic transactions and at the zero-rate in the case of exports where the actual export is arranged by the relevant LBMA member, subject to the usual satisfactory evidence of exportation being produced. Where a non-member takes physical delivery of bullion in the United Kingdom for subsequent export arranged by the non-member, the LBMA member would charge VAT at the standardrate, leaving the non-member to reclaim VAT at the time of export.

4. Under this regime, the LBMA member who relinquishes physical control of bullion when it leaves the black box will be deemed for all relevant VAT purposes to have made the supply to the non-LBMA member, irrespective of whether the member had title at that point to the bullion in question. In particular, the LBMA member will raise a VAT invoice and treat the VAT charged to the customer as their output tax. The customer will treat it as recoverable input tax provided it is attributable to other taxable supplies.

5. It is agreed that this regime will apply to all transactions involving bullion held by LBMA members with the following exceptions:

Appendix 9: Customs Industry Agreements

(a) **Safe carriage delivery to a non-member.** Where the service provided by an LBMA member receiving bullion from another member amounts only to the provisions of safe carriage, a supply will be treated as taking place when the bullion is passed to the LBMA member providing safe carriage. VAT will be charged at that point at the standard-rate by the LBMA member supplying the bullion to the non-LBMA member who is the customer (except in the case of an export or a supply to a Central Bank).

(b) **Safe custody/storage.** Where, subject to customary safeguards and checks of status, an LBMA member holds bullion for a customer which remains that customer's property and is not supplied into the black box, the return of the bullion to the customer would not give rise to a VAT charge on the metal. A charge for safe custody or storage is standard-rated irrespective of LBMA membership.

(c) **Refining.** Where bullion is to be supplied by an LBMA member to a non-member, but before it is physically delivered it is to be transferred to another LBMA member for process, the supply will be treated as taking place for VAT purposes when the bullion is released to the LBMA refiner (unless there is an earlier invoice or payment tax point). VAT will be charged to the non-LBMA customer at the standard rate at that point (except in the case of an export) by the LBMA member releasing the bullion to the LBMA refiner. The same tax point will also apply to a case when the bullion is the subject of a (physical) loan rather than a sale. The documentation to the refiner must make it clear that VAT has been accounted for by the supplier of the metal.

Where bullion is supplied by an LBMA member who is a refiner to a non-member and it is to be processed before delivery, the tax point will either be when the bullion is transferred to the customer's metal account with that refiner or, if the non-member is not required to make payment at that point, when the bullion is physically delivered following processing (unless there is an earlier payment or issue of a tax invoice). Again this will apply both to sales and physical loans.

The above rules are not intended to apply to cases where a refiner applies a process to a customer's bullion which remains the property of the customer (eg sweepings or scrap). In such cases the bullion does not enter the black box and the supply by the refiner is purely one of refining services. When bullion is made available by an LBMA member who is a refiner to a non-LBMA member for a process to be carried out, eg chain-making for and on behalf of the refiner, on the clear understanding that the finished product will be returned to the refiner, who will remain responsible for the bullion throughout, or where bullion is taken to a third party for assay, it will be regarded as remaining within the effective physical control of the refiner and therefore remaining within the black box, unless or until it is sold or otherwise disposed of, when VAT must be accounted for by the refiner.

(d) **Supplies between non-members.** In the case of supplies between parties who are not LBMA members, zero-rating will be available under the general rule in paragraph 3 above where the bullion is and remains within the black box, ie in the effective physical control of an LBMA member, and, unless the special rules in (a) to (c) above apply, VAT will be charged and accounted for by the LBMA member relinquishing that control on physical delivery from the black box. However, where the supply is to a UK resident, zero-rating is subject to the further condition that the bullion is intended for commercial use by a customer engaged in regular transactions in precious metal as part of their manufacturing or processing trade.

Appendix 9: Customs Industry Agreements

6. It is the responsibility of all LBMA members to ensure that VAT is properly accounted for under the above rules, in particular where bullion is sold or loaned and subsequently physically delivered outside the black box to non-members. In order that this responsibility can be effectively discharged it is agreed that there will be close co-operation and exchange of relevant information between members, and in any case where there may be doubt, the VAT status of bullion transferred within or outside the black box will be made clear.

7. Agreement has also been reached on the correct treatment of bullion loans. These can take two forms: purely financial 'paper' transactions, where the loan is a pure book transfer not involving any physical delivery of bullion and 'consignments', where physical bullion is made available to the customer to work on, but where payment is not required until a later date. In both cases a charge expressed as a rate of interest is made for the duration of the loan.

8. In the former case, the interest is normally calculated at a predetermined agreed rate denominated in ounces of the precious metal in question, which is then converted to sterling or US dollars at the then prevailing market rate. It is agreed that in this case, the interest should be treated as consideration for an exempt supply within item 2 of Group 5 of Schedule 9 to the VAT Act 1994. However, where the loan could be regarded as taking place within the black box, it would be zero-rated. VAT would not be chargeable on the principal amount of the loan.

9. In the latter case, where the bullion is physically consigned to the non-LBMA customer on credit, VAT will be charged at the standard-rate on the market value of the bullion, even though the actual charge to the customer of the principal amount is deferred, when the tax point arises, ie when it is physically delivered or made available to the customer (including a transfer to an LBMA member for processing), or when an invoice is issued, whichever is the earlier. This will normally mean issuing a VAT only invoice when the tax point arises. In this case the financing charge will be seen in all cases as further consideration for the supply of the bullion and taxable at the standard rate, with a tax point arising on each subsequent payment. This treatment replaces an existing concessionary* treatment previously agreed with Customs and Excise.

* The concession, which came to an end on 1 May 1991 in respect of all new loans business, allowed the 'supplier' to account for VAT only on the amount of interest charged and not on the value of the principal amount of the loan.

All physical gold loans will be subject to the VAT treatment described above with effect from 1 October 1991. Subject to the normal rules, the VAT will be recoverable by the customer as input tax, provided it relates to their taxable supplies. If at the end of the loan period when the principal amount falls to be paid, the price of the bullion has increased, the additional payment would be treated as further consideration for the supply, and taxable at the standard rate. If it has fallen, the reduction in the price would be treated as a reduction in the consideration, and a credit note could be issued adjusting the VAT, though if both parties agree the credit note need not be issued. If at the end of the loan period, the customer discharges their liability by supplying bullion back to the LBMA member, this would be a separate standard-rated supply, and again a VAT only invoice would need to be issued by the customer, with the VAT payment being remitted by the LBMA member direct to Customs and Excise if the Special Accounting Scheme applies.

10. This agreement will be subject to regular review between the parties and may be amended or withdrawn after discussion or notice in writing to the LBMA.

The concessionary treatment in respect of existing loans ended on 30 September 1991.

2. Agreement with the Association of British Factors and Discounters (formerly the Association of British Factors) about partial exemption and factors (October 1995)

(The responsibilities of this organisation were subsumed into the Factoring and Commercial Finance Association with effect from 1 April 1996).

1. These proposals contain provisions for more than one apportionment of residual input tax and for the use of calculations based on transactions counts. Any partial exemption method based on these proposals is, therefore, a special method and members will be required to seek approval of their local VAT Offices before applying the formula. Because of the variable level of taxable services in invoice discounting it will be also necessary for members to negotiate individually with their local offices a basis for recovery in this area.

Where necessary, the proposals can be incorporated in a wider partial exemption method to take account of members' other business activities.

2. Under the agreement, factors are required to sectorise the different areas of their business and the related input tax: in particular, they must identify separately the input tax incurred in relation to invoice discounting and mainline factoring.

3. Invoice discounting factoring

In this type of factoring the level of taxable services and, thus, the extent of input tax recovery can vary from business to business. For this reason we are unable to propose a set formula for dealing with input tax in this area. Members can agree with their local VAT offices any fair and reasonable basis for apportionment of the input tax attributable to invoice discounting. There would be no objection to the use of a transactions based calculation similar to that for mainline factoring, but it will be necessary for individual businesses to agree which transactions should be included.

4. Mainline factoring

Businesses must identify all the goods and services received which are used or to be used in mainline factoring (with or without credit) and the proportion of input tax thereon which may be deducted is to be determined in accordance with the following formula:

$$\frac{\text{Taxable transactions}}{\text{Taxable and exempt transactions}} \times \text{Input tax identified above as relating to the mainline factoring sector of the business}$$

The only taxable and exempt transactions which may be used in the fraction above are:

Taxable transactions

- Invoices
- Credit notes
- Debtor payments
- Payments to clients at maturity

Exempt transactions

- Prepayments to clients
- Interests

The transactions included in this calculation are those, in Customs' opinion, which are common to all your members and are fully attributable to either the taxable or exempt supplies of your members.

5. The remaining transactions with the exception of 'sales ledger adjustments' are not common to your members and in certain instances are only partly attributable to taxable or exempt supplies and their inclusion could lead to distortions. The variations in sales ledger adjustments indicate a difference in accounting methods of your members and again the inclusion could lead to distortion. Customs consider that by confining the calculation to 6 transactions it will have the merit of administrative simplicity for your members.

6. Where input tax cannot be allocated to one of the sectors of the business (eg audit fees etc) it will be recoverable only to the extent that the supply on which the input tax was charged is, or is to be, used in the making of taxable supplies. In such cases your members will need to negotiate an appropriate formula with their local VAT office (eg a straightforward outputs based proportional formula may be acceptable, provided it produces a 'fair and reasonable' result).

7. At the end of each tax year an annual adjustment should be undertaken using the figures for the whole tax year. Any difference between the amount of deductible input tax recalculated at the end of the tax year and the total amount provisionally deducted during the tax year is an over or under-declaration of VAT. The amount must be entered in the VAT account for the first tax period after the end of the tax year.

If the recalculation shows that input tax attributable to exempt supplies is below the partial exemption deminimis limit the business may be treated as fully taxable for the tax year. Any input tax not reclaimed during the year under the partial exemption rules is an overdeclaration of VAT.

8. Any agreed special method is subject to review by Customs and can be modified or withdrawn at any time.

9. Where approval is given for the use of a transactions count method by the local VAT office, the approval will be based on the numbers and frequency of transactions at that time. If,

Appendix 9: Customs Industry Agreements

however, there is any significant change in the way transactions are recorded, or the numbers or frequency of transactions, the member must advise the local VAT office so that the method can be reviewed.

10. These proposals do not constitute a partial exemption method as such but provide a framework within which the members of the Association can agree acceptable methods with their local VAT offices.

3. Agreement with the Finance Houses Association Ltd about finance houses and partial exemption (September 1984)

Cancelled with effect from 31 January 2000 – reproduced for information only

1. Outstanding balances

We are prepared to accept that outstanding balances may be used in any pro-rata calculation for each tax period; details of the outstanding balances to be used are to be agreed with the local VAT office. Deductions of input tax for each tax period are, of course, only provisional, and at the end of each tax year the annual adjustment must be made on the basis of receipts for the tax year. For this purpose, the receipts are to be calculated in the following way:

> 'Outstanding balance at the start of the year plus the value of new business written during the tax year minus the outstanding balance at the end of the tax year.'

Calculations on this basis will be subject to review at any time.

2. General principles

Discussions and exchanges have been in general terms and have not dealt specifically with the variety of supplies made by members. In fact, for purposes of simplification, we have referred only to the most common type of supply, and we think it might be helpful to set out how the deductibility of input tax is determined. The fundamental principle is that input tax related to taxable supplies is recoverable, but that related to exempt and other supplies is not. Input tax on goods bought and sold in the same state and on goods which are the subject of a taxable lease is normally recoverable in full, but the input tax on goods or plant bought in connection with an exempt leasing supply is not. Input tax related to taxable leasing is deductible, but the input tax incurred in connection with exempt leasing, exempt loans and hire purchase credit is not. How these principles are to be applied in practice is illustrated below.

3. Hire purchase receipts related to goods

We have agreed, subject to review, that 15% of the input tax related to hire purchase credit can be regarded as being properly attributable to the sale of the goods in respect of which the credit is granted. Where any member makes a variety of supplies the amount of input tax which can be regarded as related to hire purchase credit is to be identified in each tax period as follows:

$$\frac{\text{Outstanding balances for hire purchase credit}}{\text{Total outstanding balances}} \times \frac{\text{Total input tax less any tax directly}}{\text{attributable to goods or plant}}$$

4. Hire purchase only

Where only hire purchase supplies are made, the deductible input tax is as follows:

(a) all the input tax incurred on goods bought and sold in the same state; plus
(b) 15% of the remaining input tax.

5. Hire purchase and taxable leasing supplies

Where only hire purchase and taxable leasing supplies are made, the deductible input tax is as follows:

(a) all the input tax incurred on goods bought and sold in the same state;
(b) 15% of the input tax related to hire purchase credit (see above); and
(c) the residue of the total input tax after that dealt with under (a) plus the whole of the input tax related to hire purchase credit have been deducted.

6. Hire purchase, taxable and exempt leasing and exempt loans

Where the supplies made consist of hire purchase, taxable and exempt leasing and exempt loans, the deductibility of input tax is as follows:

(a) none of the input tax on goods or plant bought in connection with an exempt leasing supply is deductible;
(b) all the input tax on goods bought for sale in the same state or to be disposed of in the same state as the subject of a taxable leasing supply is deductible;
(c) 15% of the input tax related to hire purchase (see above) is deductible; and
(d) after the input tax calculated under (a) and (b) above has been determined and deducted from the total tax together with all the input tax relating to hire purchase, a further percentage may be deducted according to the following formula:

$$\frac{\text{Outstanding balance for taxable leasing supplies}}{\text{Outstanding balances for exempt loans, exempt leases and taxable leases}} \times 100$$

7. Acceptable method

The activities of members is so varied, it is not practicable to give examples which will apply to all situations.

Nevertheless, the examples set out above, together with the general principles, provide a guide to the sort of method of calculating deductible input tax which would be regarded as acceptable to this Department.

8. Annual adjustments

At the end of each tax year, the amount of input tax which a member is entitled to deduct is to be recalculated on the basis of the figures for the tax year. The deductible input tax is to be identified in precisely the same way as for each tax period, except that receipts for the tax year calculated as in the opening paragraph are to be used instead of outstanding balances in all calculations including that which is used to identify the input tax related to hire purchase credit. Any difference between the amount of input tax deducted for the tax periods in the year and the amount deductible on the basis of the figures for the tax year is to be regarded as an over or under-declaration of VAT and an entry is to be made in the VAT account for the first tax period after the end of the tax year.

4. Agreement negotiated with the Association of British Insurers (ABI) [formerly the British Insurance Association (BIA)] about recovery of input tax incurred in the UK in connection with supplies by branches outside the European Community

1. **The British Insurance Association**

Regulation 103 provides authority for insurance businesses to recover input tax incurred in the UK in connection with supplies made by their branches outside the European Community (EC). It has been accepted that insurance businesses have difficulty in identifying this input tax and, following an exercise carried out with the co-operation of some of the members of the British Insurance Association (BIA), agreement has been reached with the Association that from 1 April 1985 this input tax may be identified in the following way:

(a) **Identification of recoverable input tax related to the activities of branches and agencies outside the EC**

$$\text{Total input tax} \times \frac{\text{Expenses incurred in the UK in connection with supplies made by branches and agencies outside the EC}}{\text{Total expenses incurred in the UK}}$$

(b) **Identification of recoverable input tax related to the activities of branches and agencies outside the EC by two stages**

Stage (i)

$$\text{Total input tax} \times \frac{\text{Expenses incurred in the UK in connection with supplies made by overseas branches and agencies}}{\text{Total expenses incurred in the UK}}$$

Stage (ii)

$$\text{Product of stage (i)} \times \frac{\text{Premium income of branches and agencies outside the EC}}{\text{Total premium income of overseas branches and agencies}}$$

Appendix 9: Customs Industry Agreements

(c) **Identification of recoverable input tax related to the activities of branches outside the EC by two stages**

Stage (i)

either

$$\text{Total expenses incurred in the UK in respect of supplies made by overseas branches} \times \frac{\text{Premium income of branches outside the EC}}{\text{Total premium income of overseas branches}}$$

or

$$\text{Total expenses incurred in the UK in respect of supplies made by overseas branches and agencies} \times \frac{\text{Premium income of branches outside the EC}}{\text{Total premium income of overseas branches and agencies}}$$

Stage (ii)

$$\text{Total input tax} \times \frac{\text{Expenses incurred in the UK in connection with supplies made by branches outside the EC (ie product of Stage (i))}}{\text{Total expenses incurred in the UK}}$$

(d) **Any other formula to be agreed by an individual company with the local VAT office**

2. If formula (a) or formula (b) is used, the value of any supplies made through overseas branches and agencies must be excluded from companies' partial exemption calculations. The value of any supplies to overseas agencies must also be excluded.

3. If formula (c) is used, the value of any supplies made through overseas branches must be excluded from companies' partial exemption calculations, but the value of any supplies made through overseas agencies must be included.

4. Acceptance of any of the above options is to be confirmed to insurance businesses in writing. If an insurance business already uses a special method, a new letter of approval is to be issued covering the agreed option.

5. **Foreign-owned insurance businesses**

Foreign owned insurance businesses registered in the UK may regard the parent insurance company and any other branches of the company as 'a branch of his' for the purpose of Regulation 103. These businesses may use any of the options set out above to identify the input tax incurred in the UK in connection with the activities of any 'branch of his' located outside the EC.

5. Agreement with the Association of Investment Trust Companies about partial exemption

1. With effect from 1 April 1987 members who are currently using the present standard method or the agreed alternative may calculate deductible input tax on the following basis:

- input tax on commission on sales within the UK and EC must be isolated and treated as irrecoverable;
- the remaining input tax should be apportioned and the deductible proportion determined by applying the same ratio as the value of taxable supplies bears to the value of all supplies.

2. Members need not notify their local VAT offices if they wish to adopt the above method but where a member, after isolating the input tax on the commissions on sales within the UK and EC, wishes to apportion the remaining input tax by an alternative method they should apply to their local VAT office for approval.

3. If any obviously distortive transaction is undertaken, eg the sale of a property (which would usually be exempt), it should be isolated from the above calculation. The deductibility of any related input tax would be determined by the liability of the supply in question.

6. Arrangement allowed to marine, aviation and transport insurance underwriters who are members of a particular trade organisation in respect of claims related input tax and associated imported services

1. The collection of premiums and payment of claims by insurance underwriters who are members of a certain insurance traders association is co-ordinated by that organisation. In the course of settling claims, expenses are incurred both in the UK and abroad. The latter are often Schedule 5 (VAT Act 1994) services, which formerly came under Schedule 3 (VAT Act 1983), and subject to reverse charge provisions. Such expenses are re-allocated to individual members on the basis of the percentage of the risk underwritten by each; input tax is recoverable according to the proportion of 'taxable' supplies made and by each individual member (ie those supplies which are outside the scope of UK VAT but have the right to recovery of related input tax). Members also account under the reverse charge provisions for their proportion of qualifying services received from abroad.

2. The following procedure has been agreed between the trade organisation on behalf of the membership and Customs and Excise:

(i) The broker will supply the trade organisation with a single copy of the VAT invoice and/or other supporting documentation. The trade organisation will retain this at their central office.
(ii) Member companies will be advised by the trade organisation on a daily basis of claims processed which will show the detail of the VAT amount and where applicable the imported services.
(iii) On a monthly basis member companies will receive a tabulation showing relevant details for each item processed relating to VAT or imported services. Members will be able to use the tabulation details as evidence to substantiate entries in respect of claims related input VAT or imported services in their VAT returns.
(iv) The tabulation sheets will show individual amounts of input tax recoverable by the insurer (at the appropriate partial exemption percentage). Imported services amounts

will be shown in the original currencies so they will have to be converted using the appropriate exchange rates and VAT calculated at the standard-rate.
(v) The invoices and/or other documents supplied to the trade organisation will be retained centrally and available for inspection by Customs and Excise during normal working hours.
(vi) In the event that a member company fails to account for output tax on imported services (for whatever reason) the trade organisation will upon request from that member provide historical details of the appropriate tabulations.
(vii) In respect of these transactions or failure of a member to account correctly for them, it has been agreed with Customs and Excise that the trade organisation does not incur any liability to VAT.

7. Agreement with the Association of British Insurers, Lloyd's of London, the Institute of London Underwriters and the British Insurance and Investment Association about coding supplies of marine, aviation and transport (MAT) insurance services

1. From 5 July 1993 the liability of marine, aviation and transport (MAT) insurance services and the entitlement to input tax recovery must be based on the place of belonging of the insured person rather than on where the journey takes place.

2. The normal criteria for deciding the liability of these services are set out in Notice 741 *Place of supply of services* but there are instances where it will be difficult to determine the liability using the location criteria. As the result of a pilot study, and discussions between Customs and Excise and the representatives from the insurance industry, an agreement has been reached on VAT coding guidelines which will enable traders to determine the liability for any transactions where, for instance, there are joint insurers or where insurance is arranged through a central point for a number of subsidiary companies.

3. The Association of British Insurers, Lloyd's of London, the Institute of London Underwriters and the British Insurance and Investment Association have already issued the agreed coding guidelines to their members.

An outline of the guidelines is set out below and further guidance is available from local VAT offices. The guidelines are also available in VAT Notice 701/36 *Insurance*.

4. These guidelines apply to supplies made by both insurers and brokers or other intermediaries.

MAT Guidelines

(a) Insurers and brokers may continue to code transactions as either Z (zero-rated) with entitlement to input tax recovery, or × with no entitlement to input tax recovery.
(b) Where it is not possible to determine the VAT liability of MAT insurance services based on the place of belonging of the insured using the agreed guidelines, then the specific transactions may be coded M (mixed) with 50% of the attributable input tax being

Appendix 9: Customs Industry Agreements

recoverable and 50% irrecoverable. Transactions may be coded M only where the place of belonging of the insured cannot be determined.

(c) The insured's address is normally shown on the broker's slip or equivalent document or can be determined by the broker or other intermediary. This address is to be taken as the place of belonging of the insured. If the insured has more than one address, the one on the slip or document should be used unless it is clear that this is simply an administrative address for payment or other purposes.

(d) Where business is written in conjunction with an overseas agent and it is not possible to identify the address of each insured dealing with the agent, the agent's address may be taken as the place of belonging of the insured's.

(e) If a policy specifically covers the movement of goods from a place inside the EC to a place outside the EC then the transaction may be coded Z. Customs accept that it may be difficult for insurers to identify an entitlement to input tax recovery for policies involving the export of goods to a place outside the EC but this will be the subject of further discussions with the trade before long.

(f) The VAT liability of additional premiums and return premiums may be recorded under the new rules if the insurer wishes to do so. Alternatively all such premiums should be assigned the same code as that given to the original transaction if this is preferred.

(g) All local VAT offices have copies of the coding guidelines and any further queries should be made to the National Advice Service on 0845 010 9000.

8. Agreement with the Association of Unit Trust and Investment Managers about the VAT liability of charges made in connection with Personal Equity Plans (PEPs)

Description	Non Self-Select* (1)	Self-Select (2)
	(* The numbers in brackets refer to the notes following this list)	
(a) Unit trust manager and plan manager are the same company (ie unit trust only plan) (3)		
– Initial charge	Exempt (4)	Exempt (4)
– Periodic charge	Exempt (4)	Exempt (4)
– Additional PEP periodic administrative/ management charges (if any)	SR (4)	SR (4)
(b) Unit trust manager and plan manager are separate entities in the same VAT group (5)		
– Initial charge by the plan manager		
unit trust only plan	Exempt (5)	Exempt (6)
share linked plan	SR	Exempt/SR (6)–(7)
unit trust/share plan	SR (8)	Exempt/SR (6)–(7)
– Periodic charges by the plan manager		
unit trust only plan	SR	SR
share linked plan	SR	SR
unit trust/share plan	SR	SR

Appendix 9: Customs Industry Agreements

Description	Non Self-Select* (1)	Self-Select (2)
(c) Unit trust manager and plan manager are wholly separate entities		
– Initial charge by the plan manager		
unit trust only	Exempt (5)	Exempt (6)
share linked plan	SR	Exempt/SR (6)(7)
unit trust/share plan	SR (8)	Exempt/SR (6)(7)
– Periodic charges by the plan manager		
unit trust only plan	SR	SR
share linked plan	SR	SR
unit trust/share plan	SR	SR
(d) Other charges		
– Transaction charges	Exempt (9)	Exempt (9)
– Charge for cash withdrawal	Exempt (10)	Exempt (10)
– Charge for receiving dividend and passing this charge on to plan holder	Exempt (10)	Exempt (10)
– Charge for transfer of assets	Exempt	Exempt
– Charge for attending shareholder's meetings	SR	SR
– Charge for provision of companies' annual reports	SR	SR
– introductory fees paid to brokers/agents	SR(11)	SR(11)
– Exit charges	Exempt (12)	Exempt (12)

This agreement takes effect on 1 April 1994.

Notes

1. Non self-select covers the situation where the plan manager invests client money in a general personal equity plan, the mix of instruments within the plan being determined by the plan manager.

2. Self-select indicates where the investor selects the securities and the plan manager arranges the purchase of the securities as agent for the investor. Normally the contract will provide for the investor to bear the cost of transaction charges. These charges can be either the exact amount of brokerage charges incurred, which would be a disbursement by the plan manager (subject to the conditions laid down in Notice 700 *The VAT Guide* in the paragraph on disbursements), or the brokerage charge plus an additional amount representing the plan manager's fee for acting as an intermediary for the transaction. These transaction charges will be exempt unless they relate to sales of securities outside the EC. For further details see Notice 701/49 *Finance and Securities*, Section 8 – Intermediaries.

3. For further details see Notice 701/49 Finance and Securities, Section 7 – Investment Management, Unit Trusts, ISAs and PEPs.

Appendix 9: Customs Industry Agreements

4. Normally only the unit trust manager levies initial and periodic charges. However, if the company marketing the PEPs is the same as the unit trust management company, and the charge is no more than the normal unit trust management fee, then the PEP management fee is exempt. If an additional PEP management charge is made over and above the normal unit trust management fee, then the additional charge to the investor is standard-rated.

5. Where the plan manager makes an initial charge, the service provided by the plan manager would not normally be fund management as it is the unit trust manager who provides that service. Where such a charge is made, it will be for the plan manager to demonstrate that the services for which the charge is levied fall within Group 5 of Schedule 9 to the VAT Act 1994. Where the contract provides for the supply of intermediary services in acquiring the unit trust units for the investor and tax accounting services, Customs and Excise accept that the supply is one of acting as an intermediary for a purchase of units (item 5 of Group 5 of Schedule 9) and the charges will be exempt. If the plan manager treats this initial charge as exempt, this must be reflected in the contractual arrangements to the extent that in non self-select plans the investor is expected to bear the dealing charge. However, where any initial charge exceeds the normal bid/offer spread on units, the difference between the spread and the initial charge should be treated as a standard-rated PEP management fee.

6. Where the service provided consists of acting as an intermediary in acquiring the unit trust units or shares for the investor and incidental tax accounting services Customs accept that the service is one of acting as an intermediary for the purchase of units or shares and the charges will be treated as consideration for an exempt supply. If an initial charge for a unit trust based PEP exceeds the normal bid/offer spread, however, the difference between the spread and the initial charge should be treated as payment for a standard-rated supply of PEP management.

7. Where the initial charge exceeds the normal dealing charge for the procurement of the securities then the difference between the initial charge and the dealing charge is liable to VAT.

8. An initial charge in such circumstances includes the investment management service associated with the selection of shares to be included in the PEP and as such the charge is taxable at the standard rate.

9. Item 5 of Group 5 exempts acting as an intermediary for the issue, transfer, receipt of, or any dealing with securities. Usually such services are supplied by an intermediary who has been given instruction to acquire or dispose of securities. Transaction fees charged by a plan manager falling within the above framework are therefore exempt from VAT. With non self-select PEPs, the intermediary is not specifically instructed. However if, under the terms of the contract, the client is expected to bear dealing charges, and these charges are passed to the client by the PEP manager, these supplies may be treated as exempt.

10. Exempt under item 1 of Group 5 of Schedule 9 to the VAT Act 1994.

11. Where the PEP investor is charged an initial fee which is exempt from VAT, any commission (including renewal commission) paid to brokers/agents for the introduction of the investor will also be exempt. In other circumstances introductory commissions will be liable to VAT at the standard rate. When no initial charge is levied, any introductory fee (including

renewal fees) will be exempt as long as it is levied for the service of an introduction to a plan manager who is arranging for units to be purchased.

12. Where these charges represent the consideration for disposal of the securities held in the plan, they are exempt from VAT under item 6 of Group 5 of Schedule 9. In other circumstances exit charges are taxable at the standard rate.

9. Agreement with the British Bankers' Association about the VAT liability of electronic banking/cash management services

1. Cash management is one of the electronic banking services supplied by banks to mainly business customers, as an addition or alternative to conventional banking services. The customer uses computer equipment, sometimes leased or purchased from the bank, to obtain services which would otherwise have been provided by the bank in the course of its operation of the customer's account (such as statements of the customer's current balance or transfers of funds between accounts), as well as more general financial services (such as information about share prices or foreign exchange rates).

2. Customs and Excise and the British Bankers' Association have agreed that the liability to VAT electronic banking services should be determined by examining the status of the individual services provided and determining the liability of each of these on its merits. In principle, services which would have been treated as exempt under Group 5 of Schedule 9 to the VAT Act 1994 if they had been provided by the bank by conventional means should be treated as exempt when provided within the framework of electronic banking services; other financial services which are not covered by Group 5 should be treated as liable to VAT at the standard rate.

3. Where charges are made for the supplies detailed below they should be treated as follows:
   (a) Provision of information on share prices, foreign exchange rates, balances on accounts with other financial institutions and investment management services – are all standard-rated supplies.
   (b) Provision of information on the state of the client's accounts within the bank providing the electronic banking services, bank statements, the transfer of funds and the debiting and crediting of accounts – are all exempt supplies.
   (c) Hire of equipment and related charges, such as training, will be standard-rated if supplied and shown as a separate item on the invoice, otherwise standard-rated or exempt dependent on predominant or intended use when absorbed with other charges. Hire of equipment which can be used for other purposes (eg where the link gives access to Prestel) will always be standard-rated.
   (d) Services charges/overall services charges will be standard-rated or exempt dependent on predominant use.
   (e) Sale of equipment will be standard-rated.

4. Either Customs and Excise or the British Bankers' Association may seek discussions with the other party on amendment to or amplification of the note, bearing in mind the rapid rate of technical and commercial change in this area.

Appendix 10: Examples of Typical Banking and Financial Services

(1) Monetary financial services

As a consequence of the rules on the place of supply, many of the services to persons outside the UK are *outside the scope*. They do not, therefore, need to be included as outputs in the VAT return. They still, however, have impact on the recovery of input VAT under the partial exemption rules. The VAT liability generally depends partly on the status of the client or customer, i.e. whether inside or outside the UK and the Isle of Man and whether VAT-registered, partly on the nature of the service. The potential for recovery of underlying input VAT, which again depends partly on the status of the client and partly on the nature of the service, is denoted by the following key:

✔ = recoverable

X = not recoverable

o/s = outside the scope

References to the UK include the Isle of Man which is not outside the EU for this purpose.

	All UK		EU Non-VAT-registered[1]		EU VAT-registered		Non-EU Private Business		Non-EU Private	
Agency fees (for ongoing administration of loans)	E	X	E	X	o/s	X	–		o/s	✔
Bills of exchange										
• Collection commissions	E	X	E	X	o/s	X	–		o/s	✔
• Discounts[2]	o/s	X	o/s	X	o/s	X	–		o/s	✔
• Proceeds[3]	E	X	E	X	o/s	X	–		o/s	✔
Consortium/syndicated loans[4]										
• Arrangement fees/commissions	E	X	E	X	o/s	X	–		o/s	✔
• Commitment fees	E	X	E	X	o/s	X	–		o/s	✔
• Participation fees	E	X	E	X	o/s	X	–		o/s	✔
• Underwriting	E	X	E	X	o/s	X	–		o/s	✔
Finance for exports[5]										
• Letters of credit	E	✔	–	o/s	✔	–	o/s			✔
• Collection charges	E	✔	–	o/s	✔	–	o/s			✔
• Commitment fees	E	✔	–	o/s	✔	–	o/s			✔
• Guarantee fees	E	✔	–	o/s	✔	–	o/s			✔
• Loan interest	E	✔	–	o/s	✔	–	o/s			✔
• Confirming House commission	E	✔	–	o/s	✔	–	o/s			✔

Appendix 10: Examples of Typical Banking and Financial Services

	All UK		EU Non-VAT-registered[1]		EU VAT-registered		Non-EU Private		Non-EU Business	
Foreign exchange										
• Remittance commission	E	X	E	X	o/s	X	–		o/s	✓
• Exchange commission	E	X	E	X	o/s	X	–		o/s	✓
• Dealing profits/proceeds[6]	E	X	E	X	o/s	X	–		o/s	✓
Guarantees	E	X	E	X	o/s	X	o/s	✓	o/s	
Deposits	E	X	–	o/s	X	–	o/s	✓		
Loans	E	X	E	X	o/s	✓	o/s	✓	o/s	
Letter of credit	E	X	E	X	o/s	✓	o/s	✓	o/s	
Securities:										
(a) New issues										
• Arrangement fees[8]	E	X	E	X	o/s	X	–		o/s	✓
• Issue[9]	–	✓	–	✓	–	✓	–		–	✓
• Underwriting	E	X	E	X	o/s	X	–		o/s	✓
• Receiving bank fees	E	X	E	X	o/s	X	–		o/s	✓
(b) Existing shares										
• Arranging offers for sale[8]	E	X	E	X	o/s	X	o/s	✓	o/s	
• Underwriting	E	X	E	X	o/s	X	o/s	✓	o/s	
• Sale proceeds	E	X	E	X	o/s	X	o/s	✓	o/s	
• Receiving bank fees	E	X	E	X	o/s	X	o/s	✓	o/s	
Paying agents' services	SR	SR	o/s	✓	o/s	✓	o/s	✓		
Account operation	E	E	X	o/s	X	o/s	✓	o/s	✓	
Credit card charges and discounts	E	–	o/s	X	–	o/s	✓			

Notes

[1] Includes non-taxable businesses.

[2] Discounts on bills of exchanges are not the same as interest but are merely the difference between the face value of a bill and the price at which the bill is purchased by the Discount House.

[3] HMRC now accept there is a supply on the discounting or sale of a bill of exchange. The receipt of proceeds on the redemption of a bill remains outside the scope.

[4] Different treatment may be afforded to consortium/syndicated loans according to whether there is co-participation or sub-participation. With co-participation each member lends direct to the borrower; with sub-participation only the lead member will lend to the borrower – all the others will lend to the lead member. This can affect the availability of input VAT relief.

[5] Where the finance is in relation to the export of goods from the EU, relief for input VAT is given, whether the place of supply is in the UK or outside (e.g. to a VAT-registered business belonging in another member state).

[6] Foreign exchange profits are, arguably, not consideration for a supply, although the ECJ in First National Bank of Chicago v C & E Commrs (Case C-172/96) [1998] BVC 389 felt that the measure of the taxable amount in that case was effectively equal to the profit over-time. The Tribunal in the Willis Pension Trustees Ltd. case [2006] BVC 2,045 has also

found that the Trustee of a Pension Fund was not making a supply when entering into a transaction purely as a financial hedge. The only supply in this situation was made by the bank with whom the hedge was undertaken. See the commentary in Chapter 7 at Section 705(21).

[7] This heading does not cover loans evidenced by a security, e.g. loan stock or Eurobonds.

[8] The treatment shown is according to the normal rules on the place of supply and the recovery of input VAT (see chapters 3 and 7). However where the sale or issue is to someone outside the EU:
- the supply is zero-rated under VATA 1994, Sch. 8, Grp. 7, item 2(c) where the place of supply is in the UK;
- the supply is outside the scope but with the right of input VAT recovery where the place of supply is outside the UK (e.g. for a VAT-registered business belonging in another member state).

[9] In *Kretztechnik AG v Finanzamt Linz* (Case C-465/03) [2006] BVC 66 the ECJ held that the issue of shares is not, itself, a supply for VAT. The underlying input tax is normally, therefore, treated as *residual* and recoverable as for any other tax on overhead costs.

(2) Non-monetary financial services

	All UK		EU Non-VAT-registered[1]		EU VAT-registered		Non-EU Private Business			
Account preparation	SR	✓	–		o/s	✓	–		o/s	✓
Cheque books and printing										
• Ordinary	E	X	E	X	o/s	✓	o/s	✓	o/s	✓
• Decorative	SR	✓	SR	✓	o/s	✓	o/s	✓	o/s	✓
Data processing	SR	✓	SR	✓	o/s	✓	–		o/s	✓
Debt collection	SR	✓	SR	✓	o/s	✓	–		o/s	✓
Credit control	SR	✓	SR	✓	o/s	✓	–		o/s	✓
Executor and trustee services	SR	✓	SR	✓	o/s	✓	o/s	✓	o/s	✓
Financial advice	SR	✓	SR	✓	o/s	✓	o/s	✓	o/s	✓
Investment advice	SR	✓	SR	✓	o/s	✓	o/s	✓	o/s	✓
Investment brokerage[1]	E	X	E	X	o/s	X	o/s	✓	o/s	✓
Management[2]	SR	✓	SR	✓	o/s	✓	–		o/s	✓
Management consultancy	SR	✓	SR	✓	o/s	✓	–		o/s	✓
Merger and takeover advice	SR	✓	SR	✓	o/s	✓	–		o/s	✓
Nominee services	E	X	E	X	o/s	X	o/s	X	o/s	✓

Appendix 10: Examples of Typical Banking and Financial Services

	All UK		Client or customer EU Non-VAT-registered[1]		EU VAT-registered		Non-EU Private		Non-EU Business	
Portfolio/investment management										
• General	SR	✔	SR	✔	o/s	✔	–		o/s	✔
• Special Investment Funds[3]	E	X	E	X	o/s	✔	–		o/s	✔
Registration services	SR	✔	SR	✔	o/s	✔	–		o/s	✔
Safe custody[4]	SR	✔	SR	✔	SR	✔	SR	✔	SR	✔
Sales ledger accounting	SR	✔	SR	✔	o/s	✔	–		o/s	✔
Secretarial services[5]	SR	✔	SR	✔	SR	✔	–		SR	✔
Staff secondment	SR	✔	SR	✔	o/s	✔	–		o/s	✔
Taxation services	SR	✔	SR	✔	o/s	✔	o/s	✔	o/s	✔

Notes

[1] Includes non-taxable businesses.

[2] Investment brokerage may, alternatively, be zero-rated where the place of supply is in the UK and the buyer belongs outside the EU (VATA 1994, Sch. 8, Grp. 7, item 2(c)) – Appendix C.

[3] See commentary in Chapter 7 on Abbey National and J P Morgan.

[4] Management services are only treated as supplies outside the UK if they are of a kind described elsewhere in Sch. 5 (see Appendix E). Management as such is not within Sch. 5, para. 3 so that the service must be otherwise described as, say, advisory, consultancy, etc.

[5] Safe deposit facilities are specifically excluded from Sch. 5, para. 5.

[6] Secretarial services as such are not within VATA 1994, Sch. 5.

Appendix 11: Extracts from the Financial Services and Markets Act 2000

PART II – REGULATED AND PROHIBITED ACTIVITIES

The general prohibition

19 The general prohibition

19(1) No person may carry on a regulated activity in the United Kingdom, or purport to do so, unless he is–

(a) an authorised person; or
(b) an exempt person.

19(2) The prohibition is referred to in this Act as the general prohibition.

Requirement for permission

20 Authorised persons acting without permission

20(1) If an authorised person carries on a regulated activity in the United Kingdom, or purports to do so, otherwise than in accordance with permission–

(a) given to him by the Authority under Part IV, or
(b) resulting from any other provision of this Act, he is to be taken to have contravened a requirement imposed on him by the Authority under this Act.

20(2) The contravention does not–

(a) make a person guilty of an offence;
(b) make any transaction void or unenforceable; or
(c) (subject to subsection (3)) give rise to any right of action for breach of statutory duty.

20(3) In prescribed cases the contravention is actionable at the suit of a person who suffers loss as a result of the contravention, subject to the defences and other incidents applying to actions for breach of statutory duty.

Financial promotion

21 Restrictions on financial promotion

21(1) A person ('A') must not, in the course of business, communicate an invitation or inducement to engage in investment activity.

21(2) But subsection (1) does not apply if–

(a) A is an authorised person; or
(b) the content of the communication is approved for the purposes of this section by an authorised person.

21(3) In the case of a communication originating outside the United Kingdom, subsection (1) applies only if the communication is capable of having an effect in the United Kingdom.

21(4) The Treasury may by order specify circumstances in which a person is to be regarded for the purposes of subsection (1) as–

(a) acting in the course of business;
(b) not acting in the course of business.

21(5) The Treasury may by order specify circumstances (which may include compliance with financial promotion rules) in which subsection (1) does not apply.

21(6) An order under subsection (5) may, in particular, provide that subsection (1) does not apply in relation to communications–
(a) of a specified description;
(b) originating in a specified country or territory outside the United Kingdom;
(c) originating in a country or territory which falls within a specified description of country or territory outside the United Kingdom; or
(d) originating outside the United Kingdom.

21(7) The Treasury may by order repeal subsection (3).

21(8) 'Engaging in investment activity' means–
(a) entering or offering to enter into an agreement the making or performance of which by either party constitutes a controlled activity; or
(b) exercising any rights conferred by a controlled investment to acquire, dispose of, underwrite or convert a controlled investment.

21(9) An activity is a controlled activity if–
(a) it is an activity of a specified kind or one which falls within a specified class of activity; and
(b) it relates to an investment of a specified kind, or to one which falls within a specified class of investment.

21(10) An investment is a controlled investment if it is an investment of a specified kind or one which falls within a specified class of investment.

21(11) Schedule 2 (except paragraph 26) applies for the purposes of subsections (9) and (10) with references to section 22 being read as references to each of those subsections.

21(12) Nothing in Schedule 2, as applied by subsection (11), limits the powers conferred by subsection (9) or (10).

21(13) 'Communicate' includes causing a communication to be made.

21(14) 'Investment' includes any asset, right or interest.

21(15) 'Specified' means specified in an order made by the Treasury

Regulated activities

22 The classes of activity and categories of investment

22(1) An activity is a regulated activity for the purposes of this Act if it is an activity of a specified kind which is carried on by way of business and–
(a) relates to an investment of a specified kind; or
(b) in the case of an activity of a kind which is also specified for the purposes of this paragraph, is carried on in relation to property of any kind.

22(2) Schedule 2 makes provision supplementing this section.

22(3) Nothing in Schedule 2 limits the powers conferred by subsection (1).

22(4) 'Investment' includes any asset, right or interest.

22(5) 'Specified' means specified in an order made by the Treasury.

Offences

23 Contravention of the general prohibition

23(1) A person who contravenes the general prohibition is guilty of an offence and liable–
(a) on summary conviction, to imprisonment for a term not exceeding six months or a fine not exceeding the statutory maximum, or both;
(b) on conviction on indictment, to imprisonment for a term not exceeding two years or a fine, or both.

23(2) In this Act 'an authorisation offence' means an offence under this section.

23(3) In proceedings for an authorisation offence it is a defence for the accused to show that he took all reasonable precautions and exercised all due diligence to avoid committing the offence.

24 False claims to be authorised or exempt

24(1) A person who is neither an authorised person nor, in relation to the regulated activity in question, an exempt person is guilty of an offence if he–
(a) describes himself (in whatever terms) as an authorised person;
(b) describes himself (in whatever terms) as an exempt person in relation to the regulated activity; or
(c) behaves, or otherwise holds himself out, in a manner which indicates (or which is reasonably likely to be understood as indicating) that he is–
  (i) an authorised person; or
  (ii) an exempt person in relation to the regulated activity.

24(2) In proceedings for an offence under this section it is a defence for the accused to show that he took all reasonable precautions and exercised all due diligence to avoid committing the offence.

24(3) A person guilty of an offence under this section is liable on summary conviction to imprisonment for a term not exceeding six months or a fine not exceeding level 5 on the standard scale, or both.

24(4) But where the conduct constituting the offence involved or included the public display of any material, the maximum fine for the offence is level 5 on the standard scale multiplied by the number of days for which the display continued.

25 Contravention of section 21

25(1) A person who contravenes section 21(1) is guilty of an offence and liable–
(a) on summary conviction, to imprisonment for a term not exceeding six months or a fine not exceeding the statutory maximum, or both;
(b) on conviction on indictment, to imprisonment for a term not exceeding two years or a fine, or both.

25(2) In proceedings for an offence under this section it is a defence for the accused to show–
(a) that he believed on reasonable grounds that the content of the communication was prepared, or approved for the purposes of section 21, by an authorised person; or
(b) that he took all reasonable precautions and exercised all due diligence to avoid committing the offence.

Enforceability of agreements

26 Agreements made by unauthorised persons

26(1) An agreement made by a person in the course of carrying on a regulated activity in contravention of the general prohibition is unenforceable against the other party.

26(2) The other party is entitled to recover–
(a) any money or other property paid or transferred by him under the agreement; and
(b) compensation for any loss sustained by him as a result of having parted with it.

26(3) 'Agreement' means an agreement–
(a) made after this section comes into force; and
(b) the making or performance of which constitutes, or is part of, the regulated activity in question.

26(4) This section does not apply if the regulated activity is accepting deposits.

27 Agreements made through unauthorised persons

27(1) An agreement made by an authorised person ('the provider')
(a) in the course of carrying on a regulated activity (not in contravention of the general prohibition), but

(b) in consequence of something said or done by another person ('the third party') in the course of a regulated activity carried on by the third party in contravention of the general prohibition, is unenforceable against the other party.

27(2) The other party is entitled to recover–

(a) any money or other property paid or transferred by him under the agreement; and

(b) compensation for any loss sustained by him as a result of having parted with it.

27(3) 'Agreement' means an agreement–

(a) made after this section comes into force; and

(b) the making or performance of which constitutes, or is part of, the regulated activity in question carried on by the provider.

27(4) This section does not apply if the regulated activity is accepting deposits.

28 Agreements made unenforceable by section 26 or 27

28(1) This section applies to an agreement which is unenforceable because of section 26 or 27.

28(2) The amount of compensation recoverable as a result of that section is–

(a) the amount agreed by the parties; or

(b) on the application of either party, the amount determined by the court.

28(3) If the court is satisfied that it is just and equitable in the circumstances of the case, it may allow–

(a) the agreement to be enforced; or

(b) money and property paid or transferred under the agreement to be retained.

28(4) In considering whether to allow the agreement to be enforced or (as the case may be) the money or property paid or transferred under the agreement to be retained the court must–

(a) if the case arises as a result of section 26, have regard to the issue mentioned in subsection (5); or

(b) if the case arises as a result of section 27, have regard to the issue mentioned in subsection (6).

28(5) The issue is whether the person carrying on the regulated activity concerned reasonably believed that he was not contravening the general prohibition by making the agreement.

28(6) The issue is whether the provider knew that the third party was (in carrying on the regulated activity) contravening the general prohibition.

28(7) If the person against whom the agreement is unenforceable–

(a) elects not to perform the agreement, or

(b) as a result of this section, recovers money paid or other property transferred by him under the agreement,

he must repay any money and return any other property received by him under the agreement.

28(8) If property transferred under the agreement has passed to a third party, a reference in section 26 or 27 or this section to that property is to be read as a reference to its value at the time of its transfer under the agreement.

28(9) The commission of an authorisation offence does not make the agreement concerned illegal or invalid to any greater extent than is provided by section 26 or 27.

29 Accepting deposits in breach of general prohibition

29(1) This section applies to an agreement between a person ('the depositor') and another person ('the deposit-taker') made in the course of the carrying on by the deposit-taker of accepting deposits in contravention of the general prohibition.

29(2) If the depositor is not entitled under the agreement to recover without delay any money deposited by him, he may apply to the court for an order directing the deposit-taker to return the money to him.

29(3) The court need not make such an order if it is satisfied that it would not be just and equitable for the money deposited to be returned, having regard to the issue mentioned in subsection (4).

29(4) The issue is whether the deposit-taker reasonably believed that he was not contravening the general prohibition by making the agreement.

29(5) 'Agreement' means an agreement–
(a) made after this section comes into force; and
(b) the making or performance of which constitutes, or is part of, accepting deposits.

30 Enforceability of agreements resulting from unlawful communications

30(1) In this section–
- 'unlawful communication' means a communication in relation to which there has been a contravention of section 21(1);
- 'controlled agreement' means an agreement the making or performance of which by either party constitutes a controlled activity for the purposes of that section; and
- 'controlled investment' has the same meaning as in section 21.

30(2) If in consequence of an unlawful communication a person enters as a customer into a controlled agreement, it is unenforceable against him and he is entitled to recover–
(a) any money or other property paid or transferred by him under the agreement; and
(b) compensation for any loss sustained by him as a result of having parted with it.

30(3) If in consequence of an unlawful communication a person exercises any rights conferred by a controlled investment, no obligation to which he is subject as a result of exercising them is enforceable against him and he is entitled to recover–
(a) any money or other property paid or transferred by him under the obligation; and
(b) compensation for any loss sustained by him as a result of having parted with it.

30(4) But the court may allow–
(a) the agreement or obligation to be enforced, or
(b) money or property paid or transferred under the agreement or obligation to be retained,

if it is satisfied that it is just and equitable in the circumstances of the case.

30(5) In considering whether to allow the agreement or obligation to be enforced or (as the case may be) the money or property paid or transferred under the agreement to be retained the court must have regard to the issues mentioned in subsections (6) and (7).

30(6) If the applicant made the unlawful communication, the issue is whether he reasonably believed that he was not making such a communication.

30(7) If the applicant did not make the unlawful communication, the issue is whether he knew that the agreement was entered into in consequence of such a communication.

30(8) 'Applicant' means the person seeking to enforce the agreement or obligation or retain the money or property paid or transferred.

30(9) Any reference to making a communication includes causing a communication to be made.

30(10) The amount of compensation recoverable as a result of subsection (2) or (3) is–
(a) the amount agreed between the parties; or
(b) on the application of either party, the amount determined by the court.

30(11) If a person elects not to perform an agreement or an obligation which (by virtue of subsection (2) or (3)) is unenforceable against him, he must repay any money and return any other property received by him under the agreement.

30(12) If (by virtue of subsection (2) or (3)) a person recovers money paid or property transferred by him under an agreement or obligation, he must repay any money and return any other property received by him as a result of exercising the rights in question.

30(13) If any property required to be returned under this section has passed to a third party, references to that property are to be read as references to its value at the time of its receipt by the person required to return it.

PART XVII COLLECTIVE INVESTMENT SCHEMES

CHAPTER I INTERPRETATION

235   Collective investment schemes

235(1)   In this Part 'collective investment scheme' means any arrangements with respect to property of any description, including money, the purpose or effect of which is to enable persons taking part in the arrangements (whether by becoming owners of the property or any part of it or otherwise) to participate in or receive profits or income arising from the acquisition, holding, management or disposal of the property or sums paid out of such profits or income.

235(2)   The arrangements must be such that the persons who are to participate ('participants') do not have day-to-day control over the management of the property, whether or not they have the right to be consulted or to give directions.

235(3)   The arrangements must also have either or both of the following characteristics–
(a)   the contributions of the participants and the profits or income out of which payments are to be made to them are pooled;
(b)   the property is managed as a whole by or on behalf of the operator of the scheme.

235(4)   If arrangements provide for such pooling as is mentioned in subsection (3)(a) in relation to separate parts of the property, the arrangements are not to be regarded as constituting a single collective investment scheme unless the participants are entitled to exchange rights in one part for rights in another.

235(5)   The Treasury may by order provide that arrangements do not amount to a collective investment scheme–
(a)   in specified circumstances; or
(b)   if the arrangements fall within a specified category of arrangement.

236   Open-ended investment companies

236(1)   In this Part 'an open-ended investment company' means a collective investment scheme which satisfies both the property condition and the investment condition.

236(2)   The property condition is that the property belongs beneficially to, and is managed by or on behalf of, a body corporate ('BC') having as its purpose the investment of its funds with the aim of–
(a)   spreading investment risk; and
(b)   giving its members the benefit of the results of the management of those funds by or on behalf of that body.

236(3)   The investment condition is that, in relation to BC, a reasonable investor would, if he were to participate in the scheme–
(a)   expect that he would be able to realize, within a period appearing to him to be reasonable, his investment in the scheme (represented, at any given time, by the value of shares in, or securities of, BC held by him as a participant in the scheme); and
(b)   be satisfied that his investment would be realized on a basis calculated wholly or mainly by reference to the value of property in respect of which the scheme makes arrangements.

236(4)   In determining whether the investment condition is satisfied, no account is to be taken of any actual or potential redemption or repurchase of shares or securities under–
(a)   Chapter VII of Part V of the [1985 c.6.] Companies Act 1985;

(b) Chapter VII of Part VI of the [S.I.1986/1032 (N.I.6.)] Companies (Northern Ireland) Order 1986;
(c) corresponding provisions in force in another EEA State; or
(d) provisions in force in a country or territory other than an EEA state which the Treasury have, by order, designated as corresponding provisions.

236(5) The Treasury may by order amend the definition of 'an open-ended investment company' for the purposes of this Part.

237 Other definitions

237(1) In this Part 'unit trust scheme' means a collective investment scheme under which the property is held on trust for the participants.

237(2) In this Part–

- 'trustee', in relation to a unit trust scheme, means the person holding the property in question on trust for the participants;
- 'depositary', in relation to–

a collective investment scheme which is constituted by a body incorporated by virtue of regulations under section 262, or

any other collective investment scheme which is not a unit trust scheme, means any person to whom the property subject to the scheme is entrusted for safekeeping;

'**the operator**', in relation to a unit trust scheme with a separate trustee, means the manager and in relation to an open-ended investment company, means that company;

'**units**'
means the rights or interests (however described) of the participants in a collective investment scheme.

237(3) In this Part–

'**an authorised unit trust scheme**' means a unit trust scheme which is authorised for the purposes of this Act by an authorisation order in force under section 243;

'**an authorised open-ended investment company**' means a body incorporated by virtue of regulations under section 262 in respect of which an authorisation order is in force under any provision made in such regulations by virtue of subsection (2)(l) of that section;

'**a recognised scheme**' means a scheme recognised under section 264, 270 or 272.

CHAPTER II RESTRICTIONS ON PROMOTION

238 Restrictions on promotion

238(1) An authorised person must not communicate an invitation or inducement to participate in a collective investment scheme.

238(2) But that is subject to the following provisions of this section and to section 239.

238(3) Subsection (1) applies in the case of a communication originating outside the United Kingdom only if the communication is capable of having an effect in the United Kingdom.

238(4) Subsection (1) does not apply in relation to–
(a) an authorised unit trust scheme;
(b) a scheme constituted by an authorised open-ended investment company; or
(c) a recognised scheme.

238(5) Subsection (1) does not apply to anything done in accordance with rules made by the Authority for the purpose of exempting from that subsection the promotion otherwise than to the general public of schemes of specified descriptions.

238(6) The Treasury may by order specify circumstances in which subsection (1) does not apply.

238(7) An order under subsection (6) may, in particular, provide that subsection (1) does not apply in relation to communications–
(a) of a specified description;
(b) originating in a specified country or territory outside the United Kingdom;
(c) originating in a country or territory which falls within a specified description of country or territory outside the United Kingdom; or
(d) originating outside the United Kingdom.

238(8) The Treasury may by order repeal subsection (3).

238(9) 'Communicate' includes causing a communication to be made.

238(10) 'Promotion otherwise than to the general public' includes promotion in a way designed to reduce, so far as possible, the risk of participation by persons for whom participation would be unsuitable.

238(11) 'Participate', in relation to a collective investment scheme, means become a participant (within the meaning given by section 235(2)) in the scheme.

239 Single property schemes

239(1) The Treasury may by regulations make provision for exempting single property schemes from section 238(1).

239(2) For the purposes of subsection (1) a single property scheme is a scheme which has the characteristics mentioned in subsection (3) and satisfies such other requirements as are prescribed by the regulations conferring the exemption.

239(3) The characteristics are–
(a) that the property subject to the scheme (apart from cash or other assets held for management purposes) consists of–
   (i) a single building (or a single building with ancillary buildings) managed by or on behalf of the operator of the scheme, or
   (ii) a group of adjacent or contiguous buildings managed by him or on his behalf as a single enterprise, with or without ancillary land and with or without furniture, fittings or other contents of the building or buildings in question; and
(b) that the units of the participants in the scheme are either dealt in on a recognised investment exchange or offered on terms such that any agreement for their acquisition is conditional on their admission to dealings on such an exchange.

239(4) If regulations are made under subsection (1), the Authority may make rules imposing duties or liabilities on the operator and (if any) the trustee or depositary of a scheme exempted by the regulations.

239(5) The rules may include, to such extent as the Authority thinks appropriate, provision for purposes corresponding to those for which provision can be made under section 248 in relation to authorised unit trust schemes.

240 Restriction on approval of promotion

240(1) An authorised person may not approve for the purposes of section 21 the content of a communication relating to a collective investment scheme if he would be prohibited by section 238(1) from effecting the communication himself or from causing it to be communicated.

240(2) For the purposes of determining in any case whether there has been a contravention of section 21(1), an approval given in contravention of subsection (1) is to be regarded as not having been given.

241 Actions for damages

241 If an authorised person contravenes a requirement imposed on him by section 238 or 240, section 150 applies to the contravention as it applies to a contravention mentioned in that section.

CHAPTER III AUTHORISED UNIT TRUST SCHEMES

Applications for authorisation

242 Applications for authorisation of unit trust schemes

242(1) Any application for an order declaring a unit trust scheme to be an authorised unit trust scheme must be made to the Authority by the manager and trustee, or proposed manager and trustee, of the scheme.

242(2) The manager and trustee (or proposed manager and trustee) must be different persons.

242(3) The application–
(a) must be made in such manner as the Authority may direct; and
(b) must contain or be accompanied by such information as the Authority may reasonably require for the purpose of determining the application.

242(4) At any time after receiving an application and before determining it, the Authority may require the applicants to provide it with such further information as it reasonably considers necessary to enable it to determine the application.

242(5) Different directions may be given, and different requirements imposed, in relation to different applications.

242(6) The Authority may require applicants to present information which they are required to give under this section in such form, or to verify it in such a way, as the Authority may direct.

243 Authorisation orders

243(1) If, on an application under section 242 in respect of a unit trust scheme, the Authority—
(a) is satisfied that the scheme complies with the requirements set out in this section,
(b) is satisfied that the scheme complies with the requirements of the trust scheme rules, and
(c) has been provided with a copy of the trust deed and a certificate signed by a solicitor to the effect that it complies with such of the requirements of this section or those rules as relate to its contents,the Authority may make an order declaring the scheme to be an authorised unit trust scheme.

243(2) If the Authority makes an order under subsection (1), it must give written notice of the order to the applicant.

243(3) In this Chapter 'authorisation order' means an order under subsection (1).

243(4) The manager and the trustee must be persons who are independent of each other.

243(5) The manager and the trustee must each—
(a) be a body corporate incorporated in the United Kingdom or another EEA State, and
(b) have a place of business in the United Kingdom,and the affairs of each must be administered in the country in which it is incorporated.

243(6) If the manager is incorporated in another EEA State, the scheme must not be one which satisfies the requirements prescribed for the purposes of section 264.

243(7) The manager and the trustee must each be an authorised person and the manager must have permission to act as manager and the trustee must have permission to act as trustee.

243(8) The name of the scheme must not be undesirable or misleading.

243(9) The purposes of the scheme must be reasonably capable of being successfully carried into effect.

243(10) The participants must be entitled to have their units redeemed in accordance with the scheme at a price—
(a) related to the net value of the property to which the units relate; and
(b) determined in accordance with the scheme.

243(11) But a scheme is to be treated as complying with subsection (10) if it requires the manager to ensure that a participant is able to sell his units on an investment exchange at a price not significantly different from that mentioned in that subsection.

244 Determination of applications

244(1) An application under section 242 must be determined by the Authority before the end of the period of six months beginning with the date on which it receives the completed application.

244(2) The Authority may determine an incomplete application if it considers it appropriate to do so; and it must in any event determine such an application within twelve months beginning with the date on which it first receives the application.

244(3) The applicant may withdraw his application, by giving the Authority written notice, at any time before the Authority determines it.

Applications refused

245 Procedure when refusing an application

245(1) If the Authority proposes to refuse an application made under section 242 it must give each of the applicants a warning notice.

245(2) If the Authority decides to refuse the application—
(a) it must give each of the applicants a decision notice; and
(b) either applicant may refer the matter to the Tribunal.

Certificates

246 Certificates

246(1) If the manager or trustee of a unit trust scheme which complies with the conditions necessary for it to enjoy the rights conferred by any relevant Community instrument so requests, the Authority may issue a certificate to the effect that the scheme complies with those conditions.

246(2) Such a certificate may be issued on the making of an authorisation order in respect of the scheme or at any subsequent time.

Rules

247 Trust scheme rules

247(1) The Authority may make rules ('trust scheme rules') as to
(a) the constitution, management and operation of authorised unit trust schemes;
(b) the powers, duties, rights and liabilities of the manager and trustee of any such scheme;
(c) the rights and duties of the participants in any such scheme; and
(d) the winding up of any such scheme.

247(2) Trust scheme rules may, in particular, make provision—
(a) as to the issue and redemption of the units under the scheme;
(b) as to the expenses of the scheme and the means of meeting them;
(c) for the appointment, removal, powers and duties of an auditor for the scheme;
(d) for restricting or regulating the investment and borrowing powers exercisable in relation to the scheme;
(e) requiring the keeping of records with respect to the transactions and financial position of the scheme and for the inspection of those records;
(f) requiring the preparation of periodical reports with respect to the scheme and the provision of those reports to the participants and to the Authority; and
(g) with respect to the amendment of the scheme.

247(3) Trust scheme rules may make provision as to the contents of the trust deed, including provision requiring any of the matters mentioned in subsection (2) to be dealt with in the deed.

247(4) But trust scheme rules are binding on the manager, trustee and participants independently of the contents of the trust deed and, in the case of the participants, have effect as if contained in it.

247(5) If—

(a) a modification is made of the statutory provisions in force in Great Britain or Northern Ireland relating to companies,
(b) the modification relates to the rights and duties of persons who hold the beneficial title to any shares in a company without also holding the legal title, and
(c) it appears to the Treasury that, for the purpose of assimilating the law relating to authorised unit trust schemes to the law relating to companies as so modified, it is expedient to modify the rule-making powers conferred on the Authority by this section,

the Treasury may by order make such modifications of those powers as they consider appropriate.

248 Scheme particulars rules

248(1) The Authority may make rules ('scheme particulars rules') requiring the manager of an authorised unit trust scheme—
(a) to submit scheme particulars to the Authority; and
(b) to publish scheme particulars or make them available to the public on request.

248(2) **'Scheme particulars'** means particulars in such form, containing such information about the scheme and complying with such requirements, as are specified in scheme particulars rules.

248(3) Scheme particulars rules may require the manager of an authorised unit trust scheme to submit, and to publish or make available, revised or further scheme particulars if there is a significant change affecting any matter—
(a) which is contained in scheme particulars previously published or made available; and
(b) whose inclusion in those particulars was required by the rules.

248(4) Scheme particulars rules may require the manager of an authorised unit trust scheme to submit, and to publish or make available, revised or further scheme particulars if—
(a) a significant new matter arises; and
(b) the inclusion of information in respect of that matter would have been required in previous particulars if it had arisen when those particulars were prepared.

248(5) Scheme particulars rules may provide for the payment, by the person or persons who in accordance with the rules are treated as responsible for any scheme particulars, of compensation to any qualifying person who has suffered loss as a result of—
(a) any untrue or misleading statement in the particulars; or
(b) the omission from them of any matter required by the rules to be included.

248(6) **'Qualifying person'** means a person who—
(a) has become or agreed to become a participant in the scheme; or
(b) although not being a participant, has a beneficial interest in units in the scheme.

248(7) Scheme particulars rules do not affect any liability which any person may incur apart from the rules.

249 Disqualification of auditor for breach of trust scheme rules

249(1) If it appears to the Authority that an auditor has failed to comply with a duty imposed on him by trust scheme rules, it may disqualify him from being the auditor for any authorised unit trust scheme or authorised open-ended investment company.

249(2) Subsections (2) to (5) of section 345 have effect in relation to disqualification under subsection (1) as they have effect in relation to disqualification under subsection (1) of that section.

250 Modification or waiver of rules

250(1) In this section **'rules'** means—
(a) trust scheme rules; or
(b) scheme particulars rules.

250(2) The Authority may, on the application or with the consent of any person to whom any rules apply, direct that all or any of the rules—
(a) are not to apply to him as respects a particular scheme; or
(b) are to apply to him, as respects a particular scheme, with such modifications as may be specified in the direction.

250(3) The Authority may, on the application or with the consent of the manager and trustee of a particular scheme acting jointly, direct that all or any of the rules—
(a) are not to apply to the scheme; or
(b) are to apply to the scheme with such modifications as may be specified in the direction.

250(4) Subsections (3) to (9) and (11) of section 148 have effect in relation to a direction under subsection (2) as they have effect in relation to a direction under section 148(2) but with the following modifications—
(a) subsection (4)(a) is to be read as if the words 'by the authorised person' were omitted;
(b) any reference to the authorised person (except in subsection (4)(a)) is to be read as a reference to the person mentioned in subsection (2); and
(c) subsection (7)(b) is to be read, in relation to a participant of the scheme, as if the word 'commercial' were omitted.

250(5) Subsections (3) to (9) and (11) of section 148 have effect in relation to a direction under subsection (3) as they have effect in relation to a direction under section 148(2) but with the following modifications—
(a) subsection (4)(a) is to be read as if the words 'by the authorised person' were omitted;
(b) subsections (7)(b) and (11) are to be read as if references to the authorised person were references to each of the manager and the trustee of the scheme;
(c) subsection (7)(b) is to be read, in relation to a participant of the scheme, as if the word 'commercial' were omitted;
(d) subsection (8) is to be read as if the reference to the authorised person concerned were a reference to the scheme concerned and to its manager and trustee; and
(e) subsection (9) is to be read as if the reference to the authorised person were a reference to the manager and trustee of the scheme acting jointly.

Alterations

251 Alteration of schemes and changes of manager or trustee

251(1) The manager of an authorised unit trust scheme must give written notice to the Authority of any proposal to alter the scheme or to replace its trustee.

251(2) Any notice given in respect of a proposal to alter the scheme involving a change in the trust deed must be accompanied by a certificate signed by a solicitor to the effect that the change will not affect the compliance of the deed with the trust scheme rules.

251(3) The trustee of an authorised unit trust scheme must give written notice to the Authority of any proposal to replace the manager of the scheme.

251(4) Effect is not to be given to any proposal of which notice has been given under subsection (1) or (3) unless—
(a) the Authority, by written notice, has given its approval to the proposal; or
(b) one month, beginning with the date on which the notice was given, has expired without the manager or trustee having received from the Authority a warning notice under section 252 in respect of the proposal.

251(5) The Authority must not approve a proposal to replace the manager or the trustee of an authorised unit trust scheme unless it is satisfied that, if the proposed replacement is made, the scheme will continue to comply with the requirements of section 243(4) to (7).

252 Procedure when refusing approval of change of manager or trustee

252(1) If the Authority proposes to refuse approval of a proposal to replace the trustee or manager of an authorised unit trust scheme, it must give a warning notice to the person by whom notice of the proposal was given under section 251(1) or (3).

252(2) If the Authority proposes to refuse approval of a proposal to alter an authorised unit trust scheme it must give separate warning notices to the manager and the trustee of the scheme.

252(3) To be valid the warning notice must be received by that person before the end of one month beginning with the date on which notice of the proposal was given.

252(4) If, having given a warning notice to a person, the Authority decides to refuse approval—
(a) it must give him a decision notice; and
(b) he may refer the matter to the Tribunal.

Exclusion clauses

253 Avoidance of exclusion clauses

253 Any provision of the trust deed of an authorised unit trust scheme is void in so far as it would have the effect of exempting the manager or trustee from liability for any failure to exercise due care and diligence in the discharge of his functions in respect of the scheme.

Ending of authorisation

254 Revocation of authorisation order otherwise than by consent

254(1) An authorisation order may be revoked by an order made by the Authority if it appears to the Authority that—
(a) one or more of the requirements for the making of the order are no longer satisfied;
(b) the manager or trustee of the scheme concerned has contravened a requirement imposed on him by or under this Act;
(c) the manager or trustee of the scheme has, in purported compliance with any such requirement, knowingly or recklessly given the Authority information which is false or misleading in a material particular;
(d) no regulated activity is being carried on in relation to the scheme and the period of that inactivity began at least twelve months earlier; or
(e) none of paragraphs (a) to (d) applies, but it is desirable to revoke the authorisation order in order to protect the interests of participants or potential participants in the scheme.

254(2) For the purposes of subsection (1)(e), the Authority may take into account any matter relating to—
(a) the scheme;
(b) the manager or trustee;
(c) any person employed by or associated with the manager or trustee in connection with the scheme;
(d) any director of the manager or trustee;
(e) any person exercising influence over the manager or trustee;
(f) any body corporate in the same group as the manager or trustee;
(g) any director of any such body corporate;
(h) any person exercising influence over any such body corporate.

255 Procedure

255(1) If the Authority proposes to make an order under section 254 revoking an authorisation order ('a revoking order'), it must give separate warning notices to the manager and the trustee of the scheme.

255(2) If the Authority decides to make a revoking order, it must without delay give each of them a decision notice and either of them may refer the matter to the Tribunal.

256 Requests for revocation of authorisation order

256(1) An authorisation order may be revoked by an order made by the Authority at the request of the manager or trustee of the scheme concerned.

256(2) If the Authority makes an order under subsection (1), it must give written notice of the order to the manager and trustee of the scheme concerned.

256(3) The Authority may refuse a request to make an order under this section if it considers that—
(a) the public interest requires that any matter concerning the scheme should be investigated before a decision is taken as to whether the authorisation order should be revoked; or
(b) revocation would not be in the interests of the participants or would be incompatible with a Community obligation.

256(4) If the Authority proposes to refuse a request under this section, it must give separate warning notices to the manager and the trustee of the scheme.

256(5) If the Authority decides to refuse the request, it must without delay give each of them a decision notice and either of them may refer the matter to the Tribunal.

Powers of intervention

257 Directions

257(1) The Authority may give a direction under this section if it appears to the Authority that—
(a) one or more of the requirements for the making of an authorisation order are no longer satisfied;
(b) the manager or trustee of an authorised unit trust scheme has contravened, or is likely to contravene, a requirement imposed on him by or under this Act;
(c) the manager or trustee of such a scheme has, in purported compliance with any such requirement, knowingly or recklessly given the Authority information which is false or misleading in a material particular; or
(d) none of paragraphs (a) to (c) applies, but it is desirable to give a direction in order to protect the interests of participants or potential participants in such a scheme.

257(2) A direction under this section may–
(a) require the manager of the scheme to cease the issue or redemption, or both the issue and redemption, of units under the scheme;
(b) require the manager and trustee of the scheme to wind it up.

257(3) If the authorisation order is revoked, the revocation does not affect any direction under this section which is then in force.

257(4) A direction may be given under this section in relation to a scheme in the case of which the authorisation order has been revoked if a direction under this section was already in force at the time of revocation.

257(5) If a person contravenes a direction under this section, section 150 applies to the contravention as it applies to a contravention mentioned in that section.

257(6) The Authority may, either on its own initiative or on the application of the manager or trustee of the scheme concerned, revoke or vary a direction given under this section if it appears to the Authority–
(a) in the case of revocation, that it is no longer necessary for the direction to take effect or continue in force;
(b) in the case of variation, that the direction should take effect or continue in force in a different form.

258 Applications to the court

258(1) If the Authority could give a direction under section 257, it may also apply to the court for an order–
(a) removing the manager or the trustee, or both the manager and the trustee, of the scheme; and
(b) replacing the person or persons removed with a suitable person or persons nominated by the Authority.

258(2) The Authority may nominate a person for the purposes of subsection (1)(b) only if it is satisfied that, if the order was made, the requirements of section 243(4) to (7) would be complied with.

258(3) If it appears to the Authority that there is no person it can nominate for the purposes of subsection (1)(b), it may apply to the court for an order–
(a) removing the manager or the trustee, or both the manager and the trustee, of the scheme; and
(b) appointing an authorised person to wind up the scheme.

258(4) On an application under this section the court may make such order as it thinks fit.

258(5) The court may, on the application of the Authority, rescind any such order as is mentioned in subsection (3) and substitute such an order as is mentioned in subsection (1).

258(6) The Authority must give written notice of the making of an application under this section to the manager and trustee of the scheme concerned.

258(7) The jurisdiction conferred by this section may be exercised by–
(a) the High Court;
(b) in Scotland, the Court of Session.

259 Procedure on giving directions under section 257 and varying them on Authority's own initiative

259(1) A direction takes effect–
(a) immediately, if the notice given under subsection (3) states that that is the case;
(b) on such date as may be specified in the notice; or
(c) if no date is specified in the notice, when the matter to which it relates is no longer open to review.

259(2) A direction may be expressed to take effect immediately (or on a specified date) only if the Authority, having regard to the ground on which it is exercising its power under section 257, considers that it is necessary for the direction to take effect immediately (or on that date).

259(3) If the Authority proposes to give a direction under section 257, or gives such a direction with immediate effect, it must give separate written notice to the manager and the trustee of the scheme concerned.

259(4) The notice must–
(a) give details of the direction;
(b) inform the person to whom it is given of when the direction takes effect;
(c) state the Authority's reasons for giving the direction and for its determination as to when the direction takes effect;
(d) inform the person to whom it is given that he may make representations to the Authority within such period as may be specified in it (whether or not he has referred the matter to the Tribunal); and
(e) inform him of his right to refer the matter to the Tribunal.

259(5) If the direction imposes a requirement under section 257(2)(a), the notice must state that the requirement has effect until–
(a) a specified date; or
(b) a further direction.

259(6) If the direction imposes a requirement under section 257(2)(b), the scheme must be wound up–
(a) by a date specified in the notice; or
(b) if no date is specified, as soon as practicable.

259(7) The Authority may extend the period allowed under the notice for making representations.

259(8) If, having considered any representations made by a person to whom the notice was given, the Authority decides–
(a) to give the direction in the way proposed, or
(b) if it has been given, not to revoke the direction, it must give separate written notice to the manager and the trustee of the scheme concerned.

259(9) If, having considered any representations made by a person to whom the notice was given, the Authority decides–
(a) not to give the direction in the way proposed,
(b) to give the direction in a way other than that proposed, or
(c) to revoke a direction which has effect, it must give separate written notice to the manager and the trustee of the scheme concerned.

259(10) A notice given under subsection (8) must inform the person to whom it is given of his right to refer the matter to the Tribunal.

259(11) A notice under subsection (9)(b) must comply with subsection (4).

259(12) If a notice informs a person of his right to refer a matter to the Tribunal, it must give an indication of the procedure on such a reference.

259(13) This section applies to the variation of a direction on the Authority's own initiative as it applies to the giving of a direction.

259(14) For the purposes of subsection (1)(c), whether a matter is open to review is to be determined in accordance with section 391(8).

260 Procedure: refusal to revoke or vary direction

260(1) If on an application under section 257(6) for a direction to be revoked or varied the Authority proposes–
(a) to vary the direction otherwise than in accordance with the application, or
(b) to refuse to revoke or vary the direction, it must give the applicant a warning notice.

260(2) If the Authority decides to refuse to revoke or vary the direction–
(a) it must give the applicant a decision notice; and
(b) the applicant may refer the matter to the Tribunal.

261 Procedure: revocation of direction and grant of request for variation

261(1) If the Authority decides on its own initiative to revoke a direction under section 257 it must give separate written notices of its decision to the manager and trustee of the scheme.

261(2) If on an application under section 257(6) for a direction to be revoked or varied the Authority decides to revoke the direction or vary it in accordance with the application, it must give the applicant written notice of its decision.

261(3) A notice under this section must specify the date on which the decision takes effect.

261(4) The Authority may publish such information about the revocation or variation, in such way, as it considers appropriate.

CHAPTER IV OPEN-ENDED INVESTMENT COMPANIES

262 Open-ended investment companies

262(1) The Treasury may by regulations make provision for–
(a) facilitating the carrying on of collective investment by means of open-ended investment companies;
(b) regulating such companies.

262(2) The regulations may, in particular, make provision–
(a) for the incorporation and registration in Great Britain of bodies corporate;
(b) for a body incorporated by virtue of the regulations to take such form as may be determined in accordance with the regulations;
(c) as to the purposes for which such a body may exist, the investments which it may issue and otherwise as to its constitution;
(d) as to the management and operation of such a body and the management of its property;
(e) as to the powers, duties, rights and liabilities of such a body and of other persons, including–
   (i) the directors or sole director of such a body;
   (ii) its depositary (if any);
   (iii) its shareholders, and persons who hold the beneficial title to shares in it without holding the legal title;
   (iv) its auditor; and
   (v) any persons who act or purport to act on its behalf;
(f) as to the merger of one or more such bodies and the division of such a body;
(g) for the appointment and removal of an auditor for such a body;
(h) as to the winding up and dissolution of such a body;
(i) for such a body, or any director or depositary of such a body, to be required to comply with directions given by the Authority;
(j) enabling the Authority to apply to a court for an order removing and replacing any director or depositary of such a body;
(k) for the carrying out of investigations by persons appointed by the Authority or the Secretary of State;
(l) corresponding to any provision made in relation to unit trust schemes by Chapter III of this Part.

262(3) Regulations under this section may–
(a) impose criminal liability;
(b) confer functions on the Authority;
(c) in the case of provision made by virtue of subsection (2)(l), authorise the making of rules by the Authority;
(d) confer jurisdiction on any court or on the Tribunal;
(e) provide for fees to be charged by the Authority in connection with the carrying out of any of its functions under the regulations (including fees payable on a periodical basis);
(f) modify, exclude or apply (with or without modifications) any primary or subordinate legislation (including any provision of, or made under, this Act);
(g) make consequential amendments, repeals and revocations of any such legislation;
(h) modify or exclude any rule of law.

262(4) The provision that may be made by virtue of subsection (3)(f) includes provision extending or adapting any power to make subordinate legislation.

262(5) Regulations under this section may, in particular–
(a) revoke the [S.I. 1996/2827.] Open-Ended Investment Companies (Investment Companies with Variable Capital) Regulations 1996; and

(b) provide for things done under or in accordance with those regulations to be treated as if they had been done under or in accordance with regulations under this section.

263 Amendment of section 716 Companies Act 1985

263 In section 716(1) of the [1985 c. 6.] Companies Act 1985 (prohibition on formation of companies with more than 20 members unless registered under the Act etc.), after 'this Act,' insert 'is incorporated by virtue of regulations made under section 262 of the Financial Services and Markets Act 2000'.

CHAPTER V RECOGNISED OVERSEAS SCHEMES

Schemes constituted in other EEA States

264 Schemes constituted in other EEA States

264(1) A collective investment scheme constituted in another EEA State is a recognised scheme if–
(a) it satisfies such requirements as are prescribed for the purposes of this section; and
(b) not less than two months before inviting persons in the United Kingdom to become participants in the scheme, the operator of the scheme gives notice to the Authority of his intention to do so, specifying the way in which the invitation is to be made.

264(2) But this section does not make the scheme a recognised scheme if within two months of receiving the notice under subsection (1) the Authority notifies–
(a) the operator of the scheme, and
(b) the authorities of the State in question who are responsible for the authorisation of collective investment schemes, that the way in which the invitation is to be made does not comply with the law in force in the United Kingdom.

264(3) The notice to be given to the Authority under subsection (1)–
(a) must be accompanied by a certificate from the authorities mentioned in subsection (2)(b) to the effect that the scheme complies with the conditions necessary for it to enjoy the rights conferred by any relevant Community instrument;
(b) must contain the address of a place in the United Kingdom for the service on the operator of notices or other documents required or authorised to be served on him under this Act; and
(c) must contain or be accompanied by such other information and documents as may be prescribed.

264(4) A notice given by the Authority under subsection (2) must–
(a) give the reasons for which the Authority considers that the law in force in the United Kingdom will not be complied with; and
(b) specify a reasonable period (which may not be less than 28 days) within which any person to whom it is given may make representations to the Authority.

264(5) For the purposes of this section a collective investment scheme is constituted in another EEA State if–
(a) it is constituted under the law of that State by a contract or under a trust and is managed by a body corporate incorporated under that law; or
(b) it takes the form of an open-ended investment company incorporated under that law.

264(6) The operator of a recognised scheme may give written notice to the Authority that he desires the scheme to be no longer recognised by virtue of this section.

264(7) On the giving of notice under subsection (6), the scheme ceases to be a recognised scheme.

265 Representations and references to the Tribunal

265(1) This section applies if any representations are made to the Authority, before the period for making representations has ended, by a person to whom a notice was given by the Authority under section 264(2).

265(2) The Authority must, within a reasonable period, decide in the light of those representations whether or not to withdraw its notice.

265(3) If the Authority withdraws its notice the scheme is a recognised scheme from the date on which the notice is withdrawn.

265(4) If the Authority decides not to withdraw its notice, it must give a decision notice to each person to whom the notice under section 264(2) was given.

265(5) The operator of the scheme to whom the decision notice is given may refer the matter to the Tribunal.

266 Disapplication of rules

266(1) Apart from–
(a) financial promotion rules, and
(b) rules under section 283(1),rules made by the Authority under this Act do not apply to the operator, trustee or depositary of a scheme in relation to the carrying on by him of regulated activities for which he has permission in that capacity.

266(2) 'Scheme' means a scheme which is a recognised scheme by virtue of section 264.

267 Power of Authority to suspend promotion of scheme

267(1) Subsection (2) applies if it appears to the Authority that the operator of a scheme has communicated an invitation or inducement in relation to the scheme in a manner contrary to financial promotion rules.

267(2) The Authority may direct that–
(a) the exemption from subsection (1) of section 238 provided by subsection (4)(c) of that section is not to apply in relation to the scheme; and
(b) subsection (5) of that section does not apply with respect to things done in relation to the scheme.

267(3) A direction under subsection (2) has effect–
(a) for a specified period;
(b) until the occurrence of a specified event; or
(c) until specified conditions are complied with.

267(4) The Authority may, either on its own initiative or on the application of the operator of the scheme concerned, vary a direction given under subsection (2) if it appears to the Authority that the direction should take effect or continue in force in a different form.

267(5) The Authority may, either on its own initiative or on the application of the operator of the recognised scheme concerned, revoke a direction given under subsection (2) if it appears to the Authority–
(a) that the conditions specified in the direction have been complied with; or
(b) that it is no longer necessary for the direction to take effect or continue in force.

267(6) If an event is specified, the direction ceases to have effect (unless revoked earlier) on the occurrence of that event.

267(7) For the purposes of this section and sections 268 and 269–
(a) the scheme's home State is the EEA State in which the scheme is constituted (within the meaning given by section 264);
(b) the competent authorities in the scheme's home State are the authorities in that State who are responsible for the authorisation of collective investment schemes.

267(8) 'Scheme' means a scheme which is a recognised scheme by virtue of section 264.

267(9) 'Specified', in relation to a direction, means specified in it.

268 Procedure on giving directions under section 267 and varying them on Authority's own initiative

268(1) A direction under section 267 takes effect–
(a) immediately, if the notice given under subsection (3)(a) states that that is the case;
(b) on such date as may be specified in the notice; or
(c) if no date is specified in the notice, when the matter to which it relates is no longer open to review.

268(2) A direction may be expressed to take effect immediately (or on a specified date) only if the Authority, having regard to its reasons for exercising its power under section 267, considers that it is necessary for the direction to take effect immediately (or on that date).

268(3) If the Authority proposes to give a direction under section 267, or gives such a direction with immediate effect, it must–
(a) give the operator of the scheme concerned written notice; and
(b) inform the competent authorities in the scheme's home State of its proposal or (as the case may be) of the direction.

268(4) The notice must–
(a) give details of the direction;
(b) inform the operator of when the direction takes effect;
(c) state the Authority's reasons for giving the direction and for its determination as to when the direction takes effect;
(d) inform the operator that he may make representations to the Authority within such period as may be specified in it (whether or not he has referred the matter to the Tribunal); and
(e) inform him of his right to refer the matter to the Tribunal.

268(5) The Authority may extend the period allowed under the notice for making representations.

268(6) Subsection (7) applies if, having considered any representations made by the operator, the Authority decides–
(a) to give the direction in the way proposed, or
(b) if it has been given, not to revoke the direction.

268(7) The Authority must–
(a) give the operator of the scheme concerned written notice; and
(b) inform the competent authorities in the scheme's home State of the direction.

268(8) Subsection (9) applies if, having considered any representations made by a person to whom the notice was given, the Authority decides–
(a) not to give the direction in the way proposed,
(b) to give the direction in a way other than that proposed, or
(c) to revoke a direction which has effect.

268(9) The Authority must–
(a) give the operator of the scheme concerned written notice; and
(b) inform the competent authorities in the scheme's home State of its decision.

268(10) A notice given under subsection (7)(a) must inform the operator of his right to refer the matter to the Tribunal.

268(11) A notice under subsection (9)(a) given as a result of subsection (8)(b) must comply with subsection (4).

268(12) If a notice informs a person of his right to refer a matter to the Tribunal, it must give an indication of the procedure on such a reference.

268(13) This section applies to the variation of a direction on the Authority's own initiative as it applies to the giving of a direction.

268(14) For the purposes of subsection (1)(c), whether a matter is open to review is to be determined in accordance with section 391(8).

269 Procedure on application for variation or revocation of direction

269(1) If, on an application under subsection (4) or (5) of section 267, the Authority proposes–
(a) to vary a direction otherwise than in accordance with the application, or
(b) to refuse the application, it must give the operator of the scheme concerned a warning notice.

269(2) If, on such an application, the Authority decides–
(a) to vary a direction otherwise than in accordance with the application, or
(b) to refuse the application, it must give the operator of the scheme concerned a decision notice.

269(3) If the application is refused, the operator of the scheme may refer the matter to the Tribunal.

269(4) If, on such an application, the Authority decides to grant the application it must give the operator of the scheme concerned written notice.

269(5) If the Authority decides on its own initiative to revoke a direction given under section 267 it must give the operator of the scheme concerned written notice.

269(6) The Authority must inform the competent authorities in the scheme's home State of any notice given under this section.

Schemes authorised in designated countries or territories

270 Schemes authorised in designated countries or territories

270(1) A collective investment scheme which is not a recognised scheme by virtue of section 264 but is managed in, and authorised under the law of, a country or territory outside the United Kingdom is a recognised scheme if–
(a) that country or territory is designated for the purposes of this section by an order made by the Treasury;
(b) the scheme is of a class specified by the order;
(c) the operator of the scheme has given written notice to the Authority that he wishes it to be recognised; and
(d) either–
　(i) the Authority, by written notice, has given its approval to the scheme's being recognised; or
　(ii) two months, beginning with the date on which notice was given under paragraph (c), have expired without the operator receiving a warning notice from the Authority under section 271.

270(2) The Treasury may not make an order designating any country or territory for the purposes of this section unless satisfied–
(a) that the law and practice under which relevant collective investment schemes are authorised and supervised in that country or territory affords to investors in the United Kingdom protection at least equivalent to that provided for them by or under this Part in the case of comparable authorised schemes; and
(b) that adequate arrangements exist, or will exist, for co-operation between the authorities of the country or territory responsible for the authorisation and supervision of relevant collective investment schemes and the Authority.

270(3) 'Relevant collective investment schemes' means collective investment schemes of the class or classes to be specified by the order.

270(4) 'Comparable authorised schemes' means whichever of the following the Treasury consider to be the most appropriate, having regard to the class or classes of scheme to be specified by the order–
(a) authorised unit trust schemes;
(b) authorised open-ended investment companies;
(c) both such unit trust schemes and such companies.

270(5) If the Treasury are considering whether to make an order designating a country or territory for the purposes of this section–
(a) the Treasury must ask the Authority for a report–
  (i) on the law and practice of that country or territory in relation to the authorisation and supervision of relevant collective investment schemes,
  (ii) on any existing or proposed arrangements for co-operation between it and the authorities responsible in that country or territory for the authorisation and supervision of relevant collective investment schemes,having regard to the Treasury's need to be satisfied as mentioned in subsection (2);
(b) the Authority must provide the Treasury with such a report; and
(c) the Treasury must have regard to it in deciding whether to make the order.

270(6) The notice to be given by the operator under subsection (1)(c)–
(a) must contain the address of a place in the United Kingdom for the service on the operator of notices or other documents required or authorised to be served on him under this Act; and
(b) must contain or be accompanied by such information and documents as may be specified by the Authority.

271 Procedure

271(1) If the Authority proposes to refuse approval of a scheme's being a recognised scheme by virtue of section 270, it must give the operator of the scheme a warning notice.

271(2) To be valid the warning notice must be received by the operator before the end of two months beginning with the date on which notice was given under section 270(1)(c).

271(3) If, having given a warning notice, the Authority decides to refuse approval–
(a) it must give the operator of the scheme a decision notice; and
(b) the operator may refer the matter to the Tribunal.

Individually recognised overseas schemes

272 Individually recognised overseas schemes

272(1) The Authority may, on the application of the operator of a collective investment scheme which–
(a) is managed in a country or territory outside the United Kingdom,
(b) does not satisfy the requirements prescribed for the purposes of section 264,
(c) is not managed in a country or territory designated for the purposes of section 270 or, if it is so managed, is of a class not specified by the designation order, and
(d) appears to the Authority to satisfy the requirements set out in the following provisions of this section,make an order declaring the scheme to be a recognised scheme.

272(2) Adequate protection must be afforded to participants in the scheme.

272(3) The arrangements for the scheme's constitution and management must be adequate.

272(4) The powers and duties of the operator and, if the scheme has a trustee or depositary, of the trustee or depositary must be adequate.

272(5) In deciding whether the matters mentioned in subsection (3) or (4) are adequate, the Authority must have regard to–
(a) any rule of law, and
(b) any matters which are, or could be, the subject of rules,applicable in relation to comparable authorised schemes.

272(6) **'Comparable authorised schemes'** means whichever of the following the Authority considers the most appropriate, having regard to the nature of scheme in respect of which the application is made–
(a) authorised unit trust schemes;

(b) authorised open-ended investment companies;
(c) both such unit trust schemes and such companies.

272(7) The scheme must take the form of an open-ended investment company or (if it does not take that form) the operator must be a body corporate.

272(8) The operator of the scheme must–
(a) if an authorised person, have permission to act as operator;
(b) if not an authorised person, be a fit and proper person to act as operator.

272(9) The trustee or depositary (if any) of the scheme must–
(a) if an authorised person, have permission to act as trustee or depositary;
(b) if not an authorised person, be a fit and proper person to act as trustee or depositary.

272(10) The operator and the trustee or depositary (if any) of the scheme must be able and willing to co-operate with the Authority by the sharing of information and in other ways.

272(11) The name of the scheme must not be undesirable or misleading.

272(12) The purposes of the scheme must be reasonably capable of being successfully carried into effect.

272(13) The participants must be entitled to have their units redeemed in accordance with the scheme at a price related to the net value of the property to which the units relate and determined in accordance with the scheme.

272(14) But a scheme is to be treated as complying with subsection (13) if it requires the operator to ensure that a participant is able to sell his units on an investment exchange at a price not significantly different from that mentioned in that subsection.

272(15) Subsection (13) is not to be read as imposing a requirement that the participants must be entitled to have their units redeemed (or sold as mentioned in subsection (14)) immediately following a demand to that effect.

273 Matters that may be taken into account

273 For the purposes of subsections (8)(b) and (9)(b) of section 272, the Authority may take into account any matter relating to–
(a) any person who is or will be employed by or associated with the operator, trustee or depositary in connection with the scheme;
(b) any director of the operator, trustee or depositary;
(c) any person exercising influence over the operator, trustee or depositary;
(d) any body corporate in the same group as the operator, trustee or depositary;
(e) any director of any such body corporate;
(f) any person exercising influence over any such body corporate.

274 Applications for recognition of individual schemes

274(1) An application under section 272 for an order declaring a scheme to be a recognised scheme must be made to the Authority by the operator of the scheme.

274(2) The application–
(a) must be made in such manner as the Authority may direct;
(b) must contain the address of a place in the United Kingdom for the service on the operator of notices or other documents required or authorised to be served on him under this Act;
(c) must contain or be accompanied by such information as the Authority may reasonably require for the purpose of determining the application.

274(3) At any time after receiving an application and before determining it, the Authority may require the applicant to provide it with such further information as it reasonably considers necessary to enable it to determine the application.

274(4) Different directions may be given, and different requirements imposed, in relation to different applications.

274(5) The Authority may require an applicant to present information which he is required to give under this section in such form, or to verify it in such a way, as the Authority may direct.

275 Determination of applications

275(1) An application under section 272 must be determined by the Authority before the end of the period of six months beginning with the date on which it receives the completed application.

275(2) The Authority may determine an incomplete application if it considers it appropriate to do so; and it must in any event determine such an application within twelve months beginning with the date on which it first receives the application.

275(3) If the Authority makes an order under section 272(1), it must give written notice of the order to the applicant.

276 Procedure when refusing an application

276(1) If the Authority proposes to refuse an application made under section 272 it must give the applicant a warning notice.

276(2) If the Authority decides to refuse the application–
(a) it must give the applicant a decision notice; and
(b) the applicant may refer the matter to the Tribunal.

277 Alteration of schemes and changes of operator, trustee or depositary

277(1) The operator of a scheme recognised by virtue of section 272 must give written notice to the Authority of any proposed alteration to the scheme.

277(2) Effect is not to be given to any such proposal unless–
(a) the Authority, by written notice, has given its approval to the proposal; or
(b) one month, beginning with the date on which notice was given under subsection (1), has expired without the Authority having given written notice to the operator that it has decided to refuse approval.

277(3) At least one month before any replacement of the operator, trustee or depositary of such a scheme, notice of the proposed replacement must be given to the Authority–
(a) by the operator, trustee or depositary (as the case may be); or
(b) by the person who is to replace him.

Schemes recognised under sections 270 and 272

278 Rules as to scheme particulars

278 The Authority may make rules imposing duties or liabilities on the operator of a scheme recognised under section 270 or 272 for purposes corresponding to those for which rules may be made under section 248 in relation to authorised unit trust schemes.

279 Revocation of recognition

279 The Authority may direct that a scheme is to cease to be recognised by virtue of section 270 or revoke an order under section 272 if it appears to the Authority–
(a) that the operator, trustee or depositary of the scheme has contravened a requirement imposed on him by or under this Act;
(b) that the operator, trustee or depositary of the scheme has, in purported compliance with any such requirement, knowingly or recklessly given the Authority information which is false or misleading in a material particular;

(c) in the case of an order under section 272, that one or more of the requirements for the making of the order are no longer satisfied; or
(d) that none of paragraphs (a) to (c) applies, but it is undesirable in the interests of the participants or potential participants that the scheme should continue to be recognised.

280 Procedure

280(1) If the Authority proposes to give a direction under section 279 or to make an order under that section revoking a recognition order, it must give a warning notice to the operator and (if any) the trustee or depositary of the scheme.

280(2) If the Authority decides to give a direction or make an order under that section–
(a) it must without delay give a decision notice to the operator and (if any) the trustee or depositary of the scheme; and
(b) the operator or the trustee or depositary may refer the matter to the Tribunal.

281 Directions

281(1) In this section a **'relevant recognised scheme'** means a scheme recognised under section 270 or 272.

281(2) If it appears to the Authority that–
(a) the operator, trustee or depositary of a relevant recognised scheme has contravened, or is likely to contravene, a requirement imposed on him by or under this Act,
(b) the operator, trustee or depositary of such a scheme has, in purported compliance with any such requirement, knowingly or recklessly given the Authority information which is false or misleading in a material particular,
(c) one or more of the requirements for the recognition of a scheme under section 272 are no longer satisfied, or
(d) none of paragraphs (a) to (c) applies, but the exercise of the power conferred by this section is desirable in order to protect the interests of participants or potential participants in a relevant recognised scheme who are in the United Kingdom,it may direct that the scheme is not to be a recognised scheme for a specified period or until the occurrence of a specified event or until specified conditions are complied with.

282 Procedure on giving directions under section 281 and varying them otherwise than as requested

282(1) A direction takes effect–
(a) immediately, if the notice given under subsection (3) states that that is the case;
(b) on such date as may be specified in the notice; or
(c) if no date is specified in the notice, when the matter to which it relates is no longer open to review.

282(2) A direction may be expressed to take effect immediately (or on a specified date) only if the Authority, having regard to the ground on which it is exercising its power under section 281, considers that it is necessary for the direction to take effect immediately (or on that date).

282(3) If the Authority proposes to give a direction under section 281, or gives such a direction with immediate effect, it must give separate written notice to the operator and (if any) the trustee or depositary of the scheme concerned.

282(4) The notice must–
(a) give details of the direction;
(b) inform the person to whom it is given of when the direction takes effect;
(c) state the Authority's reasons for giving the direction and for its determination as to when the direction takes effect;

(d) inform the person to whom it is given that he may make representations to the Authority within such period as may be specified in it (whether or not he has referred the matter to the Tribunal); and
(e) inform him of his right to refer the matter to the Tribunal.

282(5) The Authority may extend the period allowed under the notice for making representations.

282(6) If, having considered any representations made by a person to whom the notice was given, the Authority decides–
(a) to give the direction in the way proposed, or
(b) if it has been given, not to revoke the direction, it must give separate written notice to the operator and (if any) the trustee or depositary of the scheme concerned.

282(7) If, having considered any representations made by a person to whom the notice was given, the Authority decides–
(a) not to give the direction in the way proposed,
(b) to give the direction in a way other than that proposed, or
(c) to revoke a direction which has effect, it must give separate written notice to the operator and (if any) the trustee or depositary of the scheme concerned.

282(8) A notice given under subsection (6) must inform the person to whom it is given of his right to refer the matter to the Tribunal.

282(9) A notice under subsection (7)(b) must comply with subsection (4).

282(10) If a notice informs a person of his right to refer a matter to the Tribunal, it must give an indication of the procedure on such a reference.

282(11) This section applies to the variation of a direction on the Authority's own initiative as it applies to the giving of a direction.

282(12) For the purposes of subsection (1)(c), whether a matter is open to review is to be determined in accordance with section 391(8).

Facilities and information in UK

283 Facilities and information in UK

283(1) The Authority may make rules requiring operators of recognised schemes to maintain in the United Kingdom, or in such part or parts of it as may be specified, such facilities as the Authority thinks desirable in the interests of participants and as are specified in rules.

283(2) The Authority may by notice in writing require the operator of any recognised scheme to include such explanatory information as is specified in the notice in any communication of his which–
(a) is a communication of an invitation or inducement of a kind mentioned in section 21(1); and
(b) names the scheme.

283(3) In the case of a communication originating outside the United Kingdom, subsection (2) only applies if the communication is capable of having an effect in the United Kingdom.

CHAPTER VI INVESTIGATIONS

284 Power to investigate

284(1) An investigating authority may appoint one or more competent persons to investigate on its behalf–
(a) the affairs of, or of the manager or trustee of, any authorised unit trust scheme,
(b) the affairs of, or of the operator, trustee or depositary of, any recognised scheme so far as relating to activities carried on in the United Kingdom, or

Appendix 11: Extracts from the Financial Services and Markets Act 2000

(c) the affairs of, or of the operator, trustee or depositary of, any other collective investment scheme except a body incorporated by virtue of regulations under section 262, if it appears to the investigating authority that it is in the interests of the participants or potential participants to do so or that the matter is of public concern.

284(2) A person appointed under subsection (1) to investigate the affairs of, or of the manager, trustee, operator or depositary of, any scheme (scheme 'A'), may also, if he thinks it necessary for the purposes of that investigation, investigate–

(a) the affairs of, or of the manager, trustee, operator or depositary of, any other such scheme as is mentioned in subsection (1) whose manager, trustee, operator or depositary is the same person as the manager, trustee, operator or depositary of scheme A;

(b) the affairs of such other schemes and persons (including bodies incorporated by virtue of regulations under section 262 and the directors and depositaries of such bodies) as may be prescribed.

284(3) If the person appointed to conduct an investigation under this section ('B') considers that a person ('C') is or may be able to give information which is relevant to the investigation, B may require C–

(a) to produce to B any documents in C's possession or under his control which appear to B to be relevant to the investigation,

(b) to attend before B, and

(c) otherwise to give B all assistance in connection with the investigation which C is reasonably able to give, and it is C's duty to comply with that requirement.

284(4) Subsections (5) to (9) of section 170 apply if an investigating authority appoints a person under this section to conduct an investigation on its behalf as they apply in the case mentioned in subsection (1) of that section.

284(5) Section 174 applies to a statement made by a person in compliance with a requirement imposed under this section as it applies to a statement mentioned in that section.

284(6) Subsections (2) to (4) and (6) of section 175 and section 177 have effect as if this section were contained in Part XI.

284(7) Subsections (1) to (9) of section 176 apply in relation to a person appointed under subsection (1) as if–

(a) references to an investigator were references to a person so appointed;

(b) references to an information requirement were references to a requirement imposed under section 175 or under subsection (3) by a person so appointed;

(c) the premises mentioned in subsection (3)(a) were the premises of a person whose affairs are the subject of an investigation under this section or of an appointed representative of such a person.

284(8) No person may be required under this section to disclose information or produce a document in respect of which he owes an obligation of confidence by virtue of carrying on the business of banking unless subsection (9) or (10) applies.

284(9) This subsection applies if–

(a) the person to whom the obligation of confidence is owed consents to the disclosure or production; or

(b) the imposing on the person concerned of a requirement with respect to information or a document of a kind mentioned in subsection (8) has been specifically authorised by the investigating authority.

284(10) This subsection applies if the person owing the obligation of confidence or the person to whom it is owed is–

(a) the manager, trustee, operator or depositary of any collective investment scheme which is under investigation;

(b) the director of a body incorporated by virtue of regulations under section 262 which is under investigation;

(c) any other person whose own affairs are under investigation.

284(11) 'Investigating authority' means the Authority or the Secretary of State.

Appendix 12: VATA 1994, Sch. 9, Grp. 5

SCHEDULE 9 – EXEMPTIONS

Sections 8 and 31

GROUP 5 – FINANCE

Item No.
1. The issue, transfer or receipt of, or any dealing with, money, any security for money or any note or order for the payment of money.
2. The making of any advance or the granting of any credit.
2A. The management of credit by the person granting it.
3. The provision of the facility of instalment credit finance in a hire-purchase, conditional sale or credit sale agreement for which facility a separate charge is made and disclosed to the recipient of the supply of goods.
4. The provision of administrative arrangements and documentation and the transfer of title to the goods in connection with the supply described in item 3 if the total consideration therefor is specified in the agreement and does not exceed £10.
5. The provision of intermediary services in relation to any transaction comprised in item 1, 2, 3, 4 or 6 (whether or not any such transaction is finally concluded) by a person acting in an intermediary capacity.
5A. The underwriting of an issue within item 1 or any transaction within item 6.
6. The issue, transfer or receipt of, or any dealing with, any security or secondary security being–

(a) shares, stocks, bonds, notes (other than promissory notes), debentures, debenture stock or shares in an oil royalty; or
(b) any document relating to money, in any currency, which has been deposited with the issuer or some other person, being a document which recognises an obligation to pay a stated amount to bearer or to order, with or without interest, and being a document by the delivery of which, with or without endorsement, the right to receive that stated amount, with or without interest, is transferable; or
(c) any bill, note or other obligation of the Treasury or of a government in any part of the world, being a document by the delivery of which, with or without endorsement, title is transferable, and not being an obligation which is or has been legal tender in any part of the world; or
(d) any letter of allotment or rights, any warrant conferring an option to acquire a security included in this item, any renounceable or scrip certificates, rights coupons, coupons representing dividends or interest on such a security, bond mandates or other documents conferring or containing evidence of title to or rights in respect of such a security; or
(e) units or other documents conferring rights under any trust established for the purpose, or having the effect of providing, for persons having funds available for investment, facilities for the participation by them as beneficiaries under the trust, in any profits or income arising from the acquisition, holding, management or disposal of any property whatsoever.

7. [Omitted by SI 1999/594, art. 4, operative in respect of supplies made on or after 10 March 1999.]
8. The operation of any current, deposit or savings account.
9. The management of–

(a) an authorised open-ended investment company; or
(b) an authorised unit trust scheme; or
(c) a Gibraltar collective investment scheme that is not an umbrella scheme; or
(d) a sub-fund of any other Gibraltar collective investment scheme; or
(e) an individually recognised overseas scheme that is not an umbrella scheme; or
(f) a sub-fund of any other individually recognised overseas scheme; or

(g) a recognised collective investment scheme authorised in a designated country or territory that is not an umbrella scheme; or
(h) a sub-fund of any other recognised collective investment scheme authorised in a designated country or territory; or
(i) a recognised collective investment scheme constituted in another EEA state that is not an umbrella scheme; or
(j) a sub-fund of any other recognised collective investment scheme constituted in another EEA state.
10. The management of a closed-ended collective investment undertaking.

Notes:
(1) Item 1 does not include anything included in item 6.
(1A) Item 1 does not include a supply of services which is preparatory to the carrying out of a transaction falling within that item.
(2) This Group does not include the supply of a coin or a banknote as a collectors' piece or as an investment article.
(2A) [Omitted by SI 2003/1569, art. 2(d).]
(2B) [Omitted by SI 2003/1568, art. 2.]
(3) Item 2 includes the supply of credit by a person, in connection with a supply of goods or services by him, for which a separate charge is made and disclosed to the recipient of the supply of goods or services.
(4) This Group includes any supply by a person carrying on a credit card, charge card or similar payment card operation made in connection with that operation to a person who accepts the card used in the operation when presented to him in payment for goods or services.
(5) For the purposes of item 5 **'intermediary services'** consist of bringing together, with a view to the provision of financial services–
(a) persons who are or may be seeking to receive financial services, and
(b) persons who provide financial services,
together with (in the case of financial services falling within item 1, 2, 3 or 4) the performance of work preparatory to the conclusion of contracts for the provision of those financial services, but do not include the supply of any market research, product design, advertising, promotional or similar services or the collection, collation and provision of information in connection with such activities.
(5A) For the purposes of item 5 a person is **'acting in an intermediary capacity'** wherever he is acting as an intermediary, or one of the intermediaries, between–
(a) a person who provides financial services, and
(b) a person who is or may be seeking to receive financial services.
(5B) For the purposes of Notes (5) and (5A) **'financial services'** means the carrying out of any transaction falling within item 1, 2, 3, 4 or 6.
(6) For the purposes of this Group–
> **'authorised open-ended investment company'** and **'authorised unit trust scheme'** have the meaning given in section 237(3) of the Financial Services and Markets Act 2000;
> **'closed-ended collective investment undertaking'** means an undertaking in relation to which the following conditions are satisfied–

(a) its sole object is the investment of capital, raised from the public, wholly or mainly in securities; and
(b) it manages its assets on the principle of spreading investment risk; and
(c) all of its ordinary shares (of each class if there is more than one) or equivalent units are included in the official list maintained by the Financial Services Authority pursuant to section 74(1) of the Financial Services and Markets Act 2000; and
(d) all of its ordinary shares (of each class if there is more than one) or equivalent units are admitted to trading on a regulated market situated or operating in the United Kingdom;

'**collective investment scheme**' has the meaning given in section 235 of the Financial Services and Markets Act 2000;

'**Gibraltar collective investment scheme**' means–

(a) a collective investment scheme to which section 264 of the Financial Services and Markets Act 2000 applies pursuant to an order made under section 409(1)(d) of that Act; or

(b) a collective investment scheme to which the Financial Services and Markets Act 2000 applies pursuant to an order made under section 409(1)(f) of that Act;

'**individually recognised overseas scheme**' means a collective investment scheme declared by the Financial Services Authority to be a recognised scheme pursuant to section 272 of the Financial Services and Markets Act 2000;

'**recognised collective investment scheme authorised in a designated country or territory**' means a collective investment scheme recognised pursuant to section 270 of the Financial Services and Markets Act 2000;

'**recognised collective investment scheme constituted in another EEA state**' means a collective investment scheme which is recognised pursuant to section 264 of the Financial Services and Markets Act 2000;

'**regulated market**' has the meaning given in section 103(1) of the Financial Services and Markets Act 2000;

'**sub-fund**' means a separate part of the property of an umbrella scheme that is pooled separately;

'**umbrella scheme**' means a collective investment scheme under which the contributions of the participants in the scheme and the profits or income out of which payments are to be made to them are pooled separately in relation to separate parts of the scheme property.

(6A) A collective investment scheme, or sub-fund, that is not for the time being marketed in the United Kingdom is to be treated as not falling within item 9(c) to (j) if–

(a) it has never been marketed in the United Kingdom, or

(b) less than 5% of its shares or units are held by, or on behalf of, investors who are in the United Kingdom.

(7) [Omitted by SI 2003/1569, art. 2(g).]

(8) [Omitted by SI 2008/2547, art. 3(6).]

(9) [Omitted by SI 2003/1569, art. 2(i).]

(10) [Omitted by SI 2008/2547, art. 3(6).]

Appendix 13: Liability of Money Brokers' Services

This appendix sets out the VAT liability of UK brokers' commission for the financial service of arranging transactions in currency. In consequence of the place of supply rules, services are outside the scope when provided to clients who belong in other EU states and who are not VAT-registered or to any clients belonging outside the EU. In some cases, services to persons in the UK or the Isle of Man or to persons not in business and belonging in other member states are zero-rated. The numbers in brackets refer to the appropriate item in VATA 1994, Sch. 8, Grp. 7. For supplies to persons outside the EU, the broker can reclaim underlying input VAT. The recoverability of input VAT is denoted below by X or ✔.

References to the UK include the Isle of Man, which is not outside the EU for this purpose.

Buyers and sellers with the EU are all taken to be taxable businesses for the purposes of this table.

Seller belonging in	VAT status of commission		Commission charged to Sells to	Buyer belonging in	VAT status of commission	
UK	Exempt	X	→	UK	Exempt	X
UK	Exempt	X	→	EC	O/scope	X
UK	Zero (2(c))	✔	→	Non-EU country	O/scope	✔
EU	O/scope	X	→	UK	Exempt	X
EU	O/scope	X	→	EC	O/scope	X
EU	O/scope	✔	→	Non-EU country	O/scope	✔
Non-EU country	O/scope	✔	→	UK	Exempt	X
Non-EU country	O/scope	✔	→	EC	O/scope	X
Non-EU country	O/scope	✔	→	Non-EU country	O/scope	✔

Notes

[1] Following the decision of the ECJ in *First National Bank of Chicago v Customs and Excise Commissioners* (Case C-172/96) [1998] BVC 389, this treatment is largely based on the assumption that the underlying client transaction involves a supply by both client counter-parties. However, this has now been somewhat tempered by the decision of the Tribunal given in July 2005 in the *Willis Pension Trustees Ltd* case [2006] BVC 2,045, where Willis, the Trustee of a Pension Fund, has been held not to be making a supply when entering into a transaction purely as a financial hedge. The only supply in this situation was made by the bank with whom the hedge was undertaken.

[2] None of the above financial services are subject to a reverse charge (under VATA 1994, s. 7) if imported from an overseas broker.

Appendix 14: VATA 1994, Sch. 9, Grp. 1

SCHEDULE 9 – EXEMPTIONS

Sections 8 and 31

GROUP 1 – LAND

Item No.
1. The grant of any interest in or right over land or of any licence to occupy land, or, in relation to land in Scotland, any personal right to call for or be granted any such interest or right, other than–
    (a) the grant of the fee simple in–
        (i) a building which has not been completed and which is neither designed as a dwelling or number of dwellings nor intended for use solely for a relevant residential purpose or a relevant charitable purpose;
        (ii) a new building which is neither designed as a dwelling or number of dwellings nor intended for use solely for a relevant residential purpose or a relevant charitable purpose after the grant;
        (iii) a civil engineering work which has not been completed;
        (iv) a new civil engineering work;
    (b) a supply made pursuant to a developmental tenancy, developmental lease or developmental licence;
    (c) the grant of any interest, right or licence consisting of a right to take game or fish unless at the time of the grant the grantor grants to the grantee the fee simple of the land over which the right to take game or fish is exercisable;
    (d) the provision in an hotel, inn, boarding house or similar establishment of sleeping accommodation or of accommodation in rooms which are provided in conjunction with sleeping accommodation or for the purpose of a supply of catering;
    (e) the grant of any interest in, right over or licence to occupy holiday accommodation;
    (f) the provision of seasonal pitches for caravans, and the grant of facilities at caravan parks to persons for whom such pitches are provided;
    (g) the provision of pitches for tents or of camping facilities;
    (h) the grant of facilities for parking a vehicle;
    (j) the grant of any right to fell and remove standing timber;
    (k) the grant of facilities for housing, or storage of, an aircraft or for mooring, or storage of, a ship, boat or other vessel;
    (l) the grant of any right to occupy a box, seat or other accommodation at a sports ground, theatre, concert hall or other place of entertainment;
    (m) the grant of facilities for playing any sport or participating in any physical recreation; and
    (n) the grant of any right, including–
        (i) an equitable right,
        (ii) a right under an option or right of pre-emption, or
        (iii) in relation to land in Scotland, a personal right,
to call for or be granted an interest or right which would fall within any of paragraph (a) or (c) to (m) above.

Notes:
(1) '**Grant**' includes an assignment or surrender and the supply made by the person to whom an interest is surrendered when there is a reverse surrender.
(1A) A '**reverse surrender**' is one in which the person to whom the interest is surrendered is paid by the person by whom the interest is being surrendered to accept the surrender.
(2) A building shall be taken to be '**completed**' when an architect issues a certificate of practical completion in relation to it or it is first fully occupied, whichever happens first; and a civil engineering

work shall be taken to be **'completed'** when an engineer issues a certificate of completion in relation to it or it is first fully used, whichever happens first.

(3) Notes (2) to (10) and (12) to Group 5 of Schedule 8 apply in relation to this Group as they apply in relation to that Group.

(4) A building or civil engineering work is **'new'** if it was completed less than three years before the grant.

(5) Subject to Note (6), the grant of the fee simple in a building or work completed before 1st April 1989 is not excluded from this Group by paragraph (a)(ii) or (iv).

(6) Note (5) does not apply where the grant is the first grant of the fee simple made on or after 1st April 1989 and the building was not fully occupied, or the work not fully used, before that date.

(7) A tenancy of, lease of or licence to occupy a building or work is treated as becoming a **'developmental tenancy'**, **'developmental lease'** or **'developmental licence'** (as the case may be) when a tenancy of, lease of or licence to occupy a building or work, whose construction, reconstruction, enlargement or extension commenced on or after 1st January 1992, is treated as being supplied to and by the developer under paragraph 6(1) of Schedule 10 (except where that paragraph applies by virtue of paragraph 5(1)(b) of that Schedule).

(8) Where a grant of an interest in, right over or licence to occupy land includes a valuable right to take game or fish, an apportionment shall be made to determine the supply falling outside this Group by virtue of paragraph (c).

(9) **'Similar establishment'** includes premises in which there is provided furnished sleeping accommodation, whether with or without the provision of board or facilities for the preparation of food, which are used by or held out as being suitable for use by visitors or travellers.

(10) **'Houseboat'** includes a houseboat within the meaning of Group 9 of Schedule 8.

(11) Paragraph (e) includes–

(a) any grant excluded from item 1 of Group 5 of Schedule 8 by Note (13) in that Group;
(b) any supply made pursuant to a tenancy, lease or licence under which the grantee is or has been permitted to erect and occupy holiday accommodation.

(12) Paragraph (e) does not include a grant in respect of a building or part which is not a new building of–

(a) the fee simple, or
(b) a tenancy, lease or licence to the extent that the grant is made for a consideration in the form of a premium.

(13) **'Holiday accommodation'** includes any accommodation in a building, hut (including a beach hut or chalet), caravan, houseboat or tent which is advertised or held out as holiday accommodation or as suitable for holiday or leisure use, but excludes any accommodation within paragraph (d).

(14) A **seasonal pitch** for a caravan is–

(a) a pitch on a holiday site other than an employee pitch, or
(b) a non-residential pitch on any other site.

(14A) In this Note and in Note (14)–

'**employee pitch**' means a pitch occupied by an employee of the site operator as that person's principal place of residence during the period of occupancy;

'**holiday site**' means a site or part of a site which is operated as a holiday or leisure site;

'**non-residential pitch**' means a pitch which–

(a) is provided for less than a year, or
(b) is provided for a year or more and is subject to an occupation restriction,

and which is not intended to be used as the occupant's principal place of residence during the period of occupancy;

'**occupation restriction**' means any covenant, statutory planning consent or similar permission, the terms of which prevent the person to whom the pitch is provided from occupying it by living in a caravan at all times throughout the period for which the pitch is provided.

(15) **'Mooring'** includes anchoring or berthing.

(16) Paragraph (m) shall not apply where the grant of the facilities is for–
(a) a continuous period of use exceeding 24 hours; or
(b) a series of 10 or more periods, whether or not exceeding 24 hours in total, where the following conditions are satisfied–
- (i) each period is in respect of the same activity carried on at the same place;
- (ii) the interval between each period is not less than one day and not more than 14 days;
- (iii) consideration is payable by reference to the whole series and is evidenced by written agreement;
- (iv) the grantee has exclusive use of the facilities; and
- (v) the grantee is a school, a club, an association or an organisation representing affiliated clubs or constituent associations.

Appendix 15: Lloyd's VAT Arrangements

CONTENTS
Paragraph
1. INTRODUCTION
2. SCOPE OF THE ARRANGEMENTS
3. REGISTRATION
4. OUTPUTS
5. LIABILITY OF SUPPLIES
6. ENTITLEMENT TO INPUT TAX RECOVERY
7. PARTIAL EXEMPTION
8. GLOBAL MARKET RATE (GMR)
9. MEMBERS' AGENTS RATE (MAR)
10. INPUT TAX – ALTERNATIVE EVIDENCE
11. IMPORTED SERVICES
12. GENERAL

1. INTRODUCTION

This document sets out administrative arrangements for operating VAT within the Lloyd's market. It was drawn up following an extensive review of the previous Lloyd's VAT Arrangements, which dated back to 1985 and a period of review and consultation with the Lloyd's market.

The Lloyd's VAT Arrangements set out in this document provide guidelines on the VAT registration and recovery treatment of entities operating within the Lloyd's market. They are intended to set out a minimum framework that Customs & Excise expect to be adopted, together with some methodology for the supporting evidence. However, the VAT methodology that is contained in these arrangements is not intended to be prescriptive or exhaustive, and so each VAT registered entity will have to formulate and agree with Customs & Excise a VAT recovery method that is suitable for its own specific circumstances and activities.

This document records arrangements that came into effect on 1 January 2000, and which have already been communicated to entities in the Lloyd's market by way of meetings and bulletins. It also records subsequent amendments to those arrangements.

In signing this agreement, Customs & Excise and the Corporation of Lloyd's underline the desirability and the benefit of the Lloyd's market's having a cohesive approach to VAT. However, these arrangements are subject to prevailing VAT law and are therefore without prejudice to the right of any entity to take an appeal to the VAT and Duties Tribunal on a matter of law.

2. SCOPE OF THE ARRANGEMENTS

2.1   The arrangements are for the use of the following entities within the Lloyd's market:
- Syndicates
- Managing agents
- Members' agents
- Lloyd's advisors
- Mixed agents

- Corporate members of Lloyd's
- Scottish Limited Partnerships (SLPs) which are members of Lloyd's
- Natural members of Lloyd's.

2.2 The arrangements exclude all other entities.

3. REGISTRATION

3.1 The following entities may register in their own right to account for VAT on their Lloyd's insurance market activities, subject to a requirement or entitlement to register:
- Syndicates (a syndicate is an unincorporated association of the participating members)
- Managing agents
- Members' agents
- Lloyd's advisors
- Mixed agents
- Corporate members (to the extent that para 3.4 applies)
- SLPs (to the extent that para 3.4 applies)

3.2 The following members may register in their own right to account for VAT on activities other than insurance underwriting, subject to a requirement or entitlement to register for VAT:
- Corporate members
- SLPs
- Natural members.

But see also paragraph 3.5 in relation to corporate members that are part of a group of companies.

3.3 Unless Customs & Excise have approved an application to render monthly returns, all registrations covered by these arrangements will render VAT returns on calendar quarters (stagger 1), that is March/June/Sept/Dec.

3.4 A corporate member or an SLP that has 100% of the underwriting capacity of a syndicate will be required to cancel the VAT registration of the syndicate as all the economic activities, including underwriting activities, are to be accounted for under the VAT registration of the corporate member or of the SLP. However, see also paragraph 3.5 in relation to corporate members that are part of groups of companies.

3.5 Whether or not a corporate member is required or permitted to register in its own right, a corporate member is eligible for membership of a VAT group, subject to the normal VAT grouping requirements being met. In the case where a corporate member has 100% of the underwriting capacity of a syndicate, and the VAT registration of the syndicate must be cancelled, the syndicate activities may be accounted for either under a single registration for the corporate member or under the registration of a VAT group of which it is a member.

3.6 Syndicates that are underwriting in the year 2000 or future years of account are entitled to register for VAT provided they do not write wholly EU business.

3.7 Syndicates that do not have a successor year of account at 31 December 1999 (that will not be underwriting for the 2000 year of account) will continue to be dealt with via the VAT registration of the managing agents. Subsequent to the 1999 year of account, syndicates that do not have a successor year of account can continue to be registered and will recover input tax at an average recovery rate calculated from the previous 3 years' underwriting premiums. For example, a syndicate that does not have a successor year of account to 2000 will have an average recovery rate based on the aggregate value of all premiums for the period from 1 January 1998 to 31 December 2000.

Appendix 15: Lloyd's VAT Arrangements

4. OUTPUTS

4.1 The outputs that will be declared by the entities within the scope of these arrangements for their activities at Lloyd's are described below. This is in addition to outputs that are derived from other activities.

4.2 *Outputs value*

The value to be declared for a supply is the total consideration for that supply. The consideration for a supply of insurance is the gross premium, including Insurance Premium Tax (IPT) and any other fiscal charges or levies, that is payable by the insured, without any deductions. The consideration for a supply of reinsurance is the gross reinsurance premium less reinsurance commission and profit commission.

4.3 The value of insurance and reinsurance premiums processed through LPSO Limited (LPSO) and notified to managing agents and syndicates will be calculated through a procedure agreed by LPSO, to reflect the full consideration.

4.4 *Syndicates*

The outputs to be declared are the total of the insurance and reinsurance premiums processed through LPSO and notified by them, plus any premiums not processed through LPSO, such as UK motor business. LPSO notification is evidence of the outputs processed through LPSO.

4.5 *Managing Agents*

The outputs to be declared are the value of supplies (fees charged for services under the managing agents' contract) by the managing agents to the syndicates that they are authorised to manage plus any other supplies made by the agent. Throughout these arrangements the term 'fees' includes profit commission.

4.6 *Members' Agents*

The outputs to be declared are the value of supplies (fees charged to members under the Lloyd's members' agents' agreement) made to members, plus any other supplies made by the members' agent.

4.7 *Lloyd's Advisors*

The outputs to be declared are the value of supplies made to corporate members, plus any other supplies made by the advisor.

4.8 *Mixed Agents*

The outputs to be declared will be a combination of the managing agent supplies and the members' agent supplies, plus any other supplies made.

4.9 *Corporate Members*

No outputs will be declared from the underwriting of insurance in the Lloyd's market as these are to be declared by the syndicate. The outputs to be declared will be those from other activities. Where, however, the corporate member has 100% of a syndicate, the outputs to be declared will include the underwriting of insurance in relation to the wholly-owned syndicate.

4.10 *SLPs*

No outputs will be declared from the underwriting of insurance in the Lloyd's market as these are to be declared by the syndicate. The outputs to be declared will be those from other activities. Where, however, the SLP has 100% of a syndicate, the outputs to be declared will include the underwriting of insurance in relation to the wholly-owned syndicate.

4.11 *Natural members*

No outputs will be declared from the underwriting of insurance in the Lloyd's market as these are to be declared by the syndicates. The outputs to be declared will be those from other activities.

5. LIABILITY OF SUPPLIES

5.1 The liability of any supply will be determined by the VAT legislation in force at the time.

6. ENTITLEMENT TO INPUT TAX RECOVERY

(underwriting related activities only, all other supplies subject to the normal rules)

6.1 *Syndicates*

Recovery will be based on the value of supplies made by the individual syndicates.

6.2 *Managing Agents*

Recovery will be based on the value of services supplied to the syndicates they manage.

6.3 *Members' Agents (to 31 December 2000)*

Recovery will be based on the Global Market Rate.

6.4 *Members' Agents (from 1 January 2001)*

Recovery will be based on the Members' Agents Rate.

6.5 *Lloyd's Advisors*

Recovery will be based on the value of services supplied to corporate members.

6.6 *Mixed Agents*

Recovery will be based on the Members' Agents Rate (for the members' agent activities) and the value of the managing agent services (for the managing agent activities).

6.7 *Corporate members*

Whilst the primary purpose of the corporate member registration is to account for their activities other than syndicate underwriting, corporate members will also incur input tax directly in relation to their syndicate underwriting. Recovery of this underwriting related input tax will be based on the supplies made by them on the syndicates on which they participate.

6.8 *Scottish Limited Partnerships*

Whilst the primary purpose of the SLP member registration is to account for their activities other than syndicate underwriting, SLPs will incur input tax directly in relation to their syndicate underwriting. Recovery of this underwriting-related input tax will be based on the supplies made by them on the syndicates on which they participate.

6.9 *Natural members*

Whilst the primary purpose of the member registration is to account for activities other than syndicate underwriting, natural members will incur input tax directly in relation to their syndicate underwriting. Please refer to section 7.11 for details of the possible methods of recovery of input tax.

7. PARTIAL EXEMPTION

7.1 Each registration making taxable and/or specified supplies (under the Specified Supplies Order 1999 [SI 1999/3121]) in addition to exempt supplies will agree a partial exemption method with Customs and Excise. The method will reflect their business activities, in relation to which they will calculate the amount of recoverable input tax. The partial exemption methods will conform to the legislation that prevails.

7.2 Input tax will be directly attributed to supplies made and recovered as appropriate. Input tax that cannot be directly attributed to supplies made will be recovered via the agreed partial exemption calculations.

7.3 The treatment of investment activities undertaken by registrations will be agreed as a separate sector within each individual partial exemption method. Input tax recovery on other activities, e.g. share issues, will be subject to the normal rules and may constitute a separate sector.

7.4 *Syndicates – Partial Exemption Method*

The tax year will be 1 January to 31 December with the annual adjustment declared in the December quarter of that tax year.

The partial exemption agreement will comprise at least the following components:

SECTOR 1 – UNDERWRITING

The calculation will be based on premiums processed, both through LPSO and elsewhere. Premiums processed by LPSO will be notified on summary reports.

Premiums will be coded by LPSO as follows,

- X = exempt and outside the scope with no input tax credit
- Z = outside the scope (O/S) with input tax (I/T)credit
- M = mixed, this will be split 50/50 to X and Z

The sector recovery calculation will be,

$$\frac{\text{Value of premiums O/S with I/T credit}}{\text{Value of total premiums}} = \text{recoverable \% to 2 decimal places}$$

SECTOR 2 – INVESTMENTS

The calculation will be based on either the number or the value of securities sales.

The sector recovery calculation will be,

$$\frac{\text{Number or value of O/S with I/T credit sales of securities}}{\text{Number or value of total sales of securities}} = \text{recoverable \% to 2 decimal places}$$

7.5 *Managing Agents – Partial Exemption Method*

The annual adjustment will be declared in the first quarter following the end of their VAT tax year.

The partial exemption agreement will comprise at least the following components:

SECTOR 1 – MANAGING AGENT

The calculation will be based upon the value of fees charged to syndicates which the managing agent is authorised to manage by Lloyd's. Where the fees relate to services supplied under the Managing Agent's Agreement (General) and Managing Agent's Agreement (Corporate Member) the liability split of the fees will be determined by the insurance business underwritten by the syndicates managed.

The sector recovery calculation will be,

$$\frac{\text{Value of O/S with I/T credit fees}}{\text{Total value of fees}} = \text{recoverable \% to 2 decimal places}$$

SECTOR 2 – INVESTMENTS

The calculation will be based on either the number or value of securities sales.

The sector recovery calculation will be,

$$\frac{\text{Number or value of O/S with I/T credit sales of securities}}{\text{Number or value of total sales of securities}} = \text{recoverable \% to 2 decimal places}$$

OTHER SUPPLIES

Recovery of input tax in relation to supplies not made under the Managing Agent's Agreement (General) and Managing Agent's Agreement (Corporate Member) will be subject to the normal rules and may constitute a separate sector.

7.6 *Members' Agents – Partial Exemption Method*

The annual adjustment will be declared in the first quarter following the end of their VAT tax year.

The partial exemption agreement will comprise at least the following components:

SECTOR 1 – MEMBERS' AGENT

This sector relates to the services provided to members under the terms of the Lloyd's Members' Agent's Agreement

Appendix 15: Lloyd's VAT Arrangements

The sector recovery calculation will be,

$$\text{Non-attributable input VAT multiplied by the Members' Agents Rate} = \text{input VAT recoverable to the nearest penny}$$

SECTOR 2 – INVESTMENTS

The calculation will be based on either the number or the value of securities sales.

The sector recovery calculation will be,

$$\frac{\text{Number or value of O/S with I/T credit sales of securities}}{\text{Number or value of total sales of securities}} = \text{recoverable \% to 2 decimal places}$$

OTHER SUPPLIES

Recovery of input tax in relation to supplies that are outside the terms of the Lloyd's Members' Agent's Agreement will be subject to the normal rules and may constitute a separate sector.

7.7 Lloyd's Advisors – Partial Exemption Method

The annual adjustment will be declared in the first quarter following the end of their VAT tax year.

The partial exemption agreement will comprise at least the following components:

SECTOR 1 – LLOYD'S ADVISOR

The calculation will be based upon the value of fees charged to individual corporate members which the advisor is authorised by Lloyd's to advise.

The sector recovery calculation will be,

$$\frac{\text{Value of taxable supplies and other supplies with I/T credit}}{\text{Total value of supplies}} = \text{recoverable \% to 2 decimal places}$$

Input tax recovery on supplies that are outside the terms of the advisor's agreement may comprise a separate sector.

SECTOR 2 – INVESTMENTS

The calculation will be based on either the number or value of securities sales.

The sector recovery calculation will be,

$$\frac{\text{Number or value of O/S with I/T credit sales of securities}}{\text{Number or value of total sales of securities}} = \text{recoverable \% to 2 decimal places}$$

7.8 Mixed Agents – Partial Exemption Method

The annual adjustment will be declared in the first quarter following the end of their VAT tax year.

The partial exemption agreement will comprise at least the following components:

SECTOR 1 – MANAGING AGENT

The calculation will be based upon the value of fees charged to syndicates which the managing agent is authorised to manage by Lloyd's. Where the fees relate to services supplied under the Managing Agent's Agreement (General) and Managing Agent's Agreement (Corporate Member) the liability split of the fees will be determined by the insurance business underwritten by the syndicates managed.

The sector recovery calculation will be,

$$\frac{\text{Value of O/S with I/T credit fees}}{\text{Total value of fees}} = \text{recoverable \% to 2 decimal places}$$

SECTOR 2 – MEMBERS' AGENT

This sector relates to the services provided to members under the terms of the Lloyd's Members' Agent's Agreement

The sector recovery calculation will be,

Non-attributable input VAT multiplied by the Members' Agents Rate = input VAT recoverable to the nearest penny

SECTOR 3 – INVESTMENTS

The calculation will be based on either the number or value of securities sales.

The sector recovery calculation will be,

$$\frac{\text{Number or value of O/S with I/T credit sales of securities}}{\text{Number or value of total sales of securities}} = \text{recoverable \% to 2 decimal places}$$

OTHER SUPPLIES

Input tax recovery on supplies that are outside the terms of the Managing Agent's Agreement (General), Managing Agent's Agreement (Corporate Member) or the Members' Agent's Agreement will be subject to the normal rules and may comprise additional separate sectors.

7.9 *Corporate Members – Partial Exemption Method*

The annual adjustment will be declared in the first quarter following the end of their VAT tax year.

The partial exemption agreement will comprise at least the following components:

SECTOR 1 – INVESTMENTS

The calculation will be based on either the number or value of securities sales.

The sector recovery calculation will be,

$$\frac{\text{Number or value of O/S with I/T credit sales of securities}}{\text{Number or value of total sales of securities}} = \text{recoverable \% to 2 decimal places}$$

SECTOR 2 – SYNDICATE UNDERWRITING

The calculation will be based on the premiums processed through LPSO and elsewhere.

The sector recovery calculation will be,

$$\frac{\text{Value of premiums O/S with I/T credit}}{\text{Total value of premiums}} = \text{recoverable \% to 2 decimal places}$$

Where the corporate member participates on a number of syndicates which makes the above calculation difficult, the Global Market Rate may be used in its place for this sector subject to agreement with Customs & Excise. However those members that participate solely on syndicates which write only EU business will not be permitted to use the Global Market Rate or recover input tax in relation to these supplies.

Where a corporate member owns 100% of the capacity on a syndicate consideration will need to be given to establishing a further sector for this activity.

7.10 *Scottish Limited Partnerships (SLPs) – Partial Exemption Method*

The annual adjustment will be declared in the first quarter following the end of their VAT tax year.

The partial exemption agreement will comprise at least the following components:

SECTOR 1 – INVESTMENTS

The calculation will be based on either the number or value of securities sales.

The sector recovery calculation will be,

$$\frac{\text{Number or value of O/S with I/T credit sales of securities}}{\text{Number or value of total sales of securities}} = \text{recoverable \% to 2 decimal places}$$

SECTOR 2 – SYNDICATE UNDERWRITING

The calculation will be based on the premiums processed through LPSO and elsewhere.

The sector recovery calculation will be,

$$\frac{\text{Value of premiums O/S with I/T credit}}{\text{Total value of premiums}} = \text{recoverable \% to 2 decimal places}$$

Where the SLP participates on a number of syndicates which makes the above calculation difficult, The Global Market Rate may be used in its place for this sector. However those members that participate solely on syndicates which write only EU business will not be permitted to use the Global Market Rate.

Where a SLP owns 100% of the capacity on a syndicate consideration will need to be given to establishing a further sector for this activity.

7.11 *Natural members – Partial Exemption Method*

Input tax arising from underwriting activities incurred by natural members who are registered for VAT as sole proprietors by virtue of business activities other than underwriting at Lloyd's may be recovered subject to the normal rules. The Global Market Rate will normally be used to calculate the recoverable amount. The exception to this will be any members who participate solely on syndicates which write only EU business. These members will be unable to recover any underwriting related input tax as they have only written insurance in respect of which there is no right to recover input tax.

Natural members who are VAT registered other than as sole proprietors are not entitled to recover input tax arising from their underwriting activities by virtue of that registration.

8. GLOBAL MARKET RATE (GMR)

8.1 The Global Market Recovery rate (GMR) will be calculated on an annual basis for each VAT tax year. During the current VAT tax year, the recoverable amount of non-attributable input VAT incurred in each quarter will be determined by reference to the GMR for the previous tax year. The actual GMR for the current year will be used to determine the annual adjustment for that year.

8.2 The GMR will be calculated using the value of all insurance business written in the Lloyd's market to include:

- the LPSO calculated gross premium VAT figures, including small pool business and IPT,
- gross premiums (including IPT) not processed through LPSO for the previous year of account,
- Records and Amendments section adjustments.

The method of calculating the GMR will be through a procedure agreed between Lloyd's and Customs and Excise and will be subject to review.

9. MEMBERS' AGENTS RATE (MAR)

9.1 The Members' Agents Recovery Rate (MAR) will be calculated on an annual basis for each VAT tax year. During the current VAT tax year, the recoverable amount of non-attributable input VAT incurred in each quarter will be determined by reference to the MAR for the previous year. The actual MAR for the current year will be used in determining the annual adjustment.

9.2 The MAR will be calculated using the value of all insurance business written in the Lloyd's market except for business written by those syndicates all of whose capacity is provided by a single corporate member or by a number of corporate members that belong to the same group. It will include:

- the LPSO calculated gross premium VAT figures, including small pool business and IPT,
- gross premiums (including IPT) not processed through LPSO for the previous year of account,
- Records and Amendments section adjustments.

The method of calculating the MAR will be through a procedure agreed between Lloyd's and Customs and Excise and will be subject to review.

10. INPUT TAX – ALTERNATIVE EVIDENCE

Input Tax – Claims expenses ('tabulation figures')

10.1 The input tax on services supplied from within the UK in relation to claims will only be regarded as recoverable by the syndicate if the supply is to the syndicate and if the insured in relation to the claim belongs outside the EU. Such input tax is directly attributable to outside the scope supplies with input tax recovery under the terms of the Specified Supplies Order 1999. The evidence to substantiate input tax claims by syndicates is the Underwriters' Signing Message (USM).

10.2 The information contained within the USMs will be substantiated by LPSO upon requests made by Customs and Excise to Lloyd's via procedures agreed with Lloyd's.

10.3 LPSO will retain the original invoices or their scanned images for the period required under prevailing VAT legislation and make them available upon request.

11. IMPORTED SERVICES

11.1 *LeBoeuf Lamb Greene & MacRae*

Fees charged by the US firm of LeBoeuf Lamb Green & MacRae are paid centrally by Lloyd's and recharged to the syndicates. The invoices produced by Lloyd's may be treated as invoices for the purposes of calculating the VAT charges under the reverse charge procedure. The fees charged to syndicates relate to a number of supplies and cannot at this time be directly attributed to specific supplies of insurance. Therefore the fees are regarded as residual and input tax may be recovered at the appropriate syndicate rate.

Gross net claims

11.2 Monthly summaries will be made of the values of claims costs processed by LPSO on behalf of syndicates.

11.3 A proportion of the services received in dealing with claims are supplied from overseas and are subject to the reverse charge procedure. To arrive at the value of the international services a survey is to be conducted periodically. The procedure and intervals will be as agreed with Lloyd's. Lloyd's will advise syndicates of the prevailing percentage figure.

11.4 Syndicates will apply the percentage to the gross net claims figures to arrive at the notional net value of reverse charge services. The VAT rate will be applied to the calculated figure to arrive at the output tax to be declared. The associated input tax will be recovered at the syndicate recovery rate.

Tax point

11.5 The tax point is taken as the last working day of the relevant month.

12. GENERAL

These arrangements are agreed as guidelines setting out a minimum framework for the operation of VAT in the Lloyd's market from 1 January 2000 onwards as amended by further agreement on 6 January 2004. Except as otherwise specifically stated, everything in these arrangements is to be governed by the VAT legislation in force at the time.

Signed .... Date..

(Corporation of Lloyd's)

Signed .... Date..

(HM Customs and Excise)

Appendix 16: VATA 1994, Sch. 9, Grp. 2

SCHEDULE 9 – EXEMPTIONS

Sections 8 and 31

GROUP 2 – INSURANCE

Item No.
1. Insurance transactions and reinsurance transactions.
2. [Deleted by the substitution of item 1 for former items 1 to 3 by SI 2004/3083, art. 3.]
3. [Deleted by the substitution of item 1 for former items 1 to 3 by SI 2004/3083, art. 3.]
4. The provision by an insurance broker or insurance agent of any of the services of an insurance intermediary in a case in which those services–
(a) are related (whether or not a contract of insurance or reinsurance is finally concluded) to an insurance transaction or a reinsurance transaction; and
(b) are provided by that broker or agent in the course of his acting in an intermediary capacity.

Notes:
(A1) [Omitted by SI 2004/3083, art. 5.]
(B1) [Omitted by SI 2004/3083, art. 5.]
(C1) [Omitted by SI 2004/3083, art. 5.]
(1) For the purposes of item 4 services are **services of an insurance intermediary** if they fall within any of the following paragraphs–
(a) the bringing together, with a view to the insurance or reinsurance of risks, of–
  (i) persons who are or may be seeking insurance or reinsurance, and
  (ii) persons who provide insurance or reinsurance;
(b) the carrying out of work preparatory to the conclusion of contracts of insurance or reinsurance;
(c) the provision of assistance in the administration and performance of such contracts, including the handling of claims;
(d) the collection of premiums.
(2) For the purposes of item 4 an insurance broker or insurance agent is acting **'in an intermediary capacity'** wherever he is acting as an intermediary, or one of the intermediaries, between–
(a) a person who provides insurance or reinsurance, and
(b) a person who is or may be seeking insurance or reinsurance or is an insured person.
(3) Where–
(a) a person (the **'supplier'**) makes a supply of goods or services to another (the **'customer'**),
(b) the supply of the goods or services is a taxable supply and is not a zero-rated supply,
(c) a transaction under which insurance is to be or may be arranged for the customer is entered into in connection with the supply of the goods or services,
(d) a supply of services which are related (whether or not a contract of insurance is finally concluded) to the provision of insurance in pursuance of that transaction is made by–
  (i) the person by whom the supply of the goods or services is made, or
  (ii) a person who is connected with that person and, in connection with the provision of that insurance, deals directly with the customer,
  and
(e) the related services do not consist in the handling of claims under the contract for that insurance,
those related services do not fall within item 4 unless the relevant requirements are fulfilled.
(4) For the purposes of Note (3) the **relevant requirements** are–
(a) that a document containing the statements specified in Note (5) is prepared;
(b) that the matters that must be stated in the document have been disclosed to the customer at or before the time when the transaction mentioned in Note (3)(c) is entered into; and

(c) that there is compliance with all such requirements (if any) as to–
   (i) the preparation and form of the document,
   (ii) the manner of disclosing to the customer the matters that must be stated in the document, and
   (iii) the delivery of a copy of the document to the customer,

as may be set out in a notice that has been published by the Commissioners and has not been withdrawn.

(5) The statements referred to in Note (4) are–

(a) a statement setting out the amount of the premium under any contract of insurance that is to be or may be entered into in pursuance of the transaction in question; and

(b) a statement setting out every amount that the customer is, is to be or has been required to pay, otherwise than by way of such a premium, in connection with that transaction or anything that is to be, may be or has been done in pursuance of that transaction.

(6) For the purposes of Note (3) any question whether a person is **connected** with another shall be determined in accordance with section 1122 of the Corporation Tax Act 2010.

(7) Item 4 does not include–

(a) the supply of any market research, product design, advertising, promotional or similar services; or

(b) the collection, collation and provision of information for use in connection with market research, product design, advertising, promotional or similar activities.

(8) Item 4 does not include the supply of any valuation or inspection services.

(9) Item 4 does not include the supply of any services by loss adjusters, average adjusters, motor assessors, surveyors or other experts except where–

(a) the services consist in the handling of a claim under a contract of insurance or reinsurance;

(b) the person handling the claim is authorised when doing so to act on behalf of the insurer or reinsurer; and

(c) that person's authority so to act includes written authority to determine whether to accept or reject the claim and, where accepting it in whole or in part, to settle the amount to be paid on the claim.

(10) Item 4 does not include the supply of any services which–

(a) are supplied in pursuance of a contract of insurance or reinsurance or of any arrangements made in connection with such a contract; and

(b) are so supplied either–
   (i) instead of the payment of the whole or any part of any indemnity for which the contract provides, or
   (ii) for the purpose, in any other manner, of satisfying any claim under that contract, whether in whole or in part.

Appendix 17: Extracts from Notice 701/21 Gold (October 2011)

11. The special accounting scheme for gold transactions

Note: the special accounting scheme for gold is compulsory.

11.1 About the special accounting scheme

The special accounting scheme for gold is to be used for the transactions in gold listed below at paragraph 11.2 between VAT registered traders.

Under normal VAT procedures, if you are a VAT registered trader selling goods you issue a VAT invoice and receive payment for the price of the goods and the VAT due on the sale. You (as the seller) then account to us for this VAT on your next VAT return.

The scheme transfers the responsibility for paying the VAT on certain transactions in gold from the seller to the buyer.

11.2 When does the scheme apply?

The special accounting scheme for gold **must** be used when:

- the seller and the buyer are both VAT registered persons, or are persons liable to be registered as a consequence of the transaction, or other transactions;
- the supply by the seller is by way of business and the buyer is making the purchase in connection with any business carried on by them; or
- you carry out treatment or processing work on your customers' goods, and the goods produced are fine gold (see section 16), gold grain of any purity, or gold coins.

The special accounting scheme for gold will apply if you supply:

- goods consisting of fine gold (see section 16), and gold coins except coins traded under the second-hand margin scheme. See Notice 718 *Margin schemes for second-hand goods, works of art, antiques and collectors' items.* Supplies of dental gold, gold targets and gold slugs are excluded;
- goods containing gold for which the amount paid or payable for the supply (apart from any VAT) does not exceed, or exceeds by no more than a negligible amount, the open market value of the gold contained in the goods. The open market value of the gold is the 'fix price' of the gold at the time of supply, this is the price set in the twice-daily meetings by London Gold Fixing Ltd. This includes supplies of scrap (including live scrap – scrapped jewellery, broken jewellery, watch cases, cigarette cases etc) and sweepings. Supplies of part manufactured or finished jewellery, gold compounds and semi manufactured carated products, are excluded (except gold grain);
- services of treating or processing goods to make fine gold (see section 16), gold grain or gold coins; or
- investment gold regardless of whether the supply is classed as a supply of goods or a supply of services where the seller has exercised the option to tax outlined at section 4, or where the supply is between a member and a non-member of the London Bullion Market Association.

11.3 How does the scheme work?

If you are liable to use the special accounting scheme, you should follow the procedure table below.

Step	Ask yourself...	Further information
1	Are you a UK VAT registered business? *If 'yes', go to step 3.* *If 'no', go to step 2.*	

Appendix 17: Extracts from Notice 701/21 Gold (October 2011)

Step	Ask yourself...	Further information
2	Are you liable to be registered for VAT? If 'yes', **apply to register**. Failure to do so may make you liable to financial penalties. If 'no', you are not making taxable supplies.	See section 13 and Notice 700/1 *Should I be registered for VAT?*
3	Is this a supply of gold of a type described in paragraph 11.2? If 'yes', go to step 5 for gold coins, or step 7 for other supplies of gold. If 'no', go to step 4.	
4	Is this a supply of gold coins? If 'yes', go to step 5. If 'no', the supply is **not** within the scope of the special accounting scheme. You **must** charge VAT to your customer who should pay it to you. You **must** issue a VAT invoice and account for the VAT to HM Revenue & Customs.	
5	Are the coins investment gold coins? If 'yes', go to step 6. If 'no', VAT may be accounted for under the margin scheme, or go to step 7.	See Notice 701/21A *Investment gold coins*. See Notice 718 *Margin scheme for second-hand goods*
6	Are you a producer or transformer of investment gold coins who has opted to tax the supply? If 'yes', go to step 7. If 'no', your supply is exempt and the special accounting scheme does not apply unless you are a member or are dealing with a member of the London Bullion Market Association.	See section 4. See paragraph 11.5.
7	Are you satisfied your buyer is a UK VAT registered business? If 'yes', the supply is within the scope of the special accounting scheme. You must issue a tax invoice as described in paragraph 11.6. The **purchaser** pays you the **VAT exclusive price** of the gold and accounts for the output tax to HM Revenue & Customs. If 'no', the special accounting scheme does not apply.	See paragraphs 11.4 and 11.6.

11.4 Accounting for output tax as a purchaser

If you purchase gold under the special accounting scheme for gold, you must account for VAT on the value of the supply of gold made by the seller. If you fail to do this, we may assess you for the VAT due on the transaction.

If you purchase manufactured goods containing gold which are held out for sale as such, and you pay over VAT to your supplier, you may be required to prove that your purchase did not fall within the provisions of the special accounting scheme for gold. If you cannot prove this, you may be treated as if you purchased gold and you will be required to account for the output tax due under the special accounting scheme.

11.5 Dealings on the terminal market in gold

Supplies which are zero-rated under the Terminal Markets Order are unaffected by the special accounting scheme for gold. However, transactions between members of the London Bullion Market Association and taxable persons who are not members of that Association are taxable at the standard rate and the special accounting scheme applies (see paragraph 10.5). In such a case the London Bullion Market Association member or non-member must raise a VAT invoice as usual. This must bear the form of words detailed in paragraph 11.6 and the buyer is responsible for accounting for the seller's output tax. See Notice 701/9 *Derivatives and terminal markets*.

11.6 Issue of VAT invoices for supplies of gold covered by the scheme

If you make a supply of gold under the special accounting scheme for gold, you must issue a VAT invoice to the buyer. This must show all of the information normally required to be shown on VAT invoices, (see Notice 700 *The VAT Guide*, and for investment gold paragraph 6.2). The seller's invoice must include a form of words to the effect that the output tax shown on the invoice is payable to Customs by the purchaser of the gold. The suggested form of words is:

'£......output tax on this supply of gold to be accounted for to HM Revenue & Customs by the buyer.'

The invoice must also show:

(a) the time of supply (or tax point). This is ordinarily the date of delivery of the gold or the date when the gold is made available for removal by the purchaser, (see Notice 700 *The VAT Guide*);

and

(b) a description sufficient to identify the goods which includes:
- the weight of the gold;
- the purity of the gold;
- the number of individual items (where possible); and
- the fix price of the gold on the day of delivery;

and

(c) the name and address of the buyer;

and

(d) the invoice date and number.

If you are approved to issue self-billed VAT invoices, you must also show all of the above details.

12. Filling in your VAT return

Box	Information to enter
1	If you have purchased gold, include the VAT due on your purchase of gold. The purchase of gold is treated as a supply by you as well as by your supplier. You must account for the output tax in the same period that you purchase the gold or it is made available for removal by you whether or not you have sold it.
	If you have sold gold under the special accounting scheme, do not show the VAT shown on your sales invoice in this box.
	In this box you must also show output tax due on your other supplies under the normal VAT accounting mechanism.
2	In this box include acquisition (see section 16) tax on any goods, including gold acquired from other EC member states.
3	Enter the sum of box 1 and box 2.

Box	Information to enter
4	Include the VAT due on your purchases of gold. In this box you must also show input tax to be reclaimed under the normal VAT accounting procedures on your other purchases and acquisitions.
5	Complete as normal.
6	Complete as normal. If you have sold gold, enter the VAT-exclusive value of the sale. If you have purchased gold include its value here. This is deemed to be a supply by you, as well as by your supplier.
7	Complete as normal. Include the value of gold you have bought.
8 & 9	Complete as normal.

13. Registration

The special accounting scheme for gold covers supplies of gold between taxable persons as outlined in paragraph 11.2. A taxable person is someone who is either registered for VAT or who is liable to be registered for VAT.

The supply of gold covered by the scheme is treated as a taxable supply by the customer as well as by the seller for the purposes of registration.

In deciding if you are liable to register for VAT you must add the value of your business *purchases* of gold to the value of other taxable supplies which you make including *sales* of gold to arrive at your taxable turnover. So, if you purchase gold in the course or furtherance of a business and you are not registered for VAT, then you must consider whether you are liable to be registered as follows if either:

- in a 12 month period your taxable supplies exceed the registration threshold, you must notify your local Business Advice Centre within 30 days of the end of the month in which the limit was exceeded;

  or

- there are reasonable grounds for believing that the taxable supplies which you will make **in the next 30 days** will exceed the threshold, then you must notify your local Business Advice Centre within 30 days of the day on which grounds first existed. However, there are special rules for persons who become liable to be registered for VAT solely by virtue of their dealings in investment gold with members of the London Bullion Market Association. If you require further advice you should contact our Helpline on 0845 010 9000.

Further information on VAT registration can be found in Notice 700/1 *Should I be registered for VAT?* **If you fail to notify Customs at the proper time you may be liable to a financial penalty.**

Appendix 18: Value Added Tax (Terminal Markets) Order 1973 (SI 1973/173)

(SI 1973/173, as amended by SI 1975/385, SI 1980/304, SI 1981/338, SI 1981/955, SI 1984/202, SI 1985/1046, SI 1987/806, SI 1997/1836, SI 1999/3117)

Made 6 February 1973 by the Treasury under s. 26 of the Finance Act 1972 [VATA 1994, s. 50].
Operative from 1 April 1973.

1 This Order may be cited as the Value Added Tax (Terminal Markets) Order 1973 and shall come into operation on 1st April 1973.

2(1) The Interpretation Act 1889 [Interpretation Act 1978] shall apply for the interpretation of this Order as it applies for the interpretation of an Act of Parliament.

2(2) This Order applies to the following terminal markets–

the London Metal Exchange,
the London Rubber Market,
the London Cocoa Terminal Market,
the London Coffee Terminal Market,
the London Sugar Terminal Market,
the London Vegetable Oil Terminal Market,
the London Wool Terminal Market,
the London Bullion Market,
the London Meat Futures Market,
the London Grain Futures Market,
the London Soya Bean Meal Futures Market,
the Liverpool Barley Futures Market,
the International Petroleum Exchange of London,
the London Potato Futures Market,
the London Platinum and Palladium Market, and
the London Securities and Derivatives Exchange Limited (OMLX).

2(3) References in this Order to a **member of a market** include any person ordinarily engaged in dealings on the market.

2(4) Notwithstanding paragraph 3 above, for the purposes of this Order a person is to be regarded as '**being a member of the London Bullion Market**' only if that person is a member of the London Bullion Market Association.

2(5) In this Order–

'**investment gold**' has the same meaning as that expression has for the purposes of Group 15 of Schedule 9 to the Value Added Tax Act 1994;
'**the Act**' means the Value Added Tax Act 1994.

3(1) The following supplies of goods or services in the course of dealings on a terminal market to which this Order applies are hereby zero-rated, subject to the conditions specified in this Article–

(a) the sale by or to a member of the market of any goods, other than investment gold, ordinarily dealt with on the market,
(b) the grant by or to a member of the market of a right to acquire such goods,
(c) where a sale of goods or the grant of a right zero-rated under sub-paragraph (a) or (b) above is made, or where a supply of a description falling within article 4 or 5 below is made, in dealings between members of the market acting as agents, the supply by those members to their principals of their services in so acting.

Appendix 18: Value Added Tax (Terminal Markets) Order 1973 (SI 1973/173)

3(2) The zero-rating of a sale by virtue of paragraph (1)(a) above is subject to the condition that the sale is either–
(a) a sale which, as a result of other dealings on the market, does not lead to a delivery of the goods by the seller to the buyer, or
(b) a sale by and to a member of the market which–
- (i) if the market is the London Metal Exchange, is a sale between members entitled to deal in the ring,
- (ii) if the market is the London Cocoa Terminal Market, the London Coffee Terminal Market, the London Meat Futures Market, the International Petroleum Exchange of London, the London Potato Futures Market, the London Soya Bean Meal Futures Market, the London Sugar Terminal Market, the London Vegetable Oil Terminal Market or the London Wool Terminal Market, is a sale registered with the International Commodities Clearing House Limited,
- (iii) if the market is the London Grain Futures Market, is a sale registered in the Clearing House of the Grain and Feed Trade Association Limited, and
- (iv) if the market is the Liverpool Barley Futures Market, is a sale registered at the Clearing House of the Liverpool Corn Trade Association Limited.

3(3) The zero-rating of the grant of a right by virtue of paragraph (1)(b) above is subject to the condition that either–
(a) the right is exercisable at a date later than that on which it is granted, or
(b) any sale resulting from the exercise of the right would be a sale with respect to which the condition specified in paragraph (2) above is satisfied.

4 Supplies between taxable persons which but for Note 4(a) to Group 15 of Schedule 9 to the Act (exemption for investment gold) would have fallen within that Group are hereby zero-rated.

5 Subject to articles 6 and 7 below, section 55(1) to (4) of the Act (customers to account for tax on supplies of gold) shall apply to any supply between taxable persons which but for Note 4(b) to Group 15 of Schedule 9 to the Act would have fallen within that Group.

6 Subject to article 7 below, where a taxable person who is not a member of the London Bullion Market Association makes or receives a supply falling within the description in article 5 is liable to be registered under Schedule 1 or under Schedule 3 to the Act solely by virtue of that supply or acquisition, paragraphs 5 to 8 of Schedule 1 or paragraph 3 of Schedule 3 to the Act (notification of liability and registration) shall not apply.

7 Notwithstanding section 55(2) of the Act, where articles 5 and 6 above apply, it shall be for the London Bullion Market Association member, on the non-member's behalf, to keep a record of the supplies and to pay to the Commissioners of Customs and Excise the net amount of VAT, and not for the person who is not a member.

Appendix 19: VATA 1994, Sch. 9, Grp. 15

SCHEDULE 9 – EXEMPTIONS

Sections 8 and 31

GROUP 15 – INVESTMENT GOLD

Item No.
1. The supply of investment gold.
2. The grant, assignment or surrender of any right, interest, or claim in, over or to investment gold if the right, interest or claim is or confers a right to the transfer of the possession of investment gold.
3. The supply, by a person acting as agent for a disclosed principal, of services consisting of–
(a) the effecting of a supply falling within item 1 or 2 that is made by or to his principal, or
(b) attempting to effect a supply falling within item 1 or 2 that is intended to be made by or to his principal but is not in fact made.

Notes:
(1) For the purposes of this Group **'investment gold'** means–
(a) gold of a purity not less than 995 thousandths that is in the form of a bar, or a wafer, of a weight accepted by the bullion markets;
(b) a gold coin minted after 1800 that–
  (i) is of a purity of not less than 900 thousandths,
  (ii) is, or has been, legal tender in its country of origin, and
  (iii) is of a description of coin that is normally sold at a price that does not exceed 180% of the open market value of the gold contained in the coin; or
(c) a gold coin of a description specified in a notice that has been published by the Commissioners for the purposes of this Group and has not been withdrawn.
(2) A notice under Note (1)(c) may provide that a description specified in the notice has effect only for the purposes of supplies made at times falling within a period specified in the notice.
(3) Item 2 does not include–
(a) the grant of an option, or
(b) the assignment or surrender of a right under an option at a time before the option is exercised.
(4) This Group does not include a supply–
(a) between members of the London Bullion Market Association, or
(b) by a member of that Association to a taxable person who is not a member or by such a person to a member.

Appendix 20: VAT: Guidance on the VAT treatment of certain Islamic products

This Information Sheet sets out guidance on the VAT treatment of certain Islamic products currently being offered to the general public, businesses and other financial institutions by various banks in the UK.

1 Introduction

1.1 What is this Information Sheet about?

HM Revenue and Customs (HMRC), providers of Islamic products and representative trade bodies have been in discussions concerning the VAT treatment of certain Islamic products currently being offered to the general public, businesses and other financial institutions by various banks in the UK. This VAT Information Sheet sets out the findings of those discussions and the VAT treatment of those products.

This VAT Information Sheet is intended to supplement, not replace, existing HMRC guidance. It is intended that the information contained herein will be included in Notice 701/49 Finance at a later date.

1.2 Who does it affect?

This VAT Information Sheet clarifies the VAT treatment of certain Islamic products currently being offered to the general public, businesses and other financial institutions by various banks in the UK and should be read by providers of those products or by those introducing customers to those providers.

1.3 When does it come into effect?

This VAT Information Sheet provides advice to providers of certain Islamic products and the VAT treatments outlined should be applied immediately.

If you are a provider of any of the Islamic products listed in this VAT Information Sheet and realise that you have treated your services incorrectly for VAT please see paragraph 5.3.

1.4 Changes in contractual details

Please be aware that the VAT treatments of the products set out in this Information Sheet have been drawn from information, including contractual details, provided by various parties. Should the details change in any way from that described HMRC reserves the right to review the VAT treatments set out in this Information Sheet and, if necessary, to change the VAT treatment from a current or future date.

1.5 Further reading

This VAT Information Sheet should be read in conjunction with the following Notices:

- 701/9 Derivatives and Terminal Markets.
- 701/49 Finance.

Appendix 20: VAT: Guidance on the VAT treatment of certain Islamic products

You may also need to read the following Notices:

- 700/6 Rulings.
- 700/9 Transfer of business as a going concern.
- 701/21 Gold.
- 701/21A Investment gold coins.
- 700/45 How to correct VAT errors and make adjustments or claims.
- 708 Buildings and construction.
- 741 Place of supply of services.
- 742 Land and Property.
- 742A Opting to tax land and buildings.

2. Sharia'a principles

Sharia'a is a body of Islamic law and is a framework regulating aspects of private and public life.

According to Sharia'a principles the following are prohibited:

- the charging or receipt of interest (riba)
- uncertainty or deception, for example an ambiguity or lack of clarity in the terms of a contract that can give rise to speculation (gharar)
- gambling or speculation, for example any transaction undertaken for purely speculative purposes (maisir)
- unethical investments, for example dealing in activities or commodities that include pork, pornography, arms or munitions, conventional financial services, cinema, tobacco, gambling or alcohol.

This has meant that many Muslims have been unable or unwilling to obtain conventional credit finance in order to purchase goods and/or services because those products are prohibited in their faith.

In order to be able to provide Sharia'a compliant products, banks and other financial institutions in the UK, along with boards of Sharia'a scholars, have worked together to create the products listed in this Information Sheet. The basic tenants under which these products operate are via a trade or rental arrangement – which are allowed under Sharia'a.

3. Description of Islamic products and their VAT treatment

3.1 Price plus 'profit'

There are three products that use the 'price plus 'profit' principle to fund purchases – a basic product (called 'Murabaha'), one that involves commodity transactions (called 'commodity Murabaha') and a reverse of this (called 'reverse Murabaha').

3.1.1 Basic price plus 'profit' ('Murabaha')

Description

This product can be used to fund the purchase of a variety of assets, including cars, fridges, televisions and property (both residential and commercial).

Example: A customer of a financial institution (eg a bank) wishes to purchase an asset but does not have the available funds. The customer therefore enters into an agreement with the bank under which the bank will purchase the asset for the sale price (eg £10,000), taking title, whilst the customer takes possession of the asset as agent for the bank. The bank will then sell the asset to the customer for sale price plus a 'profit' (eg £15,000 (being the selling price of £10,000 and £5,000 'profit')), allowing the customer to

Appendix 20: VAT: Guidance on the VAT treatment of certain Islamic products

defer payment by instalment over a set period of time or to pay the total price at a specified future date. Title to the asset will always pass from the bank to the customer at the beginning of the arrangement.

VAT treatment (goods)

Where title to the asset passes from the bank to the customer the sale is treated in the same way as a credit sale (please see paragraph 4.3 of Notice 701/49 Finance). There are two supplies being made by the bank – one of the goods and one of the facility to defer payment.

Consideration for supply of the goods will follow the normal liability rules. The 'profit' element will be treated as consideration for the facility to defer payment and will be exempt under the VAT Act 1994, Schedule 9, Group 5, item 3.

VAT treatment (property)

As with goods, the sale is treated in the same way as a credit sale (please see paragraph 4.3 of Notice 701/49 Finance). There are two supplies being made by the bank - one of the property and one of the facility to defer payment.

For the liability of the sale of the property you should read Notice 708 Buildings and construction, Notice 742 Land and Property and Notice 742A Opting to tax land and buildings.

The 'profit' element will be treated as consideration for the facility to defer payment and will be exempt under the VAT Act 1994, Schedule 9, Group 5, item 3.

When property is transferred as part of the purchase of a going concern the bank will not have operated the business. Where the consideration of in regard to the property the liability will follow the normal rules for property (see also paragraph 4.2 of this Information Sheet).

3.1.2 Price plus 'profit' involving commodity transactions ('commodity Murabaha')

Description

This product can operate in either of the following ways.

Example 1: A customer requires a loan of £10,000. The bank purchases commodities from a supplier for £10,000, taking title but not delivery, and then sells immediately to the customer for £10,500 (price and 'profit'), allowing the customer to defer payment, either over a set period or until a specified future date. The customer takes title to the commodities (but not delivery). The customer, using the bank as its agent, then immediately sells the commodities for £10,000 to a purchaser (the bank makes no charge to the customer for acting as agent). All of this is done on spot (ie it is done almost instantaneously to avoid the risk of either a rise or fall in the commodity price). The £10,000 cash is credited into the customer's account for the customer to use as he/she wishes. The £500 'profit' on the sale of the commodity by the bank to the customer is what the bank makes from the deal.

Example 2: A customer requires a loan of £10,000. The bank, using an agent, purchases commodities from a supplier for £10,000, taking title but not delivery, and sells immediately to the customer for £10,500 (price and 'profit'), allowing the customer to defer payment, either over a set period or until a specified future date. The customer takes title to the commodities. All of this is done on spot (ie it is done almost instantaneously to avoid the risk of either a rise or fall in the commodity price). The £500 'profit' on the sale of the commodity by the bank to the customer is what the bank makes from the deal.

VAT treatment

The VAT treatment of commodities is set out in Notice 701/9 Derivatives and Terminal Markets. Please note that there are separate rules covering supplies of investment gold, and these can be found in Notice 701/21 Gold.

Appendix 20: VAT: Guidance on the VAT treatment of certain Islamic products

The 'profit' element made by the bank will be treated as consideration for the facility to defer payment and will be exempt under the VAT Act 1994, Schedule 9, Group 5, item 2.

3.1.3 Reverse of the price plus 'profit' involving commodity transactions ('reverse Murabaha')

Description

This product is the reverse to the commodity Murabaha, and is normally used to affect a loan between financial institutions. As with the commodity Murabaha described above this product can operate in either of the following ways:

Example 1: Bank A requires a loan of £100m. Bank B purchases commodities from a supplier for £100m, but does not take delivery, Bank A acting as agent for Bank B but making no charge for doing this. Bank A takes title to the commodities. Bank A then sells the commodities immediately to Bank B for £105m (price and 'profit'), allowing Bank B to defer payment, either over a set period or at a specified future date. Bank B takes title to the commodities but not delivery. Bank B then immediately sells the commodities for £100m to an end-purchaser. All of this is done on spot (ie it is done almost instantaneously to avoid the risk of either a rise or fall in the commodity price). The £100m cash is credited into Bank A's account.

Example 2: Bank A requires a loan of £100m. Bank B purchases commodities from a supplier for £100m, taking title but not delivery, and sells immediately to Bank A for £105m (price and 'profit'), allowing Bank A to defer payment, either over a set period or at a specified future date. Bank A takes title to the commodities but not delivery. Bank A, with Bank B now acting as its agent, immediately sells the commodities for £100m to an end-purchaser. All of this is done on spot (ie it is done almost instantaneously to avoid the risk of either a rise or fall in the commodity price). The £100m cash is credited into Bank A's account.

VAT treatment

See the VAT treatment set out in paragraph 3.1.2.

3.2 Lease only ('Ijara')

Description

This product is a basic leasing product that can be used to lease a variety of assets, including cars, fridges, televisions and property (both residential and commercial). The financial institution (eg a bank) acquires title to the asset and leases it to its customer. At no time does title to the asset pass to the customer, nor is it expected to pass. If the customer wishes to purchase the asset at a later date a separate agreement is drawn up.

VAT treatment

Consideration for supplies made under this arrangement will be treated in the same way as other forms of leasing agreements. Where the consideration is for a supply of services, other than property, it is taxable at the standard rate of VAT. Where the consideration is in regard to property, the liability will follow the normal rules for property (please see Notice 708 Buildings and construction, Notice 742 Land and Property and Notice 742A Opting to tax land and buildings).

3.3 Lease and purchase ('Ijara-wa-Iqtina')

Description

This product is the same as the Ijara described above except that title to the asset is expected to pass to the customer at some time, usually at the end of the contract period. It can be used to purchase both goods and property.

VAT treatment (goods)

This product will be treated in the same way as a Hire Purchase/Conditional Sale (please see paragraph 4.3 of Notice 701/49 Finance). There are two supplies being made by the bank – one of the goods and one of the facility to defer payment.

Consideration for supply of the goods will follow the normal liability rules. The additional charge above the price of the goods will be treated as consideration for a deferred payment facility and thus exempt under the VAT Act 1994, Schedule 9, Group 5, item 3.

VAT treatment (property)

Where the bank is the absolute legal and beneficial owner of the property the transaction will be treated in the same way as for goods (eg Hire Purchase/Conditional Sale), except that the normal rules for property will apply for the sale of the asset (please see Notice 708 Buildings and construction, Notice 742 Land and Property and Notice 742A Opting to tax land and buildings). The additional charge above the price of the property will be treated as consideration for a deferred payment facility and thus exempt under the VAT Act 1994, Schedule 9, Group 5, item 3.

Where the bank is unlikely to be the absolute legal and beneficial owner of the property, but takes title only by way of security, the assignment of the title by the customer to the bank operates by way of a mortgage. Any payments made by the customer to the bank will be repayments of the loan and, where the amount repaid is greater than the capital sum advanced, will be consideration for a grant of credit and be exempt under the VAT Act 1994, Schedule 9, Group 5, item 2.

When property is transferred as part of the purchase of a going concern the bank will not have operated the business. Where the consideration of in regard to the property the liability will follow the normal rules for property (see also paragraph 4.2 of this Information Sheet).

3.4 Shared ownership ('diminishing Musharaka')

Description

This product involves the use of two written contracts, being a lease agreement ('Ijara') and a diminishing ownership agreement ('Musharaka'), where two or more parties share ownership of an asset.

Example: A customer wishes to purchase a residential property for £200,000. He/she pays a deposit of £20,000 to the vendor of the property and then enters into a diminishing ownership agreement with the bank, under which the bank pays the outstanding £180,000, taking title to the property by way of a sub-sale between the vendor and the bank. The bank's customer now has a 10% beneficial interest (or share) in the property, with the remainder being with the bank. The bank allows the customer to defer payment of the £180,000 over a period of twenty-five years. It does not (and cannot) add any interest to the £180,000 and so under this contract the customer pays back the exact amount paid out by the bank.

At the same time as the customer enters into the diminishing ownership agreement he also enters into a lease agreement, whereby the bank agrees to lease its share of the house to the customer for a variable amount of rent. This lease agreement runs concurrent with the diminishing ownership agreement.

The customer may also be expected to pay any outgoings related to the property as well as all administrative and legal costs, arrangements fees, Stamp Duty Land Tax, HM Registry fees and VAT (if applicable).

Both the amount repaid under the diminishing ownership agreement and the amount paid under the lease agreement are amalgamated and used to calculate how much of the bank's share of the property has been purchased per month by the customer. As the bank's share in the property decreases so does the amount paid under the lease agreement.

At the end of the twenty-five years, and if all the conditions contained within the two contracts have been met, the bank will pass title to the property to customer under the diminishing ownership agreement, normally for an additional payment.

NB - whilst some banks also require the customer to sign a third agreement under which the customer provides some form of security against payment of the amounts due under the other two contracts, other banks may also require more than three agreements to be signed.

VAT treatment

The central supplies are (i) the gradual sale of equitable interest, and (ii) lease of property. As such consideration for supplies made under this form of arrangement will follow the normal rules for property (please see Notice 708 Buildings and construction, Notice 742 Land and Property and Notice 742A Opting to tax land and buildings).

3.5 Agency ('Wakala')

Description

This is an investment product, which functions in the same way as Mudaraba, which is discussed at paragraph 3.7. The difference between the two is that with a Mudaraba all the profit is divided between the parties, whilst with a Wakala the investor receives only the agreed ratio against investment. Anything made above that ratio is kept by the financial institution and not given to the investor.

Example: an investor agrees to invest a sum with the bank for an agreed return (eg 5%). The bank pools the investor's funds with the funds of other investors and its own capital and invests in Sharia'a compliant assets. At the end of a given period (eg a month) the bank returns the invested sum to the investor along with the agreed 5%. Any additional revenue that the bank makes on the customer's money is kept by the bank (eg if the bank makes 6% then 5% is given to the customer and the additional 1% is kept by the bank). If the bank does not make the agreed percentage return then the investor gets what has been made whilst the bank gets nothing (eg if only 4% is achieved then the investor gets the full 4%).

VAT treatment

The VAT treatment depends on whether the bank or other financial institution makes the investment decisions (discretionary or 'unrestricted') or whether it follows the instructions of its clients (non-discretionary or 'restricted').

Where the bank makes the investment decisions any charges made by the bank to the investor will follow the policy set out in paragraph 2.10 of Notice 701/49 Finance. The additional profit made by the bank will be outside the scope of VAT.

Where the bank follows the instructions of its clients the additional revenue made by the bank on the investment of the capital will be taxable at the standard-rate. This is because what the bank is doing is a form of portfolio/investment management (please see paragraph 7.1 of Notice 701/49 Finance).

3.6 Islamic current accounts

Description

These operate in the same way as a conventional current account except that there is no overdraft facility and no interest added by the bank to the account for funds in credit.

VAT treatment

Any charges made by the bank will follow the policy set out in paragraph 2.10 of Notice 701/49 Finance.

3.7 Islamic savings accounts (operated under an unrestricted 'Mudaraba' contract)

Description

This product operates under Mudaraba principles whereby the bank will act as a partner and manager and applies its expertise. The bank acts in a discretionary/unrestricted capacity.

Like conventional savings accounts, the aim of the product is to give investors an agreed return on their investments. Investors normally have to keep their money in the account for a set period of time. The bank pools the investor's money with that of other investors and the bank's own money and then invests it in Sharia'a compliant equities.

At the end of each month the gross income is calculated and then various deductions are made (eg direct costs (including costs such as marketing), fees and other expenses incurred by the bank in investing the pooled funds). The bank's share of the income is then calculated and the remainder is credited to the customer's account.

VAT treatment

See the VAT treatment set out in paragraph 3.6.

4 Other VAT issues

4.1 Intermediary services

The policy for determining whether someone is acting as an intermediary for the purposes of the finance exemption is set out in section 9 of Notice 701/49 Finance.

Where you introduce customers to products that are not financial services, for example transactions in land or property, the finance exemption for intermediaries will not apply and so any fees charged will be taxable at the standard rate of VAT.

4.2 Transfers of a going concern (TOGC)

Notice 700/9 Transfers of a going concern sets out the conditions that must be met if the transfer of a business is to be treated as a going concern. If the conditions are not met then the transfer cannot be treated as a going concern and the normal VAT rules will apply to supplies of assets (note particularly paragraph 2.3.3 of the Notice on consecutive transfers of businesses).

4.3 Place of supply of services relating to land and property

If a supply consists of services that relate to land or property, the place of supply of those services is where the land itself is located, irrespective of where either the bank etc or its customer belongs. It should also be borne in mind that:

- there may be a requirement to account for the reverse charge if both the bank etc and the land are located in the UK but the supplier of those services belongs outside the UK
- if a bank etc supplies services relating to land in another member State, it might be required to register for VAT in that member State.

For further information you should read Notice 741 Place of supply of services.

4.4 Partial exemption

It is anticipated that adjustments may be needed to partial exemption methods to ensure that they achieve a fair and reasonable result. Businesses that provide Islamic products should therefore review their methods and, if necessary, contact HMRC to discuss a new fair and reasonable method going forward. Further guidance is available in VAT Notice 706 Partial exemption.

Businesses using the standard method may need to make adjustments under the standard method override, which came into effect on 18th April 2002. The override requires businesses to make an adjustment to their partial exemption calculations where the input tax deducted during the tax year differs substantially from a deduction based on use. If override adjustments are required on a regular basis then the business should certainly contact HMRC to discuss a new method going forward.

5. Frequently asked questions

[text omitted]

Appendix 21: Flowchart for Specified Bodies

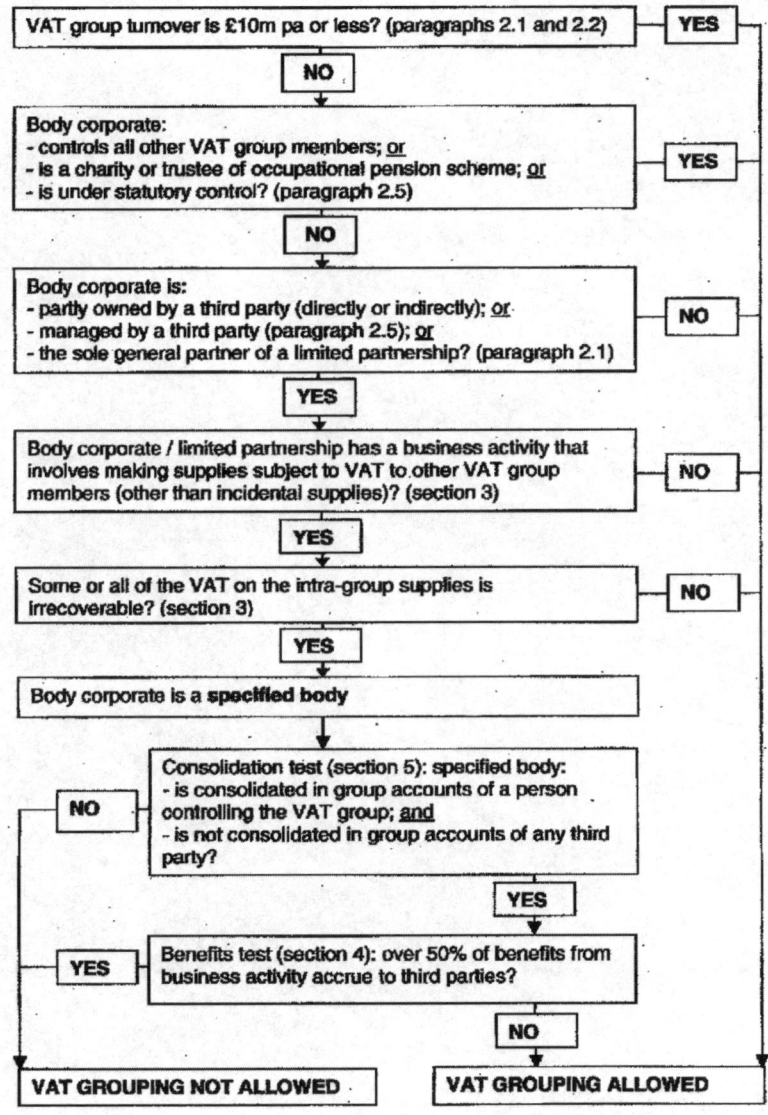

Appendix 22: VAT Finance Manual, para. VATFIN7650 – 'The Retail Distribution Review'

VATFIN7655 – The Retail Distribution Review

New regulatory rules come into force on 31 December 2012 following the FSA's Retail Distribution Review (RDR). The key objectives of the RDR are to:

- improve the clarity with which firms describe their services to consumers
- address the potential for adviser remuneration to distort consumer outcomes and
- increase the professional standards of advisers

The new rules require advisers to move from receiving commissions to fees agreed with customers in respect of all Retail Investment Products as defined by the FSA, which are:

1. a life policy; or

2. a unit; or

3. a stakeholder pension scheme; or

4. a personal pension scheme; or

5. an interest in an investment trust savings scheme; or

6. a security in an investment trust; or

7. any other designated investment which offers exposure to underlying financial assets, in a packaged form which modifies that exposure when compared with a direct holding in the financial asset; or

8. a structured capital-at-risk product;

whether or not any of a to h are held within an ISA or CTF.

Retail Investment Products do not include protection-only insurance or charges for trading in securities.

The new rules apply to all product distributors and providers across the retail investment market involved in advised-sales. They also apply to advised-sales via platforms. These rules do not apply to investment management under a discretionary mandate or to execution only transactions, which are covered in other sections of VAT guidance (see VATFIN7530 and VATFIN5800).

Appendix 22: VAT Finance Manual, para. VATFIN7650 – 'The Retail Distribution Review'

VATFIN7660 – The Retail Distribution Review – meaning of advice

It is important when considering the VAT treatment of services in this area to understand the meaning of 'advice' for regulatory purposes. From a VAT perspective general financial advice is not synonymous with the term 'advice' for the purposes of the RDR rules. The RDR is primarily concerned with the distribution (i.e. sale) of financial products to the retail market. The RDR's focus is ensuring that there is no hidden bias in product recommendations by ensuring that intermediaries (termed 'advisers') clearly disclose the nature of their service and set the level of their charges by reference to the amount of work done rather than being motivated by the level of fee associated with a particular product type or product provider.

The term 'advice' under RDR thus covers a broad range of functions including primarily recommendation, referral and intermediary work around product distribution which would continue to be VAT exempt under general principles. General financial advice would continue to be taxable in the same way.

VATFIN7665 – The Retail Distribution Review – services of an adviser

An adviser's role in the retail investment market will normally involve them entering into arrangements with the customer under which they might:

1. gather information about the customer (fact-find)

2. carry out research to find suitable investment options

3. provide the customer with reports, financial health-checks, forecasts

4. recommend specific investment products to the customer, including the prices at which these can be arranged

5. act between the product provider(s) and the customer with a view to arranging the sale of the Retail Investment Products agreed with the customer

6. and, where applicable, i.e. where the customer agrees to an ongoing review service, monitor the customer's ongoing position to ensure that the products continue to meet the requirements of the customer

Where the customer is seeking the arrangement of a Retail Investment Product and the adviser performs the arrangements as outlined at stage 5 above, (regardless of whether the sale of the product is finally concluded): and is able to evidence that they have done so; the services in stage 1-6, which fall within the agreement concluded with the customer, will be VAT exempt.

Where there is no evidence of such product arrangement services or where one or more of the stages are contracted for under a separate agreement, so that the service provided to the customer is that of general advice or recommendation only, any charges to the customer will carry VAT at the standard rate.

The VAT liability depends on what is done by the adviser and it makes no difference whether a fee is levied up front or over the life of a product (as for example with Regular Contribution products).

VATFIN7670 – The Retail Distribution Review – ongoing services

If, after the arrangements of the sale of Retail Investment Products, the customer signs up to ongoing review services, some or all of the process may occur again. The adviser should be able to determine and evidence where they are in the process with that customer. The VAT liability of ongoing services will depend upon the services the customer has agreed the adviser should perform, as outlined at VATFIN7665.

VATFIN7675 – The Retail Distribution Review – Evidence

Without prejudice to the general VAT evidential requirements, an adviser will need to keep sufficient evidence to support the tax treatment applied to the services supplied. This evidence will need to be specific to the services performed for the customer and demonstrate that the adviser acted between the customer and the product provider with a view to arranging the sale of Retail Investment Products. If an adviser is unable to provide evidence that an exempt supply has taken place, VAT will be due on that supply.

Appendix 23: Council Directive 2010/45/EU of 13 July 2010

I

(Legislative acts)

DIRECTIVES

COUNCIL DIRECTIVE 2010/45/EU

of 13 July 2010

amending Directive 2006/112/EC on the common system of value added tax as regards the rules on invoicing

THE COUNCIL OF THE EUROPEAN UNION,

Having regard to the Treaty on the Functioning of the European Union, and in particular Article 113 thereof,

Having regard to the proposal from the European Commission,

Having regard to the opinion of the European Parliament,

Having regard to the opinion of the European Economic and Social Committee,

Acting in accordance with a special legislative procedure,

Whereas:

(1) Council Directive 2006/112/EC of 28 November 2006 on the common system of value added tax ([1]) lays down conditions and rules concerning value added tax (hereinafter 'VAT') with respect to invoices, in order to ensure the proper functioning of the internal market. In accordance with Article 237 of that Directive, the Commission has presented a report which identifies, in the light of technological developments, certain difficulties with regard to electronic invoicing and which, in addition, identifies certain other areas in which the VAT rules should be simplified with a view to improving the functioning of the internal market.

(2) Since record keeping needs to be sufficient to allow Member States to control goods moving temporarily from one Member State to another, it should be made clear that record keeping is to include details of valuations on goods moving temporarily between Member States. Also, transfers of goods for valuation purposes to another Member State should not be regarded as a supply of goods for VAT purposes.

(3) The rules concerning the chargeability of VAT on intra-Community supplies of goods and on intra-Community acquisitions of goods should be clarified in order to ensure the uniformity of the information submitted in recapitulative statements and the timeliness of the exchange of information by means of those statements. It is furthermore appropriate that the continuous supply of goods from one Member State to another over a period of more than one calendar month should be regarded as being completed at the end of each calendar month.

(4) To help small and medium-sized enterprises that encounter difficulties in paying VAT to the competent authority before they have received payment from their customers, Member States should have the option of allowing VAT to be accounted using a cash accounting scheme which allows the supplier to pay VAT to the competent authority when he receives payment for a supply and which establishes his right of deduction when he pays for a supply. This should allow Member States to introduce an optional cash accounting scheme that does not have a negative effect on cash flow relating to their VAT receipts.

(5) To provide legal certainty for businesses regarding their invoicing obligations, it should be clearly stated which Member State's invoicing rules apply.

(6) With a view to improving the functioning of the internal market, it is necessary to impose a harmonised time limit for the issue of an invoice with respect to certain cross-border supplies.

(7) Certain requirements concerning the information to be provided on invoices should be amended to allow better control of the tax, to create a more uniform treatment between cross-border and domestic supplies and to help promote electronic invoicing.

([1]) OJ L 347, 11.12.2006, p. 1.

Appendix 23: Council Directive 2010/45/EU of 13 July 2010

(8) Since the use of electronic invoicing can help businesses to reduce costs and be more competitive, current VAT requirements on electronic invoicing should be revised to remove existing burdens and barriers to uptake. Paper invoices and electronic invoices should be treated equally and the administrative burden on paper invoicing should not increase.

(9) Equal treatment should also apply as regards the competences of tax authorities. Their control competences and the rights and obligations of taxable persons should apply equally whether a taxable person chooses to issue paper invoices or electronic invoices.

(10) Invoices must reflect actual supplies and their authenticity, integrity and legibility should therefore be ensured. Business controls can be used to establish reliable audit trails linking invoices and supplies, thereby ensuring that any invoice (whether on paper or in electronic form) complies with those requirements.

(11) The authenticity and integrity of electronic invoices can also be ensured by using certain existing technologies, such as Electronic Data Interchange (EDI) and advanced electronic signatures. However, since other technologies exist, taxable persons should not be required to use any particular electronic-invoicing technology.

(12) It should be clarified that, where a taxable person stores online invoices which he has issued or received, the Member State in which the tax is due, in addition to the Member State in which the taxable person is established, should have the right to access those invoices for control purposes.

(13) Since the objectives of this Directive regarding the simplification, modernisation and harmonisation of the VAT invoicing rules cannot be sufficiently achieved by the Member States and can therefore be better achieved at the level of the Union, the Union may adopt measures, in accordance with the principle of subsidiarity as set out in Article 5 of the Treaty. In accordance with the principle of proportionality, as set out in that Article, this Directive does not go beyond what is necessary in order to achieve those objectives.

(14) In accordance with point 34 of the Interinstitutional Agreement on better lawmaking ([1]), Member States are encouraged to draw up, for themselves and in the interests of the Union, their own tables illustrating, as far as possible, the correlation between this Directive and the transposition measures, and to make them public.

([1]) OJ C 321, 31.12.2003, p. 1.

(15) Directive 2006/112/EC should therefore be amended accordingly,

HAS ADOPTED THIS DIRECTIVE:

Article 1

Amendments to Directive 2006/112/EC

Directive 2006/112/EC is amended as follows:

1. in Article 17(2), point (f) is replaced by the following:

'(f) the supply of a service performed for the taxable person and consisting in valuations of, or work on, the goods in question physically carried out within the territory of the Member State in which dispatch or transport of the goods ends, provided that the goods, after being valued or worked upon, are returned to that taxable person in the Member State from which they were initially dispatched or transported;';

2. in Article 64, paragraph 2 is replaced by the following:

'2. Continuous supplies of goods over a period of more than one calendar month which are dispatched or transported to a Member State other than that in which the dispatch or transport of those goods begins and which are supplied VAT-exempt or which are transferred VAT-exempt to another Member State by a taxable person for the purposes of his business, in accordance with the conditions laid down in Article 138, shall be regarded as being completed on expiry of each calendar month until such time as the supply comes to an end.

Supplies of services for which VAT is payable by the customer pursuant to Article 196, which are supplied continuously over a period of more than one year and which do not give rise to statements of account or payments during that period, shall be regarded as being completed on expiry of each calendar year until such time as the supply of services comes to an end.

Member States may provide that, in certain cases other than those referred to in the first and second subparagraphs, the continuous supply of goods or services over a period of time is to be regarded as being completed at least at intervals of one year.';

3. in Article 66, first paragraph, point (c), and the second paragraph are replaced by the following:

'(c) where an invoice is not issued, or is issued late, within a specified time no later than on expiry of the time-limit for issue of invoices imposed by Member States pursuant to the second paragraph of Article 222 or where no such time-limit has been imposed by the Member State, within a specified period from the date of the chargeable event.

The derogation provided for in the first paragraph shall not, however, apply to supplies of services in respect of which VAT is payable by the customer pursuant to Article 196 and to supplies or transfers of goods referred to in Article 67.';

4. Article 67 is replaced by the following:

'Article 67

Where, in accordance with the conditions laid down in Article 138, goods dispatched or transported to a Member State other than that in which dispatch or transport of the goods begins are supplied VAT-exempt or where goods are transferred VAT-exempt to another Member State by a taxable person for the purposes of his business, VAT shall become chargeable on issue of the invoice, or on expiry of the time limit referred to in the first paragraph of Article 222 if no invoice has been issued by that time.

Article 64(1), the third subparagraph of Article 64(2) and Article 65 shall not apply with respect to the supplies and transfers of goods referred to in the first paragraph.';

5. Article 69 is replaced by the following:

'Article 69

In the case of the intra-Community acquisition of goods, VAT shall become chargeable on issue of the invoice, or on expiry of the time limit referred to in the first paragraph of Article 222 if no invoice has been issued by that time.';

6. in Article 91(2), the second subparagraph is replaced by the following:

'Member States shall accept instead the use of the latest exchange rate published by the European Central Bank at the time the tax becomes chargeable. Conversion between currencies other than the euro shall be made by using the euro exchange rate of each currency. Member States may require that they be notified of the exercise of this option by the taxable person.

However, for some of the transactions referred to in the first subparagraph or for certain categories of taxable persons, Member States may use the exchange rate determined in accordance with the Community provisions in force governing the calculation of the value for customs purposes.';

7. the following Article is inserted:

'Article 167a

Member States may provide within an optional scheme that the right of deduction of a taxable person whose VAT solely becomes chargeable in accordance with Article 66(b) be postponed until the VAT on the goods or services supplied to him has been paid to his supplier.

Member States which apply the optional scheme referred to in the first paragraph shall set a threshold for taxable persons using the scheme within their territory, based on the annual turnover of the taxable person calculated in accordance with Article 288. That threshold may not be higher than EUR 500 000 or the equivalent in national currency. Member States may increase that threshold up to EUR 2 000 000 or the equivalent in national currency after consulting the VAT Committee. However, such consultation of the VAT Committee shall not be required for Member States which applied a threshold higher than EUR 500 000 or the equivalent in national currency on 31 December 2012.

Member States shall inform the VAT Committee of national legislative measures adopted pursuant to the first paragraph.';

8. Article 178 is amended as follows:

(a) point (a) is replaced by the following:

'(a) for the purposes of deductions pursuant to Article 168(a), in respect of the supply of goods or services, he must hold an invoice drawn up in accordance with Sections 3 to 6 of Chapter 3 of Title XI;';

(b) point (c) is replaced by the following:

'(c) for the purposes of deductions pursuant to Article 168(c), in respect of the intra-Community acquisition of goods, he must set out in the VAT return provided for in Article 250 all the information needed for the amount of VAT due on his intra-Community acquisitions of goods to be calculated and he must hold an invoice drawn up in accordance with Sections 3 to 5 of Chapter 3 of Title XI;';

9. Article 181 is replaced by the following:

'Article 181

Member States may authorise a taxable person who does not hold an invoice drawn up in accordance with Sections 3 to 5 of Chapter 3 of Title XI to make the deduction referred to in Article 168(c) in respect of his intra-Community acquisitions of goods.';

10. in Article 197(1), point (c) is replaced by the following:

'(c) the invoice issued by the taxable person not established in the Member State of the person to whom the goods are supplied is drawn up in accordance with Sections 3 to 5 of Chapter 3.';

11. Article 217 is replaced by the following:

'Article 217

For the purposes of this Directive, "electronic invoice" means an invoice that contains the information required in this Directive, and which has been issued and received in any electronic format.';

12. in Section 3 of Chapter 3 of Title XI, the following Article is inserted:

'Article 219a

Without prejudice to Articles 244 to 248, the following shall apply:

(1) Invoicing shall be subject to the rules applying in the Member State in which the supply of goods or services is deemed to be made, in accordance with the provisions of Title V.

(2) By way of derogation from point (1), invoicing shall be subject to the rules applying in the Member State in which the supplier has established his business or has a fixed establishment from which the supply is made or, in the absence of such place of establishment or fixed establishment, the Member State where the supplier has his permanent address or usually resides, where:

(a) the supplier is not established in the Member State in which the supply of goods or services is deemed to be made, in accordance with the provisions of Title V, or his establishment in that Member State does not intervene in the supply within the meaning of Article 192a, and the person liable for the payment of the VAT is the person to whom the goods or services are supplied.

However where the customer issues the invoice (self-billing), point (1) shall apply.

(b) the supply of goods or services is deemed not to be made within the Community, in accordance with the provisions of Title V.';

13. Article 220 is replaced by the following:

'Article 220

1. Every taxable person shall ensure that, in respect of the following, an invoice is issued, either by himself or by his customer or, in his name and on his behalf, by a third party:

(1) supplies of goods or services which he has made to another taxable person or to a non-taxable legal person;

(2) supplies of goods as referred to in Article 33;

(3) supplies of goods carried out in accordance with the conditions specified in Article 138;

(4) any payment on account made to him before one of the supplies of goods referred to in points (1) and (2) was carried out;

(5) any payment on account made to him by another taxable person or non-taxable legal person before the provision of services was completed.

2. By way of derogation from paragraph 1, and without prejudice to Article 221(2), the issue of an invoice shall not be required in respect of supplies of services exempted under points (a) to (g) of Article 135(1).';

14. the following Article is inserted:

'Article 220a

1. Member States shall allow taxable persons to issue a simplified invoice in any of the following cases:

(a) where the amount of the invoice is not higher than EUR 100 or the equivalent in national currency;

(b) where the invoice issued is a document or message treated as an invoice pursuant to Article 219.

2. Member States shall not allow taxable persons to issue a simplified invoice where invoices are required to be issued pursuant to points (2) and (3) of Article 220(1) or where the taxable supply of goods or services is carried out by a taxable person who is not established in the Member State in which the VAT is due, or whose establishment in that Member State does not intervene in the supply within the meaning of Article 192a, and the person liable for the payment of VAT is the person to whom the goods or services are supplied.';

15. Articles 221, 222, 223, 224 and 225 are replaced by the following:

'Article 221

1. Member States may impose on taxable persons an obligation to issue an invoice in accordance with the details required under Article 226 or 226b in respect of supplies of goods or services other than those referred to in Article 220(1).

2. Member States may impose on taxable persons who have established their business in their territory or who have a fixed establishment in their territory from which the supply is made, an obligation to issue an invoice in accordance with the details required in Article 226 or 226b in respect of supplies of services exempted under points (a) to (g) of Article 135(1) which those taxable persons have made in their territory or outside the Community.

3. Member States may release taxable persons from the obligation laid down in Article 220(1) or in Article 220a to issue an invoice in respect of supplies of goods or services which they have made in their territory and which are exempt, with or without deductibility of the VAT paid in the preceding stage, pursuant to Articles 110 and 111, Article 125(1), Article 127, Article 128(1), Article 132, points (h) to (l) of Article 135(1), Articles 136, 371, 375, 376 and 377, Articles 378(2) and 379(2) and Articles 380 to 390b.

Article 222

For supplies of goods carried out in accordance with the conditions specified in Article 138 or for supplies of services for which VAT is payable by the customer pursuant to Article 196, an invoice shall be issued no later than on the fifteenth day of the month following that in which the chargeable event occurs.

For other supplies of goods or services Member States may impose time limits on taxable persons for the issue of invoices.

Article 223

Member States shall allow taxable persons to issue summary invoices which detail several separate supplies of goods or services provided that VAT on the supplies mentioned in the summary invoice becomes chargeable during the same calendar month.

Without prejudice to Article 222, Member States may allow summary invoices to include supplies for which VAT has become chargeable during a period of time longer than one calendar month.

Article 224

Invoices may be drawn up by the customer in respect of the supply to him, by a taxable person, of goods or services, where there is a prior agreement between the two parties and provided that a procedure exists for the acceptance of each invoice by the taxable person supplying the goods or services. Member State may require that such invoices be issued in the name and on behalf of the taxable person.

Article 225

Member States may impose specific conditions on taxable persons in cases where the third party, or the customer, who issues invoices is established in a country with which no legal instrument exists relating to mutual assistance similar in scope to that provided for in Directive 2010/24/EU (*) and Regulation (EC) No 1798/2003 (**).

(*) Council Directive 2010/24/EU of 16 March 2010 concerning mutual assistance for the recovery of claims relating to taxes, duties and other measures (OJ L 84, 31.3.2010, p. 1).
(**) Council Regulation (EC) No 1798/2003 of 7 October 2003 on administrative cooperation in the field of value added tax (OJ L 264, 15.10.2003, p. 1).';

16. Article 226 is amended as follows:

(a) the following point is inserted:

'(7a) where the VAT becomes chargeable at the time when the payment is received in accordance with Article 66(b) and the right of deduction arises at the time the deductible tax becomes chargeable, the mention "Cash accounting";';

(b) the following point is inserted:

'(10a) where the customer receiving a supply issues the invoice instead of the supplier, the mention "Self-billing";';

(c) point (11) is replaced by the following:

'(11) in the case of an exemption, reference to the applicable provision of this Directive, or to the corresponding national provision, or any other reference indicating that the supply of goods or services is exempt;';

(d) the following point is inserted:

'(11a) where the customer is liable for the payment of the VAT, the mention "Reverse charge";';

(e) points (13) and (14) are replaced by the following:

'(13) where the margin scheme for travel agents is applied, the mention "Margin scheme — Travel agents";

(14) where one of the special arrangements applicable to second-hand goods, works of art, collectors' items and antiques is applied, the mention "Margin scheme — Second-hand goods"; "Margin scheme — Works of art" or "Margin scheme — Collector's items and antiques" respectively;';

17. the following Articles are inserted:

'Article 226a

Where the invoice is issued by a taxable person, who is not established in the Member State where the tax is due or whose establishment in that Member State does not intervene in the supply within the meaning of Article 192a, and who is making a supply of goods or services to a customer who is liable for payment of VAT, the taxable person may omit the details referred to in points (8), (9) and (10) of Article 226 and instead indicate, by reference to the quantity or extent of the goods or services supplied and their nature, the taxable amount of those goods or services.

Article 226b

As regards simplified invoices issued pursuant to Article 220a and Article 221(1) and (2), Member States shall require at least the following details:

(a) the date of issue;

(b) identification of the taxable person supplying the goods or services;

(c) identification of the type of goods or services supplied;

(d) the VAT amount payable or the information needed to calculate it;

(e) where the invoice issued is a document or message treated as an invoice pursuant to Article 219, specific and unambiguous reference to that initial invoice and the specific details which are being amended.

They may not require details on invoices other than those referred to in Articles 226, 227 and 230.';

18. Article 228 is deleted;

19. Article 230 is replaced by the following:

'Article 230

The amounts which appear on the invoice may be expressed in any currency, provided that the amount of VAT payable or to be adjusted is expressed in the national currency of the Member State, using the conversion rate mechanism provided for in Article 91.';

20. Article 231 is deleted;

21. the heading of Section 5 of Chapter 3 of Title XI is replaced by the following:

'Paper invoices and electronic invoices';

22. Articles 232 and 233 are replaced by the following:

'Article 232

The use of an electronic invoice shall be subject to acceptance by the recipient.

Article 233

1. The authenticity of the origin, the integrity of the content and the legibility of an invoice, whether on paper or in electronic form, shall be ensured from the point in time of issue until the end of the period for storage of the invoice.

Each taxable person shall determine the way to ensure the authenticity of the origin, the integrity of the content and the legibility of the invoice. This may be achieved by any business controls which create a reliable audit trail between an invoice and a supply of goods or services.

"Authenticity of the origin" means the assurance of the identity of the supplier or the issuer of the invoice.

"Integrity of the content" means that the content required according to this Directive has not been altered.

2. Other than by way of the type of business controls described in paragraph 1, the following are examples of technologies that ensure the authenticity of the origin and the integrity of the content of an electronic invoice:

(a) an advanced electronic signature within the meaning of point (2) of Article 2 of Directive 1999/93/EC of the European Parliament and of the Council of 13 December 1999 on a Community framework for electronic signatures (*), based on a qualified certificate and created by a secure signature creation device, within the meaning of points (6) and (10) of Article 2 of Directive 1999/93/EC;

(b) electronic data interchange (EDI), as defined in Article 2 of Annex 1 to Commission Recommendation 1994/820/EC of 19 October 1994 relating to the legal aspects of electronic data interchange (**), where the agreement relating to the exchange provides for the use of procedures guaranteeing the authenticity of the origin and integrity of the data.

(*) OJ L 13, 19.1.2000, p. 12.
(**) OJ L 338, 28.12.1994, p. 98.';

23. Article 234 is deleted;

24. Articles 235, 236 and 237 are replaced by the following:

'Article 235

Member States may lay down specific conditions for electronic invoices issued in respect of goods or services supplied in their territory from a country with which no legal instrument exists relating to mutual assistance similar in scope to that provided for in Directive 2010/24/EU and Regulation (EC) No 1798/2003.

Article 236

Where batches containing several electronic invoices are sent or made available to the same recipient, the details common to the individual invoices may be mentioned only once where, for each invoice, all the information is accessible.

Article 237

By 31 December 2016 at the latest, the Commission shall present to the European Parliament and the Council an overall assessment report, based on an independent economic study, on the impact of the invoicing rules applicable from 1 January 2013 and notably on the extent to which they have effectively led to a decrease in administrative burdens for businesses, accompanied where necessary by an appropriate proposal to amend the relevant rules.';

25. Article 238 is amended as follows:

(a) paragraph 1 is replaced by the following:

'1. After consulting the VAT Committee, Member States may, in accordance with conditions which they may lay down, provide that in the following cases only the information required pursuant to Article 226b shall be entered on invoices in respect of supplies of goods or services:

(a) where the amount of the invoice is higher than EUR 100 but not higher than EUR 400, or the equivalent in national currency;

(b) where commercial or administrative practice in the business sector concerned or the technical conditions under which the invoices are issued make it particularly difficult to comply with all the obligations referred to in Article 226 or 230.';

(b) paragraph 2 is deleted;

(c) paragraph 3 is replaced by the following:

'3. The simplified arrangements provided for in paragraph 1 shall not be applied where invoices are required to be issued pursuant to points (2) and (3) of Article 220(1) or where the taxable supply of goods or services is carried out by a taxable person who is not established in the Member State in which the VAT is due or whose establishment in that Member State does not intervene in the supply within the meaning of Article 192a and the person liable for the payment of VAT is the person to whom the goods or services are supplied.';

26. Article 243 is replaced by the following:

'Article 243

1. Every taxable person shall keep a register of the goods dispatched or transported by him, or on his behalf, to a destination outside the territory of the Member State of departure but within the Community for the purposes of transactions consisting in valuations of those goods or work on them or their temporary use as referred to in points (f), (g) and (h) of Article 17(2).

2. Every taxable person shall keep accounts in sufficient detail to enable the identification of goods dispatched to him from another Member State, by or on behalf of a taxable person identified for VAT purposes in that other Member State, and used for services consisting in valuations of those goods or work on those goods.';

27. Article 246 is deleted;

28. in Article 247, paragraphs 2 and 3 are replaced by the following:

'2. In order to ensure that the requirements laid down in Article 233 are met, the Member State referred to in paragraph 1 may require that invoices be stored in the original form in which they were sent or made available, whether paper or electronic. Additionally, in the case of invoices stored by electronic means, the Member State may require that the data guaranteeing the authenticity of the origin of the invoices and the integrity of their content, as provided for in Article 233, also be stored by electronic means.

3. The Member State referred to in paragraph 1 may lay down specific conditions prohibiting or restricting the storage of invoices in a country with which no legal instrument exists relating to mutual assistance similar in scope to that provided for in Directive 2010/24/EU and Regulation (EC) No 1798/2003 or to the right referred to in Article 249 to access by electronic means, to download and to use.';

29. in Section 3 of Chapter 4 of Title XI, the following Article is inserted:

'Article 248a

For control purposes, and as regards invoices in respect of supplies of goods or services supplied in their territory and invoices received by taxable persons established in their territory, Member States may, for certain taxable persons or certain cases, require translation into their official languages. Member States may, however, not impose a general requirement that invoices be translated.';

Appendix 23: Council Directive 2010/45/EU of 13 July 2010

30. Article 249 is replaced by the following:

'Article 249

For control purposes, where a taxable person stores, by electronic means guaranteeing online access to the data concerned, invoices which he issues or receives, the competent authorities of the Member State in which he is established and, where the VAT is due in another Member State, the competent authorities of that Member State, shall have the right to access, download and use those invoices.';

31. in Article 272(1), the second subparagraph is replaced by the following:

'Member States may not release the taxable persons referred to in point (b) of the first subparagraph from the invoicing obligations laid down in Sections 3 to 6 of Chapter 3 and Section 3 of Chapter 4.'.

Article 2
Transposition

1. Member States shall adopt and publish, by 31 December 2012 at the latest, the laws, regulations and administrative provisions necessary to comply with this Directive. They shall forthwith communicate to the Commission the text of those provisions.

They shall apply those provisions from 1 January 2013.

When Member States adopt those provisions, they shall contain a reference to this Directive or be accompanied by such a reference on the occasion of their official publication. Member States shall determine how such reference is to be made.

2. Member States shall communicate to the Commission the text of the main provisions of national law which they adopt in the field covered by this Directive.

Article 3
Entry into Force

This Directive shall enter into force on the 20th day following its publication in the *Official Journal of the European Union*.

Article 4
Addressees

This Directive is addressed to the Member States.

Done at Brussels, 13 July 2010.

For the Council
The President
D. REYNDERS

Appendix 24: Revenue & Customs Brief 23/12 and VAT Information Sheet 07/12

Guidance on Cost Share Group Exemption - Group 16, Schedule 9 of the VAT Act 1994

Introduction

This Brief announces the introduction into law of a new group 16 to Schedule 9 of the VAT Act 1994. This follows the receipt of royal assent of the Finance Bill on 17 July 2012.

The new group 16 to Schedule 9 to the VAT Act 1994 deals primarily with the Cost Sharing Exemption provision.

Background

The exemption applies when two or more organisations (whether businesses or otherwise) with exempt and/or non-business activities join together on a co-operative basis to form a separate, independent entity, a cost sharing group (CSG), to supply themselves with certain services at cost and exempt from VAT.

The exemption applies to supplies of certain qualifying services that are made by the representative member of the CSG to other members of the CSG. These supplies must be 'directly necessary' for the exempt and/or non-business supplies made by the individual qualifying member.

Who needs to read this?

All independent businesses and organisations which have VAT exempt and/or non-business activities and may wish to set up a cost sharing arrangement with other independent businesses and organisations.

What is being published?

HM Revenue & Customs (HMRC) is initially publishing its guidance in VAT Information Sheet 07/12 which explains how the exemption can be enacted. This guidance will be incorporated as soon as possible into HMRC's appropriate book of guidance.

HMRC – 24 August 2012

Appendix 24: Revenue & Customs Brief 23/12 and VAT Information Sheet 07/12

Guidance on the Cost Sharing Exemption - from 17 Jul 2012

VAT Information Sheet 07/12

You should read this information sheet along with the following:

Revenue & Customs Brief 23/12 – Publication of Guidance on the Cost Sharing Exemption – Group 16, Schedule 9 of the VAT Act 1994

1 Introduction - what is the Cost Sharing Exemption?

The exemption applies when two or more organisations (whether businesses or otherwise) with exempt and/or non-business activities join together on a cooperative basis to form a separate, independent entity, a cost sharing group (CSG), to supply themselves with certain services at cost and exempt from VAT.

As a result a 'cooperative self-supply' arrangement (a term the EU Commission use) is created. The CSG is a separate taxable person from that of its members. It is therefore able to make supplies for VAT purposes to its members. These supplies will be exempt if the relevant conditions are met. This type of arrangement enables the creation of the same economies of scale for smaller businesses and organisations as larger businesses and organisations naturally enjoy. Thus the more members of a CSG there are the greater the potential savings and lower the costs per member of operating the relevant CSG.

The cost sharing exemption applies only in very specific circumstances and will not cover all shared service arrangements.

See diagram of the basic structure in Appendix A.

2. Does the exemption apply to supplies of goods?

No, unless the goods are an ancillary element of a single supply of services under the normal single/multiple supply principles.

3. What is meant by 'members' of a CSG?

A member of a CSG is a business or organisation that:

- is capable of jointly owning and controlling a CSG
- receives qualifying supplies from the CSG

Appendix 24: Revenue & Customs Brief 23/12 and VAT Information Sheet 07/12

4. When does the exemption apply?

As the exemption is mandatory all supplies that meet the relevant conditions will be subject to the exemption.

5. What are the conditions of the exemption?

There are five conditions attached to the exemption.

- a) There must be an 'independent group of persons' (a CSG) supplying services to persons who are its 'members'.

- b) All the members must carry on an activity that is exempt from VAT or one which is not a business activity for VAT purposes.

- c) The services supplied by the CSG, to which the exemption applies, must be 'directly necessary' for a member's exempt and/or non-business activity.

- d) The CSG only recovers, from its members, the members' individual share of the expenses incurred by the CSG in making the exempt supplies to its members.

- e) The application of the exemption to the supplies made by the CSG to its members is not likely to cause a distortion of competition.

All these conditions have to be satisfied for a supply to be exempt.

If any of the conditions are not met the supplies will be taxable.

Further details and how these conditions are to be applied are covered in more detail in this guidance. However it should be noted that the EU Commission are currently infracting a number of Member States in relation to how they have applied the exemption and the outcome of those infraction proceedings could impact on how HM Revenue & Customs (HMRC) currently view the operation of the exemption, as explained in this guidance. HMRC will monitor these infractions and consider whether or not any changes are necessary to the guidance. Should changes prove to be necessary, then transitional arrangements, as far as possible, will be put in place to facilitate an orderly move to the revised position.

Appendix 24: Revenue & Customs Brief 23/12 and VAT Information Sheet 07/12

6. Does the exemption apply to commercial outsourced services?

No, the exemption only applies to the recharges, at cost, of services supplied by a CSG to its group members. The exemption does not apply to commercial outsourced services or arrangements that amount to the provision of commercial outsourced services. Such services are generally made by specialist providers to unconnected third parties on a commercial for-profit basis and would not, therefore, meet the conditions of the exemption. They are not 'cooperative self-supply' arrangements.

7. Can a CSG make supplies to non-members?

Yes, but such supplies, unless covered by another exemption, will be taxable. If such supplies are cross border the normal place of supply and reverse charge rules apply.

8. What types of businesses and organisations can benefit from the exemption?

Any business or organisation that is capable of meeting the relevant criteria/conditions has the opportunity to use the exemption to their benefit. The types of businesses and organisations that might benefit are:

- Charities
- Banks
- Education Institutions
- Insurance businesses
- Social Housing organisations
- Betting and Gaming organisations
- Health and Welfare businesses and organisations
- Financial Services businesses
- Local Authorities, Government Departments and NDPBs

This is not an exhaustive list.

9. When did the exemption become effective in UK legislation?

The EU Directive 2006/112 (commonly referred to as the Principal VAT Directive) provides for the exemption of the services of cost sharing groups. The exemption was implemented in the UK from Royal Assent of the 2012 Finance Act with the introduction of a new Group 16 to Schedule 9 of the VAT Act 1994.

10. What is the new Group 16 to Schedule 9 of the VAT Act 1994?

Group 16 - supplies of services by groups involving cost sharing

Item No

1. The supply of services by an independent group of persons where each of the following conditions is satisfied:

- a) each of those persons is a person who is carrying on an activity ('the relevant activity') which is exempt from VAT or in relation to which the person is not a taxable person within the meaning of Article 9 of Council Directive 2006/112/EC,

- b) the supply of services is made for the purpose of rendering the members of the group the services directly necessary for the exercise of the relevant activity,

- c) the group merely claims from its members exact reimbursement of their share of the joint expenses, and

- d) the exemption of the supply is not likely to cause distortion of competition.

General provisions

11. Are all supplies made by a CSG covered by the exemption?

No, the exemption only applies to supplies of certain qualifying services (See Question 33) made by the CSG to its members which are 'directly necessary' (see Question 39) for the exempt and/or non-business supplies made by the individual qualifying member.

12. Does the exemption apply in any other circumstances?

No, the cost sharing exemption does NOT apply in any other circumstances. In all other respects the normal VAT rules will apply. So, for example, the cost sharing exemption will not apply to supplies of goods, supplies made above cost, supplies to non members or to any supplies made by members who supply services directly to other CSG members. If the CSG does make supplies which do not qualify for the exemption and which are subject to the normal VAT rules, then the CSG may have to register for VAT if it exceeds the VAT registration limits.

13. What about supplies to a CSG?

Supplies of all goods and services to a CSG (for example, the transfer of staff either permanently or temporarily to a CSG) will be subject to the normal VAT rules and any input tax which is incurred in relation to an onward exempt supply by the CSG will not be deductible by the CSG. If a CSG is partially exempt the normal partial exemption rules apply including the de minimis rule.

14. What are the normal VAT rules regarding transfers/supplies of staff?

There is a supply of staff for VAT purposes when one party makes available someone who is contractually employed by it or is a director of it to another party (either on a temporary or a permanent basis) in return for a consideration.

Where such a supply is on a temporary or secondment basis the consideration for such a supply need not necessarily be just a fee but can also constitute charges made by the contractual employer to the other party of wages, NI and other employment costs. It also includes such costs when they are paid by the recipient of the supply directly to the worker.

Whatever the nature of the business (it does not have to be an employment business), the party making the supplies of staff is normally regarded as making such supplies in the course or furtherance of business and must account for VAT at the standard rate.

There are a few exceptions to this rule, where supplies of staff are not always made in the course or furtherance of business and thus may be outside the scope of VAT.

Further information about the permanent and temporary transfer/supply of staff, the exceptions to the general rule, including joint employment contracts can be found in Notice 700/34 Staff.

If the supplying party supplies services, for example construction or care services it is not a supply of staff but a supply of those services. Such services, depending on their nature, may be zero-rated or the supply may qualify for exemption from VAT. See Notice 701/57 Health professionals and pharmaceutical products and 701/2 Welfare for more information and qualifying criteria.

15. Can a CSG benefit from the normal VAT Reliefs and special provisions?

Yes. A CSG like any other organisation, if it is able to meet the relevant conditions, can benefit from the appropriate VAT provisions and reliefs (for example, if the CSG is a charity, then charity VAT reliefs will apply where appropriate).

16. Can a UK established CSG have members in other Member States (OMS) and can a UK business or organisation belong to a CSG established in OMS?

Members of a UK established CSG can themselves be established in other EU Member States. Similarly a UK established business or organisation can be a member of a CSG established in another EU Member State.

17. Do the normal place of supply rules apply?

Yes. Cross border services will be subject to the normal EU place of supply of services rules, see Notice 741A Place of supply of service and Notice 741 Place of supply of service.

18. What is the input tax treatment in relation to supplies to overseas customers?

The normal UK policy when a UK taxpayer makes supplies to overseas customers that is outside the scope of UK tax but would have been exempt if made in the UK and which may or may not be viewed as exempt in the country where they are received, is that no UK input tax deduction on the cost components of those supplies is allowed.

This is based in UK law on s26 of the VAT Act 1994; the supplies are outside the scope of UK VAT, they would have been exempt if supplied in the UK and they are not specified supplies under the Specified Supplies Order, SI 1999/3121.

The UK cannot take tax treatments in other countries into account, irrespective of whether they are Member States or third countries.

19. What does this mean in relation to supplies received by a UK member of a CSG based in another Member State?

If the UK member is receiving the supply in relation to a business the place of supply is the UK and as the cost sharing exemption is implemented in the UK, subject to all the conditions being met, the supply will be exempt with no need to apply the reverse charge.

If the UK member is not in business for VAT purposes the place of supply will be the Member State where the CSG is established.

20. Do EU Procurement Directives apply?

The EU Procurement Directives apply to procurement by public bodies. Therefore, if a CSG member is a public body, as defined by the EU Procurement Directives, it will have to consider whether or not its purchases from the CSG are subject to the rules set out in those Directives.

How the conditions are to be interpreted

Independent group of persons

21. What is a Cost Sharing Group (CSG)?

A CSG is an independent group of persons who work together with a common purpose. The CSG is however legally separate from its members. It is established, owned and operated by the members for their cooperative benefit and is independent of any ownership, control or influence outside of the membership. It can be a group of equals or if all the members agree one or more members can have effective control and/or majority ownership of the group. In either case all members must have a legal interest in the CSG. So, for example, if the CSG was established as a limited company all members would have to be shareholders either on an equal basis or if the members agree one or more members could hold more than 50 per cent of the shares. No shares could be held by any person who was not a member of the CSG.

The CSG does not have to be a limited company, as in the example above. If it is not a limited company ownership and control will take a different form depending on the entity chosen to be the CSG. It can take any form provided it is a 'taxable person' within the Principal VAT Directive definition of 'taxable person' (see Question 22).

Appendix 24: Revenue & Customs Brief 23/12 and VAT Information Sheet 07/12

22. Must the CSG be separate from its members?

Yes. The CSG must be a separate taxable person from its members in order to be able to make exempt supplies for VAT purposes to its members. It must therefore be able to take a legal form that is capable of being a taxable person that can be registered for VAT if it were making taxable supplies, that is, it is capable of meeting the VAT registration criteria or would be if it were not wholly engaged in making exempt supplies.

Subject to the above considerations the CSG can take whatever legal form its members decide.

See V1- 28, Registration for the types of entity that would qualify.

Some particular forms of CSG

23. Partnerships have to be for profit, can they be CSG's as a CSG can only seek 'an exact reimbursement of costs'?

If a 'for profit' partnership also makes supplies that fulfil the conditions of the exemption then they can form a CSG but the exemption would only apply in respect of those services that satisfied all the conditions of the exemption, including the 'exact reimbursement of costs'. This situation might occur, for example, if the partnership (as a CSG) also made supplies to third party, non-CSG (Partnership) members, where a profit element could be added and VAT would have to be charged, at the appropriate rate.

24. What about the different legal status of partnerships in Scotland and the rest of the UK?

In Scotland a partnership has a separate legal personality from its members. In the rest of the UK that is not the case. However the effect of s45 of the VAT Act 1994 is to treat partnerships as a separate person for VAT purposes. It is possible therefore for members of a UK partnership to be treated as separate taxable persons from a partnership that is also registered for VAT.

25. What about limited partnerships?

Limited partnerships are constituted under The Limited Partnership Act 1907 and consist of general partners and limited partners. Limited partners are only liable to the extent of the amount they invest in the partnership. Limited partners may not take part in the running of the partnership business which is carried out by general partners.

For a limited partnership to be eligible to be a CSG all of the partners, both limited and general, would have to meet the qualifying test (see Question 36).

The normal procedure in the VAT Registration Units is to register limited partnerships in the names of the general partner only. Limited partnerships must register with the Registrar of Companies.

26. Can unincorporated associations be CSGs?

Where an organisation falls within s 46(2) of the VAT Act 1994 (which includes unincorporated associations) and is managed by its members in accordance with Regulation 8 of the VAT Regulations 1995 it will be eligible to be a CSG. Regulation 8 provides that:

"Anything required to be done by or under the Act, these regulations or otherwise by or on behalf of a club, association or organisation, the affairs of which are managed by its members or a committee or committees of members, shall be the joint and several responsibility of –

- a) Every member holding office as president, chairman, treasurer, secretary, or any similar office; or in default thereof,

- b) Every member holding office as a member of a committee; or in default thereof,

- c) Every member, provided that it is done by any official, committee member or member referred to above, that shall be sufficient compliance with any such requirement".

If this type of association makes taxable supplies and is required to register for VAT or wishes to voluntarily register for VAT it will be registered in the name of the association.

Proprietary associations are generally not owned by their 'members' on the same basis as members associations so would not qualify as CSGs unless ownership was shared amongst all members and the proprietor and all members received qualifying services from the association.

27. Can a CSG be a charity?

To be a charity an organisation must be, among other requirements, established for charitable purposes. So, subject to meeting that test a CSG might be able to be a charity. However, in a charity context a CSG could also be a non-charitable company limited by shares owned by a number of charities and, in practice, this model may be the more likely one. If a CSG was able to acquire charity status there are particular direct tax rules attached to the trading activities of charities that a charity CSG would have to consider, see Charity Direct Tax Guidance.

Number of members and memberships

28. Are there any limits on the number of members a CSG can have?

Each CSG must have two or more members. There is no upper limit.

Businesses and organisations can be members of more than one CSG if they so choose. This may occur where a single qualifying business or organisation requires a number of different specialist services in connection with its exempt or non-business activities and these are provided by different specialised CSGs.

29. What must a CSG consider when recruiting members?

CSGs will need to be careful when recruiting members as one of the conditions of the exemption is that it does not lead to a distortion of competition. Therefore a CSG must not have the characteristics of an independent operator seeking a customer base in order to simply generate profits. A CSG may gain members in respect of its exempt supplies by recommendation, invitation, word of mouth etc., though if it engages in promotion and marketing on a similar basis to a commercial operator there is more danger that its activities will lead to distortion of competition. CSG supplies to non-members are not covered by the exemption and can include a mark up/margin and be promoted by commercial marketing.

30. Who is responsible for the CSG's VAT affairs - the members or the CSG?

As a single taxable person it is the CSG itself not its individual members that is responsible for its VAT affairs. However, the application of the exemption is dependent on the use to which the recipient members put the services received from the CSG. This is different from many other VAT exemptions where it is the nature of the supply or the nature of the maker or receiver of it which determines its tax treatment.

CSGs must ensure that adequate controls exist to obtain the information necessary to correctly determine its VAT liability. It should be able to demonstrate to HMRC, when required to do so, that all the conditions of the exemption have been met by all of its members. Where a CSG has a member(s) in another (other) Member State(s) it may want to have particular rules covering non UK established members.

HMRC are not prescriptive about how CSGs should arrange themselves in this respect, as different CSGs will want to do so in different ways, in accordance with their members' wishes and requirements. However, HMRC will expect any system that is put in place to provide a clear audit trail of how the services received from the CSG are utilised by those individual members in their operations.

31. Will HMRC put any special process or compliance arrangements in place?

HMRC will not initially be introducing any bespoke process or compliance arrangements in respect of the exemption. However, where businesses and organisations require confirmation that their arrangements satisfy the conditions of the exemption HMRC will, where requested, provide advice in line with its standard policy.

In terms of compliance activity, HMRC deploys its resources according to risk and use of the VAT Cost Sharing Exemption will be built into risk profiling in the same way as other aspects of the VAT regime.

The primary legislation, introducing the exemption into UK law, also contains provision allowing HM Treasury to make regulations in respect of the operation of the exemption. These powers have not been immediately exercised though the operation of the exemption will be monitored and assessed to see if regulations are required in order to ensure its smooth application.

32. Must all members of a CSG receive Group 16 supplies?

Yes. All members must receive Group 16 qualifying supplies or have a realistic and genuine intention to do so.

33. What are 'qualifying supplies'?

Qualifying supplies are services which are 'directly necessary' to enable a member of the CSG to engage in the exempt and/or non-business activity for which the services are supplied.

Appendix 24: Revenue & Customs Brief 23/12 and VAT Information Sheet 07/12

34. What happens if a member of the CSG ceases to receive 'qualifying supplies'?

If an existing member ceases to receive qualifying supplies for any period of 12 months following their membership of a CSG then HMRC will presume that an intention to receive such supplies had ceased and, therefore, the member will cease to be eligible for membership of a CSG going forward. However, if the member can show that the intention to receive 'qualifying supplies' in the near future still exists then membership of the CSG can continue.

If a member ceases to be eligible for membership of the CSG there have to be at least two remaining eligible members for the CSG itself to continue to be a CSG falling within the terms of Group 16 of Schedule 9 to the VAT Act 1994 and therefore to continue to be able to make exempt supplies going forward.

35. Must all members receive the same type and volume of qualifying supplies?

No. Not all members have to receive the same services. A CSG can supply different services to each member if that is what is required. Also, members can receive different volumes of the same services, if that is what is required. However the CSG must only recover from its members, at cost, their share of the costs and expenses incurred by the CSG.

Exempt and/or non-business activities

36. Do all members have to have exempt and/or non-business activities?

Yes.

The EU Commission accept that it is legitimate, in order to facilitate the correct and straightforward application of the exemption for Member States, under Article 131 of the Principal VAT Directive, to require that the exempt and/or non-business activities of members be carried on in a regular and consistent manner rather than merely sporadically. The relevant activities need to represent a significant (not a de minimis) part of the taxpayers business.

HMRC consider that an entity would be eligible for membership if:

- 5 per cent or more of its total supplies were exempt and/or non-business supplies in the immediate 12 months prior to joining the CSG

- or 5 per cent or more of its total supplies were exempt and/or non-business supplies in its last completed partial exemption, business/non-business year prior to its membership of a CSG

- or at the time of joining a CSG, although it does not fulfil the first two tests it:
  i) has an intention to receive and does receive, qualifying services which are 'directly necessary' from the CSG, in the 12 month period starting from the date of joining
  and
  ii) those services are directly utilised within 12 months of receipt by the member to make 5 per cent or more exempt and/or non-business onward supplies.

If a member ceases to be eligible for membership of the CSG, going forward, there have to be at least two remaining eligible members for the CSG itself to continue to be a CSG falling within the terms of Group 16 of Schedule 9 to the VAT Act 1994 and therefore to continue to be able to make exempt supplies.

If a body is wholly taxable but has a clear intention to make exempt and/or non-business supplies within the next 12 months HMRC would accept it is eligible to join a CSG.

37. Can businesses and organisations that are not VAT registered join CSGs?

Yes. Businesses and organisations that are not VAT registered can also be members of a CSG provided they engage in exempt and/or non-business activity that is not de minimis. It is the activities engaged in and not registration status that determines eligibility for membership.

Businesses and organisations that are not VAT registered and engage only in taxable activity are not eligible to be members of a CSG.

38. What are exempt supplies?

Any supplies falling within Schedule 9 of the VAT Act 1994 with the exception of Groups 11, 14 and 15.

It does not include supplies with the right to recovery, for example under Article 169(c) of the PVD exempt supplies?

'Directly necessary' services

39. What are 'directly necessary' services?

Article 132(1) (f) requires that supplies made by CSGs to their members must be 'directly necessary' for their exempt and/or non-business activities. If they are not the exemption does not apply and the supplies are subject to normal VAT rules.

The word 'necessary' used alone could be interpreted on the basis that any supplies used for a CSG member's exempt and/or non-business activity would be entitled to exemption. However, the word 'necessary' is, in this case, qualified by the use of the word 'directly' meaning that the supplies received from the CSG must relate 'directly' to the exempt and/or non-business supplies made by the CSG member in their own right.

HMRC has adopted a methodology for identifying services that are 'directly necessary' which has been developed with stakeholders during the consultation process in order to provide a simple and pragmatic way of identifying qualifying supplies.

If CSGs wish to suggest alternative methodologies HMRC will give them full consideration but must be satisfied that there is a direct and exclusive link with the exempt or non-business activity on which the qualification depends.

Note - businesses and organisations considering forming CSGs should note that recently the EU Commission have commenced infraction proceedings against Luxembourg for, among other things, their application of the 'directly necessary' condition, which is similar to the 'simplification' option offered by the HMRC in this guidance. (See Question 40, point 2.)

The Commission are seeking to establish the **principle** that 'directly necessary' services are those that are used **'exclusively'** by CSG members for their exempt and/or non-business activity. The matter has been referred to the European Court and timing is now in their hands. It could perhaps take several years to come to a conclusion, although it may conclude sooner.

The EU Commission have currently decided only to commence infraction proceedings against Luxembourg in this respect although a number of other Member States have also adopted a similar approach. However further challenges cannot be ruled out.

Decisions of the European Court are binding on Member States.

HMRC will monitor the process and consider whether or not at any stage any changes need to be made to this guidance. Should changes prove to be necessary, then transitional arrangements, as far as possible, will be put in place to facilitate an orderly move to the revised position.

Appendix 24: Revenue & Customs Brief 23/12 and VAT Information Sheet 07/12

40. How may directly necessary services be identified?

HMRC will accept services are directly necessary if they are identified using the following methodology:

1. Only supplies of services received from a CSG that can be 'directly attributable' (using partial exemption methodology) to the member's exempt and/or non-business activities will be regarded as 'directly necessary' and therefore qualify for the exemption. Expenditure on services received from a CSG that is attributable to both taxable and exempt and/or non-business activities will not qualify as being 'directly necessary' as they are NOT linked exclusively to the exempt and/or non-business activities of CSG members and will consequently be subject to their normal VAT treatment.

2. On an, optional, simplification basis, where a member of a CSG has wholly exempt and/or non-business activities or low levels of taxable activity, all the supplies they receive from a CSG will be regarded as 'directly necessary' for those exempt and/or non-business activities.

A low level of taxable activity for the purposes of this test is less than 15 per cent so, where a member of a CSG has exempt (see Question 38) and/or non-business activities that form 85 per cent or more of their total activities, all the supplies they receive from their CSG will be regarded as 'directly necessary'.

41. How does the 85 per cent directly necessary test work?

A member receiving supplies from the CSG of which they are a member will have to:

- have made 85 per cent or more exempt and/or non-business supplies in the immediately preceding 12 months or completed partial exemption year end prior to their membership of a CSG (the backward look), or

- have a intention in the 12 months immediately following joining a CSG to make 85 per cent or more exempt and/or non-business supplies (the forward look)

Once this test has been met the qualifying member will be entitled to receive all of their supplies from the CSG exempt for as long as their level of exempt and/or non-business supplies remains at 85 per cent or more.

42. How can the test be applied in practice?

HMRC will accept any calculation method that produces a fair and reasonable result.

This can be done in a number of ways. For example, as members in these circumstances will be making taxable as well as exempt and/or non-business supplies they are likely to be VAT registered, partially exempt and be completing monthly or quarterly VAT returns. Their ongoing VAT return, partial exemption and, if appropriate, their business/non-business calculations could be used to determine whether or not the test has been met. Businesses and organisations that are not VAT registered could, for example, use data from their management accounts to determine whether they meet the test or not, on a monthly or quarterly basis.

43. What will happen if a member meets the 85 per cent test by having an intention to make 85 per cent or more exempt and/or non-business supplies in the following 12 month period but that intention does not materialise?

HMRC will not accept that all the CSG supplies to that member should be exempt but will permit the member to benefit from the exemption to the extent that the supplies from the CSG are 'directly attributable' (using partial exemption methodology) to their exempt and/or non-business activities. Members will only be able to use the forward look once.

44. What happens if a member fails the 85 per cent test after initially meeting the test?

If a member of a CSG is not able to meet the 85 per cent or more test, HMRC will not accept that all CSG supplies to that member are exempt but will accept exemption of supplies from their CSG which are directly attributable(using partial exemption methodology) to that member's exempt and/or non-business activities. All the supplies made by the CSG will only become exempt once the member of the CSG is able to meet the 85 per cent test again. If they fail to meet the test on the forward look, having used up their one forward look test, they will have to rely on the backward look to qualify again or the member may benefit from the exemption to the extent that the supplies from the CSG are 'directly attributable' (using partial exemption methodology) to their exempt and/or non-business activities.

45. Can the 85 per cent test be applied on a sector/account basis?

HMRC will, in certain circumstances, accept the 85 per cent test being applied to particular parts of a member's business provided the test can be reasonably applied. For example if the member has a sectorised Partial Exemption and Business/Non-Business method they can apply the test on a sector basis. If a particular sector qualifies the member can receive all supplies from their CSG that are attributable to that sector on an exempt basis. The test could also be applied on the same basis if, for example, a member can identify specific account codes in its accounting system; if the test is satisfied on that basis a member can receive all supplies from their CSG that are directly attributable to that account code on an exempt basis.

In these circumstances the test would have to be applied to external supplies and not to supplies made and received within the same VAT entity as they are neither exempt nor non-business supplies for the purpose of the Cost Sharing Exemption.

'Direct reimbursement of costs'?

46. What is meant by 'direct reimbursement of costs'?

For the exemption to apply the consideration for supplies made by the CSG to its members has to be an 'exact reimbursement' of the members' share of the joint expenses, this includes start-up costs, any general overheads incurred by the CSG in providing services to its members as well as any discounts received or input tax recovered by the CSG. Therefore there should be no profit element in the charges made by the group to its members, that is, no margin or mark-up must be factored into the cost of providing the services. So, for example, if the CSG receives discounts from its suppliers they have to on be passed to on to members by computing them into the CSGs charges to its members. If supplies to members of the CSG by the CSG do include a profit element the exemption will NOT apply and those supplies will be subject to the normal VAT rules.

CSGs can make supplies to non-members and in these circumstances the normal VAT rules apply and profit element may be included.

An expense can normally be defined as a cost incurred to generate revenue and would include for example:

- cash payments or liabilities
- costs incurred but not yet invoiced (accruals)
- amounts required to meet anticipated future expenditure
- depreciation in the value of the CSG's assets

How such costs are calculated and charged is a matter for the CSG members to agree. However HMRC expect CSGs to have a clear audit trail that can be checked if necessary.

47. What is the position if the CSG needs to raise funds?

If a CSG wishes to raise funds, for example, to make a capital purchase or to build up a contingency fund it can do so without breaching the 'at cost' condition. It is also accepted that there may be timing differences between when expenses are incurred by a CSG and when it receives income for the supplies it makes to its members. Therefore it is probable that at any point in time a CSG could be running either a deficit or a surplus. Provided the CSG can demonstrate that the 'exact reimbursement' rule has been met over a reasonable period of time, running a deficit or surplus (provided any surplus is held for future use by the CSG for the specific benefit of its members) will not affect the use of the exemption. CSGs can demonstrate whether the 'exact reimbursement' test has been met or not by using normal accounting techniques and the judgement can be made over a period of time that is reasonable given the nature and context of the supplies being made.

48. How are charges for management and similar services to be treated?

If a CSG chooses to buy in such services from third party suppliers or from a CSG member then such services will normally be taxable. If these supplies are then recharged by the CSG to its members at the appropriate proportion then they will, subject to all the conditions being met, be exempt. However if such supplies are used as a mechanism to artificially inflate costs to extract a profit from the supplies made by the CSG then they will fail to meet the 'exact reimbursement' condition and will fall to be treated as fully taxable.

49. What is transfer pricing and does it apply to services supplied by a CSG to its members?

Transfer pricing is a direct tax provision and broadly concerns the terms that connected parties use when they conduct business with each other. Where the parties to the transaction are connected, the conditions of their commercial relations will not be determined solely by market forces. The price, terms and conditions of a transaction between connected parties may not be the same as those which would have been agreed at 'arm's length' between independent parties.

Where a CSG and its members are connected parties they will often be potentially subject to transfer pricing rules for direct tax purposes.

Further information about transfer pricing can be found in the International Manual.

50. If the direct tax transfer pricing rules apply will they preclude use of the exemption as affected transactions may not comply with the 'exact reimbursement of costs' rule?

No. HMRC accept that pricing or repricing transactions under direct tax transfer pricing rules will not preclude use of the exemption.

However, if the actual pricing of the charge by the CSG to its members exceeds an arm's length figure, such transactions would not qualify for the exemption.

Where a CSG has both unconnected and connected members for transfer pricing purposes, regardless of the tax position of the connected members, the unconnected members will still have to receive qualifying supplies without a margin or mark-up to meet this condition and to benefit from the exemption.

Please note: a Transfer Pricing Adjustment is not in itself a supply nor consideration for a supply. It is an indication that transactions or arrangements may not have been undertaken at an 'arms length' price. It may therefore point to an under valuation of the underlying supply for VAT purposes. Further information regarding Transfer Pricing and VAT can be found in VAT Guidance, V1-12: Valuation.

'Distortion of competition'?

51. How can the exemption lead to a 'distortion of competition'?

A CSG is a cooperative self-supply arrangement. It is not a commercial outsourcing arrangement therefore it does not exist or compete in a market. As long as all the conditions of the exemption are met, particularly that it can only supply it's members on a 'direct reimbursement' basis, that is, it self supplies at cost, there should be little question of the exemption distorting a market and therefore little question of failing to meet this condition.

52. What does the ECJ case of Taksatorringen (C-8/01) comment on the 'distortion of competition' point?

This point was looked at by the ECJ in the case of Taksatorringen (C-8/01 [2006] STC 1842). Taksatorringen was a Danish CSG formed by a number of insurance companies to provide them with claims handling services. The point in dispute was whether or not the arrangement breached the distortion of competition condition as such services were also provided by commercial (with profit) suppliers on an outsourced basis.

Appendix 24: Revenue & Customs Brief 23/12 and VAT Information Sheet 07/12

The Advocate General in Taksatorringen case stated the following:

"121. There are two fundamental requirements that must be met in order to qualify for an exemption. First, the independent external service provider must consist only of operators carrying out an activity which is exempt from, or not subject to, VAT. Secondly, it is essential that the group does not exist for purposes of gain, in the sense that it only charges its members for expenses incurred by it in order to meet their requirements, and makes no profit whatsoever out of doing so.

122. This means that the group must be entirely transparent and that, from an economic point of view, it must not have the characteristics of an independent operator seeking a customer base in order to generate profits."

The Court itself found that the exemption can only be denied, under this condition, when it is the use of the exemption itself that gives rise to distortion of competition and a CSG cannot fail the distortion of competition condition simply because it is in a more advantageous competitive position because it complies with the requirement that it charges only an 'exact reimbursement' of costs.

"64. It follows that the grant of VAT exemption must be refused if there is a genuine risk that the exemption may by itself, immediately or in the future give rise to distortion of competition"

53. What are the practical implications of the Taksatorringen case?

Any arrangement or interaction between a CSG and a commercial operator will need to be carefully considered as such associations are more likely to lead to distortions of competition under the terms of the exemption.

HMRC would not normally expect a third party commercial supplier to be able to meet the qualifications for membership of a CSG as they are generally fully taxable organisations who would not qualify for membership. Similarly a third party commercial provider could not act as a CSG unless it was solely constituted of (was fully owned and controlled by) members who themselves qualify for CSG membership. However should a commercial outsourcer qualify for CSG membership it cannot use that membership qualification to take advantage of the exemption for its commercial outsourcing activity.

54. What is the position when a commercial operator supplies a CSG?

Normal VAT rules apply. The 'distortion of competition' condition should not affect normal customer/third party supplier arrangements. For example a CSG could, acting as an independent group of persons, freely engage a third party supplier to provide, for example, management or administrative services to the CSG and under normal commercial arrangements be able to decide to continue or not with that relationship. Such services supplied to the CSG would of course not benefit from the exemption but would be subject to the normal VAT rules and any VAT charged would be irrecoverable by the CSG to the extent that it was used for making exempt and/or non-business supplies by the CSG.

However where such charges are split so they are made directly to the individual members of a CSG as well as the CSG as a whole they may be regarded as abusive arrangements.

CSGs and VAT groups

55. Can a VAT Group Registration be a member of a CSG?

VAT grouping is a mechanism for accounting for tax and associated liabilities. Supplies of goods and services are made to individual members of the VAT group and the liability of those services depends on the status of the individual VAT group member, that member is able to join a CSG in its own right so long as its individual activities involve exempt or non-business activity.

Supplies received by a VAT group member from the CSG will be considered to be supplied to the representative member in accordance with the VAT Group Registration mechanism under the provisions s.43(1) of the VAT Act 1994.

However, s43(1AA) of the VAT Act 1994 allows the VAT group's representative member to be treated as a CSG member in relation to supplies which are treated as made to it but that are in reality made to the CSG member. Therefore it is the VAT group's member who is also a CSG member that must meet all the relevant cost share conditions and tests and be making the relevant exempt and/or non-business supplies to third parties, albeit that all such supplies are accounted for (under the VAT grouping mechanism) by the representative VAT group member. Note that supplies to other entities in the VAT group will not fulfil cost share conditions and tests, that is, they are neither exempt nor non-business, such supplies are disregarded for VAT purposes.

56. Can a CSG be a member of a VAT group?

Yes, provided all the relevant VAT grouping conditions are met, in particular the control condition. For example if the controlling entity of the VAT group was also a CSG member and had over 50 per cent of the shareholding of the CSG (with the remaining shareholding spread between the other CSG members) the CSG would meet the control condition to be a member of the VAT group.

In these circumstances the exempt supplies of the CSG would form part of those of the VAT Group Registration and input tax incurred by the CSG would form part of the VAT Group Registration's input tax.

57. How do CSGs and VAT groups interact in practice?

A CSG as a member of a VAT Group:

- All supplies made by a CSG that is a member of a VAT Group to members who are also members of the same VAT group will be outside the scope of the VAT system (they are not exempt or non-business supplies for VAT purposes).

- All supplies from other VAT Groups members to a CSG that is in the same VAT Group, whether they are CSG members or not are also outside the scope of the VAT system (they are not exempt or non-business supplies for VAT purposes).

- Supplies of qualifying services by a CSG that is a member of a VAT Group to CSG members who are outside of that VAT Group will fall within the exemption (subject to all the conditions being met) and will be form part of the VAT Groups exempt supplies.

58. How is the 5 per cent test applied to a VAT group member?

If a VAT group member wishes to become a member of a CSG it is that member who must meet the test and not the whole VAT group collectively, that is, the nature of the third party supplies made by the VAT group member determine its eligibility not the aggregated third party supplies of the VAT group. Supplies within VAT groups are outside of the scope of VAT rather than being exempt or non-business supplies so cannot be treated as exempt or non-business by the VAT group member to determine whether or not it is eligible to join a CSG.

59. How is the 85 per cent 'directly necessary' test applied to a VAT group member?

The 'directly necessary' test is applied in exactly the same way as it is by any other CSG member but only to the third party activities of the VAT group member that is the CSG member and not the aggregated activity of the VAT group as a whole. See Questions 39 to 45.

Appendix 24: Revenue & Customs Brief 23/12 and VAT Information Sheet 07/12

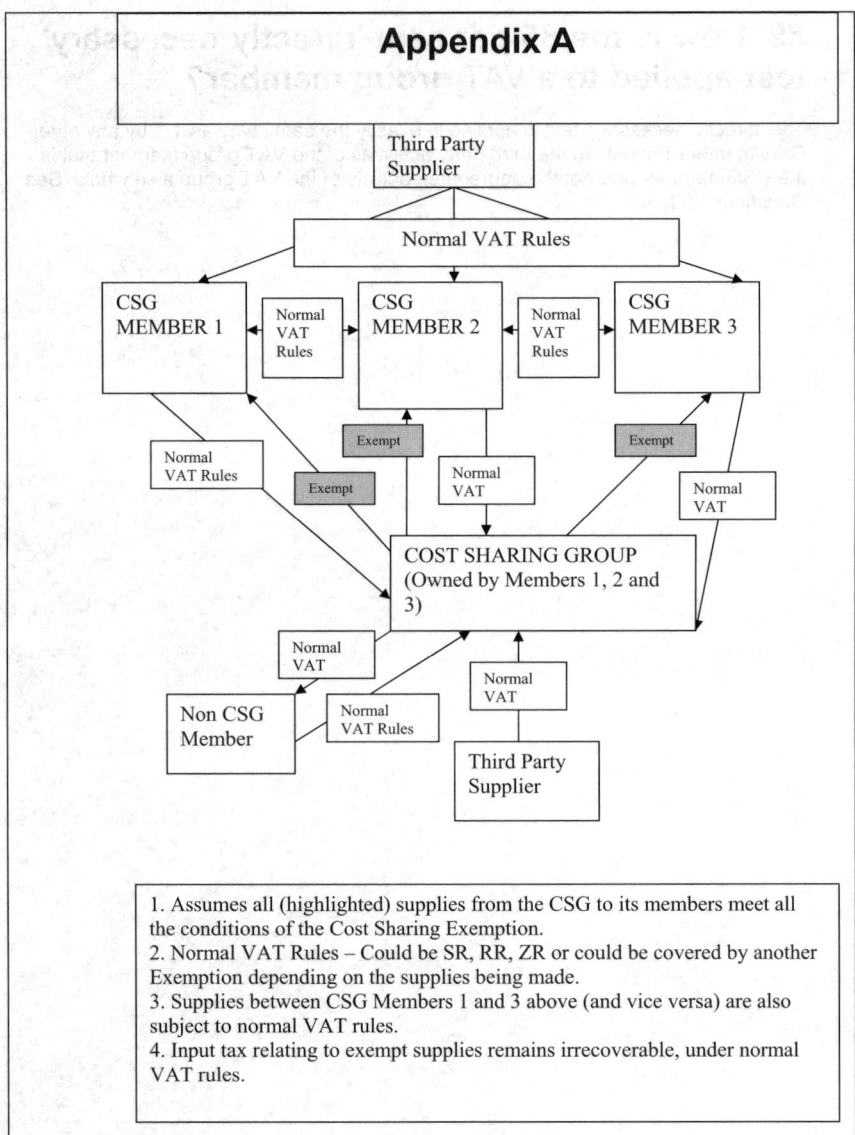

Who can I contact for further information?

If this VAT Information Sheet does not answer your question, please contact HM Revenue & Customs VAT and Excise Helpline on Tel 0845 010 9000 or +44 292 050 1261 for international enquiries.

The Helpline is available from 8.00 am to 8.00 pm, Monday to Friday. The advisers can help you with general queries.

If you have hearing difficulties, please ring the Textphone service on 0845 000 0200.

Appendix 25: VATFIN7280

Appendix 25: VATFIN7280 - Intermediaries: When is someone acting as an intermediary?: Flowchart-determining whether someone is acting as an intermediary

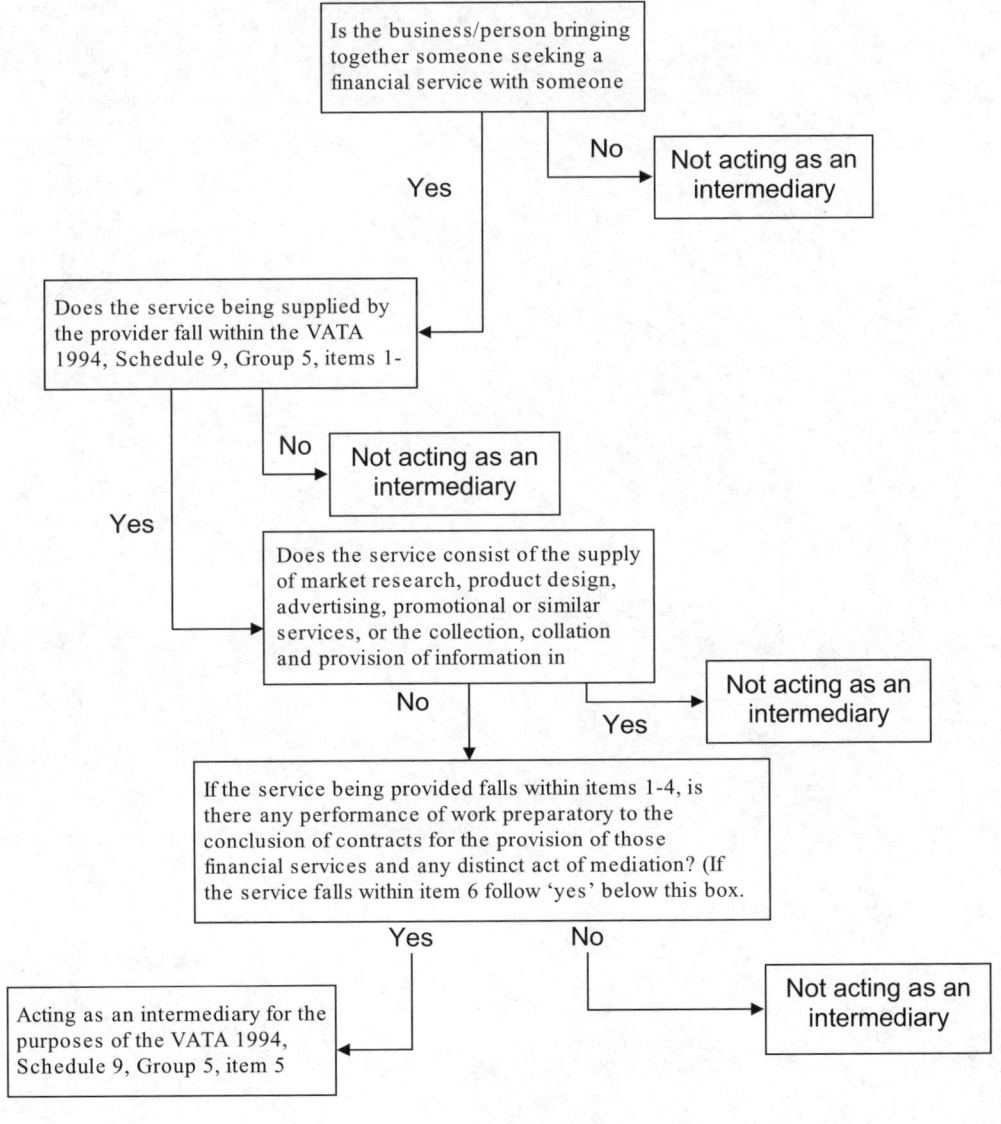

Appendix 26: VAT Finance Manual, para. VATFIN5260 – 'Actively Marketed'

Funds/sub-funds (i.e. single or umbrella schemes/sub-funds of umbrella schemes) are marketed to the gen-eral public (retail market) either directly or through retail market intermediaries such as fund platforms or 'supermarkets', IFAs, retail client stockbrokers and retail banks. A distinction is necessary here between retail investors and institutional investors such as fund of fund investment operators, pension schemes, investment companies, insurance companies, brokerage or large corporates.

We recognise that the question of whether or not a fund/sub-fund is actively marketed to UK retail investors is potentially complex. Therefore, we intend to adopt a pragmatic approach to this question in order that the ongoing administrative requirements associated with assessing and monitoring are not unduly burdensome for tax payers or HMRC.

In general, activity that is consistent with the active promotion and/or the agreement of new distribution deals in respect of individual funds/sub-funds, with the purpose of raising new assets and attracting new retail in-vestors, will be regarded as 'active marketing', including the following:

- Advertisements in UK national, consumer and/or trade press publications, or via various 'outdoor' media (e.g. posters), specifically mentioning one or more individual funds/sub-funds.
- As above, but where the publication is via a UK website or other online or digital media. For example, banner advertisements.
- Direct mail packs, specifically mentioning and promoting one or more funds/sub-funds, sent to UK retail investors and/or their advisers, for example authorised independent financial advisers (IFAs).
- Events for UK retail investors and/or their advisers featuring content relating to one or more in-dividual funds/sub-funds. For example, IFA roadshow events.
- Pro-active PR releases issued to UK publications specifically mentioning one or more individual funds/sub-funds.
- Active representation to IFA firms and/or other distributors to add one or more individual funds/sub-funds to their fund panels or available fund links.

In contrast, activity that is not consistent with the above will not be regarded as active marketing, including the following activities:

- Advertising and marketing activity where the materials do not make specific reference to an off-shore fund/sub-fund (i.e. brand advertising and promotion).
- Distribution of annual reports and other regulatory reporting requirements to existing UK retail investors.
- Communications to UK retail investors with ongoing holdings or monthly savings plans.
- General references to funds/sub-funds and prices on a promoter's/distributor's website, irrespective of whether that site carries transactional links, or on other industry information ser-vices, such as the FT fund price pages.
- The provision of general fund information to industry reference services and sites, including fund platform services, irrespective of whether that platform or service carries transactional links.
- Unsolicited PR or media coverage of a fund/sub-fund.
- The listing of an incorporated fund/sub-fund within a promoter's general information materials such as fund range brochures.

Appendix 26: VAT Finance Manual, para. VATFIN5260 – 'Actively Marketed'

- The awarding of a Fund Rating from one or more of the major UK fund rating agencies (e.g. OBSR; S&P) for one or more individual funds/sub-funds.

Certain information must be provided to UK investors in order for the manager/promoter of a CIS to comply with FSA registration requirements, and also to meet obligations relating to the 'treating customers fairly' principle and the ongoing suitability of investments. Such activity is not in itself regarded as active marketing.

Other potential indicators that a fund/sub-fund has been, or has not been, actively marketed to UK small re-tail investors are:

- Whether or not a fund/sub-fund or share class of a fund/sub-fund has distributor status (for income tax purposes);
- Whether a fund/sub-fund offers a sterling-denominated share class;

However, the key determining factor is the marketing activity undertaken by or on behalf of the fund/manager.

As noted above, for overseas CIS the change in legislation is aimed at the marketing of funds/sub-funds to the general public. Therefore, any active marketing of funds/sub-funds exclusively to institutional investors does not fall within the new rules and they can be considered to fall outside the exemption. Where, however, a fund/sub-fund is actively marketed to both UK retail investors and institutional investors, the management of that fund/sub-fund will fall within the exemption.

Appendix 27: Council Regulation (EU) No 967/2012

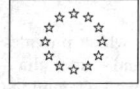 EUROPEAN COMMISSION

Brussels, XXX
[…](2011) XXX draft

Proposal for a

COUNCIL REGULATION

amending Implementing Regulation (EU) No 282/2011 as regards the special schemes for non-established taxable persons supplying telecommunications services, broadcasting services or electronic services to non-taxable persons

EN EN

EXPLANATORY MEMORANDUM

1. **CONTEXT OF THE PROPOSAL**

Grounds for and objectives of the proposal

Article 397 of Council Directive 2006/112/EC[1] (hereinafter "the VAT Directive") provides that "the Council, acting unanimously on a proposal from the Commission, shall adopt the measures necessary to implement this Directive".

On that basis, the Council adopted Council Regulation (EU) No 282/2011[2], which provides binding rules on the application of certain provisions of the VAT Directive and – inter alia – gave legal certainty to a number of non-binding guidelines agreed by the VAT Committee since 1977.

Large elements of Regulation No 282/2011 are composed of provisions which relate to the adoption of Directive 2008/8/EC[3]. Article 5 of that Directive contains legal changes concerning the special schemes for telecommunications, broadcasting or electronic services supplied to non-taxable persons by suppliers not established in the Member State of taxation. Regulation No 282/2011 currently does not provide for any implementing measure related to those provisions which will come into force as of 2015. Therefore it is necessary to adapt that Regulation in order to establish binding rules on the application of the respective provisions of the VAT Directive.

These measures should be adopted by Council as soon as possible and in any case by the middle of 2012, in order to enable the Commission and the Member States to agree on the functional and technical specifications of the IT systems that need to be built for the implementation of these special schemes.

The proposed measures only relate to those aspects (definitions, scope of the schemes, reporting obligations, identification, exclusion, VAT returns, currency, payments, records) for which a common understanding is needed before designing the IT systems. Other measures, notably relating to the determination of the location of the customer, will be proposed by the Commission at a later stage.

Only Section 2 of Chapter XI of Regulation No 282/2011 needs to be amended.

General context

On 1 January 2015, to accommodate for changes to the rules governing the place of supply, a number of substantial changes to the VAT Directive will come into effect relating to the special schemes for non-established taxable persons supplying telecommunications, broadcasting or electronic services to non-taxable persons (the so-called "mini One Stop

---

[1] Council Directive 2006/112/EC of 28 November 2006 on the common system of value added tax (OJ L 347, 11.12.2006, p. 1)
[2] Council Implementing Regulation (EU) No 282/2011 of 15 March 2011 laying down implementing measures for Directive 2006/112/EC on the common system of value added tax (recast) (OJ L 77, 23.3.2011, p. 1)
[3] Council Directive 2008/8/EC of 12 February 2008 amending Directive 2006/112/EC as regards the place of supply of services (OJ L 44, 20.2.2008, p. 11)

Shop"). Under the mini One Stop Shop, the supplier uses a web portal in the Member State in which he is identified to account for the VAT due in other Member States on supplies of such services to private consumers. A scheme is already in operation for non-EU businesses supplying electronic services.

As a result of the changes, this scheme for non-EU businesses, which currently only applies to the supply of electronic services, will be extended to telecommunications and broadcasting services. At the same time, a second special scheme which covers the same types of services will be introduced for EU businesses.

These legal changes will lead to a significant enlargement of the scope of the current mini One Stop Shop and therefore considerably more taxable persons will have the option to make use of one of the special schemes. This provides a challenge for tax administrations and businesses alike due to the need to set up administrative practices and IT systems which are duly compliant with the future legal requirements.

In order to ensure legal certainty, it is necessary to lay down clear and binding rules on the application of the provisions of the VAT Directive concerning the special schemes for non-established taxable persons supplying telecommunications services, broadcasting services or electronic services to non-taxable persons which will come into force as of 1 January 2015. The current provisions of Regulation No 282/2011 concerning the mini One Stop Shop will become outdated after 31 December 2014. Section 2 of Chapter XI of Regulation No 282/2011 should therefore be substituted by a new single set of implementing measures covering both special schemes for EU and non-EU businesses to be applied as from 1 January 2015.

2. **RESULTS OF CONSULTATIONS WITH THE INTERESTED PARTIES AND IMPACT ASSESSMENTS**

Consultation of interested parties

In order to identify the areas where implementing measures would be necessary to ensure a common application of the provisions of the VAT Directive, Member States were extensively consulted during a FISCALIS seminar and a Working Party n° 1 meeting. Exchanges of views with businesses also took place in the Business Expert Group on VAT.

Collection and use of external expertise

There was no need for external expertise.

Impact assessment

The measures concerned are of a purely technical nature and are merely setting out the application of provisions adopted by the Council. Hence there is no need for an impact assessment.

3. **LEGAL ELEMENTS OF THE PROPOSAL**

Subsidiarity principle

The subsidiarity principle applies insofar as the proposal does not fall under the exclusive competence of the EU. The objectives of the proposal cannot be sufficiently achieved by the Member States. Even though the Member States have the competence for transposition of EU law, it is essential that the provisions and incoming changes are transposed in the national legislations in a coordinated manner in order to avoid that divergent application rules adopted by the Member States could establish an obstacle to a well-functioning mini One Stop Shop scheme. For the reasons outlined above, only EU action can ensure equal treatment of business and citizens in the European Union. The proposal therefore complies with the subsidiarity principle.

Proportionality principle

The amendment of Council Regulation (EU) No 282/2011 is necessary to adapt it to the respective provisions of the VAT Directive as they will apply as from 1 January 2015. The new provisions relate to Directive 2008/8/EC amending Directive 2006/112/EC as regards the place of supply of services. These measures are necessary to implement the VAT Directive.

The proposal therefore complies with the proportionality principle.

Appendix 27: Council Regulation (EU) No 967/2012

Proposal for a

COUNCIL REGULATION

amending Implementing Regulation (EU) No 282/2011 as regards the special schemes for non-established taxable persons supplying telecommunications services, broadcasting services or electronic services to non-taxable persons

THE COUNCIL OF THE EUROPEAN UNION,

Having regard to the Treaty on the Functioning of the European Union,

Having regard to Council Directive 2006/112/EC of 28 November 2006 on the common system of value added tax[4], and in particular Article 397 thereof,

Having regard to the proposal from the European Commission,

Whereas:

(1) Directive 2006/112/EC, as amended by Directive 2008/8/EC[5], provides that as from 1 January 2015, all telecommunications, broadcasting and electronic services are to be taxed in the Member State in which the customer is established or has his permanent address or usual residence (hereinafter "Member State of consumption") regardless of where the taxable person supplying these services is established.

(2) In order to facilitate compliance with fiscal obligations where such services are supplied to non-taxable persons, a special scheme has been put in place for taxable persons established within the Community but not in the Member State where the services are supplied (hereinafter "Union scheme"). Similarly, the special scheme for taxable persons not established within the Community currently in place, should be extended to cover all of those services (hereinafter "non-Union scheme"). This should enable non-established taxable persons to designate a Member State of identification as a single point of electronic contact for value added tax (VAT) identification and declaration.

(3) A taxable person with establishments in more than one Member State should be able under the Union scheme to designate any of the Member States concerned as the Member State of identification except where he has his place of business within the Community. In that case, it should be ensured that the Member State of identification is that in which the taxable person has established his business.

(4) In order to avoid disproportionate burdens for taxable persons using the Union scheme, it should be clarified that where that taxable person has indicated a particular

---

[4] OJ L 347, 11.12.2006, p. 1
[5] OJ L 44, 20.2.2008, p. 11

Appendix 27: Council Regulation (EU) No 967/2012

Member State as his Member State of identification, he shall no longer be bound by that decision once he ceases to have a fixed establishment in that Member State.

(5) Telecommunications, broadcasting and electronic services supplied in Member States where the taxable person has established his business or has a fixed establishment are not covered by any of the special schemes. It should be made clear that such supplies should be declared directly to the Member State concerned.

(6) Since both of the special schemes are optional, a non-established taxable person may at any moment in time decide to cease use the scheme. It is necessary to establish as from when such a decision would take effect.

(7) It should be made clear that Member States must permit any taxable person to use the Union scheme where the customer is established or has his permanent address or usually resides in any Member State other than those in which the taxable person has established his business or has a fixed establishment.

(8) To keep the registration details in its data base up-to-date, the Member State of identification relies on the information received from the taxable person. In order to ensure that databases are updated without delay, it is necessary to lay down a time limit within which the taxable person should communicate any relevant information on commencement, ceasing or change of activities under the special scheme.

(9) A VAT identification number needs to be allocated to a non-established taxable person before use can be made of any of the special schemes. To prevent retroactive use by taxable persons who are already identified for VAT purposes, it is necessary to clarify from which moment the special schemes should apply.

(10) To avoid any conflict as to the jurisdiction between Member States, it should be specified which Member State may exclude a taxable person from using a special scheme, when that Member State is to take such a decision and from which moment this decision should take effect.

(11) It should be clarified when a non-established taxable person using one of the special schemes could be regarded as having ceased his activities under that scheme. It should also be clarified what, on the part of the non-established taxable person, would constitute persistent failure.

(12) To promote compliance and avoid unnecessary burden for tax authorities, a taxable person who is excluded from one of the special schemes due to persistent failure, should, for a certain period, be refused entry to any of these schemes.

(13) Where a taxable person is excluded from one of the special schemes, it should be made clear that all tax obligations must be discharged with the tax authorities of the Member State of consumption concerned, including any corrections of VAT returns previously submitted under the special scheme or payments of VAT related to those returns.

(14) Each return period should be treated separately so as to facilitate control by the Member States of consumption and amendments should only be made to the VAT return concerned. It should also be made clear that several successive amendments of the same VAT return are possible.

(15) It is appropriate, for reasons of control, to require for a VAT return to be submitted by the non-established taxable person to the Member State of identification, also where no services have been supplied during the return period. As to content, it should be clarified that the exact amount of VAT must be stated without any rounding up or down.

(16) For amendments to the VAT return, it is necessary to establish a time limit by which the return would need to be amended by the Member State of identification upon request of the non-established taxable person. The Member States of consumption should in any event be able to accept or request relevant information directly from the taxable person and process VAT assessments.

(17) Where the Member State of identification has not adopted the euro as a single currency, the non-established taxable person should be bound by the decision of that Member State as to the currency in which all VAT returns under the special schemes should be made.

(18) For a better allocation of payments, it should be ensured that amounts of VAT paid under the special schemes are specific to the VAT return submitted. Any subsequent amendments to amounts paid should be effected only by reference to that return and not allocated to another return, or adjusted on a subsequent return.

(19) In the case of non-payment, underpayment or payment in excess made by the non-established taxable person and with regard to interest, penalties and other incidental charges, it is important to specify the obligations of the Member State of identification and the Member States of consumption respectively so as to facilitate the collection of VAT and ensure that the right amount is paid on the services supplied under the special schemes.

(20) The records kept by the non-established taxable persons need to be sufficiently detailed. It should be laid down what is, as a minimum, required from these records in terms of details.

(21) To facilitate the implementation of the special schemes and with a view to enable services supplied as of 1 January 2015 to be covered by those schemes, it should be possible for non-established taxable persons to submit their registration details to the Member State which is designated by them as Member State of identification already as from 1 October 2014.

(22) Regulation (EU) No 282/2011 should therefore be amended accordingly,

HAS ADOPTED THIS REGULATION:

Article 1

In Regulation (EU) No 282/2011,

Section 2 of Chapter XI is replaced by the following:

'SECTION 2

SPECIAL SCHEMES FOR NON-ESTABLISHED TAXABLE PERSONS SUPPLYING TELECOMMUNICATIONS SERVICES, BROADCASTING SERVICES OR ELECTRONIC SERVICES TO NON-TAXABLE PERSONS

(ARTICLES 358 TO 369K OF DIRECTIVE 2006/112/EC)

SUBSECTION 1

DEFINITIONS

Article 57a

For the purposes of this Section, the following definitions shall apply:

(1) "non-Union scheme" means the special scheme for telecommunications services, broadcasting services or electronic services supplied by taxable persons not established within the Community provided for in Section 2 of Chapter 6 of Title XII of Directive 2006/112/EC;

(2) "Union scheme" means the special scheme for telecommunications services, broadcasting services or electronic services supplied by taxable persons established within the Community but not in the Member State of consumption provided for in Section 3 of Chapter 6 of Title XII of Directive 2006/112/EC;

(3) "special schemes" means "non-Union scheme" and "Union scheme";

(4) "taxable person" means a taxable person not established within the Community as defined in Article 358a(1) of Directive 2006/112/EC or a taxable person not established in the Member State of consumption as defined in Article 369a(1) of that Directive.

SUBSECTION 2

APPLICATION OF THE SPECIAL SCHEMES

Article 57b

A taxable person with more than one fixed establishment in the Community may indicate any of the Member States in which he is established as the Member State of identification pursuant to the second paragraph of Article 369a of Directive 2006/112/EC.

However, where the taxable person has established his business within the Community, the Member State in which his place of business is established shall be designated as the Member State of identification.

Article 57c

Where a taxable person using the Union scheme ceases to have a fixed establishment in the Member State indicated by that taxable person pursuant to the second paragraph of Article 369a of Directive 2006/112/EC as the Member State of identification, he shall no longer be bound by that decision.

SUBSECTION 3

SCOPE OF THE SPECIAL SCHEMES

Article 57d

The Union scheme shall not apply to telecommunications, broadcasting or electronic services supplied in a Member State where the taxable person has established his business or has a fixed establishment. Those supplies shall instead be declared to the competent tax authorities of that Member State in the VAT return as provided for under Article 250 of Directive 2006/112/EC.

Article 57e

Without prejudice to Article 57d, Member States shall permit any taxable person to use the Union scheme where the customer is established or has his permanent address or usually resides in any Member State.

SUBSECTION 4

REPORTING OBLIGATIONS

Article 57f

The taxable person shall communicate the information required under Articles 360, 361 and 369c of Directive 2006/112/EC, as well as any change of the information provided, to the Member State of identification within 30 days of that information being available to him.

SUBSECTION 5

IDENTIFICATION

Article 57g

When a taxable person states to the Member State of identification that he commences his activities covered by one of the special schemes, that scheme shall apply as from the first day of the subsequent calendar quarter.

However, where the activities are undertaken for the first time and the services are supplied prior to the first day of the subsequent calendar quarter, the scheme shall apply as from the date of that first supply, provided that supply is made during the calendar quarter of the communication.

Article 57h

Member States shall upon request permit any taxable person using one of the special schemes to cease using that scheme. The taxable person shall inform the Member State of identification at least 10 days before the end of the calendar quarter as from which he intends to cease using the scheme. Cessation shall be effective as of the first day of the next calendar quarter.

Where a taxable person decides to cease using one of the special schemes, he shall be excluded from using that scheme in any Member State for a minimum of one calendar year from the date of cessation.

SUBSECTION 6

EXCLUSION

Article 58

Where a taxable person using one of the special schemes meets at least one of the criteria for exclusion laid down in Articles 363 or 369e of Directive 2006/112/EC, the Member State of identification shall exclude that taxable person from that scheme.

Only the Member State of identification shall be authorised to exclude a taxable person from using one of the special schemes.

The Member State of identification may base its decision on exclusion on any information available, including information provided by any other Member State.

The exclusion shall be effective as from the first day of the subsequent calendar quarter.

Article 58a

Where a taxable person using one of the special schemes has made no supplies, in any Member State of consumption, of services covered by that scheme for a period of eight consecutive calendar quarters, he shall be assumed to have ceased his taxable activities within the meaning of point (b) of Article 363 or point (b) of Article 369e of Directive 2006/112/EC.

Article 58b

Where a taxable person is excluded from one of the special schemes for persistent failure to comply with the rules relating to that scheme, that taxable person shall remain excluded from using either scheme in any Member State until the end of the second calendar year following the calendar year during which the taxable person was excluded.

A taxable person shall be regarded as having persistently failed to comply with the rules relating to one of the special schemes, within the meaning of point (d) of Article 363 or point (d) of Article 369e of Directive 2006/112/EC, in at least the following cases:

(a) where he has not submitted VAT returns for a period of three consecutive calendar quarters;

(b) where he has not paid any amount of VAT due for three consecutive calendar quarters.

Article 58c

If a taxable person is excluded from one of the special schemes, that taxable person shall discharge all VAT obligations relating to supplies of telecommunications, broadcasting or electronic services directly with the tax authorities of the Member State of consumption concerned, including any corrections to be made to VAT returns submitted prior to exclusion or any payments of VAT.

SUBSECTION 7

VAT RETURN

Article 59

Any return period within the meaning of Article 364 or Article 369f of Directive 2006/112/EC shall be a separate return period.

Where a taxable person in accordance with the second subparagraph of Article 57g of this Regulation has been registered under one of the special schemes during a return period, he shall submit a VAT return covering that whole return period.

Article 59a

Where no services are supplied under the special schemes during a return period, the taxable person shall submit a VAT return indicating that no supplies have been made during that period (a nil-VAT return).

Article 60

Amounts on VAT returns made under the special schemes shall not be rounded up or down to the nearest whole monetary unit. The exact amount of VAT shall be reported and remitted.

Article 61

Once a VAT return has been submitted as provided for under Article 364 or Article 369f of Directive 2006/112/EC, any subsequent changes to the figures contained therein may be made only by means of an amendment to that return and not by an adjustment to a subsequent return. Several successive amendments of the same return shall be permitted.

Such amendments to the return shall be permitted through the special schemes for a period of up to five years after the day by which the initial return was submitted. This shall be without prejudice to the right of any Member State of consumption to accept or require the submission of such an amendment from the taxable person.

SUBSECTION 8

CURRENCY

Article 61a

Where a Member State of identification which has not adopted the euro as a single currency determines that the VAT return is to be made out in national currency, this shall apply to all taxable persons.

SUBSECTION 9

PAYMENTS

Article 62

Amounts of VAT paid under Article 367 or Article 369i of Directive 2006/112/EC shall be specific to the VAT return submitted pursuant to Article 364 or Article 369f of that Directive. Any subsequent adjustment to the amounts paid may be effected only by reference to that return and may not be allocated to another return, or adjusted on a subsequent return. Each payment shall refer to the reference number of that specific return.

Article 63

A Member State of identification which receives a payment in excess of that resulting from the VAT return submitted under Article 364 or Article 369f of Directive 2006/112/EC shall reimburse the overpaid amount directly to the taxable person concerned.

Where a Member State of identification has received an amount for a VAT return subsequently found to be incorrect, and that Member State has already distributed that amount to the Member States of consumption, those Member States shall directly reimburse any overpayment to the taxable person. In such a case, those Member States shall inform the Member State of identification of the amount of those reimbursements.

Article 63a

The taxable person shall make any payment directly to the Member State of identification.

Where the payment made does not correspond to that resulting from the VAT return submitted under Article 364 or Article 369f of Directive 2006/112/EC, the Member State of identification shall, by electronic means, remind the taxable person of any VAT overdue within 10 days of the end of the period referred to in Article 367 or Article 369i of Directive 2006/112/EC.

Any subsequent reminders and steps taken to collect the VAT shall be the responsibility of the Member State of consumption concerned.

Article 63b

Where a VAT return is incomplete or incorrect, is submitted late or the payment of VAT is late, any interest, penalties or any other charges due shall be paid directly to the Member State of consumption.

SUBSECTION 10

RECORDS

Article 63c

1. The records kept by the taxable person shall contain the following information to be regarded as sufficiently detailed within the meaning of Articles 369 and 369k of Directive 2006/112/EC:

(a) the Member State of consumption to which the service is supplied;

(b) the type of service supplied;

(c) the date of the supply of service;

(d) the taxable amount;

(e) any subsequent increase or reduction of the taxable amount;

(f) the VAT rate applied;

(g) the amount of VAT payable;

(h) the date and amount of payments received;

(i) any payments on account received before the supply of service;

(j) where an invoice is issued, the information contained on the invoice;

(k) the name of the customer, where known to the taxable person;

(l) the place where the customer is established or has his permanent address or usually resides, where known to the taxable person.

2. The information referred to in paragraph 1 shall be recorded by the taxable person in such a way that it can be made available without delay and for each single service supplied.'

Article 2

This Regulation shall enter into force on the twentieth day following that of its publication in the *Official Journal of the European Union*.

It shall apply from 1 January 2015.

However, Member States shall allow non-established taxable persons to submit the information required under Article 360 or Article 369c of Directive 2006/112/EC, as amended by Directive 2008/8/EC, for registration under the special schemes for non-established taxable persons supplying telecommunications services, broadcasting services or electronic services to non-taxable persons as from 1 October 2014.

This Regulation shall be binding in its entirety and directly applicable in all Member States.

Done at Brussels,

For the Council
The President

Appendix 28: Subsection 3 & 4 of the EU Implementing Regulation

CHAPTER V

PLACE OF TAXABLE TRANSACTIONS

SECTION 4

Place of supply of services
(Articles 43 to 59 of Directive 2006/112/EC)

Subsection 3
Location of the customer

Article 20

Where a supply of services carried out for a taxable person, or a non-taxable legal person deemed to be a taxable person, falls within the scope of Article 44 of Directive 2006/112/EC, and where that taxable person is established in a single country, or, in the absence of a place of establishment of a business or a fixed establishment, has his permanent address and usually resides in a single country, that supply of services shall be taxable in that country.

The supplier shall establish that place based on information from the customer, and verify that information by normal commercial security measures such as those relating to identity or payment checks.

The information may include the VAT identification number attributed by the Member State where the customer is established.

Article 21

Where a supply of services to a taxable person, or a non-taxable legal person deemed to be a taxable person, falls within the scope of Article 44 of Directive 2006/112/EC, and the taxable person is established in more than one country, that supply shall be taxable in the country where that taxable person has established his business.

However, where the service is provided to a fixed establishment of the taxable person located in a place other than that where the customer has established his business, that supply shall be taxable at the place of the fixed establishment receiving that service and using it for its own needs.

Where the taxable person does not have a place of establishment of a business or a fixed establishment, the supply shall be taxable at his permanent address or usual residence.

Article 22

1. In order to identify the customer's fixed establishment to which the service is provided, the supplier shall examine the nature and use of the service provided.

Where the nature and use of the service provided do not enable him to identify the fixed establishment to which the service is provided, the supplier, in identifying that fixed establishment, shall pay particular attention to whether the contract, the order form and the VAT identification number attributed by the Member State of the customer and communicated to him by the customer identify the fixed establishment as the customer of the service and whether the fixed establishment is the entity paying for the service.

Where the customer's fixed establishment to which the service is provided cannot be determined in accordance with the first and second subparagraphs of this paragraph or where services covered by Article 44 of Directive 2006/112/EC are supplied to a taxable person under a contract covering one or more services used in an unidentifiable and non-quantifiable manner, the supplier may legitimately consider that the services have been supplied at the place where the customer has established his business.

2. The application of this Article shall be without prejudice to the customer's obligations.

Article 23

1. From 1 January 2013, where, in accordance with the first subparagraph of Article 56(2) of Directive 2006/112/EC, a supply of services is taxable at the place where the customer is established, or, in the absence of an establishment, where he has his permanent address or usually resides, the supplier shall establish that place based on factual information provided by the customer, and verify that information by normal commercial security measures such as those relating to identity or payment checks.

2. Where, in accordance with Articles 58 and 59 of Directive 2006/112/EC, a supply of services is taxable at the place where the customer is established, or, in the absence of an establishment, where he has his permanent address or usually resides, the supplier shall establish that place based on factual information provided by the customer, and verify that information by normal commercial security measures such as those relating to identity or payment checks.

Article 24

1. From 1 January 2013, where services covered by the first subparagraph of Article 56(2) of Directive 2006/112/EC, are supplied to a non-taxable person who is established in more than one country or has his permanent address in one country and his usual residence in another, priority shall be given to the place that best ensures taxation at the place of actual consumption when determining the place of supply of those services.

2. Where services covered by Articles 58 and 59 of Directive 2006/112/EC are supplied to a non-taxable person who is established in more than one country or has his permanent address in one country and his usual residence in another, priority shall be given to the place that best ensures taxation at the place of actual consumption when determining the place of supply of those services.

Subsection 4
Common provision regarding determination of the status, the capacity and the location of the customer

Article 25

For the application of the rules governing the place of supply of services, only the circumstances existing at the time of the chargeable event shall be taken into account. Any subsequent changes to the use of the service received shall not affect the determination of the place of supply, provided there is no abusive practice.

Appendix 29: Guidance on the Application of Para 8A of Schedule 6 of the VAT Act Valuing Reverse Charge Supplies Due Under Section 43(2A)

Introduction

When a UK VAT group acquires services via an overseas member of the same VAT group, a VAT charge known as a 'reverse charge' must be calculated to ensure that the services are correctly taxed in the UK. This means that the VAT group has to account for output tax on an appropriate value, whilst simultaneously posting an equal amount of input tax and deducting it to the extent allowed under the law (hence the reverse charge).

How the charge should be calculated was formerly covered by a concession. That concession was given legislative effect in the Finance Act 2012. This guidance gives details of how this charge should be calculated under the new law.

The history of why the reverse charge was introduced and how we came to the current position was set out in the consultation document 'Legislating an extra-statutory Concession – ESC 3.2.2' published on 10 May 2011 and is not covered again here.

These rules are effective from Royal Assent to Finance Act 2012.

1. The basic position

1.1 When a reverse charge must be calculated

A reverse charge must be calculated when the following circumstances exist:

- There is an intra-VAT group charge for supplies of services between group members which is disregarded for VAT purposes because of the VAT group (under s43(1)(a) of the VAT Act) and which would have been taxable (as opposed to exempt) if it had not been disregarded,
- The place of supply (again if not disregarded) would have been set as the UK under the standard rule set out in s7A(2)(a) of the VAT Act (the alternative being where the place of supply is set by one of the exceptions to the standard rule set out in Schedule 4A to the VAT Act, further covered in section 2.4 below),
- Some of the cost components of the charge are services 'bought in' by an overseas establishment of the group member making the charge,
- The 'bought in' services received by the overseas establishment must have their place of supply set by the standard rule and must be 'taxable' services.

1.2 How the reverse charge must be calculated

When a reverse charge is due the values of bought in services ('taxable' and with a place of supply outside the UK under the standard rule for place of supply of services) that are cost components of the intra-VAT group charge must be determined. Unless HMRC make a direction as set out in 2.6 below, the value of the reverse charge is the total of the values of the bought in services.

The meanings of 'bought in' services, cost components, overheads and own resources are explained at 2.1 below.

2. Practicalities

2.1 Definitions of terms used above and below

This guidance uses several terms that have established VAT meanings. This section gives guidance as to what they are.

2.1.1 What is a bought in service?

A bought in service is a supply of services received by the business in question that forms a cost component of the intra-VAT group supply as identified in 1.1 and 1.2 above. However costs which are either 'overheads' of the overseas establishment or the 'own resources' of the overseas establishment are not considered bought in services for the purpose of calculating reverse charges.

2.1.2 What is a 'cost component' of a supply?

Businesses incur costs and use them to make supplies to their customers. Not all costs will be directly used to make all supplies. A cost is a cost component of the price of a supply made if it is 'directly and immediately' linked to that supply. There is further guidance on this point at 2.2 below.

However some costs, although they are directly and immediately linked to supplies made, need not be figured into the reverse charges covered by this guidance. They are overhead costs and the cost of the business's own resources.

2.1.3 What is an 'overhead' cost?

Before a business may deduct any input tax there must be a direct and immediate link between the cost it is incurred on and the taxable supplies of the business. Some costs are figured into the price of specific supplies so as to have a clear direct and immediate link to those supplies. Other costs are business costs but are not clearly figured into the price of any particular supplies made. These are overhead costs of the business. They are reckoned to be directly and immediately linked with the business as a whole and all of the supplies which it makes.

HMRC's view is that, although overhead costs are directly and immediately linked to the intra-VAT group charges, the element of any overhead related to the charges can be ignored. Overheads may include costs such as public utilities, building rent and maintenance, IT asset leasing and maintenance etc.

2.1.4 What are 'own resources'?

The reverse charge sets out to tax services bought in by the business which, via an intra-VAT group charge, become cost components of supplies made by UK establishments of VAT group members. It therefore addresses only bought in services, as opposed to the own resources of the overseas establishment making the charge. What constitutes the own resources of a business will depend on the nature of that business, but will include its staff and the basic infrastructure costs necessary for the operation of the business.

Services received by a business may be used in various ways by that business, including as 'own resources' and 'overheads'. The reverse charge only applies to 'bought in services' as defined above.

2.2 Establishing the extent to which bought in supplies are cost components of the charge

In order to be able to calculate reverse charges it is necessary to determine what bought in costs are cost components of what intra-VAT group supplies and to what extent. As set out above the legal test for determining this is 'direct and immediate link.

UK courts have said that a good way of viewing whether a direct and immediate link exists between a cost and an onward supply is to look for a sufficient link between the cost and the onward supply. Another way of looking at it is to ask whether the incurring of the cost is essential to the making of the onward supply. However looked at, a direct and immediate link is a substantial, cost component link.

The question of whether specific costs are cost components of intra-VAT group supplies in accordance with 1.1 and 1.2 above is basically one of fact, and so the individual circumstances need to be fully analysed. The identification and quantification of any such cost components may be aided by examining the accounting process of the business. Businesses will keep whatever management or accounting records they find useful and such records may set costs incurred against supplies made. HMRC will accept a system for identifying which costs are cost components of which intra group supplies, and to what extent, provided such system follows the normal cost allocation policies of the business and is not contrived to minimise the reverse charge.

However, it is important to emphasise that:

- If the cost allocation policy of the business does not directly factor specific costs into a particular charge made for intra-VAT group supplies, this cannot prevent something that is clearly a direct cost component of such supply from being liable to the reverse charge;
- Equally, the fact that certain costs may be factored into particular charges for intra-VAT group supplies does not automatically trigger a reverse charge liability where the costs represent the own resources or overheads of the business as per 2.1 above.

Examples

1. A VAT group develops software at its overseas establishment that will be used by a UK member of the VAT group. The overseas member then charges a fixed flat fee to the UK member for the use of that software. The overseas member contracts with a software company in the overseas location to maintain the software. The fee to the UK is not dependent on the level of the charge from the overseas contractor but the latter's charge to the overseas establishment is nonetheless clearly a cost component of the fee (i.e. represented in the intra-VAT group supply) to the UK.

2. A VAT group includes an overseas member which supplies various administrative and support services to members generally i.e. both in the UK and in other locations. In order to support such global activities, the overseas member incurs a number of costs locally. These include staff costs and general IT system support and maintenance from a local IT supplier. Such costs are included in the calculation of charges to all group members in order to prevent the overseas member from making a loss (and to satisfy transfer pricing requirements). Despite this cost allocation policy, the local costs above represent own resource and overheads of the business which are ignored for the purposes of the intra-VAT group reverse charge rules.

3. In the same basic scenario as 2 above, the UK member outsources the performance of a specific internal operating process to the overseas member and this requires the overseas member to incur particular local costs in order to perform the process locally e.g. new legal agreements, dedicated IT hardware and software, engagement and training costs of additional dedicated staff etc. Irrespective of whether such costs are directly factored into charges for the supply made to the UK group member, they are clearly cost components of that supply and so would potentially be liable to a reverse charge. If the new IT costs are invoiced in one charge with existing general costs then that supply would have to be analysed and only the specific cost taken into account as a bought in service.

All conclusions over whether a reverse charge is due are subject to the considerations set out in 2.3 below.

2.3 When charges can be ignored

Although the law provides that reverse charges should be applied in the circumstances set out in Para 8A(2) of Schedule 6, as described in this guidance, HMRC's view is that where the bought in element of an onward supply (i.e. the amount determined to be liable to the reverse charge) is truly minimal or trifling then calculating it is not what the provision giving rise to a charge to tax was enacted for and the law, properly construed, would not require a taxpayer to apply the rigours of section 43(2A). Also, if the net tax result would be nil (for instance because the VAT group is fully taxable, or because the intra-group supply is used wholly to make taxable supplies) it is immediately clear that no additional tax will result from calculations and HMRC's view is that no calculations are needed.

What is trifling will depend on the circumstances in each case. However HMRC agree that guidance as to the circumstances in which the calculation of reverse charges will not be required will assist in the smooth administration of the tax.

HMRC are not looking to set monetary limits below which calculated amounts of VAT on cost components of intra-group supplies need not be declared. Instead HMRC consider there is a level at which no calculation will be needed because the resultant restriction in input tax (if it had been calculated) would have been trifling in the context of a particular taxpayer's business. Indeed HMRC believes that if the work has been done and a charge calculated there is no reason not to declare it. This is so even if the resulting tax is trifling and it would thus not have been necessary to calculate a charge if this had been known prior to calculation.

In literature released when the concession which is now replaced was announced in 1997, HMRC set out that no charge needed to be applied, or that limited calculations would be accepted, in the following circumstances:

- Where the bought in services included in the cost components of an intra-VAT group supply represent less than 5% of the price of that supply (although it was made clear that this test should be applied with some common sense rather than mechanistically)
- Where the element of bought in services is greater than 5% but, because of a low overall value or a high partial exemption recovery rate, the resulting irrecoverable VAT would be very low
- Where a taxpayer is nearly fully taxable then the latitude allowed will be commensurately greater because any impact will be much lower

HMRC still considers these guidelines are sound.

A further question is whether considerations of whether charges would be trifling should be made for the VAT group as a whole, for individual VAT group members or for individual intra-VAT group charges?

The logic behind ignoring trifling charges clearly leads to the conclusion that it should be considered supply by supply i.e. by looking at the value of the cost components of the supply potentially liable to the reverse charge relative to the total value of that supply. However taxpayers breaking intra-VAT group charges down into a series of smaller charges with a view to treating each as trifling would be a strong indicator that none of those charges trifling. Similarly, amalgamating intra-VAT group charges together so that the bought in element will fall below 5% overall would a strong indicator that the reverse charge would not be trifling.

2.4 When is the place of supply of a service not set under the standard rule?

Under place of supply rules for services there is a standard rule (in s.7A(2)(a) of the Act) and a series of exceptions (in Schedule 4A to the Act). The reverse charge only applies where bought in services are received at the business's overseas establishment under the standard rule.

Some of the exceptions in Schedule 4A apply whenever a service is of the appropriate type. However there are several 'use and enjoyment' rules that only apply when the place of supply would be different because of the application of the rule.

Where a service is covered by an automatic rule then the place of supply is always set by Schedule 4A and not by the standard rule. As a consequence such services are never taken into account in calculating reverse charges. A prime example of such services is services related to land. Any services that come within the definition of services related to land can never be taken into account in VAT group reverse charge calculations.

Services which could be subject to a use and enjoyment provision will nonetheless have their place of supply set by the standard rule when the use and enjoyment provision does not apply. Consequently they may be taken into account in calculating reverse charges. Telecoms is an example of such services. Telecoms services used by an overseas establishment will be supplied there because that is where the recipient belongs and not because they are used and enjoyed there. So if such services are direct costs rather than overheads they will be included in reverse charges.

2.5 What if it is difficult to establish the value of cost components?

As an overseas establishment will always be of a company that is within the VAT group, and so under the same control as the representative member, it should normally be possible to obtain the necessary evidence over costs incurred overseas in order to calculate the reverse charges. The law does not require any particular evidence as to value, but the taxpayer must satisfy HMRC as to the value of each bought in supply. For services received an invoice is an obvious normal piece of evidence as to value. However HMRC will accept a range of other normal commercial evidence so long as it is reasonably clear and there is no reason to think that manipulation of values is occurring. If taxpayers are concerned over whether their evidence is sufficiently clear to satisfy HMRC they should contact HMRC via normal channels.

Exceptionally, it may prove impossible to arrive at a credible, evidence backed valuation. If this is so then the requirement that HMRC is satisfied as to value cannot be fulfilled. Consequently the law will value the reverse charge as the full value of the intra-VAT group charge (Paragraph 8A(1)(b) of Schedule 6).

2.6 HMRC directions

When the VAT group has been able to evidence what the values of the bought in services were, but HMRC believes that those services were undervalued, HMRC may direct that they shall be valued at their open market value. Any such direction must be made within three years of the intra-VAT group charge to the UK that causes the reverse charge. However the bought in services may have been incurred by the overseas establishment at an earlier date than that.

If the VAT group cannot evidence what the values of the bought in services are then Paragraph 8A of Schedule 6 will not apply and the value of the reverse charge will be the same as the intra-VAT group charge. If HMRC believes that this value is less than the open market value of the intra-VAT group supply, and if the other conditions required under that Paragraph are met, HMRC may direct an open market value under Paragraph 1 of Schedule 6.

2.7 Converting monetary amounts into sterling

Bought in services may well be charged in currencies other than sterling. Indeed charges between VAT group entities may be in currencies other than sterling. Because VAT must always be in sterling, calculations of reverse charges will require an amount in sterling that can be used to generate the VAT.

The business's normal arrangements for converting currencies may be used so long as they are consistently and rationally applied and are not designed to minimise reverse charges. If the business has no set policy then any meaningful, verifiable and independently compiled exchange rate may be used so long as it is consistently applied.

2.8 When reverse charges must be calculated

Where an intra-VAT group supply is represented by a clear one-off charge then the reverse charge should calculated on it immediately. However some supplies (and related charges) may be ongoing, possibly with quarterly estimates which are accurately calculated annually. Where this applies, HMRC is content for reverse charges to be similarly estimated quarterly, and for the annual calculation to correct any over or under payment of tax that may have occurred. Where charges are genuinely annual, with no charges actually made within the group until the year end, the reverse charge will only be due annually.

2.9 Overseas branches but no vat group

Although the charge requires something similar to an overseas branch to exist before it can apply (i.e. there must be a VAT group member with establishments both in the UK and overseas) it does not apply simply because there is an overseas branch but requires a VAT group and the other circumstances set out in 1.1 above.

Where there is a separately registered UK company that has an overseas branch then no reverse charges can arise under this provision. However if costs are billed to the overseas branch but used in the UK then a normal reverse charge may arise under s8 of VATA depending on circumstances. Reverse charge guidance is set out at VATPOSS14000.

2.10 Double taxation

Double taxation is something which VAT rules and HMRC seek to avoid if possible. If a cost is incurred by an overseas establishment of a group member based in another EU member state, that member state does not permit input tax on the cost to be deducted and the cost is a bought in service figurable into a reverse charge payable in the UK, then Double taxation may occur. If any taxpayer finds himself in this position he should contact HMRC via normal channels.

Appendix 30: Business Brief 30/12

Purpose of this Brief

The purpose of this Brief is to explain a change in HM Revenue & Customs' (HMRC's) position following the decision of the Tax Tribunal in the case of Robinson Family Limited ([2012] UKFTT 360 (TC), TC02046).

Readership

This Brief is for traders who enter into property transactions (other than solely as an occupier), and their advisers.

Action required

To note the contents of this Brief.

Introduction

When the assets of a business (or part of a business) are transferred as a going concern, subject to certain conditions no supply of those assets takes place for VAT purposes. For this to happen, the purchaser must have the intention of using those assets to carry on the same kind of business as the seller. This is equally the case where the business is that of property development or property rental, and the asset sold is the property, but it can sometimes be less clear when a business is being transferred in these situations.

HMRC has interpreted the law as meaning that, for there to be the transfer of a property rental or property development business as a going concern ('TOGC'), the interest in land being transferred must be the same interest as that used by the transferor in his business. It followed from this interpretation that, if what was transferred was less than the transferor's full interest in the land, then the retained interest would prevent there having been the transfer of a property business as a going concern. For example, HMRC's guidance says that where a freeholder grants a 999 year lease the freeholder's business is not transferred as a going concern because of the interest retained.

In its decision in the case of **Robinson Family Limited**, the Tax Tribunal disagreed with this interpretation of the law in the facts of that case. **HMRC will not be appealing this decision.**

Robinson Family Limited ('RFL')

RFL is a property development company which purchased a 125 year interest in a site owned by Belfast Harbour Commissioners, which it intended to develop into six units and grant sub-leases of these to third parties. The dispute between RFL and HMRC in the end concerned one unit which RFL had been negotiating to let. There was a restriction imposed by Belfast Harbour Commissioners against any subdivision of the site other than by way of the creation of sub-leases, so rather than sell its interest, RFL granted an interest of 125 years less three days to a purchaser subject to and with the benefit of the proposed letting.

HMRC relied solely on the argument that RFL could not have transferred all or part of its business as a going concern, because it did not assign the full term of its lease to the purchaser. HMRC's approach in the case reflected the guidance set out in the second bullet point in paragraph 6.3 of Notice 700/9 (April 2008): Transfer of business as a going concern:

> 'If you own the freehold of a property and grant a lease, even a 999-year lease, you are not transferring a business as a going concern. You are creating a new asset (the lease) and selling it while retaining your original asset (the freehold). This is true regardless of the length of the lease. Similarly, if you own a headlease and grant a sub-lease you are not transferring your business as a going concern.'

The Tribunal found that, although RFL retained the headlease, that distant interest in a three day reversion and the small economic interest which it represented in no way altered the substance of the transaction. The substance of the transaction was to put the transferee business in a position where it was able to continue the previous lettings business of RFL. On this basis, the Tribunal found against HMRC.

What this means

In the light of the Tribunal's decision in the **Robinson Family** case, HMRC accepts that the fact that the transferor of a property rental business retains a small reversionary interest in the property transferred does not prevent the transaction from being treated as a TOGC for VAT purposes. Provided the interest retained is small enough not to disturb the substance of the transaction, the transaction will be a TOGC if the usual conditions are satisfied. In this context, the Tribunal's decision does not as such alter any other areas of HMRC's policy on TOGCs, but we are reviewing the policy on whether the surrender of an interest in land can sometimes result in a TOGC. HMRC is also reviewing whether properties which are used in a business other than property letting are affected by this change of policy.

The second bullet point in paragraph 6.3 of Notice 700/9 should be ignored, as we now accept that the creation of a new asset (a lease or sub-lease) and the retention of the original asset (the freehold or a superior lease) is not automatically incompatible with TOGC treatment. The Notice will be updated in due course.

HMRC will accept that a reversion retained by the transferor is sufficiently small for TOGC treatment to be capable of applying if the value of the interest retained is no more than 1 per cent of the value of the property immediately before the transfer (disregarding any mortgage or charge). Where more than one property is transferred at one time, this test should be applied on a property by property basis rather than for the entire portfolio.

If the interest retained by the transferor represents more than 1 per cent of the value of the property, HMRC will regard that as strongly indicative that the transaction is too complex to be a TOGC.

Example

A Ltd owns the freehold of a building valued at £1m which A Ltd rents out commercially. A Ltd sells that property rental business by granting to B Ltd a 999 year lease under which A Ltd is entitled to receive a ground rent of £100 each year. The value of that right, together with any and all other rights retained by A Ltd, is £2,000. Provided all the normal conditions are satisfied, the transaction will be a TOGC, because HMRC will regard the 0.2 per cent interest retained as too small to disturb the substance of the transaction.

The impact of the decision

We accept there are situations where in the past customers did not regard a transaction as constituting a TOGC because of the guidance referred to. In some cases a building would have been sold where an option to tax had been exercised, and the relevant VAT charged and accounted for. SDLT would then have been payable on the VAT-inclusive amount. There are two questions to address where customers wish to retrospectively claim TOGC treatment on account of the Tribunal's decision in the **Robinson Family**.

Firstly, there is the difficulty that the relevant notification that an option to tax will not be rendered ineffective, will not have been given by the buyer to the seller. This is a legal requirement in articles 5(2A) and 5(2B) of the VAT (Special Provisions) Order 1995, and it is referred to in paragraph 11.2 of Notice 742A: Opting to tax land and buildings.

Provided the parties can satisfactorily evidence that **Article 5(2B) did not apply at the time of the transaction** and thus the requisite notification could have been given, we will accept that the legal requirement has been complied with.

Secondly, there is the question of whether an adjustment can be made to the SDLT already paid. We are considering this point and will provide further guidance on it soon.

Retrospective claims

Details of how to make any adjustments relating to previous VAT Return periods can be found in VAT Notice 700/45 How to correct VAT errors and make adjustments or claims and from the VAT Helpline on 0845 010 9000.

Where you are in any doubt about the correct VAT treatment please contact the VAT Helpline.

Issued: 16 November 2012

Case Table

(References are to paragraph numbers)

Paragraph

A

AA Insurance Services Ltd [1999] BVC
2,330 40-200

Abbey National plc [2002] BVC
2,077 80-100

Abbey National plc v C & E Commrs
[2001] BVC 581 40-200

Abbey National plc v C & E Commrs
(Case C-408/98) [2005] BVC 348 .... 30-650;
40-000; 110-400; 110-450; 110-500; 110-550

Abbey National plc v C & E Commrs
(Case C-169/04) [2006] ECR I-4027 .... 70-150;
80-100; 80-200; 80-300

Actinic plc [2003] BVC 4,096 .... 30-250;
40-000

Allied Lyons plc [1996] BVC 2,399 40-000

A1 Lofts Ltd [2011] TC 00831 10-100

A Oy, Re (Case C-33/11) 19 July 2012........ 70-400

Apple and Pear Development Council v
C & E Commrs (Case 102/86) (1988)
3 BVC 274 30-500

Aquarium Entertainments Ltd [1995]
BVC 728 80-150

ARO Lease BV v Inspecteur der
Belastingdienst Grote Ondernemingen,
Amsterdam (Case C-190/95) [1995]
BVC 547 .... 30-250;
70-150

Arsenal Football Club plc [1996] BVC
2,775 30-500

Associates Fleet Services Ltd [2001]
BVC 4,150 30-450

Association of Investment Trust Companies v
C & E Commrs (Case C-363/05) [2007]
BVC 337 .... 80-200;
80-300; 90-350

Assurandør-Societetet (acting on behalf of
Taksatorringen) v Skatteministeriet
(Case C-8/01) [2006] BVC 199 .... 90-100;
90-350

Astra Zeneca UK Ltd v R & C Commrs
(Case C-40/09) [2011] BVC 101 40-000

Auto Lease Holland BV v Bundesant fur
Finanzen (Case C-185/01) [2005]
BVC 182 .... 30-250;
70-100

Paragraph

B

BAA plc [2001] BVC 2,045 .... 70-200;
70-500

Balkan and Sea Properties ADSITs v Direktor
na Direktsia 'Obzhalvane i upravlenie na
izpalnenieto' – Varna pri Tsentralno
upravlene na Natsionalnate agentsia
za prihodite (Case C-621/10)
26 April 2012 .... 30-500;
60-050

Baltic Leasing Ltd (1986) 2 BVC 208,097;
(1986) VATTR 98 .... 30-450;
70-400

Bank of Scotland (Governor and
Company of) [1996] BVC 2,664 .... 40-200;
70-200; 70-250

Banque Bruxelles Lambert SA v
Belguim (Case C-9/03) [2007]
BVC 101 110-050

Barclays Bank plc (1988) 3 BVC 692;
(1988) VATTR 23 .... 70-100;
70-200

Barclays Bank plc (No. 2) [1991] BVC
585 .... 70-100;
70-250

Barclays Bank plc (No. 3) [1991] BVC
893 .... 90-100;
90-350

Baxi Group Ltd v R & C Commrs [2011]
BVC 1 .... 10-000;
10-100; 30-450; 40-000

Becker v Finanzamt Munster-Innenstadt
(Case 8/81) [1982] ECR 53 10-000

Belgium v Ghent Coal Terminal NV
(Case C-37/95) [1998] BVC 139;
[1998] ECR I-1 .... 40-250;
110-500

Birkdale School, Sheffield v R & C Commrs
[2008] BVC 397 90-050

Blackqueen Ltd [2002] BVC 2,221 30-000

Blandy [1996] BVC 4,075 80-150

Bloomsbury Wealth Management LLP
[2012] TC 02063 80-100

BLP Group plc v C & E Commrs
(Case C-4/94) [1995] BVC 159 .... 40-200;
70-350; 80-100;
110-050; 110-200; 110-400

Case Table

	Paragraph
Blythe Limited Partnership [1999] BVC 2,224	80-150
BMW Financial Services (GB) Ltd [2003] BVC 4,061	40-000
BMW (GB) Ltd [1997] BVC 4,090	40-200
BMW (GB) Ltd v C & E Commrs [1997] BVC 400	40-050
Bookit Ltd v R & C Commrs [2006] BVC 605	70-300; 120-150
Britannia Building Society [1997] BVC 4,106	40-200
British Airways Board No. 663 (unreported)	60-100; 80-400
British Airways Housing Trust Ltd No. 663 (unreported)	60-100; 80-400
British Broadcasting Corp v C & E Commrs (1974) VATTR 100	40-000
British Eventing Ltd [2011] TC 00664	80-150
British Hardware Federation (1975) VATTR 172	70-100
British Horse Society Ltd [2000] BVC 2,062	90-100
BUPA Hospitals Ltd and Goldsborough Developments Ltd v C & E Commrs (Case C-419/02) [2006] BVC 377	10-300; 30-350

C

	Paragraph
Cadbury Ireland Pension Trust Ltd v Revenue Commrs (Ireland) [2007] IEHC 179	10-300
Canary Wharf Ltd [1997] BVC 2,058	20-250
C & V (Advice Line) Services Ltd [2001] BVC 2,369	90-100
Capital One Bank (Europe) plc [2006] BVC 2,148	30-000; 40-200; 70-100; 70-200; 70-450; 80-200
Card Protection Plan Ltd v C & E Commrs (Case C-349/96) [1999] BVC 155	30-550; 60-050; 70-300; 70-400; 70-500; 80-100; 90-050; 90-100; 90-220; 90-350
Card Protection Plan Ltd v C & E Commrs [2001] BVC 158	30-150; 80-200; 90-100; 90-220; 90-350
Celtic Football and Athletic Co Ltd v C & E Commrs (1983) 1 BVC 554	40-050
Centralan Property Ltd v C & E Commrs (Case C-63/04) [2007] BVC 341	40-200
Central Capital Corp Ltd [1996] BVC 2,336	80-150
Centurions [1993] BVC 1,346	90-220

	Paragraph
CGI Group (Europe) Ltd [2011] TC 00678	70-500
Chalegrove Properties Ltd [2001] BVC 2,279	30-450; 80-150
Chassures Bally SA v Belgium (Case C-18/92) [1993] ECR I-2871	70-200; 70-300
Cibo Participations SA v Directeur régional des impôts du Nord-Pas-de-Calais (Case C-16/00) [2002] BVC 605; [2001] ECR I-6663	40-250; 110-100; 110-350
Citroën UK Ltd [1999] BVC 2,314	90-220
Cloud Electronics Holdings Ltd [2012] UKFTT 699 (TC)	40-250
Concept Direct Ltd [2007] BVC 4,013	70-100
Continuum (Europe) Ltd [1998] BVC 2,131	70-500; 90-350
Co-operative Insurance Society Ltd [1992] BVC 694	30-500
Co-operative Insurance Society Ltd [1997] BVC 4,100	30-000
Cornhill Management Ltd (1990) 5 BVC 901	80-300; 100-450
Costain Property Investments Ltd v Stokes [1984] BTC 92	80-150
Countrywide Insurance Marketing Ltd [1995] BVC 580	90-100; 90-350
Courts plc [2005] BVC 2,003	30-550
Cross Border Lease Management Ltd [2007] BVC 4,035	30-500
CSC Financial Services Ltd v C & E Commrs (Case C-235/00) [2002] BVC 253	80-100; 90-050
Cumbernauld Development Corp [1997] BVC 4,043	30-500
Cumbernauld Development Corp v C & E Commrs [2002] BVC 384	30-350
Curtis Edington & Say Ltd [1995] BVC 1,389	90-100; 90-350
C & E Commrs v Abbey National plc [2006] BVC 645	80-150
C & E Commrs v Apple and Pear Development Council (Case 102/86) (1988) 3 BVC 274; (1984) 2 BVC 200,029	10-300; 30-500

Case Table

	Paragraph
C & E Commrs v BAA plc [2002] BVC 463	70-200; 70-500
C & E Commrs v BAA plc [2003] BVC 112	70-300; 70-500
C & E Commrs v Barclays Bank plc [2001] BVC 606	20-250
C & E Commrs v British Railways Board (1976) 1 BVC 103	80-400
C & E Commrs v British Telecommunications plc [1999] BVC 306	30-550; 40-050
C & E Commrs v Cantor Fitzgerald International (Case C-108/99) [2002] BVC 9	80-150
C & E Commrs v Century Life plc [2001] BVC 116	90-100; 90-220; 90-350
C & E Commrs v Civil Service Motoring Association [1998] BVC 21	70-200; 70-300; 70-500; 90-100
C & E Commrs v CSC Financial Services Ltd (Case C-235/00) [2002] BVC 253	30-550; 80-200
C & E Commrs v Deutsche Ruck UK Reinsurance Co Ltd [1995] BVC 175	40-200
C & E Commrs v DFDS A/S (Case C-260/95) [1997] BVC 279	20-250; 80-100
C & E Commrs v Diners Club Ltd (1989) 4 BVC 74	70-300
C & E Commrs v Electronic Data Systems Ltd [2003] BVC 451	70-500
C & E Commrs v Euphony Communications Ltd [2004] BVC 473	30-500
C & E Commrs v FDR Ltd [2000] BVC 311	70-100; 70-300; 70-500; 90-100; 90-350
C & E Commrs v General Motors Acceptance Corporation (UK) plc [2004] BVC 611	30-500; 30-650; 70-350
C & E Commrs v Guy Butler (International) Ltd (1976) 1 BVC 84	70-200
C & E Commrs v John Dee Ltd [1995] BVC 361	40-200
C & E Commrs v Kingfisher plc [1994] BVC 3	20-250; 60-250; 110-250
C & E Commrs v Liverpool Institute for Performing Arts [2001] BVC 333	40-200
C & E Commrs v Lloyds TSB Group Ltd [1998] BVC 173	70-200; 70-500
C & E Commrs v Lord Fisher (1981) 1 BVC 392	10-300
C & E Commrs v Madgett (t/a Howden Court Hotel) (Joined Cases C-308/96 and C-94/97) [1998] BVC 458	70-300; 70-500
C & E Commrs v Midland Bank plc (Case C-98/98) [2000] BVC 229	40-200; 70-350
C & E Commrs v Mirror Group plc (Case C-409/98) [2002] BVC 16	80-150
C & E Commrs v Morrison's Academy Boarding Houses Association (1977) 1 BVC 108	10-300; 40-000
C & E Commrs v National Westminster Bank plc [2003] BVC 633	10-350
C & E Commrs v Plantiflor [2002] BVC 572	30-550; 40-000; 70-200
C & E Commrs v Primback Ltd (Case C-34/99) [2001] BVC 315	30-150; 70-200
C & E Commrs v R & R Pension Fund Trustees [1996] BVC 348	40-200; 80-150
C & E Commrs v Redrow Group plc [1999] BVC 96; [1999] BTC 5,062	10-100; 40-000; 110-450
C & E Commrs v Save & Prosper Group Ltd (1978) 1 BVC 179	20-250
C & E Commrs v Shaklee International (1981) 1 BVC 444	40-050
C & E Commrs v Svenska International plc [1999] BVC 221	110-250
C & E Commrs v Tarmac Roadstone Holdings Ltd (1987) 3 BVC 91	60-050; 60-100
C & E Commrs v Thorn Materials Supply Ltd [1998] BVC 270	110-250
C & E Commrs v Tilling Management Services Ltd (1978) 1 BVC 185	30-200; 60-050
C & E Commrs v UBAF Bank Ltd [1995] BVC 69	40-200
C & E Commrs v Venuebest Ltd [2003] BVC 444	80-150
C & E Commrs v Wellington Private Hospital Ltd [1997] BVC 251	70-300; 70-500

D

	Paragraph
Daimler AG and Widex A/S v Skatteverket (Cases C-318/11 and C-319/11) 25 October 2012	40-150

	Paragraph
d'Ambrumenil v C & E Commrs (Case C-307/01) [2005] BVC 741...........	90-220
Danfoss A/S and AstraZeneca A/S v Skatteministeriet (Case C-371/07) [2009] BVC 781	40-050
David Baxendale Ltd v R & C Commrs [2009] BVC 663	30-550
Debenhams Retail plc [2003] BVC 2,543 ...	30-000
Debouche v Inspecteur Invoerrechten en Accijnzen (Case C-302/93) [1997] BVC 332.................................	40-150
Debt Management Associates Ltd [2003] BVC 4,055...................................	70-200
Devoti (t/a Belmont Associates) [1995] BVC 1,421...................................	70-200
DFDS A/S [1995] BVC 1,184	30-250
Dial-a-Phone Ltd v C & E Commrs [2004] BVC 640............................	40-200; 70-350; 110-400
Dixons Group plc [1993] BVC 752.............	90-220
Dogbreeders Associates (1989) 4 BVC 777...	90-100
Donald Ford (Financial Services) (1987) 3 BVC 609....................................	90-100
DTZ Zadelhoff vof v Staatssecretaris van Financiën (Case C-259/11) 5 July 2012	80-100
Durham Aged Mineworkers' Homes Association v C & E Commrs [1994] BVC 145	60-050
Dyrham Park Country Club Ltd (1978) 1 BVC 1,099; (1978) VATTR 244.........	30-500; 70-200

E

Eagle Trust plc [1996] BVC 2,085	40-000
EC Commission v Germany (Case C-427/98) [2003] BVC 205	30-500
EC Commission v Greece (Case C-13/06) [2009] BVC 729	90-220
EC Commission v Italy (Case C-45/95) [1997] BVC 536	30-150; 40-050
EC Commission v United Kingdom (Case C-33/03) [2005] ECR I-1865	40-000
EC Commission v United Kingdom (Case C-583/08) [2010] ECR I-7195	40-150
ECU Group plc [2010] TC 00585	70-200
Edgemond Group Ltd [1995] BVC 627.......	40-200
Electronic Data Systems Ltd [2003] BVC 451...............................	90-350
Elida Gibbs Ltd v C & E Commrs (Case C-317/94) [1997] BVC 80............	10-350; 30-500; 30-550

	Paragraph
Empire Stores Ltd v C & E Commrs (Case C-33/93) [1994] BVC 253.............	30-500
Empresa de Desenvolvimento Mineiro SGPS SA (EDM) v Fazenda Publica (Case C-77/01) [2006] BVC 140............	10-300; 30-200; 40-150; 40-250; 60-150; 80-100
Eon Aset Menidjmunt OOD v Direktor na Direktsia obzhalvane i upravlenie na izpalnenieto (Case C-118/11) 16 February 2012..................................	70-400
Ernst & Young [1997] BVC 2,541	40-050
Everything Everywhere Ltd (Case C-276/09) [2011] BVC 44	30-150; 30-550; 120-100
Exeter Golf and Country Club Ltd v C & E Commrs (1980) 1 BVC 385	30-550

F

Fforestfach Medical Centre [2000] BVC 4,100................................	80-150
Field Fisher Waterhouse LLP v R & C Commrs (Case C-392/11) [2012] BVC 292................................	80-150
Financial and General Print Ltd [1996] BVC 2,623................................	30-500; 70-400
Finanzamt Essen-NorOst v GFKL Financial Services AG (Case C-93/10) 27 October 2011.............	70-200
Finanzamt Frankfurt am Main V-Höchst v Deutsche Bank AG (Case C-44/11) 19 July 2012	80-200
Finanzamt Groß-Gerau v MKG-Kraftfahrzeuge-Factory GmbH (Case C-305/01) [2003] BVC 616...........	70-200
Finanzamt Gummersbach v Bockemühl (Case C-90/02) [2006] BVC 95..............	40-300
Finanzamt Lüdenscheid v Christel Schriever (Case C-444/10) 10 November 2011......	30-400; 30-450
Finanzamt Offenbach am Main-Land v Faxworld Vorgründungsgesellschaft Peter Hünninghausen und Wolfgang Klein GbR (Case C-137/02) [2004] ECR I-5547.............................	40-250; 110-300; 110-350
1st Contact Ltd [2012] TC 01780	30-250
First National Bank of Chicago v C & E Commrs (Case C-172/96) [1998] BVC 389................................	70-200; 70-250; 100-000
Fischer v Finanzamt Donaueschingen (Case C-283/95) [1998] BVC 431................................	90-100

Case Table

	Paragraph
Flood v Irish Provident Assurance Co Ltd (1912) 2 Ch 597	90-100
Floridienne SA & Berginvest SA v Belgium (Case C-142/99) [2001] BVC 76	10-300; 30-200; 40-150; 40-250; 80-100; 110-100
FMCG Home Services Ltd No. 18,377; [2004] BVC 4,037	30-450
Ford (Donald) (Financial Services) (1987) 3 BVC 609	90-100
Ford Motor Co Ltd [2007] BVC 2,146	30-550
Ford Motor Co Ltd v C & E Commrs [2007] EWHC 1014 (Ch); [2007] BVC 479	30-550; 90-220
Försäkringsaktiebolaget Skandia (publ), Re (Case C-240/99) [2001] BVC 281	70-500; 90-100; 90-350
Freight Transport Leasing Ltd [1991] BVC 536	70-100; 70-200; 70-350
Furniss (HMIT) v Dawson [1984] AC 474; [1984] BTC 71	10-400

G

Gabalfrisa SL v Agencia Estatal de Administracion Tributaria (Joined Cases C-110/98 to C-147/98) [2002] BVC 333	40-000
Garsington Opera Ltd [2009] TC 00045	40-200
General Motors Acceptance Corp (UK) plc [1999] BVC 2,347	70-200
GfBk v Finanzamt Bayreuth (Case C-275/11)	80-300
GF Mercer Ltd [2011] TC 01386	10-350
Gleneagles Hotel plc (1985) 2 BVC 208,108; (1986) VATTR 196	70-200
Global Self Drive Ltd [2006] BVC 2,020	90-200
Globe Equities Ltd [1996] BVC 2,209	80-150
Granada plc [1993] BVC 792	90-220
Gulland Properties [1996] BVC 2,722	40-250

H

Halifax plc [2001] BVC 2,029	40-200
Halifax plc v C & E Commrs [2002] BVC 370	10-300
Halifax plc, Leeds Permanent Development Services Ltd, County Wide Property Investments Ltd v C & E Commrs (Case C-255/02) [2006] BVC 377	10-300; 40-000
Halladale Group plc [2003] BVC 4,140	40-000

	Paragraph
Hallborough Properties Ltd [1994] BVC 1,377	30-450
Hargreaves Landsdown Asset Management Ltd [1995] BVC 896	80-100; 80-200
Harnas & Helm v Staatssecretaris van Financiën (Case C-80/95) [1997] BVC 358	10-300; 30-200; 80-100; 110-050; 110-150
Harpur Group Ltd [1995] BVC 841	70-300
Harrison (TC) Group Ltd [1996] BVC 2,404	40-050
Haugh [1997] BVC 2,525	40-250
HBOS plc [2007] BVC 2,394	70-200
HBOS plc v R & C Commrs [2009] BVC 48	70-200
Heaton (HMIT) v Bell (1969) 46 TC 211	30-500
Heritage Venture Enterprises Ltd [1994] BVC 1,357	40-000
Higher Education Statistics Agency Ltd v C & E Commrs [2000] BVC 150	30-450; 80-150
Holiday Inns (UK) Ltd [1994] BVC 543	30-500

I

Ian Flockton Developments Ltd v C & E Commrs (1987) 3 BVC 23	40-000
Iliffe [1994] BVC 625	70-200
IR Commrs v Levene [1928] AC 217	90-100
IR Commrs v Lysaght [1928] AC 234	90-100
Inscape Investment Fund v C & E Commrs (Case C-169/04) [2006] ECR I-4027	80-200; 80-300
Institute of Chartered Accountants in England and Wales v C & E Commrs [1999] BVC 215	80-200
Institute of Directors v C & E Commrs [2003] BVC 112	70-200; 70-300; 70-500
Intercommunale voor Zeewaterontzilting (INZO) v Belgian State (Case C-110/94) [1996] BVC 326	110-500
Investment Trust Companies (in liq) v R & C Commrs [2012] BVC 109	80-100
Investrand BV v Staatsecretaris Financiën (Case C-435/05) [2009] BVC 733	4-000; 110-450
Ivory & Sime Trustlink Ltd v C & E Commrs [1998] BVC 191	80-100

J

J & W Plant and Tool Hire Ltd [2003] BVC 4,102	20-250

	Paragraph
J & W Waste Management Ltd [2003] BVC 4,102	20-250
JCM Beheer BV v Staatssecretaris van Financiën (Case C-124/07) [2011] BVC 287	90-100
Jolly Tots Ltd [1996] BVC 4,068	40-250
Joseph Nelson Investment Planning Ltd [1994] BVC 657	60-250
JP Morgan Fleming Claverhouse Investment Trust plc v R & C Commrs (Case C-363/05) [2010] BVC 337	90-350

K

	Paragraph
Kaphag Renditefinds v Finanzamt Charlottenburg (Case C-442/01) [2005] BVC 566	10-300; 30-000; 30-200; 40-000; 40-150; 80-100; 110-050
Keeping Newcastle Warm Ltd v C & E Commrs (Case C-353/00) [2003] BVC 283	30-500
Kenmir v Frizzell (1968) 1 WLR 329	30-450
Koplania Odkrywkowa Polski Trawertyn v Dyrector Izby Skarbowej w Poznanui (Case C-280/10) 1 March 2012	110-300
KPMG [1997] BVC 2,469	40-050
Kretztechnik AG v Finanzamt Linz (Case C-465/03) [2006] BVC 66	10-300; 30-000; 30-200; 40-000; 40-150; 70-100; 70-200; 80-100; 80-200; 110-450
Kwik-Fit (GB) Ltd v C & E Commrs [1998] BVC 48	40-200
Kwik Save Group plc [1996] BVC 4,004	30-450

L

Lancaster Insurance Services Ltd (1990) 5 BVC 928	90-220
Laurentian Management Services Ltd [2001] BVC 2,210	30-550
Lease Plan Luxembourg SA v Belgian State (Case C-390/96) [1998] BVC 412	30-250; 70-150
Lebara Ltd v R & C Commrs (Case C-520/10) [2012] BVC 219	70-200; 80-200
Lennartz v Finanzamt München (Case C-97/90) [1993] BVC 202	40-000
Levene v IR Commrs [1928] AC 217	90-100
Levob Verzerkeringen BV v Staatssecretaris van Financiën (Case C-41/04) [2007] BVC 155	70-400
Lincoln Assurance Ltd [2001] BVC 2,210	30-550

	Paragraph
Lindum Resources Ltd [1995] BVC 1,118	70-200
Linotype and Machinery Ltd (1978) VATTR 123	80-400
Littlewoods Retail Ltd v R & C Commrs (Case C-591/10) 19 July 2012	10-350
Lloyds Bank plc [1996] BVC 2,875	30-500; 80-150
Lubbock Fine & Co v C & E Commrs (Case C-63/92) [1993] BVC 287	30-500; 80-150
Ludwig v Finanzamt Luckenwalde (Case C-453/05) [2009] BVC 967	70-200; 90-100

M

Maierhofer v Finanzamt Augsburg-Land (Case C-315/00) [2003] BVC 325	70-400; 80-150
Manchester Ship Canal Co v C & E Commrs (1982) 1 BVC 471	80-400
Marac Life Assurance Ltd v IR Commrs [1986] 1 NZLR 694	90-100
Marks and Spencer plc v C & E Commrs (Case C-62/00) [2002] BVC 622	30-500
Marleasing SA v La Comercial Internacional de Alimentacion SA (Case C-106/89) [1990] ECR I-4135	10-000
Marston (WJ) & Son Ltd [1998] BVC 4,025	60-100
MBNA Europe Bank Ltd v R & C Commrs [2007] BVC 3	30-000; 40-200; 70-100; 70-200; 70-450; 80-200
Medical Defence Union Ltd v Department of Trade [1979] 1 All ER 421	90-100
Merchant Navy Officers Pension Fund Trustees Ltd [1996] BVC 2,924	40-200
Merchant Navy Ratings Pension Fund Trustees Ltd [1996] BVC 2,924	40-200
Merseyside Cablevision Ltd (1987) 3 BVC 596; (1987) VATTR 134	10-300; 20-100
Midland Bank plc [1991] BVC 749	20-250
Midland Bank plc v C & E Commrs (Case C-98/98) [2000] BVC 229	110-400
Ministero dell'Economia e delle Finanze and Agenzia delle Entrate v FCE Bank plc (Case C-214/04) [2006] ECR I-2803	10-100; 20-300; 30-000; 30-200; 30-500; 40-150; 50-000; 50-050

Case Table

	Paragraph
Morganash Ltd [2007] BVC 2,184	90-100; 90-220; 90-350
Morgan (JP) Fleming Claverhouse Investment Trust v R & C Commrs (Case C 363/05) [2007] BVC 337	70-150; 80-050; 80-200; 80-300; 90-350
Morpheus 2002 Ltd [2007] BVC 2,224	70-200
Muys' en De Winter's Bouw-en Aannemingsbedriif BV v Staatssecretaris van Financiën (Case C-281/91) [1993] ECR I-5405	30-150; 70-200

N

National Coal Board v C & E Commrs (1982) 1 BVC 515	80-400
National Provincial Building Society [1996] BVC 2,783	10-350
National Society for Prevention of Cruelty to Children [1993] BVC 701	10-300; 40-000; 80-100
National Westminster Bank plc [1998] BVC 2,264	20-250
National Westminster Bank plc [2003] BVC 2,003	70-200
Nationwide Anglia Building Society [1995] BVC 1,413	70-200
Naturally Yours Cosmetics v C & E Commrs (Case 230/87) (1988) 3 BVC 428	30-500
NCC Construction Danmark A/S v Skatteministeriet (Case C-174/08) [2010] BVC 1,093	40-000
Neville Russell (1987) 3 BVC 611; (1987) VATTR 194	70-200
Nightfreight plc [1998] BVC 2,232	80-100; 80-200
NM Superannuation Pty Ltd v Young 113 ALR 39	90-100
Nordea Pankki Suomi Oyj, Re (Case C-350/10) 28 July 2011	80-200; 120-150

O

Office des produits wallons ASBL v Belgium (Case C-184/00) [2001] ECR I-9115	30-500

P

P & O European Ferries (Dover) Ltd [1992] BVC 955	40-000
PARAT Automotice Cabrio [2009] ECR I-3459	40-000
Park Avenue Methodist Church Trustees [2002] BVC 4,021	40-250
Pearl Assurance plc [1999] BVC 2,176	40-200
Peugeot Motor Co plc [1999] BVC 2,314	90-220

	Paragraph
Peugeot Motor Co plc v C & E Commrs [2004] BVC 269	30-550; 70-200; 90-220
PHH Europe plc [1995] BVC 889	60-100
Plant Repair and Services (South Wales) Ltd [1991] BVC 834	40-050
Plessey Co Ltd [1996] BVC 2,074	40-000
Polysar Investments Netherlands BV v Inspecteur der Invoerrechten en Accijnzen Arnhem (Case C-60/90) [1993] BVC 88	10-300; 20-250; 30-250; 40-000; 40-250; 110-100
Portugal Telecon SGPA SA v Fazenda Pública (Case C-496/11) 6 September 2012	10-300; 40-200
Primback Ltd v C & E Commrs [1994] BVC 268	70-200
Primback Ltd v C & E Commrs [2001] BVC 315	30-550
Provadinvest OOD v Direktor na Direktsia 'Obzhalvane i upravlenie na izpalnenieto' – Varna pri Tsentralno upravlene na Natsionalnate agentsia za prihodite (Case C-129/11) 26 April 2012	30-500; 60-050
Provident Financial plc [1993] BVC 884	70-200
Prudential Assurance Co Ltd [2001] BVC 2,201	80-100; 80-300
Prudential Assurance Co Ltd [2006] BVC 4,093	20-250
Prudential Assurance Co Ltd [2006] BVC 2,340	70-200; 70-300
Purple Parking Ltd, Airparks Services Ltd v R & C Commrs (Case C-117/11) [2012] BVC 268	30-550

Q

Queen Mary, Universty of London [2011] TC 01094	70-400

R

Ravenfield Ltd [2011] TC 00641	40-050
RBS Deutschland GmbH No. 20,267; [2008] BVC 4,003	40-000; 70-150
RBS Leasing and Services (No. 1) Ltd [1998] BVC 4,141	30-500
RBS Leasing and Services (No. 2) Ltd [1998] BVC 4,141	30-500
RBS Leasing and Services (No. 3) Ltd [1998] BVC 4,141	30-500

	Paragraph
RBS Leasing and Services (No. 4) Ltd [1998] BVC 4,141	30-500
RBS Property Developments Ltd [2003] BVC 2,074	30-000; 40-000
Regie Dauphinoise – Cabinet A Forest SARL v Ministre du Budget (Case C-306/94) [1996] BVC 447	110-050
Republic National Bank of New York [1992] BVC 968	70-200
R & C Commrs v Airtours Holiday Transport Ltd [2010] BVC 1,587	40-000; 110-600
R & C Commrs v Axa UK plc [2012] BVC 1; [2011] BVC 35	70-200; 70-500
R & C Commrs v BAA Ltd [2011] BVC 1,664	40-250; 110-350; 110-400
R & C Commrs v Bryce (t/a The Barn) [2011] BVC 1,589	30-550
R & C Commrs v Debenhams Retail plc [2005] BVC 425	10-300; 70-300
R & C Commrs v IDT Card Services Ireland Ltd [2006] BVC 244	10-000
R & C Commrs v InsuranceWide.com Services Ltd [2010] BVC 606	90-100; 120-200
R & C Commrs v Jeancharm Ltd (t/a Beaver International) [2005] EWHC 839 (Ch); [2005] BVC 316	40-000
R & C Commrs v London Clubs Management Ltd [2011] BVC 406	40-200
R & C Commrs v Loyalty Management UK Ltd (Case C-53/09) [2011] BVC 1	10-000; 10-050; 10-100; 30-400; 30-450; 40-000
R & C Commrs v Rank Group plc (Joined Cases C-259/10 and C-260/10) [2011] BVC 389	30-225
R & C Commrs v RBS Deutschland Holdings GmbH (Case C-277/09) [2011] BVC 138	40-000
R & C Commrs v Volkswagen Financial Services (UK) Ltd [2012] UKUT 394 (TCC)	40-200; 70-350
R & C Commrs v Weald Leasing Ltd (Case C-103/09) [2011] BVC 118	40-000
R & C Commrs v Zurich Insurance Co [2007] BVC 283	50-150
Richardson v Worrall [1985] BTC 508	70-300
Robinson Family Ltd [2012] TC 02046	30-450
Rompelman v Minister van Financiën (Case 268/83) (1985) 2 BVC 200,157	70-350; 110-050; 110-350; 110-650
Royal & Sun Alliance Insurance Group plc v C & E Commrs [2003] BVC 341	40-250; 110-250
Royal Bank of Scotland Group plc [2001] BVC 2,275	70-200
Royal Bank of Scotland Group plc [2002] BVC 2,213	30-450
Royal Bank of Scotland Group plc [2003] BVC 2,074	30-000; 40-000
Royal Bank of Scotland Group plc [2006] BVC 4,057	40-200
Royal Bank of Scotland Group plc [2007] BVC 2,295	70-350
Royal Bank of Scotland Group plc v C & E Commrs [2002] BVC 389	70-200
Royal Bank of Scotland Group plc v R & C Commrs (Case C-488/07) [2009] BVC 248	40-200
RoyScot Leasing Ltd [1996] BVC 2,388	40-050
Rushcombe Ltd [1997] BVC 4,066	40-000

S

	Paragraph
Scottish Eastern Investment Trust plc [2001] BVC 4,058	80-200; 100-150
Scottish Exhibition Centre Ltd [2005] BVC 2,529	70-300
Secret Hotels2 Ltd v R & C Commrs [2011] BVC 1,700	10-100
Securenta G"ttinger Immobilienanlagen und Verm"gensmanagement AG v Finanzamt G"ttinger (Case C-437/06) [2011] BVC 766	40-250
Shamrock Leasing Ltd [1999] BVC 2,032	20-250; 50-000
Shell International Petroleum Co Ltd [2006] BVC 2,325	40-000
Sinclair Collis Ltd v C & E Commrs (Case C-275/01) [2003] BVC 374	80-150
Skandinaviska Enskilda Banken AB Momsgrupp v Skatteverket (Case C-540/09) 10 March 2011	80-200
Skatteministeriet v Henriksen (1990) 5 BVC 140	80-150
Skatteverket v AB SKF (Case C-29/08) [2011] BVC 359	10-300; 40-200; 80-100; 110-000;110-050; 110-150; 110-400
Skipton Building Society [2010] TC 00146	40-200

Case Table

	Paragraph
Smarter Money Ltd [2006] BVC 4,098	70-100; 70-300; 70-500
Smart Voucher Ltd [2009] TC 00131	120-250
Smith (CR) Glaziers (Dumfermline) Ltd v C & E Commrs [2003] BVC 249	90-100
Societe thermale d'Eugenie-Les-Bains v Ministere de l'Economie, des Finances et de l'Industrie (Case C-277/05) [2010] BVC 367	30-500
SOC Private Capital Ltd [2003] BVC 2,038	90-300
Sofitam v Ministre Chargé du Budget (Case C-333/91) [1993] ECR I-3513	10-300
Sovereign Finance plc [2000] BVC 4,023	40-200
Southampton Leisure Holdings plc [2003] BVC 4,010	30-200; 40-000
Sparekassernes Datacenter (SDC) v Skatteministeriet (Case C-2/95) [1997] BVC 509	70-200; 70-300; 70-500; 80-200; 90-050; 90-100; 90-350; 120-150
Staatssecretaris van Financiën v Arthur Andersen & Co Accountants c.s. (Case C-472/03) [2006] BVC 228	10-100; 60-050; 70-500; 80-100; 80-200; 90-050; 90-350
Staatssecretaris van Financiën v Shipping and Forwarding Enterprise Safe BV (Case 320/88) [1991] BVC 119	10-100
Staatssekretaris van Financien v Vereniging 'Cooperatieve Aardappelenbewaarplaats' [1981] ECR 445	110-400
Stichting 'Goed Wonen' v Staatssecretaris van Financiën (Case C-326/99) [2002] BVC 46	80-150
Svenska International plc v C & E Commrs [1999] BVC 221	30-350; 40-200

T

Telent plc [2007] BVC 2,262	40-000
Teletech UK Ltd [2003] BVC 2,514	70-200; 70-500; 90-220; 90-350
Telewest Communications plc v C & E Commrs [2005] BVC 156	30-550
Terra Baubedarf-Handel GmbH v Finanzamt Osterholz-Scharmbeck (Case C-152/02) [2006] BVC 672	40-300
Themis FTSE Fledgling Index Trust plc [2001] BVC 4,093	30-500
Thorn EMI plc [1992] BVC 867	40-050
Thorn EMI plc [1993] BVC 792	90-220

	Paragraph
Thorn Materials Supply Ltd [1996] BVC 2,095	20-250
Thorn Resources Ltd [1996] BVC 2,095	20-250
Tremerton Ltd v C & E Commrs [2000] BVC 3	40-250
Trinity Mirror plc v C & E Commrs [2001] BVC 167	10-300; 30-200; 40-000; 40-150

U

Ultimate Advisory Services Ltd [1993] BVC 743	40-000
Union Bank of Switzerland (1987) 3 BVC 654; (1987) VATTR 221	70-250
USAA Ltd [1993] BVC 1,612	90-100

V

Vereniging Noordelijke Land -en Tuinbouw Organisatie v Staatssecretaris van Financiën (Case C-515/07) [2009] ECR I-839	40-000
Viscount Reinsurance [2002] BVC 4,061	40-150
Vogtländische Straßen-, Tief- und Rohrleitungsbau GmbH Rodewisch (VSTR) v Finanzamt Plauen (Case C-587/10) 27 September 2012	30-100
Volker Ludwig v Finanzamt Luckenwalde (Case C-453/05) [2007] ECR I-5083	70-200
Volkswagen Financial Services (UK) Ltd [2011] TC 01401	40-200; 70-350
Von Coulson and Kamann v Land Nordrhein-Westfalen (Case 14/83) [1984] ECR 1891	10-000
Von Hoffman v Finanzamt Trier (Case C-145/96) [1997] BVC 562	70-200

W

Wagon Finance Ltd [2000] BVC 2,125	70-200
Walia (R) Opticians Ltd [1997] BVC 2,511	80-150
Water Hall Group plc [2003] BVC 4,085	30-200; 80-100
Weald Leasing Ltd [2007] BVC 2,321	40-000
Wellcome Trust Ltd [1995] BVC 1,011	40-000
Wellcome Trust Ltd v C & E Commrs (Case C-155/94) [1996] BVC 377	10-300; 30-200; 30-250; 80-100; 80-400; 110-050
WHA Ltd [2002] BVC 4,061	40-150

	Paragraph
WHA Ltd v C & E Commrs [2004] BVC 485	40-150; 90-100
WHA Ltd v R & C Commrs [2007] BVC 695	40-150; 90-100
Wheels Common Investment Fund Trustees Ltd [2011] TC 01381	80-300
WH Payne & Co [1996] BVC 2,551	30-250
Wiggett Construction Ltd [2001] BVC 2,159	40-250
Williams & Glyn's Bank Ltd (1974) 1 BVC 1,021; (1974) VATTR 262	70-100; 70-200
Willis Pension Trustees Ltd [2006] BVC 2,045	10-300; 30-000; 30-200; 70-150; 70-200; 70-250; 80-100; 80-400; 100-000; 100-100; 100-150; 100-300
Winterthur Life UK Ltd (formerly Provident Life Association Ltd) [1997] BVC 2,433	90-100
Winterthur Life UK Ltd [1999] BVC 2,093	80-150
Winterthur Life UK Ltd [2002] BVC 2,136	80-100; 90-220
Winterthur Swiss Insurance Co [2006] BVC 2,376	30-450; 90-220
Wright & Partners [1993] BVC 1,595	70-200; 90-100
Wright Manley Ltd [1993] BVC 1,595	70-200; 90-100

Y

	Paragraph
Yorkhurst Ltd [1997] BVC 4,004	40-200

Legislation Finding List

(References are to paragraph numbers)

Provision	Paragraph
Bills of Exchange Act 1882	70-100; 70-200
Capital Allowances Act 1990	40-200
Capital Allowances Act 2001	
See generally	70-400
Ch. 18	40-200
Companies Act 2006	
See generally	110-000
895–901	110-000
Pt. 28	110-000
1159	20-250
Consumer Credit Act 1974	70-100; 70-200; 70-350
Corporation Tax Act 2010	
Pt. 5, Ch. 5	20-250
1122	30-500; 60-050; App. 7
EC Directive 67/227	
art. 2	40-200
EC Directive 67/228	
See generally	10-000
art. 11	40-050
art. 11(1)	40-050
art. 11(4)	40-050
EC Directive 77/388	
See generally	10-000; 10-300; 40-000; 70-100; 70-150; 70-500; 100-350
art. 1	10-050
art. 2	10-050; 70-200
art. 2(1)	10-050; 30-200; 30-500
art. 4	10-300; 30-000; 40-250; 70-200
art. 4(1)	10-100; 10-250; 10-300; 30-500; 40-150; 80-100
art. 4(2)	10-300; 40-200; 40-250
art. 4(4)	20-250
art. 5(6)	30-500
art. 5(8)	30-450
art. 8	30-250
art. 9	30-250; 80-100
art. 9(1)	20-250; 30-250; 70-150
art. 9(2)	90-200
art. 9(2)(a)	90-200
art. 9(2)(c)	30-250
art. 9(2)(e)	30-450; 50-150; 70-100; 70-200; 90-220; 100-350
art. 9(3)	70-400
art. 10	30-350; 30-400
art. 10(2)	30-350
art. 11A	30-500
art. 11(A)(1)(a)	30-500; 70-200

Provision	Paragraph
art. 11(A)(2)	30-500
art. 11(C)(1)	30-650
art. 13	30-000; 30-150; 70-200; 80-100; 80-150; 90-100
art. 13(A)(1)(f)	90-350
art. 13(B)	70-200; 70-500
art. 13(B)(a)	70-500; 80-100; 90-100; 90-220; 90-300; 90-350
art. 13(B)(b)	70-400; 80-150
art. 13(B)(c)	30-150
art. 13(B)(d)	70-100; 70-200; 80-100; 100-450
art. 13(B)(d)(1)	70-100; 70-200; 70-500; 80-100
art. 13(B)(d)(3)	70-150; 70-200; 70-300; 70-500; 80-100; 90-300; 90-350; 120-150
art. 13(B)(d)(4)	70-100
art. 13(B)(d)(5)	10-300; 70-500; 80-100; 80-200; 80-300; 80-350; 120-150
art. 13(B)(d)(6)	70-150; 80-100; 80-200; 80-300
art. 13(B)(f)	30-225; 80-100; 90-100
art. 13(B)(g)	80-150
art. 13(B)(h)	80-150
art. 14–16	30-150
art. 15	30-300
art. 15(2)	80-100
art. 16	100-250
art. 17	10-300; 40-000; 40-150; 40-200
art. 17(1)–(3)	40-200
art. 17(1)	10-300; 80-100
art. 17(2)	10-300; 80-100
art. 17(2)(a)	40-000
art. 17(3)	40-150; 40-200
art. 17(3)(a)	40-150
art. 17(3)(b)	40-150; 70-100; 80-100; 90-100
art. 17(3)(c)	40-150; 70-100; 80-100; 90-100
art. 17(4)	40-150
art. 17(5)	40-200
art. 17(6)	40-050
art. 18(1)(a)	40-000
art. 19	40-200
art. 19(1)	40-200
art. 19(2)	10-300; 40-150
art. 20(1)(b)	40-250
art. 20(2)	40-200
art. 22	30-600
art. 26(2)	20-250
art. 28A(3)	30-300
EC Directive 79/1072	30-000; 30-250; 30-450; 40-150; 90-220
EC Directive 85/611	
See generally	80-300
art. 5(g)	80-300

891

Provision	Paragraph
EC Directive 86/560	
See generally	20-300; 30-250; 40-150; 50-050; 70-400; 80-200
2(1)	40-150
EC Directive 92/12	10-050
EC Directive 92/77	
See generally	90-100; 90-350
art. 2	90-100; 90-220; 90-350
art. 2(1)(b)	90-300
EC Directive 98/80	100-450
EC Directive 2001/107	80-300
EC Directive 2001/115	30-600
EC Directive 2002/92	
art. 2(1)(a), (b)	90-100
art. 3, 4	90-100; 90-350
EC Directive 2003/87	100-400
EC Directive 2003/92	100-350
EC Directive 2006/112	
See generally	10-000; 10-050; 30-000; 70-000; 70-100; 70-150; 70-500; 80-100; 120-250
art. 2	10-050
art. 2(1)	10-050; 10-100; 80-100
art. 2(1)(a)	10-100; 30-200; 30-250
art. 2(1)(d)	10-050
art. 3(1)	10-050
art. 5(1)	10-100
art. 6(1)	10-100
art. 9	10-100; 10-300; 30-000; 30-250; 30-500; 40-250
art. 9(1)	10-250; 10-300; 30-250; 40-000; 40-150; 40-200; 110-050
art. 10	30-250; 50-100; 70-500
art. 11	20-250
art. 11A(1)(a)	10-100
art. 13(B)(a)	60-050
art. 13(B)(c)	30-150
art. 13(1)	30-250
art. 14	10-100; 30-000; 30-500; 100-150
art. 16	30-500
art. 19	30-450; 80-150
art. 19(1)	10-300
art. 20	30-300
art. 22	80-200
art. 24	10-100; 30-000
art. 26	30-500
art. 29	30-450; 80-150
art. 31–36	30-250
art. 31–59	30-000
art. 33	10-050
art. 36	10-050
art. 38, 38(1)	100-350
art. 43–45	70-200
art. 43–59	30-100; 30-200
art. 43	20-250; 30-500
art. 44–45	100-150
art. 44	30-250; 50-000; 70-150; 70-400; 90-100; 100-150

Provision	Paragraph
art. 45	30-250; 50-050; 70-400; 100-150
art. 47	30-250; 90-200
art. 49	100-150
art. 56	30-450; 50-000; 50-150; 70-100; 70-200; 90-220
art. 56(1)(e)	100-350
art. 57	30-250
art. 58	50-050; 70-400
art. 59	50-150; 90-100; 90-200; 100-150; 100-350
art. 59(e)	100-150
art. 62–71	30-350
art. 63	30-350
art. 65	30-350
art. 67	30-400
art. 68	30-400
art. 69	30-400
art. 73–80	70-300
art. 73	30-500; 70-200
art. 78	30-500
art. 79	30-500
art. 80, 80(1)	30-500; 60-050
art. 90	30-500
art. 90(1)	30-650
art. 91	30-600
art. 99(1)(d)	40-200
art. 99(7)	40-200
art. 131–137	30-000; 30-150
art. 131	90-100
art. 132	30-250
art. 132(1)	60-050; 60-300
art. 132(1)(f)	60-300
art. 132(1)(q)	30-250
art. 135	80-100; 90-050; 90-100; 100-450
art. 135(1)	70-100; 70-200; 70-400; 70-500; 80-150
art. 135(1)(a)–(c)	80-100
art. 135(1)(a)–(d)	80-100
art. 135(1)(a)–(e)	80-100; 90-100; 90-350
art. 135(1)(a)–(f)	40-000; 90-050
art. 135(1)(a)–(g)	30-600; 70-100; 70-500; 80-100; 90-100; 90-350
art. 135(1)(a)	30-150; 60-050; 70-500; 80-100; 90-100; 90-220; 90-300; 90-350; 120-200
art. 135(1)(b)–(g)	30-150
art. 135(1)(b)	70-100; 70-200; 70-300; 70-450; 70-500; 80-100; 90-200; 100-300; 100-450
art. 135(1)(c)	70-200
art. 135(1)(d)	70-100; 70-150; 70-200; 70-300; 70-500; 80-100; 80-150; 80-200; 90-050; 90-300; 90-350; 100-300; 120-150
art. 135(1)(e)	70-100; 70-200
art. 135(1)(f)	10-300; 30-225; 60-250; 70-500; 80-100; 80-200; 80-250; 80-300; 80-350; 90-200; 100-300; 110-150; 120-150
art. 135(1)(g)	70-150; 80-100; 80-200; 80-300
art. 135(1)(i)	90-100
art. 135(1)(j)	30-150; 80-150
art. 135(1)(k)	30-150; 80-150
art. 135(1)(l)	30-150; 70-200; 80-100; 80-150
art. 135(2)	80-150
art. 135(2)(c)	70-400; 80-150
art. 135a	70-150; 70-500; 80-100; 90-100; 90-350

Provision	Paragraph
art. 136	30-150
art. 138–164	30-150
art. 138	30-300
art. 157	100-250
art. 167	40-000; 40-150; 40-300
art. 168	10-300; 40-000; 40-150; 80-100
art. 168a	40-000
art. 169–171	40-150
art. 169	40-000; 40-150
art. 169(b)	70-100; 80-100; 90-100
art. 169(c)	70-100; 80-100; 80-350; 90-100
art. 171	40-150
art. 173, 173(2), (2)(a), (b), (c), (d)	40-200
art. 174	40-200
art. 174(2)	40-150; 40-200
art. 175	40-200
art. 176	40-050
art. 178	40-000
art. 185(2)	40-250
art. 187(1)	40-200
art. 192(a)	30-250; 50-150
art. 196	50-000
art. 217	30-600
art. 219a, (2)(a), (b)	30-600
art. 220(2)	30-600
art. 221(2), (3)	30-600
art. 224(1)	30-600
art. 226, 226(2), (7a), (11)	30-600
art. 226b	30-600
art. 230	30-600
art. 233, 233(2)	30-600
art. 247, 248a	30-600
art. 282–292	10-050
art. 307	20-250
art. 397	10-000
Annexe A	70-400

EC Directive 2008/8
art. 2	40-000; 50-150

EC Directive 2008/9
	20-300; 40-150

EC Directive 2010/45
	30-600

EC Regulation 2005/1777
	70-100

EC Regulation 2011/282
See generally	10-000; 30-250; 120-250
art. 3	30-250; 70-400
art. 4(3)	30-250
art. 10(1), (2), (3)	30-250
art. 11(1), (2), (3)	30-250
art. 12, 13	30-250
art. 18(1), (2), (3)	30-250
art. 21, 22	30-250; 50-150
art. 38	70-400
art. 40	70-400
art. 42	70-300
art. 45	70-100
art. 53(1), (2)	30-250; 50-150
art. 54	30-250

EC Regulation 976/2012 ... App. 27

Provision	Paragraph
EC Treaty	
art. 226	40-150
Finance Act 1972	10-000
Finance Act 1991	
59	40-200
Sch. 14	40-100
Finance Act 1995	20-250
Finance Act 1999	
13	100-450
Finance Act 2000	
132(8)	70-400
Sch. 3A	70-400
Sch. 36	70-400
Finance Act 2002	
24	30-600
Finance Act 2004	
19	10-400
Sch. 2	10-400
Finance Act 2007	
97	10-350
Sch. 24	10-350
Finance Act 2008	
123	10-350
Sch. 41	10-350
Sch. 41, para. 1	20-050
Finance Act 2009	
1, 2, 4, 5, 7, 9	10-350
14, 15(2)	10-350
Finance (No. 3) Act 2011	30-500
Finance Act 2012	
196	80-150
197	60-300
201	70-200; 80-200
Sch. 26	80-150
Sch. 26, para. 1, 3, 7	80-150
Financial Services Act 1986	70-200; 80-300
Financial Services and Markets Act 2000	
See generally	80-100; 90-100
Pt. II	App. 11
19	90-100
22	100-150
Pt. IV	90-220
Pt. XVII	App. 11
235	80-100
237(3)	80-100
270	80-300
Sch. 2, Pt. I, II	100-150
Financial Services and Markets Act 2000 (Consequential Amendments and Repeals) Order 2001 (SI 2001/3649)	
art. 347	80-100

Provision	Paragraph
Financial Services and Markets Act 2000 (Regulated Activities) Order 2001 (SI 2001/544)	
Sch. 1, para. 1, 4–7, 11, 12	90-220
Financial Services (Regulated Schemes) Regulations 1991	
reg. 7(15)	80-300
Greenhouse Gas Emissions Trading Scheme Regulations 2005 (SI 2005/925)	100-400
Income and Corporation Taxes Act 1988	
839	30-350
Income Tax Act 2007	
Pt. 15, Ch. 11	60-050
Insolvency Act 1986	
See generally	110-000
110, 111	110-000
Interpretation Act 1978	
Sch. 1	80-150
Law of Property Act 1925	
105	40-000
Moneylenders Act 1927	70-200
Plannng (Listed Buildings and Conservation Areas) Act 1990	80-150
Road Vehicles (Construction and Use) Regulations 1986 (SI 1986/1078)	
See generally	40-300
reg. 6	70-400
Sale of Goods Act 1979	
See generally	100-150
16	100-150
Transfer of Undertakings (Protection of Employment) Regulations 1981	70-500
Treaty on the Functioning of the European Union 2010	
113	10-000
Value Added Tax Act 1983	
See generally	70-500
Sch. 6, Grp, 2	90-100
Sch. 6, Grp, 2, item 3	70-200; 90-100
Sch. 6, Grp, 5	70-200; 70-500
Sch. 6, Grp, 5, item 3	30-550
Sch. 6, Grp, 5, Note (5)	70-200
Value Added Tax Act 1994	
See generally	10-000
1	10-050
1(1)(a)	30-250
1(1)(b)	30-250
1(1)(c)	30-300
1(4)	10-050; 30-300; 50-000
3	10-250; 80-400
3(1)	20-000
4	10-050
4(1)	10-050; 110-050
4(2)	10-050; 30-000
4(2)(a)	30-200

Provision	Paragraph
5	30-000
5(1)	30-000
5(2)	10-100; 30-000; 40-200
5(2)(a)	20-300; 70-100
5(5)	40-100
6	20-300; 30-350
6(2)	30-350
6(2)(a)	30-650
6(3)	30-350
6(4)	30-350
6(5)	30-350
6(6)	30-350
6(7)	30-400
6(10)	30-350
7–7A	20-300
7	30-000; 30-250
7(1)	10-150
7(2)(a)	20-250
7A	30-000; 30-100; 30-200; 30-250; 70-100; 70-150; 70-400; 80-100; 80-200; 100-250
7A(2)	30-250; 100-300
7A(4)	30-250
8	20-300; 30-400; 40-300; 50-000; 50-100; 80-150; 100-150; 100-300
8(2)	50-000; 50-050
8(4)	50-000; 50-050
8(4A)	50-000
9	30-000; 30-250
9(2)(a)	30-250
9(2)(b)	30-250
9(3)	30-250
9(4)	30-250
9(5)	30-250
9(5)(a), (b), (6)	30-250
9A	100-350
10	10-050; 30-300
11	20-200
12	20-200; 30-400
13	10-200; 30-300
13(2)	30-300
13(3)	30-300
18, 18A–18F, 18A, 18B, 18C	100-250
19	30-500
19(3)	50-150
19(4)	30-450; 30-500
24	60-250
24(1)	40-000; 40-200
24(5)	60-050
24(5A), (5B)	40-000
25	60-050; 80-300; 80-400
25(2)	10-350
26	30-150; 40-150
26(2)(c)	40-200; 80-150
26(3)	40-200
26A	30-650
30	30-000; 30-100; 70-150; 70-200
30(1)	30-000; 70-050; 70-100
30(2)	30-100
30(6)	30-100; 100-250
30(7)	100-250
30(8)	30-100

Provision	Paragraph
31	30-000; 30-150
31(3)–(5)	60-300
33, 33A	80-150
36	30-650
39	40-150
41(3)	80-150
43	20-250; 30-350; 50-000; 60-250; 80-400; 90-220; 110-250; App. 2
43(1)	20-250; 50-000; 60-300
43(1AA)	20-250
43(2A)–(2E)	20-250; 50-000; 50-100
43(3)	20-250
43(6)	20-250
43(7)	20-250
43A–43D	20-250
43A(1)	20-250
43A(2)	20-250
43B	20-250
43B(2)	20-250
43B(5)	20-250
43C	20-250
43C(1)	20-250
43C(3)	20-250
43D	20-250
44	20-250; 30-450; 40-200; 70-400
44(4)	20-250; 30-450
45	60-150
49	30-450
49(1)(a)	20-050; 20-250; 30-450
49(1)(b)	30-450
50	30-100; 100-200
55	70-100; 100-450
56	30-500
57	30-500
58A	10-400
59	10-350
69	10-350
73, 74, 76, 78, 79	10-350
80	10-350; 80-100
80(3)	10-350
80A	10-350(7)
81	90-300
84(4)	40-000
94	10-300
96(1)	80-150; 90-200
Sch. 1–3	10-250
Sch. 1, para. 1	20-050
Sch. 1, para. 1(1)(a)	20-050
Sch. 1, para. 1(1)(b)	20-050
Sch. 1, para. 1(2)	20-050; 30-450
Sch. 1, para. 1(7)	20-300; 70-400
Sch. 1, para. 5	20-050
Sch. 1, para. 7	20-050
Sch. 1, para. 8	20-050
Sch. 1, para. 9	20-050; 20-100
Sch. 1, para. 10	20-100; 20-300
Sch. 1, para. 13	20-200
Sch. 1, para. 14	30-450
Sch. 1, para. 14(1)	20-150
Sch. 1, para. 16	20-050; 20-200
Sch. 1A	20-050
Sch. 1A, para. 1	20-050
Sch. 2	10-250
Sch. 3, para. 1	10-250
Sch. 3A	20-300
Sch. 3B, para. 2, 3, 4, 6, 10(3), (4)	120-250
Sch. 4	30-350
Sch. 4, para. 1	100-450
Sch. 4, para. 1(1)(a)	100-150
Sch. 4, para. 1(1)(b)	70-400
Sch. 4, para. 1(2)	70-400
Sch. 4, para. 1(2)(b)	30-650; 70-350
Sch. 4, para. 3	100-000
Sch. 4, para. 5	60-050
Sch. 4, para. 5(1)	30-500
Sch. 4, para. 5(2)	30-200; 30-500
Sch. 4, para. 5(4), (4A)	30-500
Sch. 4, para. 5(5)	30-500
Sch. 4, para. 6	30-000; 30-300; 40-150
Sch. 4, para. 7	30-500
Sch. 4, para. 8	30-500
Sch. 4A	20-300; 30-200; 30-250; 50-050; 70-150; 70-400; 80-100; 90-100; 90-200; 100-350; App. 4
Sch. 4A, Pt. 1	50-000; 50-050; 70-100
Sch. 4A, para. 1	30-250; 50-050; 90-200
Sch. 4A, para. 1(2)	30-250
Sch. 4A, para. 1(2)(c)	90-200
Sch. 4A, para. 2	30-250
Sch. 4A, para. 3	30-250; 70-150; 70-400
Sch. 4A, para. 3(1)	70-400
Sch. 4A, para. 3(3), (4)	70-150
Sch. 4A, para. 7(1), (2)	30-250; 70-150; 70-400
Sch. 4A, para. 8	30-250; 50-050
Sch. 4A, Pt. 2	50-000; 50-050; 70-100
Sch. 4A, para. 9, 9(4)	30-250; 120-250
Sch. 4A, para. 15	120-250
Sch. 4A, para. 16	70-100; 90-100; 100-150; 100-250; 100-350
Sch. 4A, para. 16(2)	80-100
Sch. 4A, para. 16(2)(d)	70-150; 70-200
Sch. 4A, para. 16(2)(e)	70-100; 70-150; 100-150
Sch. 4A, para. 16(2)(h)	70-150
Sch. 5	30-450; 40-300; 50-000; 70-100; 80-100; 80-200; 90-220; 120-250
Sch. 5, para. 2	40-200; 50-050
Sch. 5, para. 3	50-050; 90-200
Sch. 5, para. 5	50-050; 80-100; 80-200; 90-100; 90-200
Sch. 5, para. 6	50-050
Sch. 5, para. 7	70-150
Sch. 5, para. 7C	120-250
Sch. 5A	100-250
Sch. 6	30-500
Sch. 6, para. 1	30-500; 40-000; 60-050
Sch. 6, para. 8	50-100
Sch. 6, para. 8A	20-250; App. 29
Sch. 6, para. 10	30-000
Sch. 7A	30-000
Sch. 8	30-100
Sch. 8, Grp. 1	100-250
Sch. 8, Grp. 3	50-050
Sch. 8, Grp. 5	80-150; 90-200

Value Added Tax Act 1994 – continued

Provision	Paragraph
Sch. 8, Grp. 5, item 1	80-150; 90-200
Sch. 8, Grp. 5, item 2, 3	80-150; 90-220
Sch. 8, Grp. 5, Note (4)	70-100
Sch. 8, Grp. 5, Note (14)	80-150
Sch. 8, Grp. 6	80-150; 90-200
Sch. 8, Grp. 6, item 2, 3	80-150
Sch. 8, Grp. 6, Note (4)	80-150
Sch. 8, Grp. 7	70-100; 80-100
Sch. 8, Grp. 7, item 2	70-100; 90-100
Sch. 8, Grp. 7, item 2(a), (c)	100-250
Sch. 8, Grp. 8	70-150; 90-220
Sch. 8, Grp. 8, item 1	70-400
Sch. 8, Grp. 8, item 2	70-400
Sch. 8, Grp. 8, item 9	50-050
Sch. 8, Grp. 8, Note (2)	70-150
Sch. 8, Grp. 9	90-100
Sch. 8, Grp. 9, item 1	70-100
Sch. 8, Grp. 9, item 2	70-100; 80-100
Sch. 8, Grp. 10	70-100; 100-450
Sch. 8, Grp. 10, item 1	70-150
Sch. 8, Grp. 10, item 2	70-150
Sch. 8, Grp. 10, Note (2)	70-150
Sch. 8, Grp. 11	70-100; 70-200
Sch. 8, Grp. 15	70-400
Sch. 8, Note (A1), (B1), (C1)	70-400
Sch. 9	30-150; 30-600; 40-200; 50-050; 50-100; 60-300; 90-100
Sch. 9, Grp. 1	60-050; 70-100; 80-150; 80-200; 90-200; App. 14
Sch. 9, Grp. 1, item 1(a)	30-350; 30-450; 80-150; 90-200
Sch. 9, Grp. 1, item 1(a)(ii)	40-200
Sch. 9, Grp. 1, item 1(b)	80-150; 90-200
Sch. 9, Grp. 1, Note (1), (1A)	80-150
Sch. 9, Grp. 1, Note (2)	30-350
Sch. 9, Grp. 1, Note (4)	30-450
Sch. 9, Grp. 2	20-250; 40-200; 60-050; 70-100; 70-200; 70-500; 80-100; 90-100; 90-220; 90-350; 120-200; App. 16
Sch. 9, Grp. 2, item 1	90-100; 90-220
Sch. 9, Grp. 2, item 2	90-220
Sch. 9, Grp. 2, item 3	60-050; 90-100
Sch. 9, Grp. 2, item 4	40-150; 40-200; 50-050; 50-100; 70-500; 90-100; 90-220; 90-300; 90-350; 120-200
Sch. 9, Grp. 2, Note (1)(c)	90-100
Sch. 9, Grp. 2, Note (2)	80-100; 90-220
Sch. 9, Grp. 2, Note (3)–(6)	90-100
Sch. 9, Grp. 2, Note (5)(b)	90-100
Sch. 9, Grp. 2, Note (7)	70-200; 70-500; 90-350
Sch. 9, Grp. 4	100-450
Sch. 9, Grp. 5	40-000; 50-000; 50-050; 70-100; 70-200; 70-300; 70-400; 70-500; 80-100; 80-250; 90-100; 90-220; 90-350; 100-300; 100-350; 120-100; 120-150; 120-200; App. 12
Sch. 9, Grp. 5, item 1–6	40-200
Sch. 9, Grp. 5, item 1	30-250; 30-500; 40-200; 70-100; 70-150; 70-200; 70-450; 70-500; 80-100; 80-200; 90-100; 100-150; 100-300
Sch. 9, Grp. 5, item 2	70-100; 70-150; 70-200; 70-450; 80-100; 80-200; 90-200; 100-150; 100-300; 100-450
Sch. 9, Grp. 5, item 3	70-100; 70-200; 80-100
Sch. 9, Grp. 5, item 4	70-100; 70-200; 80-100; 90-100
Sch. 9, Grp. 5, item 5	40-200; 70-100; 70-150; 70-200; 70-300; 70-500; 80-100; 80-200; 80-250; 100-300; 120-150; 120-200
Sch. 9, Grp. 5, item 5A	70-150; 80-100; 80-200; 90-200
Sch. 9, Grp. 5, item 6	30-500; 40-200; 70-150; 70-200; 70-500; 80-100; 80-250; 80-300; 80-350; 80-400; 90-200; 100-300
Sch. 9, Grp. 5, item 6A	80-300
Sch. 9, Grp. 5, item 7	70-100; 70-500; 80-100; 80-350
Sch. 9, Grp. 5, item 8	40-200; 70-100; 70-200
Sch. 9, Grp. 5, item 9	70-100; 70-150; 80-100; 80-200; 80-300; 80-350
Sch. 9, Grp. 5, item 10	70-150; 80-100; 80-200; 80-300; 80-350
Sch. 9, Grp. 5, Note (1A)	70-100
Sch. 9, Grp. 5, Note (2A)	70-100; 70-200
Sch. 9, Grp. 5, Note (2B)	70-100; 70-200; 70-300; 70-500
Sch. 9, Grp. 5, Note (4)	70-300
Sch. 9, Grp. 5, Note (5)	70-200
Sch. 9, Grp. 5, Note (5A)	70-100; 70-200; 80-100
Sch. 9, Grp. 5, Note (5B)	70-100; 80-100
Sch. 9, Grp. 5, Note (6)	80-100; 80-300
Sch. 9, Grp. 5, Note (7), (8), (10)	80-300
Sch. 9, Grp. 6	20-250
Sch. 9, Grp. 9	50-050
Sch. 9, Grp. 13	40-200
Sch. 9, Grp. 14	40-050; App. 6
Sch. 9, Grp. 15	100-450; App. 19
Sch. 9, Grp. 15, item 1	40-200
Sch. 9, Grp. 15, item 2	40-200
Sch. 9, Grp. 16	60-050; 60-300
Sch. 9A	20-250
Sch. 9A, para. 1(2)	20-250
Sch. 9A, para. 1(4)	20-250
Sch. 10	80-150; 90-050
Sch. 10, Pt. 1	80-150
Sch. 10, para. 1(1)	80-200
Sch. 10, para. 2–4	30-450; 90-200
Sch. 10, para. 2	70-400; 90-220; 100-450
Sch. 10, para. 3(5)	80-150
Sch. 10, para. 3A	40-200
Sch. 10, para. 3A(4)	30-350
Sch. 10, para. 3A(8)	30-350
Sch. 10, para. 5	40-100
Sch. 10, para. 12	30-450; 80-150
Sch. 10, para. 15, 15A(4), 16	80-150
Sch. 10, para. 20, 21, 23, 25, 28	80-150
Sch. 10, Pt. 2	80-150
Sch. 10A	70-200; 80-200
Sch. 10A, para. 1(2)	70-200
Sch. 11A	10-400

Value Added Tax and Other Taxes Act 1973

Sch. 2, Grp. 2	90-220

Provision	Paragraph
Value Added Tax (Buildings and Land) Order 1999 (SI 1999/593)	80-150
Value Added Tax (Buildings and Land) Order 2008 (SI 2008/1146)	
See generally	80-150
art. 4	80-150
Value Added Tax (Buildings and Land) Order 2011 (SI 2011/86)	80-150
Value Added Tax (Cars) Order 1992 (SI 1992/3122)	
art. 4(1)(a)	30-650; 70-350
art. 5	40-100
Value Added Tax (Deemed Supply of Goods) Order 2000 (SI 2000/266)	30-500
Value Added Tax (Disclosure of Avoidance Schemes) (Designations) Order 2004 (SI 2004/1933)	10-400
Value Added Tax (Disclosure of Avoidance Schemes) Regulations 2004 (SI 2004/1929)	10-400
Values Added Tax (Finance) Order 1999 (SI 1999/594)	70-100
Values Added Tax (Finance) Order 2003 (SI 2003/1568)	70-300; 70-500
Values Added Tax (Finance) (No. 2) Order 2003 (SI 2003/1569)	70-100
Value Added Tax (General) Regulations 1985 (SI 1985/886)	
reg. 23	30-350
reg. 30	40-200
reg. 30(1)(d)	40-200
reg. 30(2)(b)	40-200
reg. 32	40-200
Value Added Tax (Groups: Eligibility) Order 2004 (SI 2004/1931)	
art. 5, 6	20-250
Value Added Tax (Imported Gas, Electricity, Heat and Cooling) Relief Order 2010 (SI 2010/2924)	100-350
Value Added Tax (Increase of Registration Limits) Order 2012 (SI 2012/883)	20-050
Value Added Tax (Input Tax) Order 1992 (SI 1992/3222)	
See generally	20-250; 40-000; 40-300; 90-220; 100-450
art. 2	70-400
art. 5	40-050
art. 5(1)	40-050
art. 5(3)	40-050
art. 7	70-350; 70-400
art. 7(2)	40-300
art. 7(2)(a)(iii)	40-300
art. 7(2A)	40-300
art. 7(2B)	40-300
art. 7(2C)	40-300

Provision	Paragraph
art. 7(2D)	40-300
art. 7(2E)	40-300
art. 7(2E)(a)	40-300
art. 7(2F)	40-300
art. 7(2G)	40-050; 40-300
art. 7(2H)	40-300
art. 7(3)(b)	40-300
Value Added Tax (Input Tax) (Amendment) Order 2011 (SI 2011/1071)	
art. 5(4)	40-050
Value Added Tax (Input Tax) (Person Supplied) Order 1991 (SI 1991/2306)	40-000
Value Added Tax (Input Tax) (Reimbursement by Employers of Employees' Business Use of Raod Fuel) Order 2005 (SI 2005/3290)	40-000
Value Added Tax (Input Tax) (Specified Supplies) Order 1999 (SI 1999/3121)	
See generally	40-000; 40-200; 40-250; 80-100; 80-200; 80-300; 90-100; 90-200; 100-450
art. 2	70-100; 80-200; 80-250; 80-350; 100-300
art. 3	40-150; 70-100; 70-150; 80-100; 80-200; 80-250; 80-350; 90-100; 90-200; 100-300
art. 3(a)	30-250; 80-100; 90-100
art. 3(b)	70-100
art. 3(c)	70-100; 70-150; 80-100; 90-100
Value Added Tax (Investment Gold) Order 1999 (SI 1999/3116)	
See generally	100-450
art. 3	100-450
Value Added Tax (Isle of Man) Order 1982 (SI 1982/1067)	10-050
Value Added Tax (Land) Order 1995 (SI 1995/282)	80-150
Value Added Tax (Payments on Account) Order 1993 (SI 1993/2001)	10-350
Value Added Tax (Payments on Account) (Amendment) Order 1995 (SI 1995/291)	10-350
Value Added Tax (Payments on Account) (Amendment) Order 1996 (SI 1996/1196)	10-350
Value Added Tax (Payments on Account) (Appeals) Order 1997 (SI 1997/2542)	10-350
Value Added Tax (Place of Supply of Goods) Order 2004 (SI 2004/3148)	100-350
Value Added Tax (Place of Supply of Services) Order 1992 (SI 1992/3121)	
art. 5	30-250
art. 16	30-250; 40-200; 50-000; 90-200
art. 17	30-250; 50-050
art. 18	20-250; 30-250; 50-050
Value Added Tax Regulations 1995 (SI 1995/2518)	
See generally	10-000

Value Added Tax Regulations 1995 (SI 1995/2518) – continued

Provision	Paragraph
reg. 6	10-350
Pt. III	30-550
reg. 24	30-650; 70-350
reg. 25	10-350
reg. 29	10-350; 30-350; 40-300; 60-250
reg. 29(1A)	40-250
reg. 29(2)	40-000
reg. 34(3)	40-300
reg. 35	40-300
reg. 36	40-300
reg. 38	30-650; 70-350
reg. 43A–43G	10-350(7)
Pt. VI	10-350
Pt. XI	30-350
reg. 82	30-350; 50-100
reg. 84	30-350
reg. 90	30-350
reg. 90(1)	30-350
reg. 93	30-350
reg. 94B	30-350
Pt. XIV	40-150; App. 8
reg. 101	40-200; 40-250; 60-050; 90-220
reg. 101(2)	40-200
reg. 101(2)(b)	40-250
reg. 101(2)(d), (e), (g)	40-200
reg. 101(3), (3)(e), (5)	40-200
reg. 101(7), (8), (10)	40-200
reg. 102, 102(1A)(b), (2), (9)–(16)	40-200
reg. 102ZA	40-200
reg. 103	40-200; 70-100; 70-150; 70-200; 70-400; 80-100; 80-300; 80-350; 90-100; 90-200; 100-150; 100-250; 100-300; 100-450
reg. 103A	40-200
reg. 103B	40-200
reg. 106(1)	40-200
reg. 107	40-200
reg. 107(2)(b)	40-200
reg. 107A, 107C	40-200
reg. 108	40-250
reg. 109	40-200; 40-250
reg. 110(5)	40-250
reg. 111	40-250
reg. 111(2), (2)(b)	40-250
reg. 111(2)(d)	10-350; 40-250
reg. 111(2)(e)	40-250
Pt. XV	40-150; 40-200; App. 8
reg. 112–116	40-200
reg. 113	30-450; 80-150
reg. 115(2)	40-200
reg. 115(3)	40-200
reg. 129	70-150
reg. 136–139	10-000
Pt. XVI(A)	100-250
Pt. XIX	30-650
reg. 170A	30-650
reg. 170(2)	30-650
Pt. XX	50-050
reg. 173–184	40-150
Pt. XXI	50-050
reg. 185–197	40-150
reg. 186	40-150

Provision	Paragraph
reg. 190	40-150
reg. 190(c)	40-150

Value Added Tax (Amendment) (No. 4) Regulations 2002 (SI 2002/3027) 30-650

Value Added Tax (Amendment) (No. 5) Regulations 2003 (SI 2003/2318) 30-350

Value Added Tax (Amendment) (No. 4) Regulations 2004 (SI 2004/3140) 40-150; 100-350

Value Added Tax (Amendment) (No. 5) Regulations 2007 (SI 2007/2085) 30-350; 30-450; 30-600

Value Added Tax (Place of Supply of Services) (Transport of Goods) Order 2012 (SI 2012/2787)
See generally .... 30-250; App. 4
art. 9C 30-250

Value Added Tax (Removal of Gas, Electricity, Heat and Cooling) Order 2010 (SI 2010/2925) 100-350

Value Added Tax (Reverse Charge) (Amendment) Order 2004 (SI 2004/3149) 100-350

Value Added Tax (Self-supply of Construction Services) Order 1989 (SI 1989/472) 40-100; 80-150

Value Added Tax (Special Provisions) Order 1992 (SI 1992/3129)
art. 5 .... 30-200; 30-450; 40-200

Value Added Tax (Special Provisions) Order 1995 (SI 1995/1268)
art. 4 .... 70-200; 90-220
art. 5 .... 30-450; 40-200; 40-250; 70-400; 80-200; 90-220
art. 5(1) 30-450; 80-150
art. 5(1)(b) 30-450; 80-150
art. 5(2) 30-450; 80-150

Value Added Tax (Supplies of Goods where Input Tax cannot be recovered) Order 1999 (SI 1999/2833) 30-150

Value Added Tax (Supply of Services) Order 1993 (SI 1993/1507) 30-200; 30-500; 60-050

Value Added Tax (Terminal Markets) Order 1973 (SI 1973/173) ...30-100; 70-100; 70-150; 100-00; 100-200; 100-250; 100-350; 100-450; App. 18

Value Added Tax (Terminal Markets) (Amendment) Order 1997 (SI 1997/1836) 100-200

Value Added Tax (Terminal Markets) (Amendment) Order 1999 (SI 1999/3117) 100-200

Value Added Tax (Tour Operators) Order 1987 (SI 1987/1806)
art. 5(2) 20-250

Value Added Tax (Treatment of Transactions) Order 1992 (SI 1992/630) 30-500

Official Publications

(References are to paragraph numbers)

Provision	Paragraph
Business Briefs	
11/91	80-200
20/93	40-000
35/93	80-150
3/94	80-150
20/94	100-150
24/94	30-650
25/94	70-300
6/95	40-000
25/95	70-200
7/96	40-200
17/96	40-200
121/96	80-100
13/97	70-500
16/97	10-350
17/98	70-300
8/99	40-000
17/99	80-150
27/99	40-000
2/01	30-550; 90-100
11/01	80-150
19/01	30-650
23/02	30-650
30/02	20-250
07/03	70-200
30/03	70-200
28/04	100-400
15/05	40-000
21/05	40-250
22/05	40-000; 40-250
18/06	70-300
Extra-Statutory Concessions	
3.18	80-150; 90-200
3.2.2.	20-250
3.22.1.	40-200
HMRC Briefs	
05/07	70-200; 100-150
06/07	90-220
31/07	70-350
58/07	80-100; 80-300
60/07	40-000
82/09	70-350
44/10	40-050
12/12	70-200; 80-200
22/12	30-250
23/12	App. 24
30/12	30-400; App. 30
Information Sheets	
04/02	40-200
02/03	80-200
14/03	30-350

Provision	Paragraph
07/04	20-250
10/04	100-350
11/06	70-200
10/07	30-600
06/11	40-200
07/12	App. 24
10/12	80-150
News Releases	
13/92	30-500
59/93	20-250
Notices	
48 – see Extra-Statutory Concessions	
700, sec. 11	40-250
700, sec. 12A	30-500
700, sec. 25.6	70-200
700/1	20-050
700/1, para. 3.11	20-150
700/2	20-250
700/2, sec. 2	20-250
700/2, sec. 3	20-250
700/2, para. 3.7	20-250
700/2, sec. 4	20-250
700/2, para. 4.2	20-250
700/2, para. 6.4	20-250
700/7	30-500
700/8	10-400
700/9, para. 2.3	30-450
700/9, para. 2.4	80-150
700/9, para. 3.2	40-200
700/9, sec. 4	20-250; 30-450
700/9, para. 4.1	30-450
700/9, para. 4.2	30-450
700/9, para. 4.3	30-450
700/9, para. 5.2	30-450
700/9, sec. 6	80-150
700/9, para. 6.2	80-200
700/9, para. 8	30-450
700/11	20-050
700/17	80-400
700/17, sec. 5	80-400
700/17, sec. 6	80-400
700/17, sec. 7	80-400
700/34	50-100; 60-050; 60-100
700/34, sec. 3	60-100
700/57	App. 9
700/64	40-050
700/64, sec. 4–6	30-500
700/65	40-050
700/65, sec. 2.6, 2.7	40-050
700/65, sec. 3.2	40-050
701/4, sec. 5.9	70-200
701/9	100-000

Notices – continued

Provision	Paragraph
701/9, para. 3.3.6.	100-450
701/21	70-100; 70-200; 100-450; App. 17
701/21, sec. 11	100-450
701/21A	70-100; 70-200; 100-450
701/36	90-100
701/36, para. 11.3	90-100; 90-220
701/48	40-300; 70-300
701/49	70-200; 80-200; 100-000
701/49, para. 2.8	70-200
701/49, para. 2.9	80-200
701/49, para. 2.12	120-100
701/49, para. 3.1	70-200
701/49, para. 3.2	70-200; 80-200
701/49, para. 4.10	70-200
701/49, para. 5.10	70-150
701/49, para. 6.8	80-200
701/49, para. 6.16	30-250; 80-100
701/49, para. 7.8	80-200
701/49, sec. 8	100-300
701/49, para. 8.3	100-300
702/1	100-000
706	40-150; 40-200
706, sec. 13	40-250

Provision	Paragraph
706, sec. 14	40-200
706/2	40-200
718	70-200
718, sec. 20	90-220
723	40-150
727	20-250
732A	40-150
741, sec. 3	30-250
741, para. 2.6	30-250
741A	80-150
741A, para. 3.3, 3.4	30-250
741A, para. 3.6, 3.7	50-150
741A, para. 15.5.3	70-150
741A, para. 15.6.1	70-150
742, para. 2.5	80-150
742, para. 3.3	80-150
742A	80-150
742A, para. 5.2	80-150
742A, para. 11.2.1	80-150
744C	70-400

Statements of Practice

B12	50-100

Index

(References are to paragraph numbers)

A

	Paragraph
Abortive assignments/supplies	80-200(5)(c); 110-500

Abuse of rights
. avoidance of VAT . . . . 40-000(6)
. . prevention, groups – see Group registration

Accounting for VAT
. imported services. . . . . 50-100(6)
. input tax claims 40-300

Acquisition of business – see Mergers and acquisitions; Transfer of business as a going concern (TOGCs)

Acquisitions
. concept. 10-050
. place of – see Place of acquisition
. statistical information – see EU sales listings
. taxable event . . . . 30-300(2)
. time of supply 30-400

Administration of VAT 10-000

Advisory services. 80-200(1)

Affinity cards. . . . . 70-300(7); 70-500(5)

Agency arrangements
. groups . . . . 60-050(2)

Agency services
. fees, exemption . . . . 70-200(1)
. financial investments
. . exemption with right of recovery. . . . 80-100(3)(b)(ii)
. . general rule . . . . 80-100(3)(b)(i)
. . zero-rate option . . . . 80-100(3)(b)(iii)
. insurance, providing or arranging
    cover . . . . 90-100(2)
. . outside the scope, exemption
    with right of recovery
    and zero-rating. 90-100(2)
. Lloyd's – see Lloyd's
. relief
. . financial investments . . . . 80-100(3)
. . monetary financial services . . . . 70-100(3)(c)
. . non-monetary financial services . . . . . . 70-150(3)(c)
. search fees . . . . 70-200(34)

Aircraft – see Equipment leasing and rental

Anti-avoidance – see Avoidance of VAT

Arbitration services. . . . . 70-200(2); 100-450(1)

Arrangement fees . . . . 80-200(30)

Assessments
. best of judgment . . . . 10-350(4)
. generally . . . . 10-350(4)

Automated teller machines (ATMs). . . . . . 70-200(3); 80-200(32)

Avoidance of VAT
. abuse of right. . . . . 40-000(6)
. connected-party transactions. . . . . 30-500(7)
. credit and debit card handling fees . . . . 70-300(8)
. generally 10-400
. in the course of business 10-300
. option to tax land and buildings . . . . . 80-150(2)(b)(ii)
. registration
. . assets supplied in UK by overseas
    businesses . . . . 20-300(3)
. . groups – see Group registration

B

Bad debt relief
. generally 30-650
. goods supplied by hire purchase or
    conditional sale 30-650
. receiverships 30-650

Banking – see Banks and financial institutions

Banknotes. . . . . 70-200(4); 70-200(9)

Banks and financial institutions
. agency and services of intermediary . . . . . . 70-200(1)
. arbitration services . . . . 70-200(2)
. automated teller machines (ATMs) . . . . 70-200(3)
. banknotes. . . . . 70-200(4); 70-200(9)
. banks
. . generally. 70-250
. . partial exemption . . . . 70-250(1)
. bills of exchange and notes or orders for
    payment of money . . . . 70-200(5)
. block discounting. . . . . 70-200(6)
. cash collection and checking and change
    services . . . . 70-200(7)
. cash-point machine replenishment . . . . 70-200(8)
. clearing and settlement . . . . 70-200(40)
. coins. . . . . 70-200(9)
. confirming houses . . . . 70-200(10)
. consortium for syndicated loans . . . . 70-200(12)
. credit, debit and charge cards –
    see Credit and charge card companies
. credit management. 70-200(13)
. current accounts. . . . . 70-200(14)
. debt collection and factoring . . . . 70-200(15)

Index

Banks and financial institutions – continued

	Paragraph
. debt (re)negotiation services	70-200(16)
. debt sales and sale of debt at discount	70-200(17)
. deferred payments	70-200(18)
. deposits, loans, overdrafts and mortgages	70-200(19)
. electronic services – see Electronic services	
. equipment leasing and rental – see Equipment leasing and rental	
. face-value vouchers	70-200(20)
. factoring of debts	
. . finance	70-450(1)
. . generally	70-450
. . partial exemption	70-450(3)
. . risk control and other services	70-450(2)
. finance houses	
. . generally	70-350
. . partial exemption	70-350(1)
. . sale of repossessed goods	70-350(2)
. financial guarantees and bonds	70-200(21)
. foreign exchange (FOREX)	70-200(22)
. forfaiting	70-200(23)
. forward rate agreements	70-200(24)
. generally	70-000
. imported services	70-200(25)
. instalment credit finance and credit provided free	70-200(26)
. interest-free finance	70-200(27)
. interest rate and currency rate swaps	70-200(29)
. interest rate caps	70-200(28)
. Islamic finance	70-200(30); App. 20
. monetary financial services – see Monetary financial services	
. money brokerage	70-200(31)
. multi-currency loans and management of currency exposure	70-200(41)
. non-monetary – see Non-monetary financial services	
. outsourcing – see Outsourcing	
. pawnbroking	70-200(32)
. pension fund management	70-200(33)
. search agencies	70-200(34)
. secured loans, securities for money (including credit guarantees)	70-200(35)
. securities dealing	70-200(36)
. securitisation	70-200(37)
. sterling commercial paper and Euronotes	70-200(38)
. travellers cheques	70-200(39)
. VAT liability generally	70-050

Belonging rules – see Place of supply of services

Best of judgment assessments – see Assessments

Bills of exchange	70-200(5)
Block discounting	70-200(6)

Blocked input tax

. business entertainment	40-050(2)
. cars	40-050(1)

	Paragraph
. . leasing and rental	70-400(5)
. staff	40-050(3)
Bonds	80-200(2)

Breakdown insurance

. consumer durables	90-220(9)

Broadcasting services – see Telecommunication and broadcasting services

Brokers and dealers – see also Agency services; Intermediaries

. commission sharing	80-200(4)
. commodities – see Derivatives	
. dealing services	80-200(6)
. financial investments	
. . exemption with right of recovery	80-100(3)(b)(ii)
. . general rule	80-100(3)(b)(i)
. . zero-rate option	80-100(3)(b)(iii)
. generally	80-250
. input tax implications	80-250(2)
. insurance	90-220(2); 90-350(2)
. . partial exemption	90-350(2)(a)
. . providing or arranging cover	90-100(2)
. money brokerage	70-200(31)
. . liability of services	App. 13
. outputs	80-250(1)
. relief	
. . financial investments	80-100(3)
. . non-monetary financial services	70-100(3)(c)
. retail investment products (RIPs)	80-250(3)

Buildings – see Land and buildings

Building services – see Construction services

Business activities

. avoidance of VAT	10-300
. what constitutes a business	10-300

Business and private use

. input tax	40-000(5)

Business assets/services

. private use	30-500(5)

Business entertainment

. blocked input tax	40-050(2)
. . business entertainment defined	40-050(2)
. . staff	40-050(3)

Business gifts

. disposal of part of business asset free of charge	30-500(5)

Business purpose test

. significance	40-000(2)

C

Call-centres – see Sales and call-centres

Capital goods scheme

. generally	40-200(8)
. relevant legislation	App. 8

Index

Paragraph

Cars
. input tax .... 40-000(4)(a)
.. blocked .... 40-050(1); 70-400(5)
. insurance policy claims .... 90-220(4)(c)
. mechanical breakdown insurance .... 90-220(9)
. roadside assistance .... 90-220(18)

Cash-point machines
. replenishment .... 70-200(8)

Central administration
. groups – see Cost sharing groups

Certificate of deposit .... 70-200(35)

Charge cards – see Credit and charge card companies

Civil engineering works – see Land and buildings

Clearing and settlement services .... 70-200(40); 80-200(3)

Clearing-house charges .... 100-450(3)

Coins .... 70-200(9)

Collection of VAT
. generally 10-350
. returns – see Returns

Commercial buildings
. zero-rating .... 80-150(3)(b)

Commission – see EU Commission

Commissions – see Investment

Commodity derivatives – see Derivatives

Communication services .... 80-100(2)(c)

Companies
. consortia and joint ventures – see Consortia and joint ventures
. groups – see Group registration; Groups of companies

Company cars – see Cars

Compensation
. consideration .... 30-500(4)

Conditional sale agreements
. bad debt relief 30-650
. generally .... 70-200(26)

Confirming houses .... 70-200(10)

Connected parties – see also Consortia and joint ventures; Groups of companies
. consideration .... 30-500(7)
. relevant legislation .... App. 7
. taxpoint .... 30-350(3)(c)

Consideration
. compensation .... 30-500(4)
. connected-party transactions .... 30-500(7)
. free-supplies .... 30-500(5)
. generally 30-500
. monetary .... 30-500(1)

Paragraph

. non-monetary .... 30-500(2)
. subsidies .... 30-500(3)
. value .... 30-500(6)

Consortia and joint ventures
. companies .... 60-150(1)
. consortia .... 60-150(2)(a)
. joint ventures/co-ownerships .... 60-150(2)(b)

Construction services
. self-supplies .... 40-100; 80-150(2)(d)
. taxpoint, special rules .... 30-350(3)(b)

Consumer durables
. breakdown insurance .... 90-220(9)

Context of VAT
. administration of VAT 10-000
. current EU developments 10-000
. exempt supplies 10-000
. generally 10-000
. interpretation of UK laws 10-000

Continuous supplies
. taxpoint .... 30-350(3)(a)

Contracts – see Derivatives

Co-ownerships – see Consortia and joint ventures

Corporate finance
. abortive assignments .... 80-200(5)
. defences against hostile takeovers .... 80-200(5)
. generally .... 80-200(5)
. possible conflict of interest .... 80-200(5)(a)
. standard-rating .... 80-100(2)(b)

Corporate purchasing cards .... 70-300(5)

Costs – see Expenses

Cost sharing groups
. central administration
.. agency .... 60-050(2)
.. cost-sharing generally .... 60-050(1)
.. exemption .... 60-050(4)
.. management charges .... 60-050(3)
.. no charges made .... 60-050(5)
. generally .... 60-300; App. 24

Court fees
. debt collectors .... 70-200(15)

Credit and charge card companies
. affinity cards .... 70-300(7)
. avoidance .... 70-300(8)
. corporate purchasing or procurement cards .... 70-300(5)
. differential prices and card handling fees ... 70-300(6)
. fuel cards .... 70-300(4)
. generally 70-300
. interchange and other fees .... 70-300(3)
. membership fees and charges .... 70-300(1)
. merchant charges and retailer discounts ..... 70-300(2)
. outsourcing .... 70-500(2)(a)

Credit management .... 70-200(13)

	Paragraph
Credit sale agreements	70-200(26)
Currency rate swaps	70-200(29)
Current accounts	70-200(14)
Customs duty or excise duty warehouses – see Warehoused goods	

D

	Paragraph
Debentures	70-200(35)

Debit cards – see Credit and charge card companies

	Paragraph
Debt collection and factoring	70-200(15)
Debt (re)negotiation services	70-200(16)
Debt sales	70-200(17)
Deemed supply of goods	30-500(5)
Default interest	10-350(3)(c)
Default surcharge	10-350(3)(c)
Deferred payments	70-200(18)

Definitions and meanings
. business entertainment .... 40-050(2)
. input tax 40-000
. supply 30-000
. supply of goods 10-100; 30-000
. supply of services 10-100; 30-000
. taxable person 10-250

	Paragraph
Depositaries	80-200(7)
Deposits	70-200(19)
De-registration	20-200

Derivatives
. Administrative agreements entered into with trade bodies (Notice 700/57) ...... App. 9
. arbitration services .... 100-450(1)
. brokers .... 100-100(1)(a)
. brokers' or agency services .... 100-150(3)(h); 100-150(8); 100-250(1)(e)
. clearing members .... 100-100(1)(b)
. clients .... 100-100(3)
. commodity fund management .... 100-450(2)
. contracts and place of supply
.. allocated goods .... 100-150(1)
.. brokers' or agency services .... 100-150(3)(h)
.. categories of contracts .... 100-150(3)
.. commodity loans .... 100-150(3)(g)
.. contracts for differences .... 100-150(3)(f)
.. forward contracts .... 100-150(3)(c)
.. futures .... 100-150(3)(b)
.. generally 100-150
.. options .... 100-150(3)(d)
.. physicals/actuals .... 100-150(3)(a)
.. swaps, physical/financial .... 100-150(3)(e)
.. unallocated or unascertained goods .. 100-150(2)
. fees and clearing house charges ..... 100-450(3)
. financial futures and options and other intangibles
.. freight derivatives .... 100-300(2)
.. generally 100-300
.. LIFFE – see London International Financial Futures and Options Exchange (LIFFE)
.. other markets and situations .... 100-300(3)
. futures contracts .... 100-150(3)(b); 100-250(1)(b)
. generally 100-000
. gold
.. Black Box .... 100-450(4)(b)
.. bullion loans .... 100-450(4)(c)
.. central banks .... 100-450(4)(a)
.. generally .... 100-450(4)
.. investment gold .... 100-450(4)(f)
.. special scheme .... 100-450(4)(d); App. 17
.. unallocated gold .... 100-450(4)(e)
. hard and soft commodities
.. foreign and warehoused supplies ... 100-250(2)
.. generally .... 100-250(1)
. IPE/ICE Brent Crude contract .... 100-450(5)
. physicals/actuals and forward sales contracts .... 100-150(3)(a), (c); 100-250(1)(a)
. power supplies – see Electricity and gas trading
. market-makers and dealers .... 100-100(1)(c)
. market members .... 100-100(1)
. markets .... 100-050(2)
. non-market member brokers .... 100-100(2)
. options .... 100-150(3)(d); 100-250(1)(d)
. products .... 100-050(1)
. relevant terminal markets legislation .... App. 18
. spread betting .... 100-450(6)
. unallocated goods .... 100-150(2); 100-250(1)(c)
. warehoused supplies .... 100-250(2)
. zero-rating and the Black Box 100-200

Developmental leases and tenancies
. standard-rating .... 80-150(2)(c)

Direct and immediate link test
. mergers and acquisitions 110-400

	Paragraph
Direct MAT insurance	90-220(6)

Dispatches
. generally .... 30-300(3)
. statistical information – see EU sales listings
. time of supply 30-400

	Paragraph
Dividends	80-200(8)

Domestic legislation
. interpretation 10-000

E

E-commerce – see Electronic services

Economic activities – see Business activities; Mergers and acquisitions

Paragraph
Electricity and gas trading
. electricity
.. Elexon Ltd charges. . . . . 100-350(1)(b)(ii)
.. energy lending . . . . .100-350(1)(b)(i)
.. generally. . . . . .100-350(1)
.. imbalance settlements . . . . 100-350(1)(b)(iii)
.. information imbalance charges . . . .100-350(1)(b)(iv)
.. options . . . . 100-350(1)(b)(v)
.. swaps . . . . .100-350(1)(b)(vi)
.. trading . . . . .100-350(1)(a)
.. transmission charges . . . . 100-350(1)(b)(vii)
. gas
.. charges and fees. . . . . .100-350(2)(b)(i)
.. generally. . . . . .100-350(2)
.. options . . . . 100-350(2)(b)(ii)
.. trading . . . . .100-350(2)(a)
. generally 100-350
. place of supply rules
.. brokerage . . . . 100-350(3)(d)
.. generally. . . . . .100-350(3)
.. place of supply . . . . .100-350(3)(a)
.. services. . . . . 100-350(3)(b)
.. third-country imports . . . . .100-350(3)(c)

Electronic services
. banking and associated services:
    e-commerce context. 120-050
. classification of exempt and standard-rated
    supplies
.. electronic messaging and payment
    services 120-150
.. internet based services of intermediary/
    comparison websites 120-200
. electronically-supplied services
.. generally. . . . . 120-250(1)
.. place of supply . . . . 30-250(6); 120-250(2)
.. registration and supplies to non-business
    customers: 'The One Stop Shop'. . . . . .120-250(3)
.. generally 120-000
. services related to banking, finance and
    insurance 120-100
. special scheme, relevant EU Regulation . . . . . App. 27

Emissions allowances
. Greenhouse Gas Emissions Trading
    Scheme . . . . .100-400(1)
. renewable energy . . . . .100-400(2)

Employee-related expenses
. input tax
.. benefits. . . . . .40-000(4)(a)
.. business entertainment. . . . . .40-050(3)
.. legal and removal expenses . . . . 40-000(4)(b)
.. luxuries. . . . . .40-000(4)(c)
.. pension costs . . . . 40-000(4)(d)
.. subsistence and travel. . . . . .40-000(4)(e)

Employees
. LIFFE locals .100-300(1)(c)(iv)

Employment arrangements
. groups and connected parties 60-100

Paragraph
Energy and emissions trading –
    see Electricity and gas trading;
    Emissions allowances

Engineering insurance . . . . .90-220(7)

Entertainment – see Business entertainment

Equipment leasing and rental
. freight containers. . . . . .70-400(4)
.. non-monetary financial services . . . . . . 70-150(3)(b)
. generally 70-400
. hiring of goods. . . . . .70-400(1)
.. place of supply of services. . . . . .30-250(4)
. input tax block. . . . . .70-400(5)
. lease termination payments . . . . .70-400(6)
. means of transport. .70-400(2)
.. non-monetary financial services . . . . . . 70-150(3)(b)
.. place of supply of services. . . . . .30-250(4)
. movable property generally . . . . .70-400(1)
. non-UK lessors . . . . .70-400(9)
. rebates . . . . .70-400(7)
. ships and aircraft . . . . .70-400(3)
. transfers/disposals of agreements . . . . 70-400(8)

EU Commission
. finance and insurance services,
    proposals . . . . 70-100(1); 70-500(7);
                             80-100(1)(a); 90-100(2);
                                       90-350(1)(b)

EU Member States . . . . App. 5

Euronotes. . . . . .70-200(38); 80-200(9)

EU sales listings. . . . . .10-350(2)

Exchange bargain charges . . . . .80-200(10)

Exemption
. groups and connected parties –
    see Cost sharing groups
. electronic banking, finance and insurance
    services
.. electronic messaging and payment
    services 120-150
.. internet based services of intermediary/
    comparison websites 120-200
. finance, relevant legislation . . . . App. 12
. financial investments
.. Commission proposals. . . . . .80-100(1)(a)
.. generally. . . . . .80-100(1)
.. insurance-related activities. . . . . .90-200(2)(a)
.. intermediary services. . . . . .80-100(1)(c)
.. transactions as principal. . . . . 80-100(1)(b)
. fiscal neutrality 30-225
. generally 10-000; 30-150
. insurance, providing or arranging cover
.. generally. . . . . .90-100(1)
.. intermediaries –
    see Insurance intermediaries
.. relevant legislation . . . . App. 16
. investment gold, relevant legislation . . . . App. 19
. land and buildings
.. generally. . . . . .80-150(1)
.. inducements . . . . .80-150(1)(a)

Exemption – continued   **Paragraph**
..insurance-related activities........... 90-200(2)(b)
..licences to occupy .... 80-150(1)(d)
..relevant legislation .... App. 14
..service charges..................... 80-150(1)(c)
..virtual assignments .... 80-150(1)(b)
.monetary financial services............. 70-100(1)
.non-monetary financial services .... 70-150(2)
.supplies of goods where input tax cannot
    be recovered, relevant legislation........ App. 6

Exemption from registration 20-150

Exempt supplies – see Exemption

Expenses – see also Legal expenses
.input tax
..business purpose test .... 40-000(2)
..employee-related – see Employee-related
    expenses
..shareholder-related costs .... 40-000(3)(a)

Export of goods
.finance .... 70-100(3)(b)
.insurance .... 90-100(2)

F

Face-value vouchers .... 70-200(20); 80-200(11)

**Factoring of debts – see Banks and
    financial institutions**

Fees
.credit and charge cards – see Credit and
    charge card companies
.dealing in commodities .... 100-450(3)

**Finance houses – see Banks and
    financial institutions**

**Financial brokerage – see Brokers and
    dealers**

Financial derivatives – see Derivatives

Financial guarantees................... 70-200(21)

Financial investments
.exemption
..Commission proposals............... 80-100(1)(a)
..generally.......................... 80-100(1)
..insurance-related activities........... 90-200(2)(a)
..intermediary services................ 80-100(1)(c)
..transactions as principal............. 80-100(1)(b)
.funded pension schemes .... 80-400(4)(a)
.generally 80-100
.outside the scope, exemption with right of
    recovery and zero-rating
..agency and brokerage and services of
    intermediaries .... 80-100(3)(b)
..generally......................... 80-100(3)
..services supplied with right of recovery
    to input tax..................... 80-100(3)(a)
.standard-rating
..investment advice and corporate
    finance .... 80-100(2)(b)
..investment management............. 80-100(2)(a)

                                                                Paragraph
..research, information and
    communication services .... 80-100(2)(c)

Financial services
.banks and financial institutions – see Banks and
    financial institutions
.electronic – see Electronic services
.incidental and related goods, partial
    exemption .... 40-200(6)(c)
.invoicing rules for exempt supplies.......... 30-600
.relevant legislation
..exemption .... App. 12
..regulated and prohibited activities........ App. 11
.VAT Finance Manual
..'Actively Marketed'................... App. 26
..'Retail Distribution Review' .... App. 22
.VAT treatment, EU proposals for Council
    Directive and Regulation......... 10-000; App. 3

Fiscal neutrality
.VAT treatment of output supplies 30-225

Fiscal warehousing
.Second Simplification Directive .... 100-250(2)(a)
..basic position .... 100-250(2)(a)(i)
..interaction with Terminal Markets
    Order .... 100-250(2)(a)(iii)
..services................... 100-250(2)(a)(ii)

Flowcharts
.intermediaries .... App. 25
.specified bodies .... App. 21

Foreign exchange (FOREX) .... 70-200(22)

Foreign supplies
.commodities .... 100-250(2)

Foreign VAT
.recovery .... 40-150(3)

FOREX – see Foreign exchange (FOREX)

Forfaiting .... 70-200(23)

Forward rate agreements .... 70-200(24)

Free supplies
.consideration .... 30-500(5)

**Freight containers – see Equipment
    leasing and rental**

Freight derivatives..................... 100-300(2)

Fuel cards........................... 70-300(4)

Funded pension schemes
.activities........................... 80-400(2)
.administration
..generally................... 80-400(2); 80-400(3)
..professional management fees......... 80-400(3)(a)
..recharge of costs................. 80-400(3)(b)
.generally 80-400
.investment
..financial investments .... 80-400(4)(a)
..generally................... 80-400(2); 80-400(4)
..other assets................... 80-400(4)(d)
..partial exemption .... 80-400(4)(e)

	Paragraph
..property	80-400(4)(c)
..share underwriting	80-400(4)(b)
.registration	80-400(1)

G

Gas trading – see Electricity and gas trading

Gold
- .Black Box .... 100-450(4)(b)
- .bullion loans .... 100-450(4)(c)
- .central banks .... 100-450(4)(a)
- .generally .... 100-450(4)
- .investment gold .... 40-200(6)(b); 100-450(4)(f)
- ..relevant legislation .... App. 19
- .special scheme .... 100-450(4)(d)
- ..Notice 701/21 .... App. 17
- .unallocated gold .... 100-450(4)(e)

Goods – see Supply of goods

Greenhouse Gas Emissions Trading Scheme .... 100-400(1)

Group registration
- .anti-avoidance and prevention of abuse
- ..exit and entry schemes .... 20-250(3)(c)
- ..group supplies using overseas member .... 20-250(3)(e)
- ..protection of revenue .... 20-250(3)(a), (b)
- ..removing companies from group ...... 20-250(3)(b)
- ..special purpose companies .... 20-250(3)(d)
- .business acquisition or merger 110-250
- .consequences .... 20-250(2)
- .eligibility and membership .... 20-250(1)
- ..established and having fixed establishment .... 20-250(1)(a)
- ..fully exempt groups .... 20-250(1)(c)
- ..limitation .... 20-250(1)(e)
- ..membership of more than one group .... 20-250(1)(d)
- ..'specified bodies' rules .... 20-250(1)(b)
- .generally 20-250; 60-250
- .imported services .... 50-000(2)
- .relevant legislation .... App. 2
- .reverse charge supplies .... App. 29
- .timing .... 20-250(4)
- .transfers of business .... 20-250(5)
- ..acquisitions by partly exempt groups ... 20-250(5)(a); 30-450(3)
- ..transfers involving tenanted property ... 20-250(5)(b)

Groups of companies
- .central administration: cost-sharing see– Cost sharing groups
- .employment 60-100
- .generally 60-000
- .registration – see Group registration

H

	Paragraph

Hire-purchase agreements
- .bad debt relief 30-650
- .generally .... 70-200(26)

Hiring of equipment – see Equipment leasing and rental

HM Revenue and Customs Notices
- .Administrative agreements entered into with trade bodies (700/57) .... App. 9
- .Gold (701/21) .... App. 17
- .list .... App. 1

Holding companies
- .activities generally 110-100
- .input tax recovery
- ..acquisition costs .... 40-250(3)(b)
- ..generally .... 40-250(3)(a)
- ..issuing shares or securities .... 40-000(3); 40-250(3)(c)

Hospitality – see Business entertainment

I

Imported goods
- .electricity and gas .... 100-350(3)(c)
- .generally 10-050
- .taxable event .... 30-300(1)

Imported services
- .accounting .... 50-100(6)
- .financial services .... 70-200(25)
- .fixed establishment 50-150
- .fully exempt businesses .... 50-000(3)
- .further simplification 50-050
- .generally 50-000
- .groups .... 50-000(2)
- .insurance .... 50-100(4)
- .land-related services .... 50-100(3)
- .limitations .... 50-000(1)
- .Lloyd's .... 90-300(6)(d)
- .management charges .... 50-100(2)
- .place of belonging 50-150
- .range of services covered 50-050
- .seconded staff .... 50-100(1)
- .taxpoint .... 30-350(3)(d)
- .telecommunications .... 50-100(5)

Indemnity payments
- .VAT treatment .... 40-000(1)(a)

Individual savings accounts (ISAs) ...... 80-200(12)

Inducements – see Reverse surrenders

Information services .... 80-100(2)(c)

Input tax
- .accounting and records: timing of claims 40-300
- .avoidance and abuse of right .... 40-000(6)
- .blocked
- ..business entertainment .... 40-050(2)
- ..cars .... 40-050(1); 70-400(5)
- ..staff .... 40-050(3)

Index

Input tax – continued	Paragraph
. brokers and dealers	80-250(2)
. business and private use	40-000(5)
. expenses	
.. business purpose test	40-000(2)
.. employee-related – see Employee-related expenses	
.. shareholder-related	40-000(3)(a)
. definition	40-000
. generally	40-000
. insurance and reinsurance companies	
.. captives and non-permitted/authorised insurers	90-250(1)(c)
.. direct attribution	90-250(1)(a)
.. generally	90-250(1)
.. residual input tax	90-250(1)(b)
.. sale of business	90-250(1)(d)
. investment and unit trusts	80-350(2)
. investment managers	80-300(4)
. recipient of supply	40-000(1)
.. direct link	40-000(1)(b)
.. indemnity situations	40-000(1)(a)
.. insurance	40-000(1)(c)
. recovery	
.. financial investments – see Financial investments	
.. generally	40-150(1)
.. holding companies – see Holding companies	
.. insurance – see Insurance and insurance services	
.. monetary financial services – see Monetary financial services	
.. non-monetary financial services – see Non-monetary financial services	
.. other adjustments after the event	40-250(2)
.. partial exemption – see Partial exemption	
.. pre-incorporation/pre-registration supplies	40-250(1)
.. taxable supplies	40-150(2)
.. tax paid abroad by persons not established in member state	40-150(3)
. self-supplies	40-100
. share issues	40-000(3)
. supplies of goods where input tax cannot be recovered, relevant legislation	App. 6

Insurance and insurance services

. block policies	90-220(1)
. breakdown situations	90-220(10)
.. mechanical	90-220(9)
.. roadside assistance	90-220(18)
. brokerage	90-220(2)
. call-centres	90-220(3)
. claims	
.. legal costs	90-220(4)(b)
.. motor policies	90-220(4)(c)
.. overseas, costs	90-220(13)
.. re-instatement costs	90-220(4)(a)
. claims-handling	90-220(5)
. Commission proposals	70-100(1); 70-500(7); 90-100(2)

	Paragraph
. direct MAT	90-220(6)
. electronic services – see Electronic services	
. engineering insurance and inspection services	90-220(7)
. exemption	
.. providing or arranging cover	90-100(1)
.. relevant legislation	App. 16
. generally	90-000
. imported services	50-100(4)
. insurance and reinsurance companies – see Insurance and reinsurance companies	
. insurance-related services	90-220(8)
. intermediaries – see Insurance intermediaries	
. invoicing rules for exempt supplies	30-600
. mechanical breakdown	90-220(9)
. medico-legal and other medical services	90-220(11)
. mixed or composite supplies	90-220(12)
. other insurance-related services	90-200
.. exemption	90-200(2)
.. outside the scope, exemption with right of recovery and zero-rating	90-200(3)
.. standard-rating	90-200(1)
. outside the scope, exemption with right of recovery and zero-rating	
.. other related services	90-200(3)
.. providing or arranging cover	90-100(2)
. outsourcing	70-500(6)
.. call-centres	90-220(3)
. overseas claims costs	90-220(13)
. pension funds	90-220(14)
. premiums	90-220(15)
. protection and indemnity (P & I) insurance	90-220(16)
. providing or arranging cover	
.. brokers or agents	90-100(2)
.. claims settlement	90-100(2)
.. Commission proposals	90-100(2)
.. exemption	90-100(1)
.. generally	90-100
.. insurance for exports	90-100(2)
.. insurance intermediaries	90-100(2)
.. insurers and reinsurers	90-100(2)
.. outside the scope/exemption with right of recovery/zero-rating	90-100(2)
.. services supplied where received	90-100(2)
.. standard-rating	90-100(3)
. recipient of supply: recovery of input tax	40-000(1)(c)
. reviewing pension policies	90-220(17)
. roadside assistance	90-220(18)
. run-off situations	90-220(19)
. salvage	90-220(20)
. services supplied where received	
.. insurance-related activities	90-200(3)(a)
.. providing or arranging cover	90-100(2)
. soft commissions	90-220(21)
. valuation	90-220(22)
. VAT liability generally	90-050
. VAT treatment, EU proposals for Council Directive and Regulation	10-000; App. 3

	Paragraph
Insurance and reinsurance companies	
. generally	90-250
. input tax	
.. captives and non-permitted/authorised insurers	90-250(1)(c)
.. direct attribution	90-250(1)(a)
.. generally	90-250(1)
.. residual input tax	90-250(1)(b)
.. sale of business	90-250(1)(d)
. Lloyd's – see Lloyd's	
Insurance intermediaries	
. brokers	90-350(2)
.. partial exemption	90-350(2)(a)
. exemption	
.. Commission proposals	90-100(2); 90-350(1)(b)
.. generally	90-350(1)
.. Intermediaries Directive (Directive 92/77)	90-350(1)(a)
.. relevant legislation	App. 16
. Intermediaries Directive (Directive 92/77)	90-350(1)(a)
. outsourcing	
.. Century Life appeal	90-350(4)(c)
.. end-result	90-350(4)(d)
.. generally	90-350(4)
.. sales and call-centres	90-350(4)(e)
.. Skandia and Arthur Anderson cases	90-350(4)(b)
.. Sparekassernes Datacenter benchmark case	90-350(4)(a)
. treatment	90-350
. underwriting managers	90-350(3)
Interest-free finance	70-200(27)
Interest rate caps	70-200(28)
Interest rate swaps	70-200(29)
Intermediaries	
. commodities – see Derivatives	
. exemption	
.. fees	70-200(1)
.. financial investments	80-100(1)(c)
.. flowchart	App. 25
. financial investments	80-100(3)
.. exemption	80-100(1)(c)
.. exemption with right of recovery	80-100(3)(b)(ii)
.. general rule	80-100(3)(b)(i)
.. zero-rate option	80-100(3)(b)(iii)
. insurance – see Insurance intermediaries	
. relief	
.. monetary financial services	70-100(3)(c)
.. non-monetary financial services	70-150(3)(c)
Investment	
. advisory and other professional services	80-200(1)
. automated teller machine (ATM) services	80-200(32)
. bonds	80-200(2)
. brokers and dealers – see Brokers and dealers	
. business purpose test, input tax	40-000(2)(a)

	Paragraph
. clearing services	80-200(3)
. commission sharing	80-200(4)
. corporate finance	
.. abortive assignments	80-200(5)
.. defences against hostile takeovers	80-200(5)
.. generally	80-200(5)
.. possible conflict of interest	80-200(5)(a)
. dealing services	80-200(6)
. depositaries or trustees	80-200(7)
. dividends	80-200(8)
. Euronotes	80-200(9)
. exchange bargain charges	80-200(10)
. face-value vouchers	80-200(11)
. financial investments – see Financial investments	
. funded pension schemes – see Funded pension schemes	
. generally	80-000
. individual savings accounts (ISAs) and related services	80-200(12)
. investment and unit trusts	
.. generally	80-350
.. input tax implications	80-350(2)
.. outputs	80-350(1)
. investment management – see Investment managers	
. Lloyd's syndicates	90-300(1)(b)
. nominee services	80-200(14)
. open-ended investment companies (OEICs)	80-200(15)
. outsourcing	80-200(16)
. PEP management and introductory fees	80-200(17)
. portfolio or fund management	80-200(18)
. property – see Land and buildings	
. redemption of securities	80-200(19)
. rent-free periods	80-200(20)
. repurchases of securities (repos)	80-200(21)
. safe custody services	80-200(22)
. securitisation	80-200(23)
. share registration	80-200(24)
. soft commissions	80-200(25)
. sterling commission paper	80-200(26)
. Stock Exchange	
.. FSA listing fees	80-200(27)
.. membership fees	80-200(28)
. stock lending	80-200(29)
. underwriting commissions/arrangement fees	80-200(30)
. valuation services	80-200(31)
. VAT liability generally	80-050
Investment gold	40-200(6)(b); 100-450(4); App. 19
Investment managers	
. generally	80-200(13); 80-300(1)
. input tax implications	80-300(4)
. special investment funds	80-300(2)
. standard-rating	80-100(2)(a)
. treatment	80-300

Index

Investment managers – continued
.unit trusts
..creating, buying, selling and
 liquidating . . . . 80-300(3)(b)
..generally. . . . . .80-300(3)
..management. .80-300(3)(a)

Invoices
.generally 30-600
.rules. . . . . .30-600; App. 23
..application in member state in which
 supply deemed made 30-600
..exempt insurance and financial supplies 30-600
.self-billed. 30-600

Islamic finance. . . . . 70-200(30); App. 20

J

Joint ventures and partnerships –
 see also Consortia and joint ventures
.LIFFE locals . . . . .100-300(1)(c)(iv)

L

Land and buildings
.exemption . . . . .80-150(1)
..inducements. . . . . .80-150(1)(a)
..insurance-related activities. . . . . 90-200(2)(b)
..licences to occupy . . . . 80-150(1)(d)
..relevant legislation. . . . . App. 14
..service charges. .80-150(1)(c)
..virtual assignments . . . . 80-150(1)(b)
.generally 80-150
.investment
..funded pension schemes . . . . .80-400(4)(c)
..standard-rating. 90-200(1)(b)
..zero-rating . . . . .90-200(3)(c)
.land-related services
..insurance . . . . 90-200(3)(b)
..place of supply of services. . . . . .30-250(3)
..reverse charge. . . . . .50-100(3)
.outside the scope transfers. . . . . .80-150(4)
.standard-rating
..developmental leases and tenancies. . . . .80-150(2)(c)
..generally. . . . . .80-150(2)
..new freehold buildings and civil
 engineering works . . . . .80-150(2)(a)
..option to tax . . . . 80-150(2)(b)
..surrenders. . . . . .80-150(2)(e)
..taxable self-supplies. . . . . 80-150(2)(d)
.taxpoint . . . . 30-350(1)(b)
.transfer/transfer of going
 concern . . . . 30-450(2); App. 30
.zero-rating
..change of use . . . . .80-150(3)(a)
..commercial buildings. . . . . 80-150(3)(b)
..generally. . . . . .80-150(3)
..investment property . . . . .90-200(3)(c)

Leasing – see Equipment leasing and rental

Legal expenses
.debt collectors . . . . .70-200(15)
.employee-related costs, input tax . . . . . . 40-000(4)(b)
.insurance claims . . . . 90-220(4)(b)

Lennartz principle .40-000(5)

LIFFE – see London International
 Financial Futures and Options
 Exchange (LIFFE)

Lloyd's
.entrance fees and subscriptions . . . . .90-300(6)(c)
.generally 90-300
.Global Market Rate . . . . .90-300(6)(a)
.imported services. . . . . 90-300(6)(d)
.managing agents . . . . .90-300(2)
.members' agents and Lloyd's advisers. . . . . .90-300(3)
.members' status . . . . 90-300(6)(b)
.mixed agents . . . . .90-300(4)
.other registrations .90-300(5)
.syndicates . . . . .90-300(1)
..investments. . . . . 90-300(1)(b)
..underwriting. . . . . .90-300(1)(a)
.VAT arrangements . . . . App. 15

Loans – see Banks and financial institutions

**London International Financial Futures and
 Options Exchange (LIFFE)**
.futures . . . . 100-300(1)(b)
.generally . . . . .100-300(1)(a)
.locals . . . . .100-300(1)(c)(iv)
..employees. . . . . .100-300(1)(c)(iv)
..joint ventures and partnerships . . . .100-300(1)(c)(iv)
..self-employed locals. . . . . .100-300(1)(c)(iv)
.options . . . . .100-300(1)(c)
..equity options. . . . . 100-300(1)(c)(ii)
..futures options . . . . .100-300(1)(c)(i)
..index options . . . . .100-300(1)(c)(iii)
..locals . . . . .100-300(1)(c)(iv)

M

Management charges
.groups and connected parties . . . . .60-050(3)
.reverse charge . . . . .50-100(2)

Managing agents
.Lloyd's. . . . . .90-300(2)

Market members – see Derivatives

Meanings – see Definitions and meanings

Means of transport – see Equipment
 leasing and rental

Mechanical breakdown insurance (MBI). . .90-220(9)

Medical services
.insurance related . . . . .90-220(11)

Medico-legal services . . . . .90-220(11)

Mergers and acquisitions
.abortive supplies 110-500
.business continuity 110-300

Index

	Paragraph
. company and tax law	110-000
. direct and immediate link	110-400
. economic activity	110-050
. generally	110-000
. holding companies	110-100
. share issues	110-450
. share purchases	
.. acquisition of business	110-150
.. use of special purpose vehicle (SPV)	110-350
. share sales – disposal of business	110-200
. third party supplies	110-600
. transfer of going concerns (TOGCs)	110-550
. VAT grouping	110-250
. VAT recovery, maximising	110-650

Mixed or composite supplies –
 see Single or multiple supplies

Monetary consideration .... 30-500(1)

Monetary financial services
. Commission proposals .... 70-100(1)
. examples .... App. 10
. exemption .... 70-100(1)
. other zero-rating .... 70-100(3)(d)
. outside the scope, exemption with right of
   recovery and zero-rating .... 70-100(3)
.. agency, brokerage and services of
   intermediary .... 70-100(3)(c)
.. finance for exports .... 70-100(3)(b)
.. services supplied where received by
   relevant business person and other
   non-EU recipients .... 70-100(3)(a)
. relevant legislation .... 70-100(1)
. standard-rating .... 70-100(2)
. VAT liability generally 70-050

Money – see Banks and financial
 institutions

Mortgages .... 70-200(19)

Motor cars – see Cars

Motor insurance policies
. claims .... 90-220(4)(c)

Multi-currency loans
. management of currency exposure ... 70-200(41)

N

Nominee services .... 80-200(14)

Non-established taxable persons
. registration .... 20-050(3)

Non-monetary consideration ...... 30-500(2)

Non-monetary financial services
. examples .... App. 10
. exemption .... 70-150(2)
. investment management –
   see Investment managers

	Paragraph
. outside the scope, exemption with right of recovery and zero-rating	70-150(3)
.. agency and services of intermediary	70-150(3)(c)
.. leasing of means of transport and freight containers	70-150(3)(b)
.. services supplied where received	70-150(3)(a)
. standard-rating	70-150(1)
. VAT liability generally	70-050

Non-UK supplies
. partial exemption .... 40-200(6)

Notices – see HM Revenue and
 Customs Notices

O

Open-ended investment companies
 (OEICs) .... 80-200(15)

Options – see Derivatives; Electricity and
 gas trading; London International
 Financial Futures and Options
 Exchange (LIFFE)

Option to tax
. extent of .... 80-150(2)(b)(i)
. generally .... 80-150(2)(b)
. restrictions and avoidance ..... 80-150(2)(b)(ii)

Outputs
. brokers and dealers .... 80-250(1)
. meaning of supply 30-000
. investment and unit trusts ...... 80-350(1)
. VAT treatment: fiscal neutrality ... 30-225

Outside the scope
. commodities .... 100-250(2)(c)
. financial investments –
   see Financial investments
. generally 30-200
. insurance – see Insurance and insurance services
. monetary financial services –
   see Monetary financial services
. non-monetary financial services –
   see Non-monetary financial services
. transfers of property .... 80-150(4)

Outsourcing
. affinity cards .... 70-500(5)
. Commission proposals on finance and
   insurance .... 70-500(7)
. generally .... 70-200(1);
                               70-500; 80-200(16)
. insurance .... 70-500(6)
.. Commission proposals .... 70-500(7)
. insurance intermediaries
.. Century Life appeal .... 90-350(4)(c)
.. end-result .... 90-350(4)(d)
.. generally .... 90-350(4)
.. sales and call-centres .... 90-220(3);
                                     90-350(4)(e)
.. Skandia and Arthur Anderson cases ... 90-350(4)(b)

Outsourcing – continued
.. Sparekassernes Datacenter
    benchmark case . . . . .90-350(4)(a)
. joint employment contracts . . . . .70-500(4)
. other back-office situations . . . . .70-500(2)
.. credit and charge card companies . . . . . .70-500(2)(a)
.. payments . . . . 70-500(2)(b)
. sales and call-centres . . . . .70-200(1);70-500(3);
    90-220(3); 90-350(4)(e)
. Sparekassernes Datacenter: services
    comprising exempt activity in
    own right . . . . .70-500(1); 90-350(4)(a)

Overdrafts . . . . .70-200(19)

Overpaid VAT
. recovery . . . . .10-350(6)
.. unjust enrichment . . . . .10-350(7)

Overseas traders
. registration
.. anti-avoidance: assets supplied in UK . . . . .20-300(3)
.. generally . . . . .20-300(1)
.. representative offices . . . . .20-300(2)

P

Partial exemption
. accounting for, and VAT periods . . . . .40-200(10)
. banks . . . . .70-250(1)
. capital goods . . . . .40-200(8)
. de minimis rules . . . . .40-200(7)
. factoring of debts . . . . .70-450(3)
. finance houses . . . . .70-350(1)
. funded pension schemes . . . . .80-400(4)(e)
. generally 40-200
. insurance and insurance companies
.. direct attribution . . . . .90-250(1)(a)
.. residual input tax . . . . 90-250(1)(b)
.. insurance brokers .90-350(2)(a)
. non-UK supplies, warehoused goods
    and other specified supplies
.. financial supplies, services and related
    goods . . . . .40-200(6)(c)
.. generally . . . . .40-200(6)(a)
.. investment gold, special rules . . . . 40-200(6)(b)
.. relevant legislation . . . . App. 8
. residual input tax
.. generally . . . . .40-200(2)
.. insurance companies . . . . 90-250(1)(b)
. residual input tax, standard method . . . . .40-200(3)
.. exclusion for certain categories of
    supplies . . . . .40-200(3)(c)
.. legislation . . . . 40-200(3)(a), (b)
. rounding-up . . . . .40-200(9)
. special methods (PESM) . . . . .40-200(5)
. standard method override . . . . .40-200(4)

Passenger transport
. place of supply of services . . . . .30-250(4)

Pawnbrokers . . . . .70-200(32)

Payment of VAT
. late
.. default interest . . . . .10-350(3)(c)
.. default surcharge . . . . .10-350(3)(c)

Penalties
. error in return . . . . 10-350(3)(d)
. late notification . . . . .10-350(3)(a)
. late returns or payments . . . . .10-350(3)(c)
. regulatory offences . . . . 10-350(3)(b)

Pension funds
. administration services . . . . .90-220(14)
. employee, input tax . . . . 40-000(4)(d)
. management, VAT treatment . . . . .70-200(33)

Pension policies
. reviewing . . . . .90-220(17)

Personal equity plan (PEP)
    management . . . . .80-200(17)

Place of acquisition . . . . . . 10-200; 30-250; 30-300(2)

Place of supply
. contracts for commodities –
    see Derivatives; Electricity and gas trading
. generally 10-150; 30-250

Place of supply of goods . . . . .30-250(1)

Place of supply of services
. basic rules . . . . .30-250(2)(a)
.. exceptions . . . . 30-250(2)(b)
. electronically-supplied services . . . . 30-250(6);
    120-250(2)
. gas and electricity . . . . 100-350(3)(b)
. generally . . . . 10-150; 30-250(2)
. hiring of a means of transport,
    passenger transport, hiring of goods . . . .30-250(4)
. land-related services . . . . .30-250(3)
. location of customer, relevant EU
    Implementing Regulation . . . . App. 28
. services supplied where received
.. insurance, providing or arranging
    cover . . . . .90-100(2)
.. monetary financial services . . . . .70-100(3)(a)
. special rules
.. electricity and gas trading –
    see Electricity and gas trading
.. relevant legislation . . . . App. 4
. supplies to person who is not a relevant
    business person . . . . .30-250(7)
. telecommunication and broadcasting . . . . . .30-250(5)

Portfolio management . . . . .80-200(18)

Pre-incorporation supplies
. input tax recovery . . . . .40-250(1)

Pre-registration supplies
. input tax recovery . . . . .40-250(1)

Private use of business assets/services . . . . .30-500(5)

Procurement cards .70-300(5)

Professional services . . . . .80-200(1)

Index

	Paragraph
Promissory notes	70-200(5); 70-200(38)

Property – see Land and buildings

Protection and indemnity (P & I) insurance ..... 90-220(16)

Protection of the revenue
. VAT group ..... 20-250(3)(a)
.. removing companies from group ..... 20-250(3)(b)

R

Receiverships
. bad debt relief 30-650

Recipient of supply
. input tax ..... 40-000(1)
.. direct link ..... 40-000(1)(b)
.. indemnity situations ..... 40-000(1)(a)
.. insurance ..... 40-000(1)(c)

Reconstructions and amalgamations – see Mergers and acquisitions

Records
. transfers of business ..... 30-450(4)

Recovery of VAT
. input tax – see Input tax
. maximising on mergers and acquisitions 110-650
. overpaid VAT ..... 10-350(6)
.. unjust enrichment ..... 10-350(7)

Redemption of securities ..... 80-200(19)

Registration
. de-registration 20-200
. effective date ..... 20-050(2)
. electronically-supplied services to non-business customers 'The One Stop Shop' ..... 120-250(3)
. exemption 20-150
. funded pension schemes ..... 80-400(1)
. generally ..... 20-000; 20-050(1)
. groups – see Group registration
. non-established taxable persons ..... 20-050(3)
. notification ..... 20-050(2)
.. late, penalty ..... 10-350(3)(a)
. overseas traders
.. anti-avoidance: assets supplied in UK ..... 20-300(3)
.. generally ..... 20-300(1)
.. representative offices ..... 20-300(2)
. pre-incorporation/pre-registration supplies, input tax recovery ..... 40-250(1)
. transfers of business ..... 30-450(4)
. voluntary 20-100

Regulatory offences
. penalties ..... 10-350(3)(b)

Removal expenses
. employees, input tax ..... 40-000(4)(b)

Rent-free-periods ..... 80-200(20)

Repayment of VAT – see Recovery of VAT

Repayment supplement ..... 10-350(5)

	Paragraph
Repossessed goods	
. finance houses	70-350(2)

Representative offices
. overseas traders, registration ..... 20-300(2)

Research services ..... 80-100(2)(c)

Retail investment products (RIPs) ..... 80-250(3)

Returns
. errors, penalty ..... 10-350(3)(d)
. generally ..... 10-350(1)
. input tax claims 40-300
. late
.. default interest ..... 10-350(3)(c)
.. default surcharge ..... 10-350(3)(c)

Reverse charge – see also Imported services
. electricity and gas trading ..... 100-350(3)(a)
. VAT group ..... App. 29

Reverse surrenders
. exemption ..... 80-150(1)(a)
. standard-rating ..... 80-150(2)(e)

Road fuel
. employees
.. free provision for private use ..... 30-500(5)
.. input tax ..... 40-000(4)(e)

Roadside assistance ..... 90-220(18)

S

Safe custody services ..... 80-200(22)

Sale and repurchase of securities (repos) ..... 80-200(21)

Sales and call-centres
. outsourcing ..... 70-500(3); 90-220(3); 90-350(4)(e)

Salvaged goods
. insurance ..... 90-220(20)

Sanctions – see Penalties

Scope of VAT
. acquisitions 10-050
. generally 10-050
. imports 10-050
. supplies 10-050

Search agencies ..... 70-200(34)

Seconded staff
. groups and connected parties 60-100
. reverse charge ..... 50-100(1)

Securities – see also Investment
. brokers and dealers – see Brokers and dealers
. dealing ..... 70-200(36)
. redemption ..... 80-200(19)
. sale and repurchase (repos) ..... 80-200(21)
. underwriting commissions/arrangement fees ..... 80-200(30)

Index

Securities for money . . . . 70-200(35)

Securitisation . . . . 70-200(37); 80-200(23)

Self-billed invoices 30-600

Self-employed locals
. LIFFE . . . . 100-300(1)(c)(iv)

Self-supplies
. construction services . . . . 40-100; 80-150(2)(d)
. input tax 40-100

Senior accounting officer (SAO)
. obligations 10-350

Service charges
. exemption . . . . 80-150(1)(c)

Services – see also Imported services; Supply of services
. distribution of gas: place of supply rules . . . . 100-350(3)(b)

Shareholder-related costs
. business purpose test, input tax . . . . 40-000(3)(a)

Share issues
. input tax recovery . . . . 40-000(3); 40-250(3)(c); 110-450

Share purchases
. acquisition of business 110-150
. use of special purpose vehicle (SPV) 110-350

Share registration . . . . 80-200(24)

Share sales
. disposal of business 110-200

Ships – see Equipment leasing and rental

Single or multiple supplies . . . . . . 30-550; 90-220(12)

Soft commissions . . . . 80-200(25); 90-220(21)

Specified bodies
. flowchart . . . . App. 21

Spread betting
. financial . . . . 100-450(6)

Staff
. expenses – see Employee-related expenses
. seconded
. . groups and connected parties 60-100
. . reverse charge . . . . 50-100(1)

Standard-rating
. electronic banking, finance and insurance services
. . electronic messaging and payment services 120-150
. . internet based services of intermediary/ comparison websites 120-200
. generally 30-050
. insurance, other related services
. . generally . . . . 90-200(1)(a)
. . property investment . . . . 90-200(1)(b)

. insurance, providing or arranging cover
. . charges for insurance made in conjunction with something else . . . . . 90-100(3)(a)
. . charges where insurance element really ancillary or incidental . . . . 90-100(3)(b)
. land and buildings
. . developmental leases and tenancies . . . . . 80-150(2)(c)
. generally . . . . 80-150(2)
. . new freehold buildings and civil engineering works . . . . 80-150(2)(a)
. . option to tax . . . . 80-150(2)(b)
. . surrenders . . . . 80-150(2)(e)
. . taxable self-supplies . . . . 80-150(2)(d)
. monetary financial services . . . . 70-100(2)
. non-monetary financial services . . . . 70-150(1)

Statistical declarations – see EU sales listings

Sterling commercial paper . . . . 70-200(38); 80-200(26)

Stock Exchange
. FSA listing fees . . . . 80-200(27)
. membership fees . . . . 80-200(28)

Stock lending . . . . 80-200(29)

Subsidies
. consideration . . . . 30-500(3)

Subsistence costs
. input tax . . . . 40-000(4)(e)

Supplies
. concept 10-100
. definition of supply 30-000
. goods – see Supply of goods
. nature of supply 10-100
. scope of VAT 10-050
. services – see Supply of services

Supply of goods
. deferred payments . . . . 70-200(18)
. definition 10-100; 30-000
. place of – see Place of supply
. time of supply – see Taxpoint

Supply of services
. deferred payments . . . . 70-200(18)
. definition 10-100; 30-000
. place of – see Place of supply of services
. time of supply – see Taxpoint

Surrenders
. standard-rating . . . . 80-150(2)(e)

Swaps
. currency rate . . . . 70-200(29)
. electricity . . . . 100-350(1)(b)(vi)
. interest rate . . . . 70-200(29)
. physical/financial . . . . 100-150(3)(e)

T

Taxable amount – see Value of supply

Taxable event
. taxpoint – see Taxpoint

Index

Taxable persons   Paragraph
. definition 10-250

Taxable supplies
. input tax recovery .... 40-150(2)

Tax invoices – see Invoices

Taxpoint
. acquisitions 30-400
. connected parties.................. 30-350(3)(c)
. construction, special rules............ 30-350(3)(b)
. continuous supplies .... 30-350(3)(a)
. dispatches 30-400
. generally 30-350
. goods
.. general rule .... 30-350(1)(a)
.. property .... 30-350(1)(b)
. services .... 30-350(2)
.. imported........................ 30-350(3)(d)

Telecommunication and broadcasting services
. imported services..................... 50-100(5)
. place of supply of services .... 30-250(5)
. special scheme, relevant EU Regulation ..... App. 27

Terminal markets – see Derivatives

Third party supplies
. mergers and acquisitions 110-600

Time of supply – see Taxpoint

Transfer of business as a going concern (TOGCs)
. acquisitions by groups....... 20-250(5)(a); 30-450(3)
. generally 110-550
. general rule .... 30-450(1)
. group registration .... 20-250(5)
.. acquisitions by partly exempt groups. . . 20-250(5)(a); 30-450(3)
.. transfers involving tenanted property . . 20-250(5)(b)
.. registration and records .... 30-450(4)
.. transfers of property .... 30-450(2); App. 30
.. outside the scope .... 80-150(4)

Transport
. direct MAT insurance .... 90-220(6)
. leasing – see Equipment leasing and rental
. passenger, place of supply of services...... 30-250(4)

Travellers cheques.................... 70-200(39)

Trustees .... 80-200(7)

U

Underwriting
. Lloyd's syndicates .... 90-300(1)(a)

                                         Paragraph
Underwriting commissions............ 80-200(30)

Underwriting managers .... 90-350(3)

Unit trusts – see Investment; Investment managers

Unjust enrichment
. recovery of overpaid VAT .... 10-350(7)

V

Valuation services .... 80-200(31); 90-220(22)

Value of supply
. consideration – see Consideration

VAT avoidance – see Avoidance of VAT

VAT groups – see Group registration

Virtual assignments
. exemption .... 80-150(1)(b)

Voluntary registration................... 20-100

W

Warehoused goods – see also Fiscal warehousing
. commodities .... 100-250(2)
. customs duty or excise duty warehouse .... 100-250(2)(b)
. partial exemption..................... 40-200(6)

Z

Zero-rating
. Black Box: commodity derivatives 100-200
.. gold and gold bullion.............. 100-450(4)(b)
. financial investments – see Financial investments
. generally 30-100
. insurance – see Insurance and insurance services
. land and buildings
.. change of use .... 80-150(3)(a)
.. commercial buildings............... 80-150(3)(b)
.. generally......................... 80-150(3)
.. investment property .... 90-200(3)(c)
. monetary financial services – see Monetary financial services
. non-monetary financial services – see Non-monetary financial services